PAPERS

RELATIVE TO

MEXICAN AFFAIRS.

COMMUNICATED TO THE SENATE JUNE 16, 1864.

WASHINGTON:
GOVERNMENT PRINTING OFFICE.
1865.

MESSAGE

FROM THE

PRESIDENT OF THE UNITED STATES,

COMMUNICATING,

IN ANSWER TO A RESOLUTION OF THE SENATE OF THE 25TH ULTIMO PAPERS RELATIVE TO MEXICAN AFFAIRS.

To the Senate of the United States:

I transmit herewith a further report from the Secretary of State, in answer to the resolution of the Senate of the 25th ultimo, relative to Mexican affairs, with the papers therein referred to.

ABRAHAM LINCOLN.

WASHINGTON, *June* 16, 1864.

DEPARTMENT OF STATE,
Washington, June 16, 1864.

Pursuant to the intimation contained in the report of the Secretary of State to the President, of the 30th ultimo, and in further reply to the resolution of the Senate of the 25th ultimo, relative to the condition of affairs in Mexico, the Secretary of State has the honor to lay before the President the papers mentioned in the annexed list.

Respectfully submitted:

WILLIAM H. SEWARD.

The PRESIDENT.

INDEX

TO

PAPERS RELATIVE TO MEXICAN AFFAIRS.

No. 1.—*Correspondence of Mr. Corwin, United States minister in Mexico.*

No. 2.—*Shipment of arms to Mexico.*

No. 3.—*Intervention in New Granada.*

No. 4.—*Case of the Steamer "Noc-Daquy."*

No. 5.—*Affairs on the frontiers of Mexico.*

No. 6.—*Claims of United States citizens against Mexico.*

No. 7.—*The temporary withdrawal of Mr. Romero from Washington.*

No. 8.—*Case of the Mexican prisoners confined at Fort Delaware.*

No. 9.—*Protection of Mexican citizens in California.*

No. 10.—*Case of the Mexican brig "Raton del Nilo."*

No. 11.—*The condition of affairs in Mexico.*

No. 12.—*Case of the Mexican brig "Oriente."*

No. 13.—*Case of the Mexican brig "Brilliante."*

No. 14.—*Correspondence of legations of the United States on Mexican affairs.*

No. 15.—*Suspension of trade with Matamoras.*

MEXICAN AFFAIRS.

No. 1.—*Correspondence of Mr. Corwin, United States minister, Mexico.*

Mr. Seward to Mr. Corwin.

No. 61.]

DEPARTMENT OF STATE,
Washington, November 26, 1862.

SIR: Your despatch of October 27 (No. 34) has been received. It presents, in a very brief yet a very comprehensive way, the political and military situation of Mexico.

Under date of the 24th instant I addressed you a despatch, (No. 61,) which was forwarded by the mail of yesterday, and for which you will please consider the present a substitute, the first of this number having been cancelled.

I am, sir, your obedient servant,

WILLIAM H. SEWARD.

THOMAS CORWIN, Esq.

Mr. Corwin to Mr. Seward.

[Extract.]

No. 34.]

LEGATION OF THE UNITED STATES,
Mexico, October 27, 1862.

SIR: Since my last despatch, Buitron, a celebrated robber-chief, sent in his adhesion to the government, and has placed himself and about 600 men under the command of the proper military officers of the republic. General Comonfort is now here with 5,000 men, on his march to the main army at Puebla. General Doblado, late secretary of state, is in Guanajuato with about the same number of men, preparing to move to Puebla in time to meet the advance of the French troops upon that place.

On the 20th of this month congress was opened. The reply to the President's speech pledges the hearty co-operation of congress and its constituents in all measures necessary to repel the invasion of the French. I see no indi cation of a party in this country favorable to intervention or invasion by the French, or any other foreign power.

The French troops are now moving from Vera Cruz to this city, by way of Jalapa. When all the troops now here, and those daily expected, are united, they can present an army of 25,000 men. Arrivals of either detachments are spoken of. If the invaders choose to attack Puebla, where the Mexican army is strongly fortified, about seventy miles from this city, the battle there will, if favorable to the French, enable them to take this city without any doubt. In the latter event, the government officials will leave with the archives and take up a position in some of the states where it will be most difficult for a military force to march and capture them. This state of things, it is believed, will only begin a war of two or three years' duration.

* * * * * * * * * * * *

Your obedient servant,

THOMAS CORWIN.

Hon. WILLIAM H. SEWARD,
Secretary of State, &c.

Exhibit B—Despatch No. 34.

[Translation.]

MEXICO, *October* 3, 1862.

MR. MINISTER: The undersigned, members of the diplomatic corps, present in the city of Mexico, have learned with regret of the arrest of several foreigners, to whom the Mexican authorities had given notice of the order to depart from the capital within forty-eight hours, with the view of betaking themselves out of the territory of the republic.

The undersigned would be pleased to believe that the government will not carry out a measure so severe without having evident proofs that these foreigners have committed hostile acts against the state, and that their presence in Mexico offers a real danger.

They hope, therefore, that the government of the republic will be pleased to communicate to them its final determination, reserving to themselves the making to it of ulterior and essential communications with respect to the same measure.

The undersigned have the honor to renew to his excellency the minister of foreign relations the assurance of their high consideration.

THOMAS CORWIN,
E. E. & M. P. of the U. S. A.
E. D. WAGNER.
FR'CO DE P. PASTOR.
AUGUSTE V. KINT DE ROODENBECK.
MANUEL NICHOLAS COPANCHO.
NARCISO DE P. MARTIN.

His Excellency Mr. JUAN ANTONIO DE LA FUENTE,
Minister of Foreign Relations, &c., &c.

Exhibit B 2—Despatch No. 34.

[Translation.]

NATIONAL PALACE,
Mexico, October 3, 1862.

The undersigned, minister of foreign relations of the Mexican republic, has received the joint note which their excellencies the members of the diplomatic corps present in the city of Mexico have done him the honor to address to him on this day, in reference to the order issued by the government of the president to arrest some foreigners, to make them depart from the capital within forty-eight hours, and to compel them to quit the Mexican territory.

Their excellencies add, that they are pleased to believe that the general government will not carry out this determination without having evident proofs that these foreigners have committed hostile acts against the state, and that their presence in Mexico was really dangerous. Finally, their excellencies manifest the desire that the government of the republic may communicate to them its resolution upon this question, reserving to themselves the transmission to it of their ulterior communications, essentially connected with the measure in question.

The undersigned, after having received the instructions from the president, hastens to reply to the points which he has just stated in the same terms employed by the honorable members of the diplomatic corps.

In truth, if the government hesitated for a moment in the full conviction, which it has, of having decreed upon good grounds this expulsion, it would avoid, indeed, the carrying of it into effect; in this respect the joint note does it justice; but the undersigned regrets very much that the presumption of uprightness in the general government should not extend to the time when it thought proper to adopt the measure which is referred to, but that it should only include the interval which may elapse between its adoption and its execution. And, nevertheless, that presumption *prima facie* would have been reasonable, because the opinion of justification is so in the resolutions which a legitimate authority takes in exercising its powers, until it is proved otherwise. But the undersigned would persuade himself that the omission, to which he has just referred, was not a deliberate one.

Recurring to the essential point of this affair, the undersigned must repeat in this note what he has already had the honor of saying verbally to some of the messieurs the ministers who have conferred with him privately and confidentially upon this affair, to wit, that the federal government, with good data examined with mature and calm deliberation, has entirely satisfied itself that the foreigners in question were violating, by their conduct, the neutrality to which they were subject, and that, for this reason, their residence in the country compromitted seriously the public tranquillity, and even with some danger to their own persons.

By the constitution and laws of Mexico, the federal government is invested, at all times, with the authority of issuing a passport to, and to cause to leave the national territory, any foreigner not naturalized, whose continued residence it may deem prejudicial to the public order. This right of the government was of itself a duty in the present very critical situation. The action of the government had to be as prompt as the circumstances in which the republic finds itself are threatening, and repressing these excesses with measures proper even of the normal times, the government of the president has desired to show once more, as on so many others, that it exercises with moderation the right of the national defence, although there is being waged against Mexico a war equally unjust in its causes, as in its means and ends.

Thus, therefore, the definitive resolution of the government is, to carry into operation the measure to which the honorable members of the diplomatic corps refer.

The undersigned takes pleasure in reiterating to their excellencies the assurances of his high consideration.

JUAN ANTONIO DE LA FUENTE.

His Excellency Mr. THOMAS CORWIN,
Envoy Extraordinary and Minister Plenipotentiary of the U. S. of America, Dean of the Diplomatic Corps.

Mr. Corwin to Mr. Seward.

[Extract.]

No. 36.] LEGATION OF THE UNITED STATES OF AMERICA,
Mexico, November 19, 1862.

SIR: * * * * * * * * * * * *

There are now about 42,000 French troops in Mexico. These are on their march from the Gulf coast to Puebla by two routes—one division by Jalapa, the other by Orizaba. It is, doubtless, their intention to concentrate their main army at the siege of Puebla. This latter is a strongly fortified city, about seventy miles from this city, and on the direct route from this to Vera Cruz. Military men suppose that the superior guns and engineering skill of the French will enable them to take Puebla. If this opinion shall be verified, then it is, I think, quite certain that this city will be quickly and easily captured, though every effort possible to a government so much in want of means as Mexico is now making to defend this capital. When the French army shall be in possession of this city, and command the entire road to Vera Cruz, I see no possibility of ending the war for one or two years, unless the French choose to treat with the present government. Mexico will obstinately adhere to her present position.

Within the last two weeks all intercourse between the Gulf and this city is forbidden by a decree of the supreme government, so that this despatch will go to Acapulco, on the Pacific, and from thence to New York by way of Panama.

I must beg the department hereafter (and until this decree shall be revoked, or the route to Vera Cruz opened by the French) to send duplicate despatches—one by way of Havana and Vera Cruz, and the other by way of Panama and Acapulco to this city.

* * * * * * * * * * * *

Your obedient servant,

THOS. CORWIN.

Hon. William H. Seward,
Secretary of State, &c., &c.

Mr. Seward to Mr. Corwin.

No. 64.]

Department of State,
Washington, January 2, 1863.

Sir: Your despatch of November 19 (No. 36) has been received. The information which it gives, concerning the military situation in Mexico, agrees with the intelligence we obtain through the press, and, as I think, with the understanding of that subject that is now accepted in Europe.

Affairs have remained unchanged, but not without prospect of change and improvement. For the moment, two opposing armies seem to be fixed on the banks of the Rappahannock. There will be, before long, a change there. Our iron-clad fleet is at last afloat, and it will, I think, be heard from soon. Our two western armies, as well as that of General Banks, at New Orleans, are becoming active.

The proclamation of the President adds a new and important element to the war. Its probable results are doubtless exaggerated by one portion of the people, but not more than they are underestimated by another. Assuming, as I believe, its policy to be an unchangeable one, it is not at all to be doubted that, sooner or later, it will find and reach a weakness in every nook and corner of the insurrectionary region. The very violence with which it will probably be met will, after a little, increase its efficiency.

I refrain from giving you information concerning the changing aspect of our foreign relations, because there is no certainty that, in the present condition of communication between this capital and the one in which you reside, my communications would be safe from visitation. I must be content, therefore, with saying that there is a manifest improvement of temper in Europe in regard to our unhappy controversy, and that with success of our armies, which may be reasonably expected, we shall probably encounter no foreign disturbance.

I am, sir, your obedient servant,

WILLIAM H. SEWARD.

Thomas Corwin, Esq.

Mr. Corwin to Mr. Seward.

[Extract.]

No. 37.] LEGATION OF THE UNITED STATES OF AMERICA,
Mexico, January 8, 1863.

SIR: No act of the French government or troops has been known here, since my last despatch, whereby it can be certainly known what the ultimate designs of the Emperor are towards Mexico.

The French forces are moving towards Puebla, on the two lines of Jalapa and Orizaba. It is now quite certain that they will attack Puebla before they march upon the capital. The Mexican officers here express the opinion that Puebla cannot be taken by the present force moving against it, while it is certain that the tried and experienced commander of the French army, being well informed as to the defences of the place, has little, if any, doubt of success.

THOMAS CORWIN.

Hon. WILLIAM H. SEWARD,
Secretary of State, &c.

Mr. Corwin to Mr. Seward.

No. 38.] LEGATION OF THE UNITED STATES OF AMERICA.
Mexico, January 27, 1863.

SIR: Since the date of my last despatch the French forces have made a forward movement. It is said they have a large train of siege guns for the purpose of bombarding Puebla. They are now within about thirty miles of the latter city. Puebla is said to be strongly fortified, and is defended by about 20,000 men. We are led to suppose that General Forey is, in his own opinion, quite sure of success, since he proceeds with great caution, and so slowly, that some have supposed he wishes to reach this city without a decisive conflict with the Mexican troops.

I have been told that the government here have received information, official or otherwise, to the effect that our government has permitted the French to purchase mules and wagons for the use of their campaign here, and has denied to Mexico a like privilege. I have made no inquiry of the government here touching this rumor, nor has anything been said about it by the secretary of foreign affairs to me. It would be very necessary, if anything of this kind has been agitated at Washington, that I should have a copy of any letter to Mr. Romero on that subject. The Mexican cabinet are very suspicious of our partiality to the French. I wish to have in my possession, therefore, official information, which may give the true state of our dealings with both belligerents.

Your obedient servant,

THOMAS CORWIN.

Hon. WILLIAM H. SEWARD,
Secretary of State, &c.

Mr. Seward to Mr. Corwin.

No. 68.] DEPARTMENT OF STATE,
Washington, February 25, 1863.

SIR: Your despatch of the 27th ultimo (No. 38) has been received.

The printed document herewith enclosed, Senate Executive No. 24, of the present session, contains correpondence upon the subject of the purchase in the

United States of munitions of war by the belligerents in Mexico, which will correctly inform you of the position taken by this government.

Besides the information thus disclosed, it is understood that the Secretary of War has since placed such a construction upon the executive order as to make it applicable to certain articles much needed by the French in the prosecution of their hostilities in Mexico.

I am, sir, your obedient servant,

WILLIAM H. SEWARD.

THOMAS CORWIN, Esq.

Mr. Corwin to Mr. Seward.

No. 39.] LEGATION OF THE UNITED STATES OF AMERICA,
Mexico, March 11, 1863.

SIR: I have received your despatch No. 63, under date of December 19, 1862, accompanied by copies of the note of Mr. Romero, chargé d'affaires for Mexico, dated December 10, 1862, and your note in reply, dated December 15, 1862, copies of which, agreeably to your instructions, I have communicated to his excellency Mr. Fuente, secretary of foreign affairs for Mexico.

The correspondence between Mr. Romero and the United States, concerning the exportation of arms by Mexico, and that of wagons and mules from New York by French agents, for the use of the French army in Mexico, had, as I am informed, been transmitted to the state department of Mexico some time before the receipt of your despatch of December 19, 1862.

This correspondence and the decision of the American government on the points it involves has, I am sure, caused quite an unfriendly feeling in the minds of the Mexican cabinet towards the United States. The decision of our government is regarded here in the very light in which Mr. Romero has endeavored to place it—that is, as simply denying to Mexico rights which we concede to France; and from this postulate they easily reach the conclusion that our government has disregarded, to the prejudice of Mexico, those obligations which international law imposes upon neutral powers. However erroneous this view may be, I have no reason to expect that it will be changed. I have had no conference with the minister of foreign affairs on the subject, nor has he named it to me, either verbally or by written communication. As I regard your note to Mr. Romero as presenting all the reasons for the course our government has adopted, I shall not, of course, seek to transfer the controversy from Washington to this city, but shall use all proper means, on proper occasions, to satisfy the Mexican authorities of the propriety of the course my government has deemed it proper to take.

On the 9th day of February the Prussian minister, being about to leave Mexico, addressed to me a note, a copy of which I transmit herewith, requesting me to assume the protection of all French, Spanish, Prussian and Belgian subjects residing in Mexico.

On the withdrawal of the French legation from Mexico, the duty of protecting the foreigners above named was committed to Baron Wagner, the Prussian minister. I thought proper, at that time, to decline the office and duties proposed, for the reasons assigned in my note to the Prussian minister under date of the 16th of February, a copy of which I send you herewith.

On the 18th day of February I received from Baron Wagner another note, a copy of which I also enclose, proposing to commit the protection of the resident subjects of the four powers named above to the whole foreign diplomatic corps remaining here. This note was dated the day before the departure of

Baron Wagner, and was not received by me until the next morning, and afte he had left the city. I deemed it proper, in compliance with his request, to inform the other members of the corps now here of it, and ask their opinion as to the course proper to be adopted by us. I have received notes on the subject from the diplomatic representatives of the republics of Ecuador and Peru, and also from the consul general of Venezuela, copies of which are herewith transmitted. It will be observed that, at this time, no European power is represented here by any agent above the rank of consul, nor have any of the American republics a diplomatic representative here, except the United States and the three governments named above. Whilst I entertain no doubt that I might have accepted the powers proposed to be conferred upon me by the Prussian minister, without giving any just cause of offence to the government of Mexico, I thought such a step on my part imprudent, under existing circumstances, unless the request to do so should first be made, through the proper channels, to the President of the United States, and his approval obtained and transmitted to me; I also entertain as little doubt that the diplomatic corps, collectively, or any one of them, might, in a proper case, and in a respectful manner, interpose to protect the rights of any foreigner, without any express power given by the government to whom the allegiance of such foreigner might be due. This, it seems to me, would be my duty, since the same course of proceeding pursued towards a Prussian or Belgian subject resident here would, under like circumstances, be adopted towards a citizen of the United States residing here.

It will be seen by the copy of a letter from the state department of Mexico, under date of December 4, 1861, which is forwarded with this despatch, that when the French minister, on withdrawal from Mexico, committed the protection of the French and Spanish subjects in Mexico to the minister of Prussia, the Mexican government accepted and approved that arrangement. It is notorious that the Prussian minister has exercised that power, without objection, up to the time of his withdrawing the Prussian legation, on the 18th of February, 1863.

On the 24th of February, 1863, and before I had informed the Mexican government of the correspondence of Baron Wagner with myself and the diplomatic corps, I received the note, a copy of which is enclosed, from Mr. Fuente. To this I have, on the 7th day of March, 1863, given a reply, a copy of which is herewith transmitted. I shall act in conformity with the principles laid down in that note till otherwise instructed. I beg the early attention of the State Department to this whole subject. I have stated the reasons by which I was guided in declining the protection of the subjects of the four powers, as proposed by the Prussian minister, and have forwarded the opinions of the several members of the diplomatic corps respecting the collective protection of those subjects, as required by the note of Mr. Wagner of the 17th of February, 1863, upon all of which I ask the opinion of the President, and such instructions as may be deemed necessary for the regulation of my future action.

The French forces are concentrated at a point about five miles from Puebla, but as late as yesterday had made no attack upon that city, nor had they made any forward movement in the direction of this place. I think, from all I can learn, that the Mexican army is quite confident of victory should Puebla be attacked.

I am your obedient servant,

THOMAS CORWIN.

Hon. WILLIAM H. SEWARD,
Secretary of State, &c., &c., &c.

[Exhibit accompanying despatch No. 39.]

MARCH 11, 1863.

A.

1. Note of Prussian minister, requesting protection of the American legation for Prussia, French, Spanish, and Belgian subjects resident in Mexico.
2. Reply to the same.
3. Note of the Prussian minister, placing said subjects under the protection of the diplomatic corps generally, and the American minister, as its dean, particularly.
4. Note of American minister, calling a meeting of the diplomatic corps, to consider the request of the Prussian minister.
5. Reply of chargé d'affaires of Peru.
6. Reply of chargé d'affaires of Ecuador.
7. Reply of the consul and confidential agent of Venezuela.

B.

1. Communication from minister of foreign affairs of Mexico, protesting against the acceptance of the powers proposed to be conferred by the Prussian minister upon the diplomatic corps.
2. Reply of the American minister.

C.

Reply of the official mayor of the department of foreign affairs of Mexico to note of the Prussian minister, informing the department that he had taken under his protection the French, Spanish, Italian, and Swiss subjects, resident in Mexico.

A 1, No. 39.

Mr. Wagner to Mr. Corwin.

PRUSSIAN LEGATION, *Mexico, February* 9, 1863.

SIR: Having solicited a temporary leave of absence, and my government having granted me permission to leave Mexico, I intend to start in a few days for Berlin.

Your excellency is aware that the protection not only of the German, but also of the French, Spanish, and Belgian subjects, has been confided to this legation.

I trust that during my absence the Prussian, Spanish, and Belgian consular authorities will be able to afford all due protection to their respective countrymen, as they have already done on many occasions; and whilst I hope that their intercession in favor of the interests confided to them will avoid the necessity of often troubling your excellency, still I beg, at the same time, to take the liberty of recommending them, in case of need, to the kind and more effective protection of the United States legation, confident, as I am, that your excellency will be pleased to grant to the above-mentioned consulates, as well as to the French residents who may appeal to your excellency, such aid and assistance as may be possible under the present critical circumstances.

The French consul, M. Morineau, having left Mexico with the imperial legation, M. Farine had previously been appointed his substitute, in order to take charge of the consular archives and to keep the civil register of marriages, births, &c., &c. The Mexican government had, at the time, been informed of this circumstance.

I have the honor to remain, with the highest consideration, sir, your excellency's most obedient, humble servant,

E. DE WAGNER.

Hon. THOMAS CORWIN, *&c., &c.*

A 2, No. 39.

Mr. Corwin to Mr. Wagner.

LEGATION OF THE UNITED STATES OF AMERICA,
Mexico, February 16, 1863.

SIR: The undersigned has the honor to acknowledge the receipt of your excellency's note, under date of the 9th instant, asking the undersigned to extend the diplomatic protection of the

United States government to the French, Prussian, Spanish, and Belgian subjects resident in Mexico. The undersigned has given to the subject of your excellency's request his earnest attention, and is compelled, under existing circumstances, to decline the acceptance of the duties and responsibilities which a compliance with your excellency's request would impose upon him. Were such request addressed to the cabinet at Washington, and its objects approved, and proper instructions given to the undersigned, he should then, and only then, deem it proper for him, in obedience to such instructions, to discharge, to the best of his ability, the duties they might impose. The undersigned has not, at this time and place, the means of searching for precedents, but his memory furnishes him with no instance where a minister of the United States has, under circumstances like the present, assumed to extend diplomatic protection to foreign citizens, resident within the territories of the government to which he is accredited, without express instructions to do so from the President of the United States. In regard to the proposed protection of the subjects of his Imperial Majesty the Emperor of the French, there are reasons for the course the undersigned has adopted, which might not apply with equal force to the other nationalities specified in your excellency's note. The French empire and Mexico are at war. Between these two belligerent powers the government of the United States occupies a purely neutral position. Should the government of the United States assume the right and duty of protecting the subjects of one of the belligerent powers against the supposed wrongs to be inflicted upon them by the government of the other, it is easy to foresee that cases might arise which would tend strongly to disturb these peaceful relations with one or both the belligerents. which it is the object of perfect neutrality to preserve inviolate.

I have the honor, also, to acknowledge the receipt of your excellency's note of the 13th instant, relating to this subject, and enclosing correspondence relating thereto between your excellency and the minister of foreign relations for Mexico. The undersigned finds nothing in this last note and accompanying papers which, in his judgment, should affect the conclusion which he had come to in relation to the proposition contained in your excellency's note of the 9th instant.

I avail myself of this (probably the last that may ever occur) occasion to renew to your excellency the assurance of my esteem.

THOMAS CORWIN.

His Excellency BARON E. D. WAGNER,
Minister of Prussia, Mexico.

A 3, No. 39.

[Translation.]

MEXICO, *February* 17, 1863.

MR. ENVOY: Your excellency having considered it your duty, by your note of to-day, to refuse the protection I had solicited in favor of Prussian subjects, and Germans, French, Spanish, and Belgians, resident in Mexico, I now find myself under the necessity of placing these foreigners under the friendly protection of the diplomatic corps, convinced that all its members, were it only from a sense of humanity, would not refuse, under the grave circumstances which may present themselves, their aid and good offices to the many foreigners whose governments have not at this time representatives in Mexico.

I pray your excellency will have the kindness to inform the representatives of the other American republics, who are now at this capital, of the very pressing instances I make to the diplomatic corps, and each of its members in particular, to lend their assistance in favoring protection to foreigners who may address them directly, or to your excellency as their dean.

As neither your excellency nor your colleagues will certainly ever ask anything unjust from the Mexican government, the latter has as much interest as the other American States, that it cannot be said that foreigners are intentionally abandoned to the discretion of the government, and without any diplomatic protection. I appeal, then, once more with earnestness, and in the most formal manner, to the feelings of humanity of your excellency, and of the other members of the diplomatic corps, in recommending the foreigners above mentioned to their special protection.

Please accept, Mr. Envoy, the assurance of my high consideration,

E. DE WAGNER.

Hon. THOMAS CORWIN,
Envoy Extraordinary and Minister Plenipotentiary of the United States of America, and Dean of the Diplomatic Corps in Mexico.

A 4, No. 39.

LEGATION OF THE UNITED STATES OF AMERICA,
Mexico, February 21, 1863.

MY DEAR COLLEAGUE: On the day of the departure of the Prussian minister, but after he had left the city, I received from him a note, a copy of which I enclose herewith.

In compliance with the request contained in the note of the Prussian minister, I have to ask that you will meet the members of the diplomatic corps, now in this city, at my rooms, (Calle Donceles, No. 23,) on Monday, the 23d instant, at 12 o'clock m., there and then to take into consideration the request contained in Mr. Wagner's note.

I have the honor to be your friend and colleague,

THOMAS CORWIN.

A 5, No. 39.

[Translation.]

MEXICO, *February* 21, 1863.

MY WORTHY COLLEAGUE: I have had the honor to receive your esteemed communication, by which you invite me to assist at a meeting of the diplomatic corps which is to take place at the United States legation on Monday at noon.

I have no certainty of being in the city on the day and hour indicated, because I must go to-morrow into the country; but made aware of the object of the meeting through the despatch of the minister of Prussia, which you were pleased to send me in copy, I can make up my opinion on the matter, which is, that the diplomatic corps, to whose good offices the minister of Prussia has appealed in favor of European subjects who are at present without a representative in Mexico, would be able to render purely friendly private services, in accordance with the laws of the republic, in cases in which, in conformity with international law, diplomatic action might be interposed, and especially when the Mexican government, by its courteous concessions, should accept such offices which do not legitimately spring from the mission of representatives of nations, to whom the subjects treated of have no relations.

Please so expound my opinion to the diplomatic corps, and accept the assurances of consideration and respect which I have the honor to subscribe myself your very respectful, humble servant,

MANUAL NICHOLAS CORPANCHO.

His Excellency the Hon. THOMAS CORWIN,
Dean of the Diplomatic Corps, &c., &c., &c.

A 6, No. 39.

[Translation.]

MEXICO, *February* 24, 1863.

Mr. MINISTER: As I proposed yesterday, I have the honor to acknowledge receipt of your communication, dated 21st instant, in which you are pleased to send in copy that which was on the 17th addressed to you by his excellency Baron Wagner, placing, for reasons expressed therein, the Prussian, Russian, French, Spanish, and Belgian subjects, resident in Mexico, under the protection of the diplomatic corps, and of each of its members.

Confining myself, Mr. Minister, to the side note of his excellency Mr. Wagner, I think that the respective consuls of the subjects to whom it relates will suffice to protect the interests of their countrymen; and for those Europeans who, by force of circumstances, find themselves without representatives, either consular or diplomatic, it is to be expected that the enlightened Mexican cabinet will grant them the proper protection given to every peaceable foreigner. Moreover, I think I ought to say to your excellency that if any of the first, as well as the second, should come to me asking aid and assistance, I shall believe myself bound to interpose, as far as might be possible, my good and friendly offices with the Mexican executive government, which I hope will look with pleasure upon the frank statements I might make to it in respect of peaceful and inoffensive foreigners.

By this occasion I have the honor to repeat to your excellency, my colleague, that I am your obedient servant,

FRAN'CO DE P. PASTER.

His Excellency THOMAS CORWIN,
Envoy Extraordinary and Minister
Plenipotentiary of the United States of America.

A 7, No. 39.

[Translation.]

CONSULATE AND CONFIDENTIAL AGENCY OF VENEZUELA,
Tacubaya, February 27, 1863.

MY ESTEEMED COLLEAGUE: In consequence of what was agreed at the meeting we had on Monday, the 23d instant, to take into consideration the contents of the note dated the 17th last month, of Mr. Wagner, minister of Prussia, asking for the protection of the diplomatic corps for the foreigners to which the same refers, a copy of which you sent me, what was stated by yourself in the matter, and what was written by the absentee, Mr. Corpancho, chargé des affaires of Peru, and also ignorant of what was written by M. Paster, representative of Ecuador, my opinion on the subject is precisely analogous with yours, and that written by the representative of Peru.

Deign to accept the assurance of my distinguished consideration,

NARCISO DE F. MARTIN.

Hon. THOMAS CORWIN, *&c., &c., &c.*

B 1, No. 39.

[Translation.]

NATIONAL PALACE,
Mexico, February 24, 1863.

MR. MINISTER: Upon leaving this capital, the Baron E. de Wagner, minister resident of his Majesty the King of Prussia, made known to the government of the federation that he had recommended to certain consular agents the protection of his countrymen, and other foreigners to whom he had dispensed it, by special commission of the respective governments, adding that for extraordinary cases he had placed them under the protection of the legation in your charge, the individuals and the consuls referred to.

I beg you will please to see in annexed documents, No. 1, the pretension of Mr. Wagner on this matter, and in No. 2 the reasons for which the government of the republic could not accept a proceeding so irregular and so dangerous. Mr. Wagner made no reply to those reasons, nor sustained his contested resolution even. But on the second day of his journey there was received at the department the note which is translated in document No. 3—a note in which Mr. Wagner, carrying to a high pitch his contempt of rules, usages and conventionalities, abandons the idea of all special protection, in order to place under the safeguard of the diplomatic corps and of the people of Mexico the foreigners who were under the protection of the legation of Prussia.

Doubtless it is unnecessary to controvert the irregular commission which at the outset that minister had confided to you from the moment that commission was not accepted by you, nor adhered to by the agent who had it to confer; and although, in fact, he may have transferred it to the diplomatic corps, I cannot for a single instant apprehend it would attain better issue, being, as it in truth is, improper, offensive to the government of Mexico, and in every view impracticable. I entertain a sincere and well-founded confidence that your excellency will not lend your respected aid in giving authority to proceedings of this nature. But my duty and the orders of the president oblige me also to declare that in order to protect Prussian subjects, and other foreigners, to whom the Baron Wagner alludes in his said communications, the government of the republic will invariably maintain what I had the honor to state to the minister himself in the official letter I addressed to him, under date 12th of the current month. Until these affairs be not arranged in some other way, with the approval of the governments which are at peace with Mexico, the protection of which I speak has in its favor the spirit of the federal government, and means adequate to make it effectual in conformity with international law and our own laws.

In confiding foreigners, in the first place, to the loyalty and honor of the people of Mexico, Mr. Wagner does this nation the justice which he has so often denied to it; but Mexico does not need this testimony, nor accept it, when presented in derogation of the government she has chosen as the depository of her confidence and authority, because this government, which he affects to cast into oblivion, is the true representative of the nation in her foreign relations; because on all sides it would be reputed a rude violation of the law of nations should a foreign minister make an innovation to the people, and not to the government near which he should be accredited; and, in fine, because this omission, in the present case, would suggest the offensive presumption that the federal government does not look to the protection of foreigners, when the whole world inclusive is spectator to the contrary. Mr. Wagner, who in his note of the 9th instant, after indicating what he had resolved to do to assure the protection of Prussian subjects and other foreigners, said to me literally these words, "I flatter myself with the hope that this measure will be no more than a simple formality, and that the foreigners referred to, who may have recourse to the good disposition of your department, will have secured to them the direct protection of your excellency."

I avail of the occasion to renew to your excellency the assurances of my most distinguished consideration.

JA. DE LA FUENTE.

His Excellency THOMAS CORWIN,
Envoy Extraordinary and Minister
Plenipotentiary of the United States of America.

B 2, No. 39.

Mr. Corwin to Mr. Fuente.

LEGATION OF THE UNITED STATES OF AMERICA,
Mexico, March 7, 1863.

SIR: I have the honor to acknowledge the receipt of your note of the 24th of February, 1863, communicating the substance of a correspondence between your excellency and Mr. Wagner touching the proposed protection of Belgian, French, Prussian, and Spanish subjects, resident in Mexico, by the diplomatic corps now in this city.

I declined the protection of those subjects, when proposed to be clothed with that power by Mr. Wagner, not, however, because I conceived my assumption of such powers would give any just cause of complaint to the supreme government of Mexico, but on the ground that in the present relations of Mexico with European powers, and also with the government of the United States, I deemed it proper that the subject should be first submitted to the cabinet at Washington, and its instructions thereupon forwarded to me.

I have deemed it my duty to inform the other members of the diplomatic corps of the request of Mr. Wagner. I have received from each of them their opinions on the subject, copies of which are accompanied herewith.

I deem it due to that candor which should characterize the intercourse between the republics of Mexico and the United States to state to your excellency the course I deem it my duty to pursue on this subject until specific instructions shall be received by me from my government.

If the action of the supreme government of Mexico should at any time be exerted upon any foreign subject or citizen to such extent as to place his life, liberty or property in danger, and where such action would, with equal propriety, be applied, under like circumstances, to an American citizen, I shall, if any such case unhappily arises, deem it my duty to offer to the supreme government such expostulation as, in my judgment, the case may seem to require. This I shall do, with the most perfect respect for the just powers of the supreme government of Mexico, and with a well-founded confidence in its upright motives, and its desire to do justice to all foreigners, with such moderation as may consist with self-respect and the dignity and safety of the Mexican republic. In adopting this course, I am sure your excellency will perceive that I am making no innovation upon the modern usage of civilized nations, nor doing anything which should interrupt the friendly relations which my government so earnestly desires to preserve with the Mexican republic.

I take this occasion to renew to your excellency the assurance of my distinguished regard.

THOS. CORWIN.

His Excellency Señor A. DE LA FUENTE, *&c., &c., &c., Mexico.*

C, No. 39.

[Translation.]

The Chief Clerk, Mexico, to Baron Wagner.

NATIONAL PALACE,
Mexico, December 4, 1862.

The undersigned, chief clerk of the department of foreign relations, in charge of the office, has had the honor to receive and make report to the first magistrate of the republic of the note of M. E. de Wagner, minister resident of his Majesty the King of Prussia, of to-day's date, in which he is pleased to advise that on parting with his excellency the minister plenipotentiary of his Majesty the Emperor of the French he invited his excellency the minister of Prussia to charge himself with the protection of the subjects and interests of his nation, as well as those of the Spaniards, Italians, and Swiss, confided till now to the French legation; Mr. Wagner adding his hope that, notwithstanding the difficult circumstances of the moment, those subjects and their interests would be patronized by the government.

In reply, the undersigned must say to his excellency that the existent emergencies do not hinder the Mexican government, in conformity with its principles of justice, and its sympathies for the civilized nations of Europe, from always watching over with the greatest solicitude these subjects and those interests confided to the honor and hospitality of the Mexican nation which distinguishes and esteems peaceable and industrious foreigners, to whom the government has always desired to extend and will extend those guarantees which a civilized country can offer.

Upon this understanding, and in courteous observance of the indication of Baron Wagner, proper orders are already issued to the respective authorities that, far from foreigners being molested in their persons or interests, they shall give them every protection, hoping they, in turn, will respond by their quietude and neutrality to the decided resolution the government holds that they be respected.

The undersigned profits by this opportunity, &c.

JUAN D. DIOS ARIAS.

His Excellency Baron Wagner,
Minister Resident of his Majesty the King of Prussia.

Mr. Seward to Mr. Corwin.

No 72.]

Department of State,
Washington, April 18, 1863.

Sir: I have submitted to the President your very interesting despatch of the 11th of March, (No. 39,) with its accompaniments.

While the misapprehension by the government of Mexico of the proceedings of the United States in regard to the question of shipments for Mexico, which you describe, is regretted by the President, he does not suffer himself to doubt that it will give way before the clear explanations which have been made upon the subject to the representative of Mexico here, and of which you have been advised.

Your proceedings with relation to the request of the late Prussian minister at Mexico, that you would assume the protection of subjects of the King of Prussia and of other European powers in that republic, during the suspension of the several European legations there, are approved by the President. The first responsibility of a minister is to practice fidelity to the interests of the state whose credentials he bears; the second is the exercise of perfect good faith, respect, and courtesy to the government of the country to which he is accredited. A minister is not only at liberty, but he is morally bound, to render all the good offices he can to other powers and their subjects, consistently with the discharge of those principal responsibilities I have described. But it belongs to the state where the minister resides to decide, in every case, in what manner and in what degree such good offices shall be rendered, and, indeed, whether they shall be tolerated at all. No abridgment of this sovereign right can be insisted upon, unless, indeed, the government of that state manifestly refuses to acknowledge or to give effect to some of the entirely admitted principles of morality recognized as constituting the basis of the laws of nature and the law of nations. Not only has this government no such complaint to make against Mexico, but, on the contrary, in all its intercourse with that republic it has been impressed with the evidences of a high degree of virtue and enlightenment. That government deservedly enjoys not only the respect but the good wishes, and, so far as natural affections are allowable, the sympathy of the United States in its present unhappy embarrassments with foreign powers. The President, therefore, remits you, for your government in regard to the questions presented, to the rules you have prescribed to yourself, so long as they shall be satisfactory to the government of Mexico.

I am, sir, your obedient servant,

WILLIAM H. SEWARD.

Thomas Corwin, Esq.

Mr. Seward to Mr. Corwin.

No. 77.] DEPARTMENT OF STATE,
Washington, May 22, 1863.

SIR: I enclose herewith a copy of a despatch, dated the 4th of March, from the United States consul at Matamoras, and a translation of the order referred to, which points out the practical discrimination in favor of the rebels in Texas, and of their illicit traffic across the frontier resulting from that order.

I have to request you to invite the attention of the Mexican government to this cause of complaint, and to request the adoption of such measures as will correct the evil.

The attention of Rear-Admiral Farragut has been called by the Secretary of the Navy to the suggestion of Consul Rice as to the importance of having a vessel-of-war in that quarter.

I am, sir, your obedient servant,

WILLIAM H. SEWARD.

THOMAS CORWIN, Esq., *&c., &c., &c., Mexico.*

Mr. Corwin to Mr. Seward.

No. 40.] LEGATION OF THE UNITED STATES OF AMERICA,
Mexico, April 16, 1863.

SIR: The American consul here having a leave of absence, the government here, as a *special favor*, have permitted me to send by him despatches to my government and letters to my friends. He will deliver them at Washington.

Your despatches up to No. 66 have been received. A few days since I had an interview with the Mexican secretary of foreign relations. He expressed much satisfaction at having received from Mr. Romero a note saying that no trade from the United States would hereafter be permitted, in articles useful in war, to either France or Mexico. This, I think, will probably soothe the irritation occasioned by the correspondence with Mr. Romero, which you forwarded to me, and which was delivered by me to the state department here.

The progress of the French war presents puzzles to all not in the cabinet secrets of the Emperor. It is conceded that he wishes to take Puebla. He has been before that city just one month. It has not surrendered. He has taken Fort St. Javier, said to be the weakest of those which protect the city, and, from that point, has made a lodgement within the walls, occupying six blocks in that suburb. According to our intelligence, any attempt made to advance has been repulsed; in one a company of zouaves was captured by the Mexican forces.

If the French *wish* to capture Puebla, the reason why it is not done seems to be because, with their present force, they cannot. Re-enforcements from France, to the number of 3,000 or 4,000, lately landed at Vera Cruz, are now on their march to join the army at Puebla. It is surmised that General Forey waits for the arrival of these troops, and will, when they reach him, make a more vigorous assault.

The Mexican people greedily devour every article of news from Europe. They hope a rupture will take place touching the further occupation of Rome by French troops, or by the Polish disturbances on the further occupation of Venetia by Austria; but, as far as I can learn, their last and surest hope lies in the establishment of our old Union, which they believe would exert a controlling influence against the occupation of this country by any monarchy of Europe.

I send duplicate despatches of those recently despatched by the Acapulco route, as the transit from here to Acapulco has proved hitherto unsafe.

Your obedient servant,

THOMAS CORWIN.

Hon. WILLIAM H. SEWARD,
Secretary of State U. S. A., Washington, D. C.

Mr. Corwin to Mr. Seward.

[Extract.]

No. 41.] LEGATION OF THE UNITED STATES OF AMERICA,
Mexico, May 1, 1863.

SIR: * * * * * *

In relation to public matters here, nothing has occurred to change the general aspects since my last letter to the department. The French army, under General Forey, has been before Puebla for forty-five days. It has obtained possession of one fort (St. Javier) and five or six blocks of the city, in the neighborhood of that fort. Small detachments of troops are reported, from day to day, to be fighting in houses and streets, hand to hand, with the Mexican troops under Ortega, within the city, whilst General Comonfort, with a force of about 15,000 of all arms, is at or near San Martin, a short distance from Puebla. The French forces under Forey are estimated at 22,000 effective men. It is a question with military men whether the French will ever take Puebla without further re-enforcements from France. Rumor, and perhaps extracts from French papers, promise still further troops from France, but I believe there is not yet anything certainly known here as to these rumored re-enforcements.

Your obedient servant,

THOMAS CORWIN.

Hon. WILLIAM H. SEWARD,
Secretary of State.

Mr. Seward to Mr. Corwin.

No. 78.] DEPARTMENT OF STATE,
Washington, June 8, 1863.

SIR: Your despatch of May 1 (No. 41) has been received, and your proceeding in relation to the case of Ignacio Loperano, as therein reported, is approved

A French steamer, which arrived at New York from Havana last week, surprised the country with the news of the surrender of Puebla, with the whole of the Mexican garrison, to the French army of occupation, after the defeat of General Comonfort in a movement which he was making for the relief of that town. Assuming this information to be true, the condition of affairs in Mexico is supposed to have become by this time exceedingly critical.

I regret that I am unable to give you any definitive information concerning military events in our own country. You will have already learned of the active operations which have been instituted by General Grant and General Banks upon the Mississippi. We are awaiting the results with much anxiety

The tone of the public mind is generally pure, and the confidence of the country in our financial system is perhaps the best possible evidence of the confidence of the people in the ultimate success of the government.

I am, sir, your obedient servant,

WILLIAM H. SEWARD.

THOMAS CORWIN, Esq., *&c., &c., Mexico.*

Mr. Seward to Mr. Corwin.

No. 82.]

DEPARTMENT OF STATE,
Washington, August 8, 1863.

SIR: Your very important despatch of the 26th of June has been received. It confirms the information, otherwise received, that the French army has entered and occupied the capital of Mexico, and that a provisional government has been inaugurated there, under the protection of the imperial forces; that the Mexican government, to which you were accredited, has retired to the city of San Luis Potosi, and established itself at that place; and that the country is now divided between two governments, which still remain in hostile attitude. The President is inclined to approve the decision you made in declining, under the circumstances, the invitation of the Mexican government to leave the ancient capital and to repair to San Luis.

What would be the most convenient and favorable position for the legation, with reference to the protection of American rights in Mexico, is a question that depends much on contingencies of war, which, though they may be imminent, cannot, at least at this distance from the theatre of conflict, be anticipated. It is not perceived how you could effectually assert those interests at the present moment by representations to the government at San Luis, which is cut off from communication with the legation, while, on the other hand, you will not be expected to address yourself, under present circumstances, to the new provisional government which bears sway at the capital.

The President fully appreciates the great and unwearied labors you have performed in your mission, and the circumstances which render a temporary relief from them desirable on your part. He has thought that probably the present juncture, when things in regard to the future of Mexico are depending on dispositions and events there, with which a minister of a foreign and friendly power cannot lawfully interfere, may, perhaps, be the most suitable one for the allowance of the indulgence which you have asked. But he desires to leave this point to your own better-informed discretion. You will, therefore, have leave of absence, to begin at such time as you may think proper after this communication reaches you, and may return to the United States to confer with this department, and to await the further directions of the President. You will make such arrangements for the custody of the archives, and the transaction of the mere routine duties of the legation during your absence, as shall seem expedient.

I am, sir, your obedient servant,

WILLIAM H. SEWARD.

THOMAS CORWIN, Esq., *&c., &c., Mexico.*

Mr. Seward to Mr. Corwin.

No. 88.]

DEPARTMENT OF STATE,
Washington, December 23, 1863.

SIR: Your despatch of October 26 (No. 47) has been received and submitted to the President, and you will accept his grateful acknowledgments for the very interesting information and judicious observations which it contains concerning the present condition of Mexico.

In reply to an inquiry contained in your despatch, I have to inform you that, in the absence of further instructions from this department, you will be expected to remain in the same relations as now towards the government of the United States of Mexico.

If for any cause your residence in the city of Mexico shall become intolerable or seriously inconvenient, you will be at liberty to resort to any other part of the country, or to return to the United States. No contingency is now anticipated in which you will be expected to address yourself to any other government than the one to which you are accredited.

I give you, for your information, a copy of an instruction that has been given to Major General Banks since his occupation of Brownsville, in Texas.

I am, sir, your obedient servant,

WILLIAM H. SEWARD.

THOMAS CORWIN, Esq., *&c., &c., &c.*

DEPARTMENT OF STATE, *Washington, November* 23, 1863.

GENERAL: I have received, and have submitted to the President, your three despatches of the 6th, 7th, and 9th, respectively.

I have great pleasure in congratulating you upon your successful landing and occupation upon the Rio Grande, which is all the more gratifying because it was effected at a moment of apparently critical interest in the national cause.

You have already found that the confusion, resulting from civil strife and foreign war in Mexico, offers seductions for military enterprise. I have, therefore, to inform you of the exact condition of our relations towards that republic at the present time. We are on terms of amity and friendship, and maintaining diplomatic relations, with the republic of Mexico. We regard that country as the theatre of a foreign war, mingled with civil strife. In this conflict we take no part, and, on the contrary, we practice absolute non-intervention and non-interference. In command of the frontier, it will devolve on you, as far as practicable consistently with your other functions, to prevent aid or supplies being given from the United States to either belligerent.

You will defend the United States in Texas against any enemies you may encounter there, whether domestic or foreign. Nevertheless, you will not enter any part of Mexico, unless it be temporarily, and then clearly necessary for the protection of your own lives against aggression from the Mexican border. You can assume no authority in Mexico to protect citizens of the United States there, much less to redress there wrongs or injuries committed against the United States or their citizens, whether those wrongs or injuries were committed on one side of the border or the other. If consuls find their positions unsafe on the Mexican side of the border, let them leave the country, rather than invoke the protection of your forces. These directions result from the fixed determination of the President to avoid any departure from lawful neutrality, and any unnecessary and unlawful enlargement of the present field of war. But, at the same time, you will be expected to observe military and political events as they occur in Mexico, and to communicate all that shall be important for this government to understand concerning them. It is hardly necessary to say that any suggestions you may think proper to give for the guidance of the government in its relations towards Mexico will be considered with that profound respect which is always paid to the opinions which you express.

In making this communication, I have endeavored to avoid entering into the sphere of your military operations, and to confine myself simply to that in which you are in contact, with the political movements now going on in Mexico.

I am, general, your obedient servant,

WILLIAM H. SEWARD.

Major General N. P. BANKS,
Commanding the Department of the Gulf, Brownsville, Texas.

No. 2.—Shipment of arms to Mexico.

Mr. Romero to Mr. Seward.

[Translation.]

MEXICAN LEGATION IN THE UNITED STATES OF AMERICA,
Washington, November 22, 1862.

MR. SECRETARY: I have the honor to inform you that my government has given me instructions to communicate to that of the United States that the Mexican government has reliable information to the effect that the chief of the French expedition, which is invading the republic, has sent emissaries to New Orleans and New York to purchase mules and wagons for transporting the cannon, war materials, and provisions to the interior of Mexico. My government thinks that if such purchases should be realized, the neutrality to which they are bound would be violated by the sellers, this being the position which the government of the United States has desired to take in the war which the Emperor of the French is waging against my country. It is not doubted, in the opinion of my government, that such a sale would be a direct assistance to one of the belligerents, since it would be given to its army, which necessarily would use it in acts of hostility. In view of the preceding considerations, the government of Mexico has instructed me to solicit from that of the United States that, if it should not already have been done, it issue the orders it may deem proper to prevent the effects indicated from leaving the ports of the United States purchased for the use of the army now invading Mexico. Before these instructions had reached me I had learned, in a most reliable manner, that the emissaries of the French destined to New York had arrived some days since at that port, and were busy in purchasing the effects which they came to procure.

I avail myself of this opportunity to renew to you, sir, the assurances of my most distinguished consideration.

M. ROMERO.

Hon. WILLIAM H. SEWARD.

Mr. Seward to Mr. Romero.

DEPARTMENT OF STATE,
Washington, November 24, 1862.

SIR: I have the honor to acknowledge the receipt of your note of the 22d instant, informing me that you have been instructed by your government to make known to that of the United States that the commanding general of the French expedition now invading the territory of Mexico has sent emissaries to the cities of New Orleans and New York for the purchase of mules and wagons with which to transport his cannon, war materials, munitions, and provisions to the interior of Mexico; that the government of Mexico thinks that citizens of the United States would, in making sales of these articles to said emissaries, violate the neutrality they are bound to observe towards Mexico, and that the government of Mexico does not doubt that such sales would be the giving of direct assistance to the French army, which would use them in acts of hostility towards your government; that prior to your receipt of said instructions, you had been reliably informed that these French emissaries had arrived at New York, and were there busily engaged in the purchase of the articles they came to procure; and, finally, that in view of these facts the government of Mexico desires that this government shall issue, if it should not already have done so, the proper orders to prevent the effects mentioned from leaving the ports of the United States, they being purchased for the use of the French invading army.

In reply, I have the honor to inform you that, prior to the receipt of your note aforesaid, information of a similar nature had reached this department through the consul general of the United States at Havana, and that the matter had been submitted to the consideration of the Secretary of the Treasury, a copy of whose reply I herewith enclose, together with the extracts from the authorities in the case; and from which it appears that no intervention with the mission of the French officers is contemplated by the Treasury Department, to whom the subject more immediately appertains.

This decision appears to be in conformity with precedents, and with the rules of international law governing the case.

I avail myself of this opportunity to renew to you, sir, the assurances of my consideration.

WILLIAM H. SEWARD.

Señor Don Matias Romero, *&c.*, *&c.*, *&c.*

Enclosures with Mr. Seward's note, November 24.

Treasury Department, *November* 20, 1862.

Sir: I have the honor to acknowledge the receipt of your letter of the 29th ultimo, covering the despatch of the consul general of Havana concerning the departure of two officers of the French army for New York to purchase supplies for that army in Mexico.

I send you enclosed authorities in this case, collected for me by Mr. Marcellus Bailey, of the office of the Solicitor of the Treasury, which may be acceptable.

No intervention with the mission of these officers is contemplated by me.

With great respect,

S. P. CHASE, *Secretary of the Treasury.*

Hon. W. H. Seward, *Secretary of State.*

Instructions to collectors of customs, issued by Alexander Hamilton, Secretary of the Treasury, August 4, 1793.

"The purchasing and exporting from the United States, *by way of merchandise*, articles commonly called contraband, being generally warlike instruments and stores, is free to all parties at war, and is not to be interfered with. If our own citizens undertake to carry them to any of these parties, they will be abandoned to the penalties which the laws of war authorize."—(*Am. State Papers, Foreign Relations, vol.* 1, *p.* 141.)

Mr. Webster to Mr. Thompson, July 8, 1842.

"It is not the practice of nations to undertake to prohibit their own subjects from trafficking in articles contraband of war. Such trade is carried on at the risk of those engaged in it under the liabilities and penalties prescribed by the law of nations or particular treaties."—(*Webster's Works, vol.* 6, *p.* 452.)

Mr. Webster's instructions of July 8, 1842, cited in Gardner's Inst., American International Law, p. 552.

"That if American merchants, in the way of commerce, had sold munitions of war to Texas, the government of the United States, nevertheless, were not bound to prevent it, and could not have prevented it without a manifest departure from the principles of neutrality."

President's message, 1st session 34th Congress.—Franklin Pierce, President; William L. Marcy, Secretary of State.

"The laws of the United States do not forbid their citizens to sell to either of the belligerent powers articles contraband of war, or take munitions of war or soldiers on board their private ships for transportation; and although, in so doing, the individual citizen exposes his property or person to some of the hazards of war, his acts do not involve any breach on national neutrality, nor of themselves implicate the government."—(*Ex. Doc.*, 1855–'56, *vol.* 1, *Pt. I, p.* 6.)

Mr. Webster to Mr. Thompson.

"As to advances, loans, or donations of money or goods made by individuals to the government of Texas or its citizens, the Mexican government hardly needs to be informed that there is nothing unlawful in this so long as Texas is at peace with the United States, and that these are things which no government undertakes to restrain."—(*Ex. Doc.*, *27th Cong.*, *2d Sess.*, 1841–'42, *vol.* 5, *Doc.* 266.)

Mr. Romero to Mr. Seward.

[Translation.]

MEXICAN LEGATION IN THE UNITED STATES,
Washington, December 10, 1862.

MR. SECRETARY: The note which you were pleased to address to me under date of the 24th of November last past, and the documents thereto annexed, have informed me that the honorable Secretary of the Treasury of the United States does not propose to interfere with the purchase of articles contraband of war which the officers of the French army invading Mexico may make in the United States, and who have come to obtain the means of transportation for the use of the same army, and to whom I alluded in the note which I had the honor to address you on the 22d day of November aforesaid. It is not possible for me to refrain from expressing the pain and surprise caused me on learning that the decision of the honorable Secretary of the Treasury was sustained by yourself, for, in truth, it is very different from that which I thought myself entitled to expect. Assuming, as my government has assumed, that that of the United States is a neutral in the war which the Emperor of the French is waging against Mexico, it was natural to hope that if, in consequence of such a condition, this government did not aid one of the belligerents, it would act in the same manner towards the other, in which it would do no more than to comply faithfully with the obligations inherent to neutrality. It is very far from my purpose to teach the government of the United States what these obligations are; but I, however, deem it my duty to make known to it my opinion and that of my government: that it is incompatible with them to permit one of the belligerent armies to provide itself, in its territory, with whatsoever it may require to carry on hostilities.

Vattel, speaking at paragraph 104, chapter VII, book III, of his "Law of Nations," upon the obligations of neutrality, says that "as long as a neutral nation wishes securely to enjoy the advantages of her neutrality, she must in all things show *a strict impartiality towards the belligerent powers.*" Examining furthermore in what the impartiality consists which a neutral power is obliged to observe, he says that "it solely relates to war, and includes two articles: 1. To give *no assistance* when there is no obligation to give it; nor voluntarily to furnish troops, arms, ammunition, or anything of direct use in war. I do not say 'to give assistance equally,' but 'to give no assistance;' for it would be absurd that a state should at one and the same time assist two nations at war with each other; and besides, it would be impossible to do it with equality. The same things, the like number of troops, the like quantity of arms, of stores, &c., furnished in different circumstances, are no longer equivalent succors."

It is therefore evident that, according to these principles, if the government of the United States permits the French army to take from this country whatever it may require to carry on hostilities against Mexico, it does not act with the impartiality which its character of neutral imposes upon it, even though it should concede to Mexico the same privilege. Among the authorities which served as a foundation for the honorable Secretary of the Treasury for adopting the decision referred to are found, in the first place, and which I consider as the principal one, the instructions which Mr. Alexander Hamilton communicated on the 4th of August, 1793, to the collectors of customs of the United States, in consequence of the proclamation which President George Washington had issued on the 22d day of April preceding, recognizing the state of war then existing between Austria, Prussia, Sardinia, Great Britain, and the Netherlands on the one part, and France upon the other, and declaring the neutrality of the United States in the same.

In these instructions Mr. Hamilton said (American State Papers, series of Foreign Affairs, vol. 1, page 141) that "the purchasing within and exporting from the United States, by *way of merchandise*, articles commonly called contraband, should not be interfered with;" and, according to this principle, the purchase and exportation of the effects purchased by the French officers should not be permitted, inasmuch as they have not been made *by way of merchandise*, but, on the contrary, for the immediate and direct use of a belligerent army. It is well understood that the government of the United States would not be willing to prevent the sale of such articles to French merchants who would purchase them to speculate upon them by selling them to a third power, or, perhaps, to their own government, for the fear that the latter should occur, ought not to authorize a general prohibition, but that it should extend these principles to the purchase of the articles referred to by officers of the French army, and for the immediate use of the same army, is a matter which cannot be conceived of, because it is equivalent to laying aside neutrality, and to open the door to all nations that be at war, in which the United States are not a party, in order that, in exchange for a small profit, they may come to provide themselves here with whatever they may require to carry on hostilities.

The authorities of Mr. Webster, which are cited in the document annexed to the communication of the honorable the Secretary of the Treasury of the 20th of November last past, of which you are pleased to transmit me a copy, are in contrariety with the instructions of Mr. Hamilton, and there cannot be given to them, in my opinion, the same weight as to the latter, for the first are fragments of communications addressed by Mr. Webster, as Secretary of State of the United States, to Mr. Thompson, minister of the United States in Mexico, to justify the government of the United States from the complaints which that of Mexico made to it for the moral and material support which the first gave, at that time, to the insurgents of Texas. It is known that all the sympathies of the administration then existing were on the side of the insurgents, which caused it to encourage them in every way, in order to accomplish the enterprise in which they were engaged, while, at the same time, the United States called themselves neutrals in the contest. The principles laid down then by Mr. Webster had for their object to reconcile that neutrality with the aid given to the insurgents; and assuredly, if the government of the United States should examine them now, when the circumstances are different, and when the administration is animated with a spirit of greater justice, it would not sustain them, nor would it be willing that foreign nations should adopt them as a basis in their relations with the United States, as it does not appear disposed to sustain, in this emergency, the principles which governed it then to recognize the independence of Texas much earlier than Mexico was disposed to make such a recognition.

There is an instance of a similar case in which the United States proceeded in accordance with the principles of Vattel, and the reason which they had for it holds good with the same force in the present case Mr. Henry Wheaton, in the 16th paragraph of chapter III, of part IV of his "Elements of International Law," referring to the principles of Vattel, which I have already cited, says: "These principles were appealed to by the American government when its neutrality was attempted to be violated on the commencement of the European war of 1793, by arming and equipping vessels and enlisting men within the ports of the United States by the respective belligerent powers to cruise against each other. It was stated that if the neutral power might not, consistently with its neutrality, furnish men to either party for their aid in war, as little could either enrol them in the neutral territory."

Applying this reasoning to the present case, it follows that the United States cannot, because of its neutrality, give to France arms, munitions of war, and other articles contraband of war, neither can it permit that the French army shall come to take them from the neutral territory.

Great Britain, which adopted the American doctrine in that which relates to the enlistment of troops in its territory by a belligerent power, has been more consistent, for it also adopted the consequences which are inferred from this principle; and when it declares itself neutral in the wars between other powers, it accompanies this declaration with the prohibition that the belligerents shall not supply themselves in their ports with articles contraband of war, unless that, by special treaties, she is under the obligation of extending them to both or either of the belligerents.

President Franklin Pierce, in his message to the thirty-fourth Congress of the United States, of the 1st of September, 1855, which is another of the authorities cited by the honorable the Secretary of the Treasury, whilst he considers as a violation of the neutrality of the United States the pretensions of any of the European powers then allied against Russia to enrol troops in the territories of these same States, follows the doctrine of Mr. Webster respecting the sale of articles contraband of war made by its citizens to any one of the belligerent powers. President Pierce forgot the condition that the sale be made *by way of merchandise*, considered as indispensable by Mr. Hamilton to make it lawful. He also says that there is no law prohibiting to the citizens of the United States the sale of articles contraband of war to either of the belligerent parties; but if there be no such secondary law, there exists the natural tendency of the law of nations, which imposes such a prohibition upon the neutral powers as one of the circumstances inherent to neutrality. If the government should extend to Mexico the same principles which govern it in its relations with France, as little satisfactory as such conduct would be, because it would thus be to abandon neutrality and to furnish to the French army the means of transportation, without which it would have been obliged to remain inactive until these could arrive from Europe, giving time to the Mexican government to organize a more vigorous resistance, yet it would not have been to so great an extent as it was on refusing to Mexico the same facilities which are conceded to France.

At the commencement of February of the present year the Mexican consul at New York informed me that several merchants of that port were sending to Vera

Cruz vessels laden with provisions and other articles for the consumption of the allied army, which was then in that city. At a conference with which you favored me on the 13th of the said month of February I had the honor to inform you of these facts, and I took the liberty to suggest to you that, if the United States held the character of a neutral in the differences between Mexico and the allies, the federal government should forbid the exportation of articles contraband of war intended to give aid directly to one of the belligerents. You were pleased to reply to me that the United States did not recognize a state of war existing between Mexico and the allies. As there had been, you said, no declaration of war, they could not, for the same reason, be governed in their conduct by the rules of neutrals, for up to that time this government considered Mexico and the allies as friends, and not as belligerents. In view of such reasonable explanations, I desisted from my first suggestion, and, as was natural, I understood that the government of the United States would not object that Mexico should take from this country what she might need whilst the state of things then existing should continue; and provided that Mexico should be permitted to make use of this right, I would make no opposition to the exercise of the same being granted to the allies.

Shortly afterwards the circumstance arose that Mexico purchased some arms in New York, which the agent commissioned to make this purchase desired to ship to a Mexican port which the honorable the Secretary of the Treasury had closed to the commerce of the United States, in violation of the rights of Mexico and in contravention of the stipulations of the treaty of friendship, navigation, and commerce, which binds the United States to Mexico, as I had the honor to make known to you in the notes which I addressed you on the 23d of July and the 10th of September, 1861. The circumstance that, in accordance with the instructions of the honorable the Secretary of the Treasury, his permit was necessary, in order that the custom-house of New York might clear vessels to the said port, was the only cause of my application to the Treasury Department, soliciting extra officially this permit. Upon doing so I determined simply to make known that these arms were for Mexico and not for the insurgents of the United States, believing that this would be sufficient for the honorable the Secretary of the Treasury to grant the proper clearance. The aspect of the affairs of Mexico had then changed with respect to that in which it was in February last. The difficulties existing were then no longer between Mexico and the European allies, but between Mexico and France; and although the war existed in fact, it had not been declared, neither did I know that such a declaration, which had not been made, had been communicated to the government of the United States, nor that this government had taken official notice of such a war, which had begun like a filibustering enterprise, in contravention of the most trivial principles of the law of nations, and least of all did I know that this government intended to remain neutral in this war. Had I known this I should not have dared to inform it of a transaction which had been entered into to the loss of its rights as a neutral, nor much less to ask it to authorize it in violation of the duties which its neutrality imposed upon it. My duty would have been to advise the agent who came to purchase the arms to go and seek them elsewhere, for here they could not be obtained without loss to the rights of the United States, which I have ever been disposed to respect in the most scrupulous manner. The honorable the Secretary of the Treasury at first showed himself willing to concede the permit asked for; he asked me for the list of the effects which were to be sent to Mexico, and, upon showing it to him, it appeared to him that the number, 36,000 muskets, was too great a one, and he said to me that he would only give the permit for exporting them in case that the honorable the Secretaries of the Navy and War should make no objection to the exportation of the arms. The honorable the Secretary of the Navy made none, and the Secretary of War said that "he refused to relax the order previously issued forbidding the exportation of arms."

Neither the collector of the customs of New York, nor the honorable the Secretary of the Treasury, seemed to be aware of the order to which the honorable the Secretary of War referred; but his decision in the present case was sufficient for them to refuse in the most positive and absolute manner the clearance of the muskets purchased by Mexico. In vain did I endeavor to show to both the honorable Secretaries that these arms were Prussian muskets, flint-locks, subsequently altered to percussion locks, and of such a quality that the army of the United States would never use them. All my efforts were in vain; and the impression which was left to me, as the result of my exertions, was that the government of the United States had opposed the departure of the arms, not because it believed that the occasion might arise when it would need them for its army—inasmuch as there was in the stores of New York a larger number and of a very superior quality—but to avoid complications with France, which, it was feared, would be consequent upon the clearance of the arms to a Mexican port. I was finally confirmed in this opinion upon learning that subsequently to my said exertions the honorable Secretary of the Treasury expressly notified the collector of the custom-house of New York on no account to clear the arms aforesaid, and that the same custom-house has cleared, subsequently to these exertions, arms to ports which are not Mexican ports. I felt, therefore, that there had not been towards me the sufficient frankness to tell me the true cause why the clearance of the arms purchased by Mexico was denied, which would have saved me many steps; for, from the moment it should have been communicated to me that the United States were neutrals in the war between France and Mexico, and that the clearance of these arms was not compatible with the duties which their neutrality imposed upon them, I should have considered the affair as concluded, conceding all the reason to this government. It is, therefore, easy to understand how great was my surprise upon learning that when France came to purchase articles contraband of war in this country, when it has made of it the base whence it supplies its invading army, in a war in which I had been made to understand that the United States were neutrals, the honorable Secretary of the Treasury, relying upon authorities in my opinion totally insufficient, should have conceded to France the same thing which he so peremptorily refused to Mexico. For Mexico it is the same thing that to it should be denied what is permitted to France, by order of the honorable Secretary of War, or by the decision of any other honorable Secretary; she cannot enter into the examination of the reasons which may have caused such an order, and she can only see the palpable and incontrovertible fact that, whilst to France it is permitted to supply herself in the market of the United States with whatever she requires to carry on her war against Mexico, without excepting the articles contraband of war, to Mexico is prohibited the exportation of the only article which she needed, and the only one she had purchased in this country. As I am considering the question under the point of view of the right only, and as I understand that the United States are neutrals in the war between Mexico and France, I refrain from entering into other considerations which would present the conduct of the United States in a light still more unfavorable. The gravity of the present case, which affects so directly the rights and interests of Mexico, causes me to believe that so soon as my government shall be informed of what has occurred in this respect, it will send me precise instructions by which to abide.

Then I shall again have the honor to communicate with you upon this same affair. For the present, I have only taken the liberty to lay before you the considerations which precede, because I do not desire that my silence be taken as an indication of acquiescence in the determination contained in your note, to which I reply.

I avail myself of this opportunity to renew to you, sir, the assurances of my very distinguished consideration.

M. ROMERO.

Hon. WILLIAM H. SEWARD, *&c.*, *&c.*, *&c.*

Mr. Seward to Mr. Romero.

DEPARTMENT OF STATE,
Washington, December 15, 1862.

The undersigned, Secretary of State of the United States, has the honor to acknowledge the reception of the note which was addressed to him by his excellency Mr. M. Romero, chargé d'affaires of the republic of Mexico, on the 10th of December instant, in which Mr. Romero states his objections to the decision of this government which permits the clearance of vessels from New York, carrying cargoes of certain wagons and other merchandise purchased and designed, as Mr. Romero says, for the use of the French forces in Mexico. Mr. Romero assumes that this decision manifests partiality on the part of this government towards France.

The undersigned has the honor to inform Mr. Romero that the trade of the United States is regulated by treaties and laws which are equal in regard to France and to Mexico, and to all other nations, without any exceptions, whether they are mutually at peace or engaged in war; that whatever merchandise is allowed to be cleared for or on account of French subjects or of the French government, is equally allowed to be cleared for the citizens or for the government of Mexico, and for all other nations.

Mr. Romero builds his argument upon the fact that clearances of arms said to be designed for the use of the Mexican government were denied in its war with France, while clearances of wagons designed for the use of the French government in the same war are allowed.

Mr. Romero is respectfully informed that prohibition of the shipment of arms, in the case referred to, was a general prohibition, including all other nations as well as Mexico, on the ground of the military necessities of the United States, which, while engaged in suppressing a formidable insurrection, cannot consent that fire-arms of any kind shall be sent out of the country as merchandise.

For these reasons—first, because the government may need all such arms; and, secondly, that they might fall into the hands of the insurgents—neither the French, who are at war with Mexico, nor any other nation which is at peace with the United States, no matter what its condition or its situation, could now be allowed to export arms of any sort from this country. Mr. Romero implies, probably with truth, that wagons are as necessary and will be as useful to the French as fire-arms would be to the Mexicans. But the pertinency of the argument is not apparent, insomuch as the shipment of arms is denied to Mexico on the ground, not of want of them on her part as a belligerent, but on the ground of the military situation of the United States; and, on the other hand, the wagons are allowed to be shipped, not on the ground that France wants them as a belligerent, but on the ground that the military situation of the United States does not demand an inhibition.

The republic of Mexico enjoys the sincere friendship and good will of the United States, and they lament the war which has arisen between that republic and France. They are not, however, a party to the war, and since it has unhappily occurred, they can act in regard to it only on the principles which have always governed their conduct in similar cases. The trade of the United States, according to these principles, is left free to both nations, just as if they were at peace with each other, and no restrictions are imposed upon it to the favor or prejudice of either nation.

The argument of the Secretary of the Treasury, which has been already submitted to Mr. Romero, renders it unnecessary to say more to elucidate the settled and traditional policy of the country. It is not easy to see how that policy could be changed so as to conform to the views of Mr. Romero, without destroying all neutral commerce whatsoever. If Mexico shall prescribe to us what merchandise we shall not sell to French subjects, because it may be employed in military operations against Mexico, France must equally be allowed to dictate to us what merchandise we shall allow to be shipped to Mexico, because it might be belligerently used against France. Every other nation which is at war would have a similar right, and every other commercial nation would be bound to respect it as much as the United States. Commerce, in that case, instead of being free or independent, would exist only at the caprice of war.

The undersigned, in thus expressing to Mr. Romero the views of this government upon the question which Mr. Romero has submitted, does not at all desire to conclude him from the further presentation of the subject, which he promises to make after he shall have received the instructions upon the subject from his government.

The undersigned avails himself of this occasion to offer to Mr. Romero a renewed assurance of his high consideration.

WILLIAM H. SEWARD,

Señor Don MATIAS ROMERO, *&c.*, *&c.*, *&c.*

Mr. Romero to Mr. Seward.

[Translation.]

MEXICAN LEGATION IN THE UNITED STATES OF AMERICA,
Washington, December 20, 1862.

The undersigned, chargé d'affaires of the United Mexican States, has had the honor to receive the note which the honorable William H. Seward, Secretary of State of the United States of America, was pleased to address to him on the 15th of the present month, in reply to the communication of the undersigned of the 10th instant, in which he stated the reasons which caused him to consider as partial in favor of France the conduct followed by the government of the United States in permitting the emissaries of the French army to purchase and export from the ports of this country whatever that army requires to carry out the military operations against Mexico, in which it is engaged, while at the same time the same privilege has been denied to the Mexican republic.

In his note referred to, the honorable Secretary of State is pleased to inform the undersigned that "the trade of the United States is regulated by treaties and laws which are equal in regard to France and to Mexico, and to all other nations, without any exception, whether they are mutually at peace or engaged in war." The undersigned was not unaware that the United States have the obligation to regulate their trade with friendly nations, by the stipulations to which they have bound themselves in the treaties which bind them to these nations, and he precisely had these considerations present when he wrote his note of the 10th instant, and in it he only proposed to himself to exact from the government of the United States the fulfilment of a duty which the United States contracted towards Mexico, in the treaty of the 5th of April, 1831, at present in force between both powers. The obligation imposed by said treaty upon the two contracting governments appeared so clear to the undersigned that he did not deem it necessary to remind the honorable Secretary of State of the articles in which it is contained; but inasmuch as he is informed that the trade of the United States is regulated by treaties, he deems it his duty to be more precise upon asking the fulfilment of the stipulations of these treaties.

Article 16th of the treaty of the 5th of April stipulates that "it shall be lawful for the citizens of the United States of America and of the United Mexican States, respectively, to sail with their vessels with all manner of security and liberty, no distinction being made who are the owners of the merchandise laden thereon, from any port to the places of those who now are or may hereafter be at enmity with the United States of America or with the United Mexican States. It shall likewise be lawful for the aforesaid citizens, respectively, to sail with their vessels and merchandise, before mentioned, and to trade with the same liberty and security from the places, ports, and havens of those who are enemies of both or either party without any opposition or disturbance whatsoever, not only directly from the places of the enemy, before mentioned, to neutral places, but also from one place belonging to an enemy to another place belonging to an enemy, whether they be under the jurisdiction of the same government or under several."

So ample a liberty of trading is found shortly after wisely restricted in article 18th, which says: "This liberty of commerce and navigation shall extend to all kinds of merchandise, excepting those only which are distinguished by the name of contraband of war." * * * * * *

If it then appears that the articles purchased in the United States by the emissaries of the French army, and carried to Vera Cruz in vessels of the United States, are of the character of those called contraband of war, it is indubitable that the commerce and navigation of such articles are unlawful, agreeably to the stipulations of the treaty which binds the United States to Mexico.

The articles referred to have consisted principally of mules and wagons, and to these the undersigned exclusively referred in his last note upon the subject. The said 18th article of the treaty of the 5th of April enumerates the articles prohibited which are comprehended under the qualification of contraband of war, and in the third section it mentions expressly *horses with their furniture;* and the fourth terminates by saying, "or of any other materials manufactured, prepared, and formed expressly to make war by sea or land."

The undersigned deems it altogether unnecessary to make any effort to show that the mules as well as the wagons which form the means of transportation, without which the military operations are impossible, are included among the articles which the treaty enumerates as of the character of contraband of war.

From what has been manifested, it appears that Mexico has not thought of perscribing to the United States what merchandise they may sell to French subjects, and what are those they cannot sell to them, as the honorable Secretary of States seems to have understood it.

It (Mexico) has only desired that the United States should comply with one of the obligations which the treaty which binds them to Mexico imposes upon them, and that they do not permit a trade which the treaty referred to declares to be illegal. This just claim is exactly the same which the government of the United States has been making for several months upon the British government, and the undersigned cannot have been less than greatly surprised upon seeing that what this government deems it just to exact from that of Great Britain, it should not deem it just to concede to that of Mexico. As the despatches upon which the opinion of the undersigned is founded are familiar to the honorable Secretary of State, he abstains from citing the precise text of them, which have been recently published by the Department of State with the President's message of the 1st instant. In adopting this course, the undersigned has been also governed by the desire of not extending too much the present note; but if the honorable Secretary of State should question this assertion, the undersigned will have the honor to further discuss this subject more lengthily hereafter in another communication.

The undersigned cannot consider that the general order which prohibits the exportation of arms from the United States is the cause that the clearance of those purchased by Mexico should have been denied; first, because the date of the only general order of prohibition which has come to his knowledge and to that of the merchants of New York is subsequent to that refusal; secondly, because subsequently to that refusal, arms have been cleared for other ports which are not Mexican ports; thirdly, because the honorable Secretary of the Treasury issued an order to the collector of the custom-house of New York expressly prohibiting the clearance of the arms referred to, which would have been entirely useless if there had been a general order forbidding such clearances; and fourthly, because the custom-house of New York granted the clearance of the same arms purchased by Mexico, when it was asked for Quebec; and when this government received notice that they would be shipped thence to a Mexican port, it ordered them to be detained and returned to New York.

The honorable Secretary of State will understand that it is not the object of the undersigned to solicit that the clearance of arms to Mexico be permitted. He believed that Mexico had the right to purchase them and export them from the United States before this government should have recognized the state of war existing between Mexico and France; but from the moment when it declared itself neutral in such war, he only asks that the same principles be applied to France which with so much rigor were applied to Mexico, even before such declaration had been made; for should it not do so, the undersigned will find himself under the painful necessity of considering the conduct of the government of the United States as but little friendly towards Mexico, and as contrary to the obligations which their character of a neutral imposes upon them.

The undersigned avails himself of this opportunity to renew to the honorable William H. Seward, Secretary of State of the United States, the assurances of his most distinguished consideration.

M. ROMERO.

Hon. WILLIAM H. SEWARD, *&c., &c., &c.*

Mr. Seward to Mr. Romero.

DEPARTMENT OF STATE,
Washington, January 7, 1863.

The undersigned, Secretary of State of the United States, has the honor to acknowledge the reception of the note of his excellency, Mr. Romero, chargé d'affaires of the republic of Mexico, which bears date of December 20, and relates to the subject of the clearances of certain articles of merchandise at the city of New York, alleged by Mr. Romero to have been made on account of French subjects, for the use of the French government in its war with Mexico.

In the note which the undersigned addressed to Mr. Romero on this subject on the 15th of December last, and also in an exposition of the same subject which was made by the Secretary of the Treasury, and which was submitted to Mr. Romero, it was explained that the clearances of which he complains were made in conformity with the laws of the United States, and with the practical construction of those laws which has prevailed from the foundation of this government—a period which includes wars, more or less general, throughout the world, and involving many states situated on the American and European continents.

The undersigned, after the most careful reading of Mr. Romero's note, is unable to concede that the government of the United States has obliged itself to prohibit the exportation of mules and wagons, for which it has no military need, from its ports, on French account, because, being in a state of war and needing for the use of the government all the fire-arms made and found in the country, it has temporarily forbidden the export of such weapons to all nations. Nor is it perceived how the treaty between the United States and Mexico, to which Mr. Romero refers, bears upon the question, since the United States have not set up, or thought of setting up, any claim that Mexico shall be required to admit into her ports any articles of merchandise contraband of war which may be exported from the United States on French or any other account.

The undersigned is equally unable to perceive the bearing of Mr. Romero's allusions to the correspondence which has occurred between this government and that of Great Britain, in which complaints have been made by the United States that Great Britain wrongfully and injuriously recognized, as a public belligerent, an insurrectionary faction which has arisen in this country; has proclaimed neutrality between that faction and this government; and has suffered armed naval expeditions to be fitted out in British ports to depredate on the commerce of the United States in violation of, as was believed, the Queen's proclamation and of the municipal laws of the United Kingdom.

The undersigned avails himself of this occasion to renew to Mr. Romero the assurances of his most distinguished consideration.

WILLIAM H. SEWARD.

Señor Don MATIAS ROMERO,
Chargé d'Affaires of the Mexican Republic, Washington, D. C.

Mr. Romero to Mr. Seward.

[Translation.]

MEXICAN LEGATION IN THE UNITED STATES OF AMERICA,
Washington, January 14, 1863.

The undersigned, chargé d'affaires of the United Mexican States, has had the honor of receiving, to-day, the note which, under date of the 7th instant, the Hon. William H. Seward, Secretary of State of the United States of America, was pleased to address to him in regard to the clearance, from ports of the United States, of articles contraband of war, purchased by emissaries of the French army invading Mexico, for the use of that army.

Although the undersigned, in compliance with his duty, has left the determination of this delicate affair to his government, as he has informed the honorable Secretary of State, he thinks he is bound to make some observations which occur to him, in view of the argument contained in the note that he has just received from the Department of State of the United States.

The honorable Secretary of State says that he has not been able to perceive what congruency there is between the articles mentioned by the undersigned in his note of December 20, 1862, of the treaty which binds Mexico and the United States to each other, and the present question, "since the United States have not set up, or thought of setting up, any claim that Mexico shall be required to admit into her ports any articles of merchandise contraband of war which may be exported from the United States on French, or any other, account." As, in the opinion of the undersigned, there can be no doubt that the present question is regulated by the stipulations which have been mentioned, he requests the honorable Secretary of State to permit him again to refer to them.

The undersigned has maintained that the exportation from the United States of articles contraband of war, purchased by emissaries of the French army invading Mexico for the use of that army, is illegal according to the stipulations of the treaty of friendship, commerce, and navigation concluded between Mexico and the United States on the 5th of April, 1831. Article 16 declares legal the most ample liberty of commerce and navigation between the two countries, and article 18 provides that such liberty of navigation and commerce is not extended to articles contraband of war. If, therefore, the traffic in these articles is illegal, it is the duty of the government of the United States not to authorize it; and in granting to it the same liberty and the same franchises as to the traffic in articles of lawful commerce, this government fails to comply with one of the obligations imposed on it by said treaty.

Nor has the honorable Secretary of State discovered any similarity between this case and that which appears in the recently published correspondence between this government and that of Great Britain, to which the undersigned referred in his said note of the 20th of December last, expressing his surprise that the government of the United States should deem it just to demand from the government of Great Britain what it is unwilling to concede to that of Mexico.

It is true that what the United States have chiefly complained of against the British government is the fitting out at and sailing from British ports of naval expeditions organized by the insurrectionary States, with which the United States are now at war; but this government has not limited itself to asking the British government not to permit the fitting out and sailing of such expeditions; it has gone further. It has demanded that it should not permit the purchase and exportation from British ports of articles contraband of war intended for insurrectionary States, which is exactly what the undersigned has thought he had a right to demand of this government.

Lord Russell, in replying on the 10th of May, 1862, to a note which on the 8th of the same month had been addressed to him by the minister of the United States accredited near the British government, in which he had proposed that the statute of George IV, of 3d July, 1819, which prohibits the enlistment of British subjects in armies of belligerent powers, when Great Britain is neutral, might be amended, said what will be found on page 93 of the diplomatic correspondence annexed to the annual message of the President of the United States of the 1st of December, 1862, which is entirely the same position in which the government of the United States has desired to place itself with respect to Mexico, and which is as follows: "The foreign enlistment act is intended to prevent the subjects of the crown from going to war when the sovereign is not at war. * * * In these cases (enlistment in a belligerent army and the fitting out of vessels) the persons so acting would carry on war, and thus might engage the name of their sovereign and of their nation in belligerent operations. But owners and freighters of vessels carrying warlike stores do nothing of the kind. If captured for breaking a blockade or carrying contraband of war to the enemy of the captor, they submit to capture, are tried, and condemned to lose their cargo." * * *

Mr. Adams replied to Lord Russell on the 12th of the said month of May, (page 94,) as follows: "The position which I did mean to take is this: that the *intent* of the enlistment act, as explained by the words of its preamble, was to prevent the unauthorized action of subjects of Great Britain, disposed to embark in the contests of foreign nations, from involving the country in the risk of a war with these countries. This view of the law does not seem to be materially varied by your lordship. When speaking of the same thing you say that the law applies to cases where 'private persons so acting would carry on war, and thus might engage the name of their sovereign and of their nation in belligerent operations.' It is further shown by that preamble, that that act was an additional act of prevention, made necessary by experience of the inefficiency of former acts passed to effect the same object.

"But it is now made plain that whatever may have been the skill with which this latest act was drawn, it does not completely fulfil its intent, because it is very certain that many British subjects are now engaged in undertakings of a hostile character to a foreign state, which, though not technically within the strict letter of the enlistment act, are as much contrary to its spirit as if they levied war directly. Their measures embrace all the operations preliminary to openly carrying on war—the supply of men and ships and arms and money to one party, in order that they may be the better enabled to overcome the other, which other is in this case a nation with which Great Britain is now under treaty obligations of the most solemn nature to maintain a lasting peace and friendship." * * * * * * *

This is exactly what the undersigned has solicited since the discussion of this affair began, in the note which he addressed to the Department of State on the 10th of December last.

This view of the question is not exclusive to Mr. Adams: the honorable Secretary of State, in the despatch which he addressed to the minister of the United States at London, on the 2d of June, 1862, (page 108,) adopts it entirely in saying to him as follows: "There has just now fallen into our hands a very extraordinary document, being a report made by Caleb Huse, who calls himself a captain of artillery, and who is an agent of the insurgents in Europe for the purchase of arms, munitions of war, and military supplies, which have been shipped by him in England and elsewhere, in the mad attempt to overthrow the federal Union. It reveals enough to show that the complaints you have made to Earl Russell fell infinitely short of the real abuses of neutrality which have been committed in Great Britain in the very face of her Majesty's government."

* * * * * * * *

In writing those lines it seems the honorable Secretary of State had forgotten the doctrine which he now says is "conformable to the laws of the United States, and to the practical application of those laws which has prevailed since the foundation of this government."

Among the so-called authorities which have governed the course of the honorable Secretary of the Treasury, and which were submitted to the undersigned, and have again been referred to by the honorable Secretary of State, is the following fragment of the instructions communicated by Mr. Webster to Mr. Thompson, on the 8th of July, 1842, that is as follows:

"As to advances, loans, or donations of money or goods, made by individuals to the government of Texas or its citizens, the Mexican government needs not to be informed that there is nothing unlawful in this, so long as Texas is at peace with the United States, and that there are things which no government undertakes to restrain."

This sentence, which in the opinion of the government of the United States is an authority that may be applied to Mexico with the same rigor as if it were an article of the international code, loses all its force when it concerns the United States. A while ago the consul of the United States at Liverpool learned that in that city a subscription was being raised of £40,000 to assist the insurgents of this country, to whom England had conceded all the rights of belligerents. Instead of the honorable Secretary of State seeing in this transaction a matter "in which there was nothing unlawful, so long as England was at peace with the southern States, and one of those things which no government thinks of prohibiting," he addressed, under date of the 1st of May, 1862, (page 78,) a despatch to Mr. Adams, recommending him to call the attention of Lord Russell to the transaction. Evidently the honorable Secretary of State did not propose that Mr. Adams should speak to Lord Russell of this affair with a view of approving of it and of manifesting that there was nothing unlawful in it, but that he should request the English government to apply a remedy to this want of neutrality.

In the archives of the United States, as in those of other nations, there are opposite opinions on all questionable points; even on those which can hardly be a subject of discussion. In the present case, it seems to the undersigned that the honorable Secretary of the Treasury has only collected those *authorities* which do not favor the just cause of Mexico. The undersigned might present, in support of his good right, another list of American authorities more numerous and more weighty than those which appear to have induced the honorable Secretary of the Treasury to concede to France what separates the United States from that neutrality which they declare that they wish to observe in the war between Mexico and the Emperor of the French.

The honorable Secretary of State is pleased to inform the undersigned that the prohibition against exporting arms from the ports of the United States, which was first adopted to the prejudice of Mexico only, and which afterwards became general, is a *temporary* measure. The opinion which the undersigned holds respecting the motives which have induced the government of the United States to prohibit the exportation of arms to Mexico—an opinion founded on undeniable facts—would fail to be justified if the prohibition against exporting arms will be raised when, on account of the French having occupied or blockaded the whole coast of Mexico, it would be entirely impossible to introduce arms into the republic.

The undersigned avails himself of this opportunity to renew to the honorable William H. Seward, Secretary of State of the United States, the assurances of his most distinguished consideration.

M. ROMERO.

Hon. WILLIAM H. SEWARD, *&c.*, *&c.*, *&c.*

Mr. Seward to Mr. Romero.

DEPARTMENT OF STATE,
Washington, January 17, 1863.

The undersigned, Secretary of State of the United States, has had the honor to receive the note which was addressed to him on the 14th instant by Mr. Romero, concerning the action of the Treasury Department in relation to shipments of goods at New York for Mexican ports.

The undersigned, while seeing no cause further to expatiate upon the reasons heretofore offered in explanation of that measure, avails himself of this occasion to offer to Mr. Romero a renewed assurance of his high consideration.

WILLIAM H. SEWARD.

Señor MATÍAS ROMERO, *&c.*, *&c.*, *&c.*

Mr. Rankin to Mr. Seward.

[Telegram.]

SAN FRANCISCO, *January* 14, 1863.

French consul desires me to prevent shipment of contraband goods to Mexico. Shall I comply? If yes, what articles deemed contraband?

IRA P. RANKIN, *Collector.*

Hon. WILLIAM H. SEWARD,
Secretary of State.

Mr. Seward to Mr. Rankin.

[Telegram.]

DEPARTMENT OF STATE,
Washington, January 15, 1863.

Your telegram of the 14th has been received. Subjoined is a copy of an executive order of the 30th November last, which will serve as an answer to your inquiry.

WILLIAM H. SEWARD.

IRA P. RANKIN,
Collector of Customs, San Francisco.

EXECUTIVE MANSION,
Washington City, November 20, 1862.

Ordered, That no arms, ammunition, or munitions of war be cleared or allowed to be exported from the United States until further order. That any clearances of arms, ammunition, or munitions of war issued heretofore by the Treasury Department be vacated, if the articles have not passed without the United States, and the articles stopped. That the Secretary of War hold possession of the arms, &c., recently seized by his order at Rouse's Point, bound for Canada.

ABRAHAM LINCOLN.

Mr. Romero to Mr. Seward.

[Translation.]

MEXICAN LEGATION IN THE UNITED STATES OF AMERICA,
Washington, January 20, 1863.

The undersigned, chargé d'affaires of the United Mexican States, has the honor to address himself to the Hon. William H. Seward, Secretary of State of the United States of America, to inform him that he has received a communication, dated the 17th of this month, from the Mexican citizen Camilo Cámara, now sojourning in New York, and of which he encloses a copy. From this communication it appears that the custom-house at New York refuses to clear, for the port of Sisal, a cargo of powder, lead, and flint-stones, intended to sustain the war which the government of Yucatan is waging against the revolted Indians of that peninsula.

As all that has come to the knowledge of the undersigned is, that the exportation of arms to Mexico is the only thing which the government of the United States has prohibited up to this time, he could not less than be surprised at seeing that the prohibition is being extended to the other articles contraband of war which Mexico is in want of, even though she does not intend to make use of them in the war which the republic is sustaining against the Emperor of the French.

The undersigned would be thankful to the honorable the Secretary of State if he would be pleased to inform him, if it be possible, what are the articles, besides arms, the exportation of which to the ports of Mexico, which are in the possession of the authorities of the republic, this government has prohibited.

The undersigned would also be pleased to know if the honorable the Secretary of State would have the goodness to inform him whether this government proposes to clear, or not, the cargo to which the said letter of Mr. Cámara refers.

The undersigned avails himself of this opportunity to renew to the Hon. Wm. H. Seward, Secretary of State of the United States, the assurances of his most distinguished consideration.

M. ROMERO.

Hon. WILLIAM H. SEWARD, *&c.*, *&c.*, *&c.*

[Translation.]

NEW YORK, *January* 17, 1863.

HONORED SIR: I, the undersigned, a Mexican citizen, a native and a merchant of Yucatan, at the present time sojourning in this city for the purpose of commercial pursuits, as is customary, most respectfully do make known to you that I have been much surprised that the custom-house in this place should not permit me to ship, in either an American or a foreign vessel, a small quantity of powder, lead, and flint-stones, which my consignees in this city, Messrs. Riera & Thébaud, merchants thereof, have endeavored to ship for my account on an English vessel, and destined to Sisal, for the use of that state. You cannot but know, sir, that we have no other means of supplying ourselves with these articles, unless it be from the United States, whence they have always been carried, and at the same time you know that in our country it is indispensable to us to have powder and other articles of war, owing most especially to the desolating war now being carried on against us by the rebellious Indians. Independently of these considerations we have to call your attention to the fact that, while we are prevented from a lawful trade in these articles of war, it is said they have permitted here the exportation of effects for the French, who are actually waging war against our republic.

My aforesaid consignees have written upon the subject to the War Department at Washington, offering to give a security until we shall send a certificate from Yucatan, in which it is certified that these articles have been landed in, and are for the use of, that country, and to the said letter, of which I enclose you a copy, no answer has as yet been received. A disposition so arbitrary and illegal, preventing the shipment of certain articles to Mexico, not only does injury to the different states of the republic, by depriving them of the revenues which these articles would produce, and necessary to their consumption, but, in a very direct manner, to the commerce and government of Yucatan, which requires them to oppose the rebellious Indians. I do not see what lawful objection there is to prevent a traffic guaranteed by the treaties which exist between the two countries; and considering that my reasons are well founded, and that your co-operation in this case is made necessary, I take the liberty to request you to take the trouble to attend to this, my petition, with the least possible delay, inasmuch as the vessel which will carry my invoice is now being loaded, by applying for this purpose to the War Department to obtain the permission for shipping these effects hence for Yucatan, with the guarantee, if they desire it, of the respectable signatures of Messrs. Riera & Thébaud, as has been done in other similar cases.

The interest you may take in this matter, as our worthy representative, is the only means of favorably settling this business for us, and I do not doubt that you will be pleased to extend your protection to me.

In the event of your needing my address, you will address me to the care of Messrs. Riera & Thébaud, and meanwhile I have the honor to place myself at your service.

Your very obedient servant,

CAMILO CAMARA.

Señor DON M. ROMERO,
Minister from the Mexican Republic, in Washington.

Mr. Seward to Mr. Romero.

DEPARTMENT OF STATE,
Washington, January 21, 1863.

SIR: In reply to your note of yesterday expressing surprise at the refusal of the custom-house authorities to clear for the port of Sisal a cargo of powder, lead, and flint-stones, and desiring to be informed what are the articles the exportation of which has been prohibited by this government, I have the honor to state that, on the 20th November last, an executive order from the President of the United States directed "that no arms, ammunition, or munitions of war be cleared or allowed to be exported from the United States until further order."

I am not aware that this order has been relaxed or rescinded, nor do I perceive the propriety or expediency of remitting it under existing circumstances.

I avail, &c., &c.,

WILLIAM H. SEWARD.

Señor MATIAS ROMERO, *&c., &c., &c.*

General Canby to Mr. Seward.

WAR DEPARTMENT,
Washington City, February 17, 1864.

SIR: The Secretary of War instructs me to submit to you the enclosed letter and accompaniments from T. Lemmen Meyer, San Francisco, soliciting, for himself and others, permission to ship blasting powder from that port, for the use of designated mines in Mexico, and to request the expression of your opinion upon the propriety and expediency of granting the privilege asked for.

I have the honor to be your obedient servant,

ED. R. S. CANBY,
Brigadier General, A. A. G.

The SECRETARY OF STATE,
Washington, D. C.

Mr. Meyer to Mr. Stanton.

SAN FRANCISCO, *January* 16, 1864.

SIR: I beg to accompany two petitions, signed by me, entreating you to allow the exportation of a certain amount of powder for the use of two mines in Mexico in which I am interested. The damages that would accrue from the want of powder are so well known to your honor that I abstain from mentioning them, and I will limit myself to state, for the sake of not occupying your valuable time, that the French consul in this city having no objection to its exportation, and the French minister in your city consenting to it, (as he will most likely do,) the only party which, in my opinion, remains with the right to either allow or prohibit its exportation is the United States government.

Allow me to offer you, honorable sir, my most sincere respects.

T. LEMMEN MEYER.

Hon. EDWIN M. STANTON,
Secretary of the United States War Department, Washington, D. C.

SAN FRANCISCO, *January* 16, 1864.

DEAR SIR: Most respectfully and earnestly do we request of you permission to make monthly shipments of twenty kegs of blasting powder to the "Agua Grande" copper mine, located at Sonora, Mexico, whereof W. Randall is superintendent. Said blasting or mining powder to be in kegs, holding 25 pounds each, purchased from Edward H. Parker, San Francisco, agent of the Hazard Powder Company, New York, and to be shipped by us to the port of Guaymas, Mexico, on board the steamer Sierra Nevada, or John L. Stephens, of B. Holladay's line.

If in the affirmative, please answer by telegraph.

Yours respectfully,

T. LEMMEN MEYER.

Hon. EDWIN M. STANTON,
Secretary of the U. S. War Department, Washington City, D. C.

Note by the Department of State.

Permits were also requested from the War Department, in letters of the same tenor as the foregoing, to make monthly shipments of powder to mines in Mexico and Lower California, by the parties whose names appear annexed, and which letters are dated January 15 and 16, 1864.

T. LEMMEN MEYER.—Twenty kegs for Panuoa silver mine, in Sinaloa, Mexico.

L. B. BENTLEY & Co.—Eighty kegs for Guadalupe silver mine, in Chihuahua, Mexico. Twenty kegs for Bella Vista gold and silver mine, in Lower California.

EGGERS & Co.—Ten kegs for Ida silver mine, in Lower California. Ten kegs for Henriette and Sophie gold and silver mine, in Lower California. Ten kegs for El Tesoro silver mine, in Lower California.

Mr. Seward to Mr. Romero.

DEPARTMENT OF STATE,
Washington, February 19, 1864.

SIR: I have the honor to communicate herewith a copy of a letter addressed to me on the 17th instant, under instructions from the Secretary of War, by Brigadier General Canby, together with a copy of the papers referred to, relating to an application from Mr. T. L. Meyer, of San Francisco, for permission to ship some blasting powder, intended for mining purposes, from that port to Mazatlan.

Under existing circumstances I conceive it necessary that such an application should first be submitted to the belligerent powers now exercising authority in Mexico, and beg therefore to refer the subject to you as the representative of one of those powers.

I avail, &c., &c., &c.,

WILLIAM H. SEWARD.

Señor MATIAS ROMERO, *&c., &c., &c.*

Mr. Romero to Mr. Seward.

[Translation.]

MEXICAN LEGATION TO THE UNITED STATES OF AMERICA,
Washington, February 20, 1864.

Mr. SECRETARY: I have received the note which, under yesterday's date, your excellency was pleased to address to me, accompanied by a communication sent to you by Brigadier General Canby, together with various copies of applications made by Mr. T. L. Meyer, of San Francisco, California, that permission may be accorded to him to ship mining gunpowder to the ports of Guaymas, La Paz, and Mazatlan.

You consider that, under existing circumstances, it is necessary for you to recur "to the belligerent powers exercising authority in Mexico," in order to be ready to come to a decision on this point, and, as the representative of one of those powers, you are pleased to ask for my opinion.

Without expressing formally any opinion on this occasion as to the necessity of consulting both belligerent parties, which in your judgment exists, whenever there may be question of the introduction into Mexico of an article which may serve the uses of warfare, and falling back upon what, in this respect, I have had the honor to state to you on other occasions, I must now say that, for my part, I do not think there can be any impropriety in carrying to the ports indicated the mining gunpowder to which these applications refer.

I avail of this opportunity to reiterate to you the assurances of my very distinguished consideration.

M. ROMERO.

Hon. WILLIAM H. SEWARD, *&c.*, *&c.*, *&c.*

No. 3—*Intervention in New Granada.*

Mr. Romero to Mr. Seward.

[Translation.]

MEXICAN LEGATION IN THE UNITED STATES OF AMERICA,
Washington, March 19, 1863.

Mr. SECRETARY: Among the diplomatic correspondence which accompanies the message which the President addressed to the 37th Congress of the United States, dated December 1, 1862, and of which I seasonably transmitted a copy to the government of Mexico, there are documents relating to a subject which has attracted its attention in a very special manner, and respecting which I have received instructions to submit its views to the government of the United States.

The Mexican government, which has always considered as an indispensable condition for the preservation of the independence and autonomy of the American nations the keeping out of them the intervention of the European powers in their domestic affairs, and which, in order to maintain this sacred principle intact to-day, finds itself involved in a most gigantic war with one of the most powerful and most warlike nations of Europe, cannot see with indifference the events occurring in other portions of the American continent, and from which there may result, sooner or later, an European intervention in these countries.

The fates of the nations of America are bound together in such a manner that if the encroachments of the despots of Europe should succeed in one of them, it would scarcely be possible to prevent their being extended to all of them. Upon this subject the opinion of the government of Mexico is in full accord with the traditional policy of the United States.

In the opinion of the government of Mexico, the result could have been none other than that of an European intervention, if the proposal which the United States made in June last to the cabinets of St. James and the Tuilleries, to send land forces to the isthmus of Panama, with a view of protecting the neutrality of the isthmus, had been accepted by the governments of Great Britain and France.

Events have come to demonstrate, in a manner which does not admit of reply, that neither the tranquillity of that region was changed, nor its transit interrupted, because of its occupation by the forces of General Mosquera, who, at that time, was already in possession of Bogota, the capital of New Granada, and who had overthrown the constitutional government of that confederation.

The petition, (request,) therefore, on the part of the late representative of the Granadian confederation, that the United States should send forces which should reoccupy for his party the possession of the isthmus, under the plea that if it fell under, or remained in, the power of General Mosquera, the security of the isthmus would not be sufficiently protected, had, it seemed, no other object than to cause the plague of a foreign intervention to recoil upon his own country, in order that, through its aid, the party which had been overthrown might thus re-establish itself into power.

The pretexts which the Mexican emigrants residing in Europe adduced to the courts of Paris and Madrid were no less inadequate to bring about a similar result in Mexico, and which determined three of the nations of that continent to sign the treaty of London of the 31st of October, 1861, which unchained against Mexico the present war with France, and the calamities resulting therefrom.

The government of Mexico has, for this same reason, seen the last resolution of the President of the United States upon this subject, which you communicated to Mr. Dayton in the despatch, No. 215, of September 15, 1862, (page 381 of said correspondence,) in which the danger of an European intervention in New Granada is made to disappear, with a satisfaction as great and as sincere as its alarm would have been intense and profound in the event of a contrary determination.

I avail myself of this opportunity to renew to you, sir, the assurances of my most distinguished consideration.

M. ROMERO.

Hon. WILLIAM H. SEWARD, *&c., &c., &c.*

Mr. Seward to Mr. Romero.

DEPARTMENT OF STATE,
Washington, March 20, 1863.

SIR: The undersigned, Secretary of State, has the honor to acknowledge the receipt of a note from his excellency Señor Matias Romero, which bears the date of the 19th of March instant, and alludes to a correspondence which occurred during the last year between his excellency Señor P. A. Herran, minister plenipotentiary of the republic of New Granada, and the government of the United States, affecting the security at that time of the Panama railroad transit route in New Granada.

While the United States not only have no disposition to controvert the general views of the government of Mexico in regard to foreign intervention in the political affairs of the American states on this continent, but freely confess their sympathy with these views, as they are communicated by Mr. Romero, the undersigned, nevertheless, feels obliged to express his regret that a misapprehension, doubtless unintentional, of the character of the correspondence referred to, has seemed to the Mexican government to render it necessary to direct that communication to be made.

The undersigned avails himself of this occasion to offer to Mr. Romero the assurance of his high consideration.

WILLIAM H. SEWARD.

Señor Don MATIAS ROMERO.

Mr. Romero to Mr. Seward.

[Translation.]

MEXICAN LEGATION IN THE UNITED STATES OF AMERICA,
Washington, March 21, 1863.

SIR: The undersigned, chargé d'affaires of the United Mexican States, has had the honor to receive the note which the honorable William H. Seward, Secretary of State of the United States of America, was pleased to address to him under date of yesterday, in reply to the one which the undersigned placed in the hands of the honorable Mr. Seward, at the interview which he had with him on the nineteenth of the present month, in relation to the proposition made last year by the United States to the governments of Great Britain and France, with the object of protecting the security of the transit across the isthmus of Panama, which the government of the United States believed to be in danger in consequence of the political events which then occurred in New Granada.

The undersigned has seen, with the liveliest satisfaction, that, according to the expression of the honorable the Secretary of State, "the United States have not only no disposition to controvert the general views of the government of Mexico in regard to foreign intervention in the political affairs of the American States on this continent, but freely confess their sympathy with these views, as they are communicated by the undersigned to the Department of State in his note aforesaid."

The satisfaction of the undersigned has been still the greater, upon seeing that the honorable the Secretary of State considers as a groundless fear the uneasiness which the government of Mexico felt on receiving notice of the proposition made by the United States to the cabinets of Saint James and the Tuilleries, believing that if it were accepted it would lead to a foreign intervention in the domestic affairs of New Granada; for this shows, in the opinion of the undersigned, that, although the result of such a proposition might have been that which the government of Mexico feared, the United States were very far from desiring it, and were looking for another wholly distinct.

The undersigned will with pleasure hasten to send a copy of the note of the honorable the Secretary of State to Mexico; and he does not doubt that it will be viewed by his government with the utmost and most sincere satisfaction; and that it will finally set at rest the fears which had been entertained in view of the proposition hereinbefore alluded to.

The undersigned believes it to be his duty to express to the honorable the Secretary of State how greatly he regrets that the communication which the undersigned made to the United States, by order of his government, should have been received with regret by the honorable the Secretary of State, who laments that the government of Mexico should have thought itself under the necessity of making such a communication. The gravity and great importance of the question of intervention, on the favorable result of the solution of which to the nations of America now depends not only the welfare but the independence itself of Mexico, the undersigned believes are motives which authorize the government of Mexico to respectfully manifest its views to the United States upon a point in which all the other nations of this continent are equally interested with themselves.

The government of Mexico must, therefore, have considered itself authorized (entitled) to make such a manifestation, especially when it was made expressing the pleasure, as heartfelt as it was sincere, with which the Mexican government had learned of the final determination of the President of the United States upon this subject.

The undersigned avails himself of this opportunity to renew to the honorable William H. Seward, Secretary of State of the United States, the assurances of his most distinguished consideration.

M. ROMERO.

Hon. WILLIAM H. SEWARD, &c., &c., &c.

No. 4.—*Case of the steamer Noc-Daquy.*

Mr. Romero to Mr. Seward.

[Translation.]

MEXICAN LEGATION,
Washington, February 23, 1863.

The Mexican consul at Havana has sent me a copy of an affidavit made at the consulate under his charge by sundry individuals of the crew of the steamer Noc-Daquy, captured by the Mexican authorities of Yucatan for being in the slave trade. If the facts be true which are narrated in that affidavit, of which I have the honor to enclose you a copy, the United States steamers Wachusett and Sonoma, which arrived at the island of Mugeres the 28th December last, under the order of Commodore Wilkes, committed the offence of taking by force from the jurisdiction of the Mexican tribunals a prize which was subject to them, and which they were passing upon in accordance with the laws.

I have no doubt that, if such facts should turn out to be proven, the government of the United States will be disposed to give to that of Mexico all the satisfaction that may be due to it for the violation of its rights, as she has done to other nations whose maritime sovereignty has not been respected by vessels of the United States. Although I have not yet received instructions from my government upon this matter—and probably they will not communicate with me until the receipt in Mexico of the reports from the governor of Yucatan—I believe it to be my duty to communicate to you at once the affidavit mentioned for the information of the government of the United States, reserving the application for what may be rightly due when I shall receive instructions from the Mexican government.

I profit by this opportunity to renew to you, sir, the assurances of my most distinguished consideration.

M. ROMERO.

Hon. WILLIAM H. SEWARD, &c., &c., &c.

[Translation.]

CONSULATE OF MEXICO, AT THE HAVANA.

I certify that on pages 243, 244, 245, and 246, of book A, protocols of this consulate, are found recorded the following documents:

CONSULATE OF MEXICO, AT THE HAVANA.

On the tenth of February, one thousand eight hundred and sixty-three, there came to me, at this consulate, and before me and the undersigned witnesses, with the aid of the interpreter of the government, Don Ramon de Aroastia, the following individuals belonging to the crew of the steamer Noc-Daquy, delivering to me a letter dated at Key West, and signed by Chief Engineer Wm. E. Hardy, of that vessel, stating at the same time, and spontaneously, that they made the affidavit that all the said machinist Hardy said in the said document, which they placed in the hands of the consul subscribing, was the plain truth as to what had occurred at the islands Mujeres with the steamer Noc-Daquy: Samuel Croply, second engineer; P'lipe Carvin, fireman; Francisco Harappy, fireman; José Maria Trias, fireman; José Colmen, fireman; Pedro Juan, mariner; Luis Cosine, mariner; Ducomte Jean, mariner; Manuel Lisboa, mariner; Caire Jaques, mariner.

The letter to which the individuals mentioned attest was written in English, at Key West, dated the 2d instant, and signed by the first engineer of the steamer Noc-Daquy, translated into Spanish by the said interpreter, and says literally as follows:

KEY WEST, *February* 2, 1863.

SIR: I hope the following narrative will be read, because it interests you, as well as your government. I embarked at the Havana on the 13th December last, to join a steamer lying at the island Mujeres, to run the blockade at Mobile. On arriving at the island we found the steamer in the hands of the Mexican authorities. The employés allowed some of us to go on board to repair the engines, one of which was broken. On the 28th December the United States steamers Wachusett and Sonoma came into port, under command of Admiral Wilkes; and, on the 29th, he sent on board a lieutenant and fifteen men, who took possession of the vessel. We still went on working, believing she was a Mexican prize, and that we would be remunerated for our labor On the 9th January, 1863, the Sonoma went to Sisal. Upon her return she brought word that the Mexican authorities at Mevida had considered the vessel ("Noc-Daquy," alias "Virginia") as a slaver. On the 18th of January, our captain, acting under the orders of Admiral Wilkes, told me to set the engine going, which I did; and while I was below obeying his orders he hoisted the banner of the Confederate States, and, on seeing this, I got the engines ready, (before the anchor was weighed,) when immediately they were set in motion by the lieutenant of marines. In fine, the United States seamen got her out of port any way, weighed anchor, appointed firemen, and the lieutenant acted as engineer. When she was at a short distance from land they took possession of her in the following ridiculous way:

Officer of the Sonoma. "What bark is that?"

Captain of the Noc-Daquy. "The confederate steamer Virginia."

Then the Wachusett fired a cannon-shot, and sent the crew on board as prize; and because we, the crew of the steamer Noc-Daguy, did not choose to work under the confederate banner, nor take part in the infamous plan for stealing the vessel, and for refusing to bring her to this port, we were taken on board the steamers Wachusett and Sonoma and treated as traitors, in which condition we now are, and we ask you to act at once in this matter, because the bark is valued at $100,000, and there are nineteen of the crew who will corroborate all aforesaid. I forgot to say the cargo of the schooner was taken on board the steamer by express order of Admiral Wilkes.

I am, respectfully,

WILLIAM E. HARDY, *Engineer*.

I certify what precedes is a faithful translation of the original in English, which I have marked.

In faith whereof, I place at foot my signature and seal, at the Havana, the 10th February, one thousand eight hundred and sixty-three.

RAMON DE AROISTIA,
Interpreter for the Public and the Government.

Seal thereto, bearing interpretation for the public and the government.

(Signed) SAMUEL CROPLY,

For Felipe Corvin, Francisco Harappy, José Colmen, Pedro Juan, Luis Cosine, Manuel Lisbon, and Caire Jacques, which individuals don't know how to write, and he does it at their request.

SAMUEL CROPLY.
(Signed) JOSÉ MA TRIAS.
(Signed) ALEX. McINTOSH.
(Signed) MICHAEL HYLAND.
(Signed) ALEX. McINTOSH.

Signed as witness: A. C. MUNOS,
A. HARTMAN.

(Signed) RAMON S. DIAZ.

Consulate of Mexico, Habana, February 11, 1863.

A copy.—Washington, February 23, 1863.

ROMERO

Mr. Seward to Mr. Romero.

DEPARTMENT OF STATE,
Washington, February 25, 1863.

SIR: I have had the honor to receive your note of the 23d instant, relative to an alleged forcible taking from the jurisdiction of the Mexican tribunals, by Acting Rear-Admiral Wilkes, of the steamer Noc-Daquy, captured by the authorities of Yucatan for being engaged in the slave trade.

In reply, I have the honor to acquaint you that a translation of your communication will be at once submitted to the Secretary of the Navy, with a request for an inquiry into the case, with a view to such further proceedings as the result may be found to call for.

I avail myself of the occasion, sir, to offer you a renewed assurance of my very high consideration.

WILLIAM H. SEWARD.

Señor Don MATIAS ROMERO, *&c.*, *&c.*

Mr. Seward to Mr. Romero.

DEPARTMENT OF STATE,
Washington, March 6, 1863.

SIR: I have to acquaint you that a report from Rear-Admiral Wilkes has been received, through the Navy Department, on the subject of the steamer Virginia, *alias* Noc-Daquy. From this report, and the accompanying proofs, it appears that that vessel, though claimed to have been intended for the slave trade, was in reality the property of insurgents in arms against the United States, and was intended to run the blockade of Mobile, with a cargo which was taken from Havana to Mugeres island, on board the Spanish schooner Pepita. It also appears that, in point of fact, the Virginia was captured beyond the maritime jurisdiction of the Mexican republic. Inasmuch, however, as the vessel has been sent to Key West for adjudication, it is not to be doubted that the prize court there will give due attention to any claim which the Mexican republic may prefer with reference to her.

I avail myself of the occasion, sir, to offer to you the assurance of my distinguished consideration.

WILLIAM H. SEWARD.

Señor Don MATIAS ROMERO, *&c.*, *&c.*, *&c.*

Mr. Romero to Mr. Seward.

[Translation.]

MEXICAN LEGATION,
Washington, March 6, 1863

Mr. SECRETARY: I have the honor to acknowledge receipt of the note you were pleased to address to me of this day's date, informing me of a despatch from Rear-Admiral Wilkes, and, from the evidence which accompanies it, the steamer Noc-Daquy, it appears, is in "reality the property of rebels against the United States, which was intended to run the blockade of Mobile with a cargo which was brought from the Havana to the island of Mugeres by the Spanish schooner Pepita, and that the steamer was captured outside of the maritime jurisdiction of the Mexican republic." In said note you are pleased to state, besides, that, supposing the Noc-Daquy had been sent to Key West for trial there, it is not to be doubted that the prize court would give due attention to any complaint which the Mexican government might present with reference to said vessel.

Not having yet received the instructions of my government on this subject, I restrict myself to sending to Mexico a copy of your note. If the Mexican government could have before them the evidence to which you make reference, I have no doubt it would contribute to making it form a just idea of what has happened.

As to what relates to the disposition the court of prizes at Key West may entertain to give due attention to the claims of the Mexican government, I must say to you that, by the reports which have reached my knowledge in respect to this matter, it appears that Rear-Admiral Wilkes forcibly withdrew from the jurisdiction of the Mexican courts a prize which was subject to them, and which they had under trial according to the laws. This constitutes a violation of the maritime sovereignty of Mexico by vessels of the government of the United States. Of this violation I complain, conditionally, in the note I had the honor to address to you on the 23d of February last past, and to obtain reparation therefor, in case it should prove to be true; I could not address myself to the court at Key West, which could not give me proper satisfaction. If from proofs existent in your department, and those Mexico may furnish me, it should appear that the sovereignty of Mexico has not been violated, no more would be left for me to say on this matter, for I should not have any ground for claim.

I avail of this opportunity to repeat to you, sir, the assurances of my most distinguished consideration.

M. ROMERO.

Hon. WILLIAM H. SEWARD, *&c., &c., &c.*

Mr. Seward to Mr. Romero.

DEPARTMENT OF STATE,
Washington, March 13, 1863.

SIR: Your note of the 6th instant was duly received. In compliance with the request which it contains, a copy of the communications of Rear-Admiral Wilkes to the Navy Department, relative to the insurgent steamer Virginia, is herewith transmitted. I adhere to the opinion, however, expressed in my note to you of the 6th instant, that if your government has any claim to that vessel, there can be no doubt that the claim would be patiently heard and justly decided by the United States prize court at Key West.

I avail myself of the occasion, sir, to offer to you a renewed assurance of my high consideration.

WILLIAM H. SEWARD.

Señor Don MATIAS ROMERO, *&c., &c., &c.*

No. 4.]

U. S. FLAG STEAMER WACHUSETT,
Off Mugeres Island, January 18, 1863.

SIR: I have to apprise you that I have this day taken possession of the fine iron steamer (propeller) Virginia, of 800 tons, whereof John Johnson is master, as a prize to the Wachusett and Sonoma, being a confederate vessel, as proved by the papers found on board, the secession flag, and other evidence of the most satisfactory kind. I have avoided any interference with international rights whatever, and abstained from making her a prize within the accustomed limits from the shore.

The engineers of the Virginia having agreed to perform their duties on board till their arrival in the United States, I have given them to understand that they will receive the usual wages for their services. I have concluded to order the Virginia to Key West for adjudication. I believe she will be found, on inspection, well fitted for a government transport or an armament. She is two hundred and twenty feet long, and well built; and from her model well calculated for speed and for maintaining the sea, having bunkers capable of containing four hundred tons of coal, with a very small consumption of fuel. Her propeller trices up. Under canvas she is reported as being very fast, and is bark-rigged.

I am, very respectfully, your obedient servant,

CHARLES WILKES,
Rear-Admiral, Commanding West India Squadron.

Hon. GIDEON WELLES, *Secretary of the Navy.*

I herewith enclose copies of papers found on board the Virginia, the originals having been forwarded to the district judge or prize commissioners at Key West, numbered 1, 2, 3, 4, 5, 6, and 7.

Very respectfully, your obedient servant,

CHARLES WILKES,
Rear-Admiral, Commanding West India Squadron.

No. 1.] HAVANA, *December* 10, 1862.

SIR: The steamer described in the enclosed building certificate belongs, as I am assured, to Francis P. Drain, a citizen of the Confederate States, now temporarily in Havana, and that said steamer is about to sail for Mobile with a cargo suited to the necessities of our army and people. Francis P. Drain is known to me to be true, loyal, and devoted to our cause, and I will add, a Virginia gentleman. His steamer goes without a register; I therefore request that you give to his captain all proper facilities in disposing of all his cargo, and in the purchase of a return cargo of cotton usual in each case. I also request that a register and other papers necessary under our laws be granted to show ownership in said Drain and confederate nationality.

I am, sir, with great respect, your obedient servant,

CH. J. HELM.

The COMMANDING OFFICER, *Confederate Forces, Mobile.*

No. 2.] HAVANA, *December* 11, 1862.

MY DEAR SIR: My personal friend, F. P. Drain, of Virginia, is largely interested in the steamer bearing the name of his State, for the purpose of running our enemy's blockade and benefiting our friends with articles so much needed by them. Should the vessel succeed in reaching your port, and her captain or any other person connected with her need your kind interference in their behalf, in the way of disposing of her present cargo, obtaining one for return or otherwise, I beg that you will do your utmost for them. With kind regards to Mrs. Scott and friends, and trusting that your home may not meet with the like fate of mine,

I remain, very truly, your friend,

W. H. ROZET.

JOHN SCOTT, Esq., *Mobile, Ala.*

Particular regards to E. O. George and lady and Miss Chandler.

No. 3.] HAVANA, *December* 13, 1862.

DEAR SIR: In accordance with the agreement entered upon between ourselves yesterday, I beg you will proceed at once to take possession of the steamer Virginia, on the coast of Yucatan, put her in seaworthy condition as early as practicable, sailing thence to Mobile, Ala.

Should you succeed in running the blockade, as I expect, you shall report the vessel to the consignment of Messrs. H. O. Brewer & Co., and so soon as the report cargo is shipped upon her by those gentlemen, you shall again endeavor to run the blockade and make sail with possible despatch and caution for this port of Havana, delivering me all papers concerning vessel and cargo.

You shall look to the satisfactory disposition of the 400 or 600 boxes claret you carry.

Herewith an introduction to John Scott, esq., of Mobile, who will assist you, as well as consignees, towards promoting my views generally.

Relying upon your good management of the adventure, which I hope may succeed,

I remain truly yours,

FRANCIS P. DRAIN.

Captain JOHN JOHNSON, *Present.*

No. 4.] HABANA, *December* 12, 1862.

GENTLEMEN: With the enclosed introductory lines from our mutual friend, J. Pemberton, I beg to accompany shipping vouchers of cargo per bearer, the steamer Virginia, amounting to $15,078 09.

I have taken the liberty of consigning both cargo and vessel to your address, upon the information I have of your promptness, ability, and sound management of the interests intrusted to your care. You will, consequently, oblige me by disposing of the cargo to best possible advantage, and invest the proceeds in a cargo of cotton, documents of which you shall establish and forward to my order, holding at my disposal, with your good selves, any surplus of funds resulting after purchase of the return cargo. The within copy of my agreement with master and engineers of the steamer Virginia will govern you in your management of that vessel's business while in your port; and in this connexion I would call your attention to the papers of the craft which I desire you shall have issued in my name, under confederate colors. The vessel, running the blockade successfully, will reach you without papers.

I rely upon your management of this affair; and looking to the success of present trial for the continuance of operations of mutual benefit,

I remain, most respectfully, gentlemen, your obedient servant,

FRANCIS P. DRAIN.

Messrs. H. O. BREWER & Co., Mobile.

[Memorandum of agreement. Vouchers of cargo.]

P. S.—Besides the goods mentioned in her invoice, the vessel carries 400 to 600 boxes claret, which you will dispose of to best advantage, investing proceeds in return cargo.

Invoice of goods shipped by Francis P. Drain, per confederate steamer Virginia, John Johnson master, for Mobile, on account of and wish of whom it may concern, and consigned to Messrs. H. O. Brewer & Co., there.

4,800 woollen blankets		$6,596 87
502 do do		596 12
5,302 woollen blankets		7,192 99
12 boxes containing 4,000 pairs shoes	$5,083 37	
10 bales leather	700 00	
		5,863 37
Provisions.		
100 bags salt	$328 98	
20 bags pepper	400 00	
80 boxes cognac	300 00	
50 jars gin	275 00	
20 boxes liquors	50 00	
20 boxes preserved fruits	200 00	
		1,553 98
		14,610 34
Shipping expenses		100 00
		14,710 34
Commission $2\frac{1}{2}$ per cent		367 75
E. E.		15,078 09

FRANCIS P. DRAIN.

HAVANA, *December* 12, 1862.

No. 5.] HAVANA, *December* 12, 1862.

GENTLEMEN: I took the liberty of addressing you a few lines recommending F. P. Drain, esq., of this place. My acquaintance with you being limited, I beg to apologize, and refer you to my friends, Messrs. Charles Welsh, Charles Libaron, Thomas S. King, Mr. Duran, of Sands & Co.

Very respectfully,

JOHN PEMBERTON.

Messrs. H. O. BREWER & Co., Mobile.

No. 6.] HAVANA, *December* 12, 1862.

GENTLEMEN: Mr. Francis P. Drain, of this place, having expressed his desire to enter into correspondence with you, I beg to say that he is a gentleman of much standing, and transactions with him will always prove highly satisfactory.

With great respect, your very obedient servant,

JOHN PEMBERTON.

Messrs. H. O. BREWER & Co., Mobile.

No. 7.] BARK PROPELLER VIRGINIA,
Off Mugeres Island, December 29, 1862.

I certify that the bark Noc-Daquy, and now the Virginia, was sold on or about the 15th of December last to Francis P. Drain, a merchant in Havana, and was bought by him for the purpose of engaging in the confederate service in carrying supplies to the confederate army, and in running the blockade; that she stopped at this place for the purpose of receiving her cargo from the Spanish schooner Pepita, now here, and that it was the intention to sail from this place for Mobile and run the blockade, when she was seized on the 21st of December by a party of people from this place, and seized upon the alleged suspicion of being a slaver. I further certify that the schooner Pepita was loaded with cargo for this steamer, which was to be put on board here, when she was also seized by the same party on her arrival here the 22d of December. I further certify that the confederate flag was hoisted on board this vessel for a day and a half, to which no objection was made until the third day, when it was hauled down on the 23d of December, and no flag was substituted until the Mexican flag was hoisted upon the day of the arrival of the United States vessels-of-war Wachusett and Sonoma at this place. I further certify that, to the best of my knowledge and belief, there is nothing in the vessel's fittings or cargo upon which to base suspicion that she was intended to engage in the slave traffic.

JOHN JOHNSON, *Master Virginia.*

Witness:
F. H. STEVENS, *Commander U. S. steamer Sonoma.*

I hereby certify that the foregoing statement is correct.

JOHN ROSS, *Mate Virginia.*

Witness:
F. H. STEVENS, *Commander U. S. steamer Sonoma.*

No. 5.] UNITED STATES FLAG STEAMER WACHUSETT,
Off Mugeres Harbor, January 18, 1863.

SIR: In my communication, No. 4, of this date, I have informed you of the capture of the iron propeller steamer Virginia. There are some circumstances connected with this vessel and a small schooner, the Pepita, under Spanish colors, which it is necessary I should now state. In cruising for the Alabama I had reason to suppose that she, with the Agrippina, store-vessel, had changed their rendezvous from Grand Cayman island to that of Mugeres, on the coast of Yucatan, a well-known place, where vessels intending to run the blockade, as well as slavers, fitted out—a harbor well adapted to their purpose, and where the notorious Walker and others fitted their fillibustering expeditions. There is no government or authority here whatever, nor is it a port of entry or clearance, but a rendezvous for plunderers, slavers, and pirates.

On our arrival off the harbor we discovered the confederate steamer Virginia, with the Spanish schooner Pepita, at anchor, and immediately anchored. The Virginia was formerly the Noc-Daquy, and has no doubt been engaged in the slave trade before being purchased by the present confederate owners. Captain Johnson came over in the schooner Pepita from the Havana with a crew, stores, and contraband articles, to take charge of her, and did so, hoisting the confederate flag, the possession having been passed over to him by the officer then in charge. At this time a Mexican, who represented himself as an officer, Urcelay by name, without authority or any commission, as I have since been informed, collected an armed force in order to take possession of the vessel as a slaver, which Captain Johnson refused to permit, although threatened by an armed force of plunderers, gathered from the island and elsewhere. This took place two days before our arrival. Captain Johnson had hoisted the confederate flag, which they took down. This Urcelay removed the Spanish crew out of her, accusing them of having been engaged in the slave trade, leaving Captain Johnson, his engineers, and part of his confederate crew. He (Captain Johnson) became apprehensive of difficulties on board, and threatening of bloodshed was made, which was repeated to me by Captain Johnson on my arrival, and a request made for me to send a guard on board to prevent violence. This I did, and made an agreement with Urcelay to hold possession of her until an examination was made relative to whether she was a slaver, of which there was no proof whatever, and to await *ten days*, that the affair might be referred to Merida, he sending some of his men on board the Spanish schooner, the Pepita. I then sailed with the Wachusett and Sonoma for the Havana to coal, and to return here within the stipulated time, which we have done. On my arrival I found no information had been received from Merida, or action taken place, although the time had elapsed as agreed upon. I have determined to send Commander Stevens in the Sonoma to Sisal, the seaport of Merida, to avoid any misunderstanding, to ascertain the cause of the delay, and what proceeding, if any, had taken place relative to her being proved to be a slaver. The Spanish crew had been examined, and no evidence had been adduced, and no further proceeding taken that he could ascertain. In the event of such being the case, Commander Stevens was directed to give notice to the authorities that I no longer felt myself bound by the agreement, the time having expired, and should act as if the steamer was, which I have abundance of evidence to prove, a confederate vessel, fitting out with contraband, and intended to run the blockade, and probably, if successful, to be fitted as a confederate privateer, for which she is thought to be well adapted.

During our absence at Havana additional testimony was obtained of her confederate character and of the cargo being shipped in the schooner Pepita for her. Captain Johnson complained, on my arrival here, that the persons left on board of the Pepita were plundering the cargo which belonged to his vessel, and consuming the provisions intended for the Virginia to a great extent. I therefore gave Captain Johnson my assent to remove what remained of it on board the Virginia, leaving the schooner, after being discharged, in the possession of those who were on board of her. The Pepita was entirely without the limits of her destination, having been cleared at Havana for Cardenas, with the contraband cargo on board. I did not consider it proper to make prize of her, as I had proof of the cargo belonging to the Virginia; not wishing to involve ourselves in any international question or make the matter more intricate, I determined to leave her in the possession of those on board, Spaniards and Mexicans.

The Virginia being thus free from the charge of being a slaver, seeing there was no escape for her, Captain Johnson concluded to go beyond the limits of the maritime jurisdiction, which I permitted when he was captured and his vessel taken a prize to the Wachusett and Sonoma. I think he is entitled to some remuneration for his services in this respect, as he avoided delay on our part and placed her beyond any controversy as to any international right, although he evidently could not do otherwise. If I had permitted him to remain here he would have fallen into the hands of the parties again and have been fitted out to run the blockade; indeed the owner or agent, Mr. Drain, was down here a few days ago with some five thousand dollars to bribe her off, but finding the condition of things he left. On the Virginia proceeding to sea we followed and made her capture under the confederate flag; I ordered a prize crew on board and have sent her to Key West for adjudication, with all the papers found on board.

I herewith enclose Commander Stevens's report to me, numbered 1, and a copy of his letter to the governor of Yucatan, numbered 2.

I am, very respectfully, your obedient servant,

CHARLES WILKES,
Rear-Admiral, Commanding West India Squadron.

Hon. GIDEON WELLES,
Secretary of the Navy, Washington, D. C.

UNITED STATES STEAMER SONOMA,
Mugeres Island, January 14, 1863.

SIR: In obedience to your orders I proceeded to Sisal in the Sonoma, and finding that the United States consul was residing at Merida, I visited that place in connexion with the duties I was charged with by you.

I found the governor of Yucatan absent from the place, and as there was no probability of his return for some week or fortnight, and no one to represent him in Merida, I addressed him the communication a copy of which I enclose

No progress towards coming to a decision, as far as I could learn, had been made in the case of the Virginia, though I understood from the consul all the Spanish crew had been examined without any evidence having been found by the judges to implicate them or the vessel as connected with the slave trade.

Very respectfully, your obedient servant,

F. H. STEVENS, *Commander*.

Rear-Admiral CHARLES WILKES,
Commanding West India Squadron.

MERIDA, *January* 11, 1863.

SIR: I am instructed by Admiral Wilkes to notify you that in consequence of the time stipulated with Captain Nicholas Ucelay having elapsed, and without receiving any answer to his communication enclosed to you through the United States consul at this place, although ample time has been afforded, he cannot permit himself to be any longer bound by that agreement that has been violated in consequence of the depredations upon the cargo committed by the parties placed in charge of the schooner Pepita, by Captain Ucelay, which vessel contained part of the supplies of the steamer Virginia and contraband articles. For this reason, and that the crew of the Virginia, who were before destitute, might possess the means of support, Rear-Admiral Wilkes has thought proper to take possession of her in order that the same may be subject to adjudication when the Virginia shall be tried before the prize courts of the United States.

That the Virginia was a confederate vessel at or before entering the anchorage of Mugeres, Admiral Wilkes had sufficient proof before proceeding to Havana, which proof has since been made conclusive; and as there is no shadow of evidence to prove her being engaged in the slave trade, he considers that she was unjustly seized and merely upon suspicion, and is therefore improperly detained.

A desire to treat the Mexican authorities as a friendly power and with good will and friendship prevented his taking immediate action in the premises; he preferred rather to wait a reasonable time, though satisfied that there could be no evidence to warrant the detention of the Virginia as a slaver; and this time having been afforded, and no proof having been adduced after the examination of the Spanish crew, he can no longer refrain.

Upon no consideration, under the circumstances, can the Virginia be permitted to fall into the hands of the confederates or escape from capture by us.

I have the honor to remain your obedient servant,

F. H. STEVENS, *Commander*.

The GOVERNOR OF YUCATAN.

Mr. Romero to Mr. Seward.

[Translation.]

MEXICAN LEGATION,
Washington, April 15, 1863.

The undersigned, chargé d'affaires of the United Mexican States, had the honor to receive, with the note which the Hon. William H. Seward, Secretary of State of the United States, was pleased to address to him on the 13th of March last past, the copies therein enclosed of two despatches and their annexes, addressed by Rear-Admiral Wilkes to the Navy Department of the United States, in regard to the steamer Noc-Daquy.

Since then there have come into the hands of the undersigned the official documents relating to the same affair, which were sent to him by the governor of Yucatan, which exhibit in full detail what happened at the island Mugeres in the affair of said steamer.

After a minute examination of these documents, and of the circumstances of the case, the undersigned regrets he finds himself obliged to consider the conduct of Rear-Admiral Wilkes as aggressive to the sovereignty of the Mexican nation, which to a certain extent the said rear-admiral admits in his despatch No. 5, of the 18th of January last, although endeavoring to extenuate the enormity of the violation of the rights of Mexico.

From the report which the governor of Yucatan made to the minister of foreign relations of Mexico under date of the 23d of February last, of which the undersigned transmits a copy, it appears that as soon as the said governor received intelligence that a steamer was at anchor at the island Mugeres, whose movements caused suspicion, and that she proved to be the Noc Daquy, he commissioned Don Nicolas Urcelay, captain of the national guard, to go to that place with an armed force in order to capture the steamer, and notified the court of the district of Yucatan for its information, and that it might order such measures as it deemed proper in the case.

This determination appears by the despatch addressed by the governor of Yucatan to the district judge the 10th of Decemher, 1862, of which the undersigned sends copy. By this action the steamer was from that moment subject to the jurisdiction of the said tribunal.

Captain Urcelay arrived with his force at island Mugeres, and took possession of the steamer without any resistance, hoisted the Mexican flag on her, and sent the crew under arrest to Sisal, whence they were sent to Merida at the disposal of the governor of the state, who turned them over to the district judge, who was already cognizant of the affair, when Captain Urcelay, in carrying out the decision of the district court, of which the undersigned encloses a copy, attempted to take the Noc Daquy, together with the Spanish schooner Pepita, which had come from the Havana with articles for said steamer, for which reason she also was taken, there appeared in the Mexican waters two ships-of-war of the United States, under the command of Rear-Admiral Wilkes, who took upon him to possess himself of the steamer, alleging that she was intended for the service of the insurgents of the south. Captain Urcelay, in view of the circumstances, coerced by superior force, and assuming authority which he had not, made an arrangement with of Rear-Admiral Wilkes, by virtue of which he took charge of the steamer, placing a guard on her, and engaging to restore her as soon as the competent Mexican authority should declare her to be a slaver.

Captain Urcelay left his force on board the steamer, and went to Merida to make report of the proceeding to the district court.

Thus far the undersigned finds accordances at the bottom of the reports of the governor of Yucatan and of Rear-Admiral Wilkes, although they may vary in some details, and although many of the expressions of Rear-Admiral Wilkes are as offensive to the dignity and good name of Mexico as they are groundless and unjust. Rear-Admiral Wilkes allows himself to say that Captain Urcelay had neither appointment nor commission; that he gathered an armed force and took possession of the steamer, as if this were done of his own motion and not under instructions from the Mexican authorities. On this point, however, the undersigned cannot doubt that the official declaration of the governor of Yucatan deserves more credit from the government of the United States than the suspicions of Rear-Admiral Wilkes, growing out of what some one or other may have told him.

The rear-admiral relates in this manner what afterwards happened: that he went to Havana to coal, and on his return to the island Mugeres he found no answer had been received from the governor of Yucatan, although the fixed time of *ten days*, which he assures us was settled in the agreement to receive such reply, had expired; that he sent Commander Stevens in the United States steamer Sonoma to Sisal for the purpose of ascertaining the cause of delay in proceedings which had been set on foot for ascertaining whether the Noc Daquy was engaged in the slave trade. The rear-admiral continues: "In such case," (that it were not proved that she was engaged in such traffic,) he notifies Commander Stevens that he must inform the authorities that "I did not consider myself bound any further by the agreement, the time having expired, and that I should act as if the vessel was * * * confederate, laden with contraband of war, and with intent to run the blockade, and if she succeeded in this, would probably be armed as a confederate corsair," for which he thought her well adapted.

In this alone there is, in the opinion of the undersigned, cause more than sufficient to regard the conduct of Rear-Admiral Wilkes not only as contrary to the teachings of international law, but as an open violation of the sovereignty of Mexico.

The undersigned does not believe that it can possibly be doubted that the island *Mugeres* belongs to Mexico—that the bay in that island where the Noc Daquy was fallen in with is among the territorial waters of the republic—still less that sovereignty over the territorial waters of a nation belongs wholly to its government. As little can the undersigned believe the fact can be questioned that on the coming of Rear-Admiral Wilkes into the waters of island *Mugeres*, the Noc Daquy was subjected to the jurisdiction of the Mexican tribunals, which placed her doubly under the shield of the Mexican sovereignty.

Under these circumstances, the taking possession of the steamer by forces of the United States is a proceeding which the undersigned permits himself to call highly irregular.

In the agreement, by virtue of which Rear-Admiral Wilkes took possession of the Noc Daquy, it was stipulated that she should rest at the disposal of the Mexican authorities, alone competent in the matter. The literal words of said agreement, of which the undersigned has the honor to transmit a copy, are as follows: "It is stipulated * * * that for the better security and protection of the steamer now at this place, of her cargo, and property on board of her, Admiral Wilkes shall take possession of her with a sufficient guard until the Mexican government may decide what is the character of said steamer, and whether or no she be a slaver; and if the government decide that she is, then the steamer shall be delivered to the Mexican government." The rear-admiral asserts that the term within which the decision was to be made was ten days; and even excluding the idea that had a time been limited, it would have been an absurd stipulation: such a term was not stipulated in the so-called agreement, for although in the second clause of such paper the expression *ten days* is mentioned, it is done with reference to the schooner Pepita, and indicating only that Rear-Admiral Wilkes would return from the Havana within the period mentioned. Rear-Admiral Wilkes, by giving, without doubt, a most forced interpretation, which nothing can justify, to the clause mentioned, adopted this pretext to keep the steamer, and sent to Sisal to Commander Stevens that he could notify the governor of Yucatan that he could not wait any longer time for the solution of the culpability or inculpability of the steamer; that he did not consider himself any longer bound by the compromise he had made with Captain Urcelay, as well because of the delay specified, as because such agreement had been violated by depredations which he averred had been committed on the cargo of the schooner Pepita, in care of a force of Captain Urcelay's which had taken possession of the schooner; that he had the certainty that the steamer was destined for the service of the insurgents; that there was no reason for regarding her as a slaver, and he had resolved to make her prize of the squadron of his command.

Commander Stevens did not go to the place where the governor of Yucatan was—absent at the time from the capital of the State; he contented himself with sending him a communication, and without awaiting any answer, went back to island *Mugeres*. Immediately after the return of Commander Stevens, Rear-Admiral Wilkes made out that he left the steamer absolutely at liberty; he made the crew take her outside of the Mexican waters and raise the insurgent's flag, captured her, and ordered her to Key West, leaving the schooner Pepita, (after having taken her cargo into possession,) which was afterwards taken to Sisal. The accuracy of these acts is confirmed by the relation Rear-Admiral Wilkes gives of them in his despatch No. 5, as cited.

After this narrative, proved by official documents, and even by the despatches of Rear-Admiral Wilkes, there can be no question the said rear-admiral violated the sovereignty of Mexico by taking from under it, through devices unworthy an officer of his rank, a prize that was in subjection to the jurisdiction of the Mexican courts, and attempting previously to impose terms and a rule of conduct, at his pleasure, upon those very tribunals.

It is not hidden from the undersigned that Rear-Admiral Wilkes alleges in justification of his inexcusable conduct that the Noc Daquy was a confederate vessel that was to run the blockade of the southern ports, and that there was no proof at all that she was engaged in the slave trade. Excluding from view that the Mexican courts were those alone which could make such a declaration, the undersigned cannot abstain from noting the contradiction into which Rear-Admiral Wilkes falls by saying in his cited despatch that the bay of island *Mugeres* is a point frequented by slavers, and that, undoubtedly, the Noc Daquy had been in the trade. Moreover, the undersigned believes it to be his duty to state to the government of the United States that not only the charge of being a slaver weighed against the Noc Daquy, but also that of having violated the revenue laws of the Mexican ports, on both which accounts the proper proceedings at law were being taken.

The honorable Secretary of State appears to entertain the same opinion as Rear-Admiral Wilkes in respect to the Noc Daquy being the property of southern insurgents, and intended to run the blockade, as appears in the note which he did the undersigned the honor to address to him, dated the 6th of March. But in such event, if fully established, and further, even in case the vessel had been armed for a cruise by the rebels, Rear-Admiral Wilkes should not have arrogated the powers which he took. His duty would have been to await the sentence of the courts of Mexico, and if in virtue of such the steamer were set at liberty, to arrange for her capture when she should have left the territorial waters of Mexico.

Rear-Admiral Wilkes, moreover, usurped powers inherent to the national sovereignty of Mexico, in taking depositions and exercising judicial acts on Mexican territory, in flagrant violation of the laws of the republic.

The said rear-admiral did not confine himself to committing violations referred to, but also took possession of the schooner Pepita, which Captain Urcelay had previously taken possession of with a Mexican force. He landed, and abusing his power, took the crew which the Pepita had brought from the Havana for the Noc Daquy, and which was under detention by the Mexican authorities, and subject to the orders of the proper courts.

In recapitulation, Rear-Admiral Wilkes has violated the rights of Mexico—

1st. By having taken possession, within Mexican territory, of a vessel held subject to the jurisdiction of the Mexican courts.

2d. In not having allowed the sentence of the Mexican court in relation to the transfer of the Noc Daquy to the port of Sisal to be carried into effect.

3d. In having deceptively taken the said steamer out of the jurisdiction of the Mexican courts.

4th. In having imposed terms on the Mexican courts.

5th. In having exercised in Mexican territory judicial acts of the competency exclusively of Mexican authorities.

6th. In having taken possession of the schooner Pepita, which was in Mexican territory, held by Mexican soldiers, and subjected to the jurisdiction of the Mexican courts.

7th. In having, by force, taken possession of the crew brought from the Havana by the schooner Pepita for the Noc Daquy, which was in Mexican territory and subject to the Mexican courts.

The undersigned cannot doubt for a moment that when the government of the United States has intelligence of the facts referred to, and the full proof by which they are accompanied, it will hasten to give to Mexico all the satisfaction she is justly entitled to for the offences committed against her sovereignty and clearest rights by Rear-Admiral Wilkes.

The undersigned profits by the occasion to repeat to the honorable William H. Seward, Secretary of State of the United States, the assurances of his most distinguished consideration.

M. ROMERO.

Hon. WILLIAM H. SEWARD, *&c., &c., &c.*

[Translation.]

GOVERNMENT OF THE STATE OF YUCATAN.

Having had news that, in the waters of the island Mugeres, a steamer was at anchor, whose movements caused suspicion, especially as to her being employed in the slave trade, I gave commission to Captain Nicolas Urcelay, of the national guard, to pass over to said point with an armed force in order to capture her; and I gave notice of this to the first judge on the civil side of the department of this capital, that he might put in exercise the functions of the district court, as well for his information as that he might order the measures which he should deem belonged to the case. Captain Urcelay arrived with his force at the island, and, availing himself of the circumstance of the coming ashore of the crew of said steamer—which is Spanish, and called Noc Daquy—took possession of her, without resistance of any kind, and hoisted the national flag on her; but when about to bring her to Sisal, together with a schooner, also Spanish, called Pepita, which came from Havana, and which he also captured, for having brought merchandise for said steamer, there came in two vessels-of-war of the United States squadron in the Antilles, and Rear-Admiral Charles Wilkes assumed to take possession of the steamer, taking ground upon his having had advice that she was sold at Havana under the name Virginia, and had come here bound for service of the rebels of the south of that nation. Captain Urcelay, in view of the circumstances in which he was placed, thought it prudent to make a stipulation with the said rear-admiral, in virtue of which he took charge of the steamer, placing a guard upon her, engaging himself to return her as soon as the proper Mexican authority should declare her to be a slaver.

The said Captain Urcelay left his force on board the captured schooner, to take care o her, and came himself to this capital, to make report of what happened to the distric court. That court sent intelligence to me of the event when I was away from the capital inspecting the fortified positions of our line of defence against the insurgent Indians, and, a soon as I received the communication, I addressed a note to Rear-Admiral Wilkes, making in the name of the supreme government, the proper reclamation against the violation h had committed of the national territory, and calling his attention to the necessity ther was that he should leave the steamer to the Mexican force which had captured her, tha she might be brought by it to the port of Sisal, that she might there be examined, an other measures taken, conducive to the clearing up of the point on which the court coul base its judgment whether she was or not a slave trader—whether she had or not contra vened the revenue laws of the republic. At a subsequent time the consul of the Unite States at Merida addressed a copy of a despatch from Rear-Admiral Wilkes, and some doc uments, by which he thought to prove the steamer to be a slaver, and also destined for th confederate service; and I sent them to the district court, that they should have their effec in the proper suit, answering the consul that I had done so, and begging him to sustai the application I had addressed to the rear-admiral.

I remained absent from the capital when Mr. J. E. Stevens, commander of one of th vessels of the aforesaid squadron, came there, and for this cause he addressed to me, a Valladolid, a communication, in the name of Rear-Admiral Wilkes, that he could not wa any longer for the determination of the culpability or inculpability of the steamer; that he no longer considered himself bound by the compromise he had made with Captain Urcelay, as well for the delay settled on as because the compromise was broken by the depredations committed on the cargo which, belonging to the steamer, was found on the schooner Pepita, guarded by a force placed there by Captain Urcelay; that he therefore had taken possession of the schooner; that the proofs he held amounted to evidence that the steamer was intended for the confederate service, to such extent that none existed of her being a slaver, and that not upon any account would he allow that vessel to fall into the hands of those in rebellion to his country, nor that she should be set at liberty from the capture by the squadron under his command. Such note was immediately answered, directly to Rear-Admiral Wilkes, and with the energy and propriety the national honor required, this government making proof of the flagrant violation of the law of nations committed by the squadron of the United States, and making the proper protests; but, despite all the steps I could take that my communication should pass to the island Mugeres with the greatest possible celerity, such was the haste of the American squadron that its commander never received it.

Rear-Admiral Wilkes did not restrict himself to extending indefinitely the possession of the steamer Noc Daquy, which Captain Urcelay, under an agreement, had conceded to him, nor the possession of the schooner Pepita, which that officer had left in the charge of the State troops, but landed, and, by an abuse of his strength, took the crew which the schooner had brought from Havana for the steamer, and which was arrested by the authorities and held subject to the order of the district court. This last operation being effected, Rear-Admiral Wilkes pretended that he left the steamer at absolute liberty, and when she left our waters he captured her, and without doubt sent her to the United States, leaving behind—although after having taken possession of her cargo—the schooner Pepita, which was brought to Sisal, and placed at the disposal of the district court.

All in relation to this appears in the official documents which I have the honor to transmit to you in copy, that the supreme government, possessing itself of the scandalous violation of the national territory committed by the said Rear-Admiral Wilkes, of the United States squadron in the Antilles, may please to issue suitable reclamations to whom it may be proper. Under which impression I send copies similar to the annexed to the citizen minister plenipotentiary of the republic near the United States, through the channel of the consul general resident at New York, that, on his part, he may take such action as he may deem opportune.

I have the honor to renew to you the assurances of my particular esteem and consideration.

Liberty and reform. Merida, February 23, 1863.

L. IRIGOYEN.
A. REJON, *Secretary.*

To the CONSUL GENERAL *of the Mexican Republic at New York.*

WASHINGTON, *April* 15, 1863.

A copy:

M. ROMERO.

[Translation.]

DIVISION OF OPERATIONS.

GENERAL-IN-CHIEF: The citizen general, military commandant and captain of the port of Sisal, tells me in an official note dated 8th instant:

CITIZEN GOVERNOR: Yesterday I copied for you the report made to me, dated 4th instant, by the head of the registration of the island Mugeres, referring to the steamer which under the Spanish flag appeared at that port on the 28th of the month last past, and to-day have ascertained, through the captain and supercargo of the English schooner Clyde, that arrived at Mugeres island the same day, (the 4th,) that the steamer in question remained in port at that date, and that it is known long time since that she is engaged in the opprobrious and infamous traffic in slaves on the coast of Africa. The captain of the Clyde assures me, as well as various other persons of this port, that the said steamer is the same which was at Campeachy two years ago, a trifle more or less, taking on board as captain a brother of Captain Galindo; that he came back to Campeachy, or the coast, about five months since, and is about to repeat his voyage to the same port or coast, as the said captain of the Clyde informed me. As it is not difficult to ascertain in what business the said vessel may be engaged by the water casks and other effects, which reveal that criminal commerce,

I think it my duty to make it known to you, that if you think proper you may denounce the fact to the authorities of Campeachy, who without doubt will act in conformity with the spirit of the treaties made between Mexico and the powers interested in pursuing and punishing that odious traffic. And as it may be considered that the investigation of the serious business, to which this note is confined, may belong to the attributes of the jurisdiction under your worthy charge, I refer it to you that you may at once act in the case as to you may seem fit, it being my duty to inform you, first, that I have enclosed this communication to the governor of Campeachy for the purposes he may judge proper on his part; and, second, that I have ordered the seizure of the vessel referred to, and also the captain and crew, by means of the revenue cutter of Sisal and citizen Nicolas Urcelay, in command of another commissioned cutter.

Liberty and reform!

LIBORIO IRIGOYEN.

MERIDA, *December* 10, 1862.

To the JUDGE OF THE COURT OF FIRST INSTANCE
of the civil and revenue branch of this capital.

MERIDA, *February* 9, 1863.

A copy:

VISTO BUENO.
IRIGOYEN.
LUIS GUTIERREZ, *Secretary.*

WASHINGTON, *April* 15, 1863.

True copy:

ROMERO.

[Translation.]

SECRETARIAT GENERAL OF THE GOVERNMENT OF YUCATAN.—GOVERNMENT OF THE STATE OF YUCATAN.

THE GENERAL-IN-CHIEF: In a despatch of to-day the first judge of the civil and revenue side in this department tells me what follows: "This court not having advice of the result of the orders which you informed me you had issued for the seizure of the slave steamer which was found at the island Mugeres, I hope you will please to order an officer, with sufficient number of troops, to bring her to Sisal for the purpose that may seem adequate to the case, and to avoid any risk at the point where she is." I send this to you, that, in passing the port of Silam, or any other on the coast, he may there obtain, through the authorities and marine officers, a cutter and ten or twelve seamen, with whom he will go to island Mugeres, and presenting this official note to the guard on board the revenue cutter and to the commissioner, Captain Nicolas Urcelay, they may obey the order which you have given to make sail on the steamer Noc Daquy, to bring her to the port of Sisal with all her crew and whatever belongs to the said vessel, as the persons employed under anterior orders are already notified, which seem to be neglected, for which reason you will give them to understand that they are liable, and if they do not discharge their duty with exactness, will be held responsible for whatever their conduct may give occasion before the citizen judge of first instance referred to, to whom I send copy of this note.

Liberty and reform!

L. IRIGOYEN.

MERIDA *December* 30, 1862.

In presence of:

THOMAS QUIJCINO,
Citizen, Commanding Battalion.

MERIDA, *January* 29, 1863.

Copy:

A. REJON, *Secretary.*

WASHINGTON, *April* 15, 1863.

A copy:

ROMERO.

[Translation.]

SECRETARIAT GENERAL OF THE GOVERNMENT OF YUCATAN.

STEAMER WACHUSETT, ISLAND OF MUGERES,
December 29, 1862.

It is stipulated, and agreeable to Admiral Wilkes, commanding the western squadron, and Captain Nicolas Urcelay, of the Mexican troops at this point, that for the better security and protection of the steamer now at this port, and also of the cargo and property aboard of said steamer, that Admiral Wilkes shall take possession of her with a sufficient guard until the Mexican government may decide what is the character of said steamer, and see if she be or not a slaver; and if the government decide that she is, then the steamer shall be delivered to the Mexican government. Also, as there is anchored here the schooner Pepita, connected with the said steamer, it is stipulated for the Mexican government, by Captain Nicolas Urcelay, that the said schooner shall remain at anchor in this port until Admiral Wilkes may return in ten, or fewer, days, or may send a substitute authorized by him.

CHARLES WILKES,
Admiral, Commanding the Squadron of the Western Islands of the United States of the North.
NICOLAS URCELAY,
Captain of the National Forces at this place.

MERIDA, *February* 23, 1863.

A copy:

A. REJON, *Secretary.*

WASHINGTON, *April* 15, 1863.

A copy:

ROMERO.

No. 5.—*Affairs on the frontiers of Mexico.*

Mr. Romero to Mr. Seward.

[Translation.]

MEXICAN LEGATION,
Washington, February 26, 1863.

Mr. SECRETARY: The Mexican consul at Crownsville, Texas, and the vice-consul of Mexico at Franklin, New Mexico, have frequently complained to this legation on account of the unjustly depressed and miserable condition in which Mexicans resident in the State of Texas and the Territory of New Mexico are held, whom it is sought to compel to serve in the army of the United States, or in that of the insurgents, or to subject to other undue burdens, in violation of the rights they hold as foreigners.

Having submitted said reports to my government, the secretary for foreign relations of the republic has communicated to me the instructions of the president on this subject, in which he recommends me to call the attention of the government of the United States to the situation of Mexican citizens resident on the frontier of the United States. He also recommends that I solicit from the government of the United States the issue of decided orders to Colonel West, commander of the expedition sent to Arizona, and to the commander of the forces of the United States in New Mexico, and to that of the expedition which is going to Texas, to act so as to preserve to the Mexicans the consideration and franchises which the universal law of nations and the conventional law between Mexico and the United States guarantee to them.

In thus complying with the instructions I have received from my government, I avail of the opportunity to repeat to you, sir, the assurances of my most distinguished consideration.

M. ROMERO.

Hon. WILLIAM H. SEWARD, *&c., &c., &c.*

Mr. Seward to Mr. Romero.

DEPARTMENT OF STATE,
Washington, March 10, 1863.

SIR: I have the honor to inform you that I have transmitted a translation of your note of the 26th ultimo, respecting the condition of the Mexican citizens on the frontier of the United States, to the Secretary of War, whose reply shall be immediately communicated to you.

I avail myself of this occasion to renew to you, sir, the assurances of my high consideration.

WILLIAM H. SEWARD.

Señor Don MATIAS ROMERO, *&c., &c., &c.*

Mr. Seward to Mr. Romero.

DEPARTMENT OF STATE,
Washington, April 2, 1863.

SIR: Referring to your note of the 26th of February ultimo, inviting the attention of this government to certain alleged hardships to which Mexican citizens residing on the frontier of Texas are subjected, I have the honor to inform you that, having submitted your communication to the Secretary of War, I have received a reply upon the subject, dated the 27th ultimo, a copy of which I herewith enclose, availing myself of this occasion to renew to you the assurances of my high consideration.

WILLIAM H. SEWARD.

Señor MATIAS ROMERO, *&c., &c., &c.*

WAR DEPARTMENT,
Washington City, March 27, 1863.

SIR: Your communication of the 10th instant, enclosing the translation of a note from the Mexican chargé d'affairs, calling attention to the situation of Mexican citizens residing on the frontiers, has been duly considered, and I have now the honor to state that this department has no information in relation to the treatment of Mexican citizens in the State of Texas, and can see no remedy for the evils complained of until that State returns to her allegiance or is occupied by the United States troops.

It is very probable that Mexican citizens, as well as citizens of the United States, in New Mexico, were ill-treated by the rebels in their invasion of that Territory, but as the government has made no draft in New Mexico, no person, either citizen or foreign, could be received into the military service of the United States except by voluntary enlistment.

The commanding generals in New Mexico and in Arizona are both intelligent and discreet officers, and, in the absence of any specific charges or evidence, it must be presumed that they have not done or permitted so unauthorized an act as to force Mexican citizens into the military service of the United States.

Officers have been and will be cautioned to carefully respect the rights and property of resident foreigners, who render no aid or assistance to the enemy.

Very respectfully, sir, your obedient servant,

EDWIN M. STANTON,
Secretary of War.

Hon. WILLIAM H SEWARD,
Secretary of State, Washington, D. C.

Mr. Seward to Mr. Corwin.

No. 74.]

DEPARTMENT OF STATE,
Washington, May 12, 1863.

SIR: In February last, Mr. Romero, chargé d'affaires of Mexico, brought to my attention certain complaints which had been made to him by the Mexican consul at Brownsville, Texas, and the vice-consul at Franklin, New Mexico, of forcible impressments of Mexican citizens, residing in the Territory of New Mexico, into the military service of the United States. The subject was immediately laid before the Secretary of War, whose reply was communicated to Mr. Romero on the 2d of April, and by him, doubtless, transmitted to his government.

The Secretary of War has, by a letter of the 5th instant, received to-day, laid before me a copy of a communication addressed to the general-in-chief by Brigadier General Carlton, commanding in New Mexico, upon the same subject, a copy of which I enclose to you, as Mr. Romero has taken leave of the government and is now *en route* to his home.

You will be pleased to communicate a copy of this document to the Mexican government.

I am, sir, your obedient servant,

WILLIAM H. SEWARD.

THOMAS CORWIN, Esq., *&c., &c., &c., Mexico.*

WAR DEPARTMENT,
Washington City, D. C., May 5, 1863.

SIR: In connexion with my communication of March 27, in relation to the complaint of the Mexican chargé d'affaires of the impressment into the United States military service of citizens of Mexico, in New Mexico, I have the honor to transmit a copy of a letter on this subject from Brigadier General J. H. Carlton, commanding department of New Mexico.

Very respectfully, sir, your obedient servant,

EDWIN M. STANTON,
Secretary of War.

The SECRETARY OF STATE, *Washington, D. C.*

HEADQUARTERS DEPARTMENT OF NEW MEXICO,
Santa Fé, N. M., April 10, 1863.

GENERAL: I have the honor to acknowledge the receipt of your letter of the 15th ultimo, and to say in reply that, to my knowledge, no citizen of Mexico has been impressed into the military service of the United States within the department of New Mexico.

A copy of your letter has been sent to Brigadier General West, commanding the district of Arizona, within this department, headquarters Hart's Mills, Texas, with these instructions: "I enclose herewith an official copy of a letter from the general-in-chief in relation to a communication made by the Mexican chargé d'affaires, complaining that citizens of Mexico had been impressed into the military service of the United States in New Mexico. You will be careful that no violation of the international rights of Mexican citizens occurs in your district."

As no soldiers of any nationality have been impressed into the military service of the United States within this department, that part of the complaint relating to New Mexico falls to the ground of its own weight.

I have the honor to be, general, very respectfully, your obedient servant,

JAMES H. CARLTON,
Brigadier General Commanding.

Major General HENRY W. HALLECK,
General-in-Chief of the Armies of the United States, Washington, D. C.

WAR DEPARTMENT, *May* 5, 1863.

Official copy:

ED. R. S. CANBY,
Brigadier General, A. A. G.

Mr. Romero to Mr Seward.

[Translation.]

MEXICAN LEGATION,
Washington, February 4, 1864.

The undersigned, envoy extraordinary and minister plenipotentiary of the United Mexican States, has the honor to call the attention of the Hon. William H. Seward, Secretary of State of the United States of America, to events which have recently taken place on the eastern frontier of Mexico and the United States.

It appears that the arrival of the United States expedition at the city of Brownsville, in the State of Texas, which had, until then, been in the possession of the secessionists, in place of producing the good results which were to be expected, because it was naturally to be supposed that a considerable force sent by this government, and operating under its direct instructions, would be the most complete safeguard of the fundamental principles of the laws of nations and of the stipulations of treaties which connect Mexico with the United States, has gone on producing disturbances and misunderstandings which neither the undersigned nor his government could anticipate or expect.

The undersigned will permit himself to call the attention of the honorable Secretary of State of the United States to a communication, and the menaces contained in it, addressed from Brownsville the 26th of December last by Major General N. J. F. Dana, who commands in chief the United States forces in Texas, to the governor of the State of Tamaulipas, in the Mexican republic, because of a loan which was said to be imposed by the said functionary on various merchants resident at Matamoras, among whom, it is averred, were found some citizens of the United States, which communication has been published by various papers in New York, running along the month of January last past.

The undersigned flatters himself with the belief that the government of the United States is very far from approving the principles of protection which that government has the right to grant to citizens of the United States resident in a foreign country in the mode in which General Dana presents them in the penultimate paragraph of his above-cited communication. The undersigned will abstain at present from comment on the proceedings of the said General Dana in respect to this incident which are related in letters published in the journals of New York from their correspondents in Matamoras, because, besides not being at present fully proven, in his opinion, in an authentic manner, he awaits instructions from his government.

There has subsequently happened, nevertheless, an incident of such nature that the undersigned considers it to be his duty to denounce it at once to the government of the United States. From the Matamoras correspondence last published in the daily papers of this country it appears that, in consequence of a local disturbance stirred up in that city, on the 12th of January last past, between two military leaders who acknowledge the authority and act under the orders of the Mexican government, General Herron, who commanded accidentally the forces of the United States at Brownsville, thought proper to send into the Mexican territory the 20th Wisconsin regiment, the 10th Iowa, and the 94th Illinois, with a battery, which troops penetrated the city of Matamoras while the disturbance was going on.

The undersigned cannot but consider this step as a flagrant violation of Mexican sovereignty; and it appears to him the less explicable because the honorable Secretary of State, in some instructions which he addressed to General Banks on the 23d November last, and which have lately been published, in relation to the manner in which he should act in difficulties which might arise with Mexico, says to him:

"You will protect citizens of the United States in Texas against all enemies, domestic or foreign, that may be met in that country. You will be on your guard, nevertheless, not to enter Mexican territory unless it be temporarily, and that the step be fully justified by the necessity of protecting the lives of our soldiers against any aggression which may come from the frontier of Mexico."

Well, then, it is certain that no aggression, proceeding from Mexican territory, menaced the lives of the soldiers of General Banks on the happening at Matamoras of the local disorder of which the undersigned has made mention.

Reserving the expectation of instructions from his government on this delicate business that he may then present to the United States government the demands he may be charged with, and ask the amends to which Mexico may have right, he now addresses himself to the honorable Secretary of State, desirous of receiving the explanations Mr. Seward may deem fit to give to him, which shall be transmitted to the Mexican government, in whose mind they will contribute to calm the bad impression which the proceedings of General Herron may have occasioned.

The undersigned avails himself of this occasion to renew to the honorable William A. Seward, Secretary of State of the United States of America, the assurances of his most distinguished consideration.

M. ROMERO.

Hon. WILLIAM H. SEWARD, *&c.*, *&c.*, *&c.*

Mr. Seward to Mr. Romero.

DEPARTMENT OF STATE,
Washington, February 9, 1864.

SIR: I have the honor to acknowledge the receipt of your note of the 4th instant, directing my attention to events which have recently taken place on the eastern frontier of the United States and Mexico.

Having no official information upon the subject referred to, I have transmitted a translation of your communication to the Secretary of War for the necessary investigation, after the receipt of which I shall be enabled to reply to your note.

I avail myself of this occasion to renew to you, sir, the assurances of my distinguished consideration.

WILLIAM H. SEWARD.

Señor Don MATIAS ROMERO, *&c.*, *&c.*, *&c.*

Mr. Seward to Mr. Romero.

DEPARTMENT OF STATE,
Washington, March 12, 1864.

SIR: I have the honor, on this occasion, to recur to the note which you addressed to me on the 4th of February last, in which, among other things, you asked for information concerning certain unusual proceedings of General Herron in sending an armed force from Brownsville, in Texas, across the Rio Grande and into the city of Matamoras, on the occasion of disturbance that occurred there on the 12th of January last, between two persons whom you represented as military leaders, each of whom acknowledges the authority and acts under the orders of the Mexican government.

In the aforementioned note you were pleased to express the opinion that the proceeding of General Herron was a flagrant violation of Mexican sovereignty, and quite inconsistent with the orders which had been previously given by this government to Major General Banks, commanding on the Mexican frontier, with reference to the republic of Mexico.

On the 9th of February last I had the honor to acknowledge the receipt of your aforementioned note, and to say that, having no official information upon the subject you had therein presented, I had transmitted it to the Secretary of War with a view to the necessary investigation of the matter. I have since that day received from the Secretary of War certain papers which bear upon the transaction, but have not yet received a full report thereupon. Desirous to act with perfect good faith and reasonable diligence in regard to the complaint you have preferred, I think it not improper to place in your hands, at this time, the papers which are now before me, namely: the report of the transaction of the 12th of January last, made by Major General Banks, together with the documents appended to the same. To these papers I annex an extract from a despatch which was transmitted to the department by L. Pierce, esquire, United States consul at Matamoras, on the 16th of January last. It appears from these papers that the movement of which you complain was made at the instance and with the consent and approval of the Mexican authorities, and was strictly limited to the protection of the United States consul at Matamoras, against apprehended assaults which the Mexican authorities were unable to prevent.

It is my duty further to inform you that the imperial government of France has now asked explanations upon the same subject, upon the ground that the proceeding of General Herron was an intervention in the interest of Mexico and against the army of France.

A copy of the note of the minister of France is herewith submitted. While this government is waiting for the more full and complete report which is necessary, in order to decide upon the conflicting claims of Mexico and France, it will cheerfully receive any information you may think it desirable to furnish to this department.

To guard against misapprehension, I think it proper to say that a complaint, which was presented by you in your aforementioned note against certain proceedings of General Dana, is left out of view in this connexion, because I am awaiting the results of an investigation which has been instituted by the Secretary of War.

I will add that General Banks has again been specially charged to do whatever is practicable to avoid any collision between the forces under his command and either of the belligerents in Mexico, and even to guard, so far as may be possible, against suffering any occasion to arise for dispute or controversy between his command or the authorities of Texas, and either or both these parties.

I avail myself of this occasion to offer to you a renewed assurance of my high consideration.

WILLIAM H. SEWARD.

Señor MATIAS ROMERO, *&c.*, *&c.*, *&c.*

WAR DEPARTMENT,
Washington City, February 10, 1864.

SIR: The Secretary of War instructs me to acknowledge the receipt of your letter of yesterday, transmitting a translation of a note addressed to you on the 4th instant by Señor Matias Romero, envoy extraordinary and minister plenipotentiary of the United Mexican States, inviting attention to a publication in the New York journals during the month of January last, purporting to be a communication containing menaces addressed from Brownsville on the 26th December by Major General N. T. J. Dana, then commanding the United States forces in Texas, to the governor of Tamaulipas, in the Mexican republic; and also to the Matamoras correspondence, published in the daily papers, in which it is stated that Major General Herron, now commanding the United States forces at Brownsville, had sent troops into the city of Matamoras during local disturbances in that city, in violation of Mexican sovereignty.

In regard to the alleged violation of the Mexican territory by United States forces acting under the orders of Major General Herron, the Secretary instructs me to transmit, for your information, the enclosed copy of a communication, this day received, addressed to the general-in-chief by Major General Banks, commanding the department of the Gulf, and its accompaniments, which present a detailed account of the circumstances under which the temporary presence of the United States troops in Matamoras was deemed imperative for the protection of the United States consulate in that city.

On the subject of the alleged letter of menace addressed by Major General N. T. J Dana from Brownsville to the governor of Tamaulipas, this department has at present no knowledge. As soon as any information on the subject is received it will be communicated to you.

I have the honor to be your obedient servant,

ED. R. S. CANBY,
Brigadier General, A. A. G.

The SECRETARY OF STATE,
Washington, D. C.

HEADQUARTERS DEPARTMENT OF THE GULF,
New Orleans, January 25, 1864.

GENERAL: I have the honor to transmit to you copies of despatches received from Major General F. J Herron, commanding the forces of the United States on the Rio Grande, and giving in detail an account of affairs occurring on the 13th of January. I enclose also a copy of letter of instructions written to General Herron, by which you will see that the despatch of the Secretary of State, with an indorsement of the Secretary of War, was given to him for his guidance before he assumed command. The movement of troops into Matamoras seems to have been necessary to enable the consul to leave the city.

N. P. BANKS,
Major General Commanding.

Major General H. W. HALLECK,
General-in-Chief U. S. A., Washington, D. C.

Official copy:

J. C. KELTON, *A. A. G.*

HEADQUARTERS UNITED STATES FORCES ON THE RIO GRANDE,
Brownsville, Texas, January 16, 1864.

GENERAL: I enclose herewith my report in reference to sending troops to the other side of the river for the protection of the United States consulate, and, believing it will interest you, I add some other facts in connexion with the matter.

Upon arriving here I found Serna established as governor of Tamaulipas; but Ruiz, who had been appointed military governor by Juarez, was moving on Matamoras with 600 men. Colonel Cortinas was in command of the Serna forces. Arriving near the town, commissioners from the two parties met and settled the matter in this way: Serna to retire to his rancho, Ruiz to take his seat as governor, the troops of both parties to unite under General Casistran (a Ruiz man) with Cortinas as second in command, and to march against the French at Tampico. Serna at once vacated; Ruiz took his seat; and the troops of both parties were camped in the town. As near as I can learn, the agreement was violated in several particulars by both parties, and considerable feeling was created. On the afternoon of the 12th, about 4 o'clock, Cardenas, an officer of Colonel Cortinas, rode to Governor Ruiz's house and insulted him; was arrested by the guard, carried into a back yard and shot within half an hour. This settled the matter, and, at 8 o'clock the same evening, the parties opened on each other with artillery in the plaza.

The fight continued throughout the night and until 12 o'clock the next day. During the night, at times, the musketry was severe, and I should say 250 shots were fired with artillery. Mr. Pierce was satisfied that an attempt would be made to rob the consulate, and had great apprehension for his family. The governor having officially notified me that he could not protect him, and believing that I could remove him without complicating matters, I sent troops over, feeling satisfied that, under the circumstances, I was only doing my duty.

During the fight the town and the road leading to the ferry were filled with robbers doing a good business, and, had Mr. Pierce attempted to cross without a guard, he would have been robbed if not murdered. Both parties are perfectly satisfied with my action, although Ruiz complains somewhat that I did not aid him, claiming that the Mexican troops once aided the citizens of Brownsville in repelling an attack of this same Cortinas.

I have the honor to be, with great respect, your obedient servant,

F. J. HERRON,
Major General Commanding.
C. P. STONE,
Brigadier General, Chief-of-Staff.

Major General N. P. BANKS,
Com'dg Department of the Gulf.

HEADQUARTERS, *February* 3, 1864.

Official copy:

J. C. KELTON, *A. A. G.*

HEADQUARTERS UNITED STATES FORCES ON THE RIO GRANDE,
Brownsville, Texas, January 15, 1864.

GENERAL: I have the honor to make the following report of circumstances that transpired on the night of the 13th instant.

About 8 o'clock in the evening we were startled by rapid cannonading and musketry firing, evidently going on in the streets of Matamoras, just across the Rio Grande, which continued without cessation, and spreading over the greater portion of the town, until 10 o'clock.

At this hour I received the following communication from Mr. L. Pierce, jr., United States consul at Matamoras:

UNITED STATES CONSULATE,
Matamoras, Mexico, January 12, 1864—10 *o'clock p. m.*

GENERAL: A battle is now raging in the streets of this city between the forces of Governor Manuel Ruiz and Colonel Juan N. Cortinas. My person and family are in great danger, as the road between here and the ferry is said to be infested with robbers. I have, also, about one million dollars in specie and a large amount of valuable property under my charge in the consulate, and, from the well-known character of Cortinas and his followers, I fear the city will be plundered. I therefore earnestly request that you will send a sufficient force to protect myself and property, and to transport the money within the limits of the United States at the earliest moment possible.

I am, sir, very respectfully, your obedient servant,

L. PIERCE, JR.,
United States Consul.

Major General F. J. HERRON,
Com'dg United States Forces, Brownsville, Texas.

Within a very few moments the following, from Governor Manuel Ruiz, was handed to me:

MATAMORAS, *January* 12, 1864—10 *o'clock p. m.*

SIR: The forces commanded by Colonel Cortinas have attacked my position in this place. As this town is very extensive, I cannot protect or guarantee the United States consulate and the large property of American citizens of different nations living in this town. For this reason I shall endeavor to repulse the enemy, and ask you the favor to send some troops over to guard and protect the said property, which it is impossible for me to protect.

I ask you, general, to take this application of mine in high consideration, and to admit my profound respects.

Your obedient servant,

MANUEL RUIZ, *Governor of Tamaulipas.*

Major General F. J. HERRON.

I had, immediately after the firing commenced, despatched an officer (Colonel Black, 37th Illinois infantry) to the United States consulate with instructions to inform me at once of the condition of affairs, and hearing from him, also, that the road was infested with robbers who were taking advantage of the fighting to rob and murder, and that the family of the consul could not get away without a guard, and the legal governor, recognized by President Juarez, having informed, officially, that he could not protect him, I deemed it not inconsistent with my instructions to send a small force into the city of Matamoras for the purpose of removing the family of Mr. Pierce and the specie to this side of the river. I therefore ordered Colonel Henry Bertram, 20th Wisconsin infantry, to send forty men to take charge of the ferry, to put one regiment under arms, and call at my headquarters for further orders. Upon reporting, I instructed him to take four companies of his regiment across the river and proceed to the United States consulate and there make proper disposition of his force to protect the United States consul and his property, and to remove them, at the earliest possible time, to this side of the river; instructing him at the same time, in the most positive manner, not to interfere in the fight.

I then replied to Governor Ruiz as follows:

HEADQUARTERS UNITED STATES FORCES ON THE RIO GRANDE,
Brownsville, Texas, January 12, 1864—10½ *o'clock p. m.*

SIR: Your note dated Matamoras, 10 o'clock p. m., is at hand. Mr. Pierce, the United States consul, wrote at 10 o'clock, urging me to send a force to protect the United States consulate, and at his request I despatched Colonel Bertram with a small force to the consul's house to protect him in moving to this side of the river.

The troops have positive instructions not to interfere with either persons or property, and to take no part in the fight. They will protect the consulate until safely removed.

Regretting exceedingly the troubles which surround you, and with the hope that you may soon quiet matters,

I have the honor to be, with great respect, your obedient servant,

F. J. HERRON,
Major General, Commanding.

Governor MANUEL RUIZ.

At the same time I wrote Mr. Pierce, informing him of the instructions given to Colonel Bertram, and requesting him to prepare for removal at once. I also sent the following notification to Governor Ruiz, sending a similar one to Colonel Cortinas:

HEADQUARTERS UNITED STATES FORCES ON THE RIO GRANDE,
Brownsville, Texas, January 12, 1864—10½ *o'clock p. m.*

SIR: I have the honor to state, that owing to a battle now raging in the streets of Matamoras, between your troops and those of Colonel Cortinas, and the danger existing to the person and family of Mr. Pierce, United States consul, I have ordered Colonel Bertram with four companies of United States troops to proceed to the house of Mr. Pierce, at his request, for the sole and only purpose of conveying them within the territory of the United States. The danger from assassins and robbers on the road between here and your city seems imperatively to demand this course, which I take reluctantly, with every assurance to you that I shall commit no hostile acts upon Mexican territory, nor interfere in any manner with the fight now going on in your city. I have intrusted Mr. Pierce to remove as quickly as possible, that I may withdraw the troops.

I have the honor to be, with great respect, your obedient servant,

F. J. HERRON,
Major General, Commanding.

Governor MANUEL RUIZ.

Colonel Bertram proceeded without delay to the other side of the river, marching by the shortest route to the consulate, and placing his troops within the yard which is attached to the house, and such arrangements were then made as would prevent any possibility of interference by our men.

At 11½ o'clock I received the following note from Colonel Bertram:

UNITED STATES CONSULATE,
Matamoras, January 12, 1864—12.30 *o'clock p. m.*

GENERAL: I have arrived at the consul's house, and I was sure he was very happy to see us. I marched the shortest route, the firing having stopped as soon as we appeared in the streets. The consul thinks Cortinas is gaining ground. I await further instructions.

Very respectfully,

H. BERTRAM, *Colonel, Commanding.*

Major General F. J. HERRON,
Commanding United States Forces.

To which I replied as follows:

HEADQUARTERS UNITED STATES FORCES ON RIO GRANDE,
Brownsville, Texas, January 12, 1864.

COLONEL: Your note from the consulate is at hand. You will remain in your position, giving the consul sufficient time to remove his family and the valuables in the consulate to this side. Again let me state that you will interfere in no way with the fight, but keep your men at their posts for the duty assigned them. Send a good officer with the troops at the ferry, and issue the most positive orders prohibiting straggling from the ranks or interference of any nature whatever with either person or property. Should a stray shot come near, or even strike one of your men, that will not be considered a sufficient reason for your firing. I have notified both Ruiz and Cortinas of your presence in Matamoras, and the purpose. Should you see either of the persons named, state fully what your instructions are.

Your mission is a delicate one. Be extremely careful.

Respectfully,

F. J. HERRON,
Major General, Commanding.

Colonel H. BERTRAM.

At 12½ o'clock I received the following from Colonel Bertram:

UNITED STATES CONSULATE,
Matamoras, January 12—12.30 *o'clock.*

GENERAL: I have received your letter. Your instructions are strictly obeyed, and I have sent the most stringent orders to Lieutenant Colonel Lauglin not to allow anything to be done that could be construed into a violation of your orders. Commissions from both Ruiz and Cortinas's parties have been here to inquire into the object of our coming over. I told them what my instructions were, and both parties went away satisfied. The consul says he has about one million in specie in his possession, and that he cannot possibly remove it or his family until morning. I have not been able to learn positively which party is gaining. Ruiz still holds the *plaza*, and I think will hold it until morning.

Respectfully,

H. BERTRAM, *Colonel, Commanding.*

Major General HERRON,
Commanding United States Forces.

The fighting ceased for an hour after the appearance of my troops; but learning that there was to be no interference, both parties went at it again, taking care, however, to keep some distance from the United States consulate.

Matters continued so until daylight, when I sent a sufficient number of wagons to remove the family of Mr. Pierce and property from the consulate.

At 7 o'clock a. m. of the 15th they were safely landed on this side and the troops withdrew. The fighting in the morning was carried on bitterly until 12 o'clock, when the Ruiz party retreated and were scattered in every direction. The casualties on both sides were about 50 killed and 100 wounded. Among the killed was Ex-Governor Alvino Lopez, a prominent Ruiz man.

Governor Ruiz's forces numbered 800 men and 4 pieces of artillery, while Cortinas's force was 600 men and 6 pieces of artillery, and the town during the fight with lawless bands plundering, &c.

Colonel Cortinas has already announced himself as governor of Tamaulipas, while Governor Ruiz, General Rojas, and some other prominent officers escaped and crossed to this side, and are now here refugees.

I have in this report given merely the facts in detail, and will not enter into any argument in justification of my course.

Notified by the governor of the State that he could not protect the United States consulate, and with an appeal from the consul directly for protection for his family and property, I felt that it was unquestionably my duty to furnish a sufficient guard to remove him from the city, taking, at the same time, every precaution to prevent collision with either of the factions. I might here state that the English consul remained during the night at the United States consulate, under our protection.

I enclose as portion of the report letters* from General Ruiz and Colonel Cortinas, the former claiming to be governor, appointed and recognized by Juarez, and complaining that I did not help him, and the latter expresses his approval of the neutrality I observed.

In conclusion, I would say that Colonel H. Bertram, of the 20th Wisconsin infantry, who commanded the troops that crossed over, performed the delicate mission in an admirable manner, and proved himself of more than ordinary judgment The officers and soldiers are entitled to thanks for their conduct.

I have the honor to be, general, with great respect, your obedient servant,

F. J HERRON, *Major General.*

Brigadier General C. P. STONE,
Chief of Staff, New Orleans.

FEBRUARY 4, 1864.

Official copy :

J. C. KELTON, *A. A. G.*

[Extract.]

UNITED STATES CONSULATE,
Matamoras, January 16, 1864.

SIR : * * * * * * * * * * * * * * *
During the night of the 12th, finding that robbing was being carried on in some parts of the town, and I having about a million of dollars in specie under my charge, at 10½ p. m. I applied to Major General Herron, commanding the forces on the Rio Grande, for sufficient men to protect our property from thieves and robbers, and he immediately crossed over a large force, who remained by us until morning, when I sent all the money to Brownsville, and the troops retired.

* * * * * * * * * * * * * * * *

I am, sir, very respectfully, your obedient servant,

L. PIERCE, JR., *Consul.*

Hon. WILLIAM H. SEWARD,
Secretary of State, Washington, D. C.

[Translation.]

LEGATION OF FRANCE IN THE UNITED STATES,
Washington, March 11, 1864.

SIR : According to the information which has reached the Emperor's government, three regiments of the federal army have lately been sent to Matamoras under pretext of protecting the consul of the United States at that point, and have there re-established the Juarists, by driving out therefrom General Cortinas, who had pronounced against it. This news, the official confirmation of which, however, it had not received, has fixed the attention of the Emperor's government. Such a fact would constitute a violation of the neutrality on which the assurances of the Cabinet at Washington have authorized it to rely on its part in regard to Mexico, and would also be entirely opposed to the instructions addressed by the Department of State to General Banks, who has been directed to favor neither of the two parties, and not to enter the Mexican territory even to protect the

---

* Not received.

American consuls and citizens there. I therefore deem it my duty, sir, to point it out to you, and would be infinitely obliged if you could furnish me with explanations on this subject.

Be pleased to accept, sir, the assurances of my high consideration,

L. DE GEOFROY.

Hon. WILLIAM H. SEWARD, *&c.*, *&c.*, *&c.*

Mr. Romero to Mr. Seward.

[Translation.]

MEXICAN LEGATION TO THE UNITED STATES OF AMERICA,
Washington, March 15, 1864.

Mr. SECRETARY: I have the honor to inform you that I have this day received the note from your department dated 12th instant, with which you were pleased to send me copies of various documents which the Secretary of War had communicated to you relative to events which happened at Matamoras on the 12th of January last, as also an extract from the communication upon the same acts addressed to your department by the consul of the United States at that city, and copy of the note in which the minister of France at this capital complains of the passage of the forces under General Herron into Mexican territory.

From the documents transmitted by the Secretary of War, it seems that the presence of such force in the city of Matamoras was requested by the governor of the State of Tamaulipas, Don Manuel Ruiz. In awaiting the more complete information which you are pleased to anounce, I shall not again touch on this matter, in my correspondence with your department, so long as I am without the instructions which I have sought from my government on this point.

I will have the pleasure of transmitting to you the explanations and reports which may be in my power on this subject, thus observing the intimation you give me in your said note.

With this occasion, it is gratifying to me to renew to you, sir, the protestation of my most distinguished consideration.

M. ROMERO.

Hon. WILLIAM H. SEWARD, *&c.*, *&c.*, *&c.*

No. 6.—*Claims of United States citizens against Mexico.*

Mr. Romero to the Minister of Foreign Affairs of the Mexican Republic, October 23, 1862.

Mr. Romero to Mr. Seward, February 26, 1863, (with enclosures.)

Mr. Seward to Mr. Romero, March 9, 1863.

Mr. Romero to the Mexican Minister of Foreign Affairs.

[Translation.]

No. 340.] MEXICAN LEGATION IN THE UNITED STATES OF AMERICA,
Washington, October 23, 1862.

At a conference which I had this day with Mr. Seward, I read to him a translation which I had prepared of the note which you addressed me, under No. 392, dated September 27 last past, in relation to the claims of the mint, which the minister of the United States, residing in your capital, had presented to the supreme government. Having concluded my reading, I stated to Mr. Seward that I had to make some explanations of details not referred to in your note.

Mr. Seward said to me that there was no necessity for my giving him such explanations; that what he had heard was sufficient for him to say that this government desired that the just claims which the loyal citizens of the United States have against foreign countries should be duly acknowledged and paid; but that, with reference to Mexico, the President, in view of the actual state of affairs in Mexico, did not propose either to exact urgently the payment of such claims, or to use force to obtain it, and that the policy of the United States in that respect had been indicated in the answer which this government gave to the allied powers against Mexico, upon being invited by them to take part in the alliance, which document is known to you.

He also stated to me that the only instructions which this government has communicated to Mr. Corwin upon the claims, which have already been published, (the first of the documents annexed to the message of the President of the 14th of April last upon the present condition of Mexico,) were so liberal and conciliatory that they would assuredly be satisfactory to the government of the Republic; that this government was entirely satisfied by the reading which I had just made to him of the good faith of the government of Mexico.

Mr. Seward asked me whether I proposed to send him said note. I answered in the affirmative. He replied, Very well; if I shall have occasion to say anything more or different upon the subject I will ask a further interview with you. We will leave it to rest under that understanding, which you may communicate to your government.

The minute of this note has been submitted to Mr. Seward, to see whether he found our conference to-day to have been faithfully recorded, and it has appeared to him correct.

I reiterate to you the assurances of my very distinguished consideration. God, liberty and reform.

M. ROMERO.

The MINISTER OF FOREIGN AFFAIRS, *Mexico*.

Mr. Romero to Mr. Seward.

[Translation.]

LEGATION OF MEXICO,
Washington, February 26, 1863.

MR. SECRETARY: In conformity with what I said to you at our interview to-day, I have the honor to send you copies of some notes exchanged between the legation of the United States in Mexico and the government of the republic respecting the nationality of Don Ignacio de Loperena, who pretends to be a citizen of the United States for the purpose of eluding the duties imposed on him in his character as a Mexican.

The certificate of the consul of the United States at Cadiz presented by Loperena seems insufficient to prove the nationality of this person, for the reasons you will see in the notes of Mr. Fuente. Mr. Corwin had, besides, intimated in his confidential note to Mr. Fuente his apprehension that the certificate was false. Loperena is a native of the State of Chiapas, in Mexico, and has never been out of the republic for five years, so that he cannot have been naturalized in the United States, because, in accordance with section third of the act of Congress of the 14th of April, 1802, entitled "An act to establish an uniform rule of naturalization and to repeal the acts heretofore passed on that subject," which is still in force, it is necessary for a foreigner who is to be naturalized that he shall have resided five years in the United States; and Loperena cannot have resided such term in this country for the reason that he has not been absent from Mexico, because he went away for the first time at the close of 1858, in company with Mr. Forsyth, who was minister of the United States to Mexico, and from that time till this five years have not passed away, besides which, he has returned some time since to the republic, and has been residing as heretofore at the capital.

I do not doubt, sir, that when you are informed of these details you will give instructions to Mr. Corwin, if he has not already done so on his own motion, that he shall cease to consider Loperena as a citizen of the United States, whereby he will avoid the inconvenience occasioned to the government of Mexico in the execution of her laws, through the protection granted until now by the legation of the United States to Loperena, and through the protests of Mr. Corwin.

I avail of this opportunity to repeat to you, sir, the assurances of my most distinguished consideration.

M. ROMERO.

Hon. WILLIAM H. SEWARD, *&c.*, *&c.*, *&c.*

CONSULATE OF THE UNITED STATES OF AMERICA.

I, Ebenezer S. Eggleston, consul of the United States of America for Cadiz and the dependences thereof, do hereby certify that Ignacio Loperena, now temporarily residing in this city of Cadiz, has this day deposited in this consulate his certificate of naturalization, duly issued out of and under the seal of the supreme court of the city of New York, declaring him to have been duly admitted and made a citizen of the United States of America.

In witness thereof, I have hereunto set my hand and the seal of this consulate this twentieth day of September, in the year of our Lord one thousand eight hundred [L. S.] and sixty-two, and of the independence of the United States the eighty-seventh.

E. S. EGGLESTON,
United States Consul.

WASHINGTON, *Febrero* 26 *de* 1863.

Es copia:

ROMERO.

CONSULATE OF THE UNITED STATES OF AMERICA,
Mexico, January 13, 1863.

I, the undersigned, consul of the United States of America for the city of Mexico and the dependences thereof, do hereby certify that the foregoing is a true and faithful copy of the original filed in this consulate, the same having been carefully examined by myself and compared with said original and found to agree therewith, word for word, and figure for figure.

In witness whereof, I have hereunto set my hand and affixed the seal of this consulate [L. S.] the day and the year above written.

MARCUS OTTERBURG,
United States Consul.

WASHINGTON, *Febrero* 26, *de* 1863.

Es copia:

ROMERO.

[Translation.]

LEGATION OF THE UNITED STATES OF AMERICA, *January* 9, 1863.

SIR: At this moment I have been shown the certificate of the consul of the United States at Cadiz, proving that Mr. Loperena is a citizen of the United States. This testimony must be conclusive with me, and, in my judgment, should be so with all it may concern.

Thus, then, I find myself under the necessity of protesting, officially, against any dispositions relating to the effects Mr. Loperena may have here, based on the idea that Mr. Loperena is not a citizen of the United States.

The consul of the United States will show you the certificate to which reference is had.

I renew to you, sir, the assurances of my respect.

THOMAS CORWIN,
Envoy Extraordinary and Minister Plenipotentiary of the United States of America.

His Excellency S'r FUENTE,
Minister of Foreign Relations, Mexico.

WASHINGTON, *February* 26, 1863.

A copy:

ROMERO.

[Translation.]

NATIONAL PALACE, MEXICO, *January* 12, 1863.

SIR: A difficulty has occurred about taking under consideration the protest contained in the note you were pleased to address to me on the 9th instant, which I have directed to be privately communicated, but as your excellency's illness has not allowed it to be brought to your knowledge, I find myself obliged to state it in writing.

This difficulty is derived from the want of the regular and customary form in the document exhibited by Don Ignacio Loperena to establish his character as a citizen of the United States, because he has brought before me the original document, and neither the signature of the American consul at Cadiz nor the seal of the consulate stamped on this paper come authenticated by the minister of the United States at Madrid, or, better still, by the department for foreign affairs at Washington. I beg you to consider that if the legation which you worthily discharge can very well certify the office, signature, and seal of a consul of the United States in the republic of Mexico, the same does not occur when treating of consuls in other countries.

Please accept the assurances of my very distinguished consideration.

JUAN A DE LA FUENTE.

His Excellency THOMAS CORWIN,
Envoy Extraordinary and Minister Plenipotentiary of the United States of America.

WASHINGTON, *February* 26, 1863.

Copy:

ROMERO.

[Translation.]

NATIONAL PALACE, MEXICO, *January* 17, 1863.

SIR: Since the letter I had the honor to address to you on the 12th instant, whose object was to offer to your consideration an important remark upon the irregularity manifest in the document shown by D. Ignacio Loperena to prove his character as North American, the chief officer of this department has received from D Juan Potts a verbal message which he was bringing to me from your excellency, and in virtue of which I must think that you no longer take interest in granting your protection to that person on account of the new nationality he attributes to himself. It is true that Mr. Potts announced a prompt answer from you on this matter, and I was expecting its receipt, not as exclusive evidence of your abandonment of this matter, but as an act which might, or not, follow the message above mentioned, without that it should be necessary for me to be thus confirmed. Still, the want of prompt reply in a case so urgent would have appeared to me, by itself alone, as a mark of acquiescence in my observations; and, nevertheless, a recent and transcendent circumstance makes a reply in every respect indispensable from your legation, therefore I beg you to send it as early as possible. A paper of this morning, "The Herald," has published the notice which appears in the printed extract annexed to this communication. The manifest tendency of this notice is to keep back the bidders on the effects of Loperena, ordered to be sold for the fiscal liabilities of this individual, and this without other reason than your excellency's protest relating to him, which interested parties suppose to be in full force. Allow me to say that I cannot question for a moment the conviction I have that your excellency does not insist upon the protest mentioned. Not only the potent want of form would oppose this, as I had the honor to point out in my previous official letter, but besides the other reasons of public notoriety of the reality of the fact, and the conclusive qualification under the laws of the United States; for D. Ignacio Loperena did not leave Mexico, to which he belongs by birth, until about the year 1859, when he went to the United States in company with Forsyth, and since then the five years, which the law of the United States determines for the residence of foreigners in their country, before they can be lawfully naturalized, have not passed.

In this reasoning I have chosen to suppose that Loperena had lived without interruption in the United States through the period elapsed since he went from Mexico until this time. For these reasons you will perceive it is impossible for this government to admit the naturalization spoken of, and that it has entire confidence in the justness of your excellency, which will prompt a declaration which will admit the manifest justice of this republic.

Be pleased, &c , &c.,

JUAN ANTONIO DE LA FUENTO.

His Excellency THOMAS CORWIN,
Envoy Extraordinary and Minister Plenipotentiary of the United States of America.

MEXICO, *January* 26, 1863.

Copy:

JUAN DE DIAS ARIAS.

WASHINGTON, *February* 26, 1863.

Copy:

ROMERO.

Mr. Seward to Mr. Romero.

DEPARTMENT OF STATE,
Washington, March 9, 1863.

SIR: I have the honor to acknowledge the receipt of your note of the 26th ultimo, in relation to the nationality of Don Ignacio de Loperena, which has already been the subject of personal conference between us.

Upon examination of the correspondence of Mr. Corwin, I do not find that he has made any communication to the department on the subject; and, in the absence of such information, it is deemed proper to request a report from him upon the case. In directing Mr. Corwin to make this report, it will be intimated to him that while he yields protection to *bona fide* citizens, he will not suffer citizenship to be fraudulently assumed for the purpose of shielding Mexican citizens from the obligations due to their own laws and government.

I avail myself of this occasion to offer to you, sir, a renewed assurance of my high consideration.

WILLIAM H. SEWARD.

Señor Don MATIAS ROMERO, &c., &c., &c.

No. 7.—*The temporary withdrawal of Mr. Romero from Washington.*

Mr. Romero to Mr. Seward.

[Translation]

MEXICAN LEGATION IN THE UNITED STATES OF AMERICA,
Washington, April 23, 1863.

Mr. SECRETARY: I have the honor to inform you that my government, acceding to the repeated applications which I have made to it to permit me to return to Mexico for the purpose of taking an active part in the defence of my country against the foreign invader, has been pleased to grant me temporary leave to return to the republic.

I have instructions from my government to leave, during my absence from Washington, the Mexican citizens resident in the United States under the protection of the representative of one of the American nations friendly to Mexico accredited to this government, to be designated to the Department of State, before I leave New York. I will also leave in the keeping of the same representative the archives of this legation in Washington.

Proposing to make immediate use of the leave granted to me by my government, I beg you to order passports to be sent to me, for myself and for Don Jesus Escobar y Armendaris, attached to this legation, who will return with me to the republic.

I avail of this opportunity to repeat to you, sir, the assurances of my most distinguished consideration.

M. ROMERO.

Hon. WILLIAM H. SEWARD, &c., &c., &c.

Mr. Seward to Mr. Romero.

DEPARTMENT OF STATE,
Washington, April 23, 1863.

SIR: I have the honor to acknowledge the receipt of your note of this date, informing me that your government, yielding to your repeated applications for permission to return to Mexico for the purpose of taking an active part in the defence of your country in the unhappy war now existing there, has granted you a temporary leave of absence, during which the interests of Mexican citizens are, under your instructions, to be placed in charge of one of the representatives of the American States, to be named hereafter, and requesting passports for yourself and for Don Jesus Escobar y Armendaris, attaché of the legation, who will return with you.

Whilst I cannot but express my sincere regrets that your relations with this government are to be temporarily suspended—relations in which, both in your official and personal character, your abilities, zeal, and amiability, have rendered you most acceptable to those who have had intercourse with you—I cannot but sympathize with and appreciate the motive which has prompted your patriotic determination, and I offer my best wishes for your safety and success in carrying it into effect. When your object shall have been accomplished, it will give me pleasure to welcome your return hither.

The passports you request are enclosed. Due respect will be paid to the representations which may be made on behalf of the interests of Mexican citizens by the person to whom that duty is delegated.

I avail myself, sir, of the occasion to repeat to you the assurances of my distinguished consideration.

WILLIAM H. SEWARD.

Señor Don MATIAS ROMERO, *&c., &c., &c.*

Mr. Romero to Mr. Seward.

MEXICAN LEGATION IN THE UNITED STATES OF AMERICA,
New York, May 8, 1863.

MR. SECRETARY: I have the honor to inform you that, in compliance with the instructions which I received from my government to return to Mexico, and which I communicated to your department in my note of the 23d of April last past, I requested of Señor Don Federico L. Barreda, the minister resident of Peru, that during my absence from Washington he should remain in charge of the protection of the Mexican citizens residing in the United States, and of the trust of the archives of the Mexican legation, which charge Mr. Barreda had the goodness to accept. I have, therefore, to request you to be pleased to recognize him as charged with the protection referred to, until such time as my government may otherwise direct.

I avail myself of this opportunity to renew to you, sir, the assurances of my most distinguished consideration.

M. ROMERO.

Hon. WILLIAM H. SEWARD, *&c., &c., &c.*

No. 8.—*Case of the Mexican prisoners confined at Fort Delaware.*

Mr. Barreda to Mr. Seward.

[Translation.]

{ Stamp of Legation of Peru. }

NEW YORK, *September* 18, 1863.

SIR: Francisco Navarro Sanchez, Julio Nores, José Antonio Candido, and Jorge D. Lustin, prisoners of war in Fort Delaware, have addressed the consul general of Mexico in this city, stating to him that they are Mexican citizens, the first a native of Reynosa, and the others natives of Matamoras; that at the beginning of the war they were in the city of New Orleans, which they could not leave on account of the blockade; that they were obliged to take up arms for the term of one year; that on this being concluded they were forced to continue in the army for the time the war should last; that they do not wish to be exchanged or to return to the south, and that their desire is to be set at liberty in order that they may return to Mexico.

Not having the means of verifying the assertions of the applicants, I address your excellency, trusting, from your equity, that you will be pleased to order the case to be investigated, and that if their statements should turn out to be true, you will direct the men who have been forced to render service that was not exacted by law to be set at liberty.

Navarro Sanchez belonged to company G of the 3d regiment of infantry of Louisiana, army of the west. He will give information of the corps in which the others have done military duty.

I avail myself of this opportunity to renew to your excellency the assurances of my esteem and respect.

F. L. BARREDA.

His Excellency the SECRETARY OF STATE
of the United States, Washington.

Mr. Seward to Mr. Barreda.

DEPARTMENT OF STATE,
Washington, September 21, 1863.

SIR: I have received and have commended to the attention of the Secretary of War your note of the 18th instant, asking for the release of certain Mexicans confined in Fort Delaware as prisoners of war.

I avail myself of the occasion to offer to you a renewed assurance of my very high consideration.

WILLIAM H. SEWARD.

Señor Don F. L. BARREDA, *&c., &c., &c.*

Mr. Seward to Mr. Barreda.

DEPARTMENT OF STATE,
Washington, September 24, 1863.

SIR: I have the honor to inform you that the Secretary of War has notified this department that your request touching certain Mexicans now in confinement as prisoners of war in Fort Delaware will receive the attentive consideration of his department.

I avail myself of this occasion to renew to you, sir, the assurance of my highest consideration.

WILLIAM H. SEWARD.

Señor Don F. L. BARREDA, *&c., &c., &c.*

Mr. Barreda to Mr. Seward.

NEWPORT, *September* 28, 1863.

SIR: I have the honor to acknowledge the receipt of your communication of the 24th instant, informing me that the Secretary of War has notified you that my request touching certain Mexicans now confined as prisoners of war in Fort Delaware will receive the attentive consideration of his department.

Thanking you, sir, for your prompt attention to this subject, I have the honor to be your excellency's obedient servant,

F. L. BARREDA.

His Excellency the SECRETARY OF STATE
of the United States, Washington.

Mr. Romero to Mr. Seward.

[Translation.]

MEXICAN LEGATION TO THE UNITED STATES OF AMERICA,
Washington, February 15, 1864.

Mr. SECRETARY: Under date of the 24th September, of the year last past, the department deemed proper to answer to Don Federico Barreda, then charged with the protection of Mexicans, that his application in regard to certain Mexicans confined as prisoners of war at Fort Delaware would be taken into consideration by the Secretary of War, as that functionary had informed you.

Very lately I have received from those interested the letter which I have the honor to enclose, in copy, from which it must be inferred that as yet the case of the individuals to whom I refer has not been solved. I beg, therefore, that it may please you to tell me whether in fact no determination has been taken about that of George D. Lustin, Julio Norris and José A. Candida, or, in case no decision has been yet made, that you will be so good as to indicate the same to me, that I may not occupy the attention of the department with this matter but so far as may be strictly necessary.

I avail of this opportunity to repeat to your excellency the assurances of my most distinguished consideration.

M. ROMERO.

Hon. WILLIAM H. SEWARD, *&c., &c., &c.*

FORT DELAWARE, *February* 10, 1864.

Señor ROMERO, *Minister to the United States:*

The undersigned, a prisoner of war, was residing in the city of New Orleans at the commencement of the present war between the northern and southern States, and was forced to enter the rebel army in 1862, and served in the same until July, 1863, when he surrendered himself a prisoner of war to the northern forces, and took the oath of allegiance to the government of the United States. He would state to your excellency that he is a citizen of Matamoras, in the State of Tamaulipas, in the republic of Mexico, which you have the honor to represent at the city of Washington, and that on the 8th day of the present month he communicated the foregoing facts to the Secretary of War of the United States and to Major General Butler, commanding at Norfolk, Va. I would be under many obligations to you if you will call the attention of the government at Washington to my case and have me released from prison. I am a loyal citizen of the Juarez government, and desire to continue so.

I would assure your excellency that there are two other citizens of Mexico now confined in prison here, whose cases are the same as mine, and would respectfully ask you to use your influence and ministerial authority to have them released also. They are named Juloi Norris and José A. Candida, both citizens of Tamaulipas, and loyal to the Juarez government.

I would have addressed this communication to you in the Spanish language, but there is no one here to interpret it to the examining officer, who examines all letters sent from this post to another post.

Hoping your excellency will give his immediate attention to this, and with my best wishes for your health and prosperity, I am your most obedient servant,

GEORGE D. LUSTIN.

WASHINGTON, *February* 15, 1864.

A true copy:

IGN. MARISCAL, *Secretary.*

Mr. Seward to Mr. Romero.

DEPARTMENT OF STATE,
Washington, March 15, 1864.

SIR: Referring to your note of the 15th ultimo relative to certain Mexican citizens confined as prisoners of war in Fort Delaware, I have the honor to inform you that, having submitted the subject to the Secretary of War, I have received from General Canby, under the Secretary's instructions, a communication dated the 11th instant, copy of which is herewith enclosed.

I avail myself of this occasion to renew to you, sir, the assurances of my high consideration.

WILLIAM H. SEWARD.

Señor Don MATIAS ROMERO, *&c., &c., &c.*

WAR DEPARTMENT, WASHINGTON CITY,
March 11, 1864.

SIR: The Secretary of War instructs me to acknowledge the receipt of your letter of the 16th ultimo, inviting attention to an enclosed translation of a note from the minister of Mexico, of the day previous, requesting information as to the determination of the government in regard to George D. Lustin, Julio Norris, and José A. Candida, alleged Mexican citizens, now in confinement as prisoners of war at Fort Delaware.

In reply thereto, the Secretary instructs me to inform you that the commissary general of prisoners has been advised that these cases will be held in reserve for the present, and the prisoners will not be sent south for exchange against their consent.

I have the honor to be your obedient servant,

EDWARD R. S. CANBY,
Brigadier General, A. A. G.

The SECRETARY OF STATE, *Washington, D. C.*

Mr. Romero to Mr. Seward.

[Translation.]

MEXICAN LEGATION TO THE UNITED STATES OF AMERICA,
Washington, March 17, 1864.

Mr. SECRETARY: I have had the honor to receive the note you were pleased to address to me on the 15th current, enclosing to me a communication from General Canby relative to four Mexican citizens who are held at Fort Delaware as prisoners of war. Those individuals represented to this legation in September last that they were residing in New Orleans when the civil war broke out in the United States; that they could not depart from that port in consequence of its blockade established by the United States navy; that they were compelled by the agents of the insurrection to take up arms against the government of the United States for the term of one year; which having come to its end, they compelled them to continue in the secessionist army during the time the war might last. As a proof of the sincerity of such representations they stated that they would not be exchanged, nor return to the south, and desired to go back to Mexico.

As they did not present proofs of the truth of their assertions, Mr. Barreda, minister of Peru, in charge at that time of the protection of Mexican citizens in the United States, thought fit to confine himself, in the note which he addressed to your department of the 18th September aforesaid, to request that an investigation of the case should be made, and that if the result showed the statements of the parties interested to be true, they should be set at liberty.

On the 24th of said September you were pleased to announce to Mr. Barreda that the Secretary of War had informed him that application relative to those Mexicans would receive due attention from his department.

On the 10th of February last past, one of the parties again addressed this legation, stating that they still remained imprisoned, and alleging circumstances which tended to prove their foregoing assertions, such as having taken the oath of fealty to the government of the United States, in consequence whereof I think it proper to address myself to your department inquiring whether the honorable Secretary of War has yet decided the case referred to. The communication to which I now reply informs me "that the Secretary of War has given instructions to the commissary general of prisoners that these cases be reserved for the present; that meantime the parties are not to be exchanged against their will." From this it appears to follow that the Department of War does not think proper to make the investigation which had been solicited, which to me seems not credible, because it would be the means most adequate to determine satisfactorily this incident, it being, besides, notorious that if the parties are left indefinitely in prison, their condition will be worse than that of those who indubitably have served voluntarily in the rebellion, who may be exchanged at any time.

According to my information in similar cases, in which prisoners have been made of subjects of other nations, and chiefly of Great Britain, they have been set at liberty when it has been shown that they served in the ranks of the insurgents by compulsion of greater force, and the justice of the government of the United States is too well known to admit belief that it will proceed in a different manner in its treatment of Mexican citizens.

I therefore deem it my duty again to beg the government of the United States to cause proper investigation to be made in this business, and in case it proves the truth of the statements made by the parties interested, that it cause them to be set at liberty.

I avail of this opportunity to renew to you, sir, the assurances of my most distinguished consideration.

M. ROMERO.

Hon. WILLIAM H. SEWARD, *&c., &c., &c.*

Mr. Romero to Mr. Seward.

[Translation.]

MEXICAN LEGATION IN THE UNITED STATES OF AMERICA,
Washington, April 25, 1864.

MR. SECRETARY: In my note dated on the 17th of March last past, I had the honor to inform you that, in my opinion, the determination adopted by the Secretary of War in the case of the Mexican prisoners confined at Fort Delaware was not entirely conformable to that which the considerations of equity demanded, which militate in their favor, inasmuch as they had suffered so long an imprisonment without any investigation having been made of the truth of the facts which they allege in their defence.

Subsequently I have received the letters of George D. Lustin, copies of which I annex to this communication. By the first of these letters it will be seen that one of the prisoners has already died while awaiting the final determination as to his fate, and that Lustin complains of being quite sick. These circumstances, I trust, will influence the government of the United States to have the cases of the three remaining prisoners attended to, by judging them by means of the investigation which they solicit, and which I have had the honor to indicate, or by putting an end otherwise to the painful situation of expectancy in which they find themselves. My object in this note is none other than to again call your attention to this business by requesting your influence, to the end that it may lead to a decision as promptly as it may be possible, and in the terms of justice which are to be expected from the government of the United States.

With this motive I renew to you, Mr. Secretary, the assurances of my very distinguished consideration.

M. ROMERO.

Hon. WILLIAM H. SEWARD, *&c., &c., &c.*

FORT DELAWARE, *April* 20, 1864.

RESPECTED SIR: Permit me again to call your attention to my case, and to request you to press it upon the government of the United States, and procure a decision as early as possible. An exchange is in progress, and having no desire or intention of ever going back to the southern army, I am the more anxious to obtain my release before the prisoners are sent from here for exchange. I presume a load will be sent off in a few days from here, and I know not how soon all may be sent. I do not know what evidence the government will require me to produce to warrant it in releasing me, and securing itself against any further service on my part in the rebel army. Having once taken the oath of allegiance, as heretofore stated, and claiming Mexican citizenship and the protection of your excellency, being able to substantiate beyond a doubt that I am a citizen of the government which your excellency has the honor to represent, I think would be a sufficient guarantee of my sincerity. I am willing to submit to any test that may be imposed upon me, compatible with honor, which your excellency may approve, whereby my allegiance to your excellency's government will not be compromised or impaired.

Hoping that your excellency may be able to procure a speedy decision by the government, I am yours, most respectfully,

GEORGE D. LUSTIN.

Señor ROMERO, *Envoy Extraordinary, &c.*

Copy:

IGN. MARISCAL.

FORT DELAWARE, *March* 27, 1864.

SIR: Yours of the 23d is to hand, and I tender you my acknowledgments for your promptness in laying my case before the government.

I am very desirous of securing my release before summer, as my health is quite delicate, and I fear that I may not be able to stand it through the season. If you can expedite my release it will confer a favor. I am not afraid of being sent south, as I have no wish to go back, and do not anticipate that I will be forced to go. The statements in mine of the 10th ultimo are strictly true, and the utmost reliance can be placed in them, and can be substantiated by indubitable testimony which will be furnished you if you can secure an investigation of my case, and it should be necessary for you to be put in possession of it. Francisco Navarro Sanches was sent to Point Lookout, Maryland, and I have learned that he died there of small-pox. The regiment to which he was attached were all sent to Point Lookout.

Again thanking you for your attention, I am, sir, your most obedient servant,

GEORGE D. LUSTIN.

Señor ROMERO, *Minister at Washington.*

Copy :

IGN. MARISCAL.

Mr. Seward to Mr. Romero.

DEPARTMENT OF STATE,
Washington, April 28, 1864.

SIR: I have the honor to acknowledge the receipt of your note of the 25th instant, with its enclosures.

I have communicated a translation of the former, and a copy of the latter, to the Secretary of War, referring, at the same time, to your previous note of the 17th ultimo upon the same subject, which had been duly submitted to the War Department without eliciting any information.

I shall hasten to communicate to you the reply which may be received to these representations.

I avail myself of this occasion to renew to you the assurances of my high consideration.

WILLIAM H. SEWARD.

Señor MATIAS ROMERO, *&c., &c., &c.*

No. 9.—*Protection of Mexican citizens in California.*

Mr. Romero to Mr. Seward.

[Translation.]

MEXICAN LEGATION TO THE UNITED STATES OF AMERICA,
Washington, March 12, 1864.

SIR: I have the honor to send to you a copy of a note I have received from the Mexican consul at San Francisco, in which he informs this legation of the illegal proceedings of which two Mexican citizens were victims at a place in the State of California called Campo Chino, which proceeding ended in the execution without form of law of the said citizens named, Luis Leyva and Cosme Nuñez. I send also to your department a slip from the newspaper "La Voz de Mexico," which is mentioned in said note, and a copy of the statement which several Mexican citizens resident at Campo Chino presented to the Mexican consul at San Francisco in relation to the same matter.

I am sure that the government of the United States, animated by its natural rectitude, will not do less than proceed in this case as justice and the good report of every civilized country demands, and will do so at once upon the facts to which I allude reaching its knowledge, even if otherwise than through me; therefore I think I am excused from urging it, beyond the hope that most effective orders be issued for the apprehension and punishment of those guilty of the assassination of the two Mexican citizens to whom I have made reference, and that also there be given to all Mexican citizens resident in the State of California the protection of the laws to which they have full right in virtue of the stipulations of the treaties which bind together the United States and the Mexican republic.

Reserving return to the submission of this painful subject to the consideration of the department, when I may receive the instructions my government may think right to give me about it, I avail myself of this opportunity to repeat to you, sir, the assurances of my most distinguished consideration.

M. ROMERO.

Hon. WILLIAM H. SEWARD, &c., &c., &c.

[Translation.]

CONSULATE OF MEXICO AT SAN FRANCISCO,
San Francisco, February 13, 1864.

Having become informed, through various channels, that on the 25th December two Mexicans, called Luis Leyva and Cosme Nuñez, were hanged at a place in this State called Campo Chino, by a mob of persons of various nations, I thought it my duty to inform you of the fact, because it is no rare thing for Mexicans to be victims of such outrages without any intervention of the authorities to repress such acts. I enclose a slip from the Mexican newspaper "La Voz de Mexico," in which publicity has been given to this matter. I also enclose a paper which has been addressed to me from that point, Campo Chino, in which appear the names of the persons who make that kind of demonstration in their way. All which I place in your knowledge, that, if you think it suitable, you may take any step in the business.

I assure you of my respectful consideration.

M. E. RODRIGUEZ.

Don MATIAS ROMERO,
Envoy Extraordinary and Minister Plenipotentiary of the Republic at Washington.

WASHINGTON, *March* 12, 1864.

A copy:

IGNO. MARISCAL.

[Translation.]

Patriotic Mexican Junta of Sonora.—Statement to Don Manuel E. Rodriguez, consul of the Mexican republic at San Francisco.

We, Mexicans, who compose this patriotic association, have assembled this day, the 7th February, 1864, to make this statement, which has the double object of congratulating our consul resident at San Francisco on the firmness with which he has commenced the discharge of his functions and to bring to his knowledge the facts which we are about to press upon him. In doing thus, we think we are discharging a sacred duty as citizens of Mexico resident in a foreign country; a duty, the fulfilment of which in this State is of especial importance, as there have been here so frequent outrages on our countrymen and so little spirit shown in their defence as to give room for the repetition of the same scandals.

Moved by this consideration, C. Alejo Ramirez has made a motion in the junta in the terms following: "Countrymen, I was anxious to see assembled a good number of my fellow-citizens for the purpose of calling their attention to a scandalous outrage committed at Campo Chino on the persons of two Mexicans, who were very lately hung without suit previously instituted or any evidence soever. I propose to you that we resort to our consul, that he may recur to the government of the State or other competent power, complaining of the act to which I refer, which we must consider as offensive to the dignity of our country. Certainly we should not advocate the impunity of criminals, but we should demand that when a Mexican deserves to be punished with any penalty he should be judged according to the laws of this country." This motion was approved by all present, and the assembly closed with the signing of this act by the following citizens:

Alejo Ramirez.
Gregorio Contreras.
José M. Hernandez.
José M. Garcia.
Ramon Osorio.
Ramon Martinez.
Amdo Cuevas.
Simon Caberut.
José M. Rosas.
Jesus Camacho.
Viviano Rubio.
Francisco R. Luvilla.
Fernando Mariscal.
Jesus Duarte.
Ignacio Carvajal.
Nicolas Gonzalez.
Casimiro Leon.
Herculano Sierra.
Luis Yañes.
Pedro Lomelin.
Gabriel Mendes.
Maximiano Nava.
Cesario Ramirez.
Antonio Castro.
Cirilo Flores.
Arcadio Vasconcelos.
Basilio Villanueva.
Lugardo Palacio.
Bonito Madigales.
Francisco Anaga.
Angel Silvas.
Refugio Gastelum.
Faustino Morelos.
José Castro.
Jesus Andado.
Fermin Antelo.
Miguel Morelos.

WASHINGTON, *March* 12, 1860.

Correct:

IGNO. MARISCAL.

[Translation.]

From the San Francisco "Voz de Mexico."

Assassination of two Mexicans, Luis Leyva and Cosme Nuñes.

We take occasion to announce in our paper the assassinations committed on two of our countrymen in disregard of the authorities who are the sole executors of the laws, and now give place to a narrative sent us by a sister of Leyva, and submit it without commentary and without modification, because we wish the ideas should be read as they are presented by the party who communicated them to us.

We urge the Mexican consul resident here to take some action in relation to indemnity for the injuries caused by such outrages, and the punishment of their perpetrators if, perchance, within the sphere of his faculty; but if not, we ask him to address our minister at Washington, that such functionary may interpose the measures which may be needful to attain those objects and that the repetition of such disorders may be averted.

All Mexicans who experience wrongs may send their complaints to this press, well assured that if well founded we will give them publicity with pleasure, because there will at least rest with us the consolation that we have not kept silence on the injustice done to our countrymen.

SONORA, *January* 31, 1864.

Messrs. Editors of "La Voz de Mexico," San Francisco:

DEAR SIRS: Annexed I send you a letter in which you will find the details of the assassination committed at Campo Chino on two of our countrymen, to the end that if you find them worthy of insertion in your esteemed paper you may do so, in order that public animadversion may fall on the perpetrators.

The subscriber, sister of one of the dead men, poor and unaided, recurs to you as the only channel through which, as advised, she can elucidate this matter, which, as you will see, is of interest to every Mexican in its publication.

I remain your obedient servant, Messrs. Editors,

ANASTASIA LEYVA.

[Translation.]

Horrid assassination committed at Campo Chino on the persons of Luis Leyva and Cosme Nuñez, by a mob of Irish, Germans, and Indians, led on by Don Alejandro Retes de Castorena.

On the 18th day of December, 1863, Luis Leyva, going drunk about the campo, entered a shop known by name as El Colorado, to pawn a pistol for five dollars, because, in that trade, money is lent upon every kind of pledge to as many as ask for it; but this El Colorado did not lend to Leyva, and greatly insulted him, and was replied to by Leyva in similar terms. Leyva went out from there and entered a bakery opposite El Colorado's shop, where he pledged the pistol. On the same day El Colorado sued Leyva for damages—some hours earlier—but the authority evaded the matter.

On the 25th of same December, El Colorado, aware that Leyva had redeemed the pistol from where it was in pawn, again sued Leyva, bringing as witness his own brother, testifying in the court that Leyva was carrying arms to attack him with. The judge ordered him to be searched, and, satisfied that he was not carrying arms of any kind, the judge demanded of him bail for five hundred dollars, as guarantee he would drink no more liquor, to which Leyva replied that he was a man with whom this was a vice, and for this reason could not give the bail he asked for, as much because he had no money as that he did not own property of any kind. The judge rejoined that if he did not give the bail he asked for he would order him to prison at Sonora for six months, to which Leyva answered he would do as he chose, but he was satisfied he was acting arbitrarily, because there had been no one sworn according to law that could cause him to be so sentenced. Notwithstanding these observations, the judge sentenced him to six months' imprisonment in the jail at Sonora, Leyva remaining in the court-room till 2 o'clock in the afternoon, at which hour the judge placed him in the custody of the sheriff, who took him to jail.

It is to be remarked that while Leyva was on trial on the 25th, Don Alejandro Retes de Castorena came in, accusing Cosme Nuñez and Amado Pacheco of robbing him of three horses.

The judge of the place ordered the arrest of Nuñez and Pacheco. The sheriff, accompanied by Retes, went to the house of the subscriber, sister of the deceased, where Nuñez and Pacheco lived. They found Nuñez asleep; the sheriff waked him and went into the street, but fearing what in effect took place, he took to his heels, because Nuñez and the campo in general know, and it is notorious, that at that place things are done arbitrarily. In fine, they overtook him, and Nuñez gave up; thence they dragged him before the judge, who told him what Retes had stated, to which Nuñez replied he was entirely innocent in this matter. The judge finding no cause against Nuñez, said to Retes, if he had no proofs on the following day he would set Nuñez at liberty. Then Alexandro threatened the judge if he would not punish the accused. The judge knowing, from what was apparent, that Retes did not tell the truth and was swearing falsely, wished to set Nuñez free, but Retes again threatened the judge, saying, that if he set said Nuñez at liberty he would put a ball through him. The judge then ordered Nuñez to jail for trial the following day.

On the 25th, between eleven and twelve at night, said Retes, with a mob, rushed upon the jail, opened the door, took out Leyva and Nuñez, and on the edge of the campo hanged them on a tree.

As evidence that an assassination had been committed, which calls for the punishment of its perpetrators, it is enough to say that the horses supposed to have been stolen were found three days afterwards at a horse-raising farm, three miles distant from Campo Chino, the owner of which farm said that the horses came there of themselves. In view of an event so lamentable, we hope the authority to whom it belongs will take cognizance of it for the purpose of punishing those who, setting themselves above the laws and those charged with their administration, constitute themselves as a court and dispose of the life and honor of the citizen at their caprice and without any regular procedure.

I, as sister of the dead Leyva, demand, in presence of God and of the civilized world, the punishment of Mr. Retes Castorena as guilty of the act, for my dead brother was, by all proof, a good man, as I will testify when I am required. So also will I prove that Retes Castorena is a man who acts and has acted dishonestly, because in general he has been in companionship with thieves.

It is attributed to me that in my house I gave shelter to men of not very good repute; but those were known to all the campo, and I heard none speak evil of them, as is shown by the fact that the judge himself and his constable were with them in the same shop, and who, if they had any ground, or even suspicion, would have advised me not to let them into my house—a thing they did not do, and which evidently proves that some would cast a calumny upon me.

ANASTASIA LEYVA.

Mr. Seward to Mr. Romero.

DEPARTMENT OF STATE,
Washington, March 17, 1864.

SIR: I have the honor to acknowledge the receipt of your note of the 12th instant, relating to outrages alleged to have been perpetrated upon the Mexican citizens Leyva and Nuñez by a mob in California, with the papers accompanying it. Deeply regretting the occasion which has prompted such a representation from you, I have to assure you that this government will countenance no disregard of the rights of foreigners living within its jurisdiction, and that I have transmitted your note, with the accompanying papers, to his excellency the governor of California, with an earnest recommendation that the perpetrators of the outrage be properly dealt with.

I avail myself of this occasion to renew to you, sir, the assurances of my distinguished consideration.

WILLIAM H. SEWARD.

Señor MATIAS ROMERO, *&c., &c., &c.*

No. 10.—*Case of the Mexican brig Raton del Nilo.*

Mr. Romero to Mr. Seward, February 18, 1864, (with one enclosure.)
Mr. Seward to Mr. Romero, February 20, 1864.
Same to same, February 24, 1864, (with one enclosure.)

Mr. Romero to Mr. Seward.

[Translation.]

MEXICAN LEGATION TO THE UNITED STATES OF AMERICA,
Washington, February 18, 1864.

Mr. SECRETARY: I have the honor to remit to you copy of a protest which I have received from the Mexican consul at the Havana against the capture, by a war steamer of the United States, of the Mexican pilot-boat Raton del Nilo, which had cleared from said port for Matamoras.

Withholding myself from seeking from the government of the United States, on account of said capture, that which the Mexican government may believe proper under the circumstances of the case, I consider it my duty to send to your department the protest mentioned, that there may appear in it the effects to which it gave cause.

I avail of this opportunity to renew to you, sir, the assurances of my most distinguished consideration.

M. ROMERO.

Hon. WILLIAM H. SEWARD, *&c., &c., &c.*

CONSULATE OF THE MEXICAN REPUBLIC AT THE HAVANA.

I, José de Cabarga, charged with the Mexican consulate at the Havana, certify that in the book A of protocols, in this consulate, at folio 266, is a document which literally says thus:

CONSULATE OF MEXICO AT THE HABANA.

On the 2d day of the month of February, of the year 1864, appeared at this consulate in my charge, Doctor Don Miguel P. Guimera, for himself and as agent for Don Isidro Maristany, and said, that on the 21st day of the month of October last past, the Mexican pilot-boat Raton del Nilo, in command of her captain, Don Gil Gelpi, with a general cargo of lawful merchandise, duly cleared at the marine administration and this consulate, sailed from this port bound to Matamoras. That the said vessel having reached her port of destination, he received a letter from her captain the 18th of November last, advising him that the vessel had anchored in the roads of Matamoras about fifteen days past and was busy discharging cargo, of which he had already sent part to its owners; and in another, of the 21st of December, he notifies me that whilst he was on shore for the purpose of getting through with the custom-house papers, on the 27th of November, a heavy gale arose which caused the vessel to disappear from the place where she was at anchor without his having any knowledge of it, for which reason he feared some unfortunate event. In this state of things, and without having been able to advance in any way in what might point out where the Raton del Nilo had brought up, on the 15th day of January last arrived, and on that day the cook of said vessel, José Suarez, presented himself to the deponent, stating to him that he had just reached this city from New Orleans, whither he had been carried with his other comrades in the vessel, adding, that while anchored in the roads of Matamoras a heavy storm came on from the north on the 27th of November, and that about ten o'clock at night the chain cable broke, by reason whereof they saw they were under the necessity, although the captain was on shore, of making sail; that after two days lying to, the wind fell and the currents carried them about thirty-five miles from Matamoras; that on the 2d of December, about ten o'clock in the morning, they hove in sight of a steamer coming towards them, and that it would be about eleven o'clock when the said steamer took them prisoners, it turning out that it was the American war steamer Nerlande; that they took out all the crew of the pilot-boat and carried them on board the steamer, sending the Raton del Nilo to Matagorda manned by sailors from the steamer, which carried them to the bay of Matamoras in the Nerlande, where the captain of the steamer neither gave information of the capture which he had made, nor allowed them to advise the captain of the Raton, or to communicate with any person whatever; that from thence they were taken in the same steamer to Matagorda, where the pilot-boat arrived the 8th or 9th of December; that at Matagorda they put on board the pilot-boat the second mate, two seamen, and the cook, who declares that at night, and without the commission of any offence, they were placed in shackles and handcuffed until the 28th, when they reached New Orleans; that on the 29th they went to make oath at the commandant's, where they were set at liberty, the captain's chest remaining at the commandant's; that in this state of things, for himself and in the name of his principal, interested as they are in the said pilot-boat Raton del Nilo, and because of the great damage they have suffered by the violent and arbitrary capture of that vessel without any cause that justifies it, he protests once, twice, and thrice, and as often as may be necessary according to law, against the capturing vessel and against every one who may be liable, to the end that they return the bark and indemnify all losses and damages they have suffered, and all interests they had therein duly estimated, to the end that through the evidence of this protest there be established at this consulate the proper reclamation on the federal government, without prejudice to the protestant availing of his rights by all lawful means.

In faith whereof these presents are signed, and by the witnesses subscribing, at the date above expressed.

MIGUEL DE GUIMERA.

As witness: G. MENENDEZ.
As witness: C. BUISSON.

Before me, acting consul in charge.

JOSÉ DE CABARGA.

And that the party interested may give it in evidence when it may be proper, I sign the present, authenticated by the seal of this consulate, at the Havana, the 8th of February, 1864.

In charge of the consulate,

JOSÉ DE CABARGA,
Mexican Consulate at the Havana.

WASHINGTON, *February* 18, 1864.

A true copy:

IGNO. MARISCAL, *Secretary.*

Mr. Seward to Mr. Romero.

DEPARTMENT OF STATE,
Washington, February 20, 1864.

SIR: I have the honor to acknowledge the receipt of your note of the 18th instant, enclosing copy of the protest from the Mexican consul at the Havana, against the capture, by a war steamer of the United States, of the pilot-boat Raton del Nilo, and to inform you that I have communicated translations of the same to the Secretary of the Navy for the necessary information.

I avail myself of this occasion to renew to you the assurance of my high consideration.

WILLIAM H. SEWARD.

Señor MATIAS ROMERO, *&c.*, *&c.*, *&c.*

Mr. Seward to Mr. Romero.

DEPARTMENT OF STATE,
Washington, February 24, 1864.

SIR: I have the honor to enclose for your information the copy of a letter, dated yesterday, from the Secretary of the Navy, in relation to the capture of the Mexican pilot-boat Raton del Nilo, which was the subject of your note of the 18th instant.

I will communicate to you such further information upon the result of the admiralty proceedings as may be received.

I avail myself of this occasion to renew to you, sir, the assurances of my high consideration,

WILLIAM H. SEWARD.

Señor MATIAS ROMERO, *&c.*, *&c.*, *&c.*

NAVY DEPARTMENT, *February* 23, 1864.

SIR: I have the honor to acknowledge the receipt of your letter of the 20th instant, enclosing a translation of a note dated the 18th instant from Mr. Romero, Mexican minister, accompanied by a protest relative to the capture by one of our naval vessels of the Mexican pilot-boat Raton del Nilo, and requesting such information on the subject as the files of this department may afford.

From a communication received by the department from Lieutenant Commander W. N. Allen, commanding the United States steamer New London, dated the 8th of December last, it appears that he captured the "Raton del Nilo" on the 3d of that month in latitude 26° 36″ N., and ten miles east of Padre island, Texas, she having neither log-book nor papers. The person at the time in charge of her stated that while at anchor in the Rio Grande the cable parted in a norther and the vessel had been driven by the wind to the locality of the capture, and had not had a fair wind to get back. Lieutenant Commander Allen transmits to the department an abstract from the log of the New London, as showing that it would have been impossible for a vessel to have drifted to the northward at the time stated. The cargo of the Raton del Nilo consisted of coffee, sugar, codfish, wine, percussion caps, &c.

The vessel was sent to New Orleans for adjudication, and the prize court there will, doubtless, properly dispose of the question as to the legality of the seizure.

Very respectfully, &c.,

GIDEON WELLES,
Secretary of the Navy.

Hon. WILLIAM H. SEWARD,
Secretary of State.

No. 11.—*Condition of Affairs in Mexico.*

Mr. Romero to Mr. Seward.

[Translation.]

MEXICAN LEGATION IN THE UNITED STATES OF AMERICA,
Washington, March 31, 1863.

MR. SECRETARY: While continuing the review of the public events which have occurred in Mexico, which I have had the honor to submit to your department since the commencement of the war which the Emperor of the French is waging against my country, I now proceed to refer to you those which occurred during the months of January and February of the present year, as they appear from the official documents which I have just received from my government, and of which I transmit you copies in English, as per form indicated in the annexed Index.

When I transmitted to you my note of the 28th of January last, in which I had the honor to submit to you the events which had occurred in the republic during the month of December previous, the French army was in possession of Jalapa and Tampico, besides the other places of the Mexican territory of which it has been in possession since the defeat which General Lorencez suffered on the 5th of May, 1862. General Forey very soon convinced himself of the impossibility of his retaining both cities in his power, and whether it was because he required the forces which garrisoned them to carry on his operations against Puebla, or because he could not maintain, with the probabilities of security, small garrisons in cities which were decidedly hostile to the intervention, he determined to evacuate both positions. General Berthier consequently abandoned Jalapa on the 15th of December, marching with the forces of his command in the direction of Puebla. General Rivera, in command of a small brigade of cavalry and some infantry of the Mexican army, prepared two ambuscades for the

French; the first at the "Parage de los Carros," and the second at "Cruz Blanca." The first encounter occurred on the 17th, and in the second he was compelled to join issue with a very superior force of the enemy in a formal battle which lasted for three hours. I enclose, under Nos. 1 and 2, the official reports of both actions. The telegraphic despatches which I sent you, marked Nos. 17 and 18, with my aforesaid note of the 28th January, referred to these reports.

The French had scarcely evacuated Jalapa, when that city was occupied by the patriot forces in its environs, as appears from the official report, also enclosed, No. 3. The pretended government which the French set up in it melted away the instant the support of foreign bayonets was withdrawn, and what occurred in Jalapa has been repeated in all the other towns which the French have occupied, and will be repeated in all the others they may hereafter occupy. The general feeling with which the Mexican people rejects the intervention cannot be more clearly manifested. The main body of the French army which was at Orizaba commenced its march on the 30th of November last in the direction of Puebla. These forces were divided into two corps; the first followed the national road from Orizaba to Puebla, and the second took the road of San Andres Chalchicomula, which town was occupied on the 4th of December, while at the same time another column entered San Augustin del Palmar.

A portion of the forces which took the road of Puebla occupied Tehuacan on the 21st of December, and shortly after abandoned it. General Forey left Orizaba on the 23d February. Shortly before doing so, he issued a proclamation in which he announced that the French army was about marching upon the city of Mexico. Up to the 2d of this month there were, however, no indications that the invading forces intended immediately to attack Puebla. Up to that time they had been engaged in marching and countermarching in all directions, in occupying defenceless towns and afterwards abandoning them, and the object of their multifarious movements seems to have been to obtain the supplies which the patriot Mexicans stationed between Vera Cruz and Orizaba do not permit freely to pass. During the month of February last past there had been no encounter of any consequence between the contending forces. While the garrison of Puebla was impatiently awaiting the attack, the pickets of the Mexican cavalry have scarcely allowed a day to pass without annoying the enemy. No column of the invaders can go in search of provisions or forage, or reconnoitre the country, without meeting in their transit with obstacles more or less serious. The Mexican pickets sometimes penetrate into the centre of the towns occupied by the French, and in the daily fights they have with them, and in which frequently the advantages are on their side, they have seen that it is possible to overcome an enemy which had been represented to them as irresistible.

In order to complete the history of the movement of the French army upon Puebla, I transmit copies of the proclamation of General Forey, to which I have previously referred, and of the other which he addressed, on the 16th of February, to the inhabitants of Orizaba, thanking them for the courtesy with which they have treated his soldiers, which he acknowledges is not due to sympathy for the cause which they defend.

The Mexican government ordered General Comonfort to place himself, with a part of the army of the centre, at San Martin Tesmelucan, distant eight leagues from Puebla, in order to protect the garrison of said city. Meantime the contingents from several of the states were arriving at the city of Mexico, which, added to the force which had remained there, would form a sufficient garrison to defend the place, even in case General Forey should determine to lay siege to it without attacking Puebla. The quotas of the state of Michoacan, and those of Guanajuato and Sinaloa, were on their march to the capital.

The military operations undertaken in other parts of the Mexican territory have not been more successful for the French arms. The forces which had occupied Tampico were defeated at Pueblo Viejo, on the 21st of December, in attempting to dislodge the Mexican army at that place. Among the documents annexed, marked No. 4, I enclose a copy of the official report of that action. About the beginning of January, the invading forces made preparations for evacuating Tampico. The Spanish vice-consul at that port, upon receiving notice thereof, addressed himself to General Garza, commanding in chief the Mexican forces in Tamaulipas, asking of him guarantees for the foreigners, and especially for the Frenchmen residing at Tampico, and even for the Mexicans who had remained at that port during the French occupation. General Garza replied by saying that the foreigners residing in Tampico, including the Frenchmen who had not joined the invaders, would enjoy all the rights which the law of nations concedes to them, and that with respect to the Mexicans who had remained in Tampico during its occupation, the interposition of the Spanish vice-consul could only be considered as in an officious light, and that, in any event, he would act with equity and moderation.

I enclose copies of the communications relating to this affair, numbered 5, 6, and 7.

On the 13th of January last the French evacuated Tampico, and on the same day it was occupied by the Mexican forces, as appears from the official report annexed, marked No. 8. The French force composing the expedition was delayed upon the bar, the bad weather not permitting them to embark in the transports. General Garza sent a section of 500 men to annoy the French upon the bar, and notwithstanding that they are there well protected by their war vessels, and by temporary fortifications which they had constructed, they were attacked on the evening of the 20th of January referred to. Subsequently the French burnt the houses at the bar, and when the section sent on the expedition again attacked them on the 21st, they found the village in ashes, and the French embarking in the war steamer La Lance and in a steam gunboat. Upon being attacked by the Mexican forces, they attempted to come down the river; the gunboat succeeded in so doing, and the steamer, losing the channel, went on shore, exposed to the fire of the Mexican forces, which, owing to the short distance at which they were, suffered much injury, without receiving any in return, as they were protected by the sand-banks on the coast, though they were opposed both by the steamer and the French squadron which was outside the bar. Night brought on a suspension of the hostilities of the 21st, which were renewed on the morning of the 22d with still greater fury. The French being unable to get off the steamer La Lance, and the losses on board of her being very considerable, they determined to set fire to her, first removing her crew and the force on board, and abandoning the provisions, armament, and other effects constituting her cargo, a part of which, notwithstanding the conflagration, were taken out by the Mexican forces. The enemy left, besides, at the mouth of the river Panuco, the American schooner Eugenia, laden with munitions of war, the hermaphrodite brig Indus, laden with provisions, and the bark France and Britain, with a cargo of coal, and two large iron lighters. The wheel-steamer Reforma, which the French had captured, was also abandoned on the bar, after having been rendered completely useless by the invaders, whose destructive propensities were fully carried out upon everything within their power. Not content with burning a defenceless village, they destroyed a steamer, the only use of which was to facilitate the entrance into Tampico of merchant vessels, and the want of which will be principally felt by foreign merchants. I enclose the official reports of the action near the bar, marked Nos. 9 and 10. Thus ended the French occupation of Tampico, and it is a fair sample of what awaits the invaders throughout the Mexican territory. They not only did not obtain the mules they had gone in search of—not only were they not able to retain a town upon the coast where their naval forces give them so great an advantage, but they were compelled to abandon precipitately the second maritime custom-house of Mexico upon the gulf, leaving to their fate the few deluded Mexicans who had followed them, destroying a war steamer belonging to the imperial navy, leaving in the hands of the Mexican army a large amount of provisions and munitions of war, and abandoning, both beaten and crestfallen, a position in which they had the aid of their powerful squadron.

A few days before the French found themselves compelled to abandon Tampico with such great disadvantages, the French navy suffered another disaster in the Pacific. A small French squadron, composed of the Pallas, bearing the flag of Rear-Admiral Bonet, the Bayonnaise, the Diamant, and the Galathée, mounting in all sixty guns, appeared on the 8th of January before the town of Acapulco, making the singular demand from the chief of the Mexican forces at that port that he should give the lie to a publication published in the Chaleco, a newspaper of Callao, in Peru, in an article relating to the excesses committed by the frigate Bayonnaise at Acapulco about the end of August, 1862, when General Ghilardi was in command of the garrison of Acapulco, and to whom the article in question had been attributed. The French squadron also demanded the no less singular privilege of being permitted to provision, coal, and water, as though Acapulco were neutral ground. The pretension that the Mexican authorities should disavow the publications of the foreign press is in itself so extraordinary a proceeding, that it can scarcely be supposed that a French rear-admiral should make of it a *casus belli*. Upon issuing that relating to the neutrality of Acapulco, it appears that Rear-Admiral Bonet had forgotten that Acapulco is an integral part of the republic of Mexico; that Mexico is at war with France, and that to propose that a hostile squadron be permitted to enter and leave freely that port, in order that it might provide itself, in one part of the territory of Mexico, with the means it requires for the purpose of attacking another portion of the same country, is the most absurd thing that can be imagined. General Alvarez replied, as it was most natural, by refusing both these demands, in consequence of which the French squadron opened its batteries upon Acapulco on the morning of the 10th, with the immense advantage of having rifled guns; its fire caused great damage, without, in return, receiving any injury, because their vessels were beyond the reach of the Mexican artillery. As the result of so unequal a contest, several pieces of the Mexican artillery, used in the defence of the place, were dismounted. The houses, which had been disoccupied, previously, by order of the military authority, were soon reduced to ruins in consequence of the three days' bombardment which they suffered. The defenders of the port remained in Fort Alvarez, the only one which could resist the fire of the enemy, ready to oppose the landing of the French, which it was believed would have taken place, for it was not possible to believe that the anger of the French should limit itself to knocking down unoccupied buildings. The forces which were to have landed did not attempt to do so, and on the 12th they withdrew from the port without having occupied it, and without obtaining water, provisions, or coal, and without having obtained the objects they had intended. The bombardment of Acapulco was therefore an act of barbarism, which effected no result whatever favorable to the French

By this bombardment the property belonging to foreigners was destroyed, and this is not the first occasion upon which they have had to lament the kind of protection which France declares she has come to give them. Among the annexed documents I transmit the official report of the action at Acapulco, from No. 11 to No. 19, inclusive. The bombardment of Acapulco is not the only act of barbarism committed by the French. The official report of the outrages which they perpetrated at Tehuacan, which I enclose under No. 20, is simply an exact account of the scenes which occur in all the towns which fall under the French yoke. The most arbitrary spoliations, the most unheard of violences, the banishment to Martinique upon the most flimsy motives, and even from the simple fact of professing opinions contrary to the intervention; the most outrageous ill-treatment, and other wrongs of this same character, are very frequent occurrences in the towns which are so unfortunate as to suffer the French rule for a shorter or longer period. Among the cases of deportation which have occurred, the more notable ones are those of Don Alberto Lopez, and of the licentiate Don Antonio Corona. The latter was at one time the governor and president of the superior tribunal of the State of Vera Cruz, and the former is a distinguished citizen of Orizaba. Both of them had retired to private life, and both were violently dragged from their homes to be deported to an island whose climate is deadly. Banishments have occurred by the wholesale, and upon the most trivial causes, of many other persons, who, though more humble in their spheres than those named, in no manner diminish the criminality of the outrage. In the document No. 4 enclosed herewith, you will see the barbarous treatment to which four Mexican citizens have been subjected, who were banished from Orizaba; the offence of one of them, Don Diego Miron, being his having defended the honor of one of his daughters, threatened by a French officer.

General Forey, knowing the necessity of giving a light coloring of legality to proceedings so arbitrary and iniquitous, issued a circular (number 22) on the 6th of January last, in which he provides that a military commission composed of French officers shall determine upon "all offences which may endanger the security of the French army," under which loose definition may be included, at the will of the French officers, any acts which may occur in the Mexican territory. There has besides been perpetrated another brutal outrage by the French army, and through which the laws of war not less than the sovereignty of the United States have been outraged. The commandant, Florian Bernardi, who served in the brigade of Rivéra, offered, in compliance with an order from General Ortega, to escort with four dragoons Mr. William H. Corwin, secretary of the United States legation in Mexico, Mr. Marcus Ottenbourgh, consul of the United States in the city of Mexico, and Mr. N. A. Cajat, the consular agent of the United States at Puebla, on the journey they made to Vera Cruz, about the end of December, 1862, with the view of taking to the city of Mexico the correspondence of the government of the United States to their minister in Mexico, which had been detained at said port of Vera Cruz. This escort, employed upon a peaceful mission, was under the protection of the United States, in the service of whose agents it was at that time. Notwithstanding this fact, and their carrying a white flag, the commandant Florian Bernardi and his dragoons were captured upon their arrival at Perote, and shortly afterwards the said commandant and one dragoon were shot to death, and the three others were banished to Martinique. This act of barbarity, which would put to the blush the tribes of the Caffres, has been committed by one of the generals of the highest grade in the army which pretends to bring civilization to Mexico. The truth of the facts which I have just related is sustained by the written declarations of the secretary of the United States legation in Mexico, and of the consul of the United States in the same city, of which I transmit copy, marked No. 23. How far this iniquitous proceeding affects the dignity and sovereignty of the United States, is a matter which it becomes their government to determine.

Many of the soldiers of the French army, who are gradually becoming satisfied that neither Mexico nor its government are in the state of disorganization which had been described to them, and who, on the contrary, find that they are used as instruments for establishing oppression and despotism in a country where the most ample liberty is enjoyed, founded upon principles in defence of which these same soldiers have fought gloriously at other periods and places, have become disgusted with so iniquitous an expedition, and have begun to abandon a flag which now only represents the cause of barbarism, oppression and conquest. Among the documents annexed, I transmit two communications, (Nos. 25 and 26) from General Ortega, in which he announces that several deserters from the French army have presented themselves to him. Many others have gone towards Oajaca, and as yet no information is had as to their numbers.

The Mexican government deemed it its duty to favor these desertions, and issued to that end the instructions of which I transmit a copy, (No. 24,) in which it recommends to the generals of the national army to extend succor to the deserters who may present themselves, to give them passports to such places at which they may desire to establish themselves, and to make known to them the friendly disposition of the Mexican government to receive them as colonists in the republic. These orders have produced the best results: ten deserters from different regiments of the invading army have publicly acknowledged, in a communication addressed to the President, (No. 27,) the kind manner in which they have been received by the authorities of the republic; and this manifestation, while it will encourage other soldiers to follow the same example, will tend to dissipate the fears which the French officers have sought to instil into the minds of their soldiers with respect to the pretended sufferings and tortures which awaited the French deserters at the hands of the Mexican authorities. The injustice and iniquity of the invasion are so clearly manifest, even to the very soldiers of France, that many of them have been compelled to resort to an expedient of which there are but very few examples in the annals of the French army, and, if the war should be prolonged for any length of time, it threatens to disband the invading army.

The government of Mexico, while it desires to favor the desertions which will weaken an army engaged in the conquest of the country, does not avail itself of any undue means, and which are not conformable to the laws of war, to bring about such a result, and has not attempted to exercise any kind of coercion upon the hostile soldiers which have come under their authority. The following case proves the truth of this assertion: Upon its becoming known in Mexico that General Forey had set at liberty some prisoners belonging to the national army, the government of the republic determined to do as much with respect to several French prisoners which it held in the capital, directing at the same time that they should be provided with the funds necessary to return to the headquarters of the invading army, or to establish themselves in some other part of the Mexican territory. The prisoners decided to accept the first-named alternative, and they were allowed to join the enemy's ranks. These are the acts of humanity which it is customary with the Mexican government to extend, and whom the agents of the Emperor of the French incessantly calumniate in Europe. I enclose herewith (marked No. 28) the documents relating to this affair.

Mr. Wagner, the minister resident of his Majesty the King of Prussia in Mexico, who jointly had under his protection the interests of the Spanish, French, and Belgian subjects, received the authority of his government to return to Berlin, and upon his departure from the city of Mexico he very properly left the said subjects under the protection of their respective consuls, but he committed the mistake of desiring to leave the said subjects and consuls under the extraordinary protection of the minister of the United States. As was most natural, neither the Mexican government nor Mr. Corwin could sanct on by their approval a proceeding which was so greatly contrary to international uses, and Mr. Wagner, in a note to the Mexican government, which was received at the department for foreign affairs two days after his departure from the capital, stated that he left the subjects referred to under the safeguard of the diplomatic corps, and "relying, above all, on the honor and loyalty of the Mexican people." By such conduct Mr. Wagner has attempted to cast reproach upon the Mexican government with the least reason for so doing, because the said government has given daily proofs that it causes the rights of foreigners to be respected, which are conceded to them by the treaties, and that it knows how to extend its humanity even to the point of continuing to guarantee these same rights to the foreigners who have forfeited them in consequence of the war, as is actually the case with the French residing in Mexico. The government of Mexico energetically repelled the insult implicated in the note of Mr. Wagner, in a note addressed to Mr. Corwin, of which I enclose a copy, and also of all the other communications which refer to this matter. Other letters have been intercepted, addressed to Mr. J. B. Jecker, by some of his friends, relatives, and partners in Europe, and which show how far the business of stock-jobbing of this speculator have influenced in causing the war which the French government is waging against Mexico. I enclose these letters, as per No. 38.

I avail myself of this opportunity to renew to you, sir, the assurances of my most distinguished consideration.

M. ROMERO.

Hon. WILLIAM H. SEWARD, *&c., &c., &c.*

Enclosures with Mr. Romero's letter of 31*st March*, 1863.

[Translation.]

Index of the documents this day transmitted by the Mexican legation to the Department of State of the United States, annexed to its note of the 31st of March, 1863, relating to events which transpired in Mexico during the months of January and February, 1863.

No.	From—To.	Date.	Contents.
1	General Rivera to General Ortega.	Dec. 17, 1862	Official report of the action at the Parage de Carros.
2	Same to same	Dec. 20, 1862	Official report of the battle of Cruz Blanca.
3	General Ortega to General Blanco.	Jan. 21, 1863	Official report of the occupation of Jalapa by the Mexican forces.
4	Colonel Lara y Solis to General Blanco.	Dec. 22, 1862	Official report of the battle of Pueblo Viejo.
5	General Garza to General Blanco.	Jan. 10, 1863	Transmits copies of the correspondence between General Garza and the vice-consul of Spain at Tampico respecting the protection of foreigners residing there.
6	Mr. Obregon to General Garza.	Jan. 9, 1863	Requesting protection for foreigners residing in Tampico.
7	General Garza to Mr. Obregon.	Jan. 10, 1863	Replies that the rights conceded by treaty to foreigners will be respected.
8	Colonel Pavon to General Blanco.	Jan. 13, 1863	Official report of the evacuation of Tampico by the French army.
9	General Garza to General Blanco.	Jan. 22, 1863	Official report of the occupation of Tampico by the Mexican army and of the action on the bar.
10	Same to same	Feb. 7, 1863	Detailed report of above action.
11	General Alvarez to General Blanco.	Jan. 10, 1863	Transmits copies of correspondence between the Mexican army and the French squadron prior to the bombardment of Acapulco.
12	Commander Bonet to Mr. Van Brunt.	Jan. 8, 1863	Proposal of conditions to prevent hostilities on his part
13	Captain Le Bris to General Alvarez.	Jan. 8, 1863	Memorandum—same subject.
14	General Alvarez to Mr. Van Brunt.	Jan. 9, 1863	He replies that he cannot accede to the conditions of Commander Bonet.
15	Captain Le Bris to General Alvarez.	Jan. 9, 1863	Respecting the conditions demanded by the French squadron.
16	General Alvarez to Captain Le Bris.	Jan. 9, 1863	Replies that he cannot accept such conditions.
17	General Alvarez to General Blanco.	Jan. 11, 1863	Official report of the battle of Acapulco, of the 10th January.

Index of documents—Continued.

No.	From—To.	Date.	Contents.
18	General Alvarez to General Blanco.	Jan. 12, 1863	Official report of the actions of 10th and 11th January at Acapulco.
19	Same to same.....	Jan. 13, 1863	Official report of the withdrawal of the French squadron from Acapulco.
20	General Ortega to General Blanco.	Dec. 31, 1862	Official report of the spoliations of the French army at Tehuacan.
21	General Carbojal to General Ortega.	Jan. 7, 1863	The outrages of the French upon four Mexican citizens sent to Vera Cruz.
22	J. D. St. Armand...	Jan. 20, 1863	Circular of the French army to have them tried by a military commission.
23	From the U. S. consul in the city of Mexico and the secretary of the U. S. legation in the same city.	Jan. 4, 1863	Official report of the assassination by the French of an officer and two soldiers of the Mexican army who were under the protection of the United States.
24	General Ortega....	Feb. 1, 1863	Instructions of the Mexican government relating to the protection to be granted to deserters from the French army.
25	General Ortega to General Blanco.	Feb. 3, 1863	Notice of his aiding and sending a French deserter to Mexico.
26	Same to same.....	Feb. 12, 1863	Notice of his aiding and sending seven French deserters to Mexico.
27	From French deserters.	Feb. 14, 1863	From ten deserters from the French army to the President of Mexico, thanking him for their kind reception.
28	Commander Tapia..	Jan. 9, 1863	Official report of his release of five French prisoners, with passports and means to return to the invading army.
29	The President to the Diario official.	Feb. 22, 1863	Denies the statement of General O'Donnell, which alleges that the President was desirous of selling two of the Mexican States to the United States.
30	Mr. Wagner to Mr. Fuente.	Jan. 22, 1863	Permission to leave Mexico, and asking for passports and escorts.
31	Mr. Fuente to Mr. Wagner.	Jan. 30, 1863	Granting his requests.
32	Mr. Wagner to Mr. Fuente.	Feb. 9, 1863	Notice that he leaves the Europeans residing in Mexico under the care of their consuls and the special protection of the legation of the United States.
33	Mr. Fuente to Mr. Wagner.	Feb. 12, 1863	The Mexican government cannot accept the above measure.
34	Mr. Wagner to Mr. Fuente.	Feb. 17, 1863	The minister of the United States declining to accept this commission, he leaves the foreigners under the protection of the diplomatic corps and the loyalty of the Mexican people.
35	Mr. Fuente to Mr. Corwin.	Feb. 24, 1863	The impropriety of the conduct of Mr. Wagner.
36	General Forey to the Mexicans.	Feb. 15, 1863	Proclamation. The invading army marching upon Mexico.
37	General Forey to the citizens of Orizaba.	Feb. 16, 1863	Proclamation; thanking them for their good treatment of the French army—not due to their sympathy for the cause of intervention.
38	....	....	Eleven intercepted letters to the friends, relatives, and partners of J. B. Jecker, residing in Europe, respecting the condition of their affairs.

ROMERO.

WASHINGTON, *March* 31, 1864.

No. 1.

[Translation.]

LIBERAL ARMY, RIVERA'S BRIGADE.

I have to communicate to you that this very moment (a quarter to 1 p. m.) a little engagement has taken place at the point called Parage de Carros, half a league from this place, caused by one of the ambuscades which, according to what I have stated in my former report, I had been preparing with my infantry, in connexion with citizen Colonel Antonio Rodriguez, with the national guard of Flacolulam.

I am not aware of the loss of the enemy at this moment. They were fearfully cut up by our fire, which was at close quarters, by about 300 infantry. A dense fog favored us, while it prevented me from ascertaining immediately the results.

The line of the ambuscade covered about three blocks, and its effects have fully satisfied me. I withdrew subsequently with my small corps of infantry and cavalry in the best order, the enemy being only at a very short distance from the latter. I consider it unnecessary to recommend to you the nations of Flacolulam, who have behaved so handsomely, in company of the citizen Lieutenant Colonel José M. Grajale, whom I personally invited to second this movement. I retire to the Cerros de Leon and of Molinos, where I intend to cause yet more damage to the invaders on his passage, as I will to-morrow make another attack.

AURELIANO RIVERA.

Citizen GENERAL-IN-CHIEF *of the Army of the East.*

LAS VIGAS, *December* 17, 1862.

WASHINGTON, *March* 31, 1863.

A true copy:

ROMERO.

No. 2.

[Translation.]

LIBERAL ARMY, BRIGADE RIVERA.

As I promised you day before yesterday evening to give you a detailed account of the action which took place the same day between the brigade which I command and the invading enemy, I have now the pleasure of fulfilling that promise.

At 9 o'clock a. m. on the 18th I evacuated the village Perote, taking direction of the Molinos and of Sierra de Agua, with the intention of attacking the enemy on his rear guard if circumstances should favor me.

I had received before positive information that the traitors, to the number of 1,500 men, were covering the rear guard of this army, and immediately I fixed my attention on them at the moment when the invading enemy had the advantage of an immense numerical superiority. I arrived at Sierra de Agua, whence I took the direction of Cerro de Leon, in order to come out near Cruz Blanca, at a point where I could break his line.

Enveloped by a thick fog which disguised the distance to such a degree that objects at fifteen or twenty paces could not be distinguished, I was induced to advance with an escort of *rifleros*, in order to assure myself with my own eyes when the enemy would pass the point indicated. The sound of artillery announced to me that the traitors were advancing upon my position, and suddenly a fierce combat began between my *rifleros* and a small detachment of the traitor cavalry, whom I sought to draw forth upon an advantageous spot, in order to put into execution my other plans.

In consequence of this, I sent word to citizen Edward Manuel Quesada that he should draw out upon an advantageous spot the corps of his command, in order to resist successfully the attack of the enemy. I afterwards saw a large body of French cavalry detaching itself, evidently with the intention of making a charge, and sent immediately to meet it the *resguardo* of Tlaxcala, under the orders of citizen Colonel Doroteo Leon, who had the glory of resisting in an admirable manner a sudden attack, by driving the French cavalry back in the greatest disorder.

At this moment, seeing myself equally supported by the *resguardo* of Huamantla, under the command of citizen Colonel Antonio Rodriguez, I was able to make a charge which drove back the enemy into the midst of the infantry and artillery. The latter I was unable to get into my possession, owing to the fact that two battalions or more were aiming to turn my right flank, at the same time that another battalion, deployed as sharpshooters, were combining in an attack on the left flank, thus placing me between three fires. I immediately ordered the citizen commandant Ugalde to proceed to the right flank at a place whence he could observe and communicate to me any movement of said battalions.

Favored as we were by the lay of the land, this action lasted three hours and a half, at the expiration of which time prudence admonished me to order a countermarch. The enemy, encouraged by this move, wished to make a new and heavy charge, but could not succeed in his object, because, at the distance of 1,000 yards, in consequence of the precaution which I had taken, the squadrons Quesada and *Esploradoes* were formed, under command of citizen Lieutenant Colonel Geronimo Fragoso, and the enemy stopped as soon as he perceived them. I at once retreated to this locality leisurely, and the brigade marching in perfect order, the rear guard being covered by the corps Quesada and Fragoso, with the sharpshooters belonging to them.

In the second charge a circumstance took place which I will not allow myself to pass unmentioned. Citizen Colonel Rodriguez encountered the traitor, Colonel Macario Silva; each recognized the other, and the latter invited Colonel Rodriguez to single combat. Rodguez accepted the challenge, and in a few moments later he had killed the traitor. I enclose with this report the epaulettes worn by Colonel Silva.

It is impossible for me to state the loss of the enemy, but I can assure you, upon my word of honor, that they were considerable. We captured eleven Arabian and five Mexican horses, beside pack-horses, a large number of arms, and five prisoners, (traitors,) who were immediately put to death.

For my part, I have to deplore the loss of the citizen commanding the squadron, Rafael Ledezma, of the force of Rodriguez; also that of citizen Lieutenant Loreto Velasco, of the corps of Fragoso, besides nineteen soldiers of different corps, more than a dozen wounded, and thirteen prisoners.

Citizen general, words fail to describe the heroic conduct of the citizen chiefs, officers, and soldiers who compose the brigade which I am proud to command. In the heat of the combat only the noble cries of "Independence forever! Liberty forever! Death to the traitors! Death to France!" were uttered.

Receive the expressions of my distinguished regards, and it will give me great satisfaction if you will congratulate in my name the citizen President upon the action which took place on the 18th of the present month on the plains of Cerro de Leon and Cruz Blanca between a party of national troops and the invading enemy.

Liberty, independence, or death!

AURELIANO RIVERA.

Citizen GENERAL-IN-CHIEF *of the Army of the East.*

TEZUITLAN DE MEJIA, *December* 20, 1862.

WASHINGTON, *March* 31, 1863.

A true copy:

ROMERO.

No. 3.

[Translation.]

The citizen military commander of Vera Cruz has communicated to me, under the date of the 15th instant, from Jalapa, what follows:

"I have the honor to inform you that to-day, noon I occupied this village with the force which is under my command two hours before it had been evacuated by the enemy, who now are two leagues from here."

I have the honor to transmit it to you, so that you may inform the supreme magistrate of the republic of the same.

Liberty and reform!

Headquarters at Zaragoza, January 21, 1863.

J. GONSALES ORTEGA.

Citizen MINISTER OF WAR, *Mexico.*

WASHINGTON, *March* 31, 1863.

A true copy:

ROMERO.

No. 4.

[Extracts.—Translation.]

* * * On the 21st we arrived at Pueblo Viejo with the object of cutting off all communication with the place occupied by the French, and of attacking them should they

present themselves. We placed several guerillas on observation at El Humo, Las Piedras, la Polvora, and San Francisco, covering with the balance of the infantry forces all the line along the beach of the Laguna de Pueblo Viejo. During that day and night following it nothing new occurred; on the 22d, about 11 o'clock in the morning, two gunboats and some Frenchmen were seen on the side of El Humo, reconnoitring our camp, and having observed our guerillas, they fired their guns and muskets in that direction; a slight skirmishing took place with them, causing the invaders to fall back. In the evening Mr. Pavon and myself went, without uncovering our lines, to reconnoiter the commanding points and to observe the movements going on at Tampico. At that moment two small steamers towing five sloops with several boats were approaching by the estero of San Francisco; the enemy was on board and intended to surprise us. A cannon shot from the enemy announced to us the attack on the side of the laguna opposite the town; we returned, and Mr. Pavon, the chief of our brigade, remained at the first point on the right wing to sustain there the fire with an enemy superior both in material and force. As he was some fifty meters from the shore, I ran over myself the line which had been attacked, and I was not further than twenty or twenty-five meters when a ball from the enemy killed my horse. I was slightly hurt, and although this embarassed my march, I went over on foot the remainder of the line. I mounted again and relieved the citizen commander-in-chief, so that he might take his turn in running over the line. After a lively and heavy fire for three hours, the enemy, unable to resist any longer, withdrew with some killed and about twenty wounded. About 10 or 11 o'clock in the night, as soon as the unjust invader gave up the fight, I ordered the reveille to be beaten all along the line, so as to let the people of the town know that we had triumphed over our oppressors. The Mexican honor has not been violated on this part of our territory, and the arms of justice have shown once more after the example of the hero of Guadalupe, who made them sparkle on the 5th of May. There are among the killed two captains and a lieutenant very much beloved by the French. Thinking that the enemy would return the following day (23d) by land, and in larger numbers, we withdrew the infantry to Tampico el Alto, leaving the cavalry at Pueblo Viejo to observe and draw the enemy into the narrow passes of the mountain, doing this at 3 o'clock in the morning in the greatest possible order. At 8 o'clock the same morning the enemy, ashamed of their defeat, occupied Pueblo Viejo by land, and not finding us there, they most outrageously pillaged the town, during which they broke open the doors which were closed. Maddened by their losses of the night previous, and knowing that we suffered none, they started for Tampico Alto to exterminate us, as they said. We, being prepared to attack them with our guerillas, advanced on the same road to meet them, but they had scarcely advanced about one league when they turned back and re-embarked for Tampico. The enthusiasm of our soldiers looking for an engagement was such that, had the enemy advanced, they would have undoubtedly suffered twice as great a loss as on the day before, and we might even have cut off their retreat. The enemy's loss is officially confirmed.

La Graviere had arrived at the bar of Tampico at the very moment we were fighting; some people assert that he brings with him more forces, some others pretend that the greatest part of the force is to withdraw, and that will only leave a small garrison.

It is also reported that the chief who attacked us is to be subjected to a court-martial, having lost the action. * * * *

WASHINGTON, *March* 31, 1863.

A true copy:

ROMERO.

No. 5.

[Translation.]

FORCES OF TAMAULIPAS, GENERAL-IN-CHIEF.

For the information of the citizen President of the republic, I enclosed to you certified copies of the communications exchanged between the Spanish vice-consul in Tampico and the undersigned respecting the evacuation of that port by the invading forces. By the copies referred to you will be advised of the guarantees that I have conceded to foreigners, and especially to the French subjects who have not mixed themselves in anything with the invader. At the same time please to inform the citizen

President that with this date I commenced the march upon that port with the forces at my command, to effectuate its occupation and to hostilize the enemy by every means that may be possible.

Country, liberty, and reform!

Headquarters in the Hacienda of Chocoy, *January* 10, 1863.

JUAN JOSÉ DE LA GARZA.

Citizen MINISTER OF WAR AND MARINE, *Mexico*.

WASHINGTON, *March* 31, 1863.

A true copy:

ROMERO.

No. 6.

[Translation.]

CONSULATE OF SPAIN AT TAMPICO,
Hacienda del Chocoy, *January* 9, 1863.

GENERAL: The undersigned, vice-consul, has the honor to inform you that M. Charles de Saint Charles, who now performs the duties of consul of France, and the commander of the French man-of-war Albatros, who actually is the superior commander of the French forces occupying the port of Tampico, have addressed to him two communications informing him, among other things, that the French forces which garrison said place of Tampico will soon evacuate it.

As you will understand, in circumstances so critical as the present ones, the undersigned has thought proper to call on you at your encampment with the object of inquiring of you if, in case said evacuation should take place, you, as the superior chief of the liberal forces which will occupy it, can grant to peaceful foreigners who find themselves in said place all guarantees, and particularly to the French subjects who are there established, and who have not taken any part with the forces of their nation.

With the same sentiments towards the peaceful Mexicans, inhabitants of said town, and who are in the same case in which are other foreigners and the French to whom I refer, the undersigned would like to know if they may rely upon the same guarantees, requesting you to take into consideration that said place was occupied unexpectedly, and that some, from reason of health, and others from want of resources, have been unable to abandon their families and interests.

Please accept on this occasion, general, the expression of my esteem and distinguished consideration. God preserve you for many years.

RAMON DE OBREGON.

General JUAN JOSÉ DE LA GARZA,
Commander-in-Chief of the forces operating against Tampico.

WASHINGTON, *March* 31, 1863.

A true copy:

ROMERO.

No. 7.

[Translation.]

FORCES OF TAMPICO, GENERAL-IN-CHIEF.

I have received the note of your vice-consulate, dated the 9th instant, which has acquainted me with the fact that you had been informed by M. Charles de Saint Charles and the commander of the French ship-of-war Albatros, commanding in chief the French forces at Tampico, that that place was to be soon evacuated, and for this reason you desired to be informed, first, whether the peaceful foreigners, and particularly the Frenchmen who have taken no part with the invaders and who are settled in that place, were to enjoy all kinds of guarantees; and, second, if the Mexicans, who find themselves in the same case, may rely on the same guarantees, taking into consideration that the place had been occupied unexpectedly, and that they could not abandon their families and interests, some on account of their health, others for want of resources.

I answer the first point by saying that peaceful foreigners or neutrals may count upon all the guarantees which international law gives them in such cases, and I say the same particularly of all the French residents who have not participated with the invaders, for your consulate well knows that through the magnanimity of our government, when their Emperor has declared war against us, the guarantees which they are to enjoy are assured by our positive and written law.

The undersigned, considering the second part of your note merely as an officious step inspired by sentiments of good will of your consulate, declines answering it, limiting himself to declare his opinion that there is room to believe that any reasons which might be given by the Mexicans who did not leave the place of Tampico, when it was occupied by the French, will be listened to and taken into consideration.

I beg you to accept the assurance of my consideration and particular esteem.

Liberty and reform!

Headquarters at the Hacienda del Chocoy, January 10, 1863.

JUAN JOSÉ DE LA GARZA.

M. RAMON DE OBREGON,
Vice-Consul of H. C. M.

WASHINGTON, *March* 31, 1863.

A true copy:

ROMERO.

No. 8.

[Translation.]

NATIONAL ARMY, PAVON'S DIVISION, COMMANDER-IN-CHIEF.

CITIZEN MINISTER: As I informed you in my communication of the 11th instant, I this day, at half past 11 a. m., occupied this town with the forces under my command, immediately upon its evacuation by the invaders, by covering at once the principal points, seeing that the enemy is still upon the bar with some 800 men. The public tranquillity was maintained in a manner highly creditable to the honor of our arms, which have brilliantly sustained their well-deserved national renown. I have, at the same time, given notice, by express courier, to the citizen general-in-chief of the forces of this State, of the occupation of this important city, in order that he may determine to do whatever he may deem proper, and cause his forces to advance, and when united to mine we may consult upon the defence of the town in the event of the return of the invaders from the bar, whence they cannot embark, there being a cross sea running, and there not being a sufficient depth of water for their steamers.

I take pleasure in felicitating you upon this event that you may communicate it to the supreme chief of the nation—the abandonment by the foreign enemy of this part of the Mexican territory.

Our country, liberty, and reform!

Tampico, January 13, 1863.

DESIDERIO PAVON.

Citizen MINISTER OF WAR, *Mexico.*

WASHINGTON, *March* 31, 1863.

A true copy:

ROMERO.

No. 9.

[Translation.]

HEADQUARTERS OF THE FORCES OF TAMAULIPAS AND HUASTECA, GENERAL-IN-CHIEF.

In conformity with what I explained previously to the ministry at war, with respect to attacking the enemy in their embarking, I ordered that a force, consisting of 100 infantry of the first battalion of the State, 200 of the battalion Hidalgo, 100 of the section Pavon, 100 lancers, and two pieces of rifled artillery, the whole commanded by citizen Colonel Rafael de la Garza, should proceed to the bar of the above-named harbor, where the enemy were, to make a slight reconnoissance, which took place on the 20th instant without anything else occurring beyond the fire of the infantry on both sides, which was kept up for some time. On the following day, the 21st, citizen Colonel Garza returned to the bar with the same force, and after our artillery had fired several times upon the steamer and gunboats which they had there to protect their infantry, the former began to move out, but through their haste to leave, and the lively fire which was kept up on our side, it ran aground in doing so on the bar.

To-day it remained yet in the same state, and in order to effect its entire destruction our artillery, placed beforehand in that place, repeated its firing upon it, and the other war steamers which form the squadron that was outside the harbor, and which there is no doubt came to protect it and save it from the danger in which it happened to be.

All that they attempted was in vain, for notwithstanding having directed all their fire of artillery upon our forces, the above-named steamer remained completely in the same state, and at last was abandoned by the enemy, who, after having set it on fire, went on board the other ships-of-war that were outside the bay.

The French forces, besides this loss that they have suffered, and which is of some importance, have left in our possession a one-masted vessel laden with materials of war, a larger one filled with provisions, and another of a similar size half laden with a cargo of coal.

To-morrow I shall order to be taken out of the above-named steamer the five pieces of artillery with which it was armed, and the other articles which are still serviceable, and as soon as I have the papers giving an account of the quantity of warlike materials and provisions which are in our possession, I will send you the necessary information, that it may be placed before the citizen President of the republic.

I must likewise mention to you, among other things, that the invaders, before effecting their embarcation, completely destroyed by fire all the property in the neighborhood, leaving it in consequence reduced to a frightful desert.

All of which I let you know, that you may be pleased to lay it before the supreme magistrate of the nation.

JUAN DE LA GARZA.

Citizen Minister of War and Marine.

Tampico, *January* 22, 1863.

Washington, *March* 31, 1863.

A true copy:

ROMERO.

No. 10.

Forces of Tampico and Huasteca.

Tampico, *February* 7, 1863.

To the Minister of War, *Mexico:*

Colonel Rafael de la Garza, commanding the second division which I ordered against the bar of this port, submits to me the following communication under date of the 23d ultimo:

"In compliance with the orders received from these headquarters to make a reconnoissance of the enemy stationed on the bar of this port, I went out on the 20th instant with 400 infantry of the first Tamaulipas, Hidalgo, and Pavon battalions, 100 lancers of the second regiment of the cavalry brigade, and two pieces of rifled ordnance. As I had the honor to inform you, on that same day I remained within gun-shot of the enemy with the greater part of my division, and I ordered fire to be directed upon him for the purpose of compelling him to come out from the breastworks and barricades which he had constructed, and to draw him at the same time from the protection of his gunboats and war vessels which were in the river; but it was all in vain, and it being already late I had to order a retreat, because the bad condition of the caissons obliged me to leave the artillery in the pass of Doña Cecilia, and to make no use of it. That being in a better state of preparation, on the 21st, in compliance with your orders, I returned to the bar, the houses of which I found already set on fire by the French and yet smoking.

"At that moment in which we saw this the whole force of the enemy that had landed re-embarked on board of the war steamer La Lance, and a gunboat. These vessels were yet in the middle of the river; and then I arranged that, until the arrival of our artillery, which had been delayed by the difficulty of getting over the sandy ground, 100 men of the first batallion should be deployed as sharpshooters, protecting themselves by the sand-banks in order to take aim. The enemy understood the movement and immediately withdrew out of range. At this time our artillery came up; fire was opened on both sides, and soon the barge was compelled to withdraw, and after her the steamer. The latter lost the channel and grounded on a sand-bank, where she was exposed to our fire, which, on account of the shortness of the distance, did her much damage, without any loss to our forces, notwithstanding that the grounded steamer as well as the squadron outside the bar cannonaded us at the time, some enfilading vessels having got range of us. This operation lasted until night had set in—when the darkness did not permit us to distinguish objects—without any other accident on our side than the dismounting of one of our pieces.

"At dawn on the following day, the 22d instant, our artillery being placed on the fortification erected on the bar, we began to open fire; nearly the whole squadron kept up a lively cannonade upon us until eleven o'clock in the morning, and we replied quite regularly on our side. The hostile steamer La Lance was set on fire by the French themselves, the crew only having escaped from her, and taking none of the provisions even with them, as is shown by the committee of officers who went on board soon after and brought off a great part of them, though the vessel was very soon wrapped in flames. For this reason the five cannons with which she was armed, which were rifled ones, according to the information which I have, as also the quartermaster's stores and other effects which she contained, have been lost with the steamer, although I believe that we can yet draw out a great part of them and render them useful.

"In addition to this, the enemy has left in the mouth of the river the American transport vessel Eugenia, loaded with munitions of war; the brigantine Indus with provisions; the bark France et Bretagne with pit-coal, two large iron tenders, and a boat with double prows. On land were found some wagons, mules, horses, and asses. A report of the number and quantity of all these things will be rendered as soon as those commissioned to draw it up have concluded it. The tow-boat Reforma, which had been captured by the enemy, was likewise abandoned in the mouth of the bar, they having afterwards set fire to it so as to render it useless.

"I deem it proper to remark, that on the second and third day the expeditionary division sent to the bar was augmented by the arrival of the first company of the third battalion volunteers, of the centre, as also that General Macedonio Capistran, at his own request, held himself in readiness to march with the first regiment of lancers of his brigade, and very opportunely took position at the bridge of Chijol for the purpose of protecting me in case of necessity.

"Such has been the result of the expedition intrusted to the undersigned, and in conclusion he considers it due to justice to declare that all the commanders and subordinate officers, as well as the soldiers composing the division, have done their duty."

And in transmitting this to you for the information of the President, I should declare that I have delayed to despatch this report, because I waited for the completion of the detailed accounts of all the articles taken from the enemy, which I have now the honor of enclosing.

In regard to the vessels, I have this day ordered that the captain of this should take possession of them as national property, in which character I think of selling them at auction if there be any bidders; and if there be none, I will arrange to have them taken up the river so far as to place them in the greatest possible security in case the enemy should again threaten this place, unless the supreme government disposes otherwise.

Liberty and reform!

JUAN J. DE LA GARZA,
General Commanding.

FORCES OF TAMAULIPAS, QUARTERMASTER'S DEPARTMENT.

Report of the munitions of war taken from the French in the transport Eugenia on the bar of Tampico, January 22, 1863.

16,520 one ounce musket balls.
1 box one-ounce musket balls, spoiled.
504 musket caps.
538 caps for cannons.
30 balls for rifled cannon, Armstrong 30-pounders.
90 bombshells with 12 charges, for same.
198 bombshells, with four charges, for same.
24 rounds of grape and canister, with 4 charges.
40 hand grenades, loaded.
10 hand grenades, not loaded.
78 little sacks for 30-pounders.
207 do. do. 12-pounders.
200 do. do. 4-pounders.
40 do. do. 22-pounders.
60 fuzes for shells for 4-pounders.
1 box with mixed, for shells.
200 fulminating matches.
10 squibs.
10 rockets.
1 fire chemise.
720 pistol cartridges a la Fosset.
1 copper fuzee for vessels, blinded.

JUAN PAITTON.

TAMPICO, *January* 27, 1863.

Report of the cargo taken from the enemy, contained in the brigantine Indus.

4 boxes cheese.
15 empty barrels.
32 empty quarter casks.
47 barrels salt meat.
26 barrels of flour.
65 boxes with jars of preserved meat.
4 boxes containing medicines.
69 large jars preserved meat.
23 sacks white beans.
6 sacks maize.
15 sacks salt.
45 casks biscuit.
5 boxes tobacco.
4 empty pipes.
53 small canisters preserved meat.
2 sacks peas.
3 barrels flour.
9 barrels flour, damaged.
1 tierce tobacco.
3 jugs oil.
1 bag mustard.
2 barrels salt.
19 oars.
1 mast.
3 barrels maize.
24 barrels red wine.
2 boxes peas.
2 boxes white beans.
3 boxes biscuits.
7 casks biscuits.
6 half-casks biscuits.
3 barrels boiled meat.
4 empty pots.
2 bedsteads with pillows.
1 bundle containing bedding.
2 bundles containing crutches.
1 cask containing apothecary's bottles.
1 jug oil.
6 uncovered barrels flour.
1 bundle stakes.
3 gridirons whereon to set caldrons.
3 small gridirons for small caldrons.
1 barrel containing salt.
1 pick-axe.
1 hatchet.
1 tierce oakum.
1 little chest with small drums.
1 large barrel containing brandy.
½ cask containing liquorice.
1 barrel flour uncovered.
3 boxes old iron.
1 copper vessel.
1 copper caldron.
7 large iron plates.
½ tierce gum arabic.
1 sack with rope's-ends.
3 kegs medicine.
78 gray coverlets.
14 white do.
397 blankets.
350 sheets.
154 pillow cases.
280 bolster cases.
46 pairs woollen stockings.
400 pointed caps.
100 aprons.
290 Rouen towels.

NOTE 1. In addition to the provisions mentioned in this report there were also those consumed by the troops, to the number of five hundred men, in three days.

NOTE 2. There is no account given of the horses, mules, and wagons taken from the enemy, because the greater part of them strayed away at the last moment, and we suceeeded in recovering only three mules and six wagons.

RAMON BARBERENA,
Commissary General.

TAMPICO, *February* 5, 1863.

A true copy:

TAMPICO, *February* 6, 1863.

D. BALANDRANO, *Secretary.*

A true copy:

WASHINGTON, *March* 31, 1863.

ROMERO.

No. 11.

FEDERAL ARMY, DIVISION OF THE SOUTH,
Headquarters, Providencia, January 10, 1863.

The MINISTER OF WAR AND MARINE, *Mexico:*

For the information of the chief magistrate of the republic, I have the honor to transmit to you the enclosed copies, which were sent to me in a private letter under date of yesterday, and which I received to-day at 12 o'clock, it not having been possible to transmit them with the regular weekly report for the reason that that could not be delayed one moment.

By the said copies you will see the course pursued by the general second in command of the division, and the demands of the enemy, wherein I have not been able to do less than approve the conduct of the former.

It is now 11 o'clock p. m., and as yet the courier has not arrived whom I expect to bring me an account of the result of the attack of this morning, which I will communicate to you as soon as I receive it.

Wherefore I offer to you and to the president the assurance of my distinguished esteem and consideration.

Liberty and reform!

J. ALVAREZ.

WASHINGTON, *March* 31, 1863.

A true copy: ROMERO.

No. 12.

[Translation.]

NAVAL DIVISION OF THE PACIFIC OCEAN, OFF ACAPULCO,
On Board the Pallas, January 8, 1863.

SIR: Convinced as I am of the great disorder which a declared hostility between the French division and the port of Acapulco (the place lacking, as the governor has informed me, sufficient means to reply to the fire of the division) would cause in the commercial relations, I am disposed to enter into an arrangement on the following conditions:

General Alvarez shall publicly contradict the false article published in the journal El Chalaco, No. 633, under the date of the 3d of November last, in the name of General Ghilardi.

The admiral will then be disposed to celebrate with the general commander of the state a convention of neutrality, wherein it will be stipulated that the French ships-of-war shall have all the desirable facilities to provide themselves with provisions, water, and coal, whenever they shall present themselves at Acapulco.

On their part, the ships of the French division of the Pacific ocean will abstain from all acts of hostility against the port of Acapulco.

On accepting these conditions I will withdraw the demand which I had made to the governor for the dismantlement of the batteries.

Please accept, sir, the assurance of my distinguished consideration.

BOUET,
The Admiral Commander-in-Chief.

The AGENT *of the Compang of American Mail Steamers.*

WASHINGTON, *March* 31, 1863.

A true copy: ROMERO.

No. 13.

Copy of the rough draught which was given in.

YOUR EXCELLENCY: I believe that the intentions of my admiral, communicated to your excellency, were properly interpreted.

Permit me to repeat to you, in order to avoid all misunderstanding, 1st. The admiral requests that the wicked passion which inspired the article against the French corvette La Bayonnaise, published in the journal known as El Chalaco, under date of the 3d of November, a wicked passion hostile in every respect and false in its particular statements, be now acknowledged, inasmuch as General Ghilardi has been removed.

The acts of the late governor, so justly disapproved by your excellency in the name of those sentiments of dignity which, alike in times of war as in times of peace, impose on every one a respect for truth, give me the assurance that you will be the first, as governor, to have this article contradicted for the good of the Mexican government itself, which cannot authorize the publication of an *injury* directed against an *absent* enemy.

The question as to stores and provisions you are already acquainted with, and I need not return to its consideration; it was properly interpreted, and inspired by an idea of humanity and of conciliation, an idea which prevails among all nations.

I have confidence in your excellency's judgment, and I await the reply, although I have not received this order from my admiral.

The removal of Señor Ghilardi is a proof of the justice of his honorable father, whose high and chivalrous character cannot receive as the feeling of his country the article of the Chalaco in reference to the Bayonnaise.

WASHINGTON, *March* 31, 1863.

A true copy: ROMERO.

No. 14.

ACAPULCO, *January* 9, 1863.

ESTEEMED SIR: I have taken into consideration the communication addressed to you by the admiral of the French squadron, informing you that, being desirous to avoid the inconveniences which the company which you represent might suffer in case of fire being opened between the naval division under his command and this place, he feels disposed to enter into an agreement with me under the conditions which he himself therein indicates, and I proceed to apprise you of my ideas on the subject.

I shall begin by setting down the fact that he has fallen into a mistake in asserting that the undersigned has confessed that he has not sufficient means to withstand the fire of his naval force, as this could not have been inferred either from the official communication which I addressed yesterday to the admiral in reply to his, or much less from the private conference which I had with Captain Le Bris, the bearer of the admiral's letter.

It is true that to the cordial protestations of that officer I replied with the politeness becoming a gentleman, deploring the unavoidable necessity which I was under of treating as enemies the sons of a nation for which I had ever the liveliest sympathies; but there was nothing beyond this, and to this act no other character can be given than that of mere urbanity.

As far as regards the proposition prior to the agreement which is pretended, an engagement to contradict the assertions of Señor Ghilardi, in reference to the corvette La Bayonnaise, published in the columns of the Chalaco newspaper, No. 633, of the 3d of November last, I can do absolutely nothing in the matter, because the fact of the incorrectness of the statements in that article would assuredly impose a responsibility only on its author, the aforesaid Señor Ghilardi, who is now removed from the command and beyond the limits of this state.

In regard to the intimations in reference to the points that should be embraced in the agreement, in order to express my opinion on the subject, I conceive it to be an indispensable formality that direct communication should be made with me, in order to avoid in the future all sinister interpretation that might be made to the dishonor of the good name of my country.

For the rest, you will permit me to tell you that I cannot conceive how neutrality can be maintained between those who belong to the armed force of two nations which are actually at war, and I would desire to have an explanation of this point in order to enable me to form a less incorrect judgment.

This same thing you can make known to the French admiral, who has initiated this negotiation.

I reiterate to you the assurance of the sincere esteem with which I sign myself

Your most affectionate friend,

D. ALVAREZ.

Mr. B. S. VAN BRUNT.

WASHINGTON, *March* 31, 1863.

A true copy: ROMERO.

No. 15.

[Translation.]

Official.

EXCELLENCY: The admiral has ordered me to inform your excellency that he presents himself before Acapulco without hostile intentions.

He appeals first to your military honor, begging you to examine the gravity of the article on the French corvette La Bayonnaise.

He demands the public retraction of an injury which could not have been made under the government of your excellency, and which you disapprove as much as the undersigned. This single fact sufficiently deserves the dismissal of M Ghilardi.

The admiral will enter with his squadron the bay of Acapulco without hostile intentions, which I have the honor to repeat to you, and will provide himself with provisions, water, and coal with all security. He will be very sorry to meet with hostility in view of his peaceful intentions, which I have been commissioned to communicate to you. The admiral confides fully in your excellency's word, and doubts not that all the French vessels which may present themselves in this port will be received with equal kindness.

I have the honor to be, with respect, your excellency's devoted servant,

E. LE BRIS.

His Excellency the GENERAL COMMANDER-IN-CHIEF, *Acapulco.*

WASHINGTON, *March* 31, 1863.

A true copy: ROMERO.

No. 16.

FEDERAL ARMY, DIVISION OF THE SOUTH,
Acapulco, January 9, 1863.

To Captain LE BRIS, *Present:*

The communication, without date, which I have just received from you, leaves me impressed with the fact that the admiral of the French naval forces commissions you to inform me that he presents himself before this port without any hostile intentions.

In regard to the affair concerning the corvette La Bayonnaise, as the communication published in the Chalaco is not a work proceeding from the undersigned, but from Señor Ghilardi, to him it belongs to give explanations in reference to the matter. As to the present writer, it should be remarked that he is not accustomed to make such exaggerated statements, but always to speak the truth, and consequently that he will never approve of anything not in accordance with the principle of truth.

In regard to entrance into the bay, and concession of provision, water, and coal, it not being within the scope of the authority of the undersigned to grant them, he refers to what he has manifested to the admiral in his communication of yesterday, and considers himself excused from any further statement, so as to avoid repeating what has been already said once for all.

I renew to you the assurance of my consideration and special esteem.

Liberty and reform !

D. ALVAREZ.

WASHINGTON, *March* 31, 1863.

A true copy:

ROMERO.

No. 17.

FEDERAL ARMY, DIVISION OF THE SOUTH,
Headquarters, Providencia, January 11, 1863.

The MINISTER OF WAR AND MARINE, *Mexico:*

It is three o'clock in the morning, and I have just received from the port of Acapulco, and from the officer intrusted with its defence, the following despatch, written yesterday, at 12½ o'clock p. m.:

"COMMANDER-IN-CHIEF: At three-quarters past eight o'clock this morning fire was opened between the French squadron and the force under my command. The following circumstances have been remarked:

"At thirty-five minutes past nine o'clock all the pieces in Fort Guerrero were dismounted and rendered useless, and consequently the fire of the fort was discontinued.

"At forty-five minutes past nine o'clock the same happened with Fort Iturbide. Fort Galeana met with the like result at ten o'clock.

"The enemy has stationed himself beyond the range of Forts Hidalgo and Morelos, from which we have as yet received no news on account of the distance.

"The national flag is yet waving on Fort Alvarez.

"The enemy is furiously bombarding this port, but the troops and the people shout enthusiastically for the supreme government, and defend with honor the good name of their country.

"We have several killed and wounded. When I receive all the details and terminate the duties of the day, I will give the particulars.

"The firing is being continued with vigor up to this moment."

I have the honor to transmit this despatch to you for your information, and that of the President of the republic, with the assurance of keeping you posted in all that occurs to the final close of the action.

Wherewith I assure you of my esteem and consideration.

Liberty and reform !

J. ALVAREZ,
General Commanding.

At 5 a. m.

WASHINGTON, *March* 31, 1863.

A true copy:

ROMERO.

No. 18.

FEDERAL ARMY, DIVISION OF THE SOUTH,
Headquarters, Providencia, January 12, 1863.

The MINISTER OF WAR :

Under date of yesterday I received the following report from the officer second in command of the division :

"GENERAL : Subsequently to what I reported to you in my communication of yesterday at 12½ o'clock p. m., from that hour until 5 o'clock in the evening, the hostile squadron continued firing upon Fort Alvarez very slowly ; but the latter has not answered, as the squadron is beyond the range of its guns.

"The fire of our artillery is entirely useless, because to the circumstance of bad mountings is added that of not being able to throw shot even to half the distance of the enemy, whilst the guns of the latter have even a longer range than that distance, as they have pieces of 64 and 80 pounds calibre, and all rifled.

"At six o'clock this morning the enemy recommenced their fire upon Fort Alvarez, and continue up to the present moment, 11 o'clock a. m. Several buildings in the city were thrown down during the bombardment of yesterday, which lasted for more than two hours. The barbarity of the enemy was remarkable, as they knew that there was not a single Mexican in it, and consequently their hostility was directed against the prosperity of the city, and their purpose was to destroy existing interests. Among the houses set on fire was that belonging to Spanish subjects, known under the style of Narvarte and Company, with the remarkable circumstance that the flag-staff, the flag having been raised upon it, was struck and cut in two, as I have been informed. It appears that about two hundred boxes of dry-goods were burnt in it, as well as some other effects.

"I cannot yet give you the particulars as to the state of affairs in the forts and other points held by the division, because I have all the troops under arms, surrounding the port, in order to prevent the disembarcation of the enemy, and especially to keep them from supplying themselves with water, as all provisions have been withdrawn beyond their reach."

This communication I received at night, about 12 o'clock, and, according to my promise to you, I transmit it, for the information of the President of the republic.

I should not permit myself to pass over in silence the barbarity which the enemy is exercising against a town wherein there is nothing but the mere houses, as is shown by the preceding communication ; a circumstance which will make known to all the world what is to be expected from our invaders, who proclaim that they come to civilize us.

Wherefore I offer you the assurance of my respect and consideration.

Liberty and reform !

J. ALVAREZ.

WASHINGTON, *March* 31, 1863.

A true copy : ROMERO.

No. 19.

[Translation.]

FEDERAL ARMY, DIVISION OF THE SOUTH, GENERAL-IN-CHIEF—CITIZEN MINISTER OF WAR.

Citizen MINISTER OF WAR AND MARINE, *Mexico:*

It is half past 9 o'clock in the morning, and I have just received the following despatch :

FEDERAL ARMY, DIVISION OF THE SOUTH,
Acapulco, January 12, 1863—7 o'clock p. m.

Second in command : Long live the republic ! Long live the constitutional government !

CITIZEN GENERAL-IN-CHIEF : At six o'clock this morning firing commenced between the French squadron and our batteries of Fort Alvarez. Its greatest activity was from one to five o'clock this afternoon, and twenty minutes after the former retired from the harbor, driven off by cannon, even though these were not effective, on account of the short range of the pieces. The enemy's fire riddled, with its projectiles, our beautiful tri-colored flag, leaving it in tatters, but it waved proudly upon its staff to the last.

With opportunity I will communicate to you the events that happened during the three days' combat against the invaders, it being sufficient now for me to assure you that all the generals, chiefs, officers, and troops of the division under my command have discharged their duties with the greatest gallantry, courage, and intrepidity.

God save the republic! and that the heroic defence of the port of Acapulco may be the dawn that precedes the more splendid triumph of our armies in Puebla de Zaragoza. I congratulate you most cordially upon so happy a result, and at the same time reiterate my respect and subordination.

Liberty and reform!

D. ALVAREZ.

Citizen general, well deserving of the country,
JUAN ALVAREZ,
Chief of this Division, La Providencia.

With the greatest satisfaction I transmit it to you, for your information and that of the
izen President of the republic, congratulating him at the same time upon the triumph
ained with so much heroism in the fortifications of Acapulco, where, notwithstanding
scarcity from which we suffer, the preparations for the defence will be continued, as
is possible to prepare for the return of the enemy's squadron, which will happen, prob-
although it had not sufficient valor to take by main force Fort Alvarez, the only one
maintained itself until the last instant. In conclusion, I inform you that the enemy's
ls did not leave in so good a condition, because they suffered some damage; and I
.erstand that they have retired to repair the damages they may have sustained, and for the purpose, also, of taking in water at some point of the coast, because in Acapulco they took nothing they need.

As soon as I receive a circumstantial report I will communicate it to you. In the interim, it is pleasing to repeat to you my esteem and respectful consideration.

Liberty and reform!

LA PROVIDENCIA, *January* 13, 1863.

JUAN ALVAREZ.

WASHINGTON, *March* 31, 1863.

A true copy: ROMERO.

No. 20.

ARMY OF THE EAST.

HEADQUARTERS ZARAGOZA, *December* 31, 1862.

The MINISTER OF WAR, *Mexico:*

The military commander of Tehuacan, under date of the 19th, just past, transmits to me the following report:

"I have the honor to inform you that the hostile force which occupied this place, composed of the 95th of the line, one hundred and sixty-five *chasseurs d'Afrique*, ninety-four traitors, under the command of the infamous Trujeque, six 8-pounder rifled cannons with their proper complement of artillerists, six large wagons and twelve small ones, formed a total fifteen hundred strong.

"The population has been subjected to serious outrages. The commercial establishments of the citizens, José Vincente Esperon, Nicolas Herrera, Severiano Benites, and Dona Josefa Espinosa, were pillaged by some soldiers of the 95th of the line, as also the chandlery of Diego Gonzales by the French advance, that honorable citizen being thereby left in utter misery.

"Several families were maltreated, among them that of Antenogenes Gonzales, whose wife, after enduring the blows inflicted upon her by a French captain, they wished to carry off to prison, because her husband was in the ranks of the Riva Palacio division.

"I would weary you if I proposed to myself to narrate, one by one, the robberies and outrages committed by the French army during the few days that it remained in this city; be it sufficient to state that the greater part of the houses, even those of the very poorest people, were robbed of their hogs, hens, and fowl of all kinds that the soldiers could lay hands on, all the lumber that was in the public square, and the wooden buildings in the suburbs were burned and destroyed.

"They committed various rapes, the most notable one being that which was perpetrated in the public square, where a multitude of them surrounded their victim and gave free scope to their licentious passion.

"From the minute investigation ordered to be instituted by this military department in order to discover who had afforded supplies to the invader, it is established that the Spanish subject, Augustin Allende, sold them more than a hundred loads of flour, abstracted from the Amarilla house, and that he left for Orizaba in company with the invaders.

"The traitors, Manuel Loaiza, Mariano Loaiza, Joaquin Arroniz, sr., Joaquin Arroniz, jr., likewise went off with the enemy, as also the French subject, Eugene Lafenètre, who had previously given them information of the state of our army and the measures which were being adopted, in this manner showing his appreciation for the hospitality and consideration which had been exhibited towards him."

I have the honor of transmitting this despatch to you for your better information.

Liberty and reform!

JESUS G. ORTEGA.

WASHINGTON, *March* 31, 1863.

A true copy: ROMERO.

No. 21.

[Translation,]

Private correspondence of General Antonio Carvajal.

SAN NICOLAS, *January* 17, 1863.

MY ESTEEMED FRIEND AND COMPANION: By one of the persons who have come from Acatzingo I have learned the following news:

The French have arrested four individuals, who are Don Vicente Vioanco, Don Diego Miron, Don N. Corres, and another whose name I do not know, all of Quecholac. They have sent three individuals in carts, shut up in boxes with only a hole through which their faces could be seen and they give them to eat.

Before this, they put Don Diego Miron in a barrel of water up to his neck, with large balls in his hands, without more fault than private disputes for not consenting to grave faults with his family. Already the court inquisition begins anew, and it is said that they will place it in Mexico as soon as the capital is taken.

As ever, your affectionate friend and obedient servant,

ANTONIO CARVAJAL.

General JESUS GONZALES ORTEGA.

WASHINGTON, *March* 31, 1863.

A true copy: ROMERO.

No. 22.

[Translation.]

VERA CRUZ, *January* 20.

SUB-PREFECTURE OF THE DISTRICT OF VERA CRUZ: The prefect of the district, in a communication of yesterday, says to the subscriber as follows:

This prefecture has to-day received the following communication, which, being translated, says: Mr. Prefect: I have the honor to transmit you a circular from the commander-in-chief, asking you to have the kindness to have it translated into Spanish, and to take the necessary steps that may conduce to giving it the greatest possible publicity.

Circular.—In conformity with the French code of military law, every individual accused as the author or accomplice of treason, spying, tampering with the army, revolt, insubordination, rebellion, violence against a French soldier, táking away, stealing or hiding military effects, money, or anything that belongs either to the state or to the army—or, in a word, of any crime or misdemeanor that affects the safety of the army, will be made to appear before a French court-martial, of whatever nation he may be. I beg of you to cause these regulations to come to the knowledge of the inhabitants. Headquarters at Orizaba, January 6, 1863. FOREY, Commander-in-Chief.

Mr. Prefect, please to accept the expression of my highest consideration.

J. DURAND ST. ARNAUD.

VERA CRUZ, *January* 17, 1863.

MR. PREFECT OF THE DISTRICT OF VERA CRUZ: I communicate the present to your honor for your information, and to the end that it may be published in the official paper, making it known to the authorities of the towns that are under your jurisdiction. The which is now published for the knowledge of the inhabitants of the district.

D. BERREAN.

A MEXICAN EXECUTION.

VERA CRUZ, *Saturday*, *January* 24, 1863.

In compliance with the orders of his excellency the commander-in-chief of the French army, on the 15th instant, there was put in force in the fortress of Ulloa the sentence of death by the court-martial against Bartolo Banderas and Justo Pasos, accused of poisoning French soldiers. The two culprits, after having received spiritual aid, were shot in the presence of the Mexican prisoners in the fortress, all the formalities prescribed by the French code of military law being carried out.

WASHINGTON, *March* 31, 1863.

A true copy. ROMERO.

No. 23.

PEROTE, *January* 4, 1863.

SIR: I have the honor to acknowlege the receipt of your communication of yesterday, begging you to excuse me if I cannot present myself before the court-martial to give you the information that you ask about the so-called Florian Bernardi, who is to be tried to-day by the court-martial. Official business may require my departure from here every moment. I will, however, give you all the information I can about the above-named individual.

On the 23d I arrived at Nopalucan, in company with Mr. W. Corwin, secretary of the American legation, and of Mr. Cajat, consular agent of the United States in Puebla. From there the secretary of legation and myself addressed a communication to the general commanding the first division, asking him to place an escort at our disposition to obtain the necessary security in order to reach the line occupied by the French army. We arrived at Tepeyahualco, accompanied by an escort of the Mexican army. Until the answer of the general commanding the first division came, we remained at Tepeyahualco, without the necessary protection to continue our journey, for we had promised General Alvarez not to make the escort go, which he had the kindness to give us, beyond the above-named place.

During this time we saw entering Tepeyahualco the so-called Florian Bernardi, with a force of 17 men. Supposing that Florian with his men belonged to the Mexican army, we presented him with the order of General Ortega, commander-in-chief of the Mexican troops, ordering the commanders of the forces that we might find in the way to furnish us with every sort of security, and to furnish us with the means of continuing our journey, and we asked him if he would escort us in order to continue our journey.

Señor Florian consented immediately to it, when the messenger whom we had sent to General Bazaine arrived with a letter from the general in command, informing us that we would find a French escort in Tenestepec.

Señor Bernardi, on seeing the general's letter, in which he informed us of the place where we would find a French escort, observed that it was very probable that the general was mistaken in the name of the place, for Tenestepec was not in our way.

After this we set out, recommending Señor Florian that he should stop as soon as he perceived the French troops, or should make use of a white flag to prevent any mistake.

More than this, Señor Bernardi thought fit to leave a part of his soldiers in San Antonio, not to arrive at the French lines with a force that might occasion a mistake.

On coming near the place which we believed Tenestepec, we warned Señor Florian to take his white flag and advance alone with one man, to let our object be known.

From this time we lost sight of Florian, and entered Perote, astonished to find ourselves there when we still imagined that we were going to stop in Tenestepec.

When I saw the French troops, the three men of the escort, who came behind our coach, manifested a fear of entering the place. We observed to them that there was greater risk in returning, being already in the French lines, and when their commander was in Perote; and we told them that we did not see that there would be the least risk for them, as they were with us, for we intended to explain to the commanding general under what conditions they had entered the town in our company.

A guard informed us at the entrance that Señor Florian had passed. What afterwards occurred will be probably known to you, and, for my part, I have nothing more to add but that the secretary of the American legation agrees to the present account, and makes it his. Accept, sir, the sincerity of my perfect consideration.

MARCUS OTTERBOURG,
Consul of the United States of America in Mexico.

Having read the above memorial, made by Mr. Marcus Otterbourg, consul of the United States in Mexico, I declare hereby that I entirely agree in all that he has said, as being a true account of the facts that have taken place.

WM. H. CORWIN,
Secretary of the Legation of the United States in Mexico.
A. M. F. GARNIER,
Colonel of the Fifty-first, and President of the Court-martial.

WASHINGTON, *March* 31, 1863.

A true copy:

ROMERO.

No. 24.

[Translation.]

ARMY OF THE EAST, COMMANDER-IN-CHIEF.

PUEBLA DE ZARAGOZA, *February* 1, 1863.

The citizen minister of war writes to me under yesterday's date as follows:

By the declarations of the greater part of the deserters from the invading army it is understood that the soldiers who compose it are becoming persuaded that neither our government nor our country is in the state of disorganization which had been described to them; on the contrary, they now comprehend that they are to be tools to establish oppression and despotism in a country in which the greatest and best regulated liberty reigns, based on a constitution that proclaims the same principles as to individual liberty that these very soldiers have formerly defended with their lives in Europe, and that have also been proclaimed by their eminent writers in their works.

In consequence, the citizen President of the republic desires that by all the means in your reach you will let the French soldier know that the government will continue affording resources, as it has hitherto done, to all who present themselves, and until they can find honest means of supporting themselves in the republic, where all enjoy complete liberty, where principally the industrious and saving foreigner finds innumerable opportunities of acquiring, as is proved by a number of examples, a fortune difficult to make in Europe, and where, besides, he is free from military service, and placed under the protection of the authorities, who are particularly careful to be just. This government recommends you, then, to transmit your orders to the commanding officers of the advanced forces and to the civil authorities, so that the French who present themselves, with the intention of leaving the invading army, may be well received and provided with everything necessary to continue their journey to the capital, where, as before said, the government will afford them resources, and attend to them till they find occupation to give them means to subsist and enjoy the quiet life of an industrious man.

And I communicate it to you that, with the above directions, you may attend to the deserters from the invading army who present themselves, and also that you may take care that the present circular shall get to the knowledge of the said army, so that those who fear being badly received by the people and government of Mexico may be convinced of the contrary, and decide to abandon a cause that Europe itself has declared dishonorable to the French people.

Liberty and reform!

ORTEGA.

WASHINGTON, *March* 31, 1863.

A true copy:

ROMERO.

No. 25.

[Translation.]

ARMY OF THE EAST, GENERAL-IN-CHIEF.

Citizen MINISTER OF WAR, *Mexico:*

These headquarters gave yesterday a passport for that capital, and provided with the necessary funds to defray his travelling expenses, to the French deserter Eugene Latremolles.

Liberty and reform!

Headquarters at Zaragoza, February 3, 1863.

ORTEGA.

WASHINGTON, *March* 31, 1863.

A true copy: ROMERO.

No. 26.

[Translation.]

ARMY OF THE EAST, GENERAL-IN-CHIEF.

Citizen MINISTER OF WAR, *Mexico* :

These headquarters gave yesterday a passport for that capital, and provided with the necessary funds to defray their travelling expenses, the deserters from the French army, Corporal Alfred Lemaire, and privates Jieng Gautrou, Joseph Coffin, Anatolio Yanseur, Edwards Picot, Poullout and Jean B. Guepet, all of them belonging to the regiment of zouaves.

I have the honor to communicate to you the foregoing for your information.

Liberty and reform!

Headquarters at Zaragoza, February12, 1863.

J. G. ORTEGA.

WASHINGTON, *March* 31, 1863.

A true copy: ROMERO.

No. 27.

[Translation.]

MONSIEUR LE PRESIDENT: We would not like to leave your capital without an acknowledgment of our gratitude for the kind treatment which we have received up to the present time from the government you have the honor to represent.

Since the day we left the invading army, where we were told that all French deserters had to suffer the most cruel tortures from the Mexican people, we have seen that it was a shameful lie; for wherever we have passed we have been received with the greatest regard, even from the superior officers, who have hastened to aid us, offering us their services, and showing that they have for us the sincerest sympathies.

Receive, Monsieur le President, our heartfelt thanks.

Done at Mexico, the 14th February, 1863.

Second Battalion Zouaves:

COQUERET, ARISTIE, *First Sergeant.*
EUGENE, PICARDE, *Corporal.*
ANATOLE, VASSEUR, *Soldier.*
CAFFIN, JOSEPH, *Soldier.*
CARTERON, JEAN, *Soldier.*
GAUTRON, PIERRE, *Soldier.*

Third Battalion Zouaves:

PICAT, EDOUARD, *Soldier.*
PERILLON, PIERRE, *Soldier.*
GUEPEL, JEAN, *Soldier*
ALFRED DE CAVAIGNAC, *First Sergeant.*

WASHINGTON, *March* 31, 1863.

A true copy:

ROMERO.

No. 28.

ARMY OF THE CENTRE, HEADQ'RS SECOND DIVISION,
Mexico, January 9, 1863.

In accordance with the supreme order of the government, communicated to me by you, I have had the French prisoners that were in Santiago to draw up the declaration of which I enclose a copy to you; and I have also procured to have their passports given them and each one supplied with five dollars, in order that they may be able to return to their ranks. I also transmit to you the copy of the receipt which they have given therefor. Their passports were issued under date of the 3d of the present month.

This I lay before you for your information.

Liberty and reform!

ANDRES L. TAPIA,
Acting Chief of Division.

MEXICAN REPUBLIC, ARMY OF THE CENTRE,
Quartermaster's Department, Mexico, December 31, 1862.

We, the undersigned, soldiers of the French army in this republic, declare that, finding ourselves in this capital, in the barracks of the corps of invalides of the army of Mexico, in the character of prisoners of war, we have been made to appear to-day before the citizen Mr. Augustin Diaz, professor of the military school, who, in the name of the quartermaster general of the Mexican army of the centre, after having communicated to us a resolution of the supreme government, ordering us to be set at complete liberty, and allowing us to return to our own camp—a sum of money necessary for that purpose being tendered us—or offering us a permit to live peaceably in this country, choosing any sort of employment that might suit us, asked us a declaration of our free will. In consequence, after mature reflection, we have resolved to ask the assistance which is offered to us, in order to return to our ranks, rendering our thanks, as in duty bound, to the supreme government of the country, which has treated us with so much deference.

P. CLECH, *Corporal.*
J. CLERC.
S. CHARLES, *Soldier of the 90th regiment.*
E. JOUVERT.
L. ALAIN. } Not knowing how to write, I have
S. CHARLES. } signed for them.—A. COUTURE.

A true copy:

ANDRES L. TAPIA.

The original French is as follows:

Nous, soussignés, soldats du régiment du corps expéditionnaire Français dans cette république, déclarons: que nous trouvant dans cette capitale, dans la caserne du corps des Invalides de l'armée Mexicaine, en qualité de prisonniers de guerre, on nous a fait comparaitre aujourd'hui devant le citoyen professeur de l'école militaire, M. Augustin Diaz, lequel, au nom de M. le général quartier-maître de l'armée Mexicaine du centre, après nous avoir fait savoir la résolution du gouvernement suprême de nous remettre en complète liberté, nous permettant de rejoindre notre quartier-générale en nous remettant la somme nécessaire à cet effet, ou nous offrant un sauf-conduit, afin de pouvoir vivre pacifiquement dans ce pays, choississant le genre d'occupation qui nous conviendrait, nous demande une manifestation de notre libre volonté. En consequence, après mure réflexion, nous avons résolu de demander l'aide que l'on nous offre, afin de pouvoir rejoindre nos rangs, remerciant comme nous le devons le gouvernement suprême du pays, qui nous a traité avec tant de déférence.

P. CLECH, *Caporale.*
J. CLERC.
S. CHARLES, 90*me régiment.*
E. JOUVERT.
L. ALAIN. } Ne sachant pas signer, j'ai
S. CHARLES. } signé pour eux.—A. COUTURE.

MEXICAN REPUBLIC, ARMY OF THE CENTRE,
Quartermaster's Department, Second Division, Mexico, January 3, 1863.

We have received from the quartermaster general twenty-five dollars for each one of us who hereunto subscribe our names, in order to enable us to return to the army to which we belong.

CLECH.
CLERC.
LEMIQUE. } By Fabre.
JOUVERT. }
LECLERC.

MEXICO, *January* 9, 1863.

A true copy:

ANDRES L. TAPIA,
Chief of Division.

WASHINGTON, *March* 31, 1863.

A true copy:

ROMERO.

No. 29.

[Translation.]

NATIONAL PALACE, MEXICO,
February 22, 1863.

MY DEAR AND MOST ESTEEMED SIR: I have just read in the Monitor Republicano of to-day the speech which M. O'Donnell, president of the council of ministers of the Spanish government, has made in the discussion which took place with a view to answer the speech of the crown, and I have seen with surprise, among several inaccurate assertions which M. O'Donnell has made about Mexican affairs, the following expressions: * * * "As for myself, Juarez, as a Mexican, has a stain which never can be washed away—that of having been willing to sell two provinces of this country to the United States. * * *" This accusation, coming from a high functionary of a nation, and while an eminently serious and solemn act was taking place, when the statesman must be careful that his words are impressed with the seal of truth, of justice, and good faith, is of the utmost importance, for one may be led to think that on account of the position which he occupies he is in possession of documents which support his assertion—a thing which is not *true*. M. O'Donnell is authorized to publish the proofs he may possess concerning this affair. Meanwhile my honor compels me to show that M. O'Donnell has made a mistake in the judgment which he has formed of my official conduct, and you are authorized, Mr. Editor, to contradict the imputation which has been made with so much injustice to the first magistrate of the nation.

I am, Mr. Editor, your humble servant,

BENITO JUAREZ.

To the EDITOR OF THE DIARIO OFFICIAL.

WASHINGTON, *March* 31, 1863.

A true copy:

ROMERO.

No. 30.

[Translation.]

MEXICO, *January* 22, 1863.

MR. MINISTER: I had solicited more than one year ago a temporary leave of absence to return to Berlin, and the despatches which I have received by the last packet have brought me the intelligence that the government of the King, yielding to my repeated requests, has granted me the permission to leave Mexico.

I should desire to take the road to Tampico; but if on the 15th proximo the health of my nephew, who is now sick, should not permit him to make so long a journey on horseback, I shall leave by carriage directly for Vera Cruz, by whatever road the general-in-chief of the army of the east may deem to be the most proper and affording me the greater safety.

Requesting your excellency to communicate to his excellency the President of the republic my intended early departure, I shall hereafter inform your excellency, Mr. Minister, of the measures I have adopted for the temporary conduct of the affairs of the legation of the King during my absence, and I shall recur to your excellency's affability for the issue of the safe-conduct and escorts required.

Be pleased, Mr. Minister, to accept the assurances of my high consideration.

E. DE WAGNER.

His Excellency Don Juan Antonio de la Fuente,
Minister for Foreign Relations of the Mexican Republic, &c., &c., &c.

WASHINGTON, *March* 31, 1863.

A true copy:

ROMERO.

No. 31.

[Translation.]

MEXICO, *January* 30, 1863.

Mr. MINISTER: I have communicated to the President the note which your excellency did me the honor to address to me on the 22d instant, limited to the permission which his Majesty the King of Prussia has been pleased to grant you to withdraw temporarily to Berlin.

In relation to what your excellency says to me in reference to your journey by way of Tampico, or by the route of Vera Cruz, your excellency will be free to take that which is most convenient to you.

I hope to receive the favor of the communication which your excellency proposes to address to me upon several points. I cannot foresee that they will involve the slightest difficulty.

Your excellency will accept the assurances of my very distinguished consideration.

JUAN ANTONIO DE LA FUENTE.

His Excellency Señor Baron E. de Wagner,
Minister resident of his Majesty the King of Prussia.

WASHINGTON, *March* 31, 1863.

A true copy:

ROMERO.

No. 32.

[Translation.]

MEXICO, *February* 9, 1863.

Mr. MINISTER: Thanking your excellency for the communication which you have been pleased to address me under date of the 30th of the past month, I have the honor to inform you that I propose to take my departure for Berlin on the 18th of this month at four o'clock a. m.

The consul of the King, Mr. Benecke, will be left, during my absence, in charge of the current affairs relating to the protection of the interests of the Prussian subjects. I hope that his intervention, that of the other German consuls, as also that of Mr. Ballerteros, the consul general of Spain, and that of the consul of Belgium, Mr. Grave, will be sufficient to guarantee the interests of their countrymen, which had been, up to this period, confided to the protection of the Prussian legation. However, in the exceptional cases which may present themselves, I have recommended these consuls and their countrymen, as also the French residents, to the kind protection of the legation of the United States of North America. I hope that this measure will be only a matter of formality, and that the direct protection of your excellency will be assured to the said foreigners who may appeal to the kindness of your department. I intend to make the trip hence to Vera Cruz in the diligence; but if the military operations should require it, I shall be enabled to go directly from San Martin to Acalcingo, leaving Puebla aside. On the 15th, at mid-day, a cart containing my equipage will leave with the escort which your excellency may be pleased to cause it to be accompanied.

I take the liberty to request your excellency to be pleased to order the issue of the passports and safe-conduct for myself and my nephew, Charles Wagner, the secretary attached to this legation, and also for our three servants. I therefore request your excellency to give the necessary orders with respect to the escorts which are to accompany us, and I would be obliged to your excellency to let me know who is the military officer in charge of them, that I may have a direct understanding with him. I will also thank your excellency to apprise the general-in-chief of the army of the east of my early departure, and to transmit to his excellency the open letter herewith enclosed, addressed to the French general commanding on the Orizaba road, in order that he may transmit it to the latter through a flag of truce, and that he may take the necessary measures with respect to my passage through the advanced lines.

If by the 18th of this month there should occur any serious battle which may prevent my passage, I will thank your excellency to communicate it to me.

Be pleased, Mr. Minister, to accept the assurances of my high consideration.

E. DE WAGNER.

His Excellency Señor Don JUAN ANTONIO DE LA FUENTE,
Minister of Foreign Relations of the Mexican Republic, &c., &c., &c.

WASHINGTON, *March* 31, 1863.

A true copy:

ROMERO.

No. 33.

[Translation.]

NATIONAL PALACE, MEXICO, *February* 12, 1863.

MR. MINISTER: I have received the communication which your excellency did me the honor to address me on the 9th instant, in reference to your departure, passports, necessary safe-conducts, and the conduct of various matters during your absence.

Agreeably to what I have on other occasions had the pleasure to say to your excellency, you can make your trip hence to Vera Cruz; and in compliance with your request upon that subject now made, the proper instructions will be issued in order that General Comonfort, now stationed at San Martin, shall inform your excellency whether the military operations do not permit your excellency to pass through Puebla. The cart which your excellency sends with your equipage will be properly escorted. With respect to the passports and safe-conducts, your excellency will receive, enclosed in this communication, those which you were pleased to ask of me.

The war department will issue the orders concerning the escorts which are to accompany your excellency on your trip, and you will receive timely notice of the military officer or officers who will be charged with this duty. The letter which your excellency transmitted to me for that purpose will be sent to-day to the general-in-chief of the army of the east, that he may cause it to reach the French general in command of the forces stationed on the Orizaba road. If by the day on which your excellency intends to set out upon your journey any battle or other occurrence should take place to prevent your excellency's passage, I shall consider myself bound to make it known to you.

In relation to the other points to which your excellency refers, I must say to you that the Mexican government at once admits the interposition of Mr. Benecke, the consul of his Majesty, in matters relating to the protection of Prussian subjects and their property; and that agreeably to our laws, consul's general may, in the absence of the minister of their nation, hold correspondence with the government of the republic respecting the protection of his countrymen. Unfortunately, the commission which your excellency says you have conferred upon the legation of the United States, to protect in extraordinary cases the Prussian subjects, the Germans, Spaniards, Belgians, and their respective consuls, as well as the Frenchmen residing in this country, is not so simple a matter. That your excellency should recommend the protection of your countrymen to the benevolence of another legation would be a thing perfectly conformable to the usages received everywhere; but to make of that protection the object of two different commissions, committed to sundry functionaries, is an expedient entirely new, and which would be fruitful of conflicts and complications of every nature. The other similar commissions conferred by your excellency, have, besides the obstacle referred to, that which emanates from not possessing any data whatsoever from which it might be inferred that the governments which had confided them to the legation of Prussia gave it also the power to transfer them. With regard to the French subjects, there exists also against this sub-delegation the circumstances of the state of war, agreeably to the law of nations.

For these reasons I hope your excellency will be pleased to modify in this sense what you have been pleased to state with respect to the protection of the Prussian and other subjects to whom your legation has extended it.

Your excellency will accept the assurances of my very distinguished consideration.

JUAN ANTONIO DE LA FUENTE.

His Excellency the BARON E. DE WAGNER,
Minister Resident of his Majesty the King of Prussia.

WASHINGTON, *March* 31, 1863.

A true copy:

No. 34.

[Translation.]

MEXICO, *February* 17, 1863.

Mr. MINISTER: The envoy extraordinary and minister plenipotentiary of the United States of America having refused to give his protection to the Prussian, French, German, and Spanish subjects, who up to this time have been confided to the legation of Prussia, unless he receives a special order from his government, upon my leaving Mexico, I place them under the safeguard of the diplomatic corps, and of each one of its members particularly. At the same time, and above all, I confide them to the honor and loyalty of the Mexican people.

Accept, Mr. Minister, the assurances of my high consideration.

E. DE WAGNER.

His Excellency Señor J. A. DE LA FUENTE,
Minister of State and for Foreign Relations of the Mexican Republic, &c., &c., &c.

WASHINGTON, *March* 31, 1863.

A true copy:

ROMERO.

No. 35.

[Translation.]

NATIONAL PALACE, MEXICO, *February* 24, 1863.

Mr. MINISTER: The Baron E. de Wagner, minister resident of his Majesty the King of Prussia, upon leaving this capital, made known to the government of the confederation that he had intrusted to certain consular agents the protection of his countrymen, and of other foreigners, to whom he had extended it through the special commission of their respective governments, adding that in extraordinary cases he had placed both the subjects and the consuls referred to under the protection of the legation which you represent.

I request your excellency to read in the annexed document, No. 1, the pretension of Mr. Wagner upon this business; and in No. 2 the reasons for which the government of the republic could not accept a measure as inexpedient as it is dangerous. Mr. Wagner made no reply to these reasons, nor did he support his fixed determination. But, on the second day after his departure, there was received at the department the note transmitted as document No. 3, a note in which Mr. Wagner, manifesting in a high degree his contempt for rules, usages, and consequences, abandons the idea of all special protection, in order to place under the safeguard of the diplomatic corps and of the Mexican people the foreigners who were under the protection of the legation of Prussia.

It is doubtless unnecessary to refute the improper commission which that honorable minister had at first confided to your excellency the moment that commission was not accepted by your excellency, nor retained either by the agent who was to have conferred it upon you; and though, in fact, he may have transferred it to the diplomatic corps, I cannot for a moment fear that it will meet with a better result, being, as in truth it is, improper, offensive to the government of Mexico, and in every point of view impracticable. I entertain a sincere and well-founded hope that your excellency will not lend your respectable countenance to authorize measures of this nature. But my duty and the orders of the President also compel me to declare that, in reference to the protection of the Prussians and of the other foreigners to whom his excellency the Baron de Wagner refers in his communications referred to, the government of the republic will invariably observe what I had the honor to state to the said minister himself in the official letter which I addressed him on the 12th of the present month. Until these matters are otherwise arranged, with the approbation of the governments which are at peace with the republic, the protection of which I speak has in its favor the spirit of the federal government, and means adequate to render it effective, agreeably to international laws and to our own laws.

By confiding the foreigners, in the first place, to the loyalty and honor of the people of Mexico, Mr. Wagner renders to this nation the justice which he had so often denied to it; but Mexico does not need this testimony, nor can it accept it when it is presented insultingly to the government which it has chosen as the depository of its confidence and of its power, because this goverment, which it is affected to forget, is the true representative of the nation in its foreign relations; because the appeal that a foreign minister should make to the people, and not to the government to which he should be accredited, would be held, with good reason, as a rude violation of the law of nations; and, finally, because this omission in the present case suggests the insulting presumption that the federal government does not attend to the protection of the foreigners, while, on the contrary, everybody knows otherwise, including Mr. Wagner himself, who, in his note of the 9th February, after stating what he had determined to do to insure the protection of the Prussian subjects and other foreigners, wrote me in the following words:

"I flatter myself with the hope that this measure shall be nothing more than a mere formality, and that the foreigners who may recur to the kindness of your department will be sure to receive the direct protection of your excellency."

I avail myself of this opportunity to renew to your excellency the assurances of my very distinguished consideration.

JUAN ANTONIO DE LA FUENTE.

His Excellency Señor THOMAS CORWIN,
Envoy Extraordinary and Minister Plenipotentiary of the United States of America.

WASHINGTON, *March* 31, 1863.

A true copy:

ROMERO.

No. 36.

[Translation.]

ORIZABA, *February* 15, 1863.

MEXICANS: After the long sojourn which the corps of expedition under my command has had to make in its camp, it is about to leave and march for Mexico.

Although its sojourn has been long, and although it has had the appearance of repose, it has not been time lost. It must have made you reflect, I doubt not, upon the falsehoods of those who have an interest in pointing us out as your enemies, and to whom the valiant soldiers that I command have given a complete denial by the order and discipline which have not failed to reign in their ranks.

If we are your enemies, we Frenchmen who protect your persons, your families, your property, then what must be those Mexicans, your fellow-countrymen, who govern you by terror, who strip you of your property; who, after ruining private individuals by unexampled exactions, ruin likewise the public property, for no other end than that of preserving a power of which they make so deplorable a use.

Yes, Mexicans, you must have discovered in our actions the sincerity and loyalty of our words, when, in the name of the Emperor, I declared to you solemnly, what I again repeat to you to-day, namely, that the soldiers of France have not come here to impose upon you a government; that they have no other mission, be it well understood, after they have dragged by force from him who pretends to be the expression of the national will, the just reparation of our wrongs, which we have not been able to obtain by negotiations; they have no other mission but that of consulting the national wish as to the form of government that it desires, and as to the election of the men who appear to it most worthy to make certain good order and liberty at home, its dignity and independence abroad.

When this task has been accomplished, there will remain to the French army the obligation to aid the government chosen by you to march resolutely in the way of progress, so that, in spite of those who despise Mexico, you may succeed in forming a nation which shall have nothing to envy in others.

Then those of us who have not contributed with their lives to the accomplishment of so noble an enterprise, will re-embark in the ships of France and return to their country, happy and proud if the great duty which they have fulfilled has had for result the regeneration of your country.

FOREY,
General of Division, Senator, Commander-in-Chief of the Expeditionary Mexican Army.

No. 37.

[Translation.]

ORIZABA, *February* 16, 1863.

INHABITANTS OF ORIZABA: Within a few days I shall leave this city to undertake military operations, the preparations for which, intended to secure success, have detained me here so long a time; but I do not desire to leave without addressing you a few words, which I trust you will comprehend, because they are from my heart. In the first place, I thank you for the reception which the expeditionary corps has met with in your city during a residence of nine months, during which time order has never ceased to reign there, and our soldiers have enjoyed the same security as in their own country. If this be not owing to your sympathy, (and I would esteem myself happy if it were so,) it is due, at least, to a good disposition, which we should always thank you for. I do not believe myself laboring under a delusion when I think that the appearance and behavior of our soldiers, who in all parts of the world have been loved and esteemed even by their enemies, must have produced the same effect upon you, who have been witnesses of their order, their discipline, and the sweetness of their manners; nor is it possible that your fellow-countrymen who have seen them at other points of the country can have failed to recognize them as the sons of La Belle France, which marches in the van of civilization. Therefore I cherish the hope that you will have understood the intentions of the Emperor, whose views in sending us to Mexico have been no other, believe me, than obtaining by arms the just reparation of insults you are aware of, and which negotiation could not arrange; and then to reconcile your country with Europe, particularly with France, your ancient sympathies for which never would have ceased had it not been for the conduct of your present government. In regard to myself, if I ask Heaven to bless our arms, it is not so much for the sake of a vain ambition of personal glory as for the prosperity of your beautiful country, to which we have come to bring, at the cost of our blood, those two precious boons, without which society cannot exist—liberty and order. Farewell, then, inhabitants of Orizaba, or rather until next time, because I hope we shall return to see you. God alone knows the future; but be what may reserved for me, I shall never forget the hospitality we have received here, and shall preserve, throughout my life, the most delightful recollections of your city.

FOREY,
General of Division, Senator, and Commander-in-Chief of the Expeditionary Corps in Mexico.

No. 38.

LETTERS OF JECKER.

Correspondence intercepted by the army of the east, and which is published with the knowledge of the department of state of the Mexican republic.

PARIS, *October* 30, 1862.

MY DEAR JAVIER: I have received your letters dated 15th of September, full of interest upon general affairs, but with gloomy estimate as regards the present and future position of the house. I have written to uncle a long letter, but, this time, I have sent it through the house of Findley & Hodgson, on account of the gravity and importance of its contents. I begged uncle to communicate it to you, to keep you informed of everything, and it will be a great satisfaction to me to know that you judge and appreciate my labors. It will be until to-morrow when I shall mail this letter; I am to have at half-past 11 an interview with No. 2 *, (consult uncle's letter,) under the auspicies of No. 3 †. Should anything of importance occur I shall write to you the substance of it on a separate leaf, that you will communicate to uncle. You will see by my letter to uncle that the position presents itself admirably here, and that all that father and I have attempted has turned out well. This morning even I received very good news. No. 3 has told me that some time since, when M. Drouyn de l'Huys was only a private individual, this personage, whose opposition has acquired, by his new position of minister of foreign affairs, so great importance for us, will have asked you (your cipher) through mere curiosity, what was the business of the bonds. You have instructed him completely upon this point, and have persuaded him of the justice of our reclamations; it is, notwithstanding, surprising that he has not spoken to me of this when knowing that the new minister was his intimate friend. I have asked him what was his opinion (the minister's) about the bonds. You see by my letter to uncle that my departure for Mexico was almost at hand some time since. No. 3 has not great confidence in the new personage whose character I describe. I shall be more or less decided after my conversation to-morrow with No 2, because No. 3 has told me that it concerned him to know if it was certain that I would place myself completely at his disposition for what he might judge opportune to do. I have now No. 3 in such a manner that he has in me—in my ability! in my gravity, above all, eh!—a confidence that I can qualify as exaggerated. If I see utility for the house in my departure, with sufficient influence to serve it well, I will depart notwithstanding the repugnance of papa and mamma, and notwithstanding that I will have to go there with incomplete knowledge of metallurgy and English—a knowledge that I could make very practicable in less than a year by my projected permanence in Pongibant ‡. You can tell uncle that No. 3 has written to L. a letter by this mail, in which he gives him the grade of confidence that he ought to grant to the personage of the letter from uncle, and informs him of his renewal of favor towards No. 1, result of the two letters, telling him things that will serve for instructions, which I hope he will not delay in receiving, and that they will determine him to protect L. energetically. *What do you say of the idea* contained in the Emperor letter of No. 3 to L. to determine T. to occupy himself immediately with B.? I have suggested it in part, and applaud myself for it. I do not comprehend what you write relative to the pretended article of "La Patria." Caricaburu is a famous tale-bearer, (canard;) that article never has existed. From that time papa receives daily "La Patria" in Porentruy for the past five months, and you know if any article of importance could escape him. I read it frequently also; I have made all the investigations possible, and I can swear to you that nothing has appeared similar to what you tell me. You have read in my penultimate letter to uncle what I say in name of Mr. Hodgson: "That they are going to undertake colossal speculations upon the mines; that uncle classes them, and amongst them for the sale a part of the shares sold immediately, leaving the expenses of the working to the acquirers, one part reserved for sale if the value rises, and some shares reserved as lottery tickets." You comprehend the importance of this advice. Do what you can, that it may have a result. We have placed all in uncle's hands, with a view that it will be saved; if it perishes, it will be his own fault. The opinion of the creditors is becoming favorable to the house—according to what Father Maguin said to me yesterday—that cousin Peter would have been able to sell his notes at fifty per centum here in Paris. Hottinguer is favorable. I refer you in the rest to my letter to uncle for this, for the petition, and for the innoxiousness of Noël, because I wrote, as I believe, to uncle that having put Father Maguin in movement to instruct No. 3, he had conducted himself very dexterously, attempting to surprise Amor Escandon, son-in-law of Subervielle, and his intimate friend, and that he had had the conviction in his conversation with him that Noël did not aspire to the hand of a Miss Subervielle, and that she did not know him even. Lately Montluc has met me and wished to salute me, but I insulted him. No. 3 writes to T. that all will be managed in Mexico, and that he will have the power. You see by my letter to uncle my conversations with Mr. Hogdson and their result. Papa returns to Paris on the 3d of November. It is time, because to many steps and my studies, it is too much. "La France" of the 27th of August contains an article upon Wyke—written carefully—one could not say more. Consider, dear brother, what may be best for our interests, and, if you have motives, not to have unlimited confidence in yourself. This is, besides, the opinion of papa and mamma. See, appreciate; our salvation is at stake.

—

PARIS, *October* 30, 1862.

Mr. J. B. JECKER, *Mexico:*

I confirm to you my letter of September 30 last, a duplicate of which I send. Afterwards I have received yours of August 27 and September 13. Contrary to what I had

---

* Marpon. † Chevarier. ‡ Emperor.

thought, it is probable that it may be in Mexico itself where your business may be arranged, and for this they will give to Mr. de S. all kinds of powers; and further, I hope that, after what I have done near his Majesty, they will send him favorable instructions. Consequently, I do not see any necessity of sending at this moment for Mr. de Ch., or to any other. It is necessary, above all, that you succeed in distributing among all the foreign merchants of your acquaintance, or of that of your friends, as many times as you can, promising them to present them to the custom-house to pay, with the benefit of the discount of twenty per cent., the duties that the merchandise accumulated in the ports since the expedition has taken place ought to satisfy, causing them to observe that if there is, as it is said, duty to pay for $2,500,000 foreign commerce, will obtain immediately a benefit of $500,000, which will represent a diminution in the tariff of twenty per cent.

It will be sufficient that there are some merchants who persist in demanding the execution of the decrees which have promised them solemnly this compensation, and that after having protested in the custom-house against the refusal of their pretensions, carry their reclamations before their respective representatives, registering their protests in the chancery of their legations, to convince the foreign ministers as much of the legitimacy of their demands as of the necessity that justice may be done them for the interest of all the European commerce. You will comprehend easily that the obstinacy of a single French merchant is sufficient, for example, that should he obtain justice in this question, to create a precedent that would bring to our opinion all the foreign ministers as well as all the other leaders of their country. And you will find easily among your creditors a merchant who is fully possessed of the conscience, of the legitimacy, of the legality of its pretension, and of that obstinate constancy that personal interest gives, insisting upon rights so incontestable. In addition, I recommend to you that you make, as soon as possible, a new petition to our minister in Mexico as soon as the French arrive there, in order to ask the execution of the decrees as being a law of the treasury granted to all the foreign commerce as a diminution of the tariff, which will not want precedent in the financial history of Mexico. The business of the canal of Nicaragua obtains the preference accidentally. I regret it on account of your lands in Tehuantepec; those that you possess in Sonora could obtain value by means of the establishment of a French colony. If you think that I can be useful to you in this negotiation, that I have the confidence of being able to conduct it to a good result, it will be necessary to send me a note of details upon this point and a power of attorney, accompanied by your particular instructions."

Accept, sir, and dear correspondent, the security of my distinguished sentiments of attachment.

By authority of Morpon.

CH. FOURNIER DES ESCURES.

PARIS, *November* 12, 1862.

I send again the 4th volume of the diplomatic archives, in which I have explained your business and analyzed your accounts—I say copied your accounts entirely. Ah, how much I should have liked to have the letter of Zarco, of May 6, 1861, of which mention is made but transitorily! As soon as I obtain it I will get it printed (Amyot, street of La Paz Leipzig, Brockaus,) in the proximo three months. I have seen Mr. de Chevarier, who fears the discord between Forey and Saligney. Notwithstanding the imperial recommendations, which would injure us, he has informed me of the conversation he had with his Majesty. From that it follows that there will be, not an Emperor, but a President. He wished that influence of Santa Anna, to whom he has spoken, might be made use of, and thought he should be named chief of the government; but his Majesty has answered: "Santa Anna has declined to be it, writing to Almonte that he take his place, as more fit for that part." In a short time we shall see Mr. Hodgson again, because I cannot go to London, and he wishes to be informed of the state of affairs, as I believe he is thinking more of the interests of English commerce, which he does not wish to abandon to France; and he is, perhaps, instructed by the capitalists to take information. He collects, takes notes, and examines. I have told him that France will undertake by herself the railroad immediately, without admitting an Anglo-French company, because of being a military road—stategic, more than commercial, and that is fully confirmed, and they have seen that my foresight was just. I believe that they have intention to sound the land. I have learned from Mr. de Becourd that Mr. Montluc, to whom he has spoken, has acquired a good deal of information about Mar, his influence, his fortune, his mines in Mexico, about those of P., &c., &c. I have answered nothing, finding myself stupefied by what he told me. It must have been that Montluc has received a good deal of money to keep saloon and to know it all. * * * Prince Murat, for whom Suberveille was banker, (&c.,) this Prince Bottomless-purse has occupied himself much with the bonds, according to Mr. de Becourd, hostilely. * * * He has no influence, but, in fine, * * * this proves. * * * It might happen that even if you were attacked they would not catch us unprepared. This time Louis will do what he can to inform you of the new method for the reduction of silver ores, and as we do not advance any money to the inventor, (with reason,) we do not run the risk of being victims of a fraud, but of having to expect for yielding to illusions. We endeavor to guarantee it by means of multiplied assays, all of which give good result. The gold separates itself naturally from the silver, and the residues are all good; but for more security Louis still wishes to speak to his professor, Cahours, rewarded with the Jecker prize. Louis wishes to depart for Chili with the inventor the 2d of December, and from there go to Mexico in April or May; but I will not sustain this project. It will be necessary that he wait until January, working steadily until then. I have the description of the proceeding that requires that ammoniac is manufactured at the place of labor. You will comprehend that it would have been necessary to be able to have an understanding with you about this, but we cannot wait for the answer to our letters

It is known here that more than 5,000 men have succumbed to the vomito. The Empress is victim to the bad news that arrived. When reading your letter about the defeat of Guadalupe, the only one that could pass, and which I have directed to Fontainebleau, the Emperor said, "Madam, behold your work!" Mr. Chevalier knows it from an ocular witness. The Empress retired to her habitation, where she wept for three days The multitude is persuaded that it is on account of a certain Jecker that the war has taken place. Louis heard it from the mouth of an old widow, whose son had departed for Mexico; but it is almost time lost to dissipate the errors of the ignorant multitude on this point. Juarez has been clever; Wyke also. The latter has made the seventy-five millions tinkle like ready money, contrary to all that has been said or done. People do not understand that it is paper, worth only from 15 to 30 per cent. I should have preferred that Louis accept one of the two employments offered to him, but he has the idea that he must do something that will save you. I shall remain alone in my old age, because Augusta will wish to get married.

Of the letters that follow we publish only extracts referring to politics, marked with commas, because they refer in the greater part to matters of family, and to a discovery in the method of reducing metals. The ministry, in this particular, has been so scrupulous that, although treating of an enemy so capital of Mexico, it wishes to limit itself to the defence of the national interests only, thus giving an additional proof of a generosity and benevolence with which it has treated this business.—(*Editors.*)

PORENTRUI, *November* 1, 1862.

MY DEAR SON JAVIER: Your letter of September 28, 1862, has arrived at length to my hands. How much your self denial has moved us; how much our desires to see you in your days of sorrow have increased. I shall be in Paris next Wednesday probably, where Luis calls me, because he needs my aid and counsel to expedite his march to Mexico by San Nazario, to take care of his own affairs and of ours. This boy has gained in his commerce a knowledge of the world and of men; he desires to go to London before his departure, but I am not of his opinion; six weeks, or even six months, for this is very little time, when he would require at the least one year. Now, to something else. I have written to your uncle with the resolution that I never did before, urging him to take advantage of the entrance of the French and of the momentary regeneration of credit which will be its consequence to liquidate. I reminded him of the appreciation of Mr. le M. de F., at this moment dying, on his mines and his business at large, a matter which I have discussed with seriousness because it is necessary to tell him. This gentleman had much disturbed and frightened me to the extreme of causing me to leave Paris. I have asked the coinciding opinion of Mr. Stuart Hogdson, with whom we have had new conferences, and who is kind-hearted with us as well as that of other persons. I have made manifest to Mr. Jecker his age, mine, the necessity of concentrating his business, the impossibility almost of exercising an efficacious supervision of all of them at fabulous distances, the robberies and depredations to which he is exposed. I reminded him of all I said to him at the time of the departure of Mr. Porter, about the limitation of his best undertakings; I tell him that if he should be sick or should die he would lose everything according to general opinion, he alone being capable of carrying on his business. Mamma writes also in this sense; here is what I propose to him: that he divides the mines and the manufactories into shares of five and ten thousand dollars, with regard to the vacant lands on the Isthmus, in Sonora, and in Matamoras; perhaps the thing may not be practicable, but that it will be necessary to endeavor to sell them. I propose to Mr. J. that he gives in payment iron, bonds, credits, houses, shares; I make him understand that the creditors will accept equivalents that will extinguish greater quantities than the debts, if, as Gautier has told me, very hard conditions are not imposed. This mode of payment would be advantageous to the house without creditors in different proportions. I calculate that a greater part of these last who originally repelled the payment in equivalencies comprehend that something is worth more than nothing. Say what they may, this plan of which we talked some time ago, was not practicable under dread, but now it can be accomplished on a scale more or less great. The creditors who have shares in the mines will be interested in supervising. I forgot to say to Mr. Jecker that I received the subsidy to take care of the business. On this we now live, or better vegetate; but for the simple lodging and the necessities, it is a small matter endeavoring to avoid what can reach his susceptibility on this point. Nothing in the world would make me insinuate to him that having filled your task you ought to return, after having placed part of our fortune in safety, because this would offend him, since I see from his correspondence that he loves you, and esteems you more every day. As for our bonds, we are two sentinels placed in the two extremities of the world, whilst we communicate events develop and make our conjectures fruitless. Here we awaited the entrance of the French, while there you awaited instructions. Now we are performing these parts, I believe, in effect; in consequence of the splendor of this business, it will be necessary that his Majesty gives intimation to Drouyn de l'Huys to send orders to Forey and Saligny, for the payment of these bonds may be in the total or in part, entering into an adjustment with the new government that perhaps restrains its course. You know already that Forey is a kind of dictator to whom Saligny is subordinate, but he can, moderating his impetuosity, influence the old sergeant; and all depends on the good harmony that exists between these two gentlemen. It will be necessary, as I have said to my brother-in-law for some time, that he dedicates himself to make Saligny more flexible; that he arranged the manner so as not to imitate the bear, but, on the contrary, that they make concessions to him. * * * Mr. De Saligny has not promised me to save the house. Tell all this to J. and ——; it is time that he is not a little interested; make a prudent use of my letters, although I have written nothing that cannot be read.

Receive kind regards from your mother, &c., &c., &c.

H. E.

PARIS, *November* 14, 1863.

Mr. J. B. JECKER, *Mexico:*

Since my last of October 31, a duplicate of which is accompanied, I have received your letter of September 27. The news that you give me of the decree of Juarez, relative to a loan of fifteen millions of dollars, has been satisfactory to me. This decree, conceived in the same terms as those of the government of Miramon, that have been criticised so much, appears to me an excellent arm placed in your hands to defend your bonds. How can the partisans of Juarez censure now what they have just imitated?

I cannot do less than confirm to you in a very especial manner the invitation to set to work the plan sent to you in my letter of October 30. This will be, in my opinion, the best means of arriving at a solution that cannot be refused.

The next mail will carry you, without doubt, a letter more in detail from Mr. de Marpon, absent at this moment I suppose, on the other hand, that Mr. Elsesser, who is now in Paris, will post you up by the packet that leaves San Nazario to-morrow of what occurs.

Receive, sir, the assurance of my distinguished sentiments,

CH. FOURNIER DES ECURES.

SAN MAURICIO, (Ch. de,) *November* 14, 1862.

MY DEAR JECKER: I arrived here yesterday afternoon in company with M. Castillo, who is always more or less infirm, which is very alarming, and causes great inquietude. Although only a few moments remain to me that I can take advantage of before the packet leaves San Nazario, I employ them with you, to give you thanks for your kind letter of the 28th of September last. Now, as you ought to understand, I have the greatest desire to know what result all these rumors have had with which you were threatened—expulsion, confiscation of property, &c., &c.—things that they will take good care not to carry into effect, particularly when they know of the proclamation of General Forey on his arrival in Mexican territory—Puebla first and Mexico afterwards. Will they have opposed his progress and his entrance? This is hardly credible, notwithstanding their preparations for defence. The army—if such a name can be given to it—the Mexican army will have retired to the side of Morelia and of Queretero, or it will have dispersed to oppose him as guerillas. But all this will soon have an end.

If, as I have written to you, and I think it, the good and honorable Mexicans (because I am not one who does not believe that there are some in Mexico) have hastened to second the chief of the French army, with whom, at the hour I write, you will probably have formed an acquaintance, or at least you will not delay in doing so, I hope, my good friend, he will do you justice, and that within a few years I shall be able to procure for you the acquaintance of some good friends I have here, and who, as well as I, desire a complete triumph to you.

As I have informed you, Subervielle, dead; Labadie, it is clear to believe so, will have modified his opinion a little about the displeasure the French expedition caused him.

As you will well understand, all the packets are waited for with great impatience. Within a few day we shall have news to the 18th of October from Vera Cruz, and at the end of the month until the 1st instant. General Forey and his army will have been able to commence their march, and it is probable that it may be with complete success. God grant it!

Yours, with all my heart,

O'LAMBELL MAURICIO.

PARIS, (via SAN NAZARIO,) *November* 15, 1862.

GENTLEMEN: We have the honor to confirm you our letter of the 30th of August last. Since then we have received yours of August 28 and September 30, the contents of which we have learned with interest. We have given a letter of recommendation to you to Messrs. Villet and Jacqueme, inspectors of the treasury, who go to Mexico with the mission to study the financial state of the country. We have believed that you could give them useful information, and at the same time it would be convenient for you to know them.

We know that a collector general, Mr. Budin, also is to start soon with a mission. We do not know him, and we cannot have occasion to direct him to you. Nevertheless, we invite you to place yourselves in relation with him if the opportunity presents itself.

Accept, gentlemen, the security of our perfect consideration,

J. FORTUIGUERO.

Messrs. J. P. JECKER & Co., *Mexico.*

PARIS, *November* 7, 1862.

MY DEAR BROTHER: I have been in Paris for some days, and it has cost me no trouble to convince myself that our protectors had neglected nothing in serving us. The opposition has been so great that to conquer it it has been necessary to work upon his Majesty; and it has been done. I have taken away the pamphlet of Luis, and amused Mr. de M.; one cannot attempt more. Messrs. Finlay have done what has been possible for them, translating and publishing your small memorial, and communicating it to John Russell. In fine, they have expedited the articles in which the question is treated, &c., &c.

As to your creditors, they hope you will take advantage of the first moment of confusion from the entrance of the French to liberate yourself by means of the payment of equivalencies, that you divide your iron-works, mines, &c., &c., into shares of $5,000 or $10,000; that you will give them in movables, estates, &c., &c. Although the situation now may be such, it cannot remain in the same state, and it will be necessary to take a step before the 1st of January, 1863. Those gentlemen of London, whom we have seen here some time before, repeat it to us, and we must respect their opinion.

The Commandant la Pierre will relieve M. de Chevardie These gentlemen could not do less than send a new agent, and, besides, the Marquis de P. is on his death-bed. * * * This has not concealed your position from us; I have taken note of all he has said, * * and without doubt he likes you, and is disinterested. He had repeated to me that protecting Villanouve near you had contributed to place him in Tasco, and, as by a great fault, your iron-works, mines, &c., &c., are so distant from one another that he could not help being robbed. It appeared to him that you embraced too much. In fine, what I encounter is that you are fifty, I fifty-eight; the Jeckers are of bronze in character but not in body. M. de Gabriac is sad. He calculated upon being the chief of the cabinet of his friend Drouyn. Oh! he is deceived. * * * Manage it so that M. de Saligny may do all he can with Forey for our house, and not for what is intended as recompense for him. His Majesty likes him, and appreciates him. Tell him I wish no other proof than the trouble he has taken to vindicate himself in the eyes of his detractors, making them understand, besides, that his recall is the triumph of Juarez. I know the exact words he has used with Forey, by which he has been obliged to subject himself to Saligny. Have you received the bulletin that contains your naturalization? Luis has sent two or three copies to you.

PORENTRUI, *November* 3, 1862.

MY DEAR BROTHER: The Marquis of P., who has painted your situation to us in sombre colors, considering above all the mines as the gnawing polypus that impedes all distribution, is very near death.

I have told you previously that I would occupy myself with the estimates of the dying marquis. I have thought that he was something of a fatalist, but I have faith in his friendship for you, and looked upon him as a frank and loyal man. Now that I see his predictions realized, now that I see two thinkers like the Finlays, twice within the interval of six months, use identical language, first with me, afterwards with my son, it is necessary that I partake of his own opinion with much more reason, as all the creditors have partaken of it. In other times I wrote to you about the danger of giving too great an extension to your business on account of the excess of the speculation; this was after the departure of Mr. Portu; now I repeat it to you, with all the world, that you have embraced too much, and that, not being able to repair the evil now, it is necessary to impede it and to diminish it. I will explain myself: Make use of a momentary credit which the entrance of the French will give you immediately to liquidate seriously, and as you will not be able even to pay in specie your just accounts the first of January, 1863, it is necessary to endeavor to arrange them in equivalencies with a dividend, &c., &c. The creditors will see themselves obliged to accept, &c., &c., &c.

I finish with some words about the bonds. It is requisite that by order of his Majesty we operate directly upon Forey or through Saligny, so that these equivalencies may be placed in way of payment immediately, because, be it Forey, be it the new government, they will repel it and will resist very naturally, and precise instructions will be necessary from M. Drouyn to conquer the resistance. Seeing the interest that all our friends have in it, I throw this case upon them, because, what could I do? Luis has the threads of all the plot. He will do his duty. Very likely I shall go to Paris very soon, either to take his place or to aid him to know, in fine, if I must sell the rest of our furniture to pay our creditors in Paris. It is absolutely necessary that the question be ventilated the first of January, 1863, because uncertainty is the worst of evils; a formal liquidation under your direction would be good. Without you it is death for us; that will replace the agony we have suffered for two years and a half. It would be beteer * * * * * * * * *

NEW INTERCEPTED CORRESPONDENCE WITH JECKER.

[*Published with the authority of the Department of Foreign Relations.*]

PARIS, *October* 27, 1862.

DEAR UNCLE: My predictions were correct in reference to the choice of the chargé d'affaires of M. M. When I wrote my opinions to you and the details which I had been able to collect from M. Chervasier in reference to M. Lapierre, Almonte's aid, and M. de Saligny's ambassador to his Majesty in July last, M. M. would have most anxiously desired that my studies had been finished, in order to intrust me personally with this mission with all the influence and all the recommendations possible; but papa, frightened at the sad fate of his agents, (the Marquis de Pierres is in his agony at this moment, and when you receive this, will certainly have ceased to exist,) would not have consented but with the greatest difficulty, especially in consequence of the malady with which I am yet convalescent; moreover, I am distrustful of my experience and of my aptitude for a mission so delicate. To be brief, an intermediary course was adopted. As the necessity for an envoy was apparent, especially in October or November, the time of the entrance of the French into Mexico, when I should be at sea, M. de M. resolved to intrust provisional power to M. Lapierre, reserving to himself the right of annulling his authority and transferring it to me if he did not attain his object. This M. Lapierre has, to a certain extent, been made acquainted with my ideas. He does not know M. de M.; but the duke has very warmly recommended him, saying that he was one who had thoroughly understood the mission of M. Pierres, and who was qualified to accomplish it, while he contented himself with the advantages which were proposed to be granted, if influence and confidence were accorded to him. I will tell you, in one word, who this personage is. The confidence and the powers granted to him by M. de M. are summed up in full in the following letter which has been written to him by M. de M. and which is his credentials and his means of making himself known to you; but he is a rascal, an intriguer, and so be careful how you act with him? He is an adventurer, who barked with hunger when he was recommended to M. de M. I copy below the letter to which I refer; he has nothing else from M. M.; he knows no other secrets than those contained in the letter itself, which in nowise compromise us;

and if he tries to persuade you of the contrary, all that he may say beyond this will be merely what his natural sagacity may have enabled him to penetrate, without any possibility on his part of showing his proofs. Do not permit yourself to be swayed by him. I have here the letter which M. M. has transmitted to me, with the request that I would transcribe it for you. It has been written under the dictation of the duke and corrected by him.

SIR: Your letter dated at Vera Cruz, August 30, has reached me, and I hasten to reply to it. Filled with sentiments of benevolence towards you and me, my friend and protector has thought that we might be mutually useful to each other, and he has spoken of our affairs in Mexico, which he knows only very superficially. Here is in what they consist:

Having had intercourse for a considerable time with M. Jecker, whom the unfortunate affairs of Mexico and the hostility of some rival houses have brought into discredit, I find myself his creditor for quite considerable sums: I have, therefore, an interest in aiding him to rise, and I am so much the more interested as I believe him to be a very able and a very honorable man; as also because many French houses and nearly all our countrymen in Mexico are, like myself, his creditors; in fine, because he is the victim of an arbitrary, unjust, and plundering system of government.

I have undertaken, in concert with M. de Elsesser, brother-in-law of M. Jecker, who has come from Switzerland to Paris for this purpose, to defend his interests by informing the government and the public as to the validity of his claims, especially in that concerning the negotiation of the bonds, known under the name of the Jecker bonds, the cause, in a great measure, of his failure, and which may likewise prove a reason for the re-establishment of his house and the restoration of his affairs.

Public opinion had totally gone astray in regard to this affair. M. Elsesser has published a memorial which I enclose to you, and which sets the affair in a new light. Hereafter, our diplomatic agents should sustain it.

For your part, sir, you can serve this cause, which is that of an honorable house odiously persecuted, in the like manner as is French and foreign commerce.

It would be suitable in this case that you should put yourself in communication with M. Jecker, with much secresy and discretion, whenever it may be necessary; in regard to which this letter will be sufficient to accredit you and to bring you to such an understanding as to cause you to work together, as well in reference to our minister in Mexico as to our general.

If the issue crowns your efforts, we can do no less than leave to the benevolent and trusty friend who has produced our intercourse, the duty of fixing the remuneration which is in justice due to you.

Receive, &c., &c., &c.

M. de Chevarrier, whom his suspicions already designated to Lapierre as his successor, regarded him with evil eye and spoke to him with coldness. He told me that Lapierre departed from Mexico under very unfavorable auspices of the French army, and left there only most odious reminiscences. Whatever there be of exaggeration in these words should be attributed to the wounded susceptibility of M. de Chevarrier. In 1849 and 1850, in the time of the republic, Lapierre was one of the editors of the *Corsaire*, a petty Bonapartist paper which every day appeared with a profusion of truisms and challenges to the republicans. Sometimes he had to support his pen with the sword, and he did it with courage. He is brave, intriguing, unscrupulous. In one word, he has all the qualities of a *chevalier d'industrie*. He is a double-edged sword that may be used with profit, but which must be handled very prudently. M. de M T. would start at the idea of seeing the doubloons that he might have in his chest in the hands of such a gentleman. Therefore it is that he authorizes me to entreat you to deliver nothing to him personally, and to send to M. Hodgson or us whatever you may have to transmit in future.

I presume you have received my last, of the 15th of October. I should regret very much if you had not, for it contained important matters. I acknowledge the receipt of all which you have sent to me. The manner in which you address them to us is so secure that I avail myself of it for the present letter, the tenor of which is of too serious a nature to be intrusted, without protection, to the fidelity of the Mexican mails. I told you in my last that I had a conversation with M. Hodgson, and I mentioned to you the pleasure and confidence which were excited in him by my assurances that the house was under a high protection.

I congratulate myself on having made to him spontaneously this act of half-confidence; because in the last visit which he made me, M. Fournier, secretary of M. de M. T., came in, charged with a commission from him to me. After I had presented him to M. de Hodgson, he spoke to me very lightly of my approaching presentation to my lord the duke, and other things of a formal nature calculated to dispel the suspicions of M. Hodgson, if he had any remaining; but which fully confirmed the little story which I had already related to him.

The evening of the departure of M. Hodgson, the Moniteur announced the appointment of M. Drouyn de l'Huys to the department of foreign affairs in place of M. de Thouvenel; and he manifested much agitation at this, and came to me to see me immediately, in order to know the degree of intimacy that might exist between our protectors and M. Drouyn de l'Huys; because, said he to me, he is, unfortunately, on intimate terms with Lord John Russell, who represented England in the congress of Vienna, and who showed himself very pliant in reference to some points of secondary interest, in order to prove to M. Drouyn de l'Huys, the French ambassador in the same congress, the spirit of conciliation with which he was animated. I could not satisfy him at the moment, because those gentlemen are temporarily absent, but I promised to write to him as soon as he should return to London. I took advantage of this opportunity to address to him, some days afterwards, a letter with an amplification of papa's defence, and of your memorial on the real interests of commerce in the negotiation of bonds, requesting him to have them translated into English, and to seek an opportunity to present them to Lord John Russell, in order to destroy his odious suspicions in regard to our affair; also, to represent to him that the interests of English commerce were likewise involved in it, and that his house was very much interested in its happy solution. In order to give more authority to my words and more latitude to my counsels, I pretended that they had been inspired into me by M. de G., in our common interest. "M. Drouyn de l'Huys," said I to them, "has not yet formed any opinion in regard to the bonds, but M. de G., who is a very intimate friend of his and of the Baron d'Andree, his chief secretary, will probably be called in a short time to the minister's house in order to give him some explanations. No one is more suitable than he is to do so, and he will use all his influence in the furtherance of our interests. The entrance of M. Drouyn de l'Huys into the cabinet is a very favorable omen for the triumph of conservative ideas It is a reaction against liberal ideas. Let us hope that the new minister will not diverge from his general course of policy in this affair only of the bonds. But you know very well, gentlemen, it will be much more easy to form the opinion of M. Drouyn if it be not already fixed, to turn it to our favor, if, perchance, it should be unfavorable, when now he is not yet beset by powerful solicitations, by hostile insinuations. In order to effect this it is necessary to combat calumny in its very source, to make an effort to enlighten John Russell. In view of an English interest he will hesitate. The bitterness which he has manifested in persecuting us will, perhaps, be somewhat diminished, and that will be an immense victory; it will be to destroy hostility ——— hostility personified by the English minister!! ———. After John Russell, ——— public opinion, ——— it would, in fact, be very useful to publish some articles in the *Times*, in concurrence with our articles in Paris, when the time shall come." These gentlemen replied to me immediately, telling me that they hastened to do what I wrote to them, and that they had been translated as soon as my letter had been received. They manifest much zeal and great confidence. I hope that their zeal will be still further quickened by the letter which I address to them with this. I tell them that we have achieved a great triumph during these few days past, but I do it in discreet terms, because it is good to acquaint them with the results in order to give them confidence and to incite them to assist in the restoration of the house; but it is useless to divulge the means to them. As their only objection against the prosperous issue of the efforts which they are going to make is, that the affair of the bonds is a private interest, I insinuate to them that it depends on them to make it one of public interest and to attain a double object at the same time; to secure its favorable settlement by changing the English policy in reference to it, in consideration of the interest that they and other English houses may take in it, and to realize great profits, since, as you say, it is an affair of two millions five hundred thousand dollars of duties to be collected at Vera Cruz, with the entrance of merchandise in its port. I think that a letter from you of a commercial and argumentative character would make a great impression on these gentlemen now that the ground is prepared.

Perhaps the result which we have obtained is the most decisive stroke of policy that has been achieved since these gentlemen have taken up the question of the bonds. Under date of August 15 or 28, M. de Saligny has addressed from Orizaba to M. de Pierres a very important letter, in which he represents Laurencez as an unfortunate individual, incapable, worthy rather of pity than of hatred, on account of the sad state of his health; but he attributes all the evil to Valaye, his chief of staff, who by his haughtiness and his incapacity had, according to him, caused the failure of the whole expedition. He says, likewise, that he has suffered so many calumnies on account of the affair of the bonds, that he will no longer be able to act so directly as heretofore; that it will be necessary to send out there some safe and skilful person to watch for the ripening of the fruit. After some incidental words against Noël, he concludes by saying that formal instructions are being sent him in order to place him in a condition to act and to regulate his position properly. M. de M. T. gave it to me in order to attend to it as far as concerned the house and Noël, and in order to present the affair as a French interest in concurrence with

English interests, an interest misrepresented by the disloyal course of Wyke, who, in order to increase the security of the English creditors, whose interests were assured by the same pledges as the bonds, was not afraid to reject this affair, notwithstanding its justice, and to make himself the official interpreter of all the calumnies of Juarez and his associates, &c., &c.

I applied myself as best I could to the performance of this task, including the greatest number of ideas in the fewest possible words, in order that it might not be supposed that, in expatiating at length on this affair, M. de Saligny gave it any other importance than that of indignation at seeing a dishonest infamy on the part of Wyke thus gained, and the efforts of French diplomacy frustrated in an affair so just. I strove, moreover, to preserve in the style its tone of military bruskness and manly indignation. The letter appeared very good to those gentlemen, and M. de M. T. hesitated whether he should give it the name of an extract, or of a copy, or should make it pass as an original, when there arrived by the last post a second letter from M. de Saligny, dated at Orizaba, September 15, and no less important than the former one. Both were put together, and on the following day my lord duke presented it to his Majesty, who read it with much interest. His confidence in M. de Saligny, already excessive, was still more augmented. "My.," said he to the duke, "it is necessary that all these difficulties in M. de Saligny's position should cease; I will make my arrangements in regard to it; but there is one thing in his letter which gives me much cause for reflection. He has strong suspicions of Noël, and yet I believe him to be an honorable man. Moved by the calumnies that were circulated, I ordered, some time ago, an investigation to be issued in the ministry of foreign affairs, and it has had no effect." "Nevertheless," interposed the duke, "I am certain of it." "Well, then," replied his Majesty, "try to collect the proof of the fact, and, if there is any certainty, he will be displaced." These gentlemen are aware of Noël's hostility to G., who has received instructions from Almonte; but this is a little vague. I have promised those gentlemen to give them all information on the subject, and I have gone to the residence of Padre Maguin in order to put him on the track, paying him off with the first reason that occurred to me, proper to excite his zeal. I have now returned, and according to what he has told me, I believe that Noël has nothing to look for in this affair. Amor Escandon, son-in-law of Subervielle, a very intimate friend of Father Maguin, came yesterday to take leave of him, because he is going, as I think, to Mexico. Dexterously enough in the course of the conversation, Father Maguin suddenly asked him: "Do you not know a person named Noël, a director in the department of foreign affairs? I have some one to whom to recommend him." "No," replied the other, "I do not know him at all." Maguin persisted in his inquiry, but he could get no other answer. I have related this conversation to M. de M. T. this morning, but he perseveres in his suspicions. I shall be presented to-morrow at mid-day (October 30) to M. de My.; he has desired to see me; I know not whether it is to judge whether I am fit for some future mission. If my letter had not to be despatched to-day, in order that the Messrs. Hodgson & Co. may have time to put it in their packet, I would wait until to-morrow to tell you the result of the conversation. If there be anything of importance, I will inform you of it in the letter which I will address to Nr. after to-morrow, (October 30,) but as it is necessary to be prudent, I shall designate his Majesty as No. 1, M. de My. as No. 2, M. de M. T. as No. 3. I am much obliged to you for the little note which you have addressed to me. I shall set out very soon for the silver mines of Sougibault, and I shall do all that may lie in my power in order to acquire connexions there that may be useful hereafter. The creditors are well disposed. As soon as papa arrives, within two or three days, we are going to present a petition entreating his Majesty to extend his protection to the house in the name of French interests. This petition, signed with the names of your creditors, will be presented directly by No. 2 to No. 1; judge of its importance!! Gabriac is somewhat slow and timorous; he has an excessive dread of compromising himself if he is urged to exertion. Mt. has acknowledged to me that he (Gabriac) shared half the profits of the bonds. I have told him in reply that he had some interest in the house; he has promised me to tell it to him as if it came from the Count de Pierres, and to urge him on, because he can be very useful to us on account of his intimacy with Drouyn. I think that instructions will be sent to M. de Saligny. Mt. desires to serve you with his Majesty in respect to your lands in Sonora. He has collected all the details that I have been able to give him. Communicate, if you please, this letter to Nr.; I have not time to speak to him of your progress.

Adieu, my dear uncle. Assuring you of all my heart's love, I remain your most affectionate nephew,

LUIS ELSESSER.

WASHINGTON, *March* 31, 1863.

A true copy:

ROMERO.

Mr. Seward to Mr. Romero.

DEPARTMENT OF STATE,
Washington, April 12, 1863.

SIR: I have the honor to acknowledge the receipt of your note of the 31st ultimo with its enclosures, in continuation of other similar communications with which you have favored me, relating to events in Mexico, growing out of the unhappy foreign war in which that republic is involved.

Thanking you for the pains you have taken in keeping me so fully informed of transactions equally vital and interesting, I avail myself of this occasion to renew to you, sir, the assurances of my distinguished consideration.

WILLIAM H. SEWARD.

Señor Don MATIAS ROMERO, *&c., &c., &c.*

Mr. Romero to Mr. Seward.

[Translation.]

MEXICAN LEGATION IN THE UNITED STATES,
Washington, November 6, 1863.

Mr. SECRETARY: I have the honor to transmit to you, for the knowledge of the department over which you preside, a translation into English of the debates which took place in the Corps Legislatif of France on the 6th and 7th of February of the present year, in relation to the Mexican question. The translation referred to has been faithfully made from the official report of the proceedings of that assembly, as published in the Moniteur Universel, Nos. 38 and 39, of the 7th and 8th of February mentioned, pages 182, 183, 184, and 185, and 191, 192, and 193.

I profit by this opportunity to convey to you, sir, the assurance of my most distinguished consideration.

M. ROMERO.

Hon. WILLIAM H. SEWARD, *&c., &c., &c.*

[Le Montieur Universel, No. 38—February 7, 1863—page 182, vol. 5th.]

Debates in the French Legislative body.

SESSION OF FRIDAY, *February* 6.

His excellency the Duke de Morny, president, in the chair.

The session was opened at a quarter past two o'clock. The minutes were read by M. the Marquis de Talhouët, one of the secretaries, and adopted.

The PRESIDENT. I have received from M. Alfred Le Roux a request for leave of absence for fifteen days. Is there no opposition? The leave is granted. Does any one desire the floor to make a report?

Count NAPOLEON DE CHAMPAGNY. I have the honor to present a report on the bill to authorize the department of Morbihan to effect a loan and to levy an extraordinary impost.

The PRESIDENT. The report will be printed and distributed. The regular order of the day is the continuation of the discussion on the address. (The government benches were occupied by Messrs. Baroche, president of the council of statè; Billault, Magne, ministers without portfolios; M. de Parieu, vice-president of the council of state; General Allard, Messrs. Boudet, Vuillefroy, Boinvilliers, and Vuitry, chairmen of committee in the council of state.)

The Chamber yesterday stopped at paragraph the third. An amendment has been proposed to this paragraph. M. Picard, one of its proposers, is entitled to the floor. The amendment is as follows:

"We admire the heroism of our soldiers combatting in Mexico under a destructive mcliate, and we send them our wishes of sincere sympathy; but the care of the national honor does not dispense a political assembly from juding an enterprise of which it can now know the cause and foresee the consequences. The forces of France ought not to be rashly engaged in ill-defined and adventurous enterprises and expeditions, and neither our principles nor our interests counsel us to proceed to inquire what government the Mexican people may desire."

M. Ernest Picard. Gentlemen, if there was needed a striking illustration in justification of the great principles of freedom enunciated here yesterday, I believe that it would be furnished to us by the history of the Mexican expedition. It has been decided upon without you, followed out without you, and I can assert, without fear of contradiction, that it has never been restrained by any excess of control or publicity; for it is to be regretted that what was done at the time when the Crimean war was most actively waged, the publication of documents relative to the war, should not have taken place with regard to the Mexican expedition.

I know that our army is repairing at this moment the faults of our diplomacy. I know that, thanks to their intrepidity, the issue is not doubtful. A year ago the honorable minister of foreign affairs without portfolio told us that our troops should, at the very moment of his speech, be entering Mexico; I would wish to be able to give the same assurance to-day. But what I do know is that, in this discussion in which such deep-rooted differences of opinion may cause us to disagree with the government, at least we are inspired with a unanimous sentiment of sympathy by the energy and the valor of our troops. It is not then exactly of the Mexican war that I desire to offer a few remarks; it is in regard to our policy, it is in regard to the undertaking which must be finally judged in public debate.

Is it proper, gentlemen, to discuss this undertaking? Is it opportune to do so at the present moment? We could not do it sooner to any useful purpose; for while the Spanish Parliament, while the English Parliament were in possession of the diplomatic documents capable of throwing a certain light on the subject, the French government had thought proper to defer laying them before the Chamber; but now, gentlemen, the documents speak, and events speak yet more loudly than the documents, and we can know what the treaty of London is worth and what the expedition undertaken in consequence of it.

The treaty of October 31 has united in one common action three great powers which seemed to have the same interest, but which were to proceed to Mexico with quite opposite sentiments.

England, who, if I may use the expression, possesses Mexico by her titles of credit; who has, by regular contracts, for many years caused the resources and the revenues of Mexico to be hypothecated to herself, and who can claim, beyond controversy, 300 millions of francs the day when Mexico will be in a condition to pay them; England, gentlemen, was the power that seemed least disposed to take part in the expedition. Spain, on the contrary, attracted by ancient reminiscences, wishing to re-establish in that country a dominion which she had formerly exercised; Spain, morever, offended at a personal insult, was more eager than England and than France, and it appears from the despatches before us that, even previous to the year 1860, she thought of the expedition. She had received a personal offence; her ambassador, Don Francesco Pacheco, at the time when Juarez held at Vera Cruz while the government of Miramon expired at Mexico, had passed through Vera Cruz and gone to find Miramon, whom he had recognized as the legitimate government almost to the eve of the day when it was to fall under the blows of the Mexican nation. He had been expelled for having taken part in the intrigues in progress at that moment; Spain had never pardoned this offence.

You see, gentlemen, how and with what interests England on the one side, and Spain on the other, were called to Mexico. England, who knows how to count, had stipulated, in the treaty of London, an arrangement according to which no nation could obtain particular advantages; she thus preserved her rights and her credits; moreover she took but a very moderate part in the expedition, for she had informed our government that she would not furnish any troops for disembarkment in the country.

As to France, gentlemen, as to French interests, the honorable minister without portfolio spoke of them in eloquent terms, in two discourses present to your memory. He said that the accumulated outrages of twenty years demanded that a French force should be sent to protect our countrymen and at last compel justice to be done to them.

Twenty years! that would be pretty long for France; and if such has been the sole motive of the expedition, if these accumulated outrages, of which the honorable minister spoke with so much eloquence, were the real cause of the enterprise, I would make you but one reproach, that of having undertaken it, not twenty years, but at least ten years too late for the responsibility of the present government.

The Chamber should understand it well, for it is the main point of debate in the question before you.

There were indeed some grievances, some claims founded on the part of our countrymen. For three years Mexico was rent by civil war, for three years especially there were two governments, and neither of the two was sufficiently powerful to restrain the marauding bands that infested the roads and attacked those who exposed themselves to meet them. We have in Mexico a little French colony composed of from 2,000 to 3,000 persons. Claims, which have not been yet sufficiently justified, had been indeed carried to the consulate. In fine, it was the state of the country which had brought on these new grievances, and with the exception of one serious case which interested the English much more than us, it might be said that if grievances existed for twenty years, they had not augmented. In these last years, there was a serious grievance. The old president, Miramon, at the moment when he was about to fall, finding no more resources to pay his last troops, had laid hands on 660,000 piastres deposited in the English legation. He had seized on it with the assistance of Marquez and certain other persons, and that was one of the reasons which decided England to interfere.

Here, gentlemen, I pause a moment. Juarez was just installed at Mexico. He was in extreme penury; in such penury that M. de La Fuente, his ambassador in France, could not leave for want of funds to pay his passage. I ask of the government if that was the moment to proceed to avenge our countrymen, and to require payment of indemnities which an exhausted treasury could not give?

Was there, however, on the part of the government of Juarez, a bad faith or ill-will to justify the expedition? That has been maintained; but an attentive scrutiny shows the reverse. If, obliged to seek resources from all quarters, he issued the decree of July 17, which suspended the payment of the indemnities due to the three powers that signed the treaty of London—if he did this, representations were made by our agents, his ministers consented to reconsider that decree, and alleged only their inability to furnish pecuniary satisfaction.

So, you will immediately see a still more complete demonstration: that was not the sole, the real motive of the enterprise which is now carried on, and of which I have to seek the causes. It is certain, and this can no longer be called in question, that there existed, in the ideas of two of the contracting powers, the design of favoring the establishment in Mexico of a monarchical form of government. This was denied in the session of March 13, 1862; it was denied also in the session of the month of June, but now a clearer light is thrown on these denials; and indeed, gentlemen, I proceed to furnish you immediately a moral proof of it which will strike your mind. I was saying just now how our little French colony, given to a very limited commerce, could not furnish the elements of a credit of such a nature as to explain, on the part of a government such as that of France, the resolution of undertaking such an expedition as this to Mexico.

Claims then were wanting; and this is so true, that the only creditor who now claims, in the ultimatum of our plenipotentiaries, a considerable sum, a sum of from sixty to seventy-five millions—this creditor is a well-known banking-house—that of Jecker.

Well, gentlemen, give me your attention, and tell me whether what I am now going to reveal to you does not show you what spirit prevailed in the organization of the Mexican expedition. The Jecker banking-house was Swiss; its chief was Swiss; he was born at Porentruy, at a period when that city did not belong to France. Do you know, gentlemen, at what time this creditor, who is going to be protected, has become French? Do you know what is the date of his naturalization? The date of his naturalization is the 26th of March, 1862. You may refer to the *Bulletin des Lois*, No. 13,441, under the date of August 31, 1862, and you will see that a decree, dated March 26 preceding, has rendered him French, in whose name we now proceed to claim an enormous sum, which claim has been one of the causes of the rupture of the treaty of London in Mexico and the departure of the allies. I have then reason to say that the causes of the expedition well studied are not those which you can read in the discourses of the honorable minister; time has advanced, and truth has advanced with time, and discloses to us to some extent the real nature of things.

As to this project of favoring the establishment of a monarchical authority, of a monarchy in Mexico, in truth if our diplomacy has conceived it, it was ignorant of what all the world knew, and did not follow those rules which I believe superior to those of diplomatic skill, namely, the rules of justice and of common sense. Who of you, gentlemen, has not already understood that, if we went with arms to Mexico, with the idea of proposing to that country to choose a government freely, Mexico, terrified by the display of these ambassadors and these mediators, would see in it an attempt at invasion, and not the benevolent mediation of powers animated by kindly sentiments? Wherefore, reason inflexibly dictated the result which has not failed to be produced—that is, one of two things: either the Mexicans, degraded as you said they were, knowing them badly, would yield to the foreigner and surrender their rights as a people; or else, uniting in one common sentiment against the invaders, and finding in the national opinion their resources for defence—poor, it is true, but the peoples that are poor are sometimes those that defend themselves most energetically—would form in effect one nation, but one nation turned against those who brought them this offensive mediation. Wherefore, also, you could not succeed except on condition that you paid yourselves the price of your triumph. Behold, gentlemen, a policy which judged itself, as it has been judged by events, and which was understood long ago by men possessed at the same time of intelligence and authority in their country. Indeed, you told the English minister what your hopes were. What did he reply to you? Or rather what did he tell you in those despatches, since published? Earl Russell wrote under date of the month of February, 1862, to the ambassador at Vienna:

"I have received your excellency's despatch on the subject of the propositions to place the Archduke Maximilian on the throne of Mexico, and you observe that this project has been conceived by the Mexican refugees at Paris. This class of people are notorious for their unfounded calculations on the strength of their partisans in their native country, and for the extravagance of their hopes of assistance. Your excellency will see by the documents laid before Parliament, that Marshal O'Donnell is of opinion that it is a chimerical idea to wish to establish a constitutional monarchy in Mexico by means of a foreign intervention."

Behold, gentlemen, what everybody repeated; behold what was understood by every one except you; and see how, when you asked English diplomacy to consent to the establishment in Mexico of a monarchy to be governed either by the Archduke Maximilian or by some other candidate, English diplomacy smiled and said to you: We are willing, but yours be the undertaking. So then, gentlemen, on this point there cannot be two opinions; and in the discourse of a man who more especially represented your policy in Spain, in the discourse of M. Mon—discourse, gentlemen, which, like that of General Prim, has not been published in the French journals that I know of—in the discourse of M. Mon we read this:

"Why this word *afrancisados*, by which it is sought to designate certain persons? Let it be clearly explained: let them tell us what are the French interests which we are going to defend in the question in debate. What are they? If there is any one who can say, he certainly knows neither the treaty, nor the negotiations, nor the motive of the expedition. What interest had Spain? Spain had greater interests involved in this question than any of the powers that have signed the treaty. Spain had the great interests which I have mentioned and which gave us a part to act superior to that of the other nations. And France, gentlemen—what are the interests of France in this question; what are the powerful motives that she had to unite with Spain in such distant countries, where so many events have happened, where we have procured her so many occasions of disgust, where she has had so many mischances? What was the interest of France? A claim for certain sums of money; the protection of some three or four thousand Frenchmen employed in a little trade.

"Such was the interest of France, who sent an expedition to which the majority of the empire was opposed, because it was contrary to its interests. As to me, when I met in the streets of Paris my particular friends, men of importance in the country, they said to me, 'We understand that you are satisfied; but we, what are we to do there? what have we to gain there? what compensation are we to obtain for all the money that we are going to spend, for all the men that we are going to lose?' Who wished Prince Maximilian to be monarch of Mexico? What interest had France in this? What matter was it to the Emperor that Prince Maximilian should be King of Mexico?"

See, gentlemen, how impossible it is to mistake the import of the treaty of London. That treaty is judged by itself; no diplomatist of character can have signed it, with the end proposed, without gravely compromising the interests of the policy of our country.

I assert it, gentlemen, in the name of reason, in the name of logic; but if I wished to rise higher, to rise to principles which the country cannot abandon without losing something of its strength and of its moral influence in the world, I would say that it is with profound regret, with profound grief, that we have seen France obliged to address to the Mexicans a proclamation which recalls that addressed in 1792 to France by the generalissimo of the armies of Prussia and Austria. (Exclamations from a great number of benches.)

Some voices: Very good.

M. Ernest Picard. Yes, gentlemen. And my words must not be misunderstood—must be taken in the sense, in the only sense, which I wish to give them. There is no doubt, gentlemen, with regard to the language which a nation, whether animated by good or by bad intentions, is obliged to use when presenting itself in arms before another nation. Do you know how the Duke of Brunswick expressed himself in 1792? "Convinced," he says, "that the sane part of the French nation abhors the excesses of a faction that holds it in subjection, and that the great majority of the inhabitants await with impatience the moment of assistance to declare themselves openly against the odious undertakings of their oppressors, his Majesty the Emperor and his Majesty the King of Prussia call upon them and invite them to return without delay to the path of reason and of justice, of order and of peace. It is with these views that I, the undersigned, commander-in-chief of the two armies, declare:

"That, drawn into the present war by irresistible circumstances, the two allied courts propose to themselves no other end than the happiness of France, without any intention of enriching themselves by conquests."

I do not wish, gentlemen, to insist on this idea, which, I am certain, is yours, too; by insisting upon it, I would fear to hurt the sentiments I experience myself; but I say that the treaty of London, thus understood, can have none but unfortunate results, and that what should come to pass can be, and ought to be, foreseen by men who should have considered what necessary consequences may flow from their acts.

And, in fact, gentlemen, what was to come to pass? The troops depart for Mexico, and from the first hour a disagreement shows itself. There is question first of settling the amount of the sums due to us; an ultimatum must be drawn up. Here, again, in the name of my country, I feel the blush rise to my cheek, when I think of what has been said in the presence of our plenipotentiaries, what they have been obliged to hear.

See how a man who, I acknowledge, does not sympathize with your policy, and who, moreover, is now irritated, see how General Prim renders account of the first conference. [Exclamations and murmurs.] Be calm, gentlemen, I take the words uttered by General Prim at a time when he was not irritated, and I take them simply to state facts.

"It was then for Admiral Jurien to give account of the ultimatum proposed by M. de Saligny, and it is here the disagreement commenced. The French claims comprise the payment of twelve millions of piastres, the figure at which the French minister has estimated those which he deems legitimate. They comprise the execution of a contract of Miramon with a commercial house originally Swiss, and afterwards become French, concluded at the moment when his government was in the agonies of dissolution.

"At the mention of the Jecker contract, the English representatives cried out in one voice that that was an inadmissible demand.

"This disagreeable incident paralyzed for the moment the progress of the negotiations, and placed us in a position of great embarrassment."

In fact, gentlemen, from this first moment, for this first motive, discord shows itself; community of action in effect ceases; each one of the nations will itself defend its own ultimatum, whereas neither the English nation nor the Spanish nation is willing to accept the pretensions of our ministers.

They talk of it in France. Now, in France, what is said, and how shall we explain the singular ignorance in which the minister of foreign affairs was left in this regard?

In a conversation between Lord Cowley and M. Thouvenel, the latter expresses himself thus, as it appears from a letter of Lord Cowley to Lord John Russell: "M. Thouvenel says that, neither in his conversations with me nor in his instructions to M. de Flahault, has he consented to abandon the Jecker claim; that he had never known so as to form an opinion on the subject; that he did not know to what point French interests were involved in it; that, consequently, he should leave the whole affair to the discretion of M. de Saligny, in whose probity he reposed entire confidence."

See how things went on; and if you will please to remember that on the 26th of March, 1862, (this despatch is dated the 14th,) at this date only, that is, ten days after this despatch, the banker Jecker obtained his letters of naturalization, you will see that there is in this affair an enigma which the lucid speech of the minister for foreign affairs without portfolio would strive to make us understand. [Murmurs of approbation and disapprobation.]

So, scarcely had this first cause of discord manifested itself, when, behold, a second arises. A vessel brings to Vera Cruz the famous Miramon, Padre Miranda, and thirty persons more or less celebrated of the last government of Mexico. Then the English minister pretends that ex-President Miramon having laid hands on 660,000 piastres which belonged to the English legation, he should be considered not as a political individual, but as an ordinary malefactor, and that, in consequence, his first duty is to demand that he should be compelled to re-embark.

Who resists this re-embarcation? At first it is General Prim, but he yields. This argument, says Sir Charles Wyke, had its weight with General Prim, but it was only half accepted by Admiral Jurien de la Gravière, and M. Dubois de Saligny always opposed it. The packet brought Miramon with thirty persons, among whom was the famous Father Miranda and other members of the clerical party. It seems that his partisans awaited him on the coast with horses and arms, and all that was necessary to renew the civil war.

You can understand, gentlemen, that in such circumstances, when the conferences were opened which are known under the name of the Preliminaries of La Soledad, it is evident that the plenipotentiaries were destined not to find themselves unanimous.

But before terminating this incident of the history of the Mexican expedition, let me be permitted to recall to your minds the remarkable speech delivered before you by the minister of foreign affairs You know how the honorable M. Billault, fascinating you by his eloquence, elicited your applause by telling you that in that country, Mexico, they called a robbery a seizure, and that the tribunals condemned only to civil reparation those who had taken away the property of others. He made allusion to a judgment of the 10th of August, 1861, rendered precisely on the occasion of the carrying off of the funds of the English legation, and of which the motive is as follows:

"Considering as being comprised in the first category the seizure of the funds destined for the payment of English creditors, effected by order of the rebel chiefs Miramon and Marquez, November 17, 1860, in the house No. 11, street of the Capuchins ——."

You understand, gentlemen, that the Mexicans, whatever confidence they may have had in our words, in our proclamations, must feel very uneasy with regard to the success of a regeneration which commenced by the introduction of Miramon, of Father Miranda, and of several others; of Marquez, gentlemen, who now fights under our flag, and who, nevertheless, was celebrated in Mexico for his ferocity; of Marquez, who is one of the principal persons concerned in those armed attacks committed on the highways against which our countrymen were to be protected.

What policy, then, gentlemen, inspired the government when it acted in this way? And to what influence did it yield? In truth, when I inquire what the conditions are of the regeneration of Mexico, and what on the point of these conditions was the real idea of the government, I find it quite hesitating, and I commence to fear that the government is committing serious errors in principle and doctrine.

When, for the first time, it addressed itself to England, asking the concurrence of the latter with it in a plan of action in common, England, gentlemen, which in matters of external policy has a fixed idea, asked two things: An amnesty and the establishment in Mexico of religious liberty. What did our government reply? I find the evidence of it in a despatch of M. Barrot of June 2, 1862. It replied that it consented to the amnesty, but that it refused the establishment of religious liberty in Mexico. It replied in the following terms, or at least its ambassador, M. Barrot, expressed himself in those terms:

"The cabinet of London desires at the same time a general amnesty and the adoption of a system of religious toleration. The first of these measures seem also to the Emperor's government indicated by the situation the day when the parties shall have been reconciled. But it has not concealed from the British government that the establishment of religious liberty in Mexico appeared to it to offer a serious objection, besides being uncalled for by any necessity in the political or moral condition of the country."

These facts being known, is it not unnecessary to say, with the English ministers who were witnesses of it, what I find in a despatch of the ambassador of London to Earl Russell, thus couched, under date of May 2, 1862:

"I would deceive your lordship," says he, "if I concealed from you my personal conviction that there exists a fixed determination, though not avowed, to overturn the government of Juarez, whatever may be the consequences of that act, and whether civil war results from it or not."

See how our policy in Mexico was understood. The honorable minister to whom I reply will say, perhaps, that it was judged severely and judged by rivals. But I would wish that, at least, the events could answer for him, and that those which have followed should not have happened.

The preliminaries of La Soledad are opened; the conferences are held, and you know how a discord breaks out. Here also I accuse, and I accuse directly, the government of an act which I find one of those acts the most to be regretted and the most painful that exist in our diplomatic history.

Arrived in Mexico, at Vera Cruz, under a climate where the yellow fever reigns, our plenipotentiaries, in the interest of the health of our troops, obtain from the government of Juarez permission for them to proceed to the upper plateau, beyond the defiles guarded by the Mexican troops, during the deliberations; on their word of honor that, when those deliberations should be terminated or broken off, if broken off they should be without result, they should resume their position and return to this side of the defiles. Well, in accordance with an order issued from hence, our troops, who would have a thousand times preferred to take these defiles which would not have resisted them, were obliged to march forward to establish themselves at Orizaba, and to assist in sorrow at the violation of the engagements made.

Oh, gentlemen, it is always imprudent to desire to regenerate the people when we are not sufficiently sure of ourselves; and, indeed, when the government pursues in Mexico such conduct as I have briefly sketched, I ask myself whether it has not understood what there is rash in this expedition, and whether it does not regret bitterly to have neglected, in undertaking it, the counsels and the control of the representatives of the nation.

So, also, you know how, on the 9th of April, the conference being broken off, according to orders issued directly from here, Admiral Jurien de la Graviere declares that he will march on Mexico; the English declare that they are going to withdraw, a thing which, I think, they had foreseen in advance; and the Spanish imitate them.

I pass no opinion on the conduct of the Spanish, and I agree with what the minister has said in regard to the English, who seem not to have deceived us. Yet I find in this rupture of the alliance, in this cessation of action in common thus coming to pass without the French government being able to make any cause of complaint out of it, to protest against its allies, or to reply to what has been said in every assembly with regard to our diplomatic conduct—I, find I say, an occasion to address a very severe reproach to those who represent our policy, a reproach for the want of foresight against which, it seems to me, they will find it difficult to defend themselves.

See, gentlemen, how the Mexican expedition has been conducted to this day. What will be the consequences of it? What will be the result? What do you wish to do in Mexico, and what, in fine, is your policy? I know that at this moment, and at this moment only, when the conferences are broken off, when all things have passed as I have said, there appears unexpectedly a system of grand policy which seems to have been kept in reserve, and which, in any case, would save appearances only at the expense of the frankness of our agents.

They tell us that there is an interest superior to this that the United States of the north should not encroach upon Mexico, that we must resist their invading power, and that it is an interest of great policy, of very great policy, which has taken us to Mexico and which keeps us there.

Oh, gentlemen, I do not examine, I shall not examine at length the after-thought scheme thus inaugurated; I find that it is in such manner judged by the facts, in such manner refuted by the first principles of political and common sense, that I am unwilling to believe that it is the foundation of the discourse which we shall hear in reply to our observations.

How, indeed! Go to Mexico in arms, that is to develop American sentiment in Mexico; to invade Mexico with the assistance of French, Spanish, or English troops; that is giving up Mexico to America. That was the opinion of one of the colleagues of the minister, when, in 1849, in the discussion on the affairs of La Plata, M. Rouher said that it was inexpedient to undertake the expedition, because this expedition would only develop the American spirit which it was not our interest to develop.

And the proof; do you wish to have it? You will find it in connexion with the course of argument which I have the honor to submit to you. The next day after that on which they are threatened by you, what steps do the Mexicans take? in what direction do they turn their eyes? to whom do they apply? where is their refuge? who is the man that becomes that day the most important in the diplomatic corps? It is the representative of the United States. And when the government of President Juarez says to us, "I have just been installed yesterday; I am without resources, without money; I cannot satisfy your claims; I cannot give you a dollar; but I am going to borrow, I am going to borrow of the United States; I will pledge to them a part of our territory;" we must reply to it, "Your territory is pledged to us; consequently we forbid you to hypothecate it in order to pay us." This argument, I am sure, ought to be appreciated by the minister as it deserves; it is an expedient of war and diplomacy; but it is no less true, and it is the only truth which I would wish to set clearly before your eyes, that from the day when France assumes a threatening attitude to Mexico, that very day Mexico turns to the United States, and, so to speak, surrenders itself up to them.

Consequently, let us lay aside this political scheme; it dates from the day of the rupture of the conferences and the departure of the allies, and I much fear that the only end sought in this is the wish to redeem a blunder by an imaginary profundity of plan and scheme

There remains then, gentlemen, the political question on which you have, in my opinion, to exercise a great and legitimate interest.

The question is submitted to you in the draught of an address, you hope that the war will have a happy and speedy termination. Who would not subscribe, gentlemen, to these expressions? But at the same time we find them quite inoffensive; that the war should have a happy and speedy termination, every one wishes that. But how should it finish? what policy should we pursue in Mexico? Should we, as the Spanish, who wish to resume the conferences, ask us, prepare ourselves for a temporary occupation? Do you wish to inaugurate in Mexico, at the distance of 2,000 leagues from us, a new Algeria, which you will try to colonize while you prepare the *senatus consultum* which is to finish the colonization of the other Algeria, which you have for thirty years so little and so badly colonized? Do you wish that the resources of France should be periodically and annually sent to aid the revolutions or the tumults of the Mexican agents who have duped you, and of whom you are only the followers in this policy of enterprise and adventure in which you have involved yourselves? Do you wish this? say so, at least; and in a question which so momentarily concerns France, its policy, its destinies, its future, its finances, let us know what is in store for us ; let us not be doomed to find, some morning, on awaking, when we least expect it, declarations of war which we could not have foreseen, declarations of policy which we cannot accept. We are, in the end, the parties who give the money and who give the men ; it is to us that account must be rendered ; it is we who are to be consulted, and consequently, when a war of this nature is undertaken, we should know what end you propose to give it.

So, gentlemen, this will doubtless be for the government an occasion to inform us about its external policy. What is it ? what does it seek to effect ? It seems to me that it has sought to apply, in its external relations, the principle which it applies so sorrowfully and so sadly in its internal policy, that of force, [vehement reprobation ;] that is to say, impotency itself. [Murmurs.]

Has it succeeded in it ? And after so much blood spilled by our soldiers, let us see and let us see closely what is your influence in Europe. We are a great nation ; we know it well, and for this reason alone that you have the honor of governing us, you can speak loudly and speak firmly. But are not your policy and your diplomacy strangely distanced by those of the neighboring powers ? When the throne of Greece becomes vacant who receives the advantages of this vacancy ? To whom are the eyes turned ? Who are the candidates that are proposed, and, above all, what are the institutions that are sought ? [To the question ! To Mexico !]

You console yourselves by giving sad counsels to those in Prussia who desire resistance, and who give to the ministers of a king, perhaps blind, the detestable counsel not to yield to the will of the nation. [Murmurs.]

Yesterday you were at Turin for Turin ; to-day you are at Rome for Rome. [Murmurs.]

M. the Baron MARIANI. Stay in Mexico, and speak of Mexico.

M. ERNEST PICARD. If this policy is an enigma we should have the clue to it. Tell us who you are ; tell us what are your names. A year ago you appealed to the nationalities ; then there was exultation through all Europe, and it seemed that France, under the impulse of its government, was going to deliver the people. [Cries of no, no.] Yesterday you heard the declaration of the minister ; you know how he treats the Polish nationality which ought never perish. [Renewed murmurings.]

I resume now, and assert, if you are for the principle of non-intervention you must explain otherwise your war in Mexico. If, on the contrary, you are for the principle of intervention, you should not be in Mexico when you ought to be elsewhere. [Noises.]

The PRESIDENT. M. David has the floor.

Baron JEROME DAVID. Gentlemen, I have been struck by one fact in the discourse which we have just heard ; it is that the Spanish, the English, and the Mexicans, everybody is right and France alone is wrong. [That's so ; good good.] I confess to you that my feelings, that my national pride revolts at this idea. [Good, good.]

I oppose the amendment which has just been defended by the honorable M. Picard. I oppose it, while acknowledging at the same time that the Mexican expedition has caused vehement excitement in the country. The distance, the nature of the obstacles, the foreseen increase of the expenses, the uncertainty of the results, must have impressed and must yet impress painfully all those who are not deeply convinced of the imperious necessity of this expedition. The discussions kept up in a neighboring nation have not contributed to the formation of an opinion favorable to the policy of the government towards Mexico. But, as I firmly approve this policy, I shall endeavor to refute such views as cannot gain credit without injury to justice and truth. [Good.]

Gentlemen, have we need of the documents placed before our eyes to know that the insinuations contained in the amendment should not be accepted ; to know, according to the expressions made use of by the honorable M. Picard, that the government can justify the expedition which it has undertaken ; to know that the Emperor's government should have accepted the Mexican war without having sought it ?

Have we forgotten that a preceding government found itself, under the same circumstances, obliged to demand by force the redress of these same grievances ? I shall not be wanting in the regard due to fallen dynasties, when I say that the government to which I allude did not usually permit itself to be carried away by exaggerated susceptibilities at a period of ultra pacific tendencies. In 1839 the address of the Chamber included these words:

"The outrages and spoliations to which our countrymen have been subjected in Mexico demand an exemplary satisfaction, and your government should have required it. The Chamber hopes that it shall have taken prompt and decisive measures to obtain it."

It was during the discussion of the same address that M Piscatory cried out : "France has descended from the rank which she occupied ; it is painful to me to say it, but I do say it, it is my duty and my right." We must not use such language under the empire.

The government of July confined itself to half measures ; the blockade of 1838, the capture of San Juan de Ulloa, the descent upon Vera Cruz, did not, in any respect, remedy the state of affairs; the actual government has been no less willing to push moderation to its utmost limits; the treaty of 1853, the conciliatory mission of Admiral Penaud in 1858, the diplomatic proceedings anterior to the treaty of October 31, 1861—are not all these undeniable proofs of our patience?

What remained to be done? Was it necessary to undertake by force of arms the reparation of our grievances? Should we have acted with inopportune timidity when there was question of the French honor? Would the second of these ways suit my opponents? In any case, I maintain that the first was the only one which becomes the Imperial government.

Gentlemen, our grievances against Mexico have been strangely slurred over by tactics habitual with parties. Some of these grievances have been omitted; the most serious have been thrown into the back-ground; the least striking have been discussed at length, so as to lose sight of the gravity of the situation, resulting from their being seen altogether. [Good; that's so.]

We have in Mexico, not 3,000, but more than 8,000 fellow-countrymen. Among them, several have been the victims of assassination, of robberies, of spoliations of all kinds. They have had to bear forced loans, military contributions, sometimes amounting to 5 per cent. of their capital. French commerce has been capriciously subjected to ruinous and abusive duties of importation and exportation. Finally, all these misdeeds have been followed by the rupture of solemn engagements guaranteed by diplomatic conventions. To remain quiet would be truly to show oneself quite regardless of national honor, unless, indeed, a person regulates his susceptibility according to the dangers of the case, or supposes the flag of France too small to extend its protecting folds to the shores of the New World. [Good, good.]

There are not many members in this assembly disposed to think that we ought to bear these injuries in silence or content ourselves with showing our indignation by an ineffectual military manifestation. After having taken up arms we cannot lay them down, we will not lay them down, but with the certitude that we will not have to recommence periodically a murderous and expensive campaign. So we will not let our most legitimate rights, I will say even our duties, be obscured in the confusion of words or ideas. We will justly interfere in the internal affairs of Mexico as often as our interests shall there be involved to a momentous extent; we will assign to them the place which is acquired for them by our efforts and by our sacrifices; we are bound by the very fact of our expedition to treat only with a government offering serious guarantees for the future; and if it is not granted to us to influence the Mexicans in the choice of their government, it will be incumbent upon us to inquire whether that government promises efficacious protection to the life, to the property of our countrymen, and a sure fulfilment of stipulated engagements.

Let us examine from this point of view the actual government of Mexico, that government recently defined in the following terms in the tribune of the Spanish Senate by the president of the counsel of the Queen's ministers. "In Mexico there is nothing but proscription of the vanquished and established anarchy in government."

The democratic, federalist party, the party of the *puros*, to which M. Juarez belongs, after having figured with various chances in all the troubles that have agitated Mexico since its independence, finally attained to power by the fall of Santa Ana, in the month of August, 1855; it maintained itself until the insurrection at Mexico, which overthrew President Comonfort in the beginning of 1858. M. Juarez, constitutional vice-president at that period, established himself at Vera Cruz, whence he kept up a contest, terminated by his attainment to power in January, 1861, after the defeat of the government at Mexico, under Miramon.

The history of Mexico remains, during these last years, what it was previously; individuals more or less audacious, causing themselves to be followed by some thousands of soldiers, proclaimed a plan, a system of government.

The principles of conservatism or progression formed the basis of these proclamations. The chiefs of each of the belligerent parties adjudged to themselves the commission of saving the nation. Meanwhile they levied imposts, extorted money from foreigners, infested the highways, pillaged the churches, devastated the country. So far did it go, gentlemen—and what I am going to say belongs to history—so far did it go, that, in the course of the year 1858 alone, there occurred in Mexico eight regular battles, twenty-four serious combats, thirty-nine secondary encounters—in all seventy-one engagements.

Therefore you will vainly seek there for roads, for canals, for works of art; you would look in vain for the slightest notion of political or social economy. Exorbitant tariffs impoverish the receipts of the government by exciting a contraband trade along the open frontier of 500 leagues which separates the United States from Mexico. There is everywhere, in Mexico, folly, disorder, want of security for strangers. To discover the least vestiges of civilization we must go back to the epoch of the empire of Montezuma, which has given place only to the tyrannical monopoly of Spain or the disastrous convulsions of the Spanish American republics.

In Mexico there are eight millions of inhabitants separated by difference of race, of manners, and of language, who know no other equality than that of oppression by ambitious upstarts who found their private fortunes on the ruin and degradation of the nation.

For the rest, I grant you, conservatives, democrats, federalists, puros, are all equivalent, [approbative laughter,] all pursue the same line of conduct; it is an incontestable fact. However, I may be permitted to state that there is a striking distinction between the conservatives and the progressionists, the puros, to whom M. Juarez belongs; it is that the conservatives have a patriotic shame entirely unknown to M. Juarez and his friends.

However strange this assertion may appear, it is confirmed by facts. The separation of Texas, its admission into the American Union, the cession of Upper California and New Mexico, were accomplished only after memorable battles sustained by the Mexican army under the orders of the conservative General Santa Anna. The conservative General Miramon, of whom mention was made a while ago, found in his patriotism, at the moment of greatest trial in 1860, the energy to protest against the odious McLane treaty, subscribed by M. Juarez and his friends, a treaty which placed all Mexico in the hands of the United States.

The compliance of M. Juarez was not useless to him. The following year the American Captain Jarvis, commanding the man-of-war Saratoga, took part with M. Juarez by forcibly seizing on two Mexican vessels which were carrying from Havana arms and munitions of war for the army of operation which was besieging Vera Cruz. It is, then, to M. Juarez and his friends and party that we should first apply the reproof justly incurred by citizens relying upon foreign assistance. It was also M. Juarez who in 1861 wished to borrow ten millions of dollars from the United States, by delivering to them the province of Sonora and other parts of the Mexican territory. Such acts call our attention to the consistency of Mexico, to the morality of the means employed by M. Juarez, in whose cause it is now sought to raise the prestige attaching to the defence of one's native land.

M. Juarez applied to the United States for money. Let us see their opinion with regard to Mexico, and then we will be forced to recognize that to borrow money of the United States is to sell Mexico to the United States.

President Buchanan said in his message of 1858: "Mexico has been in a constant state of revolution almost since the moment when it conquered its independence. Military chiefs, one after another, have usurped the government in rapid succession. The different constitutions, adopted at different periods, have been reduced to nullity almost as soon as proclaimed. The successive governments have been unable to afford effectual protection either to Mexican citizens or resident foreigners against violence and illegality."

We read further on: "The truth is, that this beautiful country, blessed with a productive soil and a beneficent climate, finds itself reduced by civil dissensions to a condition of anarchy and impotence almost irremediable."

Then the message asks that the government of the United States should assume a temporary protectorate over the northern parts of the States of Chihuahua and Sonora by establishing military posts there. Is this significant enough? President Buchanan submits to Congress the suitableness of establishing military posts, without even regarding the consent of Mexico

Mr. Buchanan says also in his message of 1859: "Is it possible that Mexico must be abandoned to anarchy and ruin without an effort to deliver and save her? Will the commercial nations of the world who have so many interests involved in Mexico remain indifferent to this result? The United States especially, which should have the greatest number of commercial relations with Mexico—will they permit this neighboring state to ruin and destroy itself? Without aid Mexico cannot resume its position among the nations, nor enter upon a career fruitful in good results. Every American citizen must be deeply moved at this. A government which cannot or will not repress such disorders deserts its duty."

Finally, we read further on: "Mexico is a ship drifting with the current of the ocean and governed only by the passions of opposing parties that dispute the government with one another."

Behold the judgment of the President of a republic. It is not out of place to contrast it with the opinions of our honorable opponents.

The messages quoted show that the United States, after having already conquered the third part of Mexico, would not be slow to seize upon the rest. Their policy in the New World was well settled. They wished to remove Spain from her ancient colonies under the pretext that the island of Cuba, by its geographical position, commands the mouth of the Mississippi, one of the principal arteries of their commerce. They sought to purchase it with thirty millions of dollars. Their attitude towards the Spanish American republics was that of expectation. Persuaded that these republics would be absorbed by the American Union, they commenced, by means of treaties, to assure to themselves the transit over the most suitable points for the connexion of the two oceans. The bases of these treaties were successively enlarged. They asked the establishment of neutral ports at the extremities of the lines of transit. Then they claimed the abolishment of all custom-house duties on American merchandise, and authority to transmit troops and munitions of war. Finally, they specified the grant to the United States of the right to assure by force the security of the transit, which thus made them masters of the great routes of commerce.

Behold the whole diplomatic history of the United States with the rest of the New World. The success has been complete as far as concerns the Isthmus of Tehuantepec. As to the republics of Costa Rica, Nicaragua, and New Granada, they yet oppose these pretensions with the assistance of England, which likewise showed itself at the time of the invasion of Central America by the Anglo-American adventurer Walker. Nevertheless, the opposition was drawing to a close, when civil war surprised the United States in the full career of the application of the celebrated doctrine of President Monroe—of that doctrine which declared that all the States of America have devolved on the Anglo-Americans, whose duty it is to oppose in every manner the interference of Europe in the affairs of the New World.

Gentlemen, the projects of the Anglo-Americans would not have failed to be soon realized, whilst placing Europe in a condition of inferiority, of which the dangers fully manifest themselves. However, the European powers that signed the treaty of October 31, 1861, now follow a different system in their policy towards Mexico. France has loyally persevered in the line of conduct originally traced out by common consent.

Let me be permitted, gentlemen, to show forth this truth whilst throwing into the background the accessory facts to which, in my opinion, too much importance has been attached in other discussions on the same subject; I shall very succinctly place in relief the principal points of the alliance of the three powers.

I select a primary point which serves as a basis for the treaty of October 31—that is, the overthrow of M. Juarez and his government. The maintenance of M. Juarez was recognized as incompatible with the end specified in the preamble of the treaty, namely, the effectual protection of persons and property, and the execution of stipulated engagements with the three powers contracting.

Whatever interpretation it may be sought to give to M. Thouvenel's despatch of October 11, 1861, addressed to our ambassador at London, after a conversation with Lord Cowley, we are forced to recognize that, twenty days before the signing of the treaty, England admitted *a priori*, as well as we did, the fall of M. Juarez and his government; the diversity of opinion concerned only the greater or less influence that was to be exercised on the form of the government that was to replace it.

As to Spain, she declared herself still more clearly; the Queen's minister of state wrote to M. Mon, ambassador to Paris, September 7, fifty-three days before the treaty of October 31: "If England and France agree to act in accord with Spain, the forces of the three powers will unite, as well to obtain reparation for outrages as to establish a regular and stable order of things in Mexico." On the 8th of October—that is to say, twenty-three days before the treaty of October 31—the minister of the Queen of Spain wrote again to M. Mon: "Far from renouncing its projects, (the action in common of Spain, France, and England,) the Spanish government is more persuaded every day that the accord of the three governments, in procuring satisfaction for offences received and the reparation of all injuries, will contribute more or less directly to create in Mexico a regular and settled state of affairs, which will permit the establishment of a government affording security and repose to the unfortunate people of that country, and guarantees for the interests and the lives of strangers."

These two despatches, gentlemen, are explicit; they speak of the establishment, of the creation, of a new order of things; this is the sense of article 11 of the treaty of October 31.

The high contracting parties engage not to exert in the internal affairs of Mexico any influence of such a nature as to attack the right of the Mexican nation to choose and to constitute freely the form of its government.

Does not this paragraph place beyond discussion, beyond doubt, the overthrow of the existing government in order to choose and constitute a new one?

I come to establish a second important point—that is, that the three powers had admitted the eventuality of a march to Mexico. England had declared from the beginning that her assistance should be limited to a display of maritime forces; but Spain, who sent the strongest contingent of forces for disembarkation, recognized, from the 6th of November, that it was possible that there might be occasion to march upon Mexico. Here is the despatch of the ambassador of France at Madrid, addressed on the 6th of November to our minister of foreign affairs:

"Monsieur le Ministre: As I have had the honor to make known to your excellency this morning by telegraph, I have communicated to Marshal O'Donnell and M. Calderon Collantes the desire expressed by your excellency that instructions should be given to the commanders-in-chief of the Spanish and French forces in Mexico, in order that these commanders may, if the circumstances appear favorable to them, march upon Mexico.

"The Duke of Tetuan agreed, without hesitation, to the opinion of the Emperor's government; he declared to me and authorized me to say, that very elastic, discretionary instructions would be given to the commander of the Spanish forces, and that he would moreover send him a private letter, signed by himself, authorizing him to act, if the case should occur in the sense of the eventual measures indicated by your excellency's despatch.

"At the close of a conversation which I had on the same subject with M. Calderon Collantes, the first secretary of state has authorized me to inform you that his opinion was conformable in every respect to that expressed by Marshal O'Donnell, and to confirm in his name the engagement entered into with me by the president of the council."

The treaty of October 31 specifies precisely the results to be attained, but in no respect limits the course of military operations; on the contrary, it says, "That the commanders of the allied forces are authorized to accomplish the operations which shall be judged, on the spot, the most suitable to realize the end specified in the preamble of the treaty." The treaty said no more, because the hope was cherished that it would suffice to seize and occupy the different fortresses and military positions of the coast, to decide the people to shake off the yoke under which they groaned.

M. Calderon Collantes, minister of foreign affairs, had said, in the commencement of October, 1861, to M. Barrot, our ambassador, "That, in his opinion, the active employment of the allied forces would be useless, and that their moral action would suffice." That was calculating too much on the spontaneous energy of populations prostrated by forty years of continual discord.

I resume, gentlemen, the consideration of the meaning and purpose of the treaty of October 31.

Spain and England appeared resolved, as well as we did, to overturn the government of M. Juarez, recognized as incompatible with the results to be attained by them in common. From the moment that the capture of San Juan de Ulloa and the occupation of Vera Cruz failed to produce the desired effects, it was necessary to march onward without waiting till the void should be formed around us, to remove from the warm country, to penetrate into the more favorable and more salubrious regions, to await re-enforcements if they should be necessary, and to plant the allied banners on the walls of Mexico.

The secondary, very secondary incidents of the exaggerated claims of M. Dubois de Saligny on the subject of the Jecker debt, to protection given to General Almonte, the hypothesis of a monarchial *regime* with an archduke of Austria, cannot be called up in good faith to explain the abandonment of which we have been the object; for they weakened in no respect the principal object of the enterprise. [Good.]

This abandonment was decided upon at the moment when, instead of acting, they parleyed; from the moment when, instead of striking the government of M. Juarez, they strengthened it, they gave it by negotiations the moral force that was wanting to it. Our plenipotentiaries have, perhaps, failed in energy, but the government has remained firm in the line of conduct which it had traced out and which it wished to pursue. As to our plenipotentiaries, we must take into account the restricted means which they had at their disposal in the beginning. Whence comes it, then, that England and Spain have withdrawn from an enterprise conducted conformably to the preliminary understanding of the three powers? I shall try to treat this delicate question—I shall treat it, if not with talent, at least patriotically, [good,] and I hope to show that France can say she has persevered loyally in the line of conduct which she has traced for herself. I shall treat this question with all the regard due to friendly nations, and at the same time with the frankness becoming our lawful rights.

Before betaking myself to this examination, I shall call attention to the general situation of the New World, in order to show clearly the conflicting interests in Mexico. It is one of those questions which becomes obscured when viewed in their petty details, but which, on the contrary, become clear and rise to their true height when they are placed on their proper level.

Passing from the frontiers of the United States to the extremities of South America you will meet only the former Spanish colonies, with the exception of Guiana and Brazil. Since their liberation, which belongs to the history of another age, these colonies have generally been given up to internal dissensions, excited in the name of federalism or of centralization. When a European nation interferes in the affairs of one of these republics, all the rest are thereby thrown into a profound excitement.

The idea of Bolivar, the liberator of South America, was that all these republics should be united in a treaty of defensive union; and so it was that in 1856 a treaty of alliance was concluded at Santiago, in Chili, between the representatives of Peru, Chili, and Ecuador. In the course of the years 1856, 1857, 1858, this treaty was submitted to the approbation of the republics of Central America, of Venezuela, and of New Granada.

In 1861, the President of Perú took the initiative in a treaty of alliance between all the American governments in order to resist all action on the part of Europe in the affairs of the New World. This treaty of alliance included the following significant phrase: "To attack the independence of one of the Spanish American republics is to wound that of all." In 1862, a deputy of Chili, M. Artega Aleamparte, asked his government, in open assembly, to take part against us. M. Leoane, minister from Peru to La Plata, strove to rouse the national feelings of the States of the Argentine Confederation, of Paraguay, and of the Oriental State; he appears to have failed in that part of his mission which consisted in obtaining effective measures. All these republics are too much embarrassed with their own affairs to seek for external complications.

Gentlemen, I desired to deduce from these facts that the question in debate in Mexico is not merely a Mexican question, but one which concerns the interests of France and of Europe in all the New World. Circumstances have brought us to undertake an expedition to Mexico, when it was necessary to show that we would support our countrymen in all regions where they might happen to be. [Good, good.]

After these preliminary explanations, let us examine, gentlemen, the conduct of the three powers.

England considerably surpasses other powers in her commercial relations with the New World; even the commercial relations of the United States are behind hers. The possessions of Belize, in the bay of Honduras, permit her to profit by the commercial transactions of the rich Mexican provinces of Yucatan and Tabasco, and to explore Central America; she has often even interfered in the events that have agitated those countries. Hence arose serious and frequent difficulties with the United States, of which difficulties the Clayton-Bulwer treaty is the best testimony. The English policy, like the American policy, has persistently striven to prevent the probable pretensions of Spain over her former colonies, in order not to see them rescued from the state of commercial and industrial infancy in which they languish in order not to lose a market. It appears evidently, from the recent discussions in the Spanish Cortes, that England decided upon the Mexican expedition solely to prevent Spain from undertaking it alone. The English policy, so justly styled a policy of material interests by the Marquis of Havana, ex-ambassador from Spain to Paris, had especially tended to participate but feebly in the expedition so as to disengage itself from the treaty of October 31 on the first occasion, whilst causing Spain to follow her example. This occasion the English plenipotentiary, Sir Charles Wyke, undertook to bring about by shuffling the cards—pardon me the expression—on minor points of detail, so as to treat separately with M. Juarez, whom they were to overturn.

As Spain took sides with England the expedition ran a chance of miscarrying, whilst leaving to Great Britain the merit of having removed the arms of the European powers from Mexico—a thing which could not fail to cause a deep sensation in America; a thing which could not but consolidate her influence; a thing which could not but extend her relations of importation and exportation and benefit her commerce. We have defeated these calculations by a perseverance which was not counted on. That was forgotten which causes our superiority, and perhaps our isolation, namely, that we subordinate our profits and our advantages to the principles of civilization and of morality, which are the marks of greatness of the times. [Applause.]

English diplomacy shows itself less accommodating than it was in Mexico, when it is alone in the case. In 1856 a *casus belli* was made with New Granada on account of a delay in the payment of some millions to an English creditor, Mr. Mackintosh. In 1859, in consequence of the detention at Assumption of an English subject, Mr. Canstalt, an English vessel, without any previous declaration of war, gave chase in the river La Plata to a Paraguayan vessel, the Tamari, which had on board the son of the President of Paraguay; M. Lopez had to return to Buenos Ayres in all haste and proceed to Assumption by way of land.

I do not ambition for my country the policy of England, however lucrative it may be. [Good, good.] We must, however, acknowledge that, in the Mexican question, it has shown itself skilful enough to escape officially the charge of disloyalty. [Sensation.]

As to Spain, gentlemen, her grievances had an exceptional importance; her resolution to have recourse to arms was anterior to ours; her military contingent was stronger, her army was commanded by a brilliant general, well known by numerous deeds of war. These different reasons explain the position assigned to Spain in the beginning of the expedition.

I shall not go back to the treaty of La Soledad; its clauses are well known to you. I shall say only that they are a symptom of the hesitancy of General Prim, a hesitancy which should be deemed merely transitory, to judge from his correspondence of March 20 and 21, 1862. The chief of the Spanish expedition said that he wished even to burn his vessels in order to march as a soldier; his warlike humor reawoke in presence of the fresh injuries committed by the Mexican government, and twenty-four hours afterwards Admiral Jurien de la Gravière received intimation that General Prim was embarking his troops.

We had never been expelled from the New World after a series of reverses once celebrated; we never had our standards suspended in testimony of defeat under the vaults of the cathedral of Mexico; the violences exercised against the French arose from the general disorder, and not at all from national hatred; our ambassador had never been expelled from Mexico, and yet we have remained faithful to our alliance, whilst the Spanish army set sail, abandoning us to a contest with an enemy numerically much superior; abandoning us to a struggle with the calamities of war, under an inexorable climate, during the worst season of the year. [Applause.]

Surely, if the Spanish army had not been already tried, if General Prim had not been renowned for his personal bravery, the retreat of the Spanish troops would be very much like a flight from danger. This supposition is inadmissible. I think we must search in another order of ideas for the origin of the facts. General Prim could not resist the illusions, the seductions, that have dazzled all the representatives of Spain charged to repress by force the excesses of the Spanish American republics. In 1856, after the sequestration of Spanish property by President Comonfort, an imposing fleet, having on board S'r de los Santos Alvarez, minister from Spain, appeared before Vera Cruz, to retire at the end of some days without having done anything and without having obtained anything. In 1860, after the massacre of some hundred Spaniards in Venezuela, some Spanish vessels again appeared. After remaining some time before La Guayra they retired, without having obtained the least satisfaction from the cabinet of Caraccas. General Prim shows, for the third time, a Spanish plenipotentiary failing to carry out the instructions of his government, in order to make more noise than work. [Good, good.]

Gentlemen, all the representatives of Spain that arrive in the New World are seized with a veritable fever of national ambition. The official language, the men who direct affairs, the manners of the population of the towns, the religious practices, the traditions, the inscriptions on the monuments, everything recalls to them the Spanish dominion; then they say to themselves that Spain might reanimate, might easily revive the elements of prosperity now hidden behind the anarchy of the moment, provided she raises no new barriers between herself and her former colonies by a recourse to violent measures. This illusion is easily worked up by the crafty diplomacy of the natives and creoles of America. Have things happened this time also in the same style in Mexico? Everything induces us to believe so.

Spain, thanks to the measures of France, now figures, in the European system, in the ranks of the great powers; thanks, also, to the wisdom of her statesmen, she has, for some years past, taken a truly remarkable flight; her preponderance in the New World would give her an *éclat* surpassing the days of her greatest splendor. Could Spain realize this grand idea she would be worthy of the gratitude, of the admiration of her citizens. But successes of this kind disdain egotism and chicanery; nations that pursue such objects should commence by raising their banners from the degradation into which the reverses of other times have thrown them. The confidence and the esteem of nations are accorded only to loyalty and the moral strength of nations. So we are permitted to doubt whether the commander-in-chief of the Spanish expedition, whatever may have been his intentions, has served his country well in withdrawing after the example of England.

For the rest, we need not regret too bitterly the withdrawal of Spain in an enterprise in which she had the honor of marching by our side; we will prove but once the more that, to have justice done us, we can do without allies. We have gone to Mexico under the impulse of necessity; we will stay there under the impulse of duty and fidelity to the end set in view. Our allies have acted differently; that is a matter that concerns them; in such cases, on each one be the responsibility of his own acts.

The honorable M. Picard asks, What is the end pursued by the government? Gentlemen, I am not in the secrets of the government; I cannot, therefore, answer him absolutely; but it is, however, an end which appears evident to me; which can be immediately understood, provided we examine it without passion, without prejudice; provided we examine with precision the state of affairs. We desire, and the treaty of October 31 says so clearly—we desire security for persons and property, with a stable and regular government; we shall soon be enabled in Mexico to second such measures as will answer this programme. How long shall we stay there? How long shall we figure in the ulterior events of Mexico? In this respect I cannot unite my wishes with those expressed in the address. For questions of this nature previsions and precise replies are difficult. In any war whatever the future belongs to the unforeseen. All that can be said at present, all that can be said for certain, is, that the difficulties which we will have to conquer will be slight beside the difficulties already surmounted by our army and navy with a degree of self-denial and courage above all praise. [Good, good.] Our fleet will no longer be stationed along the coast; the means of transportation are being organized; a railroad will shorten the distance through the hot country; our troops are encamped in the more salubrious regions; all arms of the service will rival each other in emulation and zeal, and, without any doubt, our soldiers will soon be in Mexico.

Gentlemen, there is an idea cherished with much complacency when it is desired to offer opposition to the Emperor's government. They say, "But when you are at Mexico will you be any further advanced?" It is enough to have studied, to have read the history of the transactions of Mexico for the last forty years to know, in an incontestable manner, that the occupation of Mexico, Puebla, and the seaports will comprise the whole of Mexico; there will be partial resistance here and there, which will cease of itself for want of means of propagation. The city of Mexico is the point of union where all the elements of Mexican vitality are concentrated; it is the capital and the heart of the nation; and surely it cannot be seriously said that once at Mexico we will not be further advanced than at the setting out of the expedition. At the city of Mexico we will serve as a rallying point for the reaction of the masses against the upholders of disorder. Our presence at Mexico will be an energetic and salutary act of repression; it will be felt throughout the whole of the New World. Our maritime commerce, assured of protection, will multiply its operations in America to the great advantage of international intercourse and commercial development. Our emigrants will carry with confidence the genius of the nation into the wilderness of the New World; there will be an outlet for those ardent and discontented imaginations that now turn their eyes towards the era of revolutions.

Gentlemen, what I say may be criticised; my words may be deemed quite poetical, but utterly void of the reality; it may be pretended that I place myself in a world of chimeras. Will not these assertions be refuted by considering, for example, that the Argentine Confederation, that country so rich in products of all sorts, has, for a territory of 200,000 square leagues, only 800,000 inhabitants, or four persons to the square league, whilst in France there are 1,100. And this is also the case in Mexico, in Central America, and in all the old Spanish colonies of the continent; everywhere there is an enormous disproportion between the extent of territory and the amount of population. How does it happen that the population does not increase? It is because there is no security. Adventurers, and even honorable men, can repair to these distant countries, but commercial enterprises recoil before such innumerable apprehensions. Is it not a prudent and generous undertaking to restore to native production and commercial activity an important part of the globe, of which at present the richness remains in a state of absolute sterility?

Now, if we consider the question in a purely real point of view, for at that I aim, there is not one European power that has not been injured in its relations with the Spanish American republics. To cite but one instance, which has reference to the people whom I have the honor to represent: A few years ago a Girondist emigration was attracted to Paraguay to establish a colony there, which was called New Bordeaux. Not one of the engagements entered into by the president of that state were kept, and after some months' residence most of our countrymen died, after tribulations of every kind. Others took refuge in Buenos Ayres.

In America, in La Plata especially, our diplomatic agents have continual discords and quarrels on account of serious and numerous claims against the local governments.

There are more than 100,000 Frenchmen scattered through the Spanish American republics. Before the Mexican expedition, it might be thought that we abandoned all influence beyond a certain circle; that we knew not how to afford to our countrymen any other assistance than that of protocols. When an English subject is touched, the blow that strikes him resounds throughout all England. Shall we permit it to be supposed that we are fallen into lethargy? Shall we let it be supposed that we are incapable of protecting our own?

Truly it is too easy to spread alarm and false suggestions among a public not always correctly informed as to the state of affairs; truly it is too easy to enumerate the rough labors of our soldiers and sailors whilst attacking the spirit of system or adventure which has caused them. When facts are thus distorted, when this manner is adopted, why not have the courage to be logical to the end? Why not have the boldness to say that they are satisfied with a restricted influence for their country on the European continent; that beyond this our countrymen should seek assistance under other flags, [noise,] like those eastern vessels, which shelter their fortunes and their heads under foreign protectorates? [Good, good.] If we reject this degradation and disgrace we must proclaim the Mexican expedition so much the more meritorious by how much the more arduous and difficult it is. Our worthy army, too, must be sustained in the midst of its severe trials by the consciousness that we are usefully defending the honor and the interests of France. [Good.] Our soldiers and our sailors, so admirable and so devoted, should have faith in their work; and in fine, those among them who fall in those distant regions should know well that they sleep in glorious death in serving the cause of humanity, of right, and of civilization. [Good, good.]

(The speaker was congratulated by many of his friends.)

The President. Does the Chamber desire some minutes of repose? [Cries of "Yes, yes."]

[The session is suspended for twenty minutes. It is resumed at a quarter before five o'clock.]

The PRESIDENT. Does any one of the authors of the amendment desire the floor to reply to M. David?

M. JULES FAVRE. Mr. President, I should have desired to reply to the minister.

A MEMBER. The minister will reply to you.

M. JULES FAVRE. My intention was to spare the time of the Chamber. It is well known that I am at its disposal; if it desires me to reply to the honorable M. David—[cries of "Yes, yes; speak."]

Gentlemen, the remarkable speech which you have just heard causes him who is charged with the honor of replying to it to experience an embarrassment which I can explain in a few words. I am not commissioned to defend that which has been attacked by the honorable M. David, and he does not appear to me to have justified that which was criticised by my honorable friend, M. Picard. Grant that the government of Juarez has to reproach itself with serious wrongs; that it is by no means popular in Mexico; that England has been, as opposed to us, haughty and perfidious; that Spain, our ally, has broken the treaty which united her with us—all these things, gentlemen, have, in the discussion in which we are now engaged, only a secondary importance.

I will say as much, and perhaps still more justly, of the brilliant considerations which I have remarked in the speech of our honorable colleague. His generous spirit has encountered no difficulty, no limit; and, if we believe him, France would have for her mission to spread everywhere the lights and benefits of civilization; to substitute order for anarchy; to plant the principles of morality and self-respect wherever they are badly known; and to accomplish this glorious work she should regard neither the treasures which flow from her liberal hand, nor the blood of her children which she sacrifices. This generous programme has the inconvenience of strangely involving the policy which our interests and our strength order us to restrain; and it is not to open outlets for human activity; it is not even to permit those diseased and impotent imaginations, of which M. David just spoke, to go and seek under eastern skies for realities which they have dreamed, that our soldiers can be engaged and our treasures spent.

Moreover, gentlemen, I may be allowed to add that all these things could have found a more suitable place in the discussion of last year. If the Chamber had heard them then, it would have known to what it engaged itself; it could have, with full knowledge of the question, followed the honorable M. David in those brilliant and distant expeditions, or else stopped short with those who advised it to reserve its treasures for cases exclusively personal to us And the language then held by the minister very little resembles that which we now find in the mouth of the honorable M. David.

Permit me, gentlemen, to refer back to that, for there is the real question. We have to ask ourselves how and why the expedition has been undertaken; how it seems to have deflected from its primitive design, and how it may be terminated; all which questions, I need not say, in the highest degree concern the future, the honor, and the morality of France. At the moment in which I am speaking, gentlemen, there are very few families that are not uneasy in consequence of this war—glorious undoubtedly, but already disastrous, and yet so obscure.

It is becoming, then, in the means of control that belongs to it, that the legislative body should be able to clear up that which is yet confused, and it is for this reason that I entreat you to have the kindness to hear me for a few minutes.

Well, without repeating the details given to you by my honorable *confrère*, M. Picard, [laughter,] I wished to say, my colleague, I hope the Chamber will excuse my mistake; I made use of a softer word than I am in the habit of employing. ["Yes, yes." "Go on, go on."] I was saying that it would be rash for me to repeat all the details given to you by my honorable colleague, Master Picard. [General hilarity.] I have need, gentlemen. that your indulgence should be on a level with my weakness. ["Go on, go on."] I ask your pardon for these failings. ["No, no" "Go on."]

The honorable M. Picard has explained to you in what circumstances the treaty of London was signed, and on this point I might grant to our honorable colleague, M. David, all that he has said relatively to the outrages of which our countrymen have been the object. In this respect it is a matter of public notoriety throughout the entire world that Spanish America is unhappily given up to a sort of chronic anarchy.

Mexico, on this point, is not an exception to the evil; and if we examine its neighbors in Bolivia, in the Argentine republics, we will meet examples in every respect analogous. That France should protect those who suffered thus; that she should interfere diplomatically—by arms, even, if it was necessary—no one would contest, and when the honorable M. David recalled certain discussions entered into under the monarchy of July, the military enterprises to which it resigned itself, in spite perhaps of its too pacific tendency, the honorable M. David showed us an evil on which every one is agreed, and which it was urgently sought to heal. Only all exaggerations should have been avoided. Now, permit me to say that no serious explanation has yet been rendered. For if the despatches of our chargé d'affaires have brought to our notice instances of violence to property and person, the representatives of friendly powers have replied that these violences were the consequence of a state of things engendered by the civil war; that all the successive governments should be accused of them, and the responsibility not made to fall exclusively on M. Juarez.

And in fact, gentlemen, it has been told you General Miramon, his lieutenant, Marquez, and others whom it is useless to mention, had all successively occupied the presidential chair, and the civil war was awhile ago related to you in energetic terms by the honorable speaker to whom I reply; and it is during the phases of this civil war that our countrymen have had most to suffer; for what is most remarkable is, that if the claims which have been addressed to the government date from to-day, their causes go back to yesterday, that is, to a period when Juarez was not yet established in the city of Mexico.

I have said that I did not wish to repeat what has been already shown; nevertheless, I must remark that Juarez belonged to the civil order. He was a lawyer; he afterwards became a magistrate. He was president of the supreme court at the moment when the suffrages of his fellow-citizens called him to the presidency. His election was opposed by force; he was compelled to fly; and after long wanderings in the United States, he came to seek refuge at Vera Cruz, where hi authority was recognized. It was not till towards the end of the year 1861, in the last days of December, that—the power of Miramon having crumbled away—Juarez proceeded to occupy at Mexico the place that had been regularly assigned to him by the usual method of constitutional institutions.

And it is at the moment when Juarez proceeds to take his seat that all the reclamations are addressed to him, of which the chargé d'affaires of France has spoken; and he is yet exposed to all the horrors of civil war, which the capture of Mexico has been unable to stop; he struggles amid the convulsions of a violent state. It is at this moment that we send in our complaints, and that Spain and England join in our quarrel.

Hitherto the attitude of France is irreproachable. They cannot reproach her with having too lightly received the information given to her by her agents who engage her to hold herself in a state of distrust. But what is important, and what certainly will have its influence with you, is, that the two great powers that acted in concert with us had the same interests that we had. No one, indeed, has dared to maintain that in the different acts of violence committed in Mexico there have been any specially directed against the French. If our national colony in Mexico is important, which I acknowledge, the English and the Spanish have establishments there no less considerable.

Indeed, our honorable colleague, M. David, just awhile ago told you what vigor, what vigilance, England usually displayed in the protection of her subjects. It is, then, gentlemen, for the sole purpose of protecting them that the three powers form an agreement—that they wish to form an expedition against Mexico, and obtain by main force respect for treaties hitherto most outrageously violated.

I acknowledge, gentlemen, that at this moment there was presented to the minds of the negotiators a hypothesis, which I have the right to qualify now as a chimera, which has sprung from the brain of some exiles, and which probably has been the cause of all the evil. This hypothesis was the following: that the government of Juarez was as unpopular as frail; as detested as all those which had preceded it; that as soon as an imposing force should present itself he would be immediately abandoned by all his partisans; and that it would be possible to construct a new government. Permit me, gentlemen, to say that, if this hypothesis could appear seductive when it was proposed at length by interested lips, it seems that it found from the very beginning its counteraction in the very inanity of the element that it designated, and that were to be disposed in order to reconstitute the pretended new government, which was to offer to the belligerent parties sufficient guarantees, for, after all, it was only substituting Mexican element for Mexican element. And if you introduce the foreign element there, it will be an active element of dissolution. Indeed, no one doubts but that a haughty nation like the Mexican, which, perhaps, pushes national vanity too far, might regard with suspicion and distrust the undertakings of the foreigner.

These considerations did not occur to the minds of the negotiators, so much eloquence did these refugees display when they pleaded the cause of the exile whilst pleading that of their personal interest It was thought that it was only requisite to touch the soil of Mexico in order that, at the instant, what the minister last year called the phantom of a government of Juarez should immediately vanish; and this had been announced—I appeal to your memories and to the proclamation, become famous, of the loyal officer who commanded the troops—encountering obstacles on which they had not calculated. Our soldiers were to be received with crowns of flowers. Here were lying promises, extravagant dreams, on the faith of which it was wrong to enlist the policy and the arms of France.

I acknowledge, however, that this hypothesis had been diplomatically foreseen, and under this respect our honorable colleague M. David was perfectly right to call attention to it. Only in this regard I would address a direct reproach to the member of the cabinet. Whatever be our position in the state, although it be quite modest, although it becomes none of us to exaggerate it, it must, however, be acknowledged that it transcends all positions in two respects, which are equally interesting to be recalled to mind.

In the first place, we dispose of the finances; and in the second place, having acquired the right of advising the government on its external as well as on its internal policy, we have the right to speak with frankness. Our respect ought not to arrest the truth upon our lips. It is our duty to declare the whole truth as soon as ever we are asked, and if we were convinced that a war was unjust, that it had been undertaken on false principles, we should say so, we should refuse our concurrence, for the blood of France, its treasures, cannot be lavished but with our responsibility. And it is for this reason, gentlemen, that, in similar conjunctions, the words which are pronounced by the government ought to be impressed with the most complete frankness.

I regret not to be able to make this concession to those which were pronounced in the month of March last.

You know, in fact, that at this period all was yet uncertainty and confusion, as far as concerned the Mexican expedition. Official information was wanting to us; we were convinced that in fact the little expeditionary corps, which had been directed to the shores of the Atlantic, had no other purpose than to solicit, to demand, and to obtain, in case of need by force of reparation for the grievances of our countrymen.

And yet Europe, which has a fine ear, heard rumors of various indiscretions which had transpired through the imperfectly closed doors of diplomacy, and of which the press had obtained possession. The most extraordinary things were repeated. It was said, especially, that there was an intention of overturning the republic of Mexico, not to put in the place of the deposed president a man of the country, acquainted with its language, its usages, familiar with all the necessities of the government, but, what was most strange to the south, a prince of the north, an archduke of Austria.

And you have not probably forgotten, gentlemen, the reserved manner in which he who has the honor to address you thought it his duty to explain himself in this regard whilst asking of the government such information as it interested you to obtain. For, permit me to subjoin it here, gentlemen, here was the dividing line between these two opposing policies—that of our colleague, the honorable M. David, and that of my honorable colleague, M. Picard; M. David wishing to have civilization reign in Mexico, even at the price of our millions and of our armies; M. Picard and I modestly demanding that we should confine ourselves to going to Mexico to obtain payment of the contributions which are due, and re-establish security which is threatened.

What will the minister answer? His language, gentlemen, will be perfectly clear, and it will be impossible for you not to recognize that it is the second of these policies which the minister has adopted.

"England and Spain," said he, "have joined with us. The same offers have been made to the United States . . ." Hear the sequel, gentlemen; if we may use such a word in a discussion so serious, I might say that this application is piquant. "But the United States do not seem, in regard to Mexico, to concentrate their views on a simple reparation of injury done; their policy sees things otherwise, and we have decided to act without them."

Wonderful! The United States are ambitious; they are neighbors; they have the immediate occasion of sin; we who are so very distant, who can undertake expeditions only at very great expense, we are wise of necessity, and we desire nothing further than the reparation of our grievances.

"But," added the minister, "should not this union of the three powers of itself completely reassure you against the particular suppositions on which you build your discourse? Beyond patent, declared facts, you persist in seeing I know not what secret machinations of France in favor of a foreign interest

"When such suppositions are affirmed, there should be at least some proofs, and you have none.

"The treaty made between the three powers is clear and precise. The object is to demand of Mexico: 1st, a more effectual protection for the property and persons of their subjects; 2d, the execution of the obligations entered into with them by that republic." And the second article of the treaty adds: "The three contracting parties engage themselves, &c., &c." But this is a thing already known to you, and I shall not repeat it.

"All this," said the minister also, "clearly indicates to you both what the three powers wish to effect in common, and what they forbid themselves to do."

And, after having explained that the occupation of the capital is necessary for the reparation of our grievances, the minister adds: "See why our standards are carried to Mexico. Our troops, having set out on the 20th of February, should have now arrived there." Unhappily, gentlemen, events proceed not as fast as our speeches.

It is not the orators that I attack; the intention of the minister was full of patriotism, but he did not foresee, I am sure, the obstacles of all kinds which our brave soldiers were to encounter.

The minister continued: "Now, if in the midst of this conflict, through a reaction easily conceivable, the unfortunate populations of those countries, weary at last of all the evils inflicted on them for forty years by the incessant alternatives of anarchy and tyranny, formed the wish to shake off at length the yoke of their oppressors conquered by us; if in an hour of good sense, of instinct of sovereign welfare, they endeavored to give to themselves at least a government of order and liberty, shall we hinder them?"

So we go to Mexico not to hinder it from giving itself a government.

"This case," also added the minister, "is precisely provided for by the treaty as well as by the instruction: we will not bind the people by force . . .

"We will not go to violate at Mexico the independence of the popular will; but we will leave these unfortunate people perfectly free . . . .; if they wish to continue their miserable existence, we will not impose on them a better fate."

One could not be more categorical than this; and it is here that the minister is in complete variance with our honorable colleague, M. David:

"Yes, if at the sight of our squadrons there is revealed in this Mexican people a movement attracting them towards us, we will not close our arms to them, but we will not use force; and if they prefer the miserable government under which they live, we will do nothing to cause its downfall."

These are the words that were spoken in the name of the government; here is the engagement in the face of which you have given your adhesion to its policy. And as to those allusions which I had unfortunately allowed myself to make in regard to that Austrian prince, see with what disdain the minister replies to me:

"And as to those rumors which, says the honorable member with remarkable foresight, give umbrage to the ambassador of her Britannic Majesty, permit me to decline dwelling upon them. Officers have said at parting that they were going to Mexico to enthrone a foreign prince. What! you imagine that this great secret of diplomacy, if it ever existed, would have been thus confided to the first officer that came on his way to Mexico! This is not certainly serious. If, as you say, our ally has become uneasy at these rumors, you tell us also that she applied to the proper quarter for information as to their foundation in reality; she asked our minister of foreign affairs, and you acknowledge yourselves the reply has been a denial of the truth of these rumors."

This is important, gentlemen; for if the contrary is true, what will you think of the language of the minister?

As to me, it is painful to me to suppose that the Chamber has been deceived; yet, to repel such a supposition, I must admit another equally inadmissible; it is that the minister of foreign affairs has so well kept the secret that the minister without portfolio did not know it. [Laughter.] For it is in the month of March, 1862, that this language is held to you. Now hear what was that of the minister of foreign affairs in the month of October, 1861, that is, at the very time that the treaty was signed. He gives an account of a conversation had with the English minister:

"Such an event (he speaks of the social dissolution in Mexico) cannot be a matter of indifference to England, and the principal means, in our opinion, to prevent its accomplishment would be the establishment in Mexico of a regenerative government strong enough to arrest its internal dissolution." Pursuing the development of these ideas in the form of an intimate and confidential conversation, "I have," says he, "added that, in case the contingency which I have indicated should be realized, the Emperor's government, free from all anticipations of self-interest, laid aside in advance all ideas of aspiring to the candidacy for any prince of the imperial family, and that, desirous of respecting the susceptibilities of all parties, it would see with pleasure the choice of the Mexicans and the assent of the powers fall on a prince of the house of Austria."

See, gentlemen, the value of ministerial denials. They are themselves belied by official documents. The truth has not been told to the Chamber, [murmurs of disapprobation;] indeed, its conscience has been ensnared. [Cries of No, No.] For if the Chamber had known that there was question, not of avenging our countrymen, but of destroying one government to replace it by another, its decision would certainly have been different. [Renewed marks of disapprobation.]

However it be, you see that, in this first phase of the expedition, you were assured at the same time by the concurrence of the other two powers and by the declaration made to you, that our forces and our treasures should be employed only in avenging our own injuries; and that if we ought to accept a political regeneration that might be offered to us, we ought by no means to impose it.

Three months pass away, and from the month of March I proceed to the month of June,

1862, when the same discussion continued before you, after the withdrawal of England and Spain.

Our honorable colleague, M. David, has told us that England never participated in this expedition but with reluctance; that she was well pleased to leave the burden of it to France and Spain and reap the fruits herself.

If this is so, I derive from this concession of my honorable opponent the proof, that I just sought, of the exaggeration of the pretended violences committed against resident foreigners in Mexico; and if that which has been said was true, England would never have shown, in regard to her own subjects, that strange disdain of their lives and property.

As to Spain, every one will acknowledge with me that, from this point of view, she had interests conformable to ours. Yet discord slipped in among the allies. These are, M. David has told you, secondary facts. I ask him a thousand pardons; these are, on the contrary, capital facts, not only because they leave us alone exposed to all the results of this hazardous expedition, but also because they throw a light extremely precious on the real motives which should be set forth in opposition to the apparent motives which alone the Chamber has known.

It appears from all the official documents published, that, when the plenipotentiaries met at La Soledad, the chargé d'affaires of France brought forward an ultimatum against which the chargés d'affaires of England and Spain protested; and they immediately declared that they had come, not to establish such or such a government, not to oppose such or such an individual, but to obtain serious guarantees and reparation of grievances.

Permit me, gentlemen, to say here what undoubtedly has already occurred to your minds, that this scheme, so brilliantly set off by the eloquence of him to whom I reply—that is to say, the scheme of a government inaugurated for the greater glory and the greater advantage of France—should not cause us to forget the material elements of the question. I suppose that, in fact, France entertained this view in the very beginning; I suppose that she concealed it from the eyes of the Chamber; and this point is incontestable, that, at least to accomplish it worthily, must she have been ruled by questions of principle and not by questions of person.

You tell us that you went to attack Juarez. I reply that you went to inaugurate General Almonte; you have made yourselves the champions of an individual; you had in your train the pernicious remnants of the Mexican exiles, who, deserting the true principles of nationality, appealed to the foreigner to conquer back for them the power they had lost. Here is the explanation of this moral revolt in Mexico. In all that the honorable M. David has said with regard to the elements of dissolution there is much truth. It must be acknowledged that, when a country is delivered up for many years to an anarchy, so to speak, chronic, it seems very near its dissolution; but, as my friend M. Picard said, there is a way of reuniting immediately those wills divided by miserable ambition; they can be reunited in one common sentiment, the love of country.

Does it not belong to France to awake this sentiment? Can she not take advantage of it? Consult all those who know Mexico; they will tell you that if the Spaniards were detested, the French were regarded with affection. I go so far as to assert that if the French had announced at first that they would not interfere in any way with the internal politics of the country, that they came to re-establish order, that it was a matter of little consequence to them that the presidential chair should be occupied by such or such a one, the road to Mexico would have been open to them. In place of this, they present themselves with an ultimatum, in which they say to Juarez, the choice of the national suffrage, "Depart; you are a monster and the enemy of the human race." Should we be surprised that Mexican pride revolted; that from all sides they rushed to arms; and that this people, who was supposed to have fallen into complete dissolution, resisted this French expedition? thanks certainly, I doubt not, to the advantages of a material situation, but also to prove that it wished to defend the sacred soil of the country against the invasion which threatened it.

They told Juarez to vacate his place; and there are two ways of declaring this sad truth to a government—either to say so directly, or to inform it of it by presenting an ultimatum impossible to be executed. This is what happened, and this is precisely why the ministers of England and Spain resisted this pretension of our minister. And here I cannot avoid remarking with what deplorable levity, to use no severer expression, this affair was conducted.

What was the importance of the debts due to us by Mexico as regulated by treaty? I have said, gentlemen, that Mexico was our debtor, according to treaty signed, for 750,000 piastres. There were other claims, but they were conditional; the amount did not reach 5,000,000 of francs

What does our chargé d'affaires do? Gentlemen, read the first article of his ultimatum: "Mexico engages to pay to France the sum of 12,000,000 of piastres, at which is estimated the whole of the French claim." Sixty millions of francs! If in private affairs, gentlemen, a similar process were employed, what qualification would you apply to those who had recourse to it?

Well, the minister himself was not informed of this claim; he was ignorant of it when he was advised of it by the protests of the allied powers. Behold, gentlemen, in what reserved, yet firm, terms he observes to his chargé d'affaires that perhaps he had gone too far. "The figure at which the department has been forced to value our claims did not reach that fixed by your first article."

What! Gentlemen, our chargé d'affaires, in a matter so important, acted without an understanding with his minister. A blank was given for 750,000 piastres, and by a shameful overcharge pretensions are so far raised as to demand 60,000,000 of francs.

The minister is not informed of it, and he is under the necessity, when addressing the ambassador of France at London, to acknowledge that in fact the thing is pushed very much too far. "In writing to M. Dubois de Saligny," says the same minister, "in the sense of the preceding developments, I have, moreover, left him at liberty to use further the latitude allowed him by my first instructions to modify his demands."

To modify his demands! And it is France that speaks—France that has an army at her back, that seems to have but a word to pronounce to triumph over this petty people; she demands 60,000,000, when there are due only 750,000 piastres, and perhaps 5,000,000. I shall not dwell upon this subject, gentlemen; it affects your sentiments of probity too forcibly not to be understood by you.

I might say as much, and yet more forcibly, of another article of the ultimatum, which is designated as No. 3. It is utterly inexplicable; it should draw categorical explanations from the government which has hitherto kept silence on the subject; and if I have any reproach to make to the commission, it is that they have not previously called for them. Already, indeed, gentlemen, the questions of last year had put them on the way; they knew that it was a rotten affair, and that the thing should at all events be cleared up.

Here is article 3d: "Mexico shall be bound to the entire, loyal and immediate execution of the contract concluded in the month of February, 1859, between the Mexican government and the Jecker house."

Now, what is the importance of this contract? 15,000,000 of piastres or 75,000,000 of francs; and it was required that Mexico, in the state of distress in which it was, should succumb under the weight of our armies or pay 60,000,000 at first and 75,000,000 afterwards, that is, 135,000,000 francs.

Such were the demands made. It was in a military way that Mexico was addressed; and if obedience was not rendered to these demands, war was to be declared. It is the first time, in my knowledge at least, that in a diplomatic treaty, in an ultimatum, in a summons addressed by an armed people to one whom it can invade, that there are thus found stipulated guarantees of reimbursement for an affair purely private, and I add, for an affair that was known at the time by those residing in Mexico as a shameful transaction.

Assuredly the responsibility cannot attach to the minister of foreign affairs; but if his honor is entirely acquitted in this regard, have I not the right to accuse his prudence? Was he permitted to ignore the Jecker affair? Did it not make noise enough in Mexico? When there was question of this departure for Mexico, everything was done with such carelessness that they ignored the men, the things, the realities with which they were to come in contact. Here, however, is the position assumed by the minister of foreign affairs, and you will see in what terms he expresses himself on this point:

"As to what especially concerns article 3, relatively to the Jecker affair, there is evidently a distinction to be made in this case between what directly concerns our interests and what is foreign to it. When General Miramon issued the decree which brought on his contract with the Jecker house, the communications of the legation having stated that foreign commerce derived considerable advantage from the financial measure facilitated by that house to the Mexican government, it was natural that we should regard it as of great utility to hinder, as much as possible, the revocation of this measure and of the operations which facilitated it. It is with this view that the instructions of the department have invited you, as you have already taken the initiative, to sustain the claims and maintain the complaints provoked on this question by the conduct of the government of Juarez. It would now, however, appear from the opposition with which you have met on the part of Sir Charles Wyke to your demands in respect to this affair, that no advantage, they say, would accrue to foreign commerce from the contract made with the Jecker house, but that this latter only would be exclusively benefited by the accomplishment of this contract. I do not sufficiently understand the state of the case, but I call your attention to the importance of distinguishing well in this affair between what may really involve the interests which it is our duty to defend, and what may concern others of a very different character.

"The actual government cannot pretend to deprive our countrymen of advantages assured to them by a regular measure adopted by the administration of General Miramon, for the only reason that that measure emanated from an enemy; but we, on our part, would have no foundation in reason were we to wish to impose obligations on the actual government that did not flow essentially from governmental responsibilty."

Ah, gentlemen, last year I heard the minister without portfolio repeat with complacency, "When we are a great people, when we are a great government, when we direct great affairs, we should also be a vigilant minister." I say so too; and it was not permitted thus to involve negotiations on uncertainties, on suppositions, on numbers which the least examination causes to vanish and perhaps crumble under the reprobation of the public conscience. What! the minister is not instructed; he is ignorant. At the smallest objection made by the representative of England, he stops short and says that it is possible that the government of Miramon has done a thing that was not entirely indifferent to foreign commerce.

But if all these things exist you ought to have known them; you are minister in order to know them; it was your duty to obtain information. War is not a play left to the caprices of a vain ambition; when people engage in it, when they send their fleets beyond the seas, when they deprive their country of her children and her money, we should know what they wish to do and what they wish to demand; and we should not, at the very first claim, immediately recoil as the minister of foreign affairs has done, uncertain as he was about the pretensions of his representative.

But, gentlemen, this is not enough, and it is not only on the ignorance of the minister of foreign affairs that I rely to characterize this deplorable affair as I should; it is on its own nature, and it behooves you to understand it thoroughly. These 75,000,000 that Jecker claims were, the representative of England asserted, a manifest robbery in regard to the Mexican public and government. Who, in fact, was Jecker? He was, as you have been told, a Swiss banker; he arrived poor in Mexico, and in twenty years has made a fortune of more than three millions, which, I may mention it in passing, proves that foreign commerce is not entirely abandoned to plunderers. [Laughter.] In possession of a fortune so considerable, he has plunged into great industrial schemes; he has embarked in those enterprises, objects of the dreams and the hopes of the speculators of other times as of the speculators of to-day, which sometimes hide behind diplomacy to acquire the confidence of the public. I refer to partnerships in common; Jecker engulphed considerable capital in them, and in 1859 his affairs became much embarrassed.

Beside him was another person who was not less so; I refer to General Miramon. At the end of his resources, having pillaged even the churches, as our honorable colleague, M. David, very well observed, (for this party which they call ultra-clerical, be sure, does not belie its name, and when it wishes to coin money with religion it does not spare it,) General Miramon, with empty coffers, turns to Jecker who can offer him only similar ones. But there was the public to replenish the one and the other; and it was then that they made that wonderful scheme, and that they said to one another, "If Jecker is authorized by the government to make a great loan, the public will come into it; the Mexican public (it is a little French in this respect) [laughter] will believe the fine promises that will be made to them, and when they will be told that they will derive a handsome emolument from it they will bring their capital. But there was not question only of capital. If they had authorized Jecker to issue fifteen millions in paper, and if they had thought that he would find fifteen millions of specie, they would have committed a grave error, and these gentlemen were incapable of that. [Laughter.] All who are acquainted with Mexico know to perfection that it is flooded with false money. The successive governments have wished to leave a souvenir behind them, and that souvenir is bankruptcy. They have all emitted bills of credit with which they have flooded the country, and which, to be sure, they forgot to pay when they left power. [Renewed laughter.]

There were, especially, the Peza bills, issued in 1856, if I am not mistaken, but the date is of little importance; what I am sure of is, that they circulated among the Mexican people enormously depreciated. Those who took them at 7 per cent. were considered rash; these bills sold only for 6 per cent. of their nominal value. Well, it was arranged between General Miramon and the Jecker house that the Jecker house should issue fifteen millions of paper to be guaranteed by the government. The government guaranteed its reimbursement at the end of five years by means of annuities which I need not explain; it guaranteed, moreover, the payment of the interest semi-annually, and the Jecker house was commissioned for this operation.

But the Mexican government, as I have had the honor of saying, did not expect to receive fifteen milions; far from it. It was said that the Peza bills would be received in payment at their nominal value, provided they were willing, on these bills, to pay 25 per cent. in specie. These 25 per cents, chemically disengaged (I hope the Chamber will allow me this expression) from all these *scoriæ* of stock-jobbing, formed, in reality, the net residue which was to return into the treasury of Mexico.

However, as Jecker is the associate of Miramon, Miramon will not come off best. [Laughter.] The net profit was to be 3,750,000 piastres to the Jecker house, which being commissioned for this operation, had allowed itself a commission of 20 per cent., that is, 750,000 piastres; and as it was in its counting-rooms that the semi-annual interest was to be paid, it had very prudently asked the person with whom it treated to let the money remain in its hands as a guarantee of the debt. So that Jecker first deducted 750,000 piastres for commission, and afterwards 2,250,000 piastres for guarantee; whence it followed that the residue, which really entered the coffers of the Mexican government, was only 750,000 piastres. And if you please to take notice that the Mexican government represented by Miramon borrowed 15,000,000 of piastres, you will see that it borrowed at 90 per cent. [Laughter.]

You think we are at the end? Ah! it is because you know not the usages of traffickers in Mexico. See how matters were carried on:

It has been said that the foreign merchants took a considerable number of these bills. I have here the *exposé* of the operation, and see what it states. I have made an exact estimate of the bills taken by the public, and the public were yet much too confiding, for they took about 471,275 piastres; as to the surplus, it remained in the hands of Jecker, who was unable to negotiate it, that is, fourteen millions and a fraction of a million.

I have forgotten to give the Chamber, and I ask pardon for it, but I am not as much at my ease here as at the palace. [Laughter.] I have forgotten to give the dates of the operation. This operation took place in the month of February, 1859; it was at that time that Jecker issued a part of those bills and in the course of the year 1860.

Did Jecker place in the hands of the Mexican government the 750,000 piastres for which he was accountable? No. See what he had the ingenuity to make Miramon accept. I said ingenuity; I am wrong; usurers everywhere resemble each other, and it is not only in Mexico that children are compelled to receive things of which they have the least need. [Laughter.] Miramon was to receive 1,490,414 piastres. Here is what he did receive: The public paid in money 52,541 piastres and 56 fractions. Jecker paid 566,386 piastres and 27 fractions, which in reality makes Jecker to have paid in specie on these 1,490,414 piastres only 618,927 piastres. He paid in afterwards, in bills issued by Zuloaga, 342,000 piastres; in Peza bills, 30,000 piastres; in Jecker bills, 24,750 piastres; to the order of sundries on the customs, 100,000 piastres; in equipments, 70,000 piastres; in various bills receivable, 6,750 piastres and 56 fractions; in reimbursement of the Grosso debt, 298,000 piastres; sum total, 1,490,428 piastres and 39 fractions. This Grosso, whose reimbursement is here put into account as payment for 298,000 piastres, is a nephew of Miramon. Miramon had conceded to him the exclusive privilege of clothing the Mexican troops, which, as our soldiers must be by this time convinced, is an operation costing very little to him who is charged with it. [General laughter.] This Grosso had the ingenuity to present a bill for payment of 298,000 piastres, and if the investigations which have been sent me are correct, the Mexican government has been certainly robbed of two-thirds.

It is by means of all these deductions that Jecker succeeded in charging the Mexican government with all these sums on which he paid in, in reality, only 750,000 piastres. It follows from this, that having disbursed in all 1,000,000 of piastres, in reality he retained 1,500,000, so that instead of being a creditor he should be accounted a debtor. And here is the honest capitalist in whose favor our minister interferes, for whom our ultimatum is going, perhaps, to shed the blood of the French soldiers and the Mexican soldiers; here is the reason of our intervention; here are the lessons of morality and civilization that France is going to give the world. [Expressions of dissent from many benches.]

And as a final fact, I shall add the following: It has been said, and repeated at different times in the papers, that it was the fall of Miramon that caused the failure of Jecker. Nothing more untrue. Jecker failed in the month of May, 1860. I have the record of the proceedings of the meeting held by his creditors in September, 1860, and it was in December, 1861, that Miramon was overthrown.

Gentlemen, Jecker's bills were admitted in his failure and bought at a low price. Is Jecker the keeper of them? Has he caused them to pass into the hands of third parties? Should we, in this respect, consider as furnishing information worthy of being brought before the Chamber all the data in our hands? You all know to what I allude. We have received letters emanating from members of the Jecker family, and intercepted. From these letters it would appear that Jecker flattered himself, very unreasonably, no doubt, and calumniously, that he would find (among the high personages and functionaries of France) a support which, certainly, he has never found. As for me, I am much better pleased to say that such letters cannot be mentioned here. I could have wished that the Moniteur explained itself, and that in presence of a fact so public, and which was of a nature to alarm the conscience of all honest people, it gave them a complete denial. Much more so; and it is the only fact that I wish to retain, for it is unfortunately testified by an act of the French administration, because in one of these letters, which bore the date of August 31, 1862, the correspondent informs Jecker, as a precious advantage gained, of the publication in the Bulletin des Lois of his act of naturalization.

The fact is true, and, in my opinion, it is inexplicable. How? It is in the progress of our debates, after it had been revealed that the Jecker debts concealed a veritable rascality, that Jecker is thus picked up by the administration and made a French citizen! Can we not, from this, conclude that it is an assistance given to this rotten claim? Happily, gentlemen, the developments made in this Chamber are before the world, and it will be impossible for diplomacy to obtain public sanction for such a proceeding. But, in fine, do not the honest public desire to have all this thing cleared up in a categorical manner? When I point out, in this deplorable affair, unpardonable consequences, demands which cannot be justified, this war so rashly undertaken, those ultimatums which are belied by those who ought to know them and maintain them; and when at the end of this demonstration I find the French nation offering shelter to this man who has never ceased to be a Mexican and a miserable agitator, I have a strong right, I think, to call to these facts all your attention, your entire consideration, and to ask that the government would be pleased to dispel the sad clouds that hang over the probity of its agents.

This is what I have to say in regard to this article 3 of the ultimatum, and you understand that it cannot be, especially in a French assembly, considered as secondary. Everything that touches honor, everything that touches dignity, everything that would be stigmatized in private life, everything that would be stricken down by the law, everything that would be condemned by the magistrate, cannot be let pass with impunity and admitted in public life. And now must we be astonished that this ultimatum caused England to withdraw? Must we be astonished that Spain was unwilling to accept the responsibility of it?

Do not forget—and this is also one of the characteristic traits of this deplorable enterprise—that the chargé d'affaires of France raised the pretension that each of the powers should produce its own ultimatum and its own valuation of pecuniary claims, without the other belligerent powers being allowed to discuss them, so that each one was mistress of the situation; for it sufficed, for example, for England to claim a thousand millions to render the war fatally necessary.

It is, then, on this question of money, in regard to which the government can no longer maintain the discussion which it abandons, a circumstance which bears down the responsibility of its agent; it is on this question that the bickering arises between the three powers and that war is resolved on.

Here, gentlemen, you understand I must not speak but with extreme reserve. It is not my part to say how, in a military point of view, history will judge, not the soldiers and generals who have displayed on the spot all the bravery, all the skill, all the ardor, all the resolution, that are ever found in the French armies, but those who have ordered this expedition, those who have not provided for it the materials, the means necessary for its prompt success. I desire, gentlemen, to leave all these faults in the shade. [Demonstrations in the Chamber.]

A VOICE. Leave nothing in the shade.

M. JULES FAVRE. They afflict me; they contribute no way to the solution which we seek. What we seek is a prompt termination, without any diminution of our dignity, of the war in which we are engaged; for to pretend now, after all the explanations into which I have entered, that this war is conformable with our principles, would be to deny what is evident. These principles, gentlemen, are paraded on all occasions by the minister; he everywhere repeats that the government which he serves has sprung from universal suffrage, and that this is a rule which he intends to respect among all neighboring nations.

Here is what he said on this point in your session of March 13, 1861: "The principle of non-intervention being thus laid down, there was yet, on the point of general policy, another reason which imperiously ordered us to respect it. We could not, after having proclaimed at home, as the basis of our government, national sovereignty and the suffrage of the country, fail to respect it among others. The Emperor has been elected by the people; he reigns and he glories in it, according to the national will; and you would wish him, beyond our frontiers, to employ the force confided to him by that national will, in repressing neighboring nations, in repressing their aspirations, and snatching from their hands their titles to sovereignty, thereby deny his own legitimacy!"

These, gentlemen, are the words of M. Billault. I ask him, are they ironical? Were they uttered merely to call forth our legitimate applause? Were they not the expression of the minister's political conscience? If I assume this last supposition, I say to him, By what right are you in Mexico? You have gone there to avenge national interests? In this purpose I follow you; but if these interests are avenged on the soil itself of Mexico, if at Orizaba, that is, in a salubrious position, we are offered guarantees, what good is it to overturn the government of Juarez? Is it against Juarez that you intended this war? Do you wish to overthrow him at any cost? Permit me to recall to you your own words This government, against which you precipitate your legions, was a shadow—a breath of air; it was enough for you to appear, and it would be destroyed. Well, it has resisted you; it has strengthened itself by what is most generous in the world—that is, by the blood shed by our soldiers.

Is not this enough? Do you wish to continue this cruel expedition? Do you wish, through a false point of honor, to force men thus to massacre each other in order to arrive at nothing; in order to arrive at a result which will confound your policy, I fear not to assert it, for you pursue a phantasm when you propose to raise on the sand a solid edifice not to be overturned by coming events.

You are then in opposition with justice. You did not tell the whole truth before the Chamber when you were interrogated, and you are now obliged to complete it. In vain do you take refuge, as my honorable friend M. Picard told you, behind the brilliant sophisms of a policy very seductive to some minds. You wish, it is said, to resist north America, and you do not see that you call her in! You are going to establish a point in Southern America that will become the battle-field whereon the United States and Europe will meet.

Must we yield to all your fancies? Must we find ourselves in a struggle with the north and fight beside the south? Would you thus constrain us to espouse all the quarrels of one people with another? Is this your policy? As for me, I protest against it in the name of principle, in the name of the law of nations. I say that there is no possibility for us to attack a people, who, by maintaining their nationality, by offering us satisfactory guarantees, have sufficiently honored themselves that we should not drive them contemptuously from our courts without being willing to hear them, and that we should not receive them but at the point of our bayonets.

If we have not justice on our side, gentlemen, what must we say of the final consequence of this enterprise? For it is the end, in fine, that must be regarded in all things; and when one is in a political position, when one disposes of all the forces of France, it should not be involved in a blind affair in which its dignity or its interests might have to suffer.

Last year, though well aware that in the presence of a body such as this that does me the honor to listen to me I must carefully avoid all that could wound the feeling of national honor, I deemed myself authorized to ask the immediate suspension of an expedition unfortunately undertaken, and which could in no way cause us to consider that we had experiencd a check, because our soldiers, in insufficient numbers, had broken against walls of granite. I believe that I gave you sage advice, and if it had been followed thousands of precious lives, ingloriously decimated by disease, would have been preserved. Now you persist, and you wish at all hazards, enlarging the circle of your policy, ambitious of military glory, you wish your flag to wave over the city of Mexico.

Surely, gentlemen, if France wills it, she will succeed, nothing can deter her; and when our generous children meet an obstacle, they are so prodigal of the existence which God has given them that nothing can resist them.

But should not our hearts be moved at it? Can we coolly regard these human hecatombs offered to that fantastic, confused divinity, which has never been defined by the ministers? [Interruptions and cries of disapprobation.] Can we consent to have thousands of families plunged in grief for the sterile glory of reaching the Mexican capital?

Now, gentlemen, suppose you are at the city of Mexico, what are you going to do then? You say that you will overturn the government of Juarez! Undoubtedly. But what will you do then? I hear the honorable M. David immediately cry out, "The city of Mexico is the heart of the nation; there all its military resources are concentrated." But the honorable M. David, who knows so well the history and the geography of Mexico, will permit me to reply to him with the following two facts for consideration: Mexico, he knows, has been incessantly rent by civil war, and the city of Mexico has been the sterile stake which the different pretenders conquered in turn, notwithstanding which they never possessed more than an ephemeral and limited power.

And as to the geography—but, gentlemen, only those who know it not can believe that the conquest of the city of Mexico necessarily carries along with it the conquest of Mexico. The city of Mexico is situated 69 leagues from the coast, from Vera Cruz. Do you know what is the greatest extent of Mexico in its utmost length? It is 950 leagues; and in these 950 leagues to the northwest there are rich and populous provinces with important cities.

I will mention some: Guanaxuato has 41,000 inhabitants; it is 253 kilometres to the northwest of Mexico, and the whole State has more than 520,000 inhabitants. Do you wish to proceed further? Traverse 450 kilometres, and you find the city of Guadalaxara with 60,000 inhabitants. You have then Valladolid with 18,000; you have the State of Xalisco with 800,000, and others which I shall not mention, for fear of mistake, for I do not possess the same amount of information as the honorable M. David, and mine, I acknowledge, is of very recent date. Yet it is guaranteed by all the books of geography, which know perhaps more than all of us, and which we can consult.

Well, when the French shall reach the city of Mexico, they will establish a government, I suppose; it may be Almonte, it may be the Archduke Maximilian, who is, perhaps, yet kept in reserve in spite of all asseverations to the contrary; it may be, perhaps, any other prince of Germany, for in this respect the fertility of Germany is inexhaustible. [Laughter.]

But when this German prince shall have been established, what will you do? You must support him. Juarez with his legions, with his partisans, (if not Juarez, some other representative of nationality) will retire into the provinces that remain free. Will you follow him? After having traversed sixty-nine leagues to reach the city of Mexico, will you traverse nine hundred more to come up with him who will resist you? We are at Orizaba; we have made twenty-two leagues; we have already spent more than one hundred and four millions without counting what we know nothing of, which makes five millions a league. [Demonstrations in the Chamber.] At this cost all the treasures of France would not suffice. [Interruptions. Marks of disapprobation.] And what would be the end? To regenerate Mexico, to impose a stable government on that unfortunate people? But it cannot be stable except on condition that you support it by your arms. Consult experience.

In 1848 the United States waged war with Mexico. The United States bordered upon Mexico; they had all the facilities for sending men and munitions of war. Well, notwithstanding this, the United States spent one hundred millions of dollars, and the war lasted two years.

I acknowledge, gentlemen, and it is a confession which I desire to make to the honor of France, that war costs less with us than in America; yet, whatever this concession be worth, we must acknowledge that a war, two thousand leagues from one's country, necessitates enormous sacrifices; that to defend our rights we need not place ourselves in unacceptable conditions. What you say now of the honor of your flag you will be obliged to say afterwards; the first fault will draw you into a second one, and you will find yourselves under an impossibility of withdrawing. This will be another Roman occupation, without the glory of having maintained a great principle. You will not then have the right to say that it is in the interest of the Catholic world, but only in the interests of the Mexicans, that you will spend fifty millions a year, and that you will send 30,000 men annually, of whom a great number will be cut down by the murderous effect of the climate.

This is a line of policy with which I can not agree; and when I remain convinced that this expedition has been undertaken only on the faith of lying communications, [disapprobation,] that your representatives abroad have imposed unacceptable conditions which have brought on the rupture between us, England, and Spain; when it is in opposition to the rights of the Mexicans, and the interests of France, that this deplorable war is prolonged, I can but entreat the Chamber to use the right which appertains to it to manifest its will respectfully and firmly, and to disengage, as I do solemnly by this protest, its responsibility from that of the government. [Obstreperous excitement.]

His excellency M. BILLAULT, minister without portfolio, rises to speak.

NUMEROUS VOICES. To-morrow! To-morrow!

The PRESIDENT. The minister without portfolio has the floor.

His excellency the MINISTER. Gentlemen, the lateness of the hour compels me to ask the Chamber to adjourn the discussion till to-morrow; but I make, in presence of the Chamber, the engagement to refute thoroughly all the accusations brought against the policy of France. [Good, very good.]

M. JULES FAVRE. On condition that I may reply.

The PRESIDENT. The continuation of the discussion is deferred till to-morrow.

The Chamber adjourned at 6 o'clock.

["Le Moniteur Universel," No. 39, February 8, 1863, page 191, column 4.]

SESSION OF SATURDAY, *February* 7.

His excellency the Duke of Morny, president, in the chair.

The session was opened at 2 o'clock. Baron J. David, one of the secretaries, read the minutes of the session of yesterday; the minutes were adopted.

The PRESIDENT. I lay before the Chamber a letter from M. Arnaud requesting leave of absence on account of ill health. There is no opposition? The leave is granted. Does any one desire to present a report?

M. CHABANON. I have the honor to present a report on the bill relative to an extraordinary impost by the department of Gard.

The PRESIDENT. The report will be printed and distributed. The order of the day is the continuation of the discussion on the address.

(The ministerial benches were occupied by their excellencies MM. Baroche, minister, president of the council of state; Billault, Magne, ministers without portfolio; De Parieu, vice-president of the council of state; General Allard, Boudet, Vuillefroy, Boinvilliers, and Viutry, chairmen of committees in the council of state.)

The PRESIDENT. The deliberation continues on section third, and on the amendment proposed to this section by M. Jules Favre and several other members.

His excellency M. BILLAULT, minister without portfolio. Gentlemen, as I enter upon the discussion of the amendment submitted to your deliberation, I cannot pass over in silence the first impression made upon me by reading it. In the parliamentary governments from which we have adopted the address and its political debates, it is a traditional custom that the language destined to be heard by the sovereign should always bear the impress of respectful deference. [Good, good.] The courtesy of the words does not hinder their sincerity, nor, if needs be, their firmness.

I hear frequent mention of liberty as it is in England. It would be well to consult the English practice on this point; I do not know that it would be easy to find in it any phrase borrowed from the harshness manifested by certain amendments submitted to your attention. [Renewed marks of approbation.]

I will draw from this reflection but one consequence: it is that the extreme liberty of form evidences, whatever may be said, the great liberty existing in fact. [Good, good.]

The policy which France pursues in Mexico, which our soldiers are now defending in the face of the enemy, has been the object of accusations which I yesterday promised the Chamber to refute to-day. I will trace step by step the causes which have induced the expedition, the incidents for which it has been sought to calumniate it; it will not be the fault of the explicitness of my words if each and every fact is not clearly explained to the Chamber. [Good.]

In the amendment submitted to you the legitimate causes of the expedition now commenced are denied. I proceed to enumerate them anew in brief. Is it denied that against the government of Juarez we had to complain of three treaties obligatory upon it, and all three by it violated, the treaty of 1853, that of 1859, that of 1861? Is it denied that these three treaties stipulated reparation for the outrages, the murders, the pillagings, the robberies of which our fellow-countrymen have been the victims? Is it denied that the Mexican custom-house revenues were assigned, in part, for the payment of these reparations? Is it denied that the government of Juarez, breaking these three treaties, has proclaimed the forced suspension of them, and has laid hands on the funds collected for carrying them into effect? Is it denied that, under the government of Juarez, the French population has been incessantly the victim of brutal violences, odious spoliations, robberies—ill treatment of every kind? Is this denied? That government established itself in the city of Mexico towards the end of 1860; we immediately accredited our minister; in the commencement of 1861 he arrived there with the most kindly intentions. Consigning all former wrongs to oblivion, we were disposed loyally to second the efforts of the new government to re-establish, if that were possible, a little order in the country. It has required the continuance, the constant accumulation of acts of violence and wrong, to induce us first to withdraw our kindly feelings, and then to feel the necessity of an efficacious military demonstration.

The impression was sought to be made yesterday that the wrongs of which we complain were not the act of the government of Juarez, but were the act of preceding governments. But read all the despatches of 1861, and especially those of June, July, August, September, October, and November, to the moment when our minister, by order of the French government, was forced to leave that deplorable country; there is not one that does not attest, on the part of that government, the violation of plighted faith; not one which does not attest robberies, assassinations, attacks of every kind upon our resident countrymen. This disorderly state of affairs is not attested only by French assertions. You believe more in the affirmations of the ministers of England and Spain than in those of the minister of your own country? Be it so. [Good, good] Well, Sir Charles Wyke wrote to his government, on the 27th of May, 1861, that is, at the time when the tyranny of Juarez held sway in the city of Mexico; he wrote as follows:

"The congress, instead of giving the government sufficient force to put an end to the horrible disorders that reign in all parts of the country, occupies itself with disputes on different theories of the pretended government and ultra-liberal principles. During this time the respectable part of the population is left without defence against the attacks of the robbers and assassins who swarm on the highways and in the streets of the capital. The constitutional government cannot maintain its authority in the various States of the confederation, which, in fact, are perfectly independent; so that the same causes which divided the confederation of Central America, and which are at work here, will probably produce the same results.

"The only hope of an advantageous change that I can see is in the small conservative party which may attain to power before all is lost, and which can save its country from the ruin which threatens it.

"From the moment that we shall make known our determination no longer to permit English subjects to be robbed and assassinated with impunity we will be respected. All sensible Mexicans will approve a measure, the necessity of which they are the first to recognize, in order to put an end to the excesses which, every day and every hour, are committed, under a government as corrupt as it is powerless to maintain order and to effect the execution of its own laws"

On the 28th of October he wrote again: "The experience of each day tends to prove how utterly absurd it is to seek to govern this country with the limited faculties accorded to the executive power by the present ultra-liberal constitution. I see no hope of amelioration but in the advent of a foreign intervention, or in the formation of a reasonable government, composed of the principal men of the conservative party, who, for the present, are devoid of influence, and fear to stir unless with material assistance from without."

These facts stated by our agents were evident to all the world. It is true that to acquit Juarez of them, these facts are attributed to brigandage, and it is added that brigandage is endemic in that unfortunate country. We shall probably hear on Monday, gentlemen, something on Neapolitan brigandage, severe words, and they will be well founded, but I ask how, in the face of this severity towards acts not directed against our fellow-countrymen, there is found such an abundance of indulgence for Mexican brigandage of which our citizens are the victims. [Good, good.] The government of Juarez is not only guilty for its impotence, its corruption, as the minister of England says; it is not only culpable of being unable or unwilling to prevent the brigandages committed about it; it is not only guilty of letting the brigands that surround it go unpunished; it is guilty of making of them colonels, generals, friends, confidants. [That's so; that's so; good, good.] It is, moreover, personally guilty of the direct violation of all the engagements into which it has entered.

Again, I ask, is it bound by treaties with us, treaties subscribed by its predecessors, treaties subscribed by itself? Has it not violated these treaties? Has it not forcibly seized for itself the sums collected for us, and which those treaties had assigned to us?

Here are the facts; they are incontestable. In the face of these violations and of these violences, is there one man in this assembly who does not feel the necessity for France to enforce respect for the treaties made with her and with citizens who glory in being Frenchmen? There was once in the world a people whose members had to say but one word, "I am a Roman citizen," to insure universal respect. There is another to-day which, in every quarter of the world, enforces with equal energy respect for its countrymen; acts of the greatest energy are familiar to it in this regard, and it has just very recently given a lively proof of it in the waters of Brazil. I admire its vigorous patriotism; but you will not take it ill that the government of France should imitate it, and cause its countrymen also to be respected as much as British citizens are respected. [Enthusiastic approbation.]

The cause of our offended honor, of our treaties violated, of our funds carried off, the cause of our fellow-citizens harassed, pillaged, assassinated—these causes cannot be abandoned by a government conscious of its obligations, and whose first duty it is to make its country respected.

You seek to make these causes so legitimate be forgotten by evoking I know not what scandal; of which it is hoped the mists, more or less obscure, will shade from the eyes of prejudiced public opinion all the sincerity of purpose, all the justice of the resolutions of the government. But these mists will soon be dissipated. What it imports me from the beginning to state well is, that in the face of the acts of the government of Juarez, there is no people so feeble, so timid, so pacifically inclined, that would not deem itself necessitated to have recourse to force to maintain its disregarded rights.

Is not this opinion of France, gentlemen, also that of England? Has not England judged, as we have done, that the measure was full? Has she not recalled her minister? Has she not with us signed a treaty for action in common? Has not the sentiment of England been also that of Spain? Has not Spain as well as England made common cause with us? Has she not sent her troops upon Mexican soil? Has she not judged, equally with us, that it was for her honor, that it was for the urgent interest of her citizens to resort to this great and last resort of nations, the employment of force, when their rights are violated? There is undoubtedly no occasion to accuse either England or Spain of this pretended desire to enthrone a foreign prince, or of any Jecker debt whatever to enforce. Yet the English and the Spanish have judged as well as we, for the same reasons that we have, the violation of treaties and the vexations to which their citizens have been subjected, that the occasion for the employment of force was presented, and that it was necessary to use it.

I insist on these facts, because it is important to establish well that the motives which have decided us would have decided any nation, however little desirous of making itself respected in the world, and that three great nations, identical in their complaints, have been equally so in their resolution to act.

The employment of force being found necessary, and being resolved on, what have been the steps taken by the Emperor's government in consequence? It has been asserted that its conduct has been adventurous, rash. I shall presume to show that it has been prudent, wise, and circumspect In the first place, it had an understanding with the powers which had the same interests as France. It thus avoided all cause for jealousy, difficulty, and embarrassment, and the three powers, in unison, regulated the conditions of their action. France did not even take, in the beginning, the principal part in the demonstration. The proportion of the forces had been agreed upon. Spain, whom so many memories recall into those countries, whom the most important interests in the very Gulf of Mexico command to be strong and respected, Spain had found in the traditions of her policy and the good will of ours towards her the reasons for playing the principal part, and having numerous *corps d'armée*. England, whose power is chiefly maritime, gave the assistance of her fleets. And as for us, as resolved as the Spanish, but in less number, and leaving to Spain the honor of the principal situation, we sent originally but 2,500 men.

Thus, then, driven unto the last intrenchments of her honor, France, having come to an understanding with the great powers, having the same interests as they, and regulating with common accord the concurrence of each, she who has been accustomed to take the chief parts took only the second. Assuredly, in such circumstances, she was neither rash nor adventurous; she was sensible and politic. [Very good; very good.]

Indeed, there could not well be any great degree of temerity in the fact that three powers, among the principal of the world, should proceed to demand of a savage and tyrannical government to yield at length to reason and equity. There could be nothing very venturesome in this that, preceded by Spain, followed by England, we should undertake to uphold our rights and our claims in Mexico. How, under these circumstances, can the French government be accused of having imprudently and with levity sported with the blood and treasures of its country?

But there has been brought forward another serious imputation which it behooves us to clear up. When, for the first time, in the month of March of last year, the Mexican question was brought forward in this assembly, certain explanations were given, and recalling them yesterday, the eloquent orator to whom I reply has offered us a strange dilemma: "Either you have deceived the Chamber," said he to us, "or you did not know all."

Has he well weighed the import of such words? To deceive the Chamber! If the Emperor's ministers were capable of such an infamous proceeding they should have been impeached. [Good, good.] I am not aware that the rectitude of my political life has given any one the right to throw such an imputation on my character. [No, no; good, good.]

But we might not have known all. Do you clearly understand the meaning of this? This tends, on the one side, to bring into discredit with this assembly the authoritative declarations of the government, to ruin its just authority, to destroy the faith which you have in it; it tends, on the other hand, to throw back upon him who honors us with his confidence and his instructions such insinuations as, I am sure, you would not accept. [Good, good.]

We know what we ought to have known; we said what we ought to have said. Recall to mind the facts.

I know well that, from the very first day, the efforts of the opposition have been directed to drown the popularity of a necessary chastisement in the unpopularity of the gratuitous foundation of a foreign throne. It was requisite for this purpose to substitute for the reminiscence of the violences of which our fellow-countrymen have been the object, for the reminiscence of treaties violated, the prejudice of an enterprise in which all motives of national interest would have been effaced; it was necessary to endeavor to persuade France that it was demanded of her to sacrifice her children, to expend her treasures, solely to found a throne for an archduke of Austria. But never, as you know well, has this accessory and conditional scheme, subordinate to the wishes of the Mexican people, been either the exclusive motive or purpose of the expedition undertaken.

In this discussion the honorable orator to whom I reply put forth, in effect, the assertion that France was disinterested in the affair, that entire satisfaction had been assured to her, and that the expedition was undertaken with the sole view of erecting a throne in Mexico and seating on it a foreign prince. He cited certain indications from officers who had declared it. We replied that we went to Mexico to avenge our honor, to avenge our fellow-countrymen, to compel the execution of treaties, to obtain the reparation due to us, which, whatever he may say to the contrary, Juarez was unwilling to accord to us. And then we added: "If the Mexicans, weary of the tyranny from which they suffer still more than we do, possess yet any germ of energy, if they have not been completely enervated by the forty years of anarchy and tyranny which weigh upon them, if they desire to repress all those revolutionary and counter-revolutionary hordes which harass and oppress them, profiting by the occasion which we are going to offer them, if they wish to endeavor to found a regular and reasonable government, they can reckon on our whole moral support; we will applaud their efforts, we will prosecute with our best wishes the re-edification of the social edifice in their unhappy country. We indicated plainly, as the first step in our policy, the desire to avenge the honor of France, the blood of her children, and to obtain reparation for all injuries done; and then, as a second step, in the interest also of the guarantees which we had the right to demand, the reorganization by the Mexicans themselves of a regular, responsible government, capable of respecting plighted faith. If Mexico can give herself and us this fundamental guarantee she will have, I repeat, our moral support, our approbation, our applause, and we shall be happy to have given her the occasion for the resurrection of a great and beautiful country, plunged in misery for so many years. Here is our reply. [Good.]

In what have we concealed the ideas of the government? Read all the proclamations that from the first day to the present moment have emanated from the French government. When I spoke in the month of March last you had before your eyes the instructions given by our minister of foreign affairs; they were clear, plain, precise. In the first place, our interests; in the second place, the desire for the organization of a real, effectual Mexican government. The Emperor, in his memorable letter to General De Lorencez, wrote those noble words which you have applauded: "It is against my interests, my origin, and my principles to impose any government whatever on the Mexican people; let them choose in full liberty the form that suits them." Afterwards General Forey made the same declarations; and I myself, in the month of June last, declared to you, as the last possible consequence of the line of conduct which we intended to pursue: "We appeal to the Mexican people, and if that people, free to vote as it pleases, decides even for the government of Juarez, well, be it so; let its wish be accomplished."

How, then, can we have deceived the Chamber? How have we ever concealed both the principal purpose and the conditional hypotheses? If, in these contingencies, Mexico happened to desire a monarchy, its possibilities have not remained unprovided for. Thus we have arranged everything in its proper place. We have not given a contingent hypothesis precedence of our own interests, for when a policy is pursued in the name of one's own country, it is by the interest of one's own country that we must commence. [Good, good.]

The expedition being thus resolved upon, its object being determined, the ulterior hypothesis of a foreign monarchy being reduced to its just value, the accords of the three powers, the measures for execution, and the military concurrence being regulated, what had we to do? The instructions, with which you are acquainted, specified clearly the course to be pursued. In these instructions of the 12th of November, if I remember right, it was said: "You will renew your ultimatum"—we had already made several, all without result—"you will renew your ultimatum, and then, the ultimatum being presented, you will not permit yourself to be diverted by delays and evasive promises. If the government of Juarez evacuates Vera Cruz," as it has done, "if it seeks to establish a void around you, if it seeks to draw you by artifices more or less skilful into the loss of precious time, you will avoid falling into this snare, and immediately take the most vigorous measures."

There were, gentlemen, grave reasons for recommending this active and resolute attitude. Our troops were arriving in Mexico in the month of January; we had before us, as a suitable season for transportation and war, January, February, March, and perhaps a few days of April. We knew perfectly that if at that period things were not consummated the tyranny of Juarez would receive a redoubtable and almost invincible auxiliary, the black vomit. We knew very well that it was necessary, in those few words, to characterize justly the cunning of that government as well as its violences, and to succeed in imposing upon it the solution of the question; there was no time to be lost. Behold under what inspirations the expedition set out and arrived at its destination!

The honorable orator to whom I reply has recalled the words which I uttered in the month of March, and in which I expressed my impression that our troops had already occupied the city of Mexico, and he added that the words were ahead of the soldiers. The soldiers would have been as quick as the words if the plan of the Emperor's government had been followed out. The Mexican government, at that period a prey to the most complete anarchy, without any effectual means, without any resources of consequence, offered no kind of resistance, and if, without being stopped by vain delays, the Spanish and French troops had marched upon the city of Mexico, they would have arrived there quicker than my words. [Good, good.]

See what a humane prudence had foreseen in France; it had calculated that a *corps d'armée* of about 12,000 men, supported by fleets girding the sea-coast, and having three useful months before them to bring an anarchical and disorganized government to a sense of reason, could, without striking a blow, or by the mere force of its courage, rapidly reach the city of Mexico. How has it happened that such prognostications have not been realized? How has it happened that this expedition, which the most far-sighted prudence had planned, both as to diplomatic agreement and military effectivity and means of execution, how has it happened, I say, that this expedition has momentarily but so unexpectedly miscarried? It is well to recall it to the Chamber. On the soil of Mexico the management of the affair was necessarily intrusted to the three plenipotentiaries, and there was manifested from the very first days a singular divergence of their respective opinions.

France had proclaimed, Spain and England had recognized with her, that the government of Juarez was a government without faith, without consistency, without guarantees; that it was impossible to treat seriously with it. The experience of many years, and especially of the last year, demonstrated that Mexican governments promised and never kept their promises. The three powers had recognized that force alone could master such a condition of things, and yet their representatives, having scarcely landed on the soil of Mexico, commence by recognizing the very government which had rendered itself unworthy of recognition, and by negotiating with it, when all negotiation had been recognized as useless, and all engagement on its part as illusory and superfluous. The treaty of La Soledad opens with this singular declaration, which I recall to the attention of the Chamber:

"*Preliminaries agreed upon between the Count of Reus and the Minister of Foreign Affairs of the Republic of Mexico.*

"1st. Admitting that the constitutional government which at present directs the affairs of Mexico has manifested to the commissioners of the allied powers that it has no need whatever of the assistance so kindly offered to the Mexican people, as having at its own disposal sufficient elements of force and public opinion to maintain itself against all intestine revolt, the allies, therefore, deem it their duty to enter upon the way of treaties for the purpose of drawing up the claims which they have to make in the name of their respective nations."

Thus our troops depart to combat Juarez, to impose on him by force our terms of satisfaction; our troops depart knowing that no faith can be placed in his promises; they go there to compel him to justice, and the first act of our representatives is to accept his ironical acknowledgments for a concurrence of which, he says, he has no need in order to maintain himself, and to enter into negotiations with him. Was that the policy of France? Was that in accordance with the instructions which had been given? Was that the policy prearranged with our allies? And that very same treaty of La Soledad, which recognized the government that our expedition purposed to combat, which accepted the faith of those whom we attacked as perjurers, that treaty adjourned to the 15th of April the opening of negotiations; that is, if they did not come to an agreement, and if the negotiations did not give necessary guarantees, the time for effective military action was passed, the season of rains and fevers was come, the roads were impassable, sickness decimated the soldiers, and war became impossible. And you are astonished when a conduct so dissimilar to that prescribed was adopted; you are astonished that the enterprise has not had the fortunate and rapid solution that it ought to have, and you throw the responsibility of it on those whose contrary prescriptions had regulated all with prudence and wisdom enough to bring things to a speedy and happy conclusion. [Good, good.]

Such is the true state of the case. The Emperor's government, as soon as it learned this strange magnanimity, seeing that the war would afterwards become impossible, and that there would result a prolonged and pernicious sojourn of our troops in the country, pronounced, in the Moniteur, a formal sentence of disapprobation on that unfortunate treaty, and by new despatches reminded those to whom it had given its first instructions that they had not gone there to negotiate uselessly with a perjured government, but to impose on it promptly, by its own full consent or by force, the will of our country. [Good, good.]

These new instructions reminded our representatives of the necessity of proceeding energetically, and of profiting by the little space of useful time yet remaining. And it was then that occurred that profoundly unexpected decision of Spain, withdrawing her troops, with the approbation and at the suggestion of the minister of England.

I have not to discuss that determination now. At Madrid, eminent men, speaking in view of the interests of their country, such as Mon, Bermudez de Castro, Concha, have explained it clearly and completely. As for us, it little matters now. [Good, good.] Only remark this well: by that unexpected determination France has remained alone, passing suddenly from the second place to the first. She has remained, with a handful of men, in the midst of a country in which they had allowed time to tyranny and its aids to prepare themselves, to fortify themselves, to frighten some and arouse others. [Good.]

She has remained there, in the face of the unhealthy season which was advancing—in the face of the vomito advancing with it. She has remained there; and I ask this assembly if she could recoil? [No, no.] And if she had retired, what would have been the consequences? Disgrace, in the first place, and our flag lowered in the eyes of the world. But what beside? Whilst we pursued this energetic and courageous policy, what advantages have accrued to those who have followed the opposite policy? [Good, good.] Last year I read from this desk a letter, in which a minister of Mexico, M. Doblado, congratulating General Prim on his chivalrous conduct, wrote to him: "We are going to regulate all these great affairs in half an hour; come, and in a few minutes we will have the glory of reconciling Spain and Mexico."

General Prim, as it seems, did not succeed in treating; but he sent his secretary to the city of Mexico, and that secretary, in a letter since made public, stated two things—one, the deep feeling of anger and despair of the Spaniards, abandoned in the capital of Mexico; the other, that the treaty was impossible, Juarez introducing, as the first condition, that Spain should pay the expenses of the war, [laughter,] whilst, as to him, he did not recognize himself as at war with that power. [Renewed laughter] Would you have counselled the government of your country to accept such conclusions? [Numerous voices—No, no.]

His excellency the MINISTER. The minister of England strongly approved the course of the Spanish plenipotentiary After having written to his government that he was about to leave Mexico and proceed to the Bermudas, in order not to give umbrage to France, and not to give occasion to think that he opposed her, he determined, however, to repair to the city of Mexico. [Laughter.]

A VOICE. In the English style.

His excellency the MINISTER. He has obtained a treaty. But what kind of treaty? It was easy to make promises; they have also been made to us, many of them, and they have always been violated. The difficulty was not to make Juarez promise; the difficulty was to make him keep his promise What was to be done? Sir Charles Wyke accepted as a guarantee the money which should be furnished by the United States; and in case the United States should not furnish any, and should be unwilling to ratify the treaty by which a part of the Mexican territory was pledged to them, he obtained the substitution of England in the concessions which the United States would have nothing to do with. [Laughter.]

I doubt whether such schemes as these would have been desirable to France; neither have they met with the sanction of the British government. It has not been thought proper, by accepting the money of the United States, thus tacitly to sanction this consecutive and progressive occupation of Mexico, pursued as a policy by the United States for twenty years, and which the government of Juarez only seeks to favor. [Good.] The British government refused its ratification.

Between the three courses of conduct you can judge which has been the most profitable, which has been most honorable. Spain has withdrawn her troops, the principal nucleus of the force which was to combat Juarez; the army of Spain has been re-embarked. In acknowledgment, they have plainly refused to reimburse her for the expenses of the war. [Renewed laughter.] England, with that firmness which she knows so well how to use in order to make herself respected, and which you will not take it ill that others should also practice as she does, [good, good,] England seems to have obtained a little more; but she has refused to consent to those schemes of policy which involved her against her views, and, so to speak, the final result has been negative. As for us, it is true we have remained alone, small in number, with a handful of brave men; thanks to the time lost, we have had to combat storms, fever, and Mexican bullets, but they have not inspired us with fear, and we have remained in Mexico. [Lively marks of approbation.] Under the influence of these unforeseen events we have been necessitated to lose the first military season, and endure that of rains; but the second military season is come at last, and this time there is neither desertion of allies nor parliamentary attacks to hinder us from profiting by it to insure the triumph of our flag. [Bravo, bravo.]

Behold, then, the state of the case very clearly. We might have imitated those who withdrew, but that our retreat, sad for our glory, would not have brought us, as them, any profit.

Do you find, then, as has been asserted, that this conduct is rash, adventurous, foolish? Is there, then, in all this, as was said the other day, anything dark? This is clear as the light of day. [Yes, yes; that is true.] The French government planned everything with wisdom and prudence. An unforeseen divergence, followed by a re-embarkment yet more unforeseen, has rendered the immediate success of the expedition impossible; but that which was deferred will not be lost. I know that to this rupture of the armistice of Orizaba it has been sought to assign motives which distort its character. I know that, instead of recognizing the resolute, politic line of national conduct, traced out by all our despatches, all our instructions, some persons have preferred to suppose other motives, and to endeavor to create scandal [That's so; good.] I shall not examine whether this manner of discussing the affairs of our country, when our soldiers are in face of the enemy, is very opportune. [Good, good.] I shall not examine whether it is not one of those occasions when patriotism ought at least defer the critical investigation of the opposition. [Renewed marks of approbation.] They have thought that, in spite of the military situation, they might endeavor to throw over the motives of the expedition impressions of blame and disfavor. They have thought that they might endeavor to reduce to what they call the interest of a rotten debt the cause for which the soldiers of France are at this moment combatting. I should prefer to be excused from discussing this question at the present time; but when honor is in question we must never shrink, whatever may happen. [Good, good.] I proceed, then, to examine closely whether this calumny of the Jecker debt has had any influence whatever on the conduct of the Mexican expedition.

Some persons wish to see in the expedition but two causes: a throne, which was but a secondary contingency, and the Jecker debt, of which certainly the government have scarcely thought when the expedition was decided on. But let us specify the facts. When, at the arrival of our troops in Mexico, it was requisite to establish in the ultimatum the amount of debts due us, to the total extent of our claims, as examined and reported by our consuls, the minister of England opposed a theory which, yesterday, found a supporter quite unexpected to me within this assembly. [Good.]

Sir Charles Wyke pretended that only such claims should be admitted into the ultimatum as were already liquidated by previous treaties What! Our last treaty is of the beginning of 1861 Since that, ill-treatment of every kind, all sorts of outrages, robberies, onerous and vexatious impositions, have weighed down our fellow-citizens, and we, armed to avenge them, armed to make their rights respected, and indemnify them for their losses, we should not comprise in our demands all the sums and all the reparations due to us. To what purpose, then, is the expedition? Our right was not only to compel respect for treaties and payment for the debts regulated by them, but at the same time to effect reparation of all the injuries caused since to our fellow-countrymen. Therefore, through our minister to Mexico, through our consuls at Vera Cruz, Tampico, and other places, we have caused to be made out a schedule of the sums due to our fellow-citizens.

The honorable speaker to whom I reply is astonished at these numbers: twelve millions of piastres, sixty millions of francs! He finds this amount excessive He estimates, as it seems, at a very low value the blood of our fellow-citizens, and the vexations of which they have been the victims. [Lively marks of assent from the Chamber.] The kindliness which he seems to entertain towards the government of Juarez ought not, however, make him forget that there is a government which concerns us more nearly, and that this government is that of France. [Renewed approbation] He contests the amount of these debts. Has he, then, had in his hand all the data requisite to estimate them properly? He produced many of them, but of the kind which the Mexican government might have, and I doubt whether the Mexican minister of finance possesses more than he. [Laughter.] He has made up in the greatest detail the account of the various payments made into the Mexican treasury. It would not have been bad likewise to make out the account of the outrages suffered by our fellow-citizens, and of the sums examined and settled by our consuls. [Good]

He has told you that we regulated them with a good deal of stupidity. The expression is harsh. Just before, he accused us of having deceived the Chamber, or, of having been kept in premeditated ignorance; now he accuses the government of stupidity! We are not, I confess, accustomed to such language, [good,] and if this language goes to the extreme limit of the rights of the opposition, we may be allowed, and it will be easy for us, at least, to reply to it.

Who could best appreciate the injuries done to our fellow-citizens on the soil of Mexico, if not those who witnessed them, and who were charged by their country to attend to them and state them? When a French citizen abroad is oppressed by any person whatever, to whom does he address himself? To his consul or to his minister. When he has to make proof of the injuries which he has received, who makes the official statement of them, his consul or his minister? When he has a claim against a foreign government that has violated his rights, who is his intermediary agent, his consul or his minister? Who, then, could know better than they the facts, the grievances, the character of the persons, the value of the injuries done, and fix the amount of them legitimately and fairly? Do you know the amount of documents accumulated in the archives of the legation at Mexico, and in the archives of our consuls at Vera Cruz, Tampico, and elsewhere? They were counted almost by thousands, so fruitful and active in their misdeeds are the brigands of Mexico. And there was there such a mass of claims that, to make out the official report of them in bureaucratic style, all the consular *personnel* could not suffice. For all these grievances the sum of twelve millions of piastres was fairly and conscientiously fixed. It was done by men best acquainted with the matter. And what would you wish the minister of foreign affairs to do here? Would you wish him to have all the documents, all the complaints, sent from Mexico, Vera Cruz, Tampico? And how would he have estimated them? Had he the witnesses at hand; those who had seen the robbery, the assassination, the burning; those who could attest the facts and determine the valuation? Were there not natural commissioners on the spot in the persons of the functionaries themselves who represented France? Moreover, recall to mind, since you are so anxious for the interests of our enemies, that it was proposed to submit to a complete and definite liquidation all the main points in demand comprised in the ultimatum. Is not this always the way in which these things are done? Each time that an indemnity is imposed on a country by force, is it not settled in gross, then distributed by a commission, which examines the titles of each one, and allows to each according to his rights? [Good, good.] This is what we have always offered—always understood. And, really, Mexico had no risk to run herein. It was impossible to impose on her payments in ready money. It was necessary to grant her numerous years of delay, and accept long and successive payments on her custom-house and other revenues, and the commissions would have plenty of time to verify anew and to liquidate all these debts; and if a reduction should be made on the amount, to give Mexico the benefit of it without doing any injustice. And, in truth, how is it possible to present France as seeking to speculate on claims made against an insolvent people? How does it happen that people have such feeble confidence in the representatives of the government of their country, in their sagacity, in their honor, that, without proof, without examination, without documents, they should proceed to accuse them of having overcharged the amount of reparations due? And for whose interest is this pretended overcharging? The whole was demanded exclusively for our countrymen, and for no one else than those who could justify and establish their right.

There was, I know, a protest made by Sir Charles Wyke against the amount of our claims. We have not thought proper in this respect to be reciprocal. In the arrangements made by England with Mexico, as in all those made with other nations, for the reparation of injuries done to her subjects, she does not seem to be accustomed to fall below what was legitimately due to her. [Approbative laughter.] There are before the world numerous examples on this point—the Pritchards, the Pacificos, and many others. I cannot blame the British government for making the balance, if needs be, incline on the side of its countrymen. It is well, thinks it to itself, that the world should be intimately persuaded that an English citizen is not to be touched with impunity.

Well, gentlemen, that which England puts in practice I consider wise, worthy, patriotic, politic for us to practice also. [Good, good.]

To sum up in brief, with regard to the amount of claims, the honorable gentleman to whom I reply was not informed, and we are. Moreover, no injustice was possible, for liquidation was offered, legitimate, conscientious, and fair liquidation. But in addition, gentlemen, remark that the British government itself has repudiated the pretensions of her representative, and acknowledged, on our calling attention to the subject, that none of the plenipotentiaries had any control over the amount of the claims of his colleagues, and this is the doctrine always put in force by England. When we accompanied her to China, when our flags floated there together and were even planted on the walls of Pekin, there were likewise indemnities to provide for and exact; England preserved her freedom of action, as we did ours. The facts, therefore, are in conformity with principles, and no novelty is practiced in this respect. [Approbation in the Chamber.] But I am aware that out of the mass of these legitimate claims some have wished particularly to bring forward one on which they hoped skilfully to rivet the attention of France and of the Chamber, and thereby cause all the rest to be forgotten. By means of the Jecker debt, they have striven to agitate the minds and excite the indignation of the public and make them suppose I know not what shameful imputations. These imputations, also, it is necessary to refute. [Good, good. Numerous voices: Rest awhile, rest awhile.]

(The Chamber takes a recess for a quarter of an hour. On assembling again the president announces that the minister without portfolio is entitled to the floor for the continuation of his speech.)

M. Billault, minister without portfolio. It will be easy for me, gentlemen, to show that the Jecker debt has had no influence whatever either in the declaration of war or in the rupture of the armistice of La Soledad. But that would not suffice for me; and it is necessary that, although it has had absolutely no influence on the course of events, this debt should itself be well known.

There is one thing which strikes me and makes me grieve for my country, [movement of attention;] it is the levity with which the most unseemly calumny alleged is willingly accepted as true. [Good, good.] It seems that the enunciation or imputation of any lamentable fact, made especially against persons in elevated station, is one of those strokes of good luck which make the joy and the satisfaction of every one. [Good, good.] And yet, in the end, when we look each other face to face, we know well what sentiment of honor animates us. We know well that we should respect each other reciprocally, and and that it is for no one's interest to bespatter his neighbor to-day with mire which will fall back on himself to-morrow. [Good.] Yet the people of France, so wonderful in their intellectual vivacity, are so constituted that the slightest insinuation of this kind goes on, grows big, and makes its way; and then, when the truth comes, it finds the minds of men either prejudiced or indifferent, and of that which they have accepted to-day they will not deign to hear the refutation to-morrow, or to think at all some days from hence. Governments are spared still less than individuals; but on them more than on any one it is incumbent to wage inexorable war with calumny. Honor is the life of the individual, but it is still more so the life of governments. [Good.] And in France a government that would not be jealous to excess of its honor would not long govern its country. [Enthusiastic and repeated applause] So, then, let us enter on the facts plainly.

It has been said, or at least we can conclude from what has been said, that in the Jecker affair there were some, I know not what, financial schemes of which the secret allurements might have influenced the determination of the government. What interest could the government have in this affair? How has it been produced? What advantages could flow from it? M. Jecker was a rich banker of the city of Mexico; born in France, at Porentruy, when Porentruy was part of a French department, he was classed at the French legation as French himself. He was connected with all works of French beneficence in the city of Mexico. [Interruption from the bench of M. Julius Favre.] I understand your interruption, and I doubt not but that the investigations and informations transmitted to you from Mexico by the friends of M. Juarez are hostile to M. Jecker; the men who despoil another, who throw him into prison, who drag him more than a hundred leagues under the deadly climate of Mexico in order to immure him in a murderous locality, whilst awaiting his expulsion, these men do not regard one calumny more or less. [Good, good.] We have been for some months inundated with Mexican calumnies; we have seen in circulation anonymous writings, anonymous papers, odious imputations of all kinds, furtively making their way by means of an indefatigable propaganda; it is the friends of our enemies in Mexico who thus send into France their correspondence and their poison. [Renewed and ardent approbation.] I understand that, when a person has the misfortune of having more faith in the assertions of Juarez and his friends than in those of the government of one's own country and in those of one's own fellow-citizens whom long years of honor have invested with public consideration, he accepts all imputations; but permit me to adopt a contrary course; permit me to believe rather in men of honor whom I know than in men whom I know not, or rather whom I know too well for their misdeeds. [Good.] M. Jecker, then, was the confidential depositary of nearly all the funds of the French colony, the depositary of all the funds of the French benevolent institutions, and he was not himself unconcerned in these benevolent associations. His brother, who had left him a part of his fortune, had bequeathed 100,000 francs to the hospitals of Paris and 200,000 francs to the Academy of Sciences. I do not mention this to throw any interest on M. Jecker; that is of little consequence to me; but what is of consequence to me is that it should be known that he was no less worthy of interest than others, and that if his character of Frenchman was disputable, the French engaged in consequence of their contract with the Mexican government, and who had their interests involved, had no less right to the protection of their country.

And what was the contract? Let us see. The regular government of Mexico under Miramon—and I say the regular government because it was at Mexico recognized by all the European powers, and they had their representatives near it—the government of Mexico, in 1859, fifteen months before the assistance of the United States rendered the overthrow of Miramon possible to Juarez, that government made a loan; this loan was negotiated at the nominal figure of fifteen millions of dollars with the Jecker house.

It has been asserted that the Jecker house, in its negotiation of this loan, imposed most onerous and usurious conditions. It is not my duty, in any way whatever, to justify the means of credit employed by successive governments at Mexico, and when the minister of England calculates at 12 per cent. the interest on the debts due to his countrymen, I acknowledge that high rates of interest are familiar to that country; I acknowledge, likewise, that a banker who has the boldness to lend to the government in a country in which fifty governments have succeeded each other in the space of forty years, such a banker is naturally induced to impose high terms.

I admit, then, that Miramon, on the one side, and Jecker, on the other, made a loan of which the conditions were very onerous to the Mexican nation, but that is not the question.

In order to attract the public into the scheme, the fifteen millions of Jecker bills were, by decree of the President of the Mexican republic, declared admissible, as a fifth part, in the payment of custom-house duties on all merchandise imported into Mexico. Now, as in consequence of the enormous depreciation of all Mexican securities, far from being negotiated at par, the Jecker bills were negotiated at a discount of from 70 to 75 per cent. of their nominal value, it was an advantage to pay 100 francs to the custom-house of the Mexican government in a paper currency bought at 25 or 30 francs. Consequently, all French and other merchants, who had to import into Mexico goods subject to duty, hastened to buy these bills in order to enjoy that advantage, and to pay 25 francs instead of 100 francs on the exorbitant duties imposed on foreign articles of commerce. Every Frenchman or other foreigner who, having goods to import, had bought these notes to pay the duties, was interested in having them continue to be received conformably with the engagement made; those same Frenchmen or foreigners who had further importations to make were also interested in the maintenance of that arrangement, since it was for them quite an important reduction of duties.

You see plainly, then, French or foreigner, commerce was seriously interested to have the Mexican government, which had treated with Jecker, carry into effect in regard to third persons, holders of these bills, the agreements to which it had subscribed.

This obligation was by so much the more binding on the Mexican government, as it had officially brought to the knowledge of all the foreign legations the stipulations of the contract which it had made with Jecker, and it showed that this was a diminution of duties to which it thus consented, and the sixth article of its decree of January 30, 1860, was to this effect: "As a guarantee of the execution of the preceding decree and of the decree of the 29th of October last, the supreme government will transmit copies of them to friendly legations, in order that they may inform in the ordinary way the subjects of their respective governments of the favor accorded to them by the government of the republic, and thereby give them the assurance that the present decree will be strictly executed."

It was on the faith of these promises made to the diplomatic body itself that these notes attained circulation and that foreigners received them. Had we any interest in compelling respect, as far as regarded the French holders of those notes, to the promise made to the public? [Yes, yes; that's evident. Good.] Had we any interest also in the maintenance of that agreement during the five years assigned for its duration, inasmuch as it caused a diminution of payment in the duties which our traders paid? (Yes, yes. Very good.) Had we any interest in causing to be respected, as to the present, and in maintaining, as to the future, a state of affairs which mitigated the custom-house duties on our merchandise? [Good, good.] This is the first point.

There is a second one. M. Jecker, having suffered, in the agitations of the country, a stroke which compromised his solvency, assigned some of these notes in guarantee of sums which he had received in deposit from various establishments of French benevolence. Had we any interest to have those notes respected, which were the guarantee of a French institution? [Yes, yes.] In fine, M. Jecker, the banker of nearly all the French residents in Mexico, (his house was considered as French,) had among our countrymen numerous creditors; the active principal of that house likewise depended on those notes. Had we any interest in preventing this active principal from being reduced to nothing by an act of the dictatorial will of Juarez? [Yes, yes; that's plain.] French interests, then, in this affair, were very plain and very evident.

As to M. Jecker, he made an arrangement with the Mexican government which the honorable gentleman who last spoke finds onerous, and against which he defends the government of Juarez. Be it so; Juarez will thank him for this favor. [Laughter.]

But what wrong has the French government done on this point? Accusations are brought against it, and there are some expressions which cannot be let pass.

Some persons have spoken of speculators concealing themselves behind diplomacy. Indeed, people are as fruitful in grave accusations as they are powerless to prove them. Awhile ago, the government had deceived the Chamber; it had conducted matters with the most deplorable stupidity; and now, behold, we have cloudy glimpses of speculators hiding behind diplomacy. Let us speak plainly; that means, in good French, that diplomacy has been willing to serve the illegal interests of anonymous speculators. [That's so.] Well, I give to this assertion the most solemn and the most categoric lie. [Good, good.]

That there be about the government, that there be about Juarez, people dabbling in the base depths of their private interests, I know nothing of the thing, and would not be astonished at it. Do we not see, even in this country of honor and loyalty named France, in presence of a government that keeps no measures with improbity, do we not see too often in some miserable stock-jobbing operations men boast of efficacious intrigues and potent influences, in order to obtain results from others which in reality they will never obtain. [Good, good.]

As for me, when I had the honor of being minister of the interior, I received vague denunciations of this kind quite frequently; and of those who made them I demanded, in the name of Heaven and of my country's honor, to give me the least indication, the least trace, by which I might be able to verify the facts which they denounced to me and render full and entire redress. [Good, good.] My adjurations were fruitless, and I saw the accusations, when confronted with a perspicuous and energetic interrogatory, fade away and vanish as a miserable vapor. It will be the same here, gentlemen. [Good.]

Much has been said about the seventy-five millions of the Jecker affair. Seventy-five millions! What a magnificent pasturage! What an attractive spoil for the speculators that are supposed to lurk behind diplomacy! Here is, indeed, a mirage to seduce the vulgar; but this spoil which you invent does not exist.

The seventy-five millions spoken of were in Jecker bills, negotiable at Mexico—negotiable at the depressed rate usual with the currencies of that government; that is, at a discount of about 75 per cent. on their nominal value, and acceptable only in payment of custom house duties, without ever being otherwise redeemable by the Mexican treasury. A part of them has thus returned—I know not how much, and I would gladly ask the honorable gentleman, who knows the figures so well; as to the rest, they are either partly in the hands of the merchants who procured them for the payment of duties, or held in trust by the creditors of Jecker, or thrust into his own hands as he was seized, arrested, transported, imprisoned on the shores of the Pacific, dying, perhaps, at this moment from the effects of the brutal expulsion and the forced journey which he has been compelled to undergo, but yet required to account, under the decree for the sequestration of his effects, solvent or insolvent. What possible speculations could there be in France on such notes under such circumstances? What is the possible magnificent affair capable of corrupting our diplomacy and our government? Mention it, and be specific in your accusations. [Good, good.]

Now, gentlemen, that you know the facts, one word on the action of the government in regard to that debt.

On the 31st of December, 1860, at the moment when Juarez obtained possession of the city of Mexico and overthrew Miramon, the rumor was circulated that the Jecker contract would no longer be carried out, and a considerable number of French merchants addressed a petition to the minister of France, in which they, with good reason, observed that the Jecker notes had been issued under the faith of engagements entered into by the state, and of assurances given to the legations, and that the advantages thus assured in commerce ought to be respected.

Whilst at Mexico the French, who were interested in the matter, drew up this remonstrance; at Paris other French merchants, equally numerous and honorable, themselves engaged in commerce with Mexico, and aware that the destruction of these bills of credit would entail severe losses on their own affairs, addressed themselves to the minister of foreign affairs of France in order to make the same observations to him. Under these circumstances what ought our government to do? Frenchmen in France, Frenchmen abroad, on the faith of a government recognized by France, had accepted notes of that state as payable at the custom-house. Was it not a strict duty to make representations to the new master of Mexico and to remind him that the engagements of the preceding government ought to be kept? The French minister wrote, in consequence, on the 6th of March, 1861, to our representative in Mexico; we were yet at that period on terms of friendship with M. Juarez; we were willing to hope still that his government would procure a little more security and order for foreigners living in the country.

So, what happened? The minister of President Juarez, M. Zarco, having entered into negotiations on this point with our minister at Mexico, objected the poverty of the republic, and the fact that the engagement had been made by their enemy to sustain the civil war. But we answered him, "The engagement was made by a government *de facto* existing, recognized, having our minister accredited near it. Governments that succeed each other are responsible for the pecuniary engagements of their predecessors." [Approbation.] That is a fundamental principle which we cannot permit to be ignored; it is the principle on which public credit and public faith repose in the engagements of nations. And M. Zarco, in the despatches which I have already had occasion to cite last year, recognized the principle, recognized the obligation of his government. Permit me to read to you on this subject one only of his letters.

He wrote on the 4th of May, 1861, to M. de Saligny: "My dear sir: I am obliged to you for the confidential explanations which, by your letter of the day before yesterday, you have been pleased to add to your note relative to the Jecker question, and also because you have taken into consideration the difficulties and the embarrassments by which my government is surrounded, and all that is most painful to it *in the responsibility for the fatal heritage* of the faction commanded by Miramon.

"I am, likewise, much obliged to you for the efforts that you have made to induce M. Jecker to make some concessions. In reply to your letter, I have the honor to inform you that, as soon as the question of principle involved shall be satisfactorily decided, the details of execution will be easily arranged, according to the means of the government and its powers on certain points, and taking, moreover, into consideration the propositions of M. Jecker, contained in your letter."

Here, then, behold the negotiation entered on, the basis accepted, serious hopes held out by the government of Juarez, and the duty of the French government fulfilled. This had no connexion with the Mexican war, which broke out only at a later period. Well, such being the state of affairs, when the war did break out, when the French were, in every way, more and more violently treated, when they were plundered, imprisoned, expelled, should the French government, in making out the long inventory of the ignored rights of its citizens, not mention in its ultimatum that agreement of which the enemy's government itself had recognized the principle?

And what, after all, was demanded of the Mexican government? Was it seventy-five millions in ready money? By no means; indeed, it was asked only to continue to execute fairly the engagements entered into by its predecessor—that is, to receive at the custom-houses, in payment of a fifth part of the duties, the notes that had been issued under that condition by the preceding government.

Once again: there is no trace here of any pretended speculation. Recall to mind, moreover, what a spirit of benevolent equity presided over the establishment of all these claims; permit me to remind you in what terms M de Saligny himself expressed himself at the time of estimating the various debts. He had, with advice, made out a report of them as conscientiously as possible; he gave their details, then he added, in his despatch of January 20, 1862:

"If your excellency thinks proper to adopt my views on this subject, (the liquidation of the debts,) I would propose to refer all questions relative to our claims to a commission, composed of his Majesty's consul at Vera Cruz, the secretary of the imperial legation, and a merchant. This scheme would, among other advantages, in my eyes, have that of relieving the responsibility of the Emperor's minister—a responsibility more weighty and more dangerous in Mexico than any where else, and to place his person above the recriminations and attacks of calumny."

And yet, on the question of the Jecker contract, it was not, I repeat, in the case at all to ask a dollar of the government of Juarez, it was not in the case that it should pay out the smallest sum; there was question merely that it should maintain the decree admitting the notes created by its predecessor in payment of custom-house duties; and yet the question being thus placed, the Emperor's government does not the less accept the propositions of M. de Saligny, and in several despatches it expresses the desire that all the debts due to France should be liquidated by a commission, that nothing should be paid out of the Mexican funds but what might be legally due from it, what might be regularly verified.

Such are the facts; and yet you were told yesterday, "Behold what examples of fairness France is going to give the New World." I confess that such words pronounced in this assembly have deeply grieved me. What! People in Mexico, on the authority of what is said here, may make a like imputation on the honor of our nation! They can say, "It is not we who accuse it of injustice and disregard of right; it is its own citizens; it is among its own citizens—men eminent for their talents, and elevated by the public vote to the representation of the country."

Indeed, when the facts are reduced to what you know now, those words, in my opinion, were very unjust and much to be regretted. [Approbation.]

I forgot one detail which I must not pass over. [Louder, louder.]

They spoke yesterday of some correspondence or other intercepted and published at Mexico, then numerous copies sent to Paris. The government of Mexico has sent many papers to Paris, many prints, many accusations of every kind. I thought that the calumnies against the government of France had their principal laboratories in certain neighboring countries. I see now that another laboratory, a powerful and active focus, is established beyond the seas. Hatred against the Emperor's government inspires certain ultra democrats with a fertility of accusations and calumnies inexhaustible. I shall not deign to make any further allusion to this pretended document seized by a hostile government, intercepted by it, printed by it, sent by its care through the world, without anything to testify its value or its authenticity.

I shall confine myself to reminding you that it is testified by our diplomatic documents that the party of Juarez has used all its efforts to sweep the whole French colony into this torrent of calumny, and that the great majority of this colony, in their indignation, have energetically protested.

You have in the documents distributed among you the legal protests our countrymen declare, in spite of the menaces of Juarez that they wish to absolve the French colony from the responsibility of these odious manœuvres. [Good.]

Let us then put aside all these calumnies, and let us return to the Mexican expedition, for the Jecker affair was but an odious veil that was endeavored to be thrown over it. That affair, you see, henceforth is of no account in the expedition. It is of no greater account in the rupture of the preliminaries of La Soledad. That rupture dates from the month of April, and, as early as the month of January, the difficulty arising from the valuation of the debts had been deferred by the plenipotentiaries by common consent until the solution was given by their respective governments. Moreover, in the very first stages of the difficulties, our minister had formally obtained leave to discard this debt for the time being, which General Prim approved, and which the English plenipotentiary, after having seemed to agree to it, finished by rejecting.

Yet M. de Saligny ceased not to repeat, "Well, let us defer the Jecker debt; let us not nsert it in the ultimatum; let us not speak of it; we will afterwards see what is to be done with it."

Let it not be said, then, that the Jecker debt, comprised in the French ultimatum in the month of January, has had any kind of influence on the conduct of the plenipotentiaries in the month of April. It had none for two reasons: the first, because M. de Saligny himself offered to defer it; the second, because the difficulty of that ultimatum, being referred to the examination of the governments, in no way hindered collective diplomatic action during the two months that followed.

Here, then, gentlemen, are the two things for which it was sought to complicate, darken, distort, calumniate the expedition to Mexico: the enthroning, as the sole, or at least principal end of an Austrian prince on the one side, and a pretended, shameful speculation on the Jecker notes, on the other. Behold them reduced to their just value. [Approbation.]

I forgot one final word. Yesterday they indicated as a special favor of the French government the precipitate insertion in the Bulletin des Lois of the naturalization of M. Jecker.

This precipitation, gentlemen, is presented in these terms: the decree of naturalization is of the 26th of March, and the excessive favor obtained by the petitioner is that the decree of the 26th of March was inserted in the Bulletin des Lois of the 31st of August, after five months!

I shall delay no longer on this point. I shall not examine what advantage Jecker could have in causing himself to be naturalized a Frenchman—he who was born in France in 1812; nor how his naturalization could cover, to a certain extent, his own interests at the same time as those of other Frenchmen. Let him be naturalized to-day, to-morrow, or six months hence; that makes no change whatever in the affair or in the injustice of the imputations. [Marks of assent]

Now—and remark well what I say—it is not only the Mexican expedition that is attacked in the amendment submitted to you; it is the whole policy of France; it is the general policy which you have approved, which you have received with acclamation, in which you have been intimately associated. It is in the name of a programme opposed and violently opposed to yours that the authors of the amendment present themselves.

Yesterday you heard strange words; you were asked, "Who are you, and what are your names?"

The government to which these words were addressed is that which eight millions of votes have founded. [Good, good.] It is that which a legislative body, nominated by the same number of votes, has supported for ten years, with its devotedness and its vote. [Good, good] This government, of which you ask what it is and what is its name, is all France. [Good, good.] She it is who, by means of her sovereign and her deputies, defends her honor in that New World and upholds her interests there [Good, good.]

Oh, I know well that the authors of the amendment cannnot be of the opinion of this Chamber on the great things done by the Emperor with its concurrence; I know well that there is not one glorious expedition to which they have not refused their support. [That's so; that's true.] I know well that for five years there is not an appropriation against which they have not voted. But that is no reason why the policy of the Emperor and of this Chamber should be thus treated. They qualify it as hazardous, rash. Let us say one word, in passing, with regard to the general scope of this policy; it is not only in reference to the vote on the amendment that this appears to me desirable: beyond this discussion, beyond the limits of this session, there will be rendered a solemn judgment on the policy of the country—a judgment not on your persons but on your votes—a judgment which will include the great acts in which you have shared. Now, it is not well for France, it is not well for Europe, it is not well for any one to let this great epoch be calumniated. [Good.]

The policy which France has pursued, which they dare to call rash and adventurous expeditions, is not one of those fanciful policies that a sovereign can follow one day and abandon the next, according to his caprices, and to the detriment of his country. There are, in a great nation reckoning fourteen centuries of existence, there are traditions, there are positions taken, there are necessities imposed, and it does not depend upon a government nor on its caprice to neglect the permanent interests of its country; these national and traditionary interests the government can neither ignore nor forget. [Very good.] And the greatness of its ability, its renown, and its glory—that of those who associate themselves with its course and sustain it with their vote, are proportionate to the degree in which it knows how to uphold them and render them triumphant. Let us see, then, whether they are found in these expeditions styled rash and adventurous.

There are throughout, and especially in the east, considerable rivalries, difficult situations, easily inflammable, on which Europe has her eyes perpetually fixed. There are there some of those political combinations of which the hopes of settlement are often deferred, but never abandoned. It is there in order to restrain the different influences and resume our own that we made our great Crimean expedition; we have conquered there the prestige of our ascendency; we have re-established in the world that position which, heretofore, for a moment depressed, has been, to the great joy, to the just pride of France, raised again with renewed splendor. [Ardent manifestations of assent from the Chamber.]

When, after this grand result obtained, our victorious fleet and army traversed the Black sea, we could, with legitimate satisfaction, compare this triumph to our isolation in 1840. [Very good.] Compare this glory to that check; compare this predominance to that inferiority. [Good, good]

We had nearer home, in Italy, time-honored interests: a neighboring power had, little by little, by force, and by the skill of her policy, made her influence predominant over the whole Italian peninsula. A small corner alone yet remained; but soon her standard threatened to be planted at the foot of the Alps. There was there a traditional rivalry, and so the necessity for our country to withdraw Italy from an influence singularly favored against us by the treaties of 1815. At a given day we crossed the Alps, and in two months the influence which centuries of open or hidden struggle had not succeeded in shaking disappeared from the soil of Italy. [Good, good.] Compare this glorious result with the occupation, but also with the evacuation, of Ancona.

Thousands of leagues from France, in the extreme east, there is a country where formerly great possessions belonged to us, where the French name was once powerful and glorious; but all this splendor had been effaced; some feeble reminiscences survived, nourishing some regrets for the past, but no hope in the future. Well, in accord with the power which so long had been our rival, we have penetrated into the heart of China to plant at the same time the symbol of the faith which we protect, and to open a world to our commerce: we have caused to be recognized there anew the glorious banner of France and the power of her arm. The east has resumed its ancient deference towards us; we have seen within our walls the ambassadors of Siam and Japan; between Singapore and China an immense and magnificent possession takes, under our flag, a rapid march towards a brilliant future; our packets proceed, henceforth, to furrow those seas; in face of Aden, at the mouth of the Red sea, they will find, likewise, under the flag of France a point of repose and for taking in supplies; Russia, in the northern part of the orient, gives to her influence and her possessions a series of magnificent developments; England, in the centre of Asia, has one of the most splendid seats of her power; we can, by the side of these two rival and armed powers, contemplate, without much regret, the results obtained by us and fearlessly compare them with the negative results formerly obtained by the diplomatic promenade of M. de Lagrénée. [Approbative laughter.]

Here are some of the great features of this policy of France which has been so fiercely attacked; here are the luminous beacons by which the patriotism of our fellow-citizens will recognize the deputies who have voted for that policy [Enthusiastic approbation.]

By the side of these great interests we had others also in Mexico; and it was not merely the obligation of enforcing respect for our countrymen and our rights; there, also, great political vistas are open to clear-sighted eyes; diverse interests come in contact, and it is not opportune to neglect them. [Very good.] But to avenge our rights ignored by a tyrannical government and to raise the Mexican nation, if possible, were, also, works of sound policy.

And it is at the moment when our arms seek to realize this policy that some dare within this assembly to characterize the enterprize confided to the courage of our soldiers as rash, adventurous, and inspired by detestable motives.

Under the circumstances I consider these words deplorable: happily, in opposition to the five isolated names which are subscribed to them, all France will arise—[Yes, yes]—jealous of her glory, jealous of the honor of her flag, careful of the protection which she owes to her children.

You, gentlemen, you are, by the millions of suffrages that you represent, the real organs here of the sentiments of the country. It is your part to decide solemnly on what has been said. The words, the sad words which you have heard, are going to pass the Atlantic rapidly; and, I say it with grief, they will gladden, on the soil of America, all the enemies of the renown of France. [Good, good.] Well, gentlemen, let the same vessel that carries them, carry, likewise, the protest of an entire nation. [Bravo, bravo.]

Proclaim, let us all proclaim together, in the name of the Emperor and of the people indissolubly united in a patriotic solidarity, let us proclaim that the war which we wage with Mexico is just and fair. [Yes, yes; very good, very good.]

Our soldiers go there to sustain our honor, to punish perjury, to avenge the blood of our fellow-citizens, to avenge the extortions of which they have been the victims. They go, as the Emperor has well said, to prove once more that there is in this world no country so distant that an attempt on the honor of France may remain unpunished there. [Repeated and more animated marks of assent] May they, incidentally, if they can, scatter some seeds of order and liberty in that unhappy country, crushed down by fifty years of tyranny and brigandage.

But when, after having fulfilled their duty loyally, bravely, to the glory of their country, when they return to their country I can assert, and you with me, that they will be followed by the benedictions of those thousands of Frenchmen scattered over the surface of the New World, and to whom they shall have restored security; and on the shores of their native land they will be received by the unanimous acclamations of a whole people sincerely grateful for the fatigues which they shall have braved, for the blood which they shall have spilled for the honor of France and the maintenance of her good rights. [Bravo, bravo. General acclamations. Three cheers follow the speech of his excellency the minister.]

M. JULES FAVRE. I claim the floor.

NUMEROUS VOICES. No, no. Enough, enough. Let us vote.

A MEMBER. That's not fair ; let him reply to the minister.

The PRESIDENT. No written regulation gives to a member of the opposition the right to reply to a minister, but it is a traditional right. At present, whatever be the impatience of the Chamber, the government and the men who surround it have been so shamefully calumniated in this affair, that, in my opinion, what is most proper is to permit a reply. [General marks of assent ; good, good.]

M. JULES FAVRE. Gentlemen, the expressions by which our honorable president has accorded me the floor present a double aspect. He has invoked a traditional usage which is not reproduced by any written text, and he has added that the men of the government had been calumniated, and that it was fair to permit a rejoinder. This last impeachment cannot reach those who fulfil their duty here. [Exclamations.]

A VOICE. Why not? We fulfil ours also.

M. JULES FAVRE. And as to me, if there was, in what Mr. President has said, anything whatever personal to myself, I would protest most earnestly against an insinuation of that nature. I have invoked facts, I have submitted them to the judgment of the Chamber. The minister has made a reply ; I ask permission of the Chamber to make a few brief observations.

These observations, gentlemen, are necessary in order to specify the real state oft he case, and to allow you, after becoming acquainted with each of the elements of this great debate, to resolve it with entire intelligence. And, as you may understand, I have no intention of replying to that part of the discourse of the minister without portfolio, in which, in accordance with an ancient and well known system of action, employed by the supporters of the government against the members of the opposition, he told you that those who criticised the acts of the administration were factious. [Animated reclamations.]

SEVERAL VOICES. That was not said.

M. JULES FAVRE. And that it behooved us, above all, to believe in the loyalty of its intentions, in the sincerity of its declarations, and in the justness of its views. I have said, gentlemen, similar proceedings are familiar to him who now has recourse to them, but they can have no sort of influence on your minds. [Murmurs of disapprobation.] It is of the truth of facts that there is question. These facts I endeavored, in yesterday's session, to point out precisely, with the assistance of the diplomatic documents laid before us, and it is especially relying on these documents that I characterized, as I deemed it my duty to do, the Mexican expedition in its purpose and in its consequences.

I said, as regards its purpose, that it had been concealed from the Chamber. I said that when last year the cabinet explained the intentions of the government in regard to this expedition, not only it exclusively intrenched itself behind this great and national reason of the reparation of the grievances of our countrymen, but also it energetically denied all kind of participation in any design involving a foreign prince. I do not wish to quote in this regard the texts that may at this moment be before your eyes ; you know them, and you know that, when I interrogated the cabinet on this point, the cabinet replied in the most positive manner that those who had really believed such reports had been convinced that they were calumnious, that they had no foundation in reality. And at the very moment when the minister spoke, he might have had in his hands the despatch of the minister of foreign affairs, avowing that overtures had been made to the Archduke Maximilian, and that these overtures were accepted. [Interruption.]

Allow me, gentlemen. There is, then, in this regard nothing whatever, I will not say refuted, but shaken, in the assertions which I made in the session of yesterday and in the judgment which I passed.

Now, when the minister, striving to distort and misplace the question, [animated reclamations,] repeats to you that the expedition has been exclusively undertaken in order to avenge the honor and security of our countrymen, when the minister imputes to the government, of which they have gone to demand this satisfaction, the responsibility of all the previous acts, I take the liberty to remind him of two things: the first, that Juarez did not enter the city of Mexico until the end of December, 1860, and that most of the acts on account of which our reclamations have been addressed are anterior to that date ; and the second, which is no less important, that the same men who may have been guilty of those acts of violence, of those murders, of those assassinations, of those pillagings, are precisely those whom we now shelter under our flag, who march beside our soldiers. [Denials.]

You deny it, gentlemen. [Yes, yes.] Listen on this point to the despatch just awhile ago placed before your eyes by the minister, though only in part. I refer to that which bears the date of October 28, 1861, and which was sent by Sir Charles Wyke to his government. The minister read to you that part of the despatch in which it is said that the experience of every day tends to show the impossibility of establishing a regular and stable government in Mexico, but he did not read the following :

"Marquez is at some leagues from the capital with 3,000 or 4,000 men; he has pillaged lately about $50,000 from the mine of Real del Monte, a mine in which English capitalists are largely interested."

And it is precisely Marquez, Marquez covered with European blood, Marquez who has been at times noted for his ferocity in his military executions, it is he who has come to the French camp, and who has been received by our generals. It is he who, at this very hour, with Almonte, with all the persons of the reactionary government, figures among those considered as our allies.

I have, then, the right to say that not only the purpose of the Mexican war was not that indicated by the minister, [reclamations,] but also that when they impute to Juarez all the acts inducing this war, all the acts of pillage which are but the consequences of the disorders. [Increasing noise and tumult.] You do not wish to let me speak.

SOME VOICES. Yes, yes.

M. JULES FAVRE I have to reply, and I ask the Chamber permission to do so in a few words, to what the minister has said concerning the ultimatum which I have described as having been one of the causes of the rupture of the negotiations.

I have reproached our diplomatic agents with having acted without precise instructions, and with having sent to the Mexican government a note containing demands of an intolerable nature. On this point, has the minister's reply been able to satisfy your consciences?

NUMEROUS VOICES. Yes, yes.

M. JULES FAVRE If it is so, it is, I believe, because you do not know the whole truth. [So! so!]

I said, in effect, that when the ultimatum was drawn up, the claims for money to be made by the French government on the Mexican government had been inflated in a manner extremely grievous [Murmurs.]

A VOICE Let him speak.

M. JULES FAVRE. I added that the French minister had acted in the matter without having previously the approbation of the head of his government. I supported this argument by reading the diplomatic despatches, with which you are acquainted.

The minister replies to me that there never has been an ultimatum for 12,000,000 of piastres—that is, 60,000,000 of francs—and that the possibility was always reserved of having the claims examined by a commission of merchants The minister is mistaken, gentlemen, and he is mistaken for these two reasons, which are equally explicit:

First. Because in diplomatic language the word *ultimatum* signifies a demand in which there is nothing to be retrenched; it is necessary to accept it or to prepare for battle; and when 12,000,000 of piastres were demanded as an ultimatum, it was 12,000,000 of piastres to be paid down.

The second reason, gentlemen, and which is not less explicit, but which has, I cannot explain why, escaped the sagacity of the minister, is, that in the very article in which there is question of those 12,000,000 piastres, certain debts are reserved to be taken into consideration by commissions. See, in effect, how this reserve is conceived. After setting down as an ultimatum the payment of 12,000,000 of piastres, it continues: "Saving the exceptions stipulated in articles 2 and 4, below. As far as concerns matters that have happened since the 31st of July last, and for which an express reservation is made, the amount of the claims against Mexico to which they may give rise will be afterwards settled by the plenipotentiaries of France." [Increasing tumult and murmurs.]

So the 12,000,000 of piastres are an ultimatum; it is a debt which must be immediately paid, under penalty of a declaration of war; and as for other debts, they will be the object of a future liquidation.

I had the right, then, gentlemen, to reproach the government with having thus made a means of war. [Oh! oh! renewed interruption.]

As far as concerns the Jecker bills, the minister has offered explanations very ingenious, undoubtedly, yet containing extremely important concessions, which must necessarily alarm your consciences.

The minister reproaches me with having made use of documents sent by the government of Mexico.

There was, it seems to me, a very simple means of preventing such an inconvenience; it was to furnish the committee on the address with all the documents at the disposal of the minister; for when the minister asserts his ignorance of the details of this Jecker debt, he asserts a fact which, for my part, I have considerable difficulty in believing. [Murmurs of disapprobation.]

It is impossible that the minister should not have in his hands all the data relative to this affair. He has said himself, and he was right, that it was of such a nature as to throw a disagreeable obscurity over our negotiations.

SEVERAL VOICES. He did not say that.

M. JULES FAVRE. Why did he not furnish all the information in regard to it? [Increasing disorder.] The examination of that affair might have had an opposite result; he has made none, and thereby he gives us the right—what do I say? he makes it a duty for us to institute all possible investigations. From the investigations which we have caused to be made, it appears—and this is atrocious—that the usurious rate at which the loan of 1859 was effected has been kept concealed. The minister has been compelled to acknowledge ——[To the vote; to the vote. Long interruption.] You are not willing that people should speak to you about these things; France will judge, and I will remain silent.

(M. Jules Favre sits down.)

SEVERAL VOICES. Speak; speak.

SOME MEMBERS. No; enough, enough; to the vote.

The PRESIDENT. I cannot hinder the Chamber from testifying impatience. I ask M. Jules Favre whether he desires to continue or whether he yields the floor.

M. JULES FAVRE, rising It is impossible for one as fatigued as I am, after the session of yesterday, to be able to struggle against systematic interruptions [no, no,] which have no other intention than to disturb me in the expression of my ideas. [Numerous reclamations.]

SEVERAL VOICES Speak; speak.

The PRESIDENT. Allow me. I desire merely to protest against the accusation which you make against the Chamber. Yesterday the Chamber listened to you with such attention that you cannot accuse it of designedly interrupting you to-day. It is only very natural that a question which has engaged its attention for two days should weary it to a certain extent. [Yes, yes.] I cannot, on this point, direct the sentiments of an Assembly. I ask you again whether you wish to continue your speech or whether you yield the floor. [Speak; speak]

M. JULES FAVRE. I understand very well the fatigue of the Assembly, and I ask a thousand pardons for prolonging it; I ask it to believe that mine is still greater; but this is a question of business, not a question of feelings. [Denials, confusion and disorder.] You see that I cannot speak, since at the least word you interrupt me. [No, no; speak. Silence is restored.]

I was saying, gentlemen, when I was interrupted in my explanations, that the minister was unable to conceal the disastrous terms on which the Jecker loan was negotiated; only, by explanations deeply skilful, he has presented this affair before you as possibly having in some way a direct influence on the whole commerce of Mexico; and in this way only, he tells you, France ought to sustain it.

If it were so, gentlemen, if negotiations had been commenced under such conditions, we would never have, in this regard, the slightest observation to make to the government. But the facts as well as the documents completely resist the minister's interpretation.

Documents, gentlemen; what is the question? A contract entered into between the Jecker house and the Mexican government, a contract which makes the Mexican government liable for a sum of 15,000,000 of piastres, if Jecker proves that the notes have passed out of his hands or that he has furnished them in currency. I thought I showed in yesterday's session that he had furnished all the receipts expected of him by the Mexican government. I presented figures on this point which, it seems to me, deserved the trouble of refutation. Nothing has been said in this regard; and if my reasoning stands, what is the consequence? It is that all the holders of the notes of Jecker, on closing accounts, have a right to obtain of the Mexican government the nominal value of these bills [No, no.]

You say no, and I say yes And do you know the means which I would propose to clear up this affair completely? It would be that, from now to the discussion of the Budget, the minister would please to communicate to the committee on the budget the Jecker documents as well as the others, in order that there may not be either surprise or doubt possible—in order that every one may see clearly into this affair, and know what has been, in reality, the part of each one concerned in the transaction.

As far as concerns our agents, whom we are accused of calumniating, permit me to make this observation, which has certainly struck you: the conduct of the government towards them has been very singular. I do not reproach it with having, in the beginning, blindly relied upon their communications; but, as soon as they were invested with its full powers, what did they do? They made a use of them which has been here declared contrary to the interests of the country; for the signatures of these agents are found subscribed to the treaty of La Soledad, which has been disavowed. Well, whatever praise the government may decree to itself, and whatever the complacency with which it speaks of its own acts, I ask the Chamber if it is reasonable, if it is just, if it is prudent, to keep agents at such a distance who have thus compromised the interests of France. They have been invested with sovereign powers; what use have they made of them? I have proved that in the ultimatum, so far as concerns the question of the twelve millions and the Jecker bills, they have acted with a want of reflection, blamed not only by the opposition but by the minister of foreign affairs; for the article 3, which has become the subject of discussion between the minister and myself, does not at all admit, as the minister just asserted, of any liquidation whatever of the Jecker debt. It is perfectly clear, and it contains the armed threat against the Mexican government of compelling it to pay the sum of seventy-five millions.

"Mexico shall be bound to execute fully, fairly, and immediately the contract concluded in the month of February, 1859, between the Mexican government and Mr. Jecker." [Interruption.]

Now, theminister has told you that the execution of this contract could only apply to custom-house duties. [Disorder.] Permit me, gentlemen, to tell you that nothing is more frivolous, nothing more inadmissible [Reclamations.] There is no question, assuredly, in regard to the Jecker house, of the payment more or less enfeebled of custom-house duties, of concessions which the Mexican government might have made to the holders of the notes. When there is question of the execution of a contract, we should regard the end, we must see this end; now, there *is* question of seventy-five millions claimed of the Mexican government.

Behold, gentlemen, this affair such as it is. And it is this affair which I have had the right to qualify as shameful, because it conceals under the appearance of a debt due, a real usury. I have demonstrated with positive figures, not disproved, that Jecker furnished but an insignificant sum compared to that which he claims; I have demonstrated that he wished to extortf rom the Mexican government, and that those who have associated themselves to his course merit a solemn rebuke; they have led the French government into a veritable snare. And it is not by recourse to subterfuges, but by positive explanations, that I have demonstrated that it has been sought to make the Mexican government pay seventy-five millions; and as to what has been told us awhile ago by the minister, that the bills were for the most part in the hands of Jecker—that Jecker having failed, his notes were sequestrated, nothing is more inexact: the minister was ill informed; we know it, not from the Mexicans, but from the French residents who have been included in the liabilities of the Jecker house. Jecker having been declared a bankrupt in the month of May, 1860, obtained, some time in July, a judgment replacing him at the head of his affairs, whilst according him *speranzas*—that is, hopes for the creditors who will run after their dividends, but will never realize them.

It is in this situation that Jecker negotiated with the French resident minister, in order to have his contract become an object of express stipulation in the ultimatum. He was the holder of almost all these notes; there were not 600,000 piastres in the hands of the merchants; the greater part of these notes, or 14,000,000 of piastres, are in the hands of Jecker. Jecker may have been able to assign them at any price to traffic in them; and it is precisely because there was under this affair a speculation, which was divined by the English minister, that it was brought to the notice of the minister of foreign affairs, and the minister of foreign affairs, either in his instructions or in his replies, explained that when there would be question of liquidating this affair, they would confine themselves to French interests entirely. And it is here we come upon that momentous fact over which the minister seems to me to have glided with great rapidity.

It has been declared that the Jecker debt caused a kind of uneasiness in the consciences of the merchants. Explanations were asked; the minister was alarmed himself; he wrote to M. Dubois de Saligny that it was impossible to execute anything else than what concerned the French; and then as the principal party interested in that contract was a stranger, a Swiss, in the midst of those negotiations, considered suspicious by the English and Spanish chanceries, haste was made to grant this man letters of naturalization, in order that he might be enabled to figure as a Frenchman, in order that he might be enabled to accomplish his work, and make the Mexican government the victim of his usury. Behold the truth with regard to the Jecker affair.

Had I not, then, the right to say that our diplomacy has gone astray here, that this *ultimatum* was without precedent in our history, and that, in consequence, the Chamber, which should take some position with regard to this expedition, was interested, in point of honor as well as in point of policy, to separate itself from that part of the negotiation?

As for the rest, I stop here. The minister has discoursed to you in magnificent language. He has said that French interests were to be upheld in all quarters of the world; that wherever one of our countrymen met a serious obstacle in his way, wherever his security or his fortune was compromised, the French flag should go to protect him. Never, gentlemen, have we combatted such maxims; we share in them with all our hearts; but what we desire, also, is, that the money and the blood of France should not be lavished on an ill-defined expedition which may conceal an intrigue; and this, gentlemen, is my last word. [To the vote; to the vote.]

M. Monier de la Sizeranne rises to speak.

From all sides. To the vote; to the vote.

Some voices. Speak.

M. Monier de la Sizeranne. I ask permission to say a few words.

Numerous voices. No, no; the previous question.

The President. The previous question is demanded by the great majority of the Chamber. The amendment is now to be put to the vote Ten members having demanded a ballot on the amendment, it is now to be proceeded with. The names of the deputies who have signed the demand for a ballot, are: Messrs. Roques-Salvaza, Guillaumin, Charlemagne, Count Segur-Lamoignon, Carayon-Latour, the Marquis de Chaumont-Quitry, Dabeaux, Count de Nesle, Ledier, Corneille.

SOME MEMBERS. Explain to us the vote, Mr. President.

The PRESIDENT. The Chamber is going to vote on the amendment; it is plain, then, that those opposed to it will deposit a blue ballot, and those in favor of it a white ballot.

(They proceed to ballot; then the votes are counted.)

The PRESIDENT The result of the count of the ballots is: Number of voters, 250; absolute majority, 126; for the adoption of the amendment, 5; against it, 245 Therefore the legislative body has not adopted it.

The PRESIDENT. I proceed now to put to the vote successively paragraphs 3 and 4 relative to Mexico:

"Paragraph 3. Your Majesty had concerted the Mexican expedition with two great powers whose co-operation would, undoubtedly, have had the effect of diminishing the efforts of France. Left alone to pursue a necessary satisfaction, you were justified in thinking and saying that the legislative body would not hesitate to second you.". Adopted.

"Paragraph 4. We hope for the happy and speedy termination of this war in which our army and our navy give new proofs of their constancy and their courage, and we desire that there may freely issue from it a stable government, which would respect laws and treaties, and remain the ally of France." Adopted.

The PRESIDENT. I think that at this late hour it would be suitable to adjourn the continuation of the discussion till Monday. [Yes! yes!]

The Chamber adjourned at 5½ o'clock.

Mr. F. W. Seward to Mr. Romero.

DEPARTMENT OF STATE,
Washington, November 6, 1863.

SIR: I have the honor to acknowledge the receipt of your note of this date enclosing an English translation of the debates in the corps legislatif of France, on the 6th and 7th of February ultimo, in relation to the Mexican question.

Presenting you my thanks for the interesting and valuable communication, I avail myself of the opportunity to renew to you the assurances of my most distinguished consideration.

F. W. SEWARD,
Acting Secretary.

Señor Don MATIAS ROMERO, *&c., &c., &c.*

Mr. Romero to Mr. Seward.

[Translation.]

MEXICAN LEGATION TO THE UNITED STATES OF AMERICA,
Washington, January 26, 1864.

Mr. SECRETARY: I have the honor to remit to you, translated into English, the documents relating to the affairs of Mexico, presented by the government of France to the legislative bodies of the empire on opening the sessions of 1863 and 1864.

At first sight it will appear strange that I transmit to the government of the United States documents emanating from a government which is making war on my country, and which it publishes for the purpose of justifying this very war; but as from these are deduced, in many respects, precisely the contrary of that which the French government desired to justify, I do not believe it possible to adduce proofs more conclusive in defence of the cause of my country than those which emanate from the French government, and have been produced by it in support of its policy.

It appears that the imperial government, ordinarily quite sparing enough in the publication of diplomatic documents, knew that those published in 1863 would result against those setting them forth, and desiring to avoid the repetition of the same consequence, only gave to light in 1864 three official papers in relation to a matter in which France and the whole world had the right to expect explanations less superficial on the part of the aggressor.

I avail of this opportuuity to renew to you, sir, the assurances of my most distinguished consideration.

M. ROMERO.

Hon. WILLIAM H. SEWARD, *&c.*, *&c.*, *&c.*

The Minister for Foreign Affairs to Count Flahault, Ambassador of France in London.

PARIS, *October* 11, 1861.

Monsieur le COMTE: The English ambassador has called on me to converse on Mexican affairs, and on the means of combining the action of our governments, in order to attain the common object which we have in view. Her Majesty's government, says Lord Cowley, is ready to sign a convention, together with France and Spain, to the end of obtaining redress for the offences committed against the subjects of the three nations, and of enforcing the execution of the obligations contracted by the Mexican government towards their respective governments, provided it should be declared in said convention that the forces of the three powers are not to be employed in any ulterior object, whatever it may be, and, above all, that they are not to interfere with the interior government of Mexico. The cabinet of London proposes to invite the United States to adhere to this convention, yet, without awaiting their answer, to commence active operations.

I have answered the ambassador from England, that I was perfectly agreed with his government upon one point: that I agreed with Lord Russell about the legitimacy of our coercive action towards Mexico, as it only originated from our grievances against that government, and that said grievances, together with the means of redressing them, and of preventing them in future, constituted alone the object of an ostensible convention. I admitted also, without any difficulty, that the contracting parties might bind themselves not to derive any political or commercial advantage, to the exclusion of the others or of any other power, but that it seemed to me of no use to go beyond this, and interdict, in advance, the eventual exercise of a legitimate participation in the events which our operations might originate. The government of the Emperor no more than that of her Majesty would like to assume the responsibility of a direct intervention in the domestic affairs of Mexico, but thinks it prudent for the two cabinets not to discourage the efforts which the country itself might make to put an end to the state of anarchy in which it has been plunged for so long a time—letting it know that no circumstances whatever would bring about any support or assistance from abroad. It is evidently the interest both of France and England to see there established such state of things as will secure the interest existing already, and favor the development of our exchanges with a country so richly endowed. The events just taking place in the United States add new importance and urgency to these considerations. In fact, we are led to suppose that, if the issue of the American crisis were to accomplish the definitive separation of the south from the north, both confederations would soon look after compensations, which the territory of Mexico, going to a social dissolution, would offer to their competition. Such an event could not be indifferent to England; and, in our opinion, the only obstacle which would prevent it is the constitution of a government able to redress wrongs, and strong enough to stop interior dissolution. Whether the elements of such government should be found in Mexico we cannot assure positively. Our interest in the regeneration of that country does not allow us to neglect any symptom which would give hope of the success of such an attempt. As to the form of government, provided it would afford the country and ourselves sufficient guarantees, we had not, and I suppose England herself had not, any preference, nor had chosen any. But if the Mexicans themselves, being tired of their trials, and decided to react against the disasters of the past, should draw up a new vitality from the dangers which threaten them—if, coming back and consulting the instincts of their race, for instance, they should find in the establishment of a monarchy the repose and prosperity which in vain they have looked for in republican institutions, I did not think we ought absolutely to refuse to aid them, if there was a chance, bearing, nevertheless, in mind that they were perfectly free to choose whatever means they might think best to attain their object.

In developing these ideas in the form of an intimate and confidential conversation, I added, that in case my prevision were to be realized, the government of the Emperor, freegaged from all preoccupation, rejected, in advance, the candidature for any prince of the imperial house; and that, desirous to treat gently all susceptibilities, it would see with pleasure that the election of the Mexicans and the assent of the powers should fall upon some prince of the house of Austria.

Coming back to the point of departure in this conversation, and in order to resume, I said that the convention in project, in my judgment, should indicate the end of the agreement between the contracting parties—should say, in one word, all that which we were about doing; but that, according to prudence and usage, we ought to abstain from saying what we would not do in case of uncertain events, which ought then to be met when taking place.

Such is, Monsieur le Comte, the substance of the conversation which I have had with Monsieur the ambassador from England, and of which he is to give an account to his government. I hope the cabinet of London will attentively examine these considerations, inspired by the community of our interests in Mexico, and which the frankness of our relations made a duty for me to lay before it.

THOUVENEL.

The Minister for Foreign Affairs to Mr. Barrot, French Ambassador at Madrid.

PARIS, *October* 15, 1861.

SIR: Since the last time I addressed you I have had a conversation with the ambassador of her Britannic Majesty, which you will find abridged in the annexed despatch addressed to Count Flahault. (See the foregoing despatch) As you will observe, the English government demands that, in the convention which it is about making with France and Spain, it should be stipulated that the three powers will not interfere in the domestic government of Mexico. In the mind of the Emperor such a declaration would be too absolute, and it would at least be of no use to have it figure in the conversation. You will find in my despatch to M. de Flahault the observation which, on this subject, I thought proper to present to Lord Cowley, and in which I have stated that if we are not to assume the responsibility of a direct action in the domestic affairs of Mexico, prudence dictated that we should not discourage in advance the efforts that the people themselves might make, with the moral support which the presence of our forces would afford them, to establish a regular and permanent government; that finally, while leaving the Mexicans in perfect liberty to make their own choice of government, the three powers ought not, for the sake of their interests, to interdict themselves absolutely from aiding the Mexicans in the work of their regeneration. It is in this sense that I have been led to speak to Lord Cowley about the eventuality of the re-establishment of a monarchy in Mexico, as you will see in my despatch to M. de Flahault.

The ambassador of her Catholic Majesty having yesterday come to confer with me on the same subject, I have explained myself with him in the same manner as I did with Lord Cowley. I have told him, particularly in that which refers to the eventual return of a monarchy in Mexico, that this country was, before all, to express its will as to the monarchical form and choice of a dynasty. I have also called the attention of M. Mon to the fact that the government of the Emperor, foreseeing such an eventuality, with perfect disinterestedness resigned beforehand all candidature for any prince of the imperial family, and that he did not doubt that the other two governments entertained similar dispositions. Finally, that in regard to the choice of a dynasty in the eventuality indicated, we had no candidate to propose, but that should the fact happen, an Austrian prince would meet with our assent. Such a choice, in fact, would have, besides many reasons which exist to adhere to the advantage of taking away from the common action of the three powers all motives for collision or national emulation, leaving at the same time all its authority to the moral support which they would be called upon to lend to the Mexican nation. In one word, the three powers would have to act at present as France, England, and Russia acted towards Greece, by engaging themselves not to accept for any of their princes the new throne erected through their common exertions. This precedent, in my judgment, could be brought as an example, the natural difference of the situation taken into consideration, and you may make use it of in your conversation with the minister of her Catholic Majesty.

From what M. Calderon Collantes told you in regard to the action which, in his opinion, the three powers ought to take upon the domestic organization of Mexico, it seems to me that we are very nearly agreed on that point. I would learn with pleasure that the cabinet of Madrid entertained the same opinion as the government of the Emperor as to the eventuality of Mexico's returning to monarchy. At all events, we prefer to act in this affair towards the government of her Catholic Majesty with full confidence, and we have thought that the friendly relation which now exists between both governments constituted for us a duty to deal openly upon the conduct which we ought to follow as much for the interest of Mexico as for that of the three powers.

In regard to the participation of the United States there could be no difficulty between Spain, England, and ourselves. Lord Cowley told me that his government was of opinion that operations could be commenced without awaiting the answer of the American government, and I see by your correspondence that this is also the opinion of M. Calderon Collantes.

THOUVENEL.

The French Ambassador at Madrid to the Minister for Foreign Affairs.

MADRID, *October* 21, 1861.

Monsieur le MINISTRE: I have the honor to acknowledge from your excellency the receipt of the despatch which your excellency addressed to me on the 15th of October.

I have recently held many conferences with Marshal O'Donnell and Mr. Calderon Collantes upon the Mexican question. The English minister in Madrid had already communicated to the government of Queen Isabella the project of a convention presented by England with the object of regulating the common action to be taken by the three powers in regard to the affairs of the Mexican republic. The Spanish government agrees fully with that of the Emperor about the objections made to it, and regards it as interdicting beforehand the very measures which it purposes to adopt.

It is evident, in fact, that the limitations proposed by the English project to the eventual action of the three powers are of such a nature as to destroy all its effect. M. Calderon Collantes has perfectly understood, as your excellency has, that it would be illogical and impolitic to discourage in advance, through a premature and at the least an useless declaration, the efforts of the order-loving people who are in a majority in Mexico, and to whom the presence alone of the united forces of the three nations would give that moral ascendency which they have lacked heretofore, and without which it would be impossible to dominate the bad passions of the minority.

M. Calderon Collantes sums up his opinion by saying that it would be better to abstain from going to Mexico than to go under the conditions proposed by the English project.

BARROT.

The French Ambassador at Madrid to the Minister for Foreign Affairs.

MADRID, *November* 6, 1861.

Monsieur le MINISTRE: As I have had the honor to communicate to your excellency this morning by telegraph, I have acquainted Marshal O'Donnell and M. Calderon Collantes with the wish expressed by your excellency, that instructions may be given to the commanders-in-chief of the Spanish and French forces in Mexico, so that they may march on Mexico if the circumstances would seem to them favorable.

The Duke of Tetuan unhesitatingly adhered to the opinion of the government of the Emperor. He declared to me and authorized me to inform you that very elastic instructions, in fact almost discretional, will be given to the Spanish commander, and that he, besides, would write to him privately, authorizing him to act in conformity with the measures which your excellency's despatch would indicate.

In consequence of a conversation which I have had on the same subject with M. Calderon Collantes, the first secretary of state has authorized me to inform you that his own opinion is exactly like that just expressed to me by Marshal O'Donnell, and to confirm in his name the engagement just entered into with me by the president of the council.

BARROT.

Ultimatum from the French commissioners in Mexico.

The undersigned, representatives of France, have the honor, as stated in the collective note addressed this day to the Mexican government by the plenipotentiaries of France, England, and Spain, to draw up, as follows, the ultimatum of which they have received orders in the name of the government of his Majesty the Emperor to demand the pure and simple acceptance by Mexico:

ARTICLE 1. Mexico engages to pay France a sum of $12,000,000, at which amount are calculated the total French demands, consequent upon events which have occurred up to July last, with the exceptions stipulated in articles 2 and 4, below.

As regards those events which have taken place since the 31st of July last, and of which a special reservation is here made, the amount of the claims against Mexico to which they may give rise will be fixed hereafter by the plenipotentiaries of France.

ART. 2. The sums still due under the convention of 1853, which are not included in article 1, above, shall be paid to the rightful claimants in the form, and allowing the terms of payment stipulated in the said convention of 1853.

Art 3. Mexico shall be held to the full, loyal, and immediate execution of the contract concluded in the month of February, 1859, between the Mexican government and the firm of Jecker.

Art. 4. Mexico is pledged to the immediate payment of the $11,000 forming the balance of the indemnity which was stipulated for in favor of the widow and children of M Ricke, vice-consul of France at Tepic, assassinated in October, 1859.

The Mexican government shall further, and according to the obligation already contracted by them, deprive of his rank and appointments, and punish in an exemplary manner, Colonel Rojas, one of the assassins of M. Ricke, with the express condition that Rojas shall not again be invested with any employment, command, or public functions whatsoever.

Art. 5. The Mexican government also engages to search out and to punish the authors of the numerous murders committed upon Frenchmen, and especially the murderers of M. Davesne.

Art. 6. The authors of the attacks committed on the 14th of August last against the minister of the Emperor, and of the outrages to which the representative of France has been exposed in the first part of the month of November, 1861, shall be subjected to exemplary punishment; and the Mexican government shall be bound to afford to France and to her representative the reparation and satisfaction due by reason of these deplorable excesses.

Art. 7. In order to insure the execution of the above articles 5 and 6, and the punishment for all the outrages which have been, or which may be, committed against the persons of Frenchmen residing in the republic, the minister of France shall always have the right of being present, whatever the case at issue, and by such representative as he may designate for that purpose, at all proceedings instituted by the criminal courts of the country.

The minister shall possess the same right with regard to all criminal prosecutions instituted against his countrymen.

Art. 8. The indemnities stipulated in the present ultimatum shall bear a legal annual rate of interest of 6 per cent., to date from the 17th July last, and until their complete payment.

Art 9. As a guarantee for the accomplishment of the financial and other conditions laid down in the present ultimatum, France shall have the right of occupying the ports of Vera Cruz, of Tampico, and such other ports of the republic as she shall think fit; and of there establishing commissioners designated by the imperial government, whose duty it shall be to take care that those powers which have a legal claim shall receive such funds as are to be levied for their benefit on the produce of the maritime custom-houses of Mexico, in fulfilment of the foreign conventions, and that French agents shall receive those sums which are due to France.

The commissioners in question shall, besides, be invested with the power of reducing, either by one-half or in a smaller proportion, according as they may judge advisable, the duties at present levied in the ports of the republic.

It is expressly understood that merchandise which has already paid import duty shall in no case, and on no pretext whatsoever, be subjected by the supreme government, or by the State authorities, to any additional customs duty, inland or otherwise, exceeding the proportion of fifteen per cent. on the duties paid on importation.

Art 10. All measures which shall be judged necessary for regulating the apportionment among the parties interested of the sums levied upon the produce of the customs, as well as the manner and the periods of the payment of the indemnities above stipulated, as also for guaranteeing the execution of the conditions of the present ultimatum, shall be framed in concert with the plenipotentiaries of France, England, and Spain.

Vera Cruz.

The Minister for Foreign Affairs to M. Dubois de Saligny, Minister of France at Mexico.

Paris, *February* 28, 1862.

Sir: The dispositions which Sir Charles Wyke has shown on the subject of our last claims, and which have been supported by General Prim, have put an obstacle to your presenting the ultimatum which you had formed with the view of settling the question in that which concerns us. I will take under consideration that ultimatum by and by; first, I intend to examine only the conduct which you followed. Now, in determining from the beginning the whole of the conditions in what concerns us, to which the Mexican government was to be required to assent, you proceed very reasonably, and in conformity with our intentions.

It is to be regretted that your colleagues did not think it possible to adopt a similar determination simultaneously. The disagreement between you, I should think, has been brought about by a forced interpretation of the convention of London. It was wrong that Sir Charles Wyke and General Prim should have attempted, if I do not mistake, to see in those articles the right for each one of the representatives of the three powers to exercise a binding control upon the claims presented by their colleagues in the name of their respective governments. It had never been understood, indeed, that we were to submit to a reciprocal appreciation of our grievances, and that the reparations demanded by the dignity or the injured interests of one of the powers ought to be limited to only those which the other two would think themselves authorized to admit. It was natural, undoubtedly, that having to form our ultimatum in common, the different commissioners should acquaint themselves, mutually, with the grievances for which they were to ask satisfaction, but this preliminary communication taking place only as a kind of information for the better understanding of the representatives by no means carried with it the right for any of them to discuss these grievances. The convention of the 31st of October empowers the commissioners to determine about the claims, but as the text itself says, *on the questions only which might arise from the employment and distribution of the sums of money which were recovered from Mexico, taking into consideration the respective rights of the contracting parties.* It is to each power that belongs the right to determine what it had cause to demand. Otherwise, if we had to reciprocally examine the demands drawn up on both sides, as your colleagues thought it would have to be, to expose ourselves to see several months pass, as it has been acknowledged, before having done with this task—wishing, besides, to proceed in this way, one could not (and this has been the case) arrive at an ultimatum that would authorize all the discussions for want of preciseness, and therefore it would not be very serious.

What I understand is, that, in the ulterior and effective regulation, it seems necessary or equitable to establish a classification of liquidation among the credits, to cause the payment of some of them to be made before others, to examine their quality and importance; but, what is necessary from the very beginning, is to affirm plainly and categorically what each power intends to obtain. I pretend, by no means, to say that there is an absolute obligation for the three governments to consider every demand presented by one of them as carrying with itself a right to be supported by the other two. If, in that which concerns us, our condition surpassed the measure of those which the representatives of Great Britain and Spain decided as satisfactory for them, it would be necessary for us to reflect on the attitude which was more convenient to our interests, examining whether they would not suffer much by the concessions made to maintain a common action of the three courts, or whether by remaining scrupulously faithful to the spirit of the convention of London, that is to say, not seeking in Mexico any particular advantage or territorial acquisition, we ought to separately exact the satisfaction due to France.

I come now to the observation which the reading of the ultimatum you prepared suggested to me. I am not willing to make it the text of formal instructions. I limit myself to leave them to your own reflections, so that you may pay attention to them as far as right will allow it and circumstances may demand. The amount which the department had endeavored to value our claims did not reach that which your article first fixed, but, in the absence of sufficient details to arrive at them, a great latitude was left to you on this subject. And, although I would not invite you expressly to diminish any amount which Sir Charles Wyke and General Prim should think to be exorbitant, you could be less rigorous on this subject if that was to be an evident cause of dissidence between the representatives of the three courts. The amounts to be charged to Mexico, besides the twelve millions of dollars of principal indemnity contained in the clauses of articles 2 and 4, seem to be of such a nature as to be considered as the most rigorously to be exacted. I would be inclined to think that if we fix a considerable amount of indemnity we could dispense with reparations of other kinds, although fully justified in principle that you should demand whether it be in relation to the death of our agent at Tepic, or to the criminal attempts committed against your person last August, express and additional clauses. I ask myself, also, whether the precautions which you have thought proper to take under articles 5, 6, and 7, with the object of securing the judicial pursuit and the punishment of the different outrages to which our countrymen have fallen victims, would attain, in reality, the object which they aim at, and if it would not be more advantageous to consider at once the indemnity stipulated as a satisfaction comprising all our grievances.

In what concerns, specially, article 3, in relation to the Jecker affair, there is evidently a distinction to be made between that which affects our own interests and that which is foreign. When General Miramon published the decree which brought about his contract with the house of Jecker, the information from the legation having stated that the foreign commerce derived a great relief from the financial measure brought about by this house to the Mexican government, it was natural to see a great profit in preventing as much as possible that they would go back on this measure and the operations which facilitated it. It is in this sense that instructions from the department have invited you, as you had already taken the initiative, to support the claims provoked on this point by the conduct of the Juarez government Now, the care would be, they say, on account of the opposition made by Sir Charles Wyke to that which you had proposed on this matter, that the foreign commerce would not derive any advantage from such a contract, but that the house of Jecker would be the only one to profit by its fulfilment. I do not know how the case stands, but I call your attention to the importance of separating in this affair that which I would really compromise, the interests which it is our duty to protect from that which would only affect interests of a different character. The actual government would not consent to deprive our countrymen of advantages accruing from a regular measure taken by General Miramon's administration on the only ground that it emanated from an enemy, but on our side it would be unreasonable to be willing to impose on the actual government obligations which would not essentially emanate from its responsibility as a government.

THOUVENEL.

The Minister of Foreign Affairs to the Ambassador of France at London.

PARIS, *March* 7, 1862.

Monsieur le COMTE: Lord Cowley has called to communicate to me the observations which the ultimatum, prepared in our name by M. de Saligny, and which the disposition shown by Sir Charles Wyke prevented him from presenting, had suggested to Lord Russell. I send you a copy of said ultimatum, and I think proper to inform you of my answer to the ambassador from England, so that you may be enabled to understand it in the same sense.

I reminded, first, Lord Cowly of my declaration to him from the very beginning, that the government of the Emperor could not determine in advance the amount of indemnity required for its demands in the absence of proper date to arrive at. Our legation at Mexico being in possession of all the documents of the numerous claims presented by our countrymen up to a recent period, it could alone fix the amount which would constitute an equitable and real reparation for so many grievances and damages which we have been compelled to ask from Mexico. I had, therefore, announced to Lord Cowley that we would leave this question to be settled by our representative. As soon as I learned the terms in which the ultimatum was conceived, having received only the text without any explanation in its support, I did not conceal to our plenipotentiaries, it is true, that their vigor had somewhat surpassed our previsions. But on reading afterwards the explanations sent by M. Dubois de Saligny, which I expected, I must acknowledge that, in forming this project of ultimatum, he had done so after mature reflection and formally proving the claims recommended to our case.

Our representative, in basing his conduct in this case upon the instructions which I had sent him, has tried, notwithstanding, not to exaggerate their application, and has, besides, been frank and open in his manner of proceeding towards his colleagues. The objection made by Sir Charles Wyke against our ultimatum, pretending that only claims already admitted by Mexico in virtue of treaties or conventions ought to be comprehended, must have surprised M. de Saligny no less than it does ourselves. If this were the case, we could never have attained the object of an expedition, caused by the recent acts of the government of Mexico. That which evidently led the three powers to unite their forces against Mexico has been the impossibility of permitting that the rules of right and justice should be violated with impunity towards their subjects, and the firm determination of obtaining the proper satisfaction for past injuries and security for the future, that such abuses should not be repeated. Was it then properly time to pretend that France, Great Britain, and Spain, by sending their fleets and soldiers to Mexico to secure, as the convention says, by means of a joint action, the efficacious protection of their respective subjects, did not intend to require from the Mexican government aught else than the fulfilment of conventions which, having reference only to former grievances, would leave without satisfaction our last and more serious causes of complaint?

Neither M. Dubois de Saligny nor ourselves so viewed it. Our resolution and that of the cabinets of London sand Madrid was, we are perfectly convinced, at the moment that the treaty of the 31st of October was signed, to exact from Mexico the full reparations, without leaving room to evade it, for all the wrong of which it was responsible before the three powers up to the day when they had set foot on its soil.

It does not become us to criticise the abandonment which England and Spain would be willing to make in this case of a part of their reclamations. Each of the allied powers is the judge in this respect of its own conduct; and because we always thought so, we never admitted, even for an instant, that the demands presented by one of the representatives were to have in advance the assent of the other two.

Thus the opinion enunciated by Sir Charles Wyke on this subject, though supported by General Prim, has been most properly opposed by M. Dubois de Saligny. It results from a forced interpretation of the convention of London, for it cannot be concluded, in the first place, from its clauses that each one of the representatives of the three powers has the right to exercise a binding control on the claims presented by his colleagues in the name of their respective governments It has not been understood by any means that one has to submit to a reciprocal appreciation of its claims, and that the reparations required by the dignity or injured interests of one of the governments should be limited to those which the other two would deem satisfactory. It was natural that the different commissioners, having to form simultaneously the conditions for an ultimatum, should consult each other upon the grievances for which satisfaction was to be demanded ; but this preliminary communication, made only as a simple understanding, and with the object of best showing the accord between the different representatives, could in no manner convey the right to one of them of discussing the origin and extension of the grievances themselves.

The convention of the 31st of October has conferred on the commissioners the power of giving their opinion on the subject of claims, but, as the convention properly says, on *the questions which might arise from the employment and distribution of the sums of money which will be recovered from Mexico, paying attention to the respective rights of the contracting parties.* It is in principle the right of each power to determine itself what it has to claim. Otherwise, if we were to examine reciprocally the demands made by either party, that would have been to expose ourselves to see several months elapse before the task could have been accomplished. What it is easy to understand is, that in the final and effective arrangement might have been necessary or just to establish a rank of liquidation among the credits in view of their character and importance ; but what is always necessary at the beginning is to determine frankly and categorically what it is the purpose of each power to obtain, otherwise their ultimatum gives rise to discussions, and consequently is not of a serious character. I do not pretend to say, nevertheless, that the three governments were bound to consider that all demands presented by each of them were to have the support of the other two as a right. If, in what concerns us, our conditions surpassed the measure of those with which the representatives of Great Britain and Spain were to decide or content themslves, we were to look for the attitude which would best suit our interests, and to examine whether they would not have to suffer too much from concessions made to the support of a joint action, or whether we were to prosecute separately the reparations due to France by remaining scrupulously faithful to the spirit of the convention of London—that is to say, without looking for any particular advantage or territorial acquisition. One of the clauses of our ultimatum, which seemed more than any other to have met with the opposition of Sir Charles Wyke, is that which relates to the contract made by the Mexican government with the house of Jecker. Our legation in making the claim originating from this contract has borne in mind, above all, the general interests of foreign commerce and the advantages accruing from it—as it bound the responsibility of the Mexican government, whatever it may be—no less than the enormous injury to the resident and foreign merchants which would follow its non-compliance.

Writing to M. Dubois de Saligny in the sense of the exposition which precedes, I have left him free yet to use the latitude which was accorded him by my former instructions to modify his demands. Although I have not invited him, expressly, to reduce the amount of our indemnification, he can be less rigorous on this point if this is to be an evident cause of dissidence between the representatives of the three courts.

As for the other conditions which appear in our ultimatum, I have authorized him to give way so far as new considerations may advise it. In what concerns particularly the affair of the Jecker debt, he will have again to examine, if there is not a destination to be made between the interest attached to it, and whether all of them have equally a right to our protection.

What seems to me to be essential above all is, that no room be left to the Mexican government to discuss hereafter the obligations which will be imposed upon it. This would not be the case if our exactions should not be made in a distinct manner ; if the amount of indemnity charged to the account should not be fixed at once, the power to raise objections against what she would owe us should be left to her soon after our forces had evacuated her territory. What we have experienced by recurring several times to this expediency of a liquidation, admitted in principle, but which was to be subsequently discussed and settled, proves how illusory such sort of arrangements with the Mexican government are, to expose ourselves to fall again in the situation which has followed the regulations of the kind to which, not long ago, Admiral Penana, and more recently M. Dubois de Saligny, had thought advisable to submit through a feeling of confidence in the good faith of the Mexican government—a good faith which has not been confirmed. Therefore I do not admit that an opening be left to that government to evade the obligations which it might seem to have accepted, unless I consent to have as a net loss the heavy expenses which the actual expedition has caused; I do not object, on the other hand, since the amount of our indemnity seems to be exorbitant to the English government, and since we do not pretend to establish it ourselves upon positive date at this time—I say I do not object to having a special commission to determine at a later period exactly what the amount, distinctively, of our indemnity must be which will satisfy our reclamations M. Dubois de Saligny himself first suggested the idea, and I am perfectly disposed to adopt it. We would, in such case, do what we have done in similar cases; for instance, in the indemnity of Djeddah. We would not hesitate in freeing the Mexican government from the portion of the amount primitively fixed, which would be over and above what we have a legitimate right to demand after an examination of all our injuries. It is well to remark, besides, that the importance of the demanded indemnities could not be considered as proper to render the recovery impossible after sufficient delay for payments should be granted to the Mexican government.

There is another objection to our ultimatum, made by Lord Cowley, and which it is easy to remove. Article ninth seemed to him to state that the occupation of the ports of Vera Cruz, Tampico, or others, ought to take place for the exclusive benefit of France, she only having to establish there commissioners with the indicated object. Such is not, if well understood, the sense of this disposition. The measures which this article refers to as having to be adopted to guarantee the fulfilment of the obligations imposed on Mexico must, without the least doubt, be common to the three powers. If their ultimatums were not to contain an identical clause on this head, certainly it would not be acting any longer in accordance with the spirit of the convention of London.

THOUVENEL.

The French Ambassador at London to the Minister of Foreign Affairs.

LONDON, *March* 11, 1862.

M. le MINISTRE: I waited yesterday upon the principal secretary of state, and my interview with him was almost exclusively devoted to the state of affairs superinduced by the grave dissensions among the commissioners of the allied powers in Mexico. It is too important to the success of our expedition that a good understanding should be restored as soon as possible to have authorized me to do aught else than immediately direct my efforts to exhaust the question of the difference between M. Dubois de Saligny and Sir Charles Wyke, in regard to the ultimatum drawn up by the former. I therefore immediately informed the principal secretary of state of the approbation accorded by the Emperor's government to the conduct of its commissioners. Following the spirit of your excellency's despatch of March 7, of which I thought myself authorized to read several passages, I brought Lord Russell to acknowledge that her Britannic Majesty's commissioner had mistaken the spirit of the treaty signed at London when he refused his assent to the ultimatum project of France. Like ourselves, Lord Russell does not admit, indeed, that the demands drawn up by any one of the representatives of the allied powers should preliminarily have the assent of the other two; he thinks, however, that in virtue of the solidity which binds their governments in a community of action, and the reciprocal guarantees which they give each other, each of the commissioners has a right to make observations, and to give his opinion on the ultimatum of his colleagues. The principal secretary of state, as far as he is concerned, agrees with what Sir Charles Wyke has expressed in regard to the clauses of the ultimatum presented by M. Dubois de Saligny. Our demand of twelve millions of piastres seems to him too high. The clause which exacts the execution of the contract with the Jecker house also appears to him open to most serious objections. He said to me that, in his opinion, that was not one of those engagements which deserved such a protection as that it should be necessary to lay down the execution of it as one of the conditions of an ultimatum.

I was not sufficiently acquainted, M. le Ministre, with the contract in question to be able to enter upon a profound discussion on this point. I restricted myself to replying that your excellency had left M. Dubois de Saligny free to modify his demands, and that the latter would have consented to leave the Jecker affair among the reserved questions, if Sir Charles Wyke had been willing to give his assent to the other conditions contained in the French ultimatum, and especially to the first condition. As to the pretended excessiveness of the sum of which we had fixed the amount, I maintained the right which the French plenipotentiary had of comprising in his demand not only such debts as had previously constituted the subject of treaties with the Mexican government, but also those which had not yet been recognized by that government, and which had not been liquidated; and in this connexion I let it be understood that if the pretension continued to be held forth that we ought to confine the claims which we believed ourselves justified in making upon Mexico within the limits of those with which the representatives of Great Britain and Spain had resolved to rest contented, it would perhaps be the occasion for leading us to examine whether our interests should not suffer too much from concessions made for the maintenance of common action, and whether it would not be preferable for us to proceed separately to the enforcement of the satisfaction due to us I added that it appeared essential, above all, to the Emperor's government that the Mexican government should not hereafter find itself in a position to discuss the obligations which might have been imposed upon it, and that it was chiefly with this view that it was deemed necessary to draw up the demands so as to settle now the amount of indemnity required from Mexico. "This amount," said I, "may be either insisted on or modified by our commissioner; but once accepted by the Mexican government, we will not refuse to have a special commission appointed to determine hereafter more exactly what ought to be finally paid as the sum total of our indemnities, in order to strictly satisfy our claim." And then I indicated what facilities in regard to time we were disposed to accord to the Mexican government in order to discharge its obligations. Lord Russell accepted this idea of a commission, and told me that he was going to request Sir Charles Wyke to desist from his opposition.

FLAHAULT.

The Minister of Foreign Affairs to the French Ambassador in London.

PARIS, *March* 12, 1862.

Monsieur le COMTE: I have just received the despatch which you have done me the honor of writing to me on the 11th of March. I congratulate myself on seeing that the cabinet of London admits no more than we do the primal cause of the opposition manifested by Sir Charles Wyke against the ultimatum prepared by M. Dubois de Saligny, and on learning that, Lord Russell is about to request the English minister to desist from that opposition. The opinion expressed by the principal secretary of state in regard to our claims requires of me, however, to transmit to you, in order to lay it before him, an estimate of the amount of the justice of which there can be no suspicion. This estimate is found in the article annexed, extracted from a Mexican journal, the Mexican Extraordinary, which is the accredited organ of the English interests in that country. This journal, which is far from having ever testified any very lively sympathy for our interests, does not hesitate, in an elaborate examination of the foreign debt, to place the sum total of our just claims at fifteen millions of piastres. As I already supposed, for other reasons, the amount of the English claims is still higher; since the article annexed, while allowing a reduction of twenty per centum, then fixes our claims at twelve millions of piastres, and the amount of the English claims at 16,800,000 piastres We do not propose to ourselves in any manner to examine into the origin and legitimacy of these debts, but we must think that Lord Russell himself was not perfectly informed heretofore in regard to the amount sought to be figured out in the reckoning up of England's interests by the side of ours.

THOUVENEL.

[Article annexed.]

Analysis of an article from the "Mexican Extraordinary."

The amount of the debt due by Mexico to France may, according to the writer of this article, be estimated at *fifteen millions of piastres.*

"We have," says he, "studied the question with great care, having all possible sources of information at our disposal for this investigation, and we declare that, after the minutest examination and the most rigorous research into the proofs demanded under such circumstances, the sum total of the claims of the foreign powers will not be reduced more than twenty per centum from the figure previously announced, which fixes the claims to be enforced by each power against Mexico as follows:

"English claims	16,800,000 piastres.
"French ..do	12,000,000 piastres.
"Spanish ..do	8,000,000 piastres.
"Other....do	4,000,000 piastres.
"Total	40,800,000 piastres."

The Minister of Foreign Affairs to the French Minister in Mexico.

PARIS, *March* 14, 1862.

SIR: I always regret, as I wrote to you by the last courier, that the presentation of the ultimatums did not precisely indicate, from the very first moment, the amount of satisfaction which the three powers intended, above everything else, to obtain from Mexico, and of which the common necessity had occasioned the combined expedition among themselves.

The explanations into which I have entered in this regard with Lord Cowley, and which I have requested the Count de Flahault to repeat to Lord Russell, have been conformable to all that I said to you in my last despatch, and the information since furnished to me by your correspondence has allowed me to state with more authority the perfectly well considered and justifiable character of our ultimatum. I have considered it more particularly my duty to establish the point well that neither the letter nor the spirit of the treaty of London imposed any obligation on the representatives of the three powers to submit, as Sir Charles Wyke understood it, to a reciprocal investigation of the claims which they should draw up in the name of their respective governments. As you will see by a despatch from the Count de Flahault, Lord Russell has actually admitted, in unison with us, that the demands, drawn up by any one of the representatives of the allied powers, were not subject to be approved beforehand by the other two; he added only that this did not exclude for that reason the right of expressing an opinion in reference to the ultimatum of a colleague. This is what I myself first declared, and whilst at the same time maintaining our right to consult our own interests merely on this point. Had the other two powers been willing, as far as they were concerned, to abandon a part of their claims, I did not wish to conceal from the English government the fact that we would not refuse to examine, in view of the maintenance of the common understanding between the powers, whether it was possible for us to yield up certain of our demands. I therefore called his attention to the modifications which I left you free to make in your ultimatum. I shall add, in this connexion, to what I said to you in regard to the possibility of a reduction of the amount of twelve millions of piastres due as our indemnity, that circumstances will indicate to you, better than I could do at so great a distance, whether too much rigor on our part might not, in the long run, be productive of more inconveniences than a few concessions, which might contribute to maintain an intimate concert of action between the representatives of the three courts, and which might facilitate a final arrangement. The institution of a French commission, which should be charged with the exact determination of what ought to be the amount of our indemnity, in order strictly to satisfy our claims, moreover appeared to the principal secretary of state of the Queen a happy idea, and I believe he would be disposed to adopt it also as far as the English claims are concerned. Consequently I request you to take this circumstance into consideration. In fact, I see no reason, as I have authorized the Count de Flahault to say, why we should hereafter hesitate to excuse the Mexican government from the payment of the portion of the indemnity primitively fixed upon, which might exceed what we would be legitimately authorized to demand, all our prejudices being taken into consideration. I have not failed, however, to remark to the English government that the importance of the indemnities demanded could not be considered such as to render the recovery of them impossible when sufficient delay was accorded to the Mexican government.

As far as concerns the Jecker affair, I cannot insist too much on the distinction which I recommended you not to fail to make between whatever in this affair might properly claim our protection and foreign interests, with the maintenance of which, on the contrary, we have no business.

THOUVENEL.

Preliminaries of La Soledad.

1. As the constitutional government which at present rules in the Mexican republic has made known to the commissioners of the allied powers that it is not in want of the help that they have so benevolently offered to the Mexican people, since it possesses in itself the elements of strength and of public opinion sufficient to preserve itself against any intestine revolt whatever, the allies from this time enter into negotiations ("entran en el terreno de los tratados") in order to adjust ("formalizar") all the claims that they have to make in the name of their respective nations.

2. Accordingly, and protesting, as do protest the representatives of the allied powers, that they will attempt nothing against the independence, sovereignty, and integrity of the territory of the republic, the negotiations will be opened in Orizaba, to which city will repair

the commissioners and two of the ministers of the government of the republic, except in the case that by common consent it should be arranged to name representatives delegated by both parties.

3. During the negotiations the forces of the allied powers will occupy the towns of Cordova, Orizaba, and Tehuacan, with their natural limits.

4. In order that it may not, in the most remote degree, be believed that the allies have signed these preliminaries in order to obtain the passage of the fortified positions garrisoned by the Mexican army, it is stipulated that, in the unfortunate event of the negotiations being broken off, the forces of the allies will retire from the said towns, and will place themselves in the line that is beyond the said fortifications, on the Vera Cruz side; Paso Ancho, on the Cordova road and Paso de Ovejas, on that of Jalapa, being the principal extreme points

5. Should the unfortunate event of the breaking off of negotiations take place, and the allied troops retire to the line indicated in the preceding article, the hospitals that the allies may have will remain under the protection of the Mexican nation.

6 The day on which the allied troops commence their march to occupy the places marked out in the 3d article, the Mexican flag shall be hoisted in the city of Vera Cruz and on the castle of San Juan de Ulloa.

La Soledad, *February* 19, 1862.

EL CONDE DE REUS.
MANUEL DOBLADO.

I approve these preliminaries by virtue of the full powers of which I am invested.

BENITO JUAREZ.
JESUS TERAN.

Mexico, *February* 23, 1862.

Approved:

C. LENNOX WYKE.
HUGH DUNLOP.

Approuvé les préliminaries ci-dessus:

E. JURIEN.
D. DE SALIGNY.

The Minister of Foreign Affairs to the French Minister in Mexico.

Paris, *March* 31, 1862.

Sir: I have received the despatches addressed to me by Admiral Jurien de la Gravière up to the 20th of February; yours, of which he announced to me the consignment for transmission on the same date, have not yet reached me. I regret being deprived by this delay of the information transmitted to me by you on your part at this moment. However, my last despatches will have sufficiently apprised you, without doubt, of the impression necessarily produced on the Emperor's government by the regretable preliminaries of La Soledad, to allow me to dispense myself from examining one by one all the clauses of that agreement. It is sufficient to state here, once more, that the negotiations entered into with the Mexican government did not correspond with the views of the allied powers. The annexed copy of the most recent despatches from the Count de Flahault and from M. Barrot will let you see that the cabinets of London and Madrid have not formed a judgment different from that of the Emperor's government in regard to the attitude accepted towards Mexico by the representatives of the three courts. What we demand of Mexico is, above all, I repeat it again, the redress of our grievances, and a government which will give us guarantees for the future. As to the form and *personnel* of this government, we do not pretend to impose any. What it ought or can be depends absolutely on local circumstances, and on the appreciation which may be had of it in Mexico by wise men and lovers of their country.

THOUVENEL.

[Annexed document No. 1.]

The French Ambassador at London to the Minister of Foreign Affairs.

London, *March* 28, 1862.

M. le Ministre: Yesterday I communicated to the principal secretary of state of the Queen the contents of the despatch which your excellency did me the honor of addressing to me, together with the report of Admiral Jurien de la Gravière.

I am happy to be able to inform your excellency that Lord Russell shares the opinion expressed by you in regard to the manner in which affairs have been conducted, for a difference of opinion between the governments on the course pursued by their commissioners could only aggravate, to a considerable extent, the inconveniences of the situation. Lord Russell does not hesitate to condemn the language used towards the Mexican government as in complete opposition to the facts which caused the necessity of the treaty of London; he thinks that the commissioners, after having taken possession of the ports, should have confined themselves to making the grievances of their respective courts known to the Mexican government and demanding redress for them, allowing a reasonable time for compliance, at the end of which recourse should be had to coercive measures, if the satisfaction demanded should not be obtained.

The Queen's principal secretary of state does not approve, any more than we do, the clause which permits the Mexican flag to float beside the flags of the three powers, and the engagement entered into by the commissioners to evacuate the posts occupied by our forces, if the negotiations should happen to fail. In brief, Monsieur le Ministre, Lord Russell agrees, on every point, with your excellency's opinion of the conduct adopted by our commissioners, and the state of affairs which that conduct has produced.

FLAHAULT.

[Annexed document No. 2.]

The French Ambassador at Madrid to the Minister of Foreign Affairs.

MADRID, *February* 26, 1862.

Monsieur le MINISTRE: M. Calderon Collantes coincides with the opinion expressed by your excellency in regard to the error into which the plenipotentiaries of the three powers have fallen, in opening negotiations with the government of Juarez, of which the only result possible is the loss of precious time, and the facility offered to the Mexican government to organize means of defence. In the first place, said the first secretary of state to me, the plenipotentiaries have acted contrary to the spirit and the tenor of the treaty of London; it had been decided, in fact, that each of the powers should draw up the claims which it had to make against the Mexican government, and that the other two had only to refrain from offering any opinion either on the amount or on the nature of such claims. Now the contrary has happened; the claims of the French plenipotentiary have been rejected by the English plenipotentiary, as being of such a character as not to be admissible by the Mexican government Thence the resolution adopted by common consent not to send to Mexico the details of the claims, but merely to inform the Mexican government of what it already knows too well, that the powers have claims to make against it. I cannot understand, added M. Calderon Collantes, what idea has inspired this resolution into the plenipotentiaries, nor what purpose they proposed to themselves in adopting it; it is simply a useless step, for it is evident that Juarez will tell the agents sent to him that, before replying to them, his government should know what the claims are which it is sought to enforce against him, and it will then be necessary to draw them up, a thing which it would be more simple to do at first. The Spanish government, therefore, censures General Prim for having swerved from the instructions which he received before his departure, and for having participated in an act which is a violation of one of the principal clauses of the treaty of London. However, this censure has been mitigated for the reason that General Prim acted in concert with his colleagues, with whom he had been recommended to keep always on terms of accord.

The first secretary of state entertains the same opinion that we do in regard to the demand made on the Mexican government for a healthy location where the allied troops might await the end of the negotiations. Three great powers have not combined and sent considerable forces to the shores of Mexico merely to open illusory negotiations with a government which has already given so many proofs of bad faith. The purpose of that display of military force was to compel the Mexican government, by prompt and energetic action, to give immediate and complete satisfaction for the grievances of which it has rendered itself guilty towards foreigners resident within its territory, and to prevent the repetition of them in future. Now, to attain this result, the plenipotentiaries were authorized to make all such arrangements as appeared suitable to them, and there was no reason to ask a government, which ought to be treated, and was, in fact, treated as an enemy, the very useless permission to establish themselves on such or such a point of its territory.

Negotiations being once opened with Juarez, was not the latter entitled to discuss the demands addressed to him? Suppose, said the first secretary of state, that he accepts them, and announces himself ready to give the powers all the securities which they shall be pleased to demand for the future; shall the three powers rest contented with these promises already so often made and so often violated? Is it not evident, moreover, that if Juarez acted in good faith, it would be physically impossible for him to keep the engagements which he might make? It is known, in fact, that he wished to effect a loan of six millions of dollars from the government of the United States, in order to satisfy the claims of the powers, and that, as a guarantee for this loan, he would deliver to the government of the Union the province of Sonora and other parts of the Mexican territory; now these six millions of dollars scarcely cover one-twelfth of the claims which he will have to satisfy. Will the three powers accept this state of affairs and dissolve their alliance, satisfied with having obtained what probably would not have been refused to them on an energetic note from the representative of any one of them? An enterprise such as this, which has taken the combined forces of France, Spain, and England to Mexico, is not renewed twice. We must act in such a manner as to obtain all the results which we have in view. A grave fault has been committed; we must redouble our energy and activity and essay to regain lost time. To this effect has the Spanish government already written to the Count of Reus.

In the same conversation, abandoning the positive part of the consequential results of the treaty of London, M. Calderon Collantes expatiated on the eventualities of the future. He spoke to me of the necessity in which the powers find themselves placed of substituting for the government of Juarez a stable government which may give to Mexico that prosperity of which nature has lavished all the elements on that privileged land, and which may afford security for the lives and property of foreigners. Will this be effected by treating with the government of Juarez? Shall we also submit to him the question of a change of government? One of two things will be the consequence, (I here continue to be the interpreter of the words of the first secretary of state,) either Juarez will say: My governernment is solidly established; it is the only government now possible in Mexico; the only one which can give the powers the guarantees which they demand. He has been authorized to hold this language, and we would be inconsistent with ourselves if, after having solemnly opened negotiations with his government, we were to say to him: Your government is bad; withdraw; Mexico will choose another, and we will assist her in so doing. Or, perhaps, Juarez—which is quite improbable—will accept this proposal; he will consent ostensibly to lay down his power and to consult the country. But will not this apparent abnegation give him a moral power which he does not now possess? Evidently we would deprive him momentarily of power only to see that power fall back into his hands under circumstances infinitely more favorable to him than now. Some may reply to this, that Juarez ceasing to be President of the republic, the party of order, that is to say, the great majority of the Mexican people, will bestir themselves to choose either another form of government or another man. Do not believe it. That might have happened if, on landing on the coasts of Mexico, the powers had distinctly declared that they would not treat with Juarez, and appealed to the Mexican nation to choose immediately a government with which the dignity of the allied powers would permit them to negotiate; but from the moment we openly recognized the government of Juarez by negotiating with it, we have by that alone discouraged the sane part of the people; we have repressed their aspirations for a better rule of things, and it is to be feared that it will be very difficult now to revive the hopes which were based only on the certainty of the moral and material co-operation of the three powers in case of necessity.

The situation of affairs has, therefore, become more difficult than it was at the moment that the allied troops appeared on the coasts of Mexico. We must not, however, despair of the result; we must, on the contrary, profit by the experience we have acquired. Cost what it may, France, Spain, and England cannot abandon an enterprise for which they have united their forces; they must effect in Mexico what they have proposed to themselves to effect. Spain, as far as she is concerned, is quite decided on this point.

BARROT.

[Annexed document No. 3.]

The French Ambassador at Madrid to the Minister of Foreign Affairs.

MADRID, *March* 23, 1862.

Monsieur le MINISTRE: I inform your excellency, by a telegraphic despatch, of the result of the interviews which I had yesterday with the first secretary of state, and this morning with Marshal O'Donnell.

The Queen's government has been painfully impressed on receiving intelligence of the arrangement concluded at La Soledad between General Prim and General Doblado. The marshal desired to give me a great mark of confidence by reading to me, from beginning to end, the despatch addressed by the Queen's government yesterday evening to the Count de Reus on this subject. In this despatch, the polished form of which conceals not the very pointed censure therein contained, the Queen's government expresses to the commander-in-chief of the Spanish forces in Mexico its disapproval of several of the clauses of the arrangement in question.

Thus it blames the plenipotentiaries for having given to the government of Juarez a moral force which it wanted before, by declaring in article 1 of the arrangement that that government appeared to them to present conditions of force and stability, and that they were ready to treat with it. If circumstances demanded it, said Marshal O'Donnell, they might certainly have opened negotiations with the government of Juarez, but it was not at all necessary to give it in any way a certificate of vitality ; by doing so they had compromised the attitude of the allied powers towards the other parties opposed to that of Juarez.

The Queen's government is not, any more than in the former case, satisfied with the clause relative to the withdrawal of the allied troops, in case the negotiations which were about to be opened, should not reach an amicable solution. However, it accepts, to a certain extent, the explanations given in this respect by the Count de Reus.

Marshal O'Donnell likewise censures the abandonment, in the case of the failure to which I have referred, of the hospitals which might be established by the allies in the encampments which they are going to occupy, in spite of the engagement entered into by the Mexican government to respect them, and the certitude which that government should entertain that every infraction of that engagement would be sternly punished by the forces of the allied powers.

Censure most distinct and unqualified has been pronounced by the Queen's government on the clause which imposes on France, Spain, and England the duty of flying the Mexican flag beside their own at Vera Cruz and San Juan de Ulloa.

In brief, Monsieur le Ministre, I repeat it, the government of Queen Isabella censures the arrangement of La Soledad, as that of his Majesty does, and the marshal has very decidedly expressed his opinion in this respect by saying to me that, if he had been in the place of the Count de Reus, he would not have signed it.

The Spanish government, moreover, attributes the faults which have been committed in the later stages of the proceedings to the misunderstanding which in the very beginning arose between the plenipotentiaries of France and England. General Prim had to interpose between them, and, being unable to succeed in conciliating them, he was drawn to give his sanction to the delay granted in the despatching of an ultimatum to the government of Juarez. Thence came the negotiations disapproved by the Spanish government, those negotiations entered into with the actual government of Mexico, and which resulted unfortunately in the conclusion of the arrangement of La Soledad, which the Queen's government likewise censures. It is settled, therefore, for this last, that the plenipotentiaries of the allied powers have departed from the instructions which they received from their respective governments, and that they have acted contrary to the spirit of the treaty of the 31st of October. But now that the evil is done, said Marshal O'Donnell, we must plan how to repair it

M. Calderon Collantes has sent me, as the expression of his opinion in regard to the actual state of our affairs in Mexico, the memorandum of which I enclose a copy to your excellency.

BARROT.

[Annexed document.]

MADRID, *March* 23, 1862.

The Queen's government thinks that the complications and difficulties which have arisen in Mexico spring from the fact that the claims of the three powers were not drawn up in the very beginning, of which circumstance the Spanish plenipotentiary has not been the cause ; that the first clause of the preliminaries, which gives the government of Juarez a moral force which it did not possess before, might well have been omitted ; that the fourth clause is explained by reasons of a military point of honor, and that the Mexicans, recognizing the extreme generosity with which they have been treated, should have themselves renounced its benefits.

Among the conditions laid down by the conferences of Orizaba, the last among them is that which seems least justifiable. However, the Queen's government, while addressing to General Prim, Count de Reus, such observations as are proper to this subject, as well as in reference to the spirit of conciliation with which all the plenipotentiaries were inspired, formally directs him to act with the greatest promptitude and energy, and to abandon every kind of temporizing policy if the result of the conferences has not been completely satisfactory.

The next courier will inform us of that result, and until then any decisive resolution would be premature or hazardous

---

M. Calderon Collantes, First Secretary of State, to the Plenipotentiary Commanding-in-Chief the Spanish Expeditionary Corps in Mexico.

[Extract.]

MADRID, *March* 22, 1862.

* * * * * * * * * * *

The Queen's government allows their just value to the considerations set forth by your excellency to demonstrate the necessity of all that was done previous to the 20th of February last, and of the preliminaries agreed upon with the minister of foreign affairs of Juarez; but it believes that some of them will give occasion, in Mexico itself, to interpretations of such a nature as to foment a more obstinate resistance than would have been offered if the claims had been presented immediately.

In examining the preliminaries attentively, it is seen that in virtue of the first clause the government of Don Benito Juarez acquires a moral force which it did not possess, provided that, in giving credit to its declaration that it possesses all the elements of force and of opinion necessary to maintain itself, we enter immediately on the business of treaties and negotiations. This could have been done whilst omitting the declaration, and such a course would not have produced the inconveniences presented at the very first sight. * * * *

The fourth clause has excited the most lively disapprobation on the part of the imperial government, and her Majesty's government would not approve of it without the reflections which your excellency offers to justify it, which reflections have their influence upon the government. Really that cannot be kept by force which has been obtained by treaty. The valor and justice of the allied forces, and the honor of the chiefs who command them, would recoil from such an idea; but the Mexican government should have abandoned to their generous decision the adoption of the proper course, in case the negotiations should eventuate without result, or, to speak more properly, in case the claims of the three friendly governments should fail to be accepted.

Such a manifestation of good will would not have been very great when we consider that the Mexican government had then received from the allies so many proofs of moderation and generosity. Moreover, it would be very much to be regretted that, in case the troops should have to retire, the hospitals should remain in the power of the enemy, even though they had taken a solemn engagement to respect them, and even though they possessed the means of punishing any act committed against them.

The last clause or condition of the preliminaries is that of which the application is most difficult. The city of Vera Cruz and the castle of San Juan de Ulloa have been occupied by the Spanish troops in the name of the three nations, not only as a base and starting point of operations, but also in the quality of a pledge and guarantee to compel the Mexican government to satisfy the claims which we have drawn up against it.

Inasmuch as this may not take place—inasmuch as all idea or all danger of a rupture may not have disappeared, Vera Cruz and San Juan de Ulloa, abandoned by the Mexican troops, have no other authority or power to rule over them than the authority and power of the three allied nations. * * * * * * * * * * *

The Queen's government, being assured that when this despatch shall reach you the negotiations opened will have reached a termination, and wishing to avoid giving occasion for the slightest want of concert and harmony in the resolutions of the three governments, has resolved (notwithstanding the brevity of the time past since the arrival of the courier yesterday, till the moment of the departure of the present) that I should instruct your excellency as follows:

Your excellency, acquainting yourself well with the spirit of the instructions which I have heretofore communicated to you, and with the sense of the present royal order, should proceed with the greatest promptitude and energy, and in accord with the plenipotentiaries and the commanders of the troops of the other two nations, in case the conferences of Orizaba do not have an entirely satisfactory result.

Your excellency justly recognizes that all imaginable means of conciliation having been exhausted, the necessity for hostilities, whatever may be their consequences, will be demonstrated before the world and in presence even of the Mexican people, who will not be able to preserve their confidence and their reliance, supposing that these qualities be actually banished from it in a government which has not listened to the voice of justice after having previously eschewed the sentiments which direct the actions of all civilized governments.

In this extreme case your excellency can, doubtless, count on the active co-operation of all honorable men, and the three allied nations will obtain not only the requisite satisfaction for their numerous grievances, but also the satisfaction of having contributed, by the presence of their troops and without the commission of any outrage, to favor the independence of the Mexican people, and to give them a government which may put an end to their continual sufferings by protecting equally the rights of native Mexicans and the interests of foreigners. * * * * * * * * * * *

The Minister of Foreign Affairs to the French Ambassador at Madrid.

PARIS, *April* 1, 1862.

SIR: I have the honor of acknowledging the receipt of the report under date of March 23, in which you render me an account of the recent interview which you have had with M. Calderon Collantes and with Marshal O'Donnell in regard to the affairs of Mexico.

If we could possibly have still retained the least doubt in our minds as to the conformity of views which exists between the Emperor's government and that of her Catholic Majesty, it would be completely dissipated by the declarations and assurances, equally clear and formal, which you have received from the first secretary of state and the president of the Council.

The government of her Britannic Majesty, on its part, has likewise come over to our way of thinking in regard to the course of conduct pursued by our plenipotentiaries and the preliminary articles signed at La Soledad. We are, therefore, authorized to think that the respective plenipotentiaries, now perfectly enlightened on the identical views and intentions of the three cabinets, will strive, henceforward, to establish among themselves a unanimity of action conformable to the intentions of their governments, and thus to give to their action that unity which will be for them the surest element of strength and success.

At the distance at which we are from the scene of events we could not pretend to transmit to our agents directions sufficiently prompt and precise to modify the consequences of the first acts in which they have taken part. We must hope, however, that they will have understood of themselves that, if they do not obtain from the Mexican government such engagements and guarantees as are proper to give entire satisfaction for all our grievances, they ought immediately to have recourse to the military measures dictated by circumstances.

THOUVENEL.

The Minister of Foreign Affairs to the French Minister in Mexico.

PARIS, *April* 12, 1862.

SIR: I wrote to you by the last courier that the cabinets of Madrid and London had not judged otherwise than the Emperor's government of the attitude assumed towards Mexico by the representatives of the three courts. Marshal O'Donnell, in a new conversation which he has had with his Majesty's ambassador at Madrid, has taken the trouble to explain the circumstances which should, according to him, have influenced the conduct of General Prim; but he has expressed the confidence that a perfect understanding cannot fail to be established between the Marquis de Castillejos and General de Lorencez, and he has reiterated the assurance that the commander-in-chief of the Spanish forces had orders to reject, forthwith, all dilatory measures and to march without hesitation towards the end which the allied powers have proposed to themselves. The cabinet of Madrid, it is true, posterior to that despatch, has caused its desire to be expressed to me that the plenipotentiaries of the three courts should meet in order to agree in advance on the subject of the different questions which might arise from the negotiations opened at Orizaba. I have replied that I did not think that there was any practical utility in reassembling a conference which could only deliberate from afar on eventualities more or less hypothetical; that I believed, therefore, that it was better to await the development of the situation without seeking to anticipate events. Either the negotiations will be broken off in reality, and there will remain no other course than to follow up the expedition energetically, or they will terminate in a treaty, and to appreciate it we must, necessarily, know the text of it. For the rest, I have every reason to believe that the Spanish government has already understood the value of these observations, and that it is not disposed to insist on its proposition.

The language employed to the Count de Flahault by Lord Russell authorized me to say to you heretofore, as I have done, that the English government at that time shared in our opinion in regard to the course of conduct pursued in the last negotiations with the Mexican government. But it appears from the communication to me by Lord Cowley of a despatch from the British principal secretary of state, that, though at first the cabinet judged as severely, indeed, as we did the treaty of La Soledad, the explanations since furnished by Sir Charles Wyke have modified that first impression. Lord Russell, however, does not approve of all the details of that arrangement, and especially of that one which provides for the appearance of the Mexican flag at Vera Cruz; but he appears satisfied that the grievances, for which it is proposed to obtain reparation, should become the object of negotiations, and he expresses the hope that, having entered on this course, we will attain a result such as to satisfy the powers that signed the treaty of London. I have confined myself to telling Lord Cowley, in reply to the communication which I received from him, that we could not regard matters from the same point of view, and that from the moment that the English troops should no longer find themselves engaged with ours in the interior of Mexico, the Emperor's government remained the sole judge of the exigencies that behooved, under actual circumstances, the care of its military dignity.

THOUVENEL.

The Minister of Foreign Affairs to the French Ambassador at Madrid.

PARIS, *April* 15, 1862.

SIR: After the views, so very decisive, expressed to you by the ministers of her Catholic Majesty in regard to the preliminary treaty of La Soledad, and the line of conduct pursued by the respective plenipotentiaries, and especially by General Prim, we should have thought that the cabinet of Madrid entirely shared our views on this point. Our surprise, therefore, has been no less than yours in finding in the explanations given to the Cortes by M. Calderon Collantes, in reference to the affairs of Mexico, an unreserved approval of the course pursued by General Prim and of the preliminaries of La Soledad.

However it be, sir, the Emperor's government will abstain from insisting on the regrettable phase of this incident; it prefers to hope that it will have no influence on the further conduct of the affair, and that the request lately sent to the commander-in-chief of the Spanish forces, to act with vigor in conformity with his instructions, will have the effect of impressing, henceforward, on the efforts of the respective plenipotentiaries and of the commanders-in-chief that unity of direction and of action dictated by the community of those interests which have called us to Mexico.

THOUVENEL.

The Minister of Foreign Affairs to the French Minister in Mexico.

PARIS, *May* 31, 1862.

SIR: We know now, in all its details, the rupture which has definitely taken place between the plenipotentiaries of the three powers.

I need not tell you that the Emperor's government very much regrets that this has occurred; but I think we may hope that, beyond the divergence of views which it unfortunately manifests in regard to the affairs of Mexico, it will not produce any more general political complications.

The respective governments have now approved of the conduct of their representatives. It behooves us, then, to let things take their course. The cabinet of London, as I have already told you, retains all confidence in our intentions, and that of Madrid declares that it heartily wishes our success. As far as we are concerned, I have to approve especially the terms of the proclamation which, in concert with Admiral Jurien de la Gravière, you addressed to the Mexican people on the 6th of August. It is this stand which you have taken that it behooves you to maintain. Our sentiments in regard to the internal condition of Mexico, our desire to see the country reconstituted under new conditions of order and stability, cannot be modified or enfeebled. But if it should issue transformed from the actual crisis, it is not from the French camp that the movement for its regeneration should originate; it is from the country itself, which, thanks to our presence, should resume confidence in itself and in the moral support which it should certainly have to expect from all governments, on the day when, reorganizing itself more honorably and more regularly, it would offer them all the guarantees which the combined expedition had for its object to demand. You will give your attention, I have no doubt, to observe strictly that course of conduct which has been already traced out for you by my previous instructions, and which I recall here only because we have now a much better opportunity from this circumstance that henceforward we pursue alone the end towards which we had hoped at first to proceed in concert with England and Spain.

THOUVENEL.

The Minister of Foreign Affairs to the French Ambassador at Madrid.

PARIS, *June* 10, 1862.

SIR: In shielding the responsibility of the Count De Reus by the official approbation which it has given to his conduct, the cabinet of Madrid obliges us to enter into new explanations with it, and to relieve from all ambiguity the ideas which direct our policy in the affairs of Mexico. Moreover, I cannot leave unanswered the despatch of the first secretary of state of her Catholic Majesty, of the date of the 21st of last month, of which the chargé d'affaires of Spain has permitted me a copy. In that despatch M. Calderon Collantes develops the motives which inspired the resolutions of General Prim, and he considers them fully justified by a private letter from Admiral Jurien de la Gravière to the Count De Reus, in which the latter thought he saw an insult to the dignity of his country. I regret the importance given to this document, which, in its confidential and intimate form, did not, perhaps, call for an official discussion, by an interpretation which its author would certainly have hastened to disavow if he could have foreseen it. Even though, in the freedom of private correspondence, some expressions had inexactly rendered the ideas of Admiral Jurien, his well known sympathies for our allies, his personal relations with the Count De Reus ought, it seems to me, have removed from him all suspicion of any intention to offend. General Prim seemed, for the rest, to have thought of it in the same way at first, and his reply, full of cordiality and of that affectionate brotherhood that honors the military career, scarcely permits the supposition that, at the receipt of his colleague's letter, he felt himself attacked for a moment in his dignity, still less in that of his country. As to the Emperor's government, I have not assuredly to defend it, the cabinet of Madrid knowing too well the sentiments which animate it in regard to Spain, and of which you have so often been the interpreter, to require me to renew the assurance of them. I might refuse even to admit that any doubt had arisen in this respect in the minds of the Queen's ministers, if it were possible to discover in the facts anterior to the correspondence which now occupies us the determining cause of the actual resolutions of the Spanish government. Having sometimes differed in our opinions on secondary points, the two governments have always found themselves of accord on essential questions arising from their co-operation, in the course to be pursued as well as in the end to be attained. So we should suppose that the cabinet of Madrid would be no less surprised than ourselves to learn that its plenipotentiary, on a divergence of conduct with his colleagues of France, abandoned the enterprise and, on his own responsibility, took a determination which the ministers of her Catholic Majesty have assured you never entered into their provisions.

I shall not trouble myself, sir, to recall the origin and the object of the treaty of London. France and England had not yet decided to have recourse to coercive measures against a government which ignored all its details, from which Spain, anticipating our agreement, had already prepared to claim, with arms in hand, the execution, ever refused, of the treaty signed by M. Mon and General Almonte, and the reparation which was due to her for the insult offered to her representative, M Pacheco. The conformity of interests and of circumstances quickly produced the understanding which was established at London between the three courts. Having to pursue the redress of their similar grievances, they wished to obtain their satisfactions and their guarantees in common. Resolved at the very beginning, and by force, if necessary, to seize a material pledge to answer them for the reparation of the damages suffered by their countrymen, they contemplated as an eventual result, but a very desirable one, of their operations, the establishment in Mexico of a regular and stable political *regime*, which should offer them for the future such moral sureties as they had vainly demanded from all the governments which had succeeded each other in that republic. The three powers did not hesitate, then, to recognize that the government of Juarez offered them neither at present nor in future any of those guarantees which they sought. Thus, they were unanimous in disapproving the first steps of their representatives in Mexico, which appeared to them impressed with indecision and petty arrangements which the situation did not warrant. The cabinet of Madrid was no less eager to regret an attitude which, by raising up the authority of the government of Mexico, could not but encourage its resistance, and contrasted, above all, with the ardor of which Spain had given proof in preceding her allies to Mexico, and which seemed to indicate on her part the will to do herself justice rather than to negotiate. All the incidents that have occurred since have given occasion to explanations between us and the cabinet of Madrid too complete to authorize me to return to the subject, unless it be to state once more the conformity of the judgments which we formed of them. From the confidential exchange of our ideas, from the assurances which you have received, I should have concluded the identity of our views and of the directions transmitted to our agents. Thus it is that we have been able to believe ourselves authorized to suppose that if our plenipotentiaries, enlightened by the facts which were disclosed before their eyes and relieved from the much-to-be-regretted engagements of La Soledad by the new excesses of the Mexican government, would impress on their action a more decisive appearance, the Spanish government would think, like us, that, far from authorizing the abandonment of the policy of the treaty of London, this new attitude would, on the contrary, indicate a desire to return to that policy in order to effect its final triumph. We would, necessarily, have been confirmed in this idea and in our opinion with regard to the liberty of action restored to us by the acts of the Mexican government, in reading the reply of General Prim to the letter of Admiral Jurien de la Gravière. The Count of Reus wrote on the 21st of March to the following effect: "Can we permit, while we remain quiet in our camps, that the government should continue its vexatious proceedings against our countrymen throughout the entire republic, in exacting from them the payment of the contribution of 2½ per cent. on their capitals, as is done, M. Doblado pretending that he has the right to do so? Can we permit M. Doblado to threaten us with the re-establishment of the decree preventing commercial intercourse between the custom-house of Vera Cruz and the interior of the country, in case that custom-house should not be delivered up to him? Can we permit that a forced loan of 500,000 piastres should be exacted of six houses in Mexico, of which three are Spanish, taxed at 100,000 piastres each? These are the reasons why Sir Charles Wyke and myself have assumed a more energetic attitude than that which we held when we separated. Annexed is the last letter of M. Doblado; judge, in your generous pride, whether such a cool, curt style of speech suits us. You will find, then, in the letter of M. Doblado, and in my explanations, the real cause of our warlike humor; you need seek for no other, for no other exists."

Our plenipotentiaries shared the impressions of General Prim and of Sir Charles Wyke. Freed from their engagements by the act of the Mexican government, they were impatient to emerge from a situation which suited them no more than it did the Count of Reus. But I am at a loss to understand the reproach here addressed by M. Calderon Collantes to Admiral Jurien de la Gravière, of having wished to render the direct and personal interests which had led the allies to Mexico subordinate to the preliminary establishment of a monarchy in that country. The views of the Emperor's government, in this regard, have been too often explained to the cabinet of Madrid to presume the possibility of their having been mistaken; and as to our plenipotentiaries, it suffices to read the proclamation which they addressed to the Mexican people, when, in consequence of the retirement of our allies, they had no longer to regard anything but the sentiment of their government, in order to be convinced that they strictly conformed their words and their acts to that sentiment, in disavowing all intention of imposing by force a form of government rejected by the voice of the nation.

The first secretary of state insists very much on some phrases in which Admiral Jurien de la Gravière might seem to evince a regret of the too exclusively Spanish character which the expedition might have had in the beginning, according to him, when he intimated that in future the augmentation of our effective force would assure the independence of our policy, if circumstances imposed that necessity upon us. It is evident that, as long as the accord remained complete between the allies, the expedition should have a collective character; and our plenipotentiary merely stated a fact when he recalled to mind, in a confidential communication addressed to his colleague, that the arrival of the Spanish troops before the others, their numerical superiority, the conspicuous character even of their chief, had, in that phase of the combined operations, assigned a preponderating part to Spain. Admiral Jurien did not seek by any means to complain of this. In estimating the influence exerted in the common work up to that time by the particular action of each of the combined forces, he did not overstep, it seems to me, the limits of honest discussion, and the opinion which he expressed on this point was not calculated to surprise the Count of Reus, whilst a journal printed under his eyes lost no opportunity to represent him as the soul and complete impersonation of the expedition. Did he not himself write, on the 27th of February, to the first secretary of state of her Catholic Majesty, that, "in his opinion, the Spanish element ought to predominate, as well on account of the particular situation of Spain, in regard to Mexico, as of the initiative taken by his government in this important enterprise?" Admiral Jurien, in fine, confined himself to indicating that, in certain eventualities, independent action would become the right of each one, and that, if the time came when it would be necessary to renounce the idea of obtaining by collective efforts the results which they had promised themselves, he would remain free to pursue his task as he understood it, and to attend alone to the dignity and the interests of his country. It is under this anticipation, unfortunately realized, that our plenipotentiary undertook to say that the expedition would become French

As to the particular facts which have occasioned the rupture, I wish to speak of the protection granted to General Almonte. I might, if needs be, find the justification of the conduct of our agents in the reflections, so full of wisdom and of foresight, which the expulsion of General Miramon inspired into the first secretary of state of her Catholic Majesty. After having recommended to the Count of Reus to use all his influence in order to prevent the repetition of an act of that nature, M. Calderon Collantes wrote to him, on the 7th of March—

"It might be feared that the good understanding now existing between the plenipotentiaries and the commanders of the forces of the three allied powers would be disturbed, if any one of these powers regarded itself as authorized to dictate against any Mexican such measures as that resorted to in regard to Ex-President Miramon. It would be equivalent to exercising a species of sovereignty, which, by placing itself in opposition to that of the others, might give occasion to dangerous debates, and, perhaps, even to acts of violence difficult to be justified. The representative of her Catholic Majesty has the important mission of protecting all persons without distinction, and of preventing any act that may appear dictated by passion or violence."

Finally, in his despatch of the 21st of May, M. Calderon Collantes refers to the proposition which he made, when the first differences broke out, to open a conference in order to establish between the three governments a new understanding, embracing at once accomplished facts and such eventualities as might possibly arise. The Emperor's government appreciates the sentiments which dictated that proposition, and it would have been happy to accept it if it could have hoped from it the good effects promised to itself by the cabinet of Madrid. But we had to observe that, at the distance at which we were from the scene of events, such a new understanding could exert no influence on their course; and it is enough, in fact, to compare dates, in order to convince ourselves that identical instructions, the most categorical from the three governments, could not have prevented the rupture consummated at Orizaba by their plenipotentiaries, nor rendered measures instantaneously accomplished.

I hasten, sir, to withdraw from a discussion henceforward without purpose and into which I have entered only with regret. Each government pronounces in full sovereignty on all the questions in which its dignity and its interests have been engaged. It is not our part to inquire into the motives which may determine the cabinet of Madrid to adopt now towards the government of Mexico a policy of conciliation and negotiation in which we cannot participate. We must state only, as far as we are concerned, that at the time when our plenipotentiaries separated from their colleagues of Orizaba, on the 9th of April, no insult had been avenged, no injury repaired. The object of the treaty of London had not therefore been attained, and it could not suit us to accept the results, thus far negative or illusory, of the expedition which we had sent to Mexico. We regret to have to accomplish alone a duty of which we would have been happy and proud to share the dangers with the glorious army of Spain. We will endeavor to prove equal to the effort; we will strive to obtain the reparation which is due to us; we will exact serious and lasting guarantees for the future. If, in the accomplishment of this task, which is that especially which we have imposed on ourselves, we can be of any assistance to the efforts which may be made by the country itself to emerge from the anarchy which devours it and to reconstitute itself on new and solid bases, we will not refuse our moral support to such manifestations as may appear to us to merit our sympathies. In acting thus, we confidently entertain the idea that we are serving the cause of civilization and of our own interests, which we do not separate, in those distant regions, from those of our allies who have signed the treaty of London with us.

You are authorized, sir, to read this despatch to the first secretary of state of her Catholic Majesty, and to leave with him a copy of it.

THOUVENEL.

The Minister of Foreign Affairs to the French Minister in Mexico.

PARIS, *July* 8, 1862.

SIR: The Emperor has resolved on sending considerable re-enforcements to Mexico, and his Majesty has confided the command in chief of his troops to General Forey. The re-enforcements will not delay to join the expeditionary corps, but General Forey will precede them to Mexico, his departure being to take place in a few days. His Majesty has decided that this general officer should combine in his own hands all the powers previously conferred on Admiral Jurien de la Gravière, and that consequently he should be simultaneously invested with the powers of plenipotentiary and of commander-in-chief of our expedition.

THOUVENEL.

The Emperor to General Forey.

FONTAINEBLEAU, *July* 3, 1862.

MY DEAR GENERAL: At the moment when you are about to start for Mexico, charged with political and military powers, I think it useful to make you acquainted with my ideas.

The line of conduct you will have to follow is: 1. To publish on your arrival a proclamation, the principal points of which will be indicated to you. 2. To receive with the greatest kindness all the Mexicans who shall present themselves. 3. Not to espouse the quarrel of any party; to declare that everything is provisional so long as the Mexican nation shall not have expressed its opinion; to show great deference for religion, but at the same time to tranquilize the holders of national property. 4. To feed, pay, and arm, according to your means, the Mexican auxiliary troops, and make them play principal parts in the combats. 5. To maintain among your own troops, as well as among the auxiliaries, the most severe discipline; to vigorously repress any act or word insulting to the Mexicans, for the pride of their character must not be forgotten, and it is important for the success of the enterprise to conciliate the good feelings of the people.

When you shall have reached the city of Mexico, it is to be desired that the principal persons of all political shades who shall have embraced our cause should come to an understanding with you to organize a provisional government. The government will submit to the Mexican people the question of the political *regime* which is to be definitively established. An assembly will be afterwards elected, according to the Mexican laws.

You will aid the new government to introduce into the administration, and particularly into the finances, that regularity of which France offers the best model. For that purpose, capable men will be sent to second its new organization.

The object to be attained is not to impose on the Mexicans a form of government which would be obnoxious, but to assist them in their efforts to establish, according to their own wishes, a government which may have a chance of stability, and can secure to France the settlement of the injuries of which she has to complain.

It follows, as a matter of course, that if the Mexicans prefer a monarchy, it is for the interest of France to support them in that path.

There will not be wanting people who will ask you why we expend men and money to found a regular government in Mexico.

In the present state of the civilization of the world, the prosperity of America is not a matter of indifference to Europe, for it is that country which feeds our manufactories and gives an impulse to our commerce. We have an interest in the republic of the United States being powerful and prosperous, but not that she should take possession of the whole of the Gulf of Mexico, thence command the Antilles as well as South America, and be the only dispenser of the products of the New World.

We now see, by sad experience, how precarious is the lot of a branch of manufacture which is compelled to procure its raw material in a single market, all the vicissitudes of which it has to bear.

If, on the contrary, Mexico maintains her independence and the integrity of her territory, if a stable government be there constituted with the assistance of France, we shall have restored to the Latin race on the other side the Atlantic all its strength and its prestige; we shall have guaranteed security to our West India colonies and to those of Spain; we shall have established our friendly influence in the centre of America; and that influence, by creating immense markets for our commerce, will procure us the raw materials indispensable for our manufactures.

Mexico thus regenerated will always be well-disposed towards us, not only out of gratitude, but also because her interests will be in accord with ours, and because she will find support in her friendly relations with European powers.

At present, therefore, our military honor engaged, the necessities of our policy, the interests of our industry and commerce, all conspire to make it our duty to march on Mexico, to boldly plant our flag there, and to establish either a monarchy, if not incompatible with the national feeling, or at least a government which may promise some stability.

NAPOLEON.

The French Minister in Mexico to the Minister of Foreign Affairs.

ORIZABA, *June* 23, 1862.

Monsieur le MINISTRE : I have received a copy of a protest signed by the French of th city of Mexico against the inflammatory attacks and the calumnious accusations of which the policy of the Emperor has been the object on the part of some persons who give themselves out as the interpreters of the French colony. This protest has already been signed by more than three hundred Frenchmen, among whom figure all that are in any way respectable among our colony in the capital. I am informed of two or three hundred other adhesions which it was impossible to collect for want of time. I hasten to send this document to your excellency.

DUBOIS DE SALIGNY.

[Annexed document.]

Protest of the members of the French colony in the city of Mexico.

MEXICO, *May*, 1862.

The undersigned, in obedience to the necessities of their position in the city of Mexico, and aware that it does not belong to them to take an active part in the questions and events in agitation at the present time, have abstained from protesting publicly against the injuries, the calumnies, and the insensate outrages directed against the French army, against the government of France and its representatives.

But what the undersigned consider as an imperious duty, is to protest loudly against the strange pretensions of certain persons to present themselves as the legitimate organs of the sentiments and ideas of the French population ; is, also, to protest energetically against certain publications, signed or not signed, called forth by influences now well known, and destined—so it is asserted in them—to enlighten the government of the mother country in regard to the real interests of the French colony in Mexico.

The undersigned, therefore, declare that they repudiate all sort of sympathy with the ideas expressed in these writings ; and inspired by the sentiment of national dignity, as well as by reason and justice, they await, full of hope and confidence, the accomplishment of the noble mission confided to the honor and loyalty of France.

[Here follow 314 signatures.]

The French Minister in Mexico to the Minister of Foreign Affairs.

ORIZABA, *July* 17, 1862.

Monsieur le MINISTRE : I lose no time informing you that M. Dastugnes, one of the most estimable members of the French colony at Mexico, has been recently carried off, at the very gates of the capital, by the notorious Cuellar, long a highway robber, now a colonel in the troops of Juarez, who would have threatened our countryman to shoot him unless he paid a ransom fixed at first at 2,000 piastres, subsequently at 5,000. Here is what has been written to me on this subject :

"I am authorized to bring to your knowledge a new and odious outrage committed on the person of one of our countrymen. M. P. Dastugnes, the French citizen who has been several times robbed already, as well by the liberal as by the reactionary bands, and whose claims appear in the archives of the imperial legation, was seized some eight days ago at some leagues from the city of Mexico and carried off prisoner by Cuellar.

"A sum of 2,000 piastres was first demanded for his liberation, a sum which it is utterly impossible for him to pay ; some days afterwards the ransom was raised to 5,000 piastres, a threat to shoot him if the amount stipulated was not remitted within a very short period. His family is ignorant whether these threats have been carried into execution, though there is reason to fear that they have, for these bands a short time ago hung several persons who were unable to pay the wretches.

"It has seemed proper to inform you of this new outrage committed at the gates of Mexico. Although in the present state of things your protection is powerless for us, it is well that you should know that this unfortunate government is powerless to perform the first duty imposed on every government worthy of that name, that of protecting persons and property. And yet it proclaims itself the representative of progress, the defender of guarantees, of liberty, of democracy.

"Indeed, we feel the blush rise to our cheek at the idea that people allow themselves to be carried away by these senseless words, especially when they are sincerely devoted to the cultivation of liberal ideas. Experience now is precise and positive. What individual is there of the slightest honor and intelligence who does not understand that there is no salvation possible for Mexico except by means of intervention vigorously conducted, which may organize this country, now fallen into dissolution, and rescue it from the miserable condition in which it is now deeply buried? We know that you have thus understood the question, and what efforts you have made and are making to produce a result which may assure at the same time the future of the country and that of your countrymen, not allowing yourself to be moved by the nameless injuries and outrages of which you are the object, and which are for you a source of honor at the very time that they degrade the stupid government which tolerates them, if it does not even excite them. For the rest, I believe I can affirm that these outrages have excited the disgust of the immense majority of the French population, and that they await the moment of being able to manifest the sentiments of gratitude with which they are animated towards you. You have been already enabled to know their sentiments in reading the protest of which you will probably have received a copy, and which is now signed with more than 500 signatures. It is a peremptory reply to the proceedings of some Frenchmen, very limited in number, who would willingly sacrifice to their personal interests the interests and future of the whole French population in Mexico. This population has faith in you, Monsieur le Ministre, and firmly trusts that the French government will accomplish in its entire extent the mission of justice and humanity which it has commenced."

This letter renders any reflections on my part entirely superfluous

DUBOIS DE SALIGNY.

The French Minister in Mexico to the Minister of Foreign Affairs.

ORIZABA, *August* 20, 1862.

Monsieur le MINISTRE: In spite of the denials and threats resorted to by the government to terrify the French of the capital, new signatures have been added to the protest of our countrymen enclosed to you in my despatch of June 23; a new list which has reached me, and which I have the honor herewith to transmit to you, increases to 450 the number of adhesions received up to the 22d of July.

DUBOIS DE SALIGNY.

The French Minister in Mexico to the Minister of Foreign Affairs.

ORIZABA, *October* 2, 1862.

Monsieur le MINISTRE: I wrote some time ago to your excellency that the government of Juarez, seriously excited by the protest spontaneously signed by the French of the capital, had set its police at work to prevent the circulation of the list and the addition of new signatures. A person who has recently arrived from the city of Mexico advises me of another manœuvre of the administration. For some time past the agents of government have been presenting themselves before our countrymen in order to summon them to declare categorically, and in writing, whether they are for or against the intervention, not leaving them in ignorance of the fact that on this declaration on their part depended the question of knowing whether they should be expelled or not from the territory of the republic. This question of the expulsion of the French is, moreover, the order of the day among the journals of Juarez, as also in the clubs and patriotic juntas organized by the police who proclaim themselves almost unanimously for the affirmative.

DUBOIS DE SALIGNY.

The French Minister in Mexico to the Minister of Foreign Affairs.

ORIZABA, *October* 6, 1862.

I have heretofore informed your excellency that the journals of the government and the *patriotic juntas* of the city of Mexico loudly demanded that all the French who did not publicly declare against the French intervention should be expelled, and that their goods should be confiscated. A sheet established by Juarez to excite the evil passions of the masses, *La Cuchara*, goes still further; it desires to have all our countrymen constrained, under pain of expulsion, not only to place their fortunes at the disposal of Juarez, but to take up arms to combat, under the command of Mexican officers, the flag of their country. In the fear that certain persons might be tempted to cry out at this as exaggeration, I annex here the article of that journal which proposes the measure as a very simple thing.

DUBOIS DE SALIGNY.

The French Minister in Mexico to the Minister of Foreign Affairs.

ORIZABA, *October* 8, 1862.

The Monitor Republicano of the 3d of October speaks of arrests that have been made in the capital among Mexicans and French. Chief among the former are mentioned the three generals Santiago, Miguel Blanco, and Guitian, as well as several other persons belonging to the first classes of society. As to the French, the number of those thrown into prison by Juarez is, it is said, quite considerable, and comprises some who have been his partisans. Many persons here seem to fear that extreme acts of violence may be resorted to against our unfortunate fellow-countrymen.

DUBOIS DE SALIGNY.

The French Minister in Mexico to the Minister of Foreign Affairs.

ORIZABA, *October* 11, 1862.

MONSIEUR LE MINISTRE: I hasten to transmit to you such items of information from the city of Mexico as are worthy of credit. In the evening of September 16, the festival day of independence, sixteen houses inhabited by French were assailed with stones by bands of ruffians, shouting cries of "Death to them!" Windows, doors, and fronts of shops were broken, and two Frenchmen were wounded. No measures were taken to prevent these disorders, which, however, might have been easily expected, since previously, on the night of the 15th, such cries had been raised.

We cannot in any way regard these disorders as a manifestation of public opinion. Two bands of two or three hundred individuals at most, composed of children, mob-leaders, and that rabble which it is always so easy to collect in a large city, will never prove the spontaneous and irresistible enthusiasm of a population of two hundred thousand souls. It has required the daily harangues of the newspapers and clubs, the incendiary speeches delivered on the evening of the 15th in the theatres, and on the evening of the 16th at the Alameda, and finally the excitement of the festival, to arrive at this sad result. It has required especially the carelessness or the ill-will of the administration, which, with a garrison, of two or three thousand men and a strong police, could not or would not maintain order, when a hundred men properly employed would have sufficed for the purpose.

What the Mexican government, although not disposed to recoil from any measures, be they as tyrannical or as odious as they may, cannot procure for itself, is the money necessary for the support of troops and the purchase of materials indispensable for the execution of works of defence. The people reduced to the most frightful misery, laboring under the absolute impossibility of paying the forced loans with which they crush them down every day, their property is seized and exposed to sale; but no purchasers present themselves. Then a resolution is adopted to issue about fiften millions of piasters in paper money having compulsory circulation. The question is asked, What do the representatives of England and the United States intend to do in presence of this measure which so seriously affects the English and the Americans?

The question was always agitated as to whether all our countrymen should be expelled in a body from the territory of the republic. But it has been decided to expel those who were arrested at the commencement of this month. They were to be conveyed to Acapulco, on the Pacific. It is to be feared that, for many among them at least, expulsion under such circumstances may be equivalent to a condemnation to death.

DUBOIS DE SALIGNY.

The Minister of Foreign Affairs to the French Ambassador at Madrid.

PARIS, *December* 22, 1862.

SIR: I have received the despatches which you have done me the honor to write to me, and I have laid before the Emperor those in which you give me an account of the discussion which took place in the Spanish senate in reference to the affairs in Mexico.

The speech delivered by the minister of state of her Catholic Majesty in that discussion contains, in regard to the events that have occurred in Mexico since the signing of the treaty of London, assertions and conclusions which it will not behoove us, perhaps, to leave unanswered. I might at present confine myself to saying that the explanations furnished by his excellency M. Billault to the legislative body, and since developed in the correspondence of my predecessor, retain all their effect in the eyes of the Emperor's government; and permit me, before replying to the speech of M. Calderon Collantes, to wait until the result of the debates entered upon in the Cortes has indicated the necessity of it to me.

There is one point, however, which appears to me to call forth on my part an immediate explanation; I mean the exchange of ideas which has taken place between the Marquis of Havana and myself in reference to the eventual return of Spain to a community of action with France, and I also refer to the notes exchanged between us, and in which these ideas are expressed. The words uttered by the minister of state in regard to this diplomatic incident have been variously repeated, and, as far as regards the opinion expressed by him on the dispositions of the two cabinets, and on the import of the engagements entered into, there has resulted at least an obscurity which it is our common interest to dispel. The affairs of Mexico have been the occasion of confusion and misunderstanding between us and the Queen's government too frequent not to compel me to be as precise and specific as possible in rendering the terms of the intercommunications in question, and the worth of the assurances which have been the consequences of them. M. Calderon Collantes, moreover, not having deemed it proper to lay before the Cortes the written documents of this negotiation, I believe it my duty to annex them to this despatch, although they be all well known to you already, accompanying them with such explanations as seem proper to be made.

Upon my entrance into the ministry, the Marquis of Havana, inspired with that cordiality of sentiment which he has invariably manifested during the whole course of his mission, came to acquaint me with the desire of his government to re-establish with us, in reference to the affairs of Mexico, the accord unfortunately broken, and to inquire into the conditions of the future co-operation of the two powers. In his opinion the treaty of London was not annulled by the dissension that arose between the parties signing it; it was simply suspended; the end was not obtained. To the exclusion of all particular advantages, each of the three powers was always entitled to seek the satisfaction demanded for the injuries which it had received, the indemnities due for the damages sustained by its citizens, and guarantees for the future. France would certainly accomplish, to her glory, the work of war which henceforward she supported alone; but the assistance of Spain would become necessary to her, or very useful, at least, to pacify that country and conclude a solid peace, from which the interests of none of the powers that signed the treaty of London would have to suffer. If, to obtain these results, the occupation of the capital or of some other points of Mexico was judged indispensable, the Queen's government was ready to come to an understanding with that of the Emperor in order to determine the number of troops to be furnished, and to indicate the way in which they should be employed.

These considerations, developed by the ambassador of Spain, were resumed in a note which he addressed to me in the course of the month of October, and which you will find hereunto annexed, under the designation of No. 1.

I was enabled to dispense with entering on any discussion with the Marquis of Havana in reference to anterior events, to which I had personally remained a stranger, and I have been fortunate enough, under these circumstances, to avoid any recrimination with him in regard to the past. I had found, as I said to him, France alone at war with Mexico. The question of inquiring whether the treaty which had regulated the co-operation of the three powers was yet in force, when two of them had abandoned the enterprise commenced in common, appeared to me to have become a purely theoretic investigation, and without any practical application to the circumstances. We were fully impressed with the importance of the moral and material assistance which Spain would bring in a common work, but accomplished facts had imposed a position upon us which we had accepted, and which was for the moment governed by the interests of our military dignity and honor. We did not, for the rest, contest the right of either Spain or England to follow up their claims; we thought, whilst congratulating ourselves for it, that the expedition with which we found ourselves alone charged would turn to their advantage, and we would be happy, when the proper time arrived, to come to an understanding with our allies, in order to consolidate the results. I committed these explanations to an unofficial note which I transmitted to the Marquis of Havana on the 27th of October, (annexed document, No. 2,) in reply to that which he had addressed to me.

Always anxious to efface any traces which might have been left in our relations with Spain by the dissensions that separated us in Mexico, the Marquis of Havana nevertheless persisted with the most honorable solicitude to devise some means for the renewal of the good understanding of which his high intelligence of the best interests of his country caused him to appreciate the value. He did not cease to have interviews with me on this subject full of mutual confidence.

The ambassador of Spain thought that it would be desirable that plenipotentiaries should be nominated by Spain and England before the operations of our army were accomplished; moreover, he judged it useful to suspend for the present the mode of procedure for the establishment of a national government in Mexico, and he suggested a system already indicated by his government in 1860. The Marquis of Havana desired to communicate to me a draught of an unofficial note which he had prepared on these bases. I had to decline these new proposals, and if I mention them now, though they did not produce any result, it is because one of the accounts of the part of the speech of M. Calderon Collantes, which refers to those negotiations, would tend to make us suppose that we had actually entered into engagements analogous to those which the Marquis of Havana proposed to us, whilst it is precisely for not having entered into such an engagement that I requested the ambassador of Spain to consider as not sent the note which he had desired to submit to me preliminarily. I had in fact to remind him of the rights which accrued to us from our state of war; we could not admit any control or any restriction in the exercise which we made of those rights. We were carrying on war; peace should result from it; when and how I could not tell him. At the distance at which we were from the scene of events, I could not anticipate them by hypothetical calculations. I could still less bind myself by engagements which accomplished facts in Mexico might, perhaps, have weakened before they were known there. Moreover, there was no question for us about founding and constituting a government, and the proposition even of the Marquis of Havana seemed to me, moreover, to take too little account of the part which it belongs to the Mexicans to act in such a work. We had no need of returning to what we had so often repeated, of our desire to see that country profit by the crisis through which it was passing in order to make its regeneration arise from it, and of our good will to aid it in the efforts which it might make in order to attain that object; but the work of its salvation is above all its own; it is not ours. If our troops enter the city of Mexico in triumph, we know not what influence that event may have on the country; we do not wish to exclude any combination in advance, nor to restrict the use which the Mexican nation may be able to make of its sovereign rights; if the government, whatever it may be, which it may choose to select, offers us sufficient guarantees, our clearest interests will counsel us to labor for its consolidation. Whatever may happen, Mexico will never be for us either a conquest or a colony; our interests there will consequently never be opposed to those of Spain or England. We could, therefore, only receive with eagerness their concurrence, of which we highly appreciate the potent efficacy, in order to consolidate a state of things which might assure us all the guarantees claimed on the same grounds by the interests of all the powers.

I added, finally, that before resuming with our allies of the treaty of London a negotiation destined to regulate a new understanding, it was necessary to be assured of the disposition of the English cabinet, and that I had no indication up to that time to authorize me to judge of it in advance.

The ambassador of Spain was eager to take note of these considerations, and he addressed to me, on the 29th of November, the note hereunto annexed under the designation of No. 3, in which he expressed to me a desire to see the Emperor's government indicate the time and the means which appeared to it most proper to arrive at such an agreement. I hastened to reply to the Marquis of Havana on the 1st of December, (annexed document No. 4,) "That as soon as the present phase of military operations should be terminated, the imperial government would be disposed to invite the two powers that signed with it the treaty of London to send to Mexico plenipotentiaries specially appointed for this purpose *(ad hoc,)* who had not been engaged in the previous transactions, in order to advise in concert upon the means of consolidating a state of affairs in Mexico that might insure the prosperity of the country and offer guarantees of security to the interests of foreign nations." I added that the Emperor's government would consider the declarations contained in the present note as final, as soon as the governments of Spain and England had given their adherence to them.

Such, sir, is the last act of that negotiation, the various incidents of which it has appeared useful to me to repeat, before setting forth the conclusion to be derived from them, and in order the better to illustrate their character and value. It is my duty, in conclusion, to say that the ambassador of Spain brought to the negotiation a mind entirely free from prejudice, and a frankness and straightforwardness of purpose to which I am highly pleased to be here able to render homage.

DROUYN DE LHUYS.

[Annexed Document No. 1.]

Unofficial note transmitted to the Minister of Foreign Affairs by his Excellency the Marquis of Havana, ambassador of Spain at Paris.

OCTOBER, 1862.

The government of her Catholic Majesty has declared on several occasions that it did not consider the treaty of London of the date of October 31, 1861, as annulled, but only as suspended, and that, in its opinion, it could be replaced in full force by the agreement of the powers which had signed it.

The purpose of the treaty was to obtain the satisfaction due for the offences committed against the contracting governments, indemnity for the wrongs endured by their subjects, and, as far as possible, some guarantee that similar acts should not be repeated in future.

No one of these results has yet been obtained; the disagreement supervening between the plenipotentiaries and among the chiefs of the expedition arrested their course, just at the very moment when that expedition seemed in the way of attaining the end which the powers had proposed to themselves.

Since then the French government pursues its task alone. Without the slightest doubt, it will triumph over all armed resistance that it may encounter; nevertheless it is to be feared that obstacles of another nature my prevent it from causing the Mexican republic to enter on a solid and stable career, which, by insuring internal order, may externally present a guarantee for the execution of any engagements entered into by its government; for this latter, notwithstanding all the liberty allowed to the country in order to reconstitute itself, might be considered as imposed by France.

The community of action stipulated by the treaty of London would have avoided this grave inconvenience, seeing that the three powers which signed that treaty had engaged themselves, on the one part, to abstain from all intervention in the internal affairs of Mexico calculated to infringe on the rights of the Mexican nation to choose the form of government which suited it, and on the other, not to seek for any territorial acquisitions or special advantages for themselves

Taking the existence of the treaty of London as a starting point, the contracting powers would have to settle the amount of the claims which they have to exact from the Mexican government, and the guarantees which the latter would have to give to insure the execution of its engagements and to avoid the repetition of former offences. It is evident, moreover, that if the allied governments ought to remain free to decide on the claims which they will judge it their duty to maintain, it would nevertheless be proper not to place Mexico in a state of impossibility to acquit herself of the engagements by which she may have bound herself. Moreover, this would be no more than adhering to the spirit of the treaty of London, which was not signed for the purpose of crushing out Mexican nationality, but rather, on the contrary, to aid it to recover from the state of anarchy in which the country has been so long plunged.

This suffices to explain the ideas of the government of her Catholic Majesty; however, it is not useless to add that if, in order to obtain the results indicated, the temporary occupation of the capital of the republic or of other points of its territory was judged necessary, the Queen's government would find itself ready to enter into a special agreement, having for its end to fix the forces which each power might have to send thither and the posts which they should have to occupy.

Under the influence of these ideas, her Catholic Majesty's government is disposed to take part in any new conferences destined to attain the object which the three powers proposed to themselves by the treaty of the 31st of October last.

The Emperor's government, if it shares in this way of thinking, may impart these ideas to the cabinet of her Britannic Majesty.

[Annexed Document No. 2.]

Unofficial Note addressed to the Spanish Ambassador by the Minister of Foreign Affairs.

OCTOBER 29, 1862.

The minister of foreign affairs has examined with the most serious attention the unofficial note which the ambassador of Spain has done me the honor of transmitting to me in reference to the affairs of Mexico.

After having reviewed the essential objects which the three powers proposed to themselves to realize, when signing the treaty of October 31, 1861, at London, the note expresses regret that the course of the expedition sent to Mexico should have been arrested in consequence of the disagreement supervening between the plenipotentiaries and the respective commanders at the very moment that the object was about to be attained.

His imperial Majesty's minister cannot but share this regret, but, without desiring to re-enter here on a retrospective discussion which has already been sufficiently elucidated by the correspondence of his predecessor, he will confine himself to expressing, in his turn, the conviction that the Emperor's government has faithfully interpreted the treaty of October 31, and that, if it has thought proper to act alone where it had no more ardent desire than that of operating in concert with its allies, it is because it has not depended upon it to conciliate the divergencies which have been produced, and because it has judged that the honor of its flag and the care of its interests imposed on it the obligation of continuing alone the work on which it has entered.

It appears from the note of his Excellency the Marquis of Havana that the government of her Catholic Majesty would be disposed now to come to an understanding with those of France and England, for the purpose of determining, in special conferences, the measures which it might be opportune to adopt in concert, and the number of troops which each one of the powers should have to furnish in case the temporary occupation of the city of Mexico or of other points in the country should be judged necessary to produce the results indicated by the treaty of 1860.

The Emperor's government appreciates, as becomes it, those suggestions, and his Majesty's minister of foreign affairs is pleased to acknowledge the good intentions which dictated them. Impressed with the importance of the moral and material support of its allies, it cannot, however, lose sight of the state of affairs which accomplished facts have imposed upon it. Very far, moreover, from wishing, even in the most indirect manner, to contest the right of Spain or England to pursue their legitimate claims upon Mexico, it entertains the confidence, on the contrary, that the expedition, of which, by force of circumstances, it now finds itself alone compelled to bear the burden, will turn to the advantage of those two powers at the same time as to its own. It looks with the sincerest wishes for the moment when, the efforts of its arms having obtained the success which it would have been happy to pursue in common with its allies, it will be permitted to resume serious negotiations with Mexico, to insure, with complete satisfaction of pending claims, the security which up to this time has been wanting to the persons and property of foreigners resident in that country, and to accomplish, in fine, in a new understanding with Spain and England, the enterprise commenced in common, and to the success of which their cordial co-operation can so powerfully contribute.

[Annexed Document No. 3.]

Unofficial note transmitted to the Minister of Foreign Affairs by the Spanish Ambassador.

NOVEMBER 29, 1862.

In the unofficial note concerning the affairs of Mexico, addressed to the ambassador of her Catholic Majesty, under date of the 29th of October last, by the minister of foreign affairs, his excellency declared that if, by the force of accomplished facts, France has found herself under the necessity of pursuing alone the expedition commenced in common, she did not the less long most ardently for the moment when the efforts of her arms would permit the final accomplishment of the enterprise, under a new understanding, for the success of which enterprise the cordial co-operation of the powers that signed the treaty of London can so powerfully contribute.

In thus expressing himself the minister of foreign affairs gives it to be understood that, in his opinion, it would be difficult to arrive at a new agreement before the French troops entered the capital of the Mexican republic.

Without wishing to dispute the validity of this opinion, her Catholic Majesty's ambassador thinks that it would be desirable to see the Emperor's government now indicate the time and the means which would appear to it the most suitable to come to that agreement.

It is not solely in the interest of the Spanish claims in Mexico that the ambassador of Spain proposes to the Emperor's government to make this declaration ; he thinks that its advantages would make themselves more especially felt by the confidence which it would be destined to inspire into the people of the republic, who would recognize, by this act, that the Emperor's government has not ceased to consider as still in force the declaration contained in Article 2 of the treaty of London, in accordance with which the powers signing it should abstain from exercising their influence on the right of the Mexicans to choose and freely constitute the form of their government.

[Annexed Document No. 4.]

Unofficial note transmitted to the Spanish Ambassador by the Minister of Foreign Affairs.

DECEMBER 1, 1862.

His excellency the ambassador of Spain, in a note of the 29th of November last, after having referred to the conciliatory disposition manifested by the minister of foreign affairs of France on the subject of the eventual re-establishment of a mutual understanding in regard to the affairs of Mexico as soon as circumstances will allow it, expresses the desire that the Emperor's government should now indicate the time and the means which would appear to it the most proper to come to this agreement. It is not solely in the interest of the Spanish claims that the Marquis of Havana proposes to make this declaration. According to his excellency, the advantages of it would make themselves more especially felt by the confidence which it would inspire into the Mexican people, who would by this fact recognize that the Emperor's government has not ceased to consider as yet in force the principle laid down in Article 2 of the treaty of London.

In spite of the change which has been produced in the attitude and in the conduct of his allies the Emperor has not modified his first intentions. So the minister of foreign affairs does not hesitate to reply to his excellency the ambassador of her Catholic Majesty, that as soon as the phase of military operations shall be terminated, the imperial government will be disposed to invite the two powers that signed with it the aforesaid treaty to send to Mexico plenipotentiaries named for that especial purpose, (*ad hoc*,) and who have not been engaged in any of the previous transactions, to advise in concert on the means of consolidating in Mexico a state of things which may insure the prosperity of the country, and offer guarantees of security to the interests of foreign nations.

As to the agreement on the claims which the three powers ought to exact from Mexico, it is understood that those of Spain and England cannot be any obstacle to the demands which France will have to present in consequence of the war which she has seen herself obliged to maintain.

The Emperor's government will consider the declarations contained in the present note as final as soon as the governments of Spain and England shall have given their adherence to them.

The Minister of Foreign Affairs to the French Ambassador at Madrid.

PARIS, *December* 23, 1862.

SIR: I have received the despatches which you have done me the honor to address to me; your telegraphic messages of the 19th and 20th of this month have likewise reached me, and I am therefore enabled to form an entirely correct estimate of the consequences and conclusion of the incident originated by the language used by M. Calderon Collantes, before the senate in the session of the 13th. That language was calculated to alter the sense of the explanations that took place between that minister and yourself in reference to various circumstances of the Mexican affair, and especially in regard to the estimate of which the treaty of La Soledad had been the object, and to place in doubt the perfect correctness of the advices which you had transmitted to the government of the Emperor.

The telegraphic despatch which I had the honor of addressing to you on the 18th will have shown you, sir, all the importance that the Emperor's government attached to the fact that the assertions of the first secretary of state of her Catholic Majesty, made in opposition to those which you had set down in your correspondence with my predecessor, should become on your part the object for a demand for immediate reparation. It is, then, with satisfaction that I have learned that you had anticipated in this regard the instructions which I have transmitted to you by order of his Majesty.

The Emperor, to whom I have given an account of your proceedings, has been pleased to approve of them, and, as I have hastened to announce to you by telegraph, his Majesty authorizes you to consider as a sufficient satisfaction the words which M. Calderon Collantes has pronounced before the senate, in the session of the 18th. Those explanations, in fact, under a form more or less obscure, contain an evident retraction of the allegations which had provoked our legitimate susceptibilities, and the notoriety which has not failed to follow the demand for reparation which you addressed to the first secretary of state cannot but contribute to render still more complete the satisfaction which has been given to us. You may, then, consider this affair as ended.

DROUYN DE LHUYS.

The French Minister at Washington to the Minister of Foreign Affairs.

WASHINGTON, *April* 3, 1863.

M. LE MINISTRE: Mr. Seward tells me that I may assure your excellency that I was perfectly right in representing him as having always at heart a desire to avoid giving us any cause of complaint on the Mexican question; that his policy has not ceased to be frank and open, and that in all his correspondence not one word could be found to testify the slightest participation in any combinations directed against the government of the Emperor, or which would excite his susceptibility.

MERCIER.

The Minister of Foreign Affairs to M. Mercier, at Washington.

PARIS, *April* 23, 1863.

SIR: I send you a copy of a letter from the minister of the United Statés at London, which has just been published in the English papers. Written, as you see, to the commander of the federal fleet, it has for its object to request him to allow free passage for arms and munitions of war sent from England to Matamoras by Mexican agents. This document reveals too plainly with what sentiments the representative of the United States is inspired in regard to us in this circumstance to allow me to refrain from explaining myself to Mr. Dayton on the matter. I have done so in friendly but strong terms, and I have deemed it proper, moreover, to embody the observations suggested to me by this strange incident in an unofficial note which I have transmitted to him, and of which you will find a copy enclosed. That such shipments as those in question should not be arrested by the American cruisers is not what we have to complain of, but we have reason to consider ourselves aggrieved at the conduct of Mr. Adams in giving such a preliminary assurance to the consigners, and thus contributing, as far as it depends on him, to the success of unlawful operations directed against us. Perhaps, nevertheless, I would not have bestowed so much attention on this singular document emanating from Mr. Adams if, at the same moment, your correspondence had not made me acquainted with the very different and entirely friendly language used to you by Mr. Seward. It is enough to compare it with the letter written by the minister of the United States at London in order to be struck with the contradiction which exists between the attitude of this latter agent and the disposition with which he ought to show himself animated, in order to correspond with the sentiments of his government.

DROUYN DE LHUYS.

The French Minister at Washington to the Minister of Foreign Affairs.

WASHINGTON, *May* 8, 1863.

M. LE MINISTRE: I received yesterday the despatch which your excellency has done me the honor of addressing me on the subject of the letter written by Mr. Adams to the commanders of the federal cruisers to request them to let freely pass such arms and munitions of war as are sent from England to Matamoras by Mexican agents.

On the same day I waited upon the Secretary of State to inform him of the impression made on the Emperor's government by such a proceeding on the part of the representative of the United States at London.

As he had already received advice of the unofficial note which your excellency had on that occasion placed in the hands of Mr. Dayton, he expected my call. After I had unfolded to him the observations which I had been charged to make to him, and which confirmed those which I had hastened to make to him of my own accord as soon as I had learned through the newspapers of the letter of Mr. Adams, Mr. Seward entered into some explanations tending to exonerate entirely the cabinet of Washington from any responsibility for the affair. I replied to him that, in my correspondence with your excellency I had always made it my duty to render full justice to the honorable and loyal attitude which he had at no time failed to maintain in the Mexican question.

MERCIER.

The Minister of Foreign Affairs to M. Mercier, at Washington.

PARIS, *June* 4, 1863.

Mr. Dayton has read to me a letter addressed to him by Mr. Seward in reference to that addressed by Mr. Adams to the commanders of the federal cruisers. The Secretary of State explains himself to Mr. Dayton in regard to that circumstance in the same manner that he did to you in your last interview. According to him, what Mr. Adams desired to effect was merely that the federal cruisers should prevent all transportation of arms to the south, without troubling themselves with other transportations of the same nature for a different destination, whatever that destination might be. Mr Seward, moreover, recognizes that the document emanating from the American minister at London apparently manifests an unkindly disposition, entirely at variance with the sentiments of friendship which we have reason to expect from the cabinet of Washington, and with which it is sincerely animated in our regard. Therefore he does not hesitate to consider the letter of Mr. Adams as an ill-considered proceeding.

In presence of these declarations I had no further cause to insist with Mr. Dayton on what there might be to regret in the conduct of his colleague at London.

DROUYN DE LHUYS.

The Minister of Foreign Affairs to M. Mercier, at Washington.

PARIS, *September* 15, 1863.

SIR: Mr. Dayton, who exhibits in his relations with me a great confidence, and a rectitude to which I am pleased to bear testimony, has been moved at certain rumors, propagated with a design which I have not now to inquire into, but which appear lately to have obtained some credit at Paris, and he has come to converse with me about them. According to these reports, too inconsiderately accepted, the Emperor's government has decided to recognize the States of the south, and a treaty has even been already signed, according to which the new confederacy is to cede to France, either for herself, or that she may make a retrocession of them to Mexico, Texas and a portion of Louisiana.

At the moment in which Mr. Dayton was imparting to me this information, I was exactly in a position to offer him information for information, and, before answering the questions which he addressed me, I asked him if, among the alarming symptoms for the maintenance of the good relations of the two countries, he had not, like myself, received other news, likewise diffused in public, such as, for instance, the transmission by him to me of a protest from his government against our expedition to Mexico and its consequences; the conclusion of an alliance, offensive and defensive, between the United States and Russia; the appearance of a federal fleet before Vera Cruz, &c., &c.

In regard to the protest, after remarking to me that I, better than any one else, knew that he had not transmitted to me any, Mr. Dayton said to me that, under the promptings of the general tenor of the correspondence of Mr. Seward, and of the knowledge which he himself had of the inclinations of his fellow-citizens, he had been able to speak to me of the painful impression produced on public opinion in his country by the preponderant intervention of a European power in an American republic, and by the creation of a monarchical establishment in a country adjacent to the United States; but that from that to a protest, or to any intention whatever of comminatory intermeddling. was very far, and that nothing in his instructions authorized him to overleap that distance. He knew nothing, on the other hand, of the alleged alliance of his government with Russia, and he had every reason to disbelieve it. As to the presence of a federal fleet before Vera Cruz, this news did not seem to him even to merit the honor of a contradiction.

I told Mr. Dayton that I had never attached any importance to the reports which I had pointed out to him, and that, in speaking to him of them, my object was much less to call forth explanations on his part, than to warn him against rumors of a different character; but having probably the same origin of which he had spoken to me, I could, however, contradict them categorically. In regard to the recognition of the States of the south, the intentions of the Emperor's government were known to him, and this question was still at the point where our late conversations had left it. We had not, therefore, recognized the south, and, much more, we had not signed with it any treaty for the cession of Louisiana and Texas. With respect to this, I could repeat to him, what I had so often said to him already, that we neither sought for ourselves, nor for others, any acquisition in America. I added that I trusted that the good sense of the people of the United States would do justice to exaggerations and false suppositions, by the aid of which it was endeavored to mislead and sour public opinion; and that I relied on his co-operation in trying to render prevalent a more equitable appreciation of our intentions and of the necessities which our policy obeyed.

I have thought, sir, that it was well that you should be informed of the particulars of this conversation, in order that you might, on your part, communicate it to Mr. Seward, and receive the precise words of it, in order to rectify around you false opinions and unjustifiable anticipations.

Accept, sir, assurances of my high consideration.

DROUYN DE LHUYS.

Mr. MERCIER,
Minister of the Emperor at Washington, D. C.

The Minister of Foreign Affairs to General Bazaine, commander-in-chief of the French forces in Mexico.

PARIS, *August* 14, 1863.

GENERAL: The despatches which I receive to-day from Mexico confirm the news which had already reached Europe by means of the telegraph, of the important resolutions voted by the Assembly of Notables, at Mexico, on the 10th of last July. This news could be received only with sincere satisfaction by the government of the Emperor, and we congratulate ourselves on seeing our anticipations justified by the good sense and patriotism of the assembly.

As you know, general, when the necessity of proceeding to obtain redress for accumulated wrongs conducted us to Mexico, the Emperor entertained the idea of the possibility of procuring the regeneration of that country from the very crisis brought upon it by the government of M. Juarez. According to his Majesty's ideas, no pressure should be exercised upon the Mexican nation; it alone should have the right of deciding on the form of its institutions, and in case it should adopt a monarchical constitution, on the choice of the prince who should be called to reign over it. It should only know in advance that our moral support was pledged to all honorable and serious efforts which should be used to rescue the country from anarchy and dissolution. This is what, in conformity with the orders of the Emperor, the generals and all the agents of his Majesty in Mexico have had for their mission to cause to be well understood around them. It is, then, in the plenitude of its rights and in the free exercise of its independence that the Mexican nation founds, at this moment, its new destinies. We already see, in the vote of the Assembly of Notables, a spontaneous manifestation and a most imposing one of its dispositions; but it is important that this vote should be confirmed and ratified as soon as possible by the assent of the people. We likewise applaud the choice of the eminent prince whom the assembly has called to the throne by an acclamation which must, in like manner, receive its definitive approval from the suffrages of the country.

DROUYN DE LHUYS.

The Minister of Foreign Affairs to General Bazaine.

AUGUST 17, 1863.

GENERAL: At the moment in which you find yourself invested with the plenitude of political and military power, and when, thanks to the heroism of our soldiers and the skill of our chiefs, the elaboration of a new political *régime* supersedes the clash of arms in Mexico, I deem it useful to retrace once more the ideas with which the Emperor's government is inspired. Those ideas have been most clearly indicated in the letter addressed by his Majesty to General Forey, July 3, 1862, and to this memorable document we must always refer.

I shall not return to enumerate the facts which caused our intervention, or the incidents too well known which have signalized the first phase of it, whilst we were engaged in collective action with other powers. I refer to them merely to recall to mind that, left alone, we have used our independence only to pursue the work which it was not in our power to accomplish in conjunction with the rest, and without deviating from the line which, from the beginning, we had traced out for ourselves and which we had indicated to our allies. In acting thus, we persist in believing that we serve the general interests of Europe.

We have recognized that the legitimacy of our intervention resulted solely from our grievances against the government of that country; we have declared that, whatever rights war conferred on us, we sought neither conquest nor colonial establishment, nor even any political or commercial advantage to the exclusion of other powers. Penetrated, however, with the idea, which several onerous experiences justified, that an expedition, analogous to those of which the traditional proceedings of the Mexican government have so often imposed on us and others the necessity, would assure us only very precarious satisfaction and no guarantees for the future, we have thought that it would be worthy of us and profitable for all to remind the Mexican people of the iniquities of their government, and to afford them, if they desired to avail themselves of it, the occasion and the means to react against the elements of dissolution accumulated on their soil by a deplorable succession of anarchical powers. We applaud ourselves heartily now for not having despaired of the good sense and patriotism of the Mexican nation. For the rest, we most unequivocally eschew, as you are aware, any intention of substituting our influence in place of the free resolutions of the country ; we promise it our moral support to second whatever efforts it may wish to make in its own independence ; but it is from its own loins that its regeneration must issue.

We have received with pleasure, as a symptom of favorable augury, the manifestation of the Assembly of Notables of Mexico in favor of the establishment of a monarchy, and the name of the prince called to the empire. However, as I have indicated to you in a preceding despatch, we can consider the votes of the Assembly at Mexico only as the first indication of the disposition of the country. With all the authority which attaches to the eminent men who compose it, the Assembly recommends to its fellow-countrymen the adoption of monarchical institutions, and it designates a prince for their suffrages. It belongs, however, to the provisional government to collect those suffrages in such a manner as to banish all doubt in regard to the expression of the will of the country. It is not my part to indicate to you the mode to be adopted in order that this indispensable result should be completely attained ; we must search for this in the local customs and institutions. Whether the municipalities should be called upon to declare their wishes in the different provinces according as they shall have recovered the free disposal of themselves, or whether the lists should be opened by their care in order to collect the votes, the best method will be that which shall insure the largest manifestation of the popular will in all its independence and sincerity. General, the Emperor particularly recommends this essential point to your most careful attention.

Other questions at the same time demand your solicitude. We have flattered ourselves with the idea that we represent in Mexico the cause of progress and of civilization, and our regard for our responsibility does not permit us to accept the species of provisional guardianship with which we are invested by circumstances, except on condition of serving that cause faithfully by our counsels and by our actions. From this point of view, we have to regret certain measures which contrast in an unfavorable manner with the ideas which we ought to strive to establish. Sequestrations, prohibitions, outlawries have too often been, in Mexico, the arms used by parties in straits, in their desperate contests—too often, indeed, not to interdict the use of them to a government that goes to conserve and restore. Adopted, doubtless, in view of the urgent necessities of which I cannot judge, they can have but a provisional character, and at the moment at which I write to you they are certainly revoked, if they have not been already so at the reception of the instructions sent out by the last packet.

The reorganization of the Mexican army is one of the most important questions which should, at present, occupy the attention of the provisional government and yours. It is the duty of the minister of war to transmit special instructions to you on this point. I will confine myself to saying, that, the desire of the Emperor's government being to restrict, as promptly as circumstances will permit, the extent and the duration of our occupation, it is essential that this reorganization should be pushed forward with all possible activity, and that it is desirable that in future, and in proportion to the progress realized, an honorable share of duty should be assigned to the Mexican army. In the interest of the country and its ulterior development, as well as to provide for present necessities, I recommend you to press upon the government the duty of applying its utmost care to multiply the means of communication, and to assure, on the roads which now exist, security of transportation and rapid exchange of correspondence.

Without directly substituting your initiative for that of the government, all your counsels, general, should tend to have the administration, properly so called, reconstituted in conditions of regularity and strength, such as may give confidence to the country and reassure it against all ideas of reactionary and exclusive policy. Under the shadow of our flag, all parties can be worthily reconciled, and we will induce them to this ; but as we repudiate their passions, we must never allow it to serve as a shelter for them to work out their revenges.

The same principles should preside over the reorganization of the judicial administration, and you will have to recommend to the government, to be inspired with them in the choice of magistrates and in the impulse which it will give them, the independence and honesty of the magistracy being able to contribute powerfully to elevate the moral state of a people among whom the notions of right must have been very much blunted by the contact of so many revolutions.

The existing administrative and judicial institutions appear, moreover, to answer the wants and customs of the country. Your counsels should, therefore, be directed, in this regard, rather to the choice of functionaries and the directions to be impressed upon them, than to the institutions themselves.

It is not entirely so with regard to the finances. We have there, moreover, a direct interest, which commands us to watch more closely over the execution of such regulations as ought to assure to the country the benefits of a regular system of accountability. The proper management of the public money is the guarantee of our debts, and, from this point of view, we have good reason to exercise an active control over the financial administration. We have, for the rest, as far as depended on us, facilitated its reorganization by assuring to it the precious support of special agents delegated for that purpose by the minister of finance. Under their enlightened influence, the germs of prosperity so varied and abundant which the country possesses cannot fail to be rapidly developed.

I have spoken of our claims. They are, as you know, general, of two kinds: those which are anterior to the war, and those which have their origin in the war. As to the former, they will be all referred for examination to a commission which shall be instituted in connexion with my department, and which shall be composed in such a way as to assure an unquestionable authority to its decisions. The total amount to be presented to the Mexican government will be composed of the sum of all these claims that shall be recognized by the commission as legitimately founded in justice.

As to those which proceed from the war which we are now maintaining, my colleagues in the departments of war and marine are occupied in combining such elements as will allow them to form a proper estimate of the expenses of which we shall have to claim reimbursement. We shall most likely be able to transmit to you, by the next packet, the result of this labor, and you will then have to present to the provisional government for acceptance the demand for reimbursement of the sum which shall be indicated to you.

DROUYN DE LHUYS.

The Minister of Foreign Affairs to General Bazaine.

GENERAL: I have communicated, as I announced to you my intention of doing, with my colleagues in the departments of war, marine, and finance, in order to agree upon the amount of indemnity for the war, for which we shall have to claim reimbursement from Mexico. The various items of information which were indispensable to us in order to appreciate exactly the sum total of our expenses are now in our possession. Consequently we shall not delay in settling definitely the figures of the sum at which this indemnity ought to be estimated. We had, likewise, to take into consideration, in advance, the expenses yet to be incurred before our forces shall have completely evacuated the Mexican territory. I have, therefore, conferred on this subject with my colleagues, and I shall, in all probability, be able to transmit to the Marquis de Montholon, at the moment of his departure, suitable instructions to enable him to negotiate these two arrangements immediately upon his arrival in Mexico.

DROUYN DE LHUYS.

Mr. Romero to Mr. Seward.

[Translation.]

MEXICAN LEGATION TO THE UNITED STATES OF AMERICA,
Washington, January 31, 1864.

MR. SECRETARY: I have the honor to send to you, enclosed with this note, a series of articles which contain the history of political occurrences in Mexico, interwoven with the European interference, which it is attempted to carry into effect in that republic, and which demonstrate the notorious injustice of the war which the French government is making on my country, and the complete insufficiency and inexactness of the pretexts which have been alleged by the invader to the civilized world while pretending to justify such a war. The said articles were written by Mr. Lefevre, French by birth, nationality, and sentiments, who has resided many years in the Mexican republic; who has witnessed, in person, many of the acts which he recounts; and had access to the archives of the Mexican government, while writing a more extended work on the same events, which he published in 1862. Although they are not of official character, they may serve much to illustrate the truth in a question so complicated, for which reason I send them to your department.

I avail of this opportunity to repeat to you, sir, the assurances of my most distinguished consideration,

M. ROMERO.

Hon. WILLIAM H. SEWARD, *&c.*, *&c.*, *&c.*

[From the Daily News, Wednesday, December 30, 1863.]

THE INTERVENTION IN MEXICO.

No. I.—ORIGIN OF THE QUESTION.

There are two methods of representing facts. The first and easiest, which is that followed by the panegyrists of established power, and assumes the legitimacy of what is done from the mere existence of the facts.

Writers of the fatalistic school proceed in this manner. The secret of their reasoning is found in that unlucky declaration of M. de Montalembert, "Everything which is possible is just;" and if we accepted such a doctrine without protest, we should have nothing more to do than to bow everywhere and in all things before the deification of force. All the logic of the writers of this school reduces itself, in fact, to this somewhat unintellectual glorification.

But because the head of the French empire thinks fit to overthrow the republic of Mexico, because his troops are in possession of Vera Cruz, Puebla, Mexico, and probably by this time of San Luis Potosi, is that a reason for maintaining the legitimacy of a war which all France disapproves of, and which has never had any advocates except among the fanatics paid to glorify, everywhere and always, the acts of the imperial government? Assuredly not.

The other school, on the contrary, considers itself bound to take everything into account. Its criticism maintains that every fact which takes place before our eyes proceeds logically from certain causes, which are always pre-existent, and that in no case can success destroy right. Belonging, ourselves, to this later school, it is according to its principles that we are about to study the circumstances which are taking place at this moment upon the territory of Mexico.

And, in the first place, why has the French army interfered in the internal affairs of that unhappy country, and whence comes its intervention?

This intervention, it ought to be distinctly stated, does not proceed, as is pretty generally supposed, from the causes which led to the signing of the convention of the 31st of October, 1861, and which are recorded therein.

It would be an impeachment of the good faith of the powers whose names are at the bottom of that diplomatic document to believe for an instant in the anterior necessity of an armed intervention in the affairs of the country, when all the facts, on the contrary, unite in establishing that this eventuality had been carefully repudiated in all the diplomatic documents exchanged between the official representatives of the three powers, in order to arrive at a common understanding. Search must be made elsewhere, therefore, if the origin of the present intervention is to be discovered; and however slightly we refer to what has taken place, we shall find that origin in the support which the ministers of the imperial government have constantly afforded to the reactionary parties against the liberal tendencies of nearly all the people of Mexico.

This, however, demands a word of explanation.

In 1856 Mexico, weary of a system of *pronunciamientos*, a system which had lasted for forty years, rose against General Santa Anna, the last representative of that unenlightened system, and the insurrection, soon driving before it the defenders of the despot, arrived victorious even in the capital itself, where it installed General Alvarez at first, and M. Comonfort afterwards, as provisional presidents of a *de facto* government. This was the legitimate insurrection of the interests of the many against the privileges of the few; the victory of right over might; and to put an end in future to the *pronunciamientos* which were ruining and demoralizing the country, it was resolved to solemnly proclaim in a charter the rights and duties of every one.

This charter—an expression of the ideas and of the wishes of the entire country, inasmuch as the representatives of all the people of Mexico were summoned to discuss it—was concluded on the 12th of January, 1857. After being voted by the constituent assembly, it was submitted to the ratification of the people, was voluntarily accepted by all the States of the republic, and received the special oath of M. Comonfort, appointed President in virtue of article 75, on the 1st of December of the same year.

Finally, to conclude with the reforms of this period, we ought to add that the vote of the constitution had been preceded by two laws, the object of one of which was to come to the assistance of property by bringing mortmain property into circulation; while the other suppressed all special jurisdictions known under the name of *fueros ecclesiastiques et militaires*, and subjected to the undeviating regulations of general law the members, until then privileged, of the army and the clergy.

There was, however, no spoliation. The property rights of the chapters and convents were openly recognized; and to indemnify the clergy, it was decided that the revenue of all real property should be capitalized, by taking for basis of estimate the annual value of the said property, as representing a sum lent at 6 per cent. per annum, but that the capital in question should be repaid to the chapters and convents by the principal tenant, substituted by the terms of the new law, as proprietor, for the rights of the clergy henceforth barred.

It was, however, from the army and the clergy that protests against the new order of things proceeded. These two bodies combined their intrigues in order to exert a pressure upon the honest but undecided mind of M. Comonfort, and on the 17th of December, 1857, *i. e.*, only sixteen days after having taken his oath, he overthrew the constitution that he had just sworn to. He then pronounced in favor of a reactionary plan, drawn up by himself and some of his councillors; and in order not to be opposed in these projects, he arrested M. Juarez, president of the supreme court of justice, designated in virtue of Art. 79 of the same constitution to supply the place of the *coup d'état* President until the nomination of his successor.

Nevertheless, in spite of the avowed assistance, or rather the treason of the chief magistrate of the republic, the triumphant faction had adherents in the cities of Mexico, Queretaro, and Puebla only; while the entire State of Vera Cruz, Yucatan, Oaxaca, Guerrero, Michoacan, San Luis (with the exception of a small portion of the garrison,) Guanajuato, Zacatecas, Jalisco, Colima, Durango, Coahuila, Nuevo Leon, Tabasco, Chiapas, Chihuahua, Sonora, Sinaloa, and a great part even of the district of Mexico, continued to recognize the constitution of 1857 as the fundamental law of the republic.

Nay, more, M. Gutierrez Zamora, governor of the State of Vera Cruz, deceived by a friend who had come to him on behalf of M. Comonfort, pronounced, in the first place, in favor of the *coup d'état*, in the trust that that movement had no other object than that of investing the President with powers which would enable him to accomplish, without the intervention of a congress, always slow in deciding, the reforms initiated by the last revolution. But when he learnt the truth—when he knew that M. Comonfort, instead of advancing, had, on the contrary, bound himself hand and foot to the reactionary party by throwing open the council to the famous Father Miranda, he felt that he had been trifled with; and not content with repairing his error by returning within the three days which followed his defection to the constitution of 1857, he himself assembled the legislature of his State in order to submit his conduct to it, and to surrender himself thus to the justice of his fellow-citizens.

If, therefore, in the events of this period there was a pressure of any kind of the minority upon the majority to employ expressions so often repeated recently by the agents of the imperial government, this pressure proceeded solely from the authors of the *coup d'état*, all of whom are now partisans of the intervention, except MM. Comonfort and Payno; and but for the necessity of giving a liberal coloring to an expedition the real motives of which it is not yet dared to state, we should not be able to understand how in so simple a question the ministers of the empire have been able to blind themselves so far as constantly to take the part for the whole.

M. Comonfort, nevertheless, soon perceived what a deplorable part he had been made to play. But too weak to dare to publicly admit his fault, and surrender himself, like M. Gutierrez Zamora, to the justice of the congress, he preferred to shuffle, and continued to vacillate from side to side, hoping, doubtless, in time, to oppose the credit of the president of the supreme court, then a prisoner, to the annoying influence of the leader of the *prononcés*, and the ambition of the general of the counter-revolutionary army to the well-known patriotism of the provisional president appointed by Art. 79 of the constitution. With this object he arrested General Zuloaga; but this time also his half-and-half policy failed before the pitiless logic of the spirit of the party, and he was compelled, in spite of himself, to liberate his two prisoners, M. Juarez and M. Zuloaga.

The former, restored to liberty on the 11th January, 1858, immediately repaired to Guanajuato, to organize there the constitutional government. Zuloaga, glad to be let off so easily, shut himself up in the citadel, determined to no longer trust his fortune in the hands of M. Comonfort; and the latter, abandoned by everybody, without party or prestige, unable to count upon the reactionaries, who despised him after making him their accomplice, or upon the liberal party, which he had so disgracefully betrayed only sixteen days after taking the oath of the constitution;—the latter, we repeat, soon felt that his time had come, and relinquished *de facto* the presidency, by signing on the 15th of January the decrees necessitated by the situation as general-in-chief of the troops under his orders, and no longer as President of the republic. M. Comonfort fell, therefore, before the abandonment of his own forces, rather than from the efforts of the reactionary party.

On the morning of the 22d January the national palace of Mexico was vacant. The *religionnaires* occupied it not as a conquered, but as an abandoned post.

Hence it is untrue that the reactionary party overthrew at Mexico, on the 22d January, 1858, the government established by the constitution of 1857, for that government had been sitting since the 14th of the same month at Guanajuato, and on the 19th M. Juarez had publicly taken possession, by issuing a manifesto intended to call the attention of the country and of the foreign ministers to the situation.

It is still more opposed to the truth to give to the promoters of the insurrection commenced on the 17th of December, 1857, and terminated on the 22d January, 1858, by the momentary triumph of the plan of Tacubaya, at Mexico, the name of *de facto* government, since the legitimate government had never ceased to exist, and there could not be two governments in the same country, one legitimate and the other illegitimate.

It is true that a division of the federal army, commanded by M. Comonfort, forgetting the fidelity it owed to its flag, rebelled amid the ringing of the bells which pealed forth the impious vengeance of the monks and the clergy, and at the same time abjured its flag, its oath, and the constitution. How long has the treason of the army implied the fall of the government that it had to sustain? Neither force nor treason avails against the truth, and the energy displayed by the people of Mexico for the maintenance of the constitution during the three years the civil war lasted alone suffices now to show on which side was the right then, and on which the insurrection.

Let us see, therefore, what, under these circumstances, was the conduct of the European ministers accredited to the constitutional government. There were two such ministers at that time—viz., M. de Gulnar and Mr. Lettsom; the former, minister of the imperial government, was also chargé d'affaires of the governments of Belgium, Spain, and Prussia; the latter was simply chargé d'affaires of the British government. Both were accredited to the government of the republic, and not to the individual who might happen to be at that moment dwelling in the national palace of Mexico; and, moreover, they perfectly well knew all the threads of all the intrigues that were crossing each other between the citadel and the palace, and from the palace to the convent of St. Domingo, the seat of the insurrection. They knew well how their conduct at such a moment might assist in consolidating or weakening the legitimate government. Honor, then, made it their duty to risk no step prejudicial to the authority of the government to which they were accredited. Unfortunately it was not so. Whether from party connexion, or from personal regard for the author of the *coup d'état*, or from some other motive of which I am ignorant, they recognized, on the 23d January, the insurrection, which in the capital was triumphant over the right, and it was their recognition, equally mysterious and inopportune, that, by lending a semblance of validity to what must otherwise have proved an abortion, became the sole cause of the events which afterwards brought about the convention of October 31, 1861.

The recognition of the reactionary insurrection—17th December, 1857, 21st January, 1858—by the European representatives, at a time when they had in their hands the manifesto published four days before by M. Juarez, at Guanajuato, was a grave fault, as lowering the government to which they were accredited; and it was, moreover, an absurdity. A grave fault, because the representatives of foreign states should never, under any circumstances, be mixed up with conspiracies against the government which has received them within its territory. An absurdity, because such recognition, once admitted as a doctrine, and pushed to its extreme consequences, would oblige them to recognize in the quality of a government *de facto*, the first andit who should escape from prison and prove fortunate or audacious enough to seize by a *coup de main* the seat of the government. Now I repeat, such a doctrine is absurd, and, therefore, beyond discussion.

If it be true, as I have myself heard M. de Morineau, consul of the imperial government at Mexico, declare, that the instructions of the European representatives accredited to the republic enjoined them at that time to recognize in the quality of government *de facto* the first conspirator who might succeed in seizing the capital, those instructions, let me be allowed to say, would have been an absurdity, which, out of respect to the government in question, I shall pass by without further notice.

In truth, the presence of representatives of European states in a country like Mexico is simply an act of policy necessitated by the interests of the European residents. The recognition which these ministers may think proper to bestow upon any government for the time being cannot of itself confer any right upon that government. Consequently, their recognition, however desirable it may be with respect to the daily relations of the European residents with that government, cannot convert the wrongful into the rightful possession, or set up a right where it does not exist. Thus in the case which I am discussing, after as before January 22, 1858, the constitutional government remained the true legal government of Mexico. That government, *legitimate* as long as it remained within the limits prescribed by the constitution from which it emanated, became the government *de facto* on the day when, in order to meet the exigencies of the situation, it found itself constrained to transgress those limits.

But whether a legitimate or *de facto* government, it alone had authority to represent Mexico in the eyes of the foreigner; it alone had the right to exercise sovereignty in the name of the country, and consequently to conclude contracts and treaties subject to the condition of submitting them afterwards to the sovereign sanction of the congress.

If, therefore, now that the French army is master of Mexico, the imperial government demands from that unhappy country the recognition of certain contracts—that of M. Jecker for instance, or any other of the same kind—it can only do so in the name of force, the last argument which those who have no other to offer are accustomed to invoke.

These facts clearly show that the Mexican government emanating from the constitution of 1857 never ceased to exist, and that the European ministers accredited to it committed a great fault in recognizing, on the 23d of January, 1858, the triumphant insurrection in the capital; especially as they were informed of the presence of the legitimate government at Guanajuato, and as they had received the manifesto published on the 19th, that is, four days before by the *ad interim* President, M. Benitio Juarez.

It would be easy to show that, as far as concerns the conduct of the ministers of Great Britain and France, this unusual recognition was in direct opposition to the diplomatic traditions of their countries, and was condemned beforehand by the approbation given on both sides of the channel to the policy followed under similar circumstances by the ministers of those two powers at Lisbon, under the reigns of George IV, Charles X, and Louis Philippe.

It remains for me to state how this reaction gave way, which appeared for a while so persistent, and under the pressure of what circumstances the convention of the 31st October, 1861, was produced.

E. LEFEVRE.

[From the Daily News, January 4, 1864.

No. II.—THE REACTIONARY ADMINISTRATION.

The *coup d'état* had become an established fact in Mexican history. True, the legal position of the country produced by the constitution of the 12th of February, 1857, remained the same, but the reactionists forced their yoke by arms upon the unfortunate people who submitted to it, and their action was all the more to be feared because they thoroughly understood the necessity of utilizing by all possible means the time they still had before them.

In the first place came two decrees of the 28th of January, 1858, the former of which had no other object than that of abolishing in the localities subjected to the *coup d'état* the dispositions of the law of the 25th of June, 1856, respecting the alienation of the ecclesiastical property, and the latter that of re-establishing the ecclesiastical and military jurisdictions (*fueros*) wherever they had prevailed before the 1st of January, 1853.

M. de Gabriac, the minister of the Imperial French government, forgetting that the diplomatic agents accredited at foreign courts are not considered privileged conspirators, and consequently should scrupulously abstain from fomenting and favoring conspiracies and plots against the governments which receive them, did not hesitate, in a letter of the 27th of February, 1858, which he probably did not intend for the honors of publication, to congratulate himself upon the part he had taken in the perpetration of this outrage against the sovereignty of the people of Mexico, by recalling to the archbishop of Mexico, D. Lazaro de la Garza, the trifling services (*debiles servicios*) which he had rendered to his country and to the holy churches of that ecclesiastical province.

We knew that France spent enormous sums in maintaining representatives at certain foreign courts for the purpose of sustaining the rights of her subjects there, and of protecting them when necessary against the despotism of the local authorities; but we were not previously aware that M. de Gabriac had been specially charged to protect and defend in Mexico, against the ideas of our own time, the interests of what he calls the "holy churches of that ecclesiastical province," and it is right to announce the fact to the imperial government and the people, in order that they may both know in what manner their official representative in Mexico understood the obligations of his post, and what reasons constantly prevented him from giving effect, as he ought to have done, to the legitimate complaints of his fellow-countrymen against the abuse of power of the reactionary administration.

Those, in fact, who pronounced so boldly on the night of the 16th to the 17th of December, 1857, against the constitution of their country, had counted upon the venality of part of the constituted authorities and the apathy of others, in order to seize suddenly upon a position which the undecided character of the chief magistrate of the republic rendered on all sides vulnerable.

In this plan, which had long been matured among the leaders of the conservative party, treason formed one of the principal means of action, and nothing was more natural than this hope in a country where men's consciences, governed by the priests, were accustomed to put themselves up to public auction. The clergy opened their coffers, in which they had accumulated the millions extorted from the fears of dying men; and, as Captain William C. Aldham, royal navy, indicates, in a note dated off Vera Cruz, the 20th of March, 1860, the property of the poor thus became the principal resource of a fratricidal war, undertaken for the purpose of maintaining in the republic the fatal preponderance of the army and the priests.

Nevertheless, neither the means of the clergy nor the resources they disposed of were equal to the task they had undertaken. Their attempts at seduction failed before the inflexible morality of the defenders of the constitution. The States rose with arms in their hands at the voice of those defenders to maintain the constitution they had freely accepted and sworn to; the resources became exhausted, and three months had scarcely elapsed when the victors were already reduced to expedients. In such a situation people are not particular about means. On this occasion the expedient assumed the shape of a decree, dated the 15th of May, 1858, with the signature of a certain Felix Zuloaga, formerly a *croupier* in a gambling house, but then president of the reaction by the grace of the *coup d'état*. By article 1 of this decree "a tax of one per cent."—we are not inventing, we are quoting—"was imposed for *once only* upon all capital floating or fixed, which was or might be employed in any industry whatever;" but by a prudential reservation, for which foreigners especially ought to have been grateful to M. Zuloaga, the decree of which we speak only applied to those who possessed, or who were supposed to possess, the means of satisfying the exigencies of the reaction.

This was a good deal, doubtless; it was even too much; at any rate, by touching only capital of an estimated value of £1,000 sterling and upwards, the administration gave evidence of a reserve too rare in similar cases not to be publicly recognized.

The alarm was general. Exclamations simultaneously broke forth on every hand; from high and low; from the wholesale merchant and the retail dealer; from the capitalist and the borrower; from the chief city of the republic, and from several towns in the power of the reaction, and the excitement increasing each day; at length on the 22d of the same month, that is to say, seven days after the appearance of the decree, it found expression in a diplomatic protest signed by Mr. John Forsyth, the minister of the United States.

Mr. Otway, who had recently arrived to replace Mr. Lettsom, on his part addressed to the Tacubaya administration a representation from the English residents against the tax in question, accompanied by a note in which he *begged* the above-named administration to "suspend the effects of the tax, as far as English subjects were concerned, until he had submitted the case to his government, and received instructions relative to the course he was to pursue in this matter."

Finally, M. de Gabriac himself sent a note on the 29th of the same month to M. L. G. Cuevas, * * * the preceding year with levying a tax of one per cent. upon every capital, floating or fixed, of an estimated value of £1,000 sterling and upwards. On this occasion M. Miramon acted more wisely; he fastened upon capital of £200 sterling; he assimilated the instruments of labor with productive capital, and struck a blow both at rich and poor, the capitalist and the workman, the producer and the consumer.

However, this was nothing yet. Wants every day increased in consequence of the daily waste of the public fortune. Coffers full in the morning were empty at night; and in order to fill them again in this limited administration of the *coup d'état*, there was no other resource than that of extraordinary imposts. Recourse to them again became necessary, and this time household property had its turn.

By a decree dated the 30th of May, 1859, it was decided that this property should be subjected to a tax of 10 per cent., payable by the landlord and tenant, at the rate of 5 per cent. for each, and that no one capable of being taxed might be forgotten, care was taken to include the under-tenants in the impost.

All this was but the business of a month; no less, but certainly no more. By the 1st of July the exchequer was as empty as before, and in order to replenish it recourse was had to a sort of panacea known in the history of that sad period by the name of the Peza law of the 19th of July, 1859. The assessment of the taxes was entirely changed, which was far from being a crime, but a demand, such as had never been heard of in the worst times, was made upon all the rate payers, native and foreign, of a year's taxes in advance, taking for basis the regulations newly established by the law of which we are speaking.

In demanding a year's taxes in advance, the administration had officially undertaken to satisfy, during this same period of time, all the exigencies of the situation without further recourse to the pockets of the rate payers. How this was to be done it alone knew. It is certain that if objections had then been made against the framer of the Peza law, they would not have failed to reply that their measures were all taken, and that with the sum they demanded they would undertake to meet all the eventualities of the future. The foreigners, deprived as usual of the protection of their ministers, had to accept the terms of this tacit contract, but they could not demand the strict application of it. Without respect for engagements which were all the more sacred because it had itself dictated their conditions; without pity for commerce, which it was day by day ruining by its exactions, but reckoning, doubtless, upon the forbearance of which MM. Gabriac and Otway had given so many proofs, the reactionary administration, at the commencement of the new year, published another new financial law; and this time, that nothing might be wanting to complete the hateful character of the measure, the statesmen of the reaction did not hesitate to take the 1st of January, 1860, as the starting point of a tax imposed by a law dated the 25th of March of the same year, giving it thus a retroactive effect of three months.

Let us now recapitulate a little.

M. Zuloaga, the intimate friend of MM. Gabriac and Otway, had contented himself with imposing a tax upon capital of £1,000 sterling and upwards. In February 7, 1859, M. Miramon, another and not less intimate friend of those gentlemen, had attacked (and, as usual, as an "extraordinary" measure) personal properties of £200 sterling and upwards, and had included the liberal and industrial professions in the impost. In May of the same year he had imposed 10 per cent. on real property. Then came the "Peza" law. Then, when it was found that all the financial measures above-mentioned were insufficient to fill the void of this Danaids' sieve, which was called at that time "the public treasury," the same Miramon taxed all at once, March 20, 1860—

1. Effective capital of £200 sterling and upwards;
2. The liberal and industrial professions;
3. "Moral capital."

This last was quite a local discovery; no European government had heretofore thought of availing itself of such a financial resource. It would be difficult to explain technically what these Mexican financiers of the reactionary party meant by the two words, "Moral capital;" but according to the common talk on this subject, it appears that the administration comprised under that denomination the wages of workmen and servants, and the salaries of employers of all sorts, to whatever class they might belong. By these means the exchequer managed to find even the poorest of the European residents in possession of a capital of which he had never dreamed. Nor yet was it enough to invent categories hitherto unknown of taxable persons; the greater object was to properly develop the resources of the old tax payers. To this end commissions were instituted under the title of *assessing juntas.* All these commissions vied with each other in zeal in screwing up the rate of taxation imposed upon foreigners. Thus the amount of taxation paid by them in 1855, 1856, and 1857 doubled, and in some cases tripled in 1858, under the administration of Zuloaga, was in 1859, under that of Miramon, raised fourfold, and sometimes even sevenfold in the case of certain Europeans, mostly French, for whom M. de Gabriac could never be induced to seek redress.

A simple enumeration of all the abuses of power of which, during the three years of the reactionary government, the foreign merchants established at Mexico were victims, would be an endless catalogue, which it would be materially impossible to inflict upon your readers. Enough to add, that on reading the note addressed, 29th September, 1861, by M. de Saligny to the minister of foreign affairs of the imperial government, I could not but wonder whether the writer was really aware of what had taken place before his arrival, and it appeared to me a curious study to count up the "extraordinary" taxes levied at that time by the friends of M. de Gabriac, by the men whose factitious power French bayonets are now restoring. If it were possible to be surprised at anything, I might fairly marvel at the mighty wrath of the representative of the Emperor at measures the principle of which for my own part I have never refrained from censuring, but which that gentleman's predecessor found perfectly natural, perfectly legitimate, when the reactionary party decreed and profited by them.

While, however, the financial resources of the reaction were sinking into a bottomless pit of deficits, and the complaints of the European residents were lost in the noise of official congratulations, a new insurrection, fomented by men in the very bosom of the reactionary party, disclosed on a sudden the deep dissensions existing among the pretended defenders of order. The chiefs of this insurrection were the Generals Manuel Robles, Pezuela, and Michel Maria de Echeagoray. It was called the "Christmas pronunciamiento," because it broke out December 23, 1858. The whole meaning of this movement was expressed in the third paragraph of the preamble of the decree drawn up on that occasion, stating "that it was necessary, in order to obtain the pacification of the republic, to overthrow the government of Zuloaga;" and in the following article of a new programme, "the government established at Mexico, in pursuance of the scheme of Tacubaya, lacks authority." In other words, after betraying the constitution of 1857, in company with M. Comonfort, on the pretext that that constitution was not in harmony with the wants of the country, a few subaltern military chiefs betrayed this time the government they had themselves assisted to instal eleven months before, alleging for their justification that that government wanted that physical and moral force which it required to establish peace in the republic, and transferred their mercenary swords from M. Zuloaga to M. Robles, just as they had transferred them, at the beginning of the troubles, from M. Comonfort to M. Zuloaga, and as they were shortly about to transfer them from M. Robles to M. Miramon. It would be far too lengthy and tedious a task to recount how the last-named personage, after declining the presidency offered to him by an assembly of reactionary "notables," convoked by M. Robles, succeeded in getting himself nominated substitute to General Zuloaga, thus restored just a month after his fall. Besides, Miramon, Robles, or Zuloaga, it was the reaction still—the same system, and therefore perhaps better in the hands of M. Miramon, a more thoroughgoing reactionist than M. Robles. If I dwell on the doings of this personage, then, it is not to relate how he put himself at the head of his party, but to express my astonishment at his recognition as President of the republic by the then representative of Great Britain, Mr. Otway, who had in three successive notes, dated the preceding November 20, December 1, and 4, *officially* demanded his immediate dismissal, with a statement in the official journal of the reasons for cancelling his appointment. But the situation was changed since then; M. Miramon was no longer the general whose dismissal was peremptorily demanded as a punishment for his illegal proceedings against British subjects resident at San Luis; he was now a sort of sovereign, acting as deputy for another sort of sovereign, whom Mr. Lettsom had, perhaps imprudently, recognized, but whom at any rate he had recognized; and Mr. Otway, I must acknowledge, yielded with a very good grace. He immediately recognized this coarse and ill-bred soldier; and the latter, now free in his movements, soon started for the first campaign against Vera Cruz.

At the same time M. Degollado, general-in-chief of the constitutional army, at the head of from 4,000 to 5,000 men at most, operated a diversion against the city of Mexico, for the purpose of preventing the reactionary authorities from despatching re-enforcements to the army before Vera Cruz; and he encamped at Tacubaya, a village situated some three miles from the capital.

Great was the alarm among the defenders of this good cause. General Antonio Corona, charged with the command in the absence of Miramon, called every defender of order he could lay his hands upon to the rescue; and shortly were seen to enter the capital all the "faithful" whom the reaction could depend upon, from the irregulars of the Indian Mejia to the bandits of General Marquez. This man arrived April 8, 1859. Two days after he sallied out at the head of some 6,000 men and 40 pieces of artillery to lay siege to the village held by the constitutional army, and was repulsed in an assault the same day, and twice again the day following. It was only on the third day, at 11 a. m., he succeeded in carrying the intrenchments which the constitutionalists had hastily thrown up. At the same time Miramon arrived, accompanied by his aides-de-camp only, having been obliged to raise the siege of Vera Cruz. At noon Miramon rode out to the scene of action, and between 2 and 3 p. m. effected a junction with General Marquez. Now, what passed between these two men, so well calculated to understand each other, I cannot say; all I know is, that having laid waste the village, these defenders of "order," still reeking with blood, went together straight to the hospital, where the wounded of the day before and of the day preceding lay huddled together, friends and enemies alike. There were found seven generous and devoted men doing their duty as surgeons or physicians at the bedsides of the wounded and the dying. Marquez had them seized, and that same evening ruthlessly slaughtered in cold blood, together with all the wounded officers whom the fortune of war had delivered into the hands of the reactionists that day. This atrocious massacre was executed at night by the light of lanterns under the immediate orders of General Marquez and M. Miramon. I will not undertake to examine which of these two men was the guiltier, nor whether the seven surgeons were comprised in the death warrant addressed April 11, 1859, by Miramon to Marquez, nor whether Marquez exceeded his orders in having them shot. These are secondary questions, which, in an assize court, might perhaps be worked by a skilful advocate into a plea of extenuating circumstances for his criminal clients; but before the indignant conscience of humanity they cannot change the nature of the crime committed by the orders of those men. Both Miramon and Marquez, the one equally with the other, stand accountable for the blood shed on that horrible night; the latter for having executed the assassinations, the former for having commanded them; or, if the surgeons were not put to death by his orders, for not having immediately arrested the assassins.

Let us see what the British government thought of that atrocious butchery. Not only did the resident representatives of the European governments take no steps to prevent the assassinations I have just described, not only did they make no protest against it, but it appears that in their correspondence with their governments they did not even think it worth while to mention the circumstance; for if the British government was afterwards informed of it, it was through a private correspondence; and because among the victims there happened to be one physician of English extraction, Dr John Séférino Duval.

But the reactionary administration understood too well how far it had transgressed all permissible limits not to hasten to anticipate the just reproaches to which it was liable. Accordingly, as early as June 20, it had ordered its agent at London, Mr. Murphy, to put into the hands of the British government a formal complaint of the conduct pursued during the siege of Mexico by Messrs. G. B. Matthews and Frederick Glennie, the former secretary of legation, and the latter consul of the British government at Mexico. Mr. Murphy then demanded an interview with Mr. Seymour Fitzgerald, the then under secretary for foreign affairs, who, so far from listening to the agent's complaints, declared to him, with all the indignation of a man of honor and feeling, what her Majesty's government thought of the assassinations committed at Tacubaya on the night of April 11. This reply is so honorable to the government of your country that I cannot hesitate to make it known through an extract from the despatch, marked "Very important," and "reserved," addressed by Mr. Th. Murphy, at that time diplomatic representative at the British court of the Mexican republic, to his own government.

MEXICAN LEGATION.—No. 16.

VERY IMPORTANT—RESERVED.

EXCELLENCY: I have had a conference with Mr. Seymour Fitzgerald on the contents of the despatch No. 7, marked "Very confidential," of your excellency, dated the 30th of last April, relative to the conduct of Mr G. B. Matthews, secretary of the British legation at Mexico, and to that of the British consul, Mr. Frederick Glennie, during the occupation of Tacubaya and the environs of the capital by the forces of M. Santos Dejollado.

Mr. Seymour Fitzgerald replied to me that it was somewhat out of season on my part to be bringing complaints to the government of her Majesty when they had in their hands an account written by a merchant in Mexico (whose name he would not give me) concerning Mr. John Duval, a subject of her Majesty, who, (as it was alleged,) in company with several other foreigners and natives of the country, had been assassinated in the most cruel, inhuman, and shameful manner, by order of the authorities of Mexico, solely because they had been found attending to the wounded of Tacubaya, according to their duty as surgeons.

Mr. Seymour Fitzgerald added that her Majesty's government had never known of an order so barbarous, so unworthy of a people which pretends to pass for civilized—an order, in short, which deserved the execration of the whole world. He ended by declaring that the government of her Majesty were resolved to demand a signal reparation, and a large indemnity to be paid immediately to the widow of M. Duval, and that failing this reparation and indemnity, they were resolved to recognize the constitutional government. * * * *

M. MURPHY.

His Excellency the MINISTER OF FOREIGN RELATIONS *at Mexico*.

This conversation was, in fact, followed by peremptory orders, for on the 4th August following, that is, three or four days after the arrival of the mail bringing that despatch from Mr. Murphy, Mr. Otway himself addressed to the reactionary government a note, in which he claimed, in behalf of the widow Duval, the indemnity of which Mr. Murphy had received warning; and at length some doubts of the legitimacy of the government established by the *coup d'état* began to appear. Unfortunately, the reactionary government continued to elude the demand on more or less plausible pretexts, and it was not until 1861, after the definitive triumph of the liberal party in Mexico, that the affair was settled to the satisfaction of Madame Duval and of the British government.

E. LEFEVRE.

ERRATUM.—In letter I, (Daily News, December 30,) for M. de Gulnar, read M. de Gabriac.

[From the Daily News, January 7, 1864.]

No. III.—The Jecker Bonds.

October 29, 1859, the reactionary administration, in pressing want of money, published a decree, purporting to create a paper issue of 15,000,000 piastres, or a little more than £3,000,000 sterling.

By this decree the administration suspended the issue to the same amount of bonds created by the Peza law, (Art. 2,) and decided that the new bonds should be received in the proportion of 20s. per cent. each, in payment of all the taxes or duties which the treasury should impose, (Art. 3;) that they should bear an annual interest of 6 per cent., (Art. 4;) that half that interest should be guaranteed, for five years, by the house of J. B Jecker, whose signature shall authorize the issue of the bonds, (Art 5;) and that the possessors of the old bonds should have the faculty to convert them into new bonds, by paying into the hands of the above-mentioned Jecker, as the banker who had undertaken the operation, a sum of 25 per cent., for the "revalidation" of the bonds of the old internal debt, of 27 per cent. for the bonds which have been created by the law of November 30, 1850, and of 28 per cent. for those which were created by the famous Peza law (Art. 8.)

The operation was calculated to produce a net profit of 3,750,000 piastres (£750,000.) On this amount M. Jecker received: 1. Five per cent. commission on the total issue, or, in other words, the twentieth of the total realisable profit of the operation—£150,000. 2. To payment of five years' interest, (of which he guaranteed one-half conformably with the terms of Art. 4,) £450,000; balance remaining to the government, £150.000; total, £750,000. Nevertheless, in the course of its execution, this transaction presented itself under three distinct and independent aspects. The first is that which it had naturally in virtue of the decree of October 29, above mentioned.

The second is that which it received from a private convention proposed by the house of Jecker, on the same day, October 29, 1859, to the reactionary administration, and accepted by the latter.

The third is that which it assumed, from time to time, in consequence of certain proposals or contracts presented by the above-named house of Jecker, in order to carry out the operation advantageously. Between these three aspects of the transaction the difference is so great that it would be impossible to explain it without making it demonstrable in figures.

Result of the affair of the Jecker bonds had the operation been carried out in conformity with the terms of the decree of October 29, 1859.

Product of sums expected to accrue to the treasury from the conversion, at an average of 25 per cent., of 15,000,000 piastres in bonds, issued in conformity with the decree of that day, £750,000. Product of fifteen millions of piastres in Peza bonds, which were then worth 5 per cent., and redeemable in proportion as the new bonds should be issued, £150,000. Value of the new Jecker stock, which the government was to redeem with the 20 per cent. on the State revenues, £3,000,000.

Approximate calculation of the sums that should have accrued from the fifteen half-yearly payments (at the least) required for the redemption of the whole amount of the interest on the sum of £3,000,000 sterling in bonds, in conformity with Art. 5 of the decree above mentioned.

First half-yearly payment at $6 - \frac{1}{2} = 3$ per cent. on	£3,000,000	£90,000
Second ..... do ..... do	2,800,000	84,000
Third ..... do ..... do	2,600,000	78,000
Fourth ..... do ..... do	2,400,000	72,000
Fifth ..... do ..... do	2,200,000	66,000
Sixth ..... do ..... do	2,000,000	60,000
Seventh ..... do ..... do	1,800,000	54,000
Eighth ..... do ..... do	1,600,000	48,000
Ninth ..... do ..... do	1,400,000	42,000
Tenth ..... do ..... do	1,200,000	36,000
Eleventh ..... do ..... do	1,000,000	30,000
Twelfth ..... do ..... do	800,000	24,000

Thirteenth half-yearly payment at 6 — ½ = 3 per cent. on...	£600,000	£18,000
Fourteenth..........do..................do..............	400,000	12,000
Fifteenth............do..................do..............	200,000	6,000
Total..		720,000

This sum, added to the £3,000,000 of bonds issued, made a general total of	£3,720,000
From this sum, by deducting the credit from the debit, the following result was obtained..	£3,720,000
Deduct..	900,000
Total..	£2,820,000

So that if the operation had been carried out in conformity with the prescriptions of the decree to which we referred at the beginning of this article, £900,000 would have cost the government the enormous sum of £2,820,000.

The operation, however, was not carried out on these terms, for at the moment of its execution the house of Jecker presented another proposal, which we proceed to analyse as follows:

Result of the affair of the Jecker bonds if the operation had been carried out in conformity with the second proposal of that house.

	Credit.	Debit.
Total accruing to the national treasury from the conversion of £3,000,000 sterling of bonds issued as above mentioned.......	£750,000	
Peza bonds, redeemed as above mentioned....................	150,000	
	£900,000	
Expenses of the operation.		
Commission of 5 per cent. to MM. Jecker....................	£150,000	
Deposit of 10 per cent. with MM. Jecker for payment of interest guaranteed by same..............................	300,000	
Brokerage..	30,000	
Printing bonds..	2,400	
Total to deduct from amount above mentioned................	482,400	
Difference in favor of the treasury..............................	£417,600	
From which must be deducted also the supposed value of the Peza bonds..	150,000	
Net result of the operation..............................	£267,600	
But the value of the new stock which it was proposed to redeem was......		£3,000,000
That of the interest at 3 per cent. which was also to be redeemed in fifteen half-yearly payments was..............................		720,000
Total..		£3,720,000
From which if we deduct the net sum accruing to the treasury............		267,600
The difference against the treasury was..............................		£3,452,400

So that if the operation had been carried out according to the last proposal of M. Jecker, £417,600, including even the supposed value of the Peza bonds, would have cost the state £3,720,000, or, what is the same thing, the public treasury would have received a sum of £267,600, on condition of paying interest for it from eight to ten years at the rate of something like 80 per cent. per annum

Nor is this all. The most singular feature in this operation is that to transform it from theory into practice no account was taken either of the decree which had imposed it upon the tax-payers, nor of the last proposals presented to the government by the house of Jecker itself; but it was realized any how, by means of private contracts presented one by one to the sanction of the authorities, for the public took but the smallest part in the conversion, and M. Jecker found himself obliged to complete it himself by altering each time, both in its form and in its mode of stating the figures, not only the decree of October 29, but even the very terms of his own last proposal.

Thus the first contract proposed by him to the administration bears date October 27, 1859, two days anterior to the publication of the decree.

The second presented by his nephew and partner, M. Jules Bornèque, bears date January 26, 1860.

The third, presented also by his nephew, is dated March 13 of the same year.

By virtue of these three private contracts the house of Jecker converted a part of the Peza bonds and became master of the new stock in the following proportion:

It converted, by the first contract, £400,000 ; by the second, £1,200,000 ; by the third, £1,248,322 ; total, £2,848,322 ; brokerage paid to M. Clement Caricabure, £30,000 ; converted by different persons, £121,678 ; total equal to the amount of issue £3,000,000.

It remains for us to explain how the house of Jecker undertook to convert a certain quantity of bonds bearing the signatures of MM. Peza and Zuloaga in exchange for an equal quantity of bonds which were issued by the administration of Miramon. By means of the three contracts above mentioned MM. Jecker & Co. remitted in hard cash a sum of £144,604 ; in bonds presented as cash, £49,350 ; in bills on the customs, also presented as cash, £20,000 ; in clothing and equipments for the army £73,600 ; total, £287.554.

It is true we have drawn up this statement on the proposals made by MM. Jecker & Co. themselves, and stipulated by the contracts above mentioned ; but at the moment of making the remittances to the treasury the negotiators arranged to pass as cash a certain quantity of other credits or bonds, so that this new transaction was, in fact, another variation of the primitive scheme of the operation.

The following is the result of the treasury account: MM. Jecker & Co. have remitted in cash, £123,785 ; in ordinary bonds at 3 and 5 per cent., £68,400 ; in Peza bonds, £6,000 ; M. Jecker bonds, (those of his contract,) £4,950 ; in bills on the customs, £20,000 ; in army clothing, &c., £73,600 ; in divers credits and payments, £1,350 ; total, £298,085. Difference: treasury account, £298,085 ; former account, £287,554 ; difference in favor of treasury account, £10,531.

In the second of these accounts the total sum of the remittances is augmented, as it appears, by £10,531, but it is at the same time diminished, so far as the portion which MM. Jecker & Co. were to remit in cash, contrary to their proposals, by the sum of £20,818. We remark also a difference between the quantity of bonds redeemed by M. Jecker, according to the account presented by him, and that which the registers of the treasury show. But the difference is trifling, and scarcely diminishes in any sensible degree the sum in cash which M. Jecker received for converting bonds of individual holders. We have mentioned it as a term of comparison, and as evidence that this transaction was one of those in which the profits are calculated in proportion to the risks.

We may thus easily understand the difference that exists between the conversion of stock as it was proposed by the decree of October 29, 1859, and that which was effected by the agency of MM. Jecker, a conversion for which the government received only £123,785 in specie, and £73,600 in army clothing. But even supposing that all the different fractional sums remitted by M. Jecker could be treated as cash, it would be not the less clear that for £287,554 the government (besides 3 per cent. yearly interest, which was to be redeemable in fifteen half-yearly payments, and the total of which amounted to £720,000,) mortgaged for ten years more the revenues of the republic by taking the fifth of their effective value until the complete redemption of the £300,000 remitted in bonds to M. Jecker.

In other words, for £287,554, value received in money, in clothes, in bills on the customs, and in bonds, the public treasury undertook the reimbursement of a sum of £3,720,000.

Besides, it will be observed that in these transactions no profit whatever results to the government, since M. Jecker, after having reserved out of the £3,000,000, which he had received to effect the conversion of the stock—1, 5 per cent. commission ; 2, 10 per cent., to cover the portion of the interest for which he was personally responsible, ought at least to have made good to the government, every time that a bond was redeemed, the 10 per cent. corresponding to that bond, or, at least, the surplus, whenever a half-yearly payment of interest was effected. MM. Jecker, however, in paying that half-yearly interest—that is, 1½ per cent.—considered themselves discharged from all further obligation, and retained, besides, the 8½ per cent. in addition to their commission of 5 per cent.

In this state of things, although it may be difficult to get at the precise figures, since the actual charges on the house of Jecker are not known, we may establish a commercial balance-sheet more or less accurate of what that operation must have cost, and we may here remind the reader that the expenses of brokerage to M. Caricabure, or of printing the bonds, were not borne by MM. Jecker, but by the government.

APPROXIMATE CALCULATION OF THE COST OF THE AFFAIR OF THE JECKER BONDS.

Cash paid into treasury, comprising payments for the purchase of a flotilla		123,785
Cost *sur place* of 222,000 piastres in bonds at 3, and at 5 to 6 per cent.		2,664
Ditto of 24,750 piastres in Jecker bonds at 30 per cent.		1,425
Ditto of 100,000 piastres in bills on customs at 50 per cent		10,000
Ditto of 368,000 piastres for clothing and equipments		73,600
Ditto of 14,378,700 piastres in Peza bonds employed in the conversion, at 5 per cent		143,787
Total		355,321
Deduct:		
1. Value of 554,127 piastres in bonds, which M. Jecker realized at 30 per cent	33,247	
2. Ten per cent. which M. Jecker reserved on 621,300 piastres, in bonds converted by the public	12,426	
		45,673
Actual disbursements		309,648

This, let me repeat, is only given as an approximate account, and may contain errors. But, even if we add or subtract some thousands of pounds sterling from the figures given above, it will still remain a fact that the affair was from first to last simply a banking operation, in which the reactionary government issued £3,000,000 in bonds bearing interest at 6 per cent. per annum, and that these bonds, redeemable in ten years, were sold *sur place* at 25 per cent.

In another letter we propose to consider this great operation from a political point of view.

E. LEFEVRE.

[From the Daily News, January 13, 1864.]

*No. IV.—Conclusion of the Jecker Question.

In our last article we contented ourselves with representing the affair of the Jecker bonds from a purely commercial point of view; but in order to complete it some fresh reflections are required, which appear to us of a very serious nature.

The French imperial government demanded the execution of this contract through M. de Saligny, and that agent introduced the condition into one of the articles of his ultimatum.

Now, one of two things follows from the explanations we have already given:

Either that contract was in principle an innovation, and completely independent of the decree which authorizes it; or it was a series of different contracts, which may be classed among those called in French jurisprudence *contrats bilateraux*.

If it is regarded as a single contract—which is incorrect, not to say absurd—then it was violated at every turn by M. Jecker himself. It was modified in a thousand ways. In fine, it is connected with a thousand different operations. The imperial government could not, therefore, demand from the Mexican government the full and complete execution of the decree of the 29th October, 1859, since his client had never executed his part of it.

If, on the contrary—and the evidence of this fact cannot be disputed by anybody—the deed in question is not composed of one but of several contracts concluded by the nephew of M. Jecker, rather than by M. Jecker in person, it follows that each of those contracts was distinct, and this shows that both M. Jecker and the reactionary government made and unmade, according to their interests, the conventions they signed; that they modified them; that they changed them; and above all, that they materially altered the dispositions of the legislation which served as their starting point. It was, therefore, supremely unjust on the part of the imperial commissioner to demand the full and entire execution of the clauses which were in favor of M. Jecker, since the latter had modified all those which were in favor of the treasury, by paying into it bonds, bills, goods, and drafts upon the custom-house, instead of money.

---

* See Daily News of December 30, January 4, and January 7.

But there is a still more conclusive reason. The contract in question was infringed, nay, broken, completely broken, by the Jecker firm itself.

In fact, about the middle of the month of May, 1860, that firm saw itself under the necessity of suspending payment. It cannot be said that this arose from the ill-will of the constitutional authorities, for those authorities were only re-established in Mexico on the 25th of the following December.

However, in taking this very serious step M. Jecker naturally suspended all his operations.

On the 18th or 19th of the same month he assembled his creditors and made terms with them on condition that a *conseil d'intervention* should be appointed.

Under these circumstances it became impossible for him to retain the deposit, as he had undertaken to do on commencing the *réfaction*, the 10 per cent. corresponding to the interest of the bonds issued, and which alone amounted to the enormous sum of £300,000. The contrary, however, happened, and while M. Jecker presented his 14,000,000 of bonds as part of his capital, while he mortgaged them (which he had no right to do, as he had not fulfilled the conditions of his contract,) he said nothing, and with good reason, of that £300,000 which he ought to have had in his strong box to meet the interests becoming due, and to dispose legitimately of this paper which a part of the country was paying for then with the sweat of its brow.

However, there is more yet. Under the circumstances in which M. Jecker concluded his famous contract, it was not a loan, pure and simple, undertaken by a banker unconnected with politics ; it was a real and effective society that the Jecker firm formed with a counter-revolutionary party, for the purpose of driving from Vera Cruz the government which, in conformity with all the usages of civilized nations, was the only national and legitimate government.

Thus, even before failing, M. Jecker had committed the grave fault of contracting with a government which, according to the rules of international law, was incapable of contracting, and of having by that circumstance mixed himself up in the intestine dissensions of the country.

He ought, therefore, to have known to what he exposed himself in case of reverses ; and to completely establish this fresh fact we might, if it were necessary, translate the decree rendered at Vera Cruz upon the matter on the 3d of November, 1858—that is, a year before the signing of the contract with which we are occupied.

It would be seen there, among other things, that every person convicted of having afforded aid, directly or indirectly, to the insurgents, by supplying them with money, or in any other manner, was, for that alone, to lose the integral value of the amounts he had given, and to be condemned to pay, moreover, to the treasury, as a fine, double the amount of money he had supplied.

The good faith of M. Jecker might be defended by maintaining that he might or might not have known of this decree; but this objection, which is more special than solid, would only serve to establish the insignificant value of his reclamation in the opinion even of those who sustain it; for it is publicly notorious that during the whole period of the reactionary administration the decrees rendered at Vera Cruz by the legitimate authority were disseminated in the capital by the clandestine press; and it would be insulting to the public to try to make it believe that in a matter of this importance M. Jecker alone was ignorant of the terms of a decree the rigorous dispositions of which were known to every one in Mexico.

Let us, therefore, turn from these questions, and place ourselves solely upon the ground of facts, in order to study the position occupied by the Jecker affair upon the entrance of the constitutional forces into the capital of the republic.

The counter-revolutionary authorities had disappeared, carrying away with them the hopes of all those who had attached their fortune to them; and M. Jecker was of this number. Ought the legitimate government to have sanctioned its contract with the fallen administration? We do not hesitate to reply in the negative ; in the first place, because the operations connected with it were directed against itself, and because a government could not in any case be compelled to pay for the weapons with which the insurgents had made war against it; secondly, because, in consequence of the financial organization which had again been instituted in the country, the assignment of 20 per cent. contained in the decree of the 29th of October was legally and *de facto* completely suspended.

It only remained for him in reality to conclude an engagement by private arrangement, as the government several times proposed, or to apply to the tribunals, and make them judges of the transaction.

But, urged by M. de Saligny, M. Jecker refused to follow the example given to him by several English citizens, Mr. Davidson, for instance, and he addressed himself to the French legation, which proposed a settlement, the object of which was to reduce to ten millions of piastres (£2,000,000) the sum to be paid to M. Jecker. In the event of acceptance, this debt was to be paid off by instalments, by means of a sum of 15 per cent. levied upon the custom-house revenues. Finally—to omit nothing—this proposition was preceded by a note, in which, while recognizing that *this affair was the only one which could occasion serious difficulties between France and Mexico*, M. de Saligny proceeded to add menacingly, immediately afterwards, that it would prevent the imperial government from giving free course to its friendly intentions towards the republic.

The following is this note. It is the best reply to the statements made by the late M. Billault before the corps legislatif on the 27th of June, 1862, and the 6th of February, 1863, denying that any pressure was exerted upon the relations of the imperial government with Mexico by this unfortunate affair of the Jecker bonds:

LEGATION OF FRANCE IN MEXICO,
Mexico, May 2, 1861.

Monsieur le MINISTRE: I have had the honor of frequently conversing during the last three months with your excellency upon a question in which the interests and the honor of France are seriously involved—I mean the question relating to the Jecker bonds.

After the conversations exchanged on this subject between your excellency and myself, I believe I need not for the moment enter into the details of this matter. It appears to me equally superfluous to discuss here an incontestable and undisputed principle which prevails in the relations between all civilized nations, and that your excellency yourself did not refuse to admit—the principle of the solidarity, in connexion with international engagements, of the various governments which succeed each other in a country. This principle France, throughout the various phases she has passed through during the last fifty years, has always respected—sometimes at the cost of grievous sacrifices which are still fresh in all memories. It is her right, therefore, and her duty to demand that it shall be respected by other nations; and, however sincere and ardent may be the kindly feeling with which the Emperor is animated towards the Mexican government, he cannot recognize in that government the faculty of emancipating itself from that principle, and of creating for its own advantage a new international law in formal opposition with that which has hitherto served as the rule of all international relations.

As I had given you to expect, therefore, not leaving you ignorant of the matter, I have received, first by the Tennessee, twelve days ago, and since, by the last English packet, precise and peremptory orders from my government upon this question.

I had hoped that, informed by you of the necessity and danger of the situation, as well as of the incontestable obligations imposed upon it, the government of his excellency the President would have hastened to settle this affair, the only one which can occasion grave difficulties between the two countries, and prevent France from giving free course to her friendly intentions towards Mexico. My hope, unfortunately, has been deceived. I cannot take upon myself to delay any longer the execution of the orders of the Emperor's government. Nevertheless, before notifying them to you in an official manner, I have felt bound to give you a fresh proof of the conciliatory spirit with which I am personally animated; and, guided by a sentiment that you will, I hope, appreciate, I beg of you to let me know with the shortest delay the definitive intentions of your government.

I am, &c.,

A. DE SALIGNY.

His Excellency M. FRANCISCO ZARCO,
Minister of Foreign Affairs of Mexico.

In this note M. de Saligny openly asserted, as it will be seen, a principle which no one thought of denying—the solidarity, in connexion with international engagements, of the various governments which succeed each other in the same country. But he refrained, and with good reason, from showing how the interests and the honor of France were so seriously implicated in the acceptance of the Jecker bonds, or the titles upon which, according to him, the legitimacy of the reactionary government was based. Yet it was worth the trouble.

During three years there were, in effect, two different governments in Mexico. One of these constituted powers was established at Vera Cruz, the other at Mexico. Which was to be considered as the legitimate government and which as the intruder?

M. Jecker, it is true, had concluded different contracts with one of these two governments; but in proceeding thus he had acted as a banker, not as a Frenchman, for he was then a Swiss citizen, and, try as we may, we cannot understand how the non-execution of a contract between a Swiss and the more or less legitimate government of Mexico could affect the honor and the interests of France.

M. de Gabriac, then minister of the imperial government in Mexico, had recognized, it is true, the government established in that city; but was this recognition a sufficient reason why his successor, M. de Saligny, in an affair concerning a Swiss citizen, and not a French subject, should claim, in favor of transactions between that government and that Swiss citizen, "the solidarity of international engagements?"

Surely there were two previous questions to be decided: 1. How came this Swiss citizen to claim a right to the protection of France? 2. Had the reactionary government become the legitimate government of the republic? For if M. Jecker, by reason of his nationality, had never had any right to the protection of France, if it had been decided, after a fair and careful deliberation, that the reactionary government was an usurpation, it is clear that neither the one nor the other could have claimed any right—the former to demand of France a guarantee for his jobbing speculations, the latter to make the country responsible for its acts; and in neither case could M. de Saligny be justified in quoting, in favor of the acts of his *protégé*, that principle of the solidarity of international engagements, or, in other words, the common and equal responsibility of successive governments, upon which he insisted, in order to exercise a pressure upon the legitimate government.

Now, it results from a note of M. Arnold Sutter, consul general ot the Swiss confederation in Mexico, that the citizens of that nation have never been under the protection of any foreign power, and that in extraordinary emergencies only their consuls general are authorized to claim the protection, not of the minister of the Emperor of the French, but of the envoy of the United States of America.

The following is the note written after the departure of M. de Saligny from Mexico, and addressed to the government of the republic, in consequence of the Prussian minister, M. de Wagner, having interfered in the affairs of a Swiss citizen, M. Santiago Kern, proprietor of a mill situate near the city of Mexico:

CONSULATE GENERAL OF SWITZERLAND IN MEXICO,
February 8, 1862.

The undersigned, consul general of the Swiss confederation, has the honor to acknowledge the receipt of the note addressed to him by his excellency the minister for foreign affairs, under date the 7th instant, asking whether he is still in the exercise of his consular functions, the attention of the government having been drawn to the fact that the legation of France, and subsequently that of his Majesty the King of Prussia, have taken part in questions touching the interests of Swiss citizens.

The undersigned has the honor to reply to his excellency that the instructions he has received from his government authorize him in all respects to put himself in communication with the government of the Mexican republic, and to receive all the communications which the Mexican government may transmit to him. At the same time it is his duty to inform his excellency that, in pursuance of a convention agreed to between the government of the Swiss confederation and the government of the United States of America, the *Swiss consuls are authorized to demand, in case of need, the protection of the diplomatic agents of the United States*, and that the latter are instructed to consider it their duty to protect Swiss citizens as they should their own fellow-countrymen.

The undersigned, &c.,

ARNOLD SUTTER.

His Excellency the MINISTER OF FOREIGN AFFAIRS OF MEXICO

So that, if M. Jecker had any complaint to make against the government of the Mexican republic, it was to the American and not to the French legation that he should have addressed it.

So much for the first point It remains to clear up the second According to the doctrine of international law propounded during Louis Philippe's reign by M. Rossi, at the College of France, it is understood "that an insurrection in no respect alters the relations between the government of the country in which the insurrection breaks out and foreign powers." It is even admitted that the latter ought to abstain rigorously from giving any aid, direct or indirect, to the insurgents, because, in acting otherwise, they would be acting against the presumption of the national will, which is always in favor of the established government, so long as that government exists.

The whole question, then, is, by what title M. Zuloaga first, and then M. Miramon, could have superposed the authority of the reactionary insurgents upon that of the government emanating from the constitution of 1857, and thus engage the responsibility of the latter; for it is evident that if the title invoked by M. de Saligny was not in accordance with the usages of international law, it was therefore null, and the engagements undertaken in the name of that pretended government with M. Jecker, or any other person, would fall under the category of those private engagements which are within the jurisdiction of the ordinary tribunals The constitutional government, so long as it existed alone, represented the nation in the eyes of foreign sovereigns; alone had the right to sign contracts, and, consequently, to engage the responsibility of the republic. This point is beyond all possibility of dispute. What it was essential to demonstrate was that that government had succumbed under the assaults of the reactionary party, and how and when it had succumbed.

Here the facts speak for themselves irresistibly. At the risk of repeating a part of what we stated in our first article, we may be permitted to summarize them as follows:

December 17, 1857, M. Comonfort, President of the Mexican republic, rose in insurrection, in company with a certain Zuloago, against the constitution to which sixteen days before he had sworn fidelity, and proceeded to arrest M. Juarez, who, as president of the supreme court of justice, was designated, according to the terms of article 79 of the constitution, to replace him in the functions of President till the nomination of his successor. January 11 following, perceiving that he was the tool of reactionary parties, he restored M. Juarez to liberty.

From that day forth M. Juarez was the veritable President of the republic, and M. Comonfort was so well convinced of this that, in signing the decrees required by the circumstances, he assumed the title of general-in-chief of the division of the army placed under his orders.

January 19, 1858, M. Juarez publicly took possession of the presidency at Guanajuato by a manifesto to that effect, and when, on the 22d, the insurgents entered into the national palace of Mexico, the legitimate government had, in fact, been organized three days before in the former city. Since then M. Juarez has not ceased to fulfil his duties towards the republic and towards foreign powers in every case; that is to say, where these powers had deigned to address themselves to him; and unless it is to be presumed that the recognition of the *coup d'état* by the ministers of England and of France constituted a legitimacy which before was wanting to that act of M. de Zuloaga and Miramon, a doctrine which, in M. de Saligny's own words, "*would create in their behalf a new droit de gens in formal opposition to that which has hitherto served as a rule for all international relations,*" we cannot see in virtue of what legitimate right or usage the administration of Juarez could be held responsible for the acts or contracts of the usurping administration of MM. Zuloaga and Miramon.

M. Jecker had voluntarily entered into several contracts with persons who had no lawful authority to treat in the name of the republic. This was an affair between his former partners and himself. If he had been mistaken in his calculations, it was for him to bear the consequences of his mistake, and to consider himself fortunate if the lawful government forbore to inflict upon him the penalties which he had incurred according to the terms of article 1 of the decree of November 3, 1858.

But the Mexican government never placed itself on that absolute ground of strict right. M. Zarco always manifested to M. de Saligny his desire to arrange, in a manner satisfactory to the interested parties, the questions pending between France and Mexico; and while taking into account the difficulties which beset the case of M. Jecker, both on account of its origin and the exhaustion of the public treasury, he added that as soon as the question of principle was settled the details should be speedily arranged to the satisfaction of the parties principally concerned.

If, then, M. Jecker did not come to terms on this question with the Mexican government, it is simply because, as we said above, he refused to do so; and if he refused, it is simply because M. de Saligny constantly opposed any terms of arrangement whatsoever.

E. LEFEVRE.

No. V.—Conclusion of the Reactionary Administration.—English Mediation.

There are cases in which certain governments, without being compelled to admit explicitly that they have been mistaken, may be so favored by the institutions from which they spring as to have need of the support of public opinion, and they are enabled then to react without danger against their previous decisions.

The English ministry acted thus in the Mexican question after its chargé d'affaires, Mr. Lettsom, and its official representative, Mr. Ottway, had both recognized the reactionary administration emanating from the Tacubaya project, and by degrees separated itself from that administration to draw nearer to the constitutional government.

It profited, in the first place, by the horror it felt at the assassinations committed on the 11th of April, 1859, at the village of Tacubaya, by order of Marquez and Miramon, to declare to the minister for foreign affairs of that government of bandits "that it was not sure it had done well in giving an uninterrupted preference from the commencement of the troubles to the government of which that minister was the organ."—(Note of Mr. Ottway, dated August 4, 1859.) Then, too, in reply, on the 16th of December, 1859, to certain English merchants, who begged him to declare that the sole *de facto* government was that to which he was accredited, her Britannic Majesty's minister said "it was difficult to say which was the real *de facto* government in Mexico, for while England and France recognized the authority of the President who was in possession of Mexico, the United States, on the contrary, recognized that of the President who governed at Vera Cruz."

This, if we may be allowed so to express ourselves, was the first step in the path of reparation. Then came the recall of Mr. Ottway, a gentleman so compromised by his weakness and partiality towards the reactionaries that he had become an embarrassment. Next came a despatch dated the 26th of January, 1860, in which Lord John Russell, minister of foreign affairs, requested Mr. George B. Matthews, the chargé d'affaires, to offer the mediation of England to the two belligerent parties, but on condition of "a general amnesty being at once proclaimed, together with civil and religious tolerance."

This despatch, dated, as we have said, the 26th January, 1860, arrived in Mexico about the end of February, and was not known in Mexico until the early part of March, when M. Miramon, who left on the 8th of February for the second campaign of Vera Cruz, had already arrived under the walls of that place.

It was then sent to Captain Aldham, commander of the English corvette Valorous, anchored at Sacrificios, to be communicated by him to the belligerents, and it received on the 2d March a first reply direct from Miramon, in which, without saying anything about "religious toleration," he presented, however, as a basis of an armistice, six articles, the object of which was to legitimatize the insurrection by compelling the constitutional government to take shelter under its skirts.

The constitutional government, though placed in a much more favorable position with the English government, inasmuch as by the law of 12th July, 1859, seven months before the proposition of tolerance, it had abolished religious marriages and substituted for them the civil contract, besides proclaiming liberty of worship, considered that it ought to decline all direct reply, on the ground that the moment was inopportune for answering the English proposals, and on both sides preparations were made for the struggle.

Thereupon Miramon, before opening fire against the place, addressed a last office to M. Ramon Iglesias, superior commander of the forces of Vera Cruz, in order to avoid, if possible, the effusion of blood. This time MM. Santos Degollado and José de Emparander, in the name of the constitutional government, and Isidro Diaz and Manuel Robles Pezuela, in that of the *coup d'état*, met in a railway station to discuss the basis of an armistice; but they could not agree upon the first conditions, and war followed, accompanied on the part of the reactionaries with such atrocious circumstances that the commander of the Valorous considered it his duty to interfere in the name of outraged humanity by declaring to General Miramon that he might destroy the city, and perhaps even take possession of its ruins, but he would never gain the hearts of those who inhabited it.

"If your excellency," he said at the end of his communication, "does not judge it opportune to terminate an anti-Christian war which nothing justifies, directed solely against property and foreign commerce, and which is a cause of ruin to her Majesty's subjects, in my capacity as commander-in-chief of her Britannic Majesty's naval forces in these waters I shall energetically protest against this war, and I announce to you that I shall take the first opportunity of making known to my government that your excellency has caused the ruin of English subjects and English commerce."

Miramon, in his reply, did not deny any of the charges contained in the letter of Captain Aldham. He contented himself with saddling the horrors committed by a useless bombardment upon the necessities of war, and remained profoundly silent respecting the accusation of having wickedly directed his shells towards the houses in which peaceful citizens resided, nearly all of whom were foreigners, instead of discharging them upon the fortified points held by the defenders of Vera Cruz.

Meanwhile M. Munoz Ledo addressed an official note to the foreign ministers in Mexico, announcing to them the failure of the efforts made at Vera Cruz by the representative of the reactionary party in order to bring about a reconciliation. He dwelt especially, with the chargé d'affaires of the British government, upon the causes of the failure, and induced that agent to bring to the knowledge of the London cabinet the motives which, according to him, had prevented the question from being settled in a pacific manner, and in conformity with the sense of the instructions transmitted to Mexico by Earl Russell.

But Mr. Matthews was not a man to be imposed upon by the insidious language of the reactionary diplomacy. He knew as well as M. Munoz Ledo what had passed before Vera Cruz, and how Miramon, in distorting the sense of the English proposal, had endeavored to make use of that proposal so distorted to impose the law upon his adversaries. He replied, therefore, "that he learnt with pleasure that his excellency the President had received with attention the proposals of her Britannic Majesty's government with a view to the reconciliation of the belligerent parties upon certain bases specified beforehand, because those propositions, according to M. Munoz Ledo, were in harmony with his own opinions;" but he added it was also for this reason that he "could not refrain from expressing his sincere regret that the propositions made by his excellency to the constitutional party were not in conformity with those recommended by her Majesty's government, nor with the enlightened opinion and the friendly sentiments towards Mexico with which her Majesty's secretary of state had been animated in proposing the basis suggested, as the best, the surest, and the most prudent means of re-establishing peace in the republic," &c.

On his side, Captain Aldham pursued at Vera Cruz, with a perseverance certainly worthy of better success, the generous idea of a compromise between the two parties, separated henceforth more perhaps by the blood with which the reactionaries had stained their hands since their accession to power than by the circumstances which had opened out to them the path to it. Difficulties increased his energy. Thus, when he learnt that Miramon, at the end of his resources, and unable for want of ammunition to continue longer the bombardment of the place, was preparing to raise a siege he ought never to have undertaken, he thought the occasion more favorable, and on the 28th of March, 1860, addressed to the reactionary President a fresh letter, the more prominent passages of which we cannot refrain from citing, as they show better than we can the real causes of the present disorganization of the republic.

"I think it needless to tell your excellency," he wrote, "that the greatest obstacle to the establishment of a liberal and constitutional government arises from the great power and wealth of the Mexican church. The bases of the church are good, for they were founded by the Saviour of mankind. But your clergy does not follow the path He traced. Its eyes are closed because its works are bad, and it takes pleasure in them. It will not reform itself, for to do so it must renounce its mundane pleasures. It voluntarily keeps its flocks in darkness and ignorance in order that they may be ignorant of its ways.

"If your excellency continues in the path you have hitherto chosen you will never reign in the hearts of your fellow-citizens. A small number of them may join you, but it will be from fear, not from affection.

"Do you claim to be a Christian government? Why does not your country prosper like so many others which have passed through a period of greater calamity than that which you are now passing through?

"Because they adopted civil and religious liberty, and their actions were in accordance with Christianity.

"You, on the contrary, merely know its name.

"But the time has arrived when true Christianity ought to prevail; when liberal and enlightened principles ought to take the place of darkness and ignorance.

"Your excellency has the power in your hands. You can become if you please the founder of a great work, desired by the immense majority of the people of Mexico.

"Cast off the fetters that enchain you. Unite cordially and sincerely with those who are struggling for liberty of conscience and free institutions. Once united you will be strong. Put the church in the place which belongs to it. Assign to it a fitting revenue and apply the rest of its property to the development of the national wealth. Compel the clergy, in a word, to follow the path traced out for it by its chief. Protect commerce and business with foreign powers; open your ports, reduce the taxes, and your excellency will soon see welfare and prosperity spread throughout the country, and your excellency will have been the director and the leader of this new state of things."

Thereupon Miramon, summoned by the persistence of the English commander to declare himself categorically upon the different points contained in the note of Earl Russell, and especially upon religious toleration, again glided away from the responsibility of a direct reply by sheltering his disinclination behind the congress of 1857, which, he said, although the most liberal of all that had been held, had not dared, nevertheless, to establish this toleration.

This, we admit, was convicting the liberal majority of that assembly of pusillanimity; but it will equally be admitted that some days after M. de Gabriac thought proper to take the stage in person. It was only when he had ceased to hope that the reactionists would take possession of Vera Cruz that he began to speak of mediation. But after their defeat he deemed it prudent to offer his services, if only to have the right of protecting the interests of the defeated party. So he volunteered his services in conjunction with those of Mr. Matthews, and on April 12, 1860, he offered the good offices of the imperial legation *for the conclusion of an armistice, during which they should proceed to elect a national assembly to decide the definite form of government for the country.*

The advantage of this new intervention, as it appeared to the reactionary party, was, that for the moment at least it put an end to any measure of civil and religious toleration. Accordingly M. Munoz Ledo replied to M. de Gabriac, on the 18th of the same month, that "the government of his excellency President Miramon regarded as a favor of Providence the accord of the two cabinets of London and Paris relative to the *salutary, disinterested,* and *impartial* counsels contained in the note of the minister of the Emperor." We see how unsubstantial was this accord. Indeed, the reactionary administration had so little faith in it, in spite of the assurance which it affected in its communication to M. de Gabriac, that about the same time M. Munoz Ledo, in reply to a pressing inquiry from Mr. Matthews as to the views of the cabinet to which M. Munoz Ledo belonged upon the pacification of the republic as the British cabinet had advised, returned an evasive answer, to the effect that a preliminary declaration of civil and religious liberty would be an invasion of the sovereign rights reserved to the congress whose convocation was demanded. Nothing could be falser than this reasoning, for a political assembly is no more competent to pronounce upon the relative value of this or that form of religious worship than the state to pretend to a cognizance of supernatural things; and this constitutional government, six weeks before, on proclaiming liberty of conscience as a natural consequence of the substitution of the civil contract of marriage for the purely religious sacrament, had sufficiently attested its firm resolve to make Mexico participate in the adoption of the great principles of civil and religious liberty proclaimed in France in 1789. For the constitutional government the difficulty of acceding purely and simply to the counsels of the British government, and signing an armistice of which the first condition should be the recognition of civil and religious toleration, did not (as in the case of the reactionists) consist in the adoption of that measure, which in fact it had already decreed; but it proceeded from the very conditions of its power, conditions which it could not infringe without betraying its duties and deluding the hopes of the country. Therefore it was that, in its reply, dated March 16, 1860, and addressed to Captain Aldham, R. N., to be by him transmitted to Mr. Matthews, and by the latter to the British cabinet, it pointed out the true legitimate origin and quality of the constitutional government; proved by the text of official documents the loyalty with which it had hitherto fulfilled the obligations contracted by the republic, even towards those powers whose representatives had recognized the counter-revolutionary movement of Tacubaya, and merely given it an importance which it would never otherwise have obtained, and concluding by declaring "that admitting that the constitutional President, in order to secure at once the advantages of peaceful and tranquil existence, consented to an armistice based upon the surrender of civil and religious liberty as the reactionary administration proposed, such an act of guilty complaisance would not bring the civil war to an end. On the contrary, it would result in perverting the civilizing tendencies of the great liberal party, and in weakening the elements of order which still existed by casting loose passions now under restraint and urging them to a struggle more disastrous and terrible than any before known in the country."

Since then the situation has not changed. The reactionary aspirations of M. de Gabriac have undoubtedly triumphed for a while in the capital with the aid of the intervention, but the country is up in arms, and every day's experience justifies the previsions of the government of M. Juarez.

In order to understand the causes of the rupture of the convention of London, we have thus endeavored to trace clearly the line of demarcation which, for the last four years at least, has separated the liberal policy pursued in Mexico by the British government from that of which the imperial government of France has unhappily made itself the champion.

E. LEFEVRE.

No. VI.—Conclusion of the Scandals of the Reactionary Party.—Robbery at the British Legation

While Captain Aldham denounced at Vera Cruz the savage acts of the President of the reaction, at Mexico M. de Gabriac at last received orders to return to France.

That minister communicated the news to the administration by a note, in which he asked to be allowed to "frank," in other words, to send away, without being compelled to pay the export duty, a sum of £30,000, forming the greater part of the gains he had realized in Mexico during a stay of five years, and he announced his departure for the 8th May, 1860.

He left, in fact, on that day, glad no doubt to escape the sight of the fresh scandals which were about to arise in the ranks of the pretended defenders of order.

It is impossible for me to affirm whether he was apprised of what was going to happen, but if we remember the time he lost in going to Vera Cruz, where he had, on the 24th of May, a long conference with an ambassador newly arrived from Spain, it will seem very difficult for it to have been otherwise.

However it may have been, the Tacubaya project, restored in January, 1859, under circumstances already known to the reader, definitely passed from life to death the day succeeding the departure of M. de Gabriac after a fresh freak, of which M. Miramon was again the hero; and President Zuloaga, prisoner of his substitute, was carried into the interior of the country, where his gendarme was called in consequence of the victories of Loma, Alta, and Penuelas, gained over the reactionaries by Generals Uraga and Gonzales Ortega.

This removal was kidnapping—thorough kidnapping, accompanied by all the aggravated circumstances of premeditation, violence, and ambush—and it complicated in such a grotesque manner the difficulties of a situation already tolerably involved, that everybody regarded it as an omen of the fall, more or less distant but certain, of the reactionary administration. The newsmongers immediately turned it to account in their own manner; and the public, which knew the truth only by the burdens that the clashing of subaltern ambitions caused to weigh upon it, was this time made acquainted with the last farce represented at the palace, by a document, the object of which was to declare that there was no longer a constituted power, and which had all the more effect that it bore the names of three members of the diplomatic body.

The facetious substitute had rushed into the risks of this fresh adventure with all the eagerness of an ill-bred school-boy, who considers he has a right to play tricks upon his tutor solely because the poor wretch seems ridiculous to him. But sobered by the attitude of the diplomatic corps, he reflected upon the influence that this informality might exercise upon his own position, and he thought it would be well to obtain the formal recognition at least of the power he had just seized upon in so strange a manner.

With this object he enjoined his factotum, General Antonio Corona, to elicit the opinion (paid for beforehand) of what he called his council of state. When the cards were shuffled he placed his abdication in the hands of M. Ignacio Pavon, president of the supreme tribunal of justice, and pretended to submit his conduct to the control of twenty-six notables selected from the very flower of the reactionary party, who had accepted the deplorable mission of giving to his usurpation the deceitful gloss of which a few days later the ambassador Pacheco spoke in a despatch addressed by him on the 15th of June, 1860, to M. Calderon Collantes.

The farce played out, M. Miguel Arroyo, secretary general of the ministry of foreign affairs, one of the notables who had just accorded their *satisfecit* to M. Miramon, received orders to communicate the result to the representatives of the foreign powers; but he received in exchange from Mr. G. B. Matthews, chargé d'affaires of the British government, a declaration stating "that he could not recognize by anticipation the administration established in the capital of the republic, under the presidency of the former substitute of M. Zuloaga, before receiving express orders from his government."

Thereupon, M. Lares, who had been promoted within a few days to the functions of minister of foreign affairs, intimated to him "that from the moment he refused to recognize the government of General Miramon before receiving orders from London, the general, on his part, before occupying himself with the interests of the English residents, would wait until he had nothing else to do."

The question, it will be seen, grew more embittered every day. Nevertheless, Mr. Matthews, after observing to M. Lares that his conduct in this matter had been entirely in conformity with that of the majority of the *corps diplomatique*, contented himself by replying to him "that he supposed, in expressing itself thus, the government of which General Miramon was the head had no intention of evading the responsibility devolving in such cases upon every *de facto* government, but that if it were otherwise he should receive the declaration with the utmost surprise, and that he should have the disagreeable duty of communicating it to his government."

M. Lares replied, on the 24th of September, that he could enter into no discussion upon the points advanced by Mr. Matthews, except with the minister of her Britannic Majesty, after such minister had recognized the government of M. Miramon; because the Mexican government could only treat as a *de facto* government, and that while it was unrecognized by Mr. Matthews it could not employ that title in treating with him.

Finally Mr. Matthews received the instructions of which he spoke in his note to M. Lares. They reached him in the early part of October, and on the 17th he addressed to the men who for nearly three years had taken pleasure in violating the most sacred engagements a last note, in which he repeated to them, in rather more measured terms, though similar in substance, what Captain Aldham in his note of the 28th of the previous March had already written to M. Miramon. He concluded by declaring that he had *received orders to break off his relations with the government established at Mexico*, and he retired with his legation to Jalapa, a town some ninety miles from Vera Cruz.

This was precisely what the ministers of the reaction desired, in order to proceed to the inauguration of a system entirely their own. To begin with—who would believe it?—the first two blows fell upon M. Jecker.

In the early part of August, 1860, this well-known banker, whose coffers had been so often thrown open to the necessities of M. Miramon, was informed that he had to pay into the treasury chest the modest sum of £2,000, to be devoted to the relief, in a moment of distress, of the unceasing poverty of the authors of the *coup d'état.* M. Jecker, to do him justice, resisted as well as a banker who had just failed to meet his engagements could resist. He discussed, he complained, he protested, and only when he found all his efforts unavailing, concluded that he had better come to terms. So he offered £800 ; but this sum General Corona, commanding in the absence of Miramon, inexorably declined to accept, and even carried his forgetfulness of the services M. Jecker had rendered so far as to inflict a fine of £600 upon the recalcitrant banker. Then, at length, M. Jecker understood the men he had to deal with, and sent to say that nothing should extort the sum demanded of him. Accordingly, when the police agent came in the evening with an armed force, he found the house barricaded, and entrance impossible. Next morning the doors were opened as usual, and the "defenders of order," armed some with pickaxes, some with hatchets, rushed in. The doors of the offices were opened in presence of the consul of France, whom M. Jecker had sent for, and whose protests were set at naught. The gang were going to break open the chests and safes, when M. Jecker interfered and consented to give up the keys. The safes were opened, and nothing, absolutely nothing, found in them. The knowing banker had removed all their contents in the night.

Then followed the arrest of MM. German Landa and Sanchez Navarro, and MM. Gorribar and Joaquim Rosas, who had one and all forgotten that in the hands of the heroes of Tacubaya their property was not quite so safe as in the hands of professed highwaymen and housebreakers.

But what were a few thousand pounds, more or less, to such an administration? A drop of water in the ocean. Exactions increased with difficulties, and the rapacity of the soldiery with the need of their services, until one fine day nothing was left for the defenders of the altar and of the ecclesiastical privileges but to fall upon the wealth accumulated in the churches by the piety of their fathers. In this instance, it is true, the pillage was sanctioned by the Mexican archbishop and the superior clergy.

It was reasonable enough to suppose that these ecclesiastical treasures would stop the gap for a time, and give a moment's peace. Not so ; about the middle of September M. Miramon called together a new assembly of twenty-six capitalists—just the number of "notables" who had been summoned to make him President—and demanded of them, according to his invariable custom, revolver in hand, the trifle of £100,000, with which he undertook to dispose of General Gonzalez Ortega, who had defeated him forty days before near the little town of Silao.

It was impossible to resist so polite an injunction ; but even this sum did not suffice, so the "defenders of order" resolved to seize a sum of £132,000, belonging to English bondholders, and which was deposited in the safes of the British legation, doubly protected by the place of deposit and by the seals of the legation (bearing the arms of England) affixed thereto.

General Leonardo Marquez (in Mexico commonly called *Leopardo*, in remembrance of the assassinations of Tacubaya—the man whom the imperial government of France has since decorated with the cordon of commander of the legion of honor)—was charged with this expedition ; and on November 16 the chief of the police, Lagarde, at the head of his men, occupied the residence of the legation, on the pretext of searching for a depot of arms alleged to be concealed there.

Next day, the 17th, Marquez addressed to Mr. Whitehead, the agent of the English bondholders, the following letter, in which he endeavored to put a false color on the designs of the reactionary government, by representing the object of this robbery as an act of caution against the risks which the bondholders' money might be exposed to in the event of disturbances :

NATIONAL ARMY.—MEXICAN REPUBLIC.—QUARTERMASTER GENERAL.

As the public funds deposited in your hands, and destined to the payment of the English bondholders, have not yet been paid over, and as under existing circumstances they might run great risk in case of disturbance ; and as the danger would become imminent if the forces which preserve order in the city should be unprovided for ; and as provision cannot be made for them with the resources at present at the disposal of the government, available only in periodical payments, his excellency the general-in-chief of these forces, in obedience to his duty, and desirous to clear his responsibility, *orders you to place the funds deposited in your charge at the disposal of the commissariat of the army.* It is, of course, understood that no more than the sums strictly necessary will be taken from the coffers, and that for their reimbursement the proceeds of the loan subscribed by the venerable clergy and by private persons for the payment of the garrison will be available, and that if there should be a deficit at the departure of the first conducta, this deficit will be covered by the duties to be deducted from the sums exported.

You will be so good as to deliver 200,000 piastres (£40,000) this very day, to the commissary general, who will deliver you a receipt for that amount.

God and the law.

Headquarters at Mexico, this 17th November, 1860.

L. MARQUEZ.

But it appears that Mr. Whitehead was not of opinion that the interests with which he was charged permitted him to obey this peremptory injunction, for the same day Marquez addressed to him another and still more peremptory summons.

These two notes, sent one upon the other, clearly meant that the determination of the reactionary government was taken, and that no excuses on Mr. Whitehead's part for declining to violate a deposit committed to his care would avail against it. Nevertheless, in order to clear his own responsibility in the matter, Mr. Whitehead replied once more by the following letter to the terrible quartermaster general:

MEXICO, *November* 17, 1860.

EXCELLENCY: In reply to the official note which I have had the honor to receive to-day from the hands of the commissary of the army, I deem it my duty to declare to you that the money received here on account of the foreign debt contracted at London was deposited under the protection of the legation of her Britannic Majesty, in conformity with the instructions of the foreign committee, to be forwarded as soon as circumstances should permit; and that Mr. Mathews, before his departure from Jalapa, placed the seals of the legation and his private signature on the door of the apartment in which the funds were deposited, the keys of which are in his possession. Consequently, notwithstanding the urgent circumstances which your excellency justly points out, I cannot dispose of these funds without the consent of the representative of the British government, for I have not the keys of the apartment in which they are placed, nor can I break the seal of the legation. Such is the answer that I had the honor to give to the commissary. I was obliged to give him a verbal reply, because time pressed, and I declared to him that I found it impossible to remit to him the 200,000 piastres which you demand. I trust that your excellency will be convinced that it is not from want of deference towards the government that I have not complied with your order, but simply because I have not the power to do so. As regards an observation which your excellency has addressed to me, it may not be superfluous to remark that although the funds are not distributed in dividends, they have nevertheless been legally delivered, and therefore do, in fact, belong to the bondholders. Even were they not deposited at the legation, I should have no right to touch them except to see to their being shipped for their destination. In support of this assertion, and in case your excellency should not be aware of the text of the law of January 23, 1857, I take the liberty to send him a copy enclosed herewith, and I have the honor to call his attention to the formal wording of the first three articles.

I have the honor, &c.,

CH. WHITEHEAD,
Agent of the Bondholders of the Foreign Debt.

His Excellency the QUARTERMASTER GENERAL, *Mexico.*

All this was true—physically and materially true. But Mr. Whitehead had to deal with men as well aware of the facts as himself—with needy men exasperated by their wants, and by the reiterated defeats of their party—with men, in short, who had made up their minds to listen to no remonstrances. So Colonel Jauregui, at the head of a party of Marquez's men, broke into the house, broke the seal bearing her Majesty's arms upon the doors of the apartments, and, in spite of the protest of the Spanish ambassador, M. J. F. Pacheco, took away £152,000 sterling of the sum which had been deposited there by the agent of the bondholders. The same day M. Pacheco addressed the following note to M. Teodosco Lares, minister of foreign affairs in that government of bandits:

EMBASSY OF SPAIN AT MEXICO,
November 17, 1860.

The undersigned, ambassador of her Christian Majesty, regrets to be obliged to address his excellency M. Teodosco Lares, minister of foreign affairs, concerning a deplorable event that occurred yesterday.

By order of the quartermaster general of the army, a person whom the undersigned has not the honor to know presented himself, accompanied by an armed force, at the residence of the British legation, for the purpose of demanding the remittance of a considerable sum of money which it appears had been deposited there for the payment of English creditors. So far the undersigned had no right to interfere in this matter, the chargé d'affaires of her Britannic Majesty not having recommended to his care the interests or the persons of his countrymen. But in proceeding to take possession of the sum in question the Mexican police agent must have burst open the door protected by the seals of the legation, and it is in consequence of that act that the undersigned deems himself authorized to repeat in the present note the protest which he has already made verbally, and to call the particular attention of the minister of foreign relations to the case. The undersigned, placed at the head of the diplomatic corps, cannot forbear to protest most strongly against an act which is at once a violation of the immunities which foreign representatives enjoy and of international law; for such it is to break the seals of a legation, to seize property intrusted to its protection. Were this principle liable to be disregarded with impunity, the relations existing between different countries would be deprived of all security and dignity, and public right would be abandoned to the caprices of arbitrary power and brute force. It is for these reasons that the undersigned deplores an event which he forbears to characterize in more energetic terms; but he feels himself bound to protest; and in addressing this protest to his excellency the minister of foreign relations, in the hope that he will take into his serious consideration the gravity of the facts which have occasioned it, and of the consequences it may lead to, he begs to state that he shall forward a copy of it by the next mail to the government of her Christian Majesty, and make a similar communication to his colleagues residing in the republic.

He avails himself, meanwhile, of this opportunity to, &c.

J. F. PACHECO.

The MINISTER OF FOREIGN RELATIONS.

After the minister of Spain, the minister of Prussia, who happened just then to be away at Jalapa, addressed the above named Lares a note on the same subject, warning him that the government of Mexico had entered upon a course of action which would render it impossible for foreign governments to maintain regular relations with it. The same day Mr. Mathews instructed Mr. Whitehead to write, in his name, to M Lares, insisting on the restitution, accompanied by a letter of apology, within twenty-four hours, of the sum removed by violence from his residence after breaking the seals of the legation; otherwise that he should render M. Miramon, in company with his ministers, Lares, Diaz, Corona, and Sagaseta, with General Miramon, and, conjointly, the whole Mexican nation, responsible for the attack committed, in his person, against the British nation and government. But as neither the minister of Prussia nor Mr. Mathews had recognized the strange authority of M. Miramon, the reactionary administration pretended that its dignity would not allow it to reply.

As to the ambassador of Spain, M. Miramon's administration did not even take the trouble to offer any apology for an act without excuse; it simply sent him a copy of the report of the burglarious attack upon the British legation, drawn up by a person who had been sent to assist at the operation expressly in that capacity; and without any anxiety for the consequences of an act which appeared to it perfectly regular, it calmly awaited the effect of this "report" upon the temper of European governments.

And this was the last act of the administration commonly called that of M. Miramon. A month after he was flying ignominiously, and for a second time, before the liberal forces commanded by M. Gonzalez Ortega, and was soon obliged to go and beg the protection of those very foreigners whom he had victimized and plundered incessantly as long as he was in power.

E. LEFEVRE.

No. VII.—EXPULSION OF M. PACHECO—CONDUCT OF M. DE SALIGNY.

The constitutional army arrived at Mexico without striking a blow. M. Juarez gathered the fruit of the battles won by his generals at Loma Alta, Penuelas, Calderon, Silao, and Capulalpam. He entered the capital on the 11th of January, 1861—three years, day for day, after he had left it—and immediately afterwards gave notice to the ambassador of Spain, to the Papal Nuncio, and to the ministers of Ecuador and Guatemala, to quit without delay the territory of the republic, in consequence of their declared hostility to the lawful government and to liberal institutions. This dismissal, necessitated by circumstances and justified by the conduct of those persons, was besides entirely conformable to the admitted doctrine of international law in such a case; for it is evident that if governments may on certain occasions refuse admission into their states to foreign agents simply on the ground of suspicion, they have, *à fortiori*, the right to send them away when their conduct has confirmed the suspicion and made it certainty. Yet the Spanish government made the dismissal of its ambassador a grievance against the government of the republic. Naturally enough, the dismissal of the Papal Nuncio and of the minister of Ecuador and Guatemala was scarcely noticed; but the expulsion of M. Pacheco was regarded as a more serious matter. That personage protested, not against the order he had received to quit the territory of the republic within the briefest delay necessary to complete his preparations for departure, but against a simple breach of etiquette. He protested that "he had not come to Mexico as a private individual, but in the capacity of ambassador of the Queen of Spain, as his credentials deposited in the archives of the state attested, and that therefore all communications addressed to him by the government ought to bear, as a superscription, his ambassadorial title and quality." We should certainly not have mentioned so trivial a matter as this, had not M. Pacheco repeated the terms of his protest before the senate of his country, and had not that protest foreshadowed a question far more important, viz., that of the sovereignty of the Mexican nation.

Assuredly, when M. Pacheco was sent to Mexico as ambassador of Spain, he was accredited to the lawful government of the republic, and not to a faction which, although for a moment in possession of the capital, had no lawful authority to represent the country before foreign powers.

It was to the lawful government, sprung from the constitution of 1857, and established for the moment at Vera Cruz, that M. Pacheco should have presented his credentials. Instead of this, he preferred to remit them to the chief of an oppressive faction, which for three years had covered the country with blood and ruins. In doing so, he voluntarily divested himself of his ambassadorial quality, and became the instrument of a party whose fortunes he was bound to share.

But it may be alleged that M. Pacheco had been accredited to the authorities which derived their sanction from the Tacubaya arrangement—authorities recognized by M. de Gabriac, the then chargé d'affaires of the Spanish government; and therefore that these authorities represented to the O'Donnell cabinet the sole lawful government of the republic. Was, then, the recognition of that factious combination of Tacubaya by M. de Gabriac sufficient to constitute in its favor a lawful origin? If so, it follows that the sovereignty of any country, of France, or of England, as much as of Mexico, resides in the will of a few representatives of foreign states who may according to their caprices (sometimes to their interests) transfer that sovereignty to the party they may desire to favor. It would be difficult to equal in absurdity a doctrine tending to such a conclusion as this. Common sense, not less than right usage, teaches us that before, during, and after the success of the clerico-military insurrection of December 17, 1857—January 11, 1858, the government established by the constitution was the sole lawful government of the country, and M. Pacheco, in protesting, by his recognition of a rebellious faction, against that only lawful government, deprived himself of the rights and immunities attached to the office conferred upon him by his own sovereign, and became a mere private individual in the eyes of the lawful government Indeed, this might be said equally of the new minister of France, M. Dubois de Saligny, and for the following reasons. For, while M. Pacheco was in receipt of an order of expulsion from the constitutional government, in reply to his claims for services rendered to the reactionary party, M. de Saligny, who had arrived at Mexico only on the 12th of December, 1860, and whose name was as yet untarnished by those intrigues which had rendered that of M. Pacheco so unpopular, waited patiently and apart to see what was to become of the constitutional government to which he also had been accredited by instructions dated Fontainebleau, June 28, 1860; and this silence on his part, under such circumstances, if not an actual declaration of war, was significant enough Instead of acting upon M. de Gabriac's theory, that any government whatsoever established in the capital should be recognized as the lawful government of the state, M. de Saligny remained stealthily silent and apart; while the newsmongers attributed his retreat to various causes, some pretending that the French minister wanted to be paid for his recognition of the Mexican government, some that he was not in reality accredited at all to the government of the republic.

This state of things continued until February, 1861, when M. de Saligny suddenly gave signs of life on the occasion of the visit paid to the establishment of Sisters of Charity by the authorities. M. de Saligny claimed to withdraw the establishment of the Sisters from the supervision of the local authority altogether, on the pretext that the principal foundation of the Sisterhood being in France, all these establishments were under the direct protection of the imperial government. From this strange doctrine, already adopted, in 1858, by M. de Gabriac, and of which, probably, neither M. de Gabriac nor M. de Saligny had calculated all the consequences, it would follow that any religious congregation allowed to establish itself in any country divests itself, by the mere fact of belonging to one or other of the monastic or conventual orders, of its nationality, and adopts that of the founder of the order. Thus the king of Naples, when such a potentate existed, should have been the protector of the Benedictines and the Franciscans, simply because, in the sixth century, St. Benedict, of Nursia, established the headquarters of the order at Monte Cassino, in the kingdom of Naples, and in 1208 St. François d'Assisi founded his order at Portiunçala, also in the Neapolitan territory. Such a pretension could hardly have been admitted by the government in whose name M. de Gabriac and M. de Saligny claimed to impose it upon the Mexican government, and unless on the principle of denying to a weak government, because it is weak, the sovereignty to which, as an independent power, it is entitled, by what right could the ministers of France claim for France a privilege which the imperial government would never have conceded to the Neapolitan government?

Nevertheless, in order to put an end to shifts and artifices which only seemed to keep alive the resistance of the reactionists by persuading them that the constitutional government could never be recognized by M. de Gabriac's successor, the Mexican government desisted from the exercise of its undoubted right and surveillance over a religious order of Mexican origin, and which had been established with the consent of the Mexican Congress, and proposed to the French envoy to refer the question to his own government. Thereupon M. de Saligny officially recognized, on March 17, 1861, the constitutional government. All this time the revolution, which had begun to implant reforms in the institutions of the republic, was pursuing its regular course in the midst of difficulties and trials which proved more and more the strength it derived from the support of the people who had hitherto found no escape from the retrograde tendencies of the clergy. In 1858, everybody thought it would be impossible for the constitutional government to make head against that colossal power which disposed of the conscience of the country, and relied on the indirect resources which it was in a condition to procure from the recognition of the *coup d'état* by the ministers of France and England. The struggle had been long and terrible; but it had terminated in the complete triumph of the constitutional government, and there seemed to be at length an opportunity for the latter to carry out the principles of political, social, and administrative reform. But the reactionists, beaten on every field of battle, sought to take advantage of the difficulties of the great process of reform which three years of fighting had interrupted. The reactionary party still in arms met in small bands in parts of the country beyond the reach of the rapid or regular action of authority, and these miserable gangs of no political color or creed, but whose anti-social purposes were no secret, confided in the support of men who in Mexico, as in Europe, arrogate to themselves exclusively sentiments of order and moderation. Nay, more: certain of the diplomatists who had committed the error of recognizing the abominable dictatorship of a Zuloaga and a Miramon, forgot themselves again so far as to regard with complacency the plots of these malefactors, and even received at their legations individuals most deeply compromised in the events of the three preceding years.

Meanwhile the champions of reform relaxed not in their work of social and administrative reorganization, in spite of all these obstacles and dangers, while some of the diplomatic representatives of European governments were employed in weakening the authority and assailing the character of the government, supporting conspiracies, and fomenting discord, even in the very congress. The administration, supported by public opinion, pursued the bands of malefactors who were ravaging the country, and persevered in vindicating the cause of the revolution by undeniable benefits. For, in fact, this revolution was unlike any other that had yet occurred in the Mexican republic. It was a revolution that had its source in the heart of a nation resolved to submit no longer to the lawless caprices of privileged classes, but to secure true order and civilization, by emancipating itself at once from the despotism of the sabre and the corrupting influence of the confessional. But in Mexico, as elsewhere, a new structure of reform could only be built upon the ruins of past privileges.

It was in the face of all these difficulties, inseparable from a reforming government, that European diplomacy resolved to exact the rigorous fulfilment of all the obligations contracted by the government of the republic towards foreign powers; and, as diplomacy was in a hurry to present its ultimatum, it seized the occasion of the law voted on the 17th July. And yet the question raised by this law was simple enough. The point was, whether it could ever be permitted to a government to proceed in that manner; and if so, whether the Mexican government was at that time in the condition prescribed by public law.

Now, to understand at a glance the excessive nature of these diplomatic demands, it is enough to recall the fact that all writers on international law have admitted, that whenever the impossibility of meeting an engagement arises from a change in the situation of the debtor, that impossibility changes also the nature of the obligation which he may have contracted.

Thus, according to Grotius and Cocceieus, "The obligation resulting from any convention whatsoever ceases at the same time as the impossibility of meeting it;" and, according to Wheaton, "the annulment of a treaty, even after ratification, may be demanded, on the ground of the physical and moral impossibility of fulfilling its stipulations, and there is physical impossibility in all cases where the contracting party is wanting in the means necessary to the making his contract good." According to Martens, "The physical impossibility of fulfilling a treaty discharges a State from the obligation it has contracted, but without releasing it from the indemnity which must be granted to its creditor, in case that impossibility had been provided for by the treaty, or had occurred through the fault of the debtor." Finally, to omit many more equally decisive authorities, according to Hoffter, "The party who has subscribed an obligation may refuse to execute it in cases of impossibility, even though relative only, if it arose from the force of circumstances permanently beyond his control; and he would be specially so discharged if the conflict was one between his duties as debtor on the one hand *and the rights and well-being of the country on the other.*"

So much for the law of the case. It remains to be seen whether Mexico was at that time in any one of the cases of extremity mentioned by the writers quoted above. What, then, were the conventions to which Mexico had subscribed, and under what conditions had they been accepted by the government of the republic? These conventions were two in number. They dated from the beginning of the year 1857, and had been subscribed in order to prevent the bombardment of Vera Cruz—the one in favor of certain French merchants, the other of English creditors.

By the first, the Mexican government had assigned to the payment of the creditors of the French debt:

1. As a permanent charge.	
25 per cent. on all ships of French owners	25 per cent.
2. As a temporary charge.	
8 per cent. to pay the arrears of the said convention	8 per cent.
This 8 per cent. to be raised 2 per cent., under certain circumstances provided for by the convention	2 per cent.
Total	35 per cent.

By the second, the same government had assigned to the payment of the English debt and convention:

1. By permanent assignment.	
25 per cent. in favor of debt contracted in London	25 per cent.
16 per cent. in favor of the English convention	16 per cent.
2. By temporary assignment.	
8 per cent. applicable to payment of arrears	8 per cent.
To be raised under circumstances provided for, 2 per cent	2 per cent.
Total	51 per cent.

Moreover, the expenses of management, to the amount of about 30 per cent, were charged upon the Mexican government; so that, on the revenue derived from customs dues on French imports, there remained to the Mexican government, after payment of expenses and instalments of debts, 35 per cent., and on customs dues on English imports 19 per cent. only. Considering that the greater part of the revenues of the country are derived from these customs dues, these demands appear to leave something to be desired in the way of moderation; and it cannot be denied that M. Juarez's administration, far more unfortunate than culpable in that respect, was at that time under a stress of circumstances which all authorities on international law declare to be tantamount to the impossibility of meeting its engagements.

In pronouncing against these excessive demands, we are far from supposing that the governments of Great Britain and France had for a moment calculated the difficulties which might interfere with the execution of the engagements. But the difficulties, whether foreseen or unforeseen, were not the less serious; and the government of the republic could not be fairly made liable for the delay in payment which resulted from them. Others may, perhaps, charge the Mexican government with having wilfully entered into engagements which it knew it could not fulfil. But this objection is far more specious than solid. In its struggles against the reactionary parties after the *coup d'état*, the constitutional government really represented the cause of reform in the administration and in the whole conduct of the state. It was not a few isolated individuals that succumbed, but the cause and prospects of a better government. What signified the momentary suspension of payments, if the fall of the only Mexican government that had ever represented a moral principle was in the balance? The important point was to gain time; and, as there was but one way of fairly attaining this desirable result, the government was bound to yield before a display of force which left it no other alternative possible than to fall or to submit to sign the conventions, backed by the guns of the British and French squadrons, and to wait until after a victorious entry into the capital of the republic to demand the revision of treaties, the strict execution of which was materially impossible.

E. LEFEVRE.

No. VIII.—The Convention of London.

The law of July 17, 1861, was, we have shown, in strict accordance with all the principles of right which, according to the testimony of all writers on international law, appertain to governments in such a situation of affairs. But when reasons are wanting pretexts avail, and those who were intriguing with all their might to bring about an intervention were not likely to let slip so rare an opportunity of attaching European powers to their cause.

It was Spain that commenced proceedings. Not, as might be supposed, after all the noise about the name of M. Pacheco, to punish the republic for the expulsion of that unfortunate ambassador, but to constrain the Mexican government to recognize the treaty signed in 1860, at Paris, between M. Mon, ambassador of Spain to the French court, and M. Almonte, envoy of the reactionary rebellion.

Now, to understand the conditions of this treaty it must be observed that the Mexican debt is divided into two distinct branches, which should not be confounded with one another. There is the internal debt and the external debt; the one, of course, privileged; the other subject to all the fluctuations of parties, which for the last forty years have disputed the government of the republic. The internal debt is composed of all the sums due, in any shape, by the Mexican administration to its own citizens, and the government has always maintained that nothing could divest it of its quality of a debt essentially Mexican. Nor could persons who might happen to become holders of its stock, change on any pretext its national character.

The Spaniards, on the contrary, insisted that the bonds of the foreign debt bought by foreigners should partake in the privilege accorded by the law to those same foreigners; so that being masters of a considerable portion of these bonds, which they had bought at the lowest prices, they claimed to have them treated as credits of Spanish origin in the convention destined to liquidate by instalments the Mexican debt to Spain. Thence arose between the two governments a conflict which had terminated in 1857, under M. Comonfort, in a temporary suspension of payment of the Spanish debt.

But the insurgent reaction, in order to testify gratitude to Spain, whose subjects sympathized with it on all occasions and on all points, had authorized M. Almonte to comply for the while with all the exigencies of the Spanish government; and M. Mon, on his part, in order to respond to such generous conduct, had declared that Spain would henceforward desist from availing herself of the terms of that treaty to exact from Mexico concessions of the same nature.

Unfortunately for the importance of that financial masterpiece, the fall of the reactionary party drew with it the collapse of the treaty; and Spain being warned that the constitutional government could not under any circumstances recognize the acts of the reactionary insurgents, had taken advantage of the irritation of the cabinets of London and Paris against that law of July 17 to suggest the necessity of a combined military and naval demonstration on the coast of Mexico.

How, then, did it happen that this expedition, which in its inception was purely Spanish, became transformed into an expedition exclusively French? This is a question which can only be answered satisfactorily by those who are in the secret of the communications exchanged upon that occasion between the governments of France, England, and Spain. Indeed, any answer to the point is impossible, unless we take for granted that in the preliminary negotiations of the three powers there was neither as to the motives nor as to the objects of the expedition any clear and definite understanding.

We must seek elsewhere an explanation of the nature and causes of the convention of October 31, 1861, and perhaps we cannot do better than refer to the declarations made by M. Billault to the corps legislatif.

On the 27th June, 1861, M. Billault, the minister of state, replying to a speech delivered by M. Jules Favre the day before, acknowledged, perhaps somewhat involuntarily, that in the defined scheme of the convention there was no question of an expedition into the interior of the country, the action of the allied forces being limited to the coasts. In making this avowal M. Billault stated only a part of the truth. To have stated the whole truth he should have added that the convention of October 31 had given the contracting parties no such right to undertake an expedition into the interior of the country, and that if the imperial government exceeded the terms of the convention, it was because that convention was nothing but a pretext to cover the despatch of forces destined to overthrow the republican institutions in Mexico, and replace them by an empire organized under the presence of French bayonets, and in favor of the Archduke Maximilian of Austria, or, failing his acceptance, of some other prince at the Emperor's disposal. This, at least, would have been a clear, a frank, and a definite statement of the question; and since in this nineteenth century there is a majority in the French Chambers always ready to support the strong, the corps legislatif would have had the opportunity of pronouncing upon the purely material question whether the wrongs suffered by French subjects were proportionate to the penalties exacted, or whether the military and naval expedition would not result in taxing French commerce for the profit of mostly foreign creditors. But it was not so to be. The imperial spokesman preferred to keep silence; events took their course; the expedition went on: a French army entered the city of Mexico, and "the Empire," which had been so resolutely denied on June 27, 1861, in the face of the corps legislatif, was proclaimed at Mexico on July 12, 1863, in the presence of General Forey and M. de Saligny, by a meeting of 215 individuals, without any mandate from their fellow citizens, convened by traitors, at the point of foreign bayonets, to lend a varnish of legality to measures predetermined in Paris several months before the commencement of the intervention, among certain paid dignitaries of the French empire, and some famished agents of the old reactionary factions in Mexico.

To appreciate the morality of the operations now going on in that distant country, it might be desirable to set out, side by side, the original text of the convention of the three powers, and the convention itself; but this instrument is so notorious that we need only indicate the changes which were introduced into the original draught of the scheme. That scheme defined in the simplest manner the objects of the expedition. It was "to obtain from the authorities of Mexico a more efficacious protection of the persons and property of foreigners." It appeared, as M. Billault himself acknowledged at the sitting of the corps legislatif in June 21, 1861, "that the high contracting parties engaged *beforehand* not to make use of the forces which they might employ by virtue of the said convention, for objects other than those which were specified in the preamble, and *specially* not to make use of them to interfere in the internal affairs of the republic." But the instrument added what M. Billault took very good care to suppress—"that immediately after the occupation of Vera Cruz, and of the adjacent ports, the chiefs of the allied forces should address a collective note *to the authorities established in the republic*, in order to bring to their knowledge the motives for which the allies had recourse to measures of coercion, and *to invite them to enter immediately into negotiation*."

It would appear that in presenting this handsome document for Lord Russell's sanction, the sole object of the plenipotentiaries of France and Spain was to lull the apprehensions of the British cabinet; but when once the expedition was resolved upon, and before signing the definitive convention, they referred it back to Lord Russell, with a hinted doubt of the results to which, in that form, it might lead. They declared to the British government that they had no intention of compelling the Mexicans to adopt this or that form of government; that, on the contrary, the Mexicans should be left perfectly free in that respect; all the more so that they, the plenipotentiaries, had plausible grounds for supposing that the Mexicans would themselves come forward to ask for a moral support which could not be refused them. And thus was obtained the suppression of those inconvenient paragraphs in the original draught of the convention which, as M. Billault phrased it, "might have discouraged the national movement."

Now, let no one pretend that we are inventing suppositions on behalf of the cause we have undertaken to plead. Here is a despatch from the Spanish minister of foreign affairs, M. Calderon Collantes, dated Madrid, October 22, 1861, that is, eight days before the convention at London, to the Spanish ambassadors at the courts of St. James and the Tuileries, and in which all our "suppositions" are officially recorded in the order in which we have ourselves laid them before our readers

M. Calderon Collantes, after declaring that the preamble clearly defines the nature of the united action of the three powers, continues thus:

"Article I leaves nothing to be desired by the government of her Majesty.

"Article II equally merits our approval, and *though the dispositions which it contains might perhaps be reserved for instructions which will be furnished to the commanders of the united forces*," he (M. Calderon Collantes) "believes that it is preferable to define clearly in the convention what should be their course from the moment when they present themselves on the coast of Mexico, and more particularly after their occupation of Vera Cruz, and of other important points on the coast.

"Article III of the draught convention is entirely conformable to the ideas which the Queen's government has constantly manifested. They have always thought that full liberty should be left to the Mexicans to constitute their government in the manner most agreeable to their interests, to their customs, and to their beliefs. But while he has always held, and still holds, that the Mexicans should be the sole masters of their destinies, *he equally believes that it is necessary to take measures to enable them to examine* (*qu'il est nécessaire de les mettre en état de pouvoir examiner*) without passion and without infatuation the situation to which their errors have brought them, in order to adopt the most judicious means to ameliorate it This result might be obtained by intimating to the Mexican government and to the chiefs of the belligerent forces the necessity of suspending hostilities, and concluding an armistice long enough to discuss or solve peacefully, if that be possible, their domestic differences. Otherwise, indeed, far from the presence of the combined forces suspending the struggle and arresting bloodshed, it may happen that the horrors of which the republic has so long been the theatre will even increase. Hence it might be imprudent, and perhaps somewhat hazardous, to renounce absolutely and beforehand a course of action which might be afterwards necessitated by unforeseen events.

"Article III would appear equally clear and equally precise, if the government of her Britannic Majesty would consent to suppress the last period and to terminate it at the word 'preamble.' In this way the object of the convention would not be obscure, and it would be determined *without limiting their course of action (l'action successive) which ulterior circumstances might require.* For these reasons her Majesty's government believe that article III may be drawn up in the following manner:

"'The high contracting parties mutually engage not to divert the forces they are going to make use of in virtue of the present convention, to employ them for any purpose whatever differing from that specified in the preamble.

"'And as intervention in the internal affairs of the republic is not comprehended in that preamble, it is evident that any action executed with that object would be contrary to the convention.'

* * * * * * * * * * *

"Article IV may be considered similar to the first, &c. But even if that article should retain the form given to it in the project, and not stop at the words 'special advantage,' which in the opinion of the Queen's government is all it ought to contain, its intentions and its desires would be in no way in contradiction.

"It is unnecessary to state that the Queen's government considers the monarchical preferable to any other form of government; but it will not put forward its opinion upon the advantage which would result to the Mexican people if they adopted that form in order to constitute themselves definitively. If, however, such were their desire; if they made efforts to realize it; if they consented to discuss the election of a sovereign, Spain could not remain indifferent upon such a grave question, especially if any candidate were offered to the Mexicans by one or other of the friendly governments.

"The 5th article of the project is admirably drawn up, and her Majesty's government desires nothing more, &c.

"S. CALDERON COLLANTES."

Now, what will the reader think of this juggle, by which, while great respect is professed for the sovereignty of Mexico, they are nevertheless tricked under the pretence "that it is necessary to place them in a position to examine without passion and without delusion the situation into which these errors have led them, in order to adopt the most appropriate means of ameliorating it?" and of this, in which we find "that it would be imprudent, and perhaps somewhat hazardous, to renounce in an absolute manner and beforehand a course which might be necessitated afterwards by unexpected events;" or of this appeal, finally, to the minister of foreign affairs of the British government, begging him "to permit the suppression of the last period of Article III?"

Why not under such grave circumstances apply to M. de Thouvenel as well as to Earl Russell? Was it because the consent of the former was assured beforehand, or simply because M. Calderon Collantes hoped, with or without reason, to come to an understanding with him more easily?

These are questions upon which it would be idle now to dwell, and to which we merely give a passing allusion. We search in vain through the numberless despatches written on this occasion; in vain we read and re-read the speeches upon this question delivered to this day; we find nothing, absolutely nothing, which explains, much less legitimatises, this unusual display of force against a country, the greatest crime of which was that of not despairing of its regeneration, and that of making a supreme effort without having previously filled its coffers with the indispensable sums for satisfying the greed of all those who believed themselves interested in opposing it.

It was in reality merely a question of usury, a question of hard cash, and that is why the governments of France and Spain felt from the first that the republic in that country must be destroyed, and replaced by a monarchy supported upon foreign bayonets, as this was the only means of hiding the immorality of the object by disguising it under a varnish of conventional legality.

Be it so. Let us examine the London treaty from this last point of view, and let us see if we shall discover the cause for which the Spanish minister appeared thus to mistrust the English government.

Let us imagine some merchant (the Mexican government) whose affairs, in consequence of an important circumstance over which he had no control, (the *coup d'état,*) were in a desperate position, and whose creditors, (the governments of England, Spain, and France,) instead of coming to a friendly understanding with him, so as to give him time, by means of an agreement arranged in common, to re-establish his affairs, and to pay them ultimately in full, assembled with a diametrically opposite object, and came pistol in hand to demand a payment which their unfortunate creditor, despite his willingness, could not make on the instant, and we have, commercially speaking, the exact and precise sense of the London convention.

Despite the changes effected in the original text of the project, the moral value of this diplomatic act was contained in this disposition of Article III: "Each of the contracting parties will name its general commissioner invested with full powers to conclude the arrangements, which the redivision of the sums to be received in Mexico will necessitate;" and the first paragraph of Article I, "The three powers undertake to send sufficient forces to seize upon the different fortresses and military points of all the coast of Mexico," was only the ostensible means of compelling their insolvent debtor to pay up.

Do not let us, however, forget The London convention, in giving a positive form to the mercantile object of the expedition, took care to declare beforehand that the contracting powers prohibited themselves from making it serve as the starting point of the ambition of any one of them, from seizing by armed force upon any of the provinces of the country, and from using it as a pretext for interfering in the internal dissensions of the republic. It stipulated, on the contrary, in the most formal manner, that the signatory powers meant solely to demand reparation for the outrages and injuries inflicted upon English, Spanish, and French subjects, and not to take part for or against the constitution—for or against the government of Mexico. Now, however little one may know of the institutions which govern the destinies of England, it is easy to understand that it could not have been otherwise. It was, in fact, in order to remain faithful to the principle of non-intervention recognized and proclaimed by all the powers of Europe, that England refused, in 1859, to mix in the struggle carried on at that period by the Italian people to obtain self-government and insure their independence. It was from respect for the same principle that the English government insisted with so much perseverance upon the evacuation of Syria by the French troops, and that recently in a question—we mean the American question—affecting in the highest degree the prosperity and the tranquillity of England, since the occupation and consequently the existence of several millions of English citizens were concerned in its continuance, it declared from the beginning of the struggle that it would observe the strictest neutrality between north and south. The course of the English negotiator was thus completely indicated by the precedents of his country, and despite the facility with which he agreed in the interested observations of the plenipotentiaries of France and Spain, by consenting to the suppressions above spoken of, it was impossible to suppose that Earl Russell would ever let the expedition against Mexico be turned from its object, in order to serve as the pedestal for the ambition of his allies, or as a revenge for the reactionary parties of the country.

E. LEFEVRE.

Mr. Seward to Mr. Romero.

DEPARTMENT OF STATE,
Washington, February 11, 1864.

SIR: I have the honor to acknowledge the receipt of your separate notes of the 26th and 31st ultimo, with their respective enclosures, containing the history of political occurrences in Mexico, as illustrated in contemporaneous documents.

This government cannot be indifferent to the events which are occurring in that republic, and I assure you that I appreciate your courtesy in throwing additional light upon those events from your own resources.

I avail, &c.,

WILLIAM H. SEWARD.

Señor MATIAS ROMERO, *&c., &c., &c.*

Mr. Romero to Mr. Seward.

[Translation.]

MEXICAN LEGATION TO THE UNITED STATES OF AMERICA,
Washington, February 2, 1864.

Mr. SECRETARY: Desirous to communicate to the government of the United States all the documents which may cast light upon its opinion on the conduct of the Emperor of the French in relation to Mexico, I have the honor to enclose with this note, translated into English, an official extract, published in France, of the trial to which, by order of the imperial government, the two Mexican consuls, Messrs. Montluc and Manegro, were subjected; the defence made by a French advocate in behalf of the former; and a circular issued because of this trial by the department for foreign affairs and administration of the republic. These documents of themselves, speak with sufficient clearness in favor of the cause of my country. I will allow myself, however, to call your attention briefly to the inexcusable facts that the French police assailed the consulate general of Mexico in Paris, when the consul was still in the exercise of his functions under the guarantees of the law of nations, searched his archives, and took possession of various documents, and subjected the consul general himself, and the consul residing at Havre, to a criminal trial, infringing on treaties in force which ought to have been respected, as was demonstrated by the distinguished advocate, M. Hebert, in the defence which I enclose. So manifest became the injustice of such proceedings, that the French tribunal, notwithstanding the influence of the imperial government, which, it is hidden from none, is now omnipotent in that country, absolved the accused of all responsibility, although the administration had desired they should pass judgment on these parties as disturbers of public order, and instigators of hatred and disrespect towards the government of the Emperor.

That unjust treatment of our consuls by the imperial government obliged the Mexican government to withdraw their commissions, without leaving any functionary of their class in the French territory, in order to avoid what might be the object of fresh assaults. At the same time the government of the republic withdrew its exequatur from the French consuls resident in the country as a necessary consequence of the former measure, and of the facts before referred to, as may be noted in the annexed circular from the department for foreign relations. I abstain from further commentary, assured, as I am, that the high criterion of the government of the United States renders that unnecessary; the reading of the documents I enclose being sufficient, together with the others I have communicated to it, and think of sending, for understanding on which side justice lies, and which of the two belligerent parties proceeds in open violation of the law of nations.

I avail of this opportunity to reiterate to you, sir, the protestation of my very distinguished consideration.

M. ROMERO.

Hon. WILLIAM H. SEWARD, *&c., &c., &c.*

JUDICIAL PROCEEDINGS AGAINST THE MEXICAN CONSULS, JUNE 4, 1863.

We give here the account of the proceedings in this case during the three days in which it was before the court.

COURT OF CORRECTION OF PARIS.

Sixth Chamber.—Session of the 4th of June.—Proceedings and developments within and without.—Five accused.—The Mexican consuls.

Examination of M. Montluc.

The PRESIDENT. At the time of your first examination you held the position of consul general of Mexico in Paris?

M. MONTLUC. Yes, Mr. President.

Question. You were so in fact since, in 1861, you received your *exequatur* from the French government; but this *exequatur* has since been revoked?

Answer. That is true; it has been revoked since May 3—that is, three days after the first return of the judicial writ.

Question. So you were consul general when the circumstances transpired which now bring you before the court?

Answer. Yes, sir.

Question. Have you spent any part of your life in Mexico?

Answer. Yes, sir; from 1831 to 1846; and whilst I resided in Mexico I was consul of France for eleven years.

Question. Was it in 1854 that you came to Paris and established a commercial house?

Answer. Yes, sir.

Question. When you were appointed consul from Mexico did you preserve your character of a Frenchman?

Answer. Yes, Mr. President; I esteem it too much to renounce it under any consideration.

Question. At that period were there already difficulties between the government of Mexico and the French government?

Answer. Yes, Mr. President, they commenced then.

Question. Was there in France any general agent from Mexico?

Answer. Yes; Señor Don Juan Antonio de la Fuente, who was the person that brought me my appointment as consul general.

Question. Since the departure of Señor de la Fuente there has been in France no political representative of the Mexican government; you alone remained as consul general; you had no authority to interfere with political affairs, and yet you have occupied yourself with them?

Answer. What I have done in political matters I have done openly, publicly, as a good Frenchman above all, and likewise as consul general of a country which I saw unjustly judged, unjustly threatened. I wrote to M. Billault, minister without portfolio, to inform him of the real state of affairs in Mexico. That was on the 10th of May. On the 3d of June I sought an audience of the Emperor, and on the 5th of July I sent a note to his Majesty On the 7th of the same month I received a letter from his private secretary, in which I was told that his Majesty had not time to receive me. On the 15th I received from the Mexican government a commission to address a note to the Emperor.

Question. In your communication you said that it was as a Frenchman that you had written to M. Billault?

Answer. In all the notes and letters which I have written I have always signed my name as consul general of Mexico.

Question. No fault is found with you for those acts which concerned public relations; but it is said that apart from those public relations, and independent of the exercise of your functions as consul general, which consisted in watching over the commercial interests of the government which intrusted you with such functions, you had political relations with the Mexican authorities.

Answer. That is what I positively deny. In all that I have done then and since I have had no other object in view than to make the truth known to both countries, and by such a course of action, far from injuring France, I have, on the contrary, thought to do her a great service.

Question. You received news from Mexico, news of ill will and of threatening import to France. You are charged with having propagated this news by means of those who now stand accused with you.

Answer. I sometimes communicated news to Messrs. Boué and Laverrière, recommending to them, indeed, to refute the infamous calumnies spread abroad against the Mexican government, but without ever saying anything that might hurt or offend France, always respecting the truth, without ever forgetting their character as Frenchmen.

Question. Did you not write to Señor Doblado, Mexican minister of foreign affairs, that the advices which you received from that country were published in the newspapers of Mexico?

Answer. Only those which I thought useful to publish in the interest of both governments.

Question. Did you not give information to Doblado of the military forces sent by France to Mexico?

Answer. Yes, Mr. President, and that, too, was done in the interest of both governments. All that I have done had no other purpose than to enlighten both of them, in order to conduct them to a proper appreciation of the state of affairs, since I have never written either to England, or to Belgium, or to Spain. Far from arousing angry feelings between the two powers, I only strove to bring them to an agreement.

Question. Is it not certain that through you Boué, Petit, and Laverrière have received money from the Mexican government?

Answer. Yes, Mr. President, in order to write in favor of Mexico, but not against France.

Question. The nature of your published writings proved that they were directed against France.

Answer. Never, Mr. President.

Question. Nevertheless, you yourself considered your position so delicate that, in your deposition, you have said that two or three times you were on the point of sending in your resignation of the position of consul.

Answer. That is true; in view of the difficult position in which I found myself I had doubts as to the course of conduct which I should pursue. I spoke on the subject to General Forey, to M. Drouyn de l'Huys, and to some others. What they told me set my mind at rest, and I continued in the exercise of my functions.

Question. Perhaps you would have done well in resigning. The charges laid against you intimate that you did not act by your own inspiration. In a letter from Del Rio, a member of the Mexican union, to Rodriguez, the latter is informed, "Montluc has all my instructions."

Answer. Señor Del Rio had no instructions to give me.

Question. I insist not on the character of the writings published; that is under the control of the department of state. You have said in your deposition that you approved neither the matter nor the style of those writings. The court will judge.

Answer. I cannot be responsible for all that Señor Del Rio may have written to me.

Question. So you deny the principal fact and your complicity with your four companions under accusation with you?

Answer. In what I have done, and I do not see that facts can contradict it, I have had no accomplices. As consul general I received a great many persons in my office; much conversation was indulged in; I had intercourse with Señor Maneyro, consul at Havre, a man of the highest respectability; with Señor Rodriguez, who had been appointed consul at Marseilles; with Señor Laverrière, a discreet and honorable man. I had no reason to conceal my sentiments from them. But as complicity presupposes an evil action deliberated upon and executed in common, I can in no way consider them as my accomplices.

Examination of Señor Rodriguez.

The President. Have you been a correspondent of the Republican Monitor of Mexico, edited by Vincent Torres?

Señor Rodriguez. Yes, Mr. President.

Question. Did you send information to him?

Answer. Yes, and he sent information to me.

Question. And did you communicate such information to the public?

Answer. By no means to the public; only to some fellow-countrymen.

Question. You said in your deposition that you communicated your information to every person that spoke to you on the subject.

Answer. And those persons were my friends or my fellow-countrymen.

Question. Were you in correspondence with Juarez, the President of the Mexican republic?

Answer. I wrote him one letter only.

Question. Were you in correspondence with Doblado, the minister of foreign affairs; with Del Rio, member of the union; with Ordaz, employed in the department of justice in Mexico; and, in Paris, were you in continual relations with your four co-accused friends, Montluc, Boué, Laverrière, and Maneyro?

Answer. With the three Mexicans I have had only a very slight correspondence. The others, those who are called my co-accused, I saw only rarely, and then merely for reasons of friendship.

Question. In a letter which you wrote to Doblado, did you not place yourself entirely at his disposal?

Answer. He had offered me the consulship at Marseilles On the supposition that I accepted that position—that is to say, as consul—I placed myself at his disposal, but only as consul. I never understood it, nor seek to have it understood, in any other way.

Question. You received a sum of 1,500 francs from Ordaz. Now, as Ordaz is no more than a simple employé in the department of justice in Mexico, did not the Mexican government send you that money?

Answer. I have received nothing from Señor Ordaz; I did receive a sum of 1,500 francs from Señor de la Fuente for former services rendered to the Mexican liberals.

Question. On the 29th of July, 1861, Del Rio gave you information of a sum of 2,000 francs, sent to you, and told you to obtain the assistance of Maneyro. In another letter appear the names of Boué and Maneyro. In fine, in another letter of Del Rio he tells you that he is writing to Montluc, and that he hopes from your patriotism that you will publish his manifesto. "They treat us as barbarians," he says to you, "and it is necessary to make us really known." And he concludes thus: "I wished to send this to some newspaper, but I thought that no one could render us this service better than yourself and Montluc." Thus, then, you assumed to yourself the duty of writing articles, and of having an understanding with Montluc, Boué, and Maneyro, in order to propagate information favorable to the Mexican government.

Answer. Yes, but without prejudicing France.

Question. Nevertheless, you received instructions, which, indeed, you did not always think proper to follow, but which indicate the path you pursued. Thus, on the 26th of July, Del Rio wrote to you that Ordaz announced the destruction of the priests. Did you follow those instructions?

Answer. Partly; not entirely.

Question. Did you receive on that same day a letter from the secretary of the Mexican minister of foreign affairs?

Answer. He replied to a letter of mine, and sent me some Mexican papers. I acknowledge all that, but I deny that there is any illegal information in that.

Question. You propagated the news that the Mexican war was unpopular in France.

Answer. I have not been alone in asserting that. All that I wished to express was that the Emperor had been deceived. Unfortunately, it is certain that the war is not favorably regarded in France; so I hear it said everywhere, in the streets and in the railroad cars. To say so is not to proceed to acts of sedition, nor to make oneself the echo of the public voice. Moreover, I have said so only in private conversations.

Question. Was that letter of yours to Doblado a private conversation? Remember that you have repeated the same sentiments in the newspapers.

Answer. I have done no more than express opinions with good intentions towards both countries.

Question. It is very difficult not to take you for a most active agent and propagandist when Del Rio writes to you: "Do not forget that it may be useful to us to send to England, Belgium, Spain, or Italy what cannot be published in France."

Answer. I did in fact receive that letter, but I did not follow the instructions which it gave me.

Question. Among the papers received by you there has been found a certain Mexican journal which has given information to you and which contains the most violent articles against France.

Answer. In a journal published in French in the city of Mexico; I have never published it; it was sent to all countries.

Question. Resuming the consideration of the charges against you, it is said that you have kept up relations within and without the country, such as to disturb the public peace, and that with this purpose you have come to an understanding with those accused with you.

Answer. And I deny all that in the most positive manner.

Examination of Señor Maneyro.

The PRESIDENT. Are you a Mexican?

Señor MANEYRO. Yes, Mr. President; but I have been twenty-eight years in France, as consul of Mexico at Havre.

Question. Was it not in 1836 that you received your *exequatur* as consul at Havre?

Answer. Yes, sir.

Question. Are you yet consul?

Answer. Yes, sir.

Question. Why, then, do you live in Paris?

Answer. The business of the consulate is not of frequent occurrence. Several persons of my family reside in Havre and apprise me whenever any business occurs that demands my presence.

Question. You are accused, as well as your fellow-prisoners, with——

Answer. I already know what I am accused of, but it is necessary to prove it. My fellow-prisoners! I do not know the meaning of this. M. de Montluc is an old friend of mine, one of the most honorable men that I know; I see him about every fifteen days in order to receive news from my country. Señor Boué I know no further than by having been in relations with him for the purpose of examining the qualifications of a young man who had been recommended to me. Señor Rodriguez is a worthy Mexican and a friend of mine. As to Señor Laverrière, I do not know him, except in as far as this affair is concerned. These are the men who are called my fellow-accused, and this is what I do not understand.

Question. You are accused of having had publications made for the purpose of disturbing the public peace.

Answer. Where are those publications?

Question. You have said so.

Answer. Where have I said so?

Question. Del Rio wrote to you to have an agreement with Rodriguez in order to make some publications, and you answered him that you would do what he indicated.

Answer. It is true; and what does that prove?

Question. It proves that you do something more than fulfil the duties of a consul.

Answer. That is not my conclusion, but a very different one. I received orders from my government to give publicity in France to certain official acts. I treated about publishing them in France, and I could not succeed in so doing. Then I turned my attention to the Independence Belge. I have never been in communication with any newspaper writers of Paris. My son, a youth of seventeen years, is the person who writes my correspondence and corrects my mistakes in French. I know no newspaper conductors either in Paris or in Belgium, and with the exception of the facts which I have just mentioned, I have applied neither to the Independence Belge nor to any other periodical, French or foreign. If it be sought to prove the contrary, let me be told where are my letters, where is my correspondence.

Question. You know that there has been intercepted a letter from Del Rio to you, acknowledging the receipt of despatches sent to him by you; in these letters, then, are the illegal acts complained of.

Answer. I have said no more than the truth with regard to this wretched war which has cost France more men than is imagined, and in defence of Mexico, which is my country, where I hold all my property. I believe I have merely used my rights as a private individual and as a consul.

The imperial advocate, Aubepin, then addressed the court and asked the enforcement of the law against all the accused; he mentioned Messrs. Laverrière and Boué as the persons who had played the least important part in the acts that constituted the charge.

The court, after having heard the defence of Señor Montluc, presented by the advocate Senart, adjourned the further hearing of the case to the following day.

Session of June 5.

The court of correction, (sixth Chamber,) presided over by M. Rohault de Floury, devoted the whole day to the continuation of the argument in the case of the Mexican consuls and others accused of evil practices and illegal communications within and without the empire, with the purpose of disturbing the public peace, and of bringing hatred and contempt on the Emperor's government.

M. Emanuel Arago presented the defence of M. Boué; MM. Gambetta, Leblonde, and Hebert spoke in defence of Rodriguez, Laverrière, and Maneyro.

Session of June 6.

The court pronounced its judgment in the following terms:

Considering that the five persons accused, who all had relations with Mexico, or with Mexican public men, and of them that two were agents and one now is an agent of the Mexican government, have maintained to the last moment communications with men engaged in the government and with other persons of said country; that some received instructions, others news of which they made use in France and abroad to publish and spread the contents of their instructions and periodicals;

Considering that if the accused knew each other, it is not established that they concerted with each other a common purpose; that it does not appear that their intentions were hostile, nor that they sought to bring hatred and contempt on the Emperor's government, nor to disturb the public peace;

As far as regards Montluc:

Considering that he was consul general of Mexico in France; that in that quality he received despatches from his government, wrote letters, and made communications, of which copies have been presented in court, and prove his desire to serve France, by bringing to the knowledge of his Majesty, as well as of his ministers, what he believed to be the truth

As far as regards Boué:

Considering that in the articles which he published in the French periodicals, he manifested no feeling hostile to France, and that it does not appear proved against him that he visited Montluc, and received foreign periodicals;

As far as regards Rodriguez:

Considering that, in his quality of Mexican citizen and of attaché to the Mexican legation, he kept up a continuous correspondence with the public men of his country; that the letters and papers which he received breathed great animosity against the French government; that he confesses to have permitted various persons to read those documents; but that he pretends to have acted in this way only with the view of making known the public characters and the condition of his country from their true stand-point, and that it is not proved that he had any other views;

As far as regards Laverrière:

Considering that having spent a long time in Mexico, and having returned in the month of June, 1862, his first step was to present himself before the French authorities in order to inform them of the documents which he had in his possession; that he has produced before the court copies of the communications written by him; that this course of conduct lasted until the month of April, 1863; and that he always professes a desire of making the truth known, such as he understood it, to the French government;

That what proves the good intentions both of Laverrière and Montluc is a letter from the latter to the former, dated the 10th of December, 1862, and post-marked on the same day, in which we read: "Under these circumstances, you and I should publish nothing that might bring suspicion upon us; since, if we sincerely desire that the just demands of France should be complied with, it is necessary to keep within the limits of truth. Let us always labor, then, uprightly and honestly in the consciousness of performing a duty, and let us not fear to have a bad interpretation put upon our efforts in favor of an arrangement that might re-establish peace, so desirable for all;"

That no more than this purpose can be discovered in the articles published by Laverrière in France and in his letters;

As far as regards Maneyro:

Considering that as a Mexican, as consul from Mexico in France, he has done no more than follow the instructions of his government, and that neither his action in receiving papers and the correspondence directed to him, nor any other action on his part, constitutes the crime for which he has been brought to trial;

For these reasons the court orders the release of Montluc, Boué, Rodriguez, Laverrière, and Maneyro, and the restoration to them of the documents seized upon, except the periodicals fraudulently introduced, which are to be destroyed.

Defence of the Mexican Consul, Señor Maneyro, by M. Hebert.

As soon as the court was opened M. Hebert was permitted to speak, and expressed himself in the following terms:

I have the honor of appearing for Señor Maneyro, consul of Mexico at Havre, and I ask, as well on account of his official character, as in view that there is no act of his capable of sustaining the charges brought against him, that the court be pleased to dismiss the case.

Gentlemen, in order to defend my client I shall examine three things: his personal position, that is to say, the general tenor of his conduct throughout his life; his legal and judicial character before this court, and the nature and character of the acts with which he now stands charged. As to the first point, what I have to say of this foreigner, of this agent of a foreign government, is so honorable, so satisfactory, that I would wish with all my heart, as a good Frenchman, that wherever, in any quarter of the world they exert their intelligence and their activity, they could without exception receive and take to themselves the same testimony.

Señor Maneyro is of an excellent family in Mexico On the 3d of July, 1835, he was appointed consul of the United States of Mexico at Havre. On the 18th of March, 1836, he received his *exequatur* from the late King Louis Philippe. From that time he has always represented, and now actually represents, the Mexican nation in that character. It is unnecessary to state that, in the exercise of his functions in one of our great commercial emporiums, which has very frequent relations with Mexico, he has had occasion to watch over important, numerous, and various interests; but what I have to prove is, that he always performed his duties, very difficult at times, with zeal, rectitude, and gratifying success.

It is well known that in those countries in which the republican form of government appears to be the most suitable to the customs and character of the inhabitants—in those countries which are striving to raise themselves from a chaotic condition to a stable constitution, and in the attainment of that object have to pass through a period of anarchical interregnum—it is known, I say, how frequent have been the changes since 1836 in the personal heads of the government. Under all these administrations Señor Maneyro never ceased to be consul at Havre; he retained his powers and the confidence of his country. And in order to serve those different governments, variously and widely divergent in their political character, Señor Maneyro had but one rule to follow, and that was to remain within the limits of his functions, to obey the orders given to him according to law and by law--I mean the law of nations, treaties, the course of legislation of his own country and of ours.

We likewise, since 1836, have had many political changes, which have not only affected persons, but have been deep, radical, overthrowing men and institutions in succession. Now, then, under all the governments which have succeeded each other in France during the last thirty years Señor Maneyro has always been consul of Mexico—under the government of King Louis Philippe; under the republic of 1848; under General Cavaignac; under the presidency which followed, as now under the empire.

From all this I seek merely to deduce two consequences: first, that Señor Maneyro is not the agent of a Mexican party; that he has not embraced the cause of such and such a faction, or the interests of such and such an individual in his country; that being consular agent of Mexico at Havre for thirty years, he has never been nor sought to be anything else; and, secondly, that Señor Maneyro is likewise no party man in France. A stranger to our country, totally indifferent, as he has the right to be, to the various mutations and agitations of politics, he never espoused any party among us, or participated either in the fierceness of political polemics, foreign to his character, or in the unmeasured laudations, of which he knew how to appreciate the dangers and utter insincerity. He lived in peace with all our governments and all our administrations; and when, at a former period, a conflict arose between the two countries—a conflict in which France and her government equally showed that they were not insensible to the glory of arms—when these last performed their functions and just reparation was offered, Señor Maneyro was one of those who merited well of both countries by having done all in his power that might contribute to the re-establishment of peace.

And, indeed, a course of action like this enters into the scope of consular duties, even under the restrictions and limitations imposed upon them by governmental policy. And is it not, in fact, a matter of interest to these same consuls that they should identify themselves with the interests of those whom they find themselves specially charged to represent? Is it not clear that it would be an act of folly on the part of those who are invested with the confidence of their government to consult in their conduct only their political predilections or their personal friendships or enmities? Señor Maneyro knew how to avoid all these dangers; he did at all times whatever he could to maintain friendly relations—all that he could do within the limits of his official position.

This course of conduct gained him universal approval; I have the best and most honorable testimonials of it. I have here that of the municipality of Havre, dated May 25, 1863:

"OFFICE OF THE MAYORALTY OF PARIS, *May* 25, 1863.

"We, the mayor of the city of Havre, officer of the legion of honor, certify, to whomsoever it concerns, that Señor Maneyro, consul of Mexico at Havre since 1836, is a man of excellent moral character, and that he has known, as well in private life as in the exercise of his official functions, how to gain for himself the esteem and consideration of all; that, during the period of his residence in this city, he has never ceased to be received with distinction in the most honorable houses; that, in fine, in a political point of view, he has never by word or deed attacked any of the governments that have succeeded each other since that epoch. In proof of which we have written these presents and attached to them the seal of this city.

"JUST VIEL."

To this first testimonial, so honorable to Señor Maneyro, I add another, which is no less so, given by all the consuls resident at Havre:

"HAVRE, *May* 25, 1863.

"The undersigned, consuls of the foreign powers at Havre de Grace, certify that Señor Don Luis Maneyro, consul of Mexico, has constantly enjoyed the general appreciation and esteem of all during his stay in this city, as likewise the confidence of all in the relations which they have cultivated with him; and that his political opinions have always appeared to them marked with moderation and justice."

Here follow the seals and signatures of the consuls of Prussia, Wurtemburg, Hesse, Baden, Oldenburg, Hanover, Bavaria, the Hanse Towns, Switzerland, Brazil, Spain, Belgium, Netherlands, Portugal, Sweden, and Great Britain.*

* It is to be remarked that though the Austrian consul knew Señor Maneyro in times past, he refused to sign the testimonial. Five other consuls, of modern date, could not sign it, but they attested their sympathy with Señor Maneyro.—*Note by the Editors.*

With these, and superior to them, I have another testimonial emanating from our own government. This testimonial is found in the fact of the retention of Señor Maneyro up to this time in his functions as consul at Havre. However, I draw no legal consequence from that; but I have the right morally to say that he has not been considered an upholder of disorder, an inventor of conspiracies; because here we see him consul, here we see him a man of moderation, such as he has been throughout his whole life. The indictment against him tells us that, since 1861, he has been guilty of evil practices detrimental to France and her government. Now, if this is so, how is it that the French government has, since 1861, permitted an enemy of France to perform the duties of a public employment, when it could have very easily disarmed him, by withdrawing his *exequatur*, and even expelling him as a dangerous foreigner?

Such is the personal character of Señor Maneyro. Let us now see what has been his conduct since the commencement of the war. Has it changed, perhaps? Has it belied his spotless antecedents? No, gentlemen; there is not a shadow of guilt upon him. A great error was committed in this case when it was sought to explain his coming to Paris, his determination of fixing the residence of his family in this city, as an evidence of his desire to mingle in intrigues and to aggregate himself with his pretended accomplices. This error not having been reproduced by the counsel for the government, I might have been content with this silent reparation of it if it had not become a duty for me to explain it all, in order to establish in the most incontestable manner the constant rectitude of my client.

In the month of September, 1858, it was that Señor Maneyro took a residence in Paris, long before the war with Mexico, before it was even thought of, and before any new or serious cause of dissension had arisen between the two countries. Señor Maneyro, then, came to Paris in 1858, and rented a residence in the Rue de l'Arcade, in a house of well-known character, whose proprietor, were it necessary, would give me most satisfactory certificates. That proprietor is M. the Baron de Cormenin; on the supposition that I refer to the one of to-day, [the audience smiles,*] one of the most faithful servants of the empire, and who would not have given an asylum to a man that came to Paris to intrigue against the government.

Two reasons brought Señor Maneyro to Paris, both of them serious, both of them satisfactory. He came principally for the education of his son, who is pursuing his course of studies at the Lyceum Napoleon, and I have here the proof of what I say. [M. Hebert turned around, and, smiling, pointed out to the court, with his finger, the son of Señor Maneyro, a fine youth of seventeen years, who stood up and blushed somewhat on seeing himself the object of the gaze of the spectators.] The second reason for the coming of Señor Maneyro to Paris was the change in the condition of his private fortune. Indeed, even before the war, pecuniary difficulties, of frequent occurrence in his country, had occasioned the failure of the payment of his salary as consul. I have heard the counsel for the government censure some of the accused for what he calls salaried services. I have the satisfaction of being able to say of Señor Maneyro that for several years he has served his country, and watched over the interests of his countrymen, without receiving anything, without asking anything of his salary, without complaint, and without the least diminution of zeal or efficiency.

But if this abnegation is honorable, the consequences which it produces may prove injurious to other feelings. During a space of twenty-five years Señor Maneyro kept, in Havre, what may be called a good house and respectable social relations. It is hard to descend, even with honor. The worth of the sacrifice, the thought of gratuitously serving our country, does not prevent the grief of feeling obliged, perhaps, to undergo, if not privations, at least necessary changes of life and habits.

Such, gentlemen, are the two motives which brought Señor Maneyro to Paris; not to fix there his personal residence, but to locate his wife and son modestly and temporarily, and likewise to superintend the education of the latter. For the rest, his domicile always remains in Havre; he is consul there all the time, and whenever his business calls him thither he goes immediately; he has his office there, his papers, and his secretary, who performs the part of chancellor.

In view of these explanations, either I deceive myself much, or the accused, whom I defend, is now a very different person from what prejudice may have considered him; he now stands absolved from all suspicion of clandestine practices, from a species of treason which, I do not deny, would assume the greatest gravity, on account of his character as a consul, in the exercise of his functions, because, I repeat it, he is still consul at Havre; his *exequatur* has not been withdrawn; it is not two months since he signed manifests and bills of health for two vessels bound for the coasts of Mexico in search of a cargo of dyewoods.

---

* This is satirical. The late Baron de Cormenin, likewise known by the name of Timon, and who published a biography of the orators of France of the time of Louis Philippe, was an ardent liberal; but his son is, on the contrary, devoted to the imperial policy.

Now, gentlemen, I must examine the subject in another light. I say that Mr. Maneyro is yet consul of the Mexican government at Havre, and I maintain that, in that character, he is protected by the law of nations, and clothed with certain immunities, so far that I might even question the competency of courts of correction to assume cognizance of his case. But this I shall not do; so great is the confidence which I have in truth, in the potency of the justification which I propose to lay before the court, extracted from the essence of the case itself, and which I do not desire to weaken by taking exceptions.

Gentlemen, this is the first time that judicial cognizance has been taken of a matter like this; the first time that a criminal prosecution has been commenced against consuls and for political reasons. I believe I am not mistaken when I say that it would be well to be more careful in a second attempt of the kind. Let us examine the case attentively and we will derive profit from it, for the present as well as for the future.

Two classes of privileges are united with the functions of a consul, general privileges and special privileges. The first apply to the consuls of all nations, and are founded on the law of nations; the second result from particular stipulations inserted in the treaties negotiated with each nation.

The first document which I have to consult, relative to the relations between France and Mexico, is the treaty of March 13, 1769, which was for a long time binding upon France and Spain, then mistress of all that part of America. In it we find a clause intended to settle the privileges of the consuls of both countries, which is as follows:

"Consuls, being subjects of the prince who appoints them, shall enjoy personal immunity, *without being liable to arrest or imprisonment, except in case of atrocious crimes, or when the consuls are also traders. Their papers, or those belonging to their office, can be touched under no pretext whatever*, unless the consul be also a trader, in which case, as far as regards his commercial affairs, he shall be proceeded with according to the regulations in the treaties concerning foreign merchants."

I find another treaty negotiated between the government of the Restoration and Mexico, which was then an independent power; it is an almost verbal repetition of the treaty of 1769.

On the 11th of August, 1839, a new agreement was entered into between Mexico and King Louis Philippe; I call the attention of the court to Article 3, the terms of which are these:

"Until the two nations can conclude a treaty of commerce and navigation, to settle in a definitive manner, and to their mutual advantage, the future relations of France and Mexico, *diplomatic agents and consuls*, citizens of every class, vessels and merchandise of both countries, *shall each continue to enjoy in the other whatever franchises, privileges, and immunities they have had, or may be granted, by treaty or by custom, to the most favored foreign nation.*"

Now, if I search in the various international treaties what the privileges are of the most favored nation, I find, in a great number of them, the most absolute personal immunity for consuls.

I have here one made between the present government and the republic of Salvador, and I presently find, in its 23d article, the general clause which follows:

"The consuls-general, consuls, and vice-consuls, as well as consular attachés, chancellors, and secretaries, in the performance of the duties of their mission, shall enjoy, in both countries, all the privileges, exemptions, and immunities that may be conceded, at their place of residence, to the agents of the same rank of the most favored nation," &c.

And afterwards more particularly: "Those agents shall enjoy personal immunity in all cases; *they shall not be arrested, brought to trial, or put in prison, except in case of atrocious crime.*"

By what I have specified, it is evident that this Article 23 is no more than the treaty of 1769 more elaborated. Except in case of atrocious crime, consuls can neither be *arrested nor brought to trial.* So that, in this point of view, we might have been able to maintain, in regard to two of the accused, that no proceedings could legally have been instituted against them, and, with still greater reason, that no judgment could have been pronounced against them. And then, as far as complicity is concerned, what would have become of the charge against the others? Thus, then, there is no distinction, in this respect, between consuls and diplomatic agents. In view of these immunities, conceded to them by treaties, their standing is the same, since there is no question now with regard to the simple rule of the law of nations, whence a distinction might be deduced. Here treaties constitute the law, and they make no distinction.

But I will, perhaps, be met with the objection that war dissolves all treaties, and that there is now a war with Mexico. I reply, that this would be to fall into a new confusion, which it is important that we should avoid.

If war dissolves treaties as far as they relate to diplomatic relations, it does not annul them totally as far as they regard maritime and commercial arrangements. Why this difference? Why continue the relations of nation to nation, which ought to continue notwithstanding a state of war, unless they be dissolved by express declaration to that effect and by stipulations specially opposite? The reason is because, if the governments, if their flags are at war, at least their real national interests—their commercial interests especially—are not. I repeat it, they are not, unless it be by means of blockades and absence of communication, means which begin to be considered more and more barbarous every day, and which already, in fact, no longer exist in the greater part of the wars of our times.

Commerce is the life of nations, and governments cannot seek or act to destroy that life. Now, if the consul is the essential agent of commerce, its protector, its safeguard, it is clear that, differently from the diplomatic agent, he does not disappear for the simple reason that peace has ceased.

Suppose, in fact, that war does break out; what is proposed to be done with the consul, to whom treaties have granted reciprocal immunities? Can he, perhaps, be transformed into a consul despoiled of his stipulated immunities, and, so to speak, into a half-consul? No; he is either nothing or he remains what he is according to treaties; he remains consul on the same conditions in which the two contracting parties have placed him. Is there sought a proof of this? I do not pretend to intimate that we should receive exemplifications from foreign governments; we can at least derive some instruction from them. I have here a proclamation issued by the military commandant of Puebla, under date of March 10, 1863, and addressed to the inhabitants:

"ART. 1. All the French, resident in this city, shall, three hours after the publication of this decree, present themselves before the general, second in command of the military department embracing this State, in order to obtain letters to secure their personal safety, after which *they will pass to the residence of the consul or vice-consul who represents them, and shall remain there during the attack on this place*, or during the time that the invading army remains in the neighborhood," &c., &c., &c.

"ART. 2. As the object of the preceding regulations is no other than to insure all possible security to French citizens resident in Puebla, the authorities will not be responsible for any misfortunes or accidents that may happen to the persons of such Frenchmen as refuse to conform to them."

There follows a notice from General Ortega to the consuls of foreign nations, under date of March 14, 1863, and couched in the following terms:

"This position has been very promptly assaulted by the French army, and, in view of the disastrous accidents that often ensue in such cases, *I advise you to place in a secure position whatever objects of value your government may have confided to you, as well as the interests of your consulate, and of the subjects of the nation which you represent.*

"Having, on my part, complied with what I consider my duty as commanding officer of this department, you will strive, for your part, in the way that seems *most prudent and convenient to you, for the interests which you represent.*"

Such is, gentlemen, even in war, the position of the consul. If he is consul in virtue of the law of nations, he remains consul in virtue of the law of nations; if he is consul in virtue of treaties, he remains consul in virtue of treaties.

But, then, it will be objected to me, a consul can do anything he pleases—disturb, agitate, insult with impunity, the nation to which he is accredited. No, nothing of the kind is to be feared; because the government has a very simple remedy at its disposal, of which it can always make use. It can withdraw his *exequatur* from the consul whom it considers dangerous, and even expel him if he be a foreigner, and if he has really failed in his duty, by the abuse of his official character and of his immunities. There now remains the case of atrocious crime, which destroys those immunities entirely; and doubtless it is on this ground that the commissary of police, who evidently strives to support his case on this notion, who has studied the treaties but misapplied them, acted in the beginning in virtue of Article 78 of the Penal Code. By reading that article, it will be seen, gentlemen, that the crime which it provides for and punishes is really an atrocious crime; but it will likewise be seen with what reason the government has since recognized that it was neither proper nor sensible to apply such a qualification to the acts involved in these proceedings, even should they succeed in being proved. Doubtless for this reason it was that the severe process of the examination was not resorted to in regard to Señor Maneyro, who was accused after the others, and when the 78th article of the aforesaid code was no longer held in view. Thus one of his personal immunities was recognized, but that does not suffice; we must go further and acknowledge that the two consuls, in this case, are both regarded as under the shield and protection of the immunities so expressly inserted in the treaties.

And when I defend here the rights of a foreign consul, I am not inspired only by the interests of that foreigner; I am also inspired by the regard due to justice and the honor of our country, which should give an example of respect for treaties and for the rights accruing from them to all nations, to the end that they should in their turn observe them in regard to us. I maintain, equally, that the two consuls accused are under the protection of the same immunities; I maintain it upon general principles, and for the sake of the observance of those general principles, which may not be violated without danger; and I consider it fortunate that, at the same time, those principles should be the safeguard of the fate, of the liberty, and of the honor of a venerable sire, whose merited discharge will, I hope, be decreed by the court.

But, independently of those general immunities, there is another entirely special, and even more powerful, if possible, for the protection of Señor Maneyro. This immunity results from the fact that he acted only under express orders from his government. Here I have no need of citing treaties; I may refer to the law of nations, which, I have already said, does not place consuls on the same footing with diplomatic agents. On the principles established by the law of nations, when consuls have acted under the orders of their government, they can never be prosecuted individually nor prosecuted before the courts.

Here is what Dalloz says on the subject, (General Jurisprudence; word, Foreign Consuls:)

"The jurisdiction of the French tribunals cannot extend so far as to investigate the acts of foreign consuls in France honestly performed in accordance with orders from their government. (Decree of 13th Vendemiaire, year 9; approved by official circulars from the department of foreign affairs and justice, April 18, 1818, and May 29, 1819.)

"The acts in question are considered as the acts of the foreign government, and consequently are in the category of political acts treated of between government and government. The ministerial letter of the 19th Floréal, of the year 8, is conceived in the same spirit."

Merlin (Repertory of Jurisprudence; title, Foreign Consuls,) adopts the same opinion, as also does Fælix, (Treatise on International Law,) as well as Goujet and Merget, (Dictionary; word, Consuls,) who say likewise:

"Consuls who have no treaties analogous to those which we have mentioned are treated in France like other individuals of the same nations. Nevertheless, consuls cannot be prosecuted before the courts of the country in which they reside for acts done in their consular capacity and by order of their government."

It is true that Dalloz, in the passage which I have cited from him, adds these words: "and with the approbation of the French authorities." But it is evident that he is mistaken in the law, and gives to the documents which he quotes a signification which they do not bear, since it cannot rationally be supposed that the government should cause the prosecution of an act previously known to and approved by it. For the rest, and of this I hope to convince the court, it matters little, in view of the fact that the official documents received by Señor Maneyro, and communicated by him according to orders of his government, had been previously presented to the French government and had not been disapproved by it. M. Senart established this point for my client as well as for his own.

From this the court sees that the legal *status* of Señor Maneyro is as strong as his personal *status* is interesting. I might stop here, but this would not suffice for the defence of a man of so much probity as my client, of so much consideration for thirty years at Havre, and one who stakes his honor on proving that he has not been unworthy of this good reputation. He has the right of being entirely justified, of proving that he ought not to have been prosecuted, not only on account of the letter of the law, but likewise on account of the relation of the facts themselves of which he is accused.

Let us see, then, what Señor Maneyro is blamed for doing, and let us see especially what he has really done.

The court knows that he is charged with having, in the course of the present year and of 1862, committed himself to evil practices and communications within and without the empire, for the purpose of disturbing the public peace and exciting contempt and odium against the government of the Emperor.

What I have read is the text of the law, and the summons to the accused was couched in the same terms. I do not wish to say anything of that law itself, provoked as it was by a criminal and lamentable act.* But that law does not appear, either to those who proposed it or to those who voted for it, to have for its object to punish and frustrate conspiracies against the warlike or diplomatic policy of France; it was made at a time when the motto, *the empire is peace*, already enjoyed all its prestige. More stringent laws were sought for the security of the empire; the 78th article of the penal code had provided for crimes against the security or the external power of France, and that was not what was then thought of; what was wanted was to protect a life which was believed to be conspired against by enemies who had correspondence both within and without.

Such was the intention of the law; it had no other, as I understand. Nevertheless, by implication it has been extended to correspondence with hostile journals, by the sentence of November 30, 1861, given by the court of Paris. Let us read that sentence:

"Considering that article 2 of the law of the 27th of February, 1858, in decreeing penalties against malpractices and conspiracies abroad, entered into for the purpose of disturbing the public peace or of exciting contempt and odium against the government, has necessarily had in view such correspondence and communications as feed the foreign press

---

* The attempt of Orsini.

with calumnies against the government of the Emperor; that it would even be very difficult to find any other means of propagating contempt and odium against the government, outside of France; that in view of the nature of the punishment and the similarity of the expressions employed, *it is evident that the law of* 1858 *seeks to repress the custom of fomenting the injurious attacks of the foreign press, as the ordinary legislation punishes those of the home press,*" &c., &c.

Gentlemen, I have laid a stress on these last words because—a notable fact—if the publication be made in France it will be prosecuted, as the judgment of the court with reason remarks, only in virtue of the ordinary legislation in regard to the press, and for this same reason the communications made will be culpable only in so far as that which constitutes the object of them is of such a character as should be prosecuted in case of publication in France. And how can it be otherwise with publications and communications, when there is question of foreign periodicals?

"Considering," thus proceeds the judgment of the court already quoted, "that, in fact, J——— *has maintained for several years a correspondence with periodicals whose animosity towards France is very notorious;* that the documents previous to the 22d of July, 1858, if they afford no occasion for a prosecution, constitute *an element for the moral appreciation of the political spirit and of the general tendency of the correspondence of the accused,* and that they ought, under this view, be retained in the case:

"Considering that the acts not prescribed and relative to the journals of Dresden and of Geneva *manifest a positive and continued intention to propagate odium and contempt against the imperial government;* that the sole knowledge of the *systematic ill-will of the journals in question should make known to J——— that he was contributing to a work of enmity and slander directed against the government of his country;* that the articles which form part of the correspondence *which he maintained with them,* and principally *the letters confiscated upon the institution of judicial proceedings, demonstrate that the accused had wholly associated himself to the purposes of those journals:*

"Considering *that he has thus maintained correspondence calculated to draw odium and contempt on the government of the Emperor,*" &c., &c.

This shows, gentlemen, how far it was thought, in November, 1861, possible to proceed in the application of the law of 1858. But, although it widens the range of its application, I shall say no more of what that law permitted, but more of what was then thought. The court will notice that the court of Paris traced out the essential characteristics that must constitute the crime, and these characteristics were: first, the sending to foreign journals systematically hostile to France of *calumnious writings* against the government of the Emperor; secondly, *the object,* in such writings, *of exciting odium and contempt against the government, and of disturbing the public peace;* thirdly, the habitual employment of malpractices with the constant and clearly proved intention of entering upon a culpable course of communications, as well at home as abroad, against the government of the Emperor.

Now let us see whether anything of all this can be, I shall not say established, but even alleged against Señor Maneyro.

The counsel for the government has founded the prejudice against him and against the other accused on the following four inductions:

Their presumed sentiments in regard to the politics of France and the war with Mexico; their relations with each other and with Mexico; the publications that have been sent to them by the Mexican government, and which they have communicated or transmitted; the extracts from newspapers and pamphlets that have been directed to them under their names.

To arrive at these inductions, the prosecuting officer presently took up, not the first of the accused—M. Montluc, the consul general—but a simple Mexican, Señor Rodriguez. Taking his position and his sentiments into mature consideration, it was inferred that he must be hostile to France and devoted to Mexico, and therefore that everything that he might say, do, or write, everything that he might receive or send, would be undertaken or conceived in a spirit of hostility and with a purpose of causing disturbance, in which those would be participators who would hold relations with him, and who are now his co-accused.

Against the first mode of induction I protest forthwith, not only as a lawyer but as a citizen, in the name of the liberty of human opinions. And have I not the right of doing so, particularly in the name of Señor Maneyro? Should we not excuse him for loving Mexico? It is certainly allowed to a man born at Puebla, who has yet his home there, as he himself told the court, to be afflicted at seeing that city besieged, to endeavor to remove the horrors of war, to be deeply affected at considering his native city taken by assault, his home ensanguined with the blood of his fellow-countrymen, perhaps with that of his relatives.

Let us not seek, then, inductions so far out of the way. Sentiments so natural can never serve as a pretext for making accusations, if they have led to nothing culpable in itself; because, if the prosecuting agents of the government should take as a mark of culpability the disapproval of this war with Mexico, and the ardent desire of seeing it concluded, this palace so vast could not contain all the accused. How! when the most cherished interests of numerous families are found involved in a distant war, whose causes and purposes are, to say the least of them, difficult to be understood, shall it not be permitted to those who suffer from it to deplore its existence, to express their opinions upon it, to use their endeavors to ward it off or bring it to a termination? When the heart is ready to burst must it remain dumb? Would it not be a tyrannical law that would seek to restrain the manifestations of thought and of the most irresistible emotions? Can we not speak of peace, complain of the war, without being punished for it? Ah, such rigors cannot be proposed to the justice of men; such maxims cannot be adopted; for myself, indeed, the very mention of them makes me shudder.

Oftentimes have I heard and read, outside of these sacred precincts, such charges and admonitions as were repeated yesterday. We are told, "Restrain your pacific sentiments at the bottom of your heart; it is culpable to manifest them when our banner is unfurled; let your thoughts, let your reason humble themselves and be silent before the uniform of the grenadier and the red jacket of the zouave!" Gentlemen, this is a very commonplace idea, which can doubtlessly be worked up by means of brilliant words; but it is a commonplace to which recourse is frequently had, and, for all the sense it contains, it is no more than commonplace.

At what time, it may be asked, then, shall we be allowed to talk of peace, to take counsel with each other, to show that it is possible? Before the war? But the existence of war is not known until the vessels have sailed to convey the army, until that army is already on march; and sometimes only by the roar of the cannon is it known that it has been declared. Shall it be perchance after the war? After the war, alas! we are only left to mourn over the ruins. Thus, then, during the war, and before its evils have appeared or have come to be irreparable, is it permitted, then only can it be patriotic to exclaim, in the name of reason, of humanity, and of peace: "Avoid blood and the hostile conflict of two countries that can yet be conciliated and understand each other."

These are sentiments which it is always good to propagate—means which it is always good to try. As to me, I never consider them premature or out of season; I should fear much more lest they should come too late. *Sero medicina paratur quum mala per longas invaluere moras.*

Let us derive instruction, gentlemen, from a passage of which we are permitted to speak, inasmuch as it has passed into the domain of history.

A half century ago France left on the battle-fields of Spain 200,000 men; on those of Russia 400,000; and hundreds of millions of money, and whole provinces separated from her territory, paid the penalty of her gigantic rashness. Were the wars of those times, now judged and condemned, perhaps, merely due to the eccentricities of a great genius? No; they should be attributed to the muteness, to the forced silence of such opinions as could prevent them; to the spirit of adulation and servilism which flattered every propensity, urged on every excessive trait of character, and especially to that commonplace notion which I assail, and which I shall continue to assail, that prudence and moderation should no longer seek to be heard as soon as the cannon has spoken in its thunder tones.

Let us assert it loudly: reflections, friendly counsels, censures even, provided they be dictated by good faith and expressed in temperate terms, whether they come from a Frenchman or from a foreigner, can always be uttered with freedom and honor. Let us not reject them; on the contrary, let us take charge of them. Oftentimes and ever is flattery ready to do its work; let us leave room for honest, well-meant contradiction, and, above all, let us not renew for our time, to which it is not suitable, that maxim of a period of despotism and degeneracy: "Whoever is not of the opinion of Cæsar is the enemy of Cæsar."

After this first induction, the merits of which I have just examined, Senor Maneyro is charged with his personal relations. And what were his personal relations with the four persons associated with him in this accusation? Señor Maneyro went to see M. Montluc, his consul general, twice a month; was this too frequent an intercourse with his superior, from whom he was to receive his directions and official communications? M. Boué? He only saw him twice, and he himself has told you with what motive: he wished to request M. Boué, a professor, to interest himself for a youth who was to pass his examination as a bachelor of arts. My client is not acquainted with M. Laverrière; and as to Señor Rodriguez, who has been appointed consul at Marseilles, and has consequently come to be his colleague, he saw him twice only in the house of Senor La Fuente, minister of Mexico in Paris.

To this were the relations so much censured in Señor Maneyro limited. Evidently such a species of accusation does not deserve discussion. Let us pass to the third induction.

The prosecuting agent of the government says to Señor Maneyro: You have received letters from the President of the republic of Mexico, from his secretary, from his ministers, and you have communicated their contents to others, and you have even transmitted them to the newspapers, so that you have committed the crime sought to be prevented by the law of 1858, a crime which consists in malpractices and maintaining secret relations against the government.

It is to be remarked, that Señor Maneyro might have denied these communications, as there was nothing established to prove them against him; but, being one of those men who never deny their acts, he declared them without hesitation. To whom did he communicate those documents? To a foreign journal, the Independence Belge. He himself says that he might equally have communicated them to the newspapers of France—for example, to the political director of the Siécle. Had he done so, what would have been the conclusion that could have been drawn from it? This: that he would have been considered more of a partisan of the politics of that journal; somewhat more of those of the 18,000 votes which its director obtained at a recent election. [The audience smiles.*] He might also have communicated them to the editor of the Opinion Nationale, which does not seem to approve of the war with Mexico, and which would have dealt in severe terms with it. But Señor Maneyro did not turn his attention to any French functionary, for the simple reason that he had no relations with them; and if he sent two communications to the Independence Belge, it was simply because he had, at a former period, had some accidental intercourse with one of its editors.

But here there are two observations to be made. First of all, in making these communications Señor Maneyro obeyed an order of his government. I have here a letter written to him, under date of February 27, 1861:

"NATIONAL PALACE.

"It being necessary for this government to have frequent advices of the political condition of France, and the order being yet in effect which requires consuls to transmit to this department a monthly review of such political events as transpire in the respective countries in which they reside, I recommend to you, very strongly, a strict compliance with its requisitions. His excellency the president moreover orders that you should transmit every month to this department an account of the mercantile movements of that empire, showing, in general, the condition of it with other powers, and especially in regard to its commerce with Mexico.

"Whilst bringing this subject to your notice, I desire to renew the expression of my esteem and consideration.

"ZARCO.

"The MEXICAN CONSUL *at Havre.*"

Now there follows another despatch, dated April 28, 1862:

"The President of the republic recommends to you to give the greatest possible publicity to the printed documents annexed to this communication; and this I desire to state for your information.

"TERAN.

"The MEXICAN CONSUL *at Havre.*"

Afterwards we find a letter from Señor Doblado, minister of foreign affairs of the Mexican republic, under date of May 24, 1862, and couched in the following terms:

"The supreme government has received with much interest the information which you communicate in your note of 13th ultimo, with reference to what has passed in virtue of the preliminaries signed at La Soledad, and I hope you will continue to communicate whatever information you may be able to acquire on this particular point; for which purpose you will lose no occasion or opportunity to make investigations.

"DOBLADO.

"The MEXICAN CONSUL *at Havre.*"

Such are the orders received by Señor Maneyro from his government; and in obeying them he certainly did nothing that was not legitimate. Following those same instructions, M. Montluc, the consul general, imparted, not only to the public but, above all, to the French ministers and to the Emperor himself, the official communications of his government and his own observations—documents so notable, so worthy to be taken into consideration, and which one of the honorable counsel for the defence read here yesterday. All these efforts for good having proved fruitless, there came another order, addressed to the Mexican consuls, under date of April 23, 1863. This order was sent by Señor La Fuente, the present minister of foreign affairs of Mexico, and is as follows:

* Allusion is made to the election of M. Havin, director of the Siécle, to the Chamber of Deputies.

"DEPARTMENT OF FOREIGN AFFAIRS AND GOVERNMENT,
"*National Palace, Mexico, March* 23, 1863.

"The supreme government justly acknowledges your efforts to ward off, or at least to diminish, the evils of the war which the Emperor has brought upon us. But your efforts have proved vain, before the blind resolution of attacking us, not to obtain justice, which we have never denied, but to interfere by force of arms in our politics and our national affairs. Blood has already flowed, and much more will yet flow. I do not understand the satisfaction which is had in shedding it, nor the benefits which France has to gain in kindling a war without any hope of terminating it other than by the dishonorable peace which is proposed to us, on condition of sacrificing the government which we have selected. As it is desirable to take another step, I have to tell you to suspend absolutely all proceedings that may have for their object to inform or persuade that government, which is so unwilling to listen to the truth and to the dictates of justice.

"FUENTE."

These are, gentlemen, the correspondences of Señor Maneyro with his government. And what were the printed documents sent to him by it? They were the proclamations of congress, the speeches of President Juarez and his ministers; there was also the letter of General Ortega, which was read here in court yesterday, and which did not suffer by comparison with that of General Forey. On these documents only, in this part, are the judicial proceedings against Señor Maneyro founded; and I maintain that here there is nothing serious in the proceedings, and that, by saying that he had acted by order of his government, and proving it, as he does prove, Señor Maneyro says enough to insure him from any further vexation.

Notwithstanding all this, the prosecuting agent of the government is not willing that the case should rest here. You should, says he, obey your government in all that concerns a consular agent; but that government has no right to tell you to occupy yourself with politics, and you have transcended the powers which your official position gives you, by occupying yourself with politics.

Gentlemen, I fear that a line of conduct in accordance with these principles would be open to the charge of serious disobedience. Let us figure to ourselves a functionary who would reply to his government, "No, no! I do not wish to obey such orders. I divide them, and only reply to what I please. If they ask me the price of sugars and of cochineal, very well; I will communicate all information on the subject; but I do not wish to mingle in politics—on this point I remain deaf and dumb." Would not such a man be a very stupid agent? And what would we think of the government that would employ him, and retain him in his position?

Now, I proceed further: How could that agent, in time of war especially, distinguish between political interests and commercial interests? He would be a very able man, indeed, who could trace the line which separates the two, and very secure of his pen the one who could speak of the latter without saying anything of the former. Let us remark, moreover, gentlemen, that this should have its direct and necessary application, as well in regard to our own interests as to those of foreign nations. The theory which I maintain is as much for our own consuls as for those of other nations. And now the counsel for the prosecution will allow me, not to give advice, but merely to make an intimation. I consider it proper to ask the ministers of foreign affairs and of the marine from whom they receive their information in regard to Mexico since the rupture of diplomatic relations, and they will reply that they receive them from the consuls, and almost solely from the consuls.

There is certainly in that country a commander-in-chief of our army, with other generals and a number of staff officers. If you ask them for information in regard to the military forces, the state of the fortified positions, most assuredly they will give it to you; but if you interrogate them with regard to the state of feeling, the desires of the people, the condition of parties, or, in fine, with regard to public opinion, that moral power which judges definitively and without appeal of triumphs and disasters and of their consequences, they will say nothing of all these, because they know nothing about them, and are not in a condition to know; these are matters of which nothing can be known except by means of consuls. Let us, then, let alone those men who instruct and serve their governments, because if we hinder them we may expect reprisals. Foreign governments will use against us the arms which we think we have forged against them, and we will remain in the deplorable condition of knowing nothing certain in regard to those countries into which our armies go to maintain our most important interests. Consuls, in such cases, will keep silence, as well about what is favorable as about what is adverse; and if we proclaim the reign of silence over all that most imperiously demands the exercise of thought and of word, we will extinguish all the intelligence of our agents. For what purpose, then, are those schools, those *alumni* for consulates, those examinations, and those degrees? If there is only question of watching the mercantile movement, let us take simple bookkeepers, whose functions are limited to keeping account of the arrival and departure of vessels, signing invoices and general manifests, and taking note of the component articles and the importance of cargoes.

Another charge made against Señor Maneyro by the prosecution is his correspondence with the newspapers. He is thus addressed: "You have received extracts from newspapers hostile to France, and you have communicated them to other newspapers."

In order to repel this charge I have to repeat somewhat. Let us remark immediately, in regard to Señor Maneyro, that he has not asked, sent, or received any money, nor has he been remunerated with any pleasure, nor has he manifested any exceptional zeal. If there existed anything of all this, as far as he is concerned it would, in my opinion, be a very trifling affair; but to be brief, it is less than this, because nothing of the kind exists. Let us remark, moreover, that he has had no intercourse with any French journal, nor with those of Dresden and Geneva, characterized by the edict of 1861 as hostile to the government of France. The Independence Belge alone received two communications from him, and these merely, I request the court to remember it well, on official documents sent by his government. The imperial advocate appears to have extended to other communications the fact acknowledged by Señor Maneyro; I desire to call his attention to this involuntary error, and I have no doubt his sense of justice will correct it. [Sign of assent from the imperial advocate.] But even if Señor Maneyro had sent extracts of newspapers and other communications, he had the right to do so, unless they were defamatory or culpable, in which case alone they could be prosecuted. Let us cite our precedents.

In 1857 and 1858 there was a judicial proceeding in England. Some French politicians had sent various political articles to English newspapers. A lawsuit was instituted to recover the money for inserting those articles, and the pleadings were commenced by affidavit, according to the custom of England. The incompetency of the English tribunals to decide the case was pleaded, and they declared themselves competent. The case was prosecuted no further, as it appears. I presume that this was not on account of the abandonment by the plaintiffs of the considerable sums which they claimed; it is more likely that satisfaction was made to them.

This, however, is a matter of little importance, because from this instance I infer merely that individuals, Frenchmen or foreigners, may send articles to foreign periodicals in regard to the affairs of France without thereby incurring the charge of having committed any fault. And the example comes from high quarters, since there was then question of the minister of the interior and the ambassador then in actual service. I find these details, on which I wish to insist no otherwise, in the Times of November 26, 1862.

Finally, gentlemen, I come to the last induction of the prosecuting agent for the government in reference to Señor Maneyro, and deducted from his correspondence with Señor Del Rio.

I may forthwith make an observation as simple as it is important. A correspondence supposes two persons writing to each other. Now, if Señor Del Rio has written to Señor Maneyro, Señor Maneyro is accused of the receipt of the letters of Señor Del Rio. What has really passed? Señor Del Rio, an able and influential patriot, remained some time in France, where he had dealings with various persons to whom he wrote; he did not write only to Señor Maneyro, but to a number of persons, and I am surprised that there are only five accused included in this indictment, if it suffices to have received a letter from Señor Del Rio in order to be a promoter of disorders and of public disturbances; he not only wrote to Messrs. Montluc, Rodriguez, and Maneyro—he wrote also to M. Demontel, to a brother of Señor Maneyro, who is consul at Bordeaux, to the principal editor of the Charivari, for the mention of which here I ask to be excused; it is by no means my intention to accuse it. Señor Del Rio likewise wrote to the editor of Le Nord newspaper; what is more, he wrote to Don Joaquin de Errazu. Whence, it appears that he wrote to any person he thought proper, that was a Mexican, only because Señor Del Rio thought it patriotic to distribute his writings. Wherefore, if Señor Maneyro has received documents from that indefatigable citizen, others have likewise received them, and in greater number. Why, then, has not Señor de Errazu been called up, who, being rich, would have been in a state, had he so wished, to defray the expenses of the circulation of these documents? It has not been done, and very important reasons are found for not doing so. I shall not, therefore, say that there are two sorts of weights and measures used; but I shall say that by this very fact it is recognized that such missives (which did not even reach their destination, as they were confiscated on the way) cannot, whatever be their contents, interest those who neither kept them nor sought for them. If it has been thought proper to act in a decided way in regard to Señor Maneyro, it is doubtless because he is a consul, and because he received and sent official documents appertaining to his government. But the conjunction of three actions, innocent in themselves, as I have already demonstrated, cannot constitute a culpable action. Then it is proper to acknowledge that, in regard to Señor Maneyro, the prosecuting officer has gone entirely astray.

Now, when I reflect, in general, on these judicial proceedings, after having, as I hope, cleared away the whole charge against my client, I confess I feel two causes for serious apprehension : one is the new extension given to that law of 1858, already so much enlarged by the interpretations which it has received. In presence of this new weapon in the hands of power, which menaces the safety of every individual, I ask myself who will venture in future—I shall not say to publish his dissenting opinions by means of speech, of the newspapers, or any other way of writing, but even to consign them to private correspondence? Who will venture to express his intimate thoughts to a friend, and abandon himself in his letters to that unrestrained freedom, the sweetest and most consoling of the necessities of the heart? I can no more communicate my ideas to a cherished relative, to a distant friend, and make them participators in my hopes and fears. Shall it be necessary, then, that a person should confine his sentiments, his life, within a prescribed circle? And if one passes that in his correspondence, if two letters from my friend are found in my hands, or two of mine in his, censuring and criticising what seems deserving of disapprobation, shall it be said that we have sought to disturb the public peace, and to excite odium and contempt against the government of the Emperor?

What gives me less concern is the example which we would give to the governments themselves against which we were thinking we only secured ourselves. Reference has been made to our consuls abroad ; I speak of our hundred thousand compatriots residing in Mexico, who have gone thither in search of an establishment, temporary or definitive, and who have there interests of importance. If they are harassed and disturbed, they cannot rely upon their consuls, upon their fellow countrymen, upon their government, without fear of offending the Mexican government. If, on the contrary, they are treated with humanity, they cannot then rejoice at it or speak highly of it without passing for traitors to their country.

I know that there are men who give themselves very little concern about these matters. We have the power, say they ; our fellow-countrymen will be protected by our valiant army.

Gentlemen, let us predicate nothing upon force. Moreover, that never suffices to justify and purify ; what it establishes has its vicissitudes and its terrible instabilities. Let us base everything on right, on truth, on reason, on moderation ; let us be persuaded that this is at the same time justice and good policy. In this way, gentlemen, there is no reason to fear disastrous retaliations ; good examples are given ; they are what we ought to give, and thence we shall derive honor and profit. It behooves France to take the initiative in everything ; she is great enough, sympathetic enough in the world to have her example generally imitated and followed.

(Warm manifestations of applause followed this defence, and were received by the court and audience without any attempt to restrain them.)

The case was adjourned to the following day, the 6th, for final decision.

NOTE.—On the 6th of June, on the opening of the court, a decision was rendered releasing the five persons accused from all the charges against them.

Circular from the Minister of Foreign Affairs regarding the arrest of Mexican consuls in France.

DEPARTMENT OF FOREIGN RELATIONS AND OF GOVERNMENT,
San Luis Potosi, August 15, 1863.

In addition to the grave and repeated outrages committed by the government of Napoleon III against the rights of the republic and the law of nations, he himself has just authorized still further indignities, most unworthy in their petty malice, against the consuls, Messrs. Montluc and Maneyro—the one a general of France, the other a private individual of the port of Havre—both appointed by the government of Mexico, and in the perfect exercise of their functions, by virtue of the which *exequatur* had been given to them by the imperial government.

In clear infraction of the modern code of public law, of universal practice, and of the treaties which have been celebrated between Mexico and France, (which, in so far as relates to consuls, must be considered as binding, so long as on the one side and on the other these agents are maintained,) the government of the Emperor caused the agents of the police to enter into the office of the consul general, to violate his archives, to read his books and official papers, to take from all of them such notes as they pleased, making a mockery and a jest of the consul, of his *exequatur*, and of his protests. To such exploits of force there was added a wicked and unjust trial, commenced and sustained against both consular agents by a public prosecutor, who accused them of maintaining a correspondence hostile to the government of the Emperor.

The accusation was an outrage against consular privileges, because the acts with which our consuls were principally charged had been done by them in compliance with the orders of the federal government, and, far from involving any crime or offence, were, as was declared with truth by the sentence which closed this unqualifiable proceeding, entirely inoffensive and in good faith.

I desire, on this occasion, to leave on one side all consideration of what the French government, with its prodigious invention when searching out causes of insult and of reclamation against Mexico, would have said and would have demanded of this country if this government had sanctioned such a violence and such an outrage.

The President has rightly refused to take as the regulating principle of his conduct that of a government which, in everything relative to the affairs of Mexico, has only in its words manifested any respect for the prescriptions of justice and of civilization. Although we have been terribly outraged, we still desire to leave to our aggressors their precedence in the path of crime.

This time, for example, we could well exercise the right of national reprisal, and proceed with the consular agents of France in Mexico as they have proceeded in France with ours.

But such a course would be repugnant to us, and would besides lead to an absurdity, because the Mexican consuls in France, and *vice versa*, should not be retained from the moment that, through the outrage of the imperial government, this respectable officer has been subjected to so profound a degradation.

It is, in fact, much more convenient and decorous to direct that our consuls in France cease to exercise their functions, since they can no longer continue them without insult, and that the *exequatur* of the consuls whom the French government has named in the ports and commercial cities of the republic be retired. Certainly a government which treats consular officers in this manner is neither worthy of appointing them or receiving them.

We had maintained these agents in conformity with the least rigorous usages, although the Emperor and his generals have made public the real and positive end to which this war is to lead, and that it is the destruction of our government and of our republican institutions which is sought.

To make this revelation until the last hope of peace had disappeared is to violate all the laws of war, and we are therefore free from any obligation to respect them on our part. Besides, as the government of France ignores the federal government, it cannot respect, as in fact it does not respect, any of its rights; but by this very act it declares it free of all obligations towards France, its government and its citizens.

To this extreme would the conduct of the Emperor lead us if we listened only to the voice of our great injuries, and if we sought to prove to our enemies the precise and logical consequences of their insane proceedings. But we abstain from adopting this course, because we have a respect for public law and our own dignity, not from fear of our invaders, whom we are resisting with arms, and shall resist to the end.

In one word, if in this affair it is not advisable that we should violate our traditional policy to initiate proceedings as unjust and as insulting as those of the French government, it is still proper to take others of such efficiency and energy as shall justly protect the honor of the republic.

And as this determination can be realized, as I have already intimated, by terminating the commissions of our consuls in France, and by withdrawing from the French consuls in Mexico the *exequatur* which has been obtained from the federal government, the President has been pleased to direct the adoption of this course.

And by his order I have the honor to communicate the same to you, in order that you may be pleased to cause the French consuls and vice-consuls residing in your state to be immediately notified of the said supreme resolution, the exact compliance with which you will be pleased to opportunely advise.

Liberty and reform!

FUENTE.

Mr. Romero to Mr. Seward.

[Translation.]

MEXICAN LEGATION TO THE UNITED STATES OF AMERICA,
Washington, February 20, 1864.

Mr. SECRETARY: With the object of communicating to the government of the United States authentic information upon the important political events of which the Mexican republic is at this time the theatre, I have the honor to send to you a copy in English of the documents mentioned in the index annexed, and which relate to what has been called the establishment of monarchy in Mexico.

In the report which Mr. Saligny, minister of France in Mexico, gave to General Forey, the 16th June, 1863, upon the organization of a provisional government in that country, it is declared in the face of the world that the city of Mexico, which only contains two hundred thousand (200,000) inhabitants, is of more importance than the entire republic, which contains a population of more than eight millions, and that what should be determined upon in that city (supposing it to be the spontaneous voice of its inhabitants) should be considered as obligatory on the whole nation. The no less strange declaration is also made that the indigenous population of Mexico—that is, almost two-thirds of the inhabitants there are in the republic—cannot have any political rights, and to this time are refused the character of men and Mexicans.

In conformity with the report of Mr. Saligny, General Forey issued, on the said 16th June, that is, only six days after the French army entered the city of Mexico, a decree which provided that a junta of thirty-five persons named by him, at the suggestion of Mr. Saligny, should elect other three persons, who should constitute the executive authority; and that, subsequently, this should associate to itself other two hundred and fifteen individuals, also named by General Forey, to form the Assembly of Notables, for the purpose of designating the form of government which should be adopted.

On the 18th of said month of June General Forey issued another decree, in which he appointed the so-called members of what was called the Superior Junta of government, selecting them from among the persons most addicted to ultra conservative principles.

These individuals designated the traitors Juan Nepomuseno Almonte, Pelagio Antonio de Sabaslida, and José Mariano de Salos, to exercise the executive power, and afterwards took up the organization of the Junta of Notables. Although only two hundred and fifteen persons were needed to fill up that body, there was great difficulty, and several days were passed in completing the number, which was at last not completed. The so-called Assembly of Notables appointed a committee that should decide upon the form of government which should be adopted in Mexico; and the individuals who constituted it, who knew beforehand what they were to propose, after lowering their country to such a degree as to picture it as in worse condition than the tribes of Caffres, in a report which was written in disparagement of the Mexican name, and of lasting reproach to its authors, proposed, for instance, that which it was well known, from the time the expedition left the shores of France, they were to propose—that is, the monarchy and the Archduke Maximilian of Austria.

The assembly, which had no will of its own, did not know how to act, not even with the precautions necessary to gloss over appearances, and almost without discussion adopted unanimously, on the same day, the dictation of the committee, by determining, so that there should be no doubt that the will of the Emperor of the French controlled it, that if the archduke did not accept the crown, his Majesty should name the prince who should occupy the throne.

It was by this farce, then, that the French government accomplished what it had so repeatedly declared to that of the United States on the score of its pretended wish not to force the Mexicans to accept any government, but leave them to establish that which they should think most suitable. So illy played was the farce which the French agents presented to the city of Mexico that, even, neither the French government nor the Grand Duke Maximilian considered it as satisfactory; and in degree, as they could do no less than recognize the plain fact that the decision of the so-called notables did not express the will of the country, they thought it necessary, merely to save appearances, to require other formalities, which cannot but be farces as transparent as the election by the notables. The French government has assured that of the United States at a recent period that the popular suffrage would be required throughout the republic on the question of the form of government to be established, at the same time that it was giving out that the monarchy was solidly and permanently established, as is deducible from the discourses pronounced by the organs of that government in the legislative body in the discussion of the affairs of Mexico that took place in that assembly at the close of January last past. This would, however, be a point of less importance, because the assurances given by the French government fall short of fulfilment. The measure which it is intended to substitute for universal suffrage, in order to discover what is public opinion, is to do so in places occupied by the French troops; it is true they carry acts which persons under intimidation affirm, or, by filling up with fictitious names, declarations in favor of monarchy and of the Archduke Maximilian. The French government makes believe that the occupation of the Mexican villages by the French army is necessary to the free expression of their votes; therefore, on the occupation of such villages by French bayonets, it calls it "freeing them from the tyranny of Juarez," and forgets that at the same instant it is declaring in the face of the world, and its agents are proclaiming, that the constitutional President of the Mexican republic is a wandering fugitive, that the national army has been entirely destroyed, and that there no longer remains a shadow even of the national government.

In a separate note I will explain to you in what manner this intrigue of the French government has been received by the Mexican nation, and what are the demonstrations to which it has given place. I will here only indicate that the national government and permanent deputation of the Mexican congress, the genuine representation of the nation, protested against that intrigue in the manner you will see in the documents annexed, (Nos. 11 and 12.)

I avail of this opportunity to renew to you, sir, the assurances of my most distinguished consideration.

M. ROMERO.

Hon. WILLIAM H. SEWARD, *&c., &c., &c.*

Index to the documents which the Mexican legation in Washington remits to the Department of State of the United States, annexed to its note of this date.

1. Report of Mr. Saligny to General Forey on the organization of a junta of government and an assembly of notables, June 16.
2. Decree of General Forey, in conformity with the preceding report, June 16.
3. Decree of General Forey, in which he appoints the members of the superior junta of government, June 18.
4. Decree of the junta of government upon the appointment of the so-called executive power, June 22.
5. Proclamation of General Forey upon the selection of the executive power, June 23.
6. Manifesto of the members of the so-called executive power, June 24.
7. Decree of the so-called assembly of notables on the establishment of monarchy in Mexico, July 11.
8. Decree of the junta of government providing that the so-called executive power continue in function, in the character of regency, until the arrival of Archduke Maximilian in Mexico, July 11.
9. Discourse of D. Manuel Gutierroz Estrada to the Archduke Maximilian, offering him the crown of Mexico, October 5.
10. Reply of the archduke, October 5.
11. Circular of the national government of Mexico to the governments of friendly nations upon the attempted establishment of monarchy in Mexico, July 22.
12. Protest of the permanent deputation of the national congress of Mexico against the monarchy which the French agents have sought to establish in the city of Mexico, July 22.

IGNO. MARISCAL.

WASHINGTON, *February* 20, 1864.

No. 1.

SUPERIOR JUNTA OF GOVERNMENT AND ASSEMBLY OF NOTABLES.

Communication from the Emperor's minister.

MEXICO, *June* 16, 1863.

GENERAL: The successive advantages gained by the French army over the troops of the enemy have definitively decided the fate of the Mexican nation. The government, which a few days ago occupied the capital of the republic, has not awaited the arrival before this city of the soldiers who have overthrown the strongest bulwark of its despotism. Your columns had scarcely commenced their movements to march from Puebla upon Mexico, when the government of Juarez, understanding that all resistance was useless, evacuated the capital with the remnants of its vanquished and demoralized army, leaving behind, as records of its stay, the traces of those shameful spoliations and of that abominable tyranny which constituted its sole rule of conduct.

Providence, which has so often made use of the flag of France to deliver and regenerate nations humbled by despotism, reserved to it also the glory of arresting Mexico in the headlong career which was rapidly conducting her to utter ruin by the dilapidation of her resources and the sale of her richest states to strangers. A few years more of this unexampled disorder, which has caused the intervention of the armies of the old continent, and there would remain of this country, thrice the size of France, but some few precincts that might have resisted the dissolving action of this corrupt and corrupting government: the Mexican republic would have lost its nationality.

The eagles of France have brought to this land, abysmed in the revolutionary whirlpool, the kindly sentiments of the Emperor towards this unfortunate people, and hope has been reborn in all hearts. Alone among all, an infamous faction, which, under a name of which it was unworthy, domineered over Mexico by means of terror, has in its turn trembled before the intervention. It has fled before that banner which is the symbol of civilization and justice.

Shall I consider it necessary, general, to prove what I have asserted? The sympathizing acclamations which have saluted your entry into the capital of Mexico, that triumphal march of our valiant army beneath an abundant shower of flowers, those crowns thrown in profusion to the conquerors of San Lorenzo, Puebla, and other well-known fields of combat—are not all these sufficient to testify the sentiments of the immense majority of the people towards the deliverers of Mexico? The perfect order which has ceased at no time for a single moment to reign in the capital since the flight of the fallen government—does not it say with more force than any possible amount of reasoning, that this people, so long fatigued and weary, is now in need of repose to heal the wounds inflicted upon its industry and prosperity? Now, from the generous initiative of France, Mexico hopes for the means to secure the first steps in her social regeneration and to prepare the way for the permanent establishment that is to dry up the sources of the evils which she has suffered up to this time.

These aspirations of a whole people, general, cannot be ignored, and it is to give them the satisfaction which they demand, and at the same time to carry out the benevolent intentions of the Emperor towards the Mexican nation, that I lay before you the results of the deep study which I have made of the situation of the country, of its necessities, and of the means which appear to me proper to attain the object which France proposes to herself—that is to say, the reorganization of the government—to the end that the nation, reflecting upon itself, may, in all freedom and by the organ of its most intelligent citizens and those who enjoy the most consideration, make known the form of government most suitable to it.

It is not possible to convoke a general congress to deliberate on the grave questions now pending. The state of the country does not yet permit the representatives of the great cities and of the distant states to receive any call made to them for this purpose.

Neither could we think of making the Indian population participate in this act, so important for the Mexican nation. That part of the people, so worthy of interest in every respect, has been hitherto excluded from public affairs, and would not understand either its gravity or its consequences.

The capital, in which there is not a single state not represented by its most illustrious citizens, reckons about 200,000 inhabitants. It contains a considerable number of men distinguished for their intelligence, and accustomed to political life and public affairs. Moreover, it is in the capital that that government has weighed most heavily which has just fallen. On this great population, then, it is incumbent, under present circumstances, to know the best way to conclude the era of periodic revolutions, of which Mexico has been the theatre for more than half a century.

I propose to you, then, general, to decree that a Superior Junta, composed of thirty-five citizens, chosen from among the most honorable of this great city, should be charged with the following powers:

1. To nominate three Mexican citizens, who should constitute the executive power, and two substitutes for those high functions in case of the absence or impediment of the proper incumbents.

2. To elect two hundred and fifteen members chosen from among the citizens of Mexico, to form, in conjunction with the members of the Superior Junta, the Assembly of the Notables, to whom shall be intrusted the duty of determining upon the permanent form of the government of Mexico, and deliberating upon such other questions as may be submitted to them.

3. To settle the salaries to be paid to the members of the executive department of the government.

The Superior Junta shall be divided into various committees to deliberate on the affairs of the different ministers. A general meeting will be called by its president, as often as the questions presented to it demand such a step.

The presidents and secretaries of the Superior Junta and of the committees, as well as those of the Assembly of Notables, shall be named by those bodies in their first meeting after organization. This first duty shall be directed by the president, who shall be the oldest member in each assembly or committee, accompanied by the two youngest members, is the quality of secretaries.

The members of the Superior Junta and those of the Assembly of Notables shall have no salary.

The duration of the first session of the Assembly of Notables shall be five days. It may be prorogued by the executive power.

Such are, general, the provisions contained in the constitutional decree, which is annexed, and which I request you to sign if you see proper to approve of it.

Accept, general, the assurance of my high consideration.

A. DE SALIGNY.

General FOREY,

General of Division, Senator of France, Commander-in-chief of the expeditionary army in Mexico.

No. 2.

Decree in reference to the formation of a Superior Junta of government and of an Assembly of Notables.

THE GENERAL OF DIVISION, SENATOR OF FRANCE, COMMANDER-IN-CHIEF OF THE EXPEDITIONARY CORPS IN MEXICO.

Considering that it is expedient to organize the public authorities that are to replace the intervention in the direction of the affairs of Mexico, I have thought it proper, in accordance with the communication made to me by the Emperor's minister, to decree as follows:

ART. 1. A special decree shall designate, according to the recommendation of the Emperor's minister, thirty-five Mexican citizens to constitute a Superior Junta of government.

ART. 2. This Superior Junta shall assemble in the place that shall be designated for it two days after the publication of the decree announcing the names of its members.

ART. 3. The opening session of the Junta shall be presided over by the oldest member, assisted by the two youngest members in the quality of secretaries.

ART. 4. The Superior Junta shall proceed in this first session to the nomination of its president and of his two secretaries. The election shall be valid only on condition that the elected candidates shall have obtained a majority of all the votes cast.

ART. 5. The inauguration of the dignitaries elected shall take place on the same day.

ART. 6. The Junta shall subsequently proceed to the nomination of three Mexican citizens, who shall be charged with the executive power, and of two substitutes for those high functions. A majority of the votes cast shall be necessary to a valid election.

ART. 7. The members of the executive department shall, as soon as elected, assume the direction of the affairs of Mexico.

ART. 8. The Superior Junta shall settle the salary to be paid to the members of the provisional government.

ART. 9. The Junta shall resolve itself into various committees in order to deliberate on the questions relating to the different ministers.

It shall convoke itself into general assembly by means of its president, for the discussion of business of greater importance, whenever the executive requests it.

OF THE ASSEMBLY OF NOTABLES.

ART. 10. The Superior Junta shall associate themselves, in order to constitute the Assembly of Notables, with 245 members chosen from among the citizens of Mexico, without distinction of rank or class.

ART. 11. In order to be qualified to join the Assembly of Notables, a person must be fully twenty-five years of age, and not disqualified for any office, political or civil.

ART. 12. The opening of the sessions of the Assembly of Notables shall take place immediately after the formation of that body.

ART. 13. The first session shall be devoted to the election of a president, and of two secretaries, who shall be immediately installed by the provisional organization of the eldest and the two youngest members.

ART. 14. The Assembly of Notables shall occupy itself especially with the form of the permanent government of Mexico. The vote on this question must be such that two-thirds of the ballots cast, at least, shall be necessary for a decision.

ART. 15. In case this majority of two-thirds of the votes cast cannot be obtained, after three days of balloting, the executive shall dissolve the Assembly of Notables, and the Superior Junta shall proceed, without delay, to the formation of a new assembly.

ART. 16. The members of the preceding assembly may be re-elected.

ART. 17. The Assembly of Notables shall occupy themselves, after having determined on the form of the permanent government, with such questions as may be laid before them by order of the executive department. The first session shall last five days; it may be prorogued by the executive.

GENERAL REGULATIONS COMMON TO ALL THE DELIBERATING BODIES.

ART. 18. The secretaries of the Superior Junta, and of its various committees, as also those of the Assembly of Notables, shall take down, in writing, the proceedings of the committees. They shall, together with the presidents, sign all the resolutions passed by those bodies.

ART. 19. The sessions of the Superior Junta, and of its committees, as also those of the Assembly of Notables, shall not be public. Official acts may be published in the newspapers, provided they be transmitted to them by the secretaries, under the authority of the respective presidents.

ART. 20. The members of the Superior Junta, and those of the Assembly of Notables, shall receive no salary.

OF THE EXECUTIVE POWER.

ART. 21. The members of the executive department shall divide among themselves the six ministries; they shall nominate individually to all the employments dependent on their respective offices; they shall also have the power of dispensing with such employments.

ART. 22. The executive power shall receive for promulgation, as decrees, the resolutions of the Assembly of Notables. It shall have the absolute right of vetoing such resolutions. Bills prepared by the Superior Junta shall pass to the executive for transmission to the Assembly of Notables.

ART. 23. The functions of the executive shall cease from the moment of the inauguration of the permanent government, proclaimed by the Assembly of Notables.

ART. 24. The Emperor's minister is charged with the execution of the present decree, which shall be inserted in the bulletin of the acts of the intervention, and shall be posted up in the streets of the capital.

Given at Mexico, June 16, 1863.

FOREY,
General of Division, &c., &c.

No. 3.

Decree nominating the members of the Superior Junta of government.

THE GENERAL OF DIVISION AND SENATOR OF FRANCE, COMMANDING-IN-CHIEF THE EXPEDITIONARY CORPS IN MEXICO.

In view of the decree issued on the 16th of June, relative to the establishment of a Superior Junta of government, and in accordance with the proposal of the Emperor's minister, it has seemed proper to me to decree as follows:

ART. 1. The following persons are named members of the Superior Junta of government: D. J. Ignacio Pavon, Manuel Diaz de Bonilla, Dr. J. Basilio Arellaga, Teodosio Lares, Dr. Francisco Javier Miranda, Ignacio Aguilar y Marocho, Dr. José Sollano, Joaquin Velazquez de Leon, Antonio Fernandez Monjardin, General Mora y Villamil, Ignacio Sepúlveda, José M. Andrade, Joaquin Castillo Lanzas, Mariano Dominquez, José Guadalupe Arriola, General Adrian Woll, Fernando Mangino, Agapito Munoz, José Miguel Arroyo, Teófilo Marin, General Miguel Cervantes Velasco, Crispiniano del Castillo, Alejandro Arango y Escandon, Juan Hierro Maldonado, J. Ildefonso Amable, Gerardo Garcias Rojas, Manuel Miranda, José Lopez Ortigosa, General Santiago Blanco, Pablo Vergara, General Cayetano Montolla, Manuel Tejada, Urbano Tovar, Antonio Moran, Miguel Jimenez.

ART. 2. The members of the Superior Junta, just named, shall enter upon the exercise of their functions immediately.

ART. 3. The Emperor's minister is charged with the execution of this decree.

Given at Mexico, June 18, 1863.

FOREY,
General of Division, &c., &c., &c.

No. 4.

Decree of the Junta of Government naming the persons who are to constitute the Executive

MANUEL G AGUIRRE, POLITICAL CHIEF OF THE DEPARTMENT OF MEXICO, TO THE INHABITANTS THEREOF, GREETING:

The Superior Junta of government has communicated to me the following decree:

"The Superior Junta of government, installed in conformity with the decree of the 13th of the present month, proceeded, in its session of yesterday, to the election of the executive power provided for in the sixth article of the said decree, and the following persons were chosen:

"First. His Excellency Señor Don Juan N. Almonte, general of division.

"Second. The most illustrious Señor Don Pelagio Antonio de Labastida, archbishop of Mexico.

"Third. His Excellency Don Mariano Salas, general of division.

"First substitute, the most illustrious Señor Dr. D. Juan B. de Ormaechea, bishop elect of Tulacingo

"Second substitute, his honor Don Ignacio Pavon, president of the supreme court of justice.

"This election shall be published by national edict.

"Given in the hall of the Junta at Mexico, June 22, 1863.

"TEODOSIO LARES, *President.*

"ALEJANDRO ARANGO Y ESCANDON, *Secretary.*

"JOSÉ MARIA ANDRADE, *Secretary.*"

Wherefore, I order that it be printed, published, circulated, and have full authority given to it.

MANUEL G. AGUIRRE.
MANUEL AGUILAR Y LOPEZ, *Mayor.*

PALACE OF THE POLITICAL GOVERNMENT,
Mexico, June 24, 1863.

No. 5.

Proclamation of General Forey in regard to the election of the Executive.

MEXICANS: The nation has declared its will by means of its representatives chosen according to my decree of June 16.

General Almonte, the venerable archbishop of Mexico, and General Salas, were elected, the day before yesterday, by the Superior Junta, to take upon themselves the executive authority, and to direct the destinies of the country until the establishment of a permanent government. The names which I have mentioned are well known to you: they enjoy the public esteem and all the consideration due to distinguished services and high-toned character. You can, then, rest satisfied, as I now do, with regard to the future which is to be prepared for you by this triumvirate, which will assume the reins of government from the 24th of June.

Mexicans: In placing in the hands of these three provisional chiefs of the nation the powers which circumstances have given me, in order to exercise them for your benefit, I desire to render you my thanks for the active and intelligent co-operation which I have met in you. I shall ever preserve a grateful remembrance of those relations which have caused me to appreciate, at their just value, your patriotism and your respect for order, which have made you so worthy of the interest of France and of the Emperor.

FOREY,
General of Division, &c., &c., &c

MEXICO, *June* 23, 1863.

No 6.

Manifesto of the Supreme Executive Power to the nation.

MEXICANS: Having been appointed, by the superior committee of government, to exercise the supreme powers of the nation, it is right that we should instruct you of the very grave situation in which we find ourselves, and of our designs in fulfilling the mighty charge that we have received.

Never was the Mexican nation seen with more misfortunes nor with more solid hopes. A disciplined and courageous army, a great and civilized power, have undertaken to save us from the unfathomable abyss of evils to which, as blindly as impiously, a misled minority of our countrymen have brought us. They labor for our national restoration not by the terror of arms, nor by anti-social principles.

The force that comes to protect us will only be used to conquer that which persists in destroying us; to the errors which have perverted us there will be opposed the truths that regenerate nations; to the demoralization which has overturned everything there will be applied the justice which maintains the order of nations.

We know how many sophisms and calumnies those who have persisted in our ruin have employed and employ to diffuse among you aversion or mistrust with respect to the intervention Compare their sophisms with the facts which you behold; their calumnies with the conduct which is observed; their insidious promises with the evidence of the disasters and desolation that you contemplate. Compare the deeds with the words of the magnanimous and enlightened Emperor: No hostility to the nation, and sufficient mildness even toward those who compromise it and tyrannize over it.

Driving from the capital the power which the pretended constitution of 1857 systematized in evil, by evil, and for evil, the representatives of the Emperor have made no delay in establishing the provisional Mexican government, which will govern until the nation, more amply represented, shall fix freely and definitively the form of government which Mexicans ought to have permanently. The chimeras of conquest with which it was attempted to alarm the thoughtless are made evident and vanish. Mexico has again self-government, and is able and at liberty to choose, among all the political institutions, that which suits it best, and has the most glorious titles and firmest guarantees of stability.

In the mean time it is incumbent upon us to govern *ad interim* this suffering and disorganized nation; a task immensely arduous and complicated, and much superior to our strength Can we, in our transitory administration, repair the disorders and injuries of half a century? That which was founded by three centuries of peace, and a gradual progress, is not restored in a few days; we can only aspire to take the road and guide you in the first steps. No doubt Divine Providence reserves to more competent persons the consummating all the moral, social, political, and industrial restoration of Mexico.

The work is grand, and will be the sooner realized according as your co-operation is decided and general. We shall do very little if just men of all classes, parties, and ranks of our society do not aid our intentions in their respective spheres.

We behold you vacillating and uncertain about the future of our beloved country, as dejected with cares and anxieties, as fearful of new misfortunes, anxious for peace, and distrustful of provoking new wars; ruined and panting for tranquillity to restore your fortunes, with aversion for the political and administrative theories which we have tried, and jealous of trying other new ones. Order and disorder, misery and prosperity, conciliation and discord, are at your choice. You have two powers in view—one whose long tyranny and bad passions you have so wofully experienced, and another whose measured and just behavior you are able to observe: the one which is not satisfied with all your treasures, nor with your most necessary furniture, and the other which commences by relieving you of taxes, and introducing the severest economy: the one which fled from this city without any other support than the faction whose illegitimate interests it foments, and the other which, solidly fixed in Europe, will rest upon the legitimate interest and cardinal principles of society: that, in short, which, sacrificing to personal interest, or that of party, all that was orderly, just, useful, respectable, and sacred, brought our country to wars, and this, which, by the light and unconquered force of Catholicism, according to the invincible rules of good government, and supported by the bountiful protection of France, omitted nothing, that Mexico may rise in the New World as vigorous, enlightened, and improved as corresponds to the admirable abundance of her elements of prosperity.

Very grave affairs are about to occupy our attention. Peace, which has its roots only in justice and well-defined liberty; agriculture, now so decayed, the basis of every kind of industry, and which for so long has been the common prey of revolutionists and highwaymen; commerce, so paralyzed and fallen, from the public insecurity in the country; mining, a first-rate branch of industry, in decay from the prejudices and special burden which it has suffered; the unmeasured exactions in the towns and the demoralization in agreements; the arts either destroyed or impoverished; the administration of justice, with some honorable exceptions, so corrupt and tardy; security on the highways or in the inhabited places altogether lost; the vagrancy of all classes and ranks serving as a food for disorder and national depravation; finally, the reparation of the moral and physical disasters made by the so-called system of liberty and reform, for which the two powers will co-operate together as far as concerns them, united or separate, and the tribunals in cases within their competency.

The well-deserving army will likewise merit a preferable attention, and their sufferings will be taken into consideration, proceeding, without delay, to its reorganization. The worthy mutilated of the national independence will not be forgotten, nor less the suffering widows of the honored soldiers who have died in defence of their country.

The Catholic religion is re-established and free. The church will exercise its authority without having an enemy in the government, and the state will concert with it the manner of resolving the grave questions which are pendant.

The atheism which has been planted in the establishments of instruction, and the infamous propaganda of immoral doctrines which have ruined us, must cease. Catholic instruction, solid and of the greatest possible extent, and new literary careers and guarantees for good teachers, will be the object of our labors.

We have still to get rid of the so-called constitutional government, which is only able and only knows to do evil, which courts no good in its career of innovations and destruction. Whilst it exists, we Mexicans shall have no peace, nor our fortunes security, nor commerce increase The Franco-Mexican army will, as the first act they perform, pursue it until it surrenders or is driven from the national territory, and, in proportion as the towns shake off their intolerable yoke, they will begin to feel the repose and prosperity which the people already liberated enjoy. At the same time suitable measures will be dictated to expedite the pacification of the departments, and diminish the ruin which the agents of demagogism still occasion them.

Our misdeeds, and the acts committed by terrorists against friendly nations, have discredited us in the Old World. Good and dignified relations will be opened again with injured governments and with the Sovereign Pontiff; every effort will be made to ratify the obligations of Mexico with friendly powers, and with the protection of France and the other nations that shall support the new government, we shall be respected abroad, and the honor and credit of the nation will be repaired.

We have told you frankly what we think of the new situation, and what we intend to do in the difficult commission which we have received, in spite of our insufficiency. Much will be done if eminent men of all kinds assist. Let our disgraceful discord at last end. Let the scandal which we have given to the world cease. Let there be concord, union, peace, and public spirit among us. Let the sordid speculations at public misfortunes be extirpated, and let those riches be turned to great and lucrative industrial enterprises. Let honest labor be the foundation of fortunes; let functionaries have no power over the laws, nor the laws over morality. Let religion and authority, property and liberty, order and peace, be at last precious realities for Mexicans. May the God of armies, who has so directly favored our cause, reward the generosity and sincere intervention of France, and the patriotic intention with which we good Mexicans have accepted it, with the speedy grandeur and prosperity of the nation.

Palace of the supreme executive power in Mexico, the 24th of June, 1863.

JUAN N. ALMONTE.
JOSÉ MARIANO SALAS.
JUAN B. ORMAECHEA.

No. 7.

SECRETARYSHIP OF STATE AND OF THE OFFICE OF FOREIGN RELATIONS,
PALACE OF THE SUPREME EXECUTIVE POWER,
Mexico, July 11, 1863.

The provisional supreme executive power has been pleased to address me the following decree:

"The provisional supreme executive power of the nation to the inhabitants thereof. Know ye, that the Assembly of Notables has thought fit to decree as follows:

"'The Assembly of Notables, in virtue of the decree of the 16th ultimo, that it should make known the form of government which best suited the nation, in use of the full right which the nation has to constitute itself, and as its organ and interpreter, declares, with absolute liberty and independence, as follows:

"'1. The Mexican nation adopts as its form of government a limited hereditary monarchy, with a Catholic prince.

"'2. The sovereign shall take the title of Emperor of Mexico.

"'3. The imperial crown of Mexico is offered to his imperial and royal highness the Prince Ferdinand Maximilian, Archduke of Austria, for himself and his descendants

"'4. If, under circumstances which cannot be foreseen, the Archduke of Austria, Ferdinand Maximilian, should not take possession of the throne which is offered to him, the Mexican nation relies on the good will of his Majesty Napoleon III, Emperor of the French, to indicate for it another Catholic prince.

"'Given in the Hall of Sessions of the Assembly, on the 10th of July, 1863.

"TEODOSIO LARES, *President.*

"'ALEJANDRO ARANGO Y ESCANDON, *Secretary.*
"'JOSE MARIA ANDRADE, *Secretary.*'

"Therefore, let it be printed, published by national edict, and circulated, and let due fulfilment be given thereto.

"Given at the palace of the supreme executive power in Mexico, on the 11th of July, 1863.

"JUAN N. ALMONTE.
"JOSÉ MARIANO SALAS.
"JUAN B ORMAECHEA.

"To the UNDER SECRETARY OF STATE AND OF THE OFFICE OF FOREIGN RELATIONS."

And I communicate it to you for your knowledge and consequent purposes.

J. M. ARROYO,
Under Secretary of State and of the Office of Foreign Relations.

No. 8.

SECRETARYSHIP OF STATE AND OF THE OFFICE OF FOREIGN RELATIONS,
PALACE OF THE SUPREME EXECUTIVE POWER,
Mexico, July 11, 1863.

The provisional supreme executive power has been pleased to address me the following decree:

"The provisional supreme executive power of the nation to the inhabitants thereof: Know ye that the Assembly of Notables has thought fit to decree as follows:

"'The Assembly of Notables, in view of the decree of this date, has thought fit to decree:

"'Until the arrival of the sovereign the persons appointed, by decree of 22d of June last, to form the provisional government, shall exercise the power in the very terms established by the decree referred to, with the character of regency of the Mexican empire.

"'Given in the Hall of Sessions of the Assembly on the 11th of July, 1863.

"'TEODOSIO LARES, *President.*

"'ALEJANDRO ARANGO Y ESCANDON, *Secretary*
"'JOSÉ MARIA ANDRADE, *Secretary*'

"Therefore, let it be printed, published, and circulated, and let due fulfilment be given thereto.

"Given at the palace of the supreme executive power in Mexico, on the 11th of July, 1863.

"JUAN N. ALMONTE.
"JOSÉ MARIANO DE SALAS.
"JUAN B. ORMAECHEA.

"To the Under Secretary of State and Foreign Relations, Don José Miguel Arroyo."

And I communicate it to you for your knowledge and consequent purposes.

J. M. ARROYO,
Under Secretary of State for Foreign Relations.

No. 9.

The offer of the crown.—Señor Estrada's address to Maximilian.

Prince: The powerful hand of a generous monarch had hardly restored liberty to the Mexican nation when he despatched us to your imperial highness, cherishing the sincerest wishes and warmest hopes for our mission. We shall not dwell upon the visitations Mexico has had to undergo, and which, as they are notorious, have reduced our country to the verge of despair and ruin. There is no means we have not employed, no way we have not tried, to escape a situation full of misery for the present and foreboding catastrophes for the future We have long endeavored to extricate ourselves from the fatal and ruinous position into which the country had fallen on adopting, with credulous inexperience, republican institutions, at variance with its natural arrangements, its customs and traditions; institutions which, though they resulted in the greatness and prosperity of a neighboring nation, have only become a source of trials and desperate disappointments in our case. Nearly half a century, Prince, has elapsed, carrying with it for Mexico barren tortures and intolerable humiliation, but without deadening the spark of hope and indomitable vitality in our breast. Full of unshakable confidence in the Ruler of human destinies, we never ceased to look out for a cure of our ever-growing national malady. We may say we awaited its advent true to ourselves. Our faith was not in vain. The ways of Providence have become manifest, openin gup a new era, and exciting the admiration of the greatest minds by an unexpected turn of fortune.

Once again master of her destinies, Mexico, taught by experience, is at this moment making a last effort to correct her faults. She is changing her institutions, being firmly persuaded that those now selected will be even more salutary than the analogous arrangements which existed at the time she was the colony of a European state. This will be all the more certain if we should be destined to see at our head a Catholic Prince, who, with the high and recognized worth of his character, with the nobility of his feelings, knows how to couple that firmness of will and self-sacrificing devotion which are the inheritance of those only who have been selected by God Almighty in decisive moments of public danger and social ruin, to save sinking peoples and restore them to a new life. Mexico expects much from the spirit of those institutions which have governed it for three centuries, and which, when they fell, left us a brilliant, but, alas! now spoiled inheritance. The democratic republic endeavored to do away with the traces of former grandeur. But whatever may be our confidence in such institutions, their efficiency will be only perfect when crowned in the person of your imperial highness. A king, the heir of an old monarchy, and representing solid institutions, may render his people happy, even in the absence of distinguished qualities of mind and character; but very different and exceptional qualities are required in a prince who intends to become the founder of a new dynasty and the heir of a republic.

Without you, Prince—believe it from these lips which have never served the purposes of flattery—without you, all our efforts to save the country will be in vain. Without you will not be realized the generous intentions of a great sovereign, whose sword restored us to liberty and whose powerful arm now supports us in this decisive hour. With you, however, experienced in the difficult art of government, our institutions would become what they ought to be, if the happiness and prosperity of our country are to be guaranteed. With you they would have for their foundation that genuine liberty which is coupled with justice and moderation—not the spurious counterfeit we have become conversant with during half a century's ruinous wars and quarrels. Such institutions, equally as they are in harmony with the spirit of the age, will also become the unshakable corner-stone of our national independence. These sentiments, these hopes, which have been long entertained by all true friends of Mexico, are now in the hearts of all in our country. In Europe, too, whatever sympathies or antipathies may have been roused on the occasion of our present step, there is only one voice in regard to your imperial highness and your noble consort, who, shining by personal worth and high virtues, will share your throne and rule over our hearts. The Mexicans require only to see you in order to love you.

Faithful interpreters of the longing desire and the wishes of our country, in its name we offer to your imperial highness the crown of Mexico--that crown which a solemn resolution of the Assembly of Notables has of its free will and accord handed over to your imperial highness. Even now that resolution has been confirmed by the assent of many provinces, and will soon be sanctioned by the entire nation. Nor can we forget, Prince, that by a fortunate coincidence of circumstances this great national act is taking place on the day on which Mexico celebrates the anniversary of the victorious appearance of the national army, carrying high the banner of independence and monarchy. May it please your imperial highness to fulfil our prayers and accept our choice. May we be enabled to carry the joyous tidings to a country awaiting them in longing anxiety ; joyous tidings not only for us Mexicans, but also for France, whose name is now indissolubly bound up with our history, and gratitude for England and Spain who began the work of revival, and for the illustrious house of Austria, connected by time-honored and glorious memories with a new continent.

We do not undervalue the sacrifice to be made by your imperial highness in entering upon so great a task with all its consequences, and in severing yourself from your friends in Europe--that quarter of the globe which, from its centre, diffuses civilization over the world. Yes, Prince, this crown which our love offers you is but a heavy burden to-day, but it will soon be made enviable by your virtues, our zealous co-operation, our loyal devotion and inextinguishable gratitude. Whatever may be our faults, however deep our fall, we are still the sons of those who, inspired by the sacred names of religion, king, and country, hesitated not to run the greatest risks, engage in the grandest enterprises, combat and suffer in their course. These are the sentiments which, in the name of our grateful country, we lay at the feet of your imperial highness We offer them to the worthy scion of that powerful dynasty which planted Christianity on our native soil. On that soil, Prince, we hope to see you fulfil a high task, to mature the choicest fruits of culture, which are order and true liberty. The task is great, but greater is our confidence in Providence, which has led us thus far.

No. 10.

Reply of the Archduke Maximilian, on the 3d of October, 1863, *to the Mexican deputation.*

"I am profoundly grateful for the wishes expressed by the Assembly of Notables.

"It cannot be other than flattering to our house that the thoughts of your countrymen turn to the descendants of Charles V.

"It is a proud task to assure the independence and the prosperity of Mexico under the protection of free and lasting institutions. I must, however, recognize the fact—and in this I entirely agree with the Emperor of the French, whose glorious undertaking makes the regeneration of Mexico possible—that the monarchy cannot be re established in your country on a firm and legitimate basis unless the whole nation shall confirm by a free manifestation of its will the wishes of the capital.

"My acceptance of the offered throne must, therefore, depend upon the result of the vote of the whole country.

"Further, a sentiment of the most sacred of the duties of the sovereign requires that he should demand for the proposed empire every necessary guarantee to secure it against the dangers which threaten its integrity and its independence

"If substantial guarantees for the future can be obtained, and if the universal suffrage of the noble Mexican people select me as its choice, I shall be ready, with the consent of the illustrious chief of my family, and trusting to the protection of the Almighty, to accept the throne.

"It is my duty to announce to you now, gentlemen, that in case Providence shall call me to the high mission of civilization which is attached to this crown, it is my fixed intention to open to your country, by means of a constitutional government, a path to a progress based on order and civilization, and, as soon as the empire shall be completely pacified, to seal with my oath the fundamental agreement concluded with the nation.

"It is only in this manner that a truly national policy can be established, in which all parties, forgetting their ancient quarrels, will unite to raise Mexico to the high rank which she should attain under a government whose first principle will be law based on equity.

"I beg of you to communicate these my intentions, frankly expressed, to your countrymen, and to take measures to obtain from the nation an expression of its will as to the form of government it intends to adopt."

No. 11.

Note addressed by the government of the republic to the governments of friendly powers.

NATIONAL PALACE, SAN LUIS POTOSI, *July* 22, 1863.

To His Excellency the MINISTER OF FOREIGN AFFAIRS OF ———:

The undersigned, minister of foreign affairs of the republic of Mexico, has the honor of addressing himself to his excellency the minister of foreign affairs of ———, with reference to the events which have lately taken place in the city of Mexico.

The undersigned has to commence by stating to his excellency the minister that the president, having become convinced that policy did not dictate a resistance to the invader in the former capital, ordered that the supreme powers of the federation should be transferred to this city. This decree was executed a few days after its publication, after the national congress had terminated its sessions by the expiration of the period of its second term.

Some days later, not only the president, invested with extraordinary powers by congress, but also the permanent deputation of congress which subsists during the recess of that body, and finally the supreme court of justice, which completes the *personnel* of the supreme powers of the country, were established in the new capital, where they discharge with perfect regularity the attributes conferred upon them by our organic law.

The government of the republic in all its branches receives, as is natural and due, the recognition and the obedience of the nation, excepting only the few places which the army of France hold subject and oppressed. But the power arrogated by the invader of our soil is so limited and so uncertain in its tenure, besides being so odious and so strongly resisted, that there is not held by him a single foot of ground not controlled by his military posts. However near to these other towns may be, they obey—the same as all the rest of the nation—the authorities which Mexico, in the exercise of its sovereignty, and by the free vote of its citizens, has thought proper to place at the head of its internal administration. In fine, even the line from Vera Cruz to the city of Mexico, the line which should be certain and secure to the enemy's army, is incessantly cut by the national troops.

But even if this line were not and should not be disputed by our forces, and although the French should succeed in executing their plan—which has transpired—of extending the influence of their arms to the radius of twenty leagues from the city of Mexico, there would even then have been conquered by their forces only a mere fraction of the republic, (a portion incomparably less than that which remains,) and which, animated by a sense of right and a consciousness of strength, is resolved not only to continue to resist the foreign invader, but to recover those portions where the legal order has been interrupted by the momentary triumph of force over justice and right, over patriotism the most noble, and over courage itself

Such being the actual condition of affairs, it is difficult for the undersigned properly to qualify the act which has just been committed in the former capital of the republic by the general in-chief of the invading army. Immediately upon the occupation of the city of Mexico he has thought that the hour had arrived to announce that the government of the federation had been destroyed and annihilated. He therefore proceeded to name thirty-five individuals, in order that they, in their turn, should elect a triumvirate who should be charged with the executive power, and should also name two hundred and fifteen other persons who, with the title of "notables," should be intrusted with authority to determine the form of our government. Pronouncing themselves in favor of a monarchy, they selected for emperor his royal highness the Prince Maximilian of Austria, and declared that the provisional government should take the name of regency.

Considering these acts in their true light, and deducing from them their only practical and effective consequences, it results that there is in the city of Mexico a combination of three persons, called triumvirs, and now members of a regency; and that there is a prince who has been called to reign over Mexico as emperor by two hundred and fifteen individuals, seconded, at most, by only the places occupied by the troops of the Emperor Napoleon. But as the entire party resigned to accept the foreign prince whom the invader is so anxious to give us only embraces the inhabitants dominated by the French army and a few impotent and fugitive bands, and as all this lacks very greatly of even approaching to be a majority of the people of the country, who, as a matter of fact, adhere to the constitutional government, it follows logically that the empire and the regency do not constitute a government *de facto*, nor prove anything more than a desire and an attempt to establish such a government In fine, so long as the orders of the government of Mexico are respected and obeyed throughout almost the entire nation, that is the supreme authority which international law teaches should be recognized, independent of its other legitimate titles, under the presumption that a state accepts, or at least tolerates, that government which it obeys without resistance.

Coming to the question of right, the undersigned finds a source of embarrassment in its discussion from the abundance of the reasons which demonstrate the justice with which the Mexican people reject the bastard and despicable government which General Forey seeks to impose upon them

The undersigned even fears that it may be considered an undue yielding to force to attempt the formal proof of a thing so clear and self-evident. But he feels it his duty to conform to the usage of civilized nations, and, by complying loyally with the sacred obligation imposed upon him by the vote and the confidence of the republic, provide for its defence by all the legitimate and proper means that may be within his reach.

The Emperor of the French, violating the most sacred and important of the restrictions with which civilization has tempered the right of war, has declared it against Mexico, and is making it solely on account of a miserable debt, whose payment has been offered to him, and for certain other causes equally destitute of consistency and of justice, such as the reclamation of Jecker, which has no existence, except at his hands, the mere enunciation of which causes has filled the world with astonishment.

Hostilities have been opened without waiting for the refusal of such satisfaction as might with justice be demanded of us, and only once have his agents treated of negotiations, and that was to infringe and to prove false to the stipulations of Soledad, exchanging thereby the unhealthy positions of their forces for others more salubrious and more advanced. The Emperor and his agents have not sought to obtain reparation through peace, nor have they made war upon Mexico to obtain it. Their true design, well known even before the government of France had lifted the veil with which it was covered—the design which for a long time had been openly spoken of and discussed by the politicians and the journals of Europe—was to overthrow republican institutions in Mexico, to destroy its government, and to raise a throne for the Prince Maximilian of Austria.

It is for this reason that the agents of the Emperor have declared that they would never treat with the president, which is equivalent to saying that peace should never be made; for the president, not having obtained his position through force or fraud, as have so many ambitious men in ancient and modern times, but by the free vote of his fellow-citizens, can neither reject the confidence which they have bestowed upon him, by violating his most sacred duties and obligations and abandoning his post in the day of peril for the republic, nor can they consent that the chief magistrate charged by them with the functions of government and with the duty of representing its sovereignty abroad should be removed from power to please a foreign enemy, even if that should be the sole condition required for the re-establishment of those friendly relations which have been interrupted.

As all of the events of a political character which have occurred in the city of Mexico have taken place and are sustained solely by the direction of General Forey, and as from the very nature of these events it is not possible to ascribe them to any other origin or support, it follows that France, by means of force, is intervening to the extent of her power in the administration and government of Mexico, and has therefore again inaugurated that unhappy era which it had been the glory of the nineteenth century to have terminated; for war will be full of iniquity and of interminable disasters to the nations when the power of one over the others shall have no longer the restraints of international right

The French government, in the blindness of its ambitious designs, has forgotten that this pretended right of intervention was once applied to France, although to the present imperial family this memory should be indelible.

If national sovereignty is the basis upon which rest the rights of mankind, it is easy to see how great and profound, how alarming for all the states of the globe, is this outrage which is being done to Mexico by the Emperor Napoleon III.

The undersigned will now descend to refer to the acts which the general of the invading army and his adherents have had the boldness to present as sufficient titles to attribute to their mock government a character of true nationality. They assert that the place where the empire was proclaimed has the virtue of legalizing that act both within and without the republic.

General Forey, after having occupied the city of Mexico, announced that the military question had terminated, and that they had now to decide the political question. But the truth is that the military question is scarcely commenced, and that the political question is very far from having been opened, much less closed, by the election of a monarch in that city. The city of Mexico is without doubt a very important place for us; but it by no means has the importance and influence which in some other countries is exercised by the capital. The Mexican people made war upon Spain with vigor and with success, notwithstanding the city of Mexico remained up to the last moment submissive to the colonial government; and later, when the insurrectionary party held the same city, with many others, it was only at the end of a three-years' war that they could be driven out of all by the irresistible uprising of the nation.

The consciousness of right, and the determination to sacrifice everything in the defence of our liberties, are sentiments diffused throughout the utmost bounds of the republic, and one or many cities lost cannot weaken our resolution, as it will not diminish the justice of our cause, or lessen the immense value of the objects we are defending.

It is in vain that they talk of a pretended right upon which they seek to found the appointment of the notables. In truth, even if a custom by which necessity or abuse has established among us certain governments, merely provisional, could be applicable at the time when there was a government obeyed and respected throughout all the land, and even admitting a compromise between these governments and that permanent one which the new notables imagined they could create, it would still be evident that such a custom, whether good or bad, has not been, nor can it ever be, accepted in the contingency of being invoked and used by the general of the foreign army, an invader of the country.

The organic law of Mexico, however, does not exist in abolished customs, but in the lawful constitution of the country, framed by its legitimate representatives and sustained and defended by the will and by the blood of the Mexican people. Her sovereignty, the same as that of all the nations, has for its first basis the right of Mexico to manage freely and alone her own government And what species of public right is that which commences by depriving of the equality of citizens the Indians, who form the majority of the nation?

It has been even said that the intervention has in its favor the wishes of a majority of the Mexicans; but the demonstrations of joy extorted by the police in the city of Mexico, and at other points which the enemy holds in his power, upon which alone this assertion is based, offer any appearance rather than that of a spontaneous and universal adhesion. Nor can the undersigned do more than refer to the other boasted proof of sympathy for the intervention taken from the numbers present at a ball given in Mexico by the officers of the French army. Treason, which has declared itself in Mexico, is, without doubt, a horrible crime; but it is not peculiar to the Mexican people, as is proved by history, and very especially by that of France; and neither here more than there does it justify, in any manner, the invasion of a state and the annihilation of its sovereignty.

It also appears very clear to the undersigned that to constantly repeat, as the French government and its agents have repeated, that they only desire to make us happy, is not to advance in the light of those sound principles, which certainly cannot be abolished by a phrase which any ambitious government can use, and, in fact, which has been used with eager readiness in the most iniquitous wars. Nor can it be seriously maintained that any one can by force be obliged to receive a benefit.

In one word, Mr. Minister, the intervention which the Emperor of the French is exercising in this country involves not only an immeasurable outrage to Mexico, but a menace against all other nations, while, with reference to the reality of events, it has in fact only reached the point of being a humiliation imposed by the French army upon the few towns which have fallen in their power, and remains a pure phantasy for the immense majority of the republic

The republic has not forgotten the heroism of its sons who, without other aid than their own efforts, achieved its independence and gave it the right to inscribe its name upon the honored catalogue of free nations. The defence of Puebla de Zaragoza is demonstrating to the world that our race has not degenerated, although the contrary was said when they were preparing against us this most unjust war.

We shall preserve our institutions in all their force, and the spirit of the nation will rise more and more with the passage of each day, and become more determined in its opposition and inextinguishable in its hatred against the enemies of its repose and the destroyers of its rights.

The men who have violated in the most flagrant manner the law of nations, in contriving pretexts for this war, in the employment of their means of hostilities, and in setting forth with falsehood its ends, concealing the truth, and which ends are in all points unjustifiable; the men who have conspired to rob the country of its sovereignty and to overthrow its free institutions; the men who have caused our soldiers to be murdered when prisoners and dropping with fatigue, and have forced them to hard labor in deadly climates, or to take arms in their ranks to fight against the cause of their country; the men who have stripped from the faithful servants of the government of the nation their property; those who have caused the assassination of a commander of an escort guarding a foreign consul; the men who have thought to degrade the majority of our fellow-citizens, declaring them pariahs in the land of their birth, which has been enriched by the blood their fathers shed in achieving its independence, and by their own shed in the long struggle to establish it free; the men, in fine, who have re-established the odious and abolished punishment of the lash, even for feeble women—these men never can have the love, never will receive even the tolerance, of the Mexican people, who refused to accept for their emperor even their liberator himself.

The undersigned persuades himself that these facts and these considerations will be sufficient to lead the government of your excellency to approve the protest which the government of Mexico makes, by means of this note, against whatever arrangement, treaty, or convention in which the so-called regency or the supposititious emperor of Mexico shall have part; and the government of the undersigned trusts that the enlightened government of your excellency will not recognize the said regency or empire as the government of Mexico, as it is not, with truth, either in fact or of right.

The undersigned avails himself of this occasion to offer to your excellency the assurances of his high consideration.

JUAN ANTONIO DE LA FUENTE.

No. 12.

Protest of the Permanent Deputation of the Congress of the nation.

The permanent deputation of the sovereign congress of the united Mexican States would fail in one of the most eminent and sacred of its duties, if it should maintain a criminal silence in view of the infamous and scandalous events which have recently taken place in the city of Mexico.

The nation has been outraged in all its rights. The most sacred principles of justice, of reason, and of morals have been mocked at and trampled upon under the shadow of the ephemeral power of foreign soldiers—soldiers who have not known how to conquer, and who have failed to humiliate the heroic republicans who defended the walls of Puebla de Zaragoza. Joined to these, a faction of traitors and cowards, a thousand times conquered in our intestine struggles; of cruel fanatics, who, safe from peril themselves, decree the death of the most loyal patriots; a faction of miserable egotists, who sacrifice everything to their love of gain; of degraded adventurers, the scum of all the parties in our civil wars, have pretended to despoil the nation, and forever, of the most glorious of the titles of a name engraven in the history of its independence, won and preserved by the blood of its best citizens, of its institutions the most cherished, and of its liberties the most precious.

And this small faction of abject and imbecile beings, who to-day adulate and serve the foreign power, and to-morrow will be the objects of its utmost disdain and contempt, never tire of repeating to us, with the same flagrant duplicity that has always characterized their language, that Louis Napoleon, generous and benevolent, without ulterior views, without ulterior design, without illegitimate interests, has caused his soldiers to cross the ocean, at the cost of enormous expense to the treasury of France, solely to comply with a pious and benevolent mission, solely to give us peace, liberty, all those benefits which constitute the happiness of a people, and to leave us free to enjoy in tranquillity these great benefits, without reproach to our honor, without sacrifice to our integrity, and without offence, even the slightest, to our national existence.

The foreign general, associating himself with feigned generosity with this perfidious faction of traitors, has repeated these treacherous words, which, incoherent and inexplicable as they are, have not required the evidence of the events which have occurred to prove their falsehood.

To declare himself triumphant and the victor, after he had occupied, without other resistance than that of Puebla de Zaragoza, two or three cities, abandoned from motives of policy, in a country possessed of an immense extent of territory; to assume that the military line of Vera Cruz to Mexico, incessantly attacked by the national forces, and upon which the invader holds no more than the soil upon which he stands, is equivalent to the conquest of eight millions of inhabitants, the great majority of whom were born and have lived free from the dominion of a foreign yoke; to assume to domineer over this country under such a title, and immediately to attempt to impose upon it laws and to name public functionaries; to appoint a committee of government, without other representation than the will of the self-styled conqueror, and to order it to elect another committee of so-called notables, all residents of one single town, clothed by him with authority to pronounce in an oracular manner what should be the form of government which it is the will of Mexico to have; for this committee to respond that the absurd and fantastic plan, preconceived and contrived in the Tuileries more than two years ago, is equivalent, quite equivalent, to the free vote of the nation, and that, of their free and spontaneous will, the Mexican people wish to place themselves under the monarchical system, calling for that purpose a foreign prince, a stranger, without ties, without antecedents, and without a knowledge of the country—all this, and still more, which the traitorous faction have wished to do, in testimony of their submission and blind obedience to the most iniquitous of invaders, supplanting the truth, lying in the face of the civilization of the age, and covering the country with opprobrium and reproach, is a gross tissue of absurdities and marvels, such as no history has recorded, and which would be unworthy of all credit if they were not inscribed in irrefragable documents.

Thus do they pretend that a nation can, with easy facility, abdicate its most precious prerogatives—that a state, a moral entity, distinct and independent of all other states, can transmit to another the right of establishing, of changing, or of abolishing the form and character of its government; thus it is pretended in this nineteenth century to obliterate and destroy the autonomy of a people; and thus it is hoped that the Mexicans, strong and numerous, and with the same right to be free as the most prosperous nation of the world, shall disown their political being, shall forget their most sacred traditions, lay aside their most established habits, shall outrage the memory of their greatest sons, and, cowards and ingrates, voluntarily consent to this shameful and humiliating intervention which conceals and covers up its true ends; which is founded in no legitimate motive; which has been born of allied cupidity, through falsehood, calumny, and treason; which invades even the domestic hearth, under the pretext of allotment of brutal soldiers; which sequestrates and embargoes private property, and which heaps the infamy of its odious lash upon the shoulders of feeble men and of unprotected women.

However often the traitors may repeat it, kissing the yoke that is imposed upon them, foreign intervention is not compatible, is never compatible, with the sovereignty of the nation. This right is complete, absolute, inalienable, and exclusive; it cannot be ceded nor transferred, nor given in exchange, nor held in partnership. Every sovereign nation, whatever may be its political form, governs of itself alone, and independent of any foreign control. A sovereignty, limited, modified, protected, placed in tutelage, sustained by foreign influence or by foreign arms, cannot be free, cannot live a natural life, and can have no other existence than that given to it by the power upon which it leans; and when, before the occupation by the French arms, not even one single spontaneous manifestation was heard in favor of foreign intervention, and when, in the very districts now occupied, only insignificant villages and persons of obscure position have declared in favor of this national ignominy; when nine-tenths of the Mexican people still remain under the rule of the national and legitimate authority, and multitudes of pacific families have abandoned their hearths and their connexions, in order not to remain in contact with the foreign enemy, and the valiant soldiers who fell in their power on the occupation of Puebla escape from their ranks, in order to reunite themselves to the national army—when so many explicit manifestations prove the invincible repugnance with which the invading force is viewed, yet, in the face of all this, in the capital of the republic has been improvised a phantom of government, which, from its bastard origin, from having at its head the first of traitors, has not and cannot possess either dignity or power, which is only sustained by the bayonets of France, and which has no other mission than that of strutting its little brief period of triumph, sterile and in vain, because it has no foundation in public opinion, and is neither based upon nor supported by the will of the nation, which is already inaugurating a new era in this struggle, which will be more obstinate and more bloody than any which Mexico has before sustained against her invaders.

The permanent deputation, in the name of the congress of the union, and as the faithful interpreters of the national sentiment, so energetically and universally manifested, believes that it fulfils a most solemn obligation in reproducing, as by these presents it does reproduce, all the declarations and protests before made by the sovereign congress itself, by the executive, and by the other legitimate and loyal authorities of the country—declarations which disavow and declare null and of no effect, as against the sovereignty of the Mexican people, and without force or legal value, all acts done or which may be done by virtue of the power or under the influence of the foreign invader; and it declares that, in the constitutional orbit of its functions, remaining always at the side of the government which the nation, in the exercise of its sovereign will, manifested in conformity with its organic law, has freely established, until the next session of the national assembly shall take place, it will co-operate, with all the energy and self-devotion inspired by patriotism, in repelling force by force, and in using every means to disconcert and defeat the machinations of treason and of conquest, in order to maintain secure the independence, the sovereignty, the laws, and the perfect freedom of the republic.

FRANCISCO ZARCO, *President*.
JOAQUIN M. ALCALDE.
PONCIANO ARRIAGA.
BARTOLOME E. ALMADA.
JESUS CASTANEDA.
PEDRO CONTRERAS ELIZALDE.
JOSE DIAS CORAMBIAS.
FRANCISCO P. GOCHICOA.
SEBASTIAN LERDO DE TEJADA.
GENARO I. LEYVA.
IGNACIO OROZCO.
G. PRIETO.
MANUEL POSADA.
FELIX VEGA.

IGNACIO POMBO, *Deputy Secretary*.
SIMON DE LA GARZA Y MELO, *Deputy Secretary*.

SAN LUIS POTOSI, *July* 22, 1863.

Mr. Romero to Mr. Seward.

[Translation.]

MEXICAN LEGATION TO THE UNITED STATES OF AMERICA,
Washington, February 24, 1864.

MR. SECRETARY: As further proo fof the injustice and impropriety which, with such foundation, are attributed to the intervention which the French Emperor is pretending to establish in the Mexican republic by the statesmen and political writers of France, despite the many restrictions which hold the press enchained in that empire, I have the honor to enclose with this note, for the information of the government of the United States, a translation into English of an important pamphlet published lately in Paris, under the title of "Solution of the Mexican Question," by Mr. A. Malespine, editor of L'Opinion Nationale.

The statements and deductions contained in that pamphlet respecting the policy pursued in Mexico by the imperial government are of such nature that I think it proper to commend them to the consideration of the government of the United States.

I avail of this occasion to repeat to you, sir, the assurances of my most distinguished consideration.

M. ROMERO.

SOLUTION OF THE MEXICAN QUESTION.

BY A. MALESPINE.

I.

CAUSES OF THE FRENCH INTERVENTION.

It seems, in the first place, needless to look back to the causes which led to the French intervention in Mexico. The wrongs done to our fellow-countrymen in person and property have been many, and even the government of Juarez admits in principle the justice of our demands. He disputes, however, the amount of the indemnity claimed, and complains that he is charged with not only the material responsibility, but also the moral responsibility, of crimes done by his political adversaries.

The contested indemnities are those which are named in Article 1 and in Article 3 of the ultimatum laid down by the plenipotentiaries of France. These articles are thus stated:

"ARTICLE 1. Mexico engages to pay to France a sum of $12,000,000, at which the whole of the French reclamations are valued, rating the various wrongs up to the 31st of July last, 1861, and exclusive of the exceptions stipulated in Articles 2 and 4, hereinafter stated, and which relate to what has happened since the 31st of July last, for which a special reserve is made. The amount of the reclamations against Mexico which may spring from these causes will be fixed at a later period by the plenipotentiaries of France."

"ARTICLE 3. Mexico will be held to the full, faithful, and immediate fulfilment of the contract undertaken in the month of February, 1859, between the Mexican government and the house of Jecker."

The first figure of twelve millions of dollars has seemed, in fact, excessive, for the whole number of Frenchmen permanent residents of Mexico does not exceed, according to the latest official documents, 2,048. The demand for the entire and instant execution of the contract made between Miramon and the house of Jecker, reaching the large sum of $15,000,000, has also been judged to be too rigorous

These two demands gave rise in the beginning of the expedition to a first disagreement between the plenipotentiaries of France, of England, and of Spain.

As soon as Earl Russell was informed of the nature of the French reclamations by Sir Charles Wycke, he wrote to Lord Cowley, the English ambassador at Paris:

"It is surely not possible that reclamations so excessive as that of $12,000,000 in mass and without detailed account, and that of $15,000,000 for $750,000 received, can have been made with the hope of their being entertained."

M. Thouvenal hastened, by a despatch addressed to M. Dubois de Saligny, the 28th of February, 1862, to soften the too absolute nature of these demands. He wrote as follows:

"The figure at which this department felt itself obliged to value our reclamations did not reach that fixed by your Article No. 1; but, in the absence of sufficient elements of valuation, a great latitude is now left to you on this subject. While, therefore, I do not expressly ask you to reduce a sum which Sir Charles Wycke and General Prim both seem to have thought exorbitant, you may, nevertheless, be less exacting on this point if it prove too evident a cause of difference between the representatives of the three courts."

M. Thouvenal was further of opinion that if France still insisted on a large sum of indemnity, it was no longer necessary to exact reparation of another kind, whether for the death of the French consul at Tepic, or for the attempts upon the person of M. Dubois de Saligny in the month of August, 1861.

So far as the Jecker affair was concerned, M. Thouvenel declared that there was a distinction to be drawn between what immediately concerned our interests and what was foreign to them. At the time when the Jecker contract was signed the minister of France to Mexico had informed the French government that foreign commerce would be greatly relieved by this financial measure. It was only in this view that the French government insisted on its execution. But the question would be treated very differently if the house of Jecker* was to be alone, or almost alone, benefited by the fulfilment of the contract.

"I call your attention," said M. Thouvenel, "in conclusion, to the importance of separating in this affair all that may really affect interests which it is our duty to protect from what may affect other interests of a wholly different character. The actual government (the government of Juarez) cannot assume to deprive our countrymen of advantages assured to them by a regular measure passed by the administration of General Miramon for the single reason that this measure emanated from an enemy; but it would not be just for us, on the other hand, to impose upon the actual government (upon Juarez) obligations which do not necessarily flow from his governmental responsibility."

Finally, M. Drouyn de L'huys expressed himself in the following terms in a despatch of the 17th of August, 1863, addressed to General Bazaine:

"I have spoken of our reclamations. They are, as you are aware, general, of two kinds: those which are anterior to the war, and those which spring from the war itself. As to the first, they are all referred to the examination of a commission, which will be instituted in my department, and which will be organized in a manner to secure to its decisions an indisputable authority. The total amount to present to the Mexican government will include all the reclamations which shall be recognized by the commission as legitimate."

The despatches of M. Thouvenal and of M. Drouyn de L'huys materially diminish the ultimatum given to Juarez by M. Dubois de Saligny; and there is no doubt that Juarez would have instantly received and acted upon the reclamations of France if they had been thus presented in the beginning.

---

*To this it may be objected that M. Jecker is to-day a French citizen; but he was not naturalized until by the decree of the 20th of March, 1862, while the contract signed between him and the government of Miramon was dated the 29th of October, 1859.

But these sundry pecuniary reclamations were not the only cause of intervention. France seeks redress for other wrongs which are the result of the state of anarchy in Mexico for the last forty years Many of our countrymen have been attacked, robbed, murdered, and no reparation has ever been obtained, not even the punishment of the guilty. Be it always understood, however, that when the time arrived for general expiation in 1861, the crimes of all the governments and pretenders who, during the last twelve or fifteen years, have disputed the reins of power, were unjustly ascribed to Juarez and his partisans.

SOCIAL STATE OF MEXICO.—ORIGIN OF THE CHURCH PARTY.

It is necessary to go back further than fifteen years, and even more than a century, to attain a fair, impartial understanding of the social state of Mexico. Mexico had not, like the United States, the good fortune to be colonized by intelligent and laborious men, who sought in a new land an asylum from persecution. Like all other Spanish colonies, it has been given up to debauched and quarrelsome invaders, who disdained any other occupation than war, and who sought in America a people to persecute at their leisure.

Wherever Spain planted her flag she established a licentious despotism; she degraded labor by favoring with all her power the introduction and increase of black slaves; her greatest care was to keep all ranks in ignorance and superstition; she intrusted education only to the clergy, and charged the inquisition to watch over the publication of books; lastly, she thought to retain a perpetual hold on her colonies by isolating them from the rest of mankind, and by forbidding to her colonial subjects all direct commerce with foreign nations

Populations thus governed could have neither domestic nor social virtues, and if some Mexican creoles had not found means toward the close of the 18th century to visit Europe secretly, the struggle for independence would have been delayed until our day. These hardy travellers were imbued with the teachings of Voltaire and of Rousseau, and undertook, immediately on their return to their country, a propagande. They were burned, just as they would have been in the middle ages. But the first seeds were sown, and they so fructified, that in less than a quarter of a century all the Spanish colonies had conquered their independence. Yet this emancipation was not the result of a well-studied or understood need, and in Mexico even more than elsewhere it was exclusively the work of some leading minds. It did not bring any essential change in manners, nor dissipate all prejudice. Property was not divided, and the new clergy had neither less ambition than the old, nor less influence on the spirit of the people. It formed of the remnant of the privileged classes a party which, having on its side the wealth of the country and the religious influence, was, in fact, the most powerful of all those which partitioned out Mexico among themselves.

This party, which was then designated by the name of the Spanish church party, and which is known to-day as the reactionist or conservative, gradually prepared the way for a return of Mexico to the Spanish rule, and when it failed in all its efforts, endeavored to establish an independent monarchy, and looked to France to aid it to accomplish this object. Their proposals were rejected, but they would not give up the field, and shrank from no means to render intervention inevitable.

In 1838 took place the unfortunate expedition commanded by Admiral Baudin. The causes of this expedition are frankly set forth in a book by MM. Blanchard, Dauzats & Maissin, published in 1839, by order of the French government, under the auspices of Baron Tupinier, then minister of the marine:

"It is known that it is to the clerical party that the differences which have arisen between France and Mexico must be attributed This party wishes to bring back Mexico to monarchical rule, and has pushed it to a war with us in order to arrive at this end. Since the Algerian expedition, we are supposed to fear distant expeditions and foreign conquests. It is well known that the Algerian affair has disgusted us with the rôle of dupe. It is less known in Mexico than anywhere else. The priest party thought that by injustice, insult, and outrage, it would bring France to undertake the conquest of the Mexican republic, and that a monarchy would then be established. France seemed better suited than any other nation to carry out this vast design. Her humor is warlike. She chafes under injustice, even though its redress would involve a greater injury."

It is curious to compare these lines, written in 1839, with the following extract from "The London Times," of May 27, 1862, twenty years later, and five months after the beginning of the present intervention:

"We now understand the origin of the whole affair. The monarchy, with Archduke Maximilian for Emperor, was the idea of certain Mexican refugees, members of the reactionary or clerical party in Mexico, and partisans of Marquez and other ruffians, whose misdeeds have been among the principal causes of our intervention If Ferdinand Maximilian goes to Mexico, he will find his most active friends among the men who have shot, tortured, and robbed until Europe has at last lost patience."

OUTRAGES UPON FOREIGNERS BY THE CHURCH PARTY.

The conservative party has not ceased, in fact, to be guilty of such wrongs to foreigners as were most likely to provoke the intervention of France, England, and of Spain. We will recall a few of the most recent of these. An aide de-camp of President Zuloaga, in 1858, publicly and in the grossest manner insulted M. Brasseure, captain under the first empire and attached to the chancellory of France. Shortly after, twenty high clerical officers, among whom was General Miramon, attacked and beat three Frenchmen in the streets of Mexico Later, and while himself invoking the intervention of France, Miramon ordered one of his generals, Silverio Ramirez, to throw into prison the vice-consul of France at Zacatecas, M. Lacroix, who had refused to pay an illegal tax. In 1859 General Marquez ordered the frightful massacres of Tacubaya, and robbed a *conducta* on the road to San Blas. Lastly, on the 17th of November, 1860, Miramon, in broad daylight and by main force, carried off $660,000 from the English legation. "For forty years," says the report in which the Assembly of Notables set forth the motives which determined it to proclaim the Archduke Maximilian Emperor of Mexico, "for forty years Mexico has been governed by brigands, vagabonds, and incendiaries."

The Assembly of Notables has too soon forgotten that for forty years Mexico has almost always been governed by the party which to-day proclaims the throne in Mexico It has too soon forgotten, too, that twenty-two of the thirty-five members of the superior council were formerly ministers or judges of the supreme court; that two of the three high personages who compose the regency have been ministers, and that one of them, General Salas, was at one period, in 1847, provisional president, while then belonging to the liberal party.

We do not certainly pretend that the liberal party has been without fault. M. Thouvenel had ample ground for saying in his despatch of the 30th October, 1861, addressed to M. Dubois de Saligny, that the measures of the government of Juarez in 1861, a few months before intervention, to obtain means, displayed the same disposition to abuse authority as all those which had preceded it. But the abuses with which Juarez and his ministers are reproached should not lead us to forget the excesses committed by their opponents, and we have declared to them that if we may legitimately treat the former as enemies, there is no good reason to consider the others as friends whose past is any guarantee for their future conduct.

Perhaps it is to be regretted that circumstances have not permitted us to change the situation. Suppose, for instance, that Juarez had been our ally, and that he had aided us as efficiently and energetically as he has opposed us, there is no doubt that Mexico would be to-day at peace

This hypothesis leads us to regret that the premature presence in the French camp of certain Mexicans who are too well known deprived us of the opportunity of presenting ourselves as mediators. Perhaps there is yet time to appeal anew for an agreement with conditions acceptable to all, and of a nature to put an immediate end to the civil war, and to intervention. Before stating what, in our opinion, these acceptable conditions are, we think it useful to recall all that has been said as to the purpose of the French intervention. We will then sketch a rapid picture of the existing situation, and we will deduce from this showing the only possible solution of the question.

II.

THE FRENCH PROGRAMME.—THE EMPEROR'S INSTRUCTIONS.

The end which the French government proposes to attain by intervention in Mexico may be learned by an examination of the documents published, but no declarations so precise and formal as to leave no doubt as to the intentions of the government have been made upon this subject. M. Thouvenel wrote, October 11, 1861, that the legitimacy of our coercive measures in regard to Mexico only resulted, assuredly, from our grounds of complaint against the government of that country, and that these wrongs, as well as the means to redress them and prevent their repetition, could alone be made the object of an ostensible convention. Earl Russell, taking note of this declaration, demanded that it should be absolutely stipulated that the three powers should not interfere in the internal government of Mexico; but M. Thouvenel would make no engagement on this point; he was of opinion that the intervening powers, while leaving the Mexicans free as to the choice of their government, should not interdict in advance the possible exercise of a legitimate participation in events which might spring from the military operations.

M. Thouvenel, therefore, made certain reservations before signing the convention of the 31st October, and the cabinets of London and Madrid were perfectly aware that the French government proposed to itself a triple end:

1. To obtain redress for certain wrongs.
2. To aid the Mexicans in their work of regeneration.
3. To oppose to the too great expansion of the Anglo-Saxon race in the New World an insurmountable barrier, by restoring to the Latin race in Mexico its force and prestige.

This programme was completely and very clearly laid down in the letter written by the Emperor to General Forey the 3d of July, 1862, and as constant reference must be had to this important document, we think it of use to reproduce it at length. We may afterwards better understand what has been accomplished, and what remains for us to do.

THE EMPEROR TO GENERAL FOREY.

"FONTAINEBLEAU, *July* 3, 1862.

"MY DEAR GENERAL: At the moment when you are about to leave for Mexico, charged with political and military powers, I deem it useful that you should understand my wishes.

"This is the line of conduct which you are expected to pursue: 1. To issue a proclamation on your arrival, the principal ideas of which will be indicated to you. 2. To receive with the greatest kindness all Mexicans who may join you. 3. To espouse the quarrel of no party, but to announce that all is provisional until the Mexican nation shall have declared its wishes; to show a great respect for religion, but to reassure at the same time the holders of national property. 4. To supply, pay, and arm, according to your ability, the auxiliary Mexican troops: to give them the chief part in combats. 5. To maintain among your troops, as well as among the auxiliaries, the most severe discipline; to repress with vigor every act, every design, which might wound the Mexicans, for their pride of character must not be forgotten, and it is of the first importance to the success of the undertaking to conciliate the good will of the people.

"When we shall have reached the city of Mexico, it is desirable that you should have an understanding with the notable persons of every shade of opinion who shall have espoused our cause, in order to organize a provisional government. This government will submit to the Mexican people the question of the form of political rule which shall be definitively established. An assembly will be afterwards elected in accordance with the Mexican laws.

"You will aid the new government to introduce into the administration of affairs, and especially into the finances, that regularity of which France offers the best example. To effect this, persons will be sent thither capable of aiding this new organization.

"The end to be attained is not to impose upon the Mexicans a form of government which will be distasteful to them, but to aid them to establish, in conformity with their wishes, a government which may have some chance of stability, and will assure to France the redress of the wrongs of which she complains.

"It is not to be denied that if they prefer a monarchy it is in the interest of France to aid them in this path.

"Persons will not be wanting who will ask you why we propose to spend men and money to establish a regular government in Mexico.

"In the present state of the world's civilization Europe is not indifferent to the prosperity of America; for it is she which nourishes our industry and gives life to our commerce. It is our interest that the republic of the United States shall be powerful and prosperous, but it is not at all to our interest that she should grasp the whole Gulf of Mexico, rule thence the Antilles as well as South America, and be the sole dispenser of the products of the New World. We see to-day, by sad experience, how precarious is the fate of an industry which is forced to seek its raw material in a single market, under all the vicissitudes to which that market is subject.

"If, on the contrary, Mexico preserve its independence, and maintain the integrity of its territory, if a stable government be there established with the aid of France, we shall have restored to the Latin race on the other side of the ocean its force and its prestige; we shall have guaranteed the safety of our own and the Spanish colonies in the Antilles. We shall have established our benign influence in the centre of America, and this influence, while creating immense outlets for our commerce, will procure the raw material which is indispensable to our industry.

"Mexico thus regenerated will always be favorable to us, not only from gratitude, but also because her interests will be identical with our own, and because she will find a support in the good will of European powers.

"To-day, therefore, our military honor involved, the demands of our policy, the interest of our industry and our commerce, all impose upon us the duty of marching upon Mexico, there boldly planting our flag, and establishing perhaps a monarchy, if not incompatible with the national sentiment of the country, but at least a government which will promise some stability.

"NAPOLEON."

Here, certainly, is a magnificent programme: to assure the independence of Mexico, and to render her forever favorable to us through gratitude and interest; to establish the benign influence of France in the centre of America; to open immense outlets to our commerce, and new markets, where our industry may find the raw materials which are indispensable to it; to restore to the Latin race on the other side of the ocean its power and prestige.

CAN THE FRENCH PROGRAMME BE REALIZED?

But is it possible to realize this brilliant programme? Has Mexico the necessary elements for its transformation in a day into a great power? for it will need nothing less than a first-class power to restrain the ambition of the great American republic, whenever this republic seriously wishes to extend itself over Central America. Is it possible to establish a government of the Latin race which will give promise of any stability in a country seven-eighths of whose population are of the Indian race? Is it prudent to develop a new phase of the question of race, which has been and still is a subject of so much discord in America, and thereby still further complicate its solution? Can it be seriously believed that a country without industrial resources, without capital, without roads—at least at all adequate to its population—will all at once offer to our commerce immense outlets, or to our industry the indispensable raw material?

It was at least necessary to the unanimous and loyal acceptance of our intervention that the imperial programme should be strictly conformed to. Unfortunately, when General Forey arrived at Vera Cruz the political success of this enterprise had already been long compromised by the inopportune and arbitrary acts of M. Almonte. These acts were disavowed, but it was too late

A very remarkable pamphlet, which attracted great public attention, was published about six months since, under the title "What will we do in Mexico?" To-day we may ask "What have we done in Mexico?"

III.

PROGRESS OF THE INVASION.—PROVISIONAL GOVERNMENT.

General Forey made his entry into the capital of Mexico on the 12th of June, 1863, and immediately undertook, with the aid of M. Dubois de Saligny, to organize the municipal powers and a provisional government. One of his first acts was to subject the Mexican press to the rule which governs the French press.*

A Superior Council, or Junta, composed of thirty-five members, instituted by a decree of the 16th June, designated in its turn, as members of the executive powers, General Almonte, the archbishop of Mexico, and General Salas. The same Junta afterward summoned 215 persons as an Assembly of Notables.

The provisional government was therefore composed, first, of a Superior Council or Junta, named by General Forey; second, of a Triumvirate and of an Assembly of Notables designated by the Superior Junta.†

* A decree declaring null and void, as presenting an obstacle to the law of sequestration, all sales of property or of merchandise belonging to persons hostile to intervention, was, without doubt, annulled by the simple fact of cancellation by the French government of the decree relating to sequestration, rendered at Puebla on the 21st May.

† It has been incorrectly stated that "representatives of all parties, even of the Juarists," were included in the Superior Junta. This high council was composed of the following persons: José Ignacio Pavon, president of the supreme court under the dictatorship of Santa Anna; Manuel Diaz de Bonilla, minister of foreign affairs under Santa Anna; José Basilio Arrillaga, a priest of the Jesuit order; Teodosio Lares, minister of justice under Santa Anna; Francisco Xavier Miranda, priest, minister of justice under Miramon; Ignatio Aguilar y Marocho, minister of justice under Santa Anna; José Sallano, priest; Joaquin Velasquez de Leon, minister of finance under Santa Anna; Antonio Fernandez Monjardin, minister of justice under Santa Anna; Ignacio Mora y Villamil, general director of engineers under Santa Anna; Ignacio Sepulveda, judge of Mexico under Santa Anna; José Maria Andrade; Agapito de Munoz y Muroz; José Ildofonso Amable; Gerardo Garcia Rogas; Joaquin de Castillo y Lanzas, minister under Santa Anna and under Miramon; Mariano Dominguez, judge of the supreme court under Santa Anna; José Guadalupe Arriola, priest; Teofilo Marin, minister of justice under Miramon; General Adrien Woll, Frenchman, governor of the state of Tamaulipas under Santa Anna, and of Guadalajara under Miramon; Fernando Mangino, chargé d'affaires of Mexico in France under Santa Anna; José Miguel Arroyo, director of the department of foreign affairs under Santa Anna and Miramon; Miguel Cervantes, general and marquis of Salvatierra in the time of the Spaniards; Crispiano del Castello, minister under Santa Anna and Miramon; Alessandra Arango of Escaudon, one of the leading partisans of Miramon; Juan Hierro Maldonado, minister of finance under Miramon; Manuel Miranda, a Spanish merchant; José Lopez Ortigosa; Manuel Jimenez; Gajetano Montego; Santiago Blanco, general, minister of war under Santa Anna; Pablo Vergare, member of the supreme court under Santa Anna and under Miramon; Manuel Tejada, superintendent of church property; Urbano Tovar, secretary of the treasury under Miramon; Antonio Moran, director of the department of justice under Miramon.

The Assembly of Notables, at its first session, and without debate, voted for an imperial form of government, by a majority of 213 in a vote of 215. The Archduke Maximilian was immediately proclaimed Emperor by the same majority, and it was voted at the same session that in the case of refusal by the archduke, the Emperor Napoleon be urged to designate a substitute.

We find nowhere any question of a submission of the vote of the Assembly of Notables to ratification by universal suffrage. The decree by which the Superior Junta of the Assembly of Notables was constituted nowhere refers to an appeal to the people. The articles of this law or decree which relate to the form of government are thus stated:

"ART. 14. The Assembly of Notables will discuss in the first place the form of government to be *definitively* established in Mexico. The vote upon this question must embrace at least one-half of the suffrages.

"ART. 15. In case this majority shall not be obtained, the executive power will dissolve the assembly, and the Superior Junta will proceed without delay to form a new assembly.

"ART. 16. The members of the present assembly will be eligible to re-election.

"ART. 17. After having decided upon the form of government to be *definitively* established, the Assembly of Notables will take into consideration the questions which will be submitted to it by the executive power."

"ART. 23. The functions of the executive power will cease when the Assembly of Notables shall have proclaimed the inauguration of the definitive government."

The resolution adopted by the Assembly of Notables is in effect stated in absolute terms, and undertakes the definitive settlement of the question. This resolution declares that—

"The Mexican nation, through its organ, the Assembly of Notables, chooses the empire as its form of government, and proclaims the Archduke Maximilian, of Austria, Emperor."

The Assembly of Notables has deserved the reproaches which have been cast upon it from every quarter, of having acted with too great haste. It lost neither a day nor an hour. A deputation named by it, and charged with the offer of the crown to the Archduke Maximilian, left Vera Cruz the 18th of August to proceed to Miramar with the utmost speed. This deputation was composed of the following persons:

M. Gutierrez de Estrada, formerly minister of foreign affairs and ambassador of Mexico at the court of Rome, president of the deputation; Father Miranda, formerly minister of justice; M. Aguilar y Marocho, clerk of the commission named by the Assembly of Notables; M. J. Hidalgo, formerly secretary of the embassy; General Woll, Colonel Velasquez de Leon, M. Angel Iglésias.*

DEPARTURE FROM THE IMPERIAL PROGRAMME.

But the Assembly of Notables, in pretending to be the organ of the Mexican nation, and in *definitively* choosing the empire as the form of government, did not conform to the imperial programme. The Emperor had said in his letter to General Forey:

"When we shall have reached the city of Mexico, it is desirable that you should have an understanding with the notable persons of every shade of opinion who shall have espoused our cause, in order to organize a provisional government. This government will submit to the Mexican people the question of the form of political rule which shall be definitely established—an assembly will be afterward selected, in accordance with the Mexican laws."

M. Drouyn de Lhuys consequently hastened to remind General Bazaine, who had been named commander-in-chief of the French forces, that the imperial programme should be scrupulously followed.

"We have noticed with pleasure," he wrote on the 17th of August, 1863, "as a symptom of favorable augury, the manifestation of the Assembly of Notables in Mexico in favor of the establishment of a monarchy, and the name of the prince called to the empire. But, as I indicated to you in a former despatch, we can only consider the vote of this assembly as a first indication of the inclinations of the country. With the great authority which attaches to the men of mark which compose it, the assembly recommends to its fellow-citizens the adoption of monarchical institutions, and designates a prince for their suffrages.

"It is now the part of the provisional government to collect these suffrages in such a manner that no doubt shall hang over this expression of the will of the country. I shall not indicate to you the mode to adopt to completely obtain this indispensable result. It must be found in the institutions of the country and its local customs.

"Whether the municipalities should be summoned to declare their wishes in the different provinces, as fast as they regain their independence of action, or whether the polls should be opened under their authority to receive the votes, that mode will be the best

---

* Messrs. Gutierrez de Estrada and J. Hidalgo were already in Europe.

which will assure the largest manifestation of the popular voice under the best conditions of independence and sincerity. The Emperor, general, particularly commends this essential point to your constant care."

The vote of the Assembly of Notables is, therefore, in the opinion of the French government, only a *symptom of favorable augury, a first indication of the wish of the country.*

REPLY OF THE ARCHDUKE MAXIMILIAN.

The reply made by the Archduke Maximilian on the 3d of October, 1863, to the Mexican deputation is, moreover, in the same spirit. This is his reply :

"I am profoundly grateful for the wishes expressed by the Assembly of Notables.

"It cannot be other than flattering to our house that the thoughts of your countrymen turn to the descendants of Charles V.

"It is a proud task to assure the independence and the prosperity of Mexico under the protection of free and lasting institutions. I must, however, recognize the fact—and in this I entirely agree with the Emperor of the French, whose glorious undertaking makes the regeneration of Mexico possible—that the monarchy cannot be re-established in your country on a firm and legitimate basis unless the whole nation shall confirm, by a free manifestation of its will, the wishes of the capital.

"My acceptance of the offered throne must, therefore, depend upon the result of the vote of the whole country.

"Further, a sentiment of the most sacred of the duties of the sovereign requires that he should demand for the proposed empire every necessary guarantee to secure it against the dangers which threaten its integrity and its independence.

"If substantial guarantees for the future can be obtained, and if the universal suffrage of the noble Mexican people select me as its choice, I shall be ready, with the consent of the illustrious chief of my family, and trusting to the protection of the Almighty, to accept the throne.

"It is my duty to announce to you now, gentlemen, that in case Providence shall call me to the high mission of civilization which is attached to this crown, it is my fixed intention to open to your country, by means of a constitutional government, a path to a progress based on order and civilization, and as soon as the empire shall be completely pacified, to seal with my oath the fundamental agreement concluded with the nation.

"It is only in this manner that a truly national policy can be established, in which all parties, forgetting their ancient quarrels, will unite to raise Mexico to the high rank which she should attain under a government whose first principle will be law based on equity.

"I beg of you to communicate these my intentions, frankly expressed, to your countrymen, and to take measures to obtain from the nation an expression of its will as to the form of government it intends to adopt."

EUROPEAN OPINION OF THE ARCHDUKE'S REPLY.

This wise and noble reply, which was in conformity with the line of conduct traced by the French government, disappointed no one but the Mexican deputation.

"It will be understood," said the General Correspondence of Vienna of the 5th of October, "that the Archduke could not accept the offer of the Assembly of Notables (which has as yet only received adhesion from a small number of departments occupied by the French troops) so long as certain other conditions, and chiefly the effective support of the maritime powers, are as yet in the region of possibilities. England has not yet officially promised her support, although the public opinion of that country seems to favor the project."

The London Times, in fact, said on this subject on the 1st of October :

"The Archduke expects much from France and a little from England. He will deceive himself if he expects England to take an equal part with France in the aid to be given to Mexico. It is impossible that France can recall its troops after the arrival of Maximilian in Mexico. This would be to expose him to humiliation and to the return of anarchy. But it is impossible that England should ever join in a military occupation of Mexico. We will immediately recognize the Archduke. We will be friendly to Mexico, but nothing more."

The Times only repeated in other words what Lord Russell said in all his despatches.

IV.

THE FRENCH PROGRAMME—ITS DIFFICULTIES.

It results from all the documents quoted, and especially from the despatch addressed by M. Drouyn de Lhuys to General Bazaine, the 17th of August, 1863—

1. That France seeks in Mexico "neither conquest nor colonial establishment, nor even any political or commercial advantage to the exclusion of other powers."

2. That the French government expressly disavows any intention to substitute its influence for the free will of the Mexican nation, and that the desire of the Emperor's government is to limit. as promptly as circumstances will permit, the extent and length of our occupation.

3. That the Archduke Maximilian will not definitely accept the crown until the Mexican people, being consulted, shall have freely elected him, and until he shall have obtained every guarantee, necessary to assure the proposed empire against the dangers which threaten its integrity and its independence.

It is necessary, therefore, to collect as soon as possible the suffrages of the Mexican people, and, conforming to the instructions of M. Drouyn de Lhuys, it is in the institutions and local customs of the country that the mode must be sought to obtain this indispensable result in the most thorough manner.

These institutions and local customs are quite simple. Every Mexican who has a lawful occupation, of more than eighteen years of age if married, and of more than twenty-one years of age if unmarried, exercises the privileges of a citizen, and his name is inscribed on the electoral lists of the municipality to which he belongs.

But how shall the vote be taken? Shall the poll be declared open only in the localities occupied by the French troops, or in all Mexico? If in the former manner, the vote would not be the largest manifestation of the popular will, because the whole people would not be consulted; in the latter, the appeal could not be made known to them, and would consequently fall to the ground.

The situation may be understood at a single glance by a reference to the map which is added to this pamphlet. The French occupation is only effective in the part of the Mexican territory colored in red; and even this part of the territory is overrun by seventy-two hostile guerilla bands, averaging from seventy to three hundred men each. The freedom and purity of the ballot could, therefore, only be guaranteed in a portion of the territory of Mexico, relatively very small. Seven-eighths of the population of Mexico and twenty-nine thirtieths of its territory are beyond the lines of the French protection, as may be ascertained by an examination, without reference to the map, of some of the statistical and geographical details which follow.

V.

STATES, CAPITALS, AND POPULATION OF MEXICO.

Mexico is divided into 22 States, 6 Territories, and a Federal District.*

States.	Superficial or square miles.	Population in 1858.	Capitals.	Inhabitants.
Aguascalientes	2,739	88,329	Aguascalientes	39,693
Chiapa	18,679	167,472	San Cristobal	7,649
Chihuahua	83,512	164,073	Chihuahua	12,069
Coahuila	36,572	67,590	Saltillo	19,898
Durango	48,489	144,331	Durango	22,000
Guanajuato	11,396	729,103	Guanajuato	48,954

* The Constitution of 1857, made in this political division of Mexico the following alterations:

TITLE II—SECTION 2. ART. 43. The Mexican confederation is composed of twenty-four States and one Territory, the names of which are as follows: Aguascalientes, Colima, Chiapa, Chihuahua, Durango, Guanajuato, Guerrero, Jalisco, Mexico, Michoacan, Nuevo Leon and Cohahuila, Oajaca, Puebla, Queretaro, San Luis Potosi, Sinaloa, Sonora, Tabasco, Tamaulipas, Tlaxcala, the Valley of Mexico, Vera Cruz, Yucatan, Zacatecas, and the Territory of Lower California.

ART. 44. The States of Aguascalientes, Chiapa, Chihuahua, Durango, Guerrero, Mexico, Puebla, Queretaro, Sinaloa, Sonora, Tamaulipas, and the Territory of Lower California, retain the boundaries which they have had hitherto (1857.)

ART. 45. The States of Colima and of Tlaxcala retain, being erected into States, boundaries which they had when they were only Territories of the confederacy.

ART. 46. The State of the Valley of Mexico comprises the territory which has, until now, (1857,) formed the federal district; but it will only take rank as a State when the federal government shall have been removed to some other place.

ART. 47. The State of Nuevo Leon and Cohahuila, comprises the former Territory of Nuevo Leon and Cohahuila, unless the hacienda of Bonanza, shall be re-incorporated into the State of Zacatecas.

The other States, Guanajuato, Jalisco Vera Cruz, and San Luis Potosi, make some exchanges of towns, to rectify their frontier lines.

States.	Superficial or square miles.	Population in 1858.	Capitals.	Inhabitants.
Guerrero	32,003	279,109	Tixtla	6,501
Jalisco	48,591	804,058	Guadalajara	68,000
Mexico	19,539	1,129,629	Toluca	12,000
Michoacan	22,993	554,585	Morelia	25,000
Nuevo Leon	16,688	145,779	Monterey	17,309
Oajaca	23,642	525,938	Oajaca	25,000
Puebla	8,879	658,609	Puebla	71,631
Queretaro	1,884	165,155	Queretaro	29,702
San Luis Potosi	28,142	397,189	San Luis Potosi	19,678
Sinaloa	33,722	163,714	Caliacan	9,647
Sonora	100,228	139,374	Ures	6,009
Tabasco	12,359	70,628	San Juan Bautista	5,300
Tamaulipas	30,334	109,673	Victoria	4,621
Vera Cruz	27,415	349,125	Vera Cruz	9,647
Yucatan	48,869	668,623	Merida	23,575
Zacatecas	27,768	296,789	Zacatecas	15,427
Territories.				
Lower California	60,662	12,000	La Paz	1,254
Colima	3,019	62,109	Colima	31,774
Isla de Carman	7,298	11,807	V. del Carmen	3,068
Sierra Gorda	3,127	55,358	San Luis de la Paz	4,411
Tehuantepec	12,526	82,395	Minatitlan	339
Tlaxcala	1,984	90,158	Tlaxcala	3,463
District.				
Federal District	90	260,534	City of Mexico	205,000
Total	793,179	8,400,236		

The population has increased since 1793 at the following rate:

Years.	Population.	Years.	Population.
1793	5,273,029	1839	7,065,000
1803	5,873,100	1842	7,015,509
1808	6,500,000	1851	7,867,520
1824	6,500,000	1854	7,853,395
1830	7,996,000	1858	8,287,413

The population is composed of about 1,000,000 white, descendants of Europeans, 4,000,000 Indians, 6,000 blacks, and 3,400,000 metis (part white and part Indian) or mulattoes (part white and part black.) The foreigners, to the number of 9,234 in 1838, are classed as follows: Spaniards, 5,141; French, 2,048; English, 615; Germans, 681; Americans, 444; miscellaneous, 405.

VI.

AN EXPRESSION OF MEXICAN OPINION IMPOSSIBLE.

The orders sent by Mr. Drouyn dė Lhuys to General Bazaine, the 14th of August last, could not be executed. The commander-in-chief saw the impossibility of obtaining a popular ratification of the vote of the Assembly of Notables so long as seven hundred thousand inhabitants only were under the protection of France, and more than seven millions still clung to Juarez or his partisans. Rightly or wrongly, if the polls had been declared open under such circumstances, the provisional government would have been accused of the exercise of a pressure, in the part of the country occupied by it, contrary to the freedom of the ballot. On the other hand, it would have been a strange delusion to suppose that the adversaries of intervention would permit a resort to a regular election in the immense territory not yet occupied.

Too early an announcement was made that the organization of the new political *régime* had replaced the power of arms. Such was not the opinion of General Bazaine, whose position well enabled him to survey the field, for he determined a new campaign against Juarez to be absolutely necessary. Great preparations have been made, and the latest news left the expeditionary forces masters of Queretaro. But no matter how skilfully and energetically this campaign may be managed, a prompt conclusion cannot be looked for.

Juarez will not risk everything on a single engagement. He will take good care not to er battle, and he will use every effort to avoid one. Everything leads to the belief that he will persist in the tactics which he has followed since the surrender of Puebla. He will abandon San Luis Potosi, just as he has abandoned Mexico and Queretaro. He will beat a continual retreat before the French army, confining himself to the distribution of a large part of his force into guerilla bands.

Shall we continue to pursue these forces, which ever evade our grasp, into a mountainous country, extremely difficult of access to a regular army, and in which we shall be obliged to leave garrisons in every town and village, and to distribute all along the roads flying columns to secure the safety of our communications? The effective numbers of the expeditionary corps would soon prove insufficient to such a task, and prudence would not permit us to leave too far in the rear, and exposed to a *coup de main*, Cordova, Orizaba, Puebla, and Mexico.

A MILITARY SOLUTION POSTPONED.

A solution of this question by force of arms seems, therefore, to be indefinitely postponed, unless the French expeditionary corps shall be trebled or quadrupled; and such is certainly not the intention of the French government, since M. Drouyn de l'Huys has ordered General Bazaine to take measures to limit, as promptly as circumstances will admit, the extent and length of our occupation.

These circumstances will spring up of their own accord as soon as a stable and truly national government shall have succeeded the provisional government inaugurated the 18th of June. We may then retire; the end proposed by our intervention will have been fulfilled, and we shall be finally free from our responsibility. But this result, so much desired, cannot, we fear, be obtained within any short period of time unless by the proclamation of a suspension of hostilities, during which the question of what form of political rule they shall prefer definitely to establish may be submitted to the Mexican people. The mode to obtain this is very simple:

PROPOSED SOLUTION BY AN ARMISTICE AND A BALLOT.

1. An armistice of three months.
2. During the armistice an appeal to be made to the people.
3. The electoral processes will be carried out under the supervision of an equal number of agents chosen by the provisional government in power at Mexico, and of agents named by President Juarez. Commissioners delegated by the commander-in-chief of the French forces will take care that the vote shall be surrounded by every possible guarantee of independence.
4. The people will be called upon to vote for the establishment of an empire, according to the wish expressed by the Assembly of Notables, or for the maintenance of the republic and of the constitution of 1852.
5. Juarez will engage to abide by the new order of things, or to quit the country, in case the vote of the Assembly of Notables shall be ratified by the people. If Juarez, on the contrary, or any other candidate of the liberal party, shall obtain the majority of the votes, the French occupation would no longer have any purpose.

Whatever might be the result of the vote, France would certainly obtain the redress of its wrongs. If the people pronounce in favor of the re-establishment of the empire, the Archduke Maximilian could proceed without apprehension to receive the crown which has been tendered to him, for the submission or withdrawal of Juarez would end all serious opposition. If, on the contrary, Juarez should receive the majority of the votes, his re-election under such solemn conditions would give him the moral force which he lacks, and the clerical party, knowing well that it need never count again upon a European intervention, would stop its intrigues.

The government of Juarez represents the abolition of political privileges, civil equality, the union of two races which for three centuries have been kept forcibly apart—the Indians and the creoles. What motive could be assigned for refusing to treat with him if he should be, for the third time, regularly proclaimed president? He has been reproached with a wish to dismember Mexico for the benefit of the United States. But he will not linger in the trying situation against which he has had to struggle for the last six years, and he will hereafter find his interest in maintaining the integrity of Mexico. And further, what better guarantees can the conservatives give in this respect? Did not Santa Anna sell to the United States, in 1854, the Mesilla valley for the sum of fifty millions of francs, ($10,000,000,) and did not Mr. Almonte himself, at that time minister of Mexico at Washington, approve this sale and receive the first payment, reaching the sum of thirty-five millions of francs, ($7,000,000?)

It has been falsely stated that there was a perfect unity in the views and action of the conservatives. On the contrary, the conservatives are very much divided; the archbishop of Mexico and General Salas, in tendering their resignations as members of the provisional executive power, afford a new proof of this fact.

We cannot, therefore, see what good reason there is to prefer the conservatives to the liberals.

The Emperor said in his letter to General Forey, the 3d July, 1862:

"The end to be attained is not to impose upon the Mexicans a form of government which will be distasteful to them, but to aid them to establish, in conformity with their wishes, a government which has some chance of stability, and will assure to France the redress of wrongs of which she has had to complain."

Why pursue the struggle and persist in so useless a spilling of blood, from which there cannot even result any glory to our arms? Would it not be more wise and simple not to treat with Juarez, but to proclaim on both sides a suspension of hostilities, during which the people shall freely and finally decide between the two parties in opposition—between the conservatives and the liberals? The Mexican people will be taken as the arbiter of its own destinies, and the essential part of the imperial programme will receive within a very short period its full application. We will bring to an honorable end a costly enterprise. we will avoid all danger of a collision with the United States, and we will have besides. on the eve, perhaps, of a European struggle, the free disposal of our land and naval forces

---

Mr. Romero to Mr. Seward.

[Translation.]

MEXICAN LEGATION TO THE UNITED STATES OF AMERICA,
Washington, February 25, 1864.

Mr. SECRETARY: I have the honor to transmit to you, annexed to this note, a translation into English of the discourses pronounced in the French legislative body by Mr. Gueroult, Mr. Thiers, Mr. Berryer, and Mr. Favre, during the discussions which took place in that assembly on the affairs of Mexico on the 25th, 26th, and 27th days of January last past. The speeches referred to are translated from the official text thereof as it was published in the Moniteur Universel, official paper of the French government, in the Nos. 26, 27, and 28, answering to the 26th, 27th, and 28th of the said January.

The orators of whom I have made mention had, for purpose, political censure of the course followed by the French government in its expedition against Mexico, and they considered it either in the point of view of advantage to France only, as did Mr. Thiers, or under the more elevated aspect of the justice of intervention and the motives or pretexts of the war, which engaged the attention of Mr. Favre.

I think it possible to say that, although there are in said speeches some sufficiently serious and substantial inaccuracies, which are patent to all who are well informed of the facts which had happened in Mexico, they constitute a deliberate and solemn rebuke of the imperial policy, made (and this is worthy of note) by the most distinguished and respected representatives of the nation for whose benefit it is pretended to carry out the intervention.

I do not include the speeches made by the organs of the French government in defence of the imperial policy, because, besides the supposition that the said government will take care to give them wide circulation, and that they will reach the department through other channels, they contain inaccuracies of such nature, that it would not be proper for me to send them to the government of the United States without exposing the inaccuracies to which I allude, and this would be a greater labor than I can at present undertake, being, moreover, of little use, on the supposition that the defences attempted to be made of the Napoleonic policy were so feeble that, taking for granted as true all the facts and reasons alleged by the imperial organs, that policy would forever rest condemned in the opinion of impartial and right-minded men.

I avail of this opportunity to repeat to you the assurances of my most distinguished consideration.

M. ROMERO.

Hon. WILLIAM H. SEWARD, *&c., &c., &c.*

Debate in the French legislative body, on the affairs of Mexico.

Corps Legislative, Session of the 25th of January.—Presidency of his Excellency the Duc of Morny.

The PRESIDENT. Now, gentlemen, we pass to the 6th paragraph, relative to China, Cochin-China, and Mexico. It is as follows:

"The legislative body believes with you, sire, that the most wisely-governed nations cannot flatter themselves that they will always escape external complications, and that they ought to regard them without illusions as without weakness The distant expeditions to China, Cochin-China, and Mexico, which have succeeded each other, have, in fact, disquieted many persons in France, on account of the obligations and sacrifices which they entail. We acknowledge that they ought to inspire respect afar for our countrymen and for the French flag, and that they can, therefore, develop our maritime commerce; but we will be happy to see the speedy realization of the good results which your Majesty gives us reason to hope."

The first amendment which is presented is that of Messrs. Guéroult, Magnin, A. Darimon, Jules Simon, Hénon, Havin, Jules Favre, Lanjuinais, Dorian, Eugene Pelletan, Ernest Picard, and Emile Ollivier. The amendment is couched in the following terms:

"We see with pain that the government persists in the Mexican expedition. We cannot associate ourselves with this ruinous enterprise; and we are the interpreters of public opinion when we demand that it should be brought to an immediate termination."

M. Guéroult is entitled to the floor

M. GUÉROULT Gentlemen: It has now become almost commonplace to come and criticise the Mexican expedition. That expedition is not popular. The uncertain or but little known causes which have produced it, its problematical results, the considerable sums which it has cost, the sacrifices of men mowed down by war or disease, all have brought a certain unpopularity on this expedition. So my intention, in addressing you now, is not to criticise the details of accomplished facts or actions already brought about by our generals or by the chiefs of the expedition. I am going to examine, in your presence, the causes which led to the Mexican expedition—the apparent causes and the real causes—in the hope, if we succeed in pointing out the prime idea of the expedition, to show you that this idea is wanting in justness This result would not be useless. We will not demand of an expedition to obtain results which the very nature of things does not permit it to reach; we will then show ourselves less severe and less exacting in regard to the conditions on which we can put an end to this disastrous expedition. What are the causes which gave occasion for the Mexican expedition? I speak, first, of the apparent causes. They are, outrages inflicted for a long period on our countrymen—extortions, exactions of every kind, assassinations in great number; an attempt even of assassination committed on the person of the representative of France.

It would seem, at first sight, that all these causes combined would suffice to explain the motives for a declaration of war, and yet, on a closer examination, we reach the conviction that, if there had been no other motives, the expedition should never have taken place.

In fact, gentlemen, the exactions, the extortions, the violences are real. They have been very numerous. But, seriously and sincerely, can a European power demand that, in a country given up to civil war, rent asunder by anarchy, our countrymen who go thither with full knowledge of these facts, and perfectly aware of the state of disorder into which the country is plunged, can enjoy a security which is not accorded to the people of the country themselves?

This consideration is so strong, that for a long time there were numerous causes of complaint in Mexico which never resulted in the application of any remedy, either on account of the difficulty of the expedition itself, or by reason of this general sentiment with regard to the state of the country. I do not think that these reasons were the principal reasons, the fundamental ones, of the expedition; and if you will allow me, I will proceed to seek them elsewhere, and in a higher sphere

Gentlemen, in the treaty signed between France, Spain, and England, under date of October 31, 1861, no disposition foreign to the causes which I have just enumerated is mentioned. "This expedition is undertaken to insure, by means of combined action in common, efficacious protection to the persons and property of their respective countrymen in Mexico."

In article 2 it is said that, "The high contracting parties engage not to seek for themselves, in the employment of the coercive measures provided for by the present convention, any acquisition of territory or any particular advantage, and not to exert in the internal affairs of Mexico any influence of a character calculated to infringe on the right of the Mexican nation to choose and freely establish the form of its government."

You see, gentlemen, in the commencement there is question only of reparation to be exacted.

However, it is evident that among the three contracting parties one at least entertained greater projects. In fact, when the three combined armies had arrived in Mexico, there were at first, as you know, preliminaries signed at La Soledad, subsequently disavowed by the French government; finally conferences took place at Orizaba, in which a rupture occurred. We are perfectly aware of the motives of it. The proceedings of the conference of Orizaba have been published, and from them it appears that General Almonte was present in the camp of the allies; that he asked their protection, in order to march against Mexico; that he put forth the idea that no treaty, no arrangement, should be entered into between the allies and the Mexican government. Moreover, he enunciated the idea that the allied armies were going to Mexico to overthrow the Mexican government and to establish a monarchy. He proclaimed himself as authorized for this purpose by the very words of the sovereign of France. Hereupon ensued a rupture, which is yet present to the memory of all. The Spanish army withdrew, England followed; France remained alone in Mexico, and pursued the expedition on her own account.

After some military events, on which it is useless to insist, a new commander, General Forey, was sent out. Here the idea, which, in my opinion, is the real idea of the expedition, shows itself with the greatest clearness. In a letter which you all remember, a letter addressed by the Emperor to General Forey, we read:

"There will not fail to be persons who will ask you why we proceed to expend men and money to found a regular government in Mexico.

"In the actual state of the civilization of the world, the prosperity of America is not a matter of indifference to Europe, for it is it that supports our manufactures and gives life to our commerce. We have an interest that the republic of the United States should be powerful and prosperous, but we have none that it should possess itself of the whole Gulf of Mexico, thence dominate over the Antilles as well as over South America, and be the sole dispensator of the products of the New World. We now see, by sad experience, how precarious is that sort of industry which is reduced to look for its raw material to one quarter only in all the vicissitudes of which it is thus compelled to participate.

"If, on the contrary, Mexico preserves its independence and maintains the integrity of its territory, if a stable government is established there with the assistance of France, we shall have rendered to the Latin race, on the other side of the ocean, its due strength and its prestige; we shall have guaranteed their proper security to our colonies in the Antilles and to those of Spain; we shall have established our beneficent influence in the centre of America; and that influence, in creating immense outlets for our commerce, will procure us those staples that are indispensable for our industry.

"Mexico, thus regenerated, will always be favorable to us, not only through gratitude, but also because its interests will be in unison with our own, and because it will find a powerful means of support in its friendly relations with the European powers."

There is here evidently a very grand and very lofty thought, that of opposing a barrier to the invasion of the Anglo-Saxon race.

The idea of raising up the Latin and Catholic races in opposition to the Anglo-Saxon and Protestant races is certainly a grand political idea. It only remains to be known whether this idea is as practicable as it is great. It is upon this point that I entertain doubts, which are confirmed by a residence of four years that I have spent in Mexico, and by the attentive observation which I have made of its manners and its institutions. Permit me here to enter into some details.

I commence by asserting that it appears evident to me that this idea of constituting an empire in Mexico would not have entered into the views of the French government had not a most important event, the civil war in the United States, been inaugurated a few months previously. It was in the month of January, (March,) 1861, if I am not mistaken, that the first cannon shots were exchanged at Charleston between the south and the north of the United States; it was in the month of June that complaints became urgent on the part of the French legation in Mexico; it was in the month of October that the treaty was signed between the three interfering powers.

It seems, then, that these two elementary notions, the desire of withdrawing our commerce from the preponderating influence of the United States in furnishing a precious staple, cotton, and the idea of a political equilibrium, perhaps of a religious equilibrium, combined to urge on this expedition.

Well, it is from this point of view that I propose to myself to examine the Mexican expedition, abstracting entirely, I repeat, from any criticism of details which has been already most satisfactorily done, and in regard to which I could only repeat what has been better said than I am capable of doing.

It was projected, then, gentlemen, to establish an empire in Mexico. It was evident that such an establishment could not be agreeable to the Americans of the north. Therefore, it was calculated upon, and strongly hoped, that a division should be effected between the south and the north. This desire has become so strong that it has degenerated into a mania, and that, as you remember, the whole French press friendly to the government has shown itself remarkably favorable to the cause of the south, even to the point of offending the north; and you remember that, in the course of last summer, the displeasure of the north had reached such a point that a Russian fleet, coming to rendezvous at New York, was received with an enthusiasm so great that we may be allowed to see in it a certain amount of irritation against France.

This partiality for the south, if we abstract from the reasons which I have indicated, was not really natural. France was an enemy of slavery. Now, whatever may have been said of it, there was no other cause of separation between the north and the south than slavery. [Cries of no, no, from several benches.]

Several members. Yes, yes.

M. Guéroult. Gentlemen, it is not for questions of tariffs that nations rend themselves with their own hands; they are merely transitory. It is so true that slavery was the principal and, I shall say, the only cause of war, [renewed cries of No, no,] that when President Lincoln was nominated, the southern States, which up to that time had enjoyed the privilege of furnishing Presidents to the republic, did not await the manifestation of his policy; they rushed to arms and declared war. And since that time questions of tariffs have disappeared; they are spoken of no more; there is no longer any question but that of slavery. [Manifestations of various kinds.]

Gentlemen, I do not pretend to force your convictions [No, no;] but I tell you that I have carefully examined the question, and I merely ask permission to lay before you my sentiments.

In the south slavery has become almost a religious institution; it has its philosophy and, I will say, almost its theology founded on the Bible. It is on the words pronounced against Ham, "Thou shalt serve thy brethren," that this idea is based There are preachers who preach these doctrines in the south, and who find themselves authorized to seek the sanction of slavery in that grand code of freedom for slaves, the gospel.

All this is opposed to our feelings, and yet we have inclined to the cause of the south. There is evidently a cause for this. That cause I have already declared to you. It was thought that the formation of a new state to the south of the great American republic and interposing between Mexico and the north would constitute a sort of barrier between the two nations, and that the new government which it was wished to found in Mexico might gain strength and consistency under the protection of this barrier.

If you will allow me to say so, I believe that the idea of the separation and final triumph of the south was not just. I believe that the immense disproportion which exists between the north and the south will necessarily result in the triumph of the north. I believe that this triumph will be due as well to the preponderance as to the superiority of northern industry, and then, above all, to the fact that liberty exists in the north and slavery in the south. [Marks of approbation from some benches, of disapprobation from most.]

But I go further, and I assert that, on the supposition even that the south will triumph, the south would not and could not be the sincere ally of Mexico. Gentlemen, you remember all those piratical and filibustering expeditions, undertaken by Lopez against Havana, by Walker against Nicaragua, all those attempts at conquest, that invasion of Texas, about fifteen years ago. All these attempts at aggrandizement were a political necessity for the south; slavery, left to itself and not propagated, was necessarily borne down and overthrown by the movement of ideas and of interests. It was necessary to seek recruits in order to repair the losses which were experienced. Now, I assert that, even if the south should succeed in effecting a separation, it would be found an ally of a few days perhaps, but one which, threatened on the north by its rival, would be more than ever pressed to expand itself into Mexico itself with all the energy which characterizes the race inhabiting the south of the republic, and the consequence would be that the establishment which we propose to make in Mexico would have for its first enemy that very south, on the alliance of which we had counted.

From this point of view, the idea was not well founded. But this is not all. To found an empire, the requisite elements are necessary. It is not enough to change the form of government, to change its name, in order to regenerate it.

The Mexican republic had reached a very sad condition. It is not I who assert it; it is the delegates of the Junta, or of the Assembly of Notables, as they call it, I believe, who, being sent to the Archduke Maximilian to offer him the throne, express themselves as follows in reference to their country:

"After this, it is not surprising to see highway robbers occupy the most elevated posts, to see the dilapidation of the revenues of the treasury, that of the goods of the clergy confiscated unjustly and without any profit to the country. The so-called reform has gathered around it only vagabonds and bandits, who, under this popular standard, very popular standard indeed, have ravaged, burned the harvests and villages, and sacked the large cities," &c., &c. I suppress the rest.

It is certain that there has been, and that there is yet, immense disorder in Mexico. Now, truly, it would be a very pretty thing to believe that, because in the place of a President you will have a chief who will style himself Emperor, everything will be transformed, that this chronic disorder will disappear, that prosperity will be renewed, in a word, that there will be founded a potent state of society, of such a character as to insure respect to itself. Let us not forget that the troubles, the misfortunes, the civil war, which now desolate the United States are a temporary accident. In one way or other this war will have an end, and then you may be assured that the republic or the republics of the United States will regard with evil eye the establishment of a monarchical flag on their frontiers.

It has been said that we have no concessions to make to this American prejudice which wishes that the powers of Europe should have no right to take possession of any part of the soil of any portion of American territory.

I do not examine their right in this matter, but I ask you whether it is possible for France to wage war against a republic with which we have always maintained the best understanding, against a republic which owes to us, in a great measure, its independence, which sympathizes with us, and which constitutes for us a useful and often indispensable counterpoise to the naval power of England.

However, we have gone to Mexico and we desire to create, to prepare a new government for Mexico. Mexico, you know, was divided, like most other countries, into two great factions, the clerical party and the liberal party.

The clerical party is in Mexico pretty much what it is everywhere else, powerful, rich, marvellously skilful in appropriating to itself the richest and most fertile lands, but, as a political party, behind the age, intolerant, exclusive, aiming at impossibilities. To it religious toleration is the abomination of desolation; to it liberty of worship, liberty of the press, all liberty, in a word, is the height of anarchy and disorder; it can make no compromise whatever with the principles which are now the very principles of modern society. The clerical party was for a long time dominant in Mexico, and the sad state in which this domination placed Mexico proves that its administration was not good.

Desperate efforts have been made for some years by a fraction of the country to deliver it from the brutalizing system bequeathed to it by Spain. This is what has given birth to what is called the liberal party.

I do not come here to pronounce the apology of the Mexican liberal party. That party, like the other—both almost alike in fact—bears the traces of the unfortunate condition to which the country has been reduced.

But, in the end, the principles of the liberal party are our principles; they are the principles professed by the members of this assembly, the principles of the French revolution and of modern civilization. To sustain them, that party makes efforts unfortunately combined with acts of violence which I do not wish to justify, no more than I wish to justify those of their adversaries.

But, in the end, if we were absolutely forced, which I do not believe we are, to interfere in the affairs of that country, I assert that our natural ally would be the party that professes the same principles that we do, and not the party against which we are obliged to struggle in France, against which we are obliged to struggle at Rome, [murmurs of dissatisfaction from some benches,] and which everywhere teaches, as an article of faith, the very negation of the principles which form the basis of modern public law.

Voices around the speaker. Good, good.

M. Guéroult. We have, then, gentlemen, relied on the clerical party.

I willingly pass over any reference to certain acts of the French administration, unfortunate sequestrations, irritating measures of sequestration applied to the property of persons who were only guilty, after all, of defending what they believed to be the independence of their country. For, in brief, this expedition has been commenced with the declaration that it was undertaken in order to deliver Mexico. To deliver Mexico! From whom, and from what? Where is the foreigner attacking Mexico? If they fight in Mexico, it is the Mexcans themselves that fight, and it seems to me that the species of liberation which we have undertaken in their favor singularly resembles that which the Prussians pretended to exercise in our regard when they invaded France in 1792 and in 1815.

Several voices. That's true! Good!

M. Guéroult. The Mexicans are not at all thankful to us for the service which we wish to render them. They only ask one thing of us, that is, that we should stay at home and let them attend to their own business in peace.

At present, as the country is fatigued, as a new *régime* is promised to it, as the French army, with its admirable discipline, reconciles by its presence even those whose hopes it goes to overthrow, it happens that there is a sort of pacification in Mexico, and that we have been well received there in the beginning. But the difficulties have not been slow to manifest themselves.

There has been a Junta instituted in the city of Mexico. A decree of the French authorities has instituted that Junta, which itself has nominated an Assembly of Notables. All this is done under French influence. That Assembly of Notables, which was said to contain representatives of all opinions, I have a list of here with the designation of all the members; not one of them belongs to what is called the liberal party.

But at last a provisional government composed of three members has been placed over all this machinery. This is composed of the archbishop of Mexico, General Almonte, (who has played a considerable part in this whole affair, and who, it is said, was the first instigator of the expedition,) and, lastly, General Salas.

It was not very difficult to foresee that this alliance with the clerical party would not hold together, and if you will permit me I will proceed to read to you some sentences written in the month of August last, and which are no more than an anticipated narrative of the events which I will presently lay before you:

"The presence of the archbishop of Mexico in the provisional government is indicative of a state of things full of difficulties When General Forey expresses the desire that liberty of worship should be acknowledged, he renders himself the exponent of a sentiment wholly French; but he need not count on the assistance of the archbishop of Mexico to cause it to be proclaimed. It is not in his part, nor in the nature of things. Our bishops, who have been living for seventy-four years under the *régime* of the freedom of worship, have not yet recognized it. The Pope does not recognize it; we cannot expect, then, that the Mexican clergy should recognize it merely to gratify the Emperor.

"We are proceeding, then, to find ourselves placed in the alternative either of obeying the inspirations of the party which calls us to Mexico, and then of disavowing, as far as lies in our power, all the principles for which we have been contending for three-quarters of a century, or else to proclaim French principles authoritatively, and then to turn our only partisans against us and combine in hostility towards us the liberals whom we have overthrown, and the clericals whom we have rejected.

"Doubtless France is strong enough to make her will prevail; but while consulting her own sentiments she cools those of her partisans and runs the risk of being isolated, placed as she would be between those who are already indisposed against her for having come to Mexico and those who will be indisposed against us for having come there in order to oppose them in their absurd projects of reaction.

"At bottom, it is the Roman question which is going to be reproduced on the other side of the ocean, at the distance of two thousand leagues from our frontiers."

SEVERAL MEMBERS. From what paper? Who is the author of that article?

M. GUEROULT. What I have read is an article from the *Opinion Nationale*. [Exclamations.] If I have permitted myself to read this article, it is because at this hour events have completely justified it; I shall proceed to give you the proofs of it.

Moreover, I will confess to you, after the manner in which the press has been spoken of in this hall for some time past, while the minister of state has told us that the effect of the press was to lead astray, to distort and to inflame public opinion; after having heard the press defended by arguments which appeared to me still worse and more sorry than the attacks, I am not displeased to be able to show you that the press sometimes happens to study and to see clearly into questions, to announce in advance that which is likely to happen, and to give counsels which the government would not do ill to follow.

M. GRANIER DE CASSAGNAC. That is what remains to be demonstrated.

M. GUEROULT. These conflicts, announced as likely to occur between the clerical party and the French authorities, are in course of development at this very moment.

Lastly, several judges had refused, on the intimation of certain members of the regency, to take cognizance of all cases relative to the goods of the clergy, which have been secularized in Mexico as they have been in France. An order interposed issued in a very irregular way; it was not signed by the representatives of French authority; it was signed only by an under secretary of state. This order enjoined on the judges to take cognizance in future of all such questions as they had wished to abstain from.

The archbishop of Mexico, Monseigneur Labastida, immediately protested; I have here the protest which I would read to you if I did not fear to abuse your patience.

SEVERAL MEMBERS. Read it, read it.

OTHER MEMBERS. No, no.

M. GUEROULT. And from this time forward the acts of the regency are signed only by General Almonte and General Salas The signature of "Labastida" no longer figures in them. Here, then, is a commencement of dissension.

Finally, gentlemen, we have arrived at a critical period. It is necessary to take some step. Since the expedition was undertaken, since it succeeded, since we took Puebla first and subsequently the city of Mexico itself, the candidacy of the Archduke Maximilian has been brought forward, has been affirmed, now it is considered as settled. I desire, with all my heart, that the Archduke Maximilian should accept; I admire his courage, and I would not wish to shake him; [laughter;] only I would attach a great importance to the fact that France should not be responsible for anything that might be produced under the new *régime* which is to be installed in Mexico. I would not wish her to guarantee any loans. I would not wish her to leave her army in Mexico; for, if her army should remain in Mexico, not only would she contract a kind of responsibility and identification of herself with all the events that might transpire there, but she would come in contact with an eventuality which would seem to me very much to be dreaded, and which might carry us very far beyond the sphere of the interests for which we have desired to provide. [Approbation from some benches.]

It is not doubtful, gentlemen, that as soon as the civil war shall be terminated in the United States, you will see the United States regard with a most evil eye this monarchical establishment installed on their frontiers. Governments, governments of principle especially, are jealous, and you would certainly have no more reason to be displeased with the United States for not regarding with a favorable eye a monarchical establishment on their frontiers, than you would be astonished if the imperial government of France saw with an evil eye the establishment in Belgium of a republic, for example.

SMOE VOICES. What would that have to do with us?

M. GRANIER DE CASSAGNAC. And Switzerland.

M. GUEROULT. Switzerland has not been recently established. It was anterior to our government, which found it as it was, and must have accepted the neighborhood. But I believe that the propagandism of a different principle is never acceptable or agreeable to a neighboring government.

In any case, it is incontestable that the situation in which we would be placed by this eventuality of a war with the United States is out of all proportion with what wisdom and the simplest elements of good sense would allow us to risk on that side. What interest have we in Mexico? I have examined the question in a manner rather philosophic than political. In good faith, what was it that obliged us to go to Mexico? What immediate advantage can we derive from the measure? Do you think that we can effect an establishment there which, in a given time, could cover our expenses? We have in Algeria an example which I pray you to consider. Here are thirty-four years that Algeria is in our hands; it does not pay expenses. If you are in a condition to assume the guardianship of Mexico for fifty years, and to spend there 150 millions a year, I doubt not but that at this price you would reach a favorable result; but I doubt whether any of you would be willing to engage in such an enterprise. The most reasonable step, in my opinion, would be to return and to return immediately.

Since the last accounts that reached us from Mexico, it seems that instructions more conciliatory and based on a more exact knowledge of the country have reached General Bazaine, whose excellent intentions are appreciated both by the Mexicans and by the French. I say instructions more conciliatory; in fact, less harshness is manifested towards adversaries, and if a work of conciliation could be attempted, it would certainly be under these auspices. Well, all I ask is that the government should be pleased to give us some assurances in this respect.

In the amendment which we have presented, and which I have the honor to develop before you, we demand an immediate withdrawal. I request permission to explain this expression. I did not draw up the amendment, but I signed it. I pray you to allow me to tell you how I understand it. It is clear that the immediate withdrawal of our troops cannot be demanded. [Interruption.]

A VOICE. Wherefore do you demand it for the amendment?

M. GUEROULT. It is clear that everything cannot be abandoned in twenty-four hours; but what can be done is to take immediately a firm resolution not to prolong an expedition which, it must be said, is a failure. [Vehement disapprobation.]

You may be persuaded, gentlemen, that we will obtain nothing from Mexico; you may be persuaded that if France wished to be stubborn and to remain there in order to defray the expenses of the expedition, she would do as bad a thing as she did when, to insure the payment of a debt of 60 millions, she spent 300 millions. Persist now, and you will not get clear with a thousand millions.

Gentlemen, it is no easy thing to occupy Mexico. I read in the papers that Maximilian demands, as a prerequisite to his acceptance of the crown, that the Mexican people should pronounce for him by means of universal suffrage. Gentlemen, to attain that it would be necessary to be master of Mexico; it would be necessary to occupy it. Well, permit me to tell you we do not possess the twentieth part of it. [Cries of dissent.] Mexico is an immense country cut up by plains but very little inhabited, often uncultivated, in which everything is wanting, even water.

If it is desired to have a permanent army of occupation there, it is not with 30,000 men that you will do it, nor even with 100,000 men. You will please remember that in Algeria, the surface of which is about the third part of France, we have had for a long time 100,000 men to run after Abd-el-Kader, without catching him, and restrain the Arabs.

A MEMBER. He has been caught.

M. GUEROULT. He was caught at last, but at the end of seventeen years.

Now, gentlemen, if we remain in Mexico, if we desire to occupy it in a permanent way, it will be necessary to have garrisons in all the large towns—it will be necessary to have movable colonies. The Mexican people are accustomed to partisan warfare; long years of civil war have created a population perfectly suitable for that kind of trade. If you engage in such an affair, I know not how you will be able to get out of it. I add that if the civil war ceases in the United States, the American government, without any declaration of war, without engaging in any direct struggle with France, can let loose on Mexico no less than fifty thousand volunteers, filibusters, whom peace will render disposable for such a purpose in the States of the north ; it is impossible to foresee the quantity of regular troops that would be necessary to keep the field and maintain the security of the country against predatory bands of that kind.

In my opinion, there would be a most serious danger in the prolongation of the expedition. The end that was proposed to be attained I consider as not having been reached, as I mentioned to you just now. Consequently, if you believe me, we will not make much difficulty about the conditions of evacuation ; we will leave to the government all the time necessary to prepare itself to effect it, to do it with honor and dignity, to afford protection to those who have confided in us and in the selection of whom we have sometimes committed the fault of not being severe enough ; and then we will pray the government to bring back our troops to France. As to questions of indemnity, as to any benefits that you may be able to derive thence, take my advice, do not ask any ; if with the 200 millions which we have paid this year, we have no more than 100 or 200 millions more to pay, we shall have done a good thing relatively ; for if we stay there, I tell you, it will not be by hundreds but by thousands of millions that we should have to count.

Speech of M. Thiers.

Corps Legislative, Session of the 26th of January.—Presidency of his excellency the Duc of Morny.

M. THIERS. Gentlemen : Though the amendment to which I have attached my signature is not actually in discussion, I have sought occasion to speak, because I do not come to discuss such or such an amendment, but the question itself ; and I must forthwith acknowledge to you that, attaching to that question a considerable degree of importance, and desiring to address you at some length, I have hastened to obtain the floor, for fear that I should afterwards find your attention too much fatigued. Perhaps, when you will have heard me, you will pardon me for this solicitude ; and, as to the amendments, I hasten to say that the one which will carry the truth to the foot of the throne in the most deferential and most respectful form will always be that which I shall prefer. [Good, good.]

If the only question were to pronounce an opinion on the past, I should not insist ; I would willingly imitate those merchants who carry some affairs to the account of profit and loss, in order to be no more troubled with them. But they act thus only in regard to affairs which no longer cost them any sacrifice. Unfortunately, it is not so with the Mexican expedition. We have been told that it cost twelve millions a month, and you know that, when such enterprises are in question, the months roll away rapidly. As for me, I am convinced that it will cost much more ; but that is only a minor consideration.

Gentlemen, we are at a distance of three thousand leagues from our shores—at a distance of thirty-five days' navigation—with forty thousand Frenchmen, seven or eight thousand sailors, occupied at various services, without counting some thousands of auxiliaries—and all this for what purpose? It can no longer be ignored now. The prince who has been called to reign over Mexico is soon going to pass through Paris, to embark in one of our harbors, and to find himself borne towards Vera Cruz Thus we have gone so far with a considerable part of our forces—why? To found a great empire in the New World.

Indeed, gentlemen, I confess to you that before such an enterprise my reason remains confounded. It is possible that I may have been educated in ideas of too much strictness ; but in the present state of the world, to undertake the foundation of a great monarchy, at such a distance, without any determinate end, without any certain utility, I must say confounds my reason.

Yesterday one of our young colleagues, while doing me the honor of quoting me, reminded me, or thought he reminded me, that in England no opposition was ever offered to nor difficulties thrown in the way of the great enterprises in India. Our young colleague, who is a very diligent student, will not fail to read the discussions in the English Parliament, and he will be able to see how far he has been correct in his assertion; he will learn that there never has been any great enterprise in India which has not been vehemently and severely discussed; he will find the famous trials of Lord Clive and Warren Hastings; and he will see, finally, that only a few years ago the East India Company was definitively dispossessed of its power, merely on account of its imprudent and dangerous enterprises in the kingdom of Oude. Everything is discussed in England, and practical matters never lose by it.

But since it has been granted to us, gentlemen, to strive to cause the truth to reach the foot of the throne, let us profit by the occasion; for there will never be an occasion more momentous or more useful for so doing. As to me, I regard it as a duty to make the truth known; and I request your permission to examine as briefly as possible (and that will always be too long for my convenience) the following questions: By what succession of ideas have we been led from the first act of defending our fellow-citizens to the more serious enterprise of founding a monarchy in the New World? What connexion was there between these two purposes? By what sequence of circumstances have we been led from one of these purposes to the other? And now, are there any serious chances of success; and if we succeed, what utility can be derived for France, which, after all, ought always to be the final end of all our enterprises?

M. Ernest Picard. Good.

M. Thiers. These are the questions which I wish to debate; you see that they are well worthy of discussion.

I have fortified myself with all the information that science, politics, public economy, can offer, and, perhaps, if you are willing to listen to me with patience, you will find that you will not have entirely lost the time which you may give to me. [Speak, speak.]

Gentlemen, in order that you may properly understand the exposition which I am going to make to you, I must give you some details on the nature of the relations which the states of Europe maintain with the states of America.

I may declare it at the outset, these relations are extremely difficult. We must distinguish North from South America. In North America our fellow-citizens have always found a field for an immense commerce, which, you know, has reached the value of five hundred millions. They have always, moreover, found there perfect security—I speak of the times preceding the civil war. Sometimes they have had to suffer from the rudeness of democratic manners; but a country can no more be reproached with its manners than with its climate. It is a fact, that we have always found perfect security in North America. But we must say that security was due to a vigorous government, jealous of its honor and dignity, and from which proud and potent England herself has had more than one affront to swallow. However it be, it would be very desirable that we had found in South America such relations as those which we have found in North America.

In South America, with the single exception of Brazil, of which I shall speak presently, we have found anarchy. You know that when, at the commencement of the present century, the Spanish colonies desired to separate from the mother country, they modelled their institutions on those of North America; but they were not so well prepared for republicanism. You know that when the colonists who peopled North America emigrated beyond the seas, they were already veritable republicans in their manners and their opinions; they were, moreover, industrious men, devoted to labor, and there is no better soother for the passions than labor. But those southern populations, whom, with some complacency, we style the Latin race, were scarcely prepared for republicanism when they separated from the mother country.

As far as opinions were concerned, they had only those which existed in Spain two centuries ago. They were fiery in their manners, turbulent, and disinclined to labor. Republicanism has not succeeded among them; for fifty years they have merely dragged out a miserable existence, full of inconvenience to strangers domiciled among them. Those unfortunate strangers have been harassed in a hundred ways.

In the first place, these governments of the south are always in difficulty; they borrow, and when they have borrowed they never pay. This is the first cause of claims against them. Then strangers, who spend twenty, thirty, and forty years in those countries, are soon confounded with the inhabitants themselves, and it is sought to impose on them, sometimes, military service, always forced loans and taxes for purposes of war. They complain to their native governments, and invoke their assistance. This is another subject for reclamation and demand of redress.

But the most serious of all is this: In those continually agitated countries, where there is no vigilant police, as in the old states of Europe, neither cities, nor country, nor highways offer any security. Sometimes the doors of houses are forcibly broken in; more frequently the farms are invaded and public conveyances are stopped on the highways. Violences, robberies, sometimes assassinations, are committed; and it has been recognized as so difficult not only to hunt out the guilty parties, but to bring them to punishment in a country in which the police is a nullity and justice is weak, that people have almost renounced all idea of obtaining justice, and have converted all their grievances into claims for money.

So there has been introduced into the language of the country, into diplomatic language, a certain expression; it is that of foreign agreement. Whenever European nations have had occasion to complain, treaties are made which are called foreign agreements; and what proves to you the singularity of that state of affairs is the fact that, in making a very simple calculation, I have found that foreign agreements, those demands of indemnity, were always proportioned to the extent of the commerce which each European nation carried on with that country. This is a proof, gentlemen, that in that anarchy there is at least that species of impartiality which induces it to treat all the world alike.

Well, when we desire to address ourselves to those governments we meet with very great difficulties. To whom do we address ourselves? To anarchy. If we demand security of it, it cannot give it. If we demand payment of its debts, it does not possess the means. We find ourselves, therefore, in extreme embarrassment. So people have been very circumspect, and have taken care to keep themselves within the English rule. That rule is: When those governments can be reached by the maritime way, a degree of severity is manifested, and England has always taken care to be severe; but when they cannot be so reached, people are more sparing of menaces which cannot always be carried into effect.

I will be told that this course is not a very manly one. I grant it; but allow me to say that honor stops where the means stop; and I will cite an instance to you which is some years old.

Prussia is assuredly a very proud and very brave nation. Now, you remember that a Prussian vessel, bearing the royal standard, stopped some years ago on the coasts of Riff. It experienced a terrible attack; there were many killed and wounded; the prince himself ran great risk; everybody then said, "Prussia is going to send out an expedition." But Prussia, proud and brave as she was, yet thoughtful, never sent out any expedition, because, in fact, she had neither the interest nor the means to do so.

The English rule of acting by the maritime way is, then, neither so bad nor so humble; and if I apply it to past events, you will see that it is at bottom what, up to this time, everybody has done.

For instance, you all know that on the upper Parana, in Paraguay, Dr. Francia established himself and reigned for twenty-seven years. M. Bonpland, the colleague and travelling companion of Humboldt, in whom all Europe was interested, lived there for twenty years, detained by the government of Paraguay. Learned Europe, with one voice, demanded his release, and yet it never entered into any one's mind to send out an expedition to release Dr. Bonpland.

In the lower Plata, an odious tyrant, Rosas, treated the French in an abominable manner; he had many of them massacred by his orders; and this was not in consequence of any anarchy; it was his own will, his own ferocity. Our vessels could have reached him, and sailed right into the harbor either of Montevideo or of Buenos Ayres. For my part, I advocated severe measures at that time. My opinion did not prevail, and yet force was employed. Vessels were sent out, and a treaty was obtained by the only means possible—by maritime means.

In regard to Mexico, of which there was reason to complain, in 1838 Admiral Baudin was commissioned with the execution of a vigorous stroke; it was executed, and the consequence was that, for a certain number of years, the Mexicans retained the recollection of it, and our fellow-countrymen were not guaranteed on the highways—oh no, for, whatever is done, we will not succeed in rendering the roads safe in Mexico any more than in the kingdom of Naples; but we did succeed in having our countrymen treated with more respect.

I have deemed these reflections necessary in order to let you understand what the nature is of the relations between the states of Europe and those of America, and what kind of repression we can employ there.

When our last difficulties with Mexico commenced the state of the country was this: We had, in regard to it, only very incomplete, very uncertain statistics, to which it is difficult enough to attach any credit; however, I believe we are not far from the truth in estimating the population of Mexico at eight millions. Of these eight millions there are five millions of native Indians, who are worthy people, laborious and patient, but kept in a state of deplorable abjection and ignorance. And then there are three millions of Spaniards, pure or mixed, who are the active and influential portion of the population.

What questions are agitated among those three millions of Spaniards, pure or mixed? In truth, the very questions which have been agitated in Europe for three-quarters of a century between what is called the old *régime* and the new one. There are two parties there—the party which styles itself conservative, and which its adversaries call the clerical party, the reactionary party, &c., &c.; and opposed to it, the party of the new *régime*, which styles itself liberal, and which its adversaries compliment with the names of anarchical party, revolutionary party, &c., &c., &c.

You know, by what passes under our own eyes, what courtesy parties use towards each other. [Laughter.] Well, gentlemen, as far as I am concerned I would give them both all these names, good and bad, because they deserve them all in turn, according to their conduct. But here, in your presence, I shall employ only those qualifications which will properly express my ideas, the party of the old and the party of the new *régime*.

In what position was the party of the old *régime?* There were in that party—gentlemen, these details are necessary in order to appreciate properly the situation in which we are going to find ourselves placed in Mexico—there were in that party which calls itself conservative some great families of the highest respectability. They descend from the ancient conquerors of Mexico, from the old viceroys, and from some merchants, who acquired and retained great fortunes. These are families, I repeat, of the greatest respectability, which entertain the very beautiful dream, which I would wish to see realized for them, that Mexico should become a Brazil.

I repeat it, I would gladly wish to see its realization. But let us see how Brazil has become what it is. When we took the very unfortunate notion of invading Portugal in 1808, the house of Braganza seized upon a very happy idea, that of quitting Portugal and retiring to Brazil. Thanks to that resolution, it did not lose Portugal, which was restored to it in 1815, and it preserved Brazil. How did that happen? In the simplest manner possible. There was no interruption of the royal authority, and the people of Brazil, touched at seeing their ancient royal family seek an asylum in their bosom, became most devotedly attached to it. And we must add that that royal family, when the liberal movement manifested itself very strongly in America, had the good sense to yield to it in a certain measure, and the result is that Brazil, instead of reaching republicanism, has stopped at constitutional monarchy.

I know that the expression is not in favor here, but still every one must be permitted to speak his own language; I request your permission to speak mine.

A VOICE. Constitutional monarchy is in great favor.

M. THIERS. Under that constitutional monarchy Brazil has found order in the first place—for me, that is a matter of primary importance—and then liberty and a growing prosperity.

Now, is it easy to procure for those very respectable Mexicans of whom I have spoken the blessings enjoyed by Brazil? Unfortunately it is very difficult, for whither should we go to choose a prince for them? If we followed analogies we would proceed to ask one of Spain; but, as I mentioned to you, there has been an interruption of relations there, and the recollections of the war of independence have left such profound traces that the Mexicans have an excessive dislike for Spaniards. Then if, in default of a prince naturally indicated by his origin, we proceed to make an arbitrary selection, which I would not presume to characterize as a capricious one, we expose ourselves to the choice of princes who have no recommendation.

We are, therefore, placed between these two difficulties in Mexico. If we take the one who would be the natural prince of the country, we find the recollections of the war of independence and the antipathies which it has engendered; if we proceed to take a prince outside of the Spanish royal house, we find a prince without recommendation and without support. Moreover, the people have assumed the bad habits of republicanism—not the good, but the bad habits; these habits they have, and it is very difficult to make them change. I allow myself, then, to call this very honorable wish of the rich Mexicans, this wish of which I would be much pleased to see the realization—I allow myself, I say, to call it a beautiful dream.

Moreover, that party has an ally; that ally is the clergy. Oh! if that Mexican clergy had the virtues, the enlightened minds, of our European clergy, I would have nothing to say. But that clergy, (I wish to use only the most polite expressions,) that clergy has, I shall say, the manners of tropical climes. [Laughter.] It is rich, very rich, or at least it was rich; but it was not as wise as it was rich: it has taken part in the troubles of its country; its property has been taken and sold. It was to receive, not the value of the property, but the interest. The Mexican government has sold the property at a contemptibly small price, as always happens in such cases, and in place of it it has given to the clergy an annual appropriation, which is not always paid.

What does the clergy wish? It wishes to have its property restored; and so this conservative and very respectable party, but very small in numbers, has for its only supporters a clergy which aspires to recover its property, and in opposition to it a population of three millions of souls, comprising the middle classes and the common people, and in the ranks of which are found all the purchasers of the national goods.

Well, do you imagine that it is a very easy work to rest the support of a government on one of these parties, when in the other there are included nearly the whole population, as well as the purchasers of the national goods?

Yet this is the question which was encountered in Mexico when Miramon and President Juarez found themselves in a struggle with each other, and on that occasion the two parties showed their real strength.

Miramon is a young man, celebrated for his courage, but not so much for his prudence; he was at the head of a military force and occupied the city of Mexico. President Juarez, who is of Indian origin, and a lawyer by profession, of whom his countrymen do not say that he is an unworthy man, (we must tell the truth, although it be of our enemy,) possesses a character essentially constituted of obstinacy and stubbornness. Miramon was with the army at the city of Mexico. President Juarez was at Vera Cruz, without a dollar, without any force whatever; but, with his patient character, he waited, and a short time afterwards Miramon was obliged to fly, and Juarez entered the capital of Mexico really as the chief of the party, which now is the only powerful one in Mexico.

This took place in the month of January, 1861. It was at that time that our difficulties with Mexico commenced. In the beginning all the reasonable men of Mexico desired that all enlightened and considerate people in the country should rally around President Juarez, and should form for him a moderate administration, which might govern in the name of the ideas represented by Juarez, and which might govern with that moderation which enlightened persons always bring into government. So this passed in the first days.

Juarez formed a moderate ministry, which they call the Zarco ministry, at the head of which was a man of much ability, and, as a proof of his intentions, he resisted his congress, which was composed of men of very radical opinions. So every person in those early days wished him success, as it was seen that, in fact, he sought to realize the desire of all honest people to govern moderately with the aid of the strongest party.

We had as our minister to Mexico M. De Saligny, who entered into negotiations with President Juarez in order to settle our difficulties. An agreement—one of those called foreign agreements—was effected. M. De Saligny appeared satisfied; our government was so likewise; and in those first days all went well.

But this was not all: after having signed that agreement with us, it was necessary to pay. When the day of payment came it was impossible to pay. M. De Saligny was very much excited at this refusal to execute solemn agreements. It was natural. He was entreated to wait; he did wait for a time; but whilst he was waiting he learned that congress, in spite of the president, in spite of the minister, had passed a law, in the month of July, 1861, by which they suspended the execution of all these foreign agreements for two years.

This time M. De Saligny manifested much indignation, and I can conceive how much he was justified in so doing. Nevertheless, they waited upon him; they told him all that had been done to prevent this occurrence; they promised him to use the greatest efforts with congress to have this law repealed; but they were unable to keep their word, although they succeeded afterwards.

But do you know what the motive was for this suspension of the foreign agreements? Here it is. At that time the remnants of the vanquished party, at the head of which was General Marquez, (now our ally,) committed many excesses on the highways. It was necessary to send the army in pursuit of them; the army had not been paid for a long time, and they had taken out of the treasury the sum of four hundred thousand piastres, or about two millions of francs, which were needed to pay off the army.

M. De Saligny suspended intercourse; he did not break it off entirely, but merely suspended it, and referred the question to the French government. The English minister, who had claims to make much more considerable than ours, because the English hold nearly all the debt of Mexico—the English minister, Mr. Wyke, was delighted to place himself behind the French minister; he followed his example, and, like him, referred the question to the government of London. The European governments were then intrusted with the affair.

I shall not dispute it; we had right on our side. They had signed a treaty and they had not executed it. Yet if we had opposed to us a European government, powerful, rich, able to pay, unwilling to do so, I can understand how, having right on our side, and our dignity being interested in compelling the execution of engagements assumed, we should show ourselves peremptory. But perhaps in regard to a government which had not been led into that state by any malice, which was very much embarrassed, which promised to do better when it reached a state of solvency, perhaps it would have been better to have had patience for a little while.

But there was a way of acting by which that resolution of breaking with Mexico would not have been a fault. This way was very simple; it was to adopt the English plan. The English, also, had resolved to break off relations, but they had their means already prepared, which was an easy one, and which I regret much not to have been employed; for if it had been adopted by us we would not be in the embarrassment in which we now are.

The plan is this: It was to have recourse to what the lawyers call a distress; it was simply to seize upon the ports of Tampico and Vera Cruz, (it is by these two ports that all the external commerce of Mexico is carried on,) to seize the custom-houses, and to keep them until complete payment was effected. Such was, in fact, the plan which the English had resolved to follow. They declared, indeed, from the very beginning that they were determined to take and keep the two ports of Tampico and Vera Cruz, with the aid of a few vessels and some marines accustomed to the climate, and to confine themselves to this single operation.

But it has been said: "This plan was not good, because the Mexicans by removing their custom-houses backwards could elude the measure and render it inefficacious."

I consider the objection very weak; for by removing the custom-houses backwards the Mexicans could not have removed the two ports backwards, and the English would have remained masters of the two points of arrival. They would, therefore, be in a state to insure the payment of the custom-house duties on all articles of merchandise that should be presented there for entrance. I persist, therefore, in believing that this plan was excellent and the only reasonable one.

Unfortunately, the Mexican exiles—for some of those very respectable Mexicans, composing the monarchical party at Mexico, had been obliged to leave their country—had come to Europe to endeavor to propagate their ideas there, a course of action which was assuredly very lawful.

The idea which they sought most to present before the world was that Mexico was so weary of agitation that there would be no difficulty to be met with, and that as soon as a European flag should appear on the shores of Mexico there would be an instantanecus and general uprising; that the European prince who should be sent out would be received with acclamation, and would ascend a perfectly solid throne. This is what those Mexican exiles had endeavored to circulate among European courts.

In London they would not listen to them; they were told that there was no intention to interfere in the internal affairs of Mexico, and that the English would confine themselves to occupying the ports of Tampico and Vera Cruz.

In France the ideas of the Mexican exiles had been received with more favor. People allowed themselves to be persuaded, (and the events that followed prove the truth of the assertion,) people allowed themselves to be persuaded that at the first appearance of the European flag in Mexico there would be a general uprising; that no difficulty would be encountered; that thus all the advantages would be procured for Mexico which Brazil enjoys, and that we would have the honor not only of causing justice to be rendered to our countrymen, but also of effecting the complete pacification of that fine country.

I reproach no one for having been misled by these representations. I would gladly wish the delusion had been no delusion; but unfortunately it was a veritable chimera. It was always received at Paris as truth.

At this moment Spain entered on the stage. You know how high souled and generous that nation is, whose fortune has sometimes wavered, whose heart never! She had just had considerable success in Morocco; she was very proud of it; and already the national imagination dreamed of the grandeurs of the monarchy of Charles the Fifth. It was the moment when the war in America commenced, and you remember perhaps that at that period the great republic of the north was as much decried as the republics of the south. It was said everywhere—I have heard it said, and you may have heard it also—that America was disgusted with its governments, and that all the old colonies would willingly return to their mother countries. A singular incident which occurred at the time was of such a nature as to confirm this sort of illusion. Dominica, (you know that this is the part of Santo Domingo which had always belonged to Spain,) Dominica rejected the republican form of government to re-establish and proclaim the Spanish authority.

I remember that after that incident it would have been difficult to persuade the public that this was not the sentiment of nearly all the people of America. Spain permitted herself to be led away by the idea; she accepted the proffered return to her authority, and this now costs her a fierce war in which she expends the products of Havana and her best soldiers.

Well, Spain broke off relations with Mexico for the same motives as you; she broke off for a foreign treaty to which they were unable to do honor at its failure, and she hastened to fit out a great expedition at Havana. What did Spain dream at that moment? I would not presume to say. I have read all the documents, French, English, and Spanish, and I confess that all my habits of seeking to penetrate the truth in historic documents have not yet clearly shown me what the real ideas of Spain were. What I believe is, that the nation inclined considerably towards the idea of a great enterprise against Mexico, but that the government, at the head of which was a very prudent man, Marshal O'Donnell, whilst to some extent flattering the tendencies of the nation, resisted, however, because prudence showed them the danger of engaging in such an enterprise.

Here I must say that if an adventure of this kind, which I shall always style an adventure, whoever it is that undertakes it, was excusable, it was so almost on the part of Spain.

Spain has in the Gulf of Mexico a point of immense interest—Havana. You know that Havana is a magnificent colony, one of the finest in the universe, and that it is for Spain what Java is for Holland. Spain had, therefore, an immense interest there; she had, moreover, an admirable base of operations.

That Spain, therefore, having great interests, a base of operations in Havana, should have been tempted with such an enterprise, I believe must be considered a fault; however, for my part, from the point of view of the severest policy, I should have been somewhat indulgent towards her. But frankly, it is towards her alone, I must say, that I am indulgent, in the consideration of that dream of erecting at present a great monarchy in the New World. When she learned that France and England occupied themselves with the affairs of Mexico, she hastened to open a negotiation with the English and French cabinets.

At London she was well received; she was told that they asked nothing better than to have her for an auxiliary, but that they did not wish to interfere in the internal affairs of Mexico. They declared this to her in the most formal manner. I have here the English collection, which is full of these despatches. They declared to her positively that they wished only to seize the ports of Tampico and Vera Cruz. This declaration cooled off Spain very considerably. Still she addressed herself to the French cabinet.

In France they did not tell her that they wished to confine themselves to seizing the ports of Tampico and Vera Cruz; they entered into the monarchical ideas of Spain; they only told her, and with reason, that they could not adopt a Spanish prince. They maintained, and it was natural, the principle which has prevailed in the affairs of Greece: it is that none of the powers which concurred in this enterprise should see a prince of its own race advanced.

This very reasonable declaration cooled Spain off still more, and then she gave her adhesion to the English plan. I do not say that this was done entirely without regret, entirely without ulterior intentions; I believe that Spain in adhering to the English plan said to herself, that perhaps the Spanish fortune would smile upon her, and that though they did not wish to effect any more than the English plan, some happy accident might perhaps present something better.

It is clear that she appeared resigned to do all that England wished, and they drew up the treaty of October, 1861. This treaty, although short, would be too long to read to you. I shall merely analyze it.

It was, if I may say so, but a mere negation; for England wished only a maritime expedition tending to occupy the ports of Vera Cruz and Tampico; Spain desired a monarchy, but for a prince of her own; and France, also, desired a monachy, but for an Austrian prince.

With such a disagreement, it was impossible, in signing a treaty, to sign anything but an absolutely negative treaty, but which was not the less obligatory for all that; and by that treaty they engaged to effect the mutual concurrence of the three nations for the sole purpose, says the treaty, of obtaining justice for the subjects of the three governments. They bound themselves not to make conquests, not to interfere with the internal government, to name a commission for the allotment of the indemnities, and then to inform the United States, in order that they might also unite in the intervention, if they judged it necessary.

A very singular but very significant circumstance, and one which well proves the disposition of mind in which each of the three nations was, is the number of the forces which each had offered. Spain, having already made great preparations at Havana, declared that she would send 6,000 men; and we, who now wish to create a great monarchy in Mexico offered 2,200 men, which proves that we had given full credence to the assurances of the Mexican exiles, who told us that at the very appearance of the European flags the country would immediately arise in insurrection. As to the English, who wished nothing of all this, they gave only 700 marines to occupy Vera Cruz and Tampico.

Under these circumstances it was that the three nations began their action against Mexico.

The Spaniards, who were the first on the scene of operation, and who set out from Havana, arrived at Vera Cruz towards the middle of December. For their chief they had General Prim. It was an act of courtesy on the part of France, who was opposed to the selection of a Spanish prince, to accept a Spanish officer as the generalissimo of the expedition.

All Europe knows General Prim. He is an officer of distinguished courage, of much ability, but who is fully endowed with all the Castilian haughtiness.

General Prim having arrived at Havana, set out from thence to Vera Cruz, and with his sagacity, which is very great, commenced to observe the country. He soon saw that peop had flattered themselves too much in Europe; for during the month which he spent in waiting for us, the Mexican monarchical party, which they said was to rise at the first appearance of the European flag, made no movement whatever. General Prim saw several members of this monarchical party, and to all of them he said: "We do not come here to effect a revolution; but if you effect one without our interference, we will consider it good; do it, if you can." Well, the monarchical party did nothing.

People waited, and all that was seen was a marked movement of the country in favor of the government of President Juarez, because he was threatened by foreign nations

The Mexicans retired; they abandoned to us the ports which we had set out to occupy; they established a cordon of guerillas around Vera Cruz, and formed the project, unfortunate for us, but for them very well conceived, of blockading us in some sort in the midst of the pestilence.

The French arrived in their turn about twenty or twenty-five days after the Spaniards, and disembarked at Vera Cruz. They had for their commander a very distinguished officer, a man of ability and of much common sense, Admiral Jurien de la Gravière. He set himself, like General Prim, about examining the disposition of the people's minds, and I could cite to you letters which he wrote to General Prim, and which have been published in the discussions in the Spanish senate, and in one of which I have remarked the following phrase, which proves to you what opinion he formed of the state of affairs after a careful observation:

He wrote thus to General Prim: "I have always been disposed to agree with you in recognizing the necessity we are under here to avoid embracing the cause of the party which composes the minority, and which has opposed to it the general opinion of the country."

Such was the opinion formed by Admiral Jurien de la Gravière upon seeing the country; but he acted like a prudent man, faithful to the instructions of his government, and waited.

It was in vain to wait; no one stirred. However, they could not remain indefinitely at Vera Cruz. Although it was winter, (they were in the month of January.) they suffered much in the very close encampments in which they were lodged. Already the Spaniards had 2,000 sick. We have not been told how many we had, but we had many, and especially among our marines, who are, in general, the greatest sufferers from these sorts of expeditions, in which they manifest the greatest devotedness, perhaps not always sufficiently noticed, [That's true; good;] our marine force, above all, suffered cruelly at Vera Cruz. As to the English, they had already 130 sick out of 700 sailors.

General Prim, Admiral Jurien de la Gravière, and Commodore Dunlop declared that they could not remain at Vera Cruz. They marched out from that city and encamped at some leagues' distance from thence, at Medellin and at Tegeria. They selected somewhat better quarters there; they procured provisions for themselves, and lived in somewhat better style.

However, it was necessary to do something; it was more than a month since they had arrived; it was necessary to come to some explanations with the Mexicans. They issued a proclamation, in which they announced to them that they came neither to conquer nor to revolutionize the country, but to have justice rendered to our countrymen; and as they wished to give to this declaration the form of an ultimatum, they sought to come to an agreement in regard to the amount of claims. Each one produced his own amount.

England produced hers, which was the most considerable, for the English hold nearly all the debt of Mexico. England demanded about seventeen millions of piastres, which makes about eighty-five millions of francs; Spain eight millions of piastres, or forty millions of francs; the other nations that had claims, about four millions of piastres, or twenty millions of francs; and, finally, we demanded twelve millions of piastres, or sixty millions of francs.

This figure appeared a little surprising, because, after all the talk on the subject, people thought that the amount would not exceed ten millions.

However, each party was allowed to set forth his own pretensions. But when all was added up, it was found that these sums combined amounted to forty millions of piastres, or two hundred millions of francs. They were somewhat scared at the idea of demanding such a sum from the Mexicans.

Gentlemen, I shall speak to you presently, for a moment, of their budget, if you are not too much fatigued, [no, no;] but you must forthwith know that the Mexican budget, since the separation from the mother country, has never been able to count the receipt of fifty millions of francs, or ten millions of piastres Now, to demand of a nation the sum of two hundred millions—that is to say, four years of its revenue—appeared an exorbitant and very embarrassing affair.

They were in this state of embarrassment when M. de Saligny, our minister, declared that this was not all; that there was another claim, and he produced the famous Jecker debt.

I shall not enter into the details of this debt; we would need the subtlest lawyer to disentangle the truth in the papers, for and against, that have been written on this subject. I shall confine myself to saying that it was remarkably decried in Mexico, and that, when it was necessary, for a debt universally recognized as usurious, to add seventy-five millions to the two hundred millions which were demanded, in truth, everybody recoiled. [Murmurs in the assembly.]

I confine myself to saying that the thing was decried; if it had a good reputation, the commissioners of the government have only to say so.

His excellency M. ROUHER, minister of state. Nobody interrupts you.

M. THIERS. In the state of embarrassment in which they were, they decided to refer the question to the three European governments. This was accordingly done, and they confined themselves to sending to the city of Mexico an ultimatum which could not be either precise or peremptory, because they could not actually say what they demanded. But yet it was laid down as a principle that they had not come to conquer, nor to revolutionize, but to obtain justice. Three officers of the three governments were sent to the capital; they were received with remarkable cordiality; the greatest regard was manifested for them, and they were told that if, in fact, the European governments had come to obtain justice, Mexico was ready to render it to them; and, in fact, they repealed that famous law of July 17, on account of which we had broken off relations, and which had enacted that the execution of the foreign agreements should be deferred for two years.

The three officers were, therefore, sent back to their commanders, who had sent them, with the announcement that General Doblado, who is one of the most prominent men in Mexico, and who, we are assured, would be a distinguished man in any country, would repair to the Mexican headquarters, in order to treat with the French, English, and Spanish plenipotentiaries. Such was the answer sent from the city of Mexico to Vera Cruz.

General Prim, who saw the number of the sick increase every day, said to Admiral Jurien de la Gravière, and to all the representatives of the allied powers: "But we will receive no answer from Europe for two months, and we cannot remain at Vera Cruz without seeing our armies totally swept away; (it was then verging towards the month of February.) We must obtain other places for encampment." Every one was of this opinion. They could not certainly have brought into the field, at that moment, more than 6,000 men. Mexico had 15,000. This difference of number was nothing very alarming for European troops; but the Mexicans, whose military qualities we have had occasion to see are not at all contemptible, were posted in very strong positions; and, moreover, in the confidence in which people were that at the first apparition of the European troops all Mexico would rise, Admiral Jurien de la Gravière had received no military supplies.

No means was at hand to transport a cannon, an ambulance, or a commissary wagon. It was impossible, therefore, to carry on any military operations at the moment, and to take by force the positions held by the Mexicans. They negotiated, therefore, with the Mexican general, Doblado. General Prim was intrusted with the management of the affair; he declared that, if what he wished was not done, he would break through the Mexican army, and General Doblado ended by conceding the following conditions: It was stipulated that our three small corps should be received at Orizaba—that is, at an elevated position where there was no danger of the usual diseases of the coast; that provisions and locations wherein to establish hospitals should be given to them; but that, on the other hand, if there was a failure to agree in the negotiations to be opened, the positions given us in good faith should be restored. This condition could not have been resisted; it was accepted.

General Doblado made another condition. Since you do not come to conquer, said he, why not allow the Mexican flag to wave beside the Spanish, English, and French flags, now waving over Vera Cruz? That the flags of the three nations should be there is natural enough, since their forces are there; but the Mexican flag should be found there also.

General Prim, who, notwithstanding, was not a man of very pacific temper, also accepted this proposition. There was a third demand made by General Doblado which was peremptorily rejected. That general desired to have the custom-house, which was in the hands of the allies, restored to Mexico. A very decided refusal was given to this proposition.

This is the celebrated treaty of La Soledad, which has been considered as dishonorable. Is that so, gentlemen? [Interruption.] I would like to know what my opponents would have done, in a similar case, when there were no military supplies at hand, when they had not yet taken possession of Orizaba, and when they had come to negotiate. There was nothing very dishonorable, indeed, in making such stipulations—that is to say, in asking and receiving healthy locations for encampment on condition of surrendering them again if there was a failure to agree; it seems to me, I repeat, that there was nothing dishonorable in that: anyhow, it was that treaty that saved our three little *corps d'armée*, for they would have surely perished by the pestilence if left at Vera Cruz.

M. GRANIER DE CASSAGNAC. They would not have remained there.

M. THIERS. They would not have remained there! and where would they have gone?

His excellency M. ROUHER. They would have gone to the city of Mexico.

M. JUBINAL. They had only oxen to drag the cannon.

M. the PRESIDENT. I request the different members not to interrupt the speaker.

M. THIERS. I defend here the honor of a brave French officer, whom apparently the Emperor honors with his esteem, since he has attached him to his person. He was one of the signers of that treaty. For me, I am glad to do him illustrious honor here; I am convinced that he did not compromise the honor of France in saving our soldiers.

If there were guilty parties here, do you know where they would be? They would be among those who thought it sufficient to send a few thousand men to Vera Cruz to have all Mexico uprising. [Approbation on some benches.]

When through error our soldiers have been endangered, and a brave officer saves them without compromising the dignity of our flag, I think we ought to be just towards him, and not treat men so lightly who have been placed in embarrassing circumstances.

A VOICE. Nobody is attacking him.

M. THIERS. When they obtained those locations for encampment, the Mexicans said: "Well, you have received the locations which you desired; now we must negotiate"

But answers were expected from Europe, and they were told that no negotiations could be had before the answers arrived. The answers could not arrive before the 15th of April. They agreed to adjourn to the 15th of April.

The despatches of the allied agents, addressed to the three governments in Europe, had found those governments more wedded than ever to their own ideas. Thus the English showed themselves more obstinately bent than ever to occupy only the ports of Vera Cruz and Tampico. Spain, who no longer saw any chances for herself, had given her entire adhesion to the English plan. As for us, we were more persuaded than ever that the Mexican exiles were right.

The Mexican exiles of the monarchical party had resorted to Austria. They had seen Prince Maximilian. That prince had given them a kind of consent. Then they returned to Paris, and embarked for Vera Cruz.

The French government had added 4,500 men to the expedition, and had given them for their commander a very brave and very distinguished man, General Lorencez.

At the head of the exiles of whom I have spoken, who left Europe to return to Vera Cruz, was General Almonte The part which he has played, and which he now plays, explains what his dispositions must have been and the mission which he received. When he arrived at Vera Cruz, he published the fact that he had received a commission to re establish the monarchical system in favor of an Austrian prince. The English plenipotentiary, Mr. Wyke, who was always exact in following his instructions, asked him in what government's name he spoke, and he added that it was not certainly in the name of the English government, for he had received instructions quite to the contrary. General Prim addressed him the same question, and said to him: "Assuredly, you do not come in the name of the Spanish government, for I have instructions here quite different from what you announce." General Almonte declared that he had the confidence of the French government, and that he came to re-establish monarchy in Mexico in favor of an Austrian prince.

This immediately gave rise to a very serious question. We had come to Mexico to negotiate, and we had, in fact, accepted the position of people who negotiated; we had obtained better quarters on this plea; and it was evident that our position was becoming a false one when, after having proclaimed ourselves as ready to negotiate, we received into our ranks an exile, a very respectable man assuredly, but one who proclaimed his intention of effecting a revolution.

M. GLAIS BIZOIN. As respectable as General Moreau. [Interruptions.]

The PRESIDENT. I request the members not to interrupt, and I pray the speaker not to reply to those who do interrupt, because that encourages them, and then discussion is no longer possible.

M. THIERS. I thank the president, and shall follow his advice as well as I can; but I would be glad if those interrupting would follow it also. [Approbative laughter.]

Well, the English and Spanish negotiators said to Admiral Jurien de la Gravière: "Our position is becoming entirely false." Admiral Jurien de la Gravière replied: "That is true; but I am a man of honor, and I am going to evacuate the positions that have been given to us."

This was the declaration of an honorable man, of a man who worthily represented France. [Several voices: Good!] But the English and Spanish plenipotentiaries immediately said to him: "But that is a declaration of war!" Admiral Jurien made no reply, and invariably said: "I am going to retire."

It became too evident that the representatives of France had received special orders, and that those orders were favorable to General Almonte—that is, to the ideas which he represented. They asked for a conference at Orizaba. It took place there on the 9th of April, and I regret, gentlemen, that the French government, in its publications in its yellow book, has not published the proceedings of the conference of Orizaba. These proceedings, it is said, were drawn up by the French legation. Perhaps it is because it is written in French that this conjecture has been made; but it matters little; it is signed by the French legation and by the three negotiators.

It is therefore perfectly authentic. I shall not read it; but if it had been printed, I would have been dispensed from making this long recital to you, and you would have been dispensed from hearing it; for that perfectly authentic conference, supported by the signatures of all the plenipotentiaries, offers the most complete and striking view of the state of affairs.

Here is the discussion that ensued; I proceed to resume it in a few words. The English and Spanish plenipotentiaries say: "We have all assumed the attitude of people coming to negotiate; how can we take that of people having in their camp a leader of insurrection?" The French negotiators, Messrs. Jurien de la Gravière and De Saligny, declared that it was true. M. de Saligny did not pretend to conceal the fact that, as for him, he had never wished to negotiate with Juarez, and that he had always been of opinion that a monarchy, Austrian or other, should be substituted for that of Juarez. M. Jurien de la Gravière made no such declaration, but he said that he had orders, that General Almonte had the confidence of his government, and that they could not compel him to leave the ranks of the French army. I must say that no one demanded of us, and that no one would have insulted us so far as to demand, that General Almonte should be delivered over to the Mexican army. No, no; it was demanded only that he should be treated as General Miramon had been—that is, excluded, if not from Vera Cruz, at least from the French camp. Our representatives declared that they were commissioned to interpret the treaty of the 31st of October and the treaty of La Soledad as they did; that what they owed to honor was to retire, to render up the positions temporarily allowed them; but that they could do no more. As to the impossibility of treating with Juarez, they replied to them: "You say that there is no security in treating with the government of President Juarez; but why not make the trial of treating with him, since we are now at the 9th of April, and we have appointed to meet, on the 15th, the representatives of that government, of whom the principal is a very distinguished man, General Doblado? Let us wait till the 15th; we will then see whether we can come to an understanding with them or not." Our representatives declared that they could not do so; and, in fact, Admiral Jurien de la Gravière abandoned the positions which had been lent to him.

From this time forward the English declared that they were going to re-embark in their vessels; the Spaniards declared that, in conformity with their instructions, they withdrew likewise; and we remained alone in the country. We remained there with the evident resolution—in the presence of what is passing now, it is no longer possible to throw a doubt upon it—we remained there with the resolution of founding a monarchy in Mexico in favor of an Austrian prince.

You know what has occurred since. Thanks to the very slight information given to us by the representatives of the conservative party in Mexico, we attacked Puebla. General Lorencez attacked it bravely, and he was wonderfully seconded by his soldiers, who conducted themselves heroically. (I beg the Honorable M. Beauverger's permission to use this expression, which he likes not from our lips, but which we willingly use)

M. DE BEAUVERGER. I accept the expression with the greatest pleasure.

M. THIERS. They conducted themselves heroically. But if they did not succeed, it was not their fault, nor the fault of the general who commanded them. The blame was laid upon those who had informed us so badly, and on the next day there was but a general outcry of indignation through the army against those who had so inopportunely drawn us before Puebla.

We retired to Orizaba, and a whole year was required to repair what happened at Puebla. The brave Marshal Forey has repaired that check; we have been victorious; we ought to be; no one doubted it; we entered the city of Mexico.

This, gentlemen, is an exact recital of events. I refer to the documents at hand that I have neither altered nor distorted a single fact, and that this recital is the truth itself.

I resume the account of facts, and I specify them with the utmost precision.

It was on account of the delay in carrying into effect the agreement signed with the government of Juarez—an agreement which had accepted, as they used to say in the middle ages, *the price of blood*, and converted our claims into an indemnity in money—it was on account of the delay in the execution of that agreement that we broke off relations. But in adopting the English plan it was no fault to break off relations, for by taking possession of Tampico and Vera Cruz, they could have occupied those two sources of the Mexican revenue until perfect payment should be effected. For this plan, so simple, which was the English and Spanish plan, we have substituted the plan of founding a monarchy in Mexico. This is the truth and cannot be contested; it is as clear as noonday. [Assent on several benches.]

Now, gentlemen, I ask your pardon for having detained you so long; [no, no; speak on ;] but it is not possible to clear up affairs so complicated without entering into details, and I think I have given you only indispensable details. Now I come to the practical question.

They tell us, "We are in Mexico ; how shall we get out of it ?" I confess it ; this is the practical question : How shall we get out of it?

France ought to emerge from all difficulties with honor, and without detriment to her interests. But let me tell you one thing : when people have placed themselves in a false position—and it is a somewhat false position, to be at a distance of 3,000 leagues from our own shores, with 40,000 French and a part of our navy—when people have placed themselves in a position which can be called false, if they can extricate themselves from it with honor unimpaired and interests safe, must we be intractable if our self-love suffers somewhat? for to pretend to extricate from a false position both honor and interest and self-love in safety is too much ; Providence is not so indulgent as that towards those who have committed [Various manifestations.]

What are the means of extricating ourselves with honor and interests safe? My God! The means are very simple. If it were necessary to treat as vanquished—oh, never! but to treat as conquerors is by no means dishonorable. The next day after the entrance into the city of Mexico, when we were conquerors, who hindered us from treating with the government of Juarez, which we had vanquished? What was there more simple, then, than to treat with that government?

I will be asked, "How? Treat with President Juarez!" But when we are conquerors, when those whom we have conquered are at the same time the strongest party in the country, (I am going to give you the proofs of this,) and when, moreover, that party, after all, demands nothing very unreasonable, why refuse to treat with it?

The proofs that it is the strongest party are these : Here is General Bazaine, who to great military talents joins much tact, as we are assured—I have not the honor of knowing him—and much political ability—what is he doing? He is occupied, you see, at this moment, in making a species of revolution, and inclining from the party of the old *régime*, as I have named it, towards the party of the new *régime*.

He has, in fact, consented to separate from the archbishop of Mexico on the great question of the national property ; for the question which was agitated was this : Should the entire proceedings commenced about the national property be suspended or not? If they were suspended, that would signify that there was a desire to reconsider the sale of the national property ; if they were not suspended, it would signify that the sale was confirmed. Well, no ; those proceedings were not suspended. We acknowledged, therefore, ourselves, through the ablest, the wisest of our representatives, General Bazaine, that the liberal party, which others call revolutionary—we have agreed to take no account of these appellations—that this party is the strongest, and that, moreover, it is not unreasonable, since we are doing exactly what it wishes. Was it not, then, I ask, the simplest thing in the world to treat with that party—that is to say, with its chief, President Juarez?

And, after having treated with him, gentlemen, the question was settled, because at the very instant we could have withdrawn, it being well understood that we would retain Tampico and Vera Cruz, as the English and Spaniards wished to do, in order to hold them as pledges, and to insure the execution of the treaty made with us. Then the thirteen or fourteen millions a month would not have been inscribed in your budget ; you would not have 40,000 men beyond the seas ; and this great question which occupies you, which troubles you, this great question of the detainment of our troops in Mexico would have been resolved.

I will be told, "But it would have been very disagreeable, after having announced to the world that we were going to establish a monarchy in Mexico, that we would be able to treat with a prince, to renounce that monarchy and that prince, and to treat simply with Juarez."

Gentlemen, that is what I call a sacrifice of self-love. But I assert that, when we treat with a vanquished enemy, under the conditions of which you are aware, when honor is safe, we can rise above all these petty considerations of self-love. The essential point is that honor should be unblemished.

But, gentlemen, in order to judge of the propriety of a course of action to be adopted, we must not only examine it in itself ; we must judge it from another point of view—we must judge it by comparison with the contrary course. Now, do not judge this resolution to treat with Juarez by itself only ; judge it by comparison with another resolution, that of founding a monarchy in Mexico

I shall endeavor not to detain you too long ; but we must examine this thing as serious men. I ask pardon for using this expression ; but I do not take as a serious matter this consideration of the Latin races opposed to the Anglo-Saxon races. No, this is not serious. Let us speak like statesmen. I ask you, gentlemen, is it a matter of common sense, in the present state of the universe, to think of establishing on our own account, at our own expense and on our own responsibility, a monarchy in Mexico? Truly I said to you at the beginning, my reason is confounded when I think of such an undertaking.

Let us examine, coolly, what is likely to happen. How long will you remain there? We are told that the foreign legion will be recruited, that a Mexican corps will be formed, and that we can then withdraw. But when will this be accomplished?

Some time ago we were told with great seriousness that the French debt would be paid from the resources of Mexico; now we are told with the same seriousness that, when the foreign legion and the Mexican troops shall have been recruited, we will be able to withdraw. Permit me to answer this assertion and remind you of what has passed.

We entered the city of Mexico, if I am not mistaken, on the 17th of May. Some time afterwards the rainy season began. You know that it lasts four months. We were obliged to remain quiet during all that time. Then when the rains ceased we had to take the field, and in October we commenced to make what has been wittily called an electioneering tour in favor of Prince Maximilian. [Laughter and divers manifestations.]

We commenced operations only in November, and we are probably engaged in them now. The Prince, who is announced, will not certainly reach Mexico before the month of April, for they say that he will not set out before March. He will therefore arrive in April, and he will scarcely have time before the rainy season to receive the felicitations of his subjects; for I have no doubt he will be well received. Do you remember that a new prince has ever been otherwise received anywhere? I, for my part, remember nothing of the kind. [Laughter.] He will have scarcely received the congratulations of his subjects before the rainy season will commence. We must remain quiet again; troops cannot be moved except in September or October. You will yet be obliged to protect him for some time. So you are certain, in following this plan, to remain in Mexico during the whole of the year 1864. And I set aside the expenses; I will speak of them presently; but anyhow we stay in Mexico with our whole army for the whole year 1864. Certainly this will be denied, but it is true notwithstanding; we are there for the whole of 1864, and I shall thank Heaven if we can get out of it in 1865. I shall be told: "We will recruit the troops destined for the Prince." I should be glad of it; but, in any case, the matter cannot be effected immediately, and you cannot withdraw your troops all at once; you will be obliged to withdraw them by degrees. Believe me, there is no exaggeration in what I say. You will stay in Mexico for several years, whatever you do. Now, in the actual state of the world, is it a wise resolution to remain in that position with 40,000 men beyond the seas, and when the seas might cease to be free?

Now let us also take into consideration the question of finance. Undoubtedly we are great financiers at the present day; we are rich enough to treat questions of finance with disdain. Well, gentlemen, I have adhered to the narrow ideas of former times, and I entreat you to allow me to speak briefly of the question of finances.

And to commence, how is this question of finances to be resolved? As we have heretofore done, we will pay everybody. You pay the French army now; you will have to pay the Mexican army, and I do not intend to reproach the government for so doing; it could not be otherwise; it would be absurd if it were.

In what condition will the Prince find himself on his arrival there? He will not have a dollar in his treasury. The largest part of the revenue of Mexico passes through the custom-houses. These custom-houses, gentlemen, are under sequestration now, and while we act as garnishees for our allies, the English and Spanish will receive the greatest part of these revenues. This must be the case; I blame no person for it; I blame only the state of affairs; men I blame for their obstinate persistence in such a course. So, at this moment, the Mexican government has the greatest part of its revenue sequestrated by the occupation of its two custom-houses of Tampico and Vera Cruz. Moreover, also, in extending ourselves to San Luis Potosi, we were told yesterday, with a most cavalier-like disregard of geography, that we occupy two-thirds or three-fourths of the country.

M. Jules Favre. They said seven-eighths.

M. Thiers. Ah! that is still better. The truth is that we do not occupy the twentieth part of it, not the twentieth part. It is true that we occupy some very populous provinces; but assuredly out of eight millions of people we have no more than two millions under our authority. I do not say that the Prince may not work wonders hereafter; that he may not succeed in occupying all Mexico; I should be glad if he did. I speak of the present; of the engagement which we make in remaining in Mexico. What revenues will he have? None. Then we are truly, I shall say, too honest to draw him from his family and his country [laughter] to leave him in Mexico under the impossibility of paying his own army. It will be necessary to pay everything in the beginning, and that will amount to much more than twelve millions a month.

But now I am reminded of the loans. Gentlemen, we must do ourselves justice; if loans are easily made for France, as we can convince ourselves every day—a circumstance which we regard with satisfaction not on account of the loans themselves, but on account of the public opulence which permits them to be made, which is very different [various noises]—do you think that Mexico can borrow as easily as we do? If you wished to give your guarantee it would be very soon effected; you could borrow for Mexico whatever you wished. But I imagine we are not going to bĕ asked to pass a guarantee for a loan. We, the members of the opposition, are few in number in this assembly, but on the day that such a demand should be made I should not be astonished to find ourselves much more numerous. You will not therefore ask us to guarantee any loan. When Mexico shall ask for three or four hundred millions that will be necessary for her, do you think that she will get them'? I shall enter into no details; but Mexico, you know, has very heavy debts. It has its internal debt; it does not pay it. It has its debt due to us; we do not ask it to pay it; we will allow time for that. But it has its external debt, and that we cannot treat lightly, for the debtor is a hard one, England. And you know that this external debt is about 300 millions There are besides, claimants from other nations, on whose account the war has been undertaken, and who claim 200 millions among them all. And apparently we have not gone to Mexico to have the unfortunate persons, whose rights we undertook to defend, lose their indemnity.

Well, we must collect three or four hundred millions to commence with. It is said that the Prince can obtain that sum. I have never had the honor of being near enough to him to appreciate his qualifications; I doubt not that they are very great; everybody says that he is a very estimable and engaging prince. It will not be too much to have all his talents to succeed; it would be necessary for him to have as much as his father-in-law, and that is saying much, to enable him to succeed, in a few years, in restoring order in Mexico, or in persuading the capitalists of Europe to lend him three or four hundred millions.

It might be perhaps, as I said, a very disagreeable course to treat with that Indian, Juarez; but, if you adopt the contrary course, there you are reduced to remain in Mexico for one year, two years, I do not know how long, and you are condemned during that time to pay everything. You see that I do not darken the picture; for if that happens in Mexico which has happened in Dominica, where, after the most brilliant reception extended to the Spanish authority, they have passed in a year or two to a fierce war; if that happens which has happened at Santo Domingo, the embarrassment would be great. But I lay aside these sinister auguries; I suppose that the Prince will succeed; so be it. Yet we are engaged by our policy to remain for one year, two years, three years, I know not how long, beyond the seas, and in the mean time we are obliged so pay everything. I confess, gentlemen, although our young colleague has highly admired this business, that I cannot prevail upon myself to admire it [Interruption and various movements]

M. le Baron de Beauverger. The young colleague asks to be heard.

M. Thiers. Now, have these creations of new states succeeded so well with us that we should be tempted often to renew the experiment? Can it be, perchance, that what is passing on the banks of the Danube, or in Greece, is very encouraging for the founders of new monarchies? Certainly, if there ever was a justifiable establishment, it was that of Greece. This carries me back, and carries all of us back who have reached my age, to the recollections of our youth. You know with what enthusiasm I shall say all mankind demanded the establishment of the kingdom of Greece; it was necessary to rescue those unfortunate Greeks from the sabre of the Turks. You remember the frightful massacres which we witnessed at that period.

There was a reason, not more respectable than this one, but I shall say more influential with statesmen; it was that if they had not thought to pacify Greece, the eastern question, that formidable question which, some day, if it ever comes up again, will cause so much blood to flow, the eastern question would have arisen immediately; and they acted wisely when they created the kingdom of Greece, both on principles of humanity and on principles of public policy. And then it was not really very troublesome. Which were the powers that concurred? Russia, England, France, the three powers that enveloped Greece with their navy, and covered her in some manner by their armies. That could not have been very troublesome; and at that period, when people were not yet accustomed to grand financial schemes, the money required was not very considerable; it was twenty millions for each of the three powers that co-operated in that affair. There was no danger, therefore, not much expense, and an absolute necessity. More reasons could not be combined. No regret, therefore, could be entertained for the erection of the kingdom of Greece.

And yet, has all this so well succeeded? After a reign of some years the Greeks have sent King Otho back to you. He had done no harm; he was not possessed of much ability; he interpreted the constitutional system in a certain way which did not prove successful for him, and at last he has been sent back to Europe, which had given him to Greece.

And immediately the Greeks were told: "Well, gentlemen, as you please; your king does not suit you; well, we will give you another." [General merriment.] Another was sought out and found. Here, gentlemen, I must say that I admire the wisdom which our government has manifested on this occasion. It left to England the task of finding a king, and that was not easy. England addressed herself to that Danish line, now so rudely shaken; she detached a scion from it, and of it made a king of Greece. England added to this a sacrifice which will appear to her, when she reflects upon it, more serious at bottom than it did at the first moment; she ceded the Ionian islands, and, what is more important than the Ionian islands, the fortress of Corfu.

Well, England, who sought out this king and conducted him by the hand, who made such sacrifices as these for Greece, is much more unpopular there now than we are, who did not interfere at all. [Approbative laughter.] Well, gentlemen, is it a very tempting business to proceed to erect states outside of one's own country? You are attempting a Greece at the distance of three thousand leagues from France. And with what support? When we established Greece we had the support of England and Russia, and the good wishes of all the world; I can assert that it was the general desire. Well, here we are establishing a monarchy in Mexico; with whose good wishes? It would be very embarrassing to answer. Ah! I will tell you: yes, you will have the somewhat sarcastic good wishes of England—the English papers will give you the proof of it—you will have the sarcastic good wishes of England, on one condition, and that is that the custom-houses of Tampico and Vera Cruz shall serve principally to pay her, and that you will come in last when the accounts have to be settled. [Various manifestations.] On this condition, I am convinced, she will be well disposed; she will tell you, from time to time, that she is delighted to find you yet in Mexico, as she often repeats in her newspapers. But, with the exception of this raillery, discourteous enough, perhaps, she will not at all inconvenience you in what you may do in Mexico.

But, after England, there is the Anglo-Saxon race, of which so much is said, and of which we must take proper account. Well, the United States now respect and flatter you, for it would depend on you to decide the question if France pronounced for either one of the two parties, and she will do well not to do so. For my part, I entreat her not to do so, and I strongly approve the course of the government in maintaining neutrality. [Several voices: Good!] If France declared for one of the parties the question would be decided, for all depends on her. Well, it is not very astonishing that the United States now respect you. It seems to me certain even that if you caused Prince Maximilian to pass by way of New York, the interests of the north would insure him a good reception. I grant it. But can any man seriously believe that when this civil war shall have been terminated—the termination of which we should desire, should ask of Heaven, not only in the interest of humanity, but in the interest and in the name of all Europe—can any one believe, I say, that the United States, who have proved to us on other occasions that their memories are short, will remember the careful impartiality which you have maintained? And do you believe that if you effect anything serious in Mexico they will aid you in completing it? I doubt it.

In the first place, without any interference on their part, that will happen which happened in regard to the Havana. They declared, in regard to the Havana, that they would not interfere in the matter; I am aware even that they did not interfere much, and yet all the adventurers of the southern States of America threw themselves on the Havana.

Well, you will certainly have some fifty thousand or one hundred thousand adventurers out of employment at the end of this deplorable war. Where do you wish them to go? They will only have to cross the Rio del Norte to enter Mexico. And for whom will they go? For us? Is that possible? No, no one can believe that. You see, therefore, that you have a Greece at the distance of three thousand leagues, with the coldness of England, with the inevitable hostility, sooner or later, if not of the northern States of America, at least of all the men in their service, who will find their occupation gone when the war is finished. [Cries of good! good! from several benches.]

Well, I confess it is in vain that I regard the question under all its phases; I cannot yet find a serious motive for such an enterprise. Ah! it is true that we are told, "Mexico is such a fine country; it is the finest country in the world! Read the descriptions given of it. You will find there immense resources, which will indemnify you for all your sacrifices."

Gentlemen, for a long time I have examined that question; I have had the honor of being several times minister of foreign affairs, and it was my duty to consider the question. I have considered it seriously since, and I am astonished at what is circulated in this respect.

Mexico is very rich! Well, the celebrated Humboldt, when he visited it, destroyed many illusions in reference to it. Mexico had, at the end of the last century, a colossal reputation for wealth, and this is easily explained. Spain produced for herself alone, by her colonies, nine-tenths of all the precious metals scattered throughout the world. Now, all these metals were thought to come from Mexico alone. For this reason Mexico, under the name of New Spain, had a colossal reputation. When Humboldt visited it many illusions were destroyed in his mind. And since then other travellers, who had not the sagacity and reputation of Humboldt, have found many more illusions to destroy. I do not say that Mexico is not a fine country; but look out at America; from the great lakes to Cape Horn there is not a country of which the same could not be said that has been said of Mexico. We have but to take actual facts. Consult the statistics, then, and you will see whether that wonder is as wonderful as they say.

Mention has been made of the cotton of Mexico; and certainly that which is of more importance to a country than rich mines is a large amount of agricultural productions; that is better than gold and silver.

Cotton, if Mexico could furnish it, would be a very precious product. We have been told, it has been widely circulated, that Mexico could furnish us with cotton. Well, here are the rigorous facts in this regard. I have conversed with merchants who applied themselves to the cultivation of cotton; I have consulted the directors of the agricultural school of Mexico, and here is what they have told me:

Cotton can grow only in the low lands along the Gulf of Mexico, which resemble those of Texas, but which, unfortunately, are most of the time subject to the malaria. Cotton grows there, it is true, but they have not the labor of Texas—that is, black labor; they have nothing but Indian labor, and the Indians are unwilling to descend to the low lands. They have been so badly treated there by the Spanish planters that they have retired into the mountains, where they live on little, and it is only in cases of extreme necessity that they enter into any relations with the white race. They descend only as rarely as possible into the lower regions.

Cotton, therefore, cannot be cultivated in the low lands for want of labor; and out of five crops, two or three are always lost, because the rains of the month of March attack the cotton at the moment when the cotton balls are opening. So the cultivation of cotton has been almost abandoned in Mexico; it is yet cultivated to a small extent, but this cultivation scarcely suffices for the very few cotton factories in operation in Mexico.

On the table lands it cannot grow. On the table lands there are four months of inundation and eight months of drought, and for this reason all cultivation is difficult. Cultivation is possible only in the valleys, and there it is magnificent, it is true. There, where they can collect the water and preserve it, where they can employ the means of irrigation, either natural or artificial, every class of cultivation is magnificent; that is incontestable.

Yet, there the same difficulty exists, the want of labor. At a period when Mexico is said to have been in a remarkable state of prosperity, at the end of the last century, or about 1803, when M. Humboldt wrote his work, do you know what the soil of Mexico then produced?—and certainly it is not more cultivated at the present day. It produced a hundred and forty-five millions a year. Now, compare this with the agricultural production of France, and see how much it represents. There has been great discrepancy in regard to the amount of the agricultural production of France; it has been variously estimated at about six, seven, or eight thousand millions. Well, according to Humboldt the productions of the soil of Mexico were 145,000,000 at the commencement of this century.

But they say that there are mines The mines can yield from 120,000,000 to 130,000,000. These mines, of which they talk so much, assuredly are rich, but their wealth is not the essential thing. You must know that gold and silver diggings are found everywhere—in California, for example. California presents no great amount of gold wealth in the portions of the country in the neighborhood of San Francisco, and the Californians have crossed the Sierra Nevada, and have found magnificent silver diggings beyond the Sierra Nevada, between that range and the Rocky mountains; and they have found, moreover, mercury, which is indispensable. Other miners have ascended the Fraser river, opposite Vancouver's island; diggings have been discovered there of the greatest richness. The Americans have also proceeded towards the Colorado, and they have there also found diggings extremely abundant in the precious metals.

When you are told that a country is the richest of countries, because it possesses mines of gold and silver, the assertion is not serious. The essential requisite for the prosperous working of mines is to have large capital, good managers, much continuity of effort. This is found with difficulty.

Well, in Mexico, for want of these requisites, do you know what has happened? The greater part of the capital invested in the mines of Mexico has been lost. The English have lost more than fifty millions of piastres, or two hundred and fifty millions of francs. The Germans have lost fifteen millions of piastres, or seventy-five millions of francs. Consequently we must not imagine that the mines of Mexico are anything wonderful.

Yes, there are silver diggings of considerable importance—that is undoubted; but there is no mercury at hand; it has to be bought in Europe or in California. That would contribute very much to increase the expenses of working. All the speculators of Europe that are ready to follow Prince Maximilian to Mexico have written, "I have seen letters transmitted through the most respectable houses." Do you know what replies have been returned? Not to be too confident, for that there was nothing more hazardous than working the silver mines of Mexico. They have been told, even, that it would be better to direct their attention to the copper mines.

This explains to you why Mexico, with about one hundred and fifty millions of agricultural production, one hundred and twenty, one hundred and thirty, or one hundred and forty millions of mineral production, making about three hundred millions in all, has only a commerce of one hundred and thirty or one hundred and forty millions, importation and exportation combined, in which we enter to the amount of twenty millions.

Well, gentlemen, as dreaming is the order of the day, I am going to have my dream too. I grant you the most that you can possibly imagine. I grant you that Mexico is going to succeed like Brazil. Yes, Prince Maximilian, who is a man of talent, will be, moreover, a prince of pre-eminent ability and skill; the Mexicans will all at once rally round the new monarchy; they will not act as the mulattoes are acting in Dominica—the Prince will perform the miracle of bringing the old and the new *régime* to perfect accord; he will reign; everything will turn out for the best; everything will turn out as in Brazil.

Well, how do matters go in Brazil? Do you know how long it has taken Brazil to reach the point to which it has arrived? Only fifty years. It has required princes of great wisdom, uninterrupted repose, happy relations with the whole world, and fifty years, I repeat, to attain a revenue of one hundred millions, and a commerce amounting to five or six hundred millions. Whilst we, gentlemen, see our commerce doubled in ten years—it was so said from the tribune the other day, and with justice—whilst we see it in that space of time pass from two to four and even five thousand millions, Brazil, in twenty years, has risen from about four hundred millions to six hundred millions; it has increased one-third. And how, gentlemen? By peace, by time, by labor.

God has given to man but one magic ring—that is, labor and patience. [Good, good.] Brazil has employed this means, which is more efficacious than the precious metals. I am going to give you a proof of it.

Brazil has precious metals, also; it has scarcely occupied itself with them. It has devoted itself to agriculture, and it possesses one admirable branch of agriculture, coffee. Do you know how much coffee it gives to the world every year? At the present hour, more than two hundred millions! That is better than the precious metals. With the aid of repose, calm and quiet liberty, excellent princes, not a single enemy, and a period of fifty years, Brazil has arrived at this state.

I ask you, suppose Brazil had a friend in Europe who had deeply obliged it, most sensibly obliged it, could it possibly make the fortune of that friend, or repay him for the efforts made in its favor? [Divers manifestations.] It is, then, a mere dream to pretend that Mexico, by succeeding like Brazil, could indemnify us, and pay the five or six hundred millions which we shall have spent for her.

I am well aware that people say, "Oh, yes! but you forget one thing; you forget that a miracle might be performed." A miracle! What miracle? The miracle of California.

Ah! that is true. They have talked to you of a province called Sonora, and which, it is said, must be like California. It is said, "If we had something there like California it would not be a thing to be despised, and we would have no reason to regret our sacrifices and our efforts."

Gentlemen, I have detained you very long——

SEVERAL VOICES. No, no.

M. THIERS. I shall require only a few minutes to illustrate this miracle of California. If you will allow me to speak a few words to you, you will see whether this wonder is anything so prodigious after all, or calculated to make the fortune of a government.

Well, yes, the diggings of California are very rich; are those of Sonora equally so? Nobody knows. There are some German engineers who have written on the subject, and who question it. The truth is, that we know nothing about it; and this should render everybody very cautious. As for me, it does render me very cautious; and I declare that I know nothing about it. But there is one thing that I do know, because I have studied geography, and that is that Sonora is situated about ten or fifteen degrees lower than the country where they seek for gold in California—that is, some hundreds of leagues further south, and that the climate is one of the most dangerous for Europeans; moreover, there are ferocious savages there—the Apaches—who have hitherto rendered that province almost uninhabitable.

But I am willing to concede this point; I shall make everything easy to the partisans of the Mexican monarchy. I am willing to grant them that Sonora will be the easiest province in the world to reside in. Well, things will go on as they did in California; and see how they went on in California.

When it was discovered that there were sands yielding gold, which not only offered facilities for gaining two hundred or three hundred francs a day, but that also those famous veins were found which could yield twenty, thirty, or forty thousand francs a day—oh, it was just after the termination of the European revolutions—all the outcasts of all classes, as they have been styled, rushed to California. They obtained much money at first, it is true. In the beginning, many of them killed each other—fatigue and misery killed many more; for, even whilst they possessed gold, gold in abundance, they had misery at their sides. They came to San Francisco to enjoy the treasures which they had collected.

Well, for an article of clothing which here at the Palais Royal could be procured for five francs, they were obliged to pay one hundred francs. It was very simple: the storekeepers of San Francisco profited by the condition of things and sold everything, it may be truly said, for its weight in gold. As these storekeepers themselves were obliged to pay in Europe for all that they had need of in California, and that, too, at very high prices, they did not make such extraordinary profits as some people might be induced to believe. So that the gold of California was somewhat diffused everywhere, and it is well that such was the case. For my part I do not question this; I seek merely to know whether that gold has been accumulated anywhere in such a way as to enrich a friend who might desire therewith to enrich another friend.

The gold of California was, therefore, diffused throughout the world. After a brief time what happened? The sands became less rich. The gold-seekers, who had not been prudent enough to be economical, were obliged to stop. It was necessary to open shafts; it was necessary to examine the beds of auriferous quartz; this quartz it was necessary to break up; after breaking it was necessary to employ washing to separate the gold from the stony matter. It was necessary for companies to take the matter in hand. Now only companies carry on the works in California, and the gold-seekers have become simply laborers.

There is no great evil in this, perhaps. But let us see. Has the government of California, or has the federal government, made any great fortune? The facts are these: The government of the State of California has seen its revenues increase a little, not much. As to the federal government, it was for a short time engaged in a quarrel with the State of California; it asserted and proved that the revenue from the customs, although considerably increased, was just sufficient to pay the expenses.

Consequently, the gold of California has been diffused throughout the world, it is true; but it has not been accumulated anywhere to such an extent as to provide a government with the means of handsomely recompensing a friendly government that might have rendered it great services.

There has been a wonder produced, I acknowledge, an admirable one, the only one now left, I can tell you. Who has wrought this wonder? Who has profited by it? A good creature, in truth, which makes no noise, which makes no promises, but which works—agriculture.

Do you know what has passed within twelve years in California? That province, which was entirely uncultivated, is now as well cultivated as one of the finest provinces of France. And how has this wonder been wrought? Because among the gold-seekers there was a number of men who had the good sense to buy up at very low prices some parts of that soil which is so fertile; they have cultivated these, and now California sends corn to Australia.

Here is the wonder. Yes, there is one province the more now in the United States, magnificently cultivated. But the federal government is not for all that dispensed from the necessity of using paper money, as you know; and as to the State of California, it has gained almost nothing by it.

Well, will the wonder be repeated? Suppose, I repeat, that Sonora is a California; I ask whether means will be found there to indemnify France for some hundreds of millions which she will have expended, and for the dangers which she will have run? Not at all. We must lay aside these dreams; we must come to positive realities; and I now resume this, perhaps, too long discussion, [no, no; go on,] which, if it has not exceeded your powers of endurance, begins to exceed mine.

The truth is this: The wisest course would be simply to content ourselves to maintain our honor safe, to have the interests of France so likewise, and to desist from the further pursuit of a dangerous and chimerical enterprise, in the result of which I can perceive nothing to advance any great interest of France.

Now, I shall be told: "We have addressed ourselves to Prince Maximilian; the Prince is going to set out; we have entered into engagements towards him."

That is true, gentlemen; but it is your part to come to the assistance of the government—it is your part. And beware! we are about to assume a great responsibility; for, according to the language you may use, the result may be very different. If you express yourselves in a certain way, the French government might say to that Prince, and this course would be honorable to all parties: "What do you wish? The public authorities in France are not favorable to this enterprise, and I will not be able, perhaps, as my honor would lead me, to sustain you as long and as energetically as I would wish."

Well, the Prince, who is, assuredly, a sensible man, when the French government would address him thus in accordance with your wishes, would, perhaps, decline to accept, and we might return to that President—not a very attractive personage, undoubtedly—to that President Juarez, who is at the head——[interruptions and numerous cries.]

Gentlemen, it seems that those who interrupt me find that the responsibility which we are about to assume by this language that we will use is not heavy. I congratulate them for thinking so. As for me, I do not think it so, and I believe that when you will have encouraged the government to persist in its designs, which will depend on your words, it will be entirely out of place for you hereafter to refuse to it the troops, the sailors, the millions requisite to carry out to the end what you are now going to undertake. For, reflect on it well, hitherto your honor is not engaged in the affair; but the day that the Prince shall have set out with your support and your guarantee, you must sustain him whatever happens. [Various demonstrations; applause around the speaker, who takes his seat.]

Recess for a quarter of an hour.

Speech of M. Berryer.

I have but a few words to say. On this great question I have already formed my opinion, decided both by the study which I have made of all that has transpired to this day in our Mexican expedition, and by the examination which I have made, as far as it is permitted to penetrate the future, of the consequences of the enterprise on which we have entered.

The disposition which I feel at this moment I believe is shared by the immense majority of this assembly. I see in the state of the debate only a question on which, in virtue of a right which you all assert for yourselves since it is constitutionally established, I would have wished to obtain, or that you might obtain, some explanations on the part of the organs of the government.

The question for me, in the present state of the affair, is absolutely foreign to those facts already passed and discussed, on which the speaker on the side of the government has invoked the authority of established and decided facts. I shall not, therefore, examine its antecedents, and if I refer to them at all, it will be only to deduce from them something illustrative of the troubles and difficulties which the future may have in store for us.

The question of the moment now, that in regard to which no judgment has been reached, the question on which I ask, and I presume others as well as myself will ask, some positive explanations from the government, is this: Are we soon to discontinue the occupation of Mexico? When are we to put into execution the last instructions sent to General Bazaine on the 24th of August last? This is the main question.

FROM MANY BENCHES. That is so.

M. BERRYER. That is to say, can the government assure France that it has resolved to quit Mexico soon? Or shall we be told, on the contrary, that it desires to pursue the establishment of a monarchy in Mexico, conformably to the instructions sent to General Bazaine? This, I repeat, is the real question.

In the antecedent stages of this affair, we were told that the expedition was not undertaken for ourselves alone. That is true. As to the past, I shall not discuss in any manner the motives which determined us to undertake an expedition to Mexico. We had to avenge our honor, which had been wounded and deeply outraged in the person of the representatives of France. We had to obtain legitimate reparation for material injuries done to our fellow-citizens, and reparation also for the assaults which, through a course of violence unexampled, had been made on the persons of several among them. To avenge our honor, to obtain lawful reparation on these two accounts, is assuredly a very natural motive for undertaking an expedition against the government from which these two classes of reparation are to be obtained. We had undertaken to reach this difficult result, and, it is said, we had not undertaken it alone.

Here I shall say a word about the past in order to determine precisely the condition in which we now are. On the 31st of October, 1861, a treaty was made between three powers equally or almost equally offended by Mexico. For a long time Spain had injuries to avenge, and injuries, too, of the greatest moment. In 1858, the Queen of Spain, on opening the Cortes of Madrid, pronounced a warlike speech against Mexico. The very idea of such an enterprise by Spain alone awoke all the ardor of Castilian imagination; recollections reaching backwards for three centuries and the long possession which Spain had had of that territory, all gave reasons to think that Spain would be very glad, in view of the abominable disorder which reigned in Mexico, of the anarchy which caused the fall one after another, in forty or fifty years, I do not know of how many governments, more numerous even than the years themselves—that Spain, I say, would be very glad to find an occasion to reconquer Mexico. Her ideas became more animated and her resolutions more precise when the great embarrassment of the United States occurred in consequence of the civil war which has broken out in that country.

I do not wish to read any extracts to you at this hour, but a letter, a despatch addressed to M. Mon, the Queen's ambassador at Paris, says precisely that this may be the proper occasion. Its terms are: "The government should not conceal"—that is the expression used in the despatch—"the government should not conceal that this may be a suitable occasion for awakening ancient recollections and placing on the throne of Mexico a prince of the blood of the Bourbons more or less intimately united to that house." This despatch was addressed to M. Mon in 1861.

This, then, was the position of Spain; it was known to France. I know not what passed at Vichy and under what point of view General Prim presented the ideas of his country in regard to Mexico; but what I do know is, that a despatch arrived immediately from Madrid, of the date of September 10, 1861, announcing that they desired to know whether the French government would be willing to unite with Spain in making an expedition to Mexico to demand reparation. M. Thouvenel immediately answered that France was well disposed to unite with Spain, but that she would not do so without being of accord with England, her ally. And then in that same conversation, as is stated in a despatch of October 13, M. Thouvenel indicates that it was a monarchy that was to be established in Mexico; and as to the prince that might be chosen, the three contracting parties engaging not to procure the elevation to the throne of Mexico of any prince of their own families, assuredly Prince Maximilian was the best candidate to be presented to the choice of the Mexicans. This was the position of France. As to England, she was in a quite different disposition. England thought that it was necessary to perform some vigorous act against Mexico; that it was necessary to take possession of her ports and of her outlets, to seize her custom-house revenues, and to remain satisfied with that method of obtaining a reparation which she considered sufficient; but at the same time and in the most formal terms, in her despatches to Mr. Wyke, she declared that she did not intend under any consideration to interfere in the internal affairs of the Mexican republic.

It is true, therefore, as the Hon. M. Thiers has said, that when, on the 31st of October, the three powers, in these three different dispositions, made a treaty in common, it was a veritably negative treaty; for it was impossible that, when they came to deliberate on the direction to be given to the expedition thus agreed upon, each of the plenipotentiaries should not strive to make the results of the deliberation incline towards the principle, the ruling thought, of his own government.

Thus our agent was to think of the establishment of a monarchy in Mexico in favor of Prince Maximilian; Spain could not see without pain an Austrian prince coming to occupy a position which she would have asked for a prince of her own family; and England, who did not wish to interfere in any manner in the internal affairs of the country, must necessarily have objected. I speak not of the protests made against the exaggerated nature of the debts due to us; these are details of the past which I omit. There, gentlemen, was the thing which brought on dissension, when we presented ourselves in Mexico with General Almonte in our ranks. Moreover, this dissension was in the nature of things; it was in the dispositions of the three governments, in their intentions, which were not altogether secret, at the time when the treaty of October 31, 1861, was concluded. The plenipotentiaries did all they could to come to an agreement with each other. First, the treaty of la Soledad was made, a treaty more or less blamed, more or less approved. They proceeded to Orizaba. It was there that it was necessary to pronounce the final words, and it was there that they broke off before they had opened communication with the commissioner of the government established at the city of Mexico.

Here commence our faults; here commences our resolution to undertake the whole enterprise alone, a fault into which we have been very naturally led; and to this point, in my retrospective observations, I call the attention of the assembly. We were led by false reports, by lying communications, with which we have been saturated by the press and in every possible way, to regard as an extremely easy enterprise our taking possession of the Mexican republic. There yet, gentlemen, lies our illusion; we have yet to do with the same persons, with those who have deceived us, with those who have brought our government to engage in this affair with forces entirely insufficient, and who brought us to the necessity of retiring from before the strong position of Puebla in 1862. Here is a warning; it is the only one which I would wish to deduce from the past. When faults are past, we can gratify ourselves in enumerating them.

Mention has been made of glory. Yes, the glory of our soldiers covers everything; it covers all faults. But this glory, which never fails us, will ever be the same. In all engagements it has been the same in all ages, since the first day of the French monarchy, since the first Christian king has sat on the throne of France; the French soldier has ever been the same, and unfortunately many administrations, and guilty administrations, have sought to cover their faults with the never-failing *éclat* of the valor and glory of the French soldiers. [Several voices: Good, good.]

Let us come, then, to events subsequent to their victory; let us pass over the antecedents.

You have to obtain reparation, to avenge your honor. Have you done nothing? The commissioner of the government said awhile ago that it was not a *coup de main* that could suffice for us, and that an enterprise such as that which has caused the flag of France to triumph before San Juan de Ulloa could not be a sufficient action in the estimation of the three powers. We were alone; but have you done nothing else? In what condition are we now? This is what I pray you to consider. I finish in a few words; I have but little strength to continue my address.

But you have not stopped at a *coup de main;* you have not confined yourselves, in conformity with the English policy, to seizing the ports and custom-houses; you have gone further than this: you have stormed Puebla after a heroic struggle; you have entered the city of Mexico. Have you done nothing in that capital? You have constituted a government there, a provisional government, I acknowledge—but a government, however—and you have placed at its head the very man to whom you gave admission into your ranks, whilst presenting him as a leader of revolution in opposition to Juarez and his government. This government of yours has appointed a junta, a council of notables—I know not what name they give it—an assembly of thirty members. They are, you see, in possession of power. Who are the men whom you have placed in that position? Those who told us that they were the representatives of the majority of Mexico; those who told us that we had only to show ourselves in their company on the coasts of Mexico to have all arms open to receive us, to have ourselves overwhelmed with grateful acknowledgments And you have not been contented with a portion of the territory; you have taken the city of Mexico; you have established a government there; you have done more—you have made several expeditions since your occupation of the capital; you have extended your forces over a space more or less extensive, which is a very slight matter, when I compare the points on the map over which our troops have been directed and the immense extent of Mexico. But, in fine, you have assured to yourselves a territory around the city of Mexico already subjected; you have given to that government which you created an army which you pay, which is at its disposal. It has, it says, the majority of the country, and you have no difficulty in establishing an archduke emperor or king of Mexico. You have given a capital to that government; you have conquered its enemies; you have compelled the Mexican nation to undergo the cruellest insult that a nation proud of its unity and of its existence can suffer. You are masters of the capital and of a small part of the surrounding provinces. You have constituted an army a government. You are masters of the ports, the sole outlets of that country. Who hinders you from suspending war, hostilities, further enterprises? It is not with Juarez that you must treat, but with the government which you have made. [Applause on several benches] Has that government lied? Is it composed of men who have deceived France, of men who do not represent the majority of the country? Is the approbation now given to the French enterprise by the inhabitants of Mexico a mere fiction? Are we, then, in presence of a nation now covered with falsehood, with a negation, and does not the government which we have established represent the majority of the wishes and intentions of the people of that country?

They said that we had 5,500,000 inhabitants subject to our authority. Well, when your honor has been avenged, when victory has returned to you, when you have wiped out all the affronts which those barbarians have essayed to impress for a moment on the face of France, when you have regained victory, when you are masters of the capital, when you have founded a new government which is surrounded with all the powers which it can and ought to use, all is terminated, why not stop short? Why not? Is there nothing done? Have you done nothing? This is something that you would not like to confess.

In view of this state of affairs, which appears to me to be the true one; when you can withdraw with the honors of war, when you are conquerors of your enemy, when you have overthrown Juarez in his capital, when you are masters of that capital, when you have established there a government to which you have given an army—a considerable military force organized by you; in view of this state of affairs, I say, what hinders you from treating with that government? Is there anything in it that touches the honor, the self-love, or the interests of France in any way? What, then, do you wish to do? Do you wish, on the contrary, to persist in the development of the instructions sent to General Bazaine? But you cannot now think of persisting in your enterprise, unless you recognize the insufficiency of the government which you have founded at the city of Mexico, unless you recognize that the majority of Mexicans which you boast of having obtained is a pure fiction. [Applause on several benches]

If you do not treat with that government which you have founded yourselves, it must be because that government has not the majority of the people of the country on its side, because you alone support it, because now the people of that country bow their heads merely on account of the presence of your arms, and they would rise up in insurrection on the day that your arms would be withdrawn. [Several voices: Good, good.]

And it is into such a country as that that you wish to take an Austrian prince to be there the representative of the majority of the people, to be the child of your victories! No, no; you will not do so; the undertaking would be foolish; it would be insane. You would deliver yourselves up to all sorts of adventures. You cannot honorably call Prince Maximilian to Mexico if that country is in such a state, if the government which you have placed there is not sufficiently powerful to sustain him alone. Or else, if you persist in calling him thither in spite of everything, you yourselves must maintain him there.

Maintain him!—eh! gentlemen; that may be for long years, for in order to sustain him nothing less will be required than to hold Mexico in subjection, if the majority is not really gained over to the government represented by General Almonte and the members of the junta. Think, therefore, before consolidating a kingdom, an empire, at the distance of three thousand leagues from us, think of what has happened at our doors! We received an affront from the Dey of Algiers; we avenged that affront; we reduced his capital, which is over against our ports; and we have required fifteen years of fighting to establish our authority over a nation which had within itself no causes of internal distraction, which was not broken up into hostile parties, and which we delivered from the yoke of the Turks; we have required fifteen years of struggle to succeed in the pacification of Algiers! What an enterprise, then, would not the pacification of Mexico be, the extinction there of the political passions of the parties which divide it, the rallying them around a new monarchy, after that unhappy country had been for fifty years subject to so many commotions and revolutions! How much resistance would you not have to overcome in order to make such a people pass from the republican to the monarchical state!

How do you propose to have the dissensions, manifested in the conferences of the plenipotentiaries of the three nations at Orizaba, cease all at once? Do you believe that the causes of those dissensions have disappeared, or that others will not arise? It was already something to have brought Spain to unite with you; but did she not do so because she hoped to succeed by your means in reconquering her ancient colonies? Do you believe that the English, who possess a part of the Antilles, who possess Jamaica, and who are so jealous of their interests, will ever regard with pleasure a power which may be able some day to compromise British interests in those quarters? Do you believe that they will throw no difficulties in the way?

There are other sources of difficulty which have been spoken of, and spoken of with reason: they are those respecting the position of the United States.

The actual condition of the United States is deplorable. As for me, with all the old traditions of my country, I am a devoted partisan of the American Union; I have seen it tear itself to pieces with the profoundest grief; I always hoped that in the daily increasing power of that great federal republic we should, by its commerce, by its navy, by the development of its population and power, find a powerful ally for France in certain grave conjunctures. [Several voices: Good, good.] Nothing afflicts me more than the actual division of the United States. I fondly hope to see peace restored with the least possible sacrifice to either part of that great people. But however things terminate, do not forget that the northern States will always constitute a nation of great power and influence throughout the whole American territory; do not forget that our course in this expedition to Mexico is a source of offence to them.

Numerous voices. No, no.

M. Berryer. Those who deny my assertions have not sufficiently studied the documents before our eyes and all the historic facts that cannot be denied, and which go no further back than these last three years. I speak not of that deeply rooted sentiment which is the vital principle, the nervous centre, of the political existence of the United States, of that sentiment which is called the Monroe doctrine; that is, the sentiment of impatience and hostility with which the United States consider the intervention of any European power in the affairs of America. [Divers manifestations.]

I speak not of that sentiment. But how have you commenced the Mexican expedition? By the treaty of October 31.

And what did you say in that treaty? Yielding to a desire of England, you said that the United States were invited to enter into it; you prayed them to do so; and yet, in a letter dated July 25, 1862, I have read in so many words that it was necessary to form a new establishment in Mexico precisely for the purpose of diminishing the influence of the States of the north and preventing that power, whose prosperity notwithstanding might be so useful to our commerce, from obtaining a troublesome development in South America. Thus the Mexican expedition has been partly undertaken against the United States. [Vehement denials]

I exaggerate naught, gentlemen; I speak the truth. Read over again the letter of the month of July, 1862, and you will see there, in so many words, that it is necessary to arrest the further progress of the United States.

Well, if you succeeded, when the United States—towards which such a course has been pursued, and which hold that vital principle of which I spoke just now—should see, after the termination of their war, a state which you could not sustain except at the price of immense sacrifices, (and however immense they should be, unfortunately I should be afraid they would prove useless,) when the United States, I say, should see this establishment raised up in opposition to them, hostilities would arise from all sides The republic of the north would not support the imperial monarchy of Mexico, and war would break out sooner or later. Such are the perils into which you lead Prince Maximilian by inviting him to assume an impossible and impracticable position, one which would be ruinous for France if she persisted in such an enterprise. [Applause on several benches.]

NUMEROUS VOICES. Let us adjourn.

The PRESIDENT. I presume the discussion will be adjourned till to-morrow?

NUMEROUS VOICES. Yes, yes.

The PRESIDENT. However, it is well that we should understand on what ground the discussion now stands. There are two amendments relative to Mexico.

M. JULES FAVRE. Will the president please to permit me to make a simple observation?

The PRESIDENT. With the greatest pleasure.

M. JULES FAVRE. We withdraw our amendment.

M. GLAIS BIZOIN. Yes, if the discussion is continued to-morrow.

M. JULES FAVRE. Yes, we withdraw our amendment, if the discussion continues to-morrow on the amendment supported by M. Thiers.

The PRESIDENT. The question is not on stopping the discussion, but on properly understanding the state of the debate at present and before adjourning it over until to-morrow. [Applause.]

A portion of my intended remarks is rendered unnecessary by the withdrawal of one of the amendments as just announced by M. Jules Favre. It remains to me to say that it is necessary to specify precisely the character of the amendment to be discussed to-morrow, and that we should establish the difference that exists at bottom, though it is not evident in the terms, between the amendment and the paragraph of the address. [Marks of assent.] When I read both, they appear to me perfectly concordant in thought and purpose. I hope, then, that this confusion will be cleared up to-morrow.

M. THIERS. Mr. President, please read the amendment.

FROM ALL SIDES. To-morrow.

The PRESIDENT. I will read it to-morrow.

The assembly adjourned at half past six o'clock.

DISCUSSION IN THE FRENCH CHAMBERS.

SPEECHES OF MESSRS. THIERS AND FAVRE.

Corps Legislative, session of Wednesday, 27th of January, 1864, presidency of his excellency the Duc of Morny.

President DE MORNY. As I announced yesterday, I proceed to read the amendment actually under discussion, that presented by Messrs. de Grammont, D'Andelarre, Thiers, Lambrecht, Malézieux, Ancel, Plichon, Martel:

"Whilst applauding the courage and heroic perseverance of our soldiers, France is anxious about the proportions and the duration of the expedition to Mexico; she earnestly desires a speedy conclusion to put a stop to the sacrifices which this expedition costs us, and to prevent the political complications of which it might become the occasion."

Now the paragraph of the address is as follows:

"The distant expeditions to China, Cochin-China, and Mexico, in succession, have in fact troubled the minds of many persons in France very much on account of the sacrifices and obligations which they induce. We should be happy to see the speedy realization of the good results for which your Majesty gives us reason to hope."

Gentlemen, I do not pretend to say that both are absolutely identical; only that, combining the double quality of president of the Chamber and chairman of the committee, I am so much the more entitled to demand that the questions should be well weighed. It is for the general interest, and I know the Hon. M. Thiers too well to doubt of his approbation in this respect.

M. THIERS. Certainly, certainly.

President DE MORNY. He cannot desire an equivocation; M. Berryer cannot desire it either; the Hon. M. Jules Favre, who presented an amendment still more expressive, will also be of this opinion; and I can affirm that the committee and the Chamber, no less than the government, desire on equivocation.

M. THIERS. Nobody desires it.

President DE MORNY. If no one desires it, I must say that the terms of the address and the terms of the amendment seem almost identical The difference, therefore, must appear from the developments. I say this in order that the conclusions should be well weighed and the Chamber may know what it will have to vote upon.

The committee has expressed the same wish to see the Mexican expedition come to a speedy conclusion. It expressed it after having heard the commissioners of the government. Only the committee did not deem itself authorized to propose to the Chamber to dictate a practical solution to the government, leaving to each one its responsibility. The Chambers vote supplies, or refuse them, and express their desires; but the Chambers dictate neither the management of the armies nor the diplomatic conduct of the government. [Good, good.]

What had the committee to do? It has expressed its wish to see the government withdraw as soon as possible, and with honor, from Mexico. It did not wish to go further, and the Chamber will understand why: it is because it would have thereby accepted a share of the responsibility for the consequences, supposing that in consequence of the adoption of the proposition of the honorable M. Thiers, which consists in treating with Juarez, or of the proposition of the honorable M. Berryer, which consists in treating with Almonte, a reaction should follow, and all those who have taken part for France should be persecuted, should see their goods confiscated, and should be ruined themselves, perhaps massacred. It is understood that the Chamber is not authorized to enter upon such responsibilities; the Chamber lets the government act, as it is acquainted with the question and can judge it more closely, and can come to a rational decision based on the full knowledge of all the circumstances, whilst accepting the share of responsibility that belongs to it. As to the committee, it had but one wish to express; that wish is in accord with the sentiment of the Chamber, with that of the country, and probably, as you will understand hereafter, with the desires of the government. Consequently, I return to the starting point: I request the authors of the amendment to be as precise as the honorable M. Thiers, who has spoken on the other amendment, and, in defending this one, to specify their conclusions.

M. THIERS. Gentlemen, since I have been referred to, you will consider it quite natural for me to take the floor.

Well, let us first explain clearly the principle of constitutional right. To dictate has not been for a moment in our intentions. We would be forgetful, even under the most rigorously constitutional system, of the limit of our duties, we would be forgetful of the limit of propriety, if we had intended to dictate a course of conduct to the government; and as for myself, I said some days ago that I conceded to the government the initiative in all things. So we are perfectly agreed on that point. The word *dictate* is not, to my eyes, a constitutional expression. I repudiate it, for my part; but whilst repudiating the word *dictate*, I accept from the mouth of the president—and I cannot accept a better rendition than his—I accept the word wish. [Sensation.] Do you frankly ask us our wish? Do you sincerely desire it? I will give it to you very clearly.

The PRESIDENT. That is what I ask.

M. THIERS. So we are agreed in this. The question is not to dictate on our part, but to express a wish, and a wish well deserves to be taken into consideration, for each of us here represents France in his own very slight way, and I do not propose to speak here merely as a deputy from Paris. No, we are all equal here, quite equal. [Good.] I propose to speak for my 290th part; I know not whether this is exactly the ratio of representation. Well, in my opinion, the wish of France is this: that as soon as possible, and as honorably as possible, we should withdraw from Mexico. [Interruption.] Gentlemen, it is not your wish that I propose to express.

VARIOUS VOICES. You have our approbation. Your wish is the wish of the committee.

M. THIERS. So much the better; and so when I took as the divisor of the fraction which I represent the number 290, I was mistaken; I should have taken a smaller number. I am delighted that we are somewhat more numerous than I thought.

NUMEROUS VOICES. All, all.

M. THIERS. I thank Heaven, we are all agreed.

M. BELMONTET. No, not all.

M. THIERS. Only it is necessary to endeavor to find expressions on which the agreement can be maintained. [Various manifestations.]

SOME VOICES. Ah! ah!

M. THIERS. Ah! well, we all wish to withdraw from Mexico as soon as possible.

SOME VOICES. Honorably.

M. THIERS. Eh! undoubtedly. The president did us the honor just now of telling us—or rather did me the honor of telling me, for he was pleased to address himself to me—that his text much resembled ours. [Sensation.]

President DE MORNY. It is not my text.

M. THIERS. It is not yours, Mr. President, in the same way that the amendment which I have signed is not mine.

President DE MORNY. I have not said that it was yours.

M. THIERS. Yes, Mr. President, you said so; but it does not matter. I say ours, because the necessary concurrence of several signers in the presentation of amendments requires this expression.

Well, I must tell the President that, after having read the paragraph of the address with the greatest attention and sought to find in it any likeness whatever to the text of the amendment, I have been unable to discover any. What, in fact, says the text of the address?

"The distant expeditions of China, Cochin-China, and Mexico, in succession, have in fact troubled the minds of many persons in France very much, on account of the sacrifices and obligations which they induce."

Thus far we agree.

"We acknowledge that they must inspire in distant regions respect for our countrymen and for the French flag, and that they must also develop our commerce, but we shall be happy to see the good results soon realized for which your Majesty gives us reason to hope."

If fatigue has yet left me any understanding, it seems to me that this means the following: Many wicked tongues have condemned these distant expeditions; they have said "that they trouble the minds of many persons in France very much on account of the obligations and sacrifices which they induce." Well, sire, we do not share in the opinion of these wicked tongues, for "we acknowledge that these expeditions must inspire in distant regions respect for our countrymen and for the French flag." [Interruption.]

So, the sense of the paragraph of the address is, in my opinion, thus: These distant expeditions have been blamed, but we are not of this opinion. We acknowledge that these expeditions will have such and such advantages which we are impatient to see realized.

Such is the sense of the paragraph of the address. And what is the wish that we express in the amendment? Undoubtedly, we do not pretend to say that all distant expeditions have been useless or unfortunate; but we say that in general they present great dangers, and that, in particular, the expedition to Mexico is inauspicious in itself, and destined to produce only calamitous results. [Various interruptions.] This is our idea.

Count DE LA TOUR. I request permission to speak.

M. THIERS. And see here in what terms, very different from those of the paragraph of the address, we express it:

"Whilst applauding the courage and the heroic perseverance of our soldiers, France is troubled at the proportions and duration of the Mexican expedition; she ardently desires that a speedy conclusion should put a stop to the sacrifices which this expedition costs us, and prevent the political complications of which it might become the occasion."

So, the two points of view are very different: on the one side there are persons who find that maritime expeditions, although they are attended with many disadvantages, have, however, this advantage of causing our countrymen and our flag to be respected, of promoting our commerce, and these persons desire that those results should be speedily obtained; on the other side there are persons who, without opposing all distant expeditions, specify this to Mexico, and to this attribute no possible good result, and desire to see it discontinued as soon as possible.

Now, as to treating with such or such a government, that is a distinct question.

NUMEROUS VOICES. Not at all; not at all; that is the very question itself.

M. THIERS. I retract nothing of what I said yesterday, but I state the question thus: Treat with whom you please, Juarez or anybody else, but beware of sending out a prince; for, when you send him out under such circumstances as the present, it can only be under your responsibility. [No, no.] We are honorable men; we are upright men. When you send out a prince, do you not make yourselves responsible for his subsequent fortune?

NUMEROUS VOICES. No, no.

OTHER VOICES. We do not send him out; he goes to Mexico freely and of his own accord.

M. GRANIER DE CASSAGNAC. That depends on what conditions we have made with him; we are responsible only as far as we are bound by our engagements.

M. THIERS. I would wish to be able to sum up all objections in one in order to reply to them. Let one objecter be appointed to discuss with me, and I shall take it upon myself to discuss with him; but I cannot do so with fifty persons. When fifty persons cry out all at once, they can say what they please; but I defy any man of good sense and good faith to tell me here publicly in discussion that, in sending out a prince to Mexico under our responsibility, we do not assume a moral engagement to sustain him. [Cries of No, no.] What would the contrary mean? [Noise.]

M. GRANIER DE CASSAGNAC. It is the prince himself that wishes to go to Mexico; we do not send him there.

M. ANDRÉ (de la Charente.) You cry out to him not to go, and yet he goes.

M. THIERS. You ask for light and I give it to you. I say that the integrity of France is pledged to protect a prince when you send him beyond the seas.

SEVERAL VOICES. No, no.

M. THIERS. Well, let those who think that the good faith of France is not pledged rise and proclaim it. Let them so record their votes, and then the prince will know on what conditions you send him to Mexico. [Numerous exclamations of Very good, very good.]

M. GRANIER DE CASSAGNAC. He knows the conditions.

M. THIERS. They say that we conceal ourselves behind equivocations. It is not we—— [Exclamations.]

President DE MORNY. Who does conceal himself behind equivocations?

M. THIERS That was not intended to be addressed to you, Mr. President; I shall always be courteous towards a president who shows so much courtesy to me

But I say that those who, in taking away a prince from his family and country to send him to a distant region, whilst pretending to bind themselves to no engagements towards him, conceal themselves behind equivocations. What! he goes at our call, under our protection, and yet we are under no engagement to him!

A MEMBER. Let the government explain; it is its duty to tell us.

M. THIERS. It is pretended there is no engagement. Why then were we told yesterday, that because General Almonte and his friends were at the city of Mexico, because they had formed a government with our assent, we could not now abandon them?

When I said, "Treat with any party, with Juarez if you wish," it was replied: "That would be a shame." They are not very choice in their expressions to us, you are witnesses; we are particular with them, but they are not at all particular with us. [Interruption.] For my part, I have been always particular. However, it does not matter much; I shall sacrifice, without pain, my self-love to my conscience and to moderate liberty. They may take any license they please with me; I shall suffer anything that does not attack my dignity and self-respect, and I shall never imprudently compromise the sacred cause of that moderate liberty which France now claims, and for which I shall ever struggle. [Approbation from several benches.]

Therefore, we were told yesterday that, in abandoning General Almonte and some of his friends who have compromised us, who have conducted us before Puebla, where six thousand French have been stopped, we were told that to abandon these auxiliaries would be a shame.

How! it would be a shame to abandon General Almonte and his friends, to whom we are under no obligation; and when a prince shall have been installed at Mexico, conducted thither by you, when your soldiers shall have overrun a part of Mexico to give, so they say, the Mexican people an opportunity to vote; when all this shall have been accomplished, you will dare to tell us that there will be no engagement entered into with that prince! If that be so, gentlemen, words have two meanings They have one sense to-day and to-morrow another. For us, they never have but one sense, because our words are the words of honesty, and honesty never uses but one language.

Yesterday I said, and I repeat it now—for when we treat of suchmatters as these, the quality of the persons increases still more the gravity of the engagements entered into—I repeat that, when a prince is taken from one of the greatest reigning families of Europe, when that family is asked for a prince to be delivered up to the hazards of those civil wars so frequent in Mexico, to pretend that there is no obligations contracted towards him and his, is to advance a very strange idea not at all honorable to France.

It is for this reason that I allowed myself yesterday to call the most serious attention of the Chamber to the course of action to which we are about to be dragged.

What was said yesterday on the subject? Mention was made of facts already judged; and I was astonished to hear so experienced a lawyer as the honorable M. Chaix d'Est-Auge speak of facts already judged where there is question of politics. It is all well enough when we speak of the decisions of courts; I admit that then the authority of facts already judged may be invoked, but I cannot admit it in political matters. I can admit it, for example, for the guidance of the Chamber, when it verifies the powers of its members; because, in the question of elections, gentlemen, you are supreme judges. In this case the authority of adjudged facts can be invoked; but in politics is there ever an adjudged fact? Truly, I have never before heard such a maxim advanced. It matters not, however; I accept the expression; but it should serve as a lesson to you. You may now judge of the use that will be made next year of your decision of this year. They will tell you that you have already decided, that you have authorized the establishment of the Mexican monarchy, that you cannot permit that establishment, scarcely commenced, to fall, and that it must be sustained. Well, I, who consider this expression of adjudged fact rather badly employed yesterday, I say that it will have some share of truth this time, and that it will be difficult for you to refuse your fleets and your soldiers. It is for this reason that I entreated the Chamber, and that I entreat it now again, to be on its guard as to the vote that it will give. When on the morrow of the day of your vote the prince shall set out, the situation will be very seriously changed. At present, while I am speaking, we are still free, and so is the government. Let it employ that method of solution that it may find best, for do not think that I constitute myself the patron of Juarez; I know not him or his For me, Juarez is the representative of the party reputed to be the strongest, and I say: Treat with the strongest party, with the party which you consider as such, since you seek to rally it around you, the opinions of which you recognize as good, since now the honorable General Bazaine sacrifices Monseigneur de Labastida to those opinions.

If you do not wish to treat with Juarez, treat with the prominent men of his party; demand of them the sacrifice of Juarez; that is of no consequence to me; for, fortunately, I am not charged with the management of public affairs, and in any case it would be here that the president would have reason to say that the word *dictate* would be out of place. In fine, let the government act as it pleases; still a most important point, a point most eminently evident and clear as noonday, is that, by encouraging the departure of the prince, we make an engagement to found a monarchy in the New World. Well, I say that, in the general state of affairs throughout the world, it is an engagement that I, for my part, would never wish to make, and which I never shall make. Let those make it who wish; as to me, I repudiate utterly any such responsibility. [Vociferous approbation from some benches; applause around the speaker]

President DE MORNY. It does not belong to me to discuss. If I discussed, I should request to be superseded in this presidential chair, and I would proceed to take my place on one of those benches. I have merely desired to say that, for greater clearness of debate, very precise explanations were requisite. Those explanations have been given. They have elicited the real sense of the amendment, which, if members confined themselves to criticising the expedition, both draughts would remain liable to a confusion which might be troublesome to the Chamber. [That is true; good.]

Now, it is well understood that both draughts, the paragraph of the address and the amendment, if not different in terms, are so at least in their conclusions The Chamber will, therefore, know what it has to decide upon and what it has to do. [Good, good.]

The minister of state requests permission to address you.

His excellency M. ROUHER, minister of state. Gentlemen, I do not rise to discuss the various arguments employed, either by the honorable M. Berryer or by the honorable M. Thiers. I rise now only to weigh the question, and determine in what terms we should continue the debate.

The honorable M. Thiers has said to you: "We wish to withdraw from Mexico as soon as possible; we wish to withdraw honorably." The Chamber has accepted these two declarations. In fact, these two declarations are the sentiment of the majority aud the sentiment of the government. [Good]

But the government thinks that it would not be honorable to withdraw by treating with Juarez. [Good, good.] The government thinks that it cannot treat with General Almonte, who does not represent a regularly constituted authority; that it can negotiate only with a government springing from universal suffrage, when a contract shall have been established between the Mexican nation and the Archduke Maximilian, if he is elected. In thus treating with this sovereign, the French government will not have contracted a permanent and indefinite obligation to maintain an empire in Mexico.

This is how the question stands, and in this light I shall discuss it in my turn. But, at present, there is a difference of opinion. You wish to treat with Juarez. [No, no; yes, yes.]

M. THIERS. No; I request to say a few words.

A VOICE. Yes; you proposed to do so.

The MINISTER OF STATE. Let us avoid personal reflections. The honorable M. Thiers has complained that the organs of the government sometimes attacked him with harshness. If they have done so they have acted unintentionally; they respect his character and his person alike.

M. THIERS. I thank you.

The MINISTER OF STATE. They respect him, and especially share his sentiments when he speaks of his desire to see his country enjoy a regular and rational liberty. The government believes that it has founded that liberty in France. [Good, good.]

M. THIERS. Begun. [Exclamations.]

The MINISTER OF STATE. The government believes that it has founded that liberty in France; the government is convinced that the developments which you ask would, by their precipitancy, compromise the degree of liberty now attained. [Marks of assent.]

And now, to return to the point, if I was wrong in saying that the honorable M. Thiers proposed to the Chamber to express a desire to have the government treat with Juarez, I took up the general question, and I declare, in the name of the government, that Juarez is our enemy, and that we will never treat with him.

I declare, in the name of the government, that it is equally impossible to treat with Almonte; and the question being thus laid down, I reserve to myself the right of unfolding to the Chamber the considerations which justify the principle of this expedition, which legitimate its different phases, and which should characterize its speedy solution. [Good, good.]

M. BERRYER. I ask permission to speak.

President DE MORNY. M. Jules Favre is entitled to the tribune.

A MEMBER. M. de la Tour ought to have it before him; he speaks against the amendment.

M. BERRYER. The question does not seem to me now to be on the absolute merits, but on the present phase of the question, as you have very properly observed, Mr. President, and on the difference between the paragraph of the address and the amendment. This is the point reached in the debate, which is but, in some sort, a preparatory debate to the general discussion that will ensue on the amendment. It is thus that I understood the debate to have been commenced.

President DE MORNY. I started the debate on the difference between the two texts, it is true, but that question is exhausted, and it has assumed the proportions of the real discussion by the speech of M. Thiers, which the minister of state has just answered by a simple declaration. It would be impossible for me to allow this debate to go on, which is merely based on a difference in the understanding of the two texts, which, I believe, I have demonstrated to the Chamber. The discussion should now continue on the main point, and M. Jules Favre is entitled to speak on the subject.

M. BERRYER. It is on the declaration of the minister of state that I desire to say a word, and as to the difference of the two draughts. [Interruption.]

President DE MORNY. M. Jules Favre insists on his right to speak.

M. BERRYER. I have but one word to say. [Speak, speak.]

The declaration of the minister of state is a reply to the question which I asked yesterday of the government: Is it willing to treat with the government which it has established at Mexico, or does it desire to wait and establish the authority of the Archduke Maximilian? [Interruption.]

Allow me. The minister of state has made a complete reply to the question which I submitted yesterday to the assembly. The minister of state has said: The government cannot treat with Almonte, because Almonte is only a provisional establishment which has no legal character in that country of Mexico.

The government must wait for the imperial establishment of the Emperor Maximilian, if he is elected, [noise;] the government must wait till he is recognized by means of universal suffrage in order to treat with him; and here it is—in view of the answer given to my question of yesterday by the minister of state—that the difference exists between the two draughts. There is a kind of equivocation and ambiguity in the address; there is, on the contrary, in the amendment, a very clear expression of the desire of the assembly to see a speedy conclusion put an end to the sacrifices which this expedition costs us, and prevent the political complications of which it might become the occasion.

In this state of affairs there is but one question more, and on this the assembly desires to be satisfied: Is it true that the government has made no engagement to bind the country, either in a financial point of view, or as regards its soldiers? Are we under any obligation, or are we not?

His excellency M. ROUHER. If you had read the report of the honorable M. Larrabure you would have been instructed.

M. SEGRIS. I request permission to say one word, in order to complete the remark of the minister of state in reference to the report of M Larrabure. Here is the reply of the organs of the government which I find in that report, and which I, for my part, fully accept:

"At this moment the Emperor's government declares"—

M. THIERS. At this moment!

M. SEGRIS. "At this moment the Emperor's government declares that it has made no engagement with any one either to leave a corps of French troops in Mexico, or to guarantee any loan whatever; it declares that it has no reason to think that it is necessary to increase the number of the French forces actually on the soil of Mexico; that the movements which will take place up to their withdrawal shall be for no other object than to replace the sick and those entitled to discharge."

M. THIERS. At this moment! [Various kinds of manifestations.]

M. SEGRIS. That is exactly the declaration which the minister of state has confirmed.

His excellency M. ROUHER, minister of state. I retract nothing whatever of it.

President DE MORNY. M. de la Tour is entitled to speak.

COUNT DE LA TOUR. Gentlemen, the declarations which you have just heard have enlightened us on what we have to do, and we know how our votes should be. Undoubtedly we must regret that the so rapid succession of the expeditions to China, Cochin-China, and Mexico, have occurred to weigh down our finances almost simultaneously, and to derange for a moment the equilibrium of our budget. Undoubtedly we must regret that the defection of Spain and England has constrained us to give such considerable proportions to our Mexican expedition; but it is impossible for the majority to give way to the exaggerated statements made in this assembly.

It is impossible for us to lay a formal, absolute blame on our troops engaged in a national contest against an enemy who has shown himself unworthy of our generosity, against generals who have even violated military honor, for among them there are some who had been let free on their parole, and who have again taken up arms against us.

In the first place, gentlemen, the simple examination of the situation should suffice to make us reject the amendment proposed. Whenever our army has been engaged abroad in a conflict for a just and noble cause, it is impossible for a French Chamber to desert its flag, and in a kind of a way pass over to the enemy by passing a resolution of disavowal of the acts of our soldiers. [Interruptions of various kinds.]

Yes, it is thus, gentlemen, that I believe myself authorized to interpret the amendment proposed to you; it is a formal disavowal of the expedition, a formal censure of the monarchy which we propose to establish in Mexico. Now, I believe that, from the moment we were led to Mexico, the very best course for us to adopt was precisely to endeavor to establish a monarchy in Mexico.

In fact, gentlemen, consider the necessity of establishing a certain equilibrium in Mexico. [Noise.]

Please dwell upon one consideration, certainly a most important one; it is, that one of two things must occur: either our intervention will succeed in constituting a strong, wise, honorable, and regular government in Mexico—and then it will be possible for you to derive some advantages from your expedition—or else, in a few years, Mexico will certainly be swallowed up by the States of North America, which have already, in the short period of twenty years, taken away from it three of its finest provinces—Texas, California, and New Mexico. [Increased noise.]

Gentlemen, if the Chamber is not willing to grant me a few moments of attention I shall stop. [No, no; go on.] But I believe, however, that the considerations which I have to present, and which will be brief, merit the interest of the legislative body.

What is the natural and normal fruit of the republican form of government? Revolutions. What is the natural and normal fruit of monarchy? Stability. So, on one side, we have instability; on the other, stability. Such are the respective results of monarchy and republicanism.

Now, if we allow republicanism to continue in Mexico, without any effort to organize in that country a wise and honorable government—that is to say, a monarchical government—it will be utterly impossible for us to derive from our costly expedition the advantages for which we have reason to hope.

SEVERAL MEMBERS That is true.

COUNT DE LA TOUR. It is impossible for me, therefore, to blame the government for the policy which it has pursued, and I shall urge the legislative body to vote for the address as it stands. I oppose the amendment, in the first place, because we ought to try to maintain a sort of equilibrium in the New World; because it would be dangerous hereafter, for the peace of Europe itself, that Mexico should belong to a power so important as the United States, which would very soon, by taking in the five little republics of Central America, reach the Gulf of Darien and the isthmus of Panama, whence they would rule the commerce both of the Atlantic and of the Pacific oceans. I oppose the amendment, in the second place, because it is necessary that the majority, under such grave circumstances, whilst following the dictates of conscience, should remain united. Our union is indispensable to the country—within for its peace, without for its influence and its strength. [Approbation on many benches.]

M. JULES FAVRE Gentlemen, I believe I divine the desire of the Chamber, and conform myself to it, in taking up the discussion at the point where it was left by the remarkable speeches which you heard in the session of yesterday, and by the circumstances that have occurred in that of to-day, and in rejecting, henceforth, such details as concern accomplished facts, and in regard to which many reasons might be presented for us to draw up easy but useless accusations.

Already, gentlemen, we have had occasion to express our opinions on the causes of this expedition to Mexico, which, from the very first day, we have considered as inauspicious, and as calculated to lead the country into serious embarrassment.

Succeeding events have not been such as to authorize us to change our opinion, and this opinion has received the support and defence of the eminent speakers who have laid before you such considerations, political, financial, and of national interest, as should most assuredly strike you with their gravity, and which I shall be careful not to repeat, for fear that they should become weak in my hands.

But, if you will allow me, I shall endeavor to look at the question from an entirely different point of view; and the minister of state has authorized me to do this by an expression to which he gave utterance, and which leads me back very forcibly to the natural prepossession of my mind on this subject.

This prepossession is in regard to right, superior, undoubtedly, to all considerations of policy and interest; and if this right, such as it is, revealed to us both by the eternal principles to which we can never prove recreant without loss, and by formal engagements on the part of the government--if this right, I say, completely confirms the conclusions of which you heard the brilliant developments yesterday, we shall have deduced from thence, for the security of our consciences, the support of a demonstration which we will have the right to call inflexible.

We have to consider these questions: What are we doing in Mexico? What ought we do? Should we withdraw from it, and under what conditions?

M. EDWARD DALLOZ May I be permitted to say a few words?

M. JULES FAVRE. I confess, gentlemen, I am not in any way embarrassed by that which was said to you in the session of yesterday by the honorable commissioner of the government, who sought to put forward, as his justification of the propositions which he brought before you, the support given by the votes of this Chamber.

He received for answer, in my opinion very justly, that those votes should naturally be inspired by circumstances changeable in their nature. Moreover, on this very point I ask permission of the honorable commissioner of the government to be allowed to agree with him; and, as he appeals to the formal engagements of the government, I appeal, also, to the votes of the Chamber, given only after the positive declarations of which I shall have the honor to remind you, and which really form a solemn contract between the majority and the government.

And, since mention has been made of the authority of adjudged facts, it seems to me that an authority so potential might have been invoked to qualify that which has been recognized here without dispute, that is, the judgment pronounced by public opinion on the Mexican expedition, and of which I find the traces, not in documents, of which the production might be criticised by you, but, on the contrary, in official papers, the weight of which you cannot question.

The first I borrow from the language of the sovereign himself. When the session was opened, he thought it indispensable to say a word in this regard, and that word ought to be well weighed by you.

"The distant expeditions," says the speech from the throne, "which have been the object of so much criticism, have not been undertaken in pursuance of any premeditated plan; the force of circumstances has brought them about, and yet they are not to be regretted."

For what good, gentlemen, remark those prepossessions and those criticisms in a document in which ordinarily only unanimous approbations are mentioned? It must necessarily be that those murmurs of public opinion, whatever otherwise be the difficulties which they may have to reach the throne, have been very powerful, so as to have been noticed in a document of that nature.

I wish to place by the side of that document another no less grave, but which you will perhaps find more significant. When the minister of finance saw himself under the doubly painful necessity--painful, because he is minister of finance, and painful because he had made an engagement to the contrary--of reopening the estimates of the public debt, he did not dissemble the anxieties, the uneasiness, the restlessness of the country. For this he assigned the real cause when he said:

"I had thought that it would be possible to avoid this necessity, and that a prompt settlement of the affairs of Mexico would, on the one hand, have limited our expenses to a sum inferior to that which we have disbursed, and, on the other, have brought, by means of a loan contracted for Mexico, the reimbursement of our advances. But, notwithstanding the confident hope which we entertained of seeing, within a day not far distant, a regular government established in Mexico, we cannot repose the security of our finances on the liquidation of her debt to us."

So, the minister of finance did not dissemble the gravity of that state of affairs resulting from this exceptional circumstance that has arisen to trouble our finances, at the same time that a profound emotion pervades the whole country; and I am not rash in affirming that the minister of finance is really an anonymous signer of our amendment. [Exclamations and laughter.]

But I find, gentlemen, a concurrence more explicit, more precious still, in a report emanating from one of the committees of the assembly, and which I need not recall to your recollections.

When the question of supplementary credits arose, the honorable M. Larrabure, with an ability to which every one renders homage, enters into the discussion of this question in his report, and here is the way in which he expresses himself:

"We should not seek to conceal the fact that these repeated expeditions disquiet the nation. Let us hasten, however, to say, in order to be just, that as to that of Mexico, which weighs most on the public mind and on our finances, it has attained the increased proportions which it is now seen to possess only by a chain of unfortunate incidents which the government could neither foresee nor prevent," &c., &c.

And he added: "The honor of our flag being satisfied, public opinion resumes its prepossessions. In the state of affairs in Europe, in the state of our internal necessities and of our finances, it would be pleased that the government should continue only as short a time as possible to expend at a distance those resources that may become precious to us nearer home and for our works of public utility. These expeditions will perhaps open up new horizons, new channels for trade; but, at present, we must acknowledge that the country is less struck by the possible, but uncertain or distant advantages, than by the real and actual charges which burden it."

I could multiply these quotations. You know with what persevering energy the honorable reporter of your committee solicited from the wisdom of the government and the foresight of the Chamber the cessation of a state of things which appeared to him so inauspicious.

And beside all these authorities, beside the general acknowledgment of everybody, I can also place that of the committee on the address, for our honorable and able president told you just now that this wish, of which we seek here to determine the terms of expression, is found equally earnest in all hearts Yes, we are unanimous in regretting that imperious necessities—thus it was that your committee on supplementary credits expressed themselves—should have engaged the government in a course of action, from which we hope it will withdraw as promptly as possible, on the condition, well understood, that the honor and interests of France be not compromised. [That is so; that is so.]

But permit me to tell you, it is here precisely that the difference of opinion commences. [Laughter. That is true.]

Your committee, in this respect, is filled with entire confidence in the views of the government. As to us, we respectfully request to be allowed not to share that confidence. I will proceed to give you our reasons for this, and to explain to you, in our turn, the desires which, in my opinion, might influence in a satisfactory manner the policy which we all wish, favorable to the grandeur and the dignity of the country. Well, no one will contradict me when I say that that which has occasioned, and which yet occasions, the gravity of the situation, is precisely the ambiguity which weighs upon it; it is that it was at its origin, and is yet, surrounded with obscurity. Every one feels it here, and I hope that the words of the minister of state will succeed completely in putting an end to it.

As for me, I shall strive, from my point of view, to tell what the causes are of this obscurity, how essential it is that it should disappear entirely, and on what conditions the light which alone can strike us, that of honor and probity, ought forever to succeed it.

When I say that, from the beginning, an inauspicious ambiguity hung over this situation, am I not right? You understand it perfectly, and I have no desire here to undertake a discussion which is exhausted, and belongs henceforth to the domain of history.

Was it possible to avoid war in 1861? After those dissensions that have so long agitated and ensanguined the republics of the New World, was there not beginning to appear a constitutional and civil authority to which it was possible to give our adhesion, and which, consolidated and strengthened by the protection of the European governments, should continue, more and more every day, to acquire a happy influence?

This is, also, gentlemen, a question for debate which I shall not discuss anew before you.

It has been decided by the French government. The French government thought that that new authority did not present it sufficient guarantee; it made it responsible for the iniquities of the governments which it had combated and destroyed; it has sought to lay upon it the responsibility of the bloody acts which, nevertheless, barred its passage to power.

All these things, gentlemen, I recall without even criticising them; and I say that when we allude to the interests of our countrymen which have been outraged, to crimes permitted to go unpunished, to the law of nations violated—when we allude to all these things, in order to make war on a country, we are right and just; that when France drew the sword against Mexico, supposing that, in fact, she had reason to do so, she was evidently acting within the limits of right, and no one ever denied it.

Only it is here that for me the uncertainty begins, and I take the liberty of asking the government to be pleased, if it thinks it proper, to give me an answer to the question which, at the present moment and in reference to facts, I take the liberty of proposing to it.

It is incontestable that at the same time that our *chargé d'affaires* communicated to the department of foreign affairs facts of the greatest moment, when he asked the armed protection of France, when he gave information that the indemnities were not paid, that a law of Congress had appropriated to other purposes the funds that were to be applied to them, it is perfectly certain, I say, that another influence was at work upon our government besides its own. It has been sufficiently intimated to you for me to recall it to your minds.

This influence, gentlemen, was that of persons, some condemned by the political law, others proscribed by the revolutions of their country, who had received a generous hospitality in France, who, full of illusions and hopes, as all exiles are, took their dreams for realities, and magnified their own importance to such an extent that it seemed, on nearing the coasts of Mexico, that it ought to be enough to determine the course of revolutions there.

I do not concern myself now as to whether those exiles had obtained the ear of the government, whether they had not been directly placed under its protection, and whether, to speak truly, from the first day that the expedition was resolved upon up to this time at which I am speaking, the French government has not appeared to manage their affairs.

In fact, whilst negotiations were being carried on for the reparation of our grievances, the Mexican exiles pursued their intrigues and their dreams; they entertained the French cabinet with their lamentations, and unveiled to its eyes the prospect of a revolution which might prove fortunate; for, in place of those governments of a day succeeding each other merely to lay before the eyes of the world the scandalous and pitiful spectacle of their mutual overthrows, they promised to the great French monarchy a monarchy which assuredly could not be its rival, but which, being placed in its orbit, an agent of civilization in the New World, would diffuse everywhere, with our arts and our civilization, the prosperity which is their attendant.

That these dreams were grand, gentlemen, I shall not assume to discuss; but that they were dreams, when I so affirm, who can now contradict me?

Governments should not allow themselves to be led into the opinions of persons around them; they have too great a responsibility, precisely because they have immense power, not to have demanded from them a severe account of the determination to which they may have come in an unreflecting manner.

Well, not only did the government open its ears to the words of those exiles—here it is, gentlemen, that my question rests, and that it combines itself in the strictest manner with the brilliant discussion of the honorable M. Thiers and of the honorable M. Berryer—but it is incontestable that when nothing was yet known in Europe of the resolutions of France and of the allied powers, the exiles had already opened negotiations with Prince Maximilian.

Now, gentlemen, I take the liberty of asking the government, Had it any knowledge of this? One of two things must be true: either the government was ignorant of those negotiations, or it was acquainted with them. If it was ignorant of them, you understand, gentlemen, what accusation we have a right to bring against it; for those to whom it promised its support, those for whom it lavished the blood and the treasures of France—— [Murmurs on several benches.]

Is it the case that the government was not acquainted with them? As for me, gentlemen, I am convinced that it is not so by any means. I will soon proceed to deduce my proofs from official documents. The government knew that the Archduke Maximilian had been visited by the exiles; that a negotiation had been begun.

I stop short for a moment, gentlemen, and I ask myself whether the Archduke Maximilian is the first comer; whether he is some person picked up at random in the midst of a revolution, nourished by the exaggerated hopes or by the factitious promises of the exiles; or whether, on the contrary, he does not belong in Europe to a reigning house, and whether, consequently, the designation that shall be made of him is not a designation eminently political?

The answer to this question could not be doubtful. I believe that it would be proper for the government to tell us what the negotiations have been in this respect with the house of Austria. Has the house of Austria been aware of these projects? Has it approved them? It could not have been ignorant of them. If it has not approved them, the French government finds its policy condemned by this very fact from the very first day that it sprung into existence; for, by the side of a reigning prince of a powerful sovereign who disposes of the forces of a great empire, they proceed to take him who is the nearest to him by blood, his brother. It knows that that Emperor does not approve the negotiations of which that prince is the object, and yet the French government continues them. And here, gentlemen, by the invincible logic of facts, by a chain of events through which your wisdom alone can break, the responsibility of France commences where her action commences, and her protection is extended which we could not disavow without dishonor to ourselves. [Good.]

It is certain, then, that in those first moments, when negotiations were going on, when the exiles made frequent journeys to Vienna, when they broached the matter to Prince Maximilian, the government knew all these things, and approved them. The government foresaw that eventuality; that the exiles might stir up a reactionary movement in their country, thanks to the presence of the French armies, and then it seemed opportune, if a throne was raised, to seat upon it a prince of the house of Austria.

These purposes could not continue confined to the government alone; public opinion and this Chamber are judges of them. They may be good or bad; but it is evident that you would renounce your right of initiative if you did not express some opinion on this point. I have no opinion to offer; in accordance with the ideas which I enunciate, and of which you must acknowledge the simplicity and force, I hasten to proceed with the examination to which you have been invited.

France, thus involved with these exiles, saw a double prospect opened before her. She was going to Mexico to avenge the injuries done there to our countrymen; she had the right to do this. She was going there to obey the instigations of the exiles and to establish there that eventual monarchy for which she reserved her eventual candidate also; in this I positively maintain that France had not the shadow of a right to support her—she had in her favor only an intrigue of which she made herself the instrument. [Several voices: Good, good.]

Are we, then, reduced to this remarkable degree of humiliation that we have to discuss here in your presence the question whether a great people can proceed to instigate internal changes among another friendly people by means of the appearance in its waters of an armed force unfurling there the standard of a party?

I do not wish to insult you so far as to believe that any discussion could be had on this subject within these walls. The law of nations condemns, brands, such attempts; whenever they have been tried in history, they have almost always met with the pointed condemnation of impartial and honorable minds.

M. GLAIS BIZOIN. Good, good.

M. JULES FAVRE Yes; I have the right to assert that, in this war undertaken by France, there were two motives—the one perfectly legitimate, the other not so.

Now, what has happened? These things were so well understood that, at the discussion of the address of 1862, when events were yet in a state of uncertainty, it was sought to throw a discreet veil—too discreet, perhaps, for the veracity of the French administration—over facts which now stand forth in the full light of day.

When this Mexican expedition was resolved upon, when the Chamber was called upon to take it into consideration in the discussion of the address of 1862, we, gentlemen, for our part, saw in it the germs of real misfortune to our country; we asked—and you will see in what terms—that this expedition should be restricted within what appeared to us legal limits; and certainly, gentlemen, many of those who do me the honor of listening to me, and, I am convinced, many of those even who deemed it their duty, in obedience to the dictates of their consciences, to vote against an amendment presented by the opposition, wished in the bottom of their hearts that no departure had ever been made from that policy.

"We see with regret," said we, "the Mexican expedition undertaken; its purpose seems to be to interfere in the internal affairs of a people. We request the government to prosecute only the reparation of our grievances."

This, gentlemen, was the interest of France, which we defended. As to the other object, which appeared to us involved in clouds and obscurity, we manifested our distrust and warned the government.

Now, gentlemen, rumors have reached us in Europe from the American shores which have given us to understand that there was an underground intrigue carried on, and that there was already some agreement with a prince of the house of Austria. We said so to the Chamber. Our assertions received from him who sat on that bench [the speaker points to the bench occupied by the commissioners on the part of the government] the most unqualified denial. Listen, gentlemen, to the words of the honorable M. Billault:

"And as to those rumors," said the honorable member, "which gave umbrage to the ambassador of her Britannic Majesty, permit me not to dwell upon them. Some officers, at their departure, said that they were going to Mexico to enthrone a foreign prince there. How! Do you imagine that the great secret of the diplomacy on the subject, if it ever had any existence, would have thus been intrusted to the first comer setting out to Mexico? This surely is not serious. If, as you say, our ally has been disquieted by such rumors, you told us also that she immediately applied to that quarter where she could really learn whether they were well founded; she asked our minister of foreign affairs, and you acknowledge yourselves the answer denied all these rumors.

"The facts then remain as they really are: a war legitimately imposed on us by our honor and our interests, and which, in concert with our allies, we will carry on with earnestness; a hope, a possibility, for the unfortunate Mexicans, if they have strength, or energy, or cohesion enough to desire to procure for themselves the benefits of a good government; if they know how to save themselves in that way; we will be glad of it; we will find in it the only real guarantee of the security of our countrymen; we will guide them with our counsels and with our moral support; but to constrain them to it by force, never!"

Is it clear, gentlemen? In fact, it is perfectly certain that the English ambassador applied for information to the honorable M. Thouvenel, that the *chargé d'affaires* of the United States of America made the same request, and that they were answered that there was no truth in the report of negotiations with a prince of the house of Austria. Now, the negotiations did exist; they existed before the departure of our troops; they had been made the subject of one of the secret conditions of the treaty of October 31, 1861. If you interrogate the text of that treaty, assuredly you will find there nothing of the kind; but if you go to the official documents which were unknown at that time, and which I might call the official documents of diplomacy, you will see in them, gentlemen, that the plan had been prepared in advance, that the name of Prince Maximilian had been suggested, and that he had already received the support of France. This appears, among other papers, (for I could make numerous quotations to you in this regard,) from a despatch which bears the date of October 11, 1861, addressed by the minister of foreign affairs of France to the French ambassador in London. It is, as you see, anterior to the treaty which bears the date of the 31st of the same month, and here is what we collect in it relative to the subject with which we are now occupied: "I replied," says the minister, "to the English ambassador that I was perfectly agreed with his government on one point: that I acknowledged, with Lord Russell, that the legitimacy of our coercive action in regard to Mexico evidently resulted only from our grievances against the government of that country, and that those grievances, as well as the means of redressing them and of preventing their recurrence, could constitute the only object of an ostensible treaty." There was then a treaty which was not ostensible, and the despatch proceeds to inform us on what it might turn. Here, in fact, is what I read further on:

"But that it seems to me useless to go beyond this, and to prohibit in advance the eventual exercise of a legitimate participation in the events of which our operations might be the origin," &c., &c. And further on: "We are allowed to suppose, in fact, that if the issue of the American crisis," (listen to this, and see how much reason we had yesterday to tell you that, in the forecast of the government, the Mexican expedition and the enthronement of the Archduke Maximilian were connected with the dissensions of the United States, and that about that time it was towards this end that all the wishes of the government were directed,) "we are allowed to suppose, in fact, that if the issue of the American crisis confirmed the separation of the north and the south, the two new confederations would both seek for compensation, which the Mexican territory, delivered up to social dissolution, would offer to their competition. Such an event could not be a matter of indifference to England, and the principal obstacle which could, in our opinion, prevent its accomplishment would be the establishment in Mexico of a reparative government strong enough to arrest its internal dissolution."

So, gentlemen, it is not only for the purpose of avenging our countrymen, it is not only to obtain a miserable indemnity, (which most assuredly could never be considered as a thing of very great importance in comparison with events so great as those indicated,) that the government decided to proceed against Mexico; it wished to prepare, to facilitate its own domination; it wished, in view of what was being accomplished in the United States, to have its place and its share of power by the side of the great American republic, in that great state which was going to be founded under its patronage, and which should be its vassal for long years, and thus to exercise in the New World a preponderance worthy of the great name of France.

Such, gentlemen, was the idea; I find it in the despatch which I have just read.

Now, it is not necessary that the minister of state, ignoring here the ideas which at that period were those of the government, should desert the true ground of the question—that is to say, that of the preparation of a monarchy for Mexico, that of the negotiations entered into in accordance with the suggestions of the exiles, that of the responsibility of France, which was already embarrassing.

And on this subject, also, I take the liberty of remarking to the Chamber that if the interests of France could, to a certain point, understood in a certain manner, excuse or explain utopias so dangerous as these, the government ought to be stopped by a consideration which it was not allowed to ignore: it was that of the rights of Mexico, of its nationality, which France could not attack without proving recreant to the principle on which her own government was founded, and without committing a real act of high treason against the law of nations.

SEVERAL VOICES. Good, good.

M. Jules Favre. You are acquainted, gentlemen, with the events that ensued, and I have but a few words to say of them.

You know how the alliance, which existed between Spain, England, and France, was broken at Orizaba. At that period, when those events were known in Europe, the discussion was reopened on the subject on the occasion of the voting of the budget We reproduced our observations; we said that the government had by experience learned the emptiness of the hopes entertained by the exiles; that it knew what reliance could be placed on their promises; that it was evident that they were destitute of popularity in their country; that the aggression of the French army, (even the latter had the exiles in its camp,) far from enfeebling the government of Juarez, would, on the contrary, strengthen it; and that we hoped it would be pleased to stop short and discontinue operations which thenceforward would be causeless. In fact, the reparation of the grievances which they went to obtain could then be procured, for the French had taken possession of Vera Cruz and Tampico; they were in healthy locations which they could keep secured from all kinds of epidemics, where they could not only treat, but wait until those treaties had been carried into effect.

What reply did we then receive from the government? Did it tell us, as the minister of state has just done, that we were in presence of an enemy, and that it was necessary for us to follow him up in an implacable manner; that it was impossible for us to treat with Juarez, who was branded as an odious tyrant by the animadversions of all honorable men to whom the interests of Mexico were dear?

Not at all. Here is the language used by the government, and I recommend it also to your attention:

"When the French flag, which I hope will happen soon, shall float over the walls of the city of Mexico, we shall not desist from this generous and protective policy; all, reactionists or liberals, violent men or moderate men, shall be admitted alike to this grand expression of the public will; there shall be freedom for all under the folds of the flag of France; and you know well that it will not be the first time that it shall have harbored just national manifestations under its tutelary folds. To all there shall be left entire liberty of choice, and then, if the tyranny of Juarez suits them, yes, if it suits them, they will say so!"

And you all, gentlemen, cried out, "Good, good."

As for me, I could entertain no other opinion than this, with the reservation, however, that it appears to me at least very strange that, in order thus to hold the electoral urn in which the votes of the Mexicans are to be deposited, we should be under the necessity of sending out forty thousand French. But, as to the principle, I confess that it is beyond censure. Yes, if France is willing to remain neutral in presence of the national will, I have nothing more to say, unless it be that she has continued, in spite of the official declaration, to attack it openly, since that national will manifested itself by facts the most expressive, since the government of Juarez rallied around itself, I shall not say the unanimous entirety, but a sufficient portion of the Mexican people to wage war against our brave soldiers.

Is it not true that our government and our army have been deceived? Is it necessary to remind you of that dolorous but eloquent order of the day issued by General Lorencez, who, on turning back to those who called themselves his friends, and who, in reality, were only traitors to him, said to them, You have told us that, in marching towards your cities, we would find only crowns of flowers; yet we have met with an energetic resistance, favored, it is true, by natural accidents, a resistance which certainly has not stopped our brave soldiers, by the action of which French blood has flowed, and flowed in consequence of lying promises. This was the result of the expedition in its first phase.

At the time of the discussion of the address of 1863 we renewed our opposition. In view of the events that had transpired, we demanded, in the name of justice, the cessation of that expedition which to us appeared fraught with mischief for France.

I know, gentlemen, at that time to which I refer, as you can do yourselves, the honorable minister of state replied to me in words of eloquence which sent a thrill of sympathy throughout this hall, to which I was somewhat grieved that I could not respond.

Yes, in our nation, which, above all, is generous and warlike, whenever the flag appears compromised or threatened, there are no reasons, no scruples, no opinions that can arrest us; we go where honor, danger calls, where our brethren are threatened. [Good, good.]

And yet, is it not true that alongside of these great interests for which our predilections are as strong as yours, there is another one which towers above them all? Must we not ask ourselves whether, before we seek for glory, we ought not to be most sedulously regardful of justice? And, supposing we did not have justice on our side, would it not be most impious and unchristian to assert that, because the flag of France has been not vanquished, but obliged to suspend its career of victory for a time, on account of fallacious promises, it is absolutely necessary, in order to redeem its honor, to plunge it again in human blood? [Divers manifestations.]

As to us, we have protested against that doctrine, and whilst avoiding the utterance of a single word that could wound the susceptibilities of the nation, we have thought it our duty, as it was our right, to tell the country what we believed to be the truth.

You voted, gentlemen, against the amendment which we presented. You know what resistance was encountered before the walls of Puebla; twenty-two days of struggle and conflict before an open city! If those unfortunate soldiers, who know no obstacles, who lavish their lives with an intrepidity which is wholly irresistible, yet were stopped during that fatal time which weighed on all our hearts like a mournful anxiety, it was quite necessary that they should be employed at something. It was repeated to you with the utmost complacence, in order to obtain your votes, that there was in Mexico only the phantom of a government, which would disappear at the breath of Almonte. That phantom has clothed itself with all the energy of will, of power, and of national resistance.

After that event it could no longer be doubtful to any one that that mistake, stated to be such even in 1862, had acquired all the light of evidence. We had fallen into the trap of exiles; we were carrying out their designs—that is to say, the designs of men legitimately detested, covered with crimes, and who could not do aught else than compromise our troops. [Cries of dissent.] It was forbidden to us to go any further, unless to go to the city of Mexico, whither we had made an engagement to go. The route was open. We were received there as conquerors; the official reports so assert. Many triumphs of that kind have been dearly bought by those who obtained them.

However that be, the army entered the city of Mexico. There, in my opinion, terminated the military expedition, and the political expedition commenced. How was this double mission managed?

As to the political mission, according to the report of General Forey, it appears that, from the moment our troops entered the capital, the city was in a measure encircled by a cordon of partisan rangers, who rendered the country around impracticable to such a degree that fears were entertained for the safety of our communications. In this condition of things, General Forey felt the necessity of constituting a civil power as soon as possible, and he did well.

But how did he do in order to constitute a civil power? It is here that it is important to refer to the words uttered by the honorable M. Billault, which determined your vote; for, once again, I rely on the acts of the government and on yours, asking of the government and of you no more than to apply the consequences which flow from the premises to which I refer.

Well, M. Billault told us that when we should reach the city of Mexico, we should plant there the standard of France—that is to say, the standard of liberty and of respect for nationalities; that all, without exception, would be called upon to manifest the national will. That, gentlemen, was the declaration. Ah! I do not complain of official documents, I do not complain of discourses delivered within these halls, I do not complain of programmes which are pompously announced here; I only say that facts are in flagrant contradiction with speeches and writings.

So, after you had announced to France and to Europe that the government which was to be established should rest exclusively on the national will, see what has been done.

M. Dubois de Saligny, the person on whose counsels the government much relied—too much, if I am well informed, since M. Dubois de Saligny has ceased to be in the service of the department of foreign affairs—M. Dubois de Saligny, whose predilections were well known, who could not, moreover, fail to support the success of those friends with whom he had made the campaign, nominated a junta composed of thirty-five persons. Out of these thirty-five persons there were twenty-two who had held public functions under the government overthrown by that of Juarez. And if I wished—a thing, however, which I will take care not to do—to go through their biographies, you would see how far these persons were involved in the reactionary policy, which, notwithstanding, we had assumed to ourselves no mission to reinstate.

Better still, in referring to the history of Mexico and of its late revolutions, I find that those constituent juntas and provisional governments were a kind of national custom, and that when in 1860 General Miramon, of whom I have a word to say directly, attained power by a *coup d'état*, he formed and immediately assembled a junta.

Well, I have had the consolation of finding among the members of the junta of 1863 the greater part of the members of the junta of 1860.

This, gentlemen, is the way in which the national will has been consulted. Then these 35 members named 195 others; these 195 constituted, with the 35, an assembly of 230 persons.

Is there any serious man that can have a moment's doubt as to the results of the vote of such an assembly? The papers announced that it was unanimous. Certainly; and there was something stronger still, and it must be told: that vote was dictated by the force of circumstances, and it was impossible for any of the members of that junta to have preserved a real and serious independence. But what must we say of those 230 persons thus assembled to flaunt in the eyes of Europe and the world the pretended miseries of their country, to accuse it of every crime, of every disgrace, of every indignity, when they had been themselves in the service of every preceding government which they attack !

SEVERAL VOICES. Good, good.

M. JULES FAVRE. That is a spectacle of abjection and abasement most disgraceful, from which I turn away my eyes, and on which I ask your permission to insist no longer. [Murmurs of disapprobation from some benches; approbation from others.]

But what is most serious is, that this junta, thus constituted, has not contented itself with saying that it represented the national will; it has done something much better; it has cast a vote, and what is that vote, gentlemen? It has been for a constitutional monarchy. They have not stopped there; they have chosen a prince.

Now, who could this prince be? The reply is in every mouth, and it is very certain that, as we did not for an instant doubt the unanimity of the Assembly of Notables, so there was no more reason to doubt that their candidate would be Prince Maximilian.

Well, gentlemen, permit me to say, if ever the Archduke Maximilian succeeds in reaching the throne, I hope, and you all hope, he will be the model of princes; but what I assert is that, for the present, he is the model of official candidates, [boisterous laughter from some benches; marks of disapprobation from others,] and I know not that a man has ever been presented with such a manœuvring of precautions and such a concurrence of chances of success. And when the Assembly of Notables met again, the announcement might well be made:

"The nation adopts for its form of government a limited, hereditary monarchy, with a Catholic prince.

"The sovereign shall take the title of Emperor of Mexico. The imperial crown of Mexico is offered to his Imperial Highness Prince Ferdinand Maximilian, archduke of Austria, for himself and his descendants.

"In case the Archduke Ferdinand Maximilian should not, on account of unforeseen circumstances, be able to take possession of the throne which is offered to him, the Mexican nation leaves it to the kindness of his Majesty Napoleon III, Emperor of the French, to designate another Catholic prince to whom the crown should be offered."

Let us go to the bottom of things, gentlemen; let us reason like serious men, like honorable men, and let us say this vote is not the vote of Mexico, but the vote of France, represented by her victorious army; it is the will of France that prevails, that is imposed on the Assembly of Notables, and thereupon I here replace my question. This Prince Maximilian, whom I found at the beginning of the negotiations, I find here again in the vote of the junta, which is the expression of the ideas of Marshal Forey, there representing his government, and I interrogate, gentlemen, the honorable member of the government who is now before the assembly, and I ask him: Is not that there the influence, the act, and the influence of France? Are we to be made to believe that, when the glorious eagles of France occupied Mexico, when the blood of our soldiers had flowed in streams before Puebla— [Interruption.]

His excellency the MINISTER OF STATE. You are not willing to avenge it.

M. JULES FAVRE. We all regret it alike, and I know not that we can make use of any expression of sympathy in this respect which would appear exaggerated.

What is certain is that the enterprise had succeeded; we had reached the city of Mexico, victorious, all-powerful, and once more, no reasonable man can doubt but that whatever victorious France may wish can be and will be done.

The candidacy and proclamation of Prince Maximilian were the work of France, the work of the army. Do you believe that, in an event of so much importance, there was involved the accomplishment of promises most solemnly made and engagements entered into by France? This is what it behooves us to examine well in this presence.

When General Forey departed from Europe he did not set out without instructions from his government, and we will find in the imperial letter, to which allusion has already been made, an exact and circumstantial plan of the line of conduct to be followed by the commander-in-chief of the army after his entrance into the city of Mexico; and here again we ask ourselves whether the words in this affair have not been belied by the acts.

Here is what the Emperor said: "When we shall have reached the city of Mexico, it is desirable that all the conspicuous men, of every shade of opinion, (*of every shade of opinion*,) who shall have embraced our cause, should come to an understanding with you to form a provisional government."

And listen, gentlemen: "That government shall submit to the Mexican people the question of the political *régime* that is to be definitively established. An assembly shall then be elected in accordance with the Mexican laws."

Here are the instructions which you gave, and these you have violated. [Divers exclamations.] The Mexican people have not been consulted.

His excellency the MINISTER OF STATE. They will be consulted.

M. JULES FAVRE. It was not the people that declared that the monarchical principle was re-established and that Prince Maximilian should be called to the throne; it was the junta. [Renewed exclamations.]

Thus you acted in opposition to your instructions, to the orders which you received from your sovereign to conform yourselves to the national sovereignty; these instructions you have violated, and instead of seeking for the elements of a provisional government in an assembly composed of different opinions, among all men of note, you have sought for them only in one party; that party alone has been the executor of your orders, and those orders were the destruction of the republic. [Prolonged interruption.]

SEVERAL VOICES. Now you have it. [Prolonged disturbance and various manifestations.]

M. JULES FAVRE. And it is not only the Emperor of the French who thought that there could be imposed on the Mexican people a government which was not of their choice, and that it was necessary, above all, to consult them. The Archduke Maximilian has used the same language, and this is also one of those points over which there reigns an obscurity which, for my part, I would wish with all my heart to see completely dissipated.

In fact, we have all reasoned, or at least the speakers who have preceded me have reasoned on this supposition, that the Archduke Maximilian accepted the crown. Where is his letter of acceptance? Is it in the desk of the minister of state?

As you were told, the post of king will end by becoming so difficult that no one will desire it, and whenever a crown becomes vacant it will be hard to find any one to take it. As to Prince Maximilian, do not believe that he has unconditionally accepted that which has been offered to him.

When the Mexican deputation left America to come to Europe, it was received in France with all the regard due to it; but, if I am well informed, the reception with which it met in Austria was very much cooler indeed; it had not the honor of being received into the presence of his Majesty the Emperor of Austria, although assuredly his Majesty appears extremely interested in the destinies of his brother.

His Majesty believed that this affair was of such a nature, that it partook so much of the romantic, that he would have nothing to do with it.

In fact, gentlemen, in the correspondence printed in all the journals of Europe, I find the following fact: The Emperor Francis Joseph has been asked what part he intended to take in the instalment of his brother, and here is what he answered: "What do you wish me to do? If my brother had desired to retire to a convent, I could not have prevented him from doing so; how could I hinder him from going to Mexico?"

There is, perhaps, a great difference between the two suppositions. I do not wish the Archduke Maximilian to renounce the world and enter into religion, but I do not certainly wish him any the more to try the Mexican adventure.

That which is an official fact is that the speech delivered by the young archduke at Miramar, in presence of the delegation, did not receive the honor of insertion in the Austrian Moniteur, and that speech deserves to be cited, at least in some of its points, for it complicates still more the situation which we are seeking to clear up. What does the archduke reply? "On the result of the vote of the assembly of the country, I must, therefore, in the first place, make the acceptance of the offered throne depend."

And this is not all: "If solid guarantees are obtained for the future."

Here is something for France, who is the godmother, who presents her candidate. The prince to whom she addresses her request says to her: I must have guarantees; without guarantees there can be no acceptance. Such has been the stipulation of the prince. He understands remarkably well that it is a slippery position; that the part of improvised Emperor cannot be played with impunity in Mexico unless the actor is sustained by some important power like France. He wishes France to sustain him. Such are the guarantees that he demands.

"And if the universal suffrage of the noble people of Mexico points to me, I shall be ready, with the consent of the illustrious chief of my family, and confiding in the protection of the Almighty, to accept the crown."

Well, I ask the government where is the acceptance, where are the guarantees, where is the vote of the Mexican people; and as long as all these preliminary conditions are not fulfilled, France has no right to interfere, to carry on war, to prolong an expedition which has no purpose, which has no longer any cause, unless it be a war waged against a people defending their independence and their nationality. [Numerous cries of disapprobation.]

This is the position in which we stand. I spoke to you just now of the Austrian cabinet. See how a sheet, which is not its official organ, but its officious organ, expresses itself in reference to the speech delivered at Miramar by the young archduke: "It is easily understood that the archduke could so much the less accept the offer of the Assembly of Notables, (an offer which, hitherto, has met with no adhesions except in a small number of departments occupied by the French troops,) as other conditions, such as particularly the effective support of the maritime powers, are yet only matters of doubt. England has not yet officially promised her support, although public opinion in that country is favorable to the project."

Well, England has explained her position. I do not wish to fatigue your attention with quotations already too long, but I have in my possession the words spoken by Lord Russell, in which he declares that, whatever modifications may be effected in Mexico, he will not oppose them, but that at the same time he will give them no kind of support.

So England confines herself to a strict neutrality, and isolated in the midst of the American continent, surrounded by jealous rivals, the Emperor whom we are going to install in Mexico will have no other safeguards than the guarantees which we shall have given him and which he asks in the most formal manner of us.

Well, I have reason to say that in this affair the purpose which France had in the beginning, the reparation of the grievances of our countrymen, is entirely lost to view. You can no longer say that you pursue the reparation of the grievances of our countrymen ; it is impossible. That great and legitimate object has been attained.

Now, do you wish to oppose the will of the Mexican people, and are we condemned to undergo those strange conditions made for us by this expedition which I am right to call deplorable, which, to establish a government in Mexico, to constitute an empire there, has placed us under the necessity of sacrificing French blood? [Interruption.]

They tell us that the population is unanimous; that we are not only masters of the city of Mexico, but that, from all quarters, the partisans of Juarez are abandoning him and coming over to us.

What truth is there, gentlemen, in such talk? If we must consult official documents—and I take them from the Moniteur—here is what I find, gentlemen :

"We call the attention of our readers to the correspondence from Mexico which we publish below. These documents testify to the extreme eagerness with which the Franco-Mexican troops have been received by the people of the cities and localities successively occupied, and give us reason to presume that at no distant day the greater part of Mexico will have spontaneously adhered to the empire."

The word *spontaneously*, gentlemen, deserves to figure elsewhere than in the columns of the grave *Moniteur*. It is certain, that when people are forced to acknowledge that the adhesions come only from the points occupied by our troops, to add, then, that the empire is *spontaneously* recognized is assuredly to presume a little too much on the credulity of its readers.

The truth is, that in Mexico we are really masters only of the territory which is under the wheels of our cannons, under the steps of our soldiers. [Marks of disapprobation.]

Here is something that proves it in an invincible manner: We are masters of Vera Cruz ; we have entered the city of Mexico. Instead of seeking to consult the national will, in conformity with the instructions given him, General Forey has organized an expedition ; we have resumed military operations ; and why? What can be the object of them? Who can now explain and assign a reason for this military movement, this new sacrifice of men and money? Evidently, gentlemen, there is no man who can explain it in reference to the legitimate interest of France ; and if it is not possible to explain how this military enterprise thus continues, do you know what it means? It is, that outside of the city of Mexico we meet resistance, which we are under the necessity of vanquishing, if not at the cannon's mouth, at least by the presence of our arms. Yes, wherever we tread the soil we are masters of it; but as to any adhesions whatever coming from countries not occupied, we are not informed of a single one.

As to military events, God forbid that I should come here with premature news, to throw alarm in any way through the country. [Interruption from many benches.]

BARON DE GEIGER. You are not doing anything else but that.

M. JULES FAVRE. They have spoken to you of triumphal marches ; they have told you that, wherever we have presented ourselves, we have been received as liberators. Yet we cannot conceal from ourselves that Guadalaxara resists, and that we are on the point of undertaking the siege of it ; and, if military operations are yet indispensable, I ask the government, once again, to tell us what can be the cause and the excuse for them. Is it not evident that it is because we are fighting against Mexican nationality? [Murmurs of disapprobation from several benches.]

I would much like to know what kind of a government it would be that could resist the co-operation extended to adverse parties by a victorious army in possession of its capital. As to me, I know none to which I would give the advice to make a trial of the kind.

Mexico resists, notwithstanding ; and it is here that we have to ask ourselves what we have to do ; whether it is possible for us to continue such a policy, and if we must march even to San Luis de Potosi.

You have only to cast your eyes on the map, and you will be convinced that the commissioner on the part of the government fell into an involuntary but capital error when he told you that we occupied the greater part of the Mexican territory. [Cries of disapprobation.]

SEVERAL VOICES. He did not say that. He said the greater part of the people.

M. JULES FAVRE. What we occupy—I shall not go into details—are the great centres of population; but we do not occupy all the great centres of population. To the north as well as to the west there are yet found cities of vast importance, in which the Mexican authority, which we combat, is found installed and disposed to resistance. And it will therefore be necessary for us to undertake a campaign against each of these cities. And, over and above the 40,000 men already in Mexico, we must yet send thither 10,000 or 15,000 men; that is, henceforth we must augment our effective force in Mexico, in order to carry on this deplorable expedition, to effect the conquest of Mexico for the benefit of an Austrian prince, to dissipate the clouds which the Mexican exiles have gathered, and to create that power which is repudiated by those even who have most interest in sustaining it. The country must be told that it is yet necessary to keep 50,000 or 60,000 men in Mexico, with all the materials requisite for their transportation and maintenance. Is that what you wish? [Manifestations of denial.]

Now, is it difficult to know how and why we cannot, under present conditions, constitute anything in Mexico? You were told yesterday, gentlemen, in very precise terms, the reason of our feebleness compared to our military power, which nothing resists. It comes from the fact that we rely on the support of a detested party, composing only a minority of the nation.

We have expended fifteen millions in feeding and clothing the Mexican army; we have made our generals grasp the hands of Miramon and Marquez. Miramon and Marquez! Do you know who they are—what they represent? Here are the official documents, which testify that, in 1857, Miramon and Marquez, repulsed from Vera Cruz, entered Tacubaya. There they ordered the massacre of the prisoners and of the sick who were in the hospitals.

A VOICE. And of the surgeons.

M. JULES FAVRE. They had them deliberately shot. Among the victims were seven physicians, one of them an Englishman. The seven physicians suffered the same fate as the rest. Here is the order to Marquez, signed by Miramon:

"YOUR EXCELLENCY: This very evening, and under the strictest responsibility of your excellency, you will cause to be shot all the prisoners belonging to the class of officers, subaltern and superior, and you will render me an account of the number of those who shall have met this fate. God and law.

"MIRAMON.

"MEXICO, *April* 14, 1859."

And as among these prisoners there was an English physician, England protested; and see in what energetic terms the first secretary of the department of foreign affairs in England expresses himself:

"Mr. Seymour Fitzgerald has replied to me, that it was inopportune on my part to make complaints to the government of her Majesty, when he had in his hands a remonstrance, written by a merchant of the city of Mexico, (he was not pleased to tell me his name,) concerning Mr. John Duvall, a subject of her Britannic Majesty, who, in company with several others, foreigners and natives, had been assassinated in the cruellest, most inhuman, and most shameful manner, by order of the authorities of the city of Mexico, solely because they had found them in attendance on the wounded at Tacubaya, as it was their duty to be in their quality of surgeons. He added, that her Majesty's government has never known of acts so barbarous, so unworthy of a people pretending to pass for civilized, yet meriting the execration of the whole world."

And it is through such scenes of blood, gentlemen, in the midst of such crimes, that Miramon attained the reins of power! At that period Marquez was thrown into prison. Do you know why? Why? Because he had carried off 600,000 francs belonging to the English legation.

The first act of Miramon, on attaining power, was to set him at liberty. England protested; and see in what energetic terms:

"The undersigned desires particularly to persuade his Excellency S. D. Theodosio Larès that, in conformity with the well-known sentiments of her Majesty's government, of which sentiments he is happy to be at this moment the interpreter, he will always be at his excellency's disposal, to aid him to issue from the position in which the administration, of which he forms a part, is actually placed, in case that administration should present some plan of conciliation, to put an end to the civil war which desolates the republic in so lamentable a manner, and which, if it continues, will imperil even its existence as a nation. But he would be wanting in his duty, and to the assurance which he has given to his excellency of the interest which the British government takes in the continuation of its amicable relations with Mexico, and in the honor and prosperity of the republic, if he neglected to call his excellency's attention to the rumor, mentioned in the papers, of the liberation of General Marquez, and of his being placed at the head of an important military command.

"Since the arrival of the undersigned at Mexico, that general has rendered himself guilty of several atrocious assassinations, among others, one of a British subject, (Dr. Duvall, one of the victims of Tacubaya,) who was seized at the moment that he fulfilled the duties of his profession as surgeon, duties considered sacred among all civilized nations, and he committed the still greater baseness of desiring to justify himself by calumniating his victim.

"Some weeks afterwards he rendered himself again guilty of an assassination committed on the person of an American citizen, put to death by his orders and without any form of trial.

"Subsequently he seized the money confided to his charge for transportation, and aggravated his crime by alleging, in order to exculpate himself, that he had need of money to establish the government and, the opinions which he pretended to sustain."

These are the acts of which we have demanded an account from Juarez, and for this we have become the friends and allies of those who have dishonored themselves by committing them. And you are astonished that resistance is offered to you when we place such men as this at the head of the Mexicans, who remember those abominable acts that deserve to be branded with infamy by all civilized nations.

No, no, we have deceived ourselves; let us withdraw. Our brave soldiers, our officers, men of so much delicacy of feeling, and so full of honor, have no business in the midst of such vile and bloodthirsty adventurers, among whom they find themselves astray. [Vehement applause from some benches; murmurs of disapprobation from others.]

At Mexico, how do they act? You know that General Forey was scarcely installed there when he issued that decree of sequestration which the government has been under the necessity of revoking; but it was not possible for him to escape from the inflexible law of his situation. He had come to sustain those who, after having flattered him, were going to become his masters; they tried at least to be so, and when the provisional government was established in the persons of General Almonte, General Salas, and the archbishop of Mexico, then the pretensions of the reactionists were clearly manifested; they desired to go back upon the past.

Ah, you believe that the Mexicans, whom you have gone to sustain, understand the generosity of France? They have seen in her intervention the success of their schemes, of their guilty hopes; they have wished to rescind the decree of Juarez and resume the property that had been sold. Then the general ordered in a firm tone that justice should have its course, that no change should be made as to the execution of the obligations relative to the national property. And what ensued? The provisional government resisted; it resisted the hand that had raised it from the dust, that had made it what it is, that had invested it with its ephemeral power.

General Bazaine spoke in a commanding tone; he caused a *communication* to be inserted in the papers. Out of three members of the provisional government, two humbled themselves; as to the third, it was in his conscience that he obtained his strength. Far be it from me to reproach him for having entirely separated from the government; but in the name of the dignity of France, I find my sensibilities very much hurt at seeing one of those three heads turning against us and appearing to teach us an insolent lesson by placing beside the *communication* of General Bazaine the protest which I here quote. It was printed in the official journal. Assuredly, in France, such a thing would have been impossible. General Forey says, in his proclamation, that he brings to the Mexicans the benefit of warnings in matters regarding the press; it is not certainly for that that we have made war. [Exclamations and laughter.] But, in spite of that legislation, after the *communication* of General Bazaine, Monseigneur, the archbishop of Mexico, had the following printed:

"His illustrious excellency Monseigneur the archbishop, being opposed to taking any part in the questions of the *promises to pay*, of the sales, and of the continuation of the constructions, and other points decided in accordance with the sense of the two preceding communications, published in the number of the Official Gazette to which this is a supplement, makes his dissent known to the public, in order to relieve himself from all responsibility on the subject."

So he separates from us; he declares that we have violated the divine law; that as for him he cannot follow us in such a course. He has sent in his resignation, and the papers have reported that when mass was to be heard by that army, which everywhere met with passive and due obedience, Monseigneur closed the doors of his church, and mass was heard only because cannons were planted to blow down the gates of the cathedral. [Various demonstrations and disturbances throughout the Chamber]

Such is the order which you have established in Mexico; I advise you to congratulate yourselves on it. As for me, such order appears anarchy; for you have placed in power those whom the national will had overthrown; you combat those whom it sustains. Such is your real situation, and it is for this that I earnestly ask of you to put an end to it.

The government tells us that it is going to reply. It has uttered one expression which I have received with real satisfaction: it has told you that there was no other solution than universal suffrage.

Well, if the information given to us in the session of yesterday is correct, if in reality we occupy a territory representing a population of 5,500,000 inhabitants—that is the figure given; it has been given officially, and we must keep it in mind in order that we may be able hereafter to regulate the truth of any assertions that may be made to us—if, I say, you have in your favor five millions five hundred thousand inhabitants, make them vote, and make them vote freely. The imperial order makes this a duty. It is in the name of national sovereignty that you have landed in Mexico. You have no intention of abjuring your principle; it must be propagated. This principle you consider as the source of truth and right, and according as you proclaim it, you will not certainly stifle it under the heels of your victorious generals. Well, if you wish to have a vote, you have under your hand an electoral population sufficient for the vote; make them vote. Only you are permitted—I am mistaken, you are ordered, while supervising the vote and conforming yourselves to the lofty ideas of the Emperor, you are ordered not to influence that vote. You should leave the election to the Mexican nation itself. In this peaceful accomplishment of its most sacred rights, it is necessary that Mexico should make known its wish; it is necessary that from its entrails, not torn by the knife of the sacrificers like those of the ancient victims, [noisy demonstrations,] but, on the contrary, rendered fertile by modern law, by the benefits of civilization, should issue at last that cry which will be the proclamation of its real sovereignty. Here is what the government ought to do.

But I confess, gentlemen, in view of the resolutions which have been taken, in view of consummated facts and of those now being accomplished, I frankly acknowledge my fears lest the part which it seems determined to act should prove very difficult of execution; and yet the unanimous sentiment of this assembly, the sentiment of all France, is that this occupation of Mexico should not be prolonged; it is that, as far as the honor and interests of France allow, it should cease as soon as possible; it is that our brave soldiers now in Mexico should soon again see their native land. Numerous considerations of various kinds have been laid before you to justify this opinion; permit me, in conclusion, to produce only one. [Hear, hear.]

Is it true that the lessons of history will be always lost, that they will teach nothing to those who, notwithstanding, ought constantly to draw their inspirations from them? Is it a fact that in them we shall not find, by going back to the events of bygone years, salutary warnings by which we ought to profit?

Gentlemen, fifty-six years ago, the chief of the powerful house which now reigns over France, to whom we cannot certainly refuse the possession either of genius or power, who had accustomed Europe to tremble before his slightest will, whose friendship was sought by the greatest potentates, that man one day had his Mexico also. He conceived the idea, in accordance with a policy which always appeared to me fatal, though however it has been celebrated as grand, of levelling the Pyrenees for the sake of a family alliance; and it must be granted, gentlemen, there seemed to be special pretexts in that case, as in this one of Mexico. Whom need I remind of the state of the Spanish nation at that time? Her monarchy was represented by an aged monarch almost imbecile; beside him a dissolute and violent queen, a favorite justly unpopular on account of his haughtiness and his usurped power; and to crown all, gentlemen, a son secretly conspiring, an impious son who had learned in the teachings of the Jesuits that all means are good when they can conduce to success. What did the Emperor do? The Emperor wished to regenerate Spain. He constituted himself the sovereign judge of her chiefs, summoned them before him at Bayonne, and by a stroke of his hand dashed the crown from the head of the king. He took it up to give it to his brother. The latter passed the Pyrenees. Were there ovations wanting to him? Was not he, also, able to gather up crowns of flowers? Did not courtiers throng around the triumphal car of the new king? You have been told with reason, the race of courtiers is imperishable. After success came the conflict; it lasted five years, a heroic conflict, signalized by victories that eminently displayed the valor of our soldiers; a sterile conflict, however, for their blood could never cause the tree to grow whose roots they had to fertilize on the soil of Spain. And then one day the storm lowered from the north; the tempest burst in its fury; and then the great captain saw with anguish his glorious legions sacrificed for an interest which was not a French interest, and the clash of arms on many a battle-field [louder, we cannot hear] resounded a grand lesson to the world.

Well, gentlemen, can we say, at the present time, that all is calm, that all is security around us? On casting our eyes around us, are we not struck, as the honorable M. Thiers said yesterday for Mexico, with the small number of those who declare themselves our friends? Ah! when we find before us these causes of distrust, we can all declare, with legitimate pride, they do not frighten us; for if we can be divided when there is question of internal affairs, if we cry out for liberty with earnestness, if you sometimes refuse it to us, [cries of disapprobation,] when there is need of making headway against Europe we are all united, and all united we are invincible. [Good, good.] But do you know on what condition? On condition that we always have justice on our side, and that it be not possible some day, as was done in 1813, to arouse against us the feelings of the nations, by their being told that we have violated their rights, falsified the promises of France, and oppressed their liberty. [Murmurs from some benches; applause around the speaker.]

Mr. Seward to Mr. Romero.

DEPARTMENT OF STATE,
Washington, March 8, 1864.

SIR: I have to acknowledge the receipt of your note of the 25th of February, accompanied by translations into English of the discourses pronounced in the French Chambers on the 25th, 26th, and 27th of January last, concerning Mexican affairs.

Thanking you for your courteous attention, I avail myself of the opportunity to renew to you, sir, the assurances of my very distinguished consideration.

WILLIAM H. SEWARD.

Señor MATIAS ROMERO, *&c., &c., &c.*

Mr. Romero to Mr. Seward.

[Translation.]

MEXICAN LEGATION TO THE UNITED STATES OF AMERICA,
Washington, February 26, 1864.

Mr. SECRETARY: I have the honor to enclose to you, for the information of the government of the United States, copies in English of some of the protests made by the authorities and citizens of the Mexican republic against the intervention which the Emperor of the French has been engaged in carrying through in my country.

I much regret that I have not in my possession all the protests of this kind which it would be fitting to submit to the consideration of the civilized world, that it might know without difficulty on which side the national will really lies upon the question now debated in Mexico. However, such as I have been able to collect, and which I send enclosed, are, in my opinion, sufficient to place beyond all doubt the fact that while the French and their agents have occasion for all the pressure of their bayonets to obtain in places occupied by their forces some acts of adhesion, signed by persons unknown, and often full of fictitious names, the same towns, when freed from military pressure, expressed their will against intervention, through the medium of the most distinguished citizens among the local authorities, freely and popularly chosen, who represented faithfully, therefore, the will of their constituents, and are again doing the same thing the instant they see themselves free from the foreign invaders. It is notorious that many of the protests against intervention have been made in places in which, at the time, there was no armed force of the national government. They were, therefore, the free expression of the will of those who signed them, and there cannot be the slightest suspicion that they could have been dictated by fear or violence, which there was no means of bringing into play.

I avail of this opportunity to renew to you, sir, the assurances of my very distinguished consideration.

M. ROMERO.

Hon. WILLIAM H. SEWARD, *&c.*, *&c.*, *&c.*

Manuel Doblado, governor of the state of Guanajuato, to its inhabitants.

GUANAJUATO, *July* 28, 1863.

FELLOW-CITIZENS: The honorable congress of the state, upon terminating its legislative labors, has delegated to me the exercise of its powers, amplifying the extraordinary facilities with which it had before invested me.

This new testimony of confidence imposes upon me the duty of addressing you, in order to make known to you the use that I propose to make of the authority which has been deposited in my person.

The events which have recently occurred in the city of Mexico have placed the foreign question in its true light, and presented it with a precision and an exactitude which removes all possibility of error. These events reveal nothing less than the deliberate intention of converting the republic of Mexico into a colony of France.

The theatrical farce by which it has been sought to divide and to distract public opinion has no other object than to place the country, by means of certain artificial transitions, under the domination of the French arms.

In all this there is only the good faith that a conquered people may hope to receive from their conqueror.

The invading general has affected to believe that the military question was concluded, when he yet has the intimate conviction that it has only commenced.

No one now is ignorant of the deplorable causes which contributed to bring about the disasters which occurred to the armies of the east and of the centre.

The invading general also knows them, and he knows that without the aid of those causes he would not to-day be in Mexico.

The military question begins now on the day when the country raised the flag of resistance. The solution of this question is yet known only to Providence. He will award to each that which is his just due.

The political question is a question of right, and on this field Mexico is omnipotent.

Nationality is the life of a people. The Mexicans have inherited independence from their fathers. They achieved that independence by virtue of their courage and their sacrifices, not by intrigue; nor did they purchase it with corrupt gold.

The right which exists on our side is evident; it is incontrovertible, unprescriptible. It is the right which England has, and Spain and France, under their respective nationalities; and to place this right in doubt is to reject all public law, is to imperil the very existence of nations as independent states, to attack at its very base the principle of natural right, and to introduce chaos into established international relations.

Force is not right. It is necessary to repeat this principle a thousand times, however trite it may seem. Force disposed, many years ago, of Poland, but the rights of the Poles still exist, and only burst forth the more brilliantly each time the sacred fire of insurrection appears.

The Emperor Napoleon has had the power to invade Mexico, but he has no right to convert it into a colony of France. It has been attempted to found a right upon the unhappy condition of the republic, and upon its continual revolutions.

But this is only the sophistry of bad faith, in which even its authors do not believe. It is true that we have committed many errors, and that all parties, in attempting to put in practice their respective theories, have failed, devoured by the revolutionary spirit. But only the Mexicans have a right to complain of these evils The right to reproach is exclusively our own. Foreigners have no right to take cognizance of our domestic dissensions, and still less to bring charges against us for acts done in the exercise of our national sovereignty.

The invader well knows these truths, and it is for this reason that each step he takes in the country he repeats the deceitful watchword of his designs: "We do not come to impose a government upon Mexico; we come to protect the free choice of that the Mexicans wish to give themselves." This hypocritical pretence does not merit refutation; it has already been set aside by the nation *en masse*, when it laughed with scorn at the news of the monarchy of Maximilian.

The good sense of the inhabitants of the country has comprehended that there cannot be freedom where there is compulsion; that the French army is not a protector, but a usurper; that these phrases with which it is sought to deceive the people are only the set phrases which conquerors in all times have used with lying tongues; diplomatic expedients, invented in order to paralyze resistance; involuntary confessions, but very significant of our right to freely govern ourselves without the intervention of any foreign influence whatever.

Presented thus the political question, and being clear as the light of the noonday sun the right of Mexico not to admit the protection offered to her at the point of French bayonets, the course which should be followed by all Mexicans is plainly marked out. It is to fight to the last against the invaders; to exhaust to the uttermost every resource of the country in order to make the war successful; to reject all thought of compromise as an impossible means when treating of the independence and sovereignty of the nation, which, from their very nature, are indivisible and inalienable, and to die if it is necessary, but with the consciousness that the honor of Mexico has been saved.

This is the course which the government of Guanajuato will pursue in order to correspond to the confidence which the representatives of the people have manifested in the person who exercises its functions.

For an enterprise so grand and so holy no co-operation should be refused—no individual should be rejected. Under the flag of independence, for the first time thrown to the breeze by the venerable curate Miguel Hidalgo, all political parties have a place, for under its shadow there is harm only to traitors. To-day I call upon all the inhabitants of the state, whether conservative, moderados, or liberals, to lend their services, each one in the sphere which may be possible, to the cause of independence. To-day disappear with political hatreds all the unhappy denominations born of civil war. In the bloody struggle upon which we have now to enter there are only two distinctions which can henceforth be known—Mexicans or Frenchmen and traitors; invaders or invaded; freemen or slaves. It is not a sense of peril which counsels me to this invocation to fraternity. During the three years of my administration, tolerance has been a practical truth in the state of Guanajuato, where the same respect and the same guarantees have been enjoyed by men of all shades of opinions and from all the states. If it were not unworthy of a government to pronounce its own panegyric, I could recount to you a thousand acts which testify that the idea of a universal fusion has formed one of the cardinal bases of my administration.

Nor is it fear of the great power of the French empire which incites me to make this call for reconciliation. The power of France is great. This incontestable fact will later form our glory.

But the question is not now which of the two nations has the most power, but which of the two has justice on its side. Possessing the right, we have the obligation to defend it, even when all the physical conditions of war are unfavorable to us.

What would have become of Spain in 1808 if she had stopped to consider the number and the strength of the French armies which had been perfidiously introduced into her principal cities and fortresses before she had commenced her glorious uprising?

What would Mexico now be if the father of our independence had stopped to calculate the immense resources of the crown of Spain, and the poverty with which he was surrounded at the moment when he proclaimed our emancipation?

I am very far from feeling that spirit of boastful arrogance which would preannounce triumphs and enumerate imaginary forces. Our weakness is a fact; it is a fact which itself has led to the invasion. But our duty is to defend ourselves, and when a duty is to be complied with we do not count the number of our adversaries, nor are we deterred by obstacles. We cannot lose our independence with honor without first having defended it with arms to the last extremity.

Then, and only then, shall we have a right to the consideration of the world; then, and only then, shall we transmit to our sons the right of rebellion against their oppressors whenever they shall have the power to rise; and only thus can we wash away with our blood the stain which has been thrown upon the flag of the nation by those few degraded Mexicans who, through the asperity of parties, through hunger, or from motives the most vile, have lent themselves to serve as the instruments of the invader, and have filled positions which reveal the lowest grade of abjectness.

Guanajuateneses, Providence has destined us to live in an epoch of trial.

Let us rise to the height of the situation.

Be great in the day of the struggle, as our domestic discords have made us before appear weak. Let us demonstrate to our enemies that we are not unworthy of forming an independent nation.

Let us make them feel the difference between this faction of beggars, political *chevaliers d'industrie*, who have asked the aid of the Emperor, and the immense majority of the nation with whom the love of nationality dominates as a vigorous and puissant passion, who possess that noble pride which is inspired by patriotism, and who have a sacred and inextinguishable attachment for the preservation of our independence.

The lash, the pillory, and secret executions already cause the hand of the conqueror to be felt in the city of Mexico.

Who among us has not felt his brow redden with shame on hearing of this infamous treatment applied to Mexican citizens?

Fellow-citizens, the conqueror comes boasting that his steps will be marked by peace, by security, and by abundance. Let us wait a little, and our deceived brothers will be restored to themselves when they see that all these promises are deceitful, that they are only the delusive utterances of an accomplished trickster.

Our destiny is war. Let us enter, then, upon the struggle with the dignity of freemen, with the courage of independent Mexicans, and with faith in God, who will never abandon the cause of justice.

The future is dark, because it is a future of sacrifices; but the reward is imperishable; it is the glory of Hidalgo and of Iturbide.

Posterity will judge us all; and when this epoch of passions and of hatreds shall have passed away, it will honor with posthumous impartiality these Mexicans who have died defending the independence of their country, and the traitors who have cowardly sought to deliver it over to the French covered with opprobrium and with infamy.

Viva la independencia! Viva la republica! Viva el gobierno constitucional Mexicano!

MANUEL DOBLADO.

PROCLAMATION.

Citizen Manuel Doblado, constitutional governor of the State of Guanajuato, to its inhabitants:

GUANAJUATENESES: The French and the traitors are already knocking at the gates of the State. I return, therefore, to take charge of its government, in order to fulfil my duty by defending it, and am resolved to pursue the destiny which Providence may present to me in the place where the popular will has located me.

The Frenchman proceeds, using advantageously our political antipathies, and deceiving at once progressionists and retrogressionists, in order to build up a governing power purely French on the ruin and discredit of both.

Neither the one nor the other will be persuaded of this truth, although both have been cruelly disappointed. Time alone, and the falsity of the invader's promises, evidenced by want of fulfilment, will cause the deluded to retrace their steps when it may be, perhaps, too late to remedy the evil.

The loyal Mexicans, who see clearly the object at which the conqueror aims, have marked out a path in which there can be no vacillation, and therefore pursue it with a firm step and calm conscience.

All are resolved to fight incessantly until they fall or save independence and the constitutional government of the republic. They know all the disadvantages of the situation and the resources of the enemy, but they comprehend that when the annihilation of a nation is in question, weakness is no excuse, because duty is satisfied only when all that could be has been done.

The insurrection is now an undeniable fact. Wherever there are Frenchmen and traitors there are champions of independence. They are fighting at one and the same moment from Vera Cruz to Queretaro, and in the very gutters of the city of Mexico; the upheaving of insurgents reminds the incredulous that the country is occupied militarily, but not conquered. The pacification of the country under the empire of the French flag is impossible.

The invasion will cause the state countless losses, for which neither the invaders nor false Mexicans who have called them will be responsible. The government of the state has maintained order, peace, and individual guarantees from its establishment, in the year 1860, until now, notwithstanding that it has found itself surrounded on all sides by elements of destruction. If, hereafter, it should find itself compelled to abandon that path and enter that of reprisals and coercive measures, let the blame rest on the traitors, who, to satisfy petty ambition and wretched passions, have brought upon their country the scourge of foreign war. Upon them let the tremendous responsibility of whatever may happen fall.

Fellow-citizens, the hour of struggle approaches; the time of trial has arrived. In the pages of modern history there is no glory comparable with that which Spain and Russia acquired when, at the beginning of this century, they opposed, in an insurrection, an indestructible wall to Napoleon I. Both appeared to succumb speedily to the immense power of the modern Artaxerxes; but the people arose, and those two powers overturned him who had won the prestige of invincible.

Let us imitate the heroic example of those great nations, nor allow the power and number of our enemies to affright us. It may well be that the chances of war may be adverse to us at first; but fortune will come at length to crown our constancy. The question is not between Mexico and France exclusively. There are interests and considerations of a high order, which will be developed in time, when Mexico, sustaining with courage and honor the unequal struggle, will prove to the world that she is perfectly worthy to form by herself a sovereign and independent nation.

Viva la independencia! &c., &c.

MANUEL DOBLADO.

GUANAJUATO, *November* 9, 1863.

PROTEST OF THE CONGRESS OF SONORA AGAINST FOREIGN INTERVENTION.

The protest which was made and signed at San Luis Potosi, on the 22d of July of the present year, by the permanent deputation of the congress of the Union, in the name of that sovereign body, against all acts that have taken place, or may occur hereafter, under the power or influence of French intervention, being well known throughout the republic as well as abroad, and the political importance of the same being of such a nature that it makes it useless to show forth the legitimate considerations which gave rise to it, expressing with as much truth as energy the grievances and attempts which the present government of France has committed, and contiues to commit, against the most sacred rights of the nation, allied with Mexican traitors, and violating all principles of international law, trampling under foot and scorning the individuality of Mexico as a sovereign nation, and, without any more right than that of brutal force, scandalizing the whole civilized world, pretends to arrogate to herself the authority to impose upon us the form of government which ought to rule over us and the administration we should adopt, and leaving nothing new to add to that historical monument that testifies so amply the will and sentiments of the nation, manifested by the legitimate organ of its representatives, and fixes the imprescriptible rights of the Mexican nation, sustaining its autonomy, rights that can never be ceded to a foreign power by a revengeful faction of fanactics and traitors.

Therefore the constitutional congress of the free and sovereign state of Sonora, faithful interpreter and legitimate representative of the people of the same, whose sentiments of patriotism and zeal for its independence are so well known, declares: that it makes the protest made and signed by the permanent deputation of the sovereign congress of the United Mexican States, in the city of San Luis Potosi, on the 22d of July, 1863, its own, as also any former acts and protests; that it will always consider as null and vexatious to the sovereignty of the nation and to that of the state all and every act that may have for its origin the French intervention in any of the political affairs of the Mexican republic, and that it disowns and will repel as usurper any foreign power, as well as any other created in the country which does not emanate from the legitimate federal constitution which the nation gave freely to itself on the 5th of February, 1857.

Hall of Sessions of the Congress of Sonora at Ures, on the 21st of October, 1863.

DOMINGO ELIAS, SEN.
PASCUAL ELIAS, JUN.
JESUS GUIJADA.
RAMON MARTINEZ.
FRANCISCO MORENA BUELNA.
NIEVES E. ACOSTA, *Deputy Secretary.*
JOSÉ M. REDONDO, *Deputy Secretary.*

[Annexed to Mr. Romero's letter of February 26, 1864.]

MINISTRY OF FOREIGN RELATIONS AND GOVERNMENT.

Second class—seal 5th—half a dollar. For the term of two years included in the years 1858 and 1859.—General bureau for the administration of the revenue from stamped paper.—Established for the years 1862 and 1863, conformably to the supreme order of March 16, 1861.

MANUEL GOMEZ, R. P. S.,
Principal Bureau of Stamped Paper, Sonora.

CITIZEN-GOVERNOR OF THE STATE: The undersigned, who compose the patriotic association formed in this city under the title of "Independence Club, Liberty or Death," have resolved to address ourselves to the enlightened chief magistrate of the republic, intrusted with the defence of its independence, and invested with full and complete powers by the national legislature, and to manifest to him, in the most solemn manner, as I have the honor to do through the worthy mediation of this government, our firm and decided resolution to repel with profound hatred and eternal malediction, by all the means in our power, and in every possible way becoming us as true patriots, every interventionary pretension of the French invaders, manifesting, at the same time, the closest and most sincere adherence to the wise institutions by which we are governed, and which the nation has established for itself through the instrumentality of its legitimate representatives and in the exercise of its indisputable power and sovereignty, laid down in the great constitutional charter of 1857 and in the laws of reform.

We likewise declare, as our final resolve, that, being deeply penetrated with patriotic sentiments, such as ought to animate every loyal Mexican, we are firmly resolved to co-operate with all our strength in the grand work of the national defence, and to shed our blood and that of our sons for the liberty and independence of our fatherland, most unjustly and wickedly threatened with destruction by the invading hosts of the most ambitious tyrant of Europe, the degenerate colossus of our age, the hated despot, the associate of bandits and traitors, the unprincipled Napoleon III.

Be pleased, citizen-governor, to transmit these short but truthful manifestations of our feelings to the supreme magistrate of the nation, which we are ready to reduce to practice at whatever cost.

ALAMOS, *July* 16, 1863.

A. ALMADA, *President.*
VICTORIANO ORTIZ Y RODRIGUEZ, *Vice-President.*
LEOPOLDO GIL SAMANIEGO, *Secretary.*
JUAN J. MENDOZA, *Secretary.*

Inocencio Garcia, Aurelio Garcia, Laureano Jelin, Exiquio Ordeñan, Francisco Miranda, Luis Teyechea, Juan Lopez, Saturnino Alvarez, José Maria Flores, Priciliano Orduño, Eduardo Retes, Luis Acosta, Jesus Camargo, Juan J. Zárate, Severiano Avilez, Diego Avilez, Jesus Ramirez, Leocadio Miranda, Juan J. Estrada, Ramon Ibarra, Manuel Amarillos, Antonio Gamez, E. Baldenegro, Jesus Almada, Juan S. Moreno, Rosalino Corral y S. Miguel Serrano, Cecilio Ocen. To be a free Mexican or perish: Carlos C. Avilez, Macario Escalante, Luis Acuña, R. J. Rodriguez, Jesus S. Campos, Juan Marquez, José Maria Treviña y Alvarez. Signed for the following citizens, by their request: José Maria Valenzuela, Estevan Valenzuela, Regiro Salas, Calixto Hernandez, Juan Benitez, Francisco López, Saturnino Corrales, Juan Alvarez, Ignacio Beltran, Jesus Piñuela, Porfirio Balderrama, Fulgencio Rojo, Jesus Gastelo, Adolfo Tesiseco, Miguel Salas, Ignacio Rodriguez, Concepcion Campay, Higineo Esqueo, Bernardo Camargo, Tranquilino Gutierrez, Santiago Navarro, and Manuel Campos, Leopoldo G. Samaniego, Isidoro Sonsa. For Nepomuceno Delgado, Antonio Navarro, Máximo Urias, Nemecio Alarcon, and Francisco Valenzuela, Leopoldo G. Samaniego, Jesus Maria Sanchez, Santiago Navarro, Emeterio R. Ortiz. For Liato Dominguez and Benigno Valenzuela, Victoriano Ortiz y Rodriguez, Rafael Acuña, Guadalupe Mendoza, José Maria Retes, Jesus O. Almada, Antonio Miranda, Manuel Féra, Juan J. Márquez, Florencio Cevallos, Francisco A. Cevallos. For Candido Garcia, Guadalupe Mendoza. For the citizens, Francisco Ruiz, Ramon Urbalejo, Alejandro Barreras, Manuel Valdez, Pánfilo Lugo, and Basilio Valdez, Guadupe Mendoza. For Ramon Najarratí, Leopoldo G. Samaniego, Santos Delgado. For Manuel Rodriguez, V. Ortiz y Rodriguez. For Tiburcio Valdez, Leopoldo G. Samaniego, Carlos Cevallos, Estevân Ortiz. For Eulalio Morales, Leopoldo G. Samaniego, Ramon Jácome, Jesus Cevallos, Manuel Salazar, Antonio Almada, Francisco Salido. For Agustin Gamez, José Almada, Lorenzo Ortiz, Juan de D. Tavela, J. Antonio G. Samaniego, Salvador Company, Luis G. Parada. For Porfirio Bostillos, Leopoldo G. Samaniego. For Rosendo Mendivil, Leopoldo G. Samaniego.

This is a true copy of the original which remains in the archives of the association.

V. ORTIZ Y RODRIGUEZ, *Vice-President.*
JUAN J. MENDOZA, *Secretary.*
LEOPOLDO G. SAMANIEGO, *Secretary.*

ALAMOS, *July* 17, 1863.

STATE OF SONORA,
Office of the Prefect of the district of Alamos.

VINCENTE ORTIZ, PREFECT OF THE DISTRICT OF ALAMOS.

I certify that the preceding signatures are those used by the individuals who have subscribed their names in all their affairs and business transactions, public as well as private, and therefore admitted as legal testimony in court and out of court with the credit which they deserve.

And at the request of these citizens, above mentioned, I issue these presents at Alamos, July 17, 1863, and I authorize and seal them according to law.

VINCENTE ORTIZ.

A true copy.—San Luis Potosi, August 28, 1863.

JUAN DE D. ARIAS.

OFFICE OF THE SECRETARY OF THE CONGRESS OF THE UNION,
PERMANENT COMMITTEE, BOARD OF PRIMARY INSTRUCTION OF CHIHUAHUA.

The board of instruction of this capital, deeply affected by the recent events that have transpired at the city of Zaragoza, and by the occupation of the city of Mexico by the French invaders, has deemed it proper to approve the protest which I have the honor to transmit to you, in order that you may be pleased to lay it before the permanent committee of the sovereign Congress of the Union.

In compliance with the wishes of the board, I have the honor to offer you the testimony of my profound respect and sincere attachment.

Independence and liberty!—Chihuahua, July 29, 1863.

J. M. G. DEL CAMPO, *President.* [SEAL.]
FRANCISCO ESPINOSA, *Secretary.* [SEAL.]

The SECRETARIES OF THE PERMANENT COMMITTEE OF CONGRESS.

The Board of Primary Instruction of Chihuahua to the Governor of the State:

Since the occupation of the heroic city of Zaragoza, and of the capital of Mexico, by the invading army of Napoleon III, a triumph not due to the power of its arms—resisted always and with courage by the valiant defenders of our independence—but to accidental circumstances of war or of necessity, and of regard for the great end of never compromising with the perfidious and hypocritical pretensions of the ambitious tyrant of France, and of maintaining, at all hazards, the sovereignty and liberty of our country; and since, from the fact of finding himself in the city of Mexico, followed by a disgusting crowd of infamous traitors, General Forey considers his military operations as terminated, believing himself already the conqueror of the nation; considers likewise as having arrived the moment for initiating the work of the intervention in the political reorganization of the country; has commenced to dictate laws, and has instituted a ridiculous government, counterfeiting the national will, which can never be represented by the combination of traitors resident in Mexico, who are the only persons that could second the intentions of General Forey, by this means entirely ignoring the existence of the constitutional government established by the free and spontaneous vote of the nation, which, by having its residence at present at San Luis Potosi, has thereby neither lost its legitimacy nor abdicated its authority, nor ceased to be obeyed and respected by the states; it is necessary that the voice of the country should be raised on every side, and should reach the ears of Forey, and even those of the despot of France, protesting before the world against their wicked and unjust pretensions to interfere in the politics of our republic, or to subject it to their domination; it is necessary to give them to understand, in the most energetic and conclusive manner, that, if our arms succumb, our wills are still repugnant and resist all extraneous interference, be it what it may, and whatever be the pretext or motive which it adduces in its justification; it is necessary that these gunpowder civilizers should know that, if sometimes the brutal force of arms triumphs for a period over reason and justice, the national sentiment of a free people is irresistible and its will most potent, invincible to all attacks, and unconquerable by any human power. It is necessary that all the states, all the peoples, all the authorities and corporations, and every Mexican that is not a traitor, should solemnly declare that they detest the French intervention with all their heart, as well as the interference of any other foreign nation; that they will never recognize nor acknowledge any other government than that which actually rules the nation, established in conformity with the constitution of 1857; that they consider as a mere nullity and usurpation whatever shadow of a government General Forey may establish in the city of Mexico, or whatever one may be established under the protection of the French arms; that they will also neither accept nor consider as legal any treaty that may be made with the invader, with the sacrifice of the national honor, or with the loss or alienation of any part of the Mexican territory.

These, citizen-governor, are the patriotic sentiments and the convictions of the members of the board of primary instruction, and in accordance with them they make the following declaration:

1. The members composing the board of primary instruction, individually and collectively, protest, in the most solemn manner, against the intervention of France, or of any other foreign nation whatever, and place at the disposal of the government of the state their persons and their fortunes, in order that the government may employ them in the defence of the national independence threatened by Napoleon III.

2. They consider as a nullity and a mockery the government established in the city of Mexico by General Forey or under the influence of his bayonets; and they protest against all the provisions and decrees that it may dictate or may have already dictated.

3. They will recognize no other government than that established in conformity with the constitution of 1857, nor will they obey any other laws or any other authority than those derived from that only legitimate code of the nation.

4. They protest against any treaty whatever that, by any unforeseen contingency, may come to be made with the invader, to the detriment of the honor of the nation, or the alienation of any part of its territory.

JOSÉ MARIA GOMEZ DEL CAMPO, *President.*
JOSÉ MARIA MARI, *Vice-President.*

José Maria Porras, Tomas Irigoyen, Adolfo Viard, Mariana Saenz, syndic; Roque Jacinto Moron, honorary member; José M. Telles, honorary member; José Cordero, Tomas Cordero Zuza, Eduardo Urueta, Bernardo Revilla, José M. Jaurrieta, Genaro Artalejo, Francisco Nieto, Pablo Porras; José Rodrigo Garcia, honorary member; Laureano Castañeda, Andrés Vidalva, Joaquin Campa; Victor de la Garza, honorary member; Joaquin Villalva, honorary member; Jesus Muñoz, honorary member.

FRANCISCO ESPINOSA, *Secretary.*

CHIHUAHUA, *July* 17, 1863.

This is a true copy of the original.—Chihuahua, July 30, 1863.

J. M. G. DEL CAMPO, *President.* [SEAL.]
FRANCISCO ESPINOSA, *Secretary.* [SEAL.]

A true copy.—San Luis Potosi, August 21, 1863. Signed, on account of the illness of the official superior, by

R. J. ESPINOSA DE LOS MONTEROS.

OFFICE OF THE SECRETARY OF STATE AND OF THE BUREAU OF FINANCE AND PUBLIC CREDIT.

FRONTIER CUSTOM-HOUSE OF THE PRESIDIO DEL NORTE.

The subscriber, administrator of the frontier custom-house of the Presidio del Norte, in Chihuahua, in union with the other employés of that office, declares in his name and in theirs that they comply with their duty as Mexicans in manifesting to the supreme general government of the nation, in which they recognize its legality as the only and true expression of the will of the people of the republic, that they repel, with the dignity becoming to every free and truly patriotic man, the privilege which any nation whatever may pretend to arrogate to itself, be its category what it may, to mingle or interfere in the free exercise which our nation possesses of the right to regulate itself in the manner that it thinks most suitable; that for this reason they see the present intervention with indignation, and protest—

1. Against the wicked and unjust aggression which the present Emperor of the French, Napoleon III, has made and continues to make, under pretext of interfering in our internal affairs.

2. Against all and every one of the acts that emanate from the so-called government of the capital, for the reason that it is illegitimate, inasmuch as it has been established by the invader, and formed among others of the traitors who have most distinguished themselves, and who have given most cause to be hated from the beginning of our glorious conflict with the French.

3. Against the establishment of any other system of government than the constitutional republican system which now governs us, or that which the nation may choose to adopt for itself freely and spontaneously without any sort of intervention by any foreign power whatever, and principally without that of the present invaders.

They protest, finally, that they will not recognize nor respect any other orders than those issued by the supreme government of the nation, now resident in the capital of San Luis Potosi, and by the authorities, functionaries, and agents recognized by the same supreme government.

Frontier Custom-house of the Presidio del Norte, in Chihuahua, August 3, 1863.

JUAN MUÑOZ.
FRANCISCO ESPENOSA.
JUAN JOSÉ ESCUDERO.

A true copy:

J. N. GAMBA.

The Corporation of Guadalajara to the Government and People of the State:

The invaders have planted their foul footsteps on the ruins of the heroic city of Zaragoza. The decisive moment has come; the moment in which we should show to the world our country in all her splendor, in all her majesty. Because she is no longer in the midst of triumphs, which oftentimes are solely due to the caprice of fortune, she is not, therefore, in anxiety. It is not in prosperity, nor in the peaceful and undisturbed enjoyment of their institutions and of the public will, that peoples and governments prove their power and their virtues, and achieve their greatest conquests of glory and of progress, but in suffering and in conflict with formidable enemies. The loss of the first city that resisted the assault of the French hosts is converted into an incalculable augmentation of our physical and moral strength. The hope has disappeared with which our enemies, repulsed in their first attempts, returned to their ships, and they have become convinced of their impotence. The sole result has been that the barrier banks of the channel have been burst, in which rolled the terrible wrath of a valiant and high-spirited nation, assaulted by an unjust and treacherous aggressor. The last cannon discharged on those walls, purpled with the blood of our brothers, is the signal of imminent danger, is the signal for the greatest and most sanguinary combat registered in the history of the human race. It is a universal and necessary law that from struggle results progress. Tyrants, always conquered in the arena of discussion, have recourse in their spite and rage to the power of arms. But death does not enslave, nor do the dungeons enslave in which thought is immured, nor the gag with which the voice of right and reason is stifled, nor the chains that are placed on the heroes who prefer to die rather than be conquered. Only the humiliation and homage of the will before brute force enslave; only treason and cowardice enslave. The final triumph of our arms is secure, because we not only love liberty and have a right to its enjoyment, but also know how to defend it.

This is the moment to unveil all traitors; and such are not only those who have enlisted in the ranks of the invaders, but likewise those who respond with cowardly silence to the call of their country. The uprising of a people to save their independence sanctifies the fury of their vengeance, destroys or roots up whatever obstacle it encounters in its way, and punishes selfishness and fear as crimes; for selfishness and fear are marks of treason, that therefore place men outside of the pale of the law.

The corporation urges the government, by every means in its power, to find out clearly the distinction between true Mexicans and traitors, to the end that these latter should be consigned to capital punishment, without hope of pardon, and that they should be amenable to such punishment for no other cause proved against them than their refusal to defend their country, or their entertaining any kind of relation whatever, direct or indirect, with its enemies: because this corporation, in the fulness of its conscientious persuasion, believes that, if it were practicable to penetrate the hidden thoughts of man, even the crime of thinking against the sacred rights of one's country ought to be punished with death. The corporation, likewise, urges the government to allow no other human consideration to be preferred in its mind to whatever in any way concerns the defence of our independence, and to impress on the minds of those who now have the glory of being Mexicans the immense responsibility which that character of itself imposes on them, and the duty under which they are to suppress in their hearts all affection and every obligation which cools or combats in them the sentiment of nationality. This now demands of them the sacrifice of their lives and of their fortunes; and undoubtedly they will offer both most willingly. Few, indeed, will those be from whom it will be necessary to take them by compulsion, and still fewer those who will commit the opprobrious crime of consenting to live beneath the French flag.

Let every sword be unsheathed now; let us hear no words but those of war and vengeance; in our lost cities let the invader receive only solitude and the silence of the tombs, and the devastation of our fields and the conflagration of our homes; let us imitate and excel all the free nations of the earth, as those who, like the invincible sons of Saguntum and Numantia, consigned themselves to the flames rather than submit to their enemies, or those who, like the defenders of Nasactum, slew their wives and children and then killed themselves, in order not to become slaves to the conqueror. The victory shall be ours; but if the supreme designs of Providence deny us that, let us not forget that liberty is found not only in victory, but also in death.

FELIX BARRON, *President.*
OCTAVIANO CEVALLOS.
JOSÉ MARIA BRAMBILA.
JULIO G. PEÑA.
MARTIN MUÑIZ.
ALBINO DEL MORAL
JUAN HIJAR Y HARO.
SILVERIO ALEMAN.
CALIXTO OROSCO.
MANUEL DE ZELAYETA, *Syndic.*
AURELIO HERMOSO, *Syndic.*
IRENEO PAZ, *Syndic.*
JUSTO V. TAGLE, *Secretary.*
AUGUSTIN QUEVEDO, *Assistant Secretary.*

Ignacio O. Echeverria, colonel of infantry in the regular army and major general of the division of Jalisco, to his fellow-citizens.

GUADALAJARA, *May* 27, 1863.

FELLOW-CITIZENS: A disaster sufficiently common in war has caused the heroic city of Zaragoza to fall into the power of the French, the vanguard of our valiant army being destroyed. In the height of their pride, perhaps the French cut-throats will think that the war is finished, and that the sons of Mexico will abase their heads before their vile bayonets. God forbid, fellow-citizens, that it should be so. In these final moments it will be that the whole world shall see what a free people are, who desire to be so, and who know how to defend their sacred rights of independence Yes, men of Jalisco, the sovereign day of trial has come to decide once forever the fate of the whole American continent, and the contest begins, the greatest, the most heroic, and the most sanguinary of contests. The perishable ramparts of a fortification may be overthrown and laid in ruins by the invading artillery; but those ramparts shall never be overthrown that are formed by the breasts of Mexico's brave sons, if, all united, we march to show these modern conquerors that there are millions of citizens who prefer to fall bravely in the arms of death rather than to witness the triumph of the odious flag of the tyrant of France in the country of the Hidalgos, Iturbides, and Zaragozas.

Men of Jalisco of all classes, hasten to obey the call of the chief of the state; let us offer him our lives and fortunes; and let us rush full of ardent patriotism to form the new republican army which will give our enemies to understand that in the country of Prisciliano Sanchez there are yet thousands of names to become illustrious, combating in the national defence, like those of the Montenegros, Balcazares, and many others, which are now the honor of this great state.

To you, brilliant youth of Jalisco, to you who are the hope for the future of your state, my feeble but patriotic voice calls to take up arms and worthily replace the sons whom Mexico has lost on the field of honor. Yes, you will go, my friends; in your youthful forms, full of enthusiasm, I see the hope of our country; from among you shall issue the thousands and thousands of geniuses who shall carry off the palm of victory from the hireling adventurers of France; and you will hereafter be the pride of Jalisco, for having, with your blood and the might of your arms, paid the price of her independence and liberty.

And you, wicked citizens, miserable outcasts, infamous traitors, woe be to you, if in those final moments you treacherously seek to assist the enemies of our liberty, because greater than your villany shall be the national punishment. Back! Give way to freemen and loyal citizens, who go to comply with their duty or to fall full of glory.

Fellow-citizens, let us hasten to die, if it be necessary; let us fall, borne down by brute force, if we cannot repel it; but now and ever let our war-cry be: "Long live the Mexican republic! Long live independence! Long live Jalisco! and death to the French and traitors."

IGNACIO O. ECHEVERRIA.

The officers of the supreme tribunal of justice to their fellow-citizens.

GUADALAJARA, *May* 29, 1863.

MEN OF JALISCO: The recent events of the war have proved disastrous to the national arms. It would be useless to seek to diminish the extent of the disgrace. Our loss has been great, very great, and however much the heart may feel it, its sorrow cannot equal the gravity of the situation. One of the most beautiful cities of our republic has been destroyed, many fortunes have been ruined, much of our materials of war have passed into the hands of the enemy, and, above all, the valor, the sufferings, the self-denial, the heroism of our soldiers, have proved unavailing. Are not these motives for great affliction for every Mexican and even for every man in whom there exists a sympathy for the misfortunes of a people that suffers for the holiest of causes, which are its independence and the defence of its soil, trodden by the foot of the stranger?

The understanding is unable to comprehend how the French nation, which prides itself on its intelligence and high-mindedness, can maintain that they come to insure our happiness, by means of so many calamities, and that, by rekindling the fires of our intestine broils, they labor to restore our peace; that, by favoring treason to the country, the most degrading vice that humanity has to complain of, the principles of morality and civil order are to be cemented, which are the sole salvation of all society; how, by introducing themselves into the midst of the civil war which devours us, and by raising up a vanquished party already dead through the very nature of things, we have to attain union and concord; how, amid the din of arms, is to be sought the free vote of the people.

In the condition to which the affairs of our country have arrived, when the question of justice is decided in our favor by the civilized world, it is idle to ask by what right this intervention is employed, for which we do not ask, which we resist, which we repel with all the strength of our soul. Now, at present, the Mexican desires to know why he is insulted, why he is mocked at by the invocation of such pretexts to trample on his most sacred rights.

Reverses ought not to extinguish, nor cool off, nor diminish our enthusiasm in the slightest degree. It is natural that our misfortunes should cause us grief; but let us not be dismayed in the defence of our sacred cause We are not obliged to conquer The issue of battles depends on a thousand circumstances which are not always in relation to each other, nor to the justice of the matter in question, nor to the valor of the combatants. But still it is our duty to embrace our banner and to press it to our hearts with so much the more force as our dangers are the greater, and to die in its embrace if death is the destiny which Providence designs for us.

All Mexicans, each in his proper sphere, each in the line which suits him, accept the situation, and accept it with all its consequences. Let the invader domineer over the country, if he can; but let it be after having conquered us in an obstinate contest, and when no longer any Mexican exists capable of bearing arms.

Now, then, that the danger increases, that the question is one of force, that in order to oppress us recourse is had to treason and to all sorts of means, no matter how wicked, the supreme tribunal of Jalisco undertakes to raise its voice in order to protest before the whole world against such iniquities, against such infamies, against the scandalous violation of our rights. The tribunal repeats that, in as far as it is concerned, it repels all foreign intervention and all such acts as emanate from it or from the intruding authorities which it sets up.

Men of Jalisco, the hour of sacrifice has come. Let us nerve ourselves and be faithful The people that wishes to be free, no power is able to reduce into subjection.

JESUS CAMARENA, *President.*
JOSÉ MARIA MACEDO.
JUAN ANTONIO ROBLES.
LEONARDO ANGULO.
J RAMON SOLIS.
FERMIN G. RIESTRA, *Fiscal Officer.*
PABLO IGNACIO LORETO, *Secretary of Decrees.*

DEPARTMENT OF FOREIGN AFFAIRS AND GOVERNMENT.

POST OFFICE, *San Luis Potosi.*

In the city of San Luis Potosi, on the 20th day of the month of May, in the year 1863, the employés of this department, whose names are subscribed to this document, having assembled together, have resolved to protest solemnly against the intervention of any power or potentates whatever that may seek, either singly or collectively, to interfere in the political affairs of our country, and likewise to employ the forces and the means that are within the reach of each one of them, in order to oppose, disconcert, and destroy the projects of intervention in our country manifested by the Emperor of the French, protesting likewise against the invasion of the national territory by the French troops, and against all acts emanating from the authorities that may be established under the influence of their armed forces in any quarter of the republic.

We equally testify our most firm adhesion to the constitution of 1857 and to the laws of reform, as well as to the authorities and laws that emanate from the former. Consequently, we likewise protest the firmest adhesion and obedience to the Citizen Benito Juarez, as the representative of legality, democracy, and progress.

A copy of this document shall be sent to the governor of this state, and another to the administrator general of this branch of the public service, for the ends that may follow.

JACINTO AGUILAR.
JOSÉ D. BELLO.
LUIS ASTEGUI.
CALIXTO SANCHEZ
LONGINOS RODRIGUEZ.
GERTRUDIO NIÑO.

Second Class.—For the term of two years, including 1863.—*One dollar.*

In the city of Tequisquiapan, on the twenty-fifth day of the month of May, in the year 1863, the magistrates of whom this corporation is composed having assembled in this town-hall of the municipality, there was read the communication issued by the supreme government, and dated on the nineteenth of the present month. The said magistrates, being thus made acquainted with the contents of the aforesaid communication, unanimously resolved that the supreme government has never failed to recognize the representatives of this town as true Mexicans, descendants of Hidalgo, Allende, Morelos, and various other heroes, who knew how to achieve our independence, and rescue us from the slavery in which we found ourselves oppressed. Then, at the present time, the Mexican army confronts the invading enemy, and it is an obligation upon all to assist it in the preparations which it has to make in order to attend to the necessities of a cause which our brothers defend in favor of our beloved country. We should all be branded with the name of traitors, if we did not seek to promote the cause of justice, which admits with pleasure not only the holocaust of life, but even the most trivial sacrifices, with which we should aid the cause of our national independence.

The people of Potosi have ever been the first to defend the integrity of the national territory, and have never been sparing in their efforts in favor of the independence of our country; in similar circumstances, on the present occasion, the present authorities of this town and the neighborhood find themselves, and protest solemnly to disavow the views advanced in any form by the invading enemy.

With the which this document concludes, which is signed by the following citizens: Refugio Juarez, president of the corporation; Austasio Ramirez, second magistrate; Francisco Badillo, third; Prudencio Anaya, fourth; Alvino Guerrero, syndic procurator; Andrés Lopez, popular alcalde; Damaso Manzanares, assistant alcalde; Luis Camacho, municipal treasurer; José Maria Azpeitia, civil judge; and, as assistant magistrates, the first assistant president of the corporation, Julian Najera; Juan Luna, second magistrate; Jorge Beltran, third magistrate; Secundino Lopez, fourth magistrate; Juan Beltran, syndic procurator; Juan Nepomuceno Narvaez, secretary; who all unanimously sealed these presents, leaving it for transmission with the political chief of this capital.

CONSTITUTIONAL CORPORATION OF SANTIAGO DEL RIO.

In the town of Santiago del Rio, a suburb of the capital of the state of San Luis Potosi, on the twenty-second day of the month of May, in the year 1863, there having assembled in the town-hall the citizens who compose the corporation, mayor, and treasurer of the municipal funds, under the presidency of citizen Estevan Leija, the chief of the municipality, who had previously issued a proclamation for a call for this purpose, that same citizen rose to speak, and said, that as our dear country found herself invaded by the army of the French, and as the supreme government of the nation combated with dignity this unjust invasion, directed against it without any reason whatever, it was in his opinion a very suitable time for all the people to raise their voices against the foreign invasion, which, forgetting that the time for conquests has already past, pretends to lord it over the great country of Mexico, for that purpose taking advantage of the situation in which Mexico was seen to be, from the intestine wars which it has experienced since the period of its release from the European domination, which held it in a backward state, and sunk in ignorance and slavery. It should never be forgotten that the citizens who are the inhabitants of the republic are descendants of Hidalgo, Allende, Morelos, and the other illustrious champions, who, overcoming all difficulty, proclaimed and succeeded in making us free and independent. Wherefore, all the citizens, and in particular the authorities, consider it their duty to protest against any intervention whatever, which foreigners desire or pretend to have in the affairs of our country. So it has been understood by the government of the state, when it issued its decree for the removal of the seat of government from the capital, under date of the 15th of the present month, and when it issued the circular to the other functionaries, under date of the 18th of this same month. Therefore, the citizens present here may freely speak and discuss the purpose for which they have been convoked, and resolve in the manner that may seem most suitable to them. In virtue whereof, the following resolutions have been adopted by mutual and unanimous agreement:

First. The constitutional corporation and other employés of this town, for themselves and in the name of the people whom they represent, protest in the most solemn manner against the unjust aggression made upon the republic by the army of the French

Second. They likewise protest against any intervention, whatever it may be, that foreigners wish or pretend to exercise in the affairs of Mexico; because this republic, ever and forever, whatever sacrifices may have to be made, must be free, independent, and sovereign, and does not wish, and never will consent, that its sacred rights should be usurped by any other nation in the world.

Third. A certified copy of the present resolutions is to be presented to the government of the state, by the means of the chief magistrate of the capital, for its information, and the purposes to which it may conduce.

With which declaration these resolutions are closed, and signed and sealed by the president and other citizens, who have been called to the meeting and have concurred in their passage.

ESTEVAN LEIJA, *President.*
QUIRINO MONTIEL, *Mayor.*
PANTALEON MEIZA, *Second Magistrate.*
VICTORIANO GARCIA, *Third Magistrate.*
CAMILO GONZALES, *Syndic Procurator.*
EDUWIGIS MONCADA, *Treasurer.*
CANDELARIO HERNANDEZ, *Secretary.*

I certify this to be a true copy of the original which remains in the archives of the corporation. Done at the town of Santiago del Rio, on the twenty-second day of May, in the year 1863.

ESTEVAN LEIJA, *President.*

CANDELARIO HERNANDEZ, *Secretary.*

OFFICE OF THE CONSTITUTIONAL CIVIL DEPARTMENT OF CATORCE.

In accordance with the exhortatory letter directed to this superior department, urging me, in union with the subordinate officials of the department, to manifest my opinion on the war now being maintained by the republic against foreign invasion, I have the pleasure of declaring for myself and in the name of the employés of this department, in order that it may be laid before the governor and the public, that I reprobate with all my heart and execrate the course of conduct pursued by Napoleon III towards the Mexican republic as unjust, dishonest, and derogatory to the laws of nations; and I protest that I will, as far as lies in my power, provide for the supreme government of the nation all the means that I can as a public officer and as an individual to enable it to attain the sacred end for which the glorious defenders of Zaragoza have so heroically co-operated. I desire that the cut-throats of the tyrant of France may fly in terror before the soldiers of the people, and go hide themselves in the darkness of Napoleonic servilism, while the disgrace of their rout gives to the entire world an irrefragable testimony of the enkindled patriotism and valor of my fellow-citizens May the French eagle, the symbol of monarchical retrogradism, be humbled and abased before the victorious flag of Mexico, and may the enlightened peoples of the new and old continents gaze in wonder on the regeneration of a heroic people, who, by the baptism of blood, are born again for liberty.

Our country, independence, liberty, and reform!

CATORCE, May 21, 1863.

ANTONIO PRISCILIANO HERMOSILLO.

MANUEL NARVAEZ, *Secretary*.
MARCELINO J. CASTILLO, *Clerk*.
PORFIRIO NARVAEZ. *Clerk*

In the city of Guadalcazar, on the twenty-first day of the month of May, in the year 1863, the authorities and officers whose names are hereunto subscribed, having been called together at the invitation of the political chief of the department, for the purpose of taking into consideration the circumstances into which the republic finds itself involved through the unjust war waged upon our soil by the tyrant of France, the grounds were examined on which the invaders have pretended to support their unjust aggression, and it has clearly appeared that they differ much from the humanitarian sentiments by which a strong and powerful people should strive to elevate the civilization and fraternity of their neighbors when these latter are deficient in those qualities. Very different are the views which the monarch of the warlike people of France entertains towards our race and republic, since carnage and slaughter do not constitute the sort of protection which the powerful affords to the weak in order to elevate him to an equality, and that they may both march together in unison to prosperity and greatness. It is a criminal conquest, indeed, by which it is sought to blot the name of Mexico from the catalogue of the free nations of the earth; it is by destruction that the independence is threatened which our fathers acquired with their blood and with their lives; and it is, in fine, a rude blow that is struck at our republican and democratic institutions; and for this it is that miserable renegades, branded with the mark of infamy and treason, now come leagued with that dishonored flag which, in all ages, symbolized the victories and the glory of France.

Our young republic has been villanously and cowardly assaulted by that nation, and in favor of her sacred rights she is justified in defending herself with heroism until she issues safe from the conflict or perishes with honor. We, her sons, are acquainted with the perfidy with which the conqueror, like the wolf in the skin of the sheep, brings extermination and ruin to our soil, in order to debase us and make us tributaries and slaves by means of an allied monarch, through whom he pretends to govern us. But, if such a throne should ever succeed in being established, it must be over heaps of dead bodies, accumulated in lakes of blood.

Now we are in the conflict, the precious blood of our brothers flows in torrents in the east, and their exploits and heroic resistance in the invincible city of Zaragoza place Mexico at such a height of greatness that it is the admiration of Europe, because its children have known how to conquer the strength of the first soldiers of the world, and to imprint a stigma of disgrace on the breasts of those eagles which soared in proud triumph over the turreted walls of Sebastopol and on the field of Solferino. The nation rises in a body to chastise the enemies of our independence and of our institutions, and this explains the fact that the mischievous intentions of the Emperor of the French are now laid open to the light of truth.

In the midst of this war-cry, breathed from the noble breasts of Mexicans, we should listen to the solemn protest which we should all loudly enter against this unjust invasion which is brought to attack us on our own soil, at the threshold of our own doors, and also against this monarchy, which the traitors pretend to establish with the aid of France. We, as Mexicans, lovers of our independence, and decided defenders of our liberty and of our institutions, protest solemnly, in the face of the world, against the French invasion, directed against us by the despot Napoleon III. We protest against the monarchy which it is pretended to establish on our soil, and we protest that we will sacrifice all our fortunes and shed all our blood in favor of our independence and of our liberal institutions.

In affirmance of which, and in order that our patriotic sentiments may be known to all, we sign and seal these presents, of which a copy shall be transmitted to the first magistrate of the state, in order that he may be made acquainted with the resolution of the people of Guadalcazar, manifested by their authorities and officers.

FRANCISCO ANTONIO OLAEZ,
Political Chief of the Department.
TOMAS RUIGONEZ,
First Alcalde, with the functions of a Judge of the Court of First Instance.
JOSÉ MARIA BELLOECHIO, *Second Alcalde.*
JOSÉ LEON GARCIA, *Assistant Second Alcalde.*
CRISTOBAL CORDOVA, *Civil Judge.*
JOSÉ MERCED CASTRO, *Administrator of Rents.*
NIEVES E. SALINAS, *Administrator of Stamps.*
BRUNO A. OLAVIDE, *Administrator of the Post Office.*
FELIX NOYOLA, *President of the Corporation.*
JULIO CORONADO, *Magistrate.*
ANTONIO CORDOVA, *Magistrate.*
PEDRO VEJO, *Syndic Procurator.*
JUAN TAMAYO, *Syndic Procurator.*
JOSÉ CRUZ TOSCANO,
First Deputy of the Mining Bureau.
HIGINIO CORONADO, *Second Deputy.*
CAYETANO SOTURA, *Consultor and Deputy.*
CARLOS CORONADO, *Municipal Treasurer.*
GREGORIA GOMÉZ Y CELIA.

An exact copy of the original.—Gaudalcazar, May 21, 1863.

F. A. OLAEZ.
GREGORIO GOMÉZ Y CELIA.

CONSTITUTIONAL CORPORATION OF THE MUNICIPALITY OF BOCAS.

The corporation of this municipality, over which I have the honor to preside, having been assembled in extraordinary session on this present day, has resolved that it is its duty to co-operate in the peace of our republic, as all good Mexicans and loyal sons of our adored and beloved country, and, for the greater satisfaction of your excellency, has drawn up this present document, of which, with all due respect, I transmit a certified copy with the present communication for your information. In it we protest solemnly against any foreign power whatever that proposes or thinks to invade our republic, which we will not consent that they should freely trample on until we first fall victims to their deceitful conquests, as our brothers and the heroes of liberty have pointed out the way to us.

May your excellency be pleased to accept the assurance of our consideration and distinguished esteem.

God, liberty, and reform!

Municipality of Bocas, May 22, 1863.

PORFIRIO MARTINEZ.

FELICIANO JACOBO, *Secretary.*

ILLUSTRIOUS CORPORATION OF THE CITY OF VENADO.

In the city of Venado, on the twenty-second day of the month of May, in the year 1863, the illustrious corporation of this city, having assembled in extraordinary session under the presidency of citizen Eduwigio Dominguez, and in view of a communication received from the office of the chief of the department, and issuing from the government of the state, the contents of which were received with much interest, was moved by its own instincts and the fulness of its patriotic enthusiasm to give expression to its feelings. After having seriously discussed the critical state in which our republic is situated, on account of its invasion by the French, and taking into consideration the heavy evils which may be expected if the country does not continue heroically to maintain its independence, therefor employing all its forces, as she did in the invincible city of Zaragoza, (a glorious fact and most worthy of history ;) then possessed with a true love and humanity towards ourselves in the maintenance of our independence and nationality, which constitute a sacred duty for every Mexican, and will be a source of crime to him if he shows himself indifferent to them; for which reason, with unanimous and solemn protest, this illustrious corporation records its declaration against all foreign intervention, as it also protests its desire to labor in every possible manner to carry out the views which the supreme government of the state proposes to itself to follow, according to the divers official communications in reference to this laudable object, published in the official organ of the same government. That the present protest may be brought to the knowledge of the supreme government, it was ordered that a copy of the original be taken and transmitted through the proper channel. And finally, the members of the corporation signed it before me, the secretary, who now authenticate it.

EDUWIGIO DOMINGUEZ.
FRANCISCO HERMOSILLO.
ANTONIO PUENTE.
TRINIDAD PONCE.
IRENEO MARTINEZ.
AGUSTIN OLIVEROS.
JUAN ROCHA.
LORENZO ROBLEDO, *Secretary.*

A true copy.—Venado, May 29, 1863.

EDUWIGIO DOMINGUEZ.

LORENZO ROBLEDO, *Secretary.*

OFFICE OF THE POLITICAL CHIEF OF THE DEPARTMENT OF SALIÑAS DEL PEÑON BLANCO,
SUBORDINATE BUREAU OF STAMPS AT SALIÑAS.

In the town of Salinas, on the twenty-second day of the month of May, in the year 1863, the subscribing citizens, having assembled in the hall of this office, publish the following exposition to the nation :

Great have been the events through which we have passed since December, 1857, to the present date—events as glorious as those of our independence, and perhaps to be brilliant examples in the history of the people of the globe. For what were the means on which our fathers counted to effect the independence of our country? None but the people. What were the means with which our former statesmen counted to overthrow the colossal tyranny that overshadowed us and cut the roots that had grown for three hundred years? Public opinion; the people, for they are sovereign. But what is the misfortune of our unhappy country, to shed so much blood on fields of battle? Some few spurious sons of Mexico, luxuriating in gold and honor, have called in the Frenchman to ruin his parent country, who yet has been unable, either by force or by opinion, to triumph, because on every side they have seen themselves repulsed; but on both the traitors and their abettors shall fall the malediction of the people, the malediction of the nations, and, sooner or later, the punishment of the Eternal.

Eighteen months have now passed since the foul footsteps of the invader have polluted our soil, and since, with villanous deceit, he abused the unsuspecting faith of the supreme government of the nation, by breaking the preliminary treaty of La Soledad; their intention then, as now, having been to recur to corrupt and damnable treason for success, as they knew well that it would have been very difficult for them to pass our first positions at Chiquihuite, and therefore they little regarded their treaty stipulations or their honor. Twenty days of siege did the invincible position of Zaragoza withstand, and not an inch of earth has the perfidious Frenchman gained by force, because that worthy army of the east is invincible, because it defends its country, it defends its independence, it defends its liberty, and finally, because the God of armies protects our cause, and we will triumph over Napoleon III. But if, through any caprice of war, (which will not be more than temporary,) the invaders and traitors should believe themselves triumphant in their perfidious treason, we, the subscribers, as representatives of the people, in the presence of the nation and of the entire world, sign the following protest :

1. Not to recognize any other government than that legitimately constituted, and the authorities emanating by our laws from the constitution of 1857.

2. To recognize the whole Mexican republic as a free, sovereign, and independent nation.

3. To repel and disavow all intervention by France, or by any other power, having for its object the conquest of Mexico or the establishment of a protectorate, which the Mexican republic has clearly, legally, and spontaneously expressed its purpose neither to solicit nor to allow

4. To admit no intervention, direct or indirect, physical or moral, in the internal politics of the country.

5. That it approves and recognizes the right which Mexico possesses to repel force by force, to resist the unjust invasion of the French, because their government has violated

the law of nations, and taken advantage of the honesty and good faith of the Mexican nation.

6. Neither in consequence of the occupation of the capital, nor of any of the states, nor of the whole republic, no matter for how long a period, will we consent to any treaty humiliating or dishonorable for Mexico.

7. Mexico shall always preserve her right of insurrection against Napoleon III or any other usurper whatever.

8. We declare every Mexican a traitor against the nation who directly or indirectly aids the invader.

9. At the same time we declare every Mexican a traitor who promotes or participates in associations or movements directed against the constitution of 1857, the laws of reform, and the particular constitutions of the different states, emanating from them, or against the authorities legally constituted under those laws.

To give them due effect, these resolutions are reduced to writing, ratified by the persons who participated in their passage, and signed by them with me

GERTRUDIO FERNANDEZ, *Chief of this Department.*
IRENEO DELGADO, *First Magistrate.*
JUAN C. ISAIS, *Second Magistrate.*
GAVINO HERNANDEZ, *Third Magistrate.*

In the town of San Juan de Guadelupe, on the twenty-fourth day of May, in the year 1863, in virtue of the exhortatory letter issued by the supreme government of the state, and transmitted through the hands of the political chief of the department, the commissioner, whose name is subscribed to this document, invited the authorities and citizens of this town to meet in the town hall, where, after the reading of the above-mentioned communication, being impressed with its contents, they unanimously resolved, that, being proud of their position as Mexicans and their conviction of the rights of the nation, and of the glory of Mexico, raised to the rank of a free, sovereign, and independent people, by the heroic sacrifices of Hidalgo and Morelos, and many others, who bequeathed an inestimable benefit to their posterity, which it is the sacred duty of these to preserve ; but in the present circumstances, the ambition of Napoleon III, disguised and urged on by the pitiful pretexts of some few traitors, who, in the attitude of most degrading supplication, like miserable reptiles, have gone to ask protection for their people, who need not such protection, but only those who have always desired and sometimes succeeded in effecting their desire to retard it in the way of the human perfection to which the hand of God directs it, in order that the few might live to the prejudice of the many; and when the Mexican people, victoriously traversing the path of reform, annihilates them as a mere handful of contemptible people, they hope from Napoleon III that, in exchange for the independence of their country, he will turn over to them its destinies and other things which they ambition ; that such considerations demand the expression of the frank and loyal sentiments of the inhabitants of all the communities of the republic, in order that the entire world may know the noble and natural enthusiasm of their patriotism ; that therefore, those present, representing the authorities and citizens of this town, in the name of this people, express their sentiments as follows :

1. That they protest in the most solemn manner before God, the nation, and the civilized peoples of the world, against the war so unjustly, so utterly without shadow of right, and to the scandal of the world, waged upon our soil by the Emperor of the French, Napoleon III, who hypocritically offers us a protection which we have not asked of him, and which we do not need of him, his principal end being our conquest, and that in perfidious disregard of our sacred right to independence.

2. That it is a holy duty for Mexicans to sustain, with their persons and property, the contest now waged for the preservation of our beloved country, and we protest our readiness to act in this crisis as good Mexicans.

3. That Almonte and all the traitors who have followed in the wake of the French intervention lie most villainously is the decided persuasion of all Mexicans.

With which propositions we conclude these presents, which are ordered to be transmitted through the hands of the political chief of the department to be laid before the supreme government of the state ; wherefore we sign and seal them.

MAGDALENO HERNANDEZ.
SEBASTIAN BLANCO.
LEON GARCIA.
LUCAS ARAUJO
VIVIANO PEREZ.
EDUARDO ALTAMIRA.
FAUSTINO IZQUIERDA.

CONSTITUTIONAL CORPORATION OF THE CITY OF CATORCE.

In the city of Purisima Conception de Catorce, on the twenty-second day of the month of May, in the year 1863, the corporation having assembled, on motion of the political chief of the department, the session was opened with the reading of a circular from the supreme government of the state, bearing date on the fifteenth of the present month, by which the corporations, authorities, and public functionaries of the same are called upon to manifest the sentiments which they entertain in respect to the war which is now maintained by the republic against the troops of the Emperor of the French. After proper deliberation on the part of the greater number of the individuals present, they unanimously resolved in the name of the corporation:

That they protest in the most solemn manner against the unjustifiable invasion now suffered by the republic, because it offends against all the rights and principles sanctioned and recognized in civilized countries, it attacks the independence and sovereignty of the Mexican republic, without motive, without pretext, and without the slightest appearance of justice, but merely through pure ostentation of power, since neither the French nation nor its Emperor has any grievances to demand satisfaction for, or any debts to be recovered by means of war;

That they likewise protest that they repudiate, by all the means in their power, the iniquitous and unwarrantable invasion, and therein express the consciousness entertained by the people whom they represent of the justice of the cause of their country, who will know how to sacrifice themselves in its defence.

And in order that this protest may lose nothing of its force and effect, it is signed by the citizens present on the day and date specified.

JUAN N. MATA, *President.*
FELIPE B. CABRAL, *First Magistrate.*
JOSÉ MARIA GUADIANA, *Second Magistrate.*
BARNABÉ ROCHA, *Substitute Third Magistrate.*
LUCIANO TABARES, *Fourth Magistrate.*
TIMOTEO IBARRO, *Fifth Magistrate.*
ONOFRE NIÑO, *First Syndic.*
JOSÉ ISABEL BAEZ, *Second Syndic.*

I certify that this is a faithful and legal copy taken from the original and compared with the same, to which I refer.

NESTOR MARTINEZ, *Secretary.*

CATORCE, May 25, 1863.

OFFICE OF THE PRESIDENT OF THE CORPORATION OF THE TOWN OF RAYON.

In the town of Rayon, on the twenty-fifth day of the month of May, in the year 1863, the corporation having been assembled in extraordinary session, for which it was convoked on this day at three o'clock in the evening, the president read the communication of the political chief of Rioverde, under date of the twentieth instant, and the corporation having become acquainted with its contents, unanimously resolved:

That abounding in patriotic sentiments, as they have on other occasions manifested, they solemnly protest anew against all foreign intervention, and they promise by all the means in their power to sustain the national independence at all hazards under the democratic institutions which now govern us, being fully convinced that the person possessing the executive power of the nation has displayed great ability, firmness, and good tact in the national defence, with a constancy and serenity proper to his character, which worthily entitles him to the esteem and confidence of all who, like the members of this corporation, have the honor to be Mexicans.

That a certified copy of this vote of confidence be transmitted to the office of the chief of the department, wherewith this session is brought to a close, and the present resolutions are drawn up and are signed by the members of the corporation, together with the secretary who authenticates them.

NICANOR SALAZAR, *First Magistrate, Assistant.*
ANSELMO CASTILLO, *Third Magistrate.*
PEDRO OLVERA, *Fourth Magistrate.*
PEDRO MARTINEZ, *Syndic Procurator.*
GREGORIO SANCHEZ, *Magistrate, Secretary.*

A certified copy.—Rayon, May 26, 1863.

NICANOR SALAZAR.

GREGORIO SANCHEZ, *Secretary.*

In the town of San Sebastian de San Luis Potosi, on the twenty-sixth day of the month of May, in the year 1863, the citizens composing the authorities of the same town, the officials, assistants, and other inhabitants present, having assembled in the town hall of the corporation, the citizen president of the corporation proceeded to read the circular issued by the supreme government of the state, under date of the fifteenth instant, in regard to the drawing up of a protest against the attacks of other powers, whereby the national sovereignty of the Mexican republic is endangered. Accordingly, the citizens present agreed upon the following articles :

First. That they solemnly protest against any attack whatever by a foreign power, whereby the national sovereignty is endangered ; and that they will recognize no other sovereignty than that of Mexico, which they will sustain at all hazards.

Second. That they will acknowledge no other government, be it what it may, than that which actually rules over us now, and has been established by the unanimous vote of the people ; and this they will support in like manner.

Third. That a copy of these resolutions be taken and transmitted to the secretary of the supreme government of the state, in order that the said secretary may lay the same before the governor.

Wherefore the resolutions are signed and sealed by the following citizens, present with me, the president, being unanimously agreed in all its provisions. I authenticate it.

FELICIANO MARTINEZ, *President.*
BONIFACIO BRAVO, *Assistant.*
QUIRINO PEREZ, *Second Magistrate.*
MARTIN PASTRANO, *Assistant.*
SIMON MARTINEZ, *Third Magistrate.*
FLORENCIO BUENO, *Assistant.*
ISABEL BLANCO, *Syndic Procurator.*
BERNARDINO GARCIA, *Assistant.*
BERNABÉ VAZQUEZ, *Alcalde.*
MAMERTO ELEDESMA, *Assistant.*
JULIO PEREZ,
LINO TORRES,
MERCED GONZALEZ,
VICENTE CASTILLO,
CECILIO GONZALEZ,
ENRIQUE MUGICA Y SOTO MAYOR,
MATIAS LOPEZ,
CARMEN IBARRA,
Citizens.

This is a copy of the original which remains in the archives of the office of the secretary of the corporation.

QUIRINO PEREZ,
Acting Secretary.

THE VERY ILLUSTRIOUS CORPORATION OF TLAXCALA.

In the town of Tlaxcala, on the twenty-sixth day of the month of May, in the year 1863, the honorable members of the corporation and their assistants having assembled in the town-hall of the said town, under the presidency of the first magistrate of the illustrious coporation, Norverto Suarez, in order to give effect to the supreme enactment of the government of the state, transmitted through the chief of the capital, the aforesaid enactment was taken into consideration, and the circular having been read in a loud voice by citizen Pablo Vasquez, the aforesaid president addressed the meeting in reference to the resolution to be adopted in an affair of such vital importance in defence of our independence which is sought to be taken away from us by the foreign enemy who has violated our territory and sacrificed with ruffian hand the existence of our brethren, who have preferred to die upon the battle-field rather than to bear the yoke which is sought to be imposed upon us. Whereupon, anxious for the preservation of our national sovereignty, they unanimously resolved, with one voice, to enter their solemn protest, now and forever, and in every way, against the slaves of the despot Napoleon III, and his pretensions in the wicked invasion, in reference to which these present resolutions, the original draught of which remains in the archives of this office, but of which a copy shall be transmitted to the chief of the department to be laid by him before the supreme government Wherefore, the members of the corporation have hereunto attached their signatures, and, with me, authenticate the document.

NORVERTO SUAREZ, *President.*
MARIANO MORALES, *Alcalde.*
LUCIANO ARIAS, *Assistant*
JUAN CARRIZALEZ, *Second Magistrate.*
MIGUEL PARDO, *Third Magistrate.*
CRUZ LOPEZ. *Syndic Procurator.*
PABLO VASQUEZ, *Assistant President.*
JUAN GARCIA, *Assistant Second Magistrate.*
FRANCISCO ORTEGA, *Assistant Third Magistrate.*
JUAN PABLO LOPEZ, *Assistant Procurator.*
BENITO LOPEZ, *Treasurer.*
ANTONIO DE P. SALAZAR.
JUAN LOPEZ
DIONICIO VASQUEZ.
JULIEN JARA.
JESUS CONTRERAS.
POLICARPO GONZALEZ.
JOSÉ MARIA MARTINEZ
SIMON GARCIA.
VIVIANO DE LEON.
AGAPITO TOVAR.
JUAN ALFARO.
LEON RAMIREZ.
TEOFILO RAMOS.
JOSÉ MARIA MEDINA.
PABLO ALVAREZ.
FELIPE RODRIGUEZ.
MARIANO CORPOS.
GORGONIO LOPEZ.
JUAN SOTO.
FELIX JARAMILLO.
LEONIDES MARTINEZ.
SERAPIO MACIAS.
LEANDRO NUÑEZ.

This is a true copy of the original which remains in the archives of this corporation.

NORVERTO SUAREZ, *President.*

POLITICAL AND MILITARY DEPARTMENT OF SAN LUIS POTOSI—MOCTEZUMA DEPARTMENT

LUIS GASCON, POLITICAL CHIEF OF THE MOCTEZUMA DEPARTMENT.

Considering that the war declared against Mexico by the Emperor of the French is in every way unjust, impolitic, and undeserved;

That by it he attacks in a scandalous manner the sovereignty and independence of a nation, heretofore recognized by all the European powers, in the full enjoyment of its rights, of its prerogatives, and of its privileges;

That by this extraordinary invasion a most flagrant outrage is committed against the law of nations and against international law, which all civilized nations respect;

That it is an insult to the dignity of the Mexican nation to pretend to convert it into a colony tributary to the throne of France;

That, with the most unheard-of injustice, the Emperor of the French seeks to establish an odious and repugnant intervention in the destinies of the Mexican republic, which has hitherto governed itself and will continue to govern itself, notwithstanding the wicked pretension of that tyrant to enslave it;

And that, finally, the expression of the Mexican people, freely and spontaneously given in the heroic resistance which it opposes to the enemy of its sovereignty and independence, as manifested in the defence of the unconquered city of Puebla de Zaragoza, is that the country must rule itself and be governed according to the laws and by the authorities emanating from the constitution:

I have deemed it my duty, as a good Mexican and as an officer, to protest, as I hereby do protest, for myself and in the name of the department with which I am intrusted, against the unjust war entered upon by the Emperor of the French against Mexico, my country; and I protest against all foreign intervention by which it is sought to outrage and wound our national sovereignty.

And in order that the sentiments by which I am animated may have a public manifestation, I entreat the supreme government of the state to be pleased to grant that this protest be inserted in the official periodical.

LÙIS GASCON.

MOCTEZUMA, *May* 21, 1863.

CONSTITUTIONAL CORPORATION OF THE MUNICIPALITY OF BOCAS.

In the municipality of Bocas, on the twenty-second day of the month of May, in the year 1863, the honorable corporation, composed of the citizens Porfirio Martinez, first magistrate; Estevan Niño, second magistrate; Julio Baez, third magistrate; Victoriano Chavira, syndic procurator, and Feliciano Jacobo, secretary, having assembled under the presidency of the first-named citizen, and there being present likewise the citizens Isabel Guadalupe Garcia, the only justice of the peace; Pedro Cisneros, receiver of rents and collector of direct taxes, and Crescenciano Martinez, municipal treasurer, the honorable president said that the purpose of calling the honorable body to an extraordinary session was in order to have a communication read which he had received from the secretary of the supreme government, under date of the twentieth of the present month; and thereupon, the communication having been read by the secretary, the honorable corporation considered its contents, as did also the other citizens present, and being asked their respective opinions in regard to the communication just read, all unanimously, both the members of the corporation and the officials mentioned, said that, abounding in the most ardent patriotism, both as public functionaries and as sons of our beloved country, Mexico, they express their free opinions and aspirations in the following articles:

1. We solemnly protest against all foreign intervention whatever that seeks to overthrow the actual institutions by which we are governed.
2. We likewise protest that we will support with our persons and our fortunes our independence and the integrity of our republic.
3. A certified copy of these proceedings will be transmitted to the supreme government by the ordinary channels.

Whereupon the session was closed by the reduction to writing of these resolutions for the preservation of the same; and they were signed before me, the secretary, who authenticate them, by the citizens Porfirio Martinez, first magistrate and president; Estevan Niño, second magistrate; Julio Baez, third magistrate; Victoriano Chavira, syndic procurator; Feliciano Jacobo, secretary; and the public officials, Isabel Guadalupe Garcia, justice of the peace, Pedro Cisneros, receiver of taxes, and Crescenciano Martinez, municipal treasurer.

I certify this to be a true copy.

PORFIRIO MARTINEZ.

FELICIANO JACOBO, *Secretary.*

MUNICIPALITY OF BOCA, *May* 22, 1863.

We, the subscribing citizens, having met in the hall of the honorable corporation of this town, and being made acquainted by the municipal chief with the exhortatory circular, of the date of the 15th of the current month, issued by the governor of the state, being filled with the liveliest enthusiasm as sons of Mexico, and possessed with the patriotic love which inspires our hearts and by the faith which we have in Providence that we will triumph in this unjust war made upon us by France, aided by wicked men and traitors, whose sole employment is to spill the blood of just men engaged in the defence of their nationality, and to see innocent families sacrificed, of whom so many have recently perished—with unanimous accord, and proud to record the glory which we enjoy in calling ourselves Mexicans, we enter a solemn and firm protest that we will sustain the supreme government with all the means that may be in our power, even to the shedding of the last drop of our blood on the field of honor to save our independence and to assure the liberty of our tender families. It shall, therefore, be our glory to die and never to humble ourselves beneath the proud foot of the Frenchman and of his accursed allies, those monsters of humanity.

This protestation, which we have the honor and the satisfaction of making, we have agreed to lay before the citizen chief of this municipality, in order that it may, by copy or original, or in whatever way may seem convenient, be transmitted through the usual channels to the citizen governor, to whom we offer the assurance of our sincere patriotism, and likewise our respectful esteem and consideration.

Liberty and independence, or death!—Iturbide, May 26, 1863.

VICENTE CELESTINO MARTINEZ.
ATANACIO MARTINEZ.
ANTONIO D. OROZCO.
JUAN PARTIDA.
PORFIRIO TRISTAIN.
BENITO TRISTAIN.
LIDRONIO A. AGUIRRE.
AGAPITO DE LA ROSA.
FRANCISCO M. RAMOS.
ANDRES MARTINEZ.
I. ISIDRO MARTINEZ.
SANTIAGO NIETO.
SECUNDINO CARRIZAL.
FRANCISCO TORRE BLANCA.
FRANCISCO HURTADO.

In the town of Cedral, on the twenty-ninth day of May, in the year 1863, the right honorable corporation having assembled in the town-hall, and having taken into consideration the circular issued by the governor of the state, under date of the 18th of the current month, protests in the most solemn manner, before the country and the other civilized nations of the globe, against the unjust aggression made upon our soil by the Emperor of the French, in violation of national rights and of the law of nations, purposing to destroy the liberal government which now holds Mexico constituted as a free and sovereign state and by the popular will. It likewise protests its desire to avenge the blood of our brethren unjustly shed in the defence of the heroic city of Zaragoza, and likewise offers to contribute by all the means in its power to assist the supreme magistrate of the republic to maintain the honor and dignity of the republic outraged by this invasion, until due reparation is obtained.

APOLONIO CAMARILLO.
APOLONIO FRESNILLO, *Second Magistrate.*
PROSPERO CARDENAS, *Third Magistrate.*
PEDRO LOPEZ MORALEZ, *Fourth Magistrate.*
RAMON VALERO, *Secretary.*
DOROTEO MERLO, *Secretary.*

SECOND COURT OF THE TOWN OF CEDRAL.

CITY OF CEDRAL, *May* 31, 1863.

We, the subscribers, first and second justices of the peace of this town, judge of the civil court, clerk of the courts, and alcalde of the prison, desiring not to be the last to testify our opinion before the nation, the civilized world, and the whole globe, do so in the following form:

1. We protest solemnly against the unjust invasion of our territory by Napoleon III, Emperor of the French, without reasonable cause, without declaration of war, and in the use of his power merely in favor of some traitorous Mexicans who have inspired their sinister views into him.

2. We solemnly protest against all intervention, pretended to be assumed by the French chiefs now resident in the heroic city of Zaragoza, in the actual government of Mexico legitimately constituted, as also against all foreign intervention whatever, be its designation what it may.

3. We protest loudly and solemnly that we will maintain our actual form of government, popular, federal, representative, the liberal constitution of 1857, sworn to, sanctioned, and revised by the free, explicit, and voluntary vote of the whole nation, with very rare exceptions of persons of retrograde views.

4. We protest in the most solemn manner that we will maintain the honor and dignity of the citizen president, Benito Juarez, as the only legitimate representative of the nation.

JOSÉ NICOLAS MANZANO, *First Alcalde.*
TEODORO PUENTE, *Second Alcalde.*
GUADALUPE F. PALOS, *Civil Judge.*
PABLO ROCHA, *Alcalde.*
MODESTO G. HOGUELA, *Secretary.*

In the town of Matehuela, on the thirtieth day of May, in the year 1863, the president and members of the corporation, citizens Joaquin Castillo, Isidoro Estrada, Jesus Pimentel; the syndics, Francisco Pedraza and Juan Huerta; the first and second alcaldes, citizens Francisco Soberon and Mariano Escoto; also, the administrator of the customs. Manuel Martinez; the municipal treasurer, citizen Jesus Reyes; the civil judge and administrator of the post office, citizen Jesus Vargas; the administrator of stamps, citizen Cayetano A. Gaitau; the administrator of the public granary, citizen Miguel Medrano; the master of posts, citizen Juan Gaitau; the president of the board of primary instruction, citizen Anastasio Moreno; and the secretary of the same, citizen Julio Armijo, having met in the town-hall, being invited to an extraordinary meeting therein by the citizen president above mentioned, the secretary of the corporation read the communication addressed to them, under date of the twenty-seventh of the present month, by the political chief of the city of Catorce, urging them to protest against the French invasion, which has so unjustly attacked the rights of the nation. The opinion of all the individuals present being consulted by the citizen president, full of the enthusiasm becoming every Mexican breast, they agreed, with common accord, to protest, as they do, before the nation and the entire world, against the armed intervention which the Emperor of the French has directed against our beautiful country. They protest with equal energy against all foreign intervention whatever, that has for its object the establishment of any other government than the present one, adopted by the majority of the nation, and intrusted for its administration to the worthy as well as courageous Benito Juarez. Finally, they protest that they will maintain, in every possible manner, with their lives and their fortunes, the national integrity and the public liberties, because they would prefer to suffer any misery, even to the abandonment of their homes, rather than submit to the exacting caprices of mercenary and unworthy foreigners.

These resolutions were signed by them in presence of me, the secretary. I authenticate them.

JOAQUIN CASTILLO.
ISIDORO ESTRADA.
JESUS PIMENTEL.
FRANCISCO PEDRAZA.
JUAN HUERTE.
FRANCISCO SOBERON.
MARIANO ESCOTO.
MANUEL MARTINEZ.
JESUS REYES.
JESUS VARGAS.
CAYETANO A. GAITAU.
MIGUEL MEDRANO.
JUAN GAITAU.
ANASTASIO MORENO.
JULIO ARMIJO.

I certify this to be a true copy. Office of the secretary of the corporation of Matehuela, May 31, 1863.

JESUS DELGADO,
Secretary pro tem.

The people of the capital of Tamaulipas united in publ c meeting, the political chief of the central district being president, make the following declaration of their ideas and political sentiments, in the most spontaneous, frank, and solemn manner possible:

It will adhere to liberty and reform, for that divine system makes all men equal, and grants equal rights and guarantees to all.

It is firmly convinced that peace, order, morality, and justice can only exist under democratic principles, and the aggrandizement and happiness of Mexico can be attained.

It is convinced in the same manner with regard to the causes that have retarded its progress, that they are no others than the continued revolutions that have taken place from the time of independence to the present day, all made by the clergy and the army, to defend their ridiculous privileges, and establish tyranny, by which the nation has suffered immense sacrifices, and, what is still more painful, lost thousands of innocent victims.

It is persuaded, by what has occurred in the past as well as what is occurring in the present, that the reactionary party, as infamous as it is cowardly, has crawled to the feet of Napoleon III, the tyrant, to offer him the dominion of Mexico, in exchange that the clergy should continue in the full enjoyment of the usurped mortmain property, and that they, in connexion with the army, should reconquer the sovereignty and privileges they formerly possessed, to the dishonor of the nation.

The intervention solicited by the unnatural sons of Mexico, and conceded by Napoleon, is a scandalous violation of the treaty of London, in which the principle of respecting the autonomy and independence of the republic was most solemnly stated.

The false offers of Forey, nor the vain words of the traitors that follow him, can deceive the people. The forces of France have been sent to Mexico only to establish a monarchical government, to rob and tyrannize the people in the most cruel and barbarous manner known.

The intervention is to Napoleon the pride, vanity, and ostentation of the power he has usurped; to those Mexicans that consent to it, ignominy, shame, and degradation. It will not be the people of Ciudad Victoria who will throw such an infamous stain upon their conduct; it hates despots, and will curse them eternally.

Thus it protests, before the God of nations, against all foreign intervention in the affairs of Mexico, and particularly against the infamous and unjust invasion of the French army.

It proposes, also, from its innermost heart, to place itself at the disposal of the constitutional authorities, to defend constantly the independence of the country, menaced by Frenchmen and traitors, and to sustain the democratic institutions which now govern us.

Such is the political faith and feeling of the people. It is rooted to the heart, and will never yield in any respect to tyrants. It fears not death; on the contrary, it will give it courage to fall upon a glorious tomb, to leave to their children a page in history, and to raise an everlasting malediction to all tyrants.

City of Victoria de Tamaulipas, July 7, 1863.

Antonio Perales.
Francisco Blanco.
Cipriano Guerrero.
Francisco Velasco.
Indalscio Martinez.
Antonio F. Guillen.
Dario Balandrano.
Francisco G. Rodriguez.
Juan A. Velasquez.
F. de la G. Jimenes.
Antonio Adame.
Rafael Aluña.
Juan Gonzales.
Camilo Castro.
Julio Rodriguez.
José Ma. Martinez.
Ramon Rodriguez Fernandez.
Antonio Rodriguez.
José Cortina.
Leandro Ramirez, (padre)
Juan N. G. Jimenes.
Agustin Guillen.
Fernando Cabanae.
Fernando de Vargas.
Refugio Rodriguez.
José Coronado.
Francisco Jimenes Valdez.
Lucio Castaneda.
Noverto Feran.
Cayetano Aguilera.
Priciliano F. de Cardonas.
Agaton Vargas.
Felipe Feran.
Antonio Gutierrez.
Lopez G. Reyes.
Erancisco Padilla.
Fortiz de la Garza.
José Maria Olvera.
Fito N. de Careres.
Rafael Guillen.
Francisco Carranco.
Reyes Aguirre.
Guadalupe Perales.
E. Balandramo.
Rafael del Castillo.
Albino Gomez.
Fermin Jimenes.
Juan Teran.
Gregorio Torres.
Cosme Villaseñor.
Manuel Camargo.
Lorenzo Cortina, (hijo)
Tarquino Jimenes.
Antonio Flores,
Por Francisco Gueredo.
Juan Teran.
Antonio Parreno.
Florencio Zamudio.
Ramon Rodriguez Reyes.
Juan Guerrero.
José Maria Fuentes.
Rafael Cortez.
Bernardo Gonzalez.
José Hipolito Sierra.
Marcelo Vera.
Andreo Ortega.
Francisco Abrigo.
Benito Garcia.
Ysidro Gamez.
Tranquilino Arenas.
Francisco Davila.
Trinidad de Leon.
Florentino Chavez.
Nicolas Huerta.
Agustin Gonzalez.
Rafael Linarez.
Francisco Perales.
José Luis Perez.
Leandro Valdez.
Pasenal Valvoa.
Juan Martinez.
Antonio Fuentes.
Vidal Hernandez.
Desiderio Padron.
Desiderio Lopez.
Urverno Garcia.

Emilio Castro
Francisco Guintanilla.
José Martinez
Conobio Sanchez.
Trinidad Ramirez.
Felipe Escandon.
Juan Gomez.
Antonio Romero.
José Rodriguez.
Brigido Hernandez.
Justos Adrian.
Julian Castillo.
Ventura Vasquez.
Zeferino Rojas.
Francisco Galvan.
Manuel Castillo.
Francisco Caras, (hijo.)
Felipe Rincon.
Amador Porras.
Mateo Espinosa.
Estevan Garcia.
Cresencio Ortiz.
Nieves Martinez.
Fiturcio Saldana.
Frebonio Alanis.
Pilas Soto.
Ricardo Cortez
Cayetano Guillen.
Sisto Mata.
Lorenzo Malos.
Jorge Campos.
José Sepulveda.
Silverio Ramirez.
Juan Cantor.
Joaquin Caballero.
Rafael Arredonde.
Ponciano Chavez.
Felipe Torrez.
Hilario Almaguey.
Manuel Moron
Francisco Lopez.
Francisco Vasquez.
Juan F. de Albe.
Ildefonso Velasquez.
Antonio Guevara.
Ramon Guevara.
Giro Gonzales, (hijo.)
Dimas Capetillo.
Francisco H. Flores.
Blas Bustamante.
Mauro Fernandez Garza.
Francisco Castaneda y Saldana.
Rafael Romero.
Andrez Farfan.
José Maria Cordova.
Luciano Ibarra.
Pedro Lopez.
Rosalio Zepeda.
Gregorio Garcia.
Vidal Fuentes.
Modesto Esparsa.
Felipe Barvosa.
Guadalupe de la Fuente.
Antonio Belarde.
Seberiano Hernandez.
Antonio Velasquez.

Antonio Gonzalez.
Albino Garcia.
Damaro Solano.
Ricado Bustos.
Rafael Hernandez.
Felipe Martinez.
Martin Borrego.
Bonifacio Vasquez.
Pedro Mata.
Francisco Barragan.
Juan Orta.
Tomas Moreno.
Guivino Reyesa.
Encarnacion Rodriguez.
Antonio Luna.
Luriano Hernandez.
Anacleto Mendosa.
Ignacio Gonzalez.
Macedonio Obregon.
Braulio Paz.
Francisco Esparsa.
Carmen Sanchez
Martin Isaguirre,
Julian Lopez.
Eusebio Villareal.
Simon Lopez.
Pantaleon Guintero.
Gregorio Alvarado.
Macedonio Garcia.
Justo Ramirez.
Julian Irevino.
Juan Francisco de Durein.
Julian Torrez.
Juan de la Cruz.
Antonio Portales
Inocencio Zamora.
Forivio Chavez.
Fiburcio Lopez.
Juan J. Porras.
Eduvige Puga.
Isidoro Mier.
Francisco Martinez.
Encarnacion Rangel.
Agapito Charles.
Hipolito de Velasco.
Cenobio Jimenes.
Leocadio Sanchez.
Jesus A de la Garza.
Santiago Gamez,
Por Mariano Gaspar.
Ramon Rojas.
Bernabe Garza.
Ramon Rojas.
Francisco de las Caras.
Cristobal Pisaña.
Maclorio M. Sierra.
Francisco Saldana.
Antonio Furricanday.
Miguel Guzman.
Julian Mejia.
Ascencion Pisaña.
Manuel Gonzales.
Ramon Garcia,
Por José Maria Cardenas.
Ascencion Pisaña.
Luciano Gonzales.

Francisco Balandrano.
Manuel Moreno.
Pilar Garcia.
José M. Limon.
Teofilo Losaya.
Jesus Gonzalez.
Leocardio Hernandez.
Lorenzo Pizuelo.
Maccinnano Peres.
Carlos Barres.
Juan Reyes.
Julian Rivera.
Ascencion Gil.
Francisco Ramos.
Feliciano Luna.
Natividad Cervantes.
Margarito Silguero.
Gregorio Guevara.
Brieno Rodriguez.
Bentura Reyes.
Enrique Castillo.
Cayetano Rodriguez.
José Anjel Sanchez.

In this heroic city of Matamoras, its illustrious council having met in extraordinary session on the 2d of June, 1863, Juan Fernandez presiding, being political chief of the northern district, and taking into consideration the state in which the republic has been plunged by the last events resulting in the occupation of Puebla de Zaragosa, so nobly defended by the army of the east, under command of General Jesus Gonzalez Ortega, that as these critical moments are precisely the time when true patriotism as well as the determination to defend, at all costs, the integrity of our national soil, should be shown forth, it being trampled upon by the forces of the French tyrant; that this body, representing the city of Matamoras, although it has not protested against French intervention, has clearly proved her feelings by the blood of her children shed by the invaders; that now that by all appearances our national cause has received a terrible blow, is when we should show our strength and power, teaching the audacious soldiers of the Emperor how the sons of the Mexican republic can die for their liberty. Considering that the actual form of government is the most adequate to the advances of the age, and the one chosen by the Mexican people, who, like the rest of mankind, have the right to select their mode of organization; that Benito Juarez, now president of the republic, has been made so by the free and unanimous will of his fellow-countrymen, knowing how to repay the confidence of his constituents by maintaining the constitution and developing the regenerating seeds of reform; considering all this, and by unanimity of votes, the following was resolved: The illustrious council of the city of Matamoras protests, in the most solemn manner, against all intervention or foreign dominion in the territory of the republic, and especially so against that of the French. It is determined to defend and sustain the independence and integrity of the soil, and to support, also, the democratic institutions that now govern the republic, and by which Benito Juarez, well-deserving of the country, so worthily occupies the presidency. It was also resolved to send a copy of this act to the executive of the nation, conveying it through the respectable channel of the government of state, and have it published, that the people may see, by this act, the sentiments which this corporation has always held, confirmed. The political chief and the individuals of the municipal council having signed before me, the secretary, the meeting adjourned.

JUAN FERNANDEZ.
RAFAEL QUINTERO, *First Alcalde.*
SERVANDO CAVAZOS, *Second Alcalde.*
LUIS GUERRERA, *Third Alcalde.*
JUAN MANEIRO, *First Alderman.*
CARLOS DANACHE, Jr., *Fifth Alderman.*
SEBASTIAN RODRIGUEZ, *Sixth Alderman.*
JOSÉ MARIA RAMIREZ, *First Syndic.*
JOSÉ MARIA CANTÚ, *Second Syndic.*
FELIPE ZALAZAR, *Secretary.*

Mr. Romero to Mr. Seward.

[Translation.]

MEXICAN LEGATION IN THE UNITED STATES OF AMERICA,
Washington, February 29, 1864.

MR. SECRETARY: I have the honor to enclose, with this note, several documents translated into English, which have come from Mexico, and a synopsis of which appears at the beginning. These documents reveal the absolute rupture between the Mexican clergy, on the one hand, and the invaders, on the other, together with their manikins, who form the so-called regency of the empire. It is known that the moral support on which the French invasion of Mexico relied was the high clergy of the country, who expected to recover through its medium the possession of their estates declared national and distributed among a large number of persons during the administration of the constitutional government of that republic, which acted thus for reasons of obvious public convenience, to which it is now unnecessary to refer. Well, then, the clergy having lost their expectations of being restored to the possession of those estates under French influence, now withdraws the support which they had lent to the intervention, which is reduced to the necessity of maintaining itself by the force of bayonets alone, and by material assistance from individuals, who, too much compromitted in the farce of government to be able to separate themselves from it, have blindly to obey the capricious will of their rulers. These considerations, which I take the liberty of merely pointing out, induce me to call your attention to the documents which I enclose, and the importance of which I doubt not will be duly appreciated by the government of the United States.

I avail myself of this opportunity of renewing to you, sir, assurances of my very distinguished consideration.

M. ROMERO.

Hon. WILLIAM H. SEWARD, *&c., &c., &c.*

SYNOPSIS OF DOCUMENTS

1. Protest of the archbishop of Mexico, as one of the regents, against certain orders issued in the name of the regency by Generals Almonte and Salas, under command of the French general-in chief, which orders involve a recognition of the sequestration of the church property, decreed in 1859 by the Juarez government, November 10, 1863.

2. Removal of the archbishop from his office as regent of the empire, November 17, 1863.

3. Protest of the archbishop against his removal from office as regent of the empire, November 17, 1863.

4. Official note from General Bazaine to the archbishop, acknowledging that the dismissal of the archbishop from the regency was made by his orders, November 20, 1863.

5. Reply of the archbishop to General Bazaine ; he declares his removal from the regency null and void, November 28, 1863.

6. United protest of the archbishop of Mexico, the archbishop of Michoacan, the archbishop of Guadalajara, the bishop of San Luis Potosi, and the bishop of Oajaca, against the circulars and orders issued with reference to the church property by command of the French general, and declaring against all who shall execute them, or co-operate in executing them, the excommunication decreed by the holy council of Trent ; in this protest they declare their situation to be worse than it was under the Juarez government ; December 26, 1863.

7. Adhesion of the bishops of Leon, Caladro, and Eutancingo, to the foregoing protest, December 31, 1863.

8. Protest of the supreme court of the nation, appointed by the regency, against the circulars and orders issued in relation to said church property.

9. Decree of the regents, Almonte and Salas, removing all of the judges and other officers of the supreme court, on the ground of their refusal to enforce any of the laws or orders regarding the nationalization of the church property, January 2, 1864.

10. Manifesto of Almonte and Salas, explaining this act, and declaring that they found it necessary to conform their action to "French policy," January 2, 1864.

11. Sharp letter from General Niegre to the archbishop of Mexico, complaining of the incendiary character of the publications which are being clandestinely circulated by the clergy in the capital, January 16, 1864.

12. Reply of the archbishop, declaring, categorically, that never was the church so bitterly persecuted, and that he, as chief prelate, finds himself in a worse position than under the Juarez government.

13. Further note from the archbishop to General Niegre, stating what he will address to his diocesaners when the restrictions imposed by the French on the press is removed.

No. 1.

Protest of the Archbishop of Mexico.

YOUR EXCELLENCY: Under this date I have communicated to their excellencies Regents Generals D. Juan N. Almonte and D. Mariano Salas that of which the following is a copy:

YOUR EXCELLENCIES: Being unable, in any case, to make a sacrifice of my conscience and my dignity, I find myself obliged to address to your excellencies, for your due knowledge, and publication in the official paper, the following declarations:

First. That there having been received by the regency, at the conclusion of its session, on Saturday, the 7th instant, a despatch from his excellency General Bazaine, in which he insisted that the regency should make a declaration sufficient to expedite in the courts and before the judges the course of the affairs to which the communication or notice published in the official paper of the 24th of October last refers, and which requirement is made in a manner which should strongly claim the attention of the regency, I immediately made known that the affair was, from its nature, one of the greatest gravity and of most important consequences, and that it should be treated very cautiously and not hastily, in which opinion we were of accord, the subject lying over to be treated of subsequently.

Second. That desiring to exhaust in this affair every resource which prudence should dictate, in order that it might be fitly determined, and, if it were possible, with the common accord of the regency and of his excellency General Bazaine, I had a conference with his excellency in conformity with previous notice, given the evening before to his excellency Señor Almonte, on Sunday, in the afternoon, making known to him all the reasons which, in my conception, operated in favor of laying aside the affair of the bills receivable and renting of church property, in order that its resolution should be postponed until the arrival of the Emperor, which conference took place in the presence of his excellency Señor Almonte, who sustained several of my observations.

Third. That as his excellency Señor Bazaine did not yield to my arguments, I offered, in the presence of the same Señor Almonte, to send them to him yesterday in writing, in order that he might more carefully consider them.

Fourth. That in compliance with this offer I prepared yesterday, with all precision and clearness, the reasons which operated against giving course to the said suits until a supreme resolution, dictated by the sovereign, should free from the chance of nullity and of ulterior responsibility the temporary determination which might now be given to these affairs.

Fifth. That the first of my observations demonstrated that only the first notice had been issued with the knowledge of the regency, although with my vote against it, but that the second appeared afterwards without any legal origin; and that in this first notice there appeared no recognition of any right in the unlawful holders of these *pagares* [notes given for church property.—Trans.] to avail themselves in their effort to make them good of the public tribunals, but only the declaration that the regency would hold as calumnious whatever efforts should tend to preoccupy the public judgment, causing it to be believed that the regency had the intention of putting itself forward in an affair whose resolution should be left to the sovereign; and this I stated with my natural frankness, because, in fact, the notice exhibited a meaning contrary to that which it had been desired to give it.

Sixth. That I then proceeded to demonstrate that there could not be given to said notice any other legal interpretation than that which it really bore, without deciding, in fact, the question which is sought to be postponed, and deciding it by ratifying and legalizing all that had been done in the time of Don Benito Juarez; and that such a decision could not be made because it would be anti-Catholic, immoral, scandalous, anti-economical, and impolitic with reference to the Pope, to whom it would be a most severe blow; to his Majesty the Emperor of the French, whom it would cause to represent a *rôle* diametrically opposed to his generous intentions, conciliatory disposition, and frank and loyal conduct; and to his Majesty the Emperor of Mexico, whom it would deprive of all of his resources, multiplying the obstacles before him and reducing him—such were my words—"to the deplorable and painfully fruitless task of gnawing the bleached bones of a corpse," with respect to the nation itself, because such measures would cause an immense majority to draw back, while they would not attract the opposition for whom condescensions are stimulants and concessions arms.

Seventh. That this communication was already sealed, in order to send it to his excellency Señor Bazaine, when, with a surprise and pain which I cannot express, I was informed of a document of the following tenor:

MEXICO, *November* 9, 1863.

TO THE POLITICAL PREFECT: It having arrived to the knowledge of the regency that, notwithstanding the notices inserted in No. 14 of the official paper, of which the annexed is a copy, certain judges have abstained from taking cognizance of causes which relate to the *pagares*, (notes,) and the leasing or rents of properties which have belonged to the clergy, the said regency orders me to say to your excellency that, in conformity with the notice referred to, the judges and tribunals should and must take cognizance of all causes to which they relate. By their order I communicate the same to you for its publication and due compliance.

F. RAYGOSA,
Under-Secretary of State and of the Department of Justice.

From all that has been said it appears—

First. That there has been dictated, in the name of the regency, an order which the regency has not decided upon, for I am a member of the regency, and I have not been present nor have I been cited to the deliberation upon such order.

Second. That this order, as I was afterwards informed by the under-secretary of justice when it was already in circulation, was directed to be issued on Sunday, and before I had the conference with his excellency Señor Bazaine, in the presence of Señor Almonte, as of an affair still pending, there being maintained by their excellencies the regents, my colleagues, towards me, with regard to it, a most studious reserve, which I cannot explain, and with the aggravating circumstance that the order was issued through the under-secretary of the department of justice, which is under my charge, without my having, as is seen with reference to it, either any knowledge whatever or even a simple notice on the part of this employé.

In virtue whereof, in compliance with the duty imposed upon me as regent of the empire, by the oath which I have taken to seek in all the common good, in order to decline all responsibility on my part, whether with respect to his Majesty the Emperor of Mexico, to whom I owe all fidelity, whether with respect to the nation which has honored me with its confidence, or, finally, with respect to the legitimate interests which may give way under the practical consequences of an order which I consider null, I address myself to your excellencies by the present note, making these declarations, and making known that as I do not consider said order published yesterday by the under-secretary of justice, Señor Don Felipe Raygosa, as emanating from the regency. I protest in all form that said order is entirely null, and against any effects which may flow therefrom.

God guard your excellencies many years.

PELAGIO ANTONIO,
Archbishop of Mexico, Regent of the Empire.

ARCHIEPISCOPAL PALACE, MEXICO, *November* 10, 1863.

And I transcribe the same to your excellency for your due knowledge.

God guard your excellency many years.

PELAGIO ANTONIO,
Archbishop of Mexico, Regent of the Empire.

ARCHIEPISCOPAL PALACE, MEXICO, *November* 10, 1863.

His Excellency the PRESIDENT OF THE SUPREME TRIBUNAL OF THE NATION.

No. 2.

IMPERIAL PALACE, MEXICO,
November 17, 1863.

Under this date the following communication has been addressed by this department to his grace the archbishop of Mexico by order of the regency:

"YOUR GRACE: Your grace being in open opposition to the regency, as your grace declares in your note of the 14th instant that you will no longer be present at their meetings whilst the order of the 8th instant is not revoked, as well as the decree of the same date, the regency (since the majority of it is its true representative, considering the conduct of your grace as well as that of those two gentlemen appointed substitutes who have also refused to attend) declares that your grace no longer forms a part of it. By order of the same, I have the honor to communicate it to your grace for your information and that his excellency General Bazaine, commander-in-chief of the Franco-Mexican army, concurs entirely with said resolution."

I renew to your grace the assurances, etc.

By order of the regency I inform your honor that the previously inserted communication includes your honor also, in view of your communication of yesterday.

Your excellency will accept the expression of my consideration and esteem.

J. M. ARROYO,
Honorary Sec. of State in charge of the Dep't of Foreign Affairs.

His Excellency J. YGNACIO PAVON,
President of the Supreme Tribunal of Justice of the Empire.

No. 3.

Protest of the Archbishop of Mexico against his dismissal from the Regency.

MEXICO, *November* 17, 1863.

Under this date I have said to their excellencies, Generals D. Juan N. Almonte and D. Marrano Salas, regents of the empire, the following :

YOUR EXCELLENCIES: I have just received a note from the secretary of state and ecclesiastical affairs, in which he says to me that, finding I am in open opposition to the regency, since I have declared in my note of the 14th instant that I would not again meet at its sessions until the order of the 8th instant and the decree of the same date had been repealed, the regency declare that I have ceased to form a part of it, and the same is communicated to me, with the information that his excellency Señor Bazaine concurs in the said resolution.

In answer I have to say to your excellencies :

First. That I cannot be in opposition to the regency, because I form a part of it.

Second. That I have not said I would not again meet at its sessions until the order and decree of the 8th instant had been revoked ; but that as soon as your excellencies yourselves revoke what you have done without my concurrence, I would with pleasure meet at the sessions of the regency ; two things very different, as may be seen at a glance.

Third. That I do not consider either your excellencies or General Bazaine have any right whatever to remove me from the office of regent of the empire, because General Bazaine, even under the intervention, has no power to do this, still less after the explicit, frank, loyal, and highly politic declaration of General Forey at the installation of the Mexican government ; nor can two individuals of the regency constitute and declare themselves the regency, without violating their title to legitimacy, and introducing by this act in the constitution of the government an essential change of a nature which can only be done by the Assembly of Notables.

Consequently, I ask your excellencies, in the most formal manner, in use of the right conceded to me by article 17 of the decree of the 16th July last, that for the determination of this question the Assembly of Notables be called together, this being the indispensable and legitimate resort, the question being of the essence of the government ; because the assembly is the accepted and acknowledged organ of the national will ; because it is the recognized source, even by the intervention itself, of the form of government, of legality in the country, of the power of the Emperor elect and of the regency itself ; because being obliged, according to the law, to refer to the assembly in case of grave questions, if it is not therefore convoked for this, for what other can it be called, or how can your excellencies explain your refusal to consider yourselves as the national government, or avoid your immense responsibility before God, the nation, and France ?

I conclude, therefore, protesting against my removal, on the ground of nullity, and holding in reserve all the other rights which belong to me as regent and as Mexican.

All of which I say to your excellencies for your due knowledge and that of General Bazaine, if your excellencies think proper to communicate the same to him, the said removal having been made in accord with his excellency.

God guard your excellencies many years.

PELAGIO ANTONIO,
Archbishop of Mexico and Regent of the Empire.

No. 4.

Official note from General Bazaine to the Archbishop of Mexico.

EXPEDITIONARY CORPS OF MEXICO, HEADQ'RS OF THE GENERAL-IN-CHIEF,
Mexico, November 20, 1863.

YOUR GRACE: I have received the protest which his excellency General Almonte has caused to reach me, with reference to the measures which have been adopted by the regency to remove your grace from the provisional government. I must make known to your grace that this measure was rendered necessary by the attitude of your grace, and it was taken with my accord, persuaded, as I am, that this was the only means of avoiding the interruption of the march of events.

May I be permitted to express the desire that your grace, well inspired, will accept the position as it is to-day, and will reject the advice and the suggestions of imprudent friends, against whom, notwithstanding, I am well decided to take the most rigorous measures that I am authorized to employ under the powers with which I am invested. I rely on the abnegation of your grace, and on your devotion to the country, that, at the moment I am about setting out for the interior on the work of the pacification and regeneration of Mexico, your opposition will not delay the march of the government.

Your grace will please to receive the expression of my high and respectful consideration.

BAZAINE,
General, Commanding-in-Chief.

His Grace the ARCHBISHOP OF MEXICO

No. 5.

Reply of the Archbishop to General Bazaine.

MEXICO, *November* 28, 1863.

YOUR EXCELLENCY: I have not before answered the letter of your excellency, dated the 20th instant, which I received on the afternoon of the 24th, because I have been obliged to avail myself of the time for the despatch of the packet. I do so now by stating what it appears to me proper to say to you with reference to each one of the points which in your letter relate to me.

I understand that his excellency Señor Almonte transmitted to your excellency my protest of nullity against the dismissal which his excellency and his excellency Señor Salas, and not the regency, made of me in order to remove me from the provisional government. I also understand, from the confirmation which your excellency gives me, that this act of dismissal was made with your approval, as I had already been given to understand by those gentlemen, and in answer to this point I say here to your excellency, as I have said to those gentlemen, and that is, that I do not consider either of those gentlemen or your excellency as invested with any authority whatever to remove me, and consequently I insist upon my protest of nullity. Your excellency says that this measure was required by my attitude, and that you were persuaded that my removal was the only means of avoiding the interruption of the march of events. Your excellency will permit me to reply to you that my opinion is exactly the contrary—

First. Because there is not to be found in jurisprudence any law by which the attitude of a public functionary, who legally fills his office, who defends the principles of justice, who proceeds in everything in conformity with the law, and who appeals to the substantial forms of legality for the validity of his acts, can be made the ground for such a step as his removal from office by other funtionaries who are his equals in position and authority, and who are incompetent not only to remove him, but even to call him to account or to judge him.

Second. Because this removal, far from facilitating, is just what is calculated to delay the march of events; because, say what you will, it implies the substitution of *de facto* for *de jure* in the question of legitimacy, and the destruction of the government constituted on the 25th of June last by the vote of the representatives of the nation, and accepted by the general-in-chief of the expeditionary army, who expressly declared that he placed in the hands, not of two, but of the three provisional chiefs of the nation, the powers which circumstances had intrusted to him for the benefit of the nation itself; and your excellency will see that if these powers are placed in their hands they do not remain in yours, and, consequently, that this government was terminated from the day of my removal, and that what exists to-day may be whatever you wish, but it will not be the government then announced by General Forey to the Mexican people, to France, and to the world.

Third. That not only can it not be said that my removal was the only means, but that there being many, none of them were put in practice, and the National Assembly being in existence, and the only competent means of giving a legal and national sanction to any resolution, not to apply to it, notwithstanding my formal petition in conformity with law, was to give a death blow to the government of the country.

Your excellency continues, expressing your desire that I will accept the situation as it is, and will repel the counsels and suggestions of imprudent friends, against whom your excellency is resolved to take the most rigorous measures in use of the powers with which you are invested. With reference to the first, I have to say to your excellency that I do not understand the exact meaning which you place upon the words "accept the position;" but as accepting is consenting and admitting, I have to say to your excellency that I have not, and I never will, agree to any of the steps that have been taken against the rights I have defended; but that, on the contrary, I insist upon all and each one of my protests.

If these words have a signification strictly personal, I have to say, with all frankness, that I have no aspirations of a personal character; that I entered the regency, not for pleasure, but to labor, and to sacrifice myself for the public good, and yielding to suggestions of the most elevated character. If, finally, they mean that I, in my character of archbishop, have to remain silent and impassible in view of these attacks upon the supreme authority of the church, its right to lead and its immunities, I have to say, with all frankness, that neither myself nor my illustrious brethren can maintain silence without doing violence to our consciences, and that we are disposed to suffer everything rather than prove wanting in the execution of such holy duties when the occasion shall arrive.

In the second place, I should say to your excellency, with the same ingenuousness, whoever may be those imprudent friends to whom your excellency refers, I am the sole and only one responsible for my acts. Your excellency concludes by counting upon my abnegation and my devotion to the country, that at the moment your excellency is leaving for the interior to continue the work of pacification I will not by my opposition interrupt the march of events. To this I answer, in conclusion, that your excellency can be sure that, while I am determined to defend the right, I shall not be the one to pass the bounds of a true prudence by any step contrary to the duties it imposes upon me at the times when it should be observed.

Your excellency will be pleased to accept the expression of my attentive consideration and very distinguished appreciation.

God guard your excellency many years.

PELAGIO ANTONIO,
Archbishop of Mexico.

His Excellency General BAZAINE,

No. 6.

United protest of all the prelates of Mexico.

YOUR EXCELLENCIES: Scarcely arrived in the bosom of our country, after the long and painful banishment to which we had been condemned by the government which emanated from the Plan of Ayutla, not because we had made any kind of partisan political opposition—a thing which the Mexican Episcopacy have been very far from doing—but solely on account of the conscientious and canonical defence we had made of the doctrines of the faith, the rights of religion, the principles of Christian morals, and of the prescriptions of the Holy Catholic Church; returning with the high and noble hope that we had been led to conceive, on the one hand by the intimations made at various times to the Holy Father, on the part of the Emperor of the French, that the bishops who had been banished should return to Mexico, and on the other by the highly significant fact that one of the bishops had been named a member of the executive power and afterwards of the regency; and, finally, by the solemn obligation which the said regency contracted with the church and the nation in its manifesto not to decide any of the ecclesiastical questions except in accord with the Holy Apostolic See; returning with the consoling hope of being able to dedicate our latest days in peace, and under the guarantee of a Catholic government, the restorer of sound principles, to the re-establishment of religion and of morals, and to the reform of society, through the means of our pastoral labors, we have been overwhelmed with a terrible and grievous surprise by encountering a situation in every respect exactly equal to that which preceded our banishment, in all that relates to the church, and even worse, by reason of the strange position in which we, as prelates, find ourselves placed.

The opposition, as well founded as inutile, which was made by the illustrious Archbishop of Mexico, in his quality of regent, to the communications or notices which were published in the official paper of the 24th of October last, and which placed in legal course the payments emanating from the appropriation of ecclesiastical property and the collection of rents of houses taken from the church, and expedited the continuance of the works of alteration upon the same, which has been suspended; the decision taken by your excellencies alone, without the concurrence of the other regent, that through the sub-secretary of justice the judges and tribunals should be informed that they should have and that they must take cognizance of all causes arising under the affairs to which the said notices refer; the insistance of your excellencies in this resolution, notwithstanding the protest of nullity addressed to you on the following day by his excellency Señor Labastida, in his character of regent; the formal dismissal of the illustrious archbishop from his charge of regent, made by your excellencies in concurrence with his excellency General Bazaine; the studious omission which has been made of the church in certain measures regarding the property of public charities; the resistance to the return to the religious societies of the part not yet sold of their convents, and held in lots by the government; the indifference with which it has been seen that these nuns have been reduced to the utmost poverty, without permitting them to receive even the pitiful portion which had been left to them by the despoiling government; various particular acts, which brevity will not permit us to refer to, but which show a decided determination to protect the pretended rights created by the so-called laws of reform; and, finally, the circular issued by the sub-secretary of justice, on the 15th instant, at the instance of his excellency Señor Bazaine, removing all obstacles, and declaring that there is no legal impediment to the exercise of whatever rights of action which were held with respect to the property called clergy property, on the arrival of the French intervention in the country—all these acts manifest with the most weighty evidence that the Holy Catholic Church in Mexico suffers to-day, at the hands of the government which actually exists in the capital, a compulsion in its most holy rights and in its cononical liberties entirely equal to that which it suffered when the authorities emanating from the Plan of Ayutla were in power, because such compulsion consists, not in the form of government, nor in the persons of those who compose it, but in the character and importance of its acts; and those of your excellency's tend to expedite the consummation of the work which those authorities began, for you declare in full force the rights and actions which spring from the sacrilegious and illegal laws, and from the acts committed against the immunity of the church by said authorities, and even in the same language, for the same odious expression is now used which was then employed to designate the ecclesiastical property.

Unhappy would to-day be the evils which the church suffers were they no more than these; but by a misfortune which we can never sufficiently deplore, there are peculiar circumstances which render still worse than them the situation of the church to-day in Mexico, and which increase its grief to an extraordinary degree.

Then the government frankly manifested its principles. It appeared to the view of all this Catholic people in the character of an opposition armed with power against religion and the church; and the latter, as a victim immolated by the government, defended itself heroically, suffering the consequences of a terrible persecution, and perishing nobly for the holy cause of justice. To-day's government inaugurates itself with professions eminently religious and moral, after the French army had destroyed, in the capital, that of Juarez, and it presents itself before the Mexican people as the protector of its faith, of its religion, of the church, and of the priesthood. Then we were banished; to-day we are invited and received with expressions of consideration, creating by this means among the people a feeling of confidence as regards their tenderest affections, their dearest interests. Then the prelates leaving our country carried with them the hope that the first political change which should take place would bring with it a complete moral and religious restoration. To-day, returning after such a change to be present at the immolation of all our principles, the consummation of the ruin of the church, we have received a blow such as is only received at the death of all human hope. Then the church had only one enemy—the government that persecuted it. To-day it has two—that same government which still lives in the country, which still has resources of its own; an army that contends hand to hand for every foot of ground, and that counts upon the aid of its principles and interests in the enemy's camp and in the capital—an enemy whose first occupation it is to carry into effect the destructive plans of its opponent in religious and moral affairs. Then we received the blow from the hand of an open enemy; to-day we are attacked by those who called themselves friends of the church and protectors of its liberties. Then the attack and the defence did not pass beyond strictly national bounds; to-day we have to lament the character which the intervention has given to these attacks, and that from it have come the exigencies which have obliged your excellencies to so proceed. Then we verified our episcopal acts simply as bishops; to-day we have to make our defence passive and legal, because we cannot pass that limit also as Mexicans. Then, notwithstanding the restrictions imposed by the laws of the press, we could publish our protests and our pastorals to the people, because there existed no other restraints than such as would result from the inconveniences of a trial. To-day the press is bound in such a manner that it is open only to those who favor the intervention, for there is not only the responsibility consequent upon a very strict law, but also in denial of the very epoch itself, to say nothing more, even previous censorship. The publication of a pontifical allocution, of an edifying and moral retraction, and of any paragraph copied from abroad in which allusion is made to the authority of the Holy Father with respect to the ecclesiastical questions of this country, are the subjects of formal admonitions to the press, and of prohibitions to insert in the future this class of articles, at the same time that anti-ecclesiastical, and, at some times, even scandalous doctrines, pass unnoticed.

It is for these reasons that, speaking of the situation in which circumstances have now placed us, we consider it worse than before.

The episcopacy of Mexico, considering its responsibility, save by the manifestations made by his excellency Señor Labastida, and by certain steps which have been taken by other prelates with reference to your excellencies, had remained silent up to the present time, in order that it might not be believed that it proceeded with precipitation or lack of prudence. But to-day, when affairs have reached their utmost extreme—to-day, when even the palliatives and reserve with which the first dispositions appeared have been cast aside—to-day, when the instance of a French subject has been sufficient to induce the declaration that all the rights and actions springing from the despoilment of the church property still exist in all their force and vigor—to-day, when, by this sole act, all reservation of these affairs for the decision of the government which shall be definitely established in the country has ceased, our silence would no longer be excusable; it would conceal the wrongs we suffer, and cause us to appear, in a certain measure, as accomplices, a position which it is our duty to repel at all hazards, in the name of the rights of religion, the voice of conscience, and love of our country.

What shall we say to your excellencies in this exposition, after so much that ourselves and our predecessors have said at different times against these claims and pretended rights that your excellencies have just again placed in vigor and reinvested with legal force by your circular of the 15th instant? What can we demonstrate now that is not already demonstrated, or now set forth that will be new to any Mexican ordinarily well informed as to our political history? What arguments, however specious they may be, can now be adduced by the defenders of these sacrilegious laws of spoliation that have not been already refuted and utterly demolished, either by the bishops, the ecclesiastical authorities, or the Catholic press? If the law of the 11th of January, 1847, which took possession of the ecclesiastical property only to the extent of fifteen millions, was considered by the illustrious Señor Portugal—that prelate as wise as illustrious—as a law without force, being in manifest opposition to the will of the people, and impossible of execution with justice from its repugnance to the principles of sound morality, as the inexhaustible fountain of terrible misfortunes for the church and society, as a law violative of the rights and illegal as against the immunities of the church, not less than against its canonical and even civil liberties, and, besides, as an anti-economical law, immoral and incendiary, what can we now say with reference to those laws, the pretended claims and rights under which your excellencies have revived by your circular of the 15th instant? If that virtuous prelate, with the liberty which belongs to a truly apostolic zeal, could not reconcile his Catholic professions with the approbation and execution of such laws, and who supposed, as the indispensable condition of their origin, either the grossest ignorance of the principles of religion, or its positive abjuration and a species of apostasy, what shall we say when we refer to laws which surpass infinitely, under every aspect, in arbitrariness, tyranny, immorality, violence, disasters, and ruin, those which then led to the complaints and protests of the former prelate of Michoacan?

Nothing remains to us, therefore, to say, after so much that has already been said, and still less when addressing ourselves to persons so involved in the course of events, as well as penetrated, for so we believe, with the illegal, ruinous, unpopular, and sacrilegious character of the laws so pompously called laws of reform, as your excellencies.

But we cannot do less, your excellencies, than make known to you the utter surprise and confusion into which we have been plunged by the said circulars, not merely because they have come from your excellencies, whose religious sentiments have never been placed in doubt, not merely from their character and importance, but more particularly because we cannot find any plausible reason—not to justify them, for that is impossible—but that could at least excuse them on the ground of public convenience.

That Señor Juarez with his party should enact such laws, and should work unceasingly to carry them into effect, this we can well conceive, as well as the energetic opposition of the prelates, and the conscientious resistance of all true Catholics; but that a government under the protection of France, (not as a conqueror, not as attempting to overthrow our independence, but as respecting it, and offering to save it, and instructing its commander-in-chief not to interfere with the freedom of its acts,) which has just been established as the government of a nation in virtue of a vote of a council of notables, and in opposition to the government of Señor Juarez, that such a government should work for the laws which this latter has dictated, these being, as they are, the essential and sole cause of the division among the Mexicans, and of the civil war, this we cannot understand.

What political advantages can be derived from such a course? Aside from those which will spring from the influence of the holders and immoral speculators who availed themselves of the vast riches of the church, and who are very few compared with the immense majority of the Mexican nation who detest such speculations, certainly none.

We well know that to present such proceedings in a favorable light a thousand plausible excuses are invented, principally to win over by surprise the court of France, which lacks the data which is indispensable to practically judge of the state of society here. But the truth will not be long in appearing in its true light, and to the scandal of the world it will be known that the immense majority of the Mexicans are essentially Catholic, that they respect the laws of God and of their church, that they bewail the attacks received from the government of Ayutla, and that if they manifested themselves in favor of the intervention, it was because it presented itself as their protector, not against the persons—for that would be but a childish jest—but against the acts of the government of Señor Juarez. But the attitude that the intervention to-day takes by such dispositions has transformed its triumphs to victories over the party oppressed, for it gives force and vigor to the claims and rights emanating from such acts. The impartiality and policy with which it presented itself and pretends to justify its acts consists, therefore, solely in the sterile protest of the party conquered by arms, but triumphant in its principles, and that without ceding a single hair in its opposition to France, and in the complete ruin, not only of a respectable political party—and this would be much and unjustifiable, supposing the programme was one of impartiality—but also of the nation in its moral integrity. Being a Catholic people, the Mexicans must consider as enemies all who attack their faith and their religious and moral interests; that supposing the anti-Catholic party does not yield, but, on the contrary, is strengthened by such concessions, and that the rest of the nation considers itself oppressed, the intervention may have physical force in the country, but moral, political, and national it will have none; that it will have no support but that of its arms, and that, while it might have become the possessor of the gratitude of a people, favoring them in what they hold to be most valuable and sacred, it has been left alone between an armed party who combats it, and a people unarmed and helpless who fear it.

A position such as this, however much it may be covered up or disguised, cannot be excused, and particularly when taking into consideration the spirit of the instructions given by the Emperor to his excellency General Forey.

Whatever may be the elements upon which France may count, it is clear that it did not enter into the mind of the Emperor to establish an order of things here separate and independent from the will and the great interests of the Mexican people; and this is, without doubt, the motive of those instructions, at once so circumspect and in every respect so delicate as those given to his excellency General Bazaine by the minister of foreign affairs, in the communication of the 17th of August last, which has been published in the journals of the capital.

It is there declared terminantly that nothing violent or arbitrary will be attempted or sought, not even special advantages over other nations; there the acts of the government of Señor Juarez are qualified as iniquitous, and the situation which that government created is regarded as the culminating point of dissolution; there it is declared that France, triumphant by virtue of its good intentions towards our country, rejects all idea of substituting its influence for the free determinations of the country; there the authority of the notables is considered as of great weight and authority; there the general-in-chief is prohibited from substituting his initiative for that of the government; there the principle of impartiality is proclaimed, but only as regards the passions, the vices, and the bastard interests of the parties, and where principles are involved. This is a chart full of intelligence, of reason, and of hope. Will it be possible to find here the justification for what is now passing, the support that is pretended, the reason of the resolves that have been taken?

When his excellency General Forey issued his manifesto to the nation, declaring before its face that if it were possible to give any recognition whatever to those who had acquired church property, fraudulent contracts should not be sustained, and in consonance with this, issued his decree of the 22d of May, he gave evidence of impartiality and of equity. But all this has disappeared by the issuance of the notices or communications of the 24th of October, because these, placing in legal course, without any restriction whatever, the notes given for church property, and expediting the suits for collection of rents, without the requisite of previous qualification, has destroyed entirely the moral guarantees which the manifesto and decrees before cited had given. Still, these notices, themselves establishing in principle that the measure was transitory, that it did not imply the solution of the principal questions, nor the definite legitimization of any right—because this remained reserved to the sovereign—left alive the hopes, although very feeble, that his excellency Señor Forey had caused us to conceive, and, above all, facilitated up to a certain point in the critical situation of the country the resignation of the faithful and the prudence of the pastors. But to-day, after the circular of the 15th instant, there is an end to the reign of principles, the empire of right, the encouragement of hope, confidence in the situation, and, in fine, of all promises. A step has been taken so grave that perhaps it would not have been taken even by the cabinet of the Tuileries.

And what has been the cause? What powerful motive has precipitated this crisis? Perhaps the supreme interests of society? Perhaps an extreme necessity, a sudden emergency, a tempest which could not be conjured by any other means? No! it was the most trifling cause, the most insignificant in regard to the effect.

The complaint of a French subject, and the request of the general-in-chief made to your excellencies by virtue of this complaint. This is the cause of all; this is what Mexico has to hope from the impartiality that was promised, and from the non-interference of that chief in order to leave the government free in its acts; this is the melancholy synopsis of the situation in which the Mexican church to-day finds itself.

Your excellencies, turning a glance backwards over the dispositions and acts to which we have referred, should determine to apply the remedy, which only requires from your excellencies a firm and resolute will. We ourselves ask it, with the most pressing urgency, in the name of religion, of morality, of our country, by the obligation which we have to defend the rights of the first, to guard the prescriptions of the second, and to speak under the legitimate inspiration of the third. We ask it in compliance with our most sacred duty as prelates of the church and pastors of the flock of Jesus Christ. We ask it with the confidence which is inspired by the religious and patriotic sentiments of your excellencies, and the lofty and generous views that the French government has so clearly manifested in its instructions to the two chiefs of the army in Mexico. We therefore hope that these circulars will be annulled, that this violence they inflict upon us will cease, and that all proceedings will be suspended in these affairs, which, from their character, their importance, the nature of the situation, and even from the understanding with the French government, should be postponed until they can have a solution capable of placing in harmony conscience and legitimate interests; a solution canonical and civil; a solution in which shall concur the spiritual and the temporal sovereigns; a solution upon which the hopes of religion and of the country now hang dependent.

But if, unfortunately, the said circulars are to remain in force, we, as prelates of the Mexican church, in the use of our canonical faculties, and in compliance with our duties, protest in the most solemn form against the said circulars and their effects. We hold the rights of the church reserved from the inability and nullity so protested of said circulars. We reproduce and now expressly apply our manifestation of the 30th August, 1859, of which we enclose to your excellencies four copies, issued by reason of the laws of the 12th, 13th, and 23d of July of that year, decreed by Señor Juarez, in Vera Cruz, the claims and rights under which your excellencies revive by your circular of the 15th instant, and in consonance with what we then set forth, we conclude this exposition, protesting our respect, with the following declarations:

First. That it is not lawful to obey either the communications of the 24th of October, the circulars of the 9th of November and the 15th instant, nor any disposition whatever of those that tend to the execution of the said decrees of Señor Juarez, nor to co-operate in the compliance therewith.

Second. That neither that government nor any government, whatever it may be, has any authority to take possession of the property of the church; that. therefore, as well the decrees of that government as the notices and circulars issued by order of your excellencies, involve an illegal and tyrannical disposition of the most sacred property, and are subject to the censures of the holy church, and especially to the excommunication fulminated by the Holy Council of Trent, in chapter 11 of session 22 *de reformatione.* In consequence, there are comprehended in this canonical penalty not only the authors and executors of the decrees, notices, and circulars aforesaid, but also all those who in any way co-operate or have co-operated towards their fulfilment.

Third. That the political change which has taken place in Mexico in consequence of the intervention has not altered or lessened in any respect the obligations and moral and canonical responsibilities to which those of whom we have just spoken are subject, and that therefore all of our protests, circulars, and diocesan orders, issued by reason of the so-called constitution of laws and reform, remain in all their force and vigor, and are applicable to the notices and circulars of your excellencies already mentioned, and to whatever other dispositions of your excellencies that tend to place in execution the laws, decrees, and acts to which our canonical protests said manifestation, circular, and diocesan orders refer.

Those incurring the censure of the said canon, in virtue either of the law of the 25th of July, 1856, of the decrees published in Vera Cruz by Señor Juarez in July, 1859, or afterwards in Mexico, of the communications and circulars issued by order of your excellencies, or of the disposition or orders of whatever authority or person, public or private—that is to say, the authors, executors, or co-operators in the despoliation of the church in its property, lands, rents, possessions, claims, rights, temples, objects contained therein destined to public worship, &c., are strictly obliged to make restitution and reparation for their scandalous crime; and they cannot be absolved, not even at the point of death, if they do not comply with the conditions established by the church and set forth in our circulars and diocesan decrees aforesaid.

Such are, your excellencies, the declarations and protests, which, in the unhappy case that our petition is not attended to, and the notices of the 24th of October and the circulars of the 9th November and 15th December remain in force, we shall have to make, and now, in fact, do make, not from a spirit of partisan opposition, which we are very far from feeling, but solely to comply with our duty.

Hard it is to find ourselves placed in this situation, even if we were treating of a national government and bitterly hostile. What is it, therefore, when the authorities in question have been inaugurated as protectors and have presented themselves as friends?

But, your excellencies can believe us, we cannot keep silence without making ourselves criminals by this silence before the strict justice of that government before whose tribunal we shall have to appear at the end of a life which is rapidly escaping. When these terrible occasions present themselves which call for the exercise of our pastoral charge, when we see that a soul lost through our silence will call down upon ourselves the same perdition, we tremble with terror. Not even evident knowledge of the inutility of our expostulations and protests would excuse us before God. See the fearful confirmation of this truth which the Holy Spirit gives us in chapter iii, verses 18 and 19, of Ezekiel: "When I say unto the wicked, thou shalt surely die, and thou givest him not warning, nor speakest to warn the wicked from his wicked way to save his life, the same wicked man shall die in his iniquity, but his blood or perdition will I require at thine hand. Yet, if thou warn the wicked, and he turn not from his wickedness, nor from his wicked way, he shall die in his iniquity, but thou hast delivered thy soul."

We conclude, therefore, protesting to your excellencies, with this unhappy motive, our attentive consideration and distinguished estimation.

God guard your excellencies many years.

PELAGIO A., *Archbishop of Mexico.*
CLEMENTE DE J., *Archbishop of Michoacan.*
PEDRO, *Archbishop of Guadalajara.*
PEDRO, *Bishop of San Luis Potosi.*
JOSÉ MARIA, *Bishop of Oajaca.*

Their Excellencies Generals DON JUAN L. ALMONTE and DON JOSÉ M. DE SALAS, *Regents of the Empire.*

MEXICO, *December* 26, 1863.

No. 7.

Your Excellencies the Regents:

The two first named of us, having been absent from the capital, have learned upon our return that your excellencies issued a circular, dated 15th of the present month, in which some of the impious and fatal orders emanated from the so-called reform laws, against which the venerable allocutions of our holy father, the vicar of our Lord Jesus Christ, directly operate, have been left in full force; and all the energetic protests of the illustrious Mexican episcopate, against which also, not for a vile selfish interest, but for conscientious motives, the respectable clergy of the nation have contended with such unconquerable valor, as well as ourselves personally, who have been persecuted and imprisoned, and finally, against which the public opinion of the whole country has manifestedly pronounced. But we have seen with great satisfaction at the same time the just protest, which said episcopate, on returning from banishment so gloriously suffered for the cause of the church, has addressed to your excellencies. We, who are honored more than we deserve, by forming part of the enlightened firm and compact body of Mexican prelates, constrained by our conscience and our duty, and guided only by a true Catholic spirit, make ours and do subscribe to all and every protest, circular, and orders, issued formerly by the venerable Mexican episcopate against the nefarious and heinous work of the so-called reform, which has overwhelmed our beloved country with every species of evil.

Your excellencies themselves are unexceptional witnesses that the sole and only motive the country has had in accepting willingly the French intervention, the empire, and regency, has been the feeling, or rather the profound rooted attachment to Catholic sm, whose saving principles and grave interests the nation desires to save at any sacrifice, and which it had every reason to believe could have been attained by those means.

May Divine Providence grant the pious and just wishes of the episcopate, the clergy, and the immense majority of Mexicans, who see with the utmost sorrow their beloved country and religion in danger.

Your excellencies will please to accept the assurances of our respect and personal esteem.

Mexico, December 31st, 1863.

D'R JOSÉ MARIA DIEZ DE SOLLANO, *Bishop of Leon.*
FRANCISCO DE LA C. RAMIREZ, *Bishop of Caladro, Apostolic Vicar of Tamaulipas.*
D'R JUAN B. ORMACHEA, *Bishop elect of Tulancingo.*

No. 8.

Protest of Supreme Tribunal.

The necessity, without exaggeration painful, but unavoidable, presents itself again before this supreme tribunal to address itself to that sub-secretaryship, explaining the difficulties there are to carry out the measures dictated by it; the tribunal alludes to the circular of the 15th instant, drawn by petition of his excellency General Bazaine, by which it is declared that "there is no legal obstacle to prevent the exercise of any right and acts which might be had in regard to the property *called of the clergy*, on the arrival of the French intervention to the nation."

The circular of the 9th of November upon the same subject, although not so extensive in its effects, had already obliged the tribunal to lay open the reasons given in its official communication of the 10th of the same, and since then announced that if the legal difficulty disappeared, not there set forth, the same disposition being reproduced, the case would then present itself, in which the interested parties would proceed according to the inspiration of their own conscience.

Without the legal difficulty, which the circular of the 9th November had been removed in that of the 15th instant, the conscientious case referred to has presented itself, because the tribunal cannot, either individually or collectively, keep silent upon the justness of the orders contained in said circulars, after the judgment pronounced upon them by the worthy members of the Mexican episcopate, residing at present in this capital.

The tribunal has official knowledge of the exposition, declarations, and protests which were addressed on the 26th of the present month by the said most reverend prelates to the excellencies the regents, Generals Juan N. Almonte and José Mariano de Salas, and in that document, which is a new testimony added to other thousands of the same kind, that the defence of the rights of the church involves that of nations, families, and individuals, is lost when, under religious and political aspects, it is offered to demonstrate the injustice and inconvenience of putting in vigor the iniquitous legislation called by antiphrasis reform.

No one can doubt the glorious liberty which all Catholics have to oppose their passive resistance to the attacks directed against God's church. We, members of the supreme tribunal of justice of the empire, belong to it, and preserve now the same liberty that we enjoyed in the fatal days when the administration of the reform ruled, bringing upon some violent persecutions, and plunging those who escaped best into complete obscurity and misery.

But having to speak as the superior tribunal of the empire must do, it will enter into certain considerations, casting a retrospective glance upon our public rights, upon that right in which the operations of all powers have been based, upon which the decisions of the tribunals have been constantly given, and which has been a guiding rule to every individual in the affairs of their public and private life. Everything in Mexico is explained by Catholic principles, from the conquest to the independence, and from the independence to the intervention; and without that principle nothing in it can be explained, the doors of future welfare, to which it aspires, being completely closed.

Everybody knows that the immense idea of Columbus would have remained fruitless in his brain if the immortal Ysabelle, of Castile, had not comprehended it; but everybody knows also that that queen, model of crowned heads, the first thing that she proposed to herself in the discoveries was to establish religious principles, and the development of that thought was the principal moving power of her operations upon the territories that were first discovered on this continent. Her successors followed the very same principles, either to proceed in making further conquests, or to protect the inhabitants from the violence of the conquerors, so that to conquer, or to govern with justice and equity those conquered, we have Catholic principles exercising their eminently tutelar influence.

How Spanish monarchs of Austrian dynasty understood Catholic principles history tells us, and our legislation proclaims it at every step. It was the lot of those sovereigns, especially the two first, Emperor Charles the V and King Phillip the II, to govern, whilst Europe was shaken by the frightful religious war stirred up by Protestantism; they embraced the Catholic cause, and while the Protestants endeavored to attack the church in its dogmas, principles, immunities, and all that it possessed and possesses now, they followed entirely an opposite course in Spain and the Americas. By simply stating this fact, and observing that the orders of the Holy Council of Trent were admitted and respected, it proves that in Spain and America the church preserved untouched its canonical legislation.

Later Spanish kings continued the same line of conduct, even including those of the Bourbon dynasty, who showed some slight signs of being partisans of that doctrine, which ended in the French revolution; and precisely owing to that respect to the church, that liberty left to its beneficent decision, and guaranteed by the laws and acts of the authorities, it is explained *how*, while in Europe iniquitous spoliations of riches accumulated in former ages were committed in Mexico and the other Americas belonging to Spain, they accumulated them to invest in proper objects, all in accordance with canonical legislation, especially protected by civil laws, without allowing any one for a moment to suppose that those riches, sacred in every way, would one day become the object of criminal cupidity of a few, who, to despoil its legitimate and benevolent owner, would refuse to give, not only the title of possession, but even the right to acquire that title, and that such iniquity, such absurdity, should take the haughty and ostentatious name of reform, civilization, and progress. It follows from these observations that at every step, as it is proved by our history, our code of laws, and by our public records, that during the whole time that Mexico was under the dominion of Spain, canonic legislation, supported by civil one, ruled supreme throughout the country ; that the Mexican church was governed by it for the acquirement of its prosperity, its preservation, and protection ; that the same legislation was applied by the tribunals, and formed part of the public laws of the country.

After the lapse of three centuries of continued, constant, uniform, and never contradicted practise of those laws, came the great event of independence, and while we mention it, it is also necessary that we should mention one of the principal causes which was predominant during the war, and which became the terminating one of the result. In both epochs, the fear that the cause of religion should be endangered if it continued to depend upon its former metropolis, was one of the principal chapters which caused the proclamation of independence, but particularly in the latter the idea is carried out with greater precision, making the Roman Catholic and apostolic religion the first of the three guarantees given in the immemorable Plan of Yguala.

We all know why such word was placed in said plan, and what it was intended to signify. It was done because the constitutional Spanish courts by their acts, and several of its deputies by their discourses, commenced attacking the Catholic church, not in its dogmas, because, although it is the true mark aimed at, modern tactics only commence by wounding its discipline. It was against that then that the Spanish courts made their assaults ; but Mexico, who had seen the Catholic church teaching freely its dogmas for three centuries, and exercising its discipline, Mexico—who, under the maternal rule of that church, had lived for so long a period in tranquillity and happiness, did not wish to see it endangered, and her children sought to unite with its political independence that of religious incolumity. Consequently, it was not the intention in these plans of independence, nor in the text of them, to attack that canonical legislation, by virtue of which the church holds its property, but, on the contrary, to prevent all that could possibly menace the same and give it additional support. The tribunals had the same understanding as the nation, and far from making any alteration by that great event, that part of our public laws received an additional confirmation of extraordinary solemnity in its form.

After this came a fatal succession of a series of political constitutions in the midst of our international dissensions. We have the constitution of 1824, one of 1837, another of 1843, and an act of reforms of 1847, and in all those codes of law the profession of the Catholic, apostolic, and Romish religion is textually consigned by the Mexican nation, by which it is of course understood that the church is as much mistress of her discipline as she is essentially of her dogmas, and that the nation protects it as it is, that is to say, according to its canons. The consequence of this is, that the public laws of the nation are in harmony with all political constitutions, except that of 1857, as regards the property of the church by canonical legislation.

It is true that during that period many attacks have been made against the church, and not few have been the orders issued against its rights ; but it is true, also, that almost always these triumphed at last ; for, far from considering the first as coming from a legal source, they were held for what they really were, anti-constitutional and illegitimate, the principles of that part of our public laws not suffering any alteration whatever.

The first attack made by the few enemies that the Catholic church has in Mexico, to carry out the iniquitous spoliation meditated by them for years back, took place after the triumph of the revolution of Ayutla by those who were then lords of public administration ; but all the nation impugned the novelties introduced by the reformists to that degree that the principal author of the victorious revolution, the unfortunate Don Ygnacio Comonfort, was obliged to change his ground in December, 1857.

The spurious interests created by the legislation emanated from the plan of Ayutla were never surrendered by that of the "Ciudadela," and then commenced the disastrous campaign by which all the nation fighting on one side to preserve its social constitution, (which is a religious one,) and on the other by the innovators awaking the ferocious instincts of the vulgar masses to spoliation and slaughter, the first having subjugated the last, although not definitely for one single instant ; and amidst the clash of arms, the disastrous reform laws (which are now recommended to be executed) were issued at Vera Cruz by a government that had nothing but the name, even in violation of the same constitution of 1857.

After the bloody triumph of the reformists, what we all witnessed took place, that is to say, the simultaneous banishment of the Mexican bishops, an unbounded persecution of the clergy, the imprisonment of many of them, and bloody executions of others, the savage ejection of the cloistered maidens, whose only crime was that of occupying themselves in praying for their persecutors, depriving them beforehand of all their property; the shooting down, the imprisonment, the concealment, expulsion, and wretchedness of the best citizens; the gagging of the press, using the most oppressive and overwhelming terror to suffocate the voice or complaints of the sufferer; in fact, everything was put into play by the triumphant faction to sanction their reform laws. How can those laws appear to the eyes of common sense? They are wanting in the most essential thing—justice; and to put them into practice it was necessary to have recourse to the ominous means of force. To avoid them, and for that reason only, the Mexican people were obliged to recur to the last extreme, the last supreme effort left them, and that was to solicit aid from a foreign hand; and when France extended hers she understood their true possession and felt the evils that surrounded them, helping to apply the remedy. The intervention not recognizing the administration of Don Benito Juarez as a government, (nor has it ever addressed to him one single word as such, and by that means disavowing his laws, his decrees, his acts, and everything that the idea of a government includes,) where are the antecedents, then, to suppose that the reform laws are in existence? Are they to be found in the conduct of the Mexican people, or in the genuine spirit of the intervention? In neither; and what is certain is, that the only ones that exist, and by which the church property can be administered, are the same (canonical and civil) that existed for three and a half centuries. The supreme tribunal of justice swore to obey the laws of the empire, and to cause them to be obeyed, including among these those by virtue of which the Mexican church possesses what belongs to it, and cannot withdraw its obedience to bestow it upon them that bear but the name.

The supreme tribunal of justice complies, then, with strict duty when it repeats that under no consideration will it consider the so-called reform laws in force, and adds, also, that because they wished to enslave the church, the tribunal is honored by declaring publicly and solemnly that it yields its obedience to the voice of the Mexican episcopate, who has decided that it is not lawful to comply with the circulars of the 9th of November and 15th of the present month.

If to the preceding considerations—based all upon law—we add others, which, although secondary to the duties incumbent upon the tribunals, they are, notwithstanding, of great importance in political order, and we will briefly notice some of the innumerable ones that occur to us. In the first place, the monopolist holders of the promissory notes (*pagarés*) and the monopolists of houses belonging to the church, being protected by a terrible law that admits of no procedure, delay, or form by which a defence could be made, will fall upon the hands of debtors, the greatest part of which are incapable of covering the debt in seven months, and will see their ruin consummated by the public sale of the balance of their fortune.

Secondly, such immense disaster will injure agriculture and all kinds of productive business to favor only a handful of monopolists, for it must be kept in mind that in Mexico ecclesiastic spoliation is always done in that manner, for the advantage of the few, and detriment to the multitude, whereas while they remained in the exclusive power of the church produced positive advantages everywhere.

And, finally, by carrying out the reform laws, without marking the limits and boundaries, and their revision, so solemnly promised, and which justice so imperiously demands, the revolution will increase in colossal proportions, because to the war that is now made without truce against intervention by the anti-Catholic and anti-monarchical bands, if it be not completely vanquished; the throbbings of the excited Mexican people, wounded in their religious principles and vividly outraged in their material interest, will then be added to it.

Those that may think otherwise are mistaken, for in Mexico, as well as in any other place, and with more reason than in another place, neither the consciences of the faithful nor the interests of the holders of church property will find repose unless the will of the supreme pastor of the church be made to appear in a concordat. Peace, that the immense genius of Napoleon the Great could not restore to France without the aid of the Pope, (that most elevated and respected personage on the earth,) will not return to Mexico unless he gives his assistance also.

The tribunal concludes by repeating again, with sorrow, that for the reasons it had the honor of giving in its official communication of the 10th November last, as well as for those herein set forth, cannot legally, nor is it permitted to them conscientiously to comply, or to cause the circulars of the 9th of November and 15th of the present month to be complied with.

And, by unanimous consent, we inform your honor of the same, for the knowledge of their excellencies the regents.

No. 9

Decree of the regency removing the judges of the supreme court.

DEPARTMENT OF JUSTICE AND PUBLIC INSTRUCTION.

The regency of the empire to all of its inhabitants maketh known:

That considering that the first duty of the supreme magistracy of a state consists in respecting the laws and administering justice, without ever deviating from the principles upon which social order is based;

Considering that the supreme tribunal, by its exposition addressed to the regency of the empire on the 31st of December last, has placed itself in rebellion against the legitimate government, declaring that it will never, by its acts and decisions, lend any acquiescence to, nor will it join in, decisions which have for their object the execution of the circulars and official communications ordered, or which may be ordered to be published by the regency, relative to the question of the property called clergy property, if such dispositions shall not be for the purpose of restoring the same at once and directly to the said clergy;

Considering that the tolerance observed up to the present time by the regency with respect to reprehensible acts of this order, in the hope that its efforts would be successful in changing for the better the ideas and sentiments of the individuals reinvested with that high magistracy, has been considered by them as an act of debility, and not as an idea of conciliation, by means of which it was desired to reunite the honorable men of all opinions in order to form a truly national party;

Considering that the regents of the empire would be unworthy of the confidence of their fellow-citizens and of the high mission they have received, if in the presence of this act of rebellion they delayed a longer time to reduce the magistracy to the limits of their attributes, which consist in applying the laws and administering justice without mixing themselves with acts which belong exclusively to the legislator, the regency of the empire decree—

ART. 1. All of the magistrates and secretaries of the supreme tribunal appointed in conformity with the decree issued by the regency of the empire on the 15th of July, 1863, are hereby dismissed.

ART. 2. The reorganization of the said tribunal shall be immediately proceeded with, the persons being ineligible to form any part of it who signed the exposition addressed to the regency on the 31st of December last.

The under secretary of state and of the department of justice and public instruction is charged with the execution of the present decree.

Dated in the imperial palace of Mexico the 2d day of January 1864.

JUAN N. ALMONTE.
JOSÉ MARIANO SALAS.

To the UNDER SECRETARY OF STATE AND OF THE DEPARTMENT OF PUBLIC INSTRUCTION.

And I communicate the same to you for its publication and due observance.

FELIPE RAYGOZA,
Under Secretary of State and of the Department of Justice and Public Instruction.

IMPERIAL PALACE, MEXICO, *January* 2, 1864.

No. 10.

Manifesto of the Regents Almonte and Salas.

MEXICO, *January* 21, 1864.

MEXICANS: In accepting the elevated mission which has been confided to us, of consecrating our efforts and our intelligence to preparing the way for the new destinies of our beloved country, it was our duty not to lose sight for a single moment of the intentions of the sovereign whose soldiers have come to free Mexico from tyranny in order to make it master of itself. Our line of conduct, therefore, was traced beforehand by our gratitude towards the intervention and by the interests of our country, which it was necessary not to separate from the French policy. That policy all know. In the folds of the banner which represents it are always borne the benefits of independence, and the conciliation of parties in order to scatter benefits in the midst of oppressed peoples, assuring equal justice to all and the protection of their rights by the faithful execution of the laws.

All good Mexicans have been moved with pleasure when they have seen this noble banner displayed, its colors side by side with our own. The reason was because that banner brought to our beautiful country, devoured by fifty years of revolutions, that peace and order indispensable to our true regeneration. We, ourselves, the same as the great majority of the nation, have so comprehended it, and calling to our side in the different posts of the magistracy and of the administration those men who, in other times, had been distinguished for their wisdom and their patriotism, we were persuaded that they would comprehend the new situation of Mexico, and would loyally second us in the truly patriotic work we had undertaken, which is nothing less than the reconciliation of all parties on the ground of their common interests.

What has taken place, however? The administration of justice, that first and most imperious necessity of a people freed from tyranny, has from the beginning of our reorganization proved recreant to its noble object. The supreme tribunal, that should be the natural guide of all the other courts which are inferior to it, has forgotten nothing, and nothing has it learned. The magistrates of past times, who had been again reinvested through our confidence, have carried to the sanctuary of their deliberations the spirit of party, which is opposed to justice, and which by fostering bad passions keeps alive the evils of hatred and discord. After having exhausted all means of persuasion and tolerance with respect to these magistrates whose reform is impossible, the regency, persuaded that the well-being of our country lay in the adoption of the measures pointed out to us by that generous people who are lavishing their blood and their gold without other ambition than than of elevating us to the level of the most civilized nations, has found it incumbent to resign itself to the painful duty of removing from their public functions the magistrates of the supreme court who have refused us their co-operation.

Mexicans: Be tranquil and secure. The regency, invested with authority, will watch over your interests conjointly with the chiefs of the intervention. The course of justice will not be interrupted. In making new nominations of those who are to be charged with its administration we shall not inquire of these magistrates to what party they have belonged, but we shall exact from them that they will faithfully maintain equal rights for all, without distinction of opinions, and if it be necessary we shall recall to them—if they forget it—that the dissensions of the nation were conducting it to certain ruin, when the powerful hand of the Emperor Napoleon was stretched out to arrest it on the fatal decline.

JUAN N. ALMONTE.
JOSÉ MARIANO DE SALAS.

No. 11.

Official note from General Neigre to the Archbishop of Mexico.

MEXICO, *January* 16, 1864.

YOUR GRACE: There has just been brought to my knowledge a matter of very grave import. Certain incendiary publications, which have been put under the doors of various houses and scattered clandéstinely among the public, have reached my hands.

The authors of these culpable publications magnify petty material interests which our holy religion repudiates, and appeal to the most detestable passions against the army of his Majesty, the Emperor, which has come to rescue Mexico from anarchy and to afford protection to the pastors of souls, in order to allow them the greatest liberty in their holy ministry. They forget that those prelates of whom they pretend to be the organ, and whom they make to appear as humiliated and despised, have never been surrounded with more respect and veneration.

I desire to believe, your grace, that you are ignorant of these criminal proceedings. I therefore have to denounce them to you, and to address to you an entreaty in the interest of public order and tranquillity; since, in the name of the Catholic religion, of which we Frenchmen are the eldest sons, and in the name of the prelates whom we cover with our respect, a degraded party is in movement to disturb the national repose. Tell that party, your grace, that we are watching it, and know its machinations; that the French army, in accord with the lawful government of the country, will maintain tranquillity; tell it that, although we are always reluctant to employ violent measures of repression, we shall know how, if circumstances put us under that painful obligation, to make them return again to the obscurity from which they are daring to put forth diatribes which prove them to be the real enemies of Mexico.

Be pleased to tell them this, your grace, and if they stop at your evangelical words, your grace will have done a great service to humanity, and, failing their gratitude, you will have ours.

BARON NEIGRE, *General in Command.*

His Grace the ARCHBISHOP OF MEXICO.

No. 12.

Reply of the Archbishop to General Neigre.

YOUR EXCELLENCY: In reply to the communication of your excellency of the 16th instant, I have the honor to assure you, with respect to incendiary writings distributed through the city, that I have not had, nor even now have, any knowledge of them up to the present time. It would, therefore, have been necessary that I should have read them to be able to answer you, and I would thank you sincerely if you would have the kindness to send me a copy of them.

Here I would finish my letter if you did not make in yours certain assertions that, independently of the writings referred to, you throw upon the Mexican clergy. It is, therefore, indispensable to rectify these assertions in case they are not exact.

There is an acknowledged fact—one publicly notorious—which is, that we have all protested against the two individuals who assume to be a government, and against the circulars of the 9th of November and 15th of December last, and we declare categorically that the church, in its immunities and rights, is at present the object of the same attacks that it had to suffer during the government of Juarez; that never was the church so bitterly persecuted; and that we, the chief prelate, from the position in which we have been placed, find ourselves in a worse situation than at that period.

Your excellency tells me that in the exercise of their sacred ministry the pastors of souls enjoy the greatest protection and the most complete liberty, and that they have never been held in greater respect and veneration. Your excellency, then, will perceive that the two documents quoted (our manifesto and your letter) represent, with respect to the position of the church, two propositions entirely contradictory, and that of the two propositions one is necessarily true and the other consequently false.

In conformity with this statement of facts, and the deductions of logic, it results that we, a Mexican prelate, find ourselves, according to your assertion, in the alternative of denying those writings or of retracting our words

We cannot retract, because we have spoken the truth, protested justly, and acted rightfully, and we feel in our conscience that we have been placed in the painful necessity of acting thus.

From what your excellency tells me, I infer that you are badly informed with regard to the situation of the Mexican church, and I am convinced that if you had well known the facts, the interests involved, and the motives which have determined our conduct, you would have done us justice in the opinion which you would have formed of that conduct.

I have the honor to enclose to your excellency a copy of my protest.

Your excellency will be pleased to accept the expression of my consideration.

PELAGIO ANTONIO,
Archbishop of Mexico.

His Excellency Baron NEIGRE, *General in Command.*

No. 13.

EXCELLENCY: With your excellency's note, dated yesterday, I received a manuscript cop of the publications which, in your excellency's former communication, you said had bee circulated in a clandestine manner, and having taken note thereof, I say in answer, that am exceedingly well disposed to tell my dioceseners whatever it is my duty to tell them a cording to the purpose of my pastoral charge, whenever the restriction of the press is witl drawn, with the understanding that I shall assume all legal responsibility for whatever I sa

Your excellency will accept again the assurances of esteem with which I am, genera your excellency's most obedient servant,

PELAGIO ANTONIO,
Archbishop of Mexico.

His Excellency Baron NEIGRE, *Genera in Command.*

Mr. Seward to Mr. Romero.

DEPARTMENT OF STATE,
Washington, March 2, 1864.

SIR: I have the honor to acknowledge the receipt of your note of the 29th ultimo, accompanied with various documents, translated into English, relative to the present attitude of the clergy of Mexico towards the French authorities.

I beg to renew my thanks for your attention, and at the same time to repeat the assurances of my distinguished consideration.

WILLIAM H. SEWARD.

Señor MATIAS ROMERO, *&c., &c., &c.*

Mr. Romero to Mr. Seward.

[Translation.]

MEXICAN LEGATION TO THE UNITED STATES OF AMERICA,
Washington, March 1, 1864.

MR. SECRETARY: That the government of the United States may be informed of the conduct pursued by the French army and other agents of the imperial government during the invasion which is in progress in Mexico, I have the honor to enclose, with this note, various documents translated into English, and upon which I pass on to make a slight narrative.

No. 1 is a report presented to General Forey by Mr. Budin, employed in the treasury, who was sent to Mexico by the imperial government to consult with the said general-in-chief upon measures suitable for this branch of service and to re-establish order, as was said, in the Mexican treasury. The report reduces itself to a proposition of the barbarous measure of sequestrating all the property owned by Mexican patriots who were resisting the intervention, or were perhaps showing their reprobation of it simply by leaving their domiciles upon their being occupied by the French.

No. 2 is a decree issued by General Forey at Puebla in accordance with a like consultation. It is to be noticed that the decision was carried out with the greatest cruelty as well at Puebla as in the city of Mexico, where scarcely had the invaders entered than the decree was republished and put in execution. So impolitic and cruel this must have appeared in France, where at the time the Russian sequestration decreed against the Poles was subject of censure, although that insurrection surely had not such plain foundations as the Mexican resistance to actual invasion—so impolitic and cruel, I repeat, such measures appeared, that the imperial government rebuked it officially in the Moniteur, and gave orders that it should be revoked. Nevertheless General Forey only moderated it a little in an order which he issued on the 19th of August last, (No. 10.) In that document, marked 10, it is confessed that the penalty was applicable even to individuals who had absented themselves from the capital on the entrance of the French without having part in the legitimate administration, much less taking arms against intervention, and on those who were noted simply for their liberal opinions. Even in respect of these individuals it was decided that to return to their hearths they should make a declaration never to serve either in the military or civil branch against the so-called regency which was just established. Notwithstanding this mitigation, the fact is that the properties of the patriots that were sequestered even now continue under confiscation.

No. 3 is a communication from Mr. de Saligny, proposing that there be established in Mexico the same restrictions in relation to the press which are in force in France.

No. 4 is a decree in which sanction is given to these restrictions, with exaggerations in respect to Mexico. But these are not merely the rules observed on the publication of written articles, but the liberty of the press is completely suppressed, a previous censorship existing over all offered for publication, as Archbishop Labastida and other archbishops and bishops assure us in their protest of the 26th of December last, of which I sent a copy to your department, with my communication of the 29th February last past.

Nos. 5 and 6 constitute a report by Mr. Budin, and a decree founded on it, issued by General Forey, declaring void all sales and alienations posterior to the entry of the French army into the city of Mexico, whenever made by persons subject to sequestration, in conformity to the decree which has before been spoken of. The exclusive purpose of this determination is to augment the number of sequestered properties, and of victims of the like policy, making escape from their cruel effects totally out of question for the patriots and their innocent families.

Under No. 7 I enclose a decree of the same General Forey establishing courts-martial with discretionary power to pass without appeal, and on a single hearing, upon all persons who form bands of "armed malefactors," with which name it is sought to stigmatize the Mexicans who, under previous authority of the constitutional government, united as guerillas in making war upon the invaders. Under the rigor of this decree, and even in excess of its hasty provisions, many hundreds of Mexicans have been sacrificed, condemned occasionally upon the vaguest suspicion.

The document No. 8 is an order of the so-called regency of the empire to the governor of the district of Mexico, in which, under the veil of poorly feigned piety, solicitude to please the clergy is adverted to, providing that all the old Spanish legislation upon observance of festival days, so frequent in former times in Mexico, should be strictly observed henceforward, contrary to the spirit of toleration which in latter days had been prevalent.

It is well to remember that this fanatical provision so wounded the interests of manufactures and commerce that the French general disapproved it, and the so-called regency were subjected to the humiliation of revoking it, giving another proof, among so many others, that it is merely the despised instrument of the invaders.

No. 9 is a circular from the department of foreign relations of the constitutional government, providing for the observance (as a just measure of reprisal for the sequestration decree by the invader) of the laws of the country which authorized the like measure against those guilty of treason to their native land.

Lastly, No. 11 is a letter from General Forey, published by his order in the papers of the city of Mexico, in which he relates that a French soldier had been assassinated at the village of Tlalpan, at a very short distance from said city, and that, in consequence, much inquietude prevailed there among French and traitors. To punish the delinquent, whom he vaguely accuses of other assassinations without even indicating them, he announces that he has determined to fine the whole village six thousand dollars and arrest various persons of ill report, (so he calls, it is supposed, the patriots of that village,) keeping them as hostages to answer with their lives for the lives of French soldiers and their partisans the traitors.

Following (as No. 12) appears the decree issued by the French commander at Tlalpan, in conformity with those barbarous provisions. Two things are noteworthy in this: first, that the moral influence of the French army must be very weak, when it is hardly felt at Tlalpan, in the environs of the capital, and when, notwithstanding a garrison present in the village, the French and traitors were filled with terror at any manifestation of the hatred with which they were regarded by the Mexicans. The second to be noted is that savage fury of General

Forey in punishing an entire village for the act of some unknown person, in making responsible for future occurrences an uncertain number of individuals selected at caprice, or rather to punish their patriotic opinions, and in announcing, as he has with most odious complacency, that if those measures were not sufficient for their object, he would destroy the entire settlement. These acts manifest very clearly what are the means which the invaders of Mexico employ to attain their ends, and what character of injustice and barbarism predominates in this invasion, which it is an insult to good sense to call civilizing.

The interest which, in my opinion, the government of the United States must feel in the events of grave importance which are taking place in my country, makes me hope that you will receive with satisfaction the annexed documents, and the brief remarks I have thought it proper to make in this note.

I avail of the occasion to repeat to you, sir, the assurances of my very distinguished consideration.

M. ROMERO.

Index of the documents which the Mexican legation at Washington remitted to the Department of State of the United States, annexed to its note of this date, on the attacks and outrages committed by the French in Mexico.

No.	Date.	Contents.
	1863.	
1	May 21	Report of M. Budin to General Forey, proposing that he issue a law of confiscation of the property of Mexican patriots who defend independence
2	May 21	Law of confiscation issued in consequence by General Forey.
3	June 15	Report of M. Saligny to General Forey that he subject the press in Mexico to the same restrictions that weigh upon the press in France.
4	June 15	Decree issued by General Forey in consequence, in conformity with the preceding report.
5	June 16	Report of M. Budin to General Forey, proposing that he declare void some of the sales made by the Mexican government of national property.
6	June 16	Decree issued by General Forey in consequence, in conformity with the preceding report.
7	June 20	Decree of General Forey establishing courts-martial to try some of the offences committed in Mexico.
8	July 16	Decree of the regency, so-called, that festival days be observed in Mexico in the manner provided by ancient Spanish legislation.
9	July 18	Circular of the national government of Mexico calling for the fulfilment of the Mexican laws of confiscation in respect to the property of traitors.
10	Aug 19	Explanatory order of General Forey on the decree of sequestration issued at Puebla the 15th of June previous.
11	Aug. 22	Letter of General Forey on reprisals to be made at Tlalpam for the assassination of a French soldier.
12	Aug. 27	Decree issued by the military commander at Tlalpann in virtue of the preceding letter.

IGN. MARISCAL.

WASHINGTON, *March* 1, 1864.

No. 1.

Communication made by M. Budin to General Forey in regard to the sequestration of the property of the Mexican patriots.

PUEBLA, *May* 21, 1863.

GENERAL: When you arrived in the Mexican republic with the army of which the Emperor has intrusted to you the command, in order to punish the wrongs and insults of which France and her citizens have been the object on the part of the government of Mexico, you gave ample publicity, by your proclamations and by important acts, which it is needless to repeat here, to the purpose of the intervention and the favorable views of his Imperial Majesty in regard to this country. You have not ceased to repeat that conquest was not the idea of France; that under her banner no other intentions were entertained but to cause the country to reorganize herself, by delivering it from the despotism which for so long a time has weighed upon its destinies, ruined its finances, and impeded all the material progress which its abundant resources, its rich soil, so favored by nature, should cause it to realize. In order to attain more promptly the object contemplated in the intervention, you have called for the co-operation of honorable men of all parties; you have invited the aid of all men of moderate opinions. The number of those who have come to place themselves under the loyal banner of France is relatively great, if we consider that the changes, that the revolutions, of which this unfortunate country has been the theatre for forty years, have extinguished all moral sentiment and perverted all ideas of right and wrong.

In view of your declarations, so clear and so precise, in consideration of the policy so frank and so disinterested that accompanies all the foreign expeditions of the empire, was it possible to be mistaken in regard to the intentions of France? Was Mexico authorized to treat as deceitful the words of peace addressed to her by and in the name of a power whose every aspiration is for liberty, whose forces and sacrifices have no other object than to bear the torch of civilization to an oppressed people? Clearly not; and if interested men in the support of the disorderly condition of things which you have come to attack, because it is for them a source of profit, had not interposed between a docile people whom they lead astray, and your well-meaning words which they distort, it is probable that the power which exists only by means of disorder would have been now demolished.

The time has come for the adoption against these agitators of more rigorous means—such means as, by reaching their material interests, may cause them to understand, as I trust, that the time of longanimity has passed. What the wise exhortations which you have addressed to them, what the well-meaning intentions of the Emperor which you have explained to them, has been unable to effect, will perhaps be attained by attacking the property of those men of bad faith, who persist in remaining in the hostile lines to combat the true interests of their country. The means the adoption of which appears to me necessary in regard to the men who thus far have held aloof from the intervention, has had fortunate results under other circumstances—that is, sequestration—sequestration, ransacking the entire estates appertaining to such Mexicans as yet bear arms against intervention. This means would equally reach the personal estates, as far as their incomes could be seized. You know, general, what the effect is of sequestration; it is to transfer to the hands of the state, represented here by the prefect, the administration of all the goods appertaining to those citizens who find themselves in the condition mentioned.

The conditions of sequestration may vary according to circumstances.

In the draught of a decree which I have the honor of submitting to you, and which I request you to sign if you approve its terms, I have reserved to the commander-in-chief of the army the right of mitigating its rigor in regard to such citizens as may be worthy of that favor, either because they may abandon within a fixed period the party which you have had to oppose, or because they may justify themselves for having been dragged into it by reason of force and violence.

Be pleased, general, to accept the expression of my respect and esteem.

BUDIN, *General Financial Agent.*

General FOREY,
General of Division and Senator of France,
Commander-in-Chief of the Expeditionary Corps.

No. 2.

Decree of General Forey in regard to the sequestration to which the preceding communication refers.

According to the communication submitted to me by the general financial agent of the expedition, it has seemed proper to me to decree:

ART. 1. Sequestration will be resorted to of all the estates appertaining to the citizens of the republic who bear arms against the French intervention, whether they render their services in the regular army or in the bands of guerillas, or others in a state of hostility towards France.

ART. 2. The personal property appertaining to the individuals comprised in the preceding article will also be subjected to this measure, as far as such property can be seized upon.

ART. 3. The political prefect of each state subject to the intervention shall constitute under his presidency a commission of four members, who shall be charged with designating the persons who should be comprised in the above-mentioned categories, and with drawing up a statement of the general condition of estates, both in the country and in the cities, and of personal property which may appertain to them.

ART. 4. This statement, agreeably to the model annexed to the present decree, will be signed by all the members of the commission and certified by the president prefect.

ART. 5. A copy of this statement shall be published in all the places of general resort throughout the country subject to the intervention, with a notification from the prefect informing tenants, lessees, and debtors of the goods and credits sequestrated, that they cannot exonerate themselves lawfully without satisfactory payment of the amounts due into the hands of the administrator of internal revenue of the district wherein the things sequestered are situated.

ART. 6. A copy of the above-mentioned statement, certified by the prefect, shall be, as soon as published, transmitted to the administrator of the revenue to serve as a guide for his direction.

ART. 7. The arrangements relative to rents, hiring out, or other matter whatever, that may be further entered into by the prefects to enhance the value of the personal estates that may be unoccupied, shall also be certified in writing to the same administrator, in order that they may serve him as foundations for legal proceedings against those indebted.

ART. 8. It is expressly prohibited, under the penalties prescribed by law, to the agents appointed for the collection of the internal revenue to exact from those indebted a sum greater than that set down in the lists. Exception only is made in regard to the expenses anticipated to be necessary in order to verify the collection of the sums which may be due, and which should be collected in their entirety.

ART. 9. The administrators of the revenue shall give a receipt for every sum paid to them, and shall include all receipts of this kind in a separate account, either in their books or in their monthly statements. Such account shall be entitled, "*Collections made of sequestered property.*"

ART. 10. The general-in-chief reserves to himself the right of deciding, according to the information laid before him by the prefects, upon all petitions that may be presented to him, either for exemption from the decree of sequestration, or for the restitution of the incomes received in virtue of the preceding dispositions.

ART. 11. The present decree shall be immediately published, printed, and circulated throughout the whole extent of the country subject to the intervention, and a similar course shall be pursued in succession in all the states of the republic, in order that it may be executed in its form and tenor by the prefects that may be established in those states.

ART. 12. Fifteen days after its publication the commission, mentioned in article 3, shall proceed to draw out the statement above referred to. In it shall be included all persons who shall not, at that date, have returned to their homes, or who may not be prisoners of war.

In case, after the conclusion of this document, and its transmission to the administrator, the prefect shall be informed of the emigration of one or more of such persons as may be subject to administration in his department, it shall be his duty to draw up a supplementary statement, which shall have the same legal effect as the preceding to confer title.

ART. 13. The general financial agent is charged with the execution of the present decree, which shall be notified to the commanding officer in each district and state through the chief officer in command of the staff.

Given at Puebla, May 21, 1863.

FOREY,
General of Division, Senator of France, &c., &c.

No. 3.

Communication of M. De Saligny to General Forey in regard to the liberty of the press.

MEXICO, *June* 15, 1863.

GENERAL: By an order brought to the knowledge of the public, you have for a time suspended the publication of the periodicals of the country. This exceptional means was justified by the reasons naturally arising out of the condition in which the republic of Mexico was found subsequent to the departure of the government of Juarez, and previous to the establishment of the new power. It was to be feared, in fact, that abandoned to itself, and without other control than that of its editors, the press, which in well-organized states is a powerful means by which to inculcate to the masses the ideas of order and healthy policy, would be here only an instrument in the service of evil passions to agitate the country, by misrepresenting the intentions of France, and dividing good citizens, by sowing the seeds of discord among them. Under all these points of view, it was indispensable to adopt a course which allowed time to study the situation of affairs before consigning it to the discussion of the periodicals, and tracing to the press a line of conduct such as would never place it in opposition to the direction which the constituted authorities considered proper to be impressed on public affairs. There could not exist in the life of a nation more solemn moments than those which gleam athwart Mexico under the present circumstances. Her future, her prosperity, her greatness in time to come, even her very existence, constitute the prize which is to reward the efforts that are about to be made by those honorable citizens who shall accept the laborious work of toiling in the reorganization of the country on a new basis.

If, in view of such difficulties, it is the duty of every good Mexican to preach concord, and adherence to the temporary power charged with preparing the destinies of the country, with greater reason is it that permission cannot be granted to the organs of the press to branch out into controversies, which, if they are always dangerous when they attack the spirit of governments already assented to, could at the present conjuncture paralyze the best intentions, by inspiring doubts into the mind, and disseminating doctrines that may threaten, even before they are resolved upon, the bases of the institutions which the Mexican republic anxiously hopes from the friendly intervention of the Emperor.

Confining itself within the limits of decent discussion, under the seal of moderation, and without ever attacking religion, the personal character of public men, or the private life of individuals, the press may be well occupied with the general interests of the country, and making known its aspirations, until the time when the rightful representatives of the people have determined the form of the new government which it is proposed to establish. If the press properly comprehends its mission, it is called to perform the most eminent services, by propagating good ideas among the masses, and warring upon the utopias which corrupt them.

Your intention, general, is to apply to the press of Mexico the regulations established in France; it is, therefore, a reasonable liberty which is conceded to the press. Liberty is not licentiousness. Firmly persuaded of this wise principle, which is the safeguard of all interests, the writers of the Mexican press will always rise to the level of the important mission and sacred duty to which they are called, in seconding the constituted authorities, and frequently advising them, without ever forgetting the respect which is their due.

I have prepared, and I have the honor of now submitting to your approbation, the decree which regulates, in accordance with the principles laid down, the conduct of the press of Mexico. This decree is intended to have merely a transitory effect; it will be susceptible of all the modifications which the definitive government of the country may think proper to give it.

Accept, general, the assurances of my highest esteem and regard.

A. DE SALIGNY,
Minister of the Emperor.

General FOREY,
General of Division and Senator of France,
Commander-in-Chief of the Expeditionary Army of Mexico.

No. 4.

Decree of General Forey regulating the liberty of the press.

Forey, general of division, and senator of France, commanding in chief the expeditionary army of Mexico:

Desiring to revoke the order suspending the press, which was dictated by the anomalous circumstances in which Mexico is situated, I have thought proper, in accordance with the communication made to me by the minister of the Emperor, to decree as follows:

ARTICLE 1. Every person domiciliated in Mexico for a period of one year preceding may establish a periodical, to treat of public affairs, civil, commercial, scientific, and literary matters, after having first obtained the authority of the government to that effect.

ART. 2. Each periodical will be under obligation to have a responsible editor, approved by the administration, and whose signature shall appear at the end of each number of the paper. All original articles must be signed by their authors; reproductions from other periodicals by the responsible editor.

ART. 3. All discussion of the laws and institutions established for the country by its representatives is expressly forbidden.

ART. 4. It is likewise forbidden to the press to concern itself with what appertains to religion, as such discussion may always compromise sacred interests, or impair the honor and consideration due to the clergy.

ART. 5. A moderate discussion of the acts of the administration is allowed, without any reference, however, to the persons of the representatives of authority.

ART. 6. The journals must insert, entire and without charge, the communications that may be sent to them by the department of the government intrusted with the censorship of the press. Such communications must neither be preceded nor accompanied by any reflections whatever.

ART. 7. Any person mentioned in the articles of discussion may likewise cause to be inserted, free of charge, whatever be its length, his answer or his observations on the article which concerns him, provided, always, such answer contains nothing that may call for the animadversion of the authorities, or incur a penalty provided by the laws of the country.

ART. 8. The infraction of articles 2, 3, 4, 5, and 6 will be an occasion for warnings, which shall be notified to the responsible editor of the paper and to the author of the article condemned, and which shall be inserted at the head of that number of the paper which appears on the day following that of the notification. These warnings cannot be the object of any discussion on the part of the journal to which they are given.

ART. 9. After two successive warnings, every periodical may be suspended for a certain determinate period. If occasion be given for a third warning, before being relieved from the consequences of the two preceding, the paper may be definitively suppressed.

ART. 10. The penalties laid down in article 9 will be dictated by the executive power, according to the information laid before it by the director of the press.

ART. 11. Crimes and delinquencies, qualified as such by the laws of the land, and committed by the medium of the press, either against public morality or against private persons or private interests, will be prosecuted and judged in accordance with actual legislation in effect at the time.

ART. 12. Questions relative to matters of minor importance, such as constitute misdemeanors, are reserved for the further decision of the executive power.

ART. 13. The minister of the Emperor is charged with the execution of the present decree.

Given at Mexico, June 15, 1863.

FOREY.

No. 5.

Communication of M. Budin to General Forey in relation to sales called illegal.

MEXICO, *June* 16, 1863.

GENERAL: The lieutenant colonel commanding in the city of Mexico informs me, in a communication bearing date on the present day, that the goods, movable and immovable, appertaining to the persons comprised in your decree of sequestration, are being alienated by the agents of the proprietors, who think, by acting in this way, to withdraw them from the effects of the aforesaid decree. You cannot permit, general, that the arrangements by means of which you have, with sufficient reason, calculated to inspire a great number of those who have followed the opposite party with better sentiments towards their country, should thus be eluded by persons whose first duty it is to respect the acts of the authority which protects them and affords them security. There is no difference between the venders and the purchasers. Both should be prosecuted by all the means requisite to give just effect to the acts to which reference has been made. I submit, general, the following resolutions for your approval.

1. That all sales made since the entry of the French troops into the city of Mexico, that is, from the 10th of June; all sales effected in other places occupied by France since the publication of the decree; finally, all that may henceforward be made, be null and void, and will not hinder the carrying out of the provisions of the decree of sequestration.

2. That the bureau of rental revenue, on assuming the administration of immovable goods, will be held bound to no reimbursement to purchasers.

3. That the prefect will compel purchasers to make restitution to the bureau of such movable goods as they may have purchased, or the value of them.

4. That any individual informing the prefect of a fraudulent act of this nature shall receive a reward, to be ascertained by that functionary in accordance with the importance of the effects recovered.

5. That any public functionary, notary or other, who may, after the publication of the present decree, give his official aid to draw up any instruments of writing to effectuate such sales as are herein prohibited, shall be deprived of his office and fined not less than one thousand dollars, for the benefit of the treasury.

If you approve the regulations which I have the honor of proposing to you, in order to correct the abuse which I have indicated, I request you, general, to sign the annexed decree, which will be put in execution immediately.

Please accept, general, the expression of my respectful consideration.

BUDIN,
Commissioner Extraordinary of Finance.

Certified copy:

BUDIN,
Commissioner Extraordinary of Finance.

No. 6.

Forey, general of division, senator of France, commander-in-chief of the expeditionary army in Mexico.

In view of the preceding communication from the commissioner extraordinary of finance, I have deemed it proper to decree as follows:

ARTICLE 1. All sales of goods, movable or immovable, belonging to persons comprised in the decree of sequestration which may have been effected by the agents of the proprietors since the entrance of the French troops into the city of Mexico, that is, from the 10th of June; all that may have been made in other places occupied by France since the publication of the decree; finally, all that may henceforward be made, shall be null and void and of no effect, and shall not hinder the carrying out of the provisions of the decree of sequestration.

ART. 2. The bureau of rental revenue, on assuming the administration of immovable goods, shall be held bound to no reimbursement to purchasers.

ART. 3. The political prefect of each district will compel purchasers to make restitution of movable goods, or of the value of them, to the bureau.

ART. 4. Any person informing the prefect of a fraudulent act of this nature shall receive a reward fixed by that functionary, and proportionate to the value of the objects recovered.

ART. 5. Any public functionary, notary or other, who may, after the publication of the present decree, afford his ministerial assistance to draw up instruments of writing for sales prohibited by this decree, shall incur the penalty of deprivation of office, and a fine of not less than one thousand dollars, for the benefit of the treasury.

ART. 6. The commissioner extraordinary of finance is charged with the execution of the present decree, which will be inserted in the official bulletin of the acts of the intervention.

Given at Mexico, June 16, 1863.

FOREY.

Certified copy:

BUDIN,
Commissioner Extraordinary of Finance.

No. 7.

Decree of Gen. Forey organizing a court-martial.

The general of division and senator of France, commander-in-chief of the expeditionary corps in Mexico:

Considering that it is important to put an end to the acts of vandalism committed by the bands of malefactors who overrun the country, perpetrating acts of violence on persons and property, and paralyzing commercial relations; considering, also, that the ordinary laws are insufficient to repress these disorders and cause delays prejudicial to the prompt suppression of crimes in those same places in which they are committed, I decree as follows:

1. All persons forming part of a band of armed malefactors are outside the pale of the law.
2. All persons of this description who may be arrested shall be judged by a court-martial.
3. Such court shall be invested with discretionary powers
4. It shall be composed of an official superior as president, two captains as judges, a judge advocate, and a sergeant as secretary of the court. An interpreter shall be added to the court. Persons accused may, at their own request, have counsel to defend them.
5. The court shall pronounce sentence by absolute majority of votes at the same sitting.
6. From such sentence there shall be no appeal, and it shall be executed within twenty-four hours from the time of rendering judgment.
7. A court-martial shall be established in every place in which it may be necessary.
8. The duties of each court shall be temporary, and shall begin and cease according to the orders of the commander-in-chief, or of the military commander, to whom the commander-in-chief may delegate his powers to this effect.

Headquarters in Mexico, June 20, 1863.

FOREY, *General of Division, &c., &c.*

No. 8.

Order of the regency to the governor of the district of Mexico in regard to the observance of festivals.

DEPARTMENT OF STATE AND GOVERNMENT,
Palace of the Regency of the Empire, Mexico, July 16, 1863.

The gross abuse which, with manifest violation of a sacred precept of religion, has been for a long time committed in this capital, in disregarding the observance of festival days, on which, to the scandal of all good Catholics, labor is carried on in the workshops, and stores are kept open for the sale of articles not necessary to subsistence, nor otherwise excepted in the regulations properly promulgated by the civil authorities, at different periods, has justly called for the attention of the regency of the empire, since such an abuse, which is not seen in other countries, even in those dissenting from Catholicity, demonstrates a relaxation from Christian customs, so much the more notable, as it exists in a society that loudly proclaims itself Catholic and rigorous observer of the precepts of religion.

Wherefore the regency has deemed it proper to resolve that you should issue your orders to prevent for the future this scandalous infraction, and should see that all fulfil strictly the regulations in force in respect to the observance of festival days.

Which supreme order I communicate to you for the purpose expressed.

J. I. DE ANIEVAS,
Sub-Secretary of State and of Government.

No. 9.

Circular from the Department of Foreign Affairs in regard to the sequestration of the property of traitors.

DEPARTMENT OF GOVERNMENT.

The newspapers have in a great measure published the names of such bad Mexicans as have committed the heinous crime of treason, by co-operating with the invaders of their country in the erection of a false and spurious government.

Assuredly the nation will destroy this abominable farce; but, for all that, the traitors should not remain unpunished. And when our foreign enemy and his adherents, violating all principle, arrogated to themselves the power of confiscating the goods of worthy citizens who serve the government of their country, it is not just that the action of our laws should be suspended, relative to the sequestration and alienation of property, for violation of the duties of allegiance.

Wherefore, if in the state, which you so worthily govern, such seizure should be intended to have effect, you will issue your orders to have the preliminary formalities immediately arranged, and report to this department, in order that the proper determinations should be made in regard to the alienation of the sequestered property. In view of which, after the period of fifteen days after the receipt of this supreme resolution, information may be received of overlooked or concealed goods, liable to sequestration, and the informer shall, in such case, be rewarded with the fourth part of the amount for which the goods so discovered may be sold.

Liberty and reform.

San Luis Potosi, July 18, 1863. FUENTE.

The GOVERNOR *of the State of* ———.

No. 10.

Explanation by Gen. Forey of the law of sequestration of the property of the patriots.

MEXICO, *August* 19, 1863.

To the superior officers in command of the provinces and districts in the military occupation of the intervention:

M. LE COMMANDANT: I have been informed that the commissions, instituted in conformity with the decree of May 21 last, in regard to sequestration, are accustomed to deviate, in the execution of that measure from the spirit that dictated it. The terms of that decree, and those of the preceding communication on which it was founded, should not give occasion to interpretations that in their very nature originate errors, these being so much the more serious, the more they place in doubt the good faith of the commissioners, in creating certain categories of sequestrations not contemplated in the decree.

In the main, it was not sought to affect any but those persons who oppose the arms of the intervention, and serve either in the regular army or in bands of guerillas. Posterior to the publication of the decree, and in view of the observations of the financial commissary extraordinary, I determined that those persons who take an active part in the government of the ex-president should also be comprised in the sequestration. In fact, it did not appear proper that the ministers and high functionaries, who exert a much greater influence in affairs than military men, should, whatever be their grade, be more favorably treated.

This political measure, thus understood and applied, has for its object what you have doubtless not failed to perceive, and that is, to draw off, by touching their interests, those persons who serve in one or other way, whether in a military or political capacity, the government of Juarez. This distinction made, you now understand that the sequestration need not always be imposed on the goods of those persons who assert that they are neither combatants nor public functionaries, and to whom the measure applies because they happen to be absent from their homes, or because they conceive that their ideas are different from those of the intervention. In regard to the former, it will be proper to demand from them a declaration, in virtue of which they will oblige themselves not to serve either in a military or in a civil capacity against the imperial government which has just been founded. Petitions for relief from sequestration shall not be transmitted by the prefect to the proper authorities, unless they be accompanied by the above-mentioned obligation. When, through mistake or other cause, sequestration has been applied to the goods of individuals of the second class, their petitions shall be attended to without any other requisite than the presentation of the certificate of the authorities of the place of the residence of the parties, in which certificate it shall be stated that they are neither military men nor public functionaries, or that they had retired from public affairs a considerable time previous to the decree of the 21st of May.

I request you, commander, to communicate the contents of this letter to the civil governor of N———, and recommend to him to proceed, in the way which I have indicated, in the practical details of the commission of sequestration.

Receive, commander, the assurance of my most respectful consideration.

FOREY, *Marshal of France and Commander in-Chief.*

No. 11.

Letter from Marshal Forey.

EXPEDITIONARY CORPS OF MEXICO, CABINET OF THE GENERAL-IN-CHIEF,
Mexico, August 22, 1863.

MR. EDITOR: I have read in your paper to-day that three French soldiers have been assassinated in Tlalpan recently, and that you desire to see the authorities adopt rigorous measures with reference to that locality.

There has been only one military victim; but for some time various persons, resident in that village, have perished, cowardly attacked by assassins, who, on account of the debility of the local authority, [this village is within sight of the city of Mexico, so that it is strange, if the French are so well received, order does not prevail that short distance from the principal point occupied by the French.—Translator.] evade the pursuit of justice, and find in the houses of the inhabitants an asylum which effectually conceals them.

For the rest your desires have been already anticipated, and yesterday I dictated, in accord with the government, the necessary rigorous measures to prevent the repetition of crimes which offend the public conscience, as well of French officials as of those Mexicans who have a right to my protection.

The garrison of Tlalpan has been augmented, and a high official will hereafter discharge the funtions of prefect. The ayuntamiento (common council) has been removed. The village of Tlalpan will suffer a penalty of $6,000, which will in part be distributed for the benefit of the victims who have been cowardly assassinated. A certain number of individuals of bad reputation [?] will be arrested and will serve as hostages. If the assassinations continue, these hostages shall respond for them with their heads. If this is not sufficient, the village will be destroyed. It is time that, as the Emperor said when detestable passions raged in France, the good should be tranquilized, and also the bad. The government and myself are perfectly in accord in our measures to maintain order and assure good citizens the enjoyment of their property, and of their lives, which is the first of all; and if we are disposed to forget the past and to act with clemency towards those who frankly adhere to the new order of things which the nation itself has established, we are equally decided to follow with the extremest measures of rigor all the enemies of social order.

Receive the assurances, &c.

FOREY,
Marshal of France, Commandant of the Expeditionary Corps of Mexico.

No. 12.

TLALPAN, *August* 27, 1863.

The superior military commandant and political chief of Tlalpan, in accordance with the order of the marshal commanding the French army, to the inhabitants and proprietors of this village maketh known as follows:

ARTICLE 1. The civil and administrators' authorities are temporarily suspended.

ART. 2. The superior commandant of Tlalpan will exercise all powers in the district.

ART. 3. In punishment for the assassination of the Zouave Multer, a fine of $6,000 is imposed upon the village of Tlalpan. This fine must be fully paid within four days following the publication of this decree.

ART. 4. The individuals of this town who have been conducted as prisoners to the capital will respond for the lives of the French and of those honorable persons who have adhered to the new government. For every such honorable person or soldier who shall be assassinated in Tlalpan, a reprisal will be made with the life of one of the aforesaid prisoners.

ART. 5. All the inhabitants of Tlalpan must obey exactly the orders given by the superior commandant.

If there is opposition the marshal will be obliged to adopt measures of rigor.

COUSIN,
Military Commandant and Political Chief.

No. 13.

Lodgings.

MEXICO, *June* 15, 1863.

De Poitier, lieutenant colonel, commander of the place of Mexico, to its inhabitants, know ye:

That his excellency, general of division, senator, commander-in-chief of the French expeditionary corps, with the object that the lodgings of the army and its officers should be less onerous to the inhabitants of this capital, has regulated the obligations they shall be under, declaring that all owners of houses are obliged to place at the disposal of each lieutenant and sub-lieutenant one room; to captains, two rooms; to superior officers, three rooms, of which one must be a parlor. Colonels must have at least five rooms. The officers of staff must have a number in proportion to the exigencies of the service.

It must be understood that the rooms placed at the disposal of the officers of the army will not be empty ones, but furnished by the owners; that is to say, they must supply them with beds, chairs, tables, and other furniture. Should these obligations be not complied with, the municipal authorities shall see that said lodgings are furnished at the expense of the proprietors if they choose to excuse themselves.

Those inhabitants that should have to lodge mounted officers must reserve in their stables the necessary locality and stalls for their horses.

DE POITIER.

Mr. Romero to Mr. Seward.

[Translation.]

MEXICAN LEGATION TO THE UNITED STATES OF AMERICA.
Washington, March 2, 1864.

Mr. SECRETARY: To complete the series of documents relating to the important events which are actually taking place in the Mexican republic, which I have had the honor to send to your department, I enclose with this note, translated into English, those relative to the occupation of Puebla by the French army on the evacuation of the city of Mexico by the government and national army, and on the installation of the former at the city of San Luis Potosi. I also enclose a declaration of blockade of the Mexican ports on the Gulf, and some proclamations of the French Generals Forey and Bazaine.

I avail of this opportunity to repeat to you, sir, the assurances of my most distinguished consideration.

M. ROMERO.

Hon. WILLIAM H. SEWARD, *&c., &c., &c.*

General Ortega's announcement of the surrender of Puebla.—Army of the east.—The Commander-in-chief to the Minister of War.

HEADQUARTERS AT ZARAGOZA, *May* 17, 1863.

With this date and at this hour, 4 a. m., I send the following communication to the commander-in-chief of the French army:

GENERAL: As it is impossible for me to continue defending this city, from the want of ammunition and provisions, I have disbanded the army that was under my command and destroyed its equipments, including all the artillery. The city is therefore at the order of your excellency, and you can direct it to be occupied to-day if you think fit, the measures dictated by prudence to prevent the evils that a violent occupation will bring with it when there is no motive for it. The generals, commanders, and officers of which this army consists, are at the Government House, and surrender as prisoners of war. I cannot, general, continue defending myself any longer. If I could, do not doubt that I would do so.

Please accept, &c., &c.

The above I transcribe for the information of the supreme magistrate of the republic, to whom I hope you will explain that the army—the command of which he was pleased to intrust to me—defended itself as was suitable to the honor and reputation of the republic, and that it would have continued doing so if an absolute physical impossibility had not interposed to prevent it, since some days past it had consumed all the provisions and the small quantity of ammunition which remained to it after the fierce attacks which it lately suffered, and in which, fortunately, it did not lose a single redoubt.

I believe, sir, that I have fulfilled the wishes of the supreme government, and complied with the duties imposed upon me by honor and the office intrusted to me; but if it should not be so I will with pleasure submit to a trial as soon as I am at liberty, for in a few hours I shall be a prisoner.

Libei ty and reform.

J. G. ORTEGA.

The MINISTER OF WAR, *Mexico*.

Proclamation of President Juarez.

MEXICANS: The nation has just suffered a great disaster. Puebla de Zaragoza, immortalized by numerous and glorious attacks, has just surrendered—not because of the power of the French, whom our soldiers had become accustomed to repulse, but for reasons which the government must consider without parallel for their glory alone. None of our generals, or chiefs, who have so greatly distinguished themselves in the defence of that city, have as yet sent to the government information of this deplorable event, but a variety of private accounts accredit the fact, although they are silent or vary on points of the greatest interest. But the occupation of Zaragoza, which could not be taken in any of the repeated assaults of the enemy, nor by the most formidable modes of warfare, does not in any way lessen or tarnish the glory of our brave warriors, who have known how to maintain the name of Mexico in spite of the arrogant invaders. Dishonorable and without glory has been their success, who have always been worsted in the brave combats of which the city of Zaragoza has been the theatre.

Mexicans! this calamity cannot, under any aspect, discourage the holy undertaking which you are carrying out. Prove to the French, prove to all the nations who are watching your actions in this unfortunate situation, that adversity is not a sufficient cause for fainting to the determined republicans who defend their native land and their rights. Our country is vast, and contains innumerable elements of war, which we will use against the invaders. Not only will the capital of the republic be defended to the last extremity with all the elements which we can command, but all places will be defended with like vigor. The national government will urge with energy on all sides the resistance to and attack upon the French, and will not listen to any proposition of peace from them which shall offend in the minutest particular the independence, complete sovereignty, the liberty, or the honor of the republic and its glorious antecedents in this war.

Mexicans! let us swear by the heroes killed in defending the holy walls of Zaragoza, let us swear by those who still live, victors there while able to battle, that we will wage war without ceasing, and under all sacrifices, against the odious army which is profaning the soil of Hidalgo, of Moreloz, of Zaragoza, and of Gonzalez Ortega

BENITO JUAREZ.

Close of the General Congress.

On the 31st of last month the general congress closed its sessions in conformity with the constitution. On this solemn occasion the following discourses were delivered:

The president of the republic arose and said:

CITIZEN DEPUTIES: Notwithstanding the violence and danger of the present situation, you have occupied yourself in the performance of your important duties up to the present day, on which the constitution commands you to terminate them. Although this, indeed, is nothing new and requires no great effort on the part of the worthy representatives of the Mexican people, in whom all the civic virtues are conspicuous, it will be, in truth, one proof the more of the security and firmly established dominion of our institutions presented to the view of our foreign enemy, when not only he but many politicians of Europe prophesied the utter ruin of our government at the very clash of the arms of Napoleon III.

But the influence of the army which that potentate has sent to subjugate us reaches no further than the ground which it occupies, and our enemies have no reason to be proud of an occupation that has left all the honor and the glory on our side.

The events that have transpired in Puebla de Zaragoza have filled the people of Mexico with noble pride, and have intensified their purpose of repelling the invaders of their country, who have already thrown off the mask of deceit to parade their impudence in the face of the world. The defence of Zaragoza and the glorious disaster which terminated that truly sublime drama—a contest in which the French were so often humbled, an exploit unparalleled in its heroism, and only performed under the pressure of the sternest necessity and the noble resolution of never surrendering our arms and our banners—are prodigies that proclaim the greatness of this people, examples that will not, most assuredly, be lost on the people of Mexico.

Your solicitude has been worthily employed in ameliorating the fate of our soldiers wounded and taken prisoners, and in providing for their families. The government has always employed itself in fulfilling this demand of patriotism and of the clearest justice, and the republic makes such provisions in this regard as are in its power.

Adversity, citizen deputies, dismays only contemptible nations. Our people are ennobled by great deeds, and we are far from losing sight of the immense moral and material obstacles which the country will oppose to its unjust invaders.

The vote of confidence with which you have honored me anew claims the warmest expression of my acknowledgment to the assembly of the nation, though it can no longer enhance my honor or my duty in the defence of my country.

You are now going to serve her beyond the precincts of these walls, and your love for her should, on all occasions, be animated by the assurance that the government will sustain the will of the Mexican people, maintaining, at all hazards, their autonomy and their democratic institutions.

Mr. Sebastian Lerdo de Tejada replied in the following terms:

Mr. President: The congress of the union concludes, to-day, the second yearly term of its sessions, on the day designated by the fundamental code.

While some of the representatives of the people have been defending the national honor and independence in arms, others have come from the remotest states, so that congress might not fail to assemble at the time appointed by the constitution. Thus once again has the pretext been belied for the iniquitous war waged against the republic, when it is sought to veil the ambitious purpose of usurping its sovereignty with the assumed desire to afford assistance to the Mexican people in reorganizing themselves, and to give them a protection which they have not solicited.

In these solemn moments an occasion has been presented for the display of the firm adhesion of all the states, and of the general will of the immense majority of Mexicans to sustain the institutions and the government of the republic. In the face of the invading army, in the midst of the perils of war, and in spite of the general confusion occasioned by it, the representatives of the people have come from all quarters, so that the regular course of public power might not be interrupted.

In this session congress has, justly and preferably to all else, engaged its attention in all that concerns the war. In its course it has been able to admire the heroic courage and constancy of the defenders of Puebla de Zaragoza. It justly acknowledges and declares that they have merited well of their country, and that they and the families of those who fell should be cared for with special solicitude.

There they have conquered for the republic a new glory never to be forgotten, and they have given to their fellow-citizens a noble example to imitate. They will ever serve for models to all good Mexicans, to enable them, whatever may be the vicissitudes of war, to continue it without being dismayed by any misfortune or terrified by any sacrifice, until they obtain the invader's respect for the justice of the cause of Mexico.

That the contest may be prosecuted without cessation, congress has granted to the executive a prolongation of the amplest powers that may be required.

The chief magistrate, who has defended the rights of Mexico under the most difficult circumstances, remains invested with all the plenitude of power given him by the free election of the people and the repeated votes of confidence of the national legislature. We doubt not but that, with these testimonials, with the energetic and unanimous co-operation of all the states, and with the patriotism of all good Mexicans, he will omit nothing that may be necessary to prosecute the contest worthily, until a final victory is effected for the rights, the sovereignty, and the independence of the republic.

Benito Juarez, President of the Mexican republic, to his fellow-countrymen.

MEXICANS: For grave considerations connected with the defence of the nation, I ordered our army to evacuate the city of Mexico, withdrawing the abundant materials of war which we had collected there, and I ordered that the city of San Luis Potosi should be temporarily the capital of the republic. The first of these resolutions was immediately put into execution, and the second has likewise been carried into effect by the instalment of the supreme government in this city, which possesses so many facilities for carrying on the war against the enemy of our glorious and beloved country.

In Mexico, as in Puebla de Zaragoza, we would have resisted the French, and yielded at last to invincible necessity. But it was not expedient to choose voluntarily those adverse, though glorious, situations, nor to regard our honor alone, as though we had despaired of our fortune.

Concentrated at one point, as now, the enemy will be weak outside of that; scattered, he will be weak in all quarters. He will see himself compelled to acknowledge that the republic is not confined within the limits of the cities of Mexico and Zaragoza; that life and spirit, the consciousness of justice and of strength, the love of independence and of republicanism, the noble pride aroused against the iniquitous invader of our soil, are sentiments diffused throughout the entire Mexican people; and that the silent and indefinite majority, in whose uprising Napoleen III placed the successful issue and the justification of the most astonishing enterprise which the nineteenth century has seen, will not rise above a chimera invented by a handful of traitors.

The French were mistaken when they thought they could lord it over the nation at the mere sound of their arms, and when they presumed to crown their shameless assumption by violating the laws of honor, and when they considered themselves masters of Zaragoza, because they had occupied the fort of San Javier. Now, they deceive themselves most miserably in flattering themselves that they rule over the country, when they scarcely begin to realize the enormous difficulties of their inconsiderate enterprise; since, if they have consumed so much time, invested so large sums, and sacrificed so many lives to obtain a few advantages in the glorious engagements at Puebla, what can they expect when we shall oppose them the whole people as an army and the territory of the country as a battle-field? Did Napoleon I master Spain because his troops occupied Madrid and several cities of that kingdom? What happened to the French army after having entered the capital of Russia? Were not the invaders of those countries ignominiously driven out? Did it not happen the same to the retrograde faction that held in its possession our former capital? And in what of our towns did we not overthrow the power of Spain?

Believe me, fellow-countrymen, your valor, your perseverance, your republican sentiments, your firm union and adhesion to the government which you have chosen as the depository of your confidence, of your power, and of your glorious standard, will suffice to make your unjust and perfidious enemies bite the dust. Forget your quarrels; lay aside your aspirations, be they reasonable or unreasonable, if on account of them you feel less resolute and determined in the defence of your country, because against our country we have no cause of complaint. Let us be united, then, and let us spare no sacrifices to save our independence and our liberty, those great blessings, without which all the rest are sources of sadness and shame. Let us be united, and we will be free. Let us be united, and we will cause all nations to bless and glorify the name of Mexico.

BENITO JUAREZ.

SAN LUIS POTOSI, *June* 10, 1863.

Circular to the governors of the states.

DEPARTMENT OF FOREIGN RELATIONS AND GOVERNMENT.

The President and his ministers have arrived yesterday in this city. In it the supreme government remains established, and here the chief functions of federal power will be discharged, in accordance with the decree issued to that effect.

I have the honor to transmit to you a copy of the proclamation issued by the President in regard to the aforesaid transfer, and I take the liberty of recommending to you to cause the greatest possible publicity to be given to this important document. With good reason the chief magistrate believes that his voice, on this solemn occasion, will have a faithful echo in the hearts of Mexicans.

The unequivocal and universal marks of enthusiasm with which the President has been greeted on his way and in this city, assure him more and more that the invader of our country is abhorred in all quarters, and that our defence will be terrible, unexpected, worthy of our cause, and worthy, also, of the victory which must necessarily crown our forces.

A people can be conquered only because its aggressor has in his hand an insurmountable superiority, or because discord rends its bosom, or, in fine, because it regards its danger and its future with indolent listlessness. Since the events that have transpired at Zaragoza, the French army cannot boast of its pre-eminence in combat. There remain to be considered our domestic quarrels or our unpatriotic coldness, since the impotent insurrections of the traitorous reaction scarcely merit the name of civil discords; and as to our indolence, the enemy has clearly seen that, since our great civil wars, the whole nation renounces the pleasures of an ignominious peace, to rush against the invaders of their native land.

Union, governor, union with the powers that are its bonds, ought to be promoted and affirmed with diligent solicitude; and a generous oblivion of all that prevents us from devoting ourselves with all the ardor of our nature to the sacred cause of the republic will make us great and invincible.

The President, in order that the virtues recommended in his proclamation may take deeper root with you, has requested me to address you in regard to a matter of great interest on this occasion, the first on which I have the honor of communicating with you outside of the ancient capital.

The law of nations, in treating of *de facto* governments, presumes that they really exist; but it is an evident fact that the spurious authorities imposed by Napoleon III on the people now held or hereafter to be held in subjection by them are not and cannot be the government of the country, and much less when the legitimate government exists in reality. So much for the law of nations. Now, as far as concerns our public law, those false authorities are nothing better than seditious and treasonable. Wherefore, the chief magistrate commands me so to declare, and to protest, as in his name I do protest, that the republic does not and will not recognize in these supposed functionaries any power or authority whatever to bind it by their treaties, agreements, or promises, by their acts, omissions, or other means or manner whatsoever; and that those who execute any authority or commission, conferred or consented to by the French, will most undoubtedly be punished in accordance with the laws of the country.

Please to accept the assurance of my highest consideration and esteem. Liberty and reform!

FUENTE.

San Luis Potosi, *June* 10, 1863.

Circular addressed to the foreign diplomatic body in Mexico.

National Palace, San Luis Potosi,
June 11, 1863.

I have the honor of addressing to your excellency certified copies of the proclamation just issued by the President, and of the circular addressed by his order to the governors of the states, in reference to the transfer of the seat of government of the republic to this city, now declared the temporary capital of the United States of Mexico.

It appears useless to me to repeat to your excellency what I have already officially said, that is, that whenever you consider it proper to transfer your residence to this city, you will have placed at your disposal all the escort necessary for your person and retinue, which will be stationed at proper intervals along the route from the nearest positions to the city of Mexico occupied by the constitutional government.

I am gratified, on this occasion, to be able to renew to your excellency the assurance of my consideration and esteem.

JUAN A. DE LA FUENTE.

Circular addressed to the foreign consular agent in Mexico.

National Palace, San Luis Potosi,
June 11, 1863.

For your information and convenience, I have the pleasure of transmitting to you, by direction of the President of the republic, a copy of the proclamation just issued by him, and also a copy of the circular addressed by his order to the governors of the states, in reference to the transfer of the seat of government of the nation to this city, already declared the temporary capital of the United States of Mexico.

I take this opportunity of renewing to you, &c., &c., &c.,

FUENTE

In view of the state of war existing between France and the government of Juarez, acting by virtue of the powers which belong to us, declare:

That from the 6th of September instant, the ports and their outlets, the rivers, harbors, roadsteads, creeks, &c., of the coasts of Mexico, which are not in the occupation of our troops, and which still acknowledge the power of Juarez, from the lagoon, ten leagues to the south of Matamoras, up to and including Campeche, between twenty-five degrees and twenty two minutes north, ninety-nine degrees and fifty-four minutes west, and nineteen degrees and fifty-two minutes north, and ninety-two degrees and fifty minutes west, (meridian of Paris,) shall be held in a state of effective blockade by the naval forces under our command, and that friendly or neutral vessels shall have a delay of twenty-five days to complete their cargoes and to quit the places blockaded

The points excepted from the blockade are Tampico, Vera Cruz, Alvarado, Coatzacoalcos, Tabasco, and Carmen.

Proceedings in conformity with international law and the treaties in force with neutral powers will be taken against all vessels which shall attempt to violate the said blockade.

On board of the frigate Bellona, of his Majesty the Emperor of the French, anchored in the roadstead of Sacrificios, the 5th of September, 1863.

A. BOSSE.

MEXICO, *September* 30, 1863.

MEXICANS: I have terminated the great mission which the French Emperor intrusted to me, and I am now about to leave for France.

I can assure you that no alteration has been made in the policy of the French Emperor to this day.

In departing from you, I leave you with a general in whom you may have full confidence.

To form a new constitution, that all might be happy under it, was the object of the mission; but the Emperor's intentions were not fully realized, because they are not sufficiently known.

In leaving Mexico, I hope my departure will be the means of opening the eyes of the blind (or refractory) among you, and that the false patriots in your midst will be discovered in the ruin they seek for their country. Then the true Mexican will find out there are but few false Mexicans; and that there are not many who treat with contempt or disregard the existing government. Then the true Mexican will be astonished to see the little number of mock patriots, and their proximity to the mire in which they are rapidly falling.

Be assured that God, whose Providence protects the French arms, will not allow the fratricide of the nation.

Adieu, Mexicans! I leave with full confidence in the welfare of your country. You may be proud, and you may thank Providence that your happiness has been consigned to the French Emperor. In leaving, I can say you will not regret placing your happiness in his hands.

FOREY.

HEADQUARTERS AT MEXICO, *October* 22, 1863.

MEXICANS: On taking command of the army, I must explain to you that this change of commander does not imply any change of politics.

My mission is to watch over the sincere fulfilment of the manifesto of the 12th of June, 1863, which contains the essential principles in which the provisional government must stand in the direction of public affairs.

These general principles, which belong to our epoch, and proceed from the instructions of the Emperor's government, prove how much our sovereign benevolently interests himself for the regeneration of your fine country.

My task will be easy if you assist me, and I reckon upon it, as you ought to have faith in my earnest wish to bring to fulfilment, when the time arrives, each of the promises contained in the manifesto alluded to.

Have, therefore, confidence in the future. Let every Mexican lay aside the spirit of party; let all unite to establish a stable government in harmony with the ideas of the age, protected by the French flag wherever its glorious colors wave.

BAZAINE, *Commander-in-Chief.*

Mr. Romero to Mr. Seward.

[Translation.]

MEXICAN LEGATION TO THE UNITED STATES OF AMERICA,
Washington, May 10, 1864.

MR. SECRETARY: Carrying out my purpose of remitting to you the documents which may come into my possession, and may contribute to the elucidation of the grave events which are actually taking place in my country, in the important crisis she is now passing through, I have the honor to send to you, translated into English, the annexed documents relative to the case of Don Antonio Lopez de Santa Anna, ex-general in the Mexican army. By these it seems that notwithstanding General Santa Anna had been invited by what in Mexico is now called "the regency," which congratulated him on his arrival in the country, the general-in-chief of the French army made him leave the country upon frivolous pretexts, and the so-called "regency" submitted to this determination, as it submits in everything, to the caprice of the invaders, because it has neither strength nor existence proper to itself, being merely a vile instrument of the French.

For the rest, it appears to me unnecessary to reproduce the web of calumnies against the constitutional government, the patriots, and the people of Mexico, contained in the proclamation of General Santa Anna, and by which he tries to excuse his humiliating submission to the show of government set up by the invaders of his country.

I reiterate to you, Mr. Secretary, the protestation of my most distinguished consideration.

M. ROMERO.

Hon. WILLIAM H. SEWARD, *&c.*, *&c.*, *&c.*

VERA CRUZ, *February* 28, 1864.

On the 27th instant, at 5 o'clock in the evening, I disembarked in this port, proceeding from St. Thomas, where I lived some years, receiving the hospitality which political vicissitude obliged me to seek in a foreign country.

On deciding to return to my native soil, I bring with me the intention of co-operating, in whatever way I may be able, in the consolidation of the institution which the nation has thought proper to adopt, under the beneficent shadow of the throne on which will be seated the illustrious prince designed in the sublime counsels of Divine Providence to raise the nation from the abyss of misfortune into which she has been plunged by anarchy. The regency of the empire may consider my services needless and deliver me the orders it may think proper.

On the installation of the regency I charged General Don Santiago Blanco to declare my sentiments of adhesion, and the satisfaction it gave me to know that a national government had been established under the form chosen by the will of the Mexican peple, which commission he had the goodness to discharge according to my desire. Consequently, I now do so directly from this place, to inform the regency that it may rely on my poor services and give what orders it pleases to the dean of the Mexican army.

Please to acquaint the regency with this note, and accept my protestations of consideration.

ANTONIO LOPEZ DE SANTA ANNA.

The UNDER SECRETARY OF WAR, *Mexico city.*

IMPERIAL PALACE, MEXICO, *March* 7, 1864.

MOST EXCELLENT SIR: The regency has received with the most grateful satisfaction your note of the 28th ultimo, in which you were pleased to communicate your safe arrival at that port, on the 27th, from St. Thomas, where you have lived for several years. It is also informed of the noble feelings which animate your excellency on returning to your country—feelings which were never doubted, both because they demonstrate your patriotism, and because you had made them known through General Blanco when the present government was installed.

The regency congratulates your excellency on your return to your native soil, and views with the deepest interest your decision to lend it your important services.

In having the honor to tell you this in reply, it is a satisfaction to me to offer you the assurances of my distinguished consideration.

JUAN DE D PEZA,
Under Secretary of State and War and Navy Departments.

His Excellency General of Division DON ANTONIO LOPEZ DE SANTA ANNA.

MEXICAN EXPEDITIONARY CORPS, OFFICE OF THE GENERAL-IN-CHIEF,
Mexico, March 7, 1864.

MONSIEUR LE GENERAL: His excellency General Almonte has just sent me a supplement to No. 68 of the Indicator, of Orizaba, in which I find, *in extenso*, the proclamation given by you to Mexico, which bears your signature.

You have broken the pledge signed by you on board the English steamer Conway, and have not even thought it your duty to address yourself to the commander-in chief of the Franco-Mexican army, who represents France in Mexico.

You can no longer remain on Mexican soil, and I invite you, as well as your son, to quit it without delay.

I give, in this respect, formal orders to the superior commandant of Vera Cruz, and to the admiral commanding in chief the French naval forces in the Gulf, in order that a vessel may be placed at your disposal.

BAZAINE, *General.*

VERA CRUZ, *March* 12, 1864.

GENERAL: I received with surprise your excellency's communication of the 7th instant, in which you tell me that, because I broke my pledge in causing my manifesto to be printed in Orizaba, and for not having addressed myself to your excellency, who, as commander-in-chief of the Franco-Mexican army, represents France, I must immediately leave my country.

An accusation of such a nature compels me to reply to your excellency that you are mistaken in what you say. First, because I do not remember to have pledged my word to be dumb on returning to my country. I am not acquainted with the French language, and on signing, on board the English steamer, the recognition of the intervention and the Mexican emperor, Ferdinand Maximilian, as I was directed to do by the commandant of this place, I believed myself bound by that promise alone, since I had no intention of doing anything on coming, for the reason that Marshal Forey had arranged, in an order in my possession, that nothing should be required of me on my arrival, and that I should be properly treated in every respect. Besides, it was not I who sent my manifesto to be printed. Friends from the interior who visited me, desirous of knowing my opinion under present circumstances, asked me for a copy of my manuscript, which friends, of their own accord, published it, assuredly with the best intention, since the document contained nothing unfavorable to the new system, but, on the contrary, strengthens it in every respect.

Having been informed that it could not be printed here, I directed the manuscript, signed, to General Almonte, president of the imperial regency, which is the government of the nation, recognized by it and some others, including that of your excellency, and did not direct it to you, it not being upon any military subject, and because I knew that the representative of France is his excellency the Marquis de Montholon, minister plenipotentiary of the Emperor of the French.

Wherefore your excellency will understand the profound displeasure which the supposition that I had broken my word has produced in me, and that upon this is based, in part, the abuse done me in expelling me immediately from the territory of my country, after eight years and a half of ostracism, and when my health is latterly so altered. In consequence of such a procedure, which I cannot misunderstand, and in use of my right, I protest formally against the said act of violence against my person, as being both unjust and inhuman, and I will appeal to the government of his Majesty Napoleon III, from whose wisdom and equity I do not doubt I shall obtain justice.

This is all I can say to your excellency in reply to your note; and offering you assurances of my high consideration, I remain, &c.,

ANTONIO LOPEZ DE SANTA ANNA.

Antonio Lopez de Santa Anna, well deserving of his country, and general of division of the national armies, to his fellow-countrymen:

MEXICANS: How many disturbances, how many misfortunes, have occurred in our country since I left you! Like an impetuous torrent, political passions have broken loose, destroying everything and drying up in all directions the sources of our wealth Never have I succeeded in imagining so painful a scene, nor could I ever believe that in the name of country and liberty the foundations of society could be so deeply disturbed, displaying a flag that inspired fear among its children and mistrust among strangers. The beautiful Anahuac has been torn to pieces and martyrized by the frantic ambition of a band who fancied themselves the depositories of liberty and right. It is not the conservative party which has invited to our shores the European intervention, but the error and blindness of the reformers.

Fellow-countrymen: In treading the soil where I was cradled, in incorporating myself with you, it is indispensable that I remind you of the situation in which I left the country in separating myself from the power which, by your will, I lately exercised; I wish the truth to be known by the world.

My government had placed the nation in a brilliant position; the best relations existed with friendly powers; the army was brilliant for its *morale*, arms, numbers, and discipline; the fortresses were taken care of, like all the branches of the public administration; no one presented himself at our ports with demands; the roads were free from robbers, the savages kept under, and the filibusteros frightened; the dangerous questions with the United States of the north relative to boundaries happily terminated; commerce and agriculture flourished; neither forced loans nor expropriations were known; the guarantees of peaceful citizens were not a falsehood; the religion of our fathers was venerated; no one put his hand on the property of the clergy, whose opulence we beheld with pride and credit spring up again. Only those among the discontented who live by insurrections formed mad desires, casting upon my name unjust aspersions, because I prevented them from doing mischief. And what government is forbidden from attempting its preservation, which is likewise that of society, as well as maintaining order, which is the happiness and advancement of nations? Never can I sufficiently deplore that the ambition of an ill-counselled band had reached the supreme power, taking advantage of the ignorance of the unwary.

The misdeeds of the representatives of the liberals have enveloped the church in mourning and filled the hearts of the Mexican people with bitterness; their want of good faith in treaties obliged three powerful nations to arm themselves in demand of the justice that was owing to them. The conservative party is not, therefore, responsible for the late events that have taken place in our country.

It appeared natural that, on finding me at so great a distance from the events, and keeping so profound a silence, it should be considered strange by them; but my opponents, eager to do me injury, lost no time in showing me at times the enthusiastic friend of the intervention, and at other times its enemy, according to the circle in which they acted. It would have been easy to confound them with replies and observations, but I was unwilling to direct voluntarily public attention toward myself, and resolved to be silent until I trod the soil of my country. The long wished for day has arrived, and I am consequently going to explain, so that I may be unmistakably judged in everything relating to the crisis that we are passing.

At solemn moments the good man ought to speak the truth with frankness and sincerity.

It is unquestionable that the excesses of the party who ruled brought about the armed intervention, and that it appeared at a time when our society was disturbed. Honest people feared for their lives and property, and the honor of their families; they sought, like the shipwrecked mariners, any plank whatever to save themselves That party having proclaimed an exaggerated constitution, which they carried out, despair had reached its climax.

Two of the allied nations now suspended their demands, and withdrew. Then the afflicted people had recourse to the other that remained in the country, and proffered it a friendly hand; the soldiers of the republic by hundreds joined in brotherhood with those whom they looked upon as allies to destroy the domestic tyranny and substitute a better order of things. Mexicans who had always given proofs of their patriotism appeared in the same ranks; and even the capital, despising the prohibitions and penalties imposed by the so-called constitutional government, welcomed the legions of the friendly nation with enthusiasm.

The people, wearied with the anarchy of half a century, with false promises and fine theories, anxious to have a paternal government, just and enlightened, proclaimed with enthusiasm the re-establishment of the empire of the Montezumas by a dynasty of royal extraction, voting at once for emperor the illustrious Prince Maximilian, archduke of Austria.

The demagogues, in their desperation, are exhausting the resources that they are able to use, believing that by combating they are defending Mexican independence; but the day will arrive when they will find out that patriotism was not on their side in the present struggle.

The states that have not yet made any manifestation will certainly make it as soon as they obtain any protection, and the Mexicans who are now with arms in their hands will lay them down on being convinced that nothing is attempted against the nationality, and that they are only aggravating the evils which we all lament.

A government, freely elected by Mexicans, being already installed in the capital, good patricians are under the obligation to group themselves around it, to clothe it with prestige and strength. So sacred a duty brings me here. I come, therefore, to give new proofs of the respect I owe to the national will now so in agreement with my belief and conviction. The orders that may emanate from that supreme power I shall treat with the decision and loyalty with which I have obeyed the nation on all occasions. When peace is re-established, the country settled to its satisfaction, I shall only ask as a favor that I may be allowed to enjoy, in my last days, the quiet that I have not been able to secure in any of the situations of my life.

Fellow-citizens, guard in your memory the magnanimous monarch who has extended to you his powerful hand so opportunely and generously. Without his assistance you would groan under the depressing and barbarous yoke of the most uncontrolled anarchy. Gratitude is a virtue peculiar to noble minds.

The attempts that until now have been made, under the republican form, have only brought discredit and desolation to the countries of the American continent, while constitutional monarchy has given, and continues to give, everywhere, better and more lasting fruit. If the flight of liberty is not so lofty under the monarchy as in the republic, the former has an advantage that the second does not possess, of being away from political disturbances. I am not the enemy of democracy, but of its extravagances. In our history it is shown that I was the first to proclaim the republic. I thought that I was doing a great service to our country, the object always of my adoration, and nothing stopped me until the object was attained. But the illusions of youth having passed, in presence of so many disasters produced by that system, I will not deceive anybody; the last word of my conscience and my convictions is, the constitutional monarchy.

My friends, in August, 1855, I abdicated the discretional powers with which I was invested by the free will of the people, and emigrated abroad, with the noble view of leaving you at absolute liberty to constitute yourselves as you wished, and not to appear an oppressor; by an act of so much self-denial I wished at once to contradict the imputations of the malevolent. But from my retirement, at whatever distance, I raised my humble prayers to heaven that your passions might be calmed and concord reign among you, without which the happiness of no human society is possible. At last I return to our country, without aspirations of any kind, and I assure you that all the labors of my life will be recompensed if I finish my days among you in the midst of peace and prosperity.

Mr. Seward to Mr. Romero.

DEPARTMENT OF STATE,
Washington, May 31, 1864.

SIR: I have the honor to acknowledge the receipt, yesterday, of your note dated the 10th instant, transmitting translations of documents which have reached you relating especially to the case of Don Antonio Lopez de Santa Anna, as illustrative of the political condition of Mexico.

I beg you to accept my thanks for this attention, with the renewed assurance of my most distinguished consideration.

WILLIAM H. SEWARD.

Señor M. ROMERO, *&c., &c., &c.*

Mr. Romero to Mr. Seward.

MEXICAN LEGATION,
Washington, May 23, 1864.

Mr. Romero presents his compliments to Mr. Seward, and has the honor to enclose herewith a slip taken from the New York Tribune of Saturday last, containing some letters from Monterey and Matamoras, Mexico. The impartiality and good common sense with which these letters are written, and at the same time the abundance of correct and trustworthy information that they embrace, are the reasons why Mr. Romero thinks proper to send them to Mr. Seward, calling, in a particular way, his attention towards them. They are a new proof of the great interest that the insurgents of this country have in the success of the French army invading Mexico, and show the disposition of the national government of that republic towards the United States.

FROM MEXICO.

Movements of the Mexican troops.—Vidaurri's stock at La Mesa captured.—His son-in-law, Patrick Milmo, in prison; the decree of President Juarez confiscating his cotton.—The rebel land agents and contractors in trouble.

[From our special correspondent.]

MONTEREY, MEXICO, *April* 5, 1864.

After the flight of Vidaurri, the troops of the Juarez government for a few days flocked into the city from all directions, and now appear to be moving again in detached bodies for Saltillo, it is said en route for San Luis Potosi. The cavalry and artillery sent in pursuit of Vidaurri have not yet returned, though there is now no need of their remaining longer near the Rio Grande, as all the troops of Vidaurri, except a portion of his escort, have turned over to Juarez, and have delivered up the fourteen cannon and seven mountain howitzers he carried with him when he left Monterey. It is now reported here that Vidaurri has escaped into Texas, and is at Laredo, from whence he is expected to go to the north, and perhaps to Europe. President Juarez has recovered, not only all the artillery that he lost by sending it here, but all of Vidaurri's beside, with a large stock of ammunition and n additional supply of small-arms of all sorts. Doblado sent here, after the capture of San Luis Potosi, 25 field guns, which were accompanied by 109 wagons and carts freighted with ammunition, altogether drawn by some 700 mules. These were furnished by the state of Guanajuato alone to the liberal government. These guns, with the ammunition belonging to them, have been recovered, though the mules are missing. It is said that the troops of Juarez have visited Vidaurri's stock *rancho*, called *La Mesa*, near Lampazos, and, by way of reprisal, have captured his flocks and herds there before his agents had time to drive them across the Rio Grande, and to exchange them for cotton with the rebel contrabandists of Texas. The liberals have lost nothing by this operation. The property of all sorts belonging to the following persons it is commonly thought will be confiscated for his treason: Vidaurri; Rejon, his secretary of state; Hinojoso, his general; Quiroga, his colonel of cavalry, and Yudalecio Vidaurri, his son. His son-in-law, *Patricio* (or, in plain English, Patrick) Milmo, is still in prison, and is said to be on trial before a military commission. He is reputed to be very wealthy, and to have placed most of his money beyond the seas, though he is the owner of large stocks of goods as well as other property here and in Matamoras, and, besides, has a large quantity of cotton in Texas, purchased with goods on which he paid no tariff to the United States when he sent them across the line. He may yet, by claiming its protection, cause the English government (as he is an Irishman by birth) to show what action, or rather non-action, it will consider proper in the case of a person guilty of a double violation of the laws of neutrality, viz: between the United States and the rebels, and between Mexico and her foes, who has carried on a contraband traffic with the rebels, and at the same time asserts that he has paid the duties on the cotton imported by him, not into the treasury of President Juarez, but into the treasury of a governor in armed rebellion against him.

Before this letter reaches you it is probable that you will have received a number of the *Boletin Oficial de Tamaulipas*, containing a decree of President Juarez, declaring all goods (cotton of course included) imported into Mexico at the port of Piedras Negras since March

7, at which date Vidaurri was in arms against the national government, and was collecting the national tariff on importations, without paying it over, to be forfeited for the non-payment of the legal duties into his treasury.

This decree, if enforced, will afford the Juarez government what it most needs—ready money. Not less than 12,000 bales of cotton were crossed over into Mexico at Piedras Negras about March 7, on which Vidaurri collected (as the Mexican tariff in all amounts to $8 per bale) $96,000 in coin. This cotton is worth at Matamoras $200 per bale ; that is to say, the gross amount of $2,400,000 in cash. As a matter of course, every conceivable appliance will be brought to bear to make the Juarez government recede from this decree, and instead of confiscating the cotton, as by law it can rightfully do, to let it pass upon the payment of the duties to the lawful government—or, in other words, to take $96,000, where it might take $2,400,000. What will be the result of the pressure brought to bear remains to be seen. In the mean time, the rebel lead agents and contractors are in great trouble. Murphy, who has been supplied with funds by Mr. John Trooling, of San Antonio, Texas, to forward saltpetre and lead from Mexico, and others, will now find that their contraband trade has been brought to a close. As lead for the rebels west of the Mississippi could only be had, since the fall of Vicksburg, from Mexico, and at a greatly enhanced price, their agents and sympathizers here are very uneasy at the prospect before them. Notwithstanding their hitherto openly expressed desire for the success of the French, they now are shamelessly sycophantic to the officers of President Juarez, and omit no occasion to show to the Mexican public that they know how to

"Bend the pregnant hinges of the knee,
That thrift may follow fawning."

Poor creatures ! It is rather more distressing than diverting to witness their efforts here, especially when it is to be borne in mind that every one who sees them naturally inquires why, if they are such earnest advocates of the rebellion, they are not at home fighting for it in this its hour of need. By the terms of the rebel government, all who have taken the oath to support it, if between 16 and 60 years of age, and absent without leave, are deserters, and are stigmatized as such by those who remain in Dixie. *The San Antonio Herald* says of the rebels now in Monterey, and who patronize a little sheet called *The Morning Star*, printed by Swope, whom the rebels in Matamoras assert to be a deserter from Duff's command, that "they are few in number, and mostly strapped renegades." This is the unkindest cut of all, and, besides, is incorrect. Though they are "renegades" from Dixie, they are by no means "few in number," and "the cry is, still they come." They are not in general "strapped," or, as Sheridan expressed it, "money-bound," for many of them have made more money than they ever had before, by operations in the contraband line, and others have brought off the proceeds of their property with them, but they are merely "chivalryites" of the class that resemble the war-horse in Job in only one particular : they snuff the battle *afar off*. While here they occupy a decidedly awkward position. It is, indeed, an arduous task for men who know that they are stigmatized as "deserters" by those they have left behind in Dixie, to talk in favor of the rebellion, and to satisfactorily account for their absence from the theatre of war. The Mexicans have a great deal of quiet amusement at their expense.

Runaway rebels are accumulating here to such an extent, and the prospect for an increase of their numbers is such, that a new hotel is about to be opened. No doubt it will do well for some months to come.

RIO GRANDE.

Results of the pursuit of Vidaurri.—Luna, Vidaurri's paymaster, captured.—Milmo still under arrest.—Position of the troops.—Temper of the people.—Juarez.—His cabinet. —A duel.—A military execution.

[From our special correspondent.]

MONTEREY, *April* 14, 1864.

The pursuit of Vidaurri resulted in the capture of his carriage, of a portion of the eagle dollars he took with him, together with all his artillery and ammunition, and in the pronouncing of his troops in favor of Juarez. The pursuing party has returned, bringing with it the captured guns, and accompanied by the force that joined it. Don Pepe Luna, Vidaurri's paymaster, has been taken, and is now here in person. Vidaurri's son-in-law, Milmo, is still under close arrest, and in the mean time the government is causing his account-books to be thoroughly examined, with a view of ascertaining whether he has in fact ever paid any duties into the national treasury on the immense stocks of goods imported by him, especially those he has sent into Texas, and also whether he has any funds of his father-in-law in his hands. The *Suaristas* believe that for years past Vidaurri has been a silent partner of Milmo, and will spare no effort to prove it, as, in case such should turn out to be the fact, the government will confiscate.

The cavalry force that assembled here, together with a portion of the infantry, have gone up to Saltillo, and will probably advance further, as some 7,000 troops, composed chiefly of *Reaccionarios*, commanded by Mejia, now are assembled in the city of San Luis Potosi, and appear to be preparing to make a move. General Gonzalez Ortega, with his command, is watching them, while Doblado is in Saltillo. Still, quite a considerable force remains here. The marching to and fro of the regiments through the streets, the perpetual blare of the trumpets sounding the calls, and the music of the military bands at night on the *Plaza Militar*, all remind a stranger that the country is involved in war. President Juarez has gained a very considerable accession to his army since he came here, and is daily receiving accessions to his ranks. The common people *(plebe)* of northeastern Mexico are not only patriotic, but are intensely republican. Though the mercantile class may be disposed to give up or to make terms with the French, they will never willingly bend the knee to a foreign invader. They look with a pride, blended with a personal affection, to President Juarez as a fit leader for them in their desperate struggle for the maintenance of a republican form of government. He is an Indian of unmixed race. His personal integrity has never been called in question. He is a thoroughly educated and enlightened man. He has ever stood by his country with a loyal devotion and a courageous endurance.

In coming years, when mankind shall have so progressed that individuals will take position chiefly on account of their moral worth, how much loftier place on the page of history will this Indian Juarez occupy than Napoleon III! He has never robbed his own nor sought to despoil any other country of its liberties. No blood stains his conscience, no ill-gotton wealth soils his hands. In all the relations of life, as a husband, as a father, as a private citizen, as the incumbent of high public trusts, and, lastly, as the chief magistrate of a republic, he has earned the reputation of being an honorable man. Can any sycophant of Napoleon III say as much of him?

Owing to the existing condition of affairs, President Juarez's cabinet at present consists of only three individuals, in whose hands are confided the functions of government. Sr. Lerdo de Legada is minister of foreign affairs, &c.; Sr. Iglesias is minister of finance, &c.; and Gen. Negrete is minister of war and marine. The duties which would devolve upon a cabinet, if full, are divided among out them. Sr Prieto is the postmaster general, but in Mexico the incumbent of that office does not have a seat in the cabinet.

On Monday last all the merchants interested in the contraband trade with Texas, as I am informed, held a sort of consultation as to what they should do in relation to the decree of President Juarez declaring all the cotton imported, on which the tariff has been paid to Vidaurri when in open rebellion, instead of into the national treasury, to be forfeited. They concluded to pay the tariff over again to the national government under protest. Whether President Juarez's government will accept this proposal or not remains to be seen. My own opinion is that it will, and that even after that they will go to intriguing in favor of the French. All the rebels and contrabandists here are in favor of the French. It is true that just now they pay court to Juarez and his friends, because they know that so much of Dixie as lies west of the Mississippi could not hold out for a month after the stoppage of the trade with Mexico; still written proofs against them are abundant. What position did they occupy in regard to the French while Vidaurri was in power? What ground does the rebel press of Texas hold in regard to the French even now?

It is stated that on Monday evening last a duel was fought between Colonel Juan Varra, of Juarez's forces, and *Commandante, i. e.*, Major Rafael Herrera, formerly of Vidaurri's command, at the lower suburbs of this city. The weapons used were Colt's revolvers. The ground of the quarrel is not stated, but it is supposed that Colonel Varra denounced Major Herrera because he thought that Major H. had been the cause of his having been exiled some time since by Vidaurri. My informant states that the duel was fought by permission of one of the high officers of the government, who witnessed it in person. Colonel Varra was fired at and missed three times by his antagonist without returning a shot, and, therefore, he suggested to his adversary to load up the three chambers that had been discharged, and they would proceed to fight in earnest. Upon this Major H. professed himself satisfied, and made some acknowledgments, and the officer who permitted the duel forbade it to proceed further. I tell the tale as I got it from a respectable informant, who believed it to be true, and who had conversed with one of the parties immediately after the affair was over. This is an unusual occurrence in Mexico, where the law against duelling is severe. I am told that one who fights a duel here is subject to imprisonment for life and a forfeiture of his whole estate.

On this morning, at 6 o'clock, Martin Garcia, said to have been a commandante or major under Mejia, was shot by a file of soldiers at the back of the citadel. He was executed under the sentence of a court-martial on account of his having been guilty of high treason, as well as concerned in the assassination of a late governor of San Luis Potosi. Quite a considerable body of soldiers under arms were assembled to witness the execution. The citadel (or Black Fort, as the Americans have termed it) consists of the massive walls of an unfinished church about sixteen feet high, built of an almost white stone, the abutments or square columns intended to support the arches of the roof inside being a little higher than the incomplete walls. These walls are in the middle of a field-work (lately repaired) surrounded by a dry ditch. The prisoner was made to kneel blindfold, with his face turned toward the outside of the rear wall, the bullet-marks on which showed it had been the scene of other executions, and was shot in the back of the head (chiefly) as well as through the body by a file of six men. Two stepped up after he had fallen forward on his face, and fired into him again. It is said that he was shot in the back because such is the sentence for treason, of which, as well as of assassination, he had been found guilty. A priest attended him to the last moment. As he lay a stream of blood flowed down the sloping ground beyond his feet. Quite a number of women were present. The spectators showed no levity.

Señor Don Jesus Masia Benites y Penillos went into office to-day under the appointment of President Juarez as the governor and *commandante militar* of the state of Nuevo Leon. He has hitherto been a highly respectable merchant of Linares, and has filled the office of first alcalde of that city.

Last night a refreshing rain fell on this parched and arid region, and gentle showers have continued to fall at intervals during the day. At sunset this evening the Silla mountain was still enveloped in a cloud.

RIO GRANDE.

Arrival of Señor Iglesias, Juarez's minister of finance.—Good understanding between the Mexican and American authorities.—Interesting news from the interior.—Vidaurri and the rebels of Texas.—Mr. Quintero, the rebel agent, in Monterey.—Major Simeon Hart, the rebel cotton agent, and his cotton.—Monterey the seat of the constitutional government of Mexico.

[From our special correspondent.]

MATAMOROS, *April* 25, 1864.

On yesterday afternoon the quiet of this city was interrupted by the firing of a salute. Upon inquiry it was ascertained that the cause of the salute was the arrival of Señor Iglesias, the minister of finance of President Juarez's cabinet. The objects of his visit are unknown to the public.

The recent correspondence between Major General Herron and the Mexican authorities, together with the cordial good understanding that manifestly exists between them, is a source of unutterable anguish to the rebels now in Mexico, and to the merchants engaged in the Piedras Negras trade. They are perplexed and bewildered. Their confidence is shaken; and, in short, they know not what to do. The tact and address of Major Generals McClernand and Herron, in their intercourse with Mexico, has damaged the rebel cause on this frontier almost as much as a victory.

The news from the interior is quite important. General Uraga has gained another success over the French at or near the city of Gaudalajara. General Purfirio Diaz has reappeared on the Pacific slope at the head of a well-armed and well-equipped force of 10,000 men. A movement is said to be in progress by the combined forces of Doblado and Gonzalez Ortega against San Luis Potosi, which is held by 1,200 French and 5,800 *reaccionarios* under Mejia; and, best of all, it is reported that the French have abandoned Tampico. Certain it is that the Juarez government is now in excellent spirits. It has, though they are intentionally kept scattered, almost twice as many troops in the field as the French have, and is assured of the loyalty of a vast majority of the people to a republican form of government. Besides, the despatches from General Bazaine to Almonte, which were recently intercepted, show that the Church party (*reaccionarios*) are upbraided as having deceived and misled the French government in every particular. General Bazaine appears to have given utterance to his dissatisfaction with them in very strong and emphatic terms, and to have charged that the persons at different points in Mexico, recommended by Almonte, Miramon, and others, to the confidence of the French generals, were no better than robbers and assassins, devoid of all faith and honor. The worst thing of all for the French cause is that the charges made by General Bazaine are true. What is Marquez but a cold-blooded murderer? What is Mejia but a robber, though on a large scale? What Mexican is there to be found among those that have betrayed their country that have an unblemished private character; that commands the confidence and respect due to a gentleman?

The most cheering fact of all to the republicans of Mexico is the sanction that has been given by the Emperor to the policy of General Bazaine in regard to the clergy. Now, since the clergy of the *reaccionario* party find that they will not be allowed to take the prominent position in politics they desired, and since they have ascertained from the head of the French government that the nationalized property of the church would not be restored, they have no further use for the French. From this time forward we may expect to see the troops of the church party going over to Juarez in force. What motive have they to fight against Juarez any longer? Why should they aid the French when the secular property of the church--the real bone of contention, so far as they are concerned--would not in case of success fall into the hands of the clergy (of their party,) who could reward them from its revenue?

In this connexion it is but just to remark that the parochial clergy of Mexico are in general liberals, and that the portion of the clergy that belong to the *reaccionario* or church party are in most cases either prelates or members of the monastic orders. The rank and file, if I may so express it, of the clergy of the country, to their honor be it recorded, are republicans. It was so in the revolution of Mexico against old Spain. Priests, who, instead of living in monasteries or palaces, reside among the people, must think and feel as they do. The history of Mexico shows that such have fought for the liberties of their country in times past, and hence may be expected to do so in the future.

Not only such of the clergy as belong to the *reaccionario* party, but the prominent military men on their side, are greatly disaffected. They have been and are overslaughed on all occasions. Mexican generals, even if they are traitors to their country, don't like to be put under the command of French colonels. Still, as the French place no confidence in them, such must continue to be the practice. The pride of the *reaccionario* officers must be often wounded by this course of procedure. How long they will submit to it remains to be seen. Yet it is difficult to perceive how the French can change their policy toward their Mexican confederates at this time. General Bazaine knows that their hopes for the restoration of the nationalized church property, from the revenues of which they expected to be rewarded, have been dashed. He knows that their pride has been perpetually lacerated by their higher officers having been put under the command of French officers, their inferiors in rank, and that they have ever been treated with distrust. He is aware that very many of them are only watching for a chance to make terms with President Juarez, and to turn against him. How, then, can he change his policy and treat them as equals in whom he reposes full confidence?

Since Vidaurri fled into Texas, the forces of Mejia (some 5,800 men) which were at Matelmalá and were prevented from advancing by the forces of Gonzalez Ortega, which threatened to get between them and San Luis Potosi, have fallen back to San Luis Potosi. They are now further from Monterey than before, and, as has been stated, instead of attempting to attack, are threatened with an attack from the combined commands of Doblado and Gonzalez Ortega. President Juarez has gained great advantages of late, and may well be sanguine.

It is reported that on hearing that Vidaurri had escaped on horseback, and with only the clothes he wore, to Larado, Texas, the rebel commandant at San Antonio sent a carriage and escort to bring him to that place. The rebels will now go to intriguing to get him back into power, and, before they suspect it, will probably be involved in hostilities with the government of President Juarez. They must have lead, saltpetre, sulphur, and other articles, contraband of war, which they have heretofore been only able to get through Piedras Negras. Indeed, such was the demand for lead by the rebels west of the Mississippi, that it is now worth 100 per cent. more at Monterey than formerly. Under Vidaurri's rule, as he paid no regard to the decrees of President Juarez's government, except so far as they suited his convenience, they got through Piedras Negras everything they could raise, either the cotton or credit to purchase.

The position of the rebels who have, on various pretexts, got out of the so-called southern confederacy into Mexico, is peculiarly embarrassing now since Juarez is in power at Monterey. That they are in favor of the French invasion is perfectly well known. One of their leading papers in Texas not long since, when under the delusion that Vidaurri, aided by the French, would certainly defeat Juarez, openly boasted that Mr. J. S. Quintero, the rebel lead agent residing at Monterey, had done more to bring about the invasion of Mexico by the French than any other one person. No doubt he did his best for the French. Whether his having done so, and his having made contracts with Mr. Oliver, of Monterey, for lead, in violation of the plighted faith of the Juarez government, which has never sanctioned the trade in contraband articles with the rebels, will enable him to continue at Monterey and play the same part near the constitutional government that he did at the court of Vidaurri, remains yet to be seen.

It is a little singular that so many of the leading rebels of Texas, of the class that have had to do with the cotton and money of the insurrectionary government, are now either in or very near to Mexico. The ex-collectors of Eagle Pass and Brownsville are there. Major Russell, the quartermaster of General Bee's staff, is there on a two months' sick leave. Major Simeon Hart, the Confederate States cotton agent in Texas, is at Eagle Pass; so is Captain George H. Giddings. William G. Hale, esq., is also reported to be there, engaged in forwarding cotton for a wealthy firm in Matamoras. It is well for these gentlemen to be safe. When all of their cotton is across the Rio Grande they can follow it, and the rank and file left behind will have to look out for themselves. After a season they can come in and take the oath under a special pardon, as the general one is not broad enough to cover their case, and they will then have the means at command to live handsomely where they may please; or else they can live abroad. By-the-bye, has Mr. Simeon Hart a house in your city? His brother, Mr. Henry Hart, who is reputed to be in business in New York, has been through Texas since the rebellion began, and is said to have returned. It has lately been discovered, in the course of a quarrel between Majors Russell and Hart, that a large quantity of cotton which was crossed into Mexico, marked H. H., with M. K. below, though supposed to belong to the rebel government, was really the property of one or both of the Harts and of Thomas F. McKinney, who was one of the commissioners not long since sent out to Vidaurri to negotiate for the reopening of the Piedras Negras trade. Has any of this cotton reached New York; and if so, to whom was it consigned?

By the latest arrival from Monterey the news has come that President Juarez has concluded to make that city his capital. It is, perhaps, more accessible to all the points with which he has occasion to keep up communication than Saltillo.

RIO GRANDE.

Mr. Seward to Mr. Romero.

DEPARTMENT OF STATE.
Washington, May 25, 1864.

Mr. Seward presents his compliments to Señor Romero, and acknowledges, with sincere thanks, the receipt of the slip from the New York Tribune, of last Saturday, containing very much interesting information concerning affairs in Mexico, and the sentiment of friendly sympathy which is entertained by the national government towards the United States.

Señor M. ROMERO, *&c., &c., &c.*

Mr. Romero to Mr. Seward.

[Translation.]

Private.] WASHINGTON, *May* 24, 1864.

ESTEEMED SIR: The Herald, of New York, of the 18th April last past, published an account of what occurred at a dinner which several distinguished persons of that city, friends of Mexico, had the kindness to give me on the 29th of March last. That portion of such account which relates to the remarks which I made when called upon to speak by the persons who honored me with that demonstration, attributes to me some opinions which I never even thought of uttering, and is, in general, so little exact that I think it proper to make known to you, although this can have only an indirect bearing on the official business of the department in your charge, that the enclosure herewith contains a faithful narrative, written in Spanish, of all that passed at that dinner, and an exact translation of what on that occasion I had the honor to say in English.

I am, sir, very respectfully your faithful servant,

M. ROMERO.

Hon. WILLIAM H. SEWARD, *&c., &c., &c.*

Mr. Seward to Mr. Romero.

WASHINGTON, *May* 25, 1864.

MY DEAR SIR: I beg to thank you for the authentic report, transmitted with your note of the 24th instant, of the proceedings at the banquet given to you by certain distinguished citizens of New York, and which contains an exact translation of the remarks you made on that occasion.

Although your note is unofficial, I shall place it with the printed report on the files of the legation of Mexico in the Department of State, to protect you from the misapprehensions which might result from the incorrect published reports of your remarks to which you allude.

I am, my dear sir, very truly yours,

WILLIAM H. SEWARD.

Señor MATIAS ROMERO, *&c.*, *&c.*, *&c.*

Mr. Romero to Mr. Seward.

[Translation.]

MEXICAN LEGATION IN THE UNITED STATES OF AMERICA,
Washington, May 28, 1864.

Mr. SECRETARY: I have the honor to transmit you a correct translation, in the English language, of the document of which I sent you a copy in Spanish, annexed to my letter of the 26th instant.

I also enclose you a copy, in English, for the information of your department, of some remarks which I made in New York, about the middle of last December, upon the causes which have brought about the present situation of the Mexican republic.

I renew to you, sir, the assurances of my very distinguished consideration.

M. ROMERO.

Speech delivered by Señor Romero, the Mexican minister to the United States, at a banquet given by him in New York on the 16th of December, 1863.

On the 16th day of December, 1863, a banquet was given at Delmonico's by the Mexican minister, to his friends in New York, with the object of informing them of the present condition of affairs in the Mexican republic.

It seems unaccountable, yet it is a fact, that even the most distinguished and learned men of this enlightened metropolis are not fully posted up, not only as regards the important occurrences now taking place in Mexico, but also as to the condition of affairs of that republic—its elements, its tendencies, its politics, and even its inward civilization.

It was the object of Mr. Romero to invite some of the most distinguished persons of this city, who, by their position and antecedents, occupy the front places in social life, to discuss with them, in a confidential and friendly manner, Mexican affairs, and to give them, at the same time, some important data upon the internal situation of his country. He paid special attention in inviting those who were considered as the leaders of the different political parties into which this nation is now divided, with the view that it might not appear as if any preference had been given to any one of these parties, and that the banquet might not have any other character but the one proposed.

The following persons were then invited and assisted to the banquet:

Mr. Hiram Barney, a prominent member of the republican party, friendly to the present administration, and now collector of the custom-house of New York.

Mr. Augustus Schell, a gentlemen much esteemed in this city, and a distinguished member of that portion of the democratic party who defend with the greatest warmth and interest the institution of slavery. He was formerly collector of the New York custom-house under the administration of Mr. Buchanan.

Mr. John Van Buren, son of the ex-President of the United States, Martin Van Buren, a celebrated orator and lawyer of this city, and a prominent member of that part of the democratic party which does not sympathize so strongly with slavery, and also a personal and political friend of Governor Seymour, of this State.

Mr. William C. Bryant, one of the most distinguished poets of the United States, member of the radical republican party, and chief editor of the Evening Post, of this city.

Mr. David Hoadly, president of the Panama Railroad Company, a person of conservative ideas, and high standing in this city for his integrity, honesty, and industry.

Mr. James W. Beekman, a gentleman of independence, of this city, descendant of one of the first Dutch families who colonized this island, and much respected for his honorable antecedents, and his constant desires to do good wherever his influence and his services are wanted.

Mr. William E. Dodge, jr., distinguished merchant of this city, and Mr. John H. Hamersley, one of the ancient families of this city, and a gentleman of independence and high personal qualities.

The three last-named gentlemen belong to no particular political party, and only represent the wealthy and higher classes of New York, whose ideas are above the mercantile community.

The following gentlemen were also invited, who, either by sickness, or for having previous engagements, were unable to attend the banquet: Mr. George Opdyke, mayor of the city; Major Generals George B. McClellan and John A. Dix; Mr. John C. Cisco, subtreasurer of New York; Mr. George Bancroft, the eminent historian of the United States; Mr. James T. Brady and Mr. William M. Evarts, both celebrated lawyers of this city, and a prominent member of the democratic party the former, and of the republican party the latter.

Among the Mexican gentlemen that were present at the banquet, besides Mr. Romero, were Señor Don Ignacia Mariscal, secretary of the legation; Doctor Don Juan N. Navarro, consul general of Mexico in the United States, and Señor Don José Ramon Pacheco, formerly Mexican minister at Paris, and several times secretary of state of the republic of Mexico.

The banquet was given in the handsomest apartment at Delmonico's. At the head of the dining-room the flag of Mexico on the right, and that of the United States on the left, might be seen gracefully entwined together, and under each of them respectively were placed the portraits of Presidents Juarez and Lincoln. At 6 o'clock, the hour appointed for dinner, all the guests who had accepted the invitation were present, and after a few minutes of conversation, during which Mr. Romero presented to them the Mexican gentlemen attending the banquet, and showed them a collection of engravings representing the most important views of the city of Mexico, which were upon a table of the reception room, he begged them to walk into the dining-room, where everything was already waiting for them.

They were seated in the manner which had been previously arranged as follows:

Señor Romero.

Mr. Barney.	Mr. Schell.
Mr. Van Buren.	Mr. Hamersley.
Señor Navarro.	Señor Mariscal.
Señor Pacheco.	Mr. Dodge.
Mr. Hoadley.	Mr. Bryant.

Mr. Beekman.

The service at table was the best that could be offered by Delmonico's celebrated hotel, as well as the best that could be procured in the abundant market of this city.

The wines were also abundant and of the best quality. The guests did full justice to the viands, and were perfectly satisfied with the ability and good taste displayed by the director of the culinary department. Feelings of the most perfect cordiality and good will prevailed at table.

After the dessert, Mr. BEEKMAN arose and said:

"I propose, gentlemen, that we drink the health of the gentleman who has honored us by inviting us to this agreeable meeting; the worthy representative of a neighboring and a friendly nation, which while it struggles for its independence, struggles also in defence of the principles which the people of the United States have always sustained and defended."

This toast was received with general acclamations, and then Mr. ROMERO responded to it in the following terms:

GENTLEMEN: I have never felt more embarrassed than I feel on the present occasion, in endeavoring to respond to the generous sentiments which our distinguished friend has just expressed towards my country and myself. Nor have I ever so much regretted as I do now, not possessing adequately the English language, that I might duly express the ardent and sincere desires that inspire me for your health and welfare, and for the peace, prosperity, and happiness of your great country. Since our mutual friend has made allusion to Mexico, allow me, gentlemen, to make a few remarks in regard to that nation, so favored by nature, and so little known, and so greatly misrepresented abroad.

The internal condition of Mexico is scarcely understood or appreciated in this country or in Europe. The general impression seems to be, that we are an uncivilized heterogeneous people, constantly divided by petty personal feuds and ambitions; always engaged in making pronunciamientos; entirely wanting in patriotism and high-toned sentiments; altogether unfitted for self-government; utterly incapable of developing our great natural resources, and therefore unworthy of the sympathy or respect of mankind. Gentlemen, there never has been an opinion more unjustly entertained; never a judgment more unfounded.

All of you are aware, gentlemen, that when Mexico was a colony of Spain, it was the policy of the Spanish government to rule the country through the instrumentality of the Catholic clergy. With this object in view, the clergy were clothed with every kind of personal privilege, and were allowed to monopolize a very large portion of the real estate and other property of the country. They were also the only educated class, and all instruction of the masses was left entirely in their hands. By these means they maintained a profound influence over the consciences of the ignorant people, and they constituted an aristocracy more powerful and more deeply rooted than any other upon the face of the broad earth. When, in 1810, the early Mexican patriots proclaimed the independence of their country from the Spanish yoke, the clergy became alarmed by a movement in which it had not, as an association, taken the initiative, and which, if it should terminate in the overthrow of the Spanish government and the establishment of a national government, might place in peril their numerous privileges, their immense riches, and their controlling influence. They therefore determined to oppose the movement. I do not believe it necessary to tell you, gentlemen, that so long as the Mexican clergy threw the immense weight of their influence on the side of the Spanish government, the Spaniards were everywhere triumphant. But while the struggle was going on in Mexico, a great change took place in Spain. The Spanish cortes, animated by liberal ideas, had issued various decrees, seriously diminishing the personal privileges of the clergy, and had passed laws providing for the desamortization of their immense property, for the benefit of the nation at large. The Mexican clergy then began to change their ground. They saw at once how much they would have to lose if the laws passed by the Spanish cortes should be carried into effect in Mexico; and believing at the same time that they could organize a government which would be fully under their own control, they determined to adopt the cause of independence, and with their aid the independence of Mexico was then achieved.

Since that time a fearful struggle has been going on, between the clergy on the one side, who have sought to control the national government, and, on the other, the few enlightened, patriotic men who, seeing that there was no hope that Mexico could become what nature designed her to be, unless liberal principles should be adopted, and an entire separation be effected from church influence and control, began to labor for the establishment of a liberal, popular government, which should keep down the ambition and usurpations of the clergy, always directed to the promotion of their own interests, without any regard for the welfare of the country.

The result of such a struggle in its earlier efforts could not be doubtful, taking into consideration the power, the influence, and the resources of each party respectively. Whenever the liberal party succeeded in establishing, through the ballot-box, a legal government—a government which would not favor the interests of the clergy, when these were opposed to the interests of the country—a government in favor of promoting foreign immigration, of opening highways, constructing railroads, authorizing the free and public exercise of all religions, the freedom of the press, of reducing import duties, favoring all branches of commerce—in a word, of developing all the natural wealth and vast resources of Mexico—the clergy immediately instigated a pronunciamiento against that government, and brought to bear every influence to secure its overthrow.

Such a state of affairs, however, could not last forever. While the struggle was going on, the people began to grow enlightened. Everybody saw that the money of the clergy was constantly used to foment revolutions, to subvert the public peace, and to shed the blood of the innocent people for the iniquitous purpose of maintaining interests and preserving privileges entirely incompatible with the well-being of the country.

Thus, the liberal party, which at the beginning was small in numbers and weak in power, became stronger every day, until, finally, in the year 1860, it had become strong enough to crush entirely the church party, and to re-establish, it was hoped forever, constitutional law and constitutional government throughout the whole extent of Mexican territory. This was done without foreign aid, and even against the sympathies and encouragement of European powers, who had ever lent all possible aid to the church party. At the same time all the special privileges of the clergy were repealed, and the church property was declared to be national, and was sold to the people at a low nominal price. This latter measure had a double object. While the Mexican government proposed to disarm the clergy, by taking from them the principal weapon they had used in their efforts to excite pronunciamientos and disturb the public peace, it desired to render useful to the country the immense wealth which had been accumulated by the church, and which, being withdrawn from free circulation, and monopolized by a class indisposed or incapable of making it productive, had only been a source of evil, and a perpetual barrier to the nation.

Thus, when it was generally believed abroad that we were at war without plausible motive, only to promote petty personal ambitions, we were really working out one of the most thorough of revolutions, and one of the most necessary for the true prosperity of the people of Mexico.

I desire to be distinctly understood, gentlemen, that we have never raised any issue with the church party of Mexico on spiritual questions. Our disagreement has been wholly with reference to temporal affairs, and has not, in any manner, involved the dogmas of the Catholic faith.

The church party has wished, as an association, to rule the country for their own advantage. We have sought to establish a perfect independence between church and state, to confine the church to spiritual affairs, and to make it subordinate to the state in temporal matters.

Thus, when we had reason to believe that our long civil wars had ended—for we had removed, even to the roots, the sole cause of all our past misfortunes—and that we were now about to enjoy the blessings of peace—the only thing needed by Mexico to become a prosperous nation—new misfortunes, new calamities of a different kind suddenly fell upon us.

The church party of Mexico, seeing that with their own means it was impossible to make any further resistance, or to foment any further revolutions, and having in view, as they always have had, only their own advantage, regardless of the welfare of their country, resolved to send emissaries to Europe for the purpose of interesting in their behalf some of the principal European governments, in order to be by them restored to power in Mexico.

These emissaries represented that the church party were in favor of a conservative government—a monarchical government—modelled after the European system; while the liberal party were in favor of democratic institutions, and sympathized fully with the views and principles of the United States. On this point I cannot do otherwise than acknowledge that the emissaries were right. The liberals of Mexico do believe that if we can succeed in developing there the great principles which have made the United States so great and prosperous, Mexico will reach the same end by using the same means.

These emissaries, however, exaggerated the influence of the church party in Mexico. They said the liberal government of that country was tyrannical, oppressive, and unpopular, and governed only by force; and they even affirmed that the mere moral force of Europe would be sufficient to overthrow it, and restore the church party to power. They further promised that, after overthrowing the liberal government, the church party would establish a government which should be entirely under the influence of the European nations which would aid them in their purpose.

These false representations of the emissaries led to the allied expedition of France, England, and Spain, which, assuming pretexts utterly insufficient and unjust, disembarked at Vera Cruz in December, 1861.

When the English and Spanish generals and commissioners, after having resided some time in Mexico, saw that the state of things in that country was entirely different from what the church-party emissaries had represented to their respective governments, they decided without hesitation to withdraw, with their forces, from the country; and so clear to them was the deception practiced upon their governments, that they took the delicate step of withdrawing from the alliance of their own accord, without consulting with their superiors, and without even waiting for instructions from their governments, although acting in an affair so full of difficulties and of ulterior complications.

I have reached, gentlemen, without intending it, the actual situation in Mexico; and under this head I beg to be allowed to say a few words more.

The French army did not retire from Mexico with the armies of England and of Spain, for the French government had other objects in view, and it was fully determined to accomplish them. The Emperor of the French believed at that time, and perhaps he still believes, that the United States were permanently divided, and that circumstances might take such a shape as to afford him the opportunity of acquiring Texas, of recovering Louisiana, and of possessing the mouth of the Mississippi.

To accomplish this end, it was necessary to obtain a foothold on this continent, at a point as near the United States as possible, and particularly to Louisiana and Texas—a point of departure where he could collect, securely and conveniently, a large army and a large naval force, and form a base of supplies. The Emperor of the French, therefore, directed himself, not so much against Mexico as against the United States. How far he has succeeded in his plans is now a matter which belongs to history. It is sufficient for me to say, that by means of his Mexican expedition he has been able to collect, on the American continent, almost on the southern frontier of the United States, a large French army, and has sent to the Gulf of Mexico a very considerable French squadron, larger than the objects of the expedition warrant, and much larger than could have been necessary for any purpose connected with Mexico—a country that has no navy; and all this has been accomplished, strange to say, without any remonstrance, without any protest, and even without any demonstration of interest or concern on the part of the United States.

What the end of these complications will be it is very difficult to foretell. So far as relates to the occupation of Mexico, I am entirely sure that the Emperor of the French will soon be undeceived, and will learn that he has undertaken more than he can accomplish, and that when he sees the complete failure of the farce which his agents are now playing in the city of Mexico, he will find himself compelled to retire from a country which he has so unjustly invaded. With regard to ourselves, therefore, there can be only one result, that will be verified sooner or later. It will inevitably be the triumph of the holy cause of Mexican independence.

The French will soon fail of even the aid of the church party. That party hoped, and, to a certain extent, with reason, that when the French army should occupy the city of Mexico, the imperial government would annul the laws of reform issued by the liberal government of that republic, and, the first thing, would restore to the clergy the property that had been taken from them, and nationalized and sold. But it happened that among the persons who had purchased the ecclesiastical property there were a considerable number of French subjects, who would be injured by the restitution of that property; and this consideration has led the French government not only not to abrogate the reform laws, but to prevent its satellites, who have assumed the name of regency in Mexico, from themselves attempting to abrogate them. If, then, the French government should persist in the policy which they have commenced to follow, it will not be long before the church party will begin to make as decided opposition to the intervention as they did a year ago to the constitutional government.

In conclusion, there is one remark that cannot be withheld. It appears to me, gentlemen, that there exists a striking similarity between the church party of Mexico and the pro-slavery party in the United States. The church was there a power stronger than the state; so was slavery in this country. The church has there been the only cause of our civil wars; so now is slavery here. The church party in Mexico, after being conquered by the people, solicited foreign intervention, in order to be re-established in power; so slavery in this country, as I understand, has sought foreign aid even before being conquered by the government of the United States.

This toast was also received with enthusiasm, after which some of the gentlemen present begged Mr. Hiram Barney to respond. Mr. Barney arose and said:

"GENTLEMEN: After what our friend the Mexican minister, who has given us such important information, and has so thoroughly considered the Mexican question, has said, there is nothing left that I can add. My official position does not permit me either to express my sentiments and my sympathies for Mexico with the vehemence which I feel and with the freedom that I would were I in other circumstances. We have not as yet offered Mexico the aid which it was our duty to give her in the present critical situation, and I really do not know whether it is because we would not or because we could not do it. I need not say that the sympathies of our people are in favor of the Mexican nation, and that we hope that instead of Europe being able to establish monarchies in this continent, she may see, in a short time, some of the monarchies of the Old World turned into republics." [Applause.]

Mr. Barney took his seat in the midst of acclamations of joy from those around him, when Mr. Bryant arose and made the following address:

"GENTLEMEN: Of all the atrocities committed in the world since its creation, I do not believe that there is any more mean, more base, or more vile than that of the present French Emperor, who, taking advantage of the civil war of the United States, and the wearied Mexican republic, has sent from the other continent an army of adventurers, with the object of overthrowing the republican institutions which the Mexican people had given to themselves by virtue of their sovereignty, and establishing a monarchy by force, placing at its head the stem of one of the most absolute and despotic families ever known upon earth. The baseness and villany of this action has no equal, and its lowness can only be compared with the greatness of soul, elevation of sentiments, and pure patriotism with which the Mexicans are endowed, defending the independence of their country and sustaining the constitutional government of Juarez, who is now the emblem of that holy cause. I propose, then, gentlemen, that we drink to the government of Juarez, that eminent patriot who has not hesitated to wrestle in defence of a holy cause with a European colossus, and who has become the representative of patriotism and constancy, presiding now over a government which will realize, by its triumph, the highest hopes for the welfare and prosperity of Mexico." [Applause.]

This toast was as well received as the former ones, and it met with demonstrations of great pleasure.

Several indications were then made to Doctor Navarro, Mexican consul general in the United States, to respond to Mr. Bryant's toast, and after stating the difficulty he labored under to do so in a foreign language to the eloquent and beautiful address of Mr. Bryant, he said that he drank "the health and well-being of the gentlemen present, and the prosperity and happiness of the United States."

Mr. Schell proposed that Mr. Van Buren, as the most distinguished orator, and a gentleman well versed in the politics of foreign governments, should express the sympathies of the United States in favor of Mexico—a proposition that was most favorably received, but which unfortunately could not be granted, Mr. Van Buren suffering then an indisposition which prevented him from speaking sufficiently loud for the time he thought necessary to say anything worthy to be heard by such an audience.

Mr. Dodge asked Mr. Romero several questions about the extent of Mexican territory that the French occupied; upon the so-called "Junta of Notables" who proclaimed the empire, and upon various points of importance. Mr. Romero answered, endeavoring to make himself heard by all the gentlemen present, in terms which showed that the proclamation of the empire was nothing more than a badly-managed farce, and that the French were in a difficult position, which will every day grow worse.

He availed himself also of the occasion to speak upon other points he had omitted in his address, and which were listened to by all with demonstrations of the most intense interest.

Shortly after 10 o'clock Mr. Romero arose from the table, and thus terminated a meeting in which all were highly pleased and satisfied, and which, owing to the object in view, as well as the gentlemen who composed it, cannot be less than of great importance and political transcendency, as well as of great interest to those who have any sympathy for a people who is struggling for its independence against a European tyrant, disturber of the peace of the world.

Great banquet given to the minister from the Mexican republic by several of the most distinguished persons of the city of New York, to express their sympathy for the cause of Mexico and their opposition to French intervention in that republic.

On the evening of the 29th of March last a banquet was given in this city, at Delmonico's hotel, corner of Fourteenth street and Fifth avenue, in honor of Señor Don Matias Romero, minister of the Mexican republic, by very distinguished citizens of New York, with the view of manifesting their sympathy towards the Mexican nation in the bloody struggle they are now carrying on against their invaders. The private character which it was considered proper to give to this demonstration, notwithstanding the importance with which it was invested, its spontaneity, and a thousand other circumstances, have, perhaps, been partly the cause that there has been so little comment on it in the papers.

We are going to supply this deficiency by referring to all that occurred during the entertainment so highly expressive at a time when the Archduke Maximilian (as it is asserted) is about preparing his voyage to go and sit upon a silver mountain, as Napoleon said, instead of upon a throne. Our readers will not think it strange that we enter into so minute a description of a dinner if they think that we are not only treating of a great culinary triumph of Delmonico's, of the splendid fine taste shown by those accomplished Amphytrions, but, what is far better, of a frank reproach and a terrible warning given to Europe by the people of the United States, represented by the distinguished individuals of this metropolis, of whom we shall give an idea afterwards. Now we will enter into the facts.

About a month ago some of those citizens projected a demonstration in favor of the Mexican cause, that, without taking cognizance of the policy which circumstances may have obliged the government of this country to follow, should manifest the dominant feeling in regard to the invasion of Mexico, not only among the great mass of the people of the United States, but among those classes especially favored by intelligence, learning, position, or fortune. They soon found among their friends the same disposition, and they would have collected a very large subscription if the desire they had of carrying out at the earliest opportunity their intentions, and other considerations of minor importance, had not prevented it. So that, without more delay, the following invitation was sent to Washington to Señor Romero:

NEW YORK, *February* 16, 1864.

DEAR SIR: The undersigned, in common with many loyal citizens, feel much interest in the present condition of Mexico, that important continental state.

We cordially sympathize with the people of Mexico in their unequal struggle, and, appreciating their bravery and sacrifices, and your services in maintaining the integrity of your country, we tender to you, as the faithful representative of Mexico, a dinner in this city, on Tuesday, March 29.

Your obedient servants,

Wm. C. Bryant.
Wm. H. Aspinwall.
Hamilton Fish.
John W. Hamersley.
Jonathan Sturgis.
James W. Beekman.
J. J. Astor, Jr.
Smith Clift.
W. E. Dodge, Jr.
David Hoadley.
Frederick De Peyster.
W. Butler Duncan.
Wm. Curtis Noyes.
Henry Clews.
Fred. C. Gebhard.
Geo. T. Strong.
Henry Delafield.
Henry E. Pierrepont.
George Opdyke.
David Dudley Field.
Geo. Bancroft.
C. A. Bristed.
Alex. Van Rensselaer.
Geo. Folsom.
Washington Hunt.
Chas. King.
Willard Parker.
Adrien Iselin.
Robert J. Livingston.
Samuel B. Ruggles.
James T. Brady.

His Excellency M. ROMERO,
Mexican Minister, &c., &c., &c., Washington, D. C.

For any one who is acquainted with society here, these names will suffice, and it will be seen at once that they represent the most distinguished, choice, eminent, and élite people of the city of New York, embracing every profession, every employment, and every political party in all its shades. In order, however, that foreigners and particularly the Spanish-Americans may have some idea of those persons, we will give a brief description of their antecedents in the order in which they have signed their names.

Mr. William Cullen Bryant is a most respectable elderly person, great poet, eminent literary man, and one of the first editors of the press of this city. As a poet he has been a perfect prodigy of precocity and lengthened genius, to be compared only with Lope de Vega and Voltaire. When he was only nine years old he published his first verses, and at thirteen a regular poem, in connexion with other beautiful compositions, was issued to the eyes of the world. He is now over seventy years of age, and has just given light to a new poem that has called forth the eulogy of the press, and in which his robust mental faculties have not deteriorated in the slightest degree. By the refined taste displayed in his compositions, he is considered as a poet of the most classical taste that this nation has hitherto produced. To the golden crown that girdles his venerable head may be added the respectability which Mr. Bryant enjoys for his knowledge, his well-tried probity, and his constancy in defending the most disinterested political opinions. In regard to these, Mr. Bryant belongs to the extreme portion of the republican party, being consequently an abolitionist. Septuagenary as he is, he still preserves the moral and physical vigor of youth, and is ready to defend any cause that has for a foundation liberty and justice; he has also all the necessary activity to be even now chief editor of the "New York Evening Post."

Mr. William H. Aspinwall is a rich merchant of the highest probity and possessing the most active and intelligent spirit of enterprise. The inter-oceanic communication by Panama is entirely owing to him. There he has founded the city called in New Granada "Colon," but generally known as "Aspinwall," a name that will hence be imperishable. He belongs to the firm of Howland, Aspinwall & Co. He is the owner of one of the best picture galleries in New York.

Mr. Hamilton Fish, a gentleman of the most elevated position in society by the antecedents of his family, much respected in this city as well for his personal qualities as for many other reasons. He has been governor of the State of New York, and senator for the same in the United States Congress.

Mr. John W. Hamersley, also of an ancient and notable family of this city. A man of great wealth, highly educated, and distinguished for his varied learning acquired by great reading and extensive travelling. By his exquisite taste and very fine manners he holds a place among the aristocracy which is obtained by those qualities, it being the only one that can possibly exist in republics. His independent position has hitherto prevented him from being enrolled under any political party; but his heart is entirely American, and he considers that the absolute independence of this continent from the old is (as he so eloquently expresses it) "a principle filtered in the veins of every true son of Washington by the milk that he has drawn from his mother's breast, a pass-word and countersign, and a terrible monition to Europe."

Mr. Jonathan Sturgis, a distinguished and eminent merchant, an enthusiastic philanthropist, who has already dedicated a great part of his wealth for objects of beneficence, and for the fine arts, his delicate taste for which entitles him to be an American Mæcenas. He is president of the "Union League Club," which, as it is well known, represents the most select and influential portion of the republican party.

Mr. James W. Beekman, a descendant from one of the first Dutch families, founders of the city of New York. A man of wealth, highly respected for his honesty and philanthropic sentiments, no less than for the elevated criterion revealed in all his actions. His name is always connected in every useful enterprise or in any charitable undertaking wherein the moral or physical sufferings of mankind are to be alleviated. He has been one of the most eminent senators in the State legislature.

Mr. John Jacob Astor, jr., is a nephew of the famous philanthropic millionaire, his namesake, who lavished enormous sums in objects of public benefit and instruction that bear his name, as for instance the Astor library. The town of Astoria, near this city, was also called after him. The person of whom we are now speaking, besides his illustrious name, his probity and other personal endowments, is the possessor of a fabulous fortune consisting principally of real estate in New York city, and is also a patriot of the purest and most enthusiastic kind, as the fact of his having accepted a colonelship in the volunteer army of the United States and having suffered all the privations and hazards of the campaign clearly indicate. This occasioned a malady from which he has not entirely recovered yet.

Mr. Smith Clift, a lawyer of celebrity and high reputation for his honesty and undeniable talents, is a distinguished member of the republican party.

Mr. William E. Dodge, jr., is one of the heirs to the great fortune and virtues of his father. He is a prominent merchant in this city. The Dodge family have distinguished themselves by their unstained morality and religious piety. He has spent considerable sums in philanthropic and Christian establishments, having subscribed on one occasion more than $25,000 for the founding of a college in Palestine. Mr. Dodge, partner of the house of Phelps, Dodge & Co., is a banker of high standing and great prospects.

Mr. David Hoadley is also a person of the highest respectability in this city, accredited honesty and good judgment. He is the president of the Panama Railroad Company, and has contributed largely in raising it to the height it now occupies, and is considered as one of the most lucrative and best managed enterprises in this country.

Mr. Frederick De Peyster is a much distinguished and respected literary man, as must be seen at once when he is known to be the president of the Historical Society of New York. He descends from one of the oldest and most honorable Dutch families of this city, and is held as a prominent member of the democratic party.

Mr. William Butler Duncan, a well-known and rich banker of the house of Duncan, Sherman & Co. He is a member of the extreme portion of the democratic party.

Mr. William Curtis Noyes, a prominent lawyer of high reputation, is considered one of the luminaries of the New York bar, well known as a man of probity and judgment, and is one of the principal members of the republican party.

Mr. Henry Clews is a noted merchant of the firm of Livermore, Clews & Co., United States bankers for the sale of some of its bonds.

Mr. Frederick C. Gebhard, banker of high reputation, and of an ancient and prominent family. He is a partner of the house of Schusherd, Gebhard & Co.

Mr. George T. Strong, lawyer, and treasurer of the United States Sanitary Commission, a post of great trust. He is a learned Greek scholar, of fine taste and exquisite manners.

Mr. Henry Delafield is a rich merchant, retired from business, and brother of the distinguished colonel of engineers of the same name, and of a celebrated physician of this city.

Mr. Henry E. Pierrepont is a wealthy gentleman and eminent lawyer of Brooklyn, a philanthropist, and protector of the fine arts, and belongs to one of the oldest and most respectable Huguenot families.

Mr. George Opdyke is a merchant well known and respected, having been the last mayor of the city of New York.

Mr. David Dudley Field, eminent lawyer, and one of the authors of the present civil code of New York; is a prominent member of the republican party.

Mr. George Bancroft, ex-minister from this country to England, is an eminent historian, and is now publishing a large history of the United States. He enjoys a well-deserved reputation as a literary man, and was Secretary of the Navy in a former administration.

Mr. Charles Astor Bristed, a near relation of John Jacob Astor, of whom we have already spoken, is a man well versed in sciences and letters, and has written several works of great merit upon political matters.

Mr. Alexander Van Rensselaer, son of the founder of Albany, wealthy "rentier." He is a man of much culture, and of an old Dutch family.

Mr. George Folsom, ex-minister from the United States to Holland; native of the State of Maine; connected by marriage to one of the principal families of this city. He is a person of wealth, great learning, and a distinguished member of the Ethnological Society of New York, and consequently a noted philologist. He has made a magnificent translation of the letters addressed by Hernan Cortes to Charles V upon the conquest of Mexico.

Mr. Washington Hunt, ex-governor of the State of New York, and a prominent member of the democratic party. He represents the interests of the eastern portion of the same State, of which he is a native.

Mr. Charles King is a venerable, elderly gentleman, the Nestor of that select meeting, for he is five years older than Mr. Bryant, and consequently seventy-five years of age. Notwithstanding, his features, his deportment, his voice, and, above all, his intelligent and fiery gaze, reveal an extraordinary vigor. Educated in Paris and London, where, in the beginning of the present century, his father resided as minister from the United States, he returned to his country, married into a distinguished and rich family, and was for some time engaged in a large speculating business. He excelled afterwards as a journalist, and having been appointed many years ago president of Columbia College, the most ancient and renowned institution for scientific instruction in the United States, has made great improvements there, and contributed effectively to establish its present celebrity. His good humor, that does not detract from his venerable aspect, gives him a particular attraction, and on approaching him one does not know which is the most predominent feeling of the heart, whether it be the affection inspired by his amiability, or the veneration with which his eminent intelligent qualities, his knowledge, and his purified morality subdue you.

Mr. Willard Parker is an eminent physician of New York—perhaps the most eminent in the United States, after the octogenarian Mott. To a consummate scientific knowledge that he possesses may be added the most noble character and the best qualities.

Mr. Adrien Iselin is a merchant of high standing, and whose name is advantageously known in the New York market.

Mr. Robert J. Livingston is a very wealthy man, and a descendant of an illustrious family of this country, as one of his ancestors was companion to Washington in the revolutionary war, and another one was Secretary of State and an American diplomat in Europe.

Mr. Samuel B. Ruggles, who possessed formerly a large fortune, is a very intelligent and educated person; he has been a delegate from the United States to the international statistic congress, assembled at Berlin.

Mr. James T. Brady is one of the most prominent lawyers of the New York bar, an orator of great reputation, and eminent among the democratic party. He was a candidate of the same State for governor in the election before last.

To the foregoing invitation Mr. Romero answered as follows:

MEXICAN LEGATION IN THE UNITED STATES OF AMERICA,
Washington, March 20, 1864.

GENTLEMEN: I have just had the honor to receive your kind letter of the 18th ultimo, informing me that you, in common with many loyal citizens, feel much interest in the present condition of Mexico, cordially sympathize with the people of that republic in their unequal struggle, and appreciating their bravery and sacrifices, as well as my services (you kindly add) in maintaining the integrity of my country. You are good enough to tender to me, as the representative of Mexico, a dinner in your city on the 29th instant.

Nothing could be more gratifying to myself and to my countrymen than seeing that we have with us the enlightened and uninterested sympathy of so many of the most distinguished and eminent citizens, whose virtues, learning, and persevering enterprise have made of the city of New York the great metropolis of the New World.

The demonstration with which you intend to honor the noble cause for which my country is fighting against one of the strongest and best organized military powers on earth, while it shows your high opinion of the question, and your great sense of justice, will be duly appreciated and thanked for by my government and countrymen, as well as by all unbiased and disinterested people throughout the world, who have some regard for justice, and cannot help noticing it entirely trampled down by the Emperor of the French in the policy he is pursuing towards Mexico.

I am, gentlemen, very respectfully, your obedient servant,

M. ROMERO.

Messrs. WILLIAM CULLEN BRYANT, &c., &c., and all the other gentlemen who signed this invitation.

Besides the above-copied invitation, Mr. Romero received the following one:

NEW YORK, *March* 18, 1864.

DEAR SIR: In behalf of the undersigned, who, in common with our countrymen, cordially sympathize with the people of Mexico in their unequal struggle, and with you as their faithful representative, we beg your acceptance of a dinner in this city on Tuesday, March 29, at 7 o'clock.

WILLIAM H. ASPINWALL,
Chairman Invitation Committee.

Señor ROMERO,
Envoy Extraordinary and Minister Plenipotentiary of the Republic of Mexico.

Mr. Romero's answer was this:

MEXICAN LEGATION IN THE UNITED STATES OF AMERICA,
Washington, March 25, 1864.

DEAR SIR: I have to-day had the honor of receiving the polite note you had the kindness to address to me under date of the 18th instant, proposing to me in your behalf, and in common with many of your countrymen cordially sympathizing with the people of Mexico in their unequal struggle, and with me as their representative, that I should accept a dinner in your city on Tuesday, 29th instant, at 7 o'clock p. m.

Thanking you very sincerely for the kindness of yourself and your distinguished friends in tendering me such demonstration, which, on account of the very high social standing and eminent qualities of the gentlemen from whom it originates, carries with it a great significance, I have the honor to state to you that I have already accepted said dinner in a letter dated the 20th instant, which I had the pleasure to address to the gentlemen who have honored me by their kindness in offering it to me, and that I will soon leave for your city with a view to be there on the day appointed.

I am, very respectfully, your most obedient servant,

M. ROMERO.

WILLIAM H. ASPINWALL, Esq.,
Chairman Invitation Committee, New York city.

The feast was held in the best saloons of Delmonico's hotel, occupying four of the largest. Two were set apart for the reception and convenience of the guests, one for the banquet itself, and the fourth for the orchestra and other matters indispensable to the occasion. The great dining saloon, of five hundred covers, was illuminated for the purpose of receiving a number of ladies and gentlemen belonging to the families of the guests, who assembled to see the table and its ornaments prior to the beginning of the banquet. Important additions had been made to the usual furniture and decorations of those splendid rooms; and among other things that delighted the sight there was a profusion of exquisite flowers, arranged in garlands, branches, twigs, baskets, flowerpots, &c., distributed over the doors, tables, fireplaces, at the sides of the mirrors, and wherever they could serve as graceful ornaments. The hall in which the banquet was set out displayed a most magnificent spectacle. At the head the national flags of the United States and of the republic of Mexico were placed together. On the table itself there were, besides five pyramids formed of slender branches of flowers, a splendid sugar piece, four feet high, placed in the centre, representing the arms of the Mexican republic—that is, the eagle standing in the cactus, the whole supported by a rock, which seemed to rise up in the midst of waters. The elegant table was also decorated with a palm and various kinds of cactus, as a memorial of the tropical clime and productions of Mexico. There was also a piece of pastry work in the form of a small temple, on which were distinctly written these two names: "Juarez," "Uraga," the heroic President and gallant general-in-chief who are now at the head of the Mexican patriots.

A touching and moving picture was presented by those illustrious citizens of the American Union vying with each other in entertaining and welcoming the representative of Mexico, the neighboring republic, in an hour the most difficult and critical that has ever dawned upon her. The generosity of the sentiment which inspires certain men with the desire of honoring and sustaining with demonstrations of affection those who are struggling with misfortune is something that is only within the reach of noble minds, of intelligent and well-organized hearts.

But we must come back to the prosaic but substantial and important question of the dinner itself, without going into particulars, and reserving what is technically termed the "*menu*" to be inserted afterwards. This we will take from the elegant bills of fare, printed on blue satin with golden letters, which were distributed to the guests. It is enough to say that the eatables were of the most exquisite and delicate kind, only adding that there was an abundance of excellent wines, and we will have said all that is necessary on this part of this subject.

The orchestra, which was magnificent, played a number of operatic selections, intermingled with Mexican airs, alternating with "Yankee Doodle" and "Hail Columbia." The sweet accents of the music, reverberating from the other hall without any noise or disturbance, did not prevent conversation, which flowed on in a constant and animated strain, full of friendship and cordiality.

Some of those who subscribed their names to the invitation were not able to attend the dinner in consequence of family and other matters. Mr. Aspinwall, for instance, lost his mother-in-law a day before the banquet; Mr. Fish, scarcely a week before, had received information of the death of a daughter, resident in France, and Mr. Noyes, only four days previously, lost his old and venerable mother. Other persons had unavoidable business to call them away, as in the case of Mr. Brady and Mr. Ruggles. Some of them expressed to the stewards their regrets at not being able to attend the dinner, as Mr. Brady did in the following letter:

WILLARDS' HOTEL,
Washington, D. C., March 25, 1864.

MY DEAR SIR: I am detained here by professional business, and fear that I will not be able to reach New York in time for the dinner to Señor Romero on 29th, which I would be so happy to attend, and in which I am willing in every way to participate. If I be kept away, please give my best respects to the señor, and let me wish you all the pleasure you expect from the festivity.

Yours, truly,

JAS. T. BRADY.

J. W. HAMERSLEY, Esq.

Besides Mr. Romero, Señor Don Juan N. Navarro, consul-general of the Mexican republic, residing in New York, Señor Don Ignacio Mariscal, a lawyer, highly esteemed and considered in the city of Mexico, who is now secretary of the Mexican legation in the United States, and Don Fernando de la Cuesta, second secretary of the same legation, were also invited to the banquet.

The party were seated at table in the following order:

Mr. Beekman.

Señor Romero.	Mr. Iselin.
Mr. Bryant.	Mr. Gebhard.
Mr. Delafield.	Mr. Hamersley.
Mr. Duncan.	Mr. Clews.
Mr. Astor.	Mr. Hunt.
Señor Cuesta.	Mr. Bancroft.
Mr. De Peyster.	Mr. Sturges.
Mr. Pierrepont.	Mr. Folsom.
Mr. Clift.	Mr. Bristed.
Dr. Navarro.	Mr. Dodge.
Dr. Parker.	Mr. Field.
Mr. Opdyke.	Señor Mariscal.

Mr. King.

Shortly before the dessert, Mr. BEEKMAN, the president, arose and said:

"GENTLEMEN: I am going to propose to you, by previous arrangement with some of you, what is, I know it, a complete departure from what has hitherto been customary in dinners of this kind, and which, I believe, will create quite a complete revolution in those which may be given hereafter, and that is, that before we proceed any further the first and regular toast should be made. I propose, then, gentlemen, the health of 'The President of the United States,' and I beg our distinguished friend, Mr. Field, to respond."

This toast was received with general enthusiasm, the whole assemblage rising.

Mr. DAVID DUDLEY FIELD then spoke as follows:

"Mr. CHAIRMAN: Why I should be called upon to answer this toast I do not precisely know. I hold, as you know, sir, no official position, and am in no manner entitled to speak, except as any citizen may, for the President or any member of his cabinet. So far as it is a compliment or salutation for the country of which he is the first magistrate, we who are Americans all share, both in the giving and the receiving it So far as it calls for the expression of any opinion or intention on the part of the Executive, I, of course, can say nothing. There is one respect, however, in which all of us, private citizens, may venture to speak for the Chief Magistrate, and that is when we interpret or express the judgment of the American people—here, more than anywhere else, the executive department of the popular will.

"When, therefore, we utter the opinion of the American people, we answer, in a grea measure, for the President; and in this manner any private citizen, like myself, may venture to speak. So doing, I assert, without hesitation, that, with unexampled unanimity, Americans feel a profound sympathy for the Mexican people in this day of their trial. The sentiment of the country is all but one on this subject We do not stop to inquire whether the Mexicans have not made mistakes in the management of their affairs. That is possible; all nations have done as much. We have done so in the management of our own affairs, of which we are now reaping the bitter fruits. But, whatever may have been the mistakes of the Mexicans, they give no sort of excuse to the invasion of the French, or the attempt of foreigners to impose a yoke upon their country.

"Though the minds and hearts of the American people are chiefly occupied with their own long and bloody struggle against an unnatural rebellion, they nevertheless feel deeply the wrongs of Mexico, and they will express this feeling on every proper occasion. We express it here at this festive gathering; they will express it at public meetings, in State legislatures, and in Congress; and they expect the Executive, the organ of the nation, in its intercourse with other nations, to express it also to the fullest extent, within the limits of international obligations.

"Not only do we give the Mexican people our sincerest sympathy, but we offer them all the encouragement which a neutral nation can offer. We bid them to be of good cheer; to hold fast by their integrity; to stand firm through all vicissitudes, believing in the strength of nationality, in the vitality of freedom, and in that overruling and all-wise Providence which, sooner or later, chastises wrong and casts down the oppressor.

"This is not the place to enter upon a discussion of the motives which prompted this French invasion, nor to trace the history of the parties which have divided Mexico, and been made the pretext for the intrusion of foreigners into its domestic affairs. Thus much, however, may be said, that whatever may be the incidental questions that have arisen, there is one great and controlling feature in the controversy, and that is the claim, on the one hand, of the church to interfere in the affairs of the state, and the claim of the state, on the other hand, to be freed from the interference of the church. We hear constantly of the church party in Mexico. Why should there be a church party? What can it have legitimately to do with secular affairs? With us, it has been a fundamental maxim from the formation of our government, imbedded in the organic law, that there must be forever a total separation of church and state. The Mexican people—that is to say, the true and loyal portion of them—are struggling for the same end, and in this we Americans, of all creeds and all parties, bid them God speed. Yes, all of us, excepting only the rebel, who raises his arms against his country, and the deceitful renegade, who, not daring to raise an arm against it, seeks yet to betray it—all of us, I say, with these exceptions, pray for and believe in the deliverance of Mexico. It may be sooner or later; it may come through greater misfortunes than any which she has yet suffered, but come it will. The spirit of freedom is stronger than the lances of France.

"Maximilian may come with the Austrian eagle and the French tricolor; he may come with a hundred ships; he may march on the high road from Vera Cruz to the capital, under the escort of French squadrons; he may be proclaimed by French trumpets in all the squares of the chief cities; but he will return, at some earlier or later day, a fugitive from the New World back to the Old, from which he came; his followers will be scattered and chased from the land; the titles and dignities which he is about to lavish on followers and apostates will be marks of derision; the flag of the republic will wave from all the peaks of the Cordilleras, and be answered from every mountain top, east and west, to either ocean; and the renewed country, purified by blood and fire, will resume its institutions, and be free.

"Such, Mr. Chairman, are, I am sure, the wishes and the expectations of the American people; and thus, I am bound to presume, would be the answer, if he were free to speak, of the President of the United States."

After this interesting speech, which was received with long and general applause, the dinner continued, in the manner which will appear in the bill of fare. When the dessert was served, Mr. Beekman arose and said:

"Gentlemen: The turn of the second regular toast has come. It is 'To Don Benito Juarez, constitutional president of the Mexican republic.' This illustrious personage is, gentlemen, as you are aware, of pure indigenous race. Of humble birth, his eminent virtues and exalted qualities elevated him by the votes of his fellow-citizens to the first magistracy of his country, and he has discharged his duties under the most adverse circumstances that have ever fallen to the lot of any statesman. It can be said of him, as of Bayard, that he is—

"'Without fear and without reproach.'

"I beg the illustrious president of Columbia college to respond to this toast, after which I trust we will have the pleasure of hearing our distinguished guest."

This toast was drunk with the greatest demonstrations of enthusiasm and most loudly applauded, and, at the request of one of the gentlemen, three cheers were given for the President of Mexico, after which Mr. KING spoke in the following manner:

"GENTLEMEN: The toast you have just drunk to the President of the Mexican republic is worthy of our cheers, for he is the chosen representative of the Mexican people, from whom he himself sprang, and our distinguished guest to day is accredited to our government as the representative of the government of which President Juarez is the head. In honoring the name of President Juarez, we are, then, acting in harmony with the views and policy of our own government as much as in consonance with our own feelings and convictions.

"For certainly to us, as Americans, there is much in the character and antecedents of Juarez to commend him to our regard. He is, what was the boast of the Athenians of old, (that noblest race of men that ever made a small state great,) born of the soil, and of the people, where he lives—one of those autochthones who, having no progenitors to look back to but mother earth, have all the more inducement to look forward to ennobling, as far as they may, and dignifying, that mother earth.

"Thoroughly trained and educated in all good knowledge, Juarez labors to see his country great, prosperous, and, above all, *free*—free individually and socially—free politically, and, above all, spiritually free It is there that lies the danger and the difficulty of Mexico. It is spiritual bondage even more than partisan and factious quarrels that has damaged that fine country. It is the influence of a class of religionists as a power in the state that has been most injurious there, as it must be everywhere; and I say this in the most general terms, and not as applicable to any one form of belief.

"Juarez is the avowed and bold opponent of the politico-religious hierarchy which has so largely controlled the affairs of Mexico, while monopolizing a most undue share of its wealth.

"He is proscribed by the priesthood, because he stands, as in New England our forefathers did, for liberty of conscience, for the right of every man to decide for himself in matters of faith. For the same reason he is proscribed by the imperial pro-consul of France; for it suits the present interest of the unfathomable mystery that sits upon the throne of France to cultivate the Roman Catholic hierarchy—which is a united body all over the world—wielding a sword, and that not the sword of the spirit, of which 'the hilt is at Rome, and the point everywhere.'

"We, who have tried and known how much safer and wiser it is to separate the church from the state—and where public opinion, and sometimes positive law, forbids the mingling of priests in politics—we can well sympathize with President Juarez in his brave struggle in Mexico against a domineering clergy and against the foreign allies whom they have introduced into the country, to ruin where they could no longer rule.

"In the midst of the agony of our own civil war we cannot be insensible nor indifferent to the cause of Mexico, our neighbor, our friend, our natural ally in every difficulty that shall involve the point of American nationality and American interests, as opposed to European nationality and European interests Mexico never can, with the assent of the people of the United States, become the appendage of a European nation, or furnish a peaceful throne to any scion of a European imperial house. The opportunity, so auspiciously presented by the visit of our distinguished guest, is eagerly embraced by us—private individuals, indeed, yet not unfair representatives of the popular sentiments of our fellow-citizens of all classes—to give emphatic expression to the declaration that, 'biding our time,' we will, at all hazards, when that time comes, assert and uphold the doctrine that on this continent we will not permit the interference by arms of any European nation to overthrow republican institutions and to establish monarchy. Especially as respects Mexico, (conterminous with us for so many degrees of longitude, washed on its Atlantic and Pacific shores by the same bays and seas, and anxious to model its institutions after those which have raised these United States to such power and prosperity,) with respect to Mexico, I repeat, we cannot, and we will not, consent that any archduke of Austria, be he puppet or be he principal, nor any other monarchical pretender, shall be imposed upon the Mexican people by foreign bayonets.

"True it is, alas! that, through the great crimes of slavery, we are at this moment unable to give to our firm purposes in this regard fitting outward manifestation; but, as in the inevitable course of justice, which is God, our civil war must ere long close by the extirpation of its accursed cause, and in the restoration of our national unity and territorial integrity, we shall then have disposable such a force on sea and on land as will impart unlimited power of persuasion to the diplomatic declaration we shall then make that Mexico must and shall be Mexican, that Mexico must and shall be American, and not European."

This speech was much applauded and interrupted by demonstrations of approval. Then Mr. Beekman, the chairman, announced that Mr. Romero was about to speak, alluding to him in the most honorable manner as the representative of Mexico, to whom that banquet was dedicated. Mr. Romero, being saluted by enthusiastic applause and three cheers, amid profound silence, spoke as follows:

Mr. Chairman—Gentlemen: I feel entirely unable to express to you in a sufficient manner my sincere thanks for the great honor you have bestowed upon me and my country in this refined and splendid demonstration of your sympathy for struggling Mexico. It is, indeed, particularly gratifying to me that this significant demonstration is made by so many of the most distinguished and most eminent citizens, who are an ornament to this great metropolis, and whose virtues, learning, and enterprise have contributed so much to make your city in so brief a period the first, not only of the broad United States, but of the whole American continent, as well as to make your country one of the most powerful, wealthy, and civilized on the globe.

It is, indeed, another motive which greatly adds to my gratification, and for which, in the name of my country, I beg to express to you my gratitude for the kind words with which our distinguished friend has proposed the health of Benito Juarez, the constitutional president of the republic of Mexico, and for the prompt heartiness and cordiality with which that toast has been received. I perceive, with joy and gratitude, gentlemen, that you appreciate the high qualities of that statesman and patriot, and hold a strong and pure sympathy for the noble cause of which he is the leader.

I am rejoiced that I have the opportunity to see with my own eyes the proof that the eminent French statesman, M. Thiers, was somewhat mistaken when, in a speech he recently delivered before the Corps Legislatif, of Paris, against the policy pursued by Emperor Napoleon in Mexican affairs, he stated that the United States would not, under present circumstances, object in any way to that policy; and that, should the Archduke Maximilian come to this city *en route* to Mexico, he would meet with a cordial reception at your hands. It could scarcely be possible to have a more distinguished, complete, and genuine representation of the patriotism, intelligence, and wealth of the great city of New York—the leading city of the Union—than that I see assembled here this evening; yet, if I can trust my senses, gentlemen, I venture to assert that the sympathies of your great city run in a direction very different from that imagined by M. Thiers.

I am very happy to say that the kind feeling you express for Mexico is fully reciprocated. In Mexico there are now but the sentiments of regard and admiration for the United States, and the desire to pursue such a course as will draw more closely all those powerful ties by which both nations should be united.

It has sometimes appeared to me that the gentlemen who controlled the government of the United States for thirty-five years previous to 1861 cared for nothing so much as for the acquisition of territory. Those gentlemen thus caused their country to appear in the character of a very covetous man, who, without knowing the boundaries of his own estate or endeavoring to improve it, constantly exerts himself to enlarge his limits, without being very scrupulous as to the means of its accomplishment.

Just before the war with Mexico commenced, the United States had a boundary question with England, which threatened a rupture between the two countries, and I have been informed that the same documents which were prepared as a declaration of war against Great Britain were used when war was finally declared against Mexico. Thus, while the idea of acquiring domain from Great Britain by a dubious title, to say the least, was relinquished, the same scheme was carried out against Mexico, not only without any plausible reason, but, I must say, in violation of all principles of justice.

I beg of you, gentlemen, to excuse me if I have referred to an unpleasant point in the history of late events. But I wish to forcibly present to your minds the idea that the unfair policy I have alluded to led, in a great measure, to the troubles and complications in which you are now involved, and one of the consequences of which is French intervention in Mexico, as that intervention would never have been but for the civil war in the United States.

Those who have pursued this policy appear to have been, in the main, under the influence of the slave power, and to have had in view their own political influence and personal aggrandizement, rather than the great interests of their country. They very properly thought that, by extending the area of slavery, they would extend in proportion their influence and strength. For that reason they did not insist on increasing the territory of the United States in the far northwest, where their *peculiar institution* could not be acclimated, but rather set their eyes towards the sunny regions of Mexico. By that means the institution of human slavery had so large an increase, that a short time afterwards it was strong enough to commence a gigantic war against the government of the United States. In my opinion, the leaders of the slavery party always had in view the separation of their own States from the free States of the north, and to make up for the loss they aspired to acquire territory southward.

I will not conceal from you, gentlemen, the fact that we have looked with deep apprehension upon such an aggressive policy, which threatened to deprive us of our independence and nationality—the highest and most precious rights that man can enjoy on earth. We were, of course, fully determined not to give up this precious inheritance, and we had resolved to fight to the last. In our present war with France we are giving a proof of our determination. It may appear foolish and unavailing for Mexico, that has been so often exhausted in her struggles to obtain true liberty during the last forty years, to accept war with the greatest military power in Europe ; but there are circumstances in the life of nations which cause them to overlook all secondary considerations, and determine to exert themselves to overcome all difficulties. Besides, our situation is not so bad as many think.

Fortunately, the change of policy towards Mexico operated in the United States brought up a consequent change in the feelings of my country in regard to yours. We do not wish now to have any interest antagonistical to yours, because we mean to keep peace with you, and that object could scarcely be accomplished if our respective interests were in opposition. For that reason, among other very material ones that we had, we established a republican form of government and democratic institutions, modelled on the same basis as yours.

The Emperor of the French pretends that the object of his interference in Mexican affairs is to prevent the annexation of Mexico to the United States ; and yet that very result would, most likely, be ultimately accomplished if a monarchy were established in Mexico. Fortunately for us, that scheme is by no means a feasible one.

Mexico is most bountifully blessed by nature. She can produce of the best quality and in large quantities all of the principal agricultural staples of the world—cotton, coffee, sugar, tobacco, vanilla, wheat, and corn. Her mines have yielded the largest portion of all the silver which now circulates throughout the world, and there still remain to her mountains of that precious metal, as well as of gold, which only require labor, skill, and capital to make them available and valuable. The wealth of California is nothing when compared with what still remains in Mexico.

My country, therefore, opens a most desirable field for the enterprise of a commercial nation. Farsighted England discovered this many years ago, and by establishing a line of mail steamers from Southampton to Vera Cruz and Tampico, and negotiating advantageous treaties of commerce, has, beyond all other nations, enjoyed the best of the Mexican trade. France, seeing this, and wishing to vie with England, has undertaken an enterprise which, besides being ruinous to her, will not produce the desired end, as the means adopted must surely cause the opposite result. The United States are the best situated to avail of the immense wealth of Mexico. Being a neighbor nation, they have more advantages than any other for the frontier and coasting trade, and, furthermore, being a nation second to none in wealth, activity, skill, and enterprise, they are called by nature to speculate and enjoy the resources of Mexico.

We are willing to grant to the United States every commercial facility that will not be derogatory of our independence and sovereignty. This will give to the United States all possible advantages that could be derived from annexation without any of its inconveniences. That once done, our common interests, political as well as commercial, will give us a common whole American continental policy which no European nation would dare disregard.

The bright future which I plainly see for both nations had made me forget for a moment the present troubles in which they are now involved. I consider these troubles of so transitory a nature as not to interfere materially with the common destiny I have foreshadowed ; but, as they have the interest of actuality, I beg to be allowed to make a few remarks in regard to them.

Every careful observer of events could not help noticing, when the expedition against Mexico was organized in Europe, that it would, sooner or later, draw the United States into the most serious complications, and involve them in the difficulty. The object of that expedition being no less than a direct and armed interference in the political affairs of an American nation, with a view to overthrow its republican institutions and establish on their ruins a monarchy, with a European prince on the throne, the only question to be determined by the United States and the other nations concerned was as to the time when they would be willing or ready to meet the issue thus boldly and openly held out by the antagonistic nations of Europe.

The United States could not be indifferent in this question ; just as a man who sees his neighbor's house set on fire by an incendiary could not remain an unconcerned spectator, while his own house contains his family and all his fortune, and combustible matter lies in the basement. The only alternative left to him should be whether it would be more convenient to his interests to help his neighbor in putting out the fire from the beginning, and with the same earnestness as if his own house were already caught by that destructive element, or to wait inactive until the incendiary has succeeded in making a perfect blaze of his neighbor's property, by which all will inevitably be involved in one common ruin.

This, in my opinion, is the situation in which the United States are placed with regard to Mexico. Taking into consideration the well-known sagacity of American statesmen, the often-proved devotion of the American people to republican institutions, and the patriotism and zeal of the administration that presides over the destinies of the country, I cannot entertain the slightest doubt that the United States will act in this emergency as will conduce to the best interests they and mankind at large have at stake in the Mexican question.

In the mean time, however, I consider it of the highest importance that the delusion prevailing throughout Europe that the United States do not oppose, and rather favor, the establishment of a monarchy in Mexico, by French bayonets, should be dispelled. The French government has been working steadily in causing that delusion to prevail on the other side of the water, and, so far, has succeeded more than could be expected considering the absurdity of such an idea. The war against Mexico would be ten times more unpopular in France than it is now—in fact, it could not be maintained any longer, if the French people were made to understand that the people of the United States will never tolerate, much less favor or encourage, the establishment, by force of arms, of a European monarchy upon the ruins of a sister neighboring republic. The French people are friendly to the United States; old traditions, the common love of liberty, and the absence of opposing interests, make them friendly. They would, therefore, be wholly opposed to anything that, without bringing them any real benefit, might, sooner or later, lead to a war with this country. They very well know that such a war could not but be disastrous to France, since France would have everything to lose and nothing to gain by such a war, whatever may be her influence and power in the European continental politics.

The United States may find that they are brought squarely to the issue on the Mexican question sooner than they expected, should the report, lately reached here, of any understanding between Maximilian, as so-called Emperor of Mexico, and the insurgents in this country, prove correct. The archduke, it is stated, will inaugurate his administration by acknowledging the independence of the south, and perhaps he will go further; and this, of course, by the advice, consent, and support of the French government, whose satellite, and nothing else, will the archduke be in Mexico.

The French official and semi-official papers assure us that Maximilian will soon depart for Mexico. All present appearances indicate that he is willing to change his high position in Europe for a hazardous one in Mexico. He cannot stay there unless supported by a French army, and he will not, therefore, be anything more than the shadow of the French Emperor. Should he ever have a different view or desire from the French government, or even the French general-in chief, he will be obliged to submit to the humiliating condition of forbearing to do that which he thinks best in a country where he will call himself Emperor. As far as the personality of the Austrian duke is concerned he is nothing. If he goes to Mexico to meddle in our affairs we shall consider him as our enemy, and deal with him accordingly. We hold that in the political question which is being agitated in Mexico the person of the Austrian duke is not of much account; and whether he does or does not go there, that question can ultimately have only one possible solution—namely, the triumph and maintenance of republican institutions.

As far as I am concerned, I prefer that Maximilian should go to Mexico, so as to give the European dreamers on monarchies a fair chance to realize their dreams of America. As for Mexico, I can say that nothing that has transpired in my country should surprise any one who is familiar with our affairs. It is true that we have been unfortunate during the past year; we have lost nearly all the battles we have fought with the French; they have occupied some of our principal cities; they have blockaded our ports; but all these gains on the part of the French are nothing when compared with the elements of opposition and endurance which remain with the national government of Mexico, ruling a people numbering eight millions, determinedly opposed to intervention. ready to fight, and fighting already, for their independence; a country that will require half a million of soldiers to subdue and possess; naturally strong in defences, possessing inaccessible mountains, impracticable roads, where the patriots will be able to make a perpetual warfare upon the invader, until he is persuaded of the impossibility of accomplishing the conquest or be compelled to leave for other causes. Such is the prospect before us, and that in case we could do nothing more than make a passive resistance. But we can do better than this.

Among the many events calculated to terminate immediately French intervention in Mexico, the European complications which threaten to cause a general war on that continent should be particularly mentioned. It is certainly wonderful that whilst Europe is in so insecure and agitated a condition, menaced by revolutions everywhere, and wrestling to recover its own existence and independence, the French Emperor should be thinking about arranging other people's affairs, as if his own did not require his immediate and most particular attention.

The only serious support the French intervention had among the Mexicans was that afforded by the church party, which was, in fact, the promoter and supporter of the intervention. The generals of the church party have, with the aid of the French army, been conscripting Mexican citizens to make them fight with the foreign invader against their brothers and the independence of their country. The church party expected, of course, as a small compensation for the services rendered to the intervention, that as soon as the French should take the city of Mexico they would restore the church property confiscated by the national government, and the *fueros* of the clergy, of which they had been deprived. But the French have thus far failed to do this. They discovered that the church party was the weakest, and that with that party they had no chance of subduing the country. The French now wish to conciliate the liberal party by sustaining and enforcing all the important measures and laws decreed by the national government. But the liberals of Mexico are true patriots before partisans, and will not be conciliated so long as the foot of the invader is on Mexican soil. The policy of the French so incensed the church party that they broke altogether with the French. The archbishop of Mexico, who was a member of the so-called regency, withdrew at once, and was afterwards dismissed by General Bazaine. The so-called supreme tribunal protested against those measures, and shared the fate of the archbishop. All the archbishops and bishops in the republic then joined in signing a protest, in which they declared the condition of the church to be far worse than it ever was under the rule of the liberal government; that now they are not allowed even to issue their pastorals, a right never denied to them while the liberals were in power in the city of Mexico. The protest concluded by excommunicating the French government, the French army in Mexico, all Mexicans who take sides with the French, and everybody who supports the French cause in any way. These proceedings have left the French without the support of the only part of the native population they ever had in their favor, and has combined against them all the elements of the country.

I fear that I have already imposed too much upon your kindness, and, in concluding my remarks, I beg to express my earnest and sincere desire that this demonstration may be the beginning of a new era of perpetual peace and cordiality in the relations between the United States and Mexico. [Cheers.]

Mr. Romero's speech being concluded, which was also often interrupted by prolonged and enthusiastic applause, Mr. Beekman proposed the third regular toast as follows:

"GENTLEMEN: There have not been wanting people who think there are no statesmen in Mexico. Such a thing can only happen to those who are unacquainted with the history of that country. Both during her conquest, as during her independence, and more recently during her regeneration, Mexico has had distinguished heroes as well as good statesmen: Guatimotzin, Hidalgo, and Morelos, Ocampo, Lerdo, and Dogollado, are names venerated in that country. I propose, then, gentlemen, that we drink to the statesmen of the United States and Mexico, and I beg our distinguished friend, the illustrious historian of our country, that he do us the favor of responding to the toast."

We have been unable to procure any authentic memorandum of the speech of Mr. Bancroft, as we have done with the three preceding ones, and although we will inevitably be obliged to make some alterations in his words, we are sure that we are faithful in giving his ideas. Mr. BANCROFT expressed himself substantially thus:

"GENTLEMEN: Although I am not prepared to deliver an address worthy of this auditory, I cannot refrain from replying and expressing my sentiments, as I have been called to reply to the toast which our president has just proposed to the statesmen of the two neighboring sister republics. The struggle which for many long years the Mexican people have sustained against their interior tyrants has been a heroic struggle, worthy of a civilized and cultivated people, and in which the sympathies of the whole civilized world—of all the friends of political and religious liberty—ought to have been manifested in a frank and decided manner in behalf of the Mexican people, directed by the liberal party. I believe, gentlemen, that the cause of civil wars, not only in Mexico, but throughout all Spanish America, has been the clergy alone, who, when they come to acquire power in the state, always strive to overturn the government and to subordinate the temporal interests of society to their own. This attribute seems to belong principally to the Catholic clergy.

"The struggle, then, in which up to this time the patriotic Mexicans have been engaged, was a holy struggle, and the sympathy of the whole people of the United States was with them—a people who, whatever may be their religious creeds, adopts as a fundamental principle the most complete religious liberty, and the absolute independence of the church from the state.

"But now the sympathy of the United States is increased for the Mexican people, when, in addition to the facts already mentioned, we find this people struggling for their independence and nationality against a European nation, which, taking advantage of the civil strife in which we are engaged, has sought to establish before our eyes a form of government in open antagonism to our own. We cannot do less than receive this project in the same way as Europe would receive it were we to foment revolutions and establish republics on that continent.

"Thus it is that those statesmen in the United States who aid us to emerge from our present difficulties, and to restore our power and legitimate influence, and those who in Mexico not only consummate the great work of establishing religious liberty on a solid basis, but who succeed in driving from their country the foreign invader, or at least keep the sacred fire of patriotism and of resistance to the invader burning, while we disembarrass ourselves of our complications, deserve, in the highest degree, our sincere and ardent homage.

"Gentlemen, the Egyptians used to place a burning lamp at the feet of their royal corpses. On descending to the deep vaults in which the corpses were deposited, the lamp was naturally extinguished.

"Let Europe place at Maximilian's feet the weak lamp of monarchical power. It will not burn in the free atmosphere of our continent."

This speech was listened to with great attention and applauded with enthusiasm.

Mr. BEEKMAN then arose and said :

"GENTLEMEN : Mexico has had illustrious poets of whom I cannot give the eulogy they deserve, but whose memory I am desirous you should honor, remembering the names of some of them, such as Atarcon, Heredia, Gorosteza, Carpio, Calderon, and many others. I should like our illustrious and venerable friend, Mr. Bryant, as a worthy representative of the poets of our country, to respond to this toast."

This toast having been loudly applauded, Mr. BRYANT, after some allusion to the complimentary manner in which he had been called up, remarked that there were topics of greater importance on which he desired to say a few words, and proceeded thus :

"We of the United States have constituted ourselves a sort of police of this New World. Again and again have we warned off the highwaymen and burglars of the Old World who stand at the head of its governments, styling themselves conquerors. We have said to them that if they attempted to pursue their infamous profession here they did it at their peril. But now, when this police is engaged in a deadly conflict with a band of ruffians, comes this Frenchman, knocks down an undefending bystander, takes his watch and purse, strips him of his clothing, and makes off with the booty. This act of the French monarch is as base, cowardly, and unmanly as it is criminal and cruel. There is no person acquainted even in the slightest degree with the political history of the times who does not know that it would never have been perpetrated had not the United States been engaged in an expensive and bloody war within their own borders.

"There is a proverbial phrase used by lawyers, who say of a purchaser of land who does not obtain a clear and undisputed title, that he has bought a lawsuit—paid out his money for a controversy in the courts. We may say of this Maximilian of Austria, that in accepting the crown of Mexico from the hands of Napoleon, he has accepted, not an empire, but a quarrel—a present quarrel with the people of Mexico, and a prospective quarrel with the people of the United States. The rule of a branch of the Austrian family will be no less hateful to the Mexicans than that of the Austrian monarch is to the inhabitants of Venice. Its yoke will be hated because it is a foreign yoke, laid upon their necks by strangers ; it will be hated because it is imposed by violence ; it will be hated because that violence was accompanied by fraud ; for never was there a more shallow and transparent deception than that of the convocation of notables, from whom Napoleon pretended to receive the supreme dominion over Mexico.

"Then, as to the relations of this new emperor with the United States, does any one suppose that they can possibly be amicable? Does any one suppose that, after our civil war is ended, as it soon will be, the numerous class whom it has trained to adventure, and made fond of a military life, will all remain quietly at home when the cause of liberty and independence in Mexico demands their aid? Does any man doubt that, whatever may be the course taken by our government, they will cross the Mexican frontier by thousands, to take part in favor of the people of that country? The party of liberty in Mexico will then have its auxiliaries close at hand, in a contiguous region, while the succors which the despot will need to protect his usurped dominion will be far away beyond the Atlantic.

"Yet I wonder not that Maximilian should covet the possession of so noble a principality as Mexico, provided he were allowed to govern it in peace. I remember that, a few years since, in making a voyage to Europe in one of our steamers, there was a passenger on board to whom we gave the name of the Knight of the 'Woful Countenance.' He was a thin, dark man, dressed in black, with a very broad-brimmed hat, long features, and a most sorrowful aspect. I learned that he was a Mexican, and entered into conversation with him. He described the natural advantages and resources of his country with much of that eloquence which I believe is the natural inheritance of the Latin race. He spoke of its mountains, pregnant with ores of the precious and useful metals ; its vast plains and valleys of exhaustless fertility ; its variety of climates—in some regions possessing the temperature of perpetual spring, in which were reared all the productions of the temperate zone, and in the other places basking under a torrid sun, which ripens all the fruits of the tropics to their most perfect maturity. Yet these rich mines were unwrought, these fertile fields untilled, these regions with the climate of Paradise thinly peopled by a race without enterprise, almost without arts, and living almost from hand to mouth. This unhappy state of the country he attributed to the want of a permanent, enlightened, and liberal government, which, while maintaining peace and order, and securing to every man his individual rights as a freeman, left open every path of lawful enterprise.

"We thought that we saw the dawn of this era of enlightened government in the administration of Juarez. That dawn has been overcast by the clouds of a tempest wafted hither from Europe. May the darkness which has gathered over it be of short continuance; may these clouds be soon dispelled by the sunshine of liberty and peace, and Mexico, assured in her independence, take the high place which belongs to her in the family of nations"

After the termination of this interesting speech, which, like the others, was repeatedly interrupted by prolonged applause,

Mr. BEEKMAN, rising again, said:

"GENTLEMEN: There is now among us a distinguished lawyer of Mexico, whose knowledge, probity and patriotism are acknowledged and duly appreciated in that city, the dwelling-place of so many men of culture and privileged minds. This lawyer is Señor Don Ignacio Mariscal, secretary of the Mexican legation, and one of our guests. I propose, gentlemen, that we drink his health, as well as that of his fellow lawyers of Mexico."

The preceding toast was received by acclamations and great enthusiasm, after which Mr. Mariscal said:

"GENTLEMEN: I never was more sorry than now for not having the control of your expressive language, that I might give a full utterance to my sentiments. Yet I cannot help saying a few words to thank you very warmly for the kind and splendid manner in which you are complimenting the representative of my country, as well as for the enthusiastic allusions you have made and applauded in honor of its leading patriots and distinguished men. Finally, gentlemen, the toast you have just dedicated to me, and the too benevolent terms in which it was proposed, are things which I am not able to be thankful for in a sufficient way. I am perfectly aware that the general feeling of the people of the United States is most favorable to Mexico in her present struggle to resist conquest. But when I see that feeling shared by such prominent and enlightened citizens as you are, gentlemen, I consider it is not a blind sentiment, but rather a conviction, a deep sense of right and justice, as well as the knowledge of a danger common to both republics. I cherish the idea that while this unanimous sympathy for Mexico exists, my country will not be subjugated for a long time by the brutal force of a European army. The day will soon come, I trust, in which the sympathies of this great people will be no longer disregarded by any power in the world. You know, better than I do, which are the clouds now darkening your political horizon and preventing the break of that promising day. May they be soon dispelled! The sun of America will then shine triumphant upon the end of your national disturbances and the direful sufferings of Mexico."

These remarks were much applauded and approved by demonstrations of assent.

The PRESIDENT then said:

"GENTLEMEN: We have drank to the President of Mexico, to the statesmen, poets, and lawyers of that republic: it is now time we should devote a toast to Mexican diplomats. Among them you will find an illustrious citizen who now occupies an elevated position in the army of his country. His name as a general and a diplomat is well known in Europe. It is General Don José Lopez Uraga, who, not long ago, represented his country at Berlin. I hope, gentlemen, that a toast for General Uraga will be well received, and I beg our distinguished friend, who formerly represented our country at the Hague, will respond in the name of the diplomatic corps."

This toast, like the rest, was well received, all those present partaking of the same; after which Mr. Folsom expressed himself substantially as follows, it being impossible for us to obtain from the orator any notes:

"SIR: Being at this moment invited to speak to this toast, and without preparation of any kind, it will be difficult for me to say anything worthy of my hearers. Nevertheless, although without regularity or good order, I will say a few words, for I cannot do less than accede to the request of our worthy president, Mr. Beekman—a gentleman who is worthy of all my appreciation from his antecedents in the senate of New York, as the representative of our rich and powerful city. I have always been attached to the beautiful Castilian language—to that language so robust and manly, yet so soft and insinuating, which is capable of the highest flights of eloquence, as well as of the sweetest sentiments of love. Its study has occupied a part of my life, and I declare that it would have been difficult for me to have found a more delightful task. This love of the Spanish language could not but extend to the generous people who speak it, and more especially to the people of Spanish America, among whom Mexico occupies the first place, for its extent, resources, the beauty of its climate, the fertility of the soil, and, above all, from the very essential circumstance of being our neighbor, and having, since her emancipation, adopted republican institutions similar to those which have made our happiness. Guided by these sentiments, I undertook years ago a translation of the letters which Hernan Cortez addressed to the Emperor Charles the Fifth, giving an account of the conquest of New Spain—letters which contain very important historical data, and which were then entirely unknown to us until Mr. Prescott, our immortal historian, published his history of the conquest of Mexico. I say all this that it may be seen that my sympathy for the affairs of Mexico is of long standing. And is it possible that it could cease to exist now that her sons are gloriously fighting to preserve an independence which it cost them so many sacrifices to achieve? No; certainly no. It exists in me now more actively than ever, as it does in the heart of every true American; for on this point, as some of the gentlemen have already well said, the opinion of our people is unanimous. Every one knows that on the Mexican soil a struggle is going on for a principle left us as an inheritance by one of our great statesmen, and without whose strict observance our institutions and political institutions run great danger. I wish, then, that Mexico will sustain, without rest, the struggle to which she has been so unjustly provoked, and I do not fear that I deceive myself in saying, in the name of the American people, that, as soon as our civil war is ended, our aid to Mexico will not be limited to barren sympathy."

The applause which followed this speech being ended, Mr. BEEKMAN arose and said:

"GENTLEMEN: I have the pleasure to present to you Dr. Navarro, one of our guests, and chief of the medical staff of the Mexican army during the heroical defence of the city of Puebla, when attacked by the French. At the end of the siege, Dr. Navarro delivered up all the French wounded who had been amputated and attended to by him in the best possible condition, and offering every hope of a complete cure, many of them being already in a convalescent state, as was fully testified by the surgeon in chief of the besieging army. At most none of those amputated had died, whilst at the French camp nearly every amputation made upon either French or Mexican had had an unfavorable result. Judge, then, gentlemen, of the skill of Dr. Navarro in his difficult art by that fact; and when you know that those services were given by him, on the occasion to which I allude, entirely gratis, and guided only by his patriotic feelings, you will be pleased to drink to his honor."

The toast was received with enthusiasm, and Dr. Navarro was saluted with cheers. Dr. PARKER being called upon by the president to respond, he expressed himself more or less as follows:

"GENTLEMEN: Dr. Navarro does not only deserve our consideration as a distinguished surgeon and professor of medical science, but he is still more worthy of our appreciation and our homage as a man loyal to his country—as a true patriot. I will add an important fact to what the president said, which will doubtless attract your attention. When the general-in-chief of the French army was persuaded of the ability and skill of Dr. Navarro, and of the kindness and attention he had shown to the wounded Frenchmen, he made various offers of the most advantageous kind, through trustworthy sources, to transfer his services to the medical corps of the expeditionary army, fixing himself the remuneration and advantages which he should enjoy. Then, gentlemen, Dr. Navarro, like a true member of my profession—like a loyal son of Hippocrates—energetically repelled these seductive offers. I cannot help but remember in connexion with this act the sublime action of the venerable father of medicine, who, when solicited, implored, by the conqueror Alexander to give him his services in exchange for immense treasures, replied with sublime abnegation: 'My talent, my art, my existence, all belong to Greece, and never can they be employed against my country.' Such, gentlemen, was the conduct of Dr. Navarro under circumstances analogous to those of Hippocrates. We offer him, then, the homage which he deserves; and in doing so we do not forget that in his country they are now contending, as in Greece in former days, with an invader who is aided in nothing except force and treason to carry out his ominous intentions. We hope, however, that the sons of Mexico, each one, and in the place belonging to him, will imitate the patriotism and undoubted loyalty of Dr. Navarro. [Applause.] In this way there is no doubt that that republic, our sister, will be saved from the crisis which now threatens her, and, animated by our sympathies, will succeed in carrying forward her interests and safety to the success her immense elements demand for her.

The president then announced that Dr. NAVARRO was about to speak. He spoke as follows:

"GENTLEMEN: I regret very much that my slight knowledge of your beautiful language does not permit me to duly express my feelings. I feel the greatest satisfaction in being a witness to the ardent sympathy manifested towards my dear country by persons of such a high social position and so respected for their scientific and literary knowledge. I have no words to express my gratitude for the toast and for the kind allusions which you have been pleased to make concerning me. Mexico, in defending her independence, has been struggling for a long time past with one of the most powerful monarchs of Europe, and she will struggle year after year, proving in this way the patriotic sentiments of her sons, and that she is worthy of that sympathy which all over the world every friend of justice and right share with you in extending towards her. Please to receive, gentlemen, my most sincere prayers for the ending of your civil war—of the bloody struggle which has shaken this great republic and given to European tyrants the opportunity of audaciously treading on the American continent—this sacred ground on which liberty only reigns, and in which thrones are but the sorrowful remembrances of times which will never return again. The time will come, and perhaps it is not very far off, when we shall see our republic free of all foreign intervention and your glorious Union happily restored—being once more, as it always has been, the astonishment of the civilized world and the fear of the despots of the Old World."

His discourse being loudly applauded, Mr. BEEKMAN then said;

"GENTLEMAN: There is among our invited guests a gentleman, who, having done commercial business for some years in the city of Philadelphia, we will consider as the Mexican representative of that hardworking and intelligent profession. This gentleman is Señor Fernando de la Cuesta, a member of the Mexican legation, who is at present here, and whom, I hope, we will have the pleasure of hearing to-night. I request of our friend, the ex-mayor of this city, who represents New York commerce, that he will be pleased to respond to this toast, after which I promise myself that Señor Cuesta will favor us with a speech."

Mr. OPDYKE said:

"GENTLEMEN: In the name of the merchants of this city, to whose society I have the honor to belong, and of the city itself, whose mandate and representative I had the honor to be for the last two years, although it is no longer permitted me to speak officially in its name, I have the pleasure of expressing my profound sympathy for the cause which the people of the neighboring republic are sustaining against European invasion. My attention could not but have been most strongly called to the fact which our distinguished guest referred to concerning what M. Thiers said in the corps legislatif of France on the manner in which, in his judgment, the Archduke Maximilian would be received in this city. So far would we be from making him demonstrations of regard and sympathy that, as you know, and I think it right to remark on this occasion, we have made such demonstrations precisely to those powers that are least the friends of France. When the Russian squadron arrived at this port the whole city, as you will remember, received it with enthusiasm, and the most distinguished members of our society gave it welcome and honored it, as it was right to do with the noble sailors of a great nation, which has given us so many proofs of sympathy and consideration under circumstances the most difficult that our country has ever passed through, and which, far from desiring to draw any advantage whatever from our misfortunes, magnanimously desires their speedy termination. When latterly a French squadron arrived at our port there were not wanting those who would desire that similar demonstrations to those offered to the Russians should be made to the French. I, as chief magistrate of the city, opposed myself to any such act, and, in proceeding thus, I am sure of it, and you know it well, I was only the faithful interpreter of the will and desire of the city which honored me with its confidence. If, during the time in which I was mayor, the Archduke Maximilian should have passed through here, and if there had been any one who would pretend to offer him a public demonstration of sympathy, I would not have permitted it; and I believe that no citizen who has self-respect will permit it if, by accident, Napoleon should think of sending him through here to try the sentiments of the people of the United States in reference to the enterprise which he is endeavoring to carry out in the Mexican republic. The sentiment of all our classes and all our parties is only one in this matter, as has been said with much justice. It is, then, entirely hostile to any armed intervention of Europe on this continent, and more especially to that which seeks to overthrow a republic to erect a monarchy."

After the applause brought forth by the preceding speech, Mr. DE LA CUESTA said:

"GENTLEMEN: It would be superfluous, perhaps presumptuous in me, to add one more word to what has been already said; yet I cannot help tendering you my most sincere and heartfelt thanks for the beautiful manner in which you have been pleased to express your good wishes and warm sympathy for the land where I first saw the light and breathed the sweet air of life. As the last draught of water to the camel in the desert cheers and comforts him through the dreary path that lies before him, so will the remembrance of this night cheer and comfort me, whatever may be my path in life, to sustain the liberty, independence, and integrity of our national soil. I cannot answer better the allusion made by the gentleman who so worthily occupies the chair as to my representing the commerce of Mexico, having once followed its pursuits, than by proposing the following toast:

"*The city of New York*—first in sciences, arts, commerce, wealth; in fact, in all. First, also, let me add, in extending to us her noble sympathies for our holy cause. May she always prosper as she has hitherto prospered; and may she not only be the metropolis of the United States, but the metropolis of the whole world."

This toast was saluted with loud applause.

Mr. BEEKMAN then said:

"GENTLEMEN: There has been in Mexico great advancement in the fine arts. A proof of this we find in the San Carlos Academy, where painters and sculptors of undeniable merit have been educated. We find a proof, also, in the paintings of Cabrera, Cordero, Mata and several others, as well as in the admirable buildings constructed by such Mexican architects as Tolsa, to whom Mexico owes her mining college. I propose a toast to Mexican fine arts, and let us hear what our learned friend Mr. Sturges will say about this."

This toast having renewed great applause, Mr. STURGES said:

"Mr. CHAIRMAN: I am taken quite by surprise in being called upon by you to respond to your allusion to the fine arts and architecture of Mexico. On some other occasion I should be most happy to speak upon such a theme; at present I prefer to speak a few words of encouragement to our distinguished guest, in the hope that his noble country may soon be free from her foreign and domestic enemies. When that is accomplished, we shall see everything that is beautiful, noble, and useful springing to life with new vigor, and that glorious country will become all that God intended she should be. We know what it is, sir, to have foreign and domestic enemies, although we have no foreign enemy on our soil. It is not from any love which the enemy of Mexico bears us that his armies are not in Texas and Louisiana. It is the fear of his own people that restrains him. I have the word of a French gentleman 'who knows whereof he speaks' to support this statement. He said to me, 'Rest assured, sir, the Emperor will withdraw from Mexico the moment he can do so with any kind of credit to himself. The French people are against him in his Mexican movement, as they are against any interference in your affairs.' I do not think, sir, that our honored guest can have failed to discover that the determination is as firmly fixed in the hearts of our people that no foreign government shall be established in Mexico, as it is that no separation shall take place between the States of this Union. Our own affairs settled, and it would not be sixty days before our armies would be in Mexico if her people desired it. My prayer to God is that she may hold out until we are ready for this. I respond most fully to the closing sentiment of my honorable friend, Mr. Bancroft: 'Let the Austrian lamp burn in the grave of Austria; it will not burn in the free atmosphere of America.'"

After this, Mr. BEEKMAN spoke as follows:

GENTLEMEN: Mexico too has had her illustrious governors, who have advanced the people over whom they have commanded, and who are well worthy of our homage. The actual President of the republic, before reaching that high position, was governor of the state of Oaxaca, and during the eight years that his administration lasted he accomplished so much good, and developed so well the resources of that rich state, that he succeeded in placing it in the first rank of the various states composing the Mexican confederation. General Doblado is another model governor, whose beneficent administration, even during a period of terrible intestine commotions, caused the state of Guanajuato to prosper to such a degree that it has been the astonishment of the other Mexican states. Let us drink, then, gentlemen, to the governors of Mexico, and we hope that our illustrious friend, who formerly was governor of this state, will be pleased to answer to this toast.

The toast having been received with general approbation, Mr. Washington Hunt responded to it in a lengthy speech, which we cannot give here, trusting to memory alone, for fear of not doing justice to it. With the object that there should be the greatest accuracy possible in the report of the speeches we have made, Mr. Romero requested the gentlemen who had delivered them to give him a memorandum, as far as they could recollect, of what they had said. Mr. Hunt, in reply, wrote the following letter:

ALBEMARLE HOTEL, NEW YORK, *March* 31, 1864.

DEAR SIR: It would afford me pleasure to comply with the request contained in your note of yesterday, but as my remarks were desultory and unprepared, instead of attempting an accurate sketch, I will confine myself to two leading points, which I deem of the most essential import at the present juncture.

1. I intended to utter an earnest and emphatic protest against the French invasion of Mexico, and the audacious efforts to overthrow the republic and erect upon its ruins a monarchy, to be upheld by a foreign force, acting in conjunction with a small faction of domestic traitors. I denounced it as a wanton offence against republican liberty and the independence of nations.

2. I intended to express the opinion that the United States will not permit, for any long period, the armed occupation of Mexico by a foreign power.

Our domestic conflict will terminate in the re-establishment of the national authority over all the States of the Union. The attainment of this result is not, I trust, very far distant.

Then the people of this country will manifest their sympathy for the people of Mexico in active and efficient co-operation, and if need be they will rally to your aid in a resolute and manly struggle for the recovery of your national liberty and independence.

The time approaches when our government will reassert and maintain its well-defined policy, which is, that no European power shall be allowed to subjugate the people or destroy republican institutions on any part of the American continent.

I remain, with great respect, your obedient servant,

WASHINGTON HUNT.

Hon. MATIAS ROMERO, *&c.*, *&c.*, *&c.*

Mr. BEEKMAN then said: "Gentlemen, you must know that in Mexico there have not been wanting historians of great merit. The names of Mora, Zavala, and Bustamente must be familiar to some of you. We will drink, then, to the historians of Mexico, and we hope that our illustrious friend, the president of the New York Historical Society, will say a few words on this matter."

Mr. De PEYSTER, rising, said: "I yield, sir, to your request, merely in the private character I am here this evening. I came to express, by my presence, the sympathy which I feel towards a sister republic, torn by intestine strife, brought upon her by a party that should have soothed, not inflicted, a national wound. I am reminded of the sad position of Mexico by the like sad realities which press upon my country. I know full well what would be the intensity of my feelings were my native land invaded by foreign bayonets, to compel her to change her free government for one obnoxious to her people. I came here with a further view, to testify towards our distinguished guest my deep interest in the cause which he represents—not by words—for I came to listen, not to speak; and therefore took no thought with reference to the latter.

"But, Mr. Chairman, being up, I have ideas furnished by the suggestive remarks just made by Señor Romero. I well remember the *points* presented by him in December last in a speech made on an occasion similar to the present. He considered the church party in Mexico as the direct cause of the civil war there, as slavery is of the rebellion here. He alleged that this church party sought foreign intervention to re-establish its power, as the slave power here sought the like intervention, in order to build up a confederacy based on the perpetual sacrifice of certain human rights, and designed to be destructive of our national sovereignty.

"Thus far, this parallel between the United States and Mexico truly extends. But, sir, there is a difference in the analogy of these cases not to be overlooked. Were foreign intervention to take here the course it has pursued in Mexico, the result in this country would be as a tornado is to the storm now sweeping over our land. England and France know this! It is not their good will that stays their further interference, but the danger of the risk from the blows which a free people, aroused to do their utmost at any sacrifice, could and would inflict in return.

"Educated in the school of democracy, I have, sir, adhered to the principles learned there. When our civil war broke out, I had doubts, on constitutional grounds, regarding the rights of slave-owners. But when I observed how slaves were made instruments to defend freemen striving to preserve the Union, I deemed, in a military point of view, that it was indispensable to strike from the hands of rebels their main prop; and all my constitutional scruples vanished before this military necessity. I believe, sir, all loyal men—loyal without mental reservations—deem it right to remove any obstacle for the preservation of the Union! Therefore, I have no affinity with traitors, either south or in disguise among us, who keep 'the promise to the ear;' or with 'peace democrats,'' in my judgment more alive to party interest than to our national struggle.

"What, sir, is the result thus far in *our* civil war? Why, as slavery proved itself to have been the source of all our evils, loyal men gave it its death blow. Like all monsters of great strength, determined purpose, and defiant resistance, it will die hard; but despite its struggles, die it will.

"Now, from our conflict let me for a few moments turn to our sister republic and to her accumulated ills, and contrast her purposes with our own. Mexico, with a fertile soil, genial climate, and unbounded mineral wealth, is divided into various conflicting parties. Her church party is the predominant class, intent in maintaining its present influence and recovering its lost power. There are the patriots, struggling for the government of their choice; and, if I am rightly informed, there is a class, influenced by the ecclesiastics, either hostile to or indifferent towards the present republican form of government. It is said that the church party now wavers in their appreciation of French intervention. If this be so, and Mexicans would unitedly rally as the people of our loyal States have rallied, the ills which Mexico is now experiencing would be in the condition of the monster evil that we have mortally wounded. The form of domestic treason in Mexico we know. The motives of the French Emperor are too patent to be disguised. Señor Romero has thrown ample light on both these subjects.

"Whether a recently published mention of a leave-taking between the Emperor and his Austrian *protegé* be true, or a *jeu d'esprit*, it is suggestive of probable ground of belief. 'You go,' said the former, 'to embrace a rock of silver'—a figure of speech which symbolized the mineral wealth, of which bars of silver and Mexican dollars had proved to be in Europe the best of advertisements.

"The church party in Mexico had long suffered under a disease of very great prevalence at all times and everywhere. The Emperor caught it through this party contact, and he gave it to his Austrian favorite. This disease in ancient Rome was called *auri sacra fames*. There, where the central word (*sacra*) was connected with offering to the infernal deities, or with impious or unholy purposes, it meant the reverse of its proper definition—namely, *accursed*. The tripartite association just alluded to, under the hallucination created by this disease, have this 'accursed desire of wealth,' and think to overthrow the Mexican republic, to build up in its stead a monarchy, and thus possess this 'rock of silver.'

"Sir, the snake is the emblem of evil. We took the reptile up when feeble and warmed it in the national bosom. When it gained strength it turned and stung us. It has its reward. If Mexicans will rally round their national standard, and imitate the gallant bird on their national arms, who has in his beak a malignant snake, and with his determined courage and undaunted decision extinguish, like him, the reptile's ability to do further mischief, all will yet go well in their beautiful land. In due season our rebels will have to 'succumb' to the loyal will. Then the republics of North America will shake hands in brotherly sentiment and alliance, and unitedly maintain, inviolate, 'the Monroe doctrine.'

The chairman then said: "We have among us, gentlemen, a very distinguished gentleman from Brooklyn—that sister and neighbor of ours. We would like to hear what, in her name, he will tell us in relation to a matter that has been the theme of so many speakers."

Mr. Henry E. Pierrepont then spoke, and in short and eloquent phrases said that he was sure that the feelings of the citizens of Brooklyn, with respect to the French policy in Mexico, were identical with those of the citizens of New York and of the entire country; that on that account, and fearing to tire the audience, he would not speak at length on the subject. He concluded by showing that the people of all classes and parties in the United States sympathized greatly with those Mexicans who were resisting the French invasion, and saying that he would act according to that feeling on the first opportunity offered to him.

The president again arose and solicited Mr. Clift, in the name of the lawyers of New York, to express his feelings.

Mr. CLIFT said that his voice being hoarse on account of a cold, he could only say a few words. That he, as well as all of his profession, and the entire American people, sympathized greatly with the holy cause that the Mexican people were defending at present. That he had the firm conviction that the Mexicans alone would conquer their European invaders; and in case of this not happening, they should have the powerful help of this nation, which never will allow the establishment of a European monarchy on the American continent. And lastly, that he coincided in the opinions of the distinguished persons who had preceded him, and especially with those of the venerable Mr. Bryant.

The president said that, according to his views, all the persons there present would have great pleasure in hearing some words from Mr. Charles A. Bristed, who, rising, said: "Once upon a time the Saracens—then a mighty people—took it into their heads that it would be a nice thing to conquer Old Spain, and they did conquer Spain so effectually that it took eight hundred years to drive them out. But they were driven out, and none of them are there at this day. I believe that, in like manner, the French will be driven out of Mexico, if it takes eight hundred years to do so."

A gentleman exclaimed, "We do things faster now-a-days. Say eight years."

The chairman, pointing to Mr. Dodge, said: "I think that our young and esteemed friend will have something to tell us, in the name of Young America, which he so well represents."

Mr. DODGE spoke as follows: "As perhaps the youngest, Mr. Chairman, who has been honored by an invitation on this most interesting and delightful occasion, it is my right and privilege to speak for that large and influential class in our country known as 'Young America.' and I can assure our honored guest that the full and entire sympathy of the young men of the land is with him and with his oppressed country. The tread of a French invasion on this continent is to them a direct insult; and were our own sad war over, I believe there is not a town, or village, or hamlet, where a full company would not spring to arms to aid our sister republic in her glorious struggle. I give, sir, as a sentiment, in which I know all will heartily join—The Monroe doctrine; Americans can never allow the heel of European despotism to place its imprint upon the soil of our western continent."

This toast was loudly applauded, after which Mr. Beekman proposed one in honor of the committee of stewards who had so splendidly discharged their duties, begging Mr. Hamersley to speak in behalf of the committee.

This toast was much applauded, and three cheers were given for the stewards.

Mr. JOHN W. HAMERSLEY, in the name of the stewards, (himself, Mr. Astor, and Mr. Cliros,) said:

"Sir, it is hardly fair to call on us while your hearts are beating with fervid thoughts, and your ears ringing with burning words. Had this toast been on the programme, one of my coadjutors would have prepared an address worthy of the compliment and the occasion. This committee, sir, was not chosen for their gifts of utterance, but for those humbler tastes which only lend a grace to eloquence. Our duties are æsthetic, industrial, and artistic. We have compassed the ends of the earth, the depths of the sea. We have levied contributions on the four winds of heaven, to cluster here all that can tempt the appetite or fascinate the ear and eye, and we fancied our mission accomplished. However, there is the post prandial law, the despotism of the wine cup, to which we owe allegiance—the only despotism, sir, which the descendants of the Huguenots or pilgrim fathers will ever tolerate on the continent of North America. We are here, sir, in menace to none, but firmly and respectfully in the majesty of manhood and in consciousness of power to reassert a principle imbibed with our mother's milk, a household word, a dogma of American faith; but while we cordially grasp the hand of a sister republic in the darkest hour of her trial, that grasp has due emphasis and significance. With her, sir, we have kindred traditions. Each of us has hewn an empire from the wilderness; each of us has expelled the oppressor; and both of us, with tattered banners drenched in the gore of hero martyrs, are now appealing from treachery to the God of Battles. We have a common future; for who can doubt that our successes, (and the death knell of treason has already rung)—who can doubt that the triumph of our arms will be the signal for the eagles of Austerlitz 'to change their base' from the pyramids of Puebla for their perch on the towers of Notre Dame? Permit me here, sir, to express a hope, suggested by the *season*, (God grant it may be a prophecy,) that the Easter chimes of Mexico of the coming year, with the glad tidings of a Saviour risen, shall peal from sierra to sierra, from ocean to ocean, with the glad tidings of a nation risen, a nation born again. (Cheers.)

"Sir, I would offer a toast seldom forgotten in this Eden of women. It is wise to fling the garland of chivalry over the stern realities of life, nay, over the carnage of the battle-field. It is graceful in our honored guests to seek in the bright eyes and warm hearts of those they love, in their sunset home, a solace for hope deferred. It is meet in us all, revelling amid these symbols of hope and joy, of passion and power, our twin standards nestling in each other's folds in sweet communion of the starried past and gushing hopes, (these roses and violets breathing incense to the throne of grace, their Easter hymn of thanks and praise,) to remember who it is that scatters these jewels of Paradise over our thorny path, who it is that smoothes the pillow of affliction. And when our statesman soldier shall send these our greetings to his fatherland, let him say that these are sons of sires who wielded the destinies of our country, whose names are carved on her escutcheon, like the name of Phidias on the shield of Minerva. Here are her merchant princes, whose argosies girdle the globe; here are her gifted men, whose thoughts touch the hearts or nerve the souls of the nomad in his desert and the prince upon his throne. Say, sir, that here is our western lark, who lends to devotion the muses' wings. Say, sir, that the author of 'Thanatopsis,' and these sons, worthy of their sires, send a brother's blessing to sisters bowed in grief. Fire their souls with the thrilling words of the Spartan matron giving a shield to her son: 'Return with this or upon this.' Tell them of the mother of the Gracchi, whose only jewels were her sons. Tell them of the death dirge of our red man, with 'back to the field and feet to the foe.' Tell them that the spirit of your own Guatimozin hovers around your war-path, and exhort, nay, adjure them to swear their brothers over the fresh graves of their comrades never to bury the tomahawk while the iron heel of Europe treads your soil. Sir, it is fitting, while the accents of sweet music recall tender and happy memories, (man imaged by that armed cactus, woman by that graceful palm,) it is holy to consecrate the hour to her who was last at the cross and first at the sepulchre. Sir, I propose a toast, to which your heart's pulse will echo:

"THE DAUGHTERS OF MEXICO—Fair as her sons are brave."

After the very enthusiastic and prolonged applause which Mr. Hamersley's beautiful toast brought forth, the chairman said that the audience were anxious to hear the other member of the committee of stewards then present, (Mr. CLIROS,) who, after having remarked that he had not at all been prepared to speak, said as follows:

"MR. PRESIDENT AND GENTLEMEN: Enough has been said in the speeches already made this evening to indicate most conclusively the sympathy which prevails in our midst in behalf of our sister republic, all of which I heartily indorse. The unanimous and vociferous voices show unhesitatingly the determination to oppose all encroachments of foreign powers upon any portion of this continent. Mexico, in her present struggle, needs assistance, and soon we shall be in a position to afford it. The principles of republican rule are so strongly imbedded in the minds of the people of both Mexico and America as to secure, for all time, that as the mode of government, and to cause both countries to stand in sympathy by each other."

These remarks were received with applause. It was 12 o'clock, and the enthusiasm of that interesting party had not diminished. At that time the audience took leave of Señor Romero and the Mexican gentlemen who accompanied him, expressing in earnest words the sincerity of their sentiments in favor of Mexico.

Thus ended this demonstration made by persons who undoubtedly represent the most select portion of society in this country, whilst at almost the same time the real representatives of the people, that is to say, the House of Representatives itself declared "unanimously" that the United States would never consent to the establishment of a monarchy which would arise, under the auspices of Europe, upon the ruins of a republic on the American continent.

After all this, can Maximilian ever sit quietly upon the Mexican throne, when he beholds at his feet a precipice? Can he enjoy the possession of his imperial crown, when it can only be a crown of thorns? A sad reign, indeed, awaits him; nay, more than sad, it will be but transient.

MENU.

Le mardi 29 *Mars*, 1864.

—

HUITRES.

....

POTAGES.

A la Salvator. Consommé de volaille.

HORS D'ŒUVRES.

Variés. Variés. Boudins de gibier á la Richelieu.

RELEVÉS.

Saumon de Kennebeck á la Régence. Aloses, sauce béarnaise. Filet de bœuf á l'Andalouse.

ENTRÉES.

Chapons á la Périgord. Trimbale á la Parisienne. Salmi de bécassines aux truffes. Paté de foie gras en bellevue. Chaufroid de pluviers.

SORBET.

Cardinal au vin du Rhin.

ROTIS.

Paons truffes. Canvas-back ducks.

ENTREMETS.

Petits poits. Flageolets. Artichauts farcis. Asperges.

ENTREMETS SUCRÉS.

Trimbale á la don Bazan. Pouding á la Dalbertos. Gelée muscat. Patzo di Borgo, Pain de fraise aguado. Gateau portugais. Biscuit d'Espagne. Charlotte Doria. Piéces mexicaines. Sultane aux marrons. Bombo Spongada. Napolitaine.

FRUITS ET DESSERT.

DELMONICO.

Mr. Seward to Mr. Romero.

DEPARTMENT OF STATE,
Washington, June 2, 1864.

SIR: I have the honor to acknowledge the receipt of your note of the 28th ultimo, covering a translation into the English language of the documents previously enclosed to me in your unofficial note of the 26th ultimo.

I avail, &c.

WILLIAM H. SEWARD.

Señor M. ROMERO, *&c., &c., &c.*

Mr. Romero to Mr. Seward.

[Translation.]

MEXICAN LEGATION OF THE UNITED STATES OF AMERICA,
Washington, May 31, 1864.

Mr. SECRETARY: I have the honor to transmit to you, for the information of the government of the United States, extracts of two discussions, translated into English, relating to the affairs of Mexico, which took place about the middle of the month ending this day, in the legislative assembly of Paris, in relation to the budget of the French empire. The first extract, which is translated from No. 132 of "Le Moniteur Universel," of Paris, (page 164,) under date of the 11th of May referred to, contains the portion of the speech which the deputy, Mr. Berryer, made during the session of the 10th, in reference to the resources which the French government expects to obtain from what it terms "the Mexican indemnity." From this speech it appears that the loan which the Archduke Ferdinand Maximilian of Austria, now called the Emperor of Mexico, has attempted to negotiate in Europe, would yield him, supposing the whole amount of it were negotiated, the sum of one hundred and twenty millions of francs, so that the pecuniary responsibilities which he has accepted thus far would compel him to disburse the sum of one hundred and twenty-five millions of francs. From this alone, it can readily be seen that, even should the Archduke Maximilian meet with no other difficulties in the Mexican republic than the pecuniary ones, he would find himself unable to establish, and even still more so to consolidate, the monarchical government which the Emperor of the French has sent him to set up on this continent.

The pecuniary responsibilities which the Emperor of the French has caused the said archduke to accept, and the amounts which he would have to pay for the support of an army and navy required to keep some of our cities subject to his control, and to blockade some of our ports, cannot be less than from forty to fifty millions of dollars per annum; while all the resources of the Mexican republic, supposing that he could control them all, cannot produce, under the present circumstances, more than fifteen millions of dollars.

The second extract, among those enclosed, contains those passages referring to Mexico, in the speeches delivered in the same assembly during the session of the 12th of May, by the deputy, Mr. Jules Favre, and the minister of state, Mr. Rouher.

In the first of these speeches you will find very judicious reflections upon the versatility and deep cunning of the policy adopted by the Emperor Napoleon in reference to my country.

In the second, will be noted, besides the arguments already known, and which are founded upon the misrepresentation of facts, artfully prepared and sustained by all the imperial agents, sundry allusions to the policy of the United States, and a circular from the department for foreign affairs addressed to the French diplomatic agents, which was read by Mr. Rouker, and in which an account is given of the interview between Mr. Dayton and Mr. Drouyn de l'Huys, respecting the resolution adopted by the House of Representatives of the United States, on the 4th of April last, in reference to the French intervention in Mexico, in a manner somewhat different from that given to you by Mr. Dayton himself, as appears from the correspondence recently sent by the President to the House of Representatives, on this subject.

I therefore omit the remarks to which these speeches give rise, because they cannot escape the observation of the government of the United States.

These last-mentioned speeches are taken from the No. 134, of the "Moniteur Universel," (pages 669 and 670,) dated the 13th of the said month of May.

I avail myself of this opportunity to renew to you, sir, the assurances of my most distinguished consideration.

M. ROMERO.

Hon. WILLIAM H. SEWARD, &c., &c., &c.

CORPS LEGISLATIF.

SESSION OF TUESDAY, *May* 10, 1864.

M. DE MORNY, president, in the chair.

After the reading of the journal and some preliminary proceedings, the discussion of the budget was resumed, and M. BERRYER addressed the body. The part of his speech relating to Mexican affairs was as follows:

M. BERRYER. * * * * The second resource will give us an occasion for more sad and more pointed observations. This second resource is the Mexican indemnity.

What is the state of things in this respect? We have regulated the indemnity for the war—for the war which really began in a costly manner only from the time of the departure of General Forey, if I am not mistaken, in the commencement of 1862. For two years past we have fixed the indemnity due by Mexico at a sum of two hundred and seventy millions. That is the figure set down in the convention.

Two hundred and seventy millions! Pardon me if I insist upon an assertion which I believe I did not make without due consideration, at the beginning of this year, when I said that the annual expense of our Mexican expedition could be estimated for 1864, as for the other years, at one hundred and fifty millions. Now we are told, "See, we have reached only two hundred and seventy millions."

You have made an estimate on terms extremely favorable to the government which you have established in Mexico; you have made an estimate of two hundred and seventy millions. That, for two years, is very near the sum of three hundred millions, to which I foresaw the expenses would amount—a sum to which I believe they have in fact amounted. We shall see afterwards.

However that may be, we have fixed our indemnity at two hundred and seventy millions. Out of these two hundred and seventy millions a loan has been contracted for and a creation of *rentes* decided on. By a decree issued at Miramar, on the 11th of Apr'l last, two sections of rente have been established; one of twelve millions for the wants of the new government at Mexico, and one of six million six hundred thousand francs on account of the two hundred and seventy millions due to France as an indemnity for the war; that is to say, we are assured of a sum of sixty or sixty-six millions.

Such is one of the provisions of the decree. A loan is effected; the negotiators of the loan are the English firm of Glynn & Company. I know not who has entered to participate in their enterprise, in their speculation, or at least into the commission which they receive. The negotiators announce to the public that they are going to borrow eighteen million six hundred thousand livres of rente. Pardon me, and attribute it only to the too intimate knowledge which I have of the jurisprudence of the courts that decide on the means of raising an imaginary credit; pardon me if my experience exerts too great an influence upon the estimate which I make of the manner in which the Mexican loan has been announced. I have here in my hand the prospectus of the negotiators. It announces an English and French loan. What does that mean? Has England, has France, borrowed? That England and France should contribute to the loan which is made for Mexico I can understand; and we will presently see to what extent. But such an announcement would seem to indicate to unreflecting minds that England and France are to a certain extent guarantors of the loan which is about to be issued.

This loan is announced by the negotiators as yielding a net interest of ten per cent. It is moreover announced that it is going to be issued at 63, and they promise a reimbursement of the intermediate sum of eighty francs for every six francs of rente. Finally, it is announced that there is a financial committee; that this financial committee is established at Paris; that it is composed of a Mexican commissioner, an English commissioner, and a French commissioner; and that this financial committee, sitting at Paris, has the honor of being presided over by one of the most important men in our financial affairs—a senator and former governor of the bank—the Count de Germiny. With all this show and parade it is that the loan is placed before the public. I may say even that it amounts to an abuse to employ all this superfluity of announcements.

However that be, what has become of the loan? That is a question which I address to the representatives of the government. It is important for us to know, on various accounts. There are two sections in the loan. There is, first, that of twelve millions of rente for the account of the Emperor Maximilian; then there is a second division of 6,600,000 francs of rente for the account of the French government, to which this amount of rente is remitted in place of the indemnity of two hundred and seventy millions which is acknowledged to be due to it. What has become of the loan? Is it negotiated? We need some information on the subject. It is not from the point of view of our 6,600,000 francs of rente that I spoke just now. It is from the point of view of the real resources that are going to be placed at the disposal of the Emperor Maximilian, and which are the pledge for us for several recoveries, of which it will also be necessary to speak.

In regard to these recoveries, what have we to do? This is a very important subject. The government cannot refuse to give us some information on the state of the negotiation of this loan, so important to the finances of France, in consideration of what we are to be paid hereafter. I have the honor to be in communication with some persons who are very well posted in affairs, who would not seek to mislead me, who would be indulgent towards me, and who would not expose me to the disgrace of asserting, in an assembly as respectable as this, and consequently before the whole country, a thing that would not be true. However ill, therefore, I may be informed, I can say that the loan is not negotiated, or at least that it is very far from being negotiated for twelve millions. Is it for eight millions? I have reason to think that it is not. The precise figure will be given us by the government, which is under the obligation of placing us right on this subject.

In the present state of things, I believe that we have reason to fear that in the resources which are to be placed at the disposal of the Emperor Maximilian we will not find all the security on which our treaty would give us the right to count.

Now, how is it with our rentes? The Glynn firm announced in its prospectus that it would negotiate 18,600,000 francs of rentes; that it would open subscriptions in France and in England; that is to say, that it was commissioned to make at the same time a loan of twelve millions of rentes for Mexico, and a loan of 6,600,000 francs of rentes for France. Such was the announcement of the firm of Glynn & Company.

In the secret committee I asked if we could know on what conditions the English company undertook the negotiation of our 6,600,000 livres of rentes. The minister of state told me on that day that he had not in his possession any treaty that might have existed between the French treasury and the English company. He had it not in his possession, but he promised to make it known to us afterwards. Now I believe he will not have to make it known to us, for no treaty any longer exists.

If these things are true, we offered to Mr. Glynn to intrust him with bonds at the rate of 60 francs, which he was to negotiate with the public at 63 francs, and he has thought proper to decline the bargain. Yet it was a very fine commission that we allowed him—a commission of three per cent., as we yielded to him at 60 francs what he was to negotiate in public at 63 francs; and still he has been unwilling to accept.

What is the consequence, gentlemen? If these things—this is a question which I address to the government—if these things are in the state which I have just indicated; that is to say, if Mr. Glynn has refused to undertake the negotiation of our 6,600,000 livres of rentes; if, even with a commission of three per cent., he has been unwilling to undertake to become the holder of them—well, what will become of these bonds?

They remain in the portfolio of the treasury. That is true; we have in the portfolio of the treasury 6,600,000 livres in Mexican bonds. These bonds will be negotiated hereafter as the Italian bonds have been negotiated.

You have not forgotten, gentlemen, that, after the treaty of Zurich, the government of Turin, which, perhaps, has never attached sufficient importance to that treaty, was to reimburse us for the sum of 100 millions which we had advanced for it to the Austrian government. How have these 100 millions been reimbursed? By the remittance of Italian bonds. We have had Italian bonds remitted to us at the rate of 80 francs 35 centimes. This amount in bonds represented a capital of 75 millions and some fraction—the exact figure does not matter.

We have negotiated these Italian bonds as we may be able to negotiate hereafter, I know not when, the Mexican bonds which will remain in our portfolio. But at what price have we negotiated these Italian bonds? We have negotiated them at such a price that we have lost 11,800,000 francs on the 75 millions—that is, from 15 to 16 per cent. If we are to negotiate our Mexican bonds on the same conditions, you will easily understand how, when we very exactly set down in our two budgets a certain sum of 66,900,000 francs, we shall have sadly miscalculated, and we shall be very far from an adjustment of balances.

What, in fact, is the condition of these Mexican bonds? I do not now consider the political question; I only consider the financial aspect of the case. In my opinion it is less favorable even than that of the Italian bonds. If we have lost from 15 to 16 per cent. on the Italian bonds we will lose still more on the Mexican bonds, when we shall have need of negotiating them in order to supply a deficit of 35 millions in the budget of 1864, and a deficit of 13,900,000 francs in the budget of 1865. We will therefore lose much; that is incontestable. I fear so much the more that we may lose heavily, as I cannot indulge any hopes. Yet I would gladly pray for the success of the negotiation of the Mexican bonds; for I assure you that if the 66 millions could be considered as ready money, if they could be considered as likely to restore order in our finances, I should be perfectly satisfied, although I hold here the language of a member of the opposition.

Much has been said of the financial feature of the new Mexican government; our very honorable and very eminent friend Mr. O'Quinn, the author of the report, has told us that he does not share the apprehensions which some entertain on the financial destiny of the Mexican government.

Gentlemen, I have in my hands a document which does not allow me to share those hopes, or rather which does not permit me to abandon myself or to urge my honorable colleagues to abandon themselves to such illusions. This document, which I have in my hands, is the report which M. de Araniuez, formerly minister of finance in Mexico before the presidency of Juarez, has made to the Emperor Maximilian in regard to the state of affairs in Mexico. This report has been copied for me most faithfully, and yesterday, by order of the Emperor Maximilian, it has been published in the *Morning Post*, of which a copy has been sent to me, which I have compared with the transcript previously communicated to me, of which I could therefore recognize the perfect correctness.

Now, what said the Mexican minister of finances? He said that, in the actual state of the revenues of Mexico, which amounted to a very low sum, 10 or 11 millions of piastres, that is, 50 or 55 millions of francs, it was indispensable with these revenues, in comparing them with the amount of the internal debt, the amount of the external debt, the amount of the debt due to France—and this debt he estimated only at 200 millions or 40 millions of piastres—it was indispensable to effect a loan of 750 millions.

It is for a country for which such resources are recognized as necessary by a man who was its minister of finance a few years ago, and who now makes a very complete, very clear, very methodical report to the Mexican Emperor; it is for a country which has need of 750 millions, that it is sought to effect a loan of 120 millions nearly, a loan represented by these 12 millions of bonds which it is sought to negotiate in the interest of the new government.

Such is the state of the case; I derive no hope from it to see the speedy realization of all those financial resources which Mexico, according to the fancy or the reasoning of some of our colleagues, should very soon produce.

I am so much the less disposed to entertain such a hope, as in the same report I have read, and I now read, that the new Emperor will require at least two years to re-establish civil order in the country, to assess the taxes, to organize its financial government, and to restore the *alcalas* or duties which have been suppressed, in order to replace them with monopolies which can no longer exist in a government imbued with principles of liberty, as the establishment of this new empire in Mexico ought to be, those monopolies which constituted the principal source of revenue for the Spanish government when it possessed and administered that country in 1820.

Such are the observations made by the Mexican minister. Well, gentlemen, to these observations I add mine also, such as have been suggested by the document which I have studied, a document which is well known to the government; for the copy of this report of M. de Aranjuez was transmitted to the French government before it was made known in London.

I have already said, gentlemen, that we must use the 66 millions that should proceed from the negotiation of the Mexican bonds; we must negotiate those bonds, I know not when, nor at what price; but first or last, at any price whatever, it can only be done with heavy loss. How could we be covered by what is due to us from the Emperor Maximilian? I have already said it too, and I will be corrected if, in my position as a stranger to the management of internal affairs, I am not rigorously exact in my knowledge of things; I have already said, the loan was not entirely subscribed for the Emperor Maximilian, and it was very doubtful whether he would succeed in getting the 120 millions which he hoped to obtain from the negotiation of his 6 per cent. bonds.

But suppose that this loan, which has not been subscribed to either in England or in Holland, and which has scarcely been taken anywhere else than in France, suppose that this loan is entirely taken; suppose that it will be negotiated without any loss, without any commission prejudicial to the interests of the Emperor Maximilian's finances; suppose that in consequence the Emperor Maximilian raises 120 millions. I make a very large concession here. Well, permit me now to see what the obligations of the Emperor Maximilian are, according to the terms of the treaty of Miramar.

According to that treaty the Emperor Maximilian should immediately deposit, through the agency of the committee of finance, presided over by M. de Germiny, four instalments of our rente of 6,600,000 francs in the bureau of deposits and consignments. He should, likewise, deposit four instalments of the rente negotiated in France for the 12 millions; that is to say, he should deposit four instalments of an annual rente of 18,600,000 francs. Now, if I am not mistaken, four instalments represent about 37,200,000 francs. This seems to me incontestable. It is necessary, therefore, that he should pay them down immediately, and that he should take them out of the 120 millions which he is to obtain from the very doubtful realization of his loan.

Independently of the thirty-seven millions of francs which he should deposit immediately, according to the terms of the treaty, in the French bureau of deposits and consignments, he should also arrange with England, for England has an English commissioner a member of the Mexican committee of finance, established in Paris, and this commissioner assuredly watches over the interests of his country.

What has the Emperor Maximilian done for England?

There existed a debt of English bonds to the amount of fifty-one millions of piastres, that is, two hundred and fifty millions of francs. Well, the Emperor Maximilian has consolidated this amount of English bonds into 3 per cent. rentes, at a less figure; and then, in the quality of a sovereign entering the country as a man able to pay his debts and the debts of the country of which he is going to be the sovereign, he has declared that there were twenty coupons of these English bonds which had not been discharged for a certain number of years, and that consequently he established a 3 per cent. rente similar to that in consolidation of the English bonds, that he established in favor of English creditors a rente of 3 per cent., which would amount to 3,800,000 francs.

He has, therefore, in regard to England, created a rente of 3 per cent., of which the two sections, the one a consolidation of the capital of fifty-one millions of piastres, the other a consolidation, reduced, it is true, but still a consolidation, of the amount of twenty coupons, amount in all to a rente of twelve millions and some fraction.

What is the English commissioner going to do? What he has done, and what he ought to do, most undoubtedly. He is going to demand the preliminary deposit of the interest for two years, as it has been demanded for the 18,600,000 francs.

The Emperor Maximilian must, therefore, add twenty-two or twenty-four millions for two years' interest of this rente which he has established in favor of England. Here, then, are twenty-two or twenty-four millions for England that must also be added immediately by a deposit as instantaneous as the deposit of thirty-seven millions of French interest.

Independently of these engagements, there is one other made with you, and upon which we count in our estimate of receipts for 1864, as well as for 1865. So we were told yesterday. I do not speak of the Emperor Maximilian's engagement to pay us 1,000 francs for each soldier that may be left in his territory; I do not speak of that. The Emperor Maximilian has made an engagement, embracing several matters, to pay us twenty-five millions. These twenty-five millions we have to apply to the budgets of 1864 and 1865.

Here, then, is a sum of twenty-five millions, or, taking in the semi-annual instalment of 12,500,000 francs for 1864, 37,500,000 francs in all, which the Emperor Maximilian must expend in order to discharge his obligation to pay us twenty-five millions a year; and we count so confidently upon this, that, having in the amount of the Mexican rente only fifty-four millions of which we could dispose, we dispose of sixty-six millions of this same rente, and we appropriate fifty-three millions of it in the budget of 1864, and thirteen millions in the budget of 1865; we count with entire assurance upon that money. Here, then, are twenty-five millions for 1865, and 12,500,000 francs for the half of this year, on which we count; they are our eventual resources. Thus it is 37,500,000 francs that the Emperor Maximilian must expend out of the money which is to be raised for him by the loan in the condition in which we know that to be. (Murmurs.)

There is yet another engagement made by the Emperor Maximilian. While we remain there, he ought to relieve us immediately, dating from the first of July, from the enormous expense of maintaining the Mexican army. The Mexican army, if I refer to the figures that are given us in the budget, is for us a charge of 18,600,000 francs; for I have seen in the corrected estimate, and in the report of our honorable colleague, that it was for one-half year 9,300,000 francs. It is necessary, therefore, that, for eighteen months, the Emperor Maximilian should remain charged, in our place, with this expense of 18,600,000 francs, or else he will not pay his army.

The sum of 18,600,000 francs a year, makes, for eighteen months, twenty-seven millions and some hundreds of thousands of francs which the Emperor Maximilian will have to spend. Please add up—and all these figures are incontestable—add up all that, in accordance with these decrees, with treaties, and with agreements, the Emperor Maximilian is obliged to spend immediately, before entering his empire, before being able to establish his government there, before being able to introduce there the necessary means for the establishment of order, peace, and security, and the creation of interests around him; he has to pay one hundred and twenty-five millions out of the one hundred and twenty millions which he will have borrowed. [Laughter on several benches.]

M. GLAIS-BIZOIN. Very good; very good. [Murmurs of disapprobation.]

M. BERRYER. Pardon me, gentlemen, for these long developements with which I fatigue you, [No, no. Go on.] But I consider it only my duty as a good citizen to dispel from your minds the illusions that would induce you to accept as realities what in fact are only chimeras, and nothing but chimeras.

Independently of all these external obligations which must be fulfilled in the interval of eighteen months, and the greatest part immediately, there is an internal debt. Is this new Emperor, who goes to restore peace, order, confidence in his states, to commence by bankruptcy as to the internal debt? Is he not going to be obliged to acknowledge and provide for it? What would be the condition of a new government that would commence by saying: "There are debts; I will not pay them"?

All these considerations should be weighed by you. They are true; they are of serious importance; they demand to be received as reasons determining us to recognize the impossibility of hoping for an equilibrium in the budget through the means of the income which we presume to be derivable from the Mexican indebtedness. This seems to me established by the fullest evidence. The budget is very far from finding the thirty-seven millions which Mexico owes us for eighteen months, and the 66,600,000 francs which are allotted to us, and of which we dispose as available assets. We are so far from being able with any certainty or reason to count upon that, that we must acknowledge that there will be a deficit, and a very considerable deficit, in our budget.

Most unfortunately, there will be a deficit for other reasons also, and this is still more sad; for all that I have said is only in relation to our finances abroad. As to position, attended with more or less risk, of the Archduke become Emperor, we have made the expenditure, we have balanced it; we await sufficient indemnities to cover the balance. Will those indemnities fail us? That will be a transitory misfortune; but it is not a misfortune attributable to ourselves. It is the weakness, the poverty, the chimerical illusions of other parties, that have brought us to it. We will pass over this subject. But there are other illusions which, although they do not result in figures so important, appear to me worthy to be the object of most serious reflections on the part of the government. These are the estimates which we make of the revenue derivable from taxes, and especially from indirect taxes, as available resources. As to these estimates, we are told in the report of the committee, "We need estimate for 1864 a deficit, a falling off, a diminution, of three millions in the receipt of indirect taxes."

In view of this hope, of this estimate of the committee, I look at the figures of the returns, in the Moniteur, of the revenue from our indirect taxation during the first half of the year 1864, and I see that there is a falling off of receipts, compared with 1863, of 6,673,000 francs. Now, when the first half of the year presents a deficiency of receipts to the sum of 6,673,000 francs, I ask on what grounds does the committee assert that, in the course of the whole year, there will be a diminution of receipts only of three millions?

It is a bad beginning, whereon to predict that there will be only a deficit of three millions during the whole year, when the first half alone presents a deficit of 6,673,000 francs.

* * * * * * * *

CORPS LEGISLATIF.

SESSION OF THURSDAY, *May* 12, 1864.

His excellency the DUKE DE MORNY, president, in the chair.

After the reading of the journal, in which some corrections were made, and the presentation of various reports, the order of the day came up, being the consideration of the budget for 1865. M. JULES FAVRE claimed and obtained the floor. The opening of his speech and the part relating to Mexican affairs were as follows:

M. JULES FAVRE. Gentlemen, when in the session of yesterday our honorable president advised us not to overload the discussion of the budget with irrelevant debates, it was not certainly and it could not have been his idea to debar us from the serious examination of those affairs that are involved in the regulation of finances.

In fact, gentlemen, if it is important to know the amount of our expenses and of our receipts, it is not less so to know how these expenses are incurred, and if the sacrifices which they impose upon the country turn to its welfare and its prosperity internally, to its securiy, to its repose, to its honor, to its alliances externally.

It is, therefore, gentlemen, useful to examine the condition in which our diplomacy has placed us, and I ask your permission to make this examination in your presence, throwing aside, as far as it will be possible for me, all incidental questions, and occupying myself only with those which should principally claim your attention. And if it is impossible for me, speaking in the name of the opposition, to intimate my approval of the domestic and internal policy of the government, it is no less impossible for me to show any satisfaction with its external policy, and this, gentlemen, for a reason which applies to both. In fact, we reproach both alike with appearing to be what they are not, with exciting without satisfying, and with thus creating everywhere a condition of things full of doubt, uncertainty, and danger. [Interruption.]

In order to justify this opinion, gentlemen, I must go through with you the principal questions to which I alluded just now; not that I make the rash pretension to present here the diplomatic history of the government which directs us; I desire to confine myself to a brief review of the events that have transpired and that are now transpiring since the corps legislatif has met. And it is precisely, gentlemen, in examining these events that I shall find the justification of the opinion which I have had the honor of enunciating before the chamber. And in the very beginning, gentlemen, permit me to tell you that it would be a grave error to suppose that diplomacy should restrict itself to the surveillance of facts that are being accomplished, and to the consideration of the transitory interest that might arise from them. Assuredly, gentlemen, it cannot despise either the one or the other, but in order to be really strong, it is necessary that, as for internal policy, it should have a fixed principle, a reason to direct it, a reason to serve as a lamp and guide on all important occasions whereon it may find itself engaged. Now, gentlemen, what cannot be disputed by any one that does me the honor of listening to me is, that in the contest now waged in Europe, and which, unfortunately, does not yet draw near its end, France, by her external action as well as by her internal policy, should, under pain of degenerating from her high station, represent the new spirit. And what must we understand by this expression? In my mind, here is what it means —the ancient spirit having its source in theocracy, which is the representation of the most elevated of despotism, has taken the name of divine right in order to be the more feared and the more submitted to by the people. This is the name which it has assumed in order to be able to reign without limitation, and to make all understandings be silent in its presence. But in opposition to this right to which I must restore a more logical name by calling it the imposed right, there appears the right which I name consented right, and it is this, gentlemen, which is the personification of the new spirit, that is, the liberty of the human soul which takes possession of the world, and which desires, through the power of the collective individualities called to govern their own affairs by themselves, to reveal itself and assume its proper place.

SEVERAL MEMBERS. Good.

M. JULES FAVRE. Now, it is not doubtful, and I was right in saying that upon this point I would have no person to contradict me among you, that France is the champion of this latter principle. Undoubtedly, and here again we are all of one accord, her policy ought to have a fixed rule. It ought also to avoid showing itself adventurous, utopian, and especially propagandist. It should rely for support on that which constitutes its proper force, but should not seek to impose itself abroad. It should respect the principle on which it rests, and protect that principle on all occasions when that protection is allied with possibility and the interests of the nation.

Well, gentlemen, has France been faithful to her commission in the events which have been unfolded before you? Has she respected these rules of conduct? Has she shown herself prudent, reserved, and logical? Unfortunately it is impossible for me to give her this credit.

* * * * * * * * * * * *

Italy is not the only or the most serious embarrassment in which France finds herself involved; she carries a still heavier chain: it is that of Mexico, [exclamations,] and we would be wofully wanting in our duty if we did not seek to know the truth as to our political condition on this question.

Do not fear, gentlemen, that I shall abuse your patience, which I have already, perhaps, taxed too much, but the details so clear, so authoritative, that have been given you by my illustrious colleague [M. Berryer] on the financial question, seem to me to have been left unanswered. [Cries of no, no.]

A VOICE. Read the Moniteur!

M. JULES FAVRE. It is certain, to my eyes at least, that the Emperor Maximilian, in taking possession of his new empire, assumes charges under the weight of which he will have great difficulty in establishing his government.

But here, gentlemen, I meet with an objection that has several times been urged in this debate, and to which I cannot fail to reply. Whenever a member rises here within these precincts in order to call your attention to this question, you know that he is treated as a disloyal citizen.

A VOICE. Yes, and very justly.

M. JULES FAVRE. And you have heard it asserted, in one of your recent sessions, that in the English Parliament such discussions would not be possible. [That is true, that is true!]

M. GLAIS BIZOIN. No: for no English Parliament would have ever tolerated such an expedition. [Murmurs of disapprobation.]

M. JULES FAVRE. There may be a reason for this, gentlemen; it is because the English nation is not under guardianship; [cries of disapprobation;] it is because in demanding peace it is not likely to expose itself to war; it is because it can manage its affairs, and it is for this reason, gentlemen, that it sometimes abstains from criticising them.

As to us, we are for the most part of the time called to control events that have been accomplished. And then it would be a very singular and very humiliating condition in which we would be placed, were we always to approve under pain of being wanting in patriotism. [Murmurs of disapprobation.]

And permit me, since the minister has touched upon English history, to remind you that his recollections in this respect have rather failed him; and when I revert to the end of the last century and to the commencement of the present, oh! then, gentlemen, I perceive a tremendous struggle in progress. France stands at the head of the new ideas. She is herself engaged in terrible convulsions that might terrify Europe. Yet not the less for all that does she pronounce words of emancipation and of liberty; and then the coalition of all the old despots is formed against her, and by their side is England found, England directed by a great man, by an eminent minister, but one who, in my opinion, was blinded by the contracted views of national hatred. He struggled against us and thus dragged his country into incalculable evils.

Yes, I acknowledge, he had an inflamed public opinion on his side, and in a parliament like this, one day when those irritating questions were in debate, a man arose in opposition to the common opinion, in spite of the murmurs that would have drowned his voice, and although he was forced to renounce illustrious friendships, he maintained the cause of liberty and of France. That man was Fox, and it is impossible to say what might have been the result if his wise counsels had been followed. But that which all sensible men can affirm is, that if England, instead of combating the French revolution, had sought to moderate and direct it, there would have been fifty years less of struggles, fatal struggles, battles, woe and blood, perhaps somewhat less of glory, but certainly more civilization and liberty. [Applause around the speaker.]

You see, then, that it sometimes happens that English statesmen have courageously resisted the impulse of popular opinion, believing thereby that they performed their duty, and in fact thus performing it. As to us, what have we said? I do not wish to repeat it here.

The minister has had reason to tell you that these great events had entered upon a new phase; only, perhaps, he has forgotten those different phases. The minister has traced for you a brilliant picture of the splendor reserved for America, thanks to our devotedness, to our courage, to our civilizing spirit. It is to accomplish this gigantic work that we have landed on the shores of Mexico!

Gentlemen, let the minister permit me to remind him that all this is but a poetic afterstroke; it is a grand programme that has been traced out by the victorious hand of France, but which the hand of her policy had not prepared. [Divers interruptions.]

If I refer back to the origin itself of the enterprise, I find that all this grandeur is in singular contrast with the 2,500 men that formed the first contingent of France, and with the pacific declarations which she circulated among all the cabinets of Europe!

I acknowledge it, time and events have progressed and have imposed imperious obligations upon us. Yet once more, I say I will not retrace the past, I will take things as they exist. Only, the minister will permit me to say to him: if Prince Maxamilian is traversing the ocean, and if, to use his magnificant language, the waves seem to be obedient to him, if the shores shake with joy at his approach, if he is soon to be received with unanimous acclamations, [murmurs,] ah! let them burst forth, but it is his cruellest enemies who prepare these ovations for him. [Cries of no! no!] And, as for me, I highly admire, indeed, a people that would place their patriotism, after their defeat, in wreathing crowns of glory for a foreign prince that is sent to them by a victorious enemy. [Murmurs of disapprobation.]

In fine, let us look into the reality to find out the true aspect of the question. If the Emperor Maximilian could realize all the wonders which you have heard in the eloquent speech of the minister of state, we also, gentlemen, in spite of the greatness of the sacrifices that have been imposed upon France, we also would applaud him; but the difference between the minister and ourselves consists in the confidence entertained as to the success of such an enterprise.

NUMEROUS VOICES. Wait a while.

M. JULES FAVRE. But this is not what we have now to discuss. That the Emperor Maximilian, intrusted with these new destinies, may conduct his empire to the highest summit of glory, is my sincere desire. I place no obstacle in his way; but I ask if all this is not romance, and if the reality is not otherwise; if, in reality, this great prince is no more than a lieutenant of France? [Interruption.]

This is the only true question, and it is in this way that it affects our interests, our honor, and our policy.

When the session was opened, what was the language held forth by the government? I take it from an official document, of which I ask your permission to quote some lines. The feeling was unanimous, I shall not say to blame, but at least to regret, distant enterprises. [Interruptions.]

If these enterprises were necessary, they were accepted, but the necessity was deplored which required them, and an evident desire was manifested that they should be brought to a speedy conclusion. This conclusion was very precisely indicated for the government; for here, gentlemen, is what I read in the report made by the honorable M. Larrabure:

"At this time, the Emperor's government declares that it has entered into no engagement with any one, either to leave a force of French troops in Mexico, or to guarantee any loan whatever. It declares that there is no reason whatever to suppose that it is necessary to increase the French forces now actually serving in Mexico; and that any movements that may take place up to the time of their withdrawal will have for their only object to replace the sick or those whose term of service may have expired. According to present estimates, the government hopes that the end of the year 1864 will mark the conclusion of the expedition."

There are things to be remarked in this paragraph: a hope that the expedition may end with the year 1864; a double engagement—the one that no troops will be left in Mexico and that no obligation has been incurred in this respect; the second, that no support will be given to any loan.

SEVERAL VOICES. That no guarantee will be given.

M. JULES FAVRE. Now, you know what has become of this double engagement; you know how we have been repaid for the expenses of the war. It is a new proceeding, and one which I recommend to the statesmen of our day, to make the victorious power pay the expenses of the war; for it is France that issues 66 millions of bonds, which become in her hands accommodation notes furnished with her signature. [Murmur.]

As to the engagement not to leave any troops in Mexico, how will it be compatible with the declarations which I read in the official journals?

We have sent the Emperor Maximilian across the seas we have pointed out Mexico to him as a point towards which he should proceed, because he would be received there with unanimous acclamation; such is the pompous language of eloquence. But now here is the reality of the case.

In the treaty, which is published in the Moniteur of the 17th of April, I see that "the government of his Majesty the Emperor of the French and that of his Majesty the Emperor of Mexico, animated by an equal desire to secure the restoration of order in Mexico and to consolidate the new empire, have resolved to regulate by mutual agreement the conditions of the sojourn of the French troops in that country."

So we are very far from the declarations of the honorable Mr. Larrabure, as contained for in his report.

Hope has vanished; as to engagements, it has been deemed possible to set them totally aside. Our troops will remain in Mexico, how long? They will remain there until the Emperor Maximilian is firmly established, for that is the work undertaken by France; and when she is told that the Mexican expedition is finished she is deceived; she should know this; the Mexican expedition is scarcely commenced. [Cries of disapprobation.] It is necessary to establish the new empire firmly, in the midst of difficulties of all kinds, of parties and factions. Such is the work prepared for France.

And for this, gentlemen, what are the sacrifices demanded of her? They ask her to leave at the disposal of the Emperor Maximilian a *corps d'armée* of 25,000 men, and there is no determinate period for its recall; circumstances must decide as to the time of its withdrawal, and you know how much elasticity there is in such propositions as that. It is therefore for an indeterminate time that we keep 25,000 men in Mexico.

They tell us, gentlemen, that they will be paid by the Mexican government. Permit me to say that I consider it a deplorable condition for France to have herself paid thus. [Murmurs and marks of disapprobation.]

No, France should not sell the blood of her children in order to establish a foreign empire. [Renewed murmurs.]

I find in this enterprise undertaken to Mexico detestable ideas, dynastic ideas, which I oppose with all my strength, for they are contrary to the new spirit on which the policy of France reposes. [Various manifestations of disorder.]

There is, therefore, a force of 25,000 men of which you are deprived for an indeterminate period; a force of 25,000 men is placed in the pay of a foreign prince; it will be commanded by a French officer, but it will not be the less, for all that, subject to the inspirations of a foreign policy. Now this foreign policy will gradually diverge from you in proportion as this new empire of Mexico will develop itself; it will become national, and less like to yours, and then it may involve you in enterprises, in adventures, and in dangers that we cannot now calculate. [Renewed interruption]

Is that which I say, gentlemen, a simple supposition? The minister has spoken to us of a fact, in regard to which it is impossible to maintain silence; I refer to the declaration of the Congress of the United States. [Sensation.]

M. ERNEST PICARD. That is a very serious matter!

M. JULES FAVRE. That this act has no diplomatic value, I am aware; it is not the less for that the manifestation of an opinion of which we must take notice. But what the minister knows as well as I do is, that this manifestation is not an isolated fact; that it has assumed an official character; that the United States have entered into regular and categorical explanations; and I request your permission to lay before you some lines of a despatch.

SOME MEMBERS. No, no.

OTHER MEMBERS. Yes, yes. Go on; speak

M. JULES FAVRE. Here is the despatch from the minister of foreign affairs of the United States to Mr. Dayton, their minister resident at Paris, and which has been communicated to the French minister of foreign affairs. It is of the date of the 26th of September, 1863, and here is what I read in it. After some expressions of politeness and regard for France, the American minister subjoins:

"This reserve does not prevent the government from acknowledging and declaring that the real opinion in Mexico is in favor of a domestic and republican government—" (Ah! ah!)

SEVERAL MEMBERS. Now we have it!

M. JULES FAVRE. —"in preference to any monarchical institution whatever that might be imposed upon it from without."

The expression used here may seem to you to be in bad taste; but, as to the thing, it is excellent, and for my part I believe that princes are so much the more firmly established as they are the more national, and I would never advise any state to go out of its own limits to choose one.

"Our government," adds the minister of the United States, "also acknowledges that this real opinion of the Mexican people is due in a great measure to the influence of the popular opinion in our own country, and that it continually receives a new impulse therefrom.

"The United States do not conceal that, in their opinion, their own safety, no less than the manifest and brilliant destiny to which they aspire, are intimately connected with the maintenance of free republican institutions throughout the whole of America. They have submitted this opinion to the Emperor of the French, at a proper time, and as one worthy of his serious attention, in order that he may determine in what manner he should conduct and terminate happily the war in Mexico.

"It is not any further necessary to maintain a strict reserve on that other point; if France, after mature consideration, believed it her duty to adopt in regard to Mexico a policy in opposition to the sentiments and the opinions of which I have spoken, this policy may sow the seed of jealousies which, in their development, may bring on a conflict between France, the United States, and the other American republics." (Oh! oh!)

That, gentlemen, is a diplomatic document; and unless you go so far as to say that these declarations are of no importance, and that sovereign wisdom consists in the greatest ignorance and in supreme delusion, we must take these facts into careful consideration.

Here is another despatch, under date of October 23, 1863, containing the following paragraphs:

"In consideration of these facts, M. Drouyn de Lhuys intimates that a prompt acknowledgment by the United States of the projected empire would be agreeable to France, and would free her, sooner than could otherwise be hoped for under present circumstances, from her embarrassing complications with Mexico.

"Fortunately, we have never concealed the fact from the French government that, in the opinion of the United States, the establishment of a foreign and monarchical government would be neither easy nor desirable. You will inform M. Drouyn de Lhuys that our opinion in this respect has not changed."

And further on it says: "It is, however, useful that you should inform M. Drouyn de Lhuys that the United States regard Mexico as the theatre of a war which has not yet resulted in the overthrow of the government which has for a considerable time existed in that country, and with which the United States continue to maintain relations of peace and sincere friendship. Consequently the United States are not free to take into consideration the question of the acknowledgment of a government which, in consequence of the future eventualities of this war, might be called to replace the present government."

You see, gentlemen, unless you close your eyes to the light, that we must recognize that the seeds of distrust and hostility have been sown between two countries, the union of which is so necessary to the grandeur and prosperity of both. These seeds are so much the more to be feared as the condition of the United States is the more threatened, as they are passing at the present moment through a terrible and bloody crisis, which, whatever may be the issue of it, will leave on the deserted theatres of strife numerous bands of adventurers who, sooner or later, will proceed to find work for their swords in a country to which their passion will impel them. [Various exclamations.]

Now, in view of these events, has France been sufficiently prudent? I do not wish to examine the course that she might have pursued, and should, perhaps, have pursued, in reference to the great fact of the secession. It is incontestible that, if her voice had made itself heard, if she had been able to manifest those secret sympathies which, I doubt not, exist in her heart for the triumph of human liberty and the final suppression of slavery, it would have been a very useful aid to the United States.

I add that our naval power and our commerce would have profited thereby; for, in examining the state of our relations with the New World, here is what we find and what is known to every one. The New World is our principal furnisher of that indispensable staple, for which we are at this moment making sacrifices that are becoming more and more troublesome to our monetary affairs.

In fact, in the last session, mention was made of the Bank of France. [Renewed exclations.]

On this point, gentlemen, I wish to say nothing but this—it is well understood that it is not a subject which I desire to draw into discussion—you know that in the years preceding 1859, Europe bought about five million bales—more exactly 4,872,000 bales—of cotton, of which three-quarters were furnished by America. At present, gentlemen, Europe is under the necessity not only of restricting its consumption considerably, but of looking for almost the whole of that raw staple in countries which do not return her remittances in specie; and whilst America operated with her by means of exchange, India and Egypt retain her silver and gold, the former to make idols, and the latter to bury it in her vaults.

It is thus, gentlemen, that the deposits in the Bank of France go on continually diminishing.

It has been announced to you that at the present time the deposits have increased to 240 millions. But if you choose to look at preceding years, you will see that in 1859 the minimum amount was 508 millions and the maximum 644 millions; that, in 1860, the deposits varied from 514 to 551 millions; a fact which should claim the serious attention of all financiers, and which should not be neglected by politicians, who are well aware that the great resolutions taken by prudent nations have a direct influence on their commercial relations, and that it behooves, if it be possible, to put an end, and that at the earliest moment, to the war now waged in America between the northern and the southern States.

Now, a circumstance has occurred to which, in conclusion, I desire permission to call your attention, and to provoke a reply from the government.

I said that I did not wish to examine its conduct in the general management of this affair; but I remember that, in the month of June, 1861, an official declaration was made, in presence of the world, by which France bound herself to preserve the strictest neutrality between the two belligerents.

You know, however, that in the commencement of the year 1862 France endeavored to influence the cabinet of Washington so far as to make it accept an armistice. But what is more significant is, that quite recently public opinion has been very justly moved at the revelation of facts in regard to which a categorical explanation is indispensable.

In the months of April and July, 1863, two houses received orders for the construction of six iron-clad vessels. Two of these vessels were of the class called *rams* with block-houses. And yet these houses asserted that these vessels thus constructed were simple trading vessels.

I do not examine here the question as to what the intention was. It is a point not in discussion here, and which I entirely set aside. Only these orders were given by persons whose names are well known throughout Europe, by Captain Bullock, of the Confederate States, and Mr. Slidell, who has obtained a celebrity which is yet within all recollections; and when these builders were told that these six vessels were destined to navigate between Shanghai and San Francisco, and thus to connect California and China by means of vessels armed with block-houses, I think that very serious doubts might naturally have arisen in the minds of these honorable constructors.

But I have a right to find these doubts, especially in the minds of the watchful members of the government; and when, under date of June 1, application was made to the minister of marine in order to obtain authority to put rifled cannon on board of these innocent trading vessels, then it might have been perceived that there was something serious in the matter, and the names of Bullock and Slidell were significant enough to authorize such a conclusion to be drawn.

It was drawn, for the requisite authority was granted. [Sensation and various demonstrations.]

It is true that, as some rumor of the affair had reached the other side of the Atlantic, the minister of foreign affairs of the United States wrote to Mr. Dayton; that Mr. Dayton had an interview with the minister of foreign affairs of France; that the latter made some representations on the subject to his colleague of the marine; and that, in the month of October, the authority previously granted was withdrawn.

But, gentlemen, certain journals still no less persist in asserting that these vessels are armed, that two have been launched in the port of Brest, and it is positively said will be allowed to sail.

I request the government not to leave such a question as this undecided. There is involved in it, I shall not say our honor or our safety—for here I care not to use such words—but there is involved in it our political probity.

The declaration of the month of June, 1861, is too explicit not to bind the government in the most formal manner.

Under such circumstances, gentlemen, its language should dispel every kind of doubt. There is no question here of a fact susceptible of various interpretations. You see within what limits it is restricted; and I hope that the goverment will not permit the slightest shadow of uncertitude to remain here. Such a course is absolutely indispensable; for if it could be imagined that, departing from the course which she has formally traced out for herself, France could take part for one or other of the belligerents, I leave it to your own minds to conceive what the deplorable result might be of such a state of things.

Assuredly, gentlemen, I can say with the greatest sincerity that we have no interest in augmenting our political embarrassments. I have endeavored to show you how, in my opinion, these embarrassments have been the consequence of the faults committed by diplomacy. It is because our policy has been equivocal, because its language has not been strong and precise, because it has undertaken everything without accomplishing anything, that at the same time it has compromised everything. [Cries of no, no.]

VOICES AROUND THE SPEAKER. That is true.

M. JULES FAVRE. It must renounce this system of feebleness; and do you know the remedy for this? It must have confidence in the nation, in its virility, in its expansion. Those who guide the nation must cease to be its pedagogues and its masters in order to become its inspired chiefs, counselled and directed by it, [various manifestations;] and like the divinity of the fable, instead of remaining in the clouds, they must take their stand-point on the earth which gives them strength—that is, on the soil of liberty. [Various interruptions.]

On this condition, I do not say—neither do I wish it—that they will be able to command the world and to impose laws upon it; but at least they will no longer expose themselves to see their words belied and their signatures protested. [Murmurs of disapprobation from various benches. Applause from the benches around the speaker.]

Speech of M. Rouher, Minister of State, in reply to M. Jules Favre.

[Extract.]

If I examine the speech of the honorable M. Jules Favre, taking his objections in an inverse order from that which he has adopted, the first point to which I come is this pretended violation of the rules of neutrality committed by France towards the northern States of America.

Gentlemen, questions of neutrality and the extent of the rights of neutrals have at all times been a source of difficulty and of numerous conflicts. I do not wish here to review the numerous phases through which the rights of neutrals have passed in the code of international law. But what I can say to the honor of the policy of our country is, that everything in the nature of liberal, progressive, generous ideas, introduced into the legislation of neutrals, has originated with the French government. ["That is true; that is true."]

So, at the declaration of war in America between the States of the north and the States of the south, we were not wanting to these precedents, and from the very first day we laid down the principles of neutrality that were to govern our whole conduct.

In the declaration of the 1st of June, 1861, published in the Moniteur, an official act emanating from the sovereign, it is laid down in article 3 that—

"It is forbidden to every Frenchman to take a commission from either of the two parties for the purpose of fitting out vessels-of-war, or to receive letters of marque in order to prey upon commerce, or to be concerned in any manner whatever in the equipment or armament of a vessel-of-war or privateer for either of the two belligerent parties."

In the month of June, 1863, a request was made by two French constructors for permission to build two steamers, it being indicated that these vessels were destined to navigate in the seas of China.

The Minister of the United States, in the month of December, 1863, referred to letters and documents which circumstances, the character of which we have not wished to sift, had placed in the possession of Mr. Dayton. He maintained that these vessels were intended for the confederates. An investigation was immediately commenced. The constructors were questioned, their explanations were weighed, and the authorization, temporarily given, was withdrawn by the government.

Some time afterwards doubts arose; those steamers, which are not ready to depart, were indicated as destined for Sweden. New investigations were made. This destination did not seem sufficiently demonstrated, and under date of May 1, 1864, ten days ago, the minister of marine wrote to the minister of foreign affairs: "The vessels of war to which you refer will not be permitted to sail from the French ports until it is shown in the most positive manner that their destination does not affect the principles of neutrality which the French government desires vigorously to observe in regard to the belligerents."

Such is the unequivocal course that has been pursued by the Emperor's government in the clearest and most precise manner.

And now let me be permitted to invoke the talents and eloquence of the honorable M. Jules Favre, in order to impress the United States with principles equally precise and equally clear in regard to this affair of neutrality.

At the very time that he reproaches us with not having sufficiently observed the rules laid down by the declaration of June 11, 1861, the French government is struggling with the government of the United States in order to have coal declared not contraband of war, and perhaps delivered to such of our vessels as proceed to Mexico. I hope that the considerations so very brilliant, presented by M. Jules Favre in favor of the government of the United States, will influence that government to take the representations to which I allude into most serious consideration. [Approbative laughter.] We must then reject this vain accusation. It has absolutely no foundation whatever. The French government has not deviated in the slightest degree from the most loyal neutrality. ["Very good; very good."]

Here I come to the considerations presented by the honorable M. Jules Favre in reference to the secession, in reference to the impossibility of obtaining for European industry those supplies of cotton heretofore furnished by America, and to the consequences which those difficulties have produced in regard to the deposits of the Bank of France.

Indeed, gentlemen, it requires great courage to impute to the French government any responsibility for such a condition of things—["Good, good"]—and I ask myself why we are reproached for this lamentable, fratricidal war that is now waged in the United States, and in which we have sought to intervene, not as arbiters, but as conciliators. [Renewed approbation.]

Now, I find it my duty once more to take up the Mexican question. I am compelled to weigh the arguments that have been presented.

Is it true that the treaty which has been made is a violation of previous engagements, of declarations and promises made by the government in your presence? Is it true that the threat of American intervention is ever suspended, like the sword of Damocles, over the future of Mexico?

Gentlemen, whilst the honorable M. Jules Favre spoke, whilst I listened to those ironical laudations by him of the pretended eloquence of the organ of the government, when describing with complacency the future of Mexico, its expected splendor, the pacification of that country, the manifestations of order and regularity that were to be developed there, I read patiently, without any excitement at this irony, the advices from Mexico that just reached me at the moment—[sensation]—and therein I found the following words:

"The general condition of affairs in Mexico is improving every day, in proportion as the masses understand and appreciate better the generous views of the Emperor in their regard. The resistance, localized at some points, has now lost all national color; the guerilla bands fly on the approach of our troops, and whenever they are surprised they are cut to pieces. It is becoming more and more a question of brigandage, from which the inoffensive population cruelly suffers, but to which an end will very readily be put by a well organized system of police.

"For a month or two past, especially, it is seen that confidence is reviving. The capital sees thronging from every quarter citizens of all classes and of all opinions, who intermingle with each other and forget their enmities, and seek to unite upon one sentiment, forgetfulness of the past, faith in the future. In this condition of things, with the support of the Emperor's government and the aid of European capitalists, Mexico cannot fail to enter promptly on a career of material prosperity, by which Europe will be the first to profit."

M. Ernest Picard. The signature!

The Minister of State. Such is the news which M. de Montholon, our minister to Mexico, sends to the minister of foreign affairs by the mail that has just arrived.

That is not all. I have preserved to some extent the custom of occupying myself with those commercial questions amid which I lived for eight years, and I have been desirous to know the commercial movement in the port of Vera Cruz. An account of it has been transmitted to me by this same mail, though it was not supposed that I would have to make use of it so advantageously and so very soon. [Approbative laughter.]

It appears from it that the orders brought by the mail of the Florida, which arrived yesterday in the port of Saint Nazaire, amount for tissues alone to no less than one million of piastres. Such is the condition of that country, such is the progress of its development, such is the merchandise for which it sends to Europe; such is the way in which it contradicts the statement of the lamentable condition indicated by the honorable M. Jules Favre, who experiences, in spite of himself, a sort of regret at seeing himself deprived of that patronage of Juarez, whom he had so well defended. ["Good, good." Applause.]

M. JULES FAVRE. Your client is fortune.

The MINISTER OF STATE. I did not understand M. Jules Favre.

M. JULES FAVRE. I said that your client was fortune. [Cries of disapprobation.]

The MINISTER OF STATE. Yes, gentlemen, fortune is the client of France. ["That is true."] Providence protects her and reason guides her. ["Good, good."] For that reason it is that fortune is faithful to us. [Enthusiastic approbation.[

I now come to the two fundamental objections that have been made: the treaty and America.

First, the treaty. We have, it is said, made an indefinite engagement to keep our troops in Mexico; we have guaranteed the loan proposed by the Emperor of Mexico, and thus we have violated the declarations made before the committee, the report of which was presented by the honorable M. Larrabure. Let us examine.

In truth, I ask myself first by what singular distortion of language any one can have come to the supposition that the loan has been guaranteed by France, because France has accepted sixty-six millions of negotiable bonds of the loan, and is called upon to negotiate them, not with her signature, but with that of the Emperor of Mexico, the only guarantor of the payment of the interest. How can any one come to comprehend that there is any violation of plighted faith, when, with the utmost scrupulousness and the greatest sincerity, we have maintained, observed up to the very latest moment all the declarations solemnly made before the legislative body. The loan has been contracted for by the Emperor of Mexico; it has been voluntarily subscribed for by those who judged that Mexico presented sufficient guarantees. And, indeed, your course is not very well calculated to assure the capitalists of our country who have thought proper to engage in this enterprise. [Manifestations of approbation.]

Hurried on by an impulse of fiery opposition, at a time when every consideration would have dictated respect and patience, the honorable M. Jules Favre begins by attacking everything. He declares that there is an utter impossibility of raising resources in Mexico. He declares to the voluntary holders of the Mexican bonds that there is an impossibility for them of ever realizing their value. Now, gentlemen, that is not patriotic. ["Bravo, bravo."] And when the honorable M. Jules Favre, searching in the records of the past, invoked the memory of one of England's great men, he confounded at the same time the object and the circumstances of the conflict to which he makes allusion. That great man arose in the House of Commons in order to proclaim there the great principles of humanity, of civilization, and of peace, and not to propose, under the slightest pretexts, declarations of war against all Europe. Yes, Fox at that moment performed a great duty towards civilization; he wished to arrest two nations ready to come to blows; he arose to oppose Pitt; he desired to calm the ardor of the military spirit; he did not succeed, but it is to his eternal honor that he made the attempt. On the contrary, the honorable M. Jules Favre has depreciated the credit of a new empire and paralyzed a work of civilization. Ah! if you played the part of Fox here, if your part were the same as his, believe me, I would be, with all my heart, on your side. ["Good, good."]

The treaty, it is said, might contain engagements at variance with the declarations which we have made. What does it contain? In the last months of this year the *corps d'armée* will be reduced to 25,000 men. The expedition is terminated, and, in fact, the letter which I have just read proves it. A general pacification is effected everywhere, and the return of ten thousand of our soldiers will be effected before the 1st of January, 1865.

As to the 25,000 men, whose stay has been indicated in the treaty, what is the stipulation in their regard? We declare that we will remain temporarily in Mexico, in order to protect our interests, the interests which occasioned the intervention.

M. GUEROULT. Will the minister have the goodness to read the article of the treaty? [Noise and confusion.]

SEVERAL MEMBERS. Do not interrupt.

The MINISTER OF STATE. I have not the treaty with me. If the honorable M. Gueroult will please pass it to me I will read it to the Chamber.

M. GUEROULT. I am not positive, but, as far as I can remember, I think that the treaty provides that the 25,000 men shall remain in Mexico until the Emperor Maximilian is able to do without us.

The MINISTER OF STATE. The honorable M. Gueroult is mistaken; his memory serves him badly; and from my recollections I will give him the substance, if not the precise text of the treaty and its provisions.

By article 1 it is indicated that the *corps d'armée* shall be reduced as soon as possible to 25,000 men.

By a second provision we declare that our *corps d'armée* is to remain temporarily in Mexico, in order to protect our interests.

M. ERNEST PICARD. The interests that occasioned the intervention. [Marks of disapprobation. "Do not interrupt, do not interrupt."] I merely come to the assistance of the minister.

The MINISTER OF STATE. I resume——

M. ERNEST PICARD. Give us the text.

The MINISTER OF STATE. I am going to give the honorable M. Picard the text, which has just been handed to me, and he will then permit me to comment upon it, and to demonstrate in the clearest manner the truth of my assertions.

"Article 1. The French troops that are now in Mexico will be reduced as soon as possible to a corps of 25,000 men, including therein the foreign legion.

"This corps, in order to protect our interests which occasioned the intervention, will remain temporarily in Mexico under the conditions laid down in the following articles."

So 25,000 men are to remain temporarily, the time is not fixed; no obligatory delay is determined upon; the appreciation of this delay belongs to France; she is the judge of the motives that must cause the continuance of her troops there to protect the interests that occasioned this intervention. [Noisy demonstrations.]

But this occupation cannot be indefinitely prolonged at the will of France; the Emperor of Mexico, who, to the great regret of the honorable M. Jules Favre, pays twenty-five millions a year for the stay of our troops, should have the right of requesting their evacuation. The Emperor of Mexico has, therefore, reserved to himself the right of asking the evacuation of our troops, according as the organization of the Mexican army may progress.

Article 2, in fact, adds: "The French troops will evacuate Mexico according as his Majesty the Emperor of Mexico may be able to organize the troops necessary to take their place

M. GUEROULT. But when will they be organized? In the mean time we will remain in Mexico.

The MINISTER OF STATE. I am going to answer the honorable M. Gueroult's difficulty. What says he? we will be obliged to remain there until the Mexican army is organized. That is the objection.

Well, I ask the honorable gentleman whether he knows the facts? Has he studied them? Does he not know that the Mexican army is organized, that it has a force of 25,000 men? Does he not see that there is a community of interest between the Emperor of the French and the Emperor of Mexico to put an end to a burdensome occupation?

Are there men, therefore, so much governed by their petty passions as that they do not wish to comprehend the elevated character of this agreement? Yes, undoubtedly, we may be called upon to remain in Mexico until the Mexican army is organized; but that army now exists, it is organized. Did not the honorable M. Berryer declare the day before yesterday that within the space of eighteen months that army would cost the Mexican government an expenditure of thirty-seven millions? Did he not deduct this sum from the resources of Mexico? The Mexican army, therefore, exists. So this provision laid down in article 3 is being realized every day. It is realized; the departure of the French troops has been resolved upon in advance; and the day when it shall take place we will all equally hail with satisfaction, both in France and in Mexico. ["Good, good."]

If some persons regard with chagrin the fact that the duration of the French troops in Mexico is undetermined, it is a matter of slight concern to me, because such men are revolutionists, who would like to have renewed in that unhappy country the agitations heretofore directed by Juarez. The word *temporarily* inserted in the treaty is a prudential provision to prevent the renewal of anarchical passions, for the outbreak of which the day appointed for the evacuation would be the signal.

The treaty is, therefore, above criticism, it is sincere; its entire spirit is in conformity with the purposes announced by the government in the discussion of the address. ["That is true, that is true."]

As to America, we must examine that question at some length.

It is not good thus to put between two great nations like America and France a pretended germ of discord, a pretended threat formally enunciated against our country or against Mexico, when there is at bottom nothing but a moment of transitory excitement, with which the Congress of the United States—a transitory excitement somewhat analogous to that which we have seen produced at the time of the seizure of Messrs. Mason and Slidell on the Trent, and which did not prevent the government from effecting the restitution of those two prisoners in conformity with the law of nations.

What, then, could be the afterthought of America? Would she wish to seize upon Mexico, and incorporate it with her States? Has she wished that she could have done so before. The American army was at the city of Mexico in 1847 and 1848. She had conquered the government then existing, I believe it was that of Santa Anna; she could have remained mistress of the territory; she did not even try to do so. She liquidated her condition, she determined her indemnities; she obtained, if I am not mistaken, a better settlement of the limits of Texas, the cession of New California and New Mexico, and, in virtue of these territorial arrangements, she withdrew peaceably without pretence of any annexation.

Yet the occasion was highly favorable. America was victorious; she was mistress not only of the capital, but of the entire country. Her army had been divided into two corps: one, starting from Matamoras, had seized the provinces as far as the city of Mexico; the other set out from Vera Cruz, and gained possession of Puebla before reaching the capital.

Is it solely to overturn a throne that America would design a declaration of war against Mexico? But at the present moment that great country is rent by civil war. Who can foresee the moment when that struggle shall terminate? Who can foresee the moment when cohesion shall be restored between the two parties so violently separated one from the other?

A MEMBER. Perhaps it will never be restored.

The MINISTER OF STATE. During the time that must elapse before the restoration of peace in the United States, can we not entertain a legitimate hope of seeing the new Mexican empire firmly established? When those great commotions shall have been finally settled in America, commercial interests will resume their empire; they will paralyze all desires for war between Mexico and the United States, and will produce a happy state of international relations between the two countries? [Marks of approbation.]

Assuredly, gentlemen, these temporary causes of impotence on the part of the United States I refer to only with regret. What I desire for the honor of civilization, what I desire by reason of the sympathies which animate me towards that nation by whose cradle France stood as sponsor—["Good, good"]—is that this war, which has so long desolated the American continent, should come to as speedy a solution as possible. But on the day when this war will have ceased, then I shall be more assured and more profoundly convinced that a war is impossible between Mexico and the United States of America.

Yes, such a war is impossible, gentlemen; the sympathies of France for America, of America for France, the declarations of the government of the United States, principles, interests, everything is opposed to such a consummation.

In the very outset I reject the view entertained by the honorable M. Jules Favre, to the effect that, upon the cessation of the war, it will not be the armies of the United States that may invade Mexico, but bands of adventurers, who will renew those expeditions heretofore attempted against Cuba, and which, by the way, have succeeded so badly. So, without at all compromising America, a partisan warfare would arise—a war of guerillas, who would come to trouble the Mexican empire.

You have not sufficiently studied the character of the American war, when you make such an assertion as that. If, in the beginning of the war, when the enthusiasm was great, when the population had not been decimated, there had occurred a happy arrangement of the difficulties between the south and north, if this war had been all at once arrested in its course; yes, it might have been possible that adventurers, no longer finding any occupation in the bosom of America herself, might have recklessly and boldly thrown themselves upon the Mexican territory, and carried war with them. That might have been possible, I acknowledge. But such adventurers are no more: death has mowed down their ranks. Those who are now fighting in both armies are unfortunate workmen, unhappy laborers, torn from their homes by the conscription, and compelled to fight every day under the guidance of chiefs animated with fiercest passions!

As to these unfortunate soldiers, whenever peace comes between the south and the north, they will return to their deserted workshops, they will go back to their abandoned ploughshares, and they will not go in search of Mexican adventures. Believe me, whenever the proclamation of peace comes, their only thought will be to seek remuneration in some lucrative employment; for America, exhausted by long wars, can no longer find anywhere but in commerce and industry the means of regeneration, which are—I desire it with all my soul—to restore her to the rank of great nations. [Good! good! prolonged applause.]

And now, gentlemen, by what principles is the American government actuated? The honorable M. Jules Favre has thought proper to refer to certain despatches from the government of the United States, in which he believes that he finds the proof of a kind of conformity with the declarations made by the Congress of the United States.

Gentlemen, I have the despatches in my hands. Here is what I read in that of the 23d of October, 1863:

"The United States, desiring to conform themselves to the legitimate consequences of their own principles, can only leave the destiny of Mexico in the keeping of its own inhabitants, and acknowledge their sovereignty and their independence, under whatever form it pleases them to manifest that sovereignty and independence."

Such is the language held by Mr. Seward to Mr. Dayton, and communicated to the minister of foreign affairs. Since then spontaneous explanations have been given to us in reference to that declaration of the Congress. The minister of foreign affairs has set down these explanations in a circular, addressed to all his agents, under date of May 4, 1864. I cannot do better than read it to you; from it you will be able to form an idea as to the estimate to be set upon the uneasiness and the doubts manifested by the honorable M. Jules Favre:

"The recent vote of the House of Representatives of Washington, on the subject of Mexico, has given occasion for interpretations which it may not be uninteresting to rectify. It has been presumed apparently that this vote might induce the United States to adopt towards us a new attitude of such a nature as to change the friendly relations of the two countries, or to complicate at least the affairs of Mexico by external embarrassments. It suffices, however, to take into account the circumstances under which this manifestation has been produced, in order to understand that it is very far from having such importance. It is undoubtedly the reflexion of that sentiment which the American press sedulously maintains in the United States, and of which the tendency is to have considered as an indirect attack upon their rights any intervention whatever, no matter how legitimate it may be, by a European power on any point of the American continent. But, in the United States, more even than in any other country, the legislative power is allowed such demonstrations without thereby involving the government and obliging it to make those resolutions its rule of conduct. The Emperor's government could not, therefore, have entertained any apprehension in this regard, even though the incident had not been the object of any explanation on the part of the federal government; but the cabinet of Washington has deemed it proper to prevent of its own accord any impression of the kind that might have been made by it upon us. Mr. Dayton has come to read to me a despatch addressed to him by the Secretary of State of the Union, in order to relieve the cabinet of Washington from any responsibility in this affair, and to establish the point satisfactorily that a vote of the House of Representatives or of the Senate, or even of the two houses, although naturally recommending itself to respectful attention, yet does not at all oblige the cabinet to modify its policy or take away its liberty of action.

"Mr. Seward sees no reason to adopt a different policy in the Mexican question from that which he has hitherto pursued; and if his dispositions should change at any time, we would be informed of the fact directly and at a proper time, as also of his motives for such a change.

"I replied to Mr. Dayton, that, in our opinion, there would be no justification for such a change; that our confidence in the wisdom and enlightened views of the American cabinet was too great to allow us to attribute to it any idea of compromising the veritable interests of the United States by any imprudent acts.

"In expressing to Mr. Dayton the satisfaction felt by the Emperor's government at the assurances which he had been commissioned to make to it, I added that I thought, in fact, that from the point of view of the United States themselves, the choice could not be doubtful between the establishment in Mexico of a regular and stable government and the perpetuation of an anarchy, of which they had been the first to feel the serious inconveniences. The reorganization of an immense country, destined with the return of order and security to play an important economical part in the world, ought to be, for the United States above all, a real source of advantage, since it was a new market opened to them, and of which they would be called, more than others, on account of their proximity, to profit. The prosperity of Mexico was, therefore, in unison with their best interests, and I did not certainly believe that the cabinet of Washington could fail to recognize that truth.

"This reply to Mr. Dayton's communication and the fact of that communication itself indicate to you sufficiently, Mr. ———, how it is proper to regard the circumstance to which I have deemed it my duty to call your attention."

Such is the declaration made by the American government, immediately after that of the House of Representatives. What has become of the latter declaration itself? The Senate indefinitely postponed its consideration.

And we must state, all those who have made themselves acquainted with American affairs understand the internal reasons that may have induced that resolution. A presidential contest is, at this moment, in progress in America, and every one, democrat and republican, is striving for popularity. [That is so; that is so.] And some think that they will attain their purpose by opposing the new American establishment. But, at bottom, the danger of a contest directed against Mexico is impossible, irreconcilable with the principles on which the United States rely.

How! Here is a country choosing by universal suffrage a form of government monarchical or republican, and in the name of national sovereignty, and yet the American army, it is supposed, would interfere in the states of Mexico, to impose—what? A different form from that adopted and proclaimed by the people!

Indeed, America would in that way violate the very essence of her government, liberty, and national sovereignty. She would not even have for her support that Monroe doctrine, so mistakenly quoted; for, to all those who have read the theories of President Monroe, they evidently amount only to one thing, to this declaration: that it would be regarded with disfavor if Europe established colonies in America, maintained territorial possessions there, and enjoyed such or such territories under title of conquest, and came, for instance, to convert Mexico into an Algeria placed under the sceptre of the Emperor. The Monroe doctrine is very pointedly directed against any such pretensions as these. It has established the principle—*Every one have his own; every one for himself.*

Are not the Mexicans in possession of their own? [That is it; good!] Does not Mexico, while exercising her sovereignty and choosing a prince for Emperor, perform an act of legitimate sovereignty? Is it a fact that there are any circumstances to constitute the Emperor of Mexico a mere lieutenant of the Emperor of the French? [That is clear enough.]

Let us, therefore, exclude those offensive and irritating expressions from our language. [Good!] The Emperor of Mexico is sovereign by the will of the Mexican people, and America will respect that will. Why should she not respect it? From the order, from the regularity, from the commercial prosperity of Mexico, America will derive more profit than any other nation. She it is who will most advantageously work out these industrial and commercial relations; she it is who will be able to send to the rich diggings of Sonora and Sinaloa the superfluous portion of her population to carry thither at once both labor and wealth. That which we might anticipate in our considerations, if such an anticipation should be entertained by serious and exalted minds, is in regard to the circumstances, necessary in the future, of a deep intimacy between Mexico and the United States of America. Therefore, America does not threaten the Emperor of Mexico, and that sovereign can proceed in his course; he may continue his efforts to prepare the prosperity of his country, and to mark the near approach of that prosperity by selecting the day on which to separate himself from the French flag in order to allow it to return with glory to our midst. [Good!]

This question of Mexico is now exhausted.

Mr. Seward to Mr. Romero.

DEPARTMENT OF STATE,
Washington, June 15, 1864.

SIR: I have the honor to acknowledge the receipt of your note of the 31st ultimo, transmitting translations of two discussions which have recently occurred in the corps legislatif of France, relative to Franco-Mexican affairs.

Thanking you for this attention, I have at the same time to acknowledge previous communications from you relating to the political condition of Mexico, which, with their accompanying documents, have contributed largely to my knowledge of passing events in that country. The notes, hitherto unanswered, are of the dates, respectively, of the 2d, 20th, 24th, and 26th February, and the 1st and 2d March last.

I beg to assure you of my high appreciation of the zeal and ability with which, from time to time, you have impressed this government as to the actual condition of the Mexican republic.

I avail myself of the occasion to renew to you, sir, the assurances of my distinguished consideration.

WILLIAM H. SEWARD.

Señor MATIAS ROMERO, *&c., &c., &c.*

No. 12.—*Case of the Mexican brig Oriente.*

Mr. Barreda to Mr. Seward, (with two enclosures,) June 24, 1863.
Mr. Seward to Mr. Barreda, June 30, 1863.

Mr. Barreda to Mr. Seward.

NEWPORT, *June* 24, 1863.

SIR: I have the honor to enclose a statement addressed to me by the Messrs. Echeverria & Co., of New York, agents of the owner of the Mexican schooner Oriente, with an account of the losses and damages which the latter claims.

Not knowing the antecedents of this affair, nor being in possession of documents relating to those losses and damages, my action is now limited to submitting to you the application of the claimant, trusting that you will give to it such just appreciation as it may deserve.

I reiterate to you the assurance of my distinguished consideration and respect.

F. L. BARREDA.

Hon. WILLIAM H. SEWARD,
Secretary of State of the United States, Washington, D. C.

To his Excellency FREDERICK L. BARREDA,
In charge of Mexican affairs:

The Mexican schooner Oriente, belonging to a citizen of and residing in Mexico, was seized and brought to the city of New Orleans in the month of June, 1862. The vessel was sent from that port to New York, where she arrived in the latter part of the same month.

A correspondence in relation to the schooner was had by his excellency Mr. Romero with his excellency Mr. Seward.

No libel or other proceedings in court were taken against the vessel, and, by direction of his excellency Mr. Seward, the schooner was discharged from custody about the middle of January of this year (1863) and delivered to us, the agents of the owner.

Mr. Seward informed Mr. Romero that the claim of the owner of the vessel for the damages he sustained could be ascertained by appraisers designated by the court, in case of the discharge of the vessel; but we are advised that, as the vessel was not brought into court in any manner, the court has no jurisdiction in the matter and will not assume any.

We, therefore, take the liberty of praying your excellency, in behalf of the owner of the vessel, to present to Mr. Seward the enclosed claim for damages, and request him to order the same paid.

We are your excellency's most obedient servants,

M. ECHEVERRIA & CO.,
Agents for the owners.

Claim of the owner of the Mexican schooner Oriente, for damages sustained by him by reason of the seizure of the vessel.

The vessel was seized June 18, 1862, and released from custody in January, 1863.

Loss of services of the vessel for seven months, at $2,000 per month	$14,000
Expenses of vessel and crew in New Orleans	1,000
Wages of captain and mate, board and passage to New York	1,000
Expense of sending home crew to Laguayra, there being no direct opportunity	500
Legal expenses in New York and New Orleans	500
Damage and deterioration of cargo	3,000
Damages to vessel, and expenses to place her in the same condition as when seized	2,000
Goods and articles missing from vessel	300
Charges of agent in New York	1,000
	23,300

M. ECHEVERRIA & CO.,
Agents for the owners.

Mr. Seward to Mr. Barreda.

DEPARTMENT OF STATE,
Washington, June 30, 1863.

SIR: I have the honor to acknowledge the receipt of your communication of the 24th instant, with the accompanying memorial of Messieurs. Echeverria & Company, of New York, agents of the owners of the Mexican brig Oriente, supplemental to one heretofore forwarded to this department on the 20th November, 1862, together with a statement of the items of which the alleged claim is made up, which will be duly adjusted when similar claims of American citizens against Mexico are considered.

I avail myself of this occasion to offer to you renewed assurances of my high consideration.

WILLIAM H. SEWARD.

Señor Don FEDERICO L. BARREDA, &c., &c., &c.,
Washington.

No. 13.—*Case of the Mexican brig Brilliante.*

Mr. Romero to Mr. Seward, March 6, 1862, (with one enclosure.)
Mr. Seward to Mr. Romero, March 12, 1862, (with two enclosures.)
Mr. Romero to Mr. Seward, June 23, 1862, (with two enclosures.)
Mr. Seward to Mr. Romero July 14, 1862.
Same to same, August 4, 1862, (with one enclosure.)

Mr. Romero to Mr Seward.

[Translation.]

MEXICAN LEGATION TO THE UNITED STATES OF AMERICA,
Washington, March 6, 1862.

Mr. SECRETARY: I have the honor to remit to you copy of a letter addressed by Messrs. Riera and Thébaud, merchants, of New York, to the Mexican consul at that port, upon the capture by United States cruisers of the Mexican brig Brilliante, owned by Messrs. Preciat & Gual, of Campeachy.

I beg you, sir, to communicate to me the official statements which the government of the United States may have about the circumstances which occasioned the capture of the said brig, and the situation in which the business now is, for the information of the parties interested, and that the legation may gather from those reports what may be advisable for the protection of the property of Mexican citizens.

I avail myself of this opportunity to renew to you, sir, the assurances of my very distinguished consideration.

M. ROMERO.

Hon. WILLIAM H. SEWARD, &c., &c., &c.

NEW YORK, *February* 27, 1862.

DEAR SIR: We have the honor to enclose a confidential letter from his excellency the President of Mexico to the Mexican minister at Washington, relative to the claim of Messrs. Preciat and Gual against the government of the United States, arising out of the capture and condemnation of the Mexican schooner Brilliante, with her cargo, for alleged violation of blockade, and also a letter from those gentlemen to the same. As you are aware, Messrs. Preciat and Gual are Mexican citizens, engaged in commercial affairs at Campeachy, (Yucatan,) and were the owners of said vessel and cargo at the time of their capture. They insist that the seizure and condemnation in question are illegal. We are not aware whether the grounds of imputed illegality appear in the proceedings of the prize court at Key West, or not. We beg leave to request you to place the matter in charge of the Mexican embassy at

Washington, and to make known to us what steps it will be necessary to take in behalf of the claimants in order to present their case to the favorable consideration of both governments.

We remain, dear sir, your obedient servants,

RIERA & THÉBAUD.

Señor D. JOSÉ MARIA DURAN,
Mexican Consul.

A true copy:

M. ROMERO.

WASHINGTON, *March* 6, 1862.

Mr. Seward to Mr. Romero.

DEPARTMENT OF STATE,
Washington, March 12, 1862.

SIR: Having communicated to the Secretary of the Navy a translation of your note of the 6th instant, with a copy of the letter of Messrs. Riera and Thébaud accompanying it, I have just received from him a letter upon the subject referred to, of which, and of its enclosure, I transmit you a copy.

I avail myself of this occasion to renew to you, sir, the assurances of my distinguished consideration.

WILLIAM H. SEWARD.

Señor Don MATIAS ROMERO, *&c., &c, &c.*

NAVY DEPARTMENT, *March* 11, 1862.

SIR: I have the honor to acknowledge the receipt of your letter of the 18th instant and its enclosures, and to transmit herewith an extract from a report dated June 25, 1861, made to the flag-officer of the Gulf blockading squadron by Commander Melancton Smith, which contains all the information in the possession of the department in relation to the capture of the Mexican schooner Brilliante by the United States steamer Massachusetts. I do not know what has been the result of the judicial proceedings in the case, as no information on that subject has been received by the department.

I am, very respectfully, your obedient servant,

GIDEON WELLES.

Hon. WILLIAM H. SEWARD,
Secretary of State.

[Extract.]

UNITED STATES STEAMER MASSACHUSETTS,
Off Pass à Loutre, June 25, 1861.

SIR: I have to report that on the 23d instant I captured in Mississippi sound, with the boats belonging to the vessel, five schooners—four claiming to belong to a government not recognized by the United States, and having on board the flag adopted by the States that are in rebellion, and one, a Mexican vessel, from New Orleans, that has violated the blockade.

The Mexican schooner Brilliante—cargo 600 barrels of flour, two dismounted guns, and one gun-carriage—had been warned off by the boarding officer of the steamer Brooklyn, and her register was properly indorsed. She cleared for New Orleans four days after the expiration of the notice given to neutral vessels to depart.

* * * * * * * * *

These vessels were sent forward to Key West.

* * * * * * * * *

Very respectfully, your obedient servant,

MELANCTON SMITH, *Commander.*

Flag-Officer WILLIAM MERVINE,
United States Navy.

Mr. Romero to Mr. Seward.

[Translation.]

MEXICAN LEGATION IN THE UNITED STATES OF AMERICA,
Washington, June 23, 1862.

MR. SECRETARY: I have the honor to lay before you copy of a letter which I have received from Messrs. Preciat & Gual, of Campeachy, owners, loading the Mexican brig Brilliante, which was captured on the 23d June of the year last past, in the neighborhood of New Orleans, in which they explain the reasons why the brig left the port four days after the period limited. From this letter it appears that, although, speaking absolutely, it might be said that the brig Brilliante had violated the blockade from the circumstances indicated of leaving New Orleans four days after the expiration of the time given to neutrals to pass freely, for which, most technically, she was condemned by the court at Key West, there are very important considerations in favor of the good faith of the owners of the vessel, which, perhaps, would determine the government of the United States to grant them an indemnity for the losses they would suffer in consequence of the capture of the vessel, and the judgment of the court. The parties interested estimate that seven thousand seven hundred and thirty-two dollars and twenty six cents is the amount of the loss suffered, as appears in the account which I also send in copy.

I avail myself of this opportunity to reiterate to you, sir, the assurances of my most distinguished consideration.

M. ROMERO.

Hon. WILLIAM H. SEWARD, *&c., &c., &c.*

[Translation.]

CAMPEACHY, *May* 12, 1862.

DEAR SIR: By your very obliging letter, dated 30th of March last past, we are apprised of the date when you received the documents relating to the capture of our Mexican packet-boat Brilliante, and that on the same day you addressed a note to the Secretary of the Department of State in relation thereto, of which you sent me a copy, as well as of the reply had, which you likewise sent to the Mexican consul at New York, that he might confer with Messrs. Riera and Thébaud, of that city, indicating what was suitable to be done to obtain the restoration of the vessel, or the value. We greatly appreciate your proceedings, and do not doubt, with your aid, to attain a good result.

The narration of the facts which caused the capture, for which you call upon us, should be found judicially set forth in the report from the court at Key West, where the judgment of *good prize*, founded on the declaration of blockade, and the excess of four days over the term granted for neutrals to pass freely, was given. The commander of the United States steamer Massachusetts makes reference to the term, "exceeded by four days," in his note, dated on board his ship, the 25th of June, 1861. In fact, the term set for neutrals was exceeded, and this may be a legal support of the sentence, but not a just one; for, if attention be given to the antecedents, which might have happened in each case, many, as well as ourselves, would be absolved. Don Rafael Preciat, our partner, had gone with the vessel with the single purpose of visiting his sons, who were at the college at Spring Hill, for which he set out on arrival at New Orleans, and where he was when the publication of the term limited for neutrals was made; and as, by his absence, the vessel could not be despatched by the consignees, it was necessary to wait for him. When he got back, the time limited, of which he knew nothing, had passed—no other recourse remaining to him than to hasten off from New Orleans; but before getting to sea he desired to speak one of the cruisers, and, in fact, he gave the order to come to anchor off the bay of Velopsi, where he could have taken refuge if he had had any fear, when he saw a boat coming, which he waited for in confidence, thinking he had accomplished his wish, but by which he was captured and taken to Key West. This is all that happened. Now you will understand whether the lapse of four days over time fixed for neutrals was a sufficient foundation for the sentence.

In our note of losses sent to Messrs. Riera and Thébaud we have not sought to add more expenses than we really and truly have disbursed; so much so, that the vessel, costing us much more than the sum at which she was bought in, we having been the purchasers, we have not desired to fix a higher sum than what we have disbursed to make us good for the vessel, as you will inform yourself by the copy we have the honor to send herewith, leaving to your discretion to alter it for or against us if it should be judged proper and equitable.

We have the honor to repeat that we are your very obedient servants,

PRECIAT & GUAL.

Señor Don MATIAS ROMERO, *Washington.*

A true copy: ROMERO.

WASHINGTON, *June* 23, 1862.

Expenses incurred at Key West in the matter of the Mexican pilot-boat Brilliante and her cargo, which was brought as prize into that port by an armed force of the United States of America in July, 1861.

Paid into court for value of said vessel and cargo, as per appraisal	$3,820 00
Paid to same for costs, per receipt	200 00
Paid to defendants' counsel, per receipt	100 00
Paid to English and Spanish consuls for protests, &c., there being no Mexican consul	30 71
Paid the pilot for taking the vessel out	20 00
Provisions used by the crew of said schooner, and officers and seamen of the United States who were in charge and remained on board at Key West	242 77
Costs of clerk of court, per receipt	35 60
Paid Messrs. W. H. Will & Co., commissions	149 95
Wages paid crew of said schooner	246 36
Expenses of hotel for captain and passengers	150 00
Damage to tackle and sails, appraised by experts	300 00
Damage to cargo, by detention at Key West, on 600 barrels of flour, per account sales	2,436 87
Total	7,732 26

PRECIAT & GUAL.

CAMPEACHY, *August* 20, 1861.

A true copy: ROMERO.

WASHINGTON, *June* 23, 1862.

Mr. Seward to Mr. Romero.

DEPARTMENT OF STATE,
Washington, July 14, 1862.

SIR: I have the honor to acknowledge the receipt of your note of the 23d ultimo, with its enclosures, relative to the case of the Brilliante, and to inform you that I have called on the United States district attorney at Key West for a report in the case, upon receipt of which the subject will receive due consideration.

I avail myself of this occasion to renew to you the assurances of my high consideration.

WILLIAM H. SEWARD.

Señor Don MATIAS ROMERO, *&c., &c., &c.*

Mr. Seward to Mr. Romero.

DEPARTMENT OF STATE,
Washington, August 4, 1862.

SIR: Referring to my letter of the 14th July, in answer to your communication of the 23d June last, I have the honor to transmit you, herewith, a copy of the report made to this department by the United States district attorney at Key West, Florida, setting forth the facts in relation to the seizure and condemnation of the Mexican schooner Brilliante, libelled July 20, 1861.

From this report you will perceive that the case is now pending in the Supreme Court of the United States, the claimant having appealed from the decision of the district court, while the vessel and cargo have been bonded, and are now in his possession.

I avail myself of this opportunity to renew to you, sir, the assurances of my distinguished consideration.

WILLIAM H. SEWARD.

Señor Don MATIAS ROMERO, *&c., &c., &c.*

UNITED STATES DISTRICT ATTORNEY'S OFFICE,
Key West, Florida, July 24, 1862.

SIR: Your letter of the 14th instant, requesting a brief report of the decision of the court in the case of the Mexican schooner Brilliante, is received.

The vessel was libelled as prize on the 20th of July, 1861. The evidence of the owner of the vessel, and the other witnesses, showed that the vessel's papers were indorsed with notice of the blockade by the boarding officer from the blockading vessel at the mouth of the Mississippi river. After this formal warning the vessel succeeded in getting to New Orleans by way of Lake Pontchartrain, where she proceeded to take in a load of flour. She was taken coming out.

No point except that of the authority of the President to establish the blockade was argued in this court. A decree of condemnation was rendered; the claimant appealed to the supreme court, and bonded the vessel and cargo and took them into his possession. The appeal is now pending in the supreme court.

I am, sir, very respectfully, your obedient servant,

THOMAS J. BOYNTON,
United States Attorney.

Hon. WILLIAM H. SEWARD,
Secretary of State.

No. 14.

Correspondence of Legations of the United States on Mexican affairs.

Mr. Dayton to Mr. Seward, January 23, 1863, (with one enclosure.)
Mr. Dayton to Mr. Seward, March 11, 1863.
Same to same, April 9, 1863.
Same to same, April 24, 1863, (with one enclosure.)
Mr. Seward to Mr. Dayton, April 24, 1863.
Mr. Dayton to Mr. Seward, April 27, 1863.
Same to same, May 1, 1863.
Mr. Seward to Mr. Dayton, May 8, 1863.
Same to same, May 18, 1863.
Mr. Dayton to Mr. Seward, May 29, 1863.
Same to same, May 29, 1863.
Same to same, June 11, 1863.
Mr. Seward to Mr. Dayton, June 12, 1863.
Same to same, June 12, 1863.
Mr. Dayton to Mr. Seward, June 17, 1863, (with one enclosure.)
Mr. Dayton to Mr. Seward, June 26, 1863, (with one enclosure.)
Mr. Dayton to Mr. Seward, July 2, 1863.
Mr. Seward to Mr. Dayton, July 17, 1863.
Same to same, July 25, 1863.
Mr. Dayton to Mr. Seward, August 21, 1863.
Mr. Seward to Mr. Dayton, August 31, 1863.
Same to same, September 7, 1863.
Mr. Dayton to Mr. Seward, September 14, 1863.
Same to same, September 16, 1863.
Mr. Seward to Mr. Dayton, September 21, 1863.

Mr. Dayton to Mr. Seward.

[Extract.]

No. 258.] PARIS, *January* 23, 1863.

SIR: I beg to enclose to you an extract from the Moniteur of this morning. I learned yesterday from our consul general at Alexandria, Mr. Thayer, that his highness the viceroy had put on board the French frigate La Sine, on the night of the 7th instant, several hundred negro soldiers, taken from Dalfour and Nubia, destined to join the French military expedition against Mexico. The Moniteur of this morning admits this to be so, and says that they are taken because the black race is not subject to the yellow fever, and that they are destined to be placed in garrison at Vera Cruz.

* * * * * * * * *

I am, sir, your obedient servant,

WILLIAM L. DAYTON.

Hon. WILLIAM H. SEWARD,
Secretary of State, &c., &c., &c.

From the "Moniteur" of Paris, January 23, 1863

[Translation—Bulletin.]

In consequence of the report that the viceroy of Egypt had placed a battalion of Egyptians at the disposal of the Emperor, the British press has suffered itself to indulge in suppositions which it is proper to correct. The following is the fact: Experience having taught, in the case of the negro companies from our West India possessions sent to Vera Cruz, that the negro race was not subject, like the white race, to the influence of yellow fever, the Emperor has asked from the viceroy, not the permission to recruit soldiers, as the British government did during the war in the Indies, but the temporary transfer (*cession*) of a negro regiment of 1,200 men, fully organized, with its officers and non-commissioned officers. The viceroy was unable, for the time being, to dispose of more than 450 men, who are to do garrison duty at Vera Cruz. This measure, adopted in a sense of humanity, cannot give rise to the least criticism.

Mr. Dayton to Mr. Seward.

No. 285.] PARIS, *March* 11, 1863.

SIR: I enclose you, by the present steamer, an English copy of the translation of the speech of M. Billault, "minister sans portefeuille," on the French invasion of Mexico, delivered in the corps législatif on the 7th of February last. This speech has doubtless been translated and published in England at the instance of the French government. M. Billault is, as you know, one of the most eloquent debaters in France, and on the floor of the Chambers acts, in this matter of Mexico, as the mouthpiece of the government. The Moniteur, of this morning, says that a copy of this speech has been laid on the desk of each of the members of the British Parliament. Two copies have been furnished to me, one, at least, of which was, doubtless, intended for my government. You will draw your own inferences from this course of proceeding on the part of this government.

I am, sir, your obedient servant,

WILLIAM L. DAYTON.

Hon. WILLIAM H. SEWARD,
Secretary of State, &c., &c., &c.

Mr. Dayton to Mr. Seward.

No. 297.] PARIS, *April* 9, 1863.

SIR: In a conference with Mr. Drouyn de Lhuys, had this day, he inquired particularly as to our action in reference to the issue of letters of marque.
* * * * * * * * He then said immediately there was nothing of special interest for me there; that they had no news of importance from the United States; and as to Mexico, he said again their purpose was to take the city; to give some sort of order to the condition of things there, repay themselves for debts, expenses, &c., and then leave the country; that we might rest assured they were not going to charge themselves with the government of Mexico. I told him that in the present distracted condition of that country I did not see how it was possible that France, if she got possession, could enforce the payment of the debts due her and expenses. (I suppose he meant expenses of invasion, although he did not say so.) I said that France would not be willing, I supposed, to seize on the private property of Mexican citizens for the purpose of meeting these claims, and there seemed to be no public revenues adequate. To this he answered that the wealth of Mexico was rather unused and scattered than exhausted; that there were sources of wealth, mines, &c., which, properly worked, would meet all claims upon the country. Here I think you have a view of the probable policy of this government—an intimation which will serve as an index to point out the future route which the government of France, if successful, at present designs to follow. My fear would be that, estimating for herself the debts and expenses due to her, working for herself the mines or other sources of income, and keeping both sides of the account, it would require a long possession before the profits of the adventure would fully settle the balance.

My long conference with Mr. Drouyn de Lhuys was a very pleasant and agreeable one. Our personal relations are in all respects kind. Before leaving I asked for another copy of the diplomatic correspondence of France for the past year, telling him, at the same time, that it was for Mr. Romero, the Mexican minister at Washington, who had written to me for it. He gave it to me at once, adding some other pamphlets about Mexican affairs, which I told him I should forward to Mr. Romero. I use the despatch bag for that purpose.

I am, sir, your obedient servant,

WM. L. DAYTON.

Hon. WILLIAM H. SEWARD,
Secretary of State, &c.

Mr. Dayton to Mr. Seward.

No. 301.] PARIS, *April* 24, 1863.

SIR: In pursuance of the written request of Mr. Drouyn de Lhuys, I called at the Foreign Office yesterday, and immediately learned that the French government made gave and serious complaint against us by reason of the late certificate, or, as they choose to call it, the "laissez passer" which Mr. Adams grave, as they allege, to Messrs. Howell and General Zirman, the Mexican agents in London. They assume that the cargo was arms, and that Mr. Adams knew it. I suggested that there was nothing on the face of the papers to indicate anything of the kind, and told Mr. Drouyn de Lhuys that, in giving the paper or certificate in question, I did not believe Mr. Adams had had the slightest thought or reference to France and her relations with Mexico, as Matamoras was not, I thought, blockaded by France. That he, Mr. Adams, had a difficult part to play in England, and, do what he would, he was sure to be found fault with there. I told him I much regretted that anything had occurred there to wound the sensibility of the government of the Emperor, and I was sure it was not intended. It was not so much, as it seemed to me, the fact that Mr. Adams had given the certificate in question that he complained of, as the terms or phraseology in which he had clothed it; and, assuming that the cargo was *arms* for the Mexicans, with whom France is at war, and that Mr. Adams knew it, it was perhaps justly subject to a part at least of the criticism which he placed upon it. He went on to add, too, that Mr. Adams's desire to facilitate "neutral commerce" (being arms, as he said, to kill the French) was much at variance with the action of our government at New York and New Orleans, which forbade the shipment of mules, or free laborers, and even of *timber* for the use of the French in Mexico. I told him that I knew nothing of this, and that the correspondence between yourself and Mr. Romero, the Mexican minister at Washington, indicated a policy directly the reverse of this. That while the Secretary of the Treasury had refused to interfere, on the application of Mr. Romero, to prevent the exportation of wagons, &c., for the French, he had at once stopped the exportation of 37,000 stand of muskets purchased in New York for the Mexicans, and that the Mexican minister had, in consequence, felt himself justified in making the unpleasant intimation that our government had discriminated unjustly and unfairly against Mexico and in favor of France. He wished me to send him an extract of this correspondence for the Emperor, and I have this morning sent him the correspondence itself, with the parts marked to which I desired particularly to call his attention. Before leaving this part of the subject, however, he said that he thought, in the first place, there had been some such liberty of export allowed; that even General Butler had permitted this; but that General Banks who, it was thought, was to be less severe than his predecessor at New Orleans, had been more exacting or less liberal upon these matters than even General Butler. That most serious complaints had come to him from the army and navy department here of the great inconvenience to which they had been subject by his orders limiting the export of such articles. I told him that I knew of nothing further on this subject than appeared in the published correspondence, and that if any such orders were made, they must have grown, I thought, out of some existing want or emergency of our own; but in this he did not agree with me. He said if the war in Mexico were unpleasant to us, we must remember that our war, too, was unpleasant and injurious to them: and, adverting again to Mr. Adams's certificate, he said that they had at no time, *by word or act, said or done an unkind thing towards us*; that their leaning had been rather in our favor than against us throughout, and yet here is a certificate given by a distinguished official of the United States government abroad, stating that "it gives him pleasure" to distinguish this adventure of sending a shipment of arms to their enemies as an honest and fair enterprise and for a creditable purpose, &c., (being, as he said, to kill them with!) and that he therefore "cheerfully" gave the certificate in question. That this language was calculated to excite the French people, and he should, as far as possible, keep its translation out of the French newspapers; and he hoped for something kind very shortly from the government of the United States to relieve the painful impression it had made.

In illustrating his views of the certificate, he said its manifest tendency was to encourage Mexico, and to induce the belief that if she held out the United States would, perhaps, in the end help her. He added: "Suppose Baron Gros (the present minister of France at London) had given to the owners of a ship full of arms going to the confederates, who are at war with us, such a paper, directed to the commander of the French squadron on our cost, what would our government have thought of it?" But he said that the paper was much opposed to the views you had yourself expressed very recently to Mr. Mercier, as to the purposes of our government in regard to the war of France in Mexico; and he read to me part of a despatch from Mr. Mercier, dated, I think, as late as the third of this month, on that subject. He wished me to say again to you that France had no purpose in Mexico beyond asserting her just claims against her, obtaining payment of the debt due, with the expenses of the invasion, and vindicating, by victory, the honor of her flag. He again said, expressly, that they did not mean to colonize in Mexico, or to obtain Sonora or any other section permanently, and that all such pretences, propagated through the newspapers, were untrue. In return, I assured him that all your correspondence with me, public and private, assured me that our government had no purpose to interfere in any way with the war between France and Mexico.

After this general conversation Mr. Drouyn de Lhuys said that he had, for greater certainty, put in writing the substance of his remarks as to the paper given by Mr. Adams to the Mexican agents, which he would leave with me, not as a formal communication, but as informal memoranda only of what he had said on that subject. I told him I should be happy to have the paper if I was permitted to translate and send it to my government. To this he assented. I received it without reading, and herewith send you a translation. I shall likewise send another copy to Mr. Adams. The sound judgment and great discretion which have so uniformly characterized his service in London will dictate to him whether it calls for any action on his part.

Before closing this despatch, I ought to add that I was informed that Mr. Drouyn de Lhuys has expressed himself to another person, on the subject hereinbefore referred to, in terms more decided even than to me, closing, as he did, with the remark, that if the United States aided or encouraged their enemies in Mexico, France would aid and encourage our enemies in the United States.

I am, sir, your obedient servant,

WM. L. DAYTON.

Hon. WILLIAM H. SEWARD,
Secretary of State, &c.

P. S.—I will send a copy of the original of the memoranda handed to me by Mr. Drouyn de Lhuys by the next steamer.

Translation of informal memoranda of Mr. Drouyn de Lhuys's remarks to Mr. Dayton on the 23d of April.

The government of the Emperor has not been able to read without painful surprise the document emanating from the minister of the United States at London, to which the English press have just given a publicity perhaps unexpected. A deliberate feeling only of hostility towards France can have induced Mr. Adams to deliver to the Mexican agents, who had informed him as to their projects, the strange certificate destined to facilitate the execution of them. If a doubt were possible in this respect, the terms in which is conceived the "laissez passer," addressed to the commandant of the federal fleet, would suffice to indicate with what disposition the representative of the United States in England was unfortunately inspired on this occasion.

The government of the Emperor admits perfectly that the American cruisers should abstain from molesting and seizing the vessels which have not violated, towards the United States themselves, the duties of neutrality.

But there is no necessity for setting forth the difference which exist between an abstention conformable to the attitude imposed upon every belligerent towards neutrals whose conduct does not furnish it with direct motives of complaint, and the formal assurance given to a third party engaged in operations infected with an illegal character towards another belligerent, that they will not in any way disturb their operations. There is guaranteed to these parties in this last case a security upon which they ought not to count; there is removed from them in advance certain perils which might compromise success; fears are dissipated which would perhaps have stopped them. If there is not there an effective participation in acts condemned by the right of nations, is it not, nevertheless, very evidently to accord to them an unusual guarantee, a quasi protection; and is it not, therefore, morally to associate one's self with them? In giving to M. M. Howell and Zirman the attestation which they solicited of him, and the effect of which must be to assure to them, in spite of the character of their merchandise, a free passage through the American cruisers, Mr. Adams could not be mistaken as to the concurrence which he had lent to a transaction of contraband of war, which he knew to be undertaken against us. There would then have been occasion for asking one's self by what inadvertence the minister of a friendly power had been induced thus to favor acts openly directed against France, if the tenor of the certificate signed by him did not state that it is intentionally, and because he approved of it, that Mr. Adams wished to cover them with an exceptional immunity. The expressions employed by M. the minister of the United States do not leave room for any ambiguity. It is with pleasure that he learns the end of the proposed operation. The sending of arms and ammunitions, which might have called for the most severe censure, the most rigorous repression, if they had been destined for the enemies of the federal government, assumes an entirely different character, and becomes legitimate as soon as it is to the profit of the enemies of France.

The government of the Emperor refuses to believe that such sentiments have drawn their inspiration from Washington. It is well convinced that Mr. Adams has, in this matter, only expressed opinions altogether personal.

It is easy to understand, however, that the language of the minister of the United States at London borrows, necessarily, from its diplomatic character, a particular importance, and formed as they have been, his appreciations authorize us to suppose that views hostile to France are held also by his government. The cabinet of Washington will not be astonished, then, that the government of the Emperor should see in the procedure of Mr. Adams an act gratuitously malevolent towards France, and by which it has a right to feel itself wounded. One would seek in vain a motive for excuse of the conduct of the American representative.

Nothing made it obligatory upon him to furnish to the Mexican agents a paper which was equivalent to a veritable safe-conduct, which, even had it not been a question of the transportation of contraband of war, would have contrasted with the suspicious and excessive surveillance exercised over all shipments leaving England for the same point, but which, in the form and with the conditions on which it was given, became a mark of sympathy and an altogether voluntary encouragement accorded to illegal manœuvres prejudicial to a friendly power. The government of the Emperor cannot, then, conceal the regretable impressions which it has experienced. It must think that the federal government will itself have anticipated it, and confiding in the security of the assurances of entirely another nature which it has often received from it, it believes itself authorized to expect of it an explicit disavowal of the attitude and of the language of its minister at London.

Mr. Seward to Mr. Dayton.

No. 336.] DEPARTMENT OF STATE,
Washington, April 24, 1863.

SIR: Your despatch of April 9, No. 297, has been submitted to the President.

* * * * * *

I do not care to speak often upon the war of France against Mexico. The President confidingly believes that the Emperor has no purpose of assuming, in the event of success, the government of that republic. Difficult as the exercise of self-government there has proved to be, it is, nevertheless, quite certain that the attempt to maintain foreign authority there would encounter insurmountable embarrassment. The country possesses immense, practically inexhaustible, resources. They invite foreign labor and capital from all foreign countries to become naturalized and incorporated with the resources of the country and of the continent, while all attempts to acquire them by force must meet with the most annoying and injurious hindrance and resistance. This is equally true of Mexico and of every portion of the American continent. It is more than a hundred years since any foreign state has successfully planted a new colony in America, or even strengthened its hold upon any one previously existing here. Through all the social disturbances which attend a change from the colonial state to independence, and the substitution of the democratic for the monarchical system of government, still seems to us that the Spanish-American states are steadily advancing towards the establishment of permanent institutions of self-government. It is the interest of the United States to favor this progress, and to commend it to the patronage of other nations. It is equally the interest of all other nations, if, as we confidently believe, this progress offers to mankind the speediest and surest means of rendering available to them the natural treasures of America.

I am, sir, your obedient servant,

WILLIAM H. SEWARD.

WILLIAM L. DAYTON, Esq., &c., &c., &c.,

Mr. Dayton to Mr. Seward.

[Extract.]

No. 302.] PARIS, *April* 27, 1863.

SIR: I send you herewith what, for the want of time, I could not get ready for the last steamer, to wit, a copy of the original memorandum handed to me by Mr. Drouyn de Lhuys in reference to the views taken by the French government of the certificate lately given by Mr. Adams to the Mexican agents in London. It is *not signed*, you will observe, and was given to me, as I have informed you, not as a formal communication, but as mere memoranda of conversation.

I should have added in my last despatch that Mr. Drouyn de Lhuys again observed to me, in that conversation, that it would manifestly be bad policy in the United States to adopt a course of action which would identify the policy of France with that of England; that he knows there was much exasperation of feeling in our country against England, but that heretofore France had done nothing of which we could complain. He assumes that they have been friendly throughout; says they have built no Alabamas, &c.

I am, sir, your obedient servant,

WM. L. DAYTON.

Hon. WILLIAM H. SEWARD,
Secretary of State, &c.

P. S.—It is reporteed to me that an additional loan of eight millions of francs has been effected by the confederates here. D.

Mr. Dayton to Mr. Seward.

No. 303.] PARIS, *May* 1, 1863.

SIR: Your despatches from No. 320 to No. 330, both inclusive, are received

* * * * * * * * *

Having received a note from Mr. Adams in reference to his late certificate to Messrs. Howell and Zirman, I took occasion, at his request, to say informally to Mr. Drouyn de Lhuys that he (Mr. Adams) expressly disclaimed all hostility to the French government, and all of the unfriendly motives attributed to him, in the late memoranda which had been left with me.

I am, sir, your obedient servant,

WM. L. DAYTON.

Hon. WILLIAM H. SEWARD.
Secretary of State, &c.

Mr. Seward to Mr. Dayton.

[Extract.]

No. 341.] DEPARTMENT OF STATE,
Washington, May 8, 1863.

SIR: Your despatch of the 24th of April, No. 301, has been received. It communicates the impressions which have been made upon the French government by a paper under the signature of Mr. Adams, of the date of the 9th of April last, which has appeared in the journals of London.

Candor obliges me to commence my observations upon the subject with an acknowledgment of the very generous manner in which Mr. Drouyn de Lhuys has opened the way to a dispassionate and friendly consideration of the complaint which he has preferred. He has not only reassured you of the friendly spirit of the Emperor towards the United States, but he has also, with marked decision and energy, reaffirmed to you that France has no purpose in Mexico beyond asserting just claims against her, obtaining payment of the debt due, with the expenses of the invasion, and vindicating by victory the honor of the French flag, and that France does not mean to colonize in Mexico, or to obtain Sonora or any other section permanently, and that all allegations propagated through the newspapers conflicting with these assurances are untrue.

Your reply to these remarks of Mr. Drouyn de Lhuys, namely, that in all my correspondence with you, whether public or private, I have averred that this government has no purpose to interfere in any way with the war between France and Mexico, was as truthful as it was considerate and proper. The United States have not disclaimed, and can never under existing circumstances disclaim, the interest they feel in the safety, welfare and prosperity of Mexico, any more than they can relinquish or disown their sentiments of friendship and good will towards France, which began with their national existence, and have been cherished with growing earnestness ever since. When the two nations towards which they are thus inclined are found engaged in such a war as Mr. Drouyn de Lhuys has described, the United States can only deplore the painful occurrence, and express in every way and everywhere their anxious desire that the conflict may be brought to a speedy close by a settlement consistent with the stability, prosperity and welfare of the parties concerned. The United States have always acted upon the same principle of forbearance and neutrality in regard to wars between powers with which our own country has maintained friendly relations, and they believe that this policy could not in this, more than in other cases, be departed from with advantage to themselves or to the interests of peace throughout the world. * *

The French government has justly assumed that the first knowledge which this government had of the paper of which Mr. Drouyn de Lhuys complains was derived from its publication in London. It is notorious that the insurgents of the United States derive their munitions of war and other supplies chiefly through a contraband trade of merchants and others residing or sojourning in Great Britain, carried on in vessels which pretend not a direct destination to the ports of our own country which are blockaded or held in military occupation by the government forces, but to neutral ports of Great Britain, Spain, and Mexico. Matamoras is chief among these neutral ports, and being situated on the right bank of the Rio Grande, which is our national boundary, contraband freights of vessels ascending to or approaching Matamoras through that river are with much facility transferred to the insurgents of the United States, for whose use they are designed.

The blockade has been until this moment our chief protection against this danger, although we are now obtaining a new security against it by recovering the exclusive navigation of the Mississippi river, which divides the country west of that river from the principal field of war.

We understand that two persons named Zirman and Howell appeared in London, and presented themselves to Mr. Adams, Zirman claiming American citizenship by naturalization, and Howard claiming it by birth. We do not know that they were, or that they avowed themselves to be, agents of the Mexican government, as Mr. Drouyn de Lhuys seems to have supposed. Zirman is now recognized here as an adventurer destitute of all pretensions to morality or character. We know nothing of the other's antecedents. They represented to Mr. Adams that they were freighting a British ship with British merchandise, not for the insurgents, but for the Mexicans, and that they found it difficult if not impossible to effect an insurance in London, because a general suspicion attending the Matamoras trade exposed all vessels engaged in it to seizure by the cruisers who are maintaining our blockade. They therefore asked of Mr. Adams a private note which would show that they are loyal Americans, and that their venture was not contraband as against the United States, and which being confidentially shown to the underwriters, might remove the aforementioned difficulty of insurance. Mr. Adams, acting at once upon the suggestion without waiting for further information or prolonged reflection, wrote, signed, and put into their hands the paper of which Mr. Drouyn de Lhuys complains, with no expectation that it would in any case become public.

The transaction being viewed in the light cast upon it by these circumstances, seems to me to lose something of the gravity with which it might otherwise be invested. It must certainly be allowed to be an act not of deliberation, but of inadvertence. The paper shows on its face that it had for its chief, if not its only object, to remove an embarrassment which two of his supposed countrymen had encountered in a mercantile transaction in the distant country to which Mr. Adams was accredited, which embarrassment resulted in part from proceedings in that country, and in part from the action of our own government. It seems at least possible that the bearing of the transaction upon the war between France and Mexico did not at all occur to Mr. Adams, pre-occupied as he was with its relations simply to Great Britain and the United States, for he confines himself in the paper to those relations.

The French government, however, has adopted a different conclusion. In announcing it to you Mr. Drouyn de Lhuys assumes that the cargo of Zirman and Howell was composed, or was at least understood by Mr. Adams to consist, of military stores and munitions of war. I am not able, with the light now enjoyed, to affirm or to deny this fact. Mr. Drouyn de Lhuys derives further evidence of a purpose, or at least of sentiments, on the part of Mr. Adams hostile to France, from certain expressions in the paper, namely, these: "It gives me pleasure to *distinguish* one [meaning one enterprise] which has a different and a *creditable* purpose. I therefore *very cheerfully* give them [Howell and Zirman] this certificate at their request." These expressions are grounded upon the statement which Mr. Adams makes, that these persons have presented him with evidence which is perfectly satisfactory to him that they are really bound to Matamoras with a cargo intended for the Mexicans. While I deem it possible that these expressions were conceived and used without any consciousness on the part of Mr. Adams that they would be taken as alluding to the war existing between France and Mexico, it must be admited, on the other hand, that to insist upon this point would be to stand upon a question of verbal criticism. The United States have no motive for assuming such a position. Striving to conduct their affairs frankly and cordially with all parties, and especially with France, it is enough for them that the construction put upon the expressions of Mr. Adams by Mr. Drouyn de Lhuys is by no means a violent or an unnatural one, and therefore the French government is entitled to the explanation it has asked. You will consequently say to Mr. Drouyn de Lhuys, that having taken the President's instructions upon the subject, I am of opinion that the giving of the paper complained of to Zirman and Howell was in effect an unfriendly act towards France, which was not in harmony with the sentiments and policy of this government, and which it therefore views with disfavor and with regret, while it regards the proceeding on the part of Mr. Adams as having been one of inadvertence, and not of design or motive injurious to France.

I am, sir, your obedient servant,

WILLIAM H. SEWARD.

WILLIAM L. DAYTON, Esq., *&c., &c., &c.*

Mr. Seward to Mr. Dayton.

No. 346.] DEPARTMENT OF STATE,
Washington, May 18, 1863.

SIR: Your despatch No. 303, of the 1st instant, has been received.

The department is pleased to notice that you have anticipated the instruction, No. 341, in regard to the transaction of Mr. Adams with Messrs. Howell and Zirman.

I am, sir, your obedient servant,

WILLIAM H. SEWARD.

WILLIAM L. DAYTON, Esq., *&c., &c., &c.*

Mr. Seward to Mr. Dayton.

No. 348.] DEPARTMENT OF STATE,
Washington, May 23, 1863.

SIR: Your despatch of May 8 (No. 305) has been received. It is proper for me to correct a misapprehension into which you seem to have been led by some remarks of Mr. Drouyn de Lhuys, namely, that I had suggested to Mr. Mercier, with a view to the action of the French government, a blockade of Matamoras. This is erroneous. Any suggestion of that kind that may have reached Mr. Drouyn de Lhuys from Mr. Mercier must have been made from impressions of his own, and on his own authority, although it is not improbable that he conceived the thought as the result of a free conversation with me, in which I mentioned, with some earnestness, the difficulties we sustain in seeing that the neutral port of Mexico is used as the entrepôt for munitions of war, which, if we attempt to seize them, are covered by the pretence that they are designed for another belligerent, while, if we let them pass on that ground, they are received and used for our destruction. It will not be necessary for you to make any explanations to Mr. Drouyn de Lhuys on the subject. Mr. Mercier will doubtlessly do that.

I am, sir, your obedient servant,

WILLIAM H. SEWARD.

WILLIAM L. DAYTON, Esq., *&c., &c., &c.*

Mr. Dayton to Mr. Seward.

No. 309.] PARIS, *May* 29, 1863.

SIR: Your despatch No. 341, which communicates the answer of our government to the complaint made here in respect to the paper given by Mr. Adams to Messrs. Zirman and Howell, dated 9th April last, was duly received. I immediately called upon Mr. Drouyn de Lhuys, and read to him your despatch, and likewise the copy of the one enclosed, sent to Mr. Koerner, our minister at Madrid, dated February 28, last. When I had closed reading these papers, Mr. Drouyn de Lhuys expressed himself very kindly, saying he was much gratified by the contents; and as respects the paper given by Mr. Adams, he added immediately, "Let it be forgotten." We may, therefore, consider this little diplomatic disturbance as a something passed and gone.

I am, sir, your obedient servant,

WM. L. DAYTON.

Hon. WILLIAM H. SEWARD,
Secretary of State, &c.

Mr. Dayton to Mr. Seward.

[Extracts.]

No. 311.] PARIS, *May* 29, 1863.

SIR: I wrote you some time since that I had unofficially, at the request of Messrs. Aspinwall & Forbes, asked Mr. Drouyn de Lhuys if there would be any objection to the quotation of our stocks on the French Bourse. I have not yet had any definite answer, though Mr. Drouyn de Lhuys said they (the ministers) had taken up the subject in council, and his intimation was that they were rather opposed to it. The granting of this right was, as he said, a mere arbitraryact, and *we* had not been very complying in sundry small matters towards them, viz., granting the right to export to Mexico; and Mr. Corwin, he added, has refused to take charge of the legation of France, in Mexico, when their minister was about to leave; which was, he said, a common act of international courtesy. I told him that if this privilege (quoting our stocks on their Bourse) should be denied, I hoped it would be put on no such ground. That it would surprise us very much to learn that France thought we had not been complaisant and accommodating towards them. That, in respect to exports for Mexico, I knew no more than I had previously said to him; and, as respects the action of Mr. Corwin, I knew nothing of it; but if he had declined to take charge of the French legation at Mexico, I had no doubt he had done so fearing that, in the existing state of things, it might tend to some unpleasant complications; and that I, acting under the same impulse, had, on a like application, refused, at first, to take charge of the Mexican legation here, and that that legation in Paris had, consequently, been left in the hands of the minister from Peru. This seemed to strike him, and he asked if he could mention it. I told him he could; but I must inform him, at the same time, that, after advising with others, and satisfying myself that it was a mere act of international courtesy, involving no consequence that a belligerent could complain of, I would have been willing to take charge of that legation, and so informed its minister; but that, under all the circumstances, he then thought it would be better to leave its affairs in the hands of the representatives of another government.

* * * * * *

I am, sir, your obedient servant,

WILLIAM L. DAYTON.

Hon. WILLIAM H. SEWARD,
Secretary of State.

Mr. Dayton to Mr. Seward.

[Extract.]

No. 314.] PARIS, *June* 11, 1863.

SIR: * * * * * * * *

The Emperor and court have left Paris for Fontainebleau. The unexpected news of the taking of Puebla by the French has caused great joy and gratulation, especially among the officials of the government. Illuminations occurred last night, and the cannon of the Hotel des Invalides were fired in honor of the event. The news was altogether unexpected. Even the French press had begun to admit the disastrous condition of things in Mexico, and the government, a few days since, sent off large re-enforcements.

* * * * * * * *

I am, sir, your obedient servant,

WILLIAM L. DAYTON.

Hon. WILLIAM H. SEWARD,
Secretary of State, &c.

Mr. Seward to Mr. Dayton.

No. 357.] DEPARTMENT OF STATE, *Washington, June* 12, 1863.

SIR: Your confidential despatch of May 29 (No. 311) has been received, and I have made its contents known to the Secretary of the Navy.

I have experienced the same surprise which you have confessed in learning that our recent proceedings in relation to France, in Mexico, have been regarded as illiberal by the imperial government. Mr. Corwin, in a despatch of the 11th of March, referred to complaints made by the government of Mexico to the effect that we allowed the French government to obtain supplies here, while we denied similar favors to the government of Mexico.

In the same paper Mr. Corwin informed me that, on the 9th February, he had been solicited by the retiring minister from Prussia to assume the protection of all French, Spanish, Prussian, and Belgian subjects in Mexico, and that he had declined to assume this charge without instructions from his own government. Mr. Corwin promptly set forth the circumstances of the case, and asked the President's instructions thereupon. Such instructions were duly given on the 18th of April last.

I give you, by way of extract, such portions of Mr. Corwin's despatch as bears on the subject, together with a copy of a note relating thereto, which was addressed to him by the minister for foreign relations of Mexico. I add a copy of my reply to Mr. Corwin's despatch. You are at liberty to read these papers to Mr. Drouyn de Lhuys, if it should seem to you, as it does to me, that they are calculated to show that, in respect to both of the topics mentioned by Mr. Drouyn de Lhuys, this government has acted with a scrupulous regard to its friendly relations with them, and its neutrality in the war which unhappily exists between that power and Mexico.

WILLIAM H. SEWARD.

WILLIAM L. DAYTON, Esq., *&c. &c, &c.*

Mr. Seward to Mr. Dayton.

No. 358.] DEPARTMENT OF STATE, *Washington, June* 12, 1863.

SIR: Your despatch of May 29 (No. 309) has been received. It gives me much pleasure to learn that the explanations made by me in relation to the letter written by Mr. Adams to the admirals on the blockade service were satisfactory.

I am, sir, your obedient servant,

WILLIAM H. SEWARD.

WILLIAM L. DAYTON, Esq.

Mr. Dayton to Mr. Seward.

No. 316.] PARIS, *June* 17, 1863.

SIR: I have the honor to enclose herewith a printed copy of the letter addressed by the Emperor to General Forey upon receipt of the news of the capture of Puebla.

I am, sir, your obedient servant,

WILLIAM L. DAYTON.

Hon. WILLIAM H. SEWARD,
Secretary of State, &c., &c., &c.

The Emperor to General Forey.

PALACE OF FONTAINEBLEAU, *June* 12.

GENERAL: The news of the capture of Puebla reached me the day before yesterday, *via* New York. This event has filled us with joy.

I am aware how much foresight and energy have been required of the chiefs and the soldiers to attain that importaint result. Testify in my name to the army my entire satisfaction; tell it how highly I appreciate its perseverance and its courage in so distant an expedition, in which it had to struggle against the climate, against the difficulties of the country, and against an enemy so much the more obstinate that it was deceived as to my intentions. I I bitterly deplore the probable loss of so many brave men, but I have the consolatory feeling that their death has not been useless, either to the interests or honor of France or to civilization. Our object, you well know, is not to impose a government on the Mexicans against their will, or to make our successes contribute to the triumph of any party whatever. I desire that Mexico should revive to a new life, and that, being soon regenerated by a government founded on the national will, on principles of order and of progress, and in respect for the law of nations, it shall admit by friendly relations that it is indebted to France for its repose and its prosperity.

I wait for the official reports to give to the army and to its chief their well-merited rewards; but at present, general, accept my warm and sincere congratulations.

NAPOLEON.

Mr. Dayton to Mr. Seward.

[Extracts.]

No. 321.] PARIS, *June* 26, 1863.

SIR: I herewith enclose you the translation of a communication in *La France*, and a copy of the paper itself, this journal having, it is supposed by the diplomatic corps, a certain indirect connexion with the government. As the substance of this communication was in conformity with information reported to me from other sources, I felt justified, yesterday, in asking Mr. Drouyn de Lhuys, distinctly, if any change in the policy of this government towards us was contemplated; whether anything was in agitation. He said, first, that he knew of nothing; but he added, that he had not seen the Emperor for some days, and he could not, therefore, answer for what he had said or done. He informed me, however, that he was satisfied that the Emperor had seen Mr. Slidell here, and he believed he had seen Messrs. Lindsay and Roebuck at Fontainebleau; but of the latter fact he did not speak with certainty. I have, however, no doubt of it, nor have I any doubt that their mission to Fontainebleau was to get directly from the Emperor the expression of his views, with a view to its influence in the British Parliament. I have heard it said that the conference with Mr. Slidell was mainly in reference to the policy of the confederate government in regard to the French invasion of Mexico, and its probable conduct towards them if they should wish to make the south a basis of operations against that country; upon all which Mr. Slidell, of course, gave, it is said, most satisfactory assurances.

This Mexican question has become a most prominent one in the policy of the Emperor, and the more his invasion of that country is complained of, the more anxious does he seem as to its success.

* * * * * * * *

Please let me hear from you on this subject.

I am, sir, your obedient servant,

WILLIAM L. DAYTON.

Hon. WILLIAM H. SEWARD,
Secretary of State, &c.

[Translation of extract from the journal La France.]

We understand that Mr. Slidell, envoy of the Confederate States, was received on Thursday last by the Emperor, during the short stay that his Majesty made at Paris.

We have reason to believe that the visit of Mr. Slidell was connected with the idea of recognizing the Confederate States of the south, and of thus giving new force to the peace party, which is increasing every day in the States of the north.

The sympathies of the south for France have just been manifested in a striking manner. Richmond has been illuminated upon the occasion of the capture of Puebla, while this great feat of arms was received at the north with an undissembled feeling of regret.

We are informed, also, that Messrs. Roebuck and Lindsay, members of the British Parliament, have had the honor of being received by his Majesty the Emperor.

It is known that these honorable deputies have presented a motion in Parliament, which ought to be discussed next week, and which has for its object the recognition of the southern States.

The cause of the confederates gains new sympathies every day, and their heroic resistance on the one side, on the other the impotence of the armies of the north, prove that there is in them a people strongly organized, worthy, in fine, to be admitted among the independent states.

We are assured that Spain, in particular, will show herself disposed to recognize the south upon the condition, easy to be arranged, that the new confederation would recognize, in its turn, the secular rights of the Spanish government over the island of Cuba, and would interdict itself from all aggression against this island.

A. RENAULD.

Mr. Dayton to Mr. Seward.

No. 323.] PARIS, *July* 2, 1863.

SIR: I have communicated to Mr. Drouyn de Lhuys to-day the substance of your despatch No. 357, in reference to Mexico, and the refusal of Mr. Corwin to take charge of the business of the French legation. He did not seem to consider the reasons assigned by Mr. Corwin to be very good ones.

* * * * * * * *

I am, sir, your obedient servant,

WM. L. DAYTON.

Hon. WILLIAM H. SEWARD,
Secretary of State, &c., &c., &c.

Mr. Seward to Mr. Dayton.

No. 374.] DEPARTMENT OF STATE,
Washington, July 17, 1863.

SIR: I have the honor to acknowledge the reception of your despatch of the 2d of July, No. 323, in which you have related a conversation which you had just before held with Mr. Drouyn de Lhuys upon several subjects affecting our relations with France.

Your proceeding in making the explanations concerning the action of Mr. Corwin in regard to the protection of French subjects in Mexico is approved.

* * * * * * * *

I am, sir, your obedient servant,

WILLIAM H. SEWARD.

WILLIAM L. DAYTON, Esq.

Mr. Seward to Mr. Dayton.

No. 378.] DEPARTMENT OF STATE, *Washington, July* 25, 1863.

SIR: I enclose a copy of a despatch from Mr. Burton, United States minister at Bogota, and of the correspondence to which it refers, relative to a supposed design of the French upon the independence of Ecuador. These papers may be considered sufficent to warrant an inquiry of M. Drouyn de l'Huys upon the subject, and a request for such an explanation as the answer to that inquiry may call for.

I am, sir, your obedient servant,

WILLIAM H. SEWARD.

WILLIAM L. DAYTON, Esq.

Mr. Dayton to Mr. Seward.

[Extract.]

No. 336.] PARIS, *August* 21, 1863.

SIR: Your despatch No. 378 has been duly received, and I have called Mr. Drouyn de l'Huys's attention to the subject therein referred to. He assures me that France has no purpose or design upon the independence of the republic of Ecuador; that should any change in its territory take place, or should it be absorbed in another government, as in the republic of Colombia, this would not, in the language of Baron Gowry du Roslan, their minister, pass unobserved by the government of France, but its observation of such events would apply only to such change of ministers or agents as the absorption of two governments into one might render necessary. If they had any claims against the country or territory so absorbed, they would reserve the right to press them, of course. But he said he recollected nothing of a special character in the despatches of Baron Gowry du Roslan on these subjects; he would, however, examine them further.

It is not improbable or unnatural that, in view of the course of France in Mexico, the republics of Central America may have become alarmed for their future. They look, therefore, with great suspicion and distrust upon the language of all French officials, which seems to imply a purpose upon the part of the Emperor to interfere further.

In this connexion I should add, that Mr. Drouyn de Lhuys took occasion again to say that France had no purpose in Mexico other than heretofore stated; that she did not mean to appropriate permanently any part of that country, and that she should leave it as soon as her griefs were satisfied, and she could do so with honor. In the *abandon* of a conversation somewhat familiar I took occasion to say that in quitting Mexico she might leave a *puppet* behind her. He said no; *the strings would be too long to work.* He added they had had enough of colonial experience in Algeria; that the strength of France was in her compact body and well-defined boundary. In that condition she had her resources always at command. There is much force in the suggestion, as applied to this government, which is so emphatically a military power.

You will put upon this conversation as to Mexico your own construction, and draw your own inferences. It seemed to me, however, that Mr. Drouyn de l'Huys was disposed to avail himself of the opportunity to relieve, as far as possible, the suspicion and distrust which our government might, from late events, naturally entertain of the purposes of France in that country.

* * * * * * * *

I am, sir, your obedient servant,

WM. L. DAYTON.

Hon. WILLIAM H. SEWARD,
Secretary of State.

Mr. Seward to Mr. Dayton.

No. 390.]

DEPARTMENT OF STATE,
Washington, August 31, 1863.

SIR: I have received your three despatches, namely, No. 329, under date of July 30; No. 332, of August 4, and No. 333, of August 5.

Under the uniform aspect of our domestic affairs, the matters presented by these papers may safely pass unnoticed.

You will perceive that the course of events in Mexico is giving rise to much speculation, as well in this country as in Europe, and this speculation takes a direction which may well deserve the consideration of the Emperor's government, for it indicates a disposition in some quarters to produce alienation between this country and France. This government has said nothing upon the subject, except what is contained in a previous communication made by me to yourself, and it lends no materials or encouragement to the debate to which I have referred.

I have told you in a previous despatch that the interests of the United States in Texas are not overlooked. I have now to add that preparations have been made, which, as I trust, will be effectual in establishing the national authority in that State.

I am, sir, your obedient servant,

WILLIAM H. SEWARD.

WILLIAM L. DAYTON, Esq.

Mr. Seward to Mr. Dayton.

No. 392.]

DEPARTMENT OF STATE,
Washington, September 7, 1863.

SIR: Your despatch of August 21 (No. 336) has been received. The explanations of Mr. Drouyn de Lhuys, in regard to the views of the Emperor's government concerning the Central American states, are unexceptionable; and I shall take pleasure in making them known to the parties in whose names the inquiry was instituted.

I have read with much interest the statement you have given me of the remarks which Mr. Drouyn de Lhuys made informally to you concerning the position of the imperial government in Mexico. If we were now authorized to regard them as guaranteed by the Emperor, it would go far to relieve a solicitude, not only here, but in Europe, which I cannot but believe is becoming as inconvenient to

France as it is to the United States. Before this despatch will be received you will probably have ascertained, in compliance with a previous instruction of mine, whether we are authorized to understand Mr. Drouyn de Lhuys as speaking by authority in the explanations he has thus made.

I am, sir, your obedient servant,

WILLIAM H. SEWARD.

WILLIAM L. DAYTON, Esq.

Mr. Dayton to Mr. Seward.

No. 345.] PARIS, *September* 14, 1863.

SIR: * * * * * * * *

In the course of conversation reference was made to the almost universal report that our government only awaits the termination of our domestic troubles to drive the French out of Mexico. This idea is carefully nursed and circulated by the friends of secession here, and is doing us injury with the government. The French naturally conclude that if they are to have trouble with us, it would be safest to choose their own time. M. Drouyn de Lhuys referred to these matters, and said the Emperor had recently asked him if it were true, as the public journals alleged, that the United States had made a formal protest against the action of France in Mexico, and he had told him that no such protest had been made. I told him that, so far as I was concerned, I had received no orders to make such formal protest; that, relying on the constant assurances of France as to its purposes in Mexico, and its determination to leave the people free as to their form of government, and not to hold or colonize any portion of their territories, my government had indicated to me no purpose to interfere in the quarrel; at the same time we had not at all concealed, as he well knew, our earnest solicitude for the well-being of that country, and an especial sensitiveness as to any forcible interference in the form of its government. He said that these were the same general views held by you to M. Mercier, and reported by him to this government. I told him that France must well understand that we did not want war with her; to which he answered that she did not certainly wish war with us.

When I referred to the rumored cession of Texas and part of Louisiana to the Emperor, he, in denying the fact, said these rumors were diabolical. He added that France wanted no territory there.

I enclose you a slip cut from Galignani, containing the substance of what is, I presume, a semi-official exposition of the government as to its action in respect to the rebel ship Florida at Brest.

I am, sir, your obedient servant,

WILLIAM L. DAYTON.

Hon. WILLIAM H. SEWARD,
Secretary of State.

Mr. Dayton to Mr. Seward.

No. 347.] PARIS, *September* 16, 1863.

SIR: I did not receive the communication for Mr. Mercier which Mr. Drouyn de Lhuys promised me until last night. It came then in an open envelope, with a note requesting me, after reading it, to seal it and send it by my next courier, (meaning thereby the next despatch bag.) Having sealed it according to request, I herewith send it in an envelope to you, begging that you will have it promptly delivered to Mr. Mercier. The despatch commences with a remark complimentary to myself, and then goes on to state that I had inquired of him as to the truth of certain rumors afloat, to wit, that the Emperor had decided to recognize the south, and had even already signed a treaty by which the south agreed to cede to France, for herself or to be reconveyed to Mexico, Texas and part of Louisiana, and that Mr. Drouyn de Lhuys, at the same time, asked me if I had not heard other rumors calculated to disturb the good relations existing between our two countries—as that the United States had made its protest against the action of the French government in Mexico; had sent its fleet to Vera Cruz; and made a treaty, offensive and defensive, with Russia. He goes on to say that these suggestions were made less with a view to inquiring as to their truth than for the purpose of fortifying me against a belief in the rumors I had first referred to, the truth of which rumors he expressly denied. He then tells Mr. Mercier that I said I had no knowledge of and did not believe in the report that our navy was before Vera Cruz, or that we had made a treaty, offensive and defensive, with Russia, and that if you had instructed me to make a formal protest against their proceedings in Mexico I should have done so, which I had not; although, under the influence of your general correspondence on this subject, I had made him aware of the painful impression caused in my country by European intervention in Mexico, and our anxious solicitude as to any interference with the form of government there. He then tells Mr. Mercier that he had attached little importance to the rumors he had referred to, which probably originated in the same source as those to which I had referred. He then says to Mr. Mercier, "I repeated to him (Mr. Dayton) that which I had already often said to him, that we were not seeking, either for ourselves or others, any acquisition in America. I added (says he) that I hoped the good sense of the people of the United States would do justice to the exaggerations and false suppositions by the aid of which it was sought to mislead and embitter opinion, and that I counted upon his concurrence to try and make prevail a more just appreciation of our intentions and of the necessities which our policy obeyed."

He then directs Mr. Mercier to communicate this conversation to you, and to use the text thereof to correct false judgments and unjustifiable imputations about him.

I should add that as this despatch is, in part, in reference to the intentions of France in Mexico, in which you and the country are just now so much interested, I have thought it best to avoid mistakes by sending you the above, the last twenty lines of which are little less than a translation of that part of Mr. Drouyn de Lhuys's despatch.

I am, sir, your obedient servant,

WM. L. DAYTON.

Hon. WILLIAM H. SEWARD,
Secretary of State, &c.

Mr. Seward to Mr. Dayton.

No. 400.] DEPARTMENT OF STATE,
Washington, September 21, 1863.

SIR: The French forces are understood to hold in subjection to the new provisional government established in Mexico three of the states, while all the other constituent members of the republic of Mexico still remain under its authority. There are already indications of designs, in those states, to seek aid in the United States, with the consent of this government if attainable, and without it if it shall be refused; and for this purpose inducements are held out, well calculated to excite sympathies in a border population. The United States government has hitherto practiced strict neutrality between the French and Mexico, and all the more cheerfully, because it has relied on the assurances given by the French government that it did not intend permanent occupation of that country, or any violence to the sovereignty of its people. The proceedings of the French in Mexico are regarded by many in that country, and in this, as at variance with those assurances. Owing to this circumstance, it becomes very difficult for this government to enforce a rigid observance of its neutrality laws. The President thinks it desirable that you should seek an opportunity to mention these facts to Mr. Drouyn de Lhuys, and to suggest to him that the interests of the United States, and, as it seems to us, the interests of France herself, require that a solution of the present complications in Mexico be made, as early as may be convenient, upon the basis of the unity and independence of Mexico. I cannot be misinterpreting the sentiments of the United States in saying that they do not desire an annexation of Mexico, or any part of it, nor do they desire any special interest, control, or influence there, but they are deeply interested in the re-establishment of unity, peace, and order in the neighboring republic, and exceedingly desirous that there may not arise out of the war in Mexico any cause of alienation between them and France. Insomuch as these sentiments are by no means ungenerous, the President unhesitatingly believes that they are the sentiments of the Emperor himself in regard to Mexico.

I am, sir, your obedient servant,

WILLIAM H. SEWARD.

WILLIAM L. DAYTON, Esq., &c., &c., &c.

Mr. Seward to Mr. Dayton.

No. 401.]

DEPARTMENT OF STATE,
Washington, September 22, 1863.

SIR: I enclose, for your information, a translation of a note of the 20th of July last, which has been addressed to me by Mr. J. M. Arroyo, who calls himself under-secretary of state and foreign affairs of the Mexican empire, setting forth recent proceedings, with a view to the organization of the new government at Mexico; also a copy of a memorandum which has been left with me by a person calling himself General Cortes, alleged to have been formerly governor of the Mexican state of Sonora. No reply has been, or probably will be, made to either of these papers.

I am, sir, your obedient servant,

WILLIAM H. SEWARD.

WM. L. DAYTON, Esq.

Mr. Arrogo to Mr. Seward.

[Translation.]

PALACE OF THE REGENCY OF THE EMPIRE OF MEXICO,
July 20, 1863.

The undersigned, under-secretary of state and of foreign affairs of the Mexican empire, has the honor to address the present communication to his excellency the Secretary of State and of Foreign Affairs of the United States of

America, to the end that he may be pleased to place within the knowledge of his government the recent important events which have finally resulted in the organization of an appropriate, strong, and durable government, with a view that the nation might be constituted.

This capital having been occupied on the 10th ultimo by the allied Franco-Mexican army, the first care of the general-in-chief was to issue a decree convening a superior gubernative junto of thirty-five members, composed of the most distinguished notabilities; and, moreover, another of two hundred and fifteen notables, in order that, united to the former, they might form an assembly of two hundred and fifty persons selected from all classes of society, and from all the departments, which, in conformity to public law and to the traditional usages of the country, should express the wish of the nation as to the form of government that would best suit it.

The gubernative junto having met, decreed the establishment of a provisional executive power composed of three members, appointing the most excellent the generals of divisions, Don Juan N. Almonte and Don Mariano Salas, and the most illustrious the archbishop of Mexico, Don Pelagio Antonio de Labastida, at present absent in Europe, and to act as his substitute the most illustrious Don Juan B. Ormaechea, bishop elect of Tulancingo, who, in such character, immediately took up the reins of government.

The assembly of the notables having convened in conformity to the decree of the thirteenth of June last, was engaged in causing to be made the important declaration in regard to the form of government, with a view to its permanent stability and the future happiness of the nation. The final result of their labors has been the solemn decree, a copy of which the undersigned has the satisfaction to enclose to his excellency, in which appears the following declaration:

1st. The Mexican nation adopts, as its form of government, a limited hereditary monarchy, with a Catholic prince.

2d. The sovereign shall take the title of Emperor of Mexico.

3d. The imperial crown of Mexico is offered to his imperial and royal highness the Prince Ferdinand Maximilian, Archduke of Austria, for himself and his descendants.

4th. If, under circumstances which cannot be foreseen, the Archduke of Austria, Ferdinand Maximilian, should not take possession of the throne which is offered to him, the Mexican nation relies on the good will of his Majesty Napoleon III, Emperor of the French, to indicate for it another Catholic prince.

This solemn and explicit declaration was received by all classes of society with gratification, and even with enthusiasm, manifested in such a way that the undersigned does not fear to anticipate its complete realization; and so much the more so, since he receives every day numerous manifestations of accession, notice of which his excellency will see in the official journal of the empire, which is annexed.

Consequently the undersigned relies on the moral co-operation of the governments which are friendly to Mexico, among which he has the satisfaction of enumerating that of the United States of America, which has given so many proofs of its interest in the happiness of Mexico.

The undersigned avails himself of this opportunity to offer to his excellency the Secretary of State of the United States of America the assurances of his distinguished consideration.

J. M. ARROYO.

His Excellency the SECRETARY OF STATE AND FOREIGN AFFAIRS
of the United States of America.

Mr. Arroyo to Mr. Seward.

[Translation.]

SECRETARYSHIP OF STATE AND OF THE OFFICE OF FOREIGN RELATIONS.

PALACE OF THE SUPREME EXECUTIVE POWER,
Mexico, July 11, 1863.

The provisional supreme executive power has been pleased to address me the following decree:

"The provisional supreme executive power of the nation to the inhabitants thereof: Know ye that the Assembly of Notables has thought fit to decree as follows:

"'The Assembly of Notables, in virtue of the decree of the 16th ultimo, that it should make known the form of government which best suited the nation, in use of the full right which the nation has to constitute itself, and as its organ and interpreter, declares, with absolute liberty and independence, as follows:

"'1. The Mexican nation adopts as its form of government a limited hereditary monarchy, with a Catholic prince.

"'2. The sovereign shall take the title of Emperor of Mexico.

"'3. The imperial crown of Mexico is offered to his imperial and royal highness the Prince Ferdinand Maximilian, Archduke of Austria, for himself and his descendants.

"'4. If, under circumstances which cannot be foreseen, the Archduke of Austria, Ferdinand Maximilian, should not take possession of the throne which is offered to him, the Mexican nation relies on the good will of his Majesty Napoleon III, Emperor of the French, to indicate for it another Catholic prince.

"'Given in the Hall of Sessions of the Assembly, on the 10th of July, 1863.

"'TEODOSIO LARES, *President*.

"'ALEJANDRO ARANGO Y ESCANDON, *Secretary*.
"'JOSÉ MARIA ANDRADE, *Secretary*.'

"Therefore, let it be printed, published by national edict, and circulated, and let due fulfilment be given thereto.

"Given at the palace of the supreme executive power in Mexico, on the 11th of July, 1863.

"JUAN N. ALMONTE.
"JOSÉ MARIANO SALAS.
"JUAN B. ORMAECHEA.

"To the UNDER SECRETARY OF STATE AND OF THE OFFICE OF FOREIGN RELATIONS."

And I communicate it to you for your knowledge and consequent purposes.

J. M. ARROYO,
Under Secretary of State and of the Office of Foreign Relations.

Hon. WILLIAM H. SEWARD.

Mr. Arroyo to Mr. Seward.

[Translation.]

SECRETARYSHIP OF STATE AND OF THE OFFICE OF FOREIGN RELATIONS.

PALACE OF THE SUPREME EXECUTIVE POWER,
Mexico, July 11, 1863.

The provisional supreme executive power has been pleased to address me the following decree:

"The provisional supreme executive power of the nation to the inhabitants thereof: Know ye, that the Assembly of Notables has thought fit to decree as follows:

"'The Assembly of Notables, in view of the decree of this date, has thought fit to decree:

"'Until the arrival of the sovereign the persons appointed, by decree of 22d of June last, to form the provisional government, shall exercise the power in the very terms established by the decree referred to, with the character of regency of the Mexican empire.

"'Given in the Hall of Sessions of the Assembly on the 11th of July, 1863.

"'TEODOSIO LARES, *President*.

"'ALEJANDRO ARANGO Y ESCANDON, *Secretary*.
"'JOSÉ MARIA ANDRADE, *Secretary*.'

"Therefore, let it be printed, published, and circulated, and let due fulfilment be given thereto.

"Given at the palace of the supreme executive power in Mexico, on the 11th of July, 1863.

"JUAN N. ALMONTE.
"JOSÉ MARIANO DE SALAS.
"JUAN B. ORMAECHEA.

"To the UNDER SECRETARY OF STATE AND OF THE OFFICE OF FOREIGN RELATIONS."

"DON J. MIGUEL ARROYO."

And I communicate it to you for your knowledge and consequent purposes.

J. M. ARROYO,
Under Secretary of State, and of the Office of Foreign Relations.

Hon. WILLIAM H. SEWARD.

Mr. Dayton to Mr. Seward.

No. 352.] PARIS, *September* 25, 1863.

SIR: Your despatch, No. 391, as to the proceedings of our minister resident at Salvador, in reference to French interests there, and the despatch from him to you on that subject, were at once communicated by me to the Foreign Office here. As it was evident that a copy of Mr. Partridge's despatch, stating what he had done in relation to French interests in that country, should be on the files of the Foreign Office here, I left the same temporarily with Mr. Drouyn de Lhuys, at his request, that he might have it copied, if so disposed.

I am, sir, your obedient servant,

WILLIAM L. DAYTON.

Hon. WILLIAM H. SEWARD,
Secretary of State, &c., &c., &c.

Mr. Seward to Mr. Dayton.

[Extracts.]

No. 406.] DEPARTMENT OF STATE,
Washington, September 26, 1863.

SIR: Your confidential despatch of September 7, No. 342, has been received and carefully considered. * * * * * *

It is well understood that through a long period, closing in 1860, the manifest strength of this nation was a sufficient protection, for itself and for Mexico, against all foreign states. That power was broken down and shattered in 1861, by faction. The first fruit of our civil war was a new, and in effect, though not intentionally so, an unfriendly attitude assumed by Great Britain, France, and Spain, all virtually, and the two first named powers avowedly, moving in concert. While I cannot confess to a fear on the part of this government that any one or all of the maritime powers combining with the insurgents could overthrow it, yet it would have been manifestly presumptuous, at any time since this distraction seized the American people, to have provoked such an intervention, or to have spared any allowable means of preventing it. The unceasing efforts of this department in that direction have resulted from this ever-present consideration. If in its communications the majestic efforts of the government to subdue the insurrection, and to remove the temptation which it offered to foreign powers, have not figured so largely as to impress my correspondents with the conviction that the President relies always mainly on the national power, and not on the forbearance of those who it is apprehended may become its enemies, it is because the duty of drawing forth and directing the armed power of the nation has rested upon distinct departments, while to this one belonged the especial duty of holding watch against foreign insult, intrusion, and intervention. With these general remarks I proceed to explain the President's views in regard to the first of the two questions mentioned, namely, the attitude of France in regard to the civil war in the United States.

* * * * * * *

The subject upon which I propose to remark, in the second place, is the relation of France towards Mexico. The United States hold, in regard to Mexico, the same principles that they hold in regard to all other nations. They have neither a right nor a disposition to intervene by force in the internal affairs of Mexico, whether to establish and maintain a republic or even a domestic government there, or to overthrow an imperial or a foreign one, if Mexico chooses to establish or accept it. The United States have neither the right nor the disposition to intervene by force on either side in the lamentable war which is going on between France and Mexico. On the contrary, they practice in regard to Mexico, in every phase of that war, the non-intervention which they require all foreign powers to observe in regard to the United States. But, notwithstanding this self-restraint, this government knows full well that the inherent normal opinion of Mexico favors a government there republican in form and domestic in its organization, in preference to any monarchical institutions to be imposed from abroad. This government knows, also, that this normal opinion of the people of Mexico resulted largely from the influence of popular opinion in this country, and is continually invigorated by it. The President believes, moreover, that this popular opinion of the United States is just in itself, and eminently essential to the progress of civilization on the American continent, which civilization, it believes, can and will, if left free from European resistance, work harmoniously together with advancing refinement on the other continents. This government believes that foreign resistance, or attempts to control American civilization, must and will fail before the ceaseless and ever-increasing activity of material, moral, and political forces, which peculiarly belong to the American continent. Nor do the United States deny that, in their opinion, their own safety and the cheerful destiny to which they aspire are intimately dependent on the continuance of free republican institutions throughout America. They have submitted these opinions to the Emperor of France, on proper occasions, as worthy of his serious consideration, in determining how he would conduct and close what might prove a successful war in Mexico. Nor is it necessary to practice reserve upon the point, that if France should, upon due consideration, determine to adopt a policy in Mexico adverse to the American opinions and sentiments which I have described, that policy would probably scatter seeds which would be fruitful of jealousies, which might ultimately ripen into collision between France and the United States and other American republics. An illustration of this danger has occurred already. Political rumor, which is always mischievous, one day ascribes to France a purpose to seize the Rio Grande, and wrest Texas from the United States; another day rumor advises us to look carefully to our safety on the Mississippi; another day we are warned of coalitions to be formed, under French patronage, between the regency established in Mexico and the insurgent cabal at Richmond. The President apprehends none of these things. He does not allow himself to be disturbed by suspicions so unjust to France and so unjustifiable in themselves; but he knows, also, that such suspicions will be entertained more or less extensively by this country, and magnified in other countries equally unfriendly to France and to America; and he knows, also, that it is out of such suspicions that the fatal web of national animosity is most frequently woven. He believes that the Emperor of France must experience desires as earnest as our own for the preservation of that friendship between the two nations which is so full of guarantees of their common prosperity and safety. Thinking this, the President would be wanting in fidelity to France, as well as to our own country, if he did not converse with the Emperor with entire sincerity and friendship upon the attitude which France is to assume in regard to Mexico. The statements made to you by M. Drouyn de Lhuys, concerning the Emperor's intentions, are entirely satisfactory, if we are permitted to assume them as having been authorized to be made by the Emperor in view of the present condition of affairs in Mexico. It is true, as I have before remarked, that the Emperor's purposes may hereafter change with changing circumstances. We, ourselves, however, are not unobservant of the progress of events at home and abroad; and in no case are we likely to neglect such provision for our own safety as every sovereign state must always be prepared to fall back upon when nations with which they have lived in friendship cease to respect their moral and treaty obligations. Your own discretion will be your guide as to how far and in what way the public interests will be promoted, by submitting these views to the consideration of M. Drouyn de l'Huys.

I am, sir, your obedient servant,

WILLIAM H. SEWARD.

WILLIAM L. DAYTON, Esq., *&c.*, *&c.*, *&c.*

Mr. Seward to Mr. Dayton.

No. 410.]

DEPARTMENT OF STATE,
Washington, October 5, 1863.

SIR: Your despatches of the 14th of September (No. 345) and the 16th of September (No. 347) have been received. Moreover, I have been favored by Mr. Mercier with a visit, and with a reading of the despatch addressed to him by Mr. Drouyn de Lhuys, of which special mention is made in your communications.

The explanations made by you to him are correct, and they are approved. Despatches from this department, which you must have received after writing your own, not only sustain those explanations, but they also draw very distinctly the line of policy towards France which the President has marked out under the counsels of prudence, and the traditional friendship towards her which prevails in the United States. Any statesman who has observed how inflexibly this government adheres to the policy of peace and non-intervention, would not need to be informed that the report of an alliance by us with Russia for

European war is an absurdity. So, also, no one who knows how completely the American people suffer themselves to be absorbed in the duty of suppressing the present unhappy insurrection, and restoring the authority of the Union, would for a moment believe that we are preparing for or meditating a future war against any nation, for any purpose whatever, much less that we are organizing or contemplating a future war against France, whom it is our constant desire to hold and retain as a friend, through all the vicissitudes of political fortune, and all the changes of national life.

I am, sir, your obedient servant,

WILLIAM H. SEWARD.

Hon. WILLIAM L. DAYTON, Esq., *&c., &c., &c.*

Mr. Dayton to Mr. Seward.

[Extracst.]

No. 361.] PARIS, *October* 9, 1863.

SIR: In the conference with Mr. Drouyn de Lhuys had yesterday, I communicated the general views expressed by you in despatches Nos. 395 and 400.

* * * * * * *

I brought out your views, however, in the course of a general conversation about Mexican affairs. I asked of Mr. Drouyn de Lhuys what character of test was to be adopted, with a view to learn the wishes of that country (Mexico) as to its form of government. He said that the vote of the entire country, and of all its departments, whether the French were or were not in their possession, would be taken, and if upon its registries it should appear that a large majority of the whole population (Spanish and Indian) were favorable to a monarchical form of government, he supposed that would be sufficient. He thought there would be no difficulty in applying this test, and showing a large numerical majority in favor of the Archduke, and that form of government.

Mr. Drouyn de Lhuys went on to say, that the dangers of the government of the Archduke would come principally from the United States, and the sooner we showed ourselves satisfied, and manifested a willingness to enter into peaceful relations with that government, the sooner would France be ready to leave Mexico and the new government to take care of itself, which France would, in any event, do as soon as it with propriety could; but that it would not lead or tempt the Archduke into difficulty, and then desert him before his government was settled. He added, that France could not do that. He said, that the early acknowledgment of that government by the United States would tend to shorten, or perhaps, he said, to end all the troublesome complications of France in that country; that they would thereupon quit Mexico.

* * * * * * *

I told him that, without having any authority from my government to say so, I should scarcely suppose that France, under the circumstances, would expect the United States to make haste to acknowledge a new monarchy in Mexico; but I would report his views to the government at home; not suggesting, however, that any answer would be given. In the course of conversation, he took occasion again to repeat, voluntarily, their disclaimer of any purpose to interfere with Texas, or to make or seek any permanent interest or control in Mexico. He said that our situation, as a next neighbor, entitled us to an influence there paramount to that of distant European countries, and that France, at her great distance from the scene, would not be guilty of the folly of desiring or attempting to interfere with us. He spoke highly of the conduct of Mr. Corwin, our minister in Mexico, who was reported to him as not having intrigued or interfered in these matters, but that he had always acted loyally and in good faith. Before leaving Mr. Drouyn de Lhuys, (assuming the purposes of the Emperor to be as he represented them,) I asked him why he permitted so many false reports, as to his policy, to be circulated both in Europe and America. I told him that it seemed to me the interests of both countries demanded that they should cease, and that a frank avowal in the *Moniteur* would end them. He said there were objections to using the *Moniteur* for such purposes, but that there were his despatches, which might be published. I told him that the world was given to looking at despatches as savoring too much of diplomacy. He then said that the Emperor, at the opening of the "corps legislatif," would have a proper opportunity, and he did not doubt that he would then declare his policy in Mexico, in conformity with the declarations heretofore constantly made to us.

I am, sir, your obedient servant,

WILLIAM L. DAYTON.

Hon. WILLIAM H. SEWARD,
Secretary of State.

Mr. Seward to Mr. Dayton.

No. 412.] DEPARTMENT OF STATE,
Washington, October 10, 1863.

SIR: Your despatch of the 25th of last month, No. 352, describing your proceedings in relation to Mr. Partridge's course respecting French interests at Salvador, has been received and is approved.

I am, sir, your obedient servant,

WILLIAM H. SEWARD.

WILLIAM L. DAYTON, Esq., *&c., &c., &c.*

Mr. Seward to Mr. Dayton.

No. 417.] DEPARTMENT OF STATE,
Washington, October 23, 1863.

SIR: I have the honor to acknowledge the reception of your despatch of the 9th instant, No. 361, which brings me the views expressed by Mr. Drouyn de Lhuys concerning the situation in Mexico. Various considerations have induced the President to avoid taking any part in the speculative debates bearing on that situation which have been carried on in the capitals of Europe as well as in those of America. A determination to err on the side of strict neutrality, if we err at all, in a war which is carried on between two nations with which the United States are maintaining relations of amity and friendship, was prominent among the considerations to which I have thus referred.

The United States, nevertheless, when invited by France or Mexico, cannot omit to express themselves with perfect frankness upon new incidents, as they occur in the progress of that war. Mr. Drouyn de Lhuys now speaks of an election which he expects to be held in Mexico, and to result in the choice of his Imperial Highness the Prince Maximilian of Austria to be Emperor of Mexico. We learn from other sources that the prince has declared his willingness to accept an imperial throne in Mexico on three conditions, namely: first, that he shall be called to it by the universal suffrage of the Mexican nation; secondly, that he shall receive indispensable guarantees for the integrity and independence of the proposed empire; and thirdly, that the head of his family, the Emperor of Austria, shall acquiesce.

Referring to these facts, Mr. Drouyn de Lhuys intimates that an early acknowledgment of the proposed empire by the United States would be convenient to France, by relieving her, sooner than might be possible under other circumstances, from her troublesome complications in Mexico.

Happily the French government has not been left uninformed that, in the opinion of the United States, the permanent establishment of a foreign and monarchical government in Mexico will be found neither easy nor desirable. You will inform Mr. Drouyn de Lhuys that this opinion remains unchanged. On the other hand, the United States cannot anticipate the action of the people of Mexico, nor have they the least purpose or desire to interfere with their proceedings, or control or interfere with their free choice, or disturb them in the enjoyment of whatever institutions of government they may, in the exercise of an absolute freedom, establish. It is proper, also, that Mr. Drouyn de Lhuys should be informed that the United States continue to regard Mexico as the theatre of a war which has not yet ended in the subversion of the government long existing there, with which the United States remain in the relation of peace and sincere friendship; and that, for this reason, the United States are not now at liberty to consider the question of recognizing a government which, in the further chances of war, may come into its place. The United States, consistently with their principles, can do no otherwise than leave the destinies of Mexico in the keeping of her own people, and recognize their sovereignty and independence in whatever form they themselves shall choose that this sovereignty and independence shall be manifested.

I am, sir, your obedient servant,

WILLIAM H. SEWARD.

WILLIAM L. DAYTON, Esq., *&c., &c., &c.*

Mr. Seward to Mr. Dayton.

No. 437.] DEPARTMENT OF STATE,
Washington, November 28, 1863.

SIR: I transmit for your information a copy of a communication of the 23d instant, addressed by this department to Major General Banks, and of an instruction of the same date (No. 88) to Mr. Corwin.

I am, sir, your obedient servant,

WILLIAM H. SEWARD.

WILLIAM L. DAYTON, Esq., *&c., &c., &c.*

Mr. Drouyn de Lhuys to Mr. Mercier.

[Translation.]

No. 21.] MINISTRY OF FOREIGN AFFAIRS, DIPLOMATIC DIVISION,
Paris, September 15, 1863.

SIR: Mr. Dayton, who exhibits in his relations with me a great confidence, and a rectitude to which I am pleased to bear testimony, has been moved at certain rumors, propagated with a design which I have not now to inquire into, but which appear lately to have obtained some credit at Paris, and he has come to converse with me about them. According to these reports, too inconsiderately accepted, the Emperor's government has decided to recognize the

States of the south, and a treaty has even been already signed, according to which the new confederacy is to cede to France, either for herself, or that she may make a retrocession of them to Mexico, Texas and a portion of Louisiana.

At the moment in which Mr. Dayton was imparting to me this information, I was exactly in a position to offer him information for information, and, before answering the questions which he addressed me, I asked him if, among the alarming symptons for the maintenance of the good relations of the two countries, he had not, like myself, received other news, likewise diffused in public, such as, for instance, the transmission by him to me of a protest from his government against our expedition to Mexico and its consequences; the conclusion of an alliance, offensive and defensive, between the United States and Russia; the appearance of a federal fleet before Vera Cruz, &c., &c.

In regard to the protest, after remarking to me that I, better than any one else, knew that he had not transmitted to me any, Mr. Dayton said to me that, under the promptings of the general tenor of the correspondence of Mr. Seward, and of the knowledge which he himself had of the inclinations of his fellow-citizens, he had been able to speak to me of the painful impression produced on public opinion in his country by the preponderant intervention of a European power in an American republic, and by the creation of a monarchical establishment in a country adjacent to the United States; but that from that to a protest, or to any intention whatever of comminatory intermeddling, was very far, and that nothing in his instructions authorized him to overleap that distance. He knew nothing, on the other hand, of the alleged alliance of his government with Russia, and he had every reason to disbelive it. As to the presence of a federal fleet before Vera Cruz, this news did not seem to him even to merit the honor of a contradiction.

I told Mr. Dayton that I had never attached any importance to the reports which I had pointed out to him, and that, in speaking to him of them, my object was much less to call forth explanations on his part, than to warn him against rumors of a different character; but having probably the same origin of which he had spoken to me, I could, however, contradict them categorically. In regard to the recognition of the States of the south, the intentions of the Emperor's government were known to him, and this question was still at the point where our late conversations had left him. We had not, therefore, recognized the south, and, much more, we had not signed with it any treaty for the cession of Louisiana and Texas. With respect to this, I could repeat to him, what I had so often said to him already, that we neither sought for ourselves, nor for others, any acquisition in America. I added that I trusted that the good sense of the people of the United States would do justice to exaggerations and false suppositions, by the aid of which it was endeavored to mislead and sour public opinion; and that I relied on his co-operation in trying to render prevalent a more equitable appreciation of our intentions and of the necessities which our policy obeyed.

I have thought, sir, that it was well that you should be informed of the particulars of this conversation, in order that you might, on your part, communicate it to Mr. Seward, and receive the precise words of it, in order to rectify around you false opinions and unjustifiable anticipations.

Accept, sir, assurances of my high consideration.

DROUYN DE LHUYS.

Mr. MERCIER,
Minister of the Emperor at Washington, D. C.

Mr. Pike to Mr. Seward.

[Extracts.]

No. 97.] UNITED STATES LEGATION,
The Hague, August 19, 1863.

SIR: I have had the honor to receive your despatch of July 24, (No. 111.)

Two weeks' digestion of the news from America results in no revival of hopes on this side for the rebellion. The partisans of the south seem discouraged and disheartened. The only pretence they raise, to mitigate the extremity of the situation, is the allegation that their case has seemed equally desperate before. The argument does not arrest the fall of their sinking fortunes on the exchange. Their favorite cotton loan, so lately above par, is down to 70. The complete break down of the financial system of the insurgents, demonstrated by the fall of their paper currency to 10 cents on the dollar, has, perhaps, more weight attached to it here than in the United States. It is regarded as indicating a near relapse. Dispassionate observers fail to see how the resources of the rebel government are to be replenished, or their finances even nominally administered. The melting away of its armies, from internal weakness, alone seems thus inevitable.

But beyond this, the clearing out of the Mississippi river, if its approaches be properly guarded against any sudden descent of armed iron-clads from Europe, is viewed as a fatal grip at the throat of the rebellion. The events occurring in Mexico make New Orleans looked upon more than ever as the key of our empire. Its original capture was considered in Europe a deadly blow to the insurrection. The conviction was and is that it should be made impregnable to attack by sea, which seems easy enough; the hostile action of no power in the Gulf need be feared. But should this safeguard be neglected, we might find our dear-bought triumphs suddenly brought to a disastrous termination. Our enemies tried to find consolation in the hope that we shall be less prudent to secure than we have been energetic to conquer.

That we must look to ultimate collision in that quarter with foreign powers, the action of France in Mexico does not seem to allow us to doubt.

As I took occasion to observe some months ago (I believe you thought prematurely) the cotton question is ended in Europe. We have entirely gone by that danger. Cotton is abundant. The only disturbing fact that remains is that the price is so high that manufacturers decline to spin and weave on the old scale. Distress is again setting into the manufacturing districts, but the disorder and suffering is, to a great extent, compensated by the excellent harvest which almost everywhere prevails.

Now, therefore, as heretofore, I believe we are to be unmolested from abroad. If we can furnish the troops necessary to follow up our recent great successes triumphantly, we shall have a glorious issue from our trials. Viewed at this distance, the prospects of the country have never seemed so encouraging.

I have the honor to be, with great respect, your most obedient servant,

JAMES S. PIKE.

Hon. WILLIAM H. SEWARD,
Secretary of State, &c.

Mr. Pike to Mr. Seward.

[Extract.]

No. 99.] UNITED STATES LEGATION,
The Hague, September 2, 1863.

SIR: I have to acknowledge the receipt of your despatch of the 13th of August, (No. 115,) and your circular despatch of the 12th of the same month, with an accompanying map, giving an exposition of the military situation; all of which are attentively considered.

Political affairs are comparatively quiet.

The conference of German sovereigns at Frankfort has ended; with what success in the main purpose of consolidating their power against France remains to be seen. England approves and encourages the movement. France throws cold water on the proceedings, notwithstanding the real object of the conference is veiled under other pretences.

Some of the French journals are engaged in the effort to show that the United States have no cause of hostility to the effort to establish an empire upon the ruins of Mexican independence. The argument proceeds upon the assumption that France does not desire to do any offensive political act towards the United States, and so far intimates inactivity upon the question of recognition.

It seems to be reduced to a certainty that the Polish question will not disturb the peace of Europe. Russia claims that the rebellion is exhausted.

* * * * * * * *

I have the honor to be, with great respect, your most obedient servant,

JAMES S. PIKE.

HON. WILLIAM H. SEWARD,
Secretary of State, Washington.

Mr. Seward to Mr. Pike.

No. 118.]

DEPARTMENT OF STATE,
Washington, September 5, 1863.

SIR: Your despatch of August 19 (No. 97) has been carefully considered.

What you have noticed in Europe, in regard to the political aspects of the insurrection here, has been equally observable here during the period which you have mentioned. No fortunate military incident has occurred to revive the hopes of the insurgents, while Union sieges and marches have gone on favorably. The insurgents have burned much and lost more of the cotton that they had pledged to European creditors, while the price of gold in their currency has risen, within two months, from 1,0C0 per cent. to 1,600 per cent., which is the last reported rate. The insurgent financiers last winter adopted wheat instead of gold for the standard of values, and fixed that of wheat, if I remember rightly, at five dollars per bushel. It is now reported that the farmer refuses to thresh his wheat, and the government agents are considering whether the power to appropriate at five dollars does not also include the necessary preliminary power to thresh the grain.

You have rightly assumed that the safe occupation of New Orleans, so long as it is maintained, is sufficient guarantee for the success of the government. We are, however, not without some concern on that subject; for, in the first place, we have no clearly reliable assurances that the British government will prevent the departure of the iron rams, which are being prepared in British ship yards, for that or some similar purpose. And next, notwithstanding the great energy of the Navy Department, it has not yet brought out the vessels upon which we can confidently rely for adequate defence against such an enterprise. Nevertheless, Mr. Adams is making the best possible efforts with reference to the first point, and our naval means, which certainly are neither small nor inefficient, are rapidly increasing. Your observations on this subject are so sagacious that I have thought it proper to commend them to the special attention of the Navy Department.

I thank you for the account you have given me of public opinion in Europe in regard to the condition of Mexico and its bearing on the interests of the United States. Public opinion is not embarrassed by a want of accurate knowledge of existing facts. It anticipates and assumes probable events, and thus the imagination early arrives at, and is satisfied with, premature solutions; from Mexico we have nothing in regard to the attitude or proceedings of the republican government since it withdrew before the invaders to San Luis; from France nothing in regard to the question of a new government, but reiterated assurances of an absence of any design to permanently occupy or dominate in Mexico; and from Austria, only the speculations of the press upon a condition of affairs in Mexico, too imperfectly developed to justify any decisive action by the alleged candidate for an imperial crown.

In these circumstances we see no occasion for extreme sensibility or for immediate demonstration. Mr. Corwin cannot, of course, communicate with the authorities newly instituted in the city of Mexico, while he is shut out from access to the republican one to which he is accredited. That government may, for aught we know, maintain an effectual resistance to the new one, or, on the other hand, it may even succumb. Such a resistance would relieve the people of all difficulties, while, on the other hand, it would be as unreasonable as it would be unavailing to seek to rescue a people that should voluntarily surrender itself to foreign control. The new government, if it succeeds, may respect the sovereignty and all the rights of the United States, and so give us no cause of complaint or dissatisfaction. Our opinions as to the ultimate and permanent success of an European intervention in Mexico were early expressed by way of anticipation. Until we recall them no presumption that they are abandoned can arise. But we see now, instead of a whole and normal Mexico on our southern border, a Mexico divided between Mexicans and the French. We do not know how this new condition of things might sooner or later affect the authority of the United States in Texas. Independently of that consideration, the time has arrived when that authority ought to be, and, as we think, can be, restored in that important border State, and this will be done.

I am, sir, your obedient servant,

WILLIAM H. SEWARD.

JAMES S. PIKE, Esq., *&c., &c., &c.,*

Mr. Seward to Mr. Perry.

No. 10.] DEPARTMENT OF STATE,
Washington, September 21, 1863.

SIR: Your despatch of August 26 (No. 110) has been received. The general views of the United States concerning the interests of society and government in Mexico, and on this continent, have been heretofore fully made known to all parties who officially expressed to us any concern on that subject. While adhering to these views, the President does not perceive any necessity for entering at present into the European debates which have arisen out of the changing phases of the war with France against Mexico. You will be promptly advised if it shall be deemed important to enter into explanations on that subject with the cabinet of Madrid.

I am, sir, your obedient servant,

WILLIAM H. SEWARD.

HORATIO J. PERRY, Esq., *&c., &c., &c., Madrid.*

Mr. Motley to Mr. Seward.

No. 31.] LEGATION OF THE UNITED STATES,
Vienna, August 17, 1863.

SIR: So soon as the news of the proclamation of the empire in Mexico, together with the offer of the imperial crown to the Archduke Ferdinand Maximilian, reached Vienna, I requested an interview with Count Rechberg.

I saw the minister accordingly on the 11th August. As he was to leave next day for Frankfort to attend the conference at the diet of sovereigns, and as many other members of the diplomatic corps were waiting to see him, the interview was necessarily very brief; I merely begged him to inform me what was authentically known to him in regard to the Mexican affair.

He replied that the intelligence received by the government was hardly in an authentic shape. He said: We do not consider our situation essentially altered. We are not prepared to take action on what may prove to be an ephemeral demonstration. We regard all that is reported concerning the whole affair—so far as relates to his Imperial Highness—as not having occurred; (*comme non avenu* was his expression, the conversation being in French.) I asked if he considered it true that a deputation was on the way from Mexico to offer the crown to the archduke. He replied that it was possible, but that it was very doubtful whether such a deputation would be received.

I asked if it was true that a telegram had been sent by the Emperor Napoleon congratulating the archduke on the news. He said yes; but that, from the tenor of the telegram, the Emperor Napoleon did not appear to attach much weight to the intelligence.

Under such circumstances, I said it was useless to ask whether any decision had been taken in regard to the offer, as such a question had already been answered in the negative by what he had already said.

He replied, "of course;" and I then took my leave, saying that I only wished to know the exact position of the affair up to the present moment.

I beg to be informed, at your earliest convenience, what language you wish me officially to hold on this very important subject. The recent conquest of Mexico by France seems to me fraught with future woe to our whole continent; but I cannot think it desirable, in the present condition of our own affairs, that we should hasten the evil day by taking any part in that most unhappy adventure.

It is generally supposed that the Archduke Maximilian is desirous of accepting the crown of Mexico, but I am not aware that there are many persons in this empire who regard the project with favor. It certainly is an unpopular one with all classes of society, so far as I have been able to observe.

The language of the press is, in some cases, guarded, but in general decidedly hostile on the subject.

As a specimen of Vienna journalism in this matter, I send you a translation of a portion of an article from a widely circulated journal, *Die Presse.* The tone, although bold and bitter, is not exceptionably so.

I have the honor, sir, to remain your obedient servant,

J. LOTHROP MOTLEY.

Hon. WILLIAM H. SEWARD,
Secretary of State, Washington.

[Extract from the *Presse* of August 11, 1863.]

"The journals of Paris announce to-day that the Emperor and Empress have already sent congratulations by telegraph to the Archduke Ferdinand Maximilian, on the imperial Mexican dignity which has been offered to him. Well, they may think it a piece of good fortune—and they may have their reasons for it—to obtain possession of a crown in such a way in a country like Mexico. We, however, believe that we are a faithful organ of the opinion of the Austrian people when we say, without concealment, that the acceptance of the crown by the Archduke Ferdinand Maximilian would not be looked upon by any of them as a piece of good fortune, but, on the contrary, they would look upon it as an evil destiny. An evil destiny, we say, for it would be nothing else if an Austrian prince should ever seriously think of accepting a crown from the hands of a Napoleon. In the deepest humiliation of Germany by the forcible dominion of Napoleon I, we find nothing similar to this; and shall constitutional Austria bear to-day what absolute Austria was too proud to endure? And what sort of a crown is it? Without any plausible reason, treading under foot those liberties of the people of which they are always speaking, the French soldiers have broken into Mexico, and, after shedding streams of blood, they have occupied the Mexican capital, followed by the curses of a people hitherto proud of its independence. And shall a crown of tears and blood, conquered in this forcible manner, be placed upon the head of a prince of constitutional Austria, perhaps as an indemnity for the pearl which in 1859 was broken from Austria's crown, or as a present to keep us unharmed in case of future occurrences of a similar kind? The more we lose ourselves in speculations of this kind, the more impossible, adventurous, unacceptable, and monstrous, this proposed attention of the court of Napoleon to Austria appears to us. Have those who play with the thoughts of wrapping themselves in the purple mantle of an Aztec emperor already reflected on the political consequences which would follow Austria's acceptance of this imperial crown? Have they painted to themselves the wretched, dependent relation, the vassalage in which Austria—even assuming that there is no thought of compensation at the bottom of the French offer—that it is dictated by the purest unselfishness—will find itself in regard to Napoleonic France by accepting the Mexican throne? Is Archduke Maximilian, in Mexico, to be the counterpart to King George of Greece, with only the difference that before his throne French soldiers would keep watch, as the king's crown in Athens would be protected by those of England? And even if it should be decided to give the new Emperor of Mexico an Austrian corps as an escort, has the cost of this scheme been already counted? What in the name of Heaven has Austria to do in this Mexican galley? It would be bound and exposed to France on all sides for this present of the Danaides, and particularly in regard to Poland it would be made lame and impotent in its political action; it would afford France a pretext for occupying Mexico, as the Pope affords a pretext for occupying Rome; it will have engaged its honor for specific French speculations, without satisfying a single reasonable interest. We already see the moment when the Cabinet of Washington, fortified by the Monroe doctrine, by the alliance of the states of Central and South America, and by the enormous military resources which the end of the civil war will leave at its disposition, shall call upon the French in Mexico to leave a continent on which they have no business and no right to command. Shall Austria, then, make war in company with France upon America to uphold and occupy a problematical throne in Mexico? That would be the height of the adventurous, and Austria would have then no alternative than that of a shameful fiasco or that of a vassalage, which would absorb its best powers for the interests of France. Even if the thought of ruling the old empire of the Aztecs should not be devoid of poetic charm to a romantic character, we believe that the times have gone by when such caprices are sufficient to compromise the policy of great states and to throw them into endless complications. And so we still hope that the answer of Austria to the proposition of the Mexican asamblea, received by way of Paris, will, this time, be a decided negative, and that once for all an end will be put to an intrigue which has no other aim than to shift the ignominy of the Mexican expedition—that attack on an independent people—from the shoulders of France on those of Austria, and to cover the gulf of the dirty speculations of the banker Jecker and his worthy associates in France and Mexico with the brilliant name of an Austrian prince."

Mr. Seward to Mr. Motley.

No. 41.]

DEPARTMENT OF STATE,
Washington, September 11, 1863.

SIR: Your despatch of August 17 (No. 31) has been received.

When France made war against Mexico, we asked of France explanations of her objects and purposes. She answered, that it was a war for the redress of grievances; that she did not intend to permanently occupy or dominate in Mexico, and that she should leave to the people of Mexico a free choice of institutions of government. Under these circumstances the United States adopted, and they have since maintained, entire neutrality between the belligerents, in harmony with the traditional policy in regard to foreign wars.

The war has continued longer than was anticipated. At different stages of it France has, in her intercourse with us, renewed the explanations before mentioned. The French army has now captured Puebla and the capital, while the Mexican government, with its principal forces, is understood to have retired to San Luis Potosi, and a provisional government has been instituted under French auspices in the city of Mexico, which, being supported by arms, divides the actual dominion of the country with the Mexican government, also maintained by armed power. That provisional government has neither made nor sought to make any communication to the government of the United States, nor has it been, in any way, recognized by this government. France has made no communication to the United States concerning the provisional government which has been established in Mexico, nor has she announced any actual or intended departure from the policy in regard to that country which her beforementioned explanations have authorized us to expect her to pursue. The United States have received no communications relating to the recent military events in Mexico from the recognized government of that country.

The imperial government of Austria has not explained to the United States that it has an interest in the subject, or expressed any desire to know their views upon it. The United States have heretofore, on proper occasions, frankly explained to every party having an interest in the question the general views and sentiments which they have always entertained, and still entertain, in regard to the interests of society and government on this continent. Under these circumstances, it is not deemed necessary for the representatives of the United States, in foreign countries, to engage in the political debates which the present unsettled aspect of the war in Mexico has elicited. You will be promptly advised if a necessity for any representations to the government of Austria shall arise.

I am, sir, your obedient servant,

WILLIAM H. SEWARD.

J. LOTHROP MOTLEY, Esq., *&c., &c., Vienna.*

Mr. Seward to Mr. Motley.

No. 43.]

DEPARTMENT OF STATE,
Washington, September 26, 1863.

SIR: Your interesting despatch of September 1 (No. 32) has been received. The United States are not indifferent to the events which are occurring in Mexico. They are regarded, however, as incidents of the war between France and Mexico. While the governments of those two countries are not improperly left in any uncertainty about the sentiments of the United States, the reported relations of a member of the imperial family of Austria to those events do not seem sufficient to justify this government in making any representations on that subject to the government of the Emperor. His candor and fairness towards the United States warrant the President in believing, as he firmly does, that his Majesty will not suffer his government to be engaged in any proceeding hostile or injurious to the United States.

I am, sir, your obedient servant,

WILLIAM H. SEWARD.

J. LOTHROP MOTLEY, *&c., &c., Vienna.*

Mr. Seward to Mr. Motley.

No. 45.] DEPARTMENT OF STATE,
Washington, October 9, 1863.

SIR: Your despatch of the 21st of September, No. 34, has been received.

You have proceeded very properly in giving to Count Rechberg a copy of my despatch to Mr. Dayton of the 3d of March, 1862. This government desires to practice no concealment in its intercourse with foreign states. During the discussion concerning Mexico, and France, and the United States, which has been going on in Europe, I have refrained from instructing you to speak for the United States. This reserve has been practiced because the questions immediately concern only the three states mentioned, and the personal relation to them of the Austrian grand-duke is an incident which could only bring the imperial royal government under any responsibility to the United States when that government should attempt or propose to violate some actual political right, or disregard some practical interest, which it would be the duty of the President to maintain or assert. But in this course of proceeding it has not been my intention to deny to you a full knowledge of the position of the President in regard to the questions debated. France is at war with Mexico, and at peace with the United States, and a civil war is raging in the United States. I am to speak of the attitude of France towards the United States in relation to this civil war, and also to speak of the attitude of France toward Mexico, as it bears on the United States. For the sake of perspicuity I keep the two topics distinctly separate, and I treat the last one first.

We know from many sources, and even from the direct statement of the Emperor of France, that on the breaking out of the insurrection he adopted the then current opinion of European statesmen that the efforts of this government to suppress it would be unsuccessful. To this pre-judgment we attribute his agreement with Great Britain to act in concert with her upon international questions which might arise out of the conflict, his practical concession of a belligerent character to the insurgents, his repeated suggestions of accommodations by this government with the insurgents, and his conferences on the subject of a recognition. These proceedings of the Emperor of France have been very injurious to the United States by encouraging and thus prolonging the insurrection. On the other hand, no statesman of this country is able to conceive of a reasonable motive on the part of France or the Emperor to do or to wish injury to the United States. Every statesman in the United States cherishes a lively interest in the welfare and greatness of France, and is content that she shall peacefully and in unbounded prosperity enjoy the administration of the Emperor she has chosen. We have not an acre of territory, nor a fort, which we think France could wisely covet; nor has she any possession that we could accept if she would resign it into our hands. Nevertheless, when recurring to what the Emperor of France has already done, we cannot, at any time, feel assured that, under mistaken impressions of our embarrassments in consequence of a lamentable civil war, he may not go further in the way of encouragement to the insurgents, whose intrigues in Paris we understand and do not underestimate. While the Emperor of France has held an unfavorable opinion of our national strength and unity, we, on the contrary, have as constantly indulged an entire confidence in both. Not merely the course of events, but that of time also, opposes the insurrection and reinvigorates the national strength and power. Under these convictions, we avoid everything calculated to irritate France by wounding the just pride and proper sensibilities of that spirited nation, and thus we hope to free our claim to her just forbearance in our present political emergency from any cloud of passion or prejudice. Pursuing this course, the President hopes that the pre-judgment of the Emperor against the stability of the Union may give way to considerations which will modify his course and bring him back to the traditional friendship which he found existing between this country and his own when, in obedience to her voice, he assumed the administration of her government. These desires and purposes of ours do not imply either a fear of imperial hostility, or any neglect of a prudent posture of national self-reliance, and in that posture we constantly aim to stand.

I speak next of the relation of France towards Mexico. Until 1860 our prestige was a protection to her and to all the other republican states on this continent. That prestige has been temporarily broken up by domestic faction and civil war. France has invaded Mexico, and war exists between those two countries. The United States hold, in regard to these two states and their conflict, the same principle that they hold in relation to all other nations and their mutual wars. They have neither a right nor any disposition to intervene by force in the internal affairs of Mexico, whether to establish or to maintain a republican or even a domestic government there, or to overthrow an imperial or a foreign one if Mexico shall choose to establish or accept it. The United States have not a right nor a disposition to intervene by force on either side in the lamentable war which is going on between France and Mexico. On the contrary, they practice in regard to Mexico, in every phase of the war, the non-intervention which they require all foreign powers to observe in regard to the United States. But notwithstanding this self-restraint, this government knows full well that the inherent normal opinion of Mexico favors a government there republican in form and democratic in its organization in preference to any monarchical institutions to be imposed from abroad. This government knows also that this normal opinion of the people of Mexico resulted largely from the influence of popular opinion in this country, which constantly invigorates it. The President, moreover, believes that this popular opinion of the United States is just in itself and eminently essential to the progress of civilization on the American continent, which civilization he believes can and will, if left free from European resistance, work harmoniously together with advancing refinement on the other continents. This government believes that all foreign resistance to American civilization, and all attempts to control it, must and will fail before the ceaseless and ever-increasing activity of material, moral, and political forces which peculiarly belong to the American continent. Nor do the United States deny that in their opinion their own safety and the cheerful destiny to which they aspire are intimately dependent on the continuance of free republican institutions throughout America, and that their policy will always be directed to that end. They have frankly, and on proper occasions, submitted these opinions to the Emperor of France, as worthy of his serious consideration, in determining how he would conduct and close what might prove a successful war in Mexico. Nor do we practice reserve upon the point that if France should, upon due consideration, determine to adopt a policy in Mexico adverse to the American opinions and sentiments which I have described, that policy would probably scatter seeds which would be fruitful of jealousies that might ultimately ripen into collisions between France and the United States and other American republics. An illustration of this danger has occurred already. Political rumor, which is always suspicious, one day ascribes to France a purpose to seize the Rio Grande and wrest Texas from the United States. Another day rumor advises us to look carefully to our safety on the Mississippi. Another day we are warned of coalitions to be formed under French patronage between the regency that has been recently set up at the city of Mexico and the insurgent cabal at Richmond. The President apprehends none of these things, and does not allow himself to be disturbed by suspicions. But he knows also that such suspicions will be entertained more or less extensively in this country, and will be magnified in other countries, and he knows, also, that it is out of such suspicions that the fatal web of national animosity is most frequently woven. The President, upon the assurances which he has received from the Emperor of France, expects that he will neither deprive the people of Mexico of their free choice of government nor seek to maintain any permanent occupation or dominion there.

It is true that the purposes or policy of the Emperor of France, in these respects, may change with changing circumstances. Although we are confiding, we are not therefore unobservant, and in no case are we likely to neglect such provision for our own safety as every people must always be prepared to fall back upon when a nation with which they have lived in friendship ceases to respect its moral and treaty obligations.

In giving you this summary of our positions, I have simply drawn off from the records the instructions under which Mr. Dayton is acting at Paris. I remain of the opinion that national dignity is best conserved by confining the discussion of these affairs to the cabinets of the United States, France, and Mexico, and that no public interest is to be advanced by opening it at Vienna, and, therefore, I do not direct you to communicate this despatch to the imperial royal court.

I am, sir, your obedient servant,

WILLIAM H. SEWARD.

J. LOTHROP MOTLEY, Esq., *&c.*, *&c.*, *Vienna.*

Mr. Seward to Mr. Nelson.

No. 14.]

DEPARTMENT OF STATE,
Washington, June 19, 1862.

SIR: Your despatch of May 1 (No. 33) has been received.

The change of opinion and sentiment which has taken place in Chili in regard to our domestic troubles is the attainment of an important advantage which the President early determined to secure, if possible, by frank, honorable, and generous efforts. It is certainly true that there cannot permanently exist two antagonistical systems of government upon this continent, nor can there always be two commercial systems upon this continent, one of which must have its centre here and the other in Europe. The social differences which distinguish the Latin races from those of northern stock are likely to be long perpetuated on that continent. But there is a constant and rapid tendency towards harmony and assimilation between them in America, and ultimately a constitution of society decidedly American must exist here. Such a change is necessary to secure a complete development of the resources of the continent, and necessary even to render the states which are to exist here safe against domestic divisions and foreign aggression. The change, however, is to be effected not by wars and conquests, but peacefully through the influence of moral causes. Each American state must practice justice and forbearance and cordial friendship towards every other state, and all must come to learn that political institutions, which fail to secure peace and to create prosperity, cannot be upheld even by any combination with foreign powers.

The United States want no more extended empire. The field they occupy is adequate to the employment of all their energies, and ample for the play of their just ambition. Thus content with their boundaries, they daily become more intolerant of the idea of any division of their domain, or any encroachment upon it by foreign powers. These sentiments have thus far been the great invigorating forces of the country in the present war, and have, as we believe, carried us safely to the point where the end begins. We have not been unaware that reactionary forces have manifested themselves in neighboring American states, and threaten a subversion of their republican institutions, and of course a subversion of their sovereignty and independence. It might be doubtful whether states thus menaced could in any case be benefited by material aid borrowed from any foreign nation. Every loan of that kind is ultimately repaid with the loss of a part of the independence which it was intended to save. But the Latin states of America may rest assured that the United States will maintain their own integrity and independence through the greatest trials, and thus show to the world that American institutions possess virtues and advantages which make the nations which enjoy them indissoluble and invulnerable. We invite Chili and all the other American states to cultivate the same spirit, and exhibit the same determination.

The attempt to revolutionize the American Union has already failed. The disappointed faction, if they are to be believed, will seek compensation for their failure in revenge. They have commenced what they threaten shall be a twenty years' guerilla war. The measure itself is an evidence of imbecility, and of a profound misunderstanding of the American character. Peace and harmony under the authority of the federal Union are due as a reward to the loyalty and virtue which the American people have practiced in their recent trial, and they are not now far distant.

I am, sir, your obedient servant,

WILLIAM H. SEWARD.

THOMAS H. NELSON, Esq.

Mr. Nelson to Mr. Seward.

[Extract.]

No. 48.]

LEGATION OF THE UNITED STATES,
Santiago de Chili, September 1, 1862.

SIR: Upon the 30th ultimo I addressed the secretary of foreign relations a note, having for its object a frank exposition of what I deemed the sentiments of the government of the United States towards the other American republics. In preparing this note, a copy of which is herewith transmitted, I availed myself of the views expressed in your despatch No. 14, of June 19, 1862, and in the correspondence submitted by you to the President, under date of April 14, in compliance with the resolution of the House of Representatives of February 3, 1862.

* * * * * * *

I have the honor to remain, very respectfully, your obedient servant,

THOMAS H. NELSON.

Hon. WILLIAM H. SEWARD,
Secretary of State of the United States.

Mr. Nelson to Mr. Tocornal.

LEGATION OF THE UNITED STATES,
Santiago de Chili, August 30, 1862.

SIR: Upon the 1st of May last, in a despatch to the honorable Secretary of State of the United States, I had the honor to express my gratification at the hearty manifestations of a desire evinced by a portion of the press of Chili for the suppression of the domestic dissension existing in the United States, and for a closer drawing together of the bonds uniting the other nations of America with our own. I moreover assured the honorable Secretary of my belief that these were the prevailing sentiments of the government as well as of the people of this republic, who were, to say the least, solicitous regarding the policy of some of the powers of western Europe towards the comparatively defenceless states of Spanish America. I also alluded to the gratifying circumstance that the United States and their citizens had, in my opinion, never before occupied a more favorable position in the estimation of Chili than at present—a more intimate knowledge of our people, aims and policy, having developed a true appreciation and cordial esteem, which could not but most favorably affect all our relations with this republic.

Under date of the 19th of June, 1862, the honorable Secretary addressed me, in reply to the one above alluded to, a despatch of which the relative positions of the United States of America and her sister republics, in view of the gravity of the present political situation, form the basis.

Feeling assured that a knowledge of the sentiments of my government upon this subject cannot but be most gratifying to the government of your excellency, I have believed that our official intercourse could not be more agreeably initiated than in a frank and sincere expression of such sentiments of which I am most happy in being the exponent.

I need not assure your excellency that my government has felt the most profound interest in the events now occurring in the neighboring and sister republic of Mexico, wherein reactionary forces have been threatening a subversion of her republican institutions, and, of course, a subversion of her sovereignty and independence.

The United States are deeply concerned in the peace of nations, and at the same time aim to be loyal in all their relations to European as well as American states. The President, while relying upon the good faith of the allied powers, and confident of their sincerity in disclaiming any intention to intervene to change the constitutional form of government, has deemed it his duty to express to them the opinion that no monarchical government which could be founded in Mexico, in the presence of foreign navies and armies in her waters and upon her soil, would have any prospect of security or permanency; secondly, that the instability of such a monarchy there would be enhanced if the throne should be assigned to any person not of Mexican nativity. That under such circumstances the new government must fall, unless it could draw into its support European alliances, which, relating back to the present invasion, would, in fact, make it the beginning of a permanent policy of armed European intervention, injurious and practically hostile to the most general system of government on the continent of America, and this would be the beginning, rather than the ending, of revolution in Mexico.

In such a case it is not to be doubted that the permanent interests and sympathies of the United States would be with the other American republics. It is not intended on this occasion to predict the course of events which might happen as a consequence of the proceeding contemplated, either on this continent or in Europe. It is sufficient to say that, in the opinion of the President, the emancipation of our own country from European control has been the principal feature in its history during the last century.

Between some of the South American republics and our own there has existed, not remotely, an alienation, founded partly upon an imperfect appreciation of our sentiments, partly upon errors and prejudices peculiar to themselves, and yet not altogether without fault upon our part—an alienation temporary in its character, and which I rejoice to know has yielded to a better knowledge of the government and people of the United States, and of the sincerity of their cordial interest in the integrity and welfare of sister republics.

The social differences which distinguish the Latin races from those of northern stock are likely to be long perpetuated upon the continent of Europe. But there is a constant and rapid tendency towards harmony and assimilation between them in America, and ultimately a constitution of society decidedly American must exist here. Such a change is necessary to secure a complete development of the resources of the continent, and necessary even to render the states which are to exist here safe against domestic disorders and foreign aggression. The change, however, is to be effected, not by wars and conquests, but peacefully through the influence of moral causes. Every American state must practice patience and forbearance and cordial friendship towards every other, and all must come to learn that political institutions which fail to secure peace and to create prosperity cannot be upheld, even by any combination with foreign powers. The United States want no more extended empire. The field they occupy is adequate to the employment of all their energies, and ample for the play of their just ambition. Thus content with their boundaries, they daily become more intolerant of the idea of any division of their domain or encroachment upon it by foreign powers. These sentiments have thus far been the great invigorating forces of the United States during their present domestic dissensions, and I need scarcely assure your excellency that they feel now confident of a speedy and complete re-establishment of peace within their borders. The Latin states of America may rest assured that the United States will maintain their integrity and independence through the greatest trials, and thus show to the world that American institutions possess virtues and advantages which make the nations enjoying them indissoluble and invulnerable.

We invite Chili and all other American states to cultivate the same spirit and exhibit the same determination.

These, your excellency, are the sentiments of the government and people of the United States of America, and I gladly avail myself of this opportunity of manifesting to the government of Chili how deep is their interest in the welfare of every other American republic, how disinterested their desire that the relations subsisting between these several nations and their own shall assume a spirit more elevated than one of merely commercial or conventional amity, a spirit earnestly American in the continental sense of the word, and fraternal in no mere diplomatic meaning of the term, conducive to their mutual prosperity and happiness, and ultimately auspicious to all republican states throughout the world.

Availing myself of this occasion, allow me to reiterate to your excellency the earnest assurances of distinguished consideration and high esteem with which I have the honor to remain your excellency's most obedient servant,

THOMAS H. NELSON.

His Excellency the SECRETARY OF FOREIGN RELATIONS
Of the Republic of Chili.

Mr. Nelson to Mr. Seward.

[Extract.]

No. 51.] LEGATION OF THE UNITED STATES,
Santiago de Chili, September 17, 1862.

SIR: I have the honor to enclose herein a copy of a note addressed to me by the secretary of foreign relations of Chili on the 13th instant, in reply to the one transmitted by me to his excellency on the 30th ultimo.

* * * * * *

I have the honor to remain, very respectfully, your obedient servant,

THOMAS H. NELSON.

Hon. WILLIAM H. SEWARD,
Secretary of State of the United States.

Mr. Tocornal to Mr. Nelson.

[Translation.]

SANTIAGO, *September* 13, 1862.

The undersigned, minister of foreign relations of Chili, has had the honor to receive the note which the envoy extraordinary and minister plenipotentiary of the United States was pleased to address him, under date of the 30th ultimo.

His excellency has thought proper therein to express to the undersigned how agreeable it is to him to initiate their relations by a manifestation of the sentiments which animate the government and people of the United States towards the Chilian government and nation, and towards all the other Spanish American republics.

The undersigned, while accepting the manifestation transmitted by the Hon. Mr. Nelson, highly congratulates himself that it affords him the opportunity of setting forth, in his turn, the kindly feelings entertained by the Chilian government and people towards the government and people of the United States of North America.

Nothing is more natural than that the republic of Chili should view with great interest the painful crisis at present afflicting the United States, and should pray for its early conclusion in the most satisfactory manner.

Notwithstanding the diversity of origin and of language, the United States and the Spanish American republics are mutually united by the strong bond of analogous political institutions, in whose development they found the hope of a growing prosperity, which must, of necessity, cause each to view the fate of the others as of an interest not foreign, but their own. If, heretofore, there have been at times motives which may have enfeebled the friendly relations of the Spanish American republics with the United States; if there has existed a want of confidence, either founded or unfounded; if perhaps, the principles which guided the cabinet at Washington in diplomatic affairs have not always been well appreciated, the undersigned flatters himself that the solution of the crisis through which the United States are now passing, while it will assure them the elevated rank which, in a brief period of their history, they have obtained among the great nations of the earth, thanks to the powerful resources of their territory, and, more than all, to the admirable efforts of their citizens, must contribute to draw closer together the relations of true fraternity with the Spanish American states, causing all the republics of this continent to consider themselves as the members of one and the same family.

The sincere union of all the republics of the American continent, whatever be their historical antecedents, will be a fact pregnant with great and profitable results, since it must co-operate not only to the security of republican institutions, but, also, to the moral and material progress of these states, and even to the preservation of friendly relations with European nations, which Chili, as well as the United States, desires to cultivate and foment.

The envoy extraordinary and minister plenipotentiary of the United States is also pleased to inform the undersigned that his government has viewed with especial interest the events occurring in Mexico; and the President of the United States, although confident in the good faith of the allied powers, and in the sincerity of their promises not to intervene to change the form of government of Mexico, has deemed it his duty to manifest to them his opinion that a monarchy upheld by foreign armies and navies would have no prospect of permanency in that country.

The undersigned has been especially charged by the President of the republic to manifest to the envoy extraordinary and minister plenipotentiary that he participates in the accurate opinion of the President of the United States upon the inefficacy of substituting in Mexico for the republic a monarchy constituted in favor of a Mexican citizen or foreign prince. A foreign prince would, doubtless, need the constant aid and protection of foreign forces, which would place him under a permanent tutelage, which, while it would weaken the prestige of authority, would deprive him of his true independence. A citizen of Mexico would meet with analogous difficulties and the want of those historical antecedents which, in great part, constitute the power of monarchical governments. So that it is impossible to believe that it would succeed in meriting the adhesion of the people.

Nor are social and political changes so easily effected. The constitution, in republics of the different sections of Spanish America, is, doubtless, the most prominent fact of their history, as it is in regard to the United States, as observed by his excellency the envoy extraordinary and minister plenipotentiary. And a new change in the form of government of Mexico would require radical modifications in her customs and other social elements, which, even on the hypothesis that they could be effected at the cost of immense sacrifices and in a long series of years, would give room for a movement of reorganization, slow and dangerous, which would prolong the evil condition of affairs in Mexico instead of affording a remedy therefor.

It is undoubtedly much to be regretted that the perturbations which have agitated the Spanish American republics, and especially Mexico, should have weakened the prestige of the republican system in the estimation of a few, obliging them to seek a remedy in another form of government, which, instead of being the end, would be the beginning of new and more sanguinary contests.

By an error of judgment they deem order and prosperity irreconcilable with the republican system, as though stability and the guarantees of a good government belonged alone to monarchy, without reflecting that the history of all ages has condemned the principles of absolutism, and that (both) republicanism and monarchy have given to nations prosperity and glory.

For the rest, the government of the United States ought ever to count upon the assurance of finding that reciprocity of ideas and sentiments which the undersigned has had the honor to manifest in this note to the honorable Mr. Nelson.

The undersigned likewise entertains the conviction that his excellency, who so worthily and so acceptably to the government of Chili fulfils the high mission with which he is charged, will continue, as up to the present time, co-operating in the development and increase of the cordiality and harmony which happily exist between the republics of Chili and the United States.

With this motive the undersigned takes pleasure in renewing to the envoy extraordinary and minister plenipotentiary the assurances of his high and distinguished consideration, and in subscribing himself his excellency's attentive and obsequious servant,

MANUEL A. TOCORNAL.

The ENVOY EXTRAORDINARY
and MINISTER PLENIPOTENTIARY *of the*
United States of North America.

Mr. Thayer to Mr. Seward.

[Extracts.]

No. 26.]

UNITED STATES CONSULATE GENERAL,
Alexandria, January 9, 1863.

SIR: An event of apparently grave importance has just come to light, and produces much excitement in this community.

On the morning of the 7th instant four hundred and fifty black soldiers were, by order of the viceroy of Egypt, taken by railway from the fortifications of the barrage, (about 120 miles south of Alexandria,) and at night shipped on board the French transport steamer *La Seine*, for a destination generally understood to be Mexico, with the object of aiding the French Emperor in his military operations against that country. These negroes, with others, departed early yesterday morning; it is stated that they were dressed in zouave uniform and fully armed.

In a letter from Toulon, which appeared in the *Independence Belge* of the 28th ultimo, I am told, it was reported that *La Seine* was about to sail to Alexandria with French troops *en route* for Cochin China, but that it would return with 1,000 negro troops which the viceroy had pledged to the French expedition against Mexico.

Another journal, *La France*, of Paris, confirmed the report of such a promise on the part of his highness.

* * * * * * * *

Since it has become known, the time has been too short to obtain any information from the viceroy, who is at Cairo, and his officers here profess entire ignorance, although the police under them were employed in the work of embarking the troops.

It is well understood that the French Emperor has been anxious to supply the losses which his Mexican army has suffered from climate and disease by the employment of blacks; and the viceroy, I am told, declared a month ago that he was about to send a thousand of his men to some place where their quality might be tested. His highness, it is also known, has always been proud of his army, both black and white, the effectiveness of which, except in repulsing the raids of Bedoins, has not been fairly displayed since the war in the Crimea, where his men certainly distinguished themselves, as compared with other Ottoman troops.

* * * * * * * *

I have the honor to be, sir, very respectfully, your obedient servant,

WILLIAM S. THAYER.

Hon. WILLIAM H. SEWARD,
Secretary of State, Washington, D. C.

Mr. Thayer to Mr. Seward.

[Extract.]

ALEXANDRIA, *January* 12, 1863.

SIR: The facts in my despatch No. 26 are confirmed, but as I am awaiting explanations from the viceroy, I postpone destails until the next mail, which goes in a day or two.

The European consuls general have telegraphed to their governments and are awaiting instructions.

* * * * * * * * * *

Very respectfully, your obedient servant,

WILLIAM S. THAYER.

Hon. WILLIAM H. SEWARD,
Secretary of State.

Mr. Thayer to Mr. Seward.

No. 28.] UNITED STATES CONSULATE GENERAL,
Alexandria, January 27, 1863.

SIR: I am informed that some time since the minister of foreign affairs at Paris announced to Lord Cowley the Emperor's wish to procure blacks from Egypt. This report somewhat confirms the surmise in my last despatch that the Emperor had sounded the courts of Europe before taking a step which would violate the rights of the Porte, as suzerain of Egypt. It also partially accounts for the confidence with which, in official quarters here, it was predicted that there would be no protest from the European powers against the offence. In what light the proposed measure was presented to secure in advance such an acquiescence I can only conjecture. If these reports be true, the United States is the only great power which is not hampered from protesting against the Emperor's transaction.

I have the honor to be, sir, very respectfully, your obedient servant,

WILLIAM S. THAYER.

Hon. WILLIAM H. SEWARD,
Secretary of State, Washington, D. C.

No. 15.

Suspension of trade with Matamoros.

Mr. Romero to Mr. Seward.

[Translation.]

MEXICAN LEGATION IN THE UNITED STATES OF AMERICA,
Washington, July 11, 1861.

MR. SECRETARY: Mr. B. F. Penniman, a merchant of Boston, has addressed himself to this legation, asking whether a vessel, laden with provisions and other articles of lawful commerce, will be permitted to leave said port, land her cargo in Matamoras, and sell it in that market. Mr. Penniman, who desires to send a vessel to the said port, further states that the honorable Secretary of the Treasury has notified the collector of customs at Boston not to clear any vessel whatever for Matamoras, except under certain conditions, of which I am not advised, and which, however, are not made to apply to the other ports of Mexico.

Although I believe that in the instructions which the Treasury Department may have issued upon this subject the legitimate interests of Mexico have been saved harmless, and the rights which she has acquired under the treaties which bind it to the United States have been preserved intact. I desire, nevertheless, to satisfy myself in this belief by a perusal of said instructions, and to be enabled to inform my government of them, for which purpose I would thank you to have the goodness to ask for and transmit to me a copy of the same.

I avail of this opportunity to renew to you, sir, the assurances of my very distinguished consideration,

M. ROMERO.

Mr. Seward to Mr. Romero.

DEPARTMENT OF STATE,
Washington, July 17, 1861.

SIR: Having referred your note of the 11th instant to the Secretary of the Treasury, I have the honor to transmit to you a copy of a letter addressed by him on the 19th ultimo to the collector of the customs at Boston, which contains the information you solicit.

I avail myself of this occasion to renew to you, sir, the assurances of my highest consideration.

WILLIAM H. SEWARD.

Señor DON MATIAS ROMERO, *&c., &c., &c.*

TREASURY DEPARTMENT, *July* 16, 1861.

SIR: I have the honor to acknowledge the receipt of your letter of the 13th instant, enclosing a translation of a note from Mr. Romero, the Mexican minister, requesting a copyof the instructions given to the collector at Boston in regard to clearing vessels from that port to Matamoras, Mexico. A copy of the only instructions given to the collector at Boston on the subject is herewith transmitted, dated the 19th ultimo.

I am, very respectfully,

S. P. CHASE,
Secretary of the Treasury.

Hon. WILLIAM H. SEWARD,
Secretary of State.

TREASURY DEPARTMENT, *July* 19, 1861.

SIR: I have received the letter of your deputy collector, B. F. Copeland, of the 17th instant, inquiring whether any objection should be made by you to clearing at your port a British vessel with an assorted cargo, mostly provisions for Matamoras, Mexico.

You are authorized to use your own discretion. If you are satisfied the merchandise is not intended for the insurgents you may clear. If not satisfied, you should refuse to grant a clearance. You were notified to this effect by telegraph of the 15th instant.

All official communications should be signed by you as collector.

I am, very respectfully,

S. P. CHASE,
Secretary of the Treasury.

Z. GOODRICH, Esq.,
Collector, &c., Boston, Mass.

Mr. Romero to Mr. Seward.

[Translation.]

MEXICAN LEGATION TO THE UNITED STATES OF AMERICA,
Washington, July 23, 1861.

MR. SECRETARY: I have the honor to acknowledge the receipt of your note of the 17th instant, with which you were pleased to send me a copy of the instructions communicated by the Treasury Department to the collector of the customs at Boston on the clearance of vessels for Matamoras. At the same time I received a communication from the Mexican consul at New York, of which I annex a copy. In it he informs me that the collector at that port answered the merchant who inquired if he would clear vessels for Matamoros, that he would not give a categorical reply unless the vessels should be laden and ready to sail.

Such proceedings, which, in my judgment, prejudice the mercantile relations of both countries and which are not in conformity with the stipulations of the treaty of commerce, which are obligatory, induce me to address myself anew to you on this subject, to the end that the government of the United States may please to dictate regulations such as the rights and legitimate interests of Mexico require in the present case.

You know, sir, that with respect to commercial advantages, Mexico is, in regard of the United States, on the same footing as any the most favored nations. For this reason, this merchandise, which may be lawfully exported to any port of a foreign nation, may also be exported to Vera Cruz, as well as to Matamoras or other ports of Mexico.

If by reason of especial circumstances, which at this time arise from the geographical position of Matamoras, the government of the United States should deem it convenient to make some exception in respect to that port, it would be necessary, in order to make it effective, to obtain in the first place the consent of the government of Mexico, and meantime, until this is attained, I shall hold it to be my duty to request that no difference shall be made between that port and the others of the Mexican republic,

I have the honor to renew to you, sir, the assurances of my highest consideration.

M. ROMERO.

Hon. WILLIAM H. SEWARD, *&c., &c., &c.*

[Translation.]

MEXICAN CONSULATE, *New York, July* 17, 1861.

At different times merchants of this city have approached this office, under my care, inquiring whether I would think it inexpedient to clear a vessel laden with merchandise for the port of Matamoras; and upon asking for the cause of this inquiry, they replied that the collector of the customs at this port had declared "that he will not give any categorical answer whether he will or will not clear a vessel for the said port of Matamoras until she be laden and ready to sail;" and that the parties interested understood this to be a sort of refusal, and were, therefore, not willing to incur the risk of lading their vessel, because after having done so they could not clear her. My reply was, naturally, that this office finds no difficulty in giving the consular clearance to any vessel lawfully seeking it for a Mexican port, such as Matamoras; but that, at the same time, because of the geographical position of said port, and the political state of this country at present, I would not pass any invoice which should include arms, munitions, powder and its components; that this decision was entirely spontaneous with me, and I would submit it to my government for approval, (as I do through your esteemed intervention,) so that for the future the resolution which may be adopted will serve as a rule of conduct.

In consequence of what is stated, and considering that it is a grave injury to trade that doubts of this kind be entertained. I ask your recourse, sir, to the government of the

United States, that it may issue instructions respecting it to the collector of the customs at this port, in order that he may reply decidedly that the Mexican port of Matamoras is not to be considered as comprehended in the blockade of the ports of the rebel States proclaimed by the President of the United States, because, although it is perfectly true that the bar of the Rio Bravo del Norte is at the entrance common to said port and the port of Brownsville, I also know that, by the treaty of Guadalupe Hidalgo, concluded between Mexico and the United States, the navigation of that river is neutral.

I reiterate to you, sir, my respect and consideration. God and liberty!

J. M. DURAN.

To the CHARGÉ D'AFFAIRES
Of the Mexican Legation, Washington.

A true copy.—July 23, 1861.

ROMERO.

Mr. Seward to Mr. Romero.

DEPARTMENT OF STATE,
Washington, July 31, 1861.

SIR: Having submitted your note of the 23d instant to the Secretary of the Treasury, I have the honor to communicate herewith a copy of a letter from him dated yesterday, containing his decision in reference to the subject laid before him, and which, I trust, will be regarded by the Mexican government as another proof of the disposition of the United States to facilitate as much as possible the commercial intercourse between the two countries.

I avail myself of this occasion to renew to you, sir, the assurances of my highest consideration.

WILLIAM H. SEWARD.

Señor Don MATIAS ROMERO, *&c., &c., &c.*

TREASURY DEPARTMENT, *July* 30, 1861.

SIR: I have the honor to return herewith the note of Mr. Romero, the Mexican minister, in regard to the clearance of vessels for Matamoras, Mexico, enclosed for my consideration in your communication of the 26th instant.

I can perceive no objection to the granting of clearances to vessels destined to Matamoras laden with merchandise of any kind except arms and munitions of war. Owing to the proximity of that port to Brownsville and other ports in Texas, on the Rio Grande, and the facility with which arms and munitions of war may be furnished from that point to the insurgents, it is obvious that one of the chief purposes of the blockade would be likely to be defeated if articles of that description should be freely imported into Matamoras.

But in view of the friendly relations so happily subsisting between the United States and Mexico, and which it is the desire and interest of both countries to maintain unimpaired, the restriction of the commerce of the United States with Mexican ports on the Rio Grande will be confined within the narrowest limits compatible with the maintenance of an effective blockade. No obstacle will, of course, be interposed to commercial intercourse between the United States and Mexican ports not on the Rio Grande.

Instructions to this effect will be given to collectors of the customs.

I am, very respectfully,

S. P. CHASE,
Secretary of the Treasury.

Hon. W. H. SEWARD,
Secretary of State.

Mr. Romero to Mr. Seward.

[Translation.]

MEXICAN LEGATION IN THE UNITED STATES OF AMERICA,
Washington, August 1, 1861.

Mr. SECRETARY: I have the honor to acknowledge the receipt of your note dated yesterday, in which you were pleased to enclose to me a copy of the communication of the honorable the Secretary of the Treasury of the 30th of July last, touching the clearance of vessels for Matamoras.

I this day transmit a copy of your note, aforementioned, and of the communication accompanying it, to the government of Mexico, for its information and final decision upon this subject.

I avail myself of this occasion to renew to you, sir, the assurances of my very distinguished consideration.

M. ROMERO.

Hon. WILLIAM H. SEWARD, *&c., &c., &c.*

Mr. Romero to Mr. Seward.

[Translation.]

MEXICAN LEGATION TO THE UNITED STATES OF AMERICA,
Washington, September 2, 1861.

Mr. SECRETARY: I have the honor to transmit to you a copy of a note addressed to this legation, under date of 31st August last past, by the Mexican consul at New York, stating that the custom-house at that port refuses to clear for Matamoras the schooner Alexander, which had been loading for several days, and which was already prepared to sail for her destination, not having on board arms or munitions of war.

Believing that the cause of such proceeding must be that said custom-house had not yet had notice of the resolutions of the Treasury Department of the 31st of July last, which you were pleased to communicate to me in your note of the 31st of the same month, I address myself to you, requesting that you will bring these facts to the knowledge of the honorable Secretary of the Treasury for the results that should ensue.

I avail of this opportunity, sir, to renew to you the assurances of my most distinguished consideration.

M. ROMERO.

Hon. WILLIAM H. SEWARD, *&c., &c., &c.*

[Translation.]

MEXICAN CONSULATE AT NEW YORK,
New York, August 31, 1861.

To-day Messrs. Schepeler & Co., merchants of this place, presented themselves at this office, showing that the custom-house of this port refused absolutely a clearance for Matamoras to the English schooner Alexander M., which has been loading for several days, and was to-day prepared to sail for her destination. The same gentlemen have stated to me that the cargo referred to consists solely of merchandise for the demands of Mexican trade, and contains nothing contraband of war of any kind.

The house mentioned cleared, on the 19th of the month now ending, the English schooner Brunette for the same port, and the custom-house interposed no hindrance whatever; and as much by reason of this precedent as because they obtained from this consulate the information, respectively, about the notes of the 31st July from the Department of State, and of the 30th of the same month from that of the treasury, copies of which you sent me with your communication relating to it of the 1st of the present month; for these two reasons, I say, the Messrs. Schepeler & Co. proceeded in loading the vessel to which the respective documents of clearance are now refused. I bring the matter to your knowledge for your correct information, and for the results for which it may make place, with the understanding that it seems very strange that this government, after having given its decision in the notes to which I have referred above, changes it to-day without reason and without cause—without reason, because the American government has not the right to close up a port of a friendly nation, perhaps the only one that has given proofs of friendship under existing circumstances; and without cause, because the two vessels which have sailed for Matamoras, the Brunette and the William R. Kibby, on the 19th and 28th of the month now ending, have not carried any contraband of war, at least with knowledge of this consulate, because I very decidedly stated to the shippers that I would not pass any invoice whatever which contained arms or munitions of war, and the business was in fact so carried out. I ask you to place this statement in the knowlege of the Secretary of State, and be pleased to communicate the result to me.

God and liberty!

J. M. DURAN.

To the CHARGÉ OF THE LEGATION *at Washington.*

WASHINGTON, *September* 2, 1861.

True copy:

ROMERO.

Mr. Seward to Mr. Romero.

DEPARTMENT OF STATE,
Washington, September 7, 1861.

SIR: Having transmitted to the Secretary of the Treasury a translation of your note of the 2d instant, and of its enclosure, relating to clearances of vessels from loyal ports of the United States to Matamoras, I have now the honor to communicate to you a copy of his reply, just received, dated the 5th instant.

A careful examination of the whole subject impresses me with the irresistible conviction that the course which the Secretary of the Treasury has been impelled to adopt is absolutely necessary to the public interest.

I sincerely share the regrets which he expresses that the exigencies of our condition should impose the slightest restriction upon commercial intercourse with a friendly nation, but I also anticipate, with much confidence, that the enlightened government of Mexico will not hesitate to appreciate and admit the imperative necessity which dictates the measure resorted to.

I avail myself of this occasion to renew to you, sir, the assurances of my most distinguished consideration.

WILLIAM H. SEWARD.

Señor DON MATIAS ROMERO, *&c., &c., &c.*

TREASURY DEPARTMENT, *September* 5, 1861.

SIR: I have the honor to acknowledge the receipt of your communication of the 3d instant, inviting my attention to the translation of a note, dated the 2d instant, from Mr. Romero, Mexican chargé d'affaires, upon the subject of clearances to vessels bound to Matamoras.

Having been informed, before the receipt of your communication, of the great increase of shipments to Matamoras, much beyond, it is believed, any legitimate demand in that portion of Mexico, and believing that whatever might be their ostensible destination, they were, in fact, intended for the insurgents in Texas, I directed the collector at New York to grant no more clearances for Matamoras without my special directions to that effect. This restriction I propose to make general.

I sincerely participate with you in the regret that the present condition of affairs in that section of the United States contiguous to Mexico renders it necessary to place a partial and temporary restriction over our trade with a friendly and neighboring nation. While, however, the injury which may be thus inflicted on the legitimate trade of Mexico must be slight, the continuance of commercial intercourse with Matamoras might be seriously detrimental to the United States in the contest she is now waging to restore her rightful authority in the insurgent States. The Mexican authorities, it is believed, cannot fail to perceive, and to appreciate in a liberal spirit, the necessity of this measure in the present exigency of our national affairs, although it may seem to wear an unfriendly aspect.

I am, very respectfully,

S. P. CHASE,
Secretary of the Treasury.

Hon. WILLIAM H. SEWARD,
Secretary of State.

Mr. Romeo to Mr. Seward.

[Translation.]

MEXICAN LEGATION TO THE UNITED STATES OF AMERICA,
Washington, September 10, 1861.

Mr. SECRETARY: I have had the honor to receive the note you were pleased to address to me under date of 7th instant, communicating to me the decision of the honorable Secretary of the Treasury, in relation to having ordered the suspension of the clearance of vessels from ports of the United States not under blockade, to Matamoras.

I confess, sir, that the note of the honorable Secretary of the Treasury of the 5th instant, of which you did me the favor to send me a copy, and which contains the reasons which caused that measure, has given me a painful impression.

I hold myself entirely absolved from exception in confining myself to showing the obligation which the government of the United States lies under to grant clearances of vessels from the recognized ports of this country for any port in Mexico, provided such clearances are given to the ports of any other nation. To exclude Matamoras from this right is equivalent to its partial blockade, which I do not consider the government of the United States is authorized to do in the state of peace in which we happily find ourselves.

Without prejudice to my giving an immediate report to my government of this decision of the United States, and reserving the right to act according to what may be resolved upon in Mexico upon this business, I believe it to be my duty to make some corrections of the representations which determined the action of the Treasury Department; these explanations, looked upon in a friendly manner, are, to my understanding, sufficient to determine the revocation of that measure.

Since the last demarcation of boundaries made between Mexico and the United States placed Matamoras on the dividing line, the commerce of that port has greatly increased. Now it receives not only the articles required for the consumption of the city, but many others with which it supplies Tamaulipas and other neighboring states.

Nearly one-half of the articles imported in the Mexican republic during the last six years have come in over the frontier, being brought from the United States, although, until this time, the greater part of such importations have been clandestine. The two principal places of deposit were Matamoras, which received the goods from New Orleans and Paso del Norte in Chihuahua, which received them from St. Louis, Missouri. In consequence of the blockade of the former, and of the interruption of communication between the latter with the seceding States, this great traffic on the frontier has been suspended, and for the purpose of re-establishing and following it up in a regular and lawful manner the merchants of Matamoras sent their orders to the merchants of New York and Boston.

How, then, should it cause astonishment that, when the honorable Secretary of the Treasury permitted the clearance of vessels for Matamoras, after a complete paralysis of several months, two vessels sailed from New York, with a few days only between, and a third should be getting ready for departure ?

The injury, then, which will result to Mexico from the suspension of its lawful trade is not so slight as Mr. Chase believes. The merchants of Matamoras, who find the markets of the United States closed to them, will seek what they want in Europe, and then the injury will reach also the *bona fide* commerce of this country.

I beg you, sir, to have the goodness to communicate this note to Mr. Chase, as I have no doubt from his acknowledged enlightenment, that he will find in these explanations motives which justify the revocation of that direction.

I avail of this opportunity to repeat to you, sir, the assurances of my very distinguished consideration.

M. ROMERO.

Hon. WM. H. SEWARD, *&c.*, *&c.*, *&c.*

Mr. Seward to Mr. Romero.

DEPARTMENT OF STATE,
Washington, September 13, 1861.

SIR: I have to acknowledge the receipt of your note of the 10th instant, replying to mine of the 7th, relative to the suspension of clearances for Matamoras.

After a careful perusal of your note, I am constrained to admit that I do not perceive the analogy you suggest between the measure adopted by this government for its own safety and the blockade of a port of a friendly power. There is unquestionable room for doubt as to the *bona fide* character of the traffic carried on between Matamoras and the frontier of the insurgent State of Texas, and this government would be derelict to the first principle of national existence if it failed to make the consideration of its own safety and integrity one of paramount importance.

Under these circumstances, the order for the suspension of clearances for Matamoras cannot, at this juncture, be rescinded; and it is confidently believed, indeed it cannot be doubted, that the enlightened government of Mexico will, upon mature deliberation, not only justify, but approve the measure.

A copy of this note, as well as of your own, to which it is a reply, will be transmitted to the Secretary of the Treasury.

I avail myself of this opportunity to renew to you, sir, the assurances of my most distinguished consideration.

WM. H. SEWARD.

Señor Don MATIAS ROMERO, *&c.*, *&c.*, *&c.*

www.ingramcontent.com/pod-product-compliance
Lightning Source LLC
LaVergne TN
LVHW021321110826
845150LV00003B/635

* 9 7 8 1 4 2 5 5 5 6 7 3 0 *